Asking Questions about Your Data

GW01033972

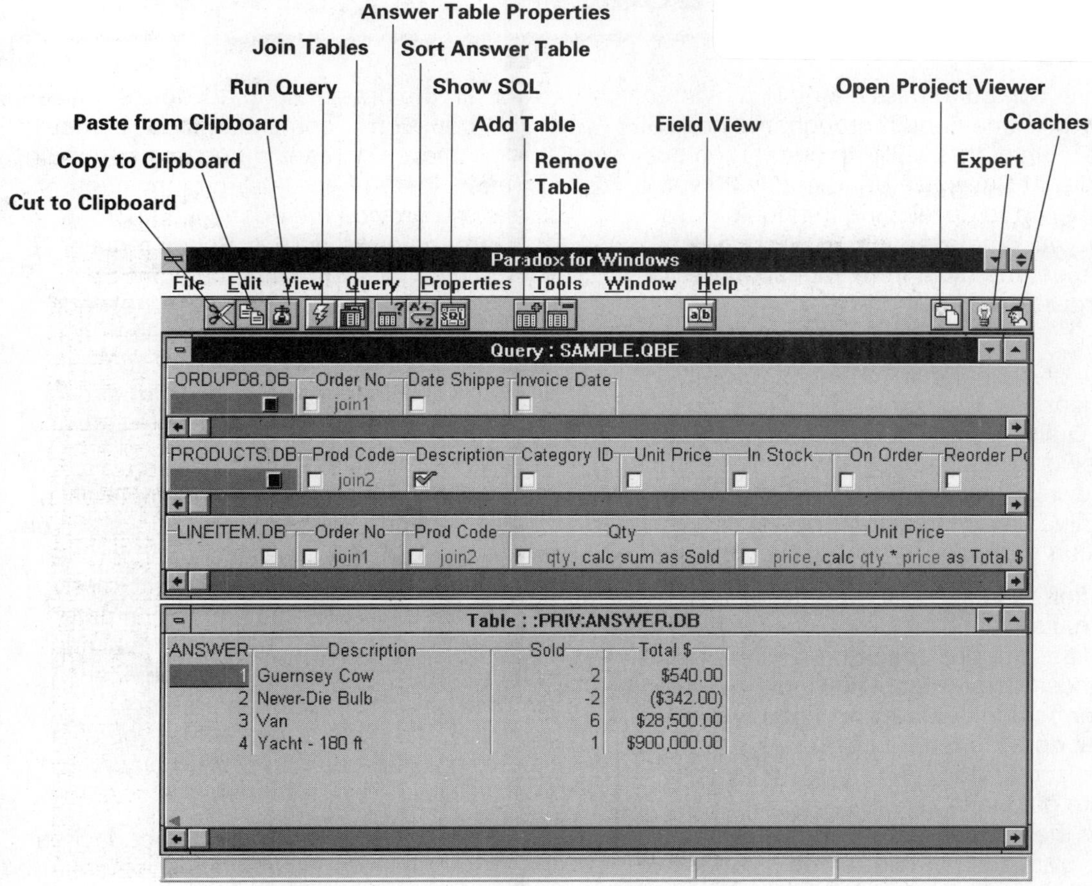

Answer Table Properties
Join Tables | **Sort Answer Table**
Run Query | **Show SQL**
Paste from Clipboard | **Add Table** | **Field View**
Copy to Clipboard | **Remove Table**
Cut to Clipboard

Open Project Viewer
Coaches
Expert

Paradox for Windows

File   Edit   View   Query   Properties   Tools   Window   Help

Query : SAMPLE.QBE

ORDUPD8.DB — Order No — Date Shippe — Invoice Date
☐ join1   ☐   ☐

PRODUCTS.DB — Prod Code — Description — Category ID — Unit Price — In Stock — On Order — Reorder P
☐ join2   ☑   ☐   ☐   ☐   ☐   ☐

LINEITEM.DB — Order No — Prod Code — Qty — Unit Price
☐ join1   ☐ join2   ☐ qty, calc sum as Sold   ☐ price, calc qty * price as Total $

Table : :PRIV:ANSWER.DB

ANSWER	Description	Sold	Total $
1	Guernsey Cow	2	$540.00
2	Never-Die Bulb	-2	($342.00)
3	Van	6	$28,500.00
4	Yacht - 180 ft	1	$900,000.00

TO DO THIS...	SEE CHAPTER
Select fields to view in the Answer table	2, 9
Run a query	2, 9
Select specific records to include in the Answer table	2, 9
Save and open a query	2, 9
Sort the Answer table and control its name and appearance	9
Change or delete records globally	9, 16, 18
Use filters to select and work with live data in an open table or form	9
Select and sort data in custom forms and reports	2, 10, 11, 12
Combine data from multiple tables	16
Display non-matching records	16
Perform calculations on fields	16
Perform statistical summaries and frequency distributions	16
Ask questions about sets of records	16
Copy fields and records from one table to another	18
Change values in one table based on values in another table	18

FOR EVERY COMPUTER QUESTION, THERE IS A SYBEX BOOK THAT HAS THE ANSWER

Each computer user learns in a different way. Some need thorough, methodical explanations, while others are too busy for details. At Sybex we bring nearly 20 years of experience to developing the book that's right for you. Whatever your needs, we can help you get the most from your software and hardware, at a pace that's comfortable for you.

We start beginners out right. You will learn by seeing and doing with our **Quick & Easy** series: friendly, colorful guidebooks with screen-by-screen illustrations. For hardware novices, the **Your First** series offers valuable purchasing advice and installation support.

Often recognized for excellence in national book reviews, our **Mastering** titles are designed for the intermediate to advanced user, without leaving the beginner behind. A **Mastering** book provides the most detailed reference available. Add our pocket-sized **Instant Reference** titles for a complete guidance system. Programmers will find that the new **Developer's Handbook** series provides a more advanced perspective on developing innovative and original code.

With the breathtaking advances common in computing today comes an ever increasing demand to remain technologically up-to-date. In many of our books, we provide the added value of software, on disks or CDs. Sybex remains your source for information on software development, operating systems, networking, and every kind of desktop application. We even have books for kids. Sybex can help smooth your travels on the **Internet** and provide **Strategies and Secrets** to your favorite computer games.

As you read this book, take note of its quality. Sybex publishes books written by experts—authors chosen for their extensive topical knowledge. In fact, many are professionals working in the computer software field. In addition, each manuscript is thoroughly reviewed by our technical, editorial, and production personnel for accuracy and ease-of-use before you ever see it—our guarantee that you'll buy a quality Sybex book every time.

To manage your hardware headaches and optimize your software potential, ask for a Sybex book.

FOR MORE INFORMATION, PLEASE CONTACT:

Sybex Inc.
2021 Challenger Drive
Alameda, CA 94501
Tel: (510) 523-8233 • (800) 227-2346
Fax: (510) 523-2373

SYBEX

Let us hear from you.

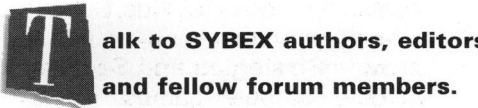

Talk to SYBEX authors, editors and fellow forum members.

Get tips, hints and advice online.

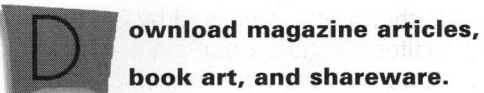

Download magazine articles, book art, and shareware.

Join the SYBEX Forum on CompuServe®

If you're already a CompuServe user, just type **GO SYBEX** to join the SYBEX Forum. If not, try CompuServe for free by calling 1-800-848-8199 and ask for Representative 560. You'll get one free month of basic service and a $15 credit for CompuServe extended services—a $23.95 value. Your personal ID number and password will be activated when you sign up.

Join us online today. Type **GO SYBEX** on CompuServe.
If you're not a CompuServe member, call Representative 560
at **1-800-848-8199**.

SYBEX

(outside U.S./Canada call 614-457-0802)

Mastering Paradox® 5
for Windows™

Special Edition

Third Edition

Alan Simpson

San Francisco ▲ Paris ▼ Düsseldorf ▲ Soest

SYBEX®

Acquisitions Editors: David Clark, Joanne Cuthbertson
Developmental Editor: David Peal
Editors: Sarah Wadsworth, Vivian Perry, Vivian Jaquette
Project Editor: Michelle Khazai
Technical Editors: Chris Campagna, Gerry Coffey, Peter Dyson
Book Designer: Suzanne Albertson
Production Artists: Charlotte Carter, Suzanne Albertson, Lucie Živny
Screen Graphics: John Corrigan, Cuong Le, Dan Schiff
Typesetters: Stephanie Hollier, Deborah Maizels, Alissa Feinberg
Production Coordinator: Sarah Lemas
Proofreader/Production Assistant: David Silva
Indexer: Matthew Spence
Cover Designer: Design Site
Cover Photographer: Mark Johann
Cover Photo Art Direction: Ingalls + Associates

SYBEX is a registered trademark of SYBEX Inc.

TRADEMARKS: SYBEX has attempted throughout this book to distinguish proprietary trademarks from descriptive terms by following the capitalization style used by the manufacturer.

Every effort has been made to supply complete and accurate information. However, SYBEX assumes no responsibility for its use, nor for any infringement of the intellectual property rights of third parties which would result from such use.

Library of Congress Card Number: 94-68436
ISBN: 0-7821-1592-6

Manufactured in the United States of America

10 9 8 7 6 5 4 3 2

To Susan, Ashley, and Alec Simpson

▶ Acknowledgments

Like all books, this one was a team effort, and much credit and my sincere appreciation go to the many people on the team.

First and foremost, credit goes to my co-author Elizabeth Olson, who almost single-handedly researched, wrote, developed, and revised the initial manuscript for most of this book. Even the great-looking sample forms and reports are Elizabeth's creations! Other writers contributing their time and talents to the earlier edition of this book were Virginia Andersen, David Rhodes, Charlie Russel, and Patricia Hartman. My thanks to Martha Mellor, whose superb coordination skills and good humor kept the entire team moving smoothly toward the finish line.

The efforts and suggestions of many people at SYBEX helped shape the original manuscript into its final form—especially Project Editor Michelle Khazai, Editors Vivian Perry, Vivian Jaquette, and Sarah Wadsworth, Developmental Editor David Peal, and Technical Editors Peter Dyson and Chris Campagna. I'm also grateful to the full production team for their hard work over the course of a very tight schedule, given the extent of the changes made to Paradox for Windows itself.

The technical support staff at Borland International deserves kudos for fielding our many questions via CompuServe and passing our suggestions along to program developers.

Many thanks to the gang at Waterside Productions, my literary agents, for managing the "business and opportunity" aspects of my writing career.

And, as always, I thank my family—Susan, Ashley, and Alec—who once again were patient and supportive while Daddy was locked away in his office during many long hours.

Contents at a Glance

*T*able of Contents

11   Creating Custom Forms   583

12 Designing and Printing Formatted Reports 647

13 Graphing Your Data

19   Automating Your Work with ObjectPAL **1053**

▶ APPENDICES

▶ *Introduction*

Simply stated, Paradox for Windows is a powerful database management system that anyone can use. Historically, database management systems have been programming language–oriented, and thus best used as tools by programmers and advanced computer users. The need to remember numerous commands, functions, data types, syntax rules, file structures, and so on made the older database management systems unwieldy for the neophyte and casual user.

Then came Paradox for DOS—a new approach to database management that freed the user from having to memorize complex commands. With Paradox, even the casual computer user could effectively store, retrieve, sort, print, change, and ask questions about data by selecting options from the menus and "filling in the blanks" on standardized questionnaires.

Now we have Paradox 5 for Windows, a dazzling, graphical database management system for the Windows environment. Incorporating all the best ideas from Paradox for DOS and earlier versions of Paradox for Windows, this latest version defines a new standard for database managers that places even more capabilities at the user's fingertips.

So what's paradoxical about Paradox for Windows? The paradox is that even though it's so easy to use, Paradox for Windows does not compromise on power or flexibility. You can still ask complex questions about many interrelated tables of data, and you can develop sophisticated forms and reports that in the past even programmers only dreamed about—and all without writing a single program or memorizing a bunch of complex commands.

▶▶ *Is This Book Right for You?*

This book is designed for experienced Windows users who are new to working with databases—those who have never used Paradox or any other database management system. Even if you're not exactly sure what a database management system *is*, or what it is used for, you're in good hands. The first chapter of this book, and the lessons in Chapter 2, will get you acquainted with what database management with Paradox for Windows is all about.

Like all books in the SYBEX *Mastering* series, this one is designed to stick to the topic at hand, namely Paradox for Windows. So we won't be spending lots of time teaching you how to use Windows, the mouse, or the keyboard. In fact, we've geared this book toward people with *some* Windows and computer experience. In particular,

- You should already be familiar with how information is organized on your hard disk in *files*, *directories*, and *drives*.

- Any prior experience with a Windows-based word processing, spreadsheet, drawing, or painting package (or any other program that's made you comfortable with the Windows environment) will be helpful. You should already have your basic Windows skills down pat.

If you're not yet up to speed in these areas, you can get a quick introduction from any small book on DOS, such as my own *Up and Running with DOS 6.2* or *The ABC's of DOS 6.2*, and my *Windows 3.1 Running Start*, also published by SYBEX.

On the other hand, you may be at the opposite end of the spectrum: perhaps you're already familiar with database management and earlier versions of Paradox. If so, there's still plenty to interest you here. The lessons in Chapter 2 will help make your transition to Paradox for Windows a smooth one, providing the basic skills necessary to proceed with the more advanced topics presented in later chapters.

▶▶ *Which Version of Paradox?*

This book is specifically written for Version 5 of *Paradox for Windows*. If you're using a DOS version of Paradox, such as Version 4.0 or 3.5, this book won't help you much because the Windows version of Paradox is really a whole new animal. If you'd like to upgrade your DOS version of Paradox to Paradox for Windows, you can do so. (The upgrade cost is subject to change, so I won't give a dollar amount here.)

For minimum hardware and memory requirements, please refer to Appendix A, "Installing Paradox for Windows." For details on using Paradox for Windows on a network, please see Appendix B, "Network, OBEX, and SQL Features."

▶▶ *Special Features of the Book*

This book is designed as both a tutorial and a reference to the many features of Paradox for Windows. Special features of the book, designed to simplify and speed your mastery of Paradox for Windows, include the following:

Endpapers Inside the front and back covers you'll find a quick reference to the Table, Query, Form, and Report windows, where you perform common tasks in Paradox for Windows.

Paradox for Windows in an Evening The lessons in Chapter 2 provide you with a quick way to get some hands-on experience with Paradox for Windows. In just a few hours, you can survey the key features of the program and develop a useful address table, data entry form, and report of your own.

Notes, Tips, Warnings, and "New" Icons Special notes throughout each chapter provide cross-references to sections of the book that cover related features, tips with insights on creative ways to use the application's features, and warnings about problems that can occur. You'll also find "new" icons sprinkled throughout the book; these point out hot new features in Paradox 5 for Windows. (You'll learn more about what's new in Chapter 1.)

Fast Tracks The Fast Tracks at the beginning of each chapter provide a quick summary of specific features and techniques. Turn to the Fast Tracks when you need a quick reminder, rather than a lengthy explanation.

▶▶ *Structure of the Book*

This book is designed to supplement the densely packed and somewhat technical manuals that came with your Paradox for Windows package. The Paradox manuals document every available feature in great detail. By contrast, *this* book is designed to show you how to use Paradox for Windows and put it to work for your own purposes.

To make things easier for you, and to help you focus on information that's relevant to your own use of Paradox, we've divided the book into five parts:

Part 1: Getting Started Provides an overview of what Paradox is all about, and includes five hands-on lessons that will help you get up to speed quickly.

Part 2: Managing Data with Paradox Shows you how to create tables, enter data, customize the appearance of tables, print simple reports, and sort and query (ask questions about) your data. You'll learn how to manage single tables (which is the easiest way to learn to use these features) and how to design multitable databases.

Part 3: Viewing and Printing Data Paradox for Windows includes powerful drawing and design features that allow you to create truly spectacular custom forms, reports, and graphs for viewing and printing your data. In this part, we first present general procedures that are common to designing both forms and reports. Then we zero in on techniques that pertain specifically to designing a custom form, report, or graph.

Part 4: Managing Your Projects This part of the book deals with more general aspects of Paradox for Windows, such as customizing Paradox and managing your files. You may use only a small portion of the many features presented in this part of the book, so feel free to refer to it on an "as-needed" basis.

Part 5: Managing Related Tables One of the real advantages that a relational database management system like Paradox for Windows offers over word processors and spreadsheets is the ability to store information efficiently in multiple related tables of information, and then "mix and match" that information as necessary. Multiple tables are essential for most business functions, such as managing orders, inventory, accounts, and so forth. In addition to discussing ways to manage multiple related tables, Part 5 also shows you how to develop *applications*, which automate and simplify all aspects of managing data stored in Paradox tables.

You'll learn special querying techniques that update data automatically, and you'll learn how to design "smart" automated forms using *ObjectPAL*, the object-oriented Paradox for Windows Application Language. This book presents the basics of ObjectPAL and provides several practical examples that you can adapt for your own needs. If you're interested in becoming an ObjectPAL programmer, you might want to "graduate" to a more advanced book on the topic, such as *Programming Paradox 5 for Windows*, also from SYBEX.

Appendices   The appendices at the back of the book present more specialized information on Paradox for installers and network administrators, for people who want to send messages and data objects to remote users on a network or other messaging system, for SQL users, and for those who want to use dBASE and Paradox for DOS tables with Paradox for Windows or who want to share Paradox data with other applications. There is also a list of properties used when designing custom forms and reports.

▶▶ *Conventions Used in This Book*

As with most Windows programs, Paradox for Windows allows you to use a mouse or the keyboard to interact with it. This book uses the following conventions to present keys, combination keys, and menu selection sequences:

$\uparrow$, $\downarrow$, $\rightarrow$, $\leftarrow$, **PgUp, PgDn**   Arrow keys and other special keys such as Ins (Insert), Del (Delete), and ⏎ (Enter) are shown with the symbol commonly displayed on the key. If your keyboard is designed so that these keys are only on the numeric keypad, remember that the Num Lock key must be turned off for these keys to work properly.

Combination Keys   Combination keys, starting with Ctrl, Alt, or Shift, are separated with a plus sign (+). To press these keystrokes, hold down the first key while pressing the second key. For instance, to press Ctrl+Ins, you hold down the Ctrl key, press Ins, then release both keys.

Menu Sequences   A series of selections that you make from the menus are shown in an abbreviated sequence with a ➤ symbol separating each selection. For example, File ➤ New ➤ Table means "Choose File from the menu bar, then choose New from the pull-down menu that appears, then choose Table from the sub-menu that appears." The *hot keys* for each menu name or option are underlined. Thus, you could also complete the menu sequence above by pressing Alt, then **F**, then **N**, then **T**. You can use either the mouse or the keyboard to choose menu options, as described in Chapter 2.

►► *A Tip for Tyros*

One of the more troublesome aspects of learning to use any new program is inadvertently choosing the wrong set of menu options and ending up in totally unfamiliar territory.

In most cases, you can simply "back out" by pressing the Escape key (labeled Esc on some keyboards, Cancel on others) until you get to more familiar territory. Clicking on any "neutral" area on the screen or clicking the Cancel button (if it's available) also serves the purpose. Also remember that online help is just an F1 keypress or the click of a "Help" button away.

Getting Started

PART ONE

► ► **CHAPTER 1**

Paradox for Windows: The Elements

*F*AST *T*RACK

▶ *A report is an object*   **12**

that retrieves information from one or more tables in whatever format you wish.

▶ *A query*   **16**

is a means of finding information in a table or isolating
(and, if you wish, changing) records that have something
in common.

▶ *A project*   **16**

is a collection of all the objects that make up a particular
database.

▶ *A relational DBMS like Paradox for Windows*   **17**

lets you store information on separate related tables and
combine that information on an as-needed basis to get answers to questions and create complex reports.

▶ *An application*   **20**

is a fully automated system that makes it easy for any user
to manage database objects, without knowing much about
Paradox or database management.

▶ ▶ **P**aradox for Windows is a relational database management system for Windows. A *database* is simply a collection of information or data, like a Rolodex file, file cabinet, or phone book filled with names and addresses. Whenever you access one of these paper databases, whether it be to add new information, retrieve information, change information, or sort information into some meaningful order, you are *managing* that database.

A computer *database management system* (DBMS) like Paradox for Windows lets you manage a database that is stored on a computer disk. The advantage to using a computer rather than a paper database is this: Tasks that may take several minutes, hours, or even days to perform with paper usually take only a few seconds or minutes to complete with Paradox.

 ▶▶**N O T E**

> **If you're already experienced with earlier versions of Paradox and general database management concepts, you might want to skip to the end of this chapter for a quick overview of what's new in Paradox 5.**

▶▶ *What Can I Do with Paradox?*

Paradox for Windows is an extremely flexible application that gives you virtually unlimited options for storing and managing information. The type of information you can store is limited only by your needs and your imagination. Here are a few of the many common uses of database management systems:

- Managing mailing lists and telephone directories
- Managing customer, sales lead, and membership information files
- Handling bookkeeping and accounting tasks, such as general ledger, accounts payable, and accounts receivable
- Managing orders and controlling inventory
- Managing a personal or professional library that includes pictures, photos, and sounds
- Managing and printing catalogs of photos, descriptions, and prices of your company's products
- Storing and updating employee information, including salary and sound data initially created in Windows applications *outside of* Paradox
- Analyzing and graphing sales performance and customer buying trends over time

▶▶ *It's All About Tables*

Regardless of the type of information you want to manage with Paradox and how you want to manage that information, there is one requirement that must be met right off the bat: The information must be organized in one or more *tables*.

A table is a single body of information that is organized in rows and columns. In database terminology, we refer to each column of information in the table as a *field* and each row of information as a *record*. For example, Figure 1.1 shows a list of names and telephone numbers organized into a table, illustrating the terms *field* and *record*.

Of course, the information you plan to store might not be arranged in a table yet, so you need to think about how you might reorganize the information into a tabular format.

For instance, suppose you have a Rolodex file, with each card in the Rolodex containing the name and address of an individual, as in Figure 1.2. Each card has four lines of information on it: (1) name, (2) address, (3) city, state, zip code, and (4) phone number.

FIGURE 1.1 ▶

*A sample table of names and telephone numbers, illustrating the terms **field** and **record**. The entire collection of information is the **table**.*

Last Name	First Name	Phone
Adams	Anthony	555-1234
Baker	Barbara	555-2345
Carlson	Cassandra	555-3212
Duvall	Muriel	555-6789
Edwards	Elizabeth	555-0101

← Field Names

← Rows (records)

↑ Columns (fields) ↑ ↑

FIGURE 1.2 ▶

Information on a Rolodex card

Sandy Smith
123 A St.
San Diego, CA 92122

(619)555-0987

To put this information into a table, think of each Rolodex card as representing one record (row) of information. Each discrete item of information on a card (name, address, city, state, zip code) represents roughly one field (column). Figure 1.3 shows how information from the Rolodex file might look when stored in a Paradox table. As you can see, we've gone one better than the simple Rolodex cards by adding a picture of each person.

Notice in Figure 1.3 that the table consists of three records (rows): one for Smith (the information shown on the sample Rolodex card), along with records for Jones and Zeepers (possibly from scraps of paper that haven't made it onto Rolodex cards). Each record contains eight fields: Last Name, First Name, Address, City, State, Zip Code, Phone, and Photo.

FIGURE 1.3

A sample table containing three records

Last Name	First Name	Address	City	State	Zip Code	Phone	Photo
Smith	Sandy	123 A St.	San Diego	CA	92122	(619) 555-0987	
Jones	Albert	P.O. Box 12	Berkeley	CA	94710	(510) 555-3232	
Zeepers	Zeke	241 Oak Ln.	Ashland	OR	89765	(123) 555-9878	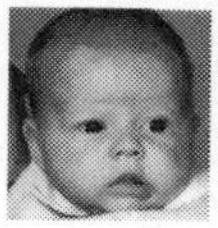

Do keep in mind that this is only a simple example. A table can store any kind of information—inventory, bookkeeping, accounts payable, receivables—just about anything that comes to mind. Furthermore, you're not limited to storing just text and numbers. With Paradox for Windows you can store pictures, graphs, even sounds.

Again, regardless of the *type* of information you plan to manage, that information must be stored in a tabular format. As you will see a little later, some data might be organized in several tables.

▶▶ *How Do I Manage a Database?*

Database management is simply the job of managing the information you've stored in tables. Common management tasks include:

- *Adding* new data to a table
- *Editing* data in a table
- *Deleting* data from a table
- *Sorting* a table into some meaningful order
- *Searching* (querying) a table for particular types of information
- *Printing* data from the table into formatted reports and graphs

Consider once more our Rolodex example. Occasionally we may need to *add* some new cards to the Rolodex. We may want to *sort* the cards (say, alphabetically or by zip code) for easy access. We might want to *search* through them and find all the people who live in Los Angeles, or all the people in the 92123 zip code area. Perhaps we just want to find out where Clark Kenney lives. If Clark Kenney moves, we may want to change (*edit*) his card to reflect his new address and phone number. (Then again, if Clark Kenney stops paying his dues, we may want to *delete* him from the Rolodex altogether and send our collection agency to recover our money.) We might want to use the data in the Rolodex to *print* various documents, such as mailing labels, form letters, or a directory.

Paradox offers many tools to help you perform these database management tasks. In fact, to simplify your work, these tools let you create *objects* that you can use over and over again to perform repetitive tasks with minimal effort. We'll talk about the various objects that you can create and use with Paradox for Windows in the sections that follow.

▶▶ *About Paradox Objects*

A database consists of many different kinds of objects, not just tables of data. Basically, an *object* is anything you create in Paradox, such as:

- A table
- A data entry form or report

- Any visible (or invisible) part of a form or report
- A graphic image or sound
- A graph
- Data created by other Windows applications, such as Excel or Paintbrush
- A query or question about your data
- A collection of related objects that make up a project
- A piece of Paradox application language code that performs some automatic operation
- Any file on the computer

Some of the more common objects are described below.

▶ Tables

Tables are the most fundamental type of Paradox object because they contain the information you want to manage. Figure 1.4 shows a table with some sample data in it on the Paradox Desktop. You'll get some practice creating a Paradox table in Chapter 2 and learn more of the details in Chapter 3.

FIGURE 1.4 ▶

A sample table on the screen. Though there may be more rows and columns in the table than can fit on the screen, you can use the scroll bars to bring other information into view.

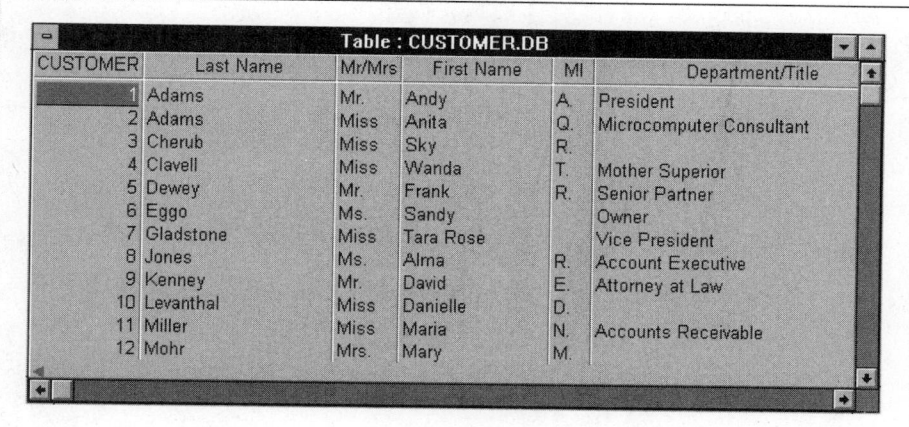

CUSTOMER	Last Name	Mr/Mrs	First Name	MI	Department/Title
1	Adams	Mr.	Andy	A.	President
2	Adams	Miss	Anita	Q.	Microcomputer Consultant
3	Cherub	Miss	Sky	R.	
4	Clavell	Miss	Wanda	T.	Mother Superior
5	Dewey	Mr.	Frank	R.	Senior Partner
6	Eggo	Ms.	Sandy		Owner
7	Gladstone	Miss	Tara Rose		Vice President
8	Jones	Ms.	Alma	R.	Account Executive
9	Kenney	Mr.	David	E.	Attorney at Law
10	Levanthal	Miss	Danielle	D.	
11	Miller	Miss	Maria	N.	Accounts Receivable
12	Mohr	Mrs.	Mary	M.	

Table : CUSTOMER.DB

▶ *Forms*

Adding new data to a table and editing and deleting existing data are common database management tasks. You can add, edit, and delete data directly in a table such as the one shown in Figure 1.4.

You can also create fancy custom *forms* to enter table data on a record-by-record basis. You can even design forms that look like the paper forms that hold the information before it is entered into the table. For example, Figure 1.5 shows a customized form for entering and editing customer information. You'll learn to create custom forms in Chapters 10 and 11.

▶ *Reports*

Another common Paradox object is the *report*. Whereas the term "forms" generally refers to information that is displayed on-screen, the term "report" generally refers to printed information.

There is virtually no limit to the number of ways in which you can organize information in a report. You can print lists, invoices, reports with

FIGURE 1.5

A custom form for entering and editing data one record at a time

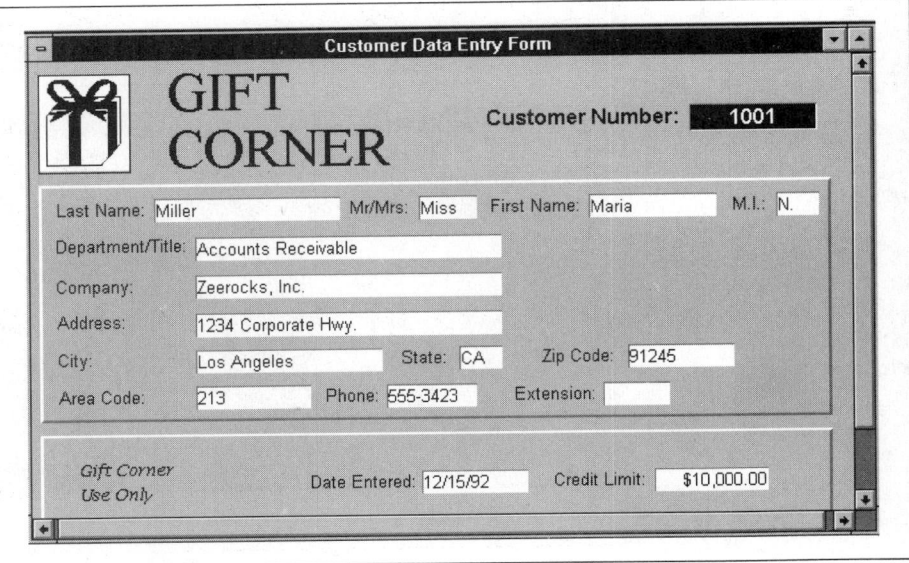

totals and subtotals, and so forth. You can even use Paradox to print form letters and mailing labels. Figure 1.6 shows some mailing labels created from the sample customer information table. Figure 1.7 shows a sample form letter printed for a customer in the table. You'll learn how to design and create reports, form letters, and mailing labels in Chapters 10, 11, and 12.

FIGURE 1.6

A report is any information printed from one or more tables. This sample report contains information organized as mailing labels.

Andy Adams
ABC Corporation
123 A St.
San Diego, CA 92122

Anita Adams
5434 Oceanic Way
Silver Spring, MD 20910

Sky Cherub
Oneness Well-Being
985 Enlightenment Way
Jefferson, SD 57038

Wanda Clavell
Westridge Convent
452 Reposo Alto
Tiverton, RI 02878

Frank Dewey
Dewey, Cheatham, and Howe
1121 Cass St, Suite 33
Bothell, WA 98011

Sandy Eggo
Pancho's Restaurant
911 Delaware Ave.
Roswell, NM 88201

Tara Rose Gladstone
Waterside Landscaping
377 Avenue of the America
New York, NY 12345

Alma Jones
Ashland Flowers
10 Shakespeare St.
Ashland, OR 98765

David Kenney
Felson and Fabian
6771 Ocean View Dr.
Anderson, SC 29621

Danielle Leventhal
Garden State Bagels
765 Tour de Force Way
Newark, NJ 02321

Maria Miller
Zeerocks, Inc.
1234 Corporate Hwy.
Los Angeles, CA 91245

Mary Mohr
6771 Baldy Vista
Herndon, VA 22071-1234

John Newell
Newell Construction
212 Riverside Way
Bernalillo, NM 88004

Elizabeth Olson
Precision Computer Arts
80486 Mill Street
Marlow, NH 03456

Rigoberto Ramirez
4323 Moonglow Dr.
Wyandotte, OK 74370

Richard Rosiello
Raydontic Labs
P.O. Box 77112
Chicago, IL 60606

Susita Schumack
Physician's Hospital
P.O. Box 11221
Philadelphia, PA 23456

John Smith
65 Overton Hwy, Box 112
Holland, MI 49423

Mary Smith
Cal State L.A.
P.O. Box 1234
Los Angeles, CA 91234

Savitha Smith
Slybacks Paperbacks
767 Ocean View Lane
Ossineke, MI 49766

Janet Smythe
P.O. Box 3384
Seattle, WA 98762

FIGURE 1.7 ▶

A sample form letter for a single record in the customer information table

8891 Gaudy Ave * West Fantasee, CA 92222
1-800-555-GIFT

Gift
Corner

Miss Maria N. Miller   October 18, 1994
Accounts Receivable
Zeerocks, Inc.
1234 Corporate Hwy.
Los Angeles, CA 91245

Dear Miss Miller :

*N*ow that the traditional gift giving season is rolling around once again, all of us at *The Gift Corner* would like to remind you that we offer a unique selection of gifts that are sure to please everyone on your list.

*O*ur new Winter catalog is chock full of great new gift items. For example, you'll find some terrific *Toys for Boys*, including hot new race cars in price ranges that are as torrid as the engines under the hoods of these babies. If you're looking for something a bit more tame, try our *Jungle Creatures Collection* -- stuffed animals that look like the real thing! And Miss Miller, if those on your gift list are itching for a winter getaway, take a look at our *Exotic Vacation Packages*. We'll guarantee some unforgettable memories! We'll even throw in a free camera, film, and developing so those memories will never be lost.

*S*o why not call your Account Representative here at *The Gift Corner* today? We'll send you a complimentary gift, just for picking up the phone and talking to us. You can reach us 24-hours a day, toll-free at **1-800-555-GIFT**. Don't delay...Call us today!

Sincerely yours,
Gondola Claplock
Gondola Claplock
The Gift Corner Customer Relations

▶ *Graphics, Graphic Images, and OLE*

Like all Windows applications, Paradox for Windows can incorporate graphical information as well as text. Paradox for Windows supports three types of graphics:

Graphs and Crosstabs You can cross-tabulate data in a table and display the results in a variety of business graph formats, or as a crosstab. Figure 1.8, for example, shows a crosstab from the sample customer table that answers the question "How many customers do we have in each state and city?"

FIGURE 1.8 ▶

A sample crosstab created by Paradox for Windows. This crosstab quickly and visually answers a question that would otherwise be difficult to answer without tedious manual tabulation.

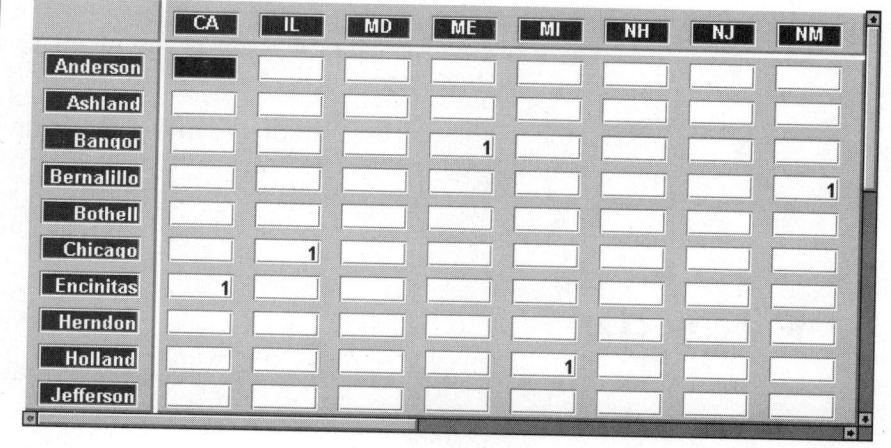

How many customers are in each state and city?

	CA	IL	MD	ME	MI	NH	NJ	NM
Anderson	■							
Ashland								
Bangor					1			
Bernalillo								1
Bothell								
Chicago		1						
Encinitas	1							
Herndon								
Holland					1			
Jefferson								

Graphic Images You can also add graphic images to your tables, forms, and reports. These graphic images may come from a variety of sources, such as clip art, scanned images, and drawing and painting applications. The sample form letter shown in Figure 1.7 included a company logo that is a graphic image.

OLE objects Object linking and embedding (OLE) lets you display and change pictures, charts, sounds, video, and other objects from other Windows products. Chapters 4, 6, 10, and 11 discuss OLE and graphics in detail.

▶ Queries

A *query* is basically a question—a way to find or isolate specific records in one or more tables. For example, with a query you can:

- quickly locate the name and address of a particular person in a table.
- print letters and labels for individuals in a particular city, state, or zip code region.
- print a "reorder report" for inventory items that need to be reordered.
- print a summary of all sales, subtotaled by product or date.
- print reminder letters for customers whose accounts are 30, 60, or 90 days overdue.

There's virtually no limit to the ways in which you can select data from a table in order to isolate the records you need. You'll learn how to query tables in Chapter 9.

Remember, you can use Paradox to manage *any* information—Paradox isn't just for business. For instance, a bird-watcher might create a table to store information about birds, including photos and sounds. Figure 1.9 shows how each "bird" record might appear on a custom form.

▶ Projects

A *project* is a collection of all the objects that make up a particular database.

The objects in a project can be stored in one or more directories on your computer. For example, you could group the tables, queries, reports, custom forms, and report formats for a customer database into a single project. The ***Project Viewer*** window, illustrated in Figure 1.10, shows all the objects in the project and lets you choose which objects to view and work with.

You may hear the terms "table" and "database" used interchangeably, but a database management purist would tell you that it is incorrect to treat the terms as synonyms. A database is actually the sum total of all

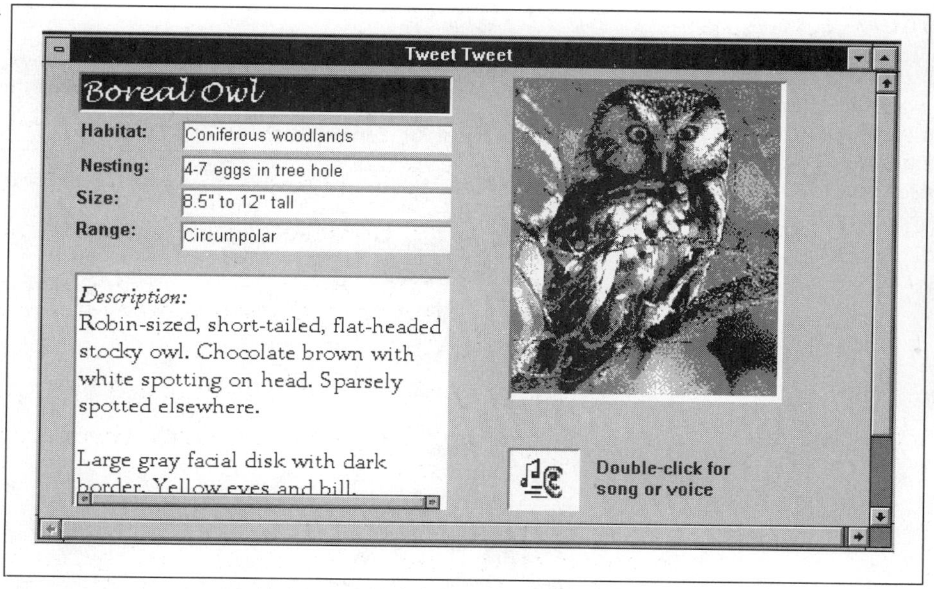

FIGURE 1.9

A custom form displaying a single record for a table of information about birds. Double-clicking the "ear" icon plays a bird song.

the tables, forms, reports, and other objects that make up a single application. Therefore it would be more accurate to define the entire project shown in Figure 1.10 as a database than to refer to any one of its objects as a database.

▶▶ *Managing Multiple Tables*

If you've ever used a word processing or spreadsheet application, you may be thinking that you can do just about anything we've described so far with one of those programs. However, a relational database management system offers some unique capabilities that are not easily duplicated in word processors or spreadsheets.

For one thing, a relational DBMS lets you store information on separate related tables and combine that information on an as-needed basis to get answers to questions and produce complex reports.

FIGURE 1.10 ▶

A sample project containing objects used to manage a customer database. The Tables objects are visible in this example.

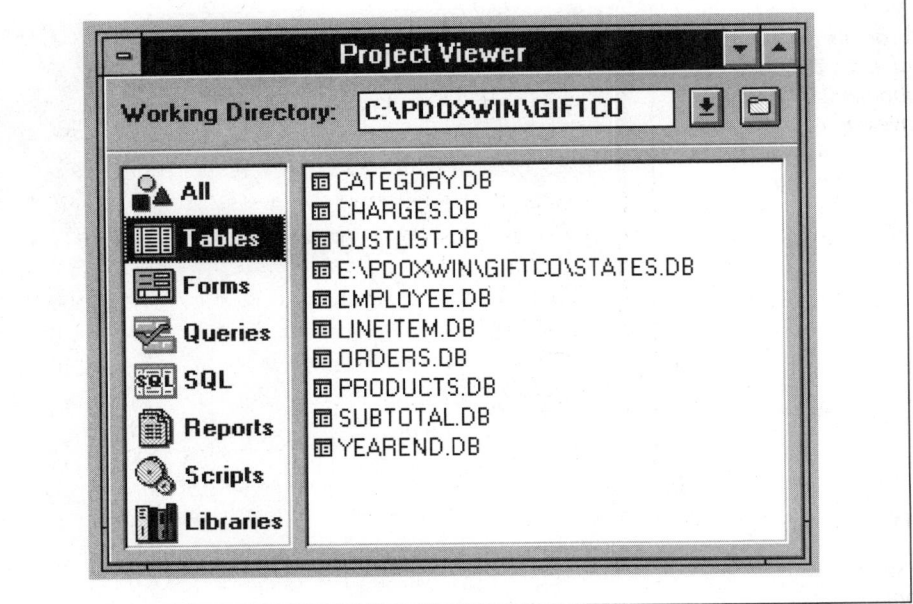

For example, let's say you want to manage an entire mail-order business, including orders, inventory, and customer accounts. These three bodies of information represent three separate entities. Since there is no convenient way to combine all that information into a single table, you would probably want to create three separate tables.

You would need one table, named *Products*, to keep track of what you have in inventory. Figure 1.11 shows an example in which each item in the inventory has a product code (Prod Code), a description, and a unit price. The table also stores the quantity of each item currently in stock. You could add any other information that pertains to products (as indicated by *etc.* in the figure), such as the reorder point, manufacturer information, or whether the product is taxable.

A second table could contain information about customers or accounts. In the example in Figure 1.12, the name and address of each customer is stored in a table.

FIGURE 1.11

A sample table containing information about the current inventory

Products Table

Prod Code	Description	Unit Price	In Stock	etc...
GC-222	Heinz 57 Puppy	150.00	13	
GC-292	White Swan	1249.00	12	
GC-321	Kangaroo	2594.00	24	
GC-360	Cowardly Lion	6422.00	15	
GC-366	Tahoe Paradise Vacation	7200.00	8	
GC-510	Archery Target	500.00	6	
GC-786	Car - Hot	34430.00	56	
GC-983	Laser Printer	4270.00	24	
GC-987	Personal Computer	3665.00	28	

FIGURE 1.12

A sample table of customers. Each customer is assigned a unique customer number (or account number).

Customers Table

Cust No	Last Name	First Name	Address	etc...
1001	Adams	Anthony	123 A St.	
1002	Baker	Barbara	234 Bollinger Way	
1003	Carlson	Cara	P.O. Box 1234	
1004	Davis	Candy	17047 E. St.	
1005	Edwards	Eddie	555 Ocean Pkwy	
1006	Fabian	Francis	6565 Tumbleweed Rd.	
1007	Gomez	Lucy	564 Washington St.	
1008	Hernandez	Harry	22 NE Norfolk Blvd.	
1009	Johnson	George	P.O. Box 2212	
1010	Lawson	Linda	8808 El Camino Real	

Finally, a third table could be used to keep track of orders. In the example shown in Figure 1.13, each record indicates who placed the order (via the customer number), what the customer ordered (via the product number), the quantity ordered, and the date that each order was placed.

Notice how compact the Orders table is. It doesn't waste a lot of disk space by repeating information that is already stored in the Customer

FIGURE 1.13 ▶

A sample table containing information about orders. The Cust No and Prod Code fields indicate who placed the order and what was ordered.

Orders Table

Cust No	Prod Code	Quantity	Date Ordered	*etc...*
1001	GC-222	1	7/1/94	
1001	GC-292	2	7/1/94	
1001	GC-360	1	7/1/94	
1001	GC-987	1	7/1/94	
1003	GC-360	5	7/1/94	
1004	GC-983	2	7/1/94	
1010	GC-366	1	7/1/94	

and Products tables. Instead, it stores only the Customer Number, Product Code, Quantity, and Date of each order.

Because it is a relational database management system, Paradox will let you combine information from these three separate tables, giving you complete flexibility in managing that information and presenting it in whatever format you wish. For example, using the information from these three tables, you could:

- print invoices and packing slips for orders by combining information from the Customer, Products, and Orders tables.

- automatically subtract the quantity of each item shipped from the Products table as orders are fulfilled, so your Products table is always up to date.

- use the Orders table to verify automatically that there are enough items in stock to fulfill the order and, if not, place the order in a "backorder list" table to be fulfilled when the stock is replenished.

You could mix and match information from various tables however you wish in order to manage data and retrieve the information you need.

▶ Building Applications

In addition to letting you manage information from multiple tables simultaneously, Paradox also allows you to develop custom *applications*.

Applications let you automate virtually all the tasks involved in managing a database, reducing even complex tasks to simple mouse clicks.

▶ ▶ N O T E

> **Applications are typically developed by programmers who have mastered the ObjectPAL programming language that comes with Paradox for Windows. Chapter 19 offers a brief introduction to ObjectPAL.**

You might think of an application as a fully automated, and much simplified, project of objects. For instance, whereas the project shown in Figure 1.10 includes all the objects used by a customer database, anyone who wants to work with that database must have some understanding of the objects in the project and how to use them.

One of the real advantages of custom applications is that they can make it easy for someone with no knowledge of tables, forms, reports, or other objects to manage a database. To illustrate this, Figure 1.14 shows the opening screen for a custom application designed to allow staff members to manage customers, inventory, orders, and receivables with ease. Note the simple options in the pull-down menu (Add New Customers, View Customers, etc.). Other options across the menu bar (Inventory, Orders, Receivables, Vendors) could provide other easy-to-use options.

▶ ▶ *For Experienced Users: What's New in Version 5?*

For you old pros who already know what databases and Paradox are all about, we offer this quick summary of new features in Paradox 5 for Windows:

- **Experts** make quick work of complex, mundane tasks.
- **Interactive coaches** help you to learn while doing, by guiding you through a task.

FIGURE 1.14 ▶

The opening screen for a custom application designed to manage a customer database. Users of this application need only choose options from this screen; they do not need to know much about Paradox or database management.

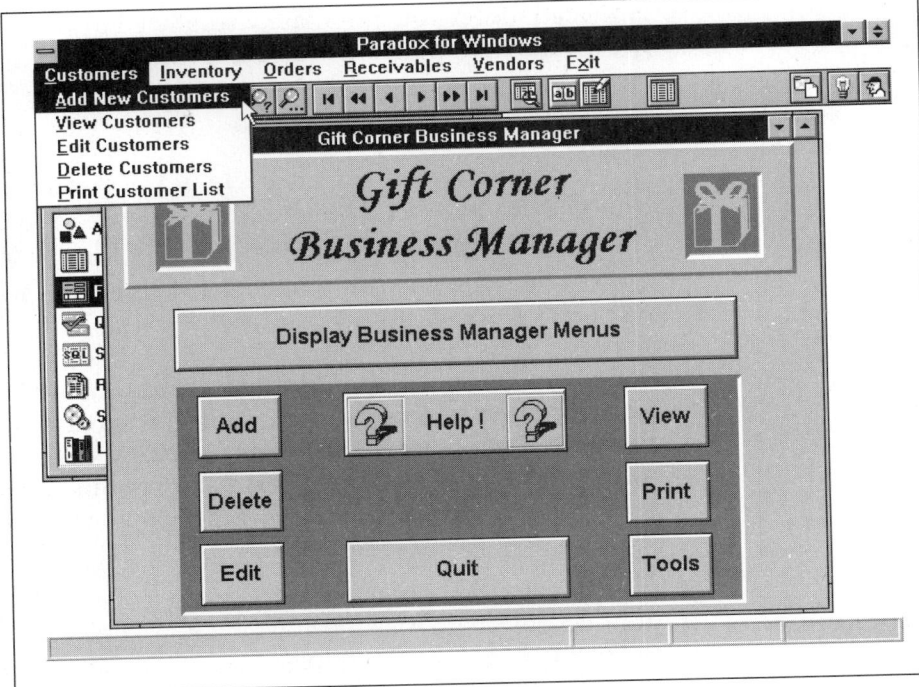

- The new **Project Viewer** lets you manage your Paradox objects visually.

- Paradox 5 for Windows is an **OLE 2.0** client and server.

- New **logical, date/time, autoincrement,** and other field types help simplify managing your data.

- You can now use **aggregate expressions** in forms and reports.

- **Filters** on tables and forms are readily available from the Toolbar. Filters on a single field can be defined with a simple right mouse click. Filters are also available for reports and no longer require a secondary index.

- Answer tables now display **live data** that you can edit on the spot.

- An improved **form and report previewer** makes it easy to format your data.

- **Crosstabs and advanced graphs** are now available in reports.

- The new **data model designer** lets you define your data model independently of forms, reports, and queries.

- You have **SQL connections** to Informix and ODBC databases.

- **Speed!** You can expect better performance in report printing, querying, ASCII import/export, and ObjectPAL.

- Dozens of **ObjectPAL enhancements,** as well as new methods, properties, and general improvements to the Integrated Development Environment (IDE).

This chapter has provided an overview of database terminology and concepts, and a quick glimpse into the many features that Paradox for Windows has to offer. You've seen that Paradox can help you manage *any* kind of information you can store on your computer—text, numbers, graphic images, sound, or data created by other programs—and it can retrieve, display, and print the information in just about any format imaginable. The only requirement is that you define the data as fields and records, which are stored in Paradox tables.

In the next chapter, you'll take Paradox for Windows for a hands-on test drive. In just five short lessons that you can easily complete in an evening, you'll create a table, add some data to it, query and sort the table, customize a data entry form, and print an attractive report of your table's records.

► ► CHAPTER **2**

Paradox for Windows in an Evening: Hands-On

▶▶ *F*AST *T*RACK

▶ ***To start Paradox for Windows***   29

once Paradox is installed on your computer, go to the
Windows Program Manager, double-click the Paradox
for Windows group icon, then double-click the Paradox
application icon.

▶ ***To exit Paradox for Windows***   31

choose File ➤ Exit. If Paradox asks if you want to save before returning to the Windows Program manager, choose
Yes and provide a file name if requested.

▶ ***To create a table***   34

choose File ➤ New ➤ Table, choose OK to accept the
suggested table type, then fill in the Field Name, Type, and
Size for each field of your table. Then choose Save As, type
a valid DOS file name, and choose OK.

▶ ***To open a table***   37

choose File ➤ Open ➤ Table or click the Open Table button
in the Toolbar, if it's available. Then click the name of the
table you want to open and choose OK. You can also click
the Tables icon in the Project viewer and then double-
click the name of the table you want to open.

▶ ***To edit data in a table***   41

switch to Edit mode by clicking the Edit Data button in
the Toolbar or pressing F9. Move the cursor to the field
you want to change, then type in your changes.

▶ ***To undo an editing change***   41

choose Edit ➤ Undo or press Alt+Backspace.

▶ ***To delete a record***   **42**

    move the cursor to the record you want to delete, then press Ctrl+Del.

▶ ***To insert a record***   **42**

    move the cursor to where you want the new record to appear and press Ins.

▶ ***To print a Quick Report of the table***   **42**

    open the table and choose File ➤ Print. Choose any options you want in the Print File dialog box and choose OK.

▶ ***To close a table***   **43**

    double-click the window's Control-menu box or press Ctrl+F4. To close all windows on the Desktop in one step, choose Window ➤ Close All.

▶ ***To create a Quick Form***   **51**

    open the table for which you want to create the form, then click the Quick Form button in the Toolbar.

▶ ***To switch between Form View and Table View***   **59**

    press F7. Or, if you're currently in Form View, click the Table View button in the Toolbar; if you're in Table View, click the Quick Form button.

▶ ▶ **W**hen you're learning Paradox for Windows, the first step is to get a feel for the program and learn how to find your way around. It's like learning the major highways in a new neighborhood before you start exploring the side streets. In this chapter you'll explore the major highways of Paradox for Windows by creating a simple table of names and addresses and using the query, form, and report objects. Once you're familiar with these important objects, subsequent chapters will lead you through the "side streets" of Paradox for Windows.

 ▶▶**T I P**

> For more practice, you can also try out the interactive Coaches that come with Paradox. There's more about Coaches in Chapter 3, but if you'd like to get a head start, choose <u>H</u>elp ➤ Coa<u>c</u>hes whenever you have a few moments to spare.

▶▶ *Before You Begin the Lessons*

Before you begin these lessons, you should already have installed Paradox for Windows on your computer. If you haven't done this, please follow the directions in Appendix A.

Also, you should already have your basic Windows skills down pat—including using a mouse, sizing, moving, opening, and closing windows, using dialog boxes, and so forth. If you're new to Windows, your best bet might be to spend *this* evening learning basic Windows skills. You can use the Windows *Getting Started* manual or some other tutorial, such as my own Windows Running Start book (also published by SYBEX) to do so. Or, for an easy crash course, follow the online Windows tutorial by choosing <u>H</u>elp and then <u>Win</u>-dows Tutorial from the Program Manager menu bar.

►► *Starting Paradox for Windows*

To start Paradox for Windows, follow the steps below.

1. Go to the Windows Program Manager and double-click the Paradox for Windows group icon.

2. Within the group window, double-click the Paradox for Windows application icon (shown at left).

Paradox for Windows

After a brief pause you should see the Paradox for Windows Desktop, looking something like Figure 2.1.

Like most Windows applications, the Paradox Desktop contains a menu bar, a tool bar, a status bar, and the standard Windows Control-menu box, title bar, and Minimize, Maximize, and Restore buttons. You also may see the Project Viewer window.

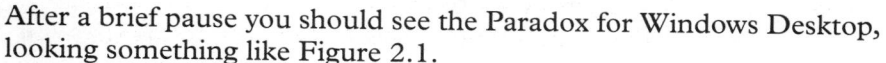

N O T E

In previous versions of Paradox for Windows, the Toolbar was called the *SpeedBar*.

►► *Following Menu Sequences*

Throughout this book, we'll represent a series of menu commands in the format: Choose <u>F</u>ile ➤ <u>W</u>orking Directory.

This is a handy shortcut for "choose File from the menu bar, then choose Working Directory from the pull-down menu." You can use any of the standard Windows techniques to choose menu commands. This means you can click the commands you want with your mouse. Alternatively, you can press the Alt key to highlight the menu bar, then press the underlined letters of the action you want (for example, press Alt, then press **F** for <u>F</u>ile, then press **W** for <u>W</u>orking Directory).

FIGURE 2.1 ▶

The Paradox for Windows Desktop

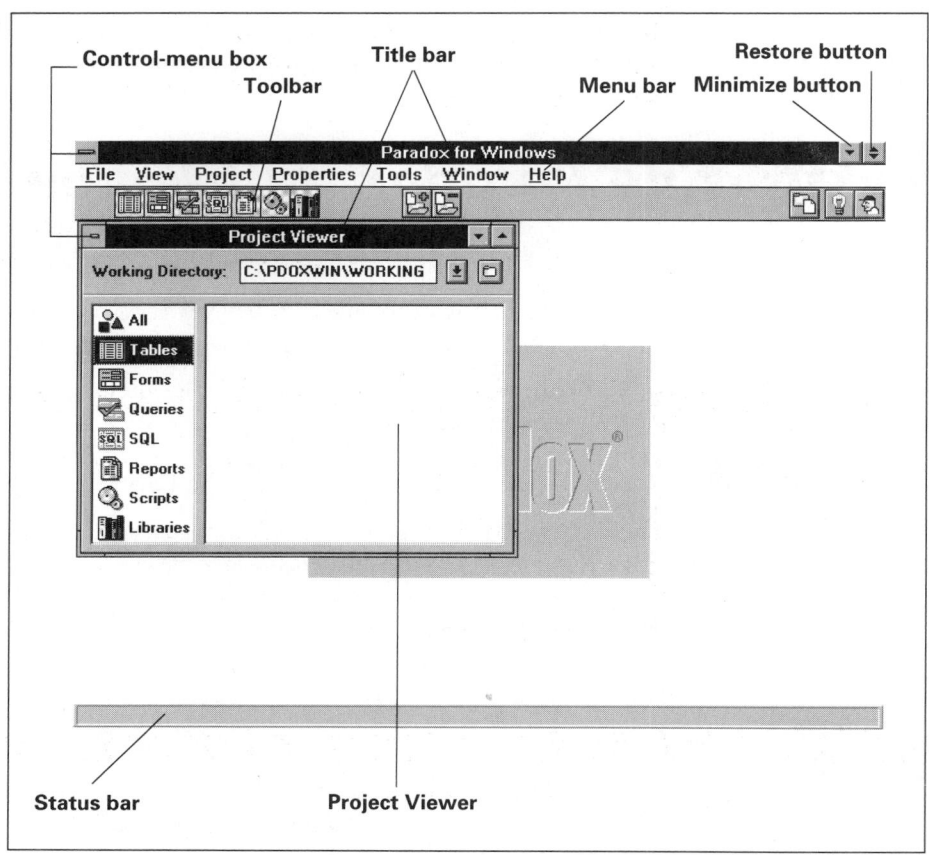

Control-menu box   Title bar   Restore button

Toolbar   Menu bar   Minimize button

Paradox for Windows

File   View   Project   Properties   Tools   Window   Help

Project Viewer

Working Directory: C:\PDOXWIN\WORKING

All
Tables
Forms
Queries
SQL
Reports
Scripts
Libraries

Status bar   Project Viewer

▶▶ *About Clicking and Right-Clicking*

As a Windows user, you're accustomed to clicking the left mouse button to choose menu and dialog box options, select text, click buttons, drag, and so forth. Paradox for Windows uses the left mouse button in all these standard ways.

Paradox for Windows also takes advantage of the *right* mouse button to inspect an object's properties. To inspect a property, you simply move the mouse pointer to an object or a specific part of an object (such as a table column) and click the right mouse button (this is called "right-clicking"). Instantly, you'll see a menu of options relevant to the object you inspected. You can use property inspection to change the color, alignment, or font of a column in a table; to open a menu for a button in the Toolbar; to customize the appearance of a field in a form or report; and much more.

 ►►N O T E

If you have a three-button mouse, be sure to click the far-right button when inspecting properties.

►► *Exiting Paradox for Windows*

If you want to take a break at any time during this brief tour of Paradox, be sure to exit Paradox before turning off your computer. To exit, choose File ➤ Exit. If you've left any unsaved work on the Desktop, Paradox will ask if you want to save before returning to the Windows Program Manager. To save your work, choose Yes and provide a file name if requested.

►► *Lesson 1: Creating a Directory and a Table*

Generally, your first step in setting up a database will be to create a directory in which to store all the tables, reports, forms, and other objects that make up the database. Then you can create a table to store your data. You'll begin your first lesson by creating a new directory using the Windows File Manager.

► *Creating a New Directory*

If Paradox for Windows Desktop is currently on your screen, you can follow these steps to get to the Windows File Manager:

1. Hold down the Alt key and press Tab until the small window for Program Manager appears in the center of the screen.

▶▶**T I P**

You can also use the Task List (Ctrl+Esc) to get to the Program Manager or return to Paradox.

2. Release the Alt and Tab keys to switch to Program Manager.

3. Open the Main group, then double-click the File Manager icon.

4. Click the drive button for the drive that Paradox is stored on (typically c:), then scroll to the *pdoxwin* directory. Alternatively, you can double-click the *pdoxwin* directory name to view the names of any subdirectories. If a subdirectory named *lessons* already exists beneath the *pdoxwin* directory, you cannot create another directory with that same name. Instead, you'll either have to create a directory with a different name (such as *lessons1*) when you get to step 6, or you can skip directly to step 7 where you'll exit the File Manager.

5. With the highlight still on the *pdoxwin* directory name, choose File ▶ Create Directory from File Manager's menu bar.

6. Type in a name, such as **lessons**, and then choose OK.

The new directory name should be listed below the *pdoxwin* directory name, as in the example shown in Figure 2.2.

FIGURE 2.2 ▶

*A new directory named **lessons**, created within the **pdoxwin** directory in File Manager*

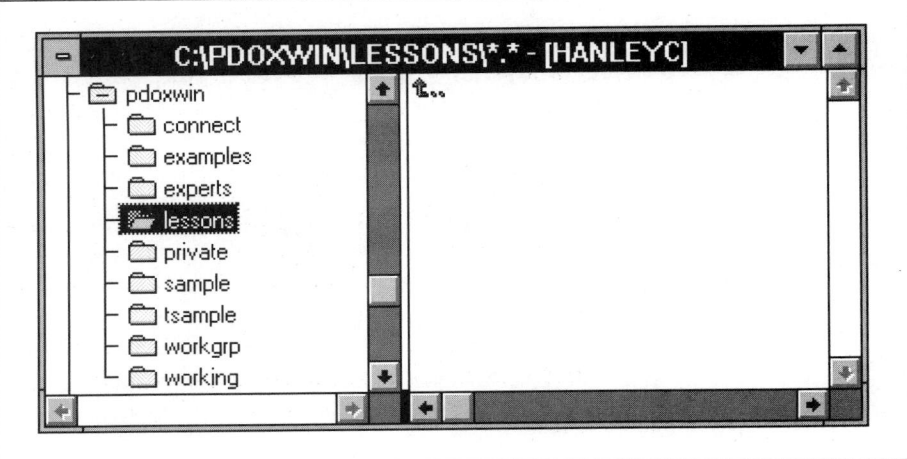

7. Now close File Manager by choosing <u>F</u>ile ➤ E<u>x</u>it from File Manager's menu bar.

8. Hold down the Alt key and press Tab until the small window for Paradox appears in the center of the screen. Then release the Alt and Tab keys to bring the Paradox Desktop to the forefront again.

▶ *Choosing the Working Directory*

Even though you've just created a new directory, you still need to tell Paradox that you want to *use* that directory to store your data. To do so, follow these steps:

1. Choose <u>F</u>ile ➤ <u>W</u>orking Directory from the Paradox menu bar. You'll see the Set Working Directory dialog box.

2. Either type the complete path to your new directory (for example, **c:\pdoxwin\lessons**) or click the <u>B</u>rowse button, double-click on the *pdoxwin* directory name, click *lessons*, and click OK. Either way, you want to make sure the text box beneath <u>W</u>orking Directory shows the complete path to the *lessons* directory you just created, as in the example shown below.

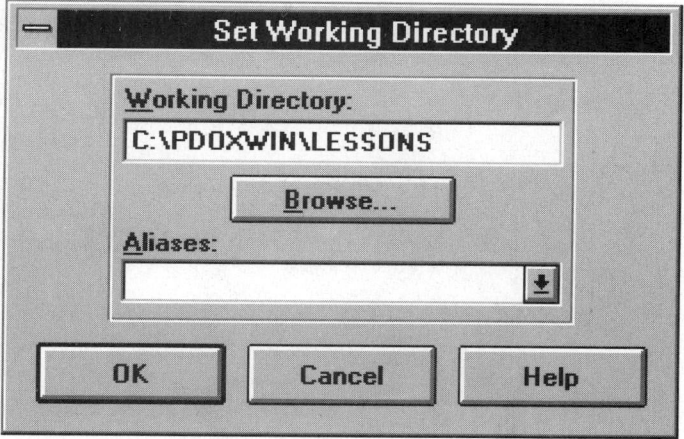

3. Choose OK. (If you see a message asking permission to close all the Desktop windows, choose OK again.)

▶ ▶ N O T E

The OK button will be dimmed and unavailable until you enter a valid path in the Working Directory text box.

▶ Creating a New Table

Now that you've created a new directory for your table and chosen your working directory, you can create a new table. Choose File ➤ New ➤ Table. In the Table Type dialog box that appears, choose OK to accept the suggested table type, Paradox 5 for Windows. You'll be taken to the Create Table dialog box shown in Figure 2.3.

▶ Defining the Fields

Now you're ready to tell Paradox what fields you want to store in this table, the type of data each field can store, and the size of each field. In this example, we'll create a small table for storing names and addresses.

FIGURE 2.3 ▶

Create Table dialog box for defining the structure of a table

Create Paradox 5.0 for Windows Table: [Untitled]

Field Roster:

	Field Name	Type	Size	Key
1				

Table Properties:

Validity Checks

Define...

☐ 1. Required Field

2. Minimum

3. Maximum

4. Default

5. Picture   Assist...

Enter a field name up to 25 characters long.

Borrow...

Save As...   Cancel   Help

Simply follow these steps:

1. Type **Last Name** then press Tab to move to the next column.

2. Now you need to give the field a data type. With the cursor and mouse pointer in the Type column, click the right mouse button or press the spacebar to view a list of available data types. Click the <u>A</u>lpha field type.

▶▶TIP

> **As a shortcut to selecting <u>A</u>lpha from the list of data types, you can just type the letter *A* when the cursor is in the Type column.**

3. Press Tab or ↵ to move to the Size column.

4. Type in a size (**20** will do for the Last Name field).

5. Press Tab or ↵ as needed to skip the Key column and move down to the Field Name column in the next row.

▶▶NOTE

> **Chapter 4 will discuss field types and the role of the key in detail. You need not concern yourself with all of that just yet.**

Following the same basic steps as above, you should be able to fill in the rest of the table structure as shown in Figure 2.4. If you make a mistake, just double-click wherever you need to make a change, use the Backspace and Delete keys to erase text, then type in your correction.

▶▶TIP

> **Notice that we've made *all* the fields the alpha (A) field type, even Zip Code and Phone. This allows you to store hyphens and parentheses in the field, as in 91234-1234 and (619)555-1929.**

FIGURE 2.4 ►

Structure of the sample table we'll be using in these lessons

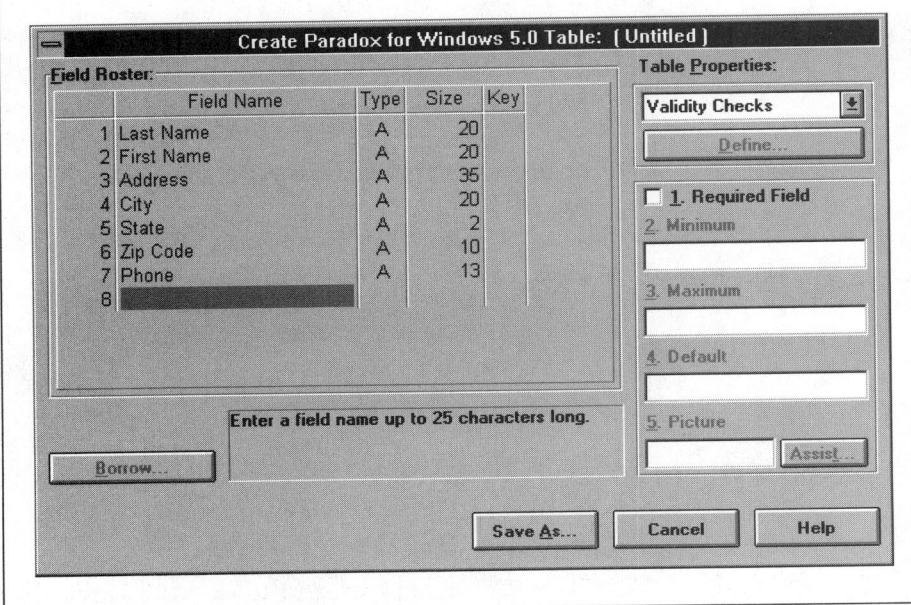

► Saving the Table Structure

Once you've defined all the fields in the table, you can follow these steps to save the table structure and give it a file name:

1. Click the Save <u>A</u>s button near the bottom of the window.

2. In the Save Table As dialog box that appears, type in a valid DOS file name—**mailings** in this example.

3. Choose OK.

Paradox saves the table structure and returns you to the Paradox Desktop.

► Taking a Break

If at any time during these lessons you want to take a break, be sure to exit Paradox before turning off your computer, as described under "Exiting Paradox for Windows," earlier in this chapter.

When you resume the lessons, your working directory will be the same as it was when you exited, and any objects that were open will automatically appear on the Desktop. However, if you share a computer with other users, you may need to choose *\pdoxwin\lessons* again as your working directory. Use the File ➤ Working Directory commands, as described earlier under "Choosing the Working Directory," to do so.

▶▶ *Lesson 2: Adding and Editing Data*

Now that you've created a table, you can start putting some data into it. First, you need to open the table.

▶ *Opening a Table*

To open the table, follow these steps:

1. Choose File ➤ Open ➤ Table, or click the Open Table button in the Toolbar (shown at left).

▶▶ T I P

To find out which button is which on the Toolbar, move the mouse pointer to any button, then look down to the status bar to see the name of the button that the mouse pointer is on.

2. Click on *Mailings.db,* then click the OK button (or double-click *Mailings.db*).

▶▶ T I P

If the Project Viewer window is open, you can open a table by clicking the Tables icon in the left side of the Project Viewer and then double-clicking the name of the table you want to open. To open the Project Viewer, choose Tools ➤ Project Viewer or click the Open Project Viewer button in the Toolbar.

The empty table appears in a Table window, with just the table name and field names across the top. Some fields will be scrolled off the right edge of the screen, as in Figure 2.5.

 ► ►**T I P**

To see as many fields as possible, click the Maximize button or double-click the title bar of the Table window.

FIGURE 2.5 ►

The new Mailings table open on the Desktop

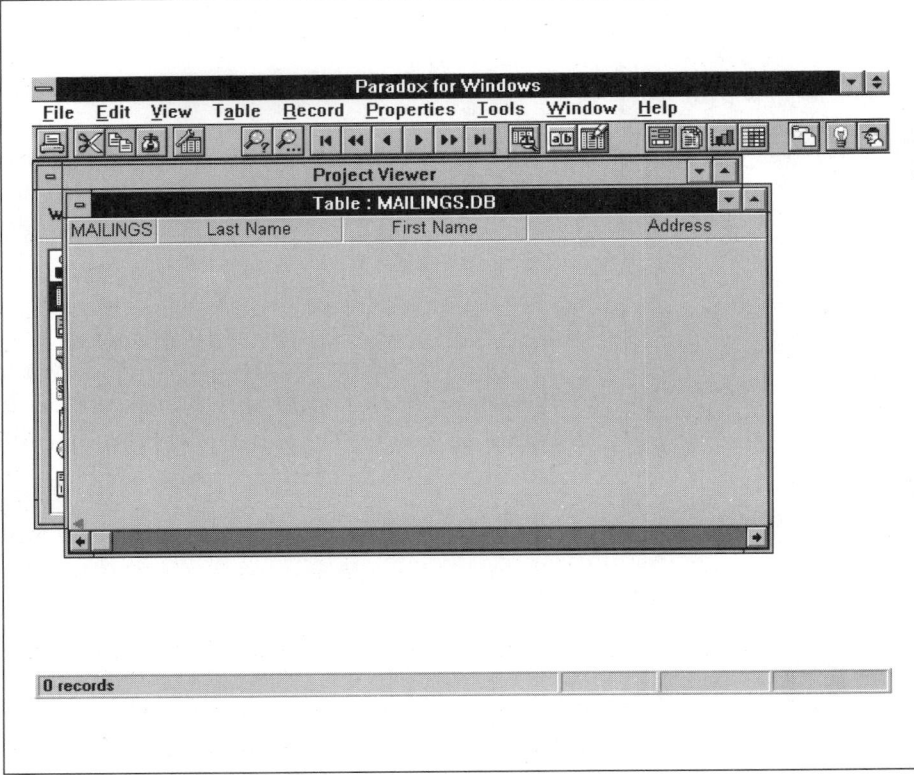

▶ *Adding New Data*

Now let's start typing in some data. If you have a Rolodex or little black book, feel free to use it for examples. Otherwise, you can just enter some fictitious names and addresses. Here's how to get started:

1. When you first open a table, it's in View mode. Before you can add or change data, you need to switch to Edit mode. To do so, click the Edit Data button in the Toolbar (shown at left), or press the F9 key, or choose <u>V</u>iew ➤ <u>E</u>dit Data from the menu bar. The word "Edit" appears down in the status bar when you're in Edit mode.

2. Type a last name, such as **Smith** or the last name of a person from your Rolodex or address book.

3. Press Tab or → or ↵ to move to the next field, or just click the next field.

4. Type in a person's first name, such as **Michael**, then move to the next field.

5. Repeat these steps to fill in the Address, City, State, Zip Code, and Phone fields.

6. After you fill in a phone number, pressing Tab or → or ↵ will automatically move the cursor to the first field of the next record.

Try entering five or ten records on your own now. Figure 2.6 shows some examples you can use. In the figure, we maximized the Table window and used techniques discussed in Chapter 7 to narrow the table columns so that more data is visible at once (you'll probably need to scroll across fields for now, unless you have a monitor that can display all the data without scrolling). Again, feel free to enter any names and addresses you wish.

Here are some pointers that will help you enter records:

*   Be sure to glance at the screen to make sure the cursor is in the correct field before typing your entry. That way you won't accidentally type a person's first name into the Last Name field or a zip code into the City field.

FIGURE 2.6 ▶

*Sample records in the
Mailings table, shown
here on a maximized
window with column
widths adjusted to
display all the data
without scrolling*

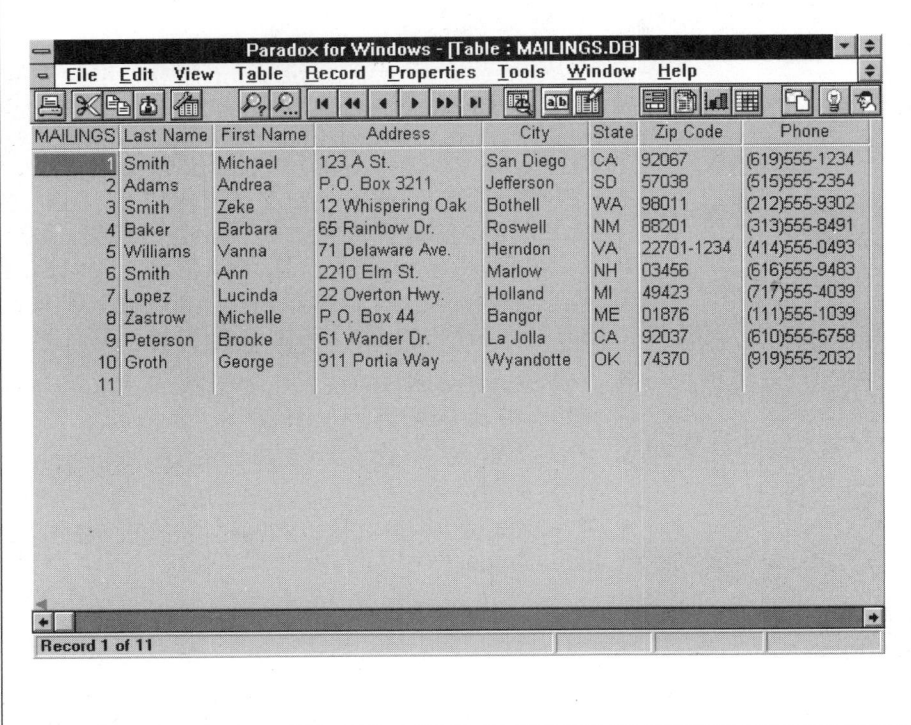

- You can make changes and corrections on the fly using the Back-space key. Or, you can use the various techniques described under "Editing Data," below, to make your changes and corrections later.

- Don't worry about entering data in alphabetical order, or any other order. As you'll see, you can sort the records into any order you want later.

- Don't worry about saving each record. Paradox saves the new data as soon as you finish filling in the fields and move to the next record.

▶ *Editing Data*

Once you've filled in some records, you may find that you need to make changes or corrections. Here are some techniques you can use to do so:

- If Paradox refuses to let you make changes, you're not in Edit mode. Press F9 or click the Edit Data button to switch to Edit mode before trying to make changes.

- To change the contents of a field, first click the field or use the Tab, Shift+Tab, ↑, ↓, ←, →, or ↵ keys to move to the field you want to edit. Then type in your changes.

- You can also use the buttons in the Toolbar to move around in the table, as shown in Figure 2.7.

- When you first move the cursor to a field, the entire field becomes selected (highlighted). Anything you type will instantly *replace* whatever is already in the field. If you want to *change* rather than replace the contents of the field, click the field a second time, or

FIGURE 2.7 ▶

Toolbar buttons for moving around in a table

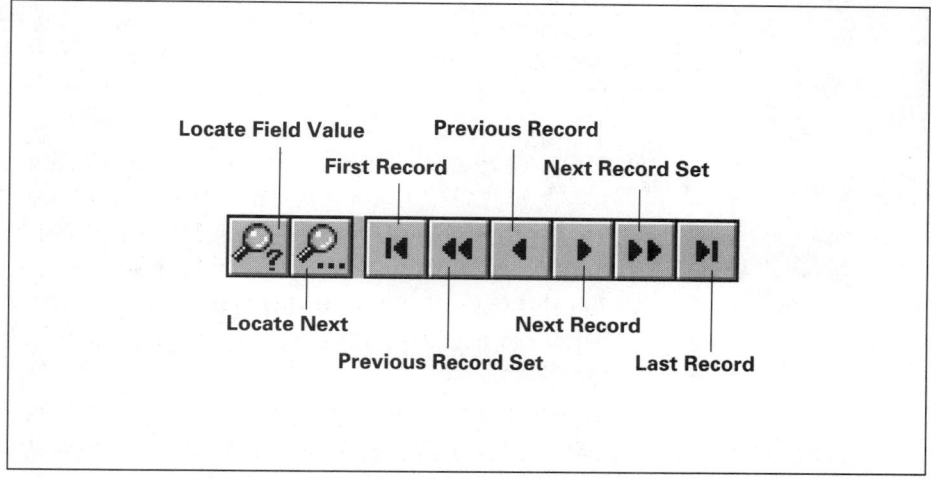

press the F2 key, or click the Field View button (shown at left) to switch to Field View. You can then use the mouse or the ← and → keys to move *within* the field to make changes and corrections. (Press ↵ or Tab when you've finished editing the field.)

> **▶ ▶ T I P**
>
> **Both the Field View button and the F2 key act as toggles, switching you into and out of Field View.**

- If you make a mistake while editing and want to undo your change, choose Edit ➤ Undo or press Alt+Backspace.

- If you want to delete an entire record, move the cursor to the record you want to delete and press Ctrl+Del. (Careful, this operation cannot be undone!)

- To insert a record into the table, move the cursor to where you want to insert a record and press Insert (Ins). The record will be inserted above the cursor.

These pointers should be enough to get any typos or other errors out of your sample table. We'll get into still more editing techniques in Chapter 6.

▶ Printing the Table

You might find it handy to keep a printed copy of your data around while working through the lessons in this chapter. Here's how to print a "Quick Report" of the data you just typed into your table:

1. Choose File ➤ Print to open the Print File dialog box.

2. If you want to print all the fields in the table, choose the Create Horizontal Overflow Pages As Needed option.

3. Choose OK to start printing the report.

After a brief delay a copy of your table will be printed. If the page isn't wide enough to print all the fields, some fields will print on a second page (if you selected the "overflow page" option in step 2).

► Saving and Closing a Table

To close the table, double-click the Control-menu box at the left end of the table's title bar, or press Ctrl+F4.

►►**T I P**

To close all windows on the Desktop at once, including the Project Viewer, choose Window ➤ Close All.

►► Lesson 3: Using a Query

Queries can play several roles in a database. Here we'll look at a few of the most common uses of queries:

- Isolating specific fields to view

- Isolating specific records to view (for example, CA residents or "Smiths")

- Determining a sort order for displaying records, such as alphabetical by name

► Creating a Query

Let's create a query that prints an alphabetized list of names and phone numbers from our Mailings table. Follow these steps to get started:

1. Choose File ➤ New ➤ Query. Or, if it's available, right-click the Open Query button in the Toolbar or the Queries icon in Project Viewer (move the mouse pointer to that button or icon and click the right mouse button); then choose New from the menu that appears.

2. Click the *Mailings.db* file name and choose OK (or just double-click *Mailings.db*).

Paradox: Hands-On

►►

Ch. 2

> ▶▶**N O T E**
>
> **The Open Query button appears in the Toolbar only when all windows (except the Project Viewer) are closed on the Desktop.**

A query window containing columns for each field in the table appears, as in Figure 2.8.

▶ Choosing Fields to View

The first step to filling in a query window is to decide which fields you want to view by marking those fields with checkmarks. Follow the steps below to mark the Last Name, First Name, and Phone fields.

1. Click the empty check box under the Last Name field name. A checkmark appears in the box.

FIGURE 2.8 ▶

A new query window for our sample Mailings table

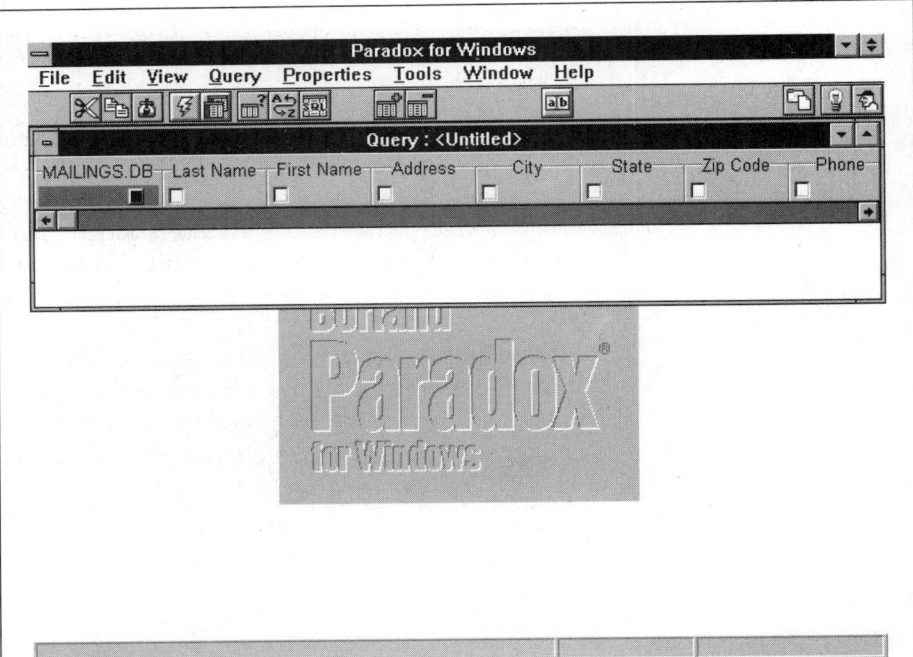

2. Now click the empty check box under the First Name field name.

3. Press Ctrl+End to scroll quickly to the last column, then click the check box under the Phone field.

Figure 2.9 shows the three fields marked with checkmarks. If you can't see all the fields, try widening the window by dragging the right border of the query window.

▶ Choosing Records to View

Suppose you're particularly interested in finding the phone number for a person named Smith. To isolate records with Smith in the Last Name field, follow the steps below.

1. Press Home to move the cursor back to the first column, then press Tab or → to move to the Last Name column (or just click the empty area beneath the Last Name field name).

FIGURE 2.9

Three fields, Last Name, First Name, and Phone, selected for viewing in the query window

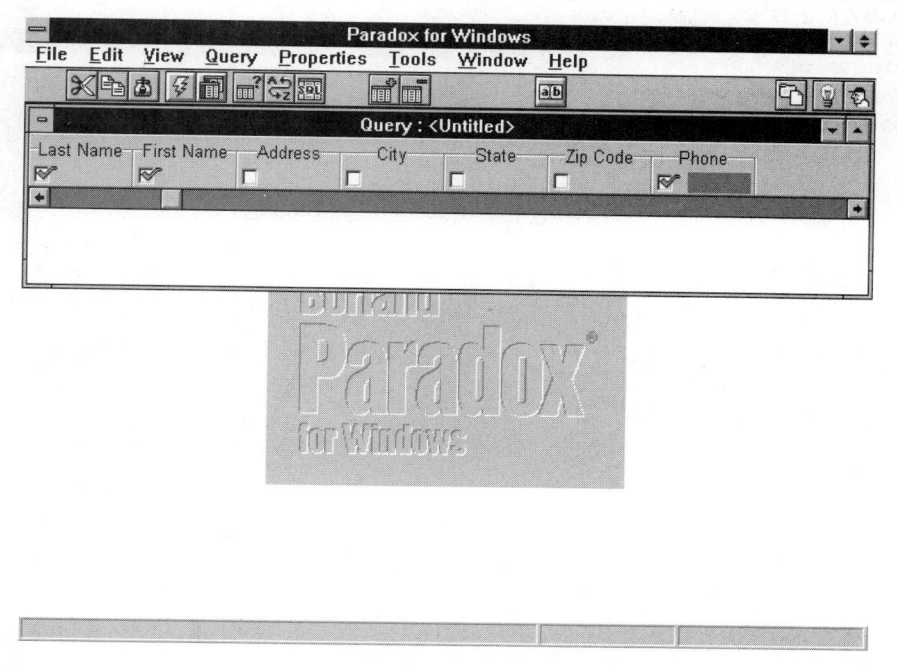

2. Type **Smith** (or some other last name that you know you've stored in your table). Be sure to use the same upper- and lower-case letters you used in the table. For example, don't type **SMITH** or **smith** if you originally entered names with an initial uppercase letter (**Smith**).

Figure 2.10 shows how the query looks with Smith entered in the Last Name column.

► Choosing the Sort Order

Whenever you run a query, the records are automatically sorted by the left-most column. In this case, Last Name is the left-most column, followed by the First Name field. Hence, if we don't do anything else to this query window, records will be sorted (alphabetized) by Last Name.

FIGURE 2.10 ►

This query will now display the Last Name, First Name, and Phone fields of records that have Smith in the Last Name field.

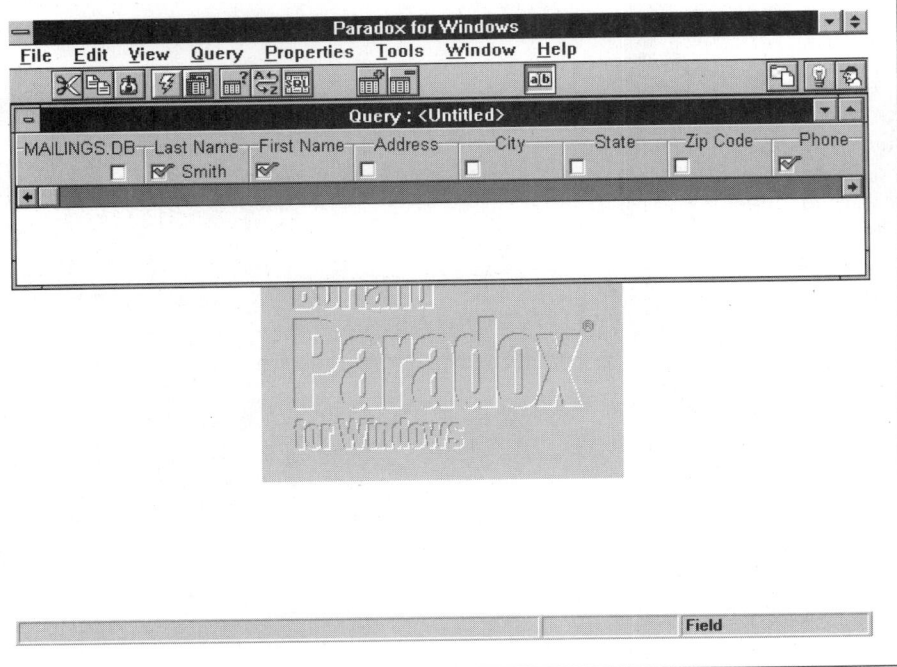

Just so you know how to control the sort order of records in a query, we'll sort records by Last Name and then by First Name. Follow these steps:

1. Choose Properties ➤ Answer Sort. You'll see the Sort Answer dialog box.

2. In the Available fields list, click on *Last Name*, then click the button with the → symbol on it (or just double-click *Last Name*).

3. Click the button with the → symbol on it again to move the highlighted First Name field name over to the Sort By list. Now the dialog box should look like this:

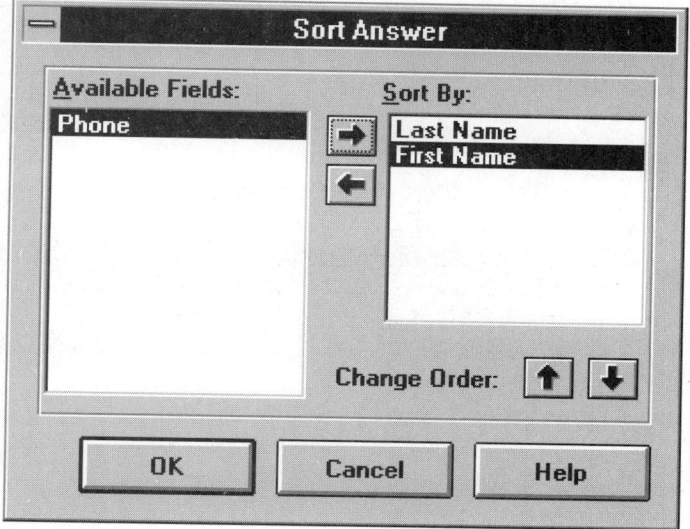

4. Because Last Name is listed first in the Sort By list, records will be alphabetized by people's last names. The First Name field will act as a tie breaker, meaning that records with identical last names will be alphabetized by first name (for example, Smith, Ann comes before Smith, Michael, which comes before Smith, Zeke).

5. Choose OK to return to the query window.

▶ ▶ **T I P**

> There are lots of ways to control the sort order of records in a table, as you'll learn in Chapter 8.

▶ Running the Query

Now let's see what the query comes up with.

1. Click the Run Query button (shown at left), or choose View ▶ Run Query, or press F8.

2. The results of the query appear in a new table named *Answer.db*, as shown in Figure 2.11.

As requested, the Answer table displays only the Last Name, First Name, and Phone fields, and only the Smiths, alphabetized by first name.

FIGURE 2.11 ▶

The results of a query appear in a table named **Answer.db**.

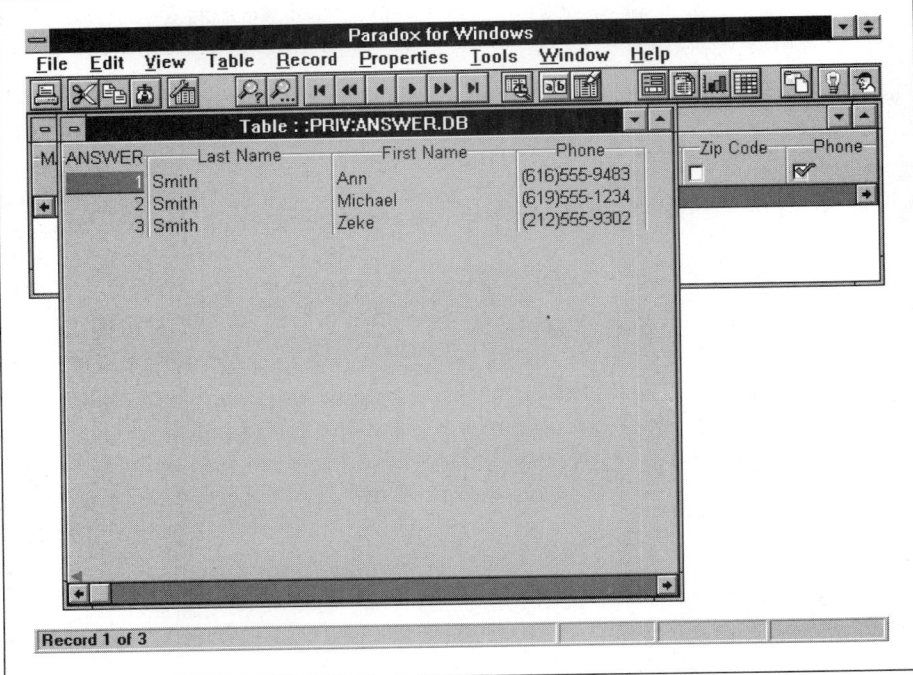

▶ Changing the Query

Now let's modify the query so that it displays an alphabetized list of all the names and phone numbers in the table.

1. If it's visible, click on the title bar for the Query window (on Query:<Untitled>), or press Ctrl+F6 as needed, or choose <u>W</u>indow and select *Query:<Untitled>* from near the bottom of the menu.

2. Scroll (if necessary) to the Last Name column, then double-click on the name Smith (or whatever name you put there).

3. Press the Backspace and Delete keys as necessary to erase Smith. Make sure the Last Name field still contains a checkmark—you just want to remove any text in that column.

4. Now run the query again by clicking the Run Query button or by pressing F8.

This time the Answer table looks like Figure 2.12. Again, records are alphabetized by name, and only the Last Name, First Name, and Phone fields appear. However, since we removed *Smith* from the query, the results of the query display all the records in the table—not just the Smiths.

▶ Printing the Answer Table

If you'd like a quick printed copy of this phone list, just follow the same steps you used to print the Mailings table. That is, make sure the Answer table is selected and appears as the front-most open window (if necessary, click the Answer table's title bar or press Ctrl+F6). Choose <u>F</u>ile ➤ <u>P</u>rint from the menu bar, then choose OK from the dialog box that appears.

▶ Saving the Query

You may want to print an updated phone list from time to time. Rather than re-creating this query each time, you can save it now and reuse it

Paradox: Hands-On

Ch. 2

FIGURE 2.12 ▶

The Answer table after removing Smith

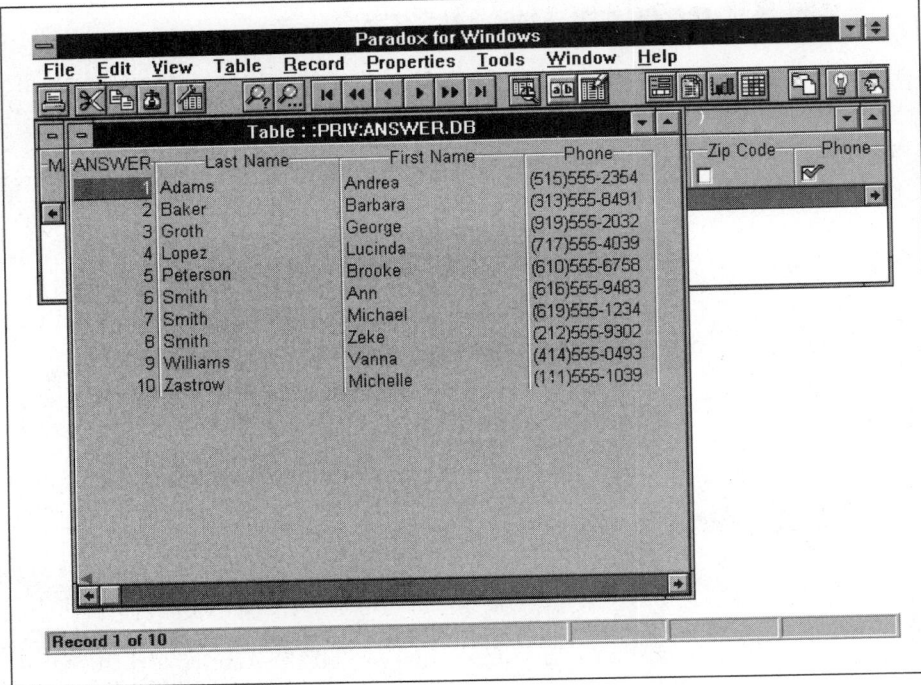

later. To save the query, follow the steps below.

1. Choose Window ➤ Close All. A dialog box will ask if you want to save the new query.

2. Choose Yes.

3. Enter a valid DOS file name, such as **phonelst**, and then choose OK.

The query, Answer table, and Project Viewer windows are removed from the Desktop, but your query is now stored on disk, with the file name *Phonelst.qbe* in this example.

If you add, delete, or change records in the Mailings table, and then run this saved query again, the Answer table produced will reflect any changes you made to the table. Thus, you can use the query as often as you wish.

▶ ▶ **N O T E**

To reuse an existing query, click the Toolbar's Open Query button, or choose File ➤ Open ➤ Query. Click the View Data option at the bottom of the Select Query dialog box, then click the name of the query you want to use and choose OK. The query will run on the latest data in your table. Choose Window ➤ Close All to tidy up the Desktop when you're done.

Though we've just experimented with some of the most frequently used features of queries, there's much, much more you can do with them. For more information on queries, please see Chapter 9.

▶ ▶ **N O T E**

In Chapter 9 you'll also learn about *filters*, which temporarily filter out unwanted data in a table so that you can focus on viewing or updating certain records only. For example, you could set up a filter that shows only the "Smiths" in your Mailings table. After updating the Smith records, you could turn off the filter and see all the records once again.

▶ ▶ *Lesson 4: Creating and Using a Form*

A *form,* in the Paradox sense of the word, is like the fill-in-the-blanks paper forms you use in the "real world," such as tax forms and order forms. A Paradox form, however, lets you view and change data right on your computer screen. In this lesson, you'll learn some of the basics of creating your own Paradox forms. Here's how to begin:

1. Open your Mailings table by clicking the Open Table button, or by choosing File ➤ Open ➤ Table.

2. In the dialog box that appears, click on the *Mailings.db* table name, then choose OK.

3. To create your Quick Form, click the Toolbar's Quick Form button (shown at left).

The new form appears on the Desktop. To see both the Mailings table and the form, as in Figure 2.13, choose Window ➤ Cascade.

Notice that the form displays the fields for the current record only. To scroll through records, you can press the PgUp and PgDn keys or use the scrolling arrows in the center of the Toolbar. To scroll from field to field within the form, use the ↑, ↓, Tab, Shift+Tab, and ↵ keys.

If you want to change an item of data that appears in the form, remember to switch to Edit mode first. You can click the Edit Data button or press F9 to do so.

FIGURE 2.13

A quick form on the Desktop

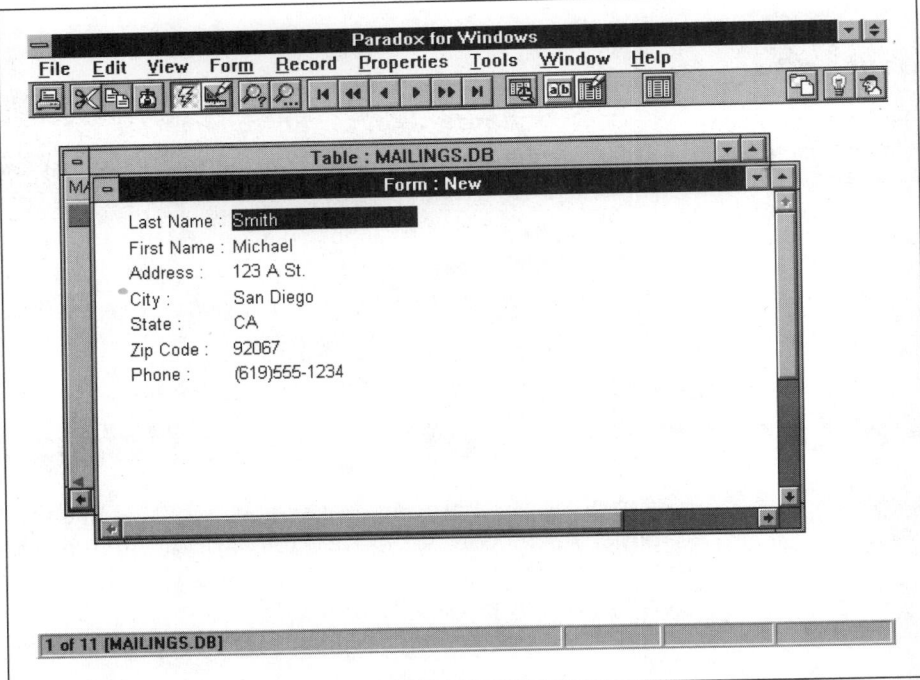

▶ *Printing a Form*

If you'd like to print a copy of the record that currently appears in the form, choose File ➤ Print, and choose OK in the Print File dialog box that appears.

▶ *Customizing the Form*

Paradox for Windows' simple black and white default form may do the trick for you. However, if you'd like to try customizing this form, follow these steps:

1. Click the Toolbar's Design button (shown at left). You'll be taken to the Form Design window, shown in Figure 2.14. You can maximize this window or resize it to make it larger if you wish.

FIGURE 2.14 ▶

The Form Design window maximized on the screen

Paradox for Windows - [Form Design : New *]

File Edit View Form Design Properties Tools Window Help

Last Name :
First Name :
Address :
City :
State :
Zip Code :
Phone :

#Form1 [Form]

2. Now let's try giving this form a real 3D "Windows" look. First, choose <u>P</u>roperties ➤ Designer.

3. Take a look at the <u>S</u>elect From Inside option that appears under Design Preferences in the dialog box. If that option isn't already selected (checked), click to select it. If <u>S</u>elect From Inside is already checked, leave it as is.

4. Similarly, make sure the <u>F</u>rame Objects option is selected (checked). If it isn't, select it now.

5. Choose OK.

The Select From Inside option affects how objects on the screen are selected when you click them. Notice how each field on the design form has a large frame around it and a smaller field within (thanks to the <u>F</u>rame Objects option). When you checked <u>S</u>elect From Inside above, you told Paradox to select the inner box when you first click within the frame. This is just a convenience for our current exercise, and we'll discuss it in more detail in Chapter 10. For now, let's just keep working on our customized form.

1. Move the mouse pointer anywhere within the empty box to the right of the Last Name field name, then click the mouse button. You should see sizing handles around that inner box, as shown below.

2. Now hold down the Shift key, and don't let go until we tell you to.

3. Carefully click within the inner, empty box for each of the remaining fields. You want to select all those inner boxes so your form looks like Figure 2.15. (Keep that Shift key held down!)

FIGURE 2.15

The inner frames of all the fields selected by clicking each while holding down the Shift key

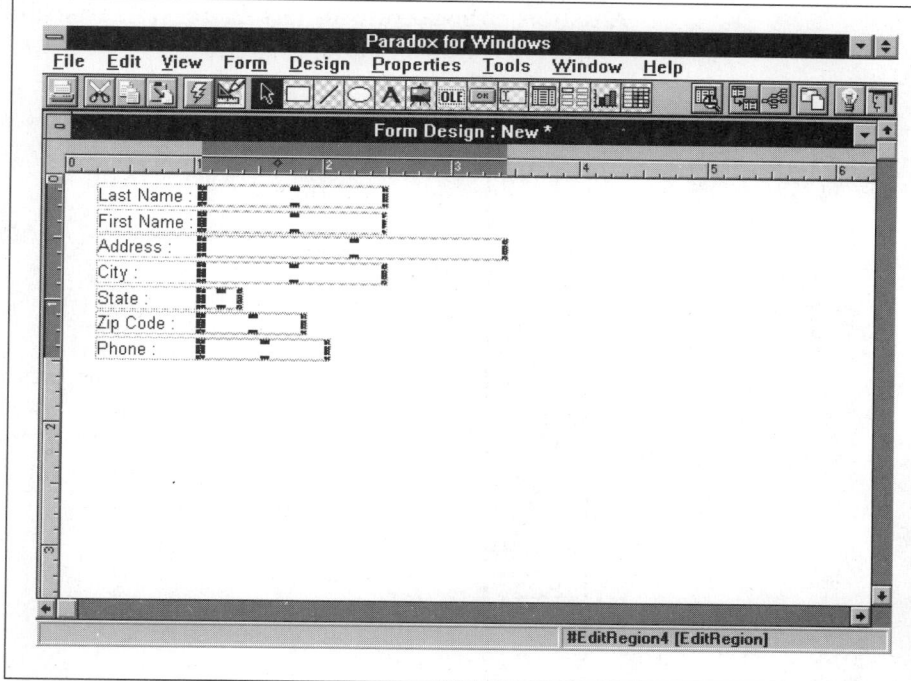

▶▶ NOTE

If you make a mistake and click the wrong box, simply click just outside all the boxes and start again at step 1 above.

4. Once all the fields are selected, release the Shift key.

5. Move the mouse pointer *inside* any selected box, then click the *right* mouse button. A menu with the title *#EditRegion* should appear on your screen.

6. Choose Frame ➤ Style from the #EditRegion menu.

7. Choose the second-to-last frame style from the options that appear, as shown below.

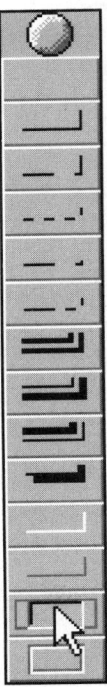

8. With the mouse pointer still *inside* any selected box, click the right mouse button again, then choose *Color*.

9. Click the *white* color in the palette that appears.

The changes might not be obvious yet, but you'll notice them in a moment, when we add some background color to this form.

1. Move the mouse pointer away from all the fields, perhaps over near the lower-right corner of the Form Design window (but not outside the window).

2. Click the right mouse button. You should see the menu shown below.

3. Choose *Color*, then select any color that suits your fancy from the options that appear. (The light blue-green and the pale gray work nicely.)

The form takes on the color you selected, and the fields appear with their 3D frames.

TIP

If you don't like the new color of the form, simply repeat the steps above, choosing a different color in step 3.

Now it's time to view your finished form. Here's how:

• Switch to View mode by clicking the View Data button in the Toolbar (shown at left), or pressing F8, or choosing <u>V</u>iew ➤ <u>V</u>iew Data.

Your form should now be whatever color you selected, with the fields you selected earlier sporting that embossed Windows look, as in Figure 2.16.

This way of doing things takes some getting used to, but once you get a little more practice, you'll wonder how you ever got along without Paradox for Windows! If you experienced any problems, or just want more information, see Chapters 10 and 11.

FIGURE 2.16

The form after coloring it and giving individual fields an embossed look

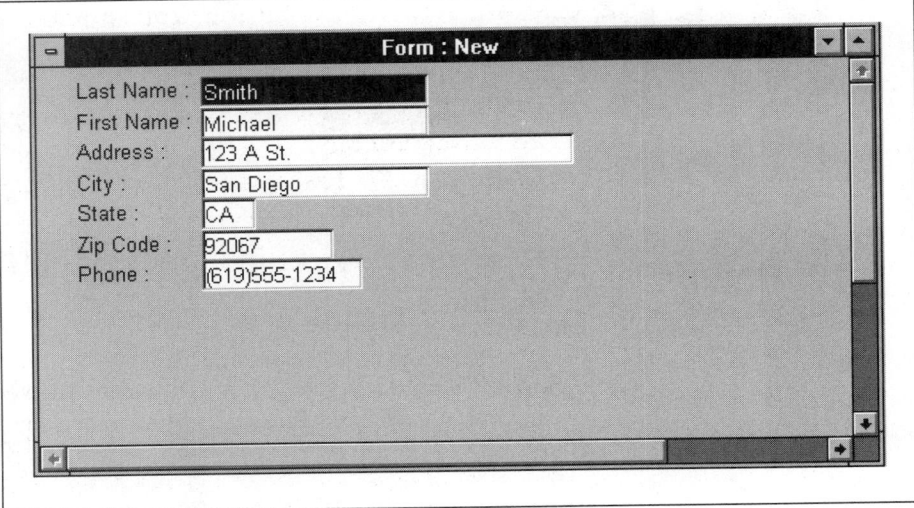

▶▶**TIP**

Here you've used the Quick Form button to create a form. Paradox also offers "Experts," which help you create forms by asking you a series of questions. See Chapters 10 and 11 for details.

▶ Saving Your New Form

To save your new form, just close it and give it a name.

1. Choose <u>W</u>indow ➤ Close <u>A</u>ll, or double-click the Form window's Control-menu box, or press Ctrl+F4.

2. Choose <u>Y</u>es when asked about saving the form.

3. Type a valid file name such as **3d-form** and then choose OK.

N O T E

> Paradox files follow the standard DOS naming
> conventions. Normally, however, you should not specify
> an extension when saving a Paradox file. Paradox
> assigns the file name extension automatically based on
> the type of file you're saving.

▶ Reusing Your Custom Form

You can reopen your custom form at any time by following these steps:

1. From the Paradox desktop, click the Open Form button in the Toolbar (if it's available), or choose File ➤ Open ➤ Form, or click the Forms icon in the Project Viewer window.

2. Double-click the form name, *3d-form.fsl* in this example.

▶ Switching between Form View and Table View

Sometimes you'll want to view a single record on a form. Other times, however, you'll want to view multiple records in your table. It's easy to switch back and forth from Form View to Table View.

- If you're currently viewing data in a form (Form View), click the Table View button in the Toolbar or press F7.

- If you're currently viewing data in Table View, click the Quick Form button in the Toolbar, or press F7 again, to switch back to Form View.

- You can also click any visible portion of the Table View or Form View window to switch between the two windows.

When you want to clean up the Desktop, choose Window ➤ Close All, or close each window individually.

▶▶ *Lesson 5: Creating a Report*

The quick report you saw in Lesson 2 can be useful for double-checking the accuracy of data you entered in a table or for printing the results of a query. But for fancier jobs like mailing labels, invoices, subtotals, and so forth, you'll need to use *reports*.

In this lesson, you'll start out with a fairly simple report, a phone list, that's based on the query you saved in Lesson 3. When you're ready to design more sophisticated reports, you can explore Chapters 10 through 13, and Chapter 17.

 ▶▶**NOTE**

> **In Lesson 2 you printed a quick report by choosing File ➤ Print from the menu bar. You can also create a quick report by clicking the Quick Report button in the Toolbar. Then, when the Quick Report appears on screen, you can switch to Design view and customize the design using techniques you learned in Lesson 4.**

Here's how to get started on the phone list:

1. If you're starting from the Desktop, you can right-click the Toolbar's Open Report button or the Project Viewer's Reports icon (shown at left) and choose <u>N</u>ew. Alternatively, choose <u>F</u>ile ➤ <u>N</u>ew ➤ <u>R</u>eport from the menu bar.

2. In the New Report dialog box that appears, click <u>D</u>ata Model/ Layout Diagram. The Data Model dialog box will open.

 ▶▶**TIP**

> **Paradox also offers a Report Expert and Labels Expert to help you create pre-designed reports and labels quickly. See Chapter 12 for more about these handy tools.**

3. Click the drop-down arrow just below the Type box, then click *<Queries>* to base your report on a saved query instead of a table. Your screen will resemble Figure 2.17.

4. Click on the *Phonelst.qbe* query name, then click OK.

FIGURE 2.17

The Data Model dialog box after selecting <Queries> from the Type list box. In Paradox, you can base your reports on tables, queries, or saved data models.

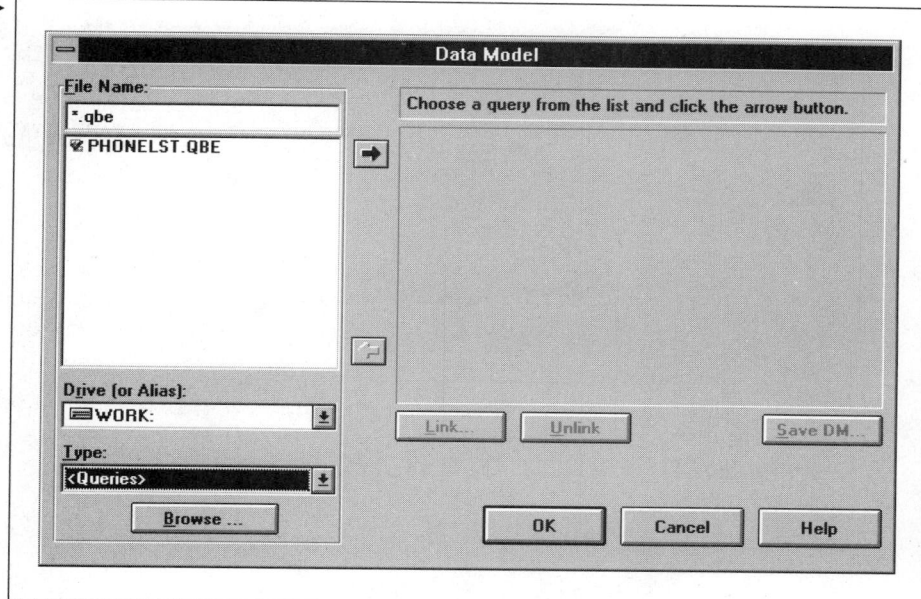

▶ Choosing a Design Layout

The Design Layout dialog box appears next. As shown in Figure 2.18, this dialog box shows a sample layout of your report. You can use the options and buttons in the Design Layout dialog box to change the initial layout, or you can just stick with the default choices.

For many reports, including our sample phone list, the defaults are just fine, so click OK to accept the basic design layout. When the Report Design window appears, maximize it by clicking the Maximize button or double-clicking the title bar.

FIGURE 2.18 ▶

The Design Layout dialog box

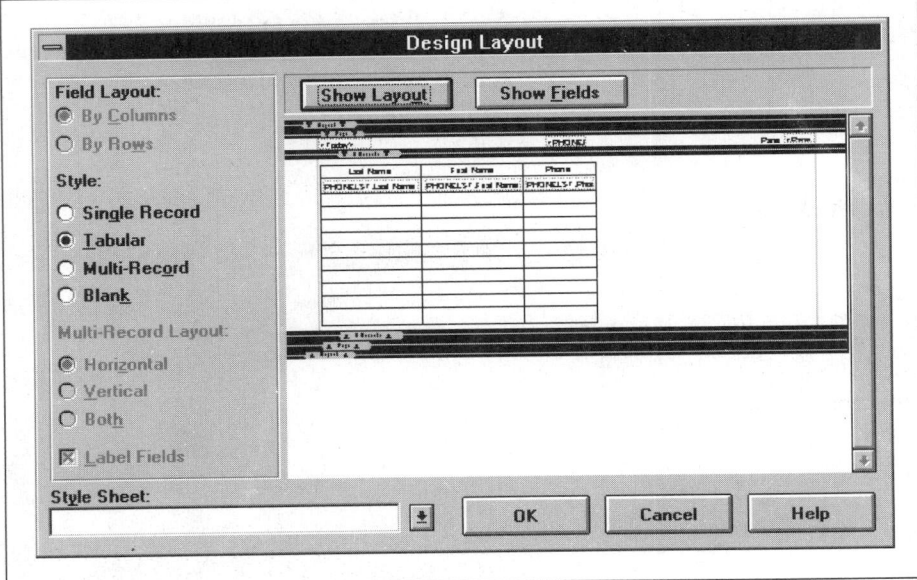

▶ Customizing the Report

The Report Design window is almost the same as the Form Design window, but with one major difference: The Report Design window includes report bands, which define the various sections of your report. Figure 2.19 shows the maximized Design Window with the report bands clearly visible.

▶▶TIP

If the report bands aren't obvious in the Report Design window on your screen, choose _Properties_ ➤ _Band Labels._

Paradox for Windows automatically adds the following bands to your report:

Report band Controls what prints at the beginning and end of the report.

FIGURE 2.19

The Report Design window with band labels visible

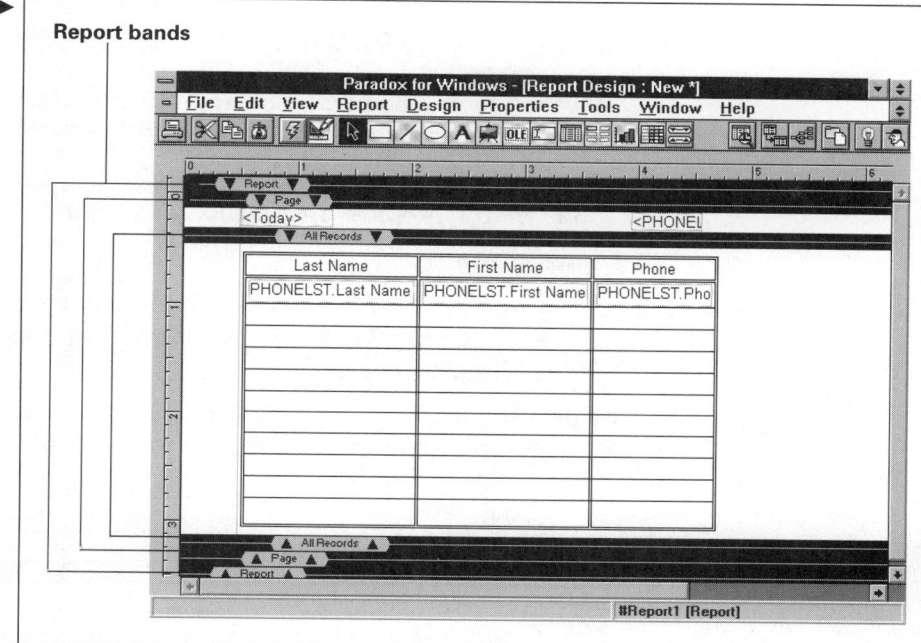

Page band   Controls what prints at the top and bottom of each page. Initially, Paradox places a special field for the date at the top-left of each page, the table or query name at the top-center, and the page number (preceded by the word *Page*) at the top-right of each page (you can use the horizontal scroll bar to see the page number information).

Record band   Controls what prints in the body of the report.

You can place any text and objects you wish in any band of the report.

NOTE

In Chapter 12 you'll learn about *group bands*, which are used to group and subtotal records in a report.

Now let's add some color to the table in the record band and give it a 3D appearance. Here's how:

1. Move the mouse pointer to an empty area in the table, below the column headers and field names but within the borders of the table.

2. Click the right mouse button to inspect the properties of the table. You'll see the property menu shown in Figure 2.20.

3. Choose *Color*.

4. If your printer can print in color, choose a pastel color from the palette. Otherwise, choose the light gray color in the second row of the second column.

5. Inspect the table again by right-clicking as in step 2 and choose Grid ➤ Grid Style ➤ 3D from the property menu.

FIGURE 2.20 ▶

The property list that appears when you inspect the properties of a table

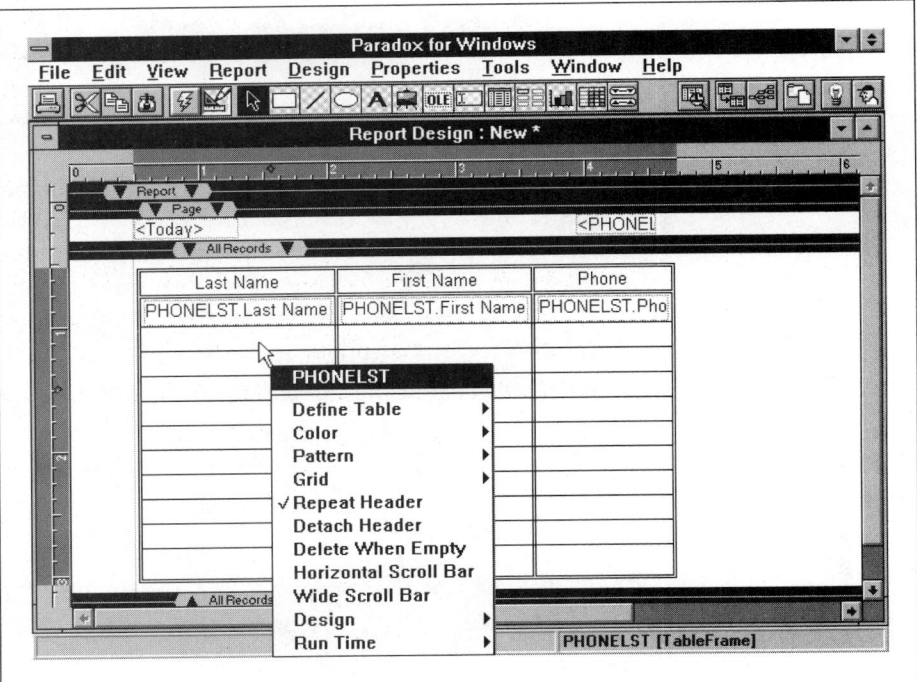

6. Inspect the table once more and choose Grid ➤ Record Divider from the property menu. You won't see an obvious change on the screen right now; however, choosing this option will place a horizontal line between records when you view or print the report.

Now change the table headings to a bold font by following these steps:

1. Click the *Last Name* heading at the top of the table's first column. Selection handles will appear around the frame.

2. Now depress the Shift key while clicking the *First Name* and *Phone* headings at the top of the second and third columns of the table. Release the Shift key when you've selected all three headings.

3. Move the mouse pointer inside any of the selected areas (remember, the pointer must be *inside* the selection handles), then click the right mouse button to open the text property menu shown in Figure 2.21.

4. Choose Font ➤ Style ➤ Bold from the property menu.

Paradox: Hands-On

Ch. **2**

FIGURE 2.21

The text property menu and selected headings

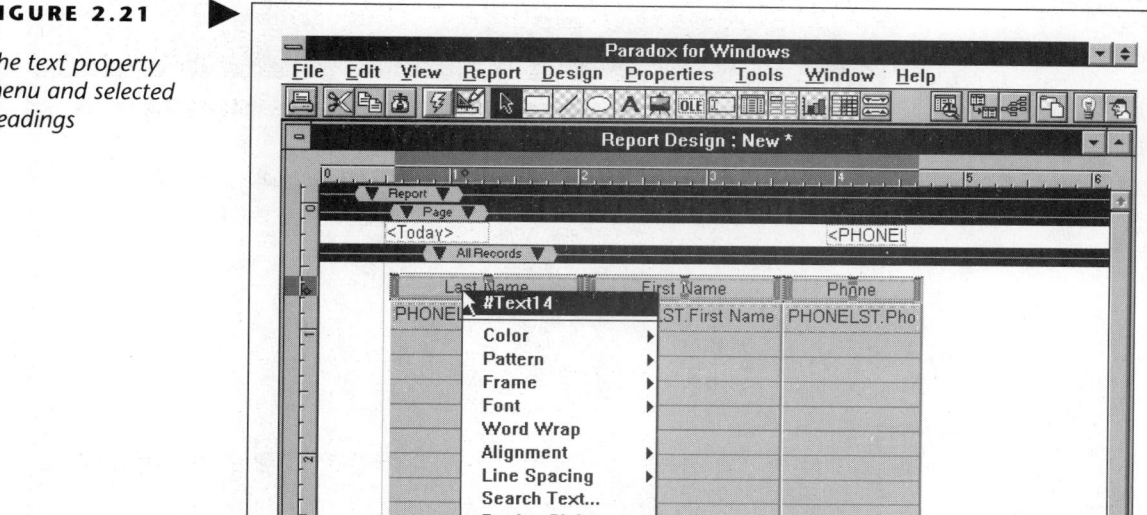

Previewing your handiwork is easy:

- Click the View Data button in the Toolbar (shown at left), or press F8.

Your report should appear with a 3D table and bold column headings, as in Figure 2.22. Because you based the report on a saved query, your report contains only the fields you want and is automatically sorted by last name and first name. You'll learn about other ways to sort data in Chapters 8 and 12.

▶ ▶ **N O T E**

If you wanted to make further changes to the report, you could click the Design button in the Toolbar or press F8 again.

FIGURE 2.22 ▶

A preview of the phone list report

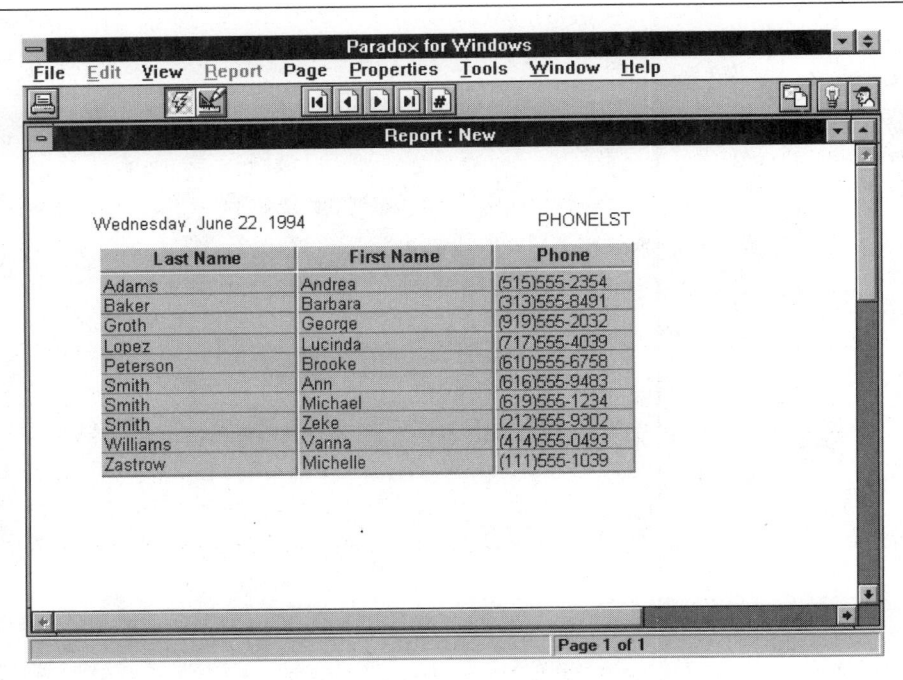

► *Printing Your Report*

Now that the design for the report is complete, you're ready to print it. Simply choose File ➤ Print (or click the Print button in the Toolbar), then choose OK to print the entire report.

T I P

If you're in the Design window, you can print the report by choosing File ➤ Print ➤ Report.

► *Saving Your New Report*

To save your new report, just close it and give it a name.

1. Choose Window ➤ Close All, or close the Report window as usual.

2. Choose Yes when asked about saving the report.

3. Type a valid file name such as **phonerpt** and choose OK.

You can reopen your custom report at any time by following these steps:

1. Click the Open Report button in the Toolbar or choose File ➤ Open ➤ Report if it's available.

2. Click the report name, *Phonerpt.rsl* in this example, and choose OK.

T I P

As a shortcut, you can open the Project Viewer, click the Reports icon, and then double-click *Phonerpt.rsl* on the right side of the Project Viewer window.

As usual, just choose Window ➤ Close All or press Ctrl+F4 when you want to clean up the Desktop.

Paradox: Hands-On

Ch. **2**

In this chapter you've seen what it's like to work with Paradox for Windows. You created a table, added and edited some names and addresses, ran queries to isolate a particular record and display a sorted phone list, and designed a custom form and report. You also learned how to inspect and change properties of objects by right-clicking the mouse. Chapter 3 expands upon many points touched on during these hands-on lessons and delves into some new areas, too. For example, you'll learn more about Paradox menus, the Toolbar, creating an *alias* or "nickname" for a directory, and personalizing the Desktop. You'll also learn how to request help at any time with just the touch of a key or a few clicks of the mouse.

Managing Data with Paradox

PART TWO

3

Getting Around
in Paradox

——

FAST TRACK

▶ **To move and size the Paradox Desktop window** **77**

   use the standard Windows techniques employed in all Windows applications.

▶ **To use the Toolbar** **81**

   move the mouse pointer to any button, then glance down at the status bar for a description of the feature. You can then click the button to activate the feature or (in some cases) right-click the button to view a menu of options for the button.

▶ **To inspect the properties of any Paradox object** **81**

   move the mouse pointer to the object and click the right mouse button; or select (highlight) the object and press F6.

▶ **To get help** **83**

   choose the Help button if it is available, or choose Help from the menu bar, or press F1 (Help) anytime.

▶ ***To switch to a new working directory***   **98**

> choose File ➤ Working Directory from the Desktop. Then
> either type in a new working directory, or use the Aliases
> drop-down list box or the Browse button to select a direc-
> tory. Choose OK. Alternatively, you can use the Project
> Viewer's Working Directory drop-down list and Browse
> button.

▶ ***To personalize the Paradox for Windows Desktop***   **104**

> choose Properties ➤ Desktop, then choose appropriate op-
> tions from the Desktop Properties dialog box that appears.

▶ ***To exit Paradox for Windows***   **112**

> choose File ➤ Exit or double-click the Paradox for Win-
> dows Control-menu box. If you're prompted to save your
> changes, choose Yes and provide additional information if
> necessary.

►► *f* you worked through the lessons in Chapter 2, you probably know all that is necessary to get around in Paradox for Windows. So you may just want to browse through this chapter now, or you can refer to it for quick reminders and additional tidbits as needed. However, if you skipped the lessons in Chapter 2, you can learn the basic skills for using the Paradox Desktop here.

►► *Starting Paradox for Windows*

The first step to using Paradox for Windows is to start the application. We'll assume that Paradox for Windows is already installed, and that its icon is available in the Windows Program Manager. (If you haven't installed Paradox yet, you will find instructions in Appendix A.) Also, as mentioned in Chapter 2, we'll assume you already have your basic Windows skills down pat. (If you need more information on using Windows and Windows applications, you should read the section "Basic Skills" or "Fundamentals" in your Windows documentation.) Now, here's how you start Paradox:

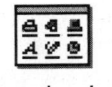

Paradox for
Windows

1. Start Windows and go to Program Manager. If the Paradox for Windows group window is open, skip to step 3. If you see the Paradox for Windows group icon (shown at left), complete step 2.

 ►►**T I P**

> **If the \ *pdoxwin* directory is in the PATH statement in your *autoexec.bat* file, you can start Windows and Paradox from the DOS prompt by typing *win pdoxwin* and pressing ⏎.**

2. Double-click the Paradox for Windows group icon to open the group window shown below.)

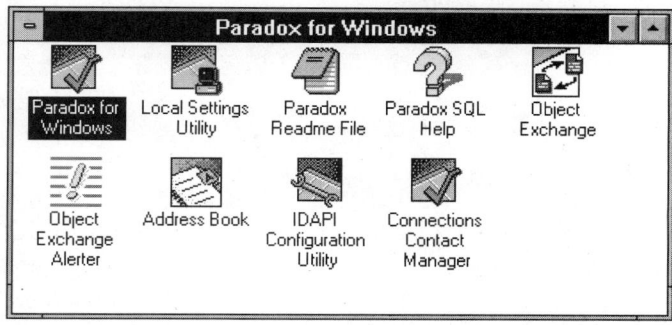

3. Double-click the Paradox for Windows program icon to start Paradox for Windows.

You'll see the Paradox for Windows *Desktop*, described in the next section.

►► *The Paradox Desktop*

Paradox for Windows follows the *Common User Access* (CUA) guidelines that most Windows applications adhere to. Therefore, if you're a seasoned Windows user, you already know how to select menu options, get help, and work with windows and dialog boxes in Paradox for Windows. All your work with Paradox for Windows takes place at the Desktop, shown in Figure 3.1. The Paradox Desktop contains the standard buttons and features that most Windows applications offer—Control menu, title bar, Minimize and Maximize buttons, and borders. Use these features to size and position the Paradox Desktop as you would any other window.

Figure 3.1 also points out the Paradox for Windows Toolbar, menu bar, status bar, and Project Viewer, which are explained later in this chapter. (The Project Viewer window offers a shortcut method for working with database objects; you can open and close it as needed.)

Like the Windows desktop, the Paradox for Windows Desktop is the *application window;* that is, the *parent window* of all Paradox objects. All other windows in Paradox are document windows (*child windows*). Any window that you open on the Paradox Desktop can be moved and sized only within the boundaries of the Paradox Desktop.

FIGURE 3.1

The Paradox for Windows Desktop with its standard Windows features and its open Project Viewer window.

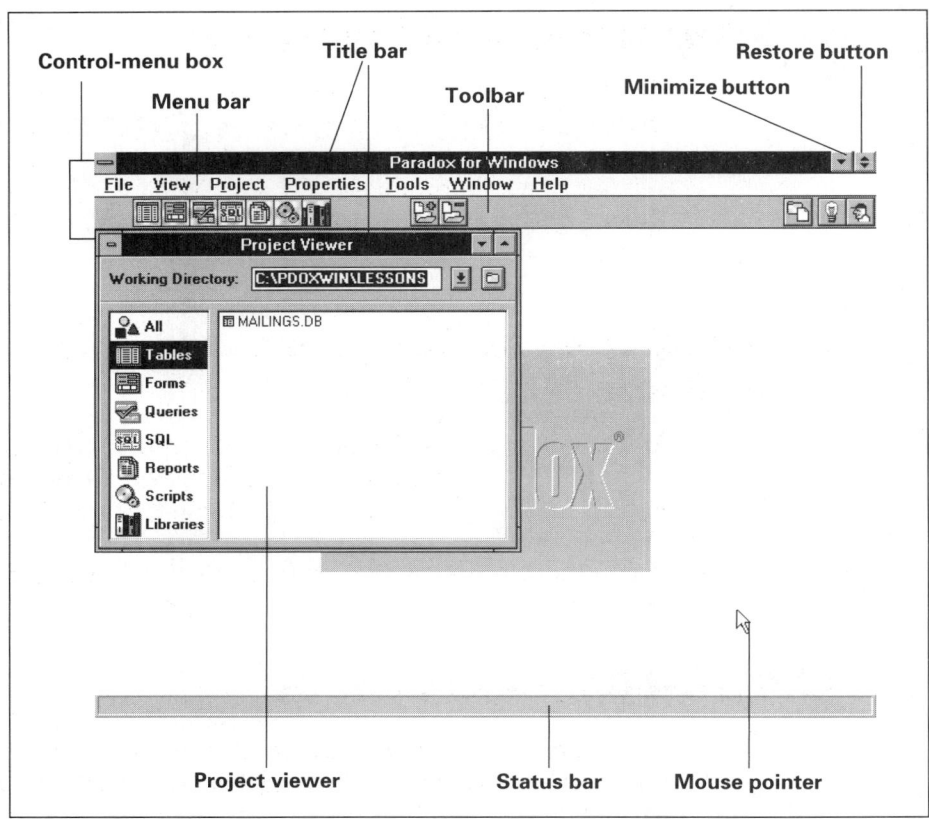

► **N O T E**

Within this book, the term *Desktop* always refers to the Paradox Desktop. We'll refer to other desktops by name (for example, the *Windows desktop*).

►► *Menus and Keystrokes*

As with all Windows applications, you can interact with Paradox for Windows through menus, keystrokes, and buttons.

▶ *Using Menus with the Mouse*

To choose menu commands with the mouse, simply click the command you want. Alternatively, you can move the mouse pointer to any command on the menu bar, hold down the mouse button, drag the highlight to the command you want, then release the mouse button. (Menu commands that appear dimmed are not available in the current situation, and can't be selected.)

▶ *Selecting Menu Commands with the Keyboard*

You can also use the keyboard to select menu commands. For instance, you can press (and release) the Alt key or F10 key to move the highlight into the menu bar. Once the highlight is in the menu bar, you can choose commands by typing the underlined letter or by using the arrow keys to move to the command you want and then pressing ↵ to select it.

▶ *Backing Out of Menus*

Occasionally, you may inadvertently choose the wrong menu options and want to back up until you get to more familiar territory. You can use any of these techniques to back out of a menu and return to the Desktop without making a selection:

- Click in any neutral area outside the menu.
- Press Alt or Esc.
- If your menu selections have taken you to a dialog box, and you want to leave that dialog box without making a selection, click the Cancel button (shown below) or press Escape.

```
   Cancel
```

Getting Around in Paradox

Ch. **3**

► Conventions Used in This Book

Throughout this book, we'll display a series of menu selections like this: Choose File ➤ New ➤ Table. This format lets you see, at a glance, the sequence of menu options you need to choose to access a particular feature. Each menu option is separated by the ➤ symbol. The "hot key" alternative for each menu option is underscored. So, the sample menu sequence above is simply a shortcut for "Choose File, then choose New, then choose Table."

For combination keystrokes, we'll use the standard *key+key* conventions. Alt+F1 means "hold down the Alt key, press F1, then release both keys."

► Understanding Paradox Menus

The menu bar lists the menus that are available at any given time. Different commands appear on the menu bar, depending on what you happen to be doing. Most windows include the File, Properties, Tools, Window, and Help menus.

The **File** menu lets you create, open, close, and save Paradox objects; print reports; change the working and private directories; set up aliases (or "nicknames") for directories; exchange messages and data with other computers and networks; and exit Paradox. We'll be discussing options on the File menu throughout this book.

The **Properties** menu contains options for controlling the appearance of the Desktop or of objects (such as tables, reports, or forms). The specific options on the Properties menu depend on what type of object you're working with. In this chapter, you'll learn how to personalize the Paradox for Windows Desktop by changing some of its properties.

The **Tools** menu lets you open the Project Viewer and Data Model Designer, and provides access to various table utilities and system settings.

The **Window** menu contains standard Windows options for controlling the appearance of windows and for switching from one Paradox child window to another.

The **Help** menu allows you to get on-screen help while you're in Paradox. See "Getting Help," later in this chapter, for more information on the Help system.

▶▶ *Using the Toolbar*

The Toolbar, just below the menu bar, offers a quick alternative to the menus as a way to access main features. When you point to a button (move the mouse pointer to it), the status bar near the bottom of the window indicates what that button does. If you're not sure what a button is for, just move the mouse pointer to the button and glance down at the status bar. Clicking the button will then activate the feature.

Like the menu bar, the buttons that are available on the Toolbar depend on what you happen to be doing at the moment. For example, the Paradox Desktop includes the buttons shown in Figure 3.1. But when you're designing a report or form, you'll see a different set of buttons that are relevant to reports and forms.

▶▶ *About Property Inspection*

Though the term *property inspection* sounds like something you need in order to get a mortgage, it actually refers to one of the handiest of all features in Paradox for Windows.

To appreciate the value of property inspection, imagine you're looking at a screen cluttered with a table, a form, and a graph. Now, suppose you want to change a particular feature, such as the alignment, font, or color, of a column in the table. *Without* property inspection, you'd either need to search through the menus until you found the appropriate commands, or use the Help system or printed documentation to find information on table columns.

With property inspection, you simply move the mouse pointer to whatever you want to change or use, then click the *right* mouse button. Alternatively, you can highlight (select) the object and then press F6. Instantly, you'll see a pop-up menu of options that are relevant to the object you selected.

For instance, Figure 3.2 shows how right-clicking the Last Name field in a sample table produces a menu of options that let you change the alignment, color, font, and other attributes of data in that field.

Getting Around in Paradox

▶ ▶

Ch.

3

FIGURE 3.2 ►

To inspect (and, if you wish, change) the properties of an object, simply move the mouse pointer to the object and click the right mouse button; or select (highlight) the object and press F6.

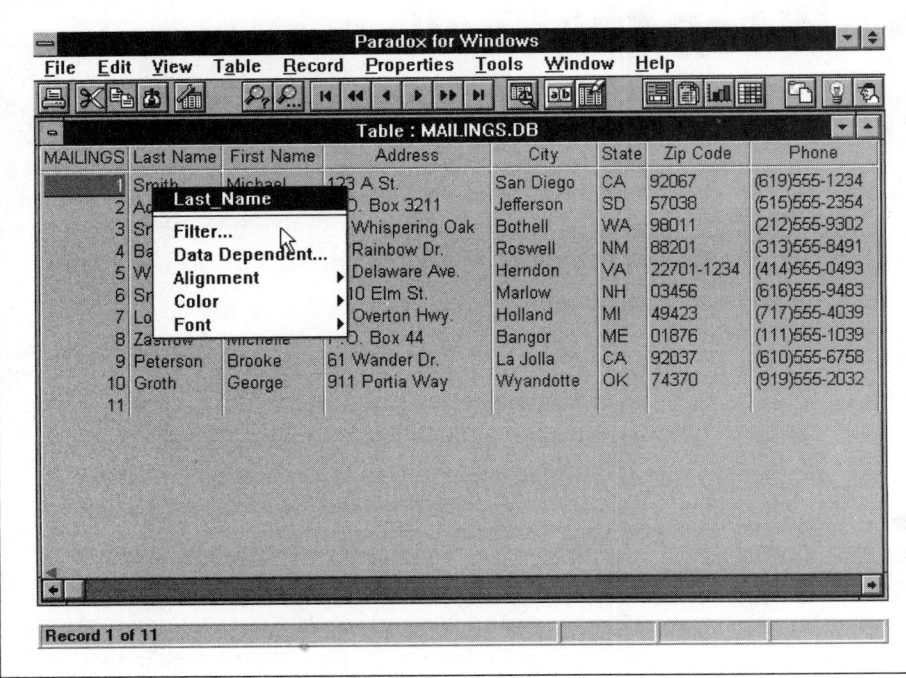

> **N O T E**
>
> **The Toolbar buttons shown in Figure 3.2 are visible only when a table is open on the Desktop, as you'll see in Chapter 4.**

We'll talk about property inspection as it pertains to various objects in upcoming chapters.

If you get confused about which mouse button is which, just keep the following in mind: You click the right mouse button only to inspect properties—to view or change some property of an object, or to open a menu for a Toolbar button or Project Viewer button. For all other operations, including choosing menu and dialog box options, selecting text, clicking a Toolbar button, dragging, and so forth, you use the left mouse button.

▶ ▶ **N O T E**

> **The roles of the left and right mouse buttons will be reversed if your mouse is configured for lefties. You can swap the roles of the buttons at any time using the Control Panel in the Windows Program Manager's Main group.**

Throughout this book we'll use the terms "click" and "double-click" to refer to left-button mouse operations. When an action requires using the right mouse button, we'll refer to that action as *right-clicking* or *inspecting the properties.*

▶ ▶ *Getting Help*

Paradox uses the standard Windows Help system to provide on-screen assistance when you need it. (The online Help provides roughly the same information as your Paradox manuals.)

Two standard types of help are available to you. *Context-sensitive help* offers information specific to whatever you happen to be doing at the time. You can get more general help by using the Help contents.

▶ ▶ **T I P**

> **Paradox also includes interactive "Coaches" to help get you up and running fast, and it offers "Experts" that will help you design forms, mailing labels, and reports in a hurry. You'll learn more about the interactive Coaches later in this chapter. The form and report Experts are covered in Chapters 10 and 12.**

► *Getting Context-Sensitive Help*

There are three ways to get context-sensitive help:

- If a Help button is available, click it.
- Any time you need help, press F1 (Help).
- To get help about a particular menu option, open the menu, use the arrow keys to highlight the option you need help with, then press F1.

A Help window will open, providing information about the task or operation you're trying to perform. For example, you can inspect the Open Table button on the Toolbar and choose New (or choose File ➤ New ➤ Table from the Desktop menus) to open the Table Type dialog box (you'll learn how to use this dialog box in Chapter 4). Clicking the Help button in that dialog box takes you directly to the Help window for creating a table, as shown in Figure 3.3.

FIGURE 3.3 ►

A sample context-sensitive Help window

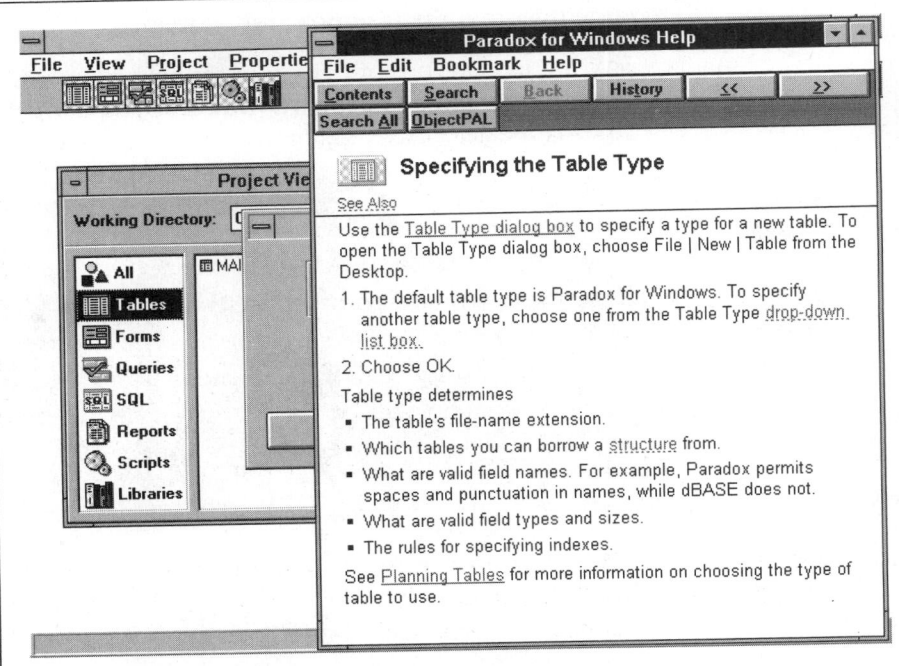

▶ *Using Jump Words, See Also, and Glossary Entries*

Some topics in the Help system are underlined with a solid line, while others are underlined with dots. Here's what it all means:

Solid underline (*jump word*)   Clicking a jump word in a Help window takes you to the Help page for that topic. (Choosing the <u>B</u>ack button would return you to the page you just left.)

Dotted underline (*See Also* or *glossary entry*)   Clicking the *See Also* message just below the Help window's buttons displays a pop-up list of solid underlined topics that you can select. You can then either click an underlined topic to jump to that topic's Help page, or you can click outside the topic (or press a key) to remain on the current Help page. Clicking a glossary word or topic within the Help text instantly shows you the definition of that word or topic. Clicking a second time (or pressing a key) removes the definition from the screen.

▶ *Getting More General Help*

If you need more general help, you can use the Help Contents. Here's how:

- Choose <u>H</u>elp ➤ <u>C</u>ontents, or click the <u>C</u>ontents button if you're already in a Help window.

▶ ▶ **T I P**

If you want to go to the Contents for the ObjectPAL programming language, choose <u>H</u>elp ➤ <u>O</u>bjectPAL Contents, or click the <u>O</u>bjectPAL button if you're already in a Help window.

The table of contents for Paradox Help will appear, as shown in Figure 3.4. You can then click on one of the icons (or underlined topics) to get more information. For example, clicking the *Tasks* icon in the Help

FIGURE 3.4

Paradox Help Contents window

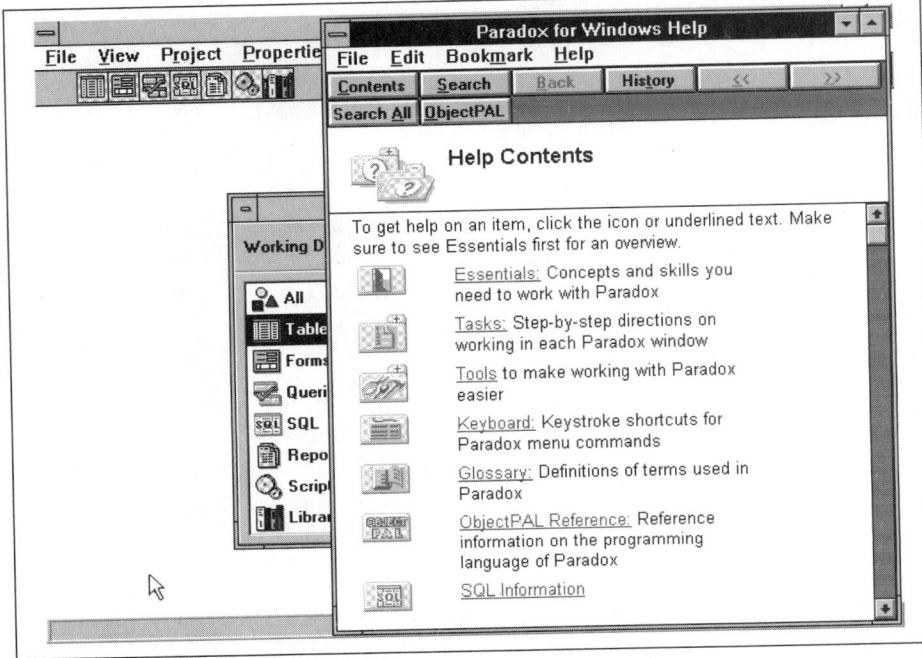

Contents takes you to a screen with more icons and underlined topics. Simply click the appropriate icons or topics until you see the information you want.

Some lists of Help topics—especially very long ones—can be expanded or collapsed like an outline. For instance, clicking the *Essentials* icon in the Help Contents takes you to an Essentials Help screen that includes a *Collapse All* topic just below the screen's title and above the horizontal line that separates the Help screen's title from its main information. You can click *Collapse All* to see a collapsed list of topics available on that screen (*Collapse All* changes to *Expand All*). When topics are collapsed, the main headings appear with broken underlining and the subtopics are hidden. To reveal and select the subtopics, simply click the appropriate broken-underlined topic, then click a solid-underlined subtopic from the pop-up menu that appears. If you want to expand the topic outline again, click *Expand All* beneath the screen's title.

▶ *Using the Help Buttons*

The Help window includes several buttons to help you navigate the Help system more quickly and zero in on specific topics. Table 3.1 explains each of these buttons.

▶ **TABLE 3.1:** *Help Buttons in the Help System*

BUTTON	WHAT IT DOES
Contents	Displays the Help Contents for Paradox.
Search	Lists all the words you can use to search for topics in either the Paradox or the ObjectPAL help lists. After choosing Search, type or select a word, then choose Show Topics. Select a topic from the list and choose Go To.
Back	Displays the last topic you viewed. You can back up one topic at a time, in the reverse order that you viewed the topics.
History	Displays the last 40 topics you've viewed, with the most recent topic listed first. Double-click a topic to revisit it.
<<	Displays the previous topic in a series of related topics. You can click this button repeatedly until you reach the first topic in the series.
>>	Displays the next topic in a series of related topics. You can click this button repeatedly until you reach the last topic in a series.

▶ **TABLE 3.1:** *Help Buttons in the Help System (continued)*

BUTTON	WHAT IT DOES
Search All	Lists all the words you can use to search for topics in both the Paradox and the ObjectPAL help lists. After choosing Search <u>A</u>ll, type or select a word, then choose <u>S</u>how Topics. Select a topic from the list and choose <u>G</u>o To.
ObjectPAL	Displays the Help Contents for ObjectPAL, the object-oriented programming language that comes with Paradox. To return to the Help Contents for Paradox, click the <u>P</u>aradox button (which replaces the <u>O</u>bjectPAL button).

▶ *Keeping the Help Window Visible*

While viewing a Help topic on the screen, you can click *outside* the Help window to return to the Desktop without closing the Help window. However, doing so may cover the Help window. If you want to see the Help window while working on the Desktop, follow these steps:

1. Go back to the Help window by clicking on any visible portion of that window, or by pressing Alt+Tab, or by opening the Task List (Ctrl+Esc) and double-clicking the name of the Help window.

2. Within the Help window, choose <u>H</u>elp ➤ Always On <u>T</u>op.

 ▶ ▶ T I P

> **The Always On <u>T</u>op option in the Help window is a**
> ***toggle*. Choosing the option once activates the feature;**
> **choosing the option a second time deactivates it.**

Now when you click on the Paradox Desktop, the Help window will remain visible. You can move and size the Help window as necessary to see whatever it is you're working on.

The Always On <u>T</u>op setting remains active until you exit the Help system, as described in the next section, or until you choose <u>H</u>elp ➤ Always On <u>T</u>op again.

▶ *Learning More about Help*

Learning to use the Help system is largely a matter of exploring. The Paradox Help system offers all the features that other Windows applications offer, such as the ability to print a Help topic (by choosing <u>F</u>ile ➤ <u>P</u>rint Topic), copy a topic to the Windows Clipboard (<u>E</u>dit ➤ <u>C</u>opy), search for topics (by clicking the <u>S</u>earch or Search <u>A</u>ll button in the Help window), and add bookmarks and annotations. For more information on these topics, refer to your Windows documentation or choose <u>H</u>elp ➤ <u>H</u>ow To Use Help from the Help window's menu bar.

▶ *Exiting Help*

When you've finished using the Help system, you can close it using any of the following techniques:

- Choose <u>F</u>ile ➤ E<u>x</u>it from the Help window's menu bar (*not* the Paradox Desktop menu bar).
- Double-click the Control-menu box in the upper-left corner of the Help window.
- Click the Help window's Control-menu box once, then choose <u>C</u>lose.
- Press Alt+F4 when the Help window is the current window.

- Press Esc (Escape).

You'll be returned to whatever you were doing when you accessed the Help system.

▶▶ *Using the Interactive Coaches*

The interactive Coaches can take you on a soup-to-nuts tour through Paradox for Windows' essential features. With the help of Coaches, you can try whatever features you want, using sample data or your own. So not only will you learn how to use a feature, but you'll also produce something that works immediately. Using the Coaches is pretty much a point-and-click affair, and Coaches are always available to assist you.

 To start the Coaches, choose <u>H</u>elp ➤ Coac<u>h</u>es or click the Coaches button in the Toolbar (the Coach is the ugly little guy shown here in the left margin). Figure 3.5 portrays the main Coaches screen.

As the left side of Figure 3.5 illustrates, you can choose a Coach in any of the following categories:

> **Paradox Basics** This category leads to the following Coaches: A Quick Look At Paradox, Getting Around In Paradox, and Creating An Alias.

FIGURE 3.5

The interactive Coaches let you take Paradox for a test drive.

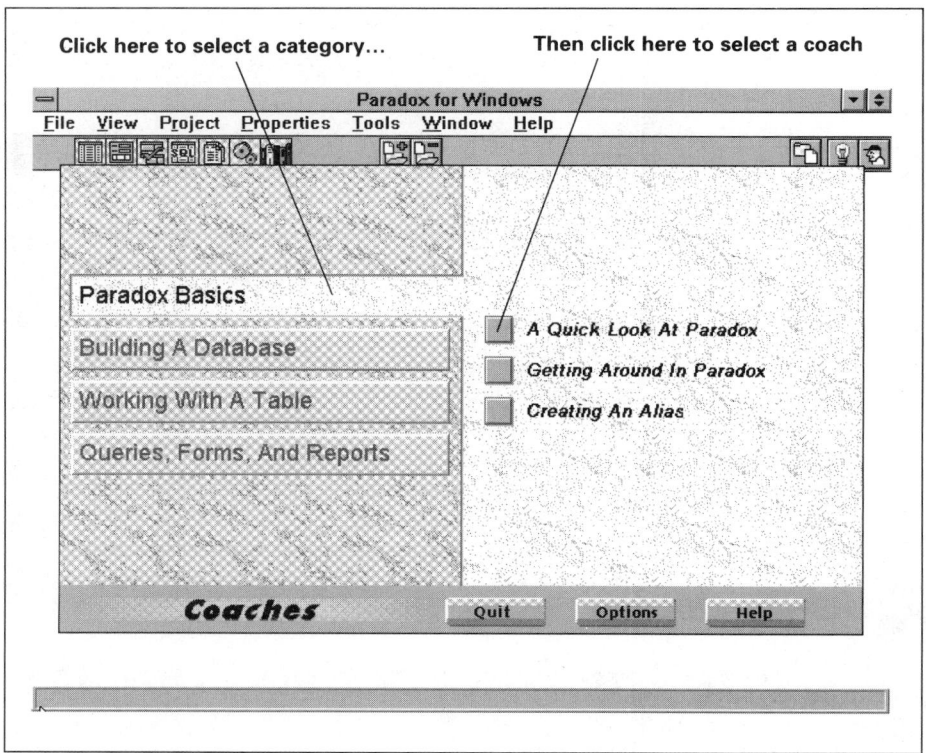

Building a Database   These Coaches take you through Database And Table Basics, Planning A Database, Creating A Table, and Adding A Key.

Working with a Table   Coaches in this category are: Viewing A Table, Editing Records, and Inserting And Deleting Records.

Queries, Forms, and Reports   From this category you can choose Coaches on Creating A Query, Creating A Standard Form, and Creating A Standard Report.

To select a Coach, simply click the button for the category you want (in the left side of the Coaches screen). Then click the appropriate button for the Coach (in the right side of the Coaches screen). From here, the Coach will lead you step by step.

The following tips will help you work with Coaches:

- Each Coach screen will tell you what to do next. To find the Coach's instruction, look for an arrow, as in the example below:

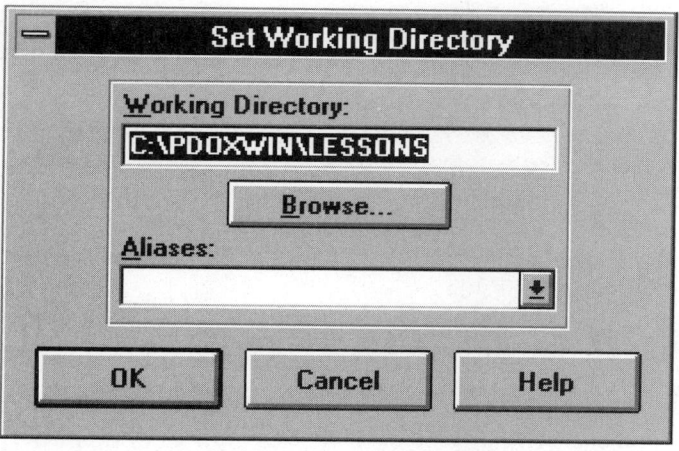

- To continue with the next Coach screen, click the Next button (which is marked with →) or carry out whatever instruction the Coach has given. To return to the previous Coach screen, click the Previous button, which is marked with ←.

- To interrupt the Coach and return to the main Coaches screen at any time, click the Cancel button (which is marked with an X) and then click Yes when asked if you want to cancel the Coach.

- For more help with the Coaches, click the Help button in the main Coaches screen.

When you complete a coaching session successfully, you'll be returned to the main Coaches screen. The completed Coach will be checked as a reminder that you've already mastered its concepts. You can then choose another category and Coach, or you can click the Quit button to return to the Paradox Desktop.

 ▶ ▶ **T I P**

To control whether Paradox saves the checkmarks that appear after you complete a Coach, click the Options button in the main Coaches screen. Then select either Save Coach Checkmarks or Clear Coach Checkmarks. If you'd like to clear whatever checkmarks are currently set, select (check) Clear Current Checkmarks. Then choose OK.

▶▶ *Creating a Directory*

It's usually best to keep your database objects together in a single directory. By organizing your database objects this way, you can group objects that belong together and prevent them from being mixed up with objects from unrelated databases.

Strange as it might sound, the terms *directory, database,* and *project* are often used interchangeably in Paradox. This is because all the objects that make up a database (i.e., tables, queries, forms, and reports) are stored on a single directory. You can also think of all the objects that make up a database as being a *project*.

▶▶ **N O T E**

> **Through the magic of *projects* and the *Project Viewer*, you can work with many objects at once, even if they aren't all stored on the same directory. But your life will be easier if you store related objects in a single directory. There is more about projects later in this chapter, and in Chapter 15.**

While Paradox itself offers no particular command for creating a directory, you can easily pop out to the Windows File Manager at any time to do this job. Lesson 1 in the last chapter provided an example, detailing the steps required to create a directory.

▶▶ *Using the Project Viewer*

new

The Project Viewer window makes it easy to display and manage objects in your working directory, the Paradox *private directory,* and other directories that you add yourself. All these related objects are called a *project.* The Project Viewer window usually appears on the Desktop whenever you open Paradox, looking something like Figure 3.6.

▶▶ **N O T E**

> **The *working* directory contains all the objects you're working with at the moment. The *private directory* stores temporary objects that aren't meant to be shared on a network. In Chapter 15, you'll learn how to add objects from other directories to the Project Viewer window.**

If the Project Viewer isn't visible on the Desktop, you can use either of these methods to display it:

- Click the Open Project Viewer button in the Toolbar (shown at left).

Getting Around in Paradox

Ch. **3**

FIGURE 3.6

The Project Viewer window

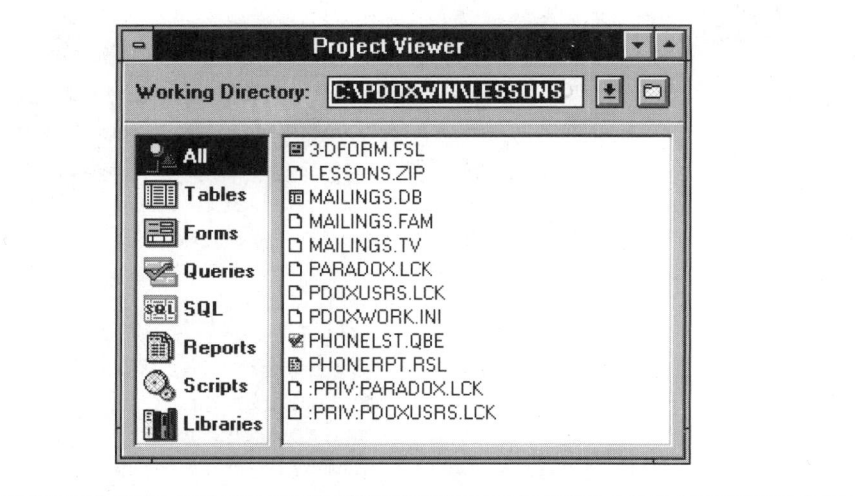

• Choose <u>T</u>ools ➤ Project <u>V</u>iewer from the Desktop menu bar.

Once the Project Viewer window is visible, you can use all the standard Windows techniques to resize, minimize, maximize, restore, or close it.

▶ ▶**TIP**

> **To control whether the Project Viewer appears when you start Paradox, open the Project Viewer, then choose <u>P</u>roperties ➤ <u>P</u>roject. Then, if you want to hide the window at startup, deselect (clear) <u>O</u>pen Project Viewer On Startup. To show the Project Viewer, select (check) that option instead. Choose OK to return to the Desktop. Your new setting will take effect the next time you start Paradox.**

▶ *Using the Project Viewer*

The Project Viewer is divided into two main areas. On the left side, you see icons representing the *types of objects* you can display (All, Tables,

Forms, Queries, SQL, Reports, Scripts, and Libraries). On the right side, you see the names of files in the currently selected object type. For example, if you chose Tables in the left side of the Project Viewer, the right side of the viewer would display only the names of tables (files with the extensions .db and .dbf).

Here are some tips for using the Project Viewer.

- To display objects of a certain type, click the appropriate icon in the left side of the window, or choose options from the <u>V</u>iew menu. For example, click the *Tables* icon or choose <u>V</u>iew ➤ <u>T</u>ables to see a list of table names. To display all the objects in the current project, click the *All* icon or choose <u>V</u>iew ➤ <u>A</u>ll.

- To work with an object, first select the type of object you want from the left side of the Project Viewer window. Then, in the right side of the window, inspect (right-click) the object's file name or click (or highlight) the object and press F6. Finally, choose an option from the pop-up menu that appears. For example, you can inspect a table file and then choose <u>V</u>iew from the top of the pop-up menu to open that table.

- As a shortcut to inspecting an object and choosing the first option on the pop-up menu, you can just double-click the object's file name in the Project Viewer window (or highlight the object name and choose <u>P</u>roject ➤ <u>O</u>pen Current Item). Thus, double-clicking a table name is the same as inspecting it and choosing <u>V</u>iew or highlighting its name and choosing <u>P</u>roject ➤ <u>O</u>pen Current Item.

- To create a new object or open an existing object of a certain type, right-click the appropriate icon in the left side of the Project Viewer window (you cannot inspect the All icon). You can then choose either <u>N</u>ew or <u>O</u>pen from the menu that appears. This offers a convenient alternative to inspecting the "Open" buttons on the Toolbar or choosing <u>F</u>ile ➤ <u>N</u>ew ➤ ....

- You can easily copy, rename, or delete an object using the Project Viewer. Simply inspect the object you're interested in, then choose the appropriate <u>C</u>opy, <u>R</u>ename, or <u>D</u>elete option and respond to any prompts that appear. There's more about managing objects in Chapter 15.

▶▶ *Creating an Alias for a Directory*

One of the handy little features of Paradox for Windows is its ability to give a directory name a descriptive, "user-friendly" *alias* or nickname. For instance, you can give a directory like *c:\pdoxwin\giftco* an alias such as *Gifts* or *Gift_Corner*. Then, whenever you're using Paradox, you can simply designate that new name as the directory without having to use the DOS syntax or rummage through drives and directories to locate the correct path.

Aliases also make your databases more flexible. For example, you could develop your database in a directory named *c:\pdoxwin\giftco* and always refer to that directory by its *Gift_Corner* alias. Later, you could move that database to a different directory on your network—*e:\dbapps\giftco*, for example. Then you could simply update the alias to point to the new directory. All your reports, forms, queries, and other objects would continue to work perfectly.

▶▶ **WARNING**

> If you develop your database using absolute path names, rather than aliases, and then move the original files to another directory, your forms, reports, tables, queries, and other objects may be unable to find one another. Therefore, we *strongly* recommend that you always use aliases.

To assign an alias to an existing directory, follow the procedures below.

1. Choose File ➤ Aliases from the Paradox for Windows menu bar, or click the Aliases button in any dialog box that offers it. You'll see the dialog box shown in Figure 3.7.

2. Click the New button.

3. In the Database Alias text box, type the alias you want to give to the directory. You can include blank spaces (though they'll be converted to underscores), and you can use any combination of

FIGURE 3.7

The Alias Manager dialog box lets you assign "nicknames" to existing directories.

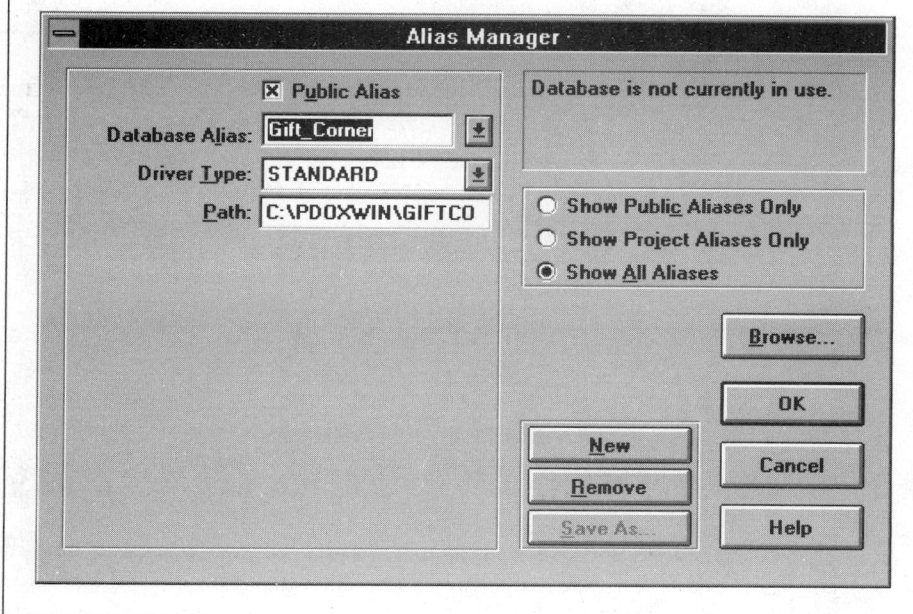

upper- and lowercase letters. For instance, *Gift_Corner* is a perfectly acceptable alias name.

4. Press Tab twice to highlight the name in the P̲ath text box.

5. Type the name of the directory you're assigning the alias to (e.g., **c:\pdoxwin\giftco**).

6. Click the Keep N̲ew button. You can repeat steps 2–6 until you've added all the aliases you want.

7. To make the alias permanent (so that it's available in future sessions of Paradox), choose Save A̲s.

8. From the Save Configuration File dialog box that appears, choose OK to save the current aliases in the suggested initialization file (typically *idapi.cfg*). Then choose Y̲es when asked for permission to overwrite.

9. Choose OK to return to the Desktop.

Getting Around in Paradox

Ch.

3

▶ ▶ **N O T E**

> **If you try to create an alias for a nonexistent directory, Paradox displays an Invalid Path error message. Click OK to return to the Alias Manager window and specify a different directory. See Chapter 15 for more information on the Alias Manager, including details about public, private, and project aliases.**

Next we'll talk about how you can choose a working directory in Paradox, using either an alias or the standard DOS and Windows syntax.

▶▶ *Choosing a Working Directory*

When you start Paradox, its *working directory* usually will be the same one you were using the last time you exited Paradox. If you're starting Paradox for the first time, the working directory will be a default working directory that was set up when Paradox was installed (usually *c:\pdoxwin\working*). Paradox will automatically use the working directory when it searches for tables, reports, and other objects that you've created.

You'll typically want to start by choosing a working directory for your data, particularly if you share a computer with other people or you have created several databases on separate directories.

Be aware that before switching to the new directory, Paradox automatically closes and saves any work in progress on the current directory. Therefore, it is particularly important to create and choose a directory before creating a new database or application. We'll remind you of this in later chapters when it's appropriate.

Whenever you're ready to switch to a new directory, just follow these steps:

1. Choose File ➤ Working Directory. You'll see the Set Working Directory dialog box, shown below. Notice that the entry in the Working Directory text box is selected (highlighted) automatically.

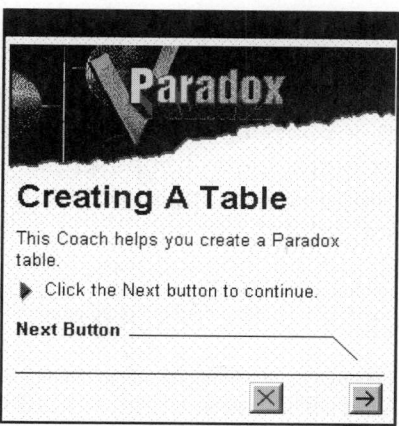

2. Select a different directory using any of these techniques:

   • If the directory you want to switch to has an alias, use the Aliases drop-down list box to select an alias, or type the alias name, as described under "Selecting a Directory by its Alias," below.

   • Click the Browse button, and use the Directory Browser as described under "Using the Browser to Choose a Working Directory," below.

   • Type the complete path name of the directory you want to switch to in the Working Directory text box, as described under "Typing the Working Directory Entry."

3. Choose OK (which is only possible if you've correctly specified an existing directory).

Paradox will switch to that directory and return you to the Desktop. Any new objects you create and save will be placed in that directory. When you ask Paradox to open an object, it will search only the current working directory.

If the Project Viewer window is open (see Figure 3.6), you can use any method below to select a different working directory:

   • Click in the Project Viewer's Working Directory text box, then type the alias name or full path name of the new working directory and press ↵.

- Click the Project Viewer's file folder button (shown at left) and select the appropriate directory from the Directory Browser dialog box that appears.

- Click the Project Viewer's drop-down arrow (shown at left), and then click any of the ten most recently used working directory names shown in the list.

▶ *Selecting a Directory by Its Alias*

If the working directory you want to switch to has an alias, you can select it from the Aliases drop-down list box or type its alias name.

To select a name from the Aliases drop-down list:

1. Click the Aliases list box (or click the ↓ just to the right of the list box) in the Set Working Directory dialog box. A list of aliases will appear, as below.

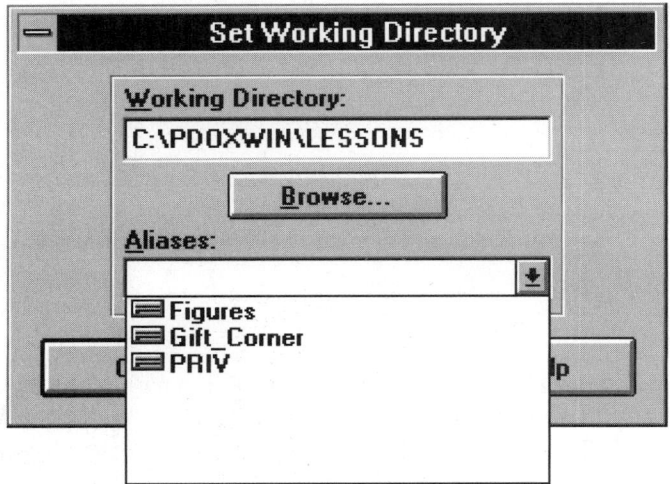

2. Now click the alias for the directory you want to switch to. The list box will close and the alias you chose will appear in the Aliases list box of the Set Working Directory dialog box. The alias name will be surrounded by colons, as below:

:Gift_Corner:

3. Click OK to return to the Desktop with the new working directory selected.

Instead of selecting an alias from an Aliases drop-down list, you can type the alias into the Working Directory text box (in the Set Working Directory dialog box or the Project Viewer). Be sure that a colon precedes and follows the alias name. For instance, you'd enter the Gift_Corner alias as **:Gift_Corner:** (without any spaces before or after the colons).

▶ *Using the Browser to Choose a Working Directory*

If the directory you want to switch to doesn't have an alias, you can use the Browse button to search through and choose a directory. When you choose the Browse button, you'll see a Directory Browser dialog box like the one in Figure 3.8. Inside this dialog box, your existing directories appear as folders in a hierarchical arrangement. To choose a directory, follow the steps below.

FIGURE 3.8 ▶

The Directory Browser dialog box shows the directory tree for the current drive. You can double-click the folders to view the names of subdirectories. Double-click the folder again to hide the subdirectories once more.

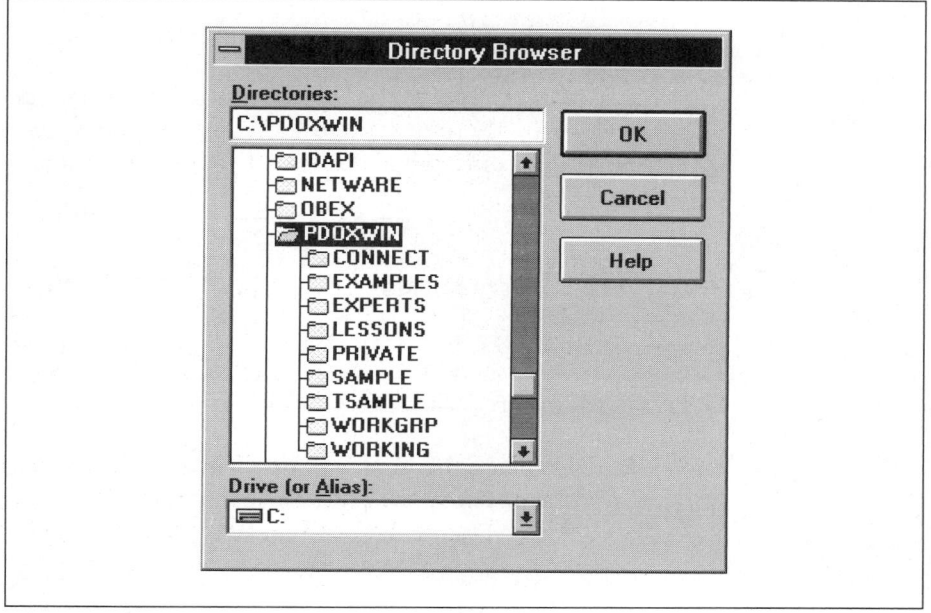

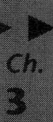

►►**N O T E**

The Browse button that appears in other Paradox windows leads to an expanded Browser window with additional buttons and options. Please see Chapter 15 for more information on browsing.

1. If you want to switch to a different disk drive, click the drop-down list button under Drive (or <u>A</u>lias), then click the drive you want to switch to. The directory tree changes to reflect all the directories on the drive you specified.

2. In the directory tree, use the scroll bars (if necessary) to scroll to the directory you want to switch to.

3. If you want to switch to a subdirectory that isn't visible, first expand the parent directory by double-clicking its name or folder icon. For instance, in Figure 3.8 we scrolled down to the *\pdoxwin* directory, then double-clicked it to reveal *connect, examples, lessons,* and other subdirectories beneath *\pdoxwin.*

4. Click on the folder or directory name you want to select.

5. Choose OK.

You'll be returned to the Set Working Directory dialog box. Now, you can choose OK to complete the switch to a new working directory (or choose Cancel to return to the Desktop without changing the working directory).

► *Typing the Working Directory Entry*

If the directory you want to switch to has no alias and you know its exact name, you can type that name into the Working Directory text box using standard Windows techniques, as summarized below.

- To replace the current entry with a new one, simply type the new entry anytime the entire entry is selected (highlighted).

- To change the current entry, click the mouse to position the insertion point where you want to start making changes, or use positioning keys (such as Home, End, ←, or →) *before* you start typing text.

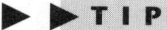

> The OK button appears dim as long as the Working Directory text box contains an *invalid* (nonexistent) directory name. As soon as you fill in the name of an existing directory, the OK button is "undimmed" to indicate that you can use the directory as the new directory.

To change to a subdirectory of the current entry (for example, to change *c:\pdoxwin* to *c:\pdoxwin\giftco*), click the mouse at the end of the text in the Working Directory text box (or press End), then type the text you want to add (**\giftco** in this example).

Choose OK or press ↵ after entering a valid directory name.

▶ *"Paradox Lost All My Data!"*

Keep in mind that if you want to open a table but can't find it, chances are that you're simply looking in the wrong directory. Before you panic, choose File ➤ Working Directory or open the Project Viewer window to find out which directory you're currently in. Then, if necessary, choose the appropriate directory using any of the techniques just described.

If you've switched to the correct working directory, but you don't see the objects you're looking for in the Project Viewer, try these techniques:

- First, choose View and make sure that the Only References option is *not* checked. If it is checked, select Only References to remove the checkmark. If it isn't checked, press the Alt key or click outside the View menu to avoid making a selection.

- Next, click the appropriate icon in the Project Viewer window, or click the All icon to see all files for the current project.

▶▶ *About the Private Directory*

You've probably noticed that the File menu lets you choose both a working directory and a *private directory*. Paradox uses the private

Getting Around in Paradox

Ch. 3

directory to store temporary tables "behind the scenes." By default, the private directory is *\pdoxwin\private*, nicknamed *:PRIV:*.

In most cases, you need not change, or even concern yourself with, the private directory. If you're on a network and have a hard disk, chances are your network administrator has already defined a private directory for your workstation. If you're using Paradox on a network and your workstation does not have a hard disk, you may need to create a private directory on the server to prevent your temporary tables from being intermingled with other users' temporary tables. See your network administrator (or Appendix B) if you need more information on this topic.

▶▶ *Personalizing the Desktop*

You can personalize the Paradox Desktop simply by changing its properties. These steps will get you started.

1. Choose <u>P</u>roperties ➤ <u>D</u>esktop from the Paradox for Windows menu bar. You'll see the dialog box shown in Figure 3.9.

2. Make your changes (as described in the sections that follow), then choose OK.

In the next few sections, we'll discuss the more important Desktop properties you can change. As always, you can click the Help button to get more information about any property you're especially interested in.

 ▶▶ N O T E

> **Paradox stores your changes to Desktop Properties in the file *pdoxwin.ini* (typically located in the *c:\windows* directory).**

▶ *Changing the Window Title*

The title bar for the Paradox window normally contains the title *Paradox for Windows*. If you want to change that title, simply type in a new title under <u>T</u>itle in the Desktop Properties dialog box.

FIGURE 3.9

*The Desktop Proper-
ties dialog box lets
you personalize the
Paradox Desktop.*

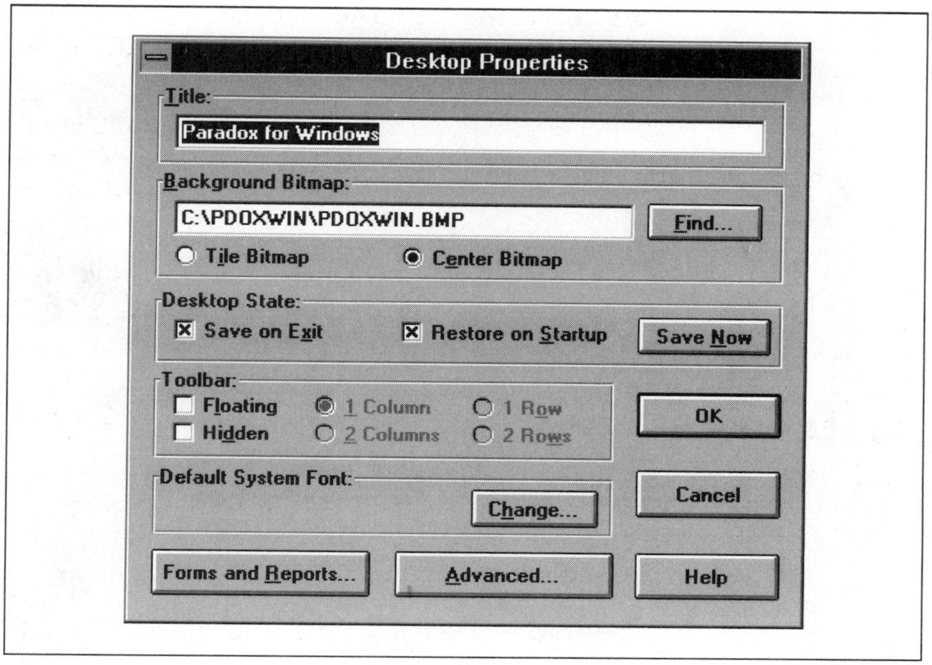

▶ *"Wallpapering" the Paradox Desktop*

You can add a wallpaper image to the Paradox Desktop just as you can
to the Windows desktop. The wallpaper image can be any existing
graphic or any printed image that you've scanned and saved in one of
the following formats:

File Type	File Name Extension
Bitmap (Windows)	.bmp
Compuserve Graphic	.gif
Encapsulated Postscript	.eps
Paintbrush	.pcx
Tagged Image File Format	.tif

**Getting Around
in Paradox**

▶ ▶

Ch.

3

Paradox centers the image by default, so if the image is smaller than the Desktop, you'll see lots of white space on the Desktop. If you want to see multiple copies of a small image on the screen (in a mosaic tile arrangement), select Tile Bitmap in the Desktop Properties window.

 ▶ ▶

When scanning an image to use as wallpaper, you can usually scale the image to near full-screen size to fill the Desktop. Common full-screen sizes (in pixels) include 640 × 480 (VGA), 800 × 600 (Super VGA), and 1024 × 768 (XGA and others).

To choose or change wallpaper, follow the steps below.

1. If you know the exact name and location of the bitmap image you want to use, type in the path and file name, then skip to step 5.

2. To look for images, click the Find button. You'll see a list of file names of possible .bmp, .pcx, .tif, .gif, and .eps images on the current directory.

3. In the Select File dialog box, you can explore multiple drives and directories with the usual techniques:

- Under Drive (or Alias), choose a drive letter or alias to view all the directories there.
- In the directory tree, double-click any file folder to view subdirectory names (if any). When you see the folder for the directory you want, click it.

4. When you find the name of the file you want to use, click its name, then click OK.

5. To view the wallpaper image, choose OK from the Desktop Properties dialog box.

NOTE

To remove an existing wallpaper image, delete the file name from the **B**ackground Bitmap text box in the Desktop Properties dialog box.

Figure 3.10 illustrates what happened after we chose as the background bitmap the graphics file stored in *c:\windows\arcade.bmp*, and asked Paradox to tile the bitmap. We also set up the Toolbar in a floating, two-row arrangement, as described next.

FIGURE 3.10

Sample graphic used as the Paradox for Windows wallpaper

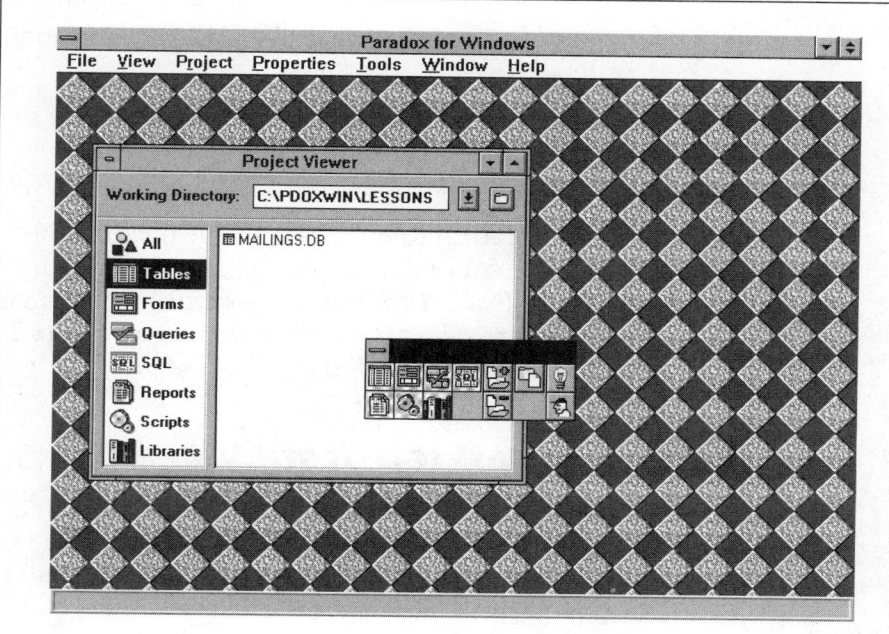

► Moving the Toolbar

Normally, the Toolbar stays fixed just below the menu bar on the Paradox Desktop. However, you can change it to a "floating" Toolbar that you can move anywhere on the screen:

1. If you haven't already done so, choose Properties ➤ Desktop to get to the Desktop Properties dialog box.

2. Under Toolbar, click the Floating option if you want a movable Toolbar.

3. Choose any one of the options to the right:

   - 1 Column (vertical Toolbar, one column of buttons)
   - 2 Columns (vertical bar with two columns)
   - 1 Row (horizontal bar, one row)
   - 2 Rows (horizontal bar with two rows as in Figure 3.10)

4. Choose OK to return to the Paradox Desktop.

When you return to the Desktop, the floating Toolbar appears in a separate palette. You can move the Toolbar by dragging the title bar (next to the Control-menu box) to any position on the screen. To return to a fixed Toolbar, click the Control-menu box on the Toolbar and choose Fix, or just double-click the Control-menu box.

► Saving the Desktop State

Normally the current state of the Desktop is saved when you exit Paradox and restored whenever you restart Paradox. For example, if you open a table and then exit Paradox, that table will reopen automatically when you start Paradox again.

To change this behavior, open the Desktop Properties dialog box (choose Properties ➤ Desktop) and then select (check) or deselect (clear) the appropriate options under Desktop State. Choose OK when you're ready to return to the Desktop. Your new settings will take effect as soon as you exit or restart Paradox.

▶ *Changing the Screen Colors*

For its default color scheme, Paradox uses whatever color scheme you've selected for Windows. If you want to change the colors of the Desktop, you need to go through the Colors dialog box in the Windows Control Panel (available in the Main group of Program Manager). See your Windows documentation for more information. (We'll talk about how to control the color of various Paradox objects as we present those objects in upcoming chapters.)

 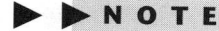 **N O T E**

Changing the color scheme of the Paradox Desktop has no effect on the color of your wallpaper.

▶ *Changing the Default System Font*

Data in tables, forms, and reports typically appears in the default system font for Windows. If you find the standard font difficult to read, or you just want something jazzier to appear on your screen, you can change this font. Start in the Desktop Properties dialog box as usual, then click the Change button in the Default System Font area. You'll see the Change Font dialog box shown below.

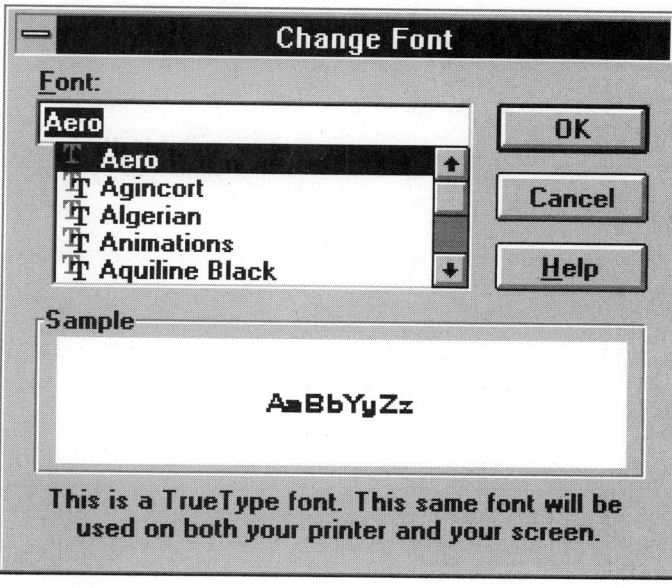

Use the scroll bar to locate the font you want, then click on the font name. A sample will appear in the Sample area. When you've highlighted the font you want, choose OK. Paradox will warn you that the new font won't take effect until the next time you start Paradox. Choose OK to clear the warning, then choose OK again to accept your changes. Your new font will take effect the next time you start Paradox.

▶ Changing the Forms and Reports

You can click the Forms and Reports button in the Desktop Properties dialog box to change default settings for new forms and reports, to determine whether forms and reports will initially open in Design mode, and more. We'll get to this when we discuss forms and reports in Chapters 10 through 12.

▶ Choosing Advanced Settings

Paradox offers some advanced preferences for those who really like to tinker. To change those settings, start in the Desktop Properties dialog box, click the Advanced button, and then select (check) or deselect (clear) the options as desired. (Click the Help button for more information on each option.)

When you're finished changing the options, choose OK until you return to the Desktop. Figure 3.11 illustrates the available preferences.

 ▶ ▶ **T I P**

If you would like the Browser dialog boxes to indicate expandable directory branches (those with subdirectories below them), check the Indicate Expandable Directory Branches option in the Advanced Preferences dialog box. With this option selected, a plus sign (+) will mark directories that you can expand by double-clicking; a minus sign (–) will mark directories that you can collapse, again by double-clicking.

FIGURE 3.11 ▶

The Advanced Preferences let you set additional properties for the Paradox Desktop.

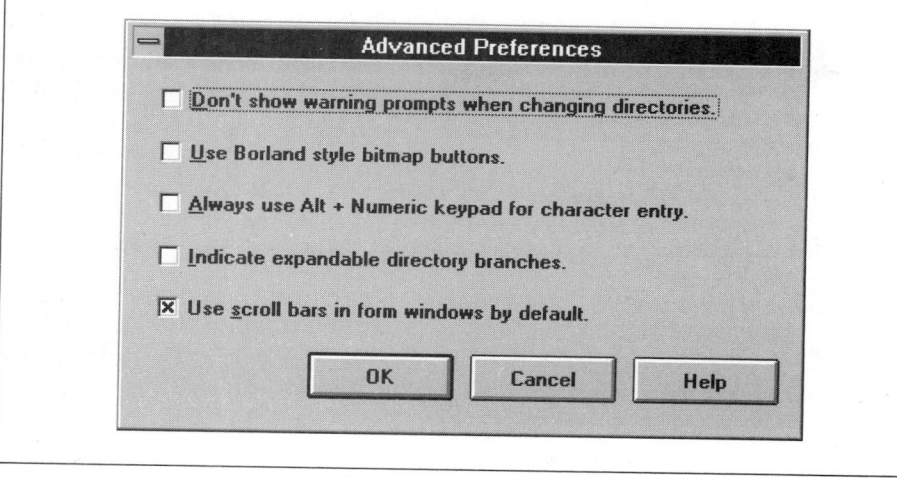

Paradox comes with some sample databases that you can experiment with and analyze to figure out "how'd they do that?" You'll especially want to try the sample forms and scripts that use ObjectPAL to automate and even animate the form's behavior.

To use the sample data, change your working directory to one of the directories described below:

\pdoxwin\connect   A complete prospecting and contact management application developed in ObjectPAL, the programming language that comes with Paradox. To start up the application in this directory, open the script named *start.ssl*. For example, click the Scripts icon in the Project Viewer or choose File ▶ Open ▶ Script, then double-click *start.ssl*. There's more about ObjectPAL in Chapter 19.

\pdoxwin\examples   Offers handy forms to help you manage an online address book (*address.fsl*) and check register (*checks.fsl*). You'll also find a simple painting application (*pdxpaint.fsl*) and a "slot machine" gambling game (*slots.fsl*).

Getting Around in Paradox

Ch. 3

\pdowxin\sample Sample forms in this directory manage customer data, provide simple order entry, summarize orders by customer, and manage vendor information. In this directory you'll also find a *biolife.db* table with colorful pictures of underwater denizens.

Once you've switched to the correct working directory, you can work with the sample objects as you would any Paradox object. For instance, to play the slots gambling game in the *examples* directory, follow these general steps:

1. Use the File ➤ Working Directory options, or the Project Viewer, to change your working directory to *\pdoxwin\examples*.

2. Click the Forms icon in the Project Viewer, or choose File ➤ Open ➤ Form. Then double-click the *slots.fsl* form name.

3. Play the slots game and have some fun. If you need help along the way, just click the Help button.

4. When you're done playing the game, choose Game ➤ Quit ➤ Yes, or double-click the form's Control-menu box.

If you can't find the sample data on your computer, or your experiments have messed it up, you'll need to install or reinstall part of Paradox. To do so, exit Paradox, grab your original installation disks, and do a Custom installation as explained in Appendix A. When the Windows Installation Options dialog box appears, deselect (clear) all but the Samples, Examples, and Connections Application options and continue the installation normally.

►► *Exiting Paradox*

Before turning off your computer, and even before exiting Windows, you should *always* exit Paradox. This ensures that any new data or changes to existing data will be stored properly on disk. If you ignore this advice, you're likely to lose data and any work you've done in the current Paradox session.

You can exit Paradox in a number of ways:

- Choose File ➤ Exit from the Paradox Desktop.
- Click the Control-menu box in the upper left-hand corner of the Paradox Desktop and choose Close from the menu that appears.
- Double-click the Paradox Desktop's Control-menu box.
- Press Alt+F4.

If you've changed any objects without saving them, Paradox will prompt you to save. You can choose Yes to save the current changes, No to abandon any current changes, or Cancel to stay in Paradox. If you choose Yes or No, you'll be returned to the Windows Program Manager.

This chapter has provided a general introduction to interacting with Paradox for Windows. In Chapter 4, we'll take a close look at designing and creating tables.

► ► CHAPTER **4**

Designing and Creating Tables

▶▶ **F**AST **T**RACK

►► *I*n Chapter 2 we whipped quickly through creating a table. However, that's not to suggest that creating a table is a trivial matter. On the contrary, the table is the most fundamental object in Paradox for Windows, since tables are what you'll use to store your data. In fact, virtually everything you do in Paradox for Windows will revolve around how you've structured your tables.

You can store any kind of information in a table: names and addresses, inventory information, orders, a check register, pictures and sounds, a personal library, photographs—any information at all. The only requirement is that the data be organized in a tabular format, that is, in columns and rows.

All but the simplest applications will require that you store data in several separate tables, rather than in a single table. In this chapter we'll examine the factors that go into designing individual tables. The information here will carry over to Chapter 5, where you'll learn about designing a database with multiple tables.

 ►►**TIP**

For some hands-on practice using techniques discussed in this chapter, try out the "Building A Database" Coach. Coaches were introduced in Chapters 2 and 3.

►► *Planning a Table*

The first step in designing a table is to plan its *structure*. That is, you've got to figure out how you're going to divide the information into separate fields, and decide how you're going to name and define each field.

Your best bet might be to do this with paper and pencil, rather than online, so you can play around with your table structure before creating it in Paradox for Windows.

▶ Planning the Field Names

When deciding what fields to place in a table, keep in mind the following rules for defining field names:

- The maximum width of a field name is 25 characters.

- A field name can *contain* blank spaces, but cannot *start* with a blank space.

- A field name can *contain* the number symbol (#), but you cannot use the number symbol alone as the field name.

- A field name cannot contain quotation marks ("), brackets([]), parentheses (()), braces ({}), or a hyphen followed by a greater-than sign (->).

- Avoid using periods and underscores in the field names. This is especially important if you plan to add calculated fields to forms and reports (see Chapter 17) or you plan to use the ObjectPAL programming language (see Chapter 19).

- No two fields in the same table can have the same name. Changing the capitalization or adding a space to the end of the field name will not make field names different from one another.

Using the example of names and addresses, you might come up with the list of fields shown in Figure 4.1 for the table.

Now, you might be wondering why we would bother to split people's names into four fields: Mr/Mrs (or Ms), Last Name, First Name, and MI (middle initial). The reason is that the more fields you break the information into, the easier it will be to manage the data later on. For example, storing each person's last name in a separate field will make it easier to tell Paradox to "put the information into alphabetical order by last name" or to "find all the records for people named Smith."

Separating the fields also makes it easier to determine exactly how you might want to print them later. For example, if you wanted to print an

FIGURE 4.1 ▶

The field names for a table of customer names, addresses, and other information, sketched out on a scratch pad.

	Field Name
1	Last Name
2	Mr/Mrs
3	First Name
4	MI
5	Department/Title
6	Company
7	Address
8	City
9	State
10	Zip Code
11	Area Code
12	Phone
13	Extension
14	Credit Limit
15	Start Date

alphabetical customer list, you could tell Paradox to list Last Name followed by a comma, followed by First Name, like this:

Adams, Andy
Baker, Barbara
Carlson, Cara

When using the same table to print formal correspondence, it would be just as easy to have Paradox put the names in a different format—Mr. or Mrs. followed by First Name, Middle Initial, and then Last Name, like this:

Mr. Andy A. Adams
Ms. Barbara B. Baker
Mrs. Cara C. Carlson

Similarly, breaking the area code and telephone number into two separate fields will allow us to analyze data by area code later on. For instance, we might want to count the number of customers in the 512 area code (one of several area codes in Texas), or find out which products sell best in that part of the country. Or we might want our sales representatives to service customer accounts based on the customer's area code.

As you can see, while your first inclination might be to combine several pieces of information into a single field, in the long run you're better off dividing the information into many separate fields.

▶ *Planning the Field Types*

Paradox stores different types of information in different formats. When defining your table, therefore, you need to think about what type of information will be stored in each field. There is a field type for storing just about any kind of data you can possibly imagine; these types are listed below. As you'll learn in Chapter 7, you can customize most field types for convenient data entry and display.

N O T E

These field types are for Paradox for Windows tables only. If you use Paradox for Windows to create tables for other applications, the field types available to you may be different. (See Appendix D.)

Alpha   Use alpha fields for textual data containing any combination of letters, numerals, spaces, and other characters. The contents of an alpha field can be anywhere from 1 to 255 characters in length. (In older versions of Paradox, the alpha field was called *alphanumeric*.) Examples: names, addresses, titles, product codes—basically, any short piece of text.

An alpha field can also store links to data in files created by another "DDE-capable" application such as a Windows spreadsheet (for example, Excel or Quattro Pro for Windows), word processor (for example, Microsoft Word), or other applications. The links are created through *Dynamic Data Exchange* or *DDE*. As you'll learn later in the chapter, Paradox for Windows can act as a DDE client or server.

new

Autoincrement (+)   This field type is perfect for generating unique values in a field. Each table can have only one autoincrement field. Autoincrement values start at 1, are incremented automatically by 1 whenever you create a new record, and cannot be changed. Paradox does not change the values in autoincrement fields when you delete records. Autoincrement data are stored as long integers. Examples: Use this field type to generate unique customer numbers, invoice numbers, and product numbers. (See "The Beauty of Autoincrement Fields" and "The Downside of Autoincrement Fields," later in this chapter.)

new

BCD (#)   This field type is for ObjectPAL programmers who need to perform calculations at a very high level of precision. It is mainly for compatibility with other databases that support BCD fields. (BCD stands for Binary Coded Decimal.) When Paradox performs a calculation on BCD data, it first converts the data to a numeric float type, performs the calculation, and then converts the results back to BCD.

Binary   Stores data that Paradox can't interpret. This field type is for ObjectPAL programmers and advanced users only. Example: a sound file that can be played only using a non-Windows application.

new

Bytes   Stores data that Paradox can't read or interpret. This field type is for ObjectPAL programmers and advanced users only, and it provides compatibility with other database managers. Examples: bar codes or magnetic strips.

Date   This field type stores dates. Paradox automatically validates any entry, rejecting a date like 06/31/95 (June has only 30 days), and it correctly handles leap years and leap centuries. Date fields allow date arithmetic, where you can calculate the number of days between two dates, add or subtract days from a date, and so forth. Examples: hiring dates, billing dates, and due dates.

Formatted memo   This field type is the same as a memo field, but allows you to embellish text with attributes such as varied fonts, styles (e.g., **bold** or *italic*), and alignment options (centered, flush-right, etc.). Formatted memo fields have basically the same uses as memo fields (described below).

Graphic   Use graphic fields for pictures. Examples: clip art, personal art work, scanned photos, video frames, screen captures, and charts.

Logical Use Logical fields to store true or false (yes or no) values. Examples: gender (male or female), marital status (single or married), or any other data that can have only one of two values (0 or 1, yes or no, and so on).

Long Integer Long integer fields are 32-bit signed integers in the range 2147483647 to -2147483647 (plus or minus 2^{31}). Examples: Use long integers to reference Customer numbers, invoice numbers, or product numbers that are stored in other tables with the autoincrement field type. (See "The Beauty of Autoincrement Fields" later in this chapter and "Using Autoincrement Fields in Related Tables" in the following chapter.)

Memo Like alphanumeric fields, memo fields contain textual data—letters, numerals, spaces, and other characters. However, a memo field can contain text of any length, limited only by the amount of disk space available on your hard drive. Examples: résumés, job descriptions, product descriptions, journal abstracts—any text that requires more than 255 characters.

Money ($) These fields store numeric data representing monetary amounts. Money data is like number data, except that all numbers are automatically rounded off to two decimal places, and negative values are enclosed in parentheses. (In earlier versions of Paradox, the money field type was called *currency*.) Examples: unit prices, salaries, and hourly wages.

> **► ► N O T E**
>
> **Money values are initially displayed with the currency symbol selected in the Windows Control Panel. You can change this to another symbol, if you wish, using methods described in Chapter 7.**

Number Use Number fields to store numbers that you'll use to perform mathematical operations such as totals, subtotals, averages, and so forth. Number fields can accept only numeric characters (0–9), decimal points, commas, and minus signs. The range of values possible for a number field is anywhere from -10^{307} to 10^{308} with 15 significant digits. Alphabetic characters are not allowed in number fields. Examples: quantities and measurements.

OLE   Object linking and embedding (OLE) fields contain objects that are placed in your table from other Windows 3.1 server applications that support OLE. Examples: spreadsheet cells, entire spreadsheets, written documents from a word processor, pictures, charts, graphics, animations, and sounds.

Paradox for Windows acts as an OLE *client* (or *container* in OLE2) for tables, forms, and reports (that is, it can receive data from other applications). It can also act as an OLE *server* for tables (that is, it can send tables to other OLE applications). We'll describe OLE in more detail in a moment.

Short   Like number fields, short number fields contain numbers; however, they're used only for whole numbers in the range of −32,767 to 32,767. No decimal point is allowed. (In older versions of Paradox, the Short field was called *Short Number*.) Examples: quantities (whole number only), account numbers, and product identification numbers that don't require letters or punctuation.

Time   This field type uses a 24-hour sequence to store the time of day. You can enter the current time by pressing the spacebar repeatedly in a time field. Examples: *1:44:22 PM* or *3:44:22 AM*.

Timestamp (@)   This field type combines the Time and Date field types. You can enter the current time and date by pressing the spacebar repeatedly in a timestamp field. Examples: *1:44:22 PM, 6/9/95* or *3:44:22 AM, 6/9/95*.

▶▶ **N O T E**

> The following field types are stored in separate .mb files that have the same name as the table (for example, *CustList.mb*): binary, formatted memo, graphic, memo, and OLE. It takes Paradox longer to access fields that are stored in .mb files.

Table 4.1 summarizes field types that you can fill in by typing at your keyboard. In Chapter 6, you'll learn more about filling in formatted memo, graphic, memo, and OLE fields.

▶ **TABLE 4.1:** *Paradox Field Types That You Can Fill in by Typing*

FIELD TYPE	ALLOWABLE VALUES	SAMPLE DATA
Date	any valid date *	10/25/95
Logical	Yes or Y, No or N; Male or M, Female or F; True or T, False or F (allowable values depend on the Logical Format setting)	Yes
Long Integer	2147483647 to −2147483647 (no decimal points)	999999999
Money	Any monetary amount, rounded to 2 decimal points	$35,555.47
Number	-10^{307} to 10^{308} with 15 significant digits	3,500.55
Short	−32,767 to 32,767 (no decimal points)	9999
Time	Any valid time (hh:mm:ss AM or hh:mm:ss PM) *	12:47:47 AM
Timestamp	Any valid time and date (hh:mm:ss AM, mm/dd/yy or hh:mm:ss PM, mm/dd/yy) *	12:47:47 AM, 5/30/95

* The date and time formats will depend on the current settings in the International option of Windows Control Panel.

Referring back to our sample CustList table, you might jot down the field types shown in Figure 4.2.

You may be thinking, "Wait a minute—you just said that the number field type is for numbers. Yet you defined Zip Code and Phone as alpha fields." The reason for making these fields alpha is that neither zip codes nor phone numbers are true numbers (that is, they don't represent quantities or numeric values). Defining either of these as numbers would prevent us from putting letters, leading zeros, and most punctuation into the entries.

FIGURE 4.2 ▶

Field types assigned to each of the fields sketched out for our sample CustList table

	Field Name	Type
1	Last Name	Alpha
2	Mr/Mrs	Alpha
3	First Name	Alpha
4	MI	Alpha
5	Department/Title	Alpha
6	Company	Alpha
7	Address	Alpha
8	City	Alpha
9	State	Alpha
10	Zip Code	Alpha
11	Area Code	Number
12	Phone	Alpha
13	Extension	Alpha
14	Credit Limit	$ (Money)
15	Start Date	Date

For example, if you defined Zip Code as a number field, you couldn't store a hyphenated zip code like *92067-3384*, or a foreign post code like *MJ3 OH4*, or a zip code with a leading zero like *01234* in that field. Nor could you store phone numbers in a hyphenated format, as in *555-1212*.

▶ Planning Alpha Field Sizes

You must decide how much space each alpha field will need. You don't want to shortchange yourself when making these decisions, nor do you want to waste disk space by overdoing a good thing. For example, if you allot ten characters to the Last Name field, you couldn't store a long last name like *Claplock-Strappman* in your table, since that requires 18 characters. On the other hand, there's no point in allowing 100 characters per last name, since nobody's last name is that long.

Figure 4.3 suggests a reasonable length for each alpha field in the sample CustList table. Field types without sizes assigned don't require you to assign a size.

Designing and
Creating Tables

Ch.
4

FIGURE 4.3

Field sizes assigned to alpha fields in the sample CustList table

	Field Name	Type	Size
1	Last Name	Alpha	20
2	Mr/Mrs	Alpha	4
3	First Name	Alpha	20
4	MI	Alpha	2
5	Department/Title	Alpha	25
6	Company	Alpha	25
7	Address	Alpha	25
8	City	Alpha	20
9	State	Alpha	2
10	Zip Code	Alpha	10
11	Area Code	Number	
12	Phone	Alpha	8
13	Extension	Alpha	5
14	Credit Limit	$ (Money)	
15	Start Date	Date	

NOTE

If you plan to store links to values in files created by DDE server applications, your alpha field should be long enough to store the full path name of the file you're linking to, plus about 25 characters.

▶ Planning Memo and Formatted Memo Field Sizes

Memo fields can have a length within the range of 1 to 240 characters. Formatted memo fields can have a length of 0 to 240 characters. Regardless of the size you assign to the memo or formatted memo field, you can store any amount of text in that field. The table itself will contain only the number of characters you specify, with the remaining characters stored in a separate file outside the table (this file has a .mb extension).

For example, if you give a memo field a length of 25, the first 25 characters of the memo will be stored in the table, with the remainder stored in the .mb file. You don't need to worry about where the text is stored; Paradox will take care of that for you and will let you store and display text of any length within that field.

► ►**N O T E**

Chapter 6 explains how to enter and edit memo data.

The size of the memo field determines how much text will appear when you scroll through the records in the table. You might want to start by assigning a modest size to memo fields, say 5 or so. You can always increase the sizes later if you wish.

► *When to Use the Graphic and OLE Field Types*

You can use the graphic and OLE field types to store pictures and sounds in a table. OLE (object linking and embedding) is a Windows 3.1 feature that allows multiple applications to share data. If you're not familiar with OLE, you might want to learn more about it from your Windows documentation before deciding whether to use this field type. The next few sections provide tips about field types for pictures, sounds, and even lengthy text.

What Can Go into an OLE Field?

An OLE field can contain any type of information. However, that information must come from a Windows 3.1 application that acts as an OLE server. For instance, the Windows 3.1 Paintbrush and Sound Recorder accessories are server applications, as is Microsoft Excel.

The only sure way to find out whether or not a Windows application is an OLE server is to check the documentation for that application.

Storing Pictures and Sound

You'll want to use OLE fields (rather than graphic fields) for pictures if you want to view or change those pictures "on the fly," without leaving

Paradox for Windows. OLE provides an instant link to the application used to create the picture (for example, Paintbrush for a bitmap image, or Excel for a chart). OLE field types are also perfect for sounds (.wav files). Once a sound is stored in an OLE field, you can hear the sound simply by double-clicking the field when it's visible on the screen. Similarly, you can double-click a picture or chart in an OLE field to display or change the image.

 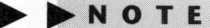

> **N O T E**
>
> **You can only record and play back sounds on a computer that is equipped with appropriate hardware, such as a sound card.**

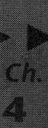

When there is no way to bring a picture into an application that acts as an OLE server, you'll need to use a graphic field type to store the pictures. For instance, if you want to store GIF (Graphic Information File) images in a field, and you don't have any applications that act as an OLE server for GIF files, you'll need to store those images in a graphic field.

But even if a graphic can't be put directly into an OLE field, you may be able to bring the image into Paintbrush first and then put it into an OLE field. For instance, Paintbrush can interpret bitmap (.bmp), device independent bitmap (.dib), Microsoft Paint (.msp), or early Paintbrush (.pcx) formats directly. It also can store pasted images from formats such as Tagged Image File Format (.tif), Windows MetaFile (.wmf), or WordPerfect Graphic (.wpg). We'll discuss this in more detail in Chapter 6.

Our sample CustList table didn't require any of these fancy field types. But let's say you're designing a database for a modeling agency and you want to store the name and address of each model, as well as a résumé, photo, and voice sample, in a table. Figure 4.4 shows how you might structure that table.

Figure 4.5 shows a sample record from this table displayed on the screen using a custom form. The Resume field shows only part of the résumé in this example. Double-clicking on it and scrolling through the field shows more of the résumé, which can contain any amount of text. The small microphone icon represents a sound (a recorded voice in

FIGURE 4.4 ▶

Sample table that a modeling agency might use to store name and address, résumé, photo, and voice sample of each model

	Field Name	Type	Size
1	Last Name	Alpha	20
2	First Name	Alpha	20
3	Address	Alpha	35
4	City	Alpha	20
5	State	Alpha	2
6	Zip Code	Alpha	10
7	Phone	Alpha	13
8	Resume	Formatted Memo	1
9	Photo	OLE	1
10	Voice	OLE	1

FIGURE 4.5 ▶

A sample custom form showing data in alpha, formatted memo, and OLE fields

this example). Double-clicking the microphone icon plays back the model's lilting voice.

You'll learn how to put memos, pictures, and sound into these field types in Chapter 6. For now, let's look at some other possibilities for OLE.

Using OLE to Store Text and Numbers

You can also use the OLE field type to store text and numbers from external applications in a Paradox for Windows table. For instance, suppose you keep salary data in a Quattro Pro or Excel spreadsheet. If you create a field named *Salary* in a Paradox table, and then give it the OLE field type, you can paste numbers from the spreadsheet into the Paradox table.

The big disadvantage of storing numbers in OLE fields is that you won't have as much flexibility in formatting and querying those numbers as you would if you stored them in money or number fields. In fact, if you need to perform any math whatsoever on the numbers in your Paradox table, you're better off defining that field as one of the numeric field types rather than as an OLE field.

You can also use the OLE field type as an alternative to the memo or formatted memo field types to store lengthy text in a Paradox table. For instance, suppose you run an employment service, and you've created a table to track clients' names, addresses, skills, and résumés.

If you want to print and edit those résumés with a word processing program, such as Microsoft Word for Windows or WordPerfect for Windows, you can store résumés in an OLE field. Then, you can paste résumés from the word processing document into the Paradox table as needed. If you want to edit a résumé, you can often just double-click its field and be taken to the word processing application with the résumé on the screen ready for editing.

▶▶ **N O T E**

An OLE field can only store text from applications that support OLE or OLE2. For example, Microsoft Word for Windows Version 6.0 supports OLE2, and WordPerfect for Windows Version 6.0 supports OLE. The behavior of the OLE object when you double-click it in Paradox depends on whether the object is linked via OLE or OLE2. We'll talk more about editing OLE objects in Chapter 6.

The disadvantage of using an external word processor to create and edit lengthy text fields is that you might not be able to see or print text in that field while you're in Paradox (the exact appearance of the OLE field depends on the word processor). Instead, you might see an icon for the application used to create the text. Thus, OLE is best for storing lengthy text that you only need to access occasionally. Normally, you'll want to use the formatted memo or memo field type to store lengthy text in your Paradox tables.

In a moment, we'll take a look at how these field types might look in a Paradox table. But first, we'll compare OLE links with their close cousins, DDE links.

▶ *OLE and DDE Links*

DDE is a Windows feature that, like OLE, lets you exchange and update data in another application. However, there are some subtle differences between the two techniques that you should know about. Understanding these differences can help you decide which type of field to use.

▶▶ **N O T E**

You'll learn how to put DDE and OLE links into Paradox tables in Chapter 6. In Chapter 16, you'll learn how to create queries that employ DDE links. And in Chapter 10, you'll learn how to add OLE links to forms and reports.

In general, you'll use *DDE* to send field values from a Paradox table to another application, or to send data from another application to a Paradox table or query. You can even use DDE to send information between a *Paradox* table and query, so that the query results are updated dynamically as you move the cursor through the table's records.

You'll typically use *OLE* to embed files from an OLE source application into a Paradox table, form, or report. You can then update data in the OLE source application without ever leaving Paradox. You can also use OLE to embed an entire Paradox table into another application's document. This allows you to update the Paradox table in the *other* application, without leaving that application.

Let's quickly look at some hypothetical examples:

- **Using Paradox as a DDE server in a spreadsheet**: Suppose you have an Employee table in Paradox that includes an Annual Salary field. You could link the Annual Salary in your table to cell A1 in an Excel or Quattro Pro for Windows spreadsheet. In spreadsheet cell A2, you calculate an hourly rate based on the annual salary in cell A1. Now, if you place the spreadsheet and Paradox applications side by side on the screen and move the cursor through the records in the Paradox Employee table, you'll see that the currently highlighted employee's annual salary and hourly rate are updated instantly in the spreadsheet. (See Chapter 6 for an example.)

- **Using Paradox as a DDE client in a query:** You could create and run a query that links your Customer and Orders tables and uses DDE to pull out orders for the current customer record only. You could then place the Customer table and the query results window side by side. Now, if you move the cursor through your Customer table, the query results will be updated automatically to show orders for the currently highlighted customer. (See Chapter 16 for an example.)

- **Using Paradox as an OLE client:** You can link a document (or part of a document) from an OLE application, such as Paintbrush, into an OLE field in your table. Then you can simply double-click the OLE field in Paradox to open Paintbrush and update the painting without leaving Paradox. Alternatively, you can go to Paintbrush to make your changes. Either way, the linked document will reflect your changes automatically, whether you view it in Paradox or in Paintbrush. (See Chapter 6 for an example.)

- **Using Paradox as an OLE2 server:** You can embed a Paradox table into a document in a word processor (such as Microsoft Word 6) or spreadsheet (such as Quattro Pro for Windows) that supports OLE2. Then you can update the Paradox table either from Paradox itself, or by double-clicking the table in the word processor or spreadsheet document. (See Chapter 6 for an example.)

▶▶ **N O T E**

If the client and server applications support OLE2, you can double-click the OLE object and edit it "in place." With in-place editing, you stay in the client application window; however, the client application's menus and other tools are temporarily replaced by those of the server until you click outside the OLE object.

Here are some other similarities and differences between DDE and OLE that you should know about.

- DDE links always point to original, "live" data. Therefore, whether you edit the data in another application or in Paradox, your changes are made to the *original* data. When you use OLE, you can either embed a *copy* of the original data file (changes made in Paradox will *not* be reflected in the original file), or you can link to the original data file (changes made in Paradox *will* be reflected in the original file).

- OLE can store just about any type of data in an *OLE field* of a Paradox table. DDE, however, is limited to linking text and numeric values from another application into an *alpha field*. For this reason, DDE is most often used to exchange small, discrete chunks of data stored in selected cells of a spreadsheet or fields of a table.

- You cannot perform math calculations on DDE-linked or OLE-linked data in Paradox.

If you use both OLE and DDE, you'll quickly notice that OLE fields and alpha fields containing DDE links look very different from one another (see Figure 4.6). After pasting data into an OLE field, you'll see an icon (or a picture), which represents the embedded data file, or you'll see the actual text of the file, depending on the server application. After using DDE to link data to an alpha field, you'll see only a pointer, or *reference*, to the data.

Figure 4.6 shows a sample Paradox for Windows table with text in a memo, formatted memo, and OLE field, and with a DDE link in an alpha field. Here's a description of each field:

Memo field   The first column shows a sample memo field. Text can be any length, but no formatting is allowed.

Formatted memo field   The second column shows text in a formatted memo field. Text can be any length and can use different fonts, alignment (centering, for example), and styles such as **boldface** and *italic*.

FIGURE 4.6 ▶

A single record of a Paradox table with a memo field, a formatted memo field, and an OLE field containing text from a Word for Windows document. Because Paradox can display Word for Windows text, you can see it in the OLE field (sometimes you'll see only an icon for the server application). The alpha field contains a DDE link to an Excel spreadsheet.

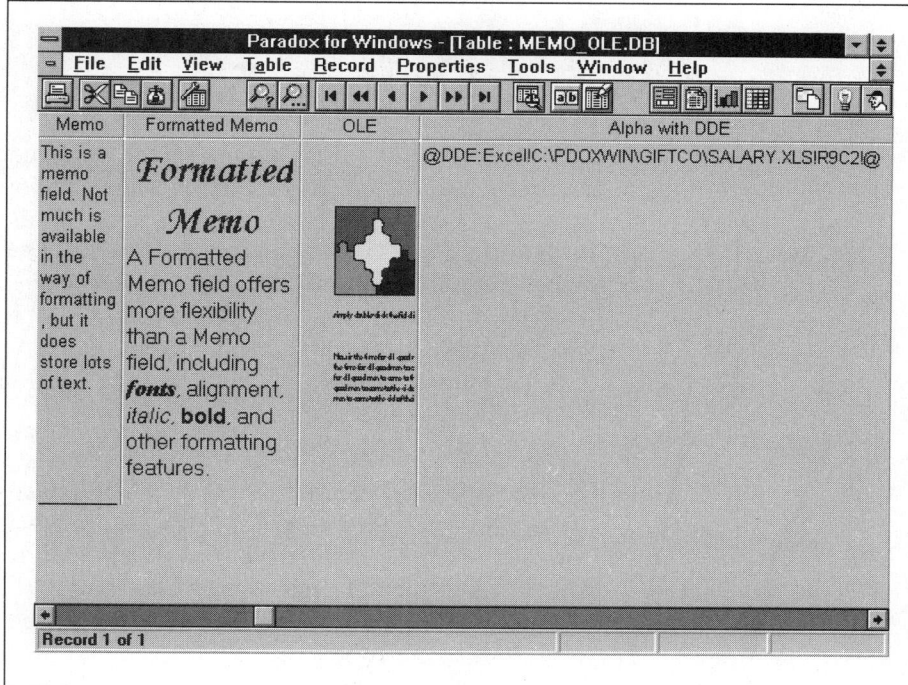

Lengthy text in OLE field The third column contains a Word for Windows Version 6 document stored in an OLE field. (Depending on the server application, you may see only the application's icon in the OLE field.)

Alpha with DDE The fourth column contains a DDE link to a Microsoft Excel spreadsheet. The link reference in the field specifies the name of the application (Excel), the file name (*c:\pdox-win\giftco\salary.xls*), and the cell (row 9, column 2) containing the linked data.

 ►►N O T E

Paradox offers two more ways to share data with other users and applications. To send snapshots of Paradox objects to other users on a network, you use Object Exchange (OBEX), which is described in Appendix B. To export Paradox tables to a variety of formats, you use the Export utility (see Appendix C).

►► *What NOT to Put in Tables*

While you're designing your *field roster* (the names and types of fields that define the table's structure), try to follow the guidelines below.

- **Avoid creating fields to store the results of calculations.** Putting such fields in a table wastes disk space and increases the likelihood of errors since you'll have to do all the calculations yourself. Instead, you need only define fields for the raw data, then let Paradox do all the calculations. We'll talk more about calculated fields in Chapters 16 and 17.

- **Never include a field that will contain the same information in every record.** Suppose you're storing customer names and addresses and you plan to print form letters with your company's logo at the top of each letter. You don't need to include a field for your logo with each customer's name and address. Instead, you can just put your company logo on the form letter design (once) when you're ready to print the letters.

- **Include only fields that are directly relevant to the table you're designing.** Don't try to throw everything, including the kitchen sink, into one table. For instance, in CustList, there's one address, city, state, zip code, and phone number for every name—a perfect correspondence between fields and the customers they describe. Don't put anything into the table that isn't directly relevant to customers. We'll get into this topic in more depth in Chapter 5.

- **Don't exclude fields for information you'll need.** You certainly don't want to exclude any fields that would hold information you might need later. For instance, our CustList table is sufficient for names and addresses within the United States. But if your customer list contains people outside the United States, you'll need to include a field for the country name. Also, you'll need to widen the State field to avoid limiting your data to two-letter abbreviations.

Figure 4.7 shows an "internationalized" version of our sample CustList table that can store both U.S. and non-U.S. names and addresses.

FIGURE 4.7

A modified version of the CustList table, which can store both U.S. and foreign names and addresses

	Field Name	Type	Size
1	Last Name	Alpha	20
2	Mr/Mrs	Alpha	4
3	First Name	Alpha	20
4	MI	Alpha	2
5	Department/Title	Alpha	25
6	Company	Alpha	25
7	Address	Alpha	25
8	City	Alpha	20
9	State/Province	Alpha	20
10	Zip/Postal Code	Alpha	10
11	Country	Alpha	15
12	Area Code	Number	
13	Phone	Alpha	8
14	Extension	Alpha	5
15	Credit Limit	$ (Money)	
16	Start Date	Date	

▶▶ *Table Structure Limitations*

Paradox for Windows offers a lot of leeway in designing tables, and your tables can be monstrously large. Here are some guidelines for planning large tables:

- A single record can contain a maximum of 255 fields.

- A single record without a primary key index (described in a moment) can contain a maximum of about 32K characters, excluding formatted memo and memo fields, which can contain any number of characters.

- Indexed tables can contain a maximum of about 10K characters per record.

- A single table can contain a maximum of about 2 gigabytes (~2 billion characters).

Since you can link up to 24 tables in a single query, the real limitation of a database (that is, all the tables within a single database) is about 24 times the limitation of a single table. Chapters 5 and 16 explain how to join tables.

▶ ▶ **N O T E**

Of course, the practical size of your databases is limited to the amount of available disk space on your computer or network hard disk.

Once you've planned the field names, types, and sizes for your table, you *could* go online and create the table in Paradox for Windows. On the other hand, you might want to add some optional enhancements to your table design, as described next.

▶▶ *Planning Keys to Manage Data Efficiently*

A primary key (often just called a *key*) is a field or group of fields containing data that uniquely identifies each record of a table. When a primary key is defined for a table, values in the primary key fields of each record must be unique, and duplicate records are not allowed. Although primary keys are entirely optional, they can be great time savers because they help Paradox manage data more efficiently.

> **▶▶NOTE**
>
> **Tables that have primary keys are called *keyed tables*. dBASE tables do not use keys.**

In many ways, keys are analogous to street addresses. Just as no two buildings in a city can have the same street address, no two records in your table can have the same values in their key fields. And, just as unique street addresses help the mail carrier locate your home more quickly, keys provide an extremely efficient way to locate records in your table.

Keys also establish the default sort order for the table. Whenever you add a new record to the table, Paradox automatically places that record in sorted order, based on the value of the key field or fields.

Paradox for Windows stores each table's primary key in a special *index* file, called the *primary index*. The primary index contains the primary key values and corresponding record numbers. Paradox uses the index file to locate and display the records in a table.

If you've defined a primary key for a table, you can also define additional indexes called *secondary indexes*. These are used on an as-needed basis to speed queries and display data with a different sort order. Although primary index values must be unique for each record, the values in secondary indexes are not restricted in this way.

In this chapter, we'll focus on the primary index, since this is the only index that you must define while designing the table's structure. We'll explain how to create secondary indexes in Chapter 8.

▶ *Planning the Primary Index*

The primary index plays three important roles in Paradox for Windows:

- Paradox ensures that no two records in a table have the same information in the primary key. This prevents you from making duplicate entries by inadvertently putting the same information into a table twice.

- Paradox uses the primary index, as appropriate, to speed up searches and other operations.

- Paradox uses the primary index to maintain an ongoing sort order based on the field or fields that define the primary key. This saves the time required to re-sort the table whenever new records are added.

 ▶ ▶ **N O T E**

Paradox offers other ways to sort (alphabetize) records, which you'll learn about in Chapter 8.

To define a primary key for a table, you place an asterisk next to the field type in the table structure. When planning your table on paper, follow suit by jotting down an asterisk next to the field or fields that make up the primary key.

You should keep these rules in mind when planning the primary index:

- All the fields marked with an asterisk (*) in the table structure make up the *primary key*. (A primary key that is composed of more than one field is sometimes called a *composite key.*)

- The primary key must be the first field in the table. If you're defining a composite key, the fields must be grouped together at the top of the table structure. Examples will be presented shortly.

- No two records in a table can contain the same primary key values. If you use multiple fields to define the primary key, only records that have indentical data in *all* the primary key fields are considered duplicates.

Designing and
Creating Tables

Ch.
4

N O T E

Only one record's key can be blank. Paradox will consider all subsequent blanks to be duplicates and won't accept records that contain them.

- Paradox automatically sorts the table based on the primary key. The first field defines the main sort order, the second field defines the secondary ("tie-breaker") sort order, and so forth.

This last item is important because it defines the initial order in which records will appear in your table. Suppose you make Last Name and First Name the first two fields in your table structure, and you mark them each with an asterisk, like this:

	Field Name	Type	Size	Key
1	Last Name	Alpha	20	⋆
2	First Name	Alpha	20	⋆
3	Mr/Mrs	Alpha	4	
4	etc.			

Because the Last Name field comes before the First Name field in the table structure, records will be alphabetized by Last Name, then by first name in the case of identical last names. Thus, regardless of the order in which you *type* the following records into the table, Paradox will always *display* those records in the order shown below.

Last Name	First Name
Adams	Zeke
Smith	Arlene
Smith	Bob
Smith	Roger
Zeppo	Bob

Notice how the records are alphabetized by Last Name, then by First Name when the last names are identical (for example, Arlene Smith comes before Bob Smith).

Now let's suppose you put the First Name field *above* the Last Name field in the table structure, and again mark both fields with an asterisk, like this:

	Field Name	Type	Size	Key
1	First Name	Alpha	20	★
2	Last Name	Alpha	20	★
3	Mr/Mrs	Alpha	4	
4	etc.			

This tells Paradox to alphabetize records by First Name, and then by Last Name in the case of identical first names. You can see the result below.

First Name	Last Name
Arlene	Smith
Bob	Smith
Bob	Zeppo
Roger	Smith
Zeke	Adams

Here records are alphabetized by First Name, with the Last Name field acting as the tie-breaker. That is, when the First Names are identical, names are alphabetized by Last Name (Bob Smith comes before Bob Zeppo).

Obviously, this latter sort order is not the customary way to alphabetize people's names. The example illustrates the importance of the order in which you list key fields at the top of the table structure.

 **TIP**

> If you're still a little fuzzy on the concept of sorting or the role played by a "tie-breaker," see "Sorts within Sorts," in Chapter 8 for more information and examples.

Now let's look at some different ways you could define a primary key in a table like our CustList example.

▶ Using Existing Fields for the Primary Key

Always remember that the primary key plays the dual role of maintaining a sort order *and* preventing duplicate entries. Thus, if you wanted to keep the records in CustList in alphabetical order by Last Name and First Name, as described above, you could simply move the Last Name and First Name fields to the top of the table structure and mark them both with an asterisk, as we did earlier.

▶ ▶ W A R N I N G

You cannot mark a binary, bytes, formatted memo, graphic, logical, memo, or OLE field as a primary key.

While this technique *would* keep records sorted by Last Name and by First Name within common last names, it also might present a problem. Any two records with the same entry in the Last Name and First Name fields would be considered duplicates, and Paradox would reject the newer record. Thus, you couldn't add a record for John Smith in Omaha if the table already contained a record for John Smith in Honolulu.

Therefore, you need to think about what constitutes a duplicate entry. In this example, we might decide that any two records with the same entries in the Last Name, First Name, Middle Initial, Zip Code, and Address fields are probably duplicate entries.

If you want to keep records alphabetized by name, and only reject a new record if it has the same name, zip code, and address as some other record, you'd need to arrange and key the fields as in Figure 4.8.

The primary key definition in Figure 4.8 has one slight disadvantage. The combined length of the keyed fields, 77 characters, creates a fairly large key. As the table grows and the index grows in proportion, Paradox may not be able to fit the entire index into memory. Therefore, it will need to keep portions of the index on disk, which, in turn, can slow down processing as the table grows.

FIGURE 4.8 ▶

Defining Last Name, First Name, Middle Initial, Address, and Zip Code as the primary key keeps records sorted into alphabetical order by name.

Field Name	Type	Size	Key
1 Last Name	Alpha	20	*
2 First Name	Alpha	20	*
3 MI	Alpha	2	*
4 Zip Code	Alpha	10	*
5 Address	Alpha	25	*
6 Mr/Mrs	Alpha	4	
7 Company	Alpha	25	
8 etc...			

▶ Using a Single Field as the Primary Key

If you're more concerned about preventing duplicate entries and getting quick access to information than you are about keeping names alphabetized, and you want to keep the primary key small, you might want to consider using a single field that uniquely identifies each record as the primary index.

Many businesses use customer phone numbers as a primary key. For instance, when I call to order a pizza, the guy on the other end of the phone always asks for my phone number, which uniquely identifies me in his database. If all your customers are local (within one area code), you could follow suit and define the Phone field as the primary key, like this:

	Field Name	Type	Size	Key
1	Phone	Alpha	8	★
2	Last Name	Alpha	20	
3	Mr/Mrs	Alpha	4	
4	First Name	Alpha	20	
5	etc.			

If your table includes customers from several area codes, you'd need to include the area code as part of the primary key, since any two customers might have the same phone number but different area codes. In that case, you'd need to arrange and mark the fields like this:

	Field Name	Type	Size	Key
1	Area Code	Number		★
2	Phone	Alpha	8	★
3	Last Name	Alpha	20	
4	Mr/Mrs	Alpha	4	
5	First Name	Alpha	20	
6	etc.			

Either way, the beauty of using the phone number as the primary key is that you can find all the information you need about a customer simply by typing in the customer's phone number, the way my pizza guy does.

Of course, this primary key means that records will always be sorted by phone number. But, as you'll see, if you need to re-sort the records into alphabetical order by name in order to print a customer list, or into zip code order for bulk mailing, you can do so quite easily at any time.

▶ Creating a Field for the Primary Key

A third option for defining a primary key is to create a new field that uniquely identifies each record in the table. This method is handy when there is no field, or even a combination of fields, in the table that is guaranteed to identify each record uniquely.

Many businesses do things this way, which explains why you have a social security number and umpteen different bank, credit card, and other account numbers. Those numbers uniquely identify you, or your accounts, in somebody's database.

Even the phone number, which might be a handy way for a small business to identify customers in a local community, is not a sure-fire way to identify customers correctly. After all, people move and change their phone numbers all the time.

If your table will be large, and you plan to keep customers around for a long time, you might want to assign each customer a unique identifying number by creating a new field, perhaps named *Customer Number* (or *Cust No* for short). You'd want to make sure this new Cust No field is the first one in the table structure, and then mark it as the primary key, as shown in Figure 4.9.

FIGURE 4.9 ▶

A new field, named Cust No, added to the CustList table. Each customer will need to have a unique customer identification number in this field, since it's the primary key.

	Field Name	Type	Size	Key
1	Cust No	Number		*
2	Last Name	Alpha	20	
3	Mr/Mrs	Alpha	4	
4	First Name	Alpha	20	
5	MI	Alpha	2	
6	Department/Title	Alpha	25	
7	Company	Alpha	25	
8	Address	Alpha	25	
9	City	Alpha	20	
10	State	Alpha	2	
11	Zip Code	Alpha	10	
12	Area Code	Number		
13	Phone	Alpha	8	
14	Extension	Alpha	5	
15	Credit Limit	$ (Money)		
16	Start Date	Date		

The Beauty of Autoincrement Fields

As mentioned earlier, the autoincrement (+) field type is ideal for automatically generating unique identifying numbers, such as customer numbers, order numbers, and invoice numbers. Each time you add a new record, Paradox automatically bumps the value in an autoincrement field ahead by one (Paradox will make sure the numbers remain unique even if several people are updating the table on a network). Thus the first value will be 1, then next value 2, and so on.

You can save some time and avoid brain strain during data entry by using the autoincrement field type as the key field in customer tables,

invoice tables, product tables, and other tables that require unique identifying numbers in a key field.

The Downside of Autoincrement Fields

At first glance, autoincrement fields may seem to offer the perfect solution to all your numbering problems. Unfortunately, autoincrement
field types do have some drawbacks that you should consider before using them.

- Only one autoincrement field is allowed in each record. Typically,
  you'll want this to be the key field in the table.

- You cannot choose the starting value for the field when you create
  the table—you're stuck with starting at 1. However, in Chapters 5
  and 18, we'll present workarounds that let you choose whatever
  starting value you want.

- You cannot change the value in an autoincrement field.

- If you delete a record, you'll be left with a "hole" in the numbering scheme (often that's what you want, but you should be aware
  of it). Suppose you're using an autoincrement type for the Cust
  No (customer number) field. If you delete the second record in
  your table, your customer numbers will now be 1, 3, 4, etc. Customer number 2 is gone forever and cannot be assigned to anyone else.

As you can see, there are no hard-and-fast rules for choosing the "best"
fields or field types for a primary key. It all depends on what fields are
in the table and how you'll be using the table. You'll see additional examples of primary keys in upcoming chapters, and you'll learn much
more about setting up multitable databases in Chapter 5.

Now let's look at another feature you can build into your table structure—validity checks.

▶▶ *Planning Validity Checks*

One of the oldest acronyms in the computer world is GIGO, which
stands for Garbage In, Garbage Out. In database management terms,
this means that if you put meaningless information into the database,

you will get meaningless information right back out when printing data later.

The most common cause of entering meaningless information into a table is simply not paying attention to the screen while typing. For instance, a data-entry person might type a zip code into a Last Name field, or an account number into a credit limit field, simply because he or she is not watching the screen while typing.

Validity checks help minimize such errors by checking the data *before* it's accepted into the table. While validity checks can't prevent every imaginable error, they certainly can reduce the likelihood of errors occurring. Validity checks can also speed your data entry efforts by automatically filling in all, or part, of certain fields. Paradox for Windows offers the validity checking options summarized in Table 4.2. Each option is described in more detail in the sections that follow.

▶ Planning a Required Field

Required fields cannot be left blank in any record. For example, you might want to make the Cust No field in the CustList table shown in Figure 4.9 a required field to ensure that each customer is assigned a customer number.

▶ **TABLE 4.2:** *Summary of Paradox Validity Checks*

VALIDITY CHECK	PURPOSE
Required Field	The field cannot be left blank.
Minimum	The value entered in the field must be greater than or equal to the specified minimum value.
Maximum	The value entered in the field must be less than or equal to the specified maximum value.
Default	The specified value is placed in the field automatically when entering records but can be changed if necessary.
Picture	Provides a template for the format of data entered into the field, can limit entry to letters or numbers, and can insert repetitive text automatically.

> ▶▶ **N O T E**
>
> At least one field in any table must *not* be defined as Required.

▶ *Planning Minimum and Maximum Entries*

You can define a minimum or maximum value for any alpha, date, long integer, money, number, short number, time, or timestamp field in your table. You can also specify a *range* of acceptable values by defining both a minimum and a maximum value for any of these field types. For example, you could specify that the Credit Limit field accept no value less than zero, nor greater than 10,000.

▶ *Planning a Default Value*

A *default value* appears automatically in a field while you're entering data into the table. A default is only a *suggested* value, and you can change it whenever you want.

Suppose our sample CustList table is for a business in California, and the majority of customers are California residents. You could make CA the default value for the State field. When entering data into the table later, CA would automatically appear as the entry for the State field. You could either leave that entry as it is or change it to the abbreviation for another state.

Similarly, you could make TODAY the default value for the Start Date field, so that the current date is automatically placed in that field when you're entering new records.

> ▶▶ **N O T E**
>
> The command TODAY is a special validity check that can be used only in a date field to define the current date as the default entry for that field. Unfortunately, Paradox offers no such validity check for automatically putting the current time or time and date into time and timestamp fields.

▶ *Planning a Picture Template*

A picture lets you define a format, or *template*, for the contents of a field. The template limits the type of data you can enter in a field; it can also insert certain characters into the field for you automatically. The special characters used to define a picture are summarized in Table 4.3.

▶▶ **TIP**

When you go online to create your table, you can use an Assist button to help you create and test picture templates.

Any character other than one of the symbols listed in Table 4.3 is a *constant* (also called a *literal*). Constants are interpreted as text to be inserted into a field.

Here's an example. Suppose you define the picture for a field named *Social Security No* as ###-##-####. The # symbol ensures that only

▶ **TABLE 4.3:** *Symbols Used in Picture Formats*

SYMBOL	ACCEPTS
#	Numeric digits (0–9, comma, hyphen)
?	Any letter A–Z or a–z
&	Any letter, but automatically converts it to uppercase
@	Any character
!	Any character, but converts a letter to uppercase
*	The symbol that follows can be repeated any number of times
;	Interprets the symbol that follows as a literal character, not as a picture character
[ ]	Optional entry
{}	Specifies a group of acceptable entries
,	Separates acceptable values within a group

numeric digits will be allowed into the field. Since hyphens (-) are not one of the symbols in Table 4.3, typing **123456789** into the Social Security No field would result in *123-45-6789,* because Paradox would automatically insert these constants. With this picture template, it would be impossible to omit a number or type a letter in place of a number since the picture requires nine numeric digits.

Another handy template might be #####[-####] used in a Zip Code field. The # symbols would allow only numeric characters into the field. The square brackets after the first five digits indicate that the rest of the entry is optional. The hyphen would be inserted automatically before a sixth character was typed. Therefore, this template would accept both five-digit zip codes, like 91234, and nine-digit zip codes, like 91234-4321.

T I P

You *wouldn't* use a template like #####[-####] if you wanted your table to accept foreign zip codes with letters. The # symbol will accept only numbers.

You can do some pretty complicated things with picture templates. For instance, if you want to use a symbol as a literal character in a field, precede the symbol with a semicolon. Suppose you have an inventory system that uses the # symbol in part codes, as in the part number ABC-#1234. If you tried using the picture &&&-#@@@@, then an entry such as ABC-1234 would be considered incomplete because Paradox interprets -#@@@@ as requiring five characters to the right of the hyphen. However, if you define the picture as &&&-;#@@@@, Paradox knows that the # symbol is to be placed into the entry as a constant. So when you typed **ABC1234,** Paradox would convert that entry to *ABC-#1234.*

You can also use a picture template to convert the case of letters. For example, the picture template &*? allows an entry of any length and converts the first letter to uppercase. Thus, if you define the picture template for the Last Name field as &*@, you can type **smith** as the contents of that field and Paradox will automatically convert that entry to *Smith.* The picture template !*@ also allows an entry of any length and converts the first letter to uppercase. However, unlike the picture

&*@, which requires the first character to be a letter, the !*@ picture would let you enter a number or other symbol as the first character.

The curly brace symbols let you define a group of acceptable values for a field. When typing an entry into a field with a picture that includes curly braces, you need only type the first letter of any valid entry. Paradox will then fill in the rest of the field for you.

▶▶TIP

If your field can only have one of two values, you can assign it the *logical* field type. Then, during data entry, you can choose a *logical format* that displays values such as Yes or No, Male or Female, and so on. You'll learn how to do this in Chapter 7.

To illustrate, suppose your table contains an alpha field named *Member*, which you want to fill with *Yes* for people who are members, *No* for people who aren't, and *Unknown* if you don't know their status. You could assign the picture template {Yes,No,Unknown} to that field. Later, when entering data into that table, typing the letter **Y** would fill in the field with *Yes*; typing **N** would fill in *No*; and typing **U** would fill in *Unknown*. Any other entry would be unacceptable. If you wanted the Member field to contain one of the single characters **Y** or **N** or **U**, you'd define the picture as {Y,N,U} rather than {Yes,No,Unknown}.

▶▶NOTE

As a shortcut to typing the first value in the picture during data entry, you can press the spacebar. Thus, pressing spacebar in a field that has the picture format {Yes,No,Unknown} would automatically fill in *Yes*.

The pictures that support alternative choices can be *nested*—that is, placed inside one another—to allow multiple choices with the same first letter. You need to nest options whenever two or more options in the list start with the same letter.

For instance, take a look at this picture:

{Mon,Tue,Wed,Thu,Fri}

When entering data into a field with this picture, typing the letter **T** would automatically fill in the field as *Tue* because *Tue* comes before *Thu* in the list of alternatives.

To provide the options *ue* and *hu* within the common *T* entry, nest these choices within the *T* entry, like this:

{Mon,T{ue,hu},Wed,Fri}

Translated into English, the above picture reads, "Accept **M**, **T**, **W**, or **F** entries. If a **T** is entered, accept either **u** or **h** before filling in the rest of the field."

▶ ▶ **T I P**

> **To define a large list of acceptable entries, such as two-letter state abbreviations or valid part numbers from an inventory table, you can use the Table Lookup validity check described in Chapter 6.**

Notice that the above example has as many open curly braces as closed curly braces. When entering your own pictures, make sure that yours also have an equal number of open and closed braces.

Curly braces can also be used to force entry of a particular character instead of filling in that character automatically. For example, if you use the template ###-##-#### for a Social Security field, Paradox will automatically fill in the two hyphens when you enter the number. If you prefer to type in the hyphens yourself (but still want Paradox to reject any other character), you can enter the picture ###{-}##{-}####. In a sense, {-} means, "The only option allowed here is a hyphen."

▶ ▶ **W A R N I N G**

When creating picture templates of your own, avoid using symbols that conflict with the field type. For example, you would not want to use the ? or @ symbol in a numeric field since these symbols require alphabetic characters, and numeric fields allow only numbers.

Figure 4.10 shows some sample validity checks jotted down on the scratchpad structure of the sample CustList table. Notice that Cust No is the primary key that uniquely identifies each customer. It's also a required field that is never left blank. Finally, by assigning the picture #### to the field, we've made sure that each ID number is exactly four digits long.

FIGURE 4.10 ▶

Sample validity checks for the CustList table jotted down on our scratchpad table design

	Field Name	Type	Size	Key	Validity Check
1	Cust No	Number		*	Required, ####
2	Last Name	Alpha	20		
3	Mr/Mrs	Alpha	4		.
4	First Name	Alpha	20		
5	MI	Alpha	2		
6	Department/Title	Alpha	25		
7	Company	Alpha	25		
8	Address	Alpha	25		Required
9	City	Alpha	20		
10	State	Alpha	2		!!
11	Zip Code	Alpha	10		#####[-####]
12	Area Code	Number			###
13	Phone	Alpha	8		###-####
14	Extension	Alpha	5		
15	Credit Limit	$ (Money)			$0.00 - $10,000
16	Start Date	Date			Default=Today

▶ ▶ **T I P**

If you want to prevent customers from being assigned awkward customer numbers like 6 or 42, you can define a minimum validity check of 1001. Then you can assign customer numbers starting at 1001, followed by 1002, 1003, and so forth.

The #### template will limit the number of customer records in the table since the largest customer number that fits the pattern is 9999. To allow for more customers, we could just increase the picture to #####, which can accept any number up to 99,999.

In Figure 4.10, we've made Address a required field and devised picture templates to help verify the zip code, area code, and phone number entries and to convert any two-letter state abbreviations to uppercase letters. We've also limited the entry in the Credit Limit field to a number between 0 and $10,000, and made the current date (TODAY) the default in the Start Date field.

The examples here should provide some food for thought as you design your own validity checks. Of course, you can always try working without the validity checks for a while. If data entry errors become a problem, you can always update the table structure with validity checks that will minimize those errors.

▶ ▶ *Creating a Table*

After planning your table and deciding what fields the table will require, you can fire up Paradox for Windows and create the table online. Remember to keep all the tables and other objects that belong together in a single directory. If you haven't already created the directory, do so first, using the Windows File Manager, as presented in Lesson 1 of Chapter 2. (Wouldn't it be nice if Paradox could create directories for you? Sigh.)

►►N O T E

If you want several network users to share data in a table, you must create the table in a shared directory.

Now you're ready to create a table. Follow these steps:

1. If you haven't already done so, choose File ➤ Working Directory. Then switch to the directory where you want to store the new table.

2. Choose File ➤ New ➤ Table. Or inspect (right-click) the Open Table button on the Toolbar or the Tables icon in the Project Viewer, then choose New from the menu that appears. You'll see the Table Type dialog box shown below.

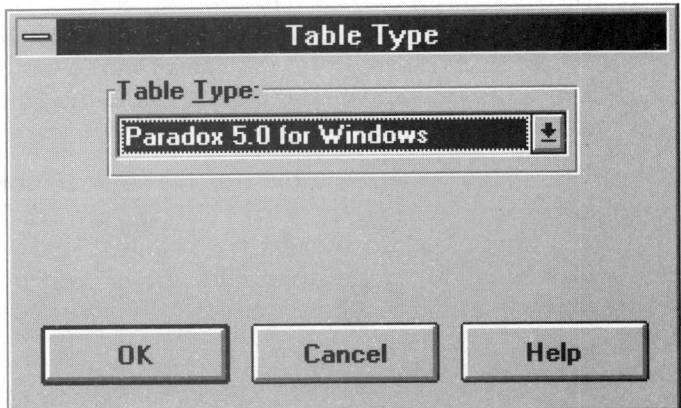

3. Assuming you want to use the standard Paradox format, choose OK to select the suggested table type, Paradox for Windows. You'll see the Create Table dialog box shown in Figure 4.11.

►►N O T E

You can define tables in a variety of formats. The format of the table you're creating (e.g., Paradox for Windows) always appears in the title bar of the Create Table dialog box. Non-Paradox formats are covered in Appendix D.

FIGURE 4.11

*Use the Create Table
dialog box to define
the structure of a new
table.*

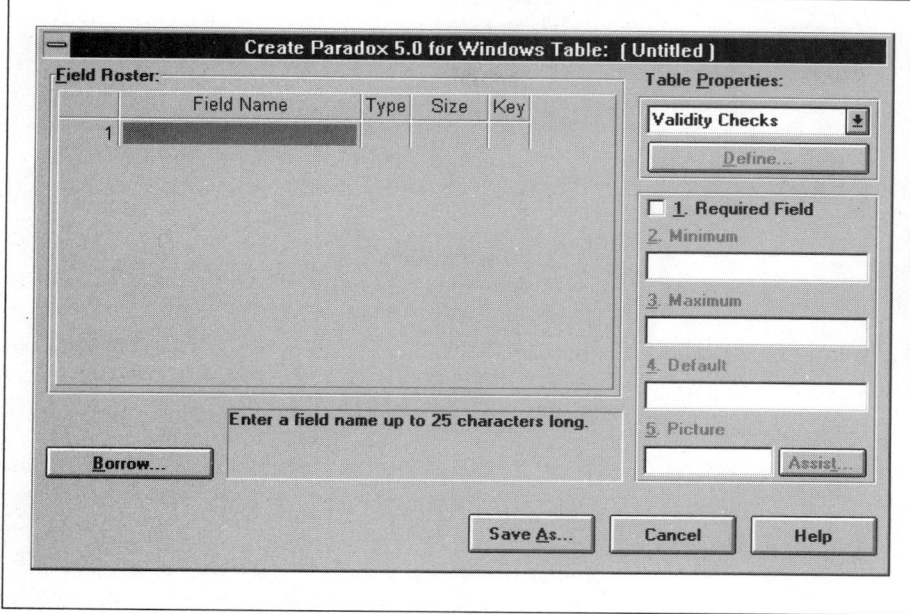

4. Type a field name (up to 25 characters long), then press Tab or ↵
or → to move the cursor into the Type column.

▶ ▶ TIP

**If the Field Roster is empty, and you'd like to copy the
structure of another table for use as the starting point
for your new table, click the Borrow button. Then
select the table you want to borrow from, check any
options for table properties you want to copy, and
choose OK.**

5. When the cursor is in the Type column, use one of the following
techniques to define the field type:

- Click the right mouse button or press the spacebar to view a
menu of field types (shown below). Then choose the field
type you want.

Type
Alpha
Number
$ [Money]
Short
Long **I**nteger
[BCD]
Date
Time
@ [Timestamp]
Memo
Formatted Memo
Graphic
OLE
Logical
± [Autoincrement]
Binary
B**y**tes

- Type the one-letter abbreviation for the field type (the under-lined letter or character in the menu above).

▶ ▶ **T I P**

> **While defining your table structure, check the message area below the field names for tips on filling in each column. This area also will tell you when entries in a column are optional or not allowed.**

6. Press Tab or ↵ or →. If the cursor lands in the Size column, you can define a size; if it lands in another column, skip to step 7.

- If you've defined the current field as # (BCD), alpha, bytes, or memo, type in a size.

- If you've defined the field as binary, formatted memo, graphic, memo, or OLE, you can either type in a size or leave the Size entry blank. If you're not sure yet what size will best suit your needs, enter 1 as the size (you can change it later, if necessary).

N O T E

> **You cannot choose the size for a $ (money), + (auto-increment), @ (timestamp), date, logical, long integer, number, short, or time field.**

7. Press Tab or ↵ or →. If the cursor lands in the Field Name column, skip to step 8 now. If the cursor lands in the Key column, you can assign the field as a key. To make the field a primary key field, double-click or press the spacebar. An asterisk (*) appears in the column. Remember, the fields you define as the primary key must be grouped together at the top of the table structure. To remove the asterisk, simply double-click or press the spacebar again.

N O T E

> **You cannot mark a binary, bytes, formatted memo, graphic, logical, memo, or OLE field as a primary key.**

8. If necessary, press ↵ or Tab or → to move down to the Field Name column in the next row.

9. Repeat steps 4–8 until you've defined all the fields for your table. If you need to make changes or corrections along the way, use any of the techniques listed in Table 4.4.

T I P

> **Instead of pressing Tab, ↵, or → to move through the Field Roster, you can click in the column you want to change. However, using the keyboard method offers an advantage over the mouse method: Paradox will automatically skip over columns that aren't valid for the current field.**

Figure 4.12 shows how the sample CustList customer table would look after you entered the first 11 field names, types, and sizes. (If you want

▶ **TABLE 4.4:** *Techniques for Making Changes and Corrections while Defining a Table Structure*

IF YOU WANT TO...	DO THIS...
Delete text in a column entry	Click where you want to start deleting, and use the Backspace or Delete key to delete characters. Or, select text by dragging the mouse pointer through the text, then press the Delete key. To delete characters from the cursor position to the start of the current word in the entry, press Ctrl+Backspace.
Delete entire field	Move the cursor to the field you want to delete, then press Ctrl+Delete.
Insert new field	To insert a new field between two existing fields, move the cursor to the lower of the two existing fields and press Insert.
Change field name	Click wherever you want to start changing text. Type new text, or use Backspace or Delete to delete existing text. Or, select text by dragging the mouse pointer through the text, then type the replacement text.
Move field	Click the row number in the leftmost column of the field you want to move. Hold down the mouse button, drag the field definition to its new location, and release the mouse button.
Start over from scratch	Choose Cancel to abandon current table structure.
Select/deselect primary key	Move the cursor to the Key column for the field and press the spacebar or double-click. An asterisk (*) appears in the Key column for the field when the key is on.
Undo a change to a column	Press Escape (Esc).

to duplicate that table structure exactly, refer to Figure 4.10 for field types and sizes of additional fields in the table.)

When you've finished typing the field names, types, and sizes (as appropriate), you can either save the table and start using it right away or, if you want to define validity checks, you can do so as explained in the next section.

FIGURE 4.12

The first 11 fields from the sample CustList table in the Create Table dialog box

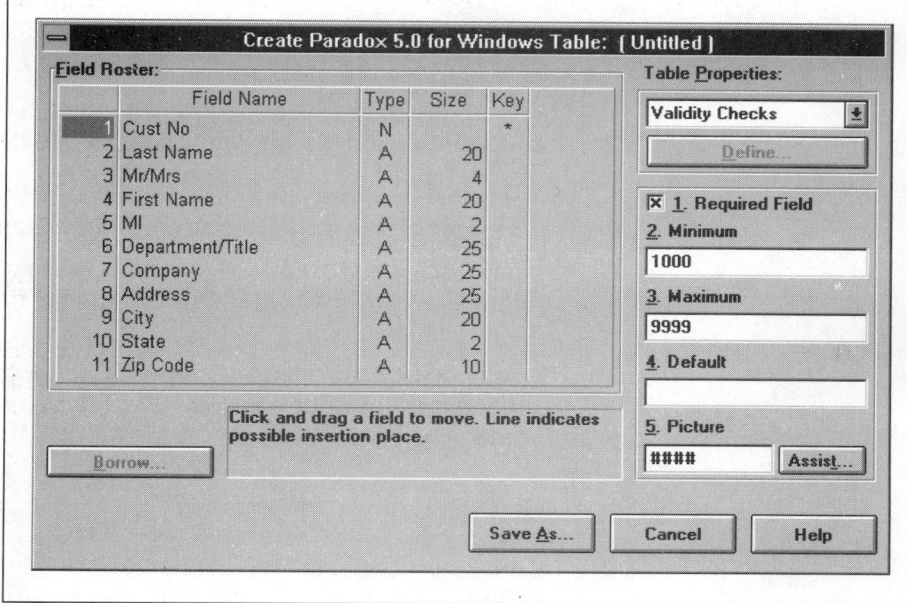

Defining Validity Checks

To define validity checks while you have the table structure on your screen, follow these steps:

1. First (and most important), highlight the field that you want to define the validity checks for. You can click the field with your mouse or use the arrow keys to position the cursor.

N O T E

You cannot define validity checks for autoincrement, BCD, binary, bytes, formatted memo, graphic, logical, memo, or OLE fields.

2. Under Table Properties near the upper-right corner of the dialog box, make sure *Validity Checks* appears in the text box. If it doesn't, click the drop-down list button and choose *Validity Checks* from the list that appears.

3. Fill in the following validity checks as needed:

- To make the current field a required field (one that can't be left blank), click the Required Field check box.
- To specify a minimum acceptable value for the current field, click the text box under Minimum and type in the smallest acceptable value.
- To specify a maximum acceptable value for the field, click the text box under Maximum and type in the largest acceptable value.

►►**TIP**

If you want to specify a range of acceptable values for a field, just fill in both the Minimum and Maximum validity check options.

- To specify a default value for the current field, click the text box under Default, then type in the default value.

►►**TIP**

If you're defining a validity check for a date field and want to make the current date the default value, type the word TODAY in the Default text box.

- To define a picture template for the current field, click the text box under Picture. Then type in the template or click the Assist button (described below) for help.

4. Repeat steps 1–3 as necessary for additional fields.

After defining your validity checks, you might want to double-check them before saving the table structure. Just use the ↑ and ↓ keys to move the cursor from field to field, and make sure that the validity checks that appear next to the highlighted field names are appropriate for that field. For instance, in Figure 4.12, the Cust No field is highlighted. Its Required Field validity option is checked, its minimum and maximum values are defined, and the #### picture template is defined.

Using the Assist Button to Define a Picture

If you need help defining a picture validity check, follow these steps:

Assist...

1. Click the Assist button (shown at left). You'll see the Picture Assistance dialog box shown in Figure 4.13.

2. If you'd like to use one of the sample picture formats, click the drop-down list button under Sample Pictures. Then select an example by clicking it. A description of the picture you selected will appear in the message area above the picture. Now click the Use button to copy the sample picture into the Picture text box.

FIGURE 4.13

You can use the Picture Assistance dialog box to help define and test picture validity checks. In this example, we also typed in a sample value, which is acceptable to the currently defined picture.

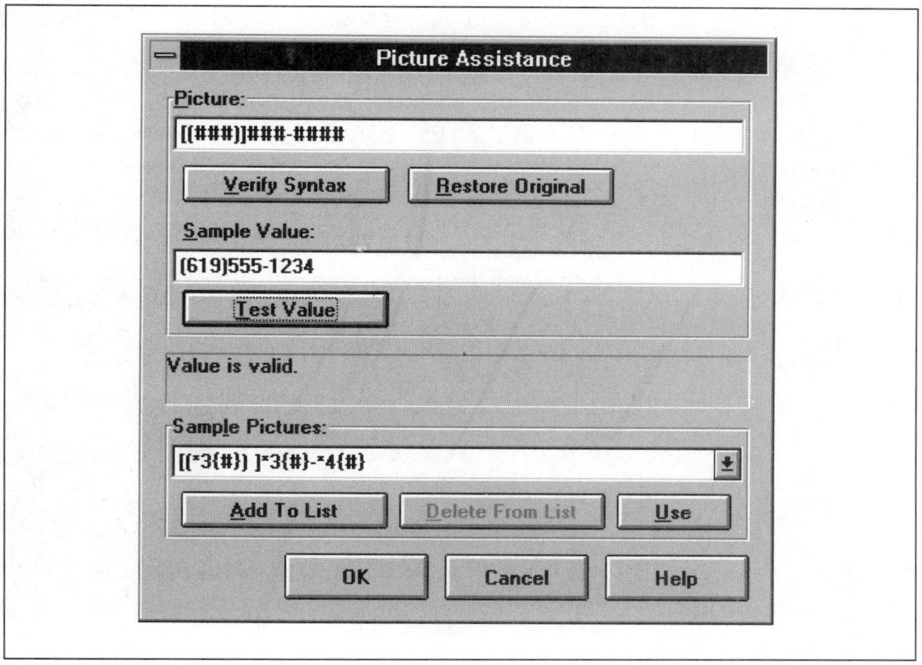

3. To complete or customize the picture further, position the insertion point in the Picture text box and make changes using the standard Windows editing techniques.

4. Use any of the techniques described below to test, change, or save the current picture. When you're satisfied with the picture template you've selected, choose OK.

When a picture appears in the Picture text box, you can check to see whether it contains any errors by clicking the Verify Syntax button. If Paradox reports errors in the message area, make any needed corrections, then click Verify Syntax again. If the picture has gone hopelessly awry and you can't fix it, you can erase the entire picture string or click the Restore Original button to return to the picture you had before clicking the Assist button.

You can also try out some sample values to see whether they'll work during data entry. Type a sample value into the Sample Value text box, then click the Test Value button. If the value is acceptable according to the currently defined picture, you'll see a *Value is Valid* message in the message area. Otherwise, you'll see an error message. If necessary, you can correct your sample value or the picture template until you're sure the picture you've entered in the Picture text box will do the trick as a validity check during data entry.

If you'd like to save the currently displayed picture in the Sample Pictures list so that you can quickly choose it as a starting point for other picture templates, click the Add To List button. A Save Picture dialog box, like the one below, will appear.

Enter a description for the picture format, then choose OK. The next time you open the Sample Pictures list box, the picture you added will appear in the list and you can select and copy it as described earlier.

To delete a picture template from the Sample Pictures list, click on the list to open it, click on the picture template you want to delete, then click the Delete From List button.

 ▶ ▶**N O T E**

> **Paradox only lets you delete pictures added to the Sample Pictures list through the Add To List button. You cannot delete the predefined picture formats.**

▶ *Deleting or Changing Validity Checks*

If you change your mind about a validity check you've assigned to a field, highlight that field. The validity checks for that field will appear in the dialog box.

To deactivate a Required Field validity check, click the check box to re-move the checkmark. To deactivate a Minimum, Maximum, Default, or Picture validity check, double-click the text box for the validity check you want to clear, then press the Delete or Backspace key. To change the Minimum, Maximum, Default, or Picture assigned to the field, click the text box for the validity check and make changes and correc-tions using the standard text editing keys and techniques for Windows text boxes.

▶ *Saving the Table Structure*

When you're satisfied with the table structure, follow the steps below to save it.

1. Click the Save As button. If you failed to complete any necessary steps, or you've entered invalid or conflicting field information, or you've left any blank rows in the table structure, Paradox will prompt you to correct the problem. You'll need to fix the prob-lems before proceeding.

2. When you've entered a valid table structure, you'll see the dialog box shown in Figure 4.14.

3. If you want to start entering data immediately, select (check) the Display Table option.

4. If you want to save the table on a different drive or directory, select the appropriate location from the Drive (or Alias) drop-down list box and the Directories area. The techniques are similar to those for changing the working directory, as described in Chapter 3.

5. In the New File Name text box, type a valid DOS file name for the table (omit the file name extension, since Paradox will add the proper extension automatically).

6. Choose OK.

You'll be returned to the Paradox Desktop. If you chose the Display Table option in step 3 above, the open, empty table will appear on the screen. (Otherwise, the table will not appear on the Desktop until you use the standard methods to open it.)

FIGURE 4.14 ▶

Use the Save Table As dialog box to save your table.

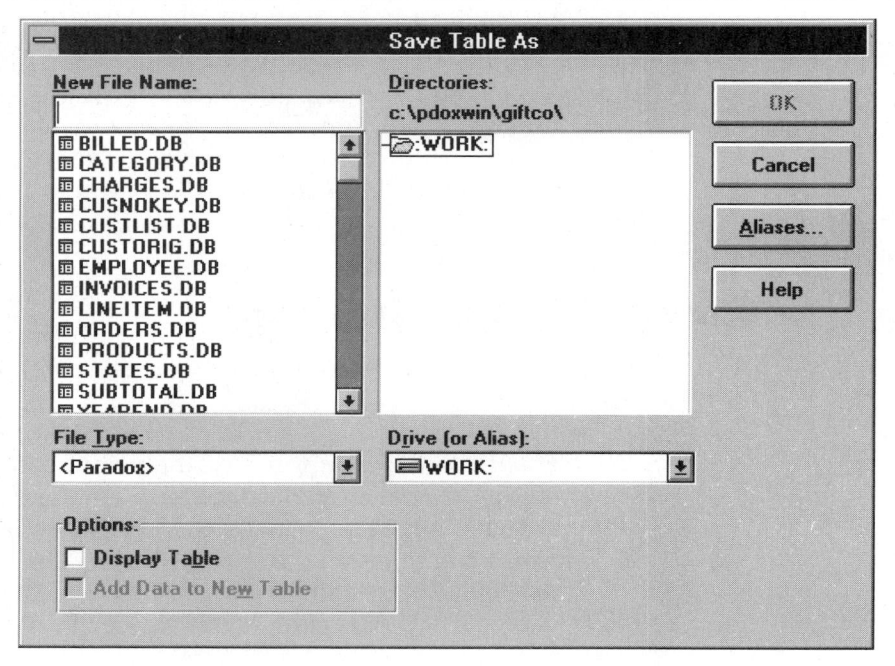

► ► **N O T E**

> If your table doesn't use any Paradox 5 for Windows
> features, Paradox will save it as a Paradox 4 table. This
> lets older versions of Paradox for Windows (that is,
> Paradox 4.*x*) use your table. If you later change your
> table structure to one that *does* use Paradox 5 for
> Windows features, Paradox will upgrade the table to
> Paradox 5 for Windows format automatically (after
> asking permission to do so).

► ► *Changing a Table Structure*

For future reference, be aware that you can change the structure of a table at any time. However, if you want to change the table structure *after*
you've added a lot of data to it, you'd do well to take a look at Chapter 15
before restructuring. If at all possible, plan your table carefully *before*
adding data to it and before designing forms, reports, and queries for
it. If your table is empty now and you'd like to restructure it, you can
open the Restructure Table dialog box in any of the following ways:

- Right-click the table name in the Project Viewer and choose
  Res<u>t</u>ructure.

- Choose <u>T</u>ools ➤ <u>U</u>tilities ➤ Res<u>t</u>ructure and double-click the
  table name in the Select File dialog box that appears.

- Open the table on the Desktop and choose T<u>a</u>ble ➤ Restructure
  <u>T</u>able, or click the Restructure button in the Toolbar. (Some restructure operations aren't possible when the table is open, so you
  may prefer to use the other methods above to begin restructuring
  your table.)

From here, you can define new fields or change existing fields as explained earlier in this chapter.

►► *Files That Paradox Creates*

When you save a Paradox table, Paradox for Windows automatically adds the extension .db to the file name you provide. (dBASE tables have the extension .dbf.) Paradox might also create several auxiliary files, depending on the features used in your table design. Table 4.5 lists the file name extensions of table and auxiliary files.

► **TABLE 4.5:** *File Name Extensions for Tables and Related Files*

FILE NAME EXTENSION	CONTENTS
.db	Paradox table
.dbf	dBASE table
.dbt	Memos for dBASE table
.mb	Binary, formatted memo, graphic, memo, and OLE data for a Paradox table
.mdx	Maintained index of a dBASE table
.ndx	Non-maintained index of a dBASE table
.px	Primary index for a Paradox table
.tv	Table view settings for a Paradox table (if different from default Table View; see Chapter 7)
.tvf	Table view settings for a dBASE table
.val	Validity checks for a Paradox table
.x*nn*	Secondary single-field index for a Paradox table (where *nn* is a number)
.y*nn*	Secondary single-field index for a Paradox table (where *nn* is a number)
.xg*n*	Secondary multiple-field (composite) index for a Paradox table (where *n* is a number)
.yg*n*	Secondary multiple-field (composite) index for a Paradox table (where *n* is a number)

▶▶ **WARNING**

> When copying a table to a floppy disk or sending it through a modem, you must include any auxiliary files for that table. These auxiliary files have the same file name with different extensions; to include all of them, use the "wildcard" search operator *. For example, to copy all of the necessary files for a table named *customer,* you would want to copy *customer.*,* not just *customer.db.*

▶▶ *Planning an Entire Database*

In this chapter we've discussed all the nitty-gritty details of designing and creating a single Paradox table. But, as mentioned earlier, a complete database might require several *related* tables of information.

If you're new to database management, your best bet might be to keep working with a single table for the time being, since this is the ideal way to learn the basic skills. In this case, you might want to skip ahead to Chapter 6, which explains how to add and change data in tables. If you're experienced with database management systems, or are sure that you need to design a database with multiple tables, continue with the next chapter for more information on that topic.

CHAPTER 5

Database Design
with Multiple Tables

FAST TRACK

exist and from deleting a customer when outstanding orders exist for that customer. It also governs how Paradox handles updates to the key field of the customer table.

▶ **To define referential integrity**   198

choose *Referential Integrity* from the Table Properties list in the Create Table or Restructure Table dialog box.

▶ **A data model**   202

provides a diagram of relationships between tables and lets you link tables graphically. You can define a *reference data model* in the Data Model Designer and then save it as a separate file. Later, you can reuse the model when you create queries and design documents (forms and reports). You can also create (and have the option to save) a data model when you create a design document.

▶ **To create and save a reference data model**   204

choose Tools – Data Model Designer. To add tables to the model, click the Add Table button in the Toolbar, select one or more tables or queries (using click or Ctrl-click as needed), and choose OK. To link two tables, use your mouse to draw a line between the master table (parent) and the detail table (child); if necessary, specify the common fields that link the two tables. To save your reference data model, click the Save Data Model button in the Toolbar, enter a file name (without an extension), and choose OK.

▶ **To load a saved reference data model**   216

open the Data Model Designer, click the Load Data Model button in the toolbar, and then double-click the data model file you want.

► ► **P**aradox for Windows allows you to manage data stored in separate, related tables. Determining when and how to divide data into separate, related tables is an important element of *database design*.

Sometimes it's obvious when data needs to be stored in separate tables. For instance, it makes little sense for a business to store all of its customer information and all of its inventory information in a single table. However, other situations are less obvious, and knowing exactly how to separate information into multiple tables can be tricky.

In this chapter, we'll look at basic multitable design concepts. The examples you'll find should serve as food for thought when deciding how best to store information for your own needs. We'll discuss the clues that can help you determine when two or more tables might be better than one. We'll also explain how to make the most of referential integrity, a feature of Paradox for Windows that preserves the ties between related tables. Finally, we'll show you how to define and save a data model that ties together all your related tables in a nice neat package. Once you've set up a data model, you can reuse it anytime you want to set up multitable queries, forms, and reports.

► ► *Types of Relationships between Tables*

Three types of relationships can exist between tables: the *one-to-many* relationship, the *many-to-many* relationship, and the *one-to-one* (or many-to-one) relationship. The most common of these is the one-to-many relationship.

▶ *The One-to-Many Relationship*

The one-to-many relationship describes a situation in which for every *one* record in a table, there may be *many* records of related information in another table. The classic example of a one-to-many relationship involves the task of managing customers and the orders they place. Because any *one* customer might place *many* orders over time, you have a natural one-to-many situation.

Figure 5.1 shows one way you could divide information about customers and orders into two tables. The Cust No field acts as the *common field* (also called the *key field*) that relates information from one table to another. We can easily tell which customer a particular order belongs to by locating the customer number in the Orders table, then locating the same customer number in the CustList table.

FIGURE 5.1 ▶

Example of a one-to-many relationship between tables. The common field, Cust No, appears in both tables and indicates which customer placed each order.

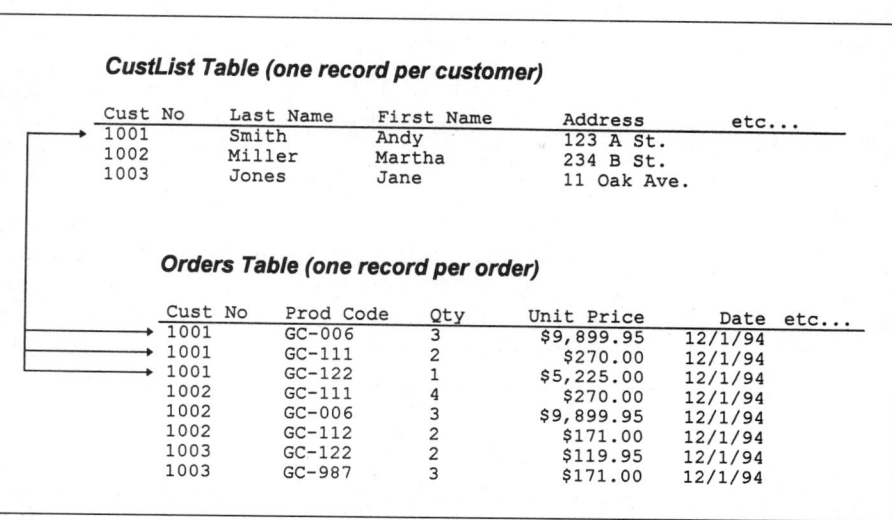

When defining the common field that links two tables, you must keep these important points in mind:

- The common field must have the same field type in both tables. Or, if one table uses an autoincrement field type for the common field, the corresponding field in the other table must be a long integer.

Design with Multiple Tables

Ch. 5

- If the common field is alphanumeric, it must be the same size in both tables.

- In the table that's on the "one" side of the one-to-many relationship, the common key field is generally called the *primary key*.

- In the table that's on the "many" side of the one-to-many relationship, the common field is called the *foreign key*.

Figure 5.2 shows the underlying structure of the CustList and Orders tables shown in Figure 5.1. The common field, Cust No, is the Number field type in both tables.

FIGURE 5.2

►

Structure of the sample CustList and Orders tables shown in Figure 5.1

Structure of the CustList Table

Field Name	Type	Size	Key
Cust No	Number		*
Last Name	Alpha	20	
First Name	Alpha	15	
Address	Alpha	35	
City	Alpha	20	
State	Alpha	2	
Zip Code	Alpha	10	
etc...			

Structure of the Orders Table

Field Name	Type	Size	Key
Cust No	Number		
Prod Code	Alpha	8	
Qty	Number		
Unit Price	$ (Money)		
Date	Date		
etc...			

In the CustList table shown in Figure 5.2, Cust No is marked as a primary key (*). Making Cust No the primary key in the CustList table will prevent us from assigning two different customers the same customer number, and will also speed things along down the road. (Chapter 4 explains how to define and use primary keys.)

We did not make Cust No a primary key in the Orders table because we wanted to ensure that customers could order as many items as they want. If we had made Cust No a primary key in the Orders table, we would be able to enter only one order for each customer.

The relationship between products and orders provides another example of a one-to-many relationship, as illustrated in Figure 5.3. In this example, the Products table stores one record for each inventory item.

FIGURE 5.3

The Products table keeps track of items in the inventory. The Orders table keeps track of individual orders.

Products Table (one record per product)

Prod Code	Description	In Stock	Unit Price etc...
GC-006	Van	100	$9,899.95
GC-111	Guernsey Cow	50	$270.00
GC-112	Wooly Wombat (Male)	25	$171.00
GC-122	Mountain Bicycle	100	$5,225.00
GC-987	Wooly Wombat (Female)	47	$171.00

Orders Table (one record per order)

Cust No	Prod Code	Qty	Unit Price	Date etc...
1001	GC-006	3	$9,899.95	12/1/94
1001	GC-111	2	$270.00	12/1/94
1001	GC-122	1	$5,225.00	12/1/94
1002	GC-111	4	$270.00	12/1/94
1002	GC-006	3	$9,899.95	12/1/94
1002	GC-112	2	$171.00	12/1/94
1003	GC-122	2	$119.95	12/1/94
1003	GC-987	3	$171.00	12/1/94

Once again, we're using a common field to relate the two tables. Each product in the Products table has a unique product code (Prod Code) assigned to it. That code is used in the Orders table to identify the products each customer has ordered. As Figure 5.4 illustrates, Prod Code is an alpha field with a length of eight in both tables.

Paradox for Windows has automatic updating features you can use to ensure that the Products table is always up-to-date. For example, you can have Paradox subtract the quantities of items sold from the in-stock quantities in the Products table as orders are filled. This way, the Products table will always accurately reflect the quantity of each item in stock. Chapter 18 discusses automatic updating in detail.

FIGURE 5.4 ▶

Structure of the sample Products and Orders tables shown in Figure 5.3. Here, Prod Code is the key field and is the same field type and size in both tables.

Structure of the Products Table

Field Name	Type	Size	Key
Prod Code	Alpha	8	*
Description	Alpha	30	
In Stock	Number		
Unit Price	$ (Money)		
etc...			

Structure of the Orders Table

Field Name	Type	Size	Key
Cust No	Number		
Prod Code	Alpha	8	
Qty	Number		
Unit Price	$ (Money)		
Date	Date		
etc...			

▶ The Many-to-Many Relationship

The many-to-many relationship occurs when *many* records from one table might be related to *many* records in another table. Suppose you're designing a database for a school and need to schedule students and courses. In this situation, there is a many-to-many relationship between students and the courses in which they enroll: The school offers many courses, and any given course will have many students enrolled in it.

So how do you set up tables for this many-to-many relationship between students and courses? As illustrated in Figure 5.5, you create one table of students, one table of courses, and then use a third table to place students in courses.

Notice how concise the tables are. The Students table contains information about students only. The Courses table contains information about courses only. (Both the Students and Courses tables could store much more information—they're summarized to fit on the page.) The third table, Schedule, links students to courses in a simple, direct manner.

If you look closely at Figure 5.5, you'll discover that the many-to-many relationship actually consists of several one-to-many relationships between tables. There's a one-to-many relationship between the Students

FIGURE 5.5

The many-to-many de-sign is used to keep track of which students are enrolled in which courses in a school.

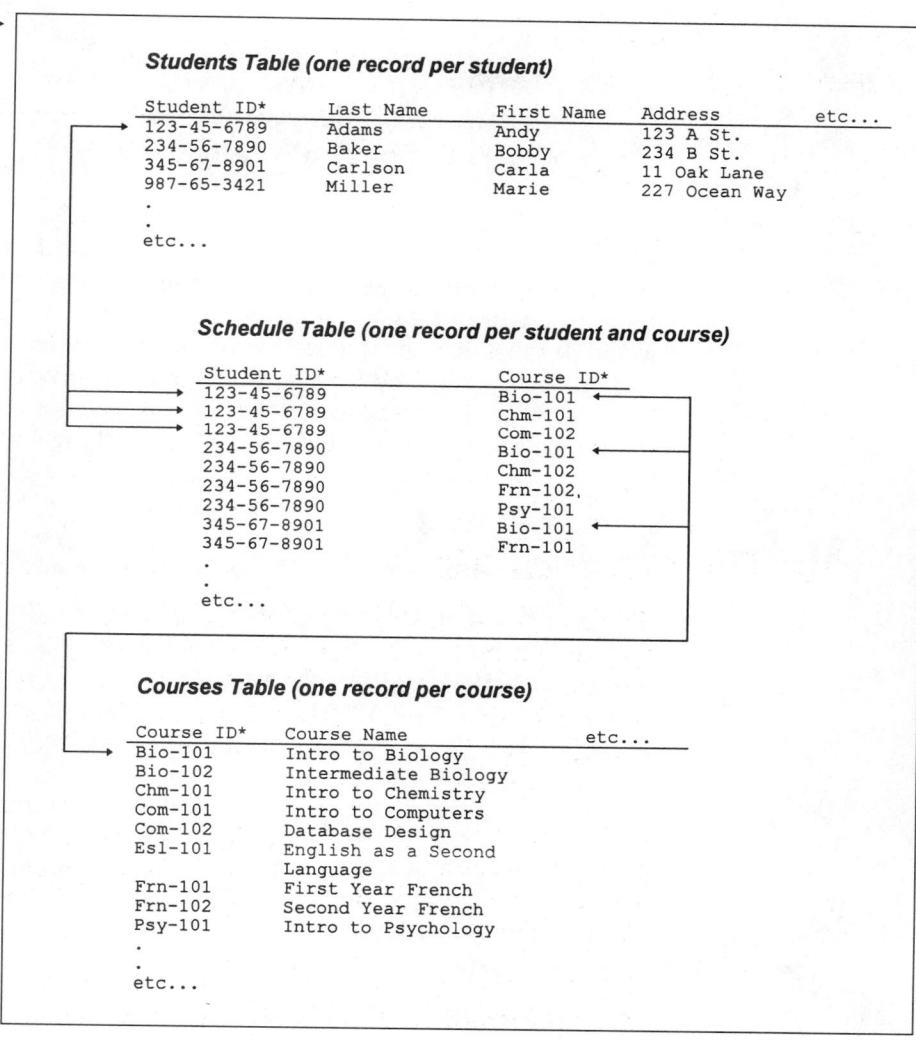

Students Table (one record per student)

Student ID*	Last Name	First Name	Address	etc...
123-45-6789	Adams	Andy	123 A St.	
234-56-7890	Baker	Bobby	234 B St.	
345-67-8901	Carlson	Carla	11 Oak Lane	
987-65-3421	Miller	Marie	227 Ocean Way	
.				
.				

etc...

Schedule Table (one record per student and course)

Student ID*	Course ID*
123-45-6789	Bio-101
123-45-6789	Chm-101
123-45-6789	Com-102
234-56-7890	Bio-101
234-56-7890	Chm-102
234-56-7890	Frn-102.
234-56-7890	Psy-101
345-67-8901	Bio-101
345-67-8901	Frn-101
.	
.	

etc...

Courses Table (one record per course)

Course ID*	Course Name	etc...
Bio-101	Intro to Biology	
Bio-102	Intermediate Biology	
Chm-101	Intro to Chemistry	
Com-101	Intro to Computers	
Com-102	Database Design	
Esl-101	English as a Second Language	
Frn-101	First Year French	
Frn-102	Second Year French	
Psy-101	Intro to Psychology	
.		
.		

etc...

Design with Multiple Tables

Ch. **5**

and Schedule tables and a one-to-many relationship between the Courses and Schedule tables. The Schedule table creates the many-to-many rela-tionship between Students and Courses. In fact, a many-to-many relation-ship is always a pair of one-to-many relationships between two tables, with a third table creating the many-to-many link.

▶ ▶ **N O T E**

> There is also a many-to-many relationship between the CustList and Products tables described earlier. The Orders table acts as the linking table.

In Figure 5.5, we've placed an asterisk next to field names that are keyed in the underlying table structures. *Student ID* is keyed in the Students table to ensure that each *student* has a unique Student ID. *Course ID* is keyed in the Courses table to ensure that each *course* has a unique ID. Together, Student ID and Course ID form the primary key in the Schedule table. This prevents students from being enrolled in the same course more than once and will speed things up when working with the data.

▶ ▶ **N O T E**

> When two or more fields in a table define the primary key, only records that have identical entries in all the keyed fields are considered duplicates. This type of key is called a *composite key*.

Of course, even with data spread across three tables, you can combine the information into data-entry forms, printed reports, and queries (see Chapters 16 and 17). With the Students, Schedule, and Courses tables, for instance, you can print student schedules and class roll sheets.

▶ *The One-to-One Relationship*

In the one-to-one relationship, for every *one* record in a table, there's exactly one corresponding record in another table. Figure 5.6 provides an example of a one-to-one relationship: For every record in the Employee table, there is exactly one corresponding record in the EmpInfo table.

A one-to-one relationship like this usually indicates a flawed database design. After all, if an exact one-to-one relationship exists between every record in two different tables, why not just put all the information into one table? In the rare cases listed below, the one-to-one design might make sense.

FIGURE 5.6

A one-to-one relation-ship exists between records in the Employee and EmpInfo tables.

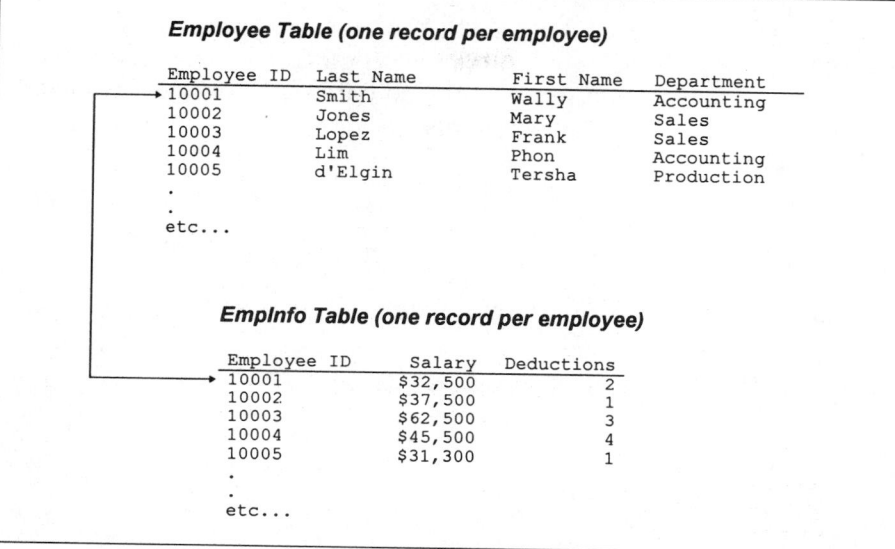

```
                    Employee Table (one record per employee)

         Employee ID    Last Name        First Name   Department
    →    10001          Smith            Wally        Accounting
         10002          Jones            Mary         Sales
         10003          Lopez            Frank        Sales
         10004          Lim              Phon         Accounting
         10005          d'Elgin          Tersha       Production
         .
         .
         etc...


                    EmpInfo Table (one record per employee)

             Employee ID       Salary     Deductions
    →        10001             $32,500         2
             10002             $37,500         1
             10003             $62,500         3
             10004             $45,500         4
             10005             $31,300         1
             .
             .
             etc...
```

Design with
Multiple Tables

Ch
5

- If you need more fields or characters than a single record can store, you can split the fields into two tables. You still must use a common field (like Employee ID in Figure 5.6) to link records from one table to the other. (This case is unlikely, because Paradox records can be very large and include many fields; see Chapter 4 for details.)

- If you need to limit access to some (but not all) fields, a one-to-one design can be useful. For instance, you could provide full access to all fields in the Employee table, but password protect the EmpInfo table, which contains salary information. However, a better solution is to place all fields in the Employee table, then assign auxiliary passwords with appropriate field rights to each field you want to protect. Chapter 15 explains how to assign passwords to tables and fields.

▶ Categorizing Information

In general, it is *not* a good idea to use multiple tables to categorize information. Imagine, for example, that you want to manage personnel information for a company with several different departments. Your first inclination might be to create one table for people in the accounting department, then create a second table for people in the marketing department, and so on. This might be handy when you want to work with personnel data for people in a given department only, but it will be a pain when you need data for all employees or for employees from several departments.

You'd be much better off creating one table, perhaps named *Employee*, to store data for all employees in the company. Include a Department field to describe the department in which the employee works. When you need to retrieve records for people in a single department, a query, form, or report can easily extract those records.

 ▶ ▶ **N O T E**

Queries are discussed in Chapters 9, 16, and 18. Chapter 17 explains how to design multitable forms and reports.

▶ *Maintaining Historical Information*

Sometimes it does make sense to store categorized data in different tables. For example, an order processing application might require two tables with identical structures to store orders. You could use one table (*NewOrds*) for new, unfulfilled orders. A second table (*OldOrds*) could contain old, fulfilled orders.

When an order is fulfilled, you could move its record from the NewOrds table to the OldOrds table. Doing so would keep the NewOrds table down to a small and manageable size. OldOrds would act as a *history table*, keeping track of old fulfilled orders. If you needed to check on a problem in an old order, you would be able to find it in the OldOrds table. We'll look at examples that use history tables in Chapter 18.

▶▶ *Clues That Indicate When Multiple Tables Might Be Better*

Understanding the relationships that can exist between tables will give you a head start on designing databases.

In many cases, your data will seem to fall naturally into separate, related tables. At other times, it won't be obvious when two or more tables would be better than one.

Suppose your starting point for designing a database is a printed form, like the order form shown in Figure 5.7. You've already learned why it's a good idea to put information about customers in one table and information about customer orders in another. However, you may not realize that you'll probably want to break up the order information into separate tables as well. In the sections that follow, we'll analyze the order form in Figure 5.7, looking for ways to store order information more efficiently. We'll also identify problems you might encounter when using tables that are poorly designed. In particular, we'll discuss how you can use repeating groups of fields and redundant data as clues that two or more tables might be better than one.

FIGURE 5.7

A sample printed order form filled in by a customer

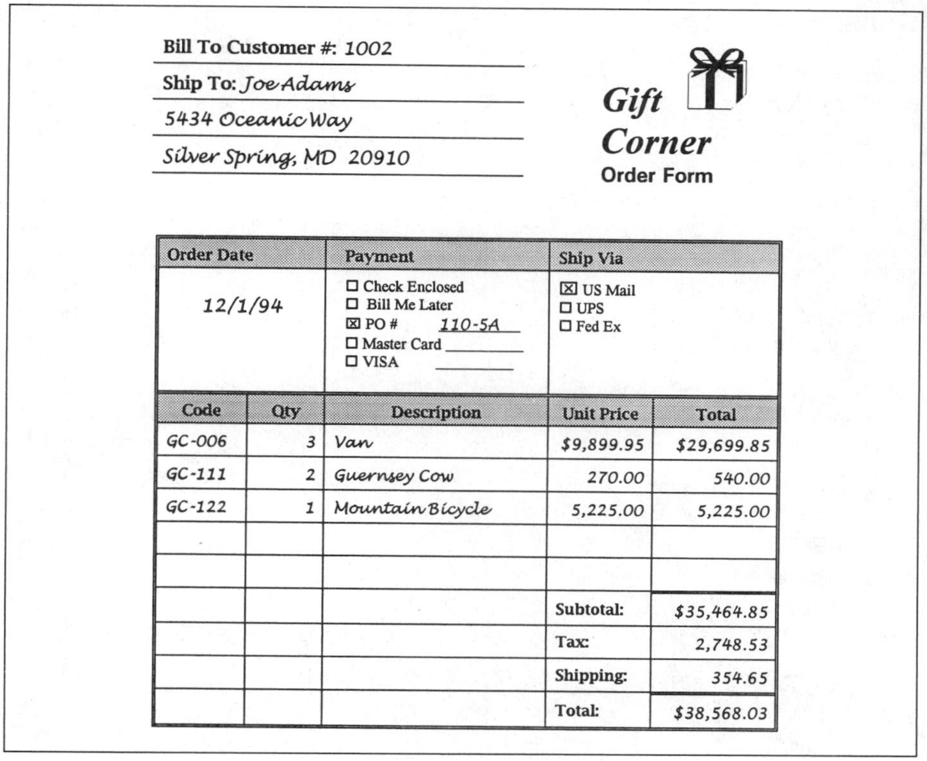

Bill To Customer #: 1002

Ship To: *Joe Adams*

5434 Oceanic Way

Silver Spring, MD 20910

Gift Corner
Order Form

Order Date	Payment	Ship Via
12/1/94	☐ Check Enclosed ☐ Bill Me Later ☒ PO # 110-5A ☐ Master Card _____ ☐ VISA _____	☒ US Mail ☐ UPS ☐ Fed Ex

Code	Qty	Description	Unit Price	Total
GC-006	3	Van	$9,899.95	$29,699.85
GC-111	2	Guernsey Cow	270.00	540.00
GC-122	1	Mountain Bicycle	5,225.00	5,225.00
			Subtotal:	$35,464.85
			Tax:	2,748.53
			Shipping:	354.65
			Total:	$38,568.03

▶ *Eliminating Repeating Groups of Fields*

When using the sample form as the basis for a table design, your first inclination might be to store fields for the order as a whole (Cust No, Order Date, Ship Via, and so forth), then use repeating groups of fields to store the order details, as shown in Figure 5.8. Notice how the Prod Code, Qty, and Unit Price fields are repeated in the table design, using #1, #2, and so forth to identify each field group uniquely.

What's wrong with this design? For one thing, since a table can contain a maximum of 255 fields, the number of line items you can assign to each order is limited. A second problem arises when you want to analyze, perform calculations on, print, or sort information about orders. You're sure to find these tasks quite difficult with the orders spread across several fields in this manner.

FIGURE 5.8 ▶

This table contains repetitive groups of fields to store information about orders.

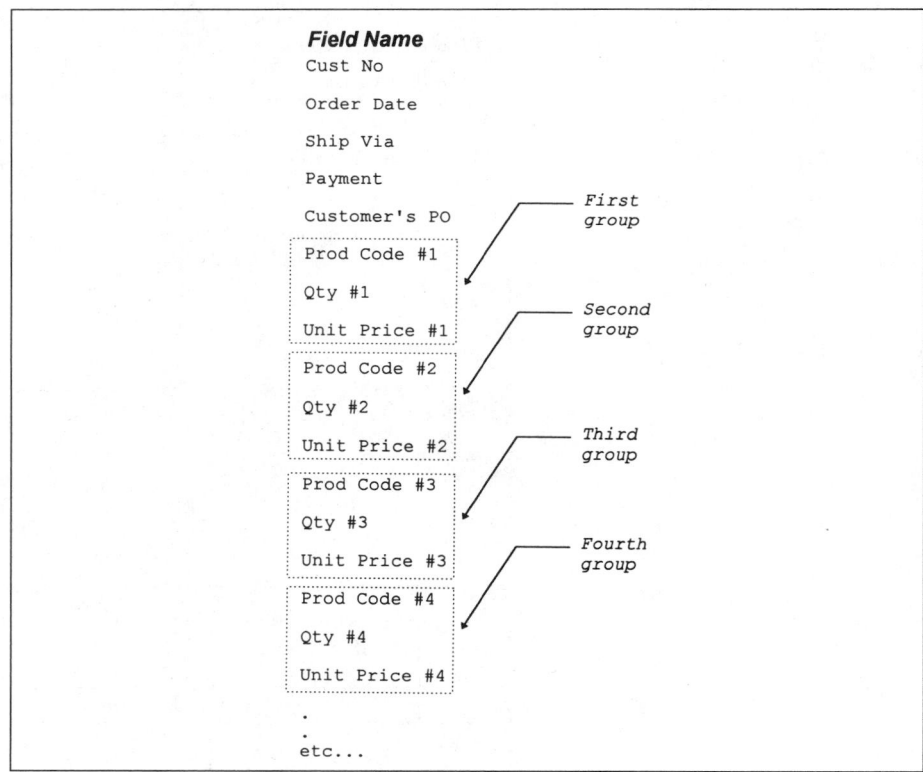

Field Name
Cust No

Order Date

Ship Via

Payment

Customer's PO

Prod Code #1 ⎤
Qty #1   ⎬ *First group*
Unit Price #1 ⎦

Prod Code #2 ⎤
Qty #2   ⎬ *Second group*
Unit Price #2 ⎦

Prod Code #3 ⎤
Qty #3   ⎬ *Third group*
Unit Price #3 ⎦

Prod Code #4 ⎤
Qty #4   ⎬ *Fourth group*
Unit Price #4 ⎦

.
.
.
etc...

Repetitive groups of fields like those in Figure 5.8 indicate that you're probably better off splitting the data into two tables. Use one set of field names in a group as the field names for a separate table. Then create a common field to link the two tables. You'll see an example in a moment.

▶ Removing Redundant Data

Another clue to problems in an existing table design are fields that store the same information repeatedly. For instance, suppose you try to use the design shown in Figure 5.9 to store information about orders.

Imagine how this table will look when you start filling it with data. If a particular order requires five line items, the Order Date, Ship Via, Payment, and Customer's PO data will be repeated in each record, as shown in Figure 5.10.

Why does this present problems? For one thing, you'll get tired of retyping the same Order Date, Ship Via, Payment, and Customer's PO number for every single item a customer orders. For another, if you need to

FIGURE 5.9

Another attempt to combine information about orders and customers in a single table

Field Name

```
Cust No
Prod Code
Qty
Unit Price
Order Date
Ship Via
Payment
Customer's PO
```

FIGURE 5.10

Storing information about Orders in the single table design shown in Figure 5.9 leads to redundant data.

Cust No	Prod Code	Qty	Unit Price	Order Date	Ship Via	Payment	Customer's PO
1001	GC-006	1	$9,899.95	12/1/94	USMail	Invoice	
1001	GC-111	2	$270.00	12/1/94	USMail	Invoice	
1001	GC-122	1	$5,225.00	12/1/94	USMail	Invoice	
1009	GC-006	1	$9,899.95	12/2/94	UPS	PO	1234
1009	GC-093	1	$119.95	12/2/94	UPS	PO	1234
1009	GC-987	1	$3,665.00	12/2/94	UPS	PO	1234
1009	GC-164	1	$3,333.00	12/2/94	UPS	PO	1234
1009	GC-122	1	$5,225.00	12/2/94	UPS	PO	1234

change the payment method or some other information in the order, you must be sure to make the same change in each relevant record.

The cure for both the repeating fields problem and the redundant data problem is simply to use two tables to store information about orders, as follows:

1. Place the data for the order as a whole—Cust No, Order Date, Ship Via, Payment, Customer's PO, and so on—in one table, named *Orders*.

2. Create a second table with fields for the individual line items— Prod Code, Qty, and Unit Price—and name the table *LineItem*.

 ▶ ▶ **N O T E**

> **You don't need to include calculated fields, such as Extended Price, to store the results of multiplying the quantity by the unit price for each line item. Because calculations are easy to perform "on the fly" in a form or report, there's no point in wasting valuable disk space simply to store a calculation result. As you'll see, we've ignored this advice for teaching purposes and have included an Extended Price field in our sample LineItem table. This allows us to show you (in Chapter 16) how to create queries that store calculation results in a table field, just in case you should ever want to do so.**

3. Finally, create a common field (Order No) that links the Orders table to the LineItem table, and define this field as the primary key for the Orders table. To prevent duplicate line items for any given order, you can make the Order No and Prod Code fields the primary key for the LineItem table.

Figure 5.11 displays the structures of these two tables. Figure 5.12 shows how the two tables might look after adding some data to each one.

FIGURE 5.11

Structures of the Orders and LineItem tables

Structure of the Orders Table

Field Name	Type	Size	Key
Order No	Number		*
Cust No	Number		
Date Sold	Date		
Ship Via	Alpha	10	
Payment	Alpha	10	
Sold By	Alpha	3	
etc...			

Structure of the LineItem Table

Field Name	Type	Size	Key
Order No	Number		*
Prod Code	Alpha	8	*
Qty	Number		
Unit Price	$ (Money)		
Extended Price	$ (Money)		
etc...			

FIGURE 5.12

The Orders and LineItem tables with some sample data added. The arrows show how the Order No field links the two tables.

Orders Table (one record per order)

Order No	Cust No	Date Sold	Ship Via	Payment	Sold By	etc...
2000	1002	12/1/94	USMail	Invoice	ACS	
2001	1001	12/1/94	UPS	PO	EAO	
2002	1007	12/1/94	FedEx	Check	KAO	

LineItem Table (many records per order)

Order No	Prod Code	Qty	Unit Price	Extended Price
2000	GC-006	3	$9,899.95	$29,699.85
2000	GC-111	2	$270.00	$540.00
2000	GC-122	1	$5,225.00	$5,225.00
2001	GC-111	4	$270.00	$1,080.00
2002	GC-006	3	$9,899.95	$29,699.85
2002	GC-112	2	$171.00	$342.00

▶▶ *The Bigger Picture*

The final design for a database might include several tables, with numerous one-to-many relationships among them. Figure 5.13 shows the structures of all the tables in a sample database, with lines indicating the one-to-many relationships between the tables. (A *1* appears next to the table on the "one" side of the relationship, and an *M* appears next to the table on the "many" side of the relationship.) The asterisks (★) next to field names indicate fields that are marked as keys.

Note that the First Name, Last Name, Address, City, State, Zip Code, Area Code, and Phone fields in the Orders table refer to the customer's *shipping* address and phone. Those same fields in the CustList table refer

FIGURE 5.13

A "clean" database design with five related tables of information

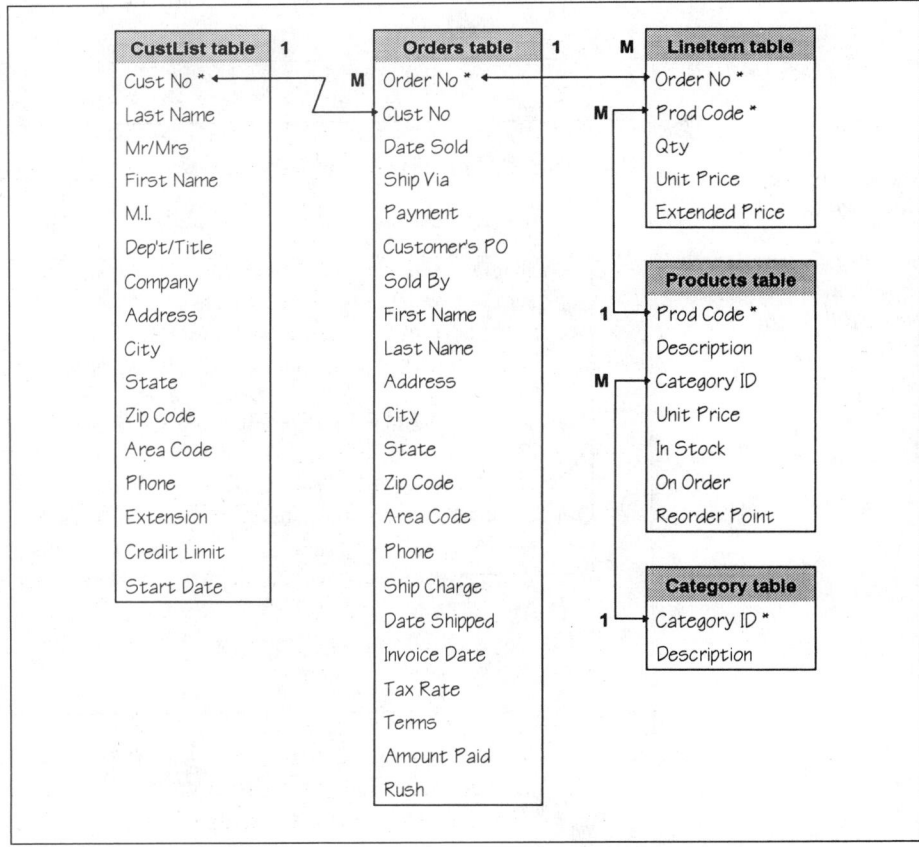

to the customer's *billing* address and phone. We've used the same field names in the CustList and Orders tables so that we can take advantage of table lookups during data entry. Chapter 6 explains how to define and use table lookup.

Though we've included only the field names, Figure 5.13 should give you a good idea of how to break up the information for a business into several tables, without using repetitive groups of fields or storing redundant data.

▶ *Achieving Database Nirvana*

The design sketched out in Figure 5.13 represents a kind of "database design nirvana" because every field in every table describes information that's relevant only to its own table.

 ▶ ▶ N O T E

The process used to achieve "database nirvana" (a database design in which duplicate data and repetitive fields are minimized) is known as *normalization*.

We intentionally omitted most totals from the order form in Figure 5.7, since Paradox can calculate that information on the fly. The product description in the order form is already stored in the Products table, so there's no need to add a field for that information to the LineItem table.

For every table in your design, you still need to determine the field type, length (for alpha fields), and any validity checks, as we did with the sample CustList table in Chapter 4. Here are some additional points to consider when designing related tables:

- When defining fields that link two or more tables (for example, Cust No, Order No, and Prod Code in Figure 5.13), give the fields the same field type and, if they're alpha, the same length in all tables.

- If you plan to use table lookups to fill in fields automatically during data entry, corresponding fields must have the same name in both the lookup table and the table for which the lookup is defined. See "Using Table Lookups" in the next section.

- When a one-to-many relationship exists between two tables, identify the common field on the "one" side of the relationship as the primary key for that table. Doing so will speed operations, prevent duplicate entries in that field, and allow you to define referential integrity between the table on the "one" side and the table on the "many" side (as discussed later). Figure 5.13 identifies ideal primary key fields with an asterisk (*) next to appropriate field names.

new

- If you want to generate numeric keys automatically in tables with a one-to-many relationship, use the *autoincrement* field type for the primary key of the table on the "one" side of the relationship. Then use the *long integer* field type for the linking field of the table on the "many" side. For example, in the Customer, Orders, and LineItem relationship, you'd use the autoincrement field type for the primary key fields Cust No in the CustList table and Order No in the Orders table. In the Orders table, you'd define Cust No as a long integer, non-key field. Similarly, in the LineItem table, you'd define Order No as a long integer, non-key field. See "Using Autoincrement Fields in Related Tables" later in the chapter for more details.

It is important to remember that although you may be splitting your data into many separate tables, you can always pull it back together when creating queries, forms, and reports. Figure 5.14 shows a custom form built from the Orders, LineItem, and Products tables shown in Figure 5.13. The information on this form describes a customer's order completely. Figure 5.15 illustrates an invoice for this order. The "Bill To" address and phone on the invoice are taken from the CustList table. Chapters 16 through 18 will explain how to mix and match data from multiple tables in your queries, forms, and reports.

Keep in mind that regardless of whether your tables have one-to-one or one-to-many relationships, you can use the basic techniques discussed in Chapter 4 to create them. In many cases you'll also want to define secondary indexes for your tables, as discussed in Chapter 8.

FIGURE 5.14

A custom order-entry form, displaying information from the Orders, LineItem, and Products tables.

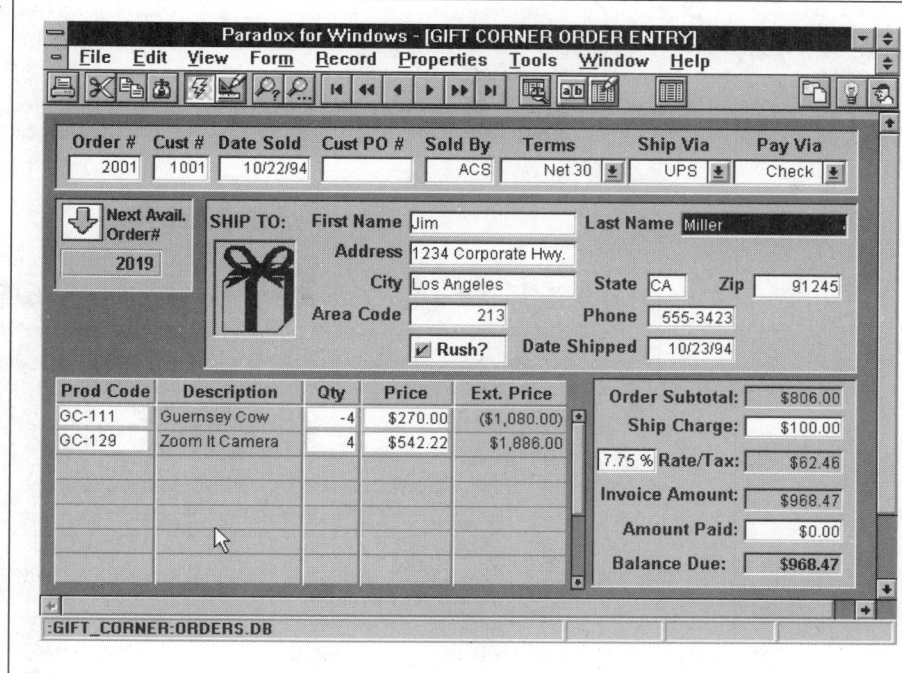

 ▶▶**TIP**

The \pdoxwin\sample directory includes sample tables that are similar to the ones used in this book. These tables are copied to your computer automatically when you do a full installation of Paradox. The sample tables Customer, LineItem, Orders, and Stock generally correspond to our CustList, LineItem, Orders, and Products tables. There's also a Vendors table that ties each Vendor to a particular Stock item. You can use the provided sample tables to experiment with any of the multitable concepts presented in this book.

FIGURE 5.15 ▶

An invoice for the order shown in Figure 5.14. The "Bill To" information is taken from the CustList table.

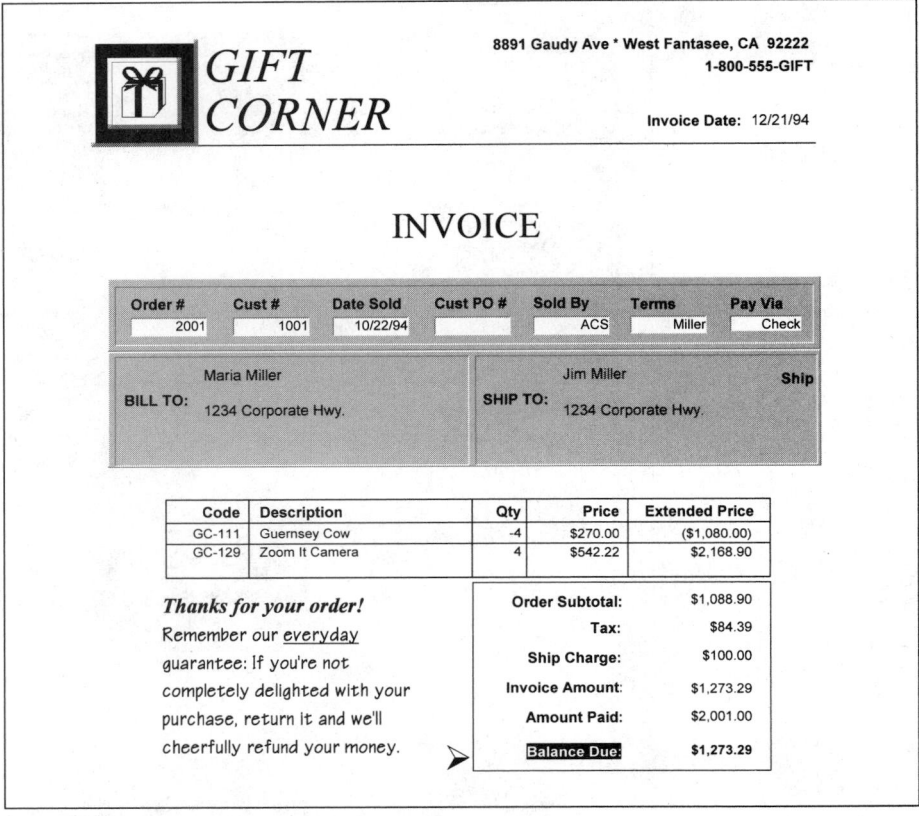

▶ Using Table Lookups

Table lookups can speed up data entry and improve accuracy in multi-table forms by filling in fields with corresponding data from another table. As you'll learn in Chapter 6, the table lookup feature provides the following capabilities:

- Allows you to require that values entered into a field exist in the first field of another table.

- Locates acceptable values for a field in another table.

- Lets you automatically copy values from fields with *matching names* in the lookup table to the table you're editing.

▶ ▶ **N O T E**

> In the order entry form shown in Figure 5.14, table lookup automatically fills in the Ship To information (First Name, Last Name, Address, City, State, Zip Code, Area Code, and Phone) after a valid customer number is entered. We can modify the Ship To information if we wish.

You can define table lookups when creating your tables or just before designing a multitable data entry form. The first field of the lookup table must be the primary key for the lookup table, and any fields to be copied automatically must have matching names in both tables.

▶ *Using Autoincrement Fields in Related Tables*

Recall that the autoincrement field type makes it easy to automatically enter unique sequential numbers into a table, starting with 1. To see how you might use the autoincrement field type (and its faithful companion, the long integer field type), let's take a closer look at the relationship between customers and orders. We know that each customer number in the CustList table and each order number in the Orders table must be unique. That is, each customer must appear only once in the CustList table, and each order must appear only once in the Orders table. And since it is common to assign sequential numbers to customers and orders, the autoincrement type is ideal for the key field of each table.

Of course, you'll certainly want to let each customer place many orders. To identify which customer has placed which order, you'll need to include a customer number field in the Orders table, using the long integer field type (no other field type will do).

Here are the essential pieces of the Customer and Orders tables in this example:

> **CustList table**   The first field, Cust No, is an autoincrement field and is the table's key field. The remaining fields are the same as for the CustList table described earlier in the chapter. When

you enter a new customer, Paradox will assign a sequential value to Cust No automatically.

Orders table   The first field, Order No, is an autoincrement field and the table's key field. The second field, Cust No, is a long integer. The remaining fields are the same as for the Orders table already described. When you enter a new order, Paradox will assign a sequential value to Order No automatically. You'll then need to enter in the Cust No field the number of the customer who placed the order.

► *Initializing an Autoincrement Field*

Now all this autoincrementing sounds just wonderful, almost too good to be true. But what if you want the first customer number (or order number) to begin at some number other than 1? Are you out of luck? Of course not.

Assigning an initial value to an autoincrement field is easy if you plan ahead and follow the simple procedure given below.

► ► **N O T E**

If you've already put some data into a table that has its primary key defined as a Number, and you want to change it to an Autoincrement, use an "insert query," as discussed in Chapter 18.

For this example, let's suppose you want the first customer number in the Cust No field of CustList to begin at 1001, rather than 1. Here are the basic steps to follow:

1. Create your table as described in Chapter 4. Make Cust No the first field, assign it a type of long integer (I), and make it a primary key (*).

2. Add other fields as desired and save the CustList table.

3. Open the new CustList table, press F9 to go into Edit mode, then fill in one "dummy" record. In the Cust No field, type the desired starting value for your customer numbers, minus 1. For example, type **1000** if you want your real customer numbers to begin at

1001. You can leave the other fields blank if you haven't defined them with the "Required Field" validity check.

4. Close the CustList table and restructure it as explained in Chapter 4. For example, choose Tools ➤ Utilities ➤ Restructure and double-click the CustList table in the File Name list.

5. In the Restructure Table dialog box, highlight the Type column for the Cust No field and change its type from long integer to autoincrement (+), then click Save to save the table and return to the Desktop.

6. Open the CustList table again, move the cursor to the first (dummy) record, press F9 and then press Ctrl+Del to delete the record.

7. Now you can add new customer records as desired, leaving the Cust No field blank in each record. Paradox will fill in the Cust No field automatically. The Cust No field in the first new record will have a value of 1001; the next Cust No value will be 1002, and so on. Pretty slick!

 ▶ ▶ **N O T E**

> **See the quick tour in Chapter 2, the "Working With A Table" Coaches, and Chapter 6 for details about adding and editing records in a table.**

▶ ▶ *Using Referential Integrity*

Like table lookup, referential integrity ensures that information entered in one table automatically appears in another table. However, referential integrity goes beyond table lookup because it also prevents the ties between data in separate tables from being broken.

Consider again the CustList and Orders example. When entering an order, you want to be absolutely sure that the customer number associated with the order also exists in the CustList table. Otherwise you might be unable to bill that customer later. Similarly, you wouldn't want Paradox to let you delete a customer record from the CustList table while an order for that customer is still outstanding. By defining referential integrity between the key field of the CustList table (Cust No) and the Cust No field of the Orders table, you can enforce the desired relationships.

►►**NOTE**

You can establish referential integrity with a single-field key or a composite key.

In the CustList and Orders example, CustList is the *parent table* (or *master table*) and Orders is the *child table* (or *detail table*). Notice that the parent table is on the "one" side of a one-to-many relationship, while the child table is on the "many" side of the relationship. The key field of the parent table in a referential integrity relationship is called the *foreign key* because it is foreign to (outside of) the child table.

► Choosing an Update Method

Imagine what would happen if you were to change the customer number in the CustList table. If referential integrity didn't exist between CustList and Orders, this change to CustList would create an "orphaned" order, since the Cust No field in Orders would no longer refer to the original customer. However, if referential integrity *did* exist between the CustList table and the Orders table, Paradox could treat this change to the parent table in one of two ways, depending on how you define the update method.

One method is to *prohibit* the update, so that you cannot change the key field in the parent table (CustList) if any orders are still associated with that field in the child table (Orders). This method is the more restrictive because you must delete that customer's records in the Orders table before changing the key field values in the CustList table.

The second method is to *cascade* the update, so that any change made to the key field in the parent table automatically flows down or "cascades" to the associated records in the child table. Thus, whenever you change the Cust No field value in CustList, Paradox will change the corresponding values in the Cust No field of the Orders table. Cascaded updates (the default method) keep data consistent between tables and provide flexibility during data entry.

▶ *Restrictions on Referential Integrity*

Paradox for Windows imposes the following restrictions on referential integrity:

- The field used to tie the two tables together must be a primary key field in the parent table (for example, Cust No is the primary key for the CustList table).

- The child table must also have a primary key. However, the child table's key field need not be the same field you're using to tie the child and parent tables together.

- You can establish referential integrity only between like fields that contain matching values. The field *names* don't have to be the same, but the field *types* must be identical (and they must be the same length if you're using alpha fields).

▶ ▶ **N O T E**

You can establish referential integrity between an autoincrement field type and a long integer field type. This doesn't break the rule about requiring field types to be the same, since the autoincrement field type is a special kind of long integer.

- You can establish referential integrity only between two tables in the same directory.

- You cannot define referential integrity between binary, formatted memo, graphic, memo, or OLE fields.

- Referential integrity is available between Paradox tables only.

- If your tables contain data, be sure to define referential integrity from the "top down." If you try to define from the "bottom up," Paradox may refuse to carry out your request. Thus, for our sample CustList, Orders, and LineItem tables, define the referential integrity between Orders and CustList before you define it between LineItem and Orders.

If your tables do not conform to these restrictions, you will need to restructure them before defining referential integrity.

▶ ▶ **W A R N I N G**

> **If your tables already contain data, don't dive into the restructure operation without fully understanding the effects of doing so. Also be aware that you cannot delete or rename the parent table if any records exist in the child table. Chapter 15 explains table restructuring in detail.**

In the sample database shown in Figure 5.13, we've defined the referential integrity relationships listed below.

This Field	Ties Child Table	To Parent Table
Cust No	Orders	CustList
Order No	LineItem	Orders
Prod Code	LineItem	Products

▶ Defining Referential Integrity between Tables

When you're ready to define referential integrity, close the child table for which you're defining the relationship (if it exists and is open) and close any tables that are (or will be) tied through referential integrity. If you forget to close tables, you may receive a "Table is Busy" message when you try to save your changes. Now proceed as follows:

1. Go to the Create Table or Restructure Table dialog box for the *child* table (for example, Orders is the child table for CustList).

▶ ▶ **N O T E**

> **If you're *creating* a new child table, define all of its fields and specify the primary key before continuing with step 2.**

2. Choose *Referential Integrity* from the Table Properties drop-down list.

3. Click the <u>D</u>efine button to open the Referential Integrity dialog box shown in Figure 5.16. The Fields list on the left displays all eligible fields from the child table. The Table list on the right displays all tables in the working directory.

4. In the <u>F</u>ields list, click the field you want to tie to the parent table, then click the → button above the list (or double-click the field name). The field you selected will appear under the Child Fields heading in the dialog box. If you choose the wrong field, click the ← button below the <u>F</u>ields list (or press Alt+R), then select another field.

5. In the <u>T</u>able list, click the name of the parent table, then click the ← button above the list (or double-click the table name). The parent's key field or fields will appear under the *Parent's Key* heading in the dialog box. (If you choose the wrong table, just repeat step 5 and select a different parent table.)

6. From the lower-left corner of the dialog box, choose the <u>U</u>pdate Rule you want. Your options are <u>C</u>ascade for cascaded updates (the default setting) or <u>P</u>rohibit to prevent updates to the parent table's key field if corresponding records exist in the child table.

Design with Multiple Tables

Ch.
5

FIGURE 5.16 ▶

The Referential Integrity dialog box

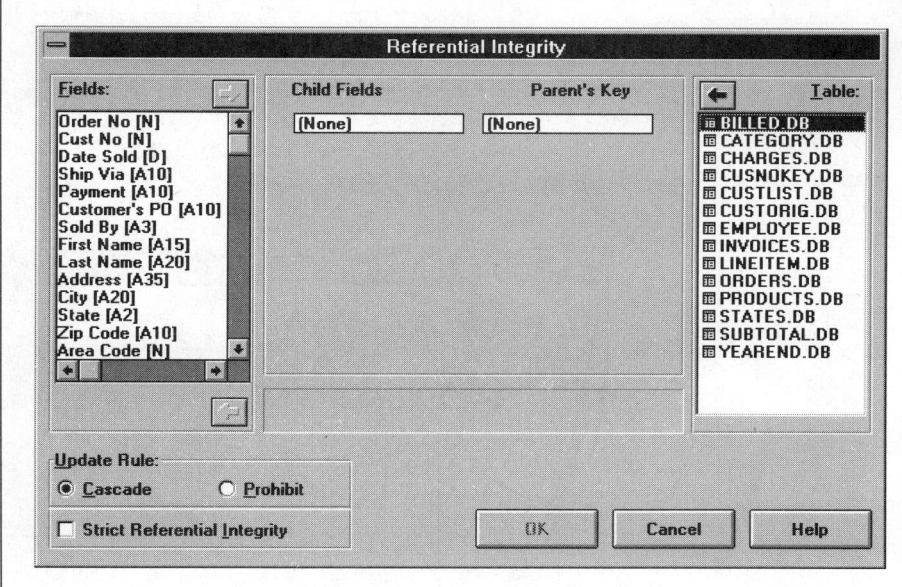

7. If you want to enforce strict referential integrity when old versions of Paradox (prior to 4.5) access this table, check the Strict Referential Integrity option. (Checking this option prevents Paradox 3.5 or 4.0 users from corrupting your data.) Clear the Strict Referential Integrity option if you do not want to prevent old versions of Paradox from opening this table.

 ▶ ▶ **N O T E**

> **Unlike Paradox for Windows, versions of Paradox before 4.5 did not completely enforce referential integrity. When Strict Referential Integrity is checked, earlier versions of Paradox will interpret the referential integrity definition as a password, which effectively prevents anyone from opening the table and adding data that could break the tie between parent and child tables.**

8. Choose OK to name and save the referential integrity, as described below.

9. Choose <u>S</u>ave or Save <u>A</u>s to save the table structure.

▶ *Saving the Referential Integrity Definition*

When you choose OK in step 8, you'll see the Save Referential Integrity As dialog box shown below.

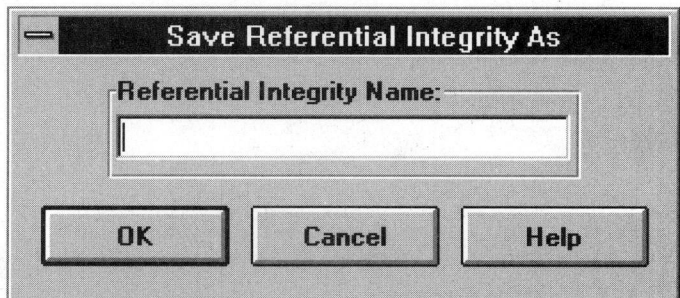

Type the name you want to give the referential integrity relationship (for example, **Orders To CustList**), then choose OK. Referential integrity names can be up to 31 printable characters and require no file extension. The name you assign will appear in the list area below the <u>D</u>efine button in the Create Table or Restructure Table dialog box. Paradox saves referential integrity definitions in a file with the table's name and the .val extension.

When you save the referential integrity rule, Paradox creates a secondary index on the child field(s) if one doesn't exist already. The index will have the name of the child field if you're using a single-field key to tie the tables together, or the name you gave the referential integrity definition if the tables are tied by a multifield key. You'll see the index name when you choose *Secondary Indexes* from the Table <u>P</u>roperties list in the Create Table or Restructure Table dialog box.

N O T E

Secondary indexes allow you to sort and link tables, and can speed up queries. You'll learn other ways to create secondary indexes in Chapter 8.

If you define referential integrity on a table that contains data already, Paradox will place child records that have no parent record into the temporary *Keyviol* table in your private directory. Considering the Orders and LineItem tables, any existing LineItem records without a corresponding record in the Orders table would be moved to Keyviol when you defined referential integrity between the tables. To restore the moved records to the LineItem table, first enter all the missing parent records into the Orders table, and then choose <u>T</u>ools ➤ <u>U</u>tilities ➤ <u>A</u>dd to add the child records from the Keyviol table to the LineItem table (see Chapter 15 for information on using Add).

N O T E

If you delete the referential integrity, Paradox will not delete the secondary index automatically. If you wish, you can use the Restructure Table dialog box to delete the secondary index (see Chapter 8).

► Changing or Erasing Referential Integrity

You can change or disable referential integrity via the Create Table or Restructure Table dialog box. (Though it's unlikely that you would ever want to totally disable referential integrity, since its purpose is to prevent faulty data from being entered in the table!) To begin, choose *Referential Integrity* from the Table Properties list, then click the referential integrity relationship you want to change or erase. The Modify and Erase buttons will be undimmed and available for use. Now perform either of the steps listed below.

- To change the selected referential integrity relationship, click the Modify button and complete the Referential Integrity dialog box as explained earlier.

- To erase the referential integrity relationship, click the Erase button.

 ►► **WARNING**

To avoid "Table is Busy" messages, be sure to close the related tables before changing or removing referential integrity.

►► Creating a Data Model

A *data model* is a graphical diagram of relationships between tables. Paradox for Windows offers a powerful *Data Model Designer* that makes it easy to create and work with data models.

You might ask, "why should I bother to create and save data models?" The answer, in a word, is convenience. Suppose you've defined the CustList, Orders, LineItem, and Products tables described in this chapter. You've also defined your primary keys and set up referential integrity between tables. Now you want to create some queries and design documents for your database.

Paradox cannot read your mind when it comes to setting up queries and designing documents. Instead, you'll need to tell it which tables and fields to use and how they relate to one another. You can do this the hard way—once for each query or design document you create.

Or you can do it the easy way, by loading in a saved data model. You can set up as many data models as you need.

There are two basic ways to design a data model:

- You can define a *reference data model* in the Data Model Designer and then save it as a separate file. Later, you can reuse the model when you create queries and design documents.

▶ ▶ **N O T E**

> A *design document* is a form, report, or chart that you create in Paradox for Windows. Chapters 10 through 13 and Chapter 17 explain how to create design documents.

- You can define a data model "on the fly" in a query or design document. If you wish, you can save this model as a separate, reusable data model file.

Figure 5.17 illustrates a reference data model. Notice how the data model graphically illustrates the relationships among these tables, using a double-headed arrow to point to the table that's on the "many" side of a one-to-many relationship. For example, in Figure 5.17 you can see that for any one customer in the CustList.db table, there might be many records in the Orders.db table.

Design with Multiple Tables

Ch. ▶ ▶
5

FIGURE 5.17 ▶

The Reference Data Model window for the Data Model Designer

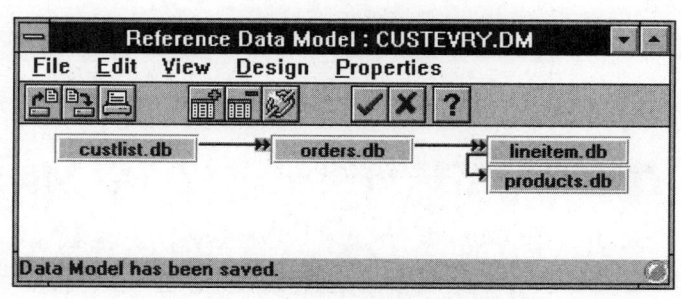

Figure 5.18 shows the same data model as it would appear if you were designing a query, form, or report. The model is the same, but here you can see that the model has been saved with the name *custevry.dm*.

In this chapter, you'll learn how to work with the Data Model Designer to create and save reference data models. In Chapters 10, 16, and 17, we'll discuss data models as they pertain to design documents and queries. As you'll discover, the techniques for designing data models are similar, whether you start in the Reference Data Model window (Figure 5.17) or from a query or design document (Figure 5.18).

Now let's take a closer look at reference data models.

FIGURE 5.18 ▶

You can use the Data Model dialog box to define or load in a data model when you're designing a query, form, or report.

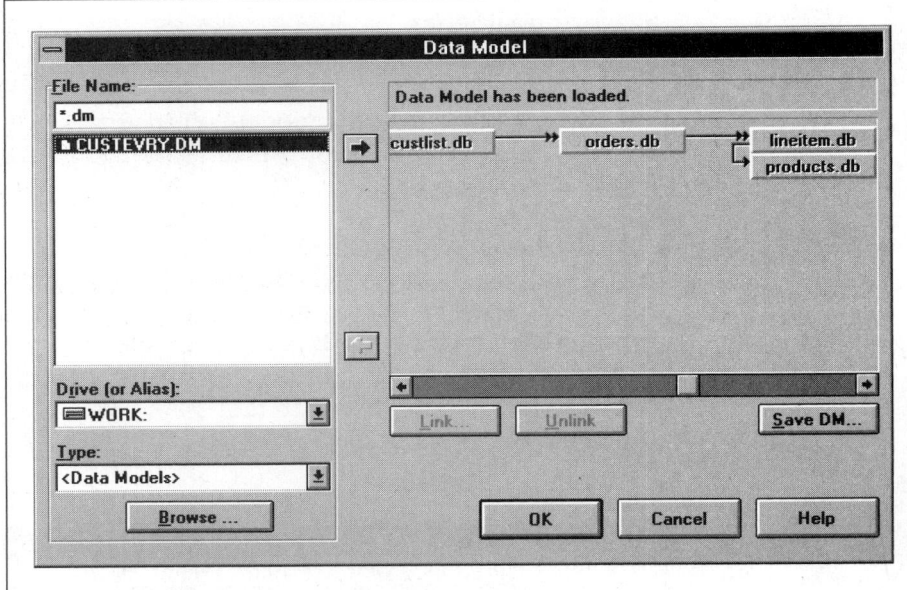

▶ Opening the Reference Data Model Window

To start defining a reference data model, choose Tools ➤ Data Model Designer. You'll see an empty Reference Data Model window like the one shown below.

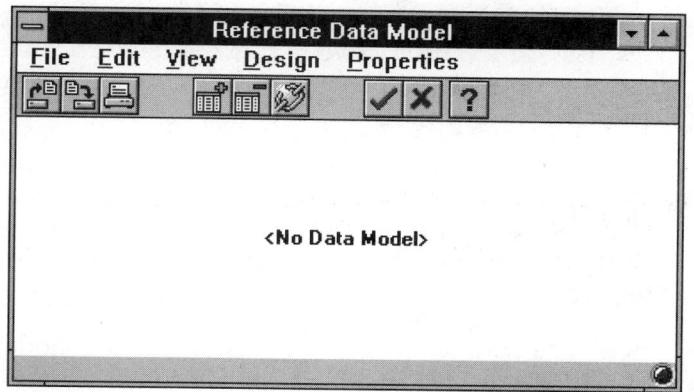

▶▶N O T E

If you've changed the default properties for the Data Model Designer, the Reference Data Model window might not be empty. See "Setting the Data Model Designer Properties" near the end of the chapter.

Once you've opened the Reference Data Model window, you'll follow the general steps below to set up your model.

1. Add the tables (or queries) you want to include.

2. Link any tables that should be tied together. For example, you'd want to link CustList to Orders, Orders to LineItem, and LineItem to Products.

3. If you wish, you can print your data model.

4. Save your data model.

5. Use your data model anytime you need to define multitable queries (Chapters 9 and 16) and design documents (Chapters 10 and 17).

We'll discuss these steps and a few other ones in the sections that follow. But first, here are some helpful tips that might come in handy while you're using the data model window:

• To get help using the Data Model Designer any time the data model window is open, click the Help button (shown at left) in the Toolbar, or press F1.

- If you need to back out of any changes that you've made since the last time you saved your data model, click the Cancel Changes button (shown at left) in the Toolbar, or choose Design ➤ Cancel Changes, or press Esc.

▶ Adding Tables to the Data Model

The first step in creating a data model is to add all the tables (or queries) you want Paradox to "know about" when you use this data model later to create queries or design documents.

To get started, click the Add Table button (shown at left) in the Toolbar. Or choose Design ➤ Add Table from the menus, or press Alt+A. You'll see a Select File dialog box like the one in Figure 5.19.

You can use any of these techniques in the Select File dialog box to select tables or queries to include in the model:

- If you want to base the data model on a query result, rather than a table, click the drop-down list below File Type and then click <Queries>. Otherwise, leave the File Type set to <Tables>.

FIGURE 5.19 ▶

The Select File dialog box lets you choose one or more tables or queries for your data model. In this example, four tables are selected. After selecting the files you want to include, choose OK.

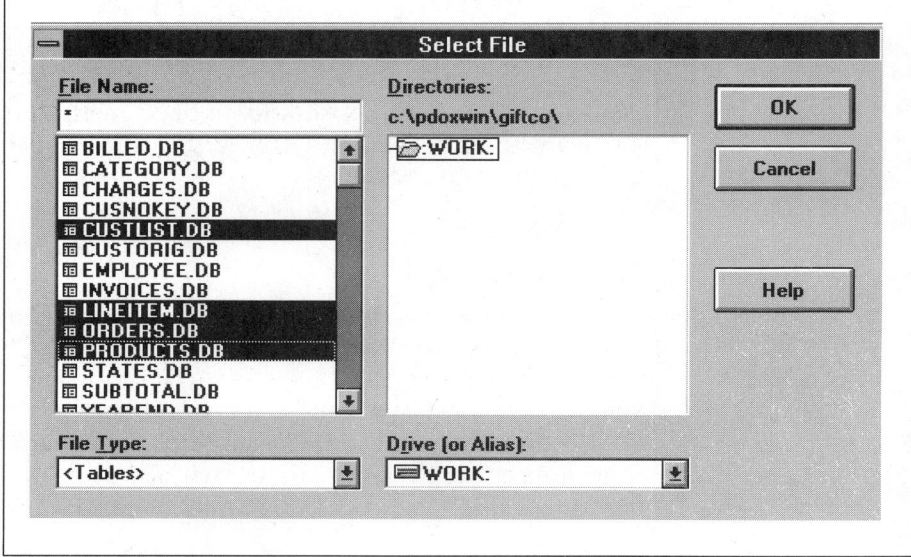

▶▶ WARNING

Because queries do not usually work on "live" table data, you probably shouldn't use them for data models that will be the basis for data entry forms or other queries. They are, however, ideal for setting up reports that show only certain fields or data. You'll learn more about queries in Chapters 9 and 16.

- If the table or query is on another disk drive or directory, use the Drive (or Alias) drop-down list and the Directories list to switch to a different location, as explained in Chapter 3.

- To select one table or query, click on it in the list below File Name, or type its name into the File Name text box.

- To select multiple tables or queries, click on the first one in the list below File Name. Then hold down the Ctrl key while you click additional names. (If you select a file name by accident, simply hold down the Ctrl key and click that name again.)

When you're finished selecting tables, choose OK. The table names will appear in the data model window, as shown below:

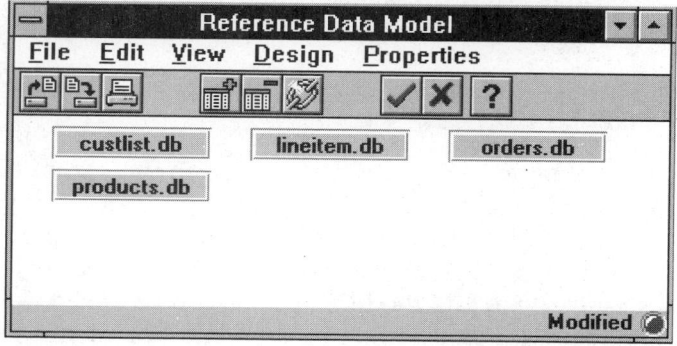

Repeat the steps above until you've added all the tables you want.

Design with Multiple Tables

▶▶

Ch. **5**

▶▶**TIP**

As an alternative to adding all the tables to the data model and then linking them, you may prefer to link each pair of tables as you add them.

▶ *Removing Tables from the Data Model*

 If you need to remove a table from the data model, begin by clicking on it to select it. (If the table you want to delete is linked, you must first unlink it, as described a bit later in this chapter.) Then press the Delete key, or click the Remove Selected Table button (shown at left) in the Toolbar, or choose <u>E</u>dit ➤ <u>D</u>elete. The table will disappear from the data model. But don't worry. The table you deleted from the data model will still remain on the hard disk, safe and sound.

 ▶▶**TIP**

To clear the entire data model from the screen in one fell swoop, inspect (right-click) an empty area of the data model, then click New Data Model in the menu that appears. You'll see the message <No Data Model> in the center of the window.

▶ *Rules for Creating Links*

Linked tables tie a particular record in the parent table to its associated records in the child table, and they're essential for setting up multitable queries and design documents. To understand the beauty of linked tables, suppose you create a "customers and orders" data entry form that is based on a data model in which you've linked the CustList and Orders tables. If you scroll in the form to the record for customer number 1001, Paradox will instantly display only the orders for customer 1001. If you then scroll to customer number 2001, Paradox will display orders for that customer instead.

Before linking Paradox tables, you should understand the important points listed below.

▶▶ **N O T E**

The rules for linking tables in the data model are basically the same as for defining referential integrity between two tables.

- Linked tables *must* have a common field. Although the field names needn't be the same, the field type and size must match and the fields must contain corresponding data. (As usual, if the field type for the common field in one table is *autoincrement*, the field type for the common field in the related table can be *long integer*.)

▶▶ **T I P**

You can right-click a table name in the data model area for a reminder of the table's field names, types, and sizes.

- The table you're linking *from* is called the *master table* (or parent). The table you're linking *to* is called the *detail table* (or child).

- The detail table must be indexed on the field you want to use in the link. This index can be the primary index, or a secondary index that you defined or Paradox created when you set up a referential integrity relationship. (See Chapters 4 and 8 for information on primary and secondary indexes, respectively.)

- Linked tables can have one-to-one, many-to-one, or one-to-many relationships, as discussed earlier in this chapter.

Design with Multiple Tables

▶▶

Ch. 5

▶ *Drawing a Link*

After placing the tables into the data model, you can link them. The following steps explain how to link two Paradox tables. (See Appendix D for information on linking dBASE tables.)

1. Move the mouse pointer to the master table in the data model. The mouse pointer changes to a linking tool (shown at left) when you pass it over a table.

2. Click and drag the linking tool from the master table to the detail table, then release the mouse button.

If you haven't established referential integrity between the two tables, Paradox will display the Define Link dialog box shown in Figure 5.20, and you can define the link as described below. If you *have* established referential integrity, Paradox will complete the link automatically and bypass the Define Link dialog box. In this case, the link will appear as a line with two arrowheads when pointing to the table on the "many" side of a one-to-many relationship, or with one arrowhead when pointing to the table on the "one" side of a relationship, as shown earlier in Figures 5.17 and 5.18. (You can override the automatic link if you wish; see "Changing and Removing Links," below.)

FIGURE 5.20 ►

The Define Link dialog box

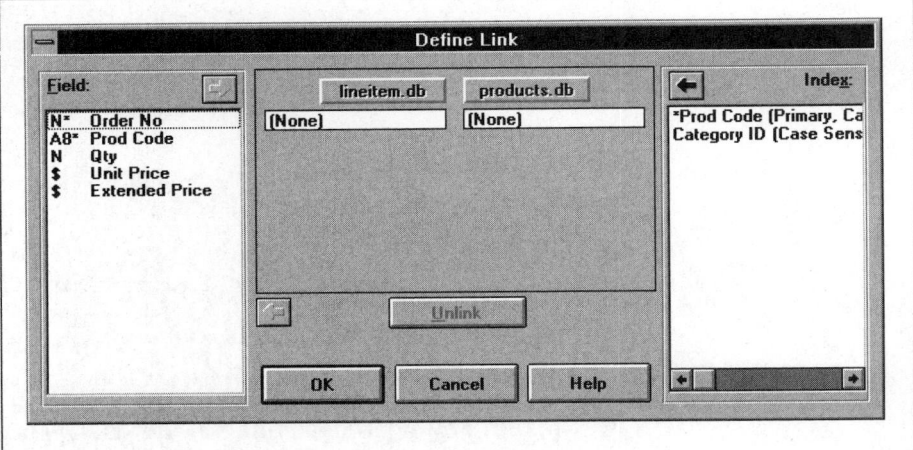

Defining the Link

If Paradox can determine which fields to use for the link, it will create the link automatically when it opens the Define Link dialog box. If you want to accept the automatic link, click OK. If you want to redefine the link, click the Unlink button.

To define the master table field you want to link, double-click the field in the Field list (see Figure 5.20), or click the field and then click the → button. If Paradox finds an index of the detail table that matches the name and type of the master table field you've chosen, it will complete the link for you automatically, as shown in Figure 5.21. (You can choose a different index, if you wish, as described next.)

▶ ▶ **N O T E**

If you've chosen the wrong field from the master table, simply click the ← button near the F͟ield list. The word *(None)* **will appear under the master table name and you can select another master table field.**

FIGURE 5.21

The Define Link dia-log box after a link is completed

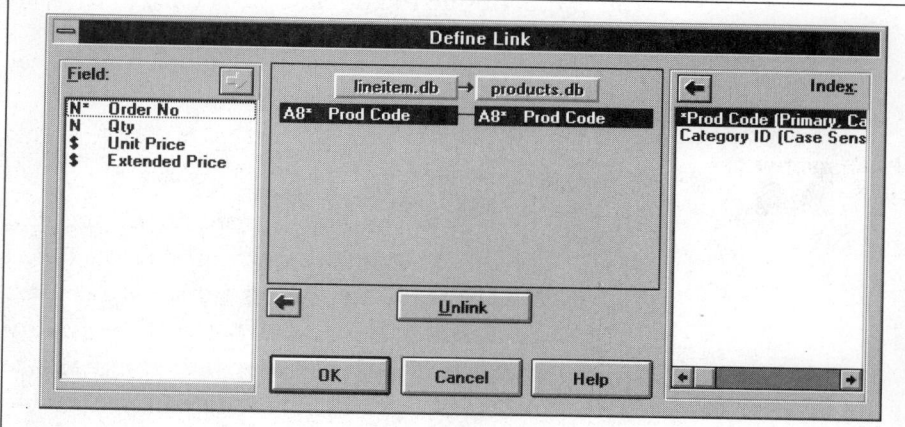

To link the selected master table field to an index field of the detail ta-ble, double-click the detail table's index name in the Inde͟x list (or click the index name and then click the ← button above the list). After you define the master field and detail index, Paradox creates a link between the two tables and displays a diagram of the link below the title bar of the dialog box.

If you wish to change the link, you can double-click a different master field or detail index, or click the U͟nlink button and redefine the mas-ter field and detail index from scratch. When you're satisfied with the link, choose OK to return to the data model window. The data model will reflect the type of link you created, as shown earlier in Figures 5.17 and 5.18.

When viewing the data model, keep the following points in mind:

- When two tables appear side by side, with a double-headed arrow between them, you've created a one-to-many link (for example, orders->>lineitem, as in Figure 5.17).

- When two tables are stacked, with an arrow joining them, you've created a one-to-one or a many-to-one relationship (for example, lineitem->products).

- The direction of the arrow indicates the direction of the link (master->detail or master->>detail).

You can continue to add and link tables in the data model window for as long as the relationships make sense. In this way, you can build complex data models that combine data from many tables into a logically connected whole.

▶ ▶ **T I P**

To review the links in the data model quickly, select a detail table in the data model area of the window. (In Figure 5.17, the detail tables are Orders, LineItem, and Products.) The status bar in the window will show the fields and indexes that link the master table to the selected detail table. You can use the arrow keys to move the selection from table to table in the diagram.

▶ *Changing and Removing Links*

You can easily change the way tables are linked in the data model. Simply select (click on) the *detail table* in the data model, then choose Design ▶ Link or press Alt+L to return to the Define Link dialog box described above.

To remove an existing link in the data model window, select the *detail table* in the data model area and click the Unlink Selected Table button (shown at left) in the Toolbar, or choose Design ▶ Unlink, or press Alt+U.

▶ *Getting Information About Tables in the Data Model*

You can inspect any table in the data model to view its field names, field types and sizes, and any associated lookup tables and referential integrity relationships. Figure 5.22 illustrates the screen after we right-clicked the Orders table in our sample data model and then clicked the ➤ symbol next to Cust No to display the lookup table and referential integrity information for the Cust No field. The small box to the left of that field shows CUSTLIST.DB as the Lookup and Ref. Int (referential integrity) table.

FIGURE 5.22 ▶

You can inspect a table to reveal its field names, field types and sizes, lookup tables, and referential integrity.

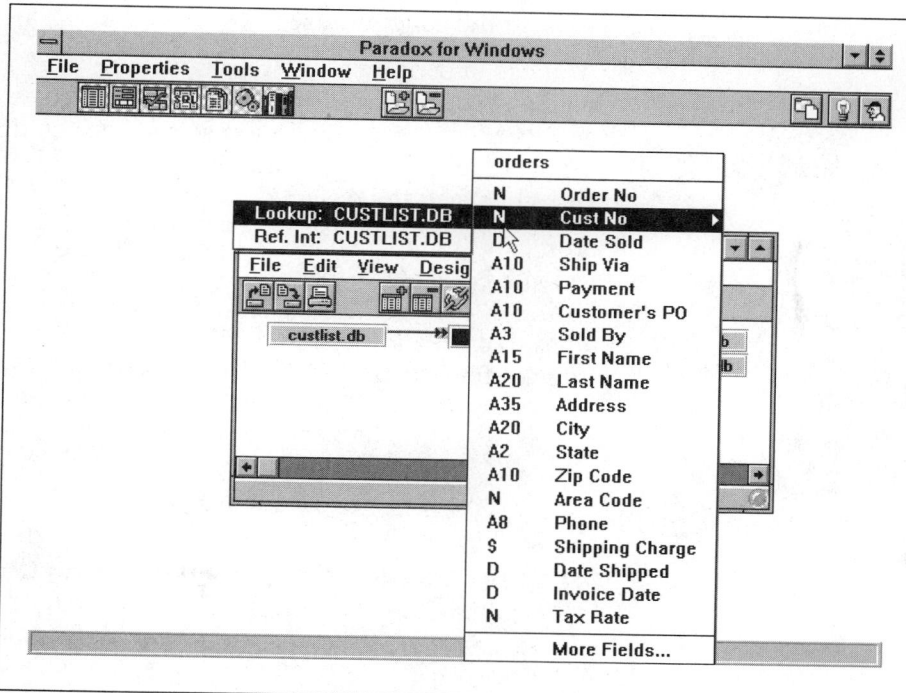

Design with
Multiple Tables

▶ ▶

Ch.
5

► Setting Up a Table Alias

Recall from Chapter 3 that you can set up alias names (nicknames) for directories. You can do the same for tables in a data model. This can provide several benefits:

- In data models that use the same table more than once (yes, you can do this), an alias will help you know which table is which.

- Your design documents will be more portable. For example, you can change table aliases to conform to the naming conventions required by SQL servers. In addition, your ObjectPAL programs can reference table aliases, rather than table names. This lets you change the table referenced by the program without having to change the program itself.

- You can substitute a different table into your data model and assign it an alias that is the same as the table you removed. This fools Paradox into thinking that your design document has not changed and prevents Paradox from asking you to re-establish links between the design document and its data model.

- You can use table aliases instead of table names when you create calculated fields in forms and reports. Then, if you need to change tables in the data model, simply assign the new table the same alias that the old table had. The calculations will still work (providing the field names used for the calculation are the same).

 ►► **N O T E**

If these benefits don't seem relevant to you now, don't worry about them. Table aliases are mainly of interest to programmers who are developing ObjectPAL applications, to people who are designing complex databases, and to people who move and rename tables frequently.

To set up a table alias, inspect the table in the data model, then click on the table name at the top of the menu that appears. The Table Name dialog box, shown below, appears next.

In the <u>N</u>ame of Table text box, type the alias name for the table and choose OK. (The alias cannot include spaces or punctuation characters. For example, *MyCustomer* is a valid alias, but *My Customer* and *My-Customer* are not.) Note that assigning an alias *does not* change the table's file name on the disk. It simply allows you to reference the table by a nickname.

If you need to delete the table's alias, inspect the table in the data model, click the table name at the top of the pop-up menu, press Del to delete the highlighted alias in the Table Name dialog box, then choose OK. The original table name will appear in the dialog box.

▶ *Printing a Data Model*

You can print a graphical report of your data model at any time. Simply click the Print Data Model button (shown at left) in the Toolbar, or choose <u>F</u>ile ▶ <u>P</u>rint in the data model window. In a flash, a printed representation of the data model will pop out of your printer.

Design with
Multiple Tables

▶▶
Ch.
5

► *Saving a Data Model*

Once you've finished designing your data model, you should save it as follows:

1. Choose File ➤ Save from the data model window's menus, or click the Save Data Model button (shown at left) in the Toolbar.

2. If you haven't saved this data model before, the Save File As dialog box will appear. In the New File Name text box, type a valid DOS file name (without the extension) and choose OK.

Paradox will save your data model and return you to the data model window. The data model file will have the name you assigned, and a .dm (data model) extension. For example, if you named your data model *custevry* in the File Save As dialog box, Paradox will save the file as *custevry.dm*.

► ►TIP

After saving your data model, you can repeat step 1 above whenever you've made changes that you want to keep. Paradox will not prompt you for the file name again.

► *Loading a Reference Data Model*

Suppose you'd like to load a data model and make some changes to it. That's easy. Just open the data model window (choose Tools ➤ Data Model Designer) and use any of the techniques below:

- Inspect (right-click) any empty area in the data model window, then click on a data model file name.

- Click the Load Data Model button (shown at left) in the Toolbar, or choose File ➤ Load, or inspect an empty area in the data model and click <Browse>. When the Select File dialog box appears, highlight the file name of the data model you want to load and choose OK (or just double-click the file name).

The data model you selected will appear in the window. After making changes, you can save them with the usual File ➤ Save menu options or by clicking the Save Data Model button in the Toolbar. Or, if you prefer to save the data model with a different name, choose File ➤ Save As, type in a new data model file name, and choose OK.

▶ Setting the Data Model Designer Properties

Paradox can display a specific data model whenever you open the Reference Data Model window, and show the window with a specific size and position. To make this happen, set up the data model window the way you want it, then choose Properties ➤ Save As Default from the data model menus. The next time you open the window, it will look just as it did when you chose Save As Default.

 ▶▶**N O T E**

> The default Reference Data Model window's appearance is saved to *pdoxwin.ini*, usually in your *c:\windows* directory. If you've chosen a default data model and now prefer to see a blank data model window instead, exit Paradox and use Windows Notepad (or another text-only editor) to change *pdoxwin.ini*. Scroll down to the [Data Model] section and CAREFULLY remove the *Reference* = ... line. Save your changes, exit Notepad, and then restart Paradox. See Chapter 14 for more about *pdoxwin.ini*.

After changing the data model window's size, position, or view, you can quickly restore those settings to their default appearance. Just choose Properties ➤ Restore Default.

► Closing the Data Model

When you're finished using the Data Model Designer, you can close the window. Choose F̲ile ➤ C̲lose from the data model window's menus, or double-click the data model window's Control-menu box. If you've made changes to the data model and haven't saved them yet, Paradox will ask if you're sure you want to exit. If you do want to exit now, choose OK; otherwise, choose Cancel (or press Esc), save your changes, and then close the window again.

► Using a Data Model in Queries and Design Documents

Once you've saved a data model, you can use it to set up queries, forms, and reports. You'll learn more about this later in the book. But for the curious, here's a quick summary of techniques you can use:

- **To base a query on a saved data model,** choose F̲ile ➤ N̲ew ➤ Query. In the Select File dialog box, click the Data M̲odel button, then open the T̲ype drop-down list and choose <Data Models>. Finally, click the appropriate data model in the list below F̲ile Name, then choose OK. All the tables in your data model will appear in the Query window, and they'll be linked automatically. (See Chapters 9 and 16).

- **To base a form or report on a saved data model**, choose File
  ➤ New ➤ Form or File ➤ New ➤ Report (as appropriate). Click
  the Data Model/Layout Diagram button, then open the Type
  drop-down list and choose <Data Models>. Next, click the appropriate data model in the list below File Name, and choose OK.
  Proceed with the Design Layout dialog box that is discussed in
  Chapter 10. (See Chapters 10 and 17.)

This chapter has covered the fundamentals of designing databases that
contain multiple related tables. We discussed one-to-many, many-to-
many, and one-to-one relationships, focused on ways to eliminate redundant data and repetitive fields, and explained how to define fields
that tie separate tables together. We also covered referential integrity,
which enforces strict ties between related tables and prevents orphan
records. Finally, we explained how to use Paradox's powerful Data
Model designer to link tables simply by drawing lines to connect them.

In the next chapter, you'll learn how to add data to a table and how to
make changes and corrections as needed.

► ► CHAPTER **6**

Entering and Editing Table Data

━━━━━

FAST TRACK

▶ ▶ **To open a table**   **224**

    choose File ➤ Open ➤ Table or click the Open Table button in the Toolbar (if it's available). Or open the Project Viewer window, switch to the appropriate working directory, and click the Table icon in the viewer; then double-click the name of the table you want to open.

▶ **To switch between Table View and Form View**   **227**

    click the Quick Form button in the Toolbar, or press F7, or choose Tools ➤ Quick Form.

▶ **To close a table**   **229**

    click the Control-menu box for Table or Form View and choose Close, or double-click the Control-menu box, or press Ctrl+F4.

▶ **To add new data or edit existing data**   **230**

    switch to Edit mode by clicking the Edit Data button in the Toolbar, or pressing F9, or choosing View ➤ Edit Data.

▶ ***To add new data to the bottom of a table*** **230**

> make sure the table is open and in Edit mode. Then click the LastRecord button in the Toolbar, or press Ctrl+F12 or Ctrl+End, or choose <u>R</u>ecord ➤ <u>L</u>ast. Then, if you're in Table View, press ↓ or F12; if you're in Form View, press PgDn or F12 to create a new blank record. Type the contents of each field, pressing ↵ or Tab (or clicking the next field) to move to the next field.

▶ ***To insert a new record above an existing record*** **243**

> choose <u>R</u>ecord ➤ <u>I</u>nsert or press the Ins (Insert) key.

▶ ***To delete the current record from the table*** **244**

> choose <u>R</u>ecord ➤ <u>D</u>elete or press Ctrl+Del.

▶ ***To switch to Field View before changing the contents of a field*** **246**

> click the current field again, or click the Field View button, or press F2, or choose <u>V</u>iew ➤ <u>F</u>ield View.

▶ ***To enter or edit data in a special field*** **259**

> (formatted memo, graphic, memo, or OLE field), your first step is usually to switch to Field View. From here, specific techniques depend on the field type.

▶ ***To format text in a formatted memo field*** **263**

> first select the text you want to format, then right-click the mouse to access the formatting options.

►► **O**nce you create a new Paradox for Windows table, you'll want to put some data in it. Of course, you'll also need to make changes and corrections to the table from time to time. This chapter explains how to open a Paradox table, add data to it, make changes and corrections, and save your work.

 ►►**TIP**

For some hands-on practice using techniques discussed in this chapter, take a lesson from the "Working With A Table" Coaches. Coaches were introduced in Chapter 3.

►► *Opening a Table*

To open a table so you can add new data to it or edit it, follow these steps:

1. If you haven't already done so, choose File ➤ Working Directory to switch to the table's working directory. (See Chapter 3 for other ways to change your working directory.)

 2. Click the Open Table button in the Toolbar (if it's available), or choose File ➤ Open ➤ Table. You'll see the Open Table dialog box, shown in Figure 6.1.

3. If necessary, use the scroll bar to the right of the table names to scroll the name of the table you want into view.

4. Click the name of the table you want to open, then choose OK (or just double-click the name of the table you want to open).

FIGURE 6.1 ▶

The Open Table dialog box lets you open an existing Paradox table.

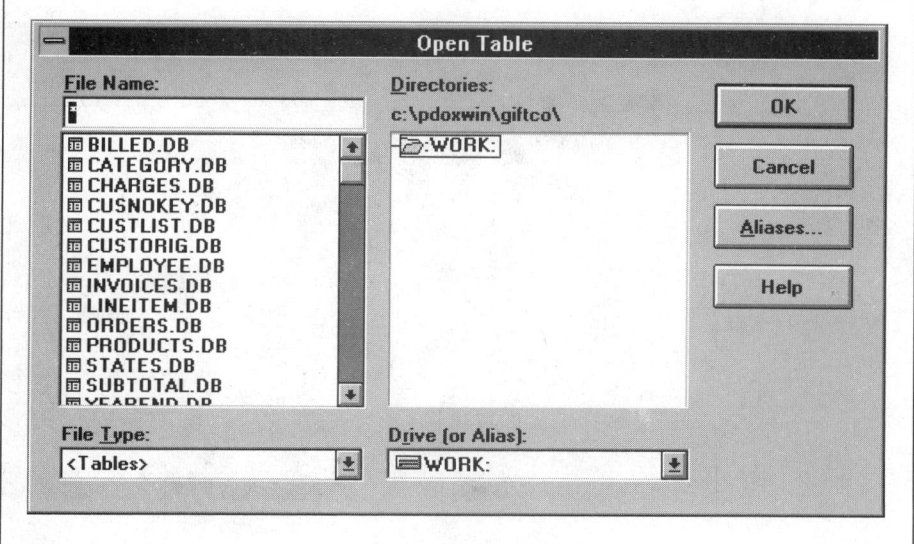

 ▶ ▶ **N O T E**

You can also type the table's file name in the File Name text box, and you can use the Drive (or Alias) drop-down list and Directories list to locate a table that's not in the current working directory (see Chapter 3).

For a quicker way to open a table, open the Project Viewer window, and change the working directory if necessary (see Chapter 3). Click the Tables icon in the left side of the viewer and then double-click the table's file name in the right side.

If the table already contains some data, you'll see whatever amount of information fits in the current window. If you haven't added data to the table yet, only the field names at the top of the table structure will appear in the table, as in Figure 6.2.

The status bar near the lower-left corner of the screen indicates how many records are in the table. Notice that once you've opened a table, the options in the menu bar change, and a new Toolbar, shown in Figure 6.3, appears below the menu bar. We'll describe the roles of many of those buttons as we progress through this chapter.

Entering/Editing
Table Data

▶ ▶

Ch.
6

FIGURE 6.2

An empty table open on the Desktop. Since we haven't entered any data into the table yet, only the field names appear across the top of the table.

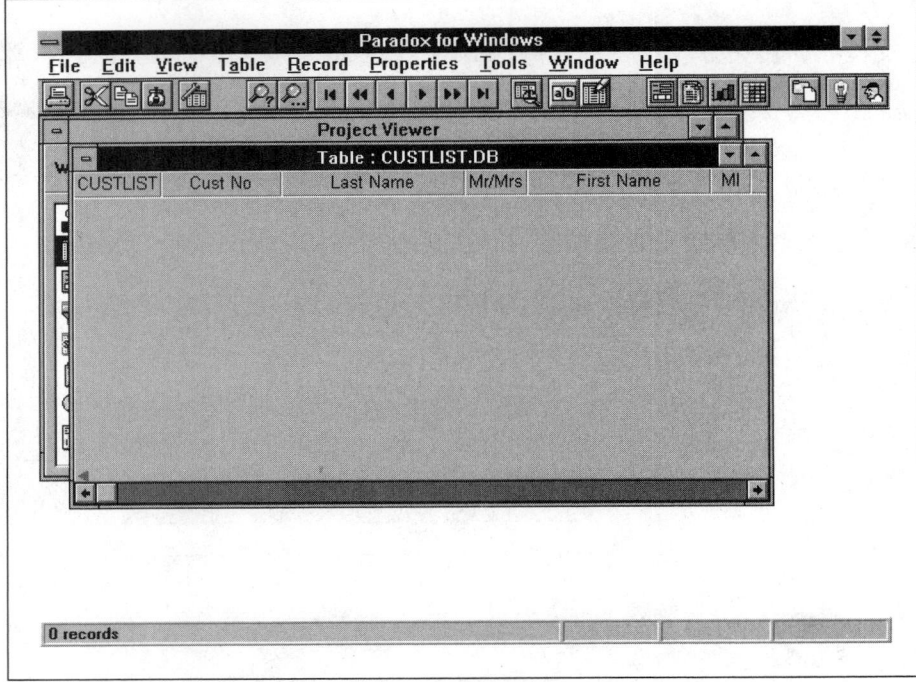

FIGURE 6.3

Once you open a table, the Toolbar offers new buttons for working with the table.

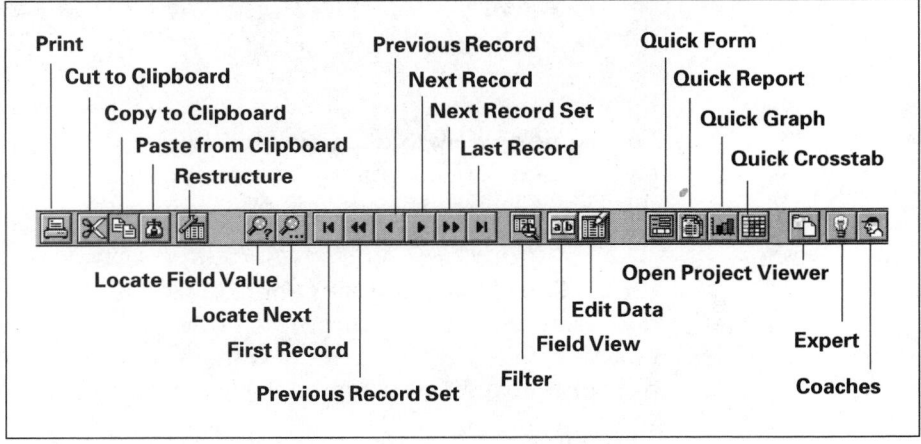

TIP

Remember, when you move the mouse pointer to a Toolbar button, the status bar describes the function of that button. To choose a button, click it. You can also right-click some buttons to view a menu.

▶▶ *Choosing a View*

Once a table is opened, you can display it in either of two views:

Table View Shows the table in tabular format, with as many rows and columns as will fit into the current window. When you're working in Table View, the window is called a *Table window*.

Form View Shows a single record at a time, as in Figure 6.4. When you're working in Form View, the window is called a *Form window*.

NOTE

Technically speaking, the "quick form" options use *preferred* form settings, which you set by choosing Properties ➤ Preferred ➤ Form in Table View. The "default form" options use *Paradox's default* form settings. If you haven't defined a preferred form for the table, Paradox will use the default form settings; therefore, a table's "quick form" and "default form" usually look the same. You'll learn more about creating preferred forms in Part 3.

Here are some simple techniques for switching between Table View and Form View:

- If you're in Table View, click the Quick Form button in the Toolbar (shown at left), or choose Tools ➤ Quick Form (or Tools ➤ Default Form), or press F7 to switch to Form View.

Entering/Editing
Table Data

▶ ▶

Ch.
6

FIGURE 6.4

A table record displayed in Form View, which lets you enter and edit data one record at a time

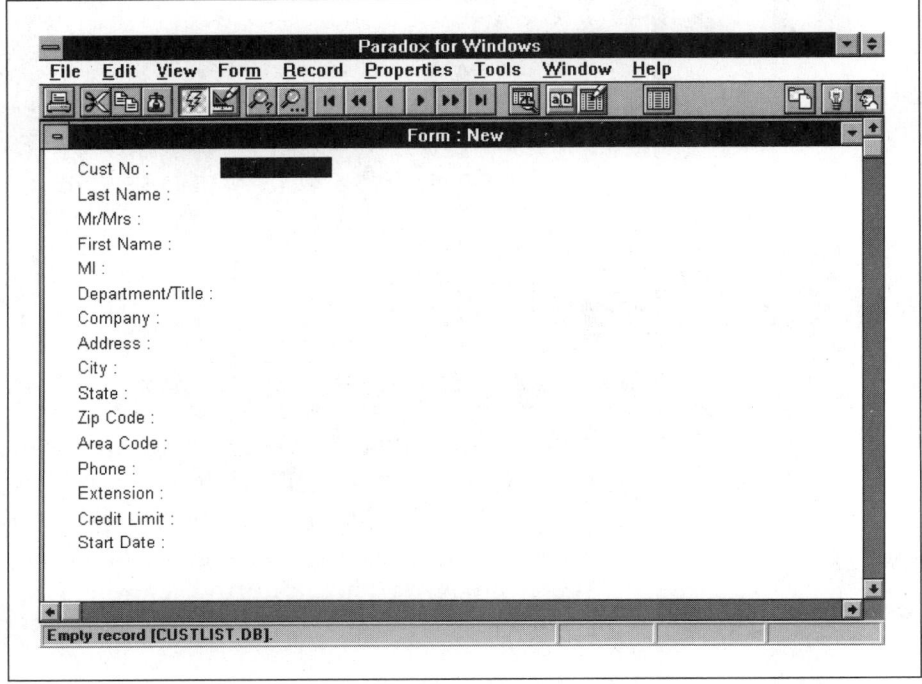

- If you're in Form View, click the Table View button in the Toolbar (shown at left), or choose View ➤ Table View (or press F7) to switch to Table View.

When you switch from Table View to Form View, Paradox opens a new Form window without closing the Table window. Therefore, you can also just click on any visible portion of whichever window is obscured to bring that window to the foreground. (To arrange the open windows neatly on the Desktop, so that each window is visible, choose Window ➤ Cascade or Window ➤ Tile.)

Whenever you switch from Table View to Form View, the menu bar changes slightly (the Table menu is replaced by a Form menu in Form View), and the Form View contains two additional buttons—a Design button (for designing custom forms, as described in Chapters 10 and 11) and a Table View button (replaces the Quick Form button, so you can quickly switch back to Table View).

▶▶ **N O T E**

> **Both the Form window and Table window act as standard document windows which you can move and size within the Paradox Desktop window.**

▶▶ *Closing a Table*

When you're done working with a table, you'll want to close it to remove clutter from the Desktop and to make sure all your data is saved to disk. You close a table simply by closing the window it's displayed in, using any of the standard Windows techniques.

Keep in mind that if you've used both Form View and Table View, you must close both those windows in order to close the table fully. The typical steps for closing your table are:

1. If you've used Form View to enter or edit data, click anywhere in the Form window or press Ctrl+F6 until the form is in full view.

2. Double-click the Control-menu box in the upper-left corner of the Form window (*not* the Control-menu box for the Paradox Desktop), or click the Control-menu box and choose Close, or press Ctrl+F4. If Paradox asks you to save the form, you can choose Yes to save it or No to discard it. (If it's a Quick Form or Default Form, you can discard it without losing anything important.)

3. You'll probably be taken to the Table View for the current table. If not, click anywhere on the Table window of the table you want to close, or press Ctrl+F6 until the table you want to close is in view.

4. Double-click the Control-menu box for the Table View's window (*not* the Control-menu box for the Paradox Desktop), or click the Control-menu box and choose Close, or press Ctrl+F4.

▶▶ **T I P**

> **The quickest way to close all the windows on the Desktop is to choose Window ➤ Close All.**

When you've closed all the tables, the Desktop will be clear (or it may show just the Project Viewer window). You can, of course, re-open the table at any time (for example, using File ➤ Open ➤ Table), as described at the beginning of this chapter.

▶▶ *Switching to Edit Mode*

When you first open a table, whether in Table View or Form View, you're in *View mode*, which means you can view data, but not add to or change it. If you try to type data into a field or make changes, Paradox will display the message "Not in Edit mode. Press F9 to edit data" and ignore your keystrokes.

To add data to a table, you must first switch to Edit mode using one of the following techniques:

- Click the Edit Data button in the Toolbar (shown at left).
- Choose View ➤ Edit Data.
- Press F9.

The status bar near the bottom of the Desktop will display "Edit" indicating that you can now add data or change data in the table. When you are finished editing data, simply click the Edit Data button, or choose View ➤ Edit Data, or press F9 again.

▶▶ *Adding Records to a Table*

The steps for adding data to alpha, numeric, and date fields are listed below. See "Entering and Editing Special Field Types," later in this chapter, for information on entering data in formatted memo, graphic, memo, and OLE fields, and for details on creating DDE links.

1. First make sure the table is open and in Edit mode, as described above (you can be in either Table View or Form View—it doesn't matter which).
2. If the table is currently empty, skip to step 5 below.

3. Move the cursor to the last record using any of these methods:

- Click the Last Record button in the Toolbar (shown at left).
- Choose <u>R</u>ecord ➤ <u>L</u>ast from the menus.
- Press Ctrl+F12.
- Press Ctrl+End.

4. If you're in Table View, press ↓ or F12 to create a new blank record. If you're in Form View, press PgDn or F12 to create a new blank record.

► ► **T I P**

> **You can also press *Insert* to insert a new blank record at the current position in the table.**

5. Type the contents of the current field. (You cannot enter data into autoincrement fields, since Paradox updates those fields automatically.)

6. After filling in the current field, click the next field or press Tab or ↵ to move to the next field. (You won't be able to do this if the current field fails a validity check—more on this in a moment.)

► ► **N O T E**

> **Number fields automatically appear with commas and two decimal places of accuracy (for example, 1,001.00 for customer number 1001; 619.00 for area code 619). Dates appear in mm/dd/yy format, as in 12/31/94. Don't worry about that. It's easy to change those formats at any time without re-entering data or changing the table's structure, as you'll see in the next chapter.**

7. Repeat steps 5 and 6 to fill in all the fields of the current record.

8. In Table View, the highlight (cursor) will automatically move to a new blank record after you fill in the last field for the current record and press Tab or ↵. In Form View, you must press F12 or

PgDn to move to the next blank record. (Pressing Tab or ↵ when the cursor is positioned in the last field of a record in Form View simply moves the cursor back up to the first field in the record.)

▶ ▶ **T I P**

If a new record that you've entered seems to disappear, it's probably just Paradox re-sorting the table on the spot.

Figure 6.5 shows some sample records added to the CustList table (though part of the table is scrolled out of view). Adding records is simply a matter of typing the contents of each field, then pressing ↵ to move to the next field.

If you need to make a correction, simply click on the field that you want to correct and type in a new entry. We'll discuss more editing techniques in a moment.

FIGURE 6.5

Sample data added to the CustList table. Part of the table is scrolled off the screen.

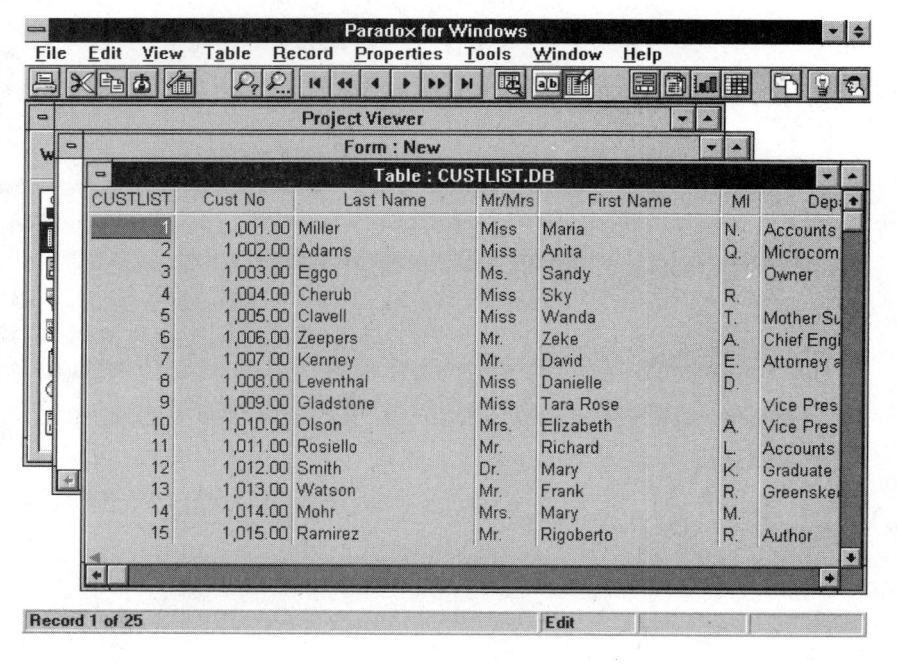

▶ *How Much Data Will Fit on the Screen?*

The amount of data you can see depends on the resolution of your screen. Therefore, your screen may not look like the ones shown in this book. For instance, if you have a 1024 × 768 high-resolution monitor, you'll see much more data at once, but the characters will appear smaller.

We'll stick with the standard VGA resolution of 640 × 480 pixels to show screens in this book, so you don't need a magnifying glass to see the figures.

▶ *Typing Special Characters*

If you need to display a foreign currency sign in a currency field, you can just change the Number Format property for that field (see Chapter 7).

When typing data in an alpha field, you can type foreign and other special characters from the IBM extended character set. The basic technique is to turn on the Num Lock key (though this isn't required on all keyboards), hold down the Alt key, type the three-digit code for the character you want *using the numbers on the numeric keypad*, then release the Alt key.

Table 6.1 lists the special characters that are available on most printers and the codes used to access them. However, codes may vary depending on your printer and the currently selected font. The table shows the commonly used PC-8 symbol set, which many printers allow you to choose (see your printer manual).

 ▶ ▶ **T I P**

To control whether the Num Lock key must be turned on when typing special characters with the numeric keypad, choose Properties ➤ Desktop, then click the Advanced button. Now, either select (check) or deselect (clear) the Always Use Alt + Numeric Keypad For Character Entry option, and choose OK twice. When deselected, Num Lock must be on; when selected, the Num Lock key need not be on.

▶ **TABLE 6.1:** *Special Characters from IBM Extended Character Set*

CODE	CHAR	CODE	CHAR	CODE	CHAR	CODE	CHAR
128	Ç	160	á	192	∟	224	α
129	ü	161	í	193	⊥	225	ß
130	é	162	ó	194	┬	226	Γ
131	â	163	ú	195	├	227	π
132	ä	164	ñ	196	—	228	Σ
133	à	165	Ñ	197	+	229	σ
134	å	166	ª	198	╞	230	μ
135	ç	167	º	199	╟	231	τ
136	ê	168	¿	200	╚	232	Φ
137	ë	169	⌐	201	╔	233	Θ
138	è	170	¬	202	╩	234	Ω
139	ï	171	½	203	╦	235	δ
140	î	172	¼	204	╠	236	∞
141	ì	173	¡	205	=	237	φ
142	Ä	174	«	206	╬	238	ε
143	Å	175	»	207	╧	239	∩
144	É	176	▒	208	╨	240	≡
145	æ	177	▓	209	╤	241	±
146	Æ	178	▓	210	╥	242	≥
147	ô	179	│	211	╙	243	≤
148	ö	180	┤	212	╘	244	⌠
149	ò	181	╡	213	╒	245	⌡
150	û	182	╢	214	╓	246	÷
151	ù	183	╖	215	╫	247	≈
152	ÿ	184	╕	216	╪	248	°
153	Ö	185	╣	217	┘	249	•
154	Ü	186	║	218	┌	250	·
155	¢	187	╗	219	█	251	√
156	£	188	╝	220	▄	252	η
157	¥	189	╜	221	▌	253	²
158	₧	190	╛	222	▐	254	■
159	ƒ	191	┐	223	▀	255	

You can also use special characters from the Windows Character Map; however, you're limited to characters in whatever font is used to display the entire field (that is, you can change fonts for a single field, but not part of a field). There's more about Character Map under "Using True-Type Special Characters," later in this chapter.

▶ Entering Data in Validated Fields

If you assigned any validity checks to a field, the entry you place in that field must conform to the rules specified by the validity check. Otherwise, the cursor will seem "stuck"; you won't be able to move out of the field until you enter some data that satisfies the validity check. When this happens, look to the status bar for information on why your entry fails the validity check. Below are some possibilities.

- If you try to move the cursor to another record before filling in a required field, the message "Field value required" will appear in the status bar, and the cursor will remain in the record until you fill the field with some value. You'll need to move to the empty field that requires an entry, and then fill in some data.

- If you try to enter a value that is less than the minimum acceptable value assigned to the field or greater than the largest acceptable value for the field, the status bar will display the message "A value no less than x is expected" or "A value no more than x is expected," where x is the minimum or maximum value specified in the validity checks for that field. You can't leave the field until you've entered a value that satisfies the validity check.

- If you've assigned a default value to a field, the default value will appear as soon as you create the new record. When you get to that field, you can retain the default entry by pressing Tab or ↵ to move to the next field. Or you can type a new entry into the field before pressing Tab or ↵.

- If the field contains a picture template, you can only enter characters specified within the template. Paradox will beep and ignore any characters that don't fit the template, or, when you try to leave the field, you'll see the message "The field value fails picture validity check." You must re-enter the field's contents to match the picture template before you can move to the next field.

Entering/Editing
Table Data

▶ ▶

Ch.
6

Of course, the job of a validity check is to prevent you from entering bad data into a table. So, in most cases you'll simply want to fix (or complete) the entry so that it passes the validity check before moving on to the next field or record.

 ▶ ▶ **N O T E**

> **If the error message in the status bar is "Key violation," see "Entering Data In Primary Key Fields" below.**

▶ Getting "Unstuck" from Validated Fields

In some cases, a value you enter into a field may fail a validity check because your validity check is wrong. Suppose you inadvertently entered $10,000.00 as the *minimum* instead of the *maximum* acceptable value in a field. In that case, you might end up in a situation where you can neither enter valid data into the field or record, nor get out of the record to change the validity check. Here's how to solve the problem:

1. First try to enter valid data into every field, and make sure all required fields contain some data. Or, delete the entry in the current field by pressing Ctrl+Backspace.

2. If you can't seem to get valid data into the record, delete the entire record by choosing Record ▶ Delete, or by pressing Ctrl+Del.

Once you get the cursor freed up, you can correct the validity check, if need be, by restructuring the table. This topic is discussed at length in Chapter 15. Basically, all you need to do is this:

1. Starting from Table View, choose Table ▶ Restructure Table or click the Restructure button in the Toolbar. You'll be taken to the Restructure Table dialog box.

2. Choose *Validity Checks* from the Table Properties drop-down list.

3. Highlight the field that contains the pesky validity check.

4. Make whatever changes are required to correct the problem with the validity check, or delete the validity check by double-clicking it and pressing Delete. (To delete a required field validity check, click the Required Field option once to deselect it.)

5. Choose <u>S</u>ave to save the structure with the new validity checks, and respond to any dialog boxes that appear.

▶ ▶ **T I P**

> **If you're having problems entering data into a validated field, chances are that the validity check needs to be *less* stringent, not more stringent.**

Paradox may ask you whether existing records must conform to the new validity checks when you try to save the table. If you have any problems, see Chapter 15 for details about table restructuring.

After saving the new table structure, you'll be returned to the table, in View mode. If you want to add, edit, or delete data, switch to Edit mode (click the Edit Data button or press F9).

▶ Entering Data in Primary Key Fields

In Chapter 4, you learned that primary keys prevent you from entering duplicate data in the primary key fields. Paradox will reject any new record that duplicates the data in the keyed fields of an existing record. For instance, suppose you've made Cust No the primary key and assigned the customer number 1009 to a new customer. Paradox will reject the whole record if an existing customer record already has that customer number. Similarly, if you've defined Last Name and First Name (only) as the primary key, Paradox will reject a new record with the name *Granolabar Wanda* if an existing record already contains that name.

Paradox won't reject a record until you complete it. That is, you can go to all the trouble of filling in the entire record; but when you try to move the cursor to some other record, the cursor will stick in the current record and you will see the message "Key violation" in the status bar.

The easy fix in such cases is to move the cursor to the keyed field and type in a unique value. For instance, if 1009 is a duplicate entry, move to the Cust No field and type in some new number, such as 1010 or whatever the next available number is.

TIP

You can use the *autoincrement* field type to ensure that all primary keys in a table are unique. With an autoincrement type, Paradox automatically assigns and fills in the next available number for the field. Note, however, that you can't type a value into an autoincrement field, and you can't change the field's value. Chapters 4 and 18 explain ways to control the starting values in an autoincrement field.

If the way you've defined the primary key is too "picky," you'll probably want to restructure the table to make the definition of a duplicate less stringent. You can usually do so by adding more fields to the primary key. For instance, suppose we defined Last Name, First Name, Address, and Zip combined as the primary key field. In that case, Paradox would reject a new record as a duplicate only if some other record had the identical data in all four of those fields, rather than in just the Last Name and First Name fields. Another option is to set up a new primary key, such as a Customer Number, that doesn't rely on other data in the record.

If you do need to change the primary key, you must first get rid of the *Key violation* error. Simply change the data in one of the key fields so that it's no longer a duplicate of another record; or, if you're really stuck, delete the entire record with Record ➤ Delete or Ctrl+Del.

Then you can restructure the table using Table ➤ Restructure Table. Chapter 4 provides help with defining a primary key. See Chapter 15 for details about restructuring a table.

"My New Records Keep Disappearing!"

When you're using a table for which you've defined a primary key, Paradox will instantly re-sort a new record into its proper sort-order position in the table when you finish entering the record. So the record may seem to disappear from the screen as soon as you've typed it!

If you want to make sure the new record is in the table, you can scroll to the position of the new record using any of the techniques described in the next section. For instance, if the table is keyed on the Last Name and First Name fields, and you just entered a record for Bilbo Bowser, you'll need to scroll to the B's to find the record in its proper sort-order position.

▶ *Entering Data when Referential Integrity is in Effect*

Recall from Chapter 5 that you can set up referential integrity relationships between tables in a multitable database. Here are some points to remember when working with tables that have referential integrity relationships:

- You cannot delete a record from the parent table if the child table contains associated records. For example, you cannot delete a customer from CustList if an order for that customer exists in the Orders table. Such attempts are refused with the message "Master has detail records. Cannot delete or modify."

- If you've selected the Prohibit update rule, you cannot change the key field of the parent table if any associated records exist in the child table. Again, the message "Master has detail records. Cannot delete or modify" will appear when you try to move the cursor to another record. (You must choose Edit ➤ Undo or type in the previous key field value to clear the message.)

- You cannot insert a record into the child table unless a corresponding record exists in the parent table. For instance, you cannot insert a record into the LineItem table unless the Orders table already includes a record with the same value for the Order No field.

- You also cannot delete or rename the parent table if any records exist in the child table.

Paradox offers a neat feature called "Move Help," which makes data entry easier in tables that are tied together with referential integrity. You can learn more about it at the end of the chapter (see "Using Move Help When Referential Integrity is in Effect").

▶ *Data Entry Shortcuts*

The following shortcuts will help you enter data in date, money, number, time, and timestamp fields:

- To enter a period automatically in number and money fields, press the spacebar instead of typing a period. (This works in Table View only. In Form View, pressing the spacebar inserts a comma in a number field and a space in a money field. Weird but true.)

- To fill in the leading currency sign in a money field automatically when you finish your entry, simply omit the currency sign.

- To fill in the ".00" portion of a money amount automatically, simply omit it.

- To fill in the current system month, day, year, hour, minute, second, AM, PM and appropriate punctuation in a date, time, or timestamp field, press the spacebar at the spot to be filled in automatically (try this and you'll see what we mean). *Examples:* The current date and time are *September 30, 1994* at *1:47:44 PM*. In a date field, pressing the spacebar three times will enter the date *9/30/94*. Typing **6**, pressing the spacebar, typing **25**, and pressing the spacebar twice will enter *6/25/94*. In a time field, pressing the spacebar four times will enter *1:47:44 PM*. In a timestamp field, pressing the spacebar eight times will enter the time and date *1:47:44 PM, 9/30/94*. Typing **2:25:** and pressing the spacebar six times would enter *2:25:44 PM, 9/30/94*.

- To automatically fill in a logical field with "True" or "Male" or "Yes" (depending on the currently selected logical format), press the spacebar. (You'll learn how to adjust the logical format in Chapter 7.)

- To duplicate the field entry from the same field in the previous record, press Ctrl+D.

- To erase the word to the left of the insertion point, press Ctrl+Backspace.

- To move to the first field in a record, press the Home key.

- To move to the last field in a record, press the End key.

You can also use the standard cut, copy, and paste techniques to move or copy data from one field to another (provided that any data within the record meets validity checks). To select data to move or copy, use any of these techniques:

- Click the field that contains the data you want to select (so the entire field is highlighted).

- Drag the mouse pointer through the portion of a field that you want to select.

- Move the mouse pointer to where you want to start selecting, then hold down the mouse button and drag the mouse pointer through multiple fields. You can also select multiple fields by holding down the Shift key while moving the cursor with the arrow, PgUp, PgDn, Home, End, Ctrl+Home, and Ctrl+End keys.

N O T E

If the message "In field view..." appears in the status bar while you're trying to select multiple fields, click some other field, then try again. You should briefly see the message "Selecting Fields" in the status bar, and the mouse pointer should change to a four-headed arrow when you've done it correctly.

- To select all the fields and records in the table, choose Edit ➤ Select All (this works in Table View only).

Once you've selected data to copy, you can use any of these techniques to move or copy the data to the Windows Clipboard:

Cut To Clipboard   Deletes selected data and places it in the Windows Clipboard. (Same as choosing Edit ➤ Cut or pressing Shift+Del.) Use this to *move* data from the current field to another field.

Copy To Clipboard   Copies selected data to the Windows Clipboard. (Same as choosing Edit ➤ Copy or pressing Ctrl+Ins.) Use this to *copy* data to another field.

Once you've cut or copied data to the Clipboard, you can paste the data from the Clipboard into another field or even into another Windows application. If you're continuing in Paradox, move the cursor to the field that you want to paste the data into (the type of data you're moving or copying must have the same field type as the field you're moving or copying to). Now use the third button to complete the job:

Paste From Clipboard   Pastes data from the Clipboard to the insertion point position in the current field. (Same as choosing Edit ➤ Paste or pressing Shift+Ins.)

If you want to paste the selected data to another application, run that application and choose Edit ➤ Paste from that application's menu.

▶▶ *Moving around in a Table*

You can go to any field in a table simply by moving the mouse pointer to that field and clicking the mouse button. You can also use the scroll bars to scroll through a table. And, you can use any of the keys, buttons, and techniques listed in Table 6.2 to get around a table.

▶ **TABLE 6.2:** *Techniques for Moving through a Table*

TO GO TO	CLICK	OR CHOOSE	OR PRESS
First record	◄	Record ➤ First	Ctrl+Home or Ctrl+F11
Last record	►|	Record ➤ Last	Ctrl+End or Ctrl+F12
Next record	►	Record ➤ Next	F12 (or ↓ in Table View or PgDn in Form View)
Previous record	◄	Record ➤ Previous	F11 (or ↑ in Table View or PgUp in Form View)

▶ **TABLE 6.2:** *Techniques for Moving through a Table (continued)*

TO GO TO	CLICK	OR CHOOSE	OR PRESS
Next record set	▸▸	Record ➤ Next Set	Shift+F12
Previous record set	◂◂	Record ➤ Previous Set	Shift+F11
Next field	Field		Tab, →, or ↵
Previous field	Field		Shift+Tab or ←
First field			Home
Last field			End
Left one screen	Scroll bar		Ctrl+PgUp
Right one screen	Scroll bar		Ctrl+PgDn
Locate field value	🔍?	Record ➤ Locate ➤ Value	Ctrl+Z
Locate next	🔍...	Record ➤ Locate Next	Ctrl+A

▶▶ *Inserting a Record*

Don't worry about the order in which you enter records into a table, because you can easily re-sort the records into any order you wish at any time. Most people just add new records to the end of the table as needed.

If you want to insert a new record between two existing records, move the cursor to the record that's *below* the place where you want to insert a new record, then choose Record ➤ Insert, or press the Ins (Insert) key.

Paradox inserts a new blank record above the current record and moves the cursor to the first field in that new record, so you can start typing immediately.

 ▶ ▶ N O T E

> **When you insert a new record into a keyed table, Paradox will still move the new record to its proper sort-order position!**

▶▶ Deleting a Record

You can delete an entire record from the current table. However, you should be *very* careful about doing this because you can't recover a deleted record. If you're sure you want to delete an entire record, move the cursor to the record you want to delete, then choose Record ➤ Delete, or press Ctrl+Del.

The entire record is removed from the table, and Paradox instantly closes the gap between existing records.

 ▶ ▶ N O T E

> **You can delete several records in a single operation using queries (see Chapter 9).**

▶▶ Editing Table Data

Only the rarest of birds can type a bunch of new records into a table without making a mistake. We mere mortals must make changes and corrections as we go along. Of course, correcting mistakes isn't the only reason you'd want to edit a table. Sometimes you'll need to change information just to bring it up to date (for instance, to change a customer's address after he or she moves).

You can easily change the contents of any field in any record at any time. Just open the table and switch to Edit mode (if you haven't already done so). Then move to the data you want to change by clicking on the field or by using the various cursor-positioning keys, such as ↑, ↓, →, ←, PgUp, PgDn, Tab, and Shift+Tab.

▶ ▶ **N O T E**

> **Remember that you can only edit the contents of a field while you're in Edit mode. If you're in View mode, click the Edit Data button or press F9 to switch to Edit mode.**

When you reach the field you want to edit, the entire field will be *selected* (highlighted). Any new text you type will completely replace the text that's in that field. You can use any of the techniques listed in Table 6.3 to change the field.

▶ **TABLE 6.3:** *Techniques for Changing Field Contents while in Table View or Form View*

TYPING/CHOOSING...	HAS THIS EFFECT...
New text	Any new text you type completely replaces all existing text in the field.
Alt+Backspace (or <u>E</u>dit ➤ <u>U</u>ndo or Escape)	Undoes the last change or deletion in a field.
Shift+Del (or <u>E</u>dit ➤ Cu<u>t</u> or the Cut To Clipboard button in the Toolbar)	Deletes the field entry and copies it to the Windows Clipboard.
Ctrl+Ins (or <u>E</u>dit ➤ <u>C</u>opy or the Copy To Clipboard button in the Toolbar)	Copies the field entry to the Windows Clipboard.
Shift+Ins (or <u>E</u>dit ➤ <u>P</u>aste or the Paste From Clipboard button in the Toolbar)	Pastes the previously cut or copied text from the Clipboard to the current field.

► **TABLE 6.3:** *Techniques for Changing Field Contents while in Table View or Form View (continued)*

TYPING/CHOOSING...	HAS THIS EFFECT...
Delete (or Edit ➤ Delete)	Deletes the field entry but does not copy it to the Windows Clipboard.
↵ or Tab	Completes the change and moves the cursor to the next field.
F2 (or second click, or click the Field View button in the Toolbar)	Switches to Field View.

► Using Field View to Make More Refined Corrections

If you want to *change* the contents of the field that the cursor is in, rather than *replace* them, you must first switch to Field View. Here's how:

1. Make sure you're in Edit mode, and then move the cursor to the field you want to change (you can be in either Table View or Form View).

2. Activate Field View using any of the methods below:

   ● Move the mouse pointer to where you want to make a change, then click the mouse button again. (Or, just click twice at exactly the place you want to start making changes.)

   ● Click the Field View button in the Toolbar (shown at left).
   ● Choose View ➤ Field View.
   ● Press F2.

Once you've switched to Field View, the cursor, which normally highlights the entire field, becomes an insertion point (blinking vertical bar), and the mouse pointer changes to an I-Beam. The message "Field" appears at the right side of the status bar.

The roles of the arrow keys and mouse now apply to the contents of the current field only, rather than the entire record. The mouse and keyboard functions are summarized in Table 6.4.

▶ **TABLE 6.4:** *Keys and Techniques Used in Field View*

TYPING/CHOOSING...	HAS THIS EFFECT...
← and →	Moves insertion point one character left or right.
Mouse click	Moves insertion point to the I-Beam.
Home	Moves insertion point to beginning of field.
End	Moves insertion point to end of field.
Backspace	Deletes character to left of insertion point.
Delete	Deletes character to right of insertion point.
New text	Any new text you type is inserted at the insertion point.
Drag	Selects (highlights) text.
Shift+←, Shift+→	Selects character to the left or right of insertion point.
Shift+Home	Selects text from insertion point to beginning of field.
Shift+End	Selects text from insertion point to end of field.
Delete (or Edit ➤ Delete) with text selected	Deletes all selected text.
Backspace with text selected	Deletes all selected text.
New text with text selected	Replaces all selected text.
Alt+Backspace (or Edit ➤ Undo or Escape)	Undoes last change or deletion.
Shift+Del (or Edit ➤ Cut or Cut To Clipboard button in the Toolbar)	Deletes selected text and copies it to Windows Clipboard.

▶ **TABLE 6.4:** *Keys and Techniques Used in Field View (continued)*

TYPING/CHOOSING...	HAS THIS EFFECT...
Ctrl+Ins (or Edit ➤ Copy or Copy To Clipboard button in the Toolbar)	Copies selected text to Windows Clipboard.
Shift+Ins (or Edit ➤ Paste or the Paste From Clipboard button in the Toolbar)	Pastes previously cut or copied text from Clipboard to current field.
F2 (or Field View button in the Toolbar)	Toggles in and out of Field View.

When you've finished making your changes, move to another field or press F2 again.

▶ *Making Field View Stick*

If you don't like the way Paradox starts replacing data as soon as you start typing in a field, you can use *Persistent Field View* to make Paradox stay in Field View. To do so, press Ctrl+F2, or choose View ➤ Persistent Field View.

You'll then need to use Tab and Shift+Tab, Alt and an arrow key, or the mouse to move from field to field. Notice that the Field View button on the Toolbar stays depressed even as you move from field to field, the keys listed in Table 6.4 remain active within each field, and the word "Persist" appears at the right edge of the status bar.

To end Persistent Field View, just press Ctrl+F2 or choose View ➤ Persistent Field View again, or click the Field View button.

▶▶ **N O T E**

Persistent Field View is turned off when you close the table or return to View mode.

▶▶ *Locking a Record*

If you share data with other users on a network, and don't want anyone
to edit a record while you're trying to edit or view it, you can lock that
record. Here's how:

1. Switch to Edit mode, then move the cursor to the record you
   want to lock.

2. Choose <u>R</u>ecord ➤ <u>L</u>ock (or press F5).

The message "Locked" appears in the status bar. Other users on the
network can view the record, but they can't change it as long as you
have it locked. If they try to change the record, they'll see the message
"Record Locked" in the status bar.

You'll rarely need to lock records because Paradox automatically locks
the current record when you begin to change any field. As soon as you
move the cursor to a different record, Paradox automatically posts
(saves) the change and unlocks the record.

 ▶▶**N O T E**

> **If you're locked out of a record by another user, you
> can find out who has locked the record. Choose <u>T</u>ools ➤
> <u>M</u>ultiuser ➤ <u>D</u>isplay Locks, then double-click the table
> with the locked record.**

To unlock a record that you've locked, choose <u>R</u>ecord ➤ Unl<u>o</u>ck, or
press Shift+F5, or move the cursor to a different record.

If you want to post (save) the record while continuing to lock it, choose
<u>R</u>ecord ➤ Post/<u>K</u>eep Locked or press Ctrl+F5. If the table is keyed,
the record will automatically move to its proper sort position. Other
users can then see the record, but it will remain locked so you can
continue editing it. As soon as you move the cursor to a new record,
Paradox will post your changes and release the record lock.

▶ ▶ T I P

> **Use Post/Keep Locked to be sure there is no key violation before you fill in the rest of the record, and to put the record in its final sort position in the table.**

▶▶ *Locating Records*

In a small table, it's pretty easy to locate a record simply by scrolling around. But as your table grows, you'll probably want to use the Locate feature to help you zip to a specific record or field quickly. As you'll see, Locate lets you enter all or part of the text you're searching for.

▶ ▶ T I P

> **You can also use queries and filters (Chapter 9) to locate data that you want to edit. Queries and filters are especially handy for editing very large tables.**

Here's how to use Locate:

1. Move the cursor anywhere in the table, to whatever field you want to search. (The search always begins in the current field and starts at the top of the table; in step 4 you can change the field that Paradox will search.)

2. Click the Locate Field Value button in the Toolbar (shown at left), or choose <u>R</u>ecord ➤ Lo<u>c</u>ate ➤ <u>V</u>alue, or press Ctrl+Z. You'll see the Locate Value dialog box, shown in Figure 6.6.

3. Type the text or number you want to search for in the <u>V</u>alue text box.

4. If the name of the field you want to search does not appear under <u>F</u>ields in the dialog box, use the drop-down list to choose a field to search. Once the drop-down list is open, you can use the ↑ and ↓, PgUp, and PgDn keys to scroll, or type the first letter of a field name until the highlight bar lands on the field you want. Then click the field name to select it.

FIGURE 6.6

FIGURE 6.6

The Locate Value dialog box lets you quickly move the cursor to a record containing a specific value.

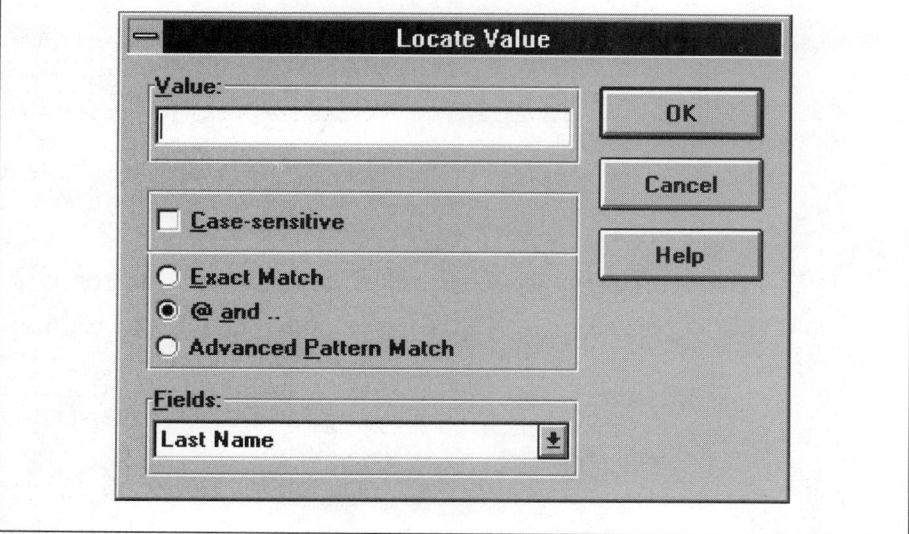

Locate Value

Value:

OK

Cancel

Help

☐ Case-sensitive

○ Exact Match
◉ @ and ..
○ Advanced Pattern Match

Fields:

Last Name ▼

5. If you want to match uppercase and lowercase letters exactly during the search, check the Case sensitive box (if it isn't already checked).

6. Choose the type of match you want:

- If you want to search for an exact match, click Exact Match.
- If you want to match a simple pattern, click the @ And .. option (described below).
- If you want to match a more complex pattern, click Advanced Pattern Match (described below).

7. Choose OK to start the search.

Paradox will take you to the first record that contains the value or pattern in the field you specified. If no records contain the value you're searching for, a message in the status bar will tell you that the value was not found.

If Paradox does find a record that matches the value you specified, but it's not the one you're looking for (say, Paradox finds Anita Smith, but you're looking for Wanda Smith), perform this simple step to find the next record that matches:

● Click the Locate Next button in the Toolbar (shown at left), or choose <u>R</u>ecord ➤ Locate Nex<u>t</u>, or press Ctrl+A.

You can repeat the above step as many times as necessary until you've either located the record you're looking for or the search fails.

Using @ And .. Wildcards to Locate a Record

If you chose *@ And* .. in step 6 above, you can use the following wildcard characters to broaden your search:

..   Matches any series of characters

@   Matches any single character

►▶ **N O T E**

> **If you use wildcards and have not checked <u>C</u>ase-sensitive, uppercase and lowercase letters will be treated the same.**

For example, if you type **Smith** as the value to search for, your search will only find the exact word *Smith*. However, if you enter

     ..smith..

(or **..sMith..** or **..SMITH..**, assuming <u>C</u>ase-sensitive is not checked), Paradox will find records that have the word *smith* embedded within the field you're searching (Smith, SMITH, sMiTh, locksmith, Smith and Wesson, and so on). Similarly, a search value of

     Sm@th

matches any text that starts with *sm*, has any single character in the third position, and ends with *th*, including Smith, smith, smyth, SMITH, and so forth.

▶▶NOTE

If you don't include wildcard characters in the search value, the value is always treated as an exact match, regardless of your choice in step 6 above. Thus, a value of *Smith* only matches "Smith" (or SMITH, smith, etc., if *Case-sensitive* is not checked).

Using Advanced Patterns to Locate a Record

When you choose *Advanced Pattern Match* in step 6, the value you're searching for can include any of the wildcard operators listed in Table 6.5. (Note that the @ And .. wildcards are treated the same in the Advanced Pattern Match option as they are in the "@ And .." option discussed above.)

▶ **TABLE 6.5:** *Advanced Wildcard Operators for Locating Values*

WILDCARD...	OPERATION
..	Matches any series of characters (same as .. in the @ and .. option).
@	Matches any single character (same as @ in the @ and .. option).
[ ]	Matches any character within the brackets.
[^]	Matches any character not contained within the brackets.
¦	Matches either the character before or after the vertical bar.
()	Groups the values within the parentheses.
^	Beginning of field.
$	End of field.
\	Treats following wildcard symbol as a regular character.

▶ **TABLE 6.5:** *Advanced Wildcard Operators for Locating Values (continued)*

WILDCARD...	OPERATION
\f	Matches a form feed.
\n	Matches a line feed.
\r	Matches a carriage return.
\t	Matches a tab.

Let's suppose we're using the Advanced Pattern Match option to locate values in the Last Name field of the CustList table. The search value

S[cm]..

matches any last name beginning with *s*, having a second letter of *c* or *m*, and any other series of characters. Thus, this pattern matches last names of Smith, Smythe, and Schumack.

The search value

..s$

matches any last name that ends with *s*. In our sample table, Adams, Jones, and Zeepers fit this pattern.

Finally, the search value

^[cow]..

matches any last name beginning with *c*, *o*, or *w* followed by any series of characters. This pattern matches Cherub, Clavell, Olson, Watson, and Wilson.

▶ *Locating a Record by Its Position*

If you happen to know the record number (i.e., the sequential position) of the record you want to edit, you can quickly move the cursor to that record by following these steps:

1. Choose <u>R</u>ecord ➤ Lo<u>c</u>ate ➤ Record <u>N</u>umber. You'll see the dialog box below.

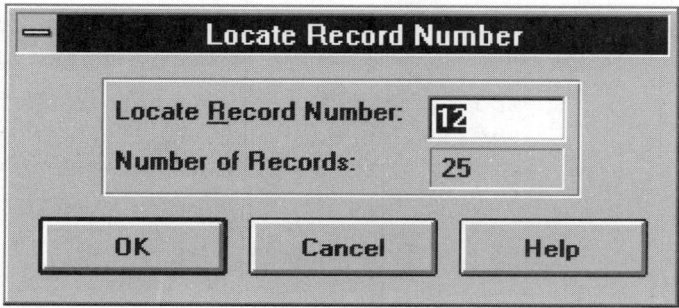

2. Type the number of the record that you want to search for. This can be any number in the range of 1 to whatever value is shown next to Number of Records in the dialog box.

3. Choose OK.

The cursor jumps to the record you specified, remaining in whatever column you were in before moving to the new record.

▶ Editing Multiple Records Simultaneously

If you need to change several records in a table in exactly the same way, you can use Locate with the "and Replace" option. Suppose that while entering records, you inadvertently typed **Lost Angles** rather than **Los Angeles** into the City field for a record. Then, you used Ctrl+D to copy that entry to other records. What a mess! But it's really no problem for the Locate And Replace feature, which can change all the misspelled entries in one fell swoop. (You can use queries, discussed in Chapter 9, to make more refined global changes to a table—for example, increasing a unit price in an inventory by 10%.)

Here's how to use Locate And Replace:

1. Make sure you're in Edit mode (press F9 or click the Edit Data button). If you like, move the cursor to the field you want to change.

2. Choose Record ➤ Locate ➤ And Replace (or press Shift+Ctrl+Z). You'll see the dialog box in Figure 6.7.

3. Choose the field that you want to search from the Fields drop-down list. (Initially, the Fields list shows whichever field the cursor is in, just as for the Locate feature.)

4. If you want to match uppercase and lowercase letters exactly during the search, check the Case-sensitive box.

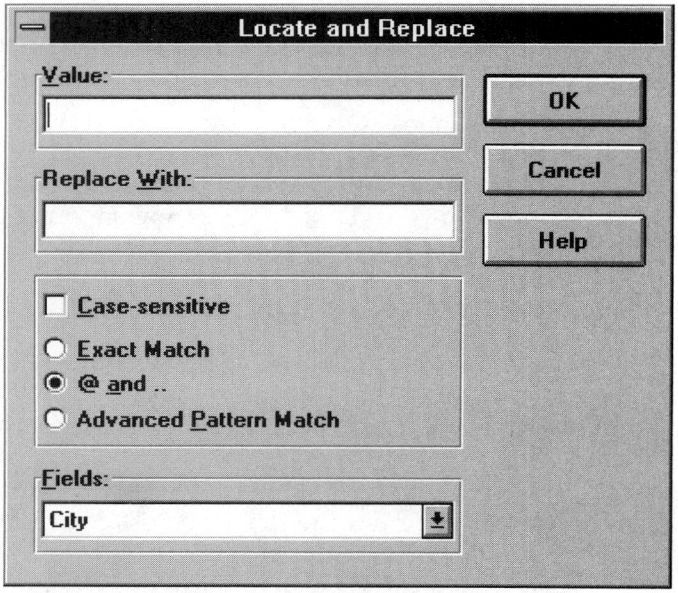

FIGURE 6.7

The Locate And Replace dialog box lets you find values and change them to new ones throughout a table.

5. Choose the type of match you want:

- To search for an exact match, click <u>E</u>xact Match.
- To match a simple pattern, click the @ <u>A</u>nd .. option.
- To match a more complex pattern, click Advanced <u>P</u>attern Match.

▶ ▶ N O T E

Recall that the .. wildcard matches a series of characters and the @ wildcard matches any single character. Table 6.5 summarizes the Advanced <u>P</u>attern Match options.

6. In the <u>V</u>alue text box, type the text you want to locate. If you checked the <u>C</u>ase-sensitive box in step 4 and selected the <u>E</u>xact Match option in step 5, be sure to type the *exact* value you want to locate (including the correct uppercase and lowercase letters and any punctuation or spaces). If you left the <u>C</u>ase-sensitive option unchecked and chose either the "@ <u>A</u>nd .." option or Advanced <u>P</u>attern Match, you can broaden your search with the wildcard characters, as described earlier.

7. In the Replace <u>W</u>ith text box, type the new text that you want to replace the old text.

8. Choose OK.

▶ ▶ T I P

Before starting the search, move the dialog box out of the way so that you can see the text highlighted as it is found.

Paradox will start its search from the beginning of the table. If Paradox finds a record that contains the text you entered in step 6, you'll see this dialog box:

Here's what to do next:

1. Choose one of the options below:

- Choose Change <u>T</u>his Occurrence to replace the text in the current record and search for the next record.
- Choose <u>S</u>kip This Occurrence if you don't want to replace text in the current record, but want to continue searching through additional records.
- Choose Change <u>A</u>ll Occurrences if you want to replace the text in the current record and in any other records where a match occurs.

2. Choose OK to carry out the deed; or choose Cancel or press Esc to leave the current record unchanged and abandon the search for more matches.

Repeat the preceding two steps if necessary, until Paradox has finished the job of replacing the values in the selected field.

▶ *Moving to a Particular Field*

Once the cursor is in the record that contains the data you want to view or edit, you can move to a particular field using any of the following techniques:

- Move the mouse pointer to the field you want to edit and click the mouse button.

- Press Tab to move to the next field or Shift+Tab to move to the previous field.

- Use the ↑, ↓, →, and ← keys to move from field to field.

- Press Home to move to the first field; press End to move to the last field.

- If the table has more fields than will fit into the current Table window (in Table View), or the fields are wider than will fit into the Form window (in Form View), you can use the scroll bars at the bottom edge of the window or press Ctrl+PgDn and Ctrl+PgUp to move a screen at a time. In Table View, pressing Ctrl+PgDn moves right through the fields a screen at a time, while pressing Ctrl+PgUp moves left through the fields. In Form View, pressing Ctrl+PgUp scrolls the screen to the right, and pressing Ctrl+PgDn scrolls the screen to the left.

- Choose <u>R</u>ecord ➤ Lo<u>c</u>ate ➤ <u>F</u>ield, highlight the name of the field you want to move to, then choose OK. (This option is available in Table View only.)

This last method is particularly handy for moving to a specific field when each record contains lots of fields.

▶▶ *Entering and Editing Special Field Types*

You'll need to use some special techniques to enter data in formatted memo, graphic, memo, and OLE fields. Since our sample CustList table doesn't contain any such fields, we'll refer to a different table, named *Employee*, for our examples. This table contains data about employees (what else?). Its structure is shown in Figure 6.8.

▶ ▶ **N O T E**

Table 4.1 in Chapter 4 shows sample data that you can enter in a variety of field types besides those described next.

FIGURE 6.8 ▶

The Employee table structure includes formatted memo, graphic, and OLE fields.

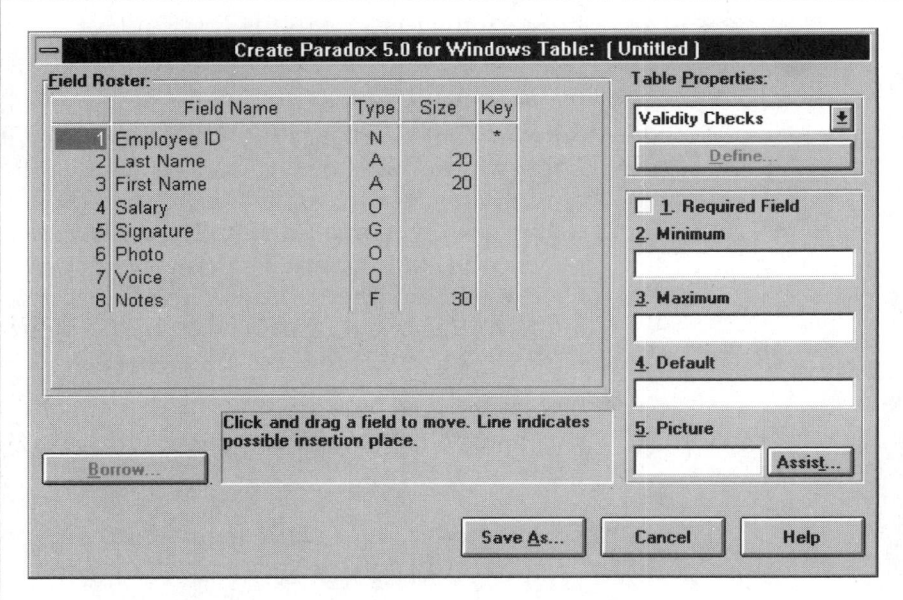

▶ Entering and Editing Memo Field Text

Memo and formatted memo fields can contain any amount of text. In Table View and Form View, only a portion of the text appears on the screen. To add text to, view, or change the contents of a memo field, follow these steps:

1. Move the cursor to the formatted memo or memo field you want to change.

2. Make sure you're in Edit mode if you want to add text to the memo field or change its contents (press F9 or click the Edit Data button).

3. Switch to Field View. To do so, you can press F2 or Shift+F2, or click the Field View button, or double-click the memo field (Table View only), or click in the field to remove the highlighting (Form View only).

In Table View, a new *Memo View* window displays the current contents of the field, as in Figure 6.9. In addition, the status bar displays the message "In Memo View, press Shift+F2 to leave memo view," and the mouse pointer changes to an I-Beam. No separate window appears in Form View.

FIGURE 6.9

Window for entering and editing text in a memo field

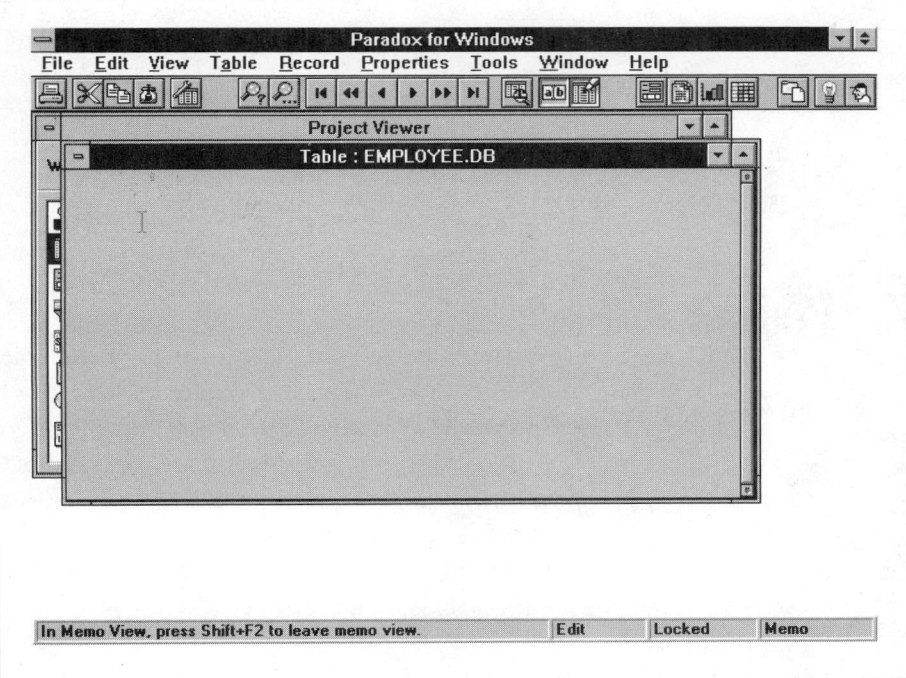

Regardless of whether you're using Table View or Form View, you can type and edit text using the basic techniques supported by all Windows applications. These are summarized below.

- Press ↵ *only* to end short lines of text and entire paragraphs, or when you want to insert a blank line.

- Use Backspace and Delete to make changes and corrections as you type.

- Select text by dragging the mouse pointer through that text, or by holding down the Shift key while pressing the various cursor-positioning keys (Home, End, PgUp, PgDn, ←, → and so forth).

- Delete selected text by pressing Delete or Backspace.

- Replace selected text by simply typing the new text.

- To move selected text, choose <u>E</u>dit ➤ Cu<u>t</u> (or press Shift+Del or click the Cut To Clipboard button in the Toolbar). Then move the insertion point to the new location for the text and choose <u>E</u>dit ➤ <u>P</u>aste (or press Shift+Ins or click the Paste From Clipboard button).

- To copy selected text, choose <u>E</u>dit ➤ <u>C</u>opy (or press Ctrl+Ins or click the Copy To Clipboard button). Then move the insertion point to the destination for the copied text, and choose <u>E</u>dit ➤ Paste (or press Shift+Ins or click the <u>P</u>aste From Clipboard button).

When you're finished typing or editing your text, you can save your work and return to Table or Form View using any of the techniques described under "Saving Memo Field Text," below.

 ▶ ▶ **W A R N I N G**

Watch out! In Form View, moving the cursor to a memo field that already contains text instantly selects all the text in that memo. Therefore, anything you type while in Edit mode will *replace* all the selected text. To avoid this, make sure you are in Field View (step 3 above) *before* you start typing. If you've already deleted the chunk of text, choose <u>E</u>dit ➤ <u>U</u>ndo, or press Alt+Backspace or Escape immediately to cancel your changes.

> **TIP**
>
> In Table View, pressing Escape cancels your changes and leaves you in the Memo View window. Choosing Edit ➤ Undo or pressing Alt+Backspace cancels your changes and returns you to the Table window.

▶ Copying Text into a Memo Field

You can copy an external file into a memo field, as long as that external file is in text (.txt), rich text (.rtf), or Paradox text (.pxt) format. To do so, edit the memo field and position the insertion point where you want the text to appear (or select text in the memo field if you want to replace it with the external file). Now, choose Edit ➤ Paste From (or right-click the mouse and choose Paste From). Specify the directory location and complete name of the file you want to copy (for example, *c:\windows\wanda.txt*), then choose OK.

Depending on the word processor you use, you might also be able to copy text from a word processing document to the Windows Clipboard, then paste it into a memo field. However, Paradox can't read all formats from the Clipboard, so this might not work. The easiest way to find out whether or not it *will* work is to try it.

If Paradox can't read the text from the Clipboard, you'll just get an error message. In that case, you'll need to export the word processing document to rich text format or text format. Then use Edit ➤ Paste From while editing the memo field to bring in the exported file.

▶ Formatting Memo Text

If you're working in a formatted memo field, you can dress it up with fancy text formatting attributes such as fonts, alignment, and line spacing. Here are the steps for formatting text in a formatted memo field:

1. If you want to apply the formatting to all text beyond the insertion point (text you're about to type), just move the insertion point to where you want the change to take effect. If you want to apply the formatting to a portion of existing text, select that chunk of text.

2. Click the right mouse button to inspect the text properties. You'll see the property menu for a formatted memo field, as shown in Figure 6.10. The basic formatting options are summarized below.

- To change the alignment of the text, choose Alignment, then one of the following options: *Left* (aligns at the left edge of the window, leaving an uneven right margin), *Right* (aligns at the right edge of the window, leaving an uneven left margin), *Center* (centers the text between the left and right edges of the window), or *Justify* (text is even at both the left and right margins).

FIGURE 6.10

Text selected in a formatted memo field, with the property menu displayed

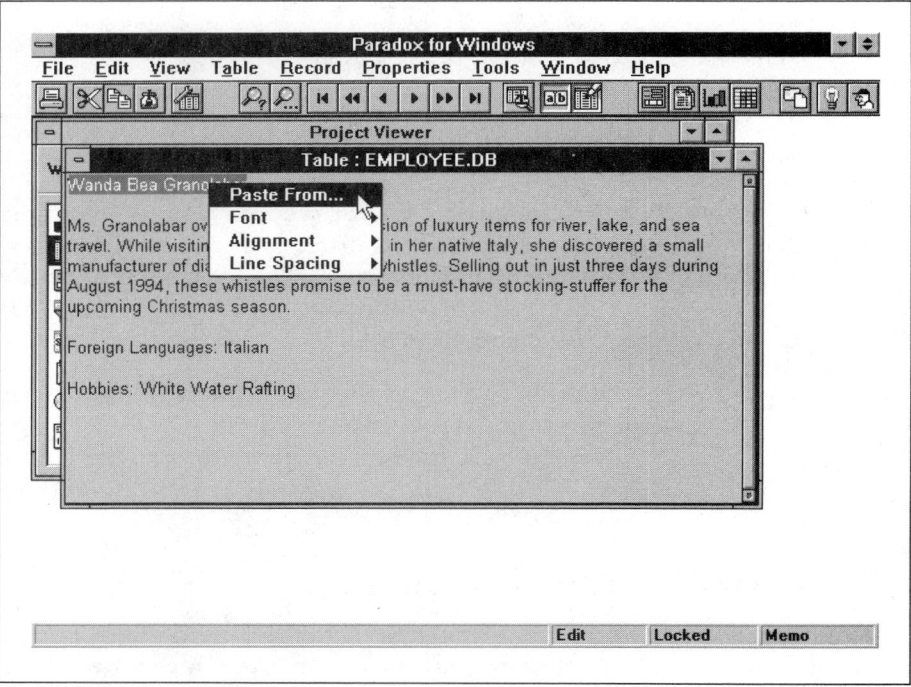

- To change the line spacing of the text, choose Line Spacing and any one of the spacing options that appears on the sub-menu. Your options are *1 line, 1.5 lines, 2 lines, 2.5 lines,* and *3 lines*.

- To change the typeface, size, style, or color of the text, choose Font and any of the font options, which are described in the next section.

TIP

To keep the property menu from covering text you want to see, move the mouse pointer to an out-of-the-way place within the memo field before you click the right mouse button.

Using Fonts and Styles

Choosing *Font* from the formatted memo property menu leads to the menu shown below.

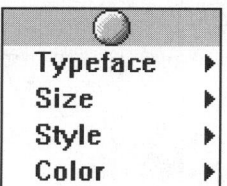

Choose the Typeface, Size, or Style option and then click on the attribute you want. If you want to assign the typeface, size, and style to the text all at once, click the little snap button at the top of the menu. You'll see a dialog box like the one below. (The list of fonts depends on the fonts installed on your system.)

Entering/Editing
Table Data

Ch.
6

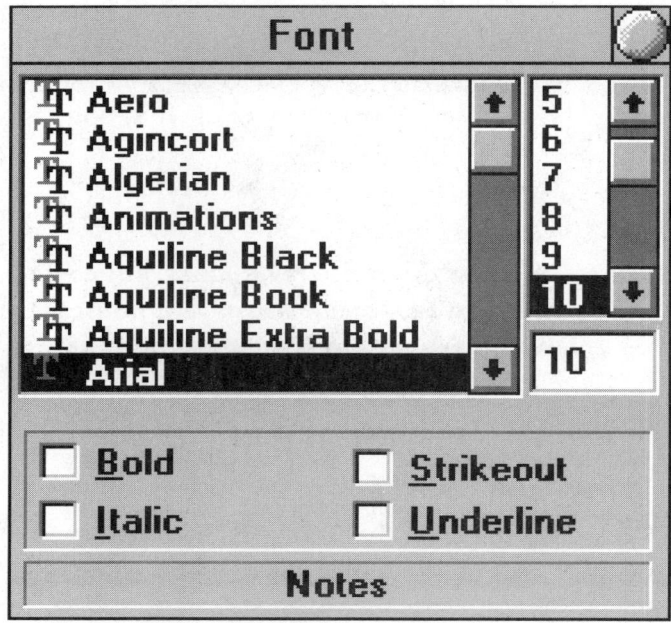

Choose whatever combination of attributes you want to apply to the text.

Changing the Color of Text

You can use the technique described above to change the color of text as well. Select the text you want to color or position the insertion point where you want the color to begin, then right-click. Choose Font ➤ Color, and you'll see a palette of colors, as shown below:

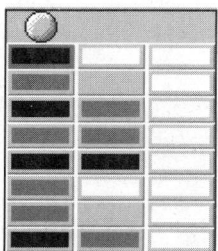

Click on the color you want, and the selected text will change to that color. (Selected text will appear in a different color until you deselect it by clicking the mouse button again.)

Floating Dialog Boxes

The snap button that appears at the top of certain Paradox menus or palettes (including Font and Color) is a handy tool indeed. Clicking the snap changes the menu or palette to a floating dialog box. You can move that dialog box if it's in the way simply by dragging the title bar.

You can click anywhere in your formatted memo to select text or reposition the insertion point without losing the floating dialog box. When you're ready to choose a new font or color, just make your selections from the floating dialog box.

To close the floating dialog box, click its snap button again.

▶ A Sample Formatted Memo Field

Figure 6.11 shows a sample formatted memo field. Following are the steps we used to type and format it.

1. First we typed the entire memo as shown in Figure 6.10. (To insert a blank line, we put the cursor where we wanted the blank line to appear and pressed ↵.)

2. To center the heading, we selected *Wanda Bea Granolabar* by dragging the mouse pointer through the text. Next we right-clicked and chose Alignment ➤ Center.

3. With the text still selected, we right-clicked and chose *Font*. Then we clicked the snap button and chose Arial as the typeface and 18 as the size.

4. We selected all remaining text below the centered title by dragging the mouse pointer through it.

5. Then we chose Times New Roman as the typeface and 12 as the size from the floating Font dialog box. We then clicked the snap button to close the floating dialog box.

6. To italicize *must-have stocking stuffer,* we dragged the mouse pointer through that text to select it. Then we right-clicked and chose Font ➤ Style ➤ Italic.

FIGURE 6.11 ▶

Sample formatted memo field with fonts, centered heading, bold-face, and italics

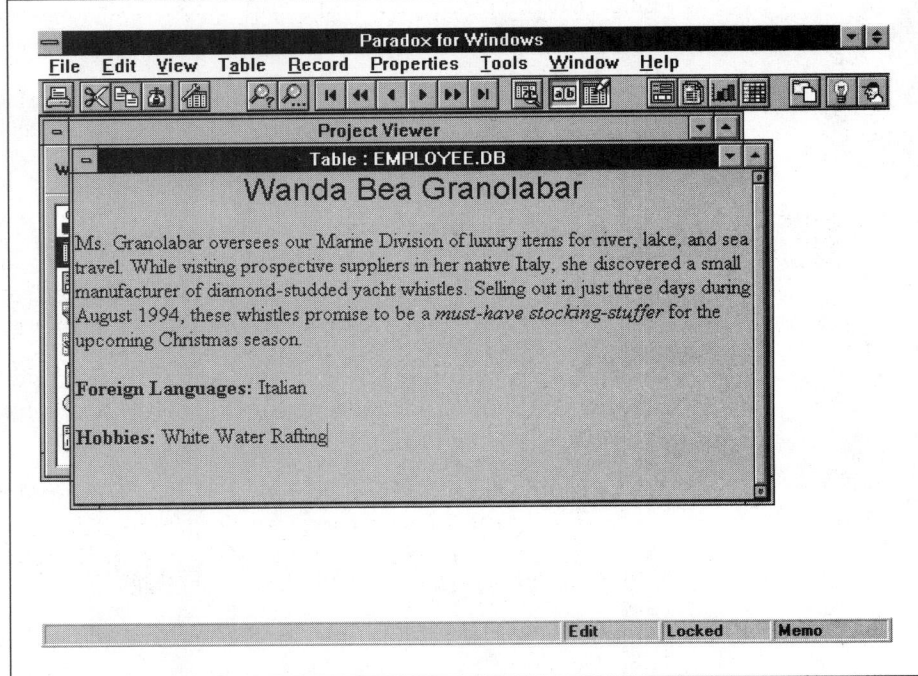

7. Finally, we boldfaced *Foreign Languages* and *Hobbies* following the same basic procedure used in the previous step to italicize *must-have stocking stuffer*. (This time we chose Font ➤ Style ➤ Bold).

It's all remarkably quick and easy once you get the hang of it. What's really great is that the whole business of property inspection is used throughout Paradox for Windows. As you'll see in upcoming chapters, custom *anything* is just a quick right-click away.

▶ Using TrueType Special Characters

A formatted memo field can contain any of the Windows TrueType special characters. To insert a special character, you can use the Windows Character Map:

1. Make sure the formatted memo field is open (in Field View) and you're in Edit mode.

2. Move the insertion point to where you want to place the special character.

3. Go to the Windows Character Map. (You can press Alt+Tab until Program Manager appears, then open the Accessories group and double-click the Character Map icon.)

> **N O T E**
>
> **If you're not already familiar with Character Map, see your Windows documentation for more information and other ways to insert special characters into a document.**

4. In Character Map, choose any TrueType font (identified with the TT symbol) from the Font drop-down list. Figure 6.12 shows an example in which Character Map appears with Wingdings as the selected font.

FIGURE 6.12

The Windows Character Map, displaying special characters in the TrueType Wingdings font

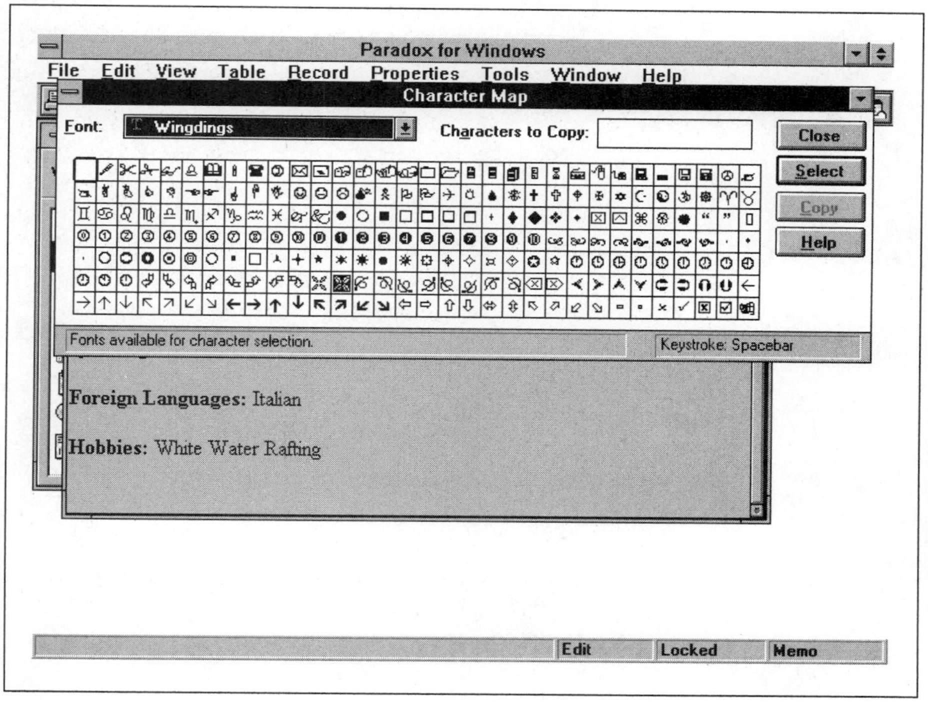

Entering/Editing Table Data

Ch. 6

5. To magnify a character, move the mouse pointer to the character and hold down the mouse button.

6. To choose a special character, click it, then click the Select button. A copy of the character will appear in the Characters to Copy text box.

7. Repeat steps 5 and 6 to select as many characters as you want.

8. Click the Copy button to copy the character(s) to the Clipboard.

9. Either minimize the Character Map window (if you think you'll need it again soon), or click its Close button to close it. You can also minimize Program Manager to get it out of the way if you want. Now you will be back in the memo field.

10. Choose Edit ➤ Paste, or press Shift+Ins, or click the Paste From Clipboard button in the Toolbar.

If the wrong character appears, or it isn't large enough, you can adjust its font. Select the character or characters by dragging the mouse pointer through them or holding down the Shift key while pressing ←. Then right-click, choose *Font*, and click the snap button. Choose the same font you chose in Character Map (for instance, Wingdings), then choose a size and click the snap button to close the Font dialog box. Press → or click elsewhere in the memo to deselect the character(s).

 ▶ ▶ **T I P**

You can also use Character Map to insert a special character into an alpha field. However, you can only use characters in the font used to display the rest of the column. That is, you can't change the font for just a single character or record in an alpha field.

▶ *Using Search And Replace in a Memo*

If you're editing a particularly large memo (or formatted memo) field, you can use *Search* or *Search And Replace* within that field to locate text throughout several records, and, if you wish, change it. The procedure is basically the same as using the Record ➤ Locate ➤ Value (Ctrl+Z) and Record ➤ Locate ➤ And Replace (Shift+Ctrl+Z) options discussed earlier.

With the memo field open, move the insertion point to where you want to begin the search (press Ctrl+Home if you want to start the search from the top of the memo). If you want to search and replace through a portion of the memo only, select that portion of text.

Next choose Edit ➤ Search Text. Type the text you want to search for in the Search For text box. If you want to match a pattern instead of exact text, select Advanced Pattern Match and use any of the wildcards listed in Table 6.5 in your Search For text. You can select or deselect the Case-sensitive option to determine whether you want the search to be case-sensitive. If you want to replace that text with some other text, type the replacement text into the Replace With text box. Then click the Search button to begin the search.

> **TIP**
>
> **If the Search And Replace dialog box is covering your text, simply drag the title bar to move it out of the way.**

When Paradox finds a match, you'll see the message "Match found" in the status bar, and the text you're searching for will be selected. If you entered a replacement value and want to replace the selected text, click the Replace button. You can continue clicking the Search and Replace buttons until Paradox displays the message "No match found." (Or, if you're sure you want to replace all remaining matches at once, click Replace All.) When you're finished using the Search And Replace dialog box, choose Cancel, or press Esc, or double-click the Control-menu box.

▶ Saving Memo Field Text

When you're finished entering or editing text, close the memo and save your work by pressing F2 or Shift+F2, or clicking the Field View button in the Toolbar, or choosing View ➤ Field View. In Table View, you can also close the memo field's window by double-clicking its Control-menu box, or pressing Ctrl+F4, or clicking the window's Control-menu box and choosing Close. In Form View, simply click on another field. (Whew! So many choices, so little time.)

▶▶ *Entering and Editing Data in a Graphic Field*

You can store a graphic image in either a graphic field or an OLE field. You use the graphic field type when you can't or don't want to maintain links to the application that was used to create the graphic image.

▶▶ **TIP**

Use a graphic field when you *don't* want to give all users access to the application used to create or edit a graphic image, or when you'll be distributing copies of the table to people.

You can store virtually any kind of graphic in a Paradox for Windows table. Figure 6.13 shows some examples. Table 6.6 lists the graphic file formats that you can place in a Paradox graphic field.

▶ **TABLE 6.6:** *Graphic File Formats Supported by Paradox, with Typical File Name Extensions*

FORMAT	FILE NAME EXTENSION
Windows Bitmap	.bmp
Encapsulated PostScript	.eps
CompuServe "GIF"	.gif
Paint	.pcx
Tagged Image File Format (TIFF)	.tif

FIGURE 6.13

Examples of graphic images

Clip art

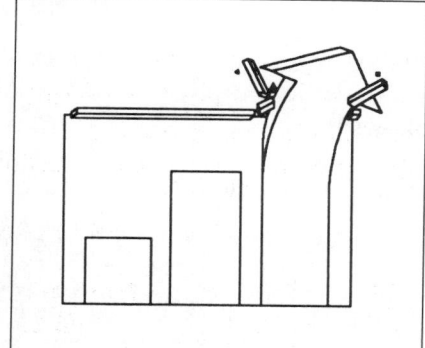

Scanned images

Business graphic

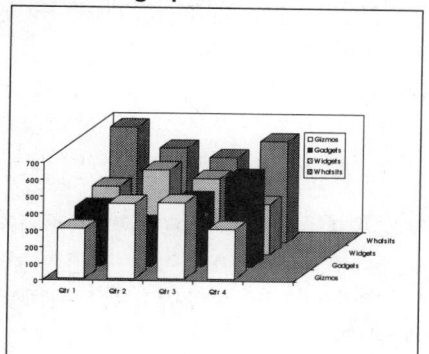

Free-form graphic

Photo/video frame

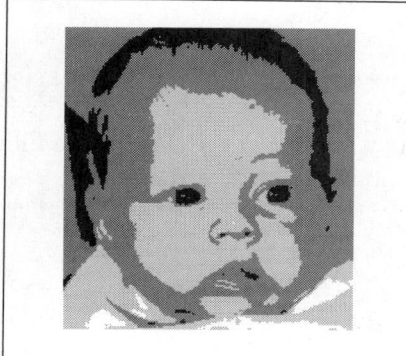

Screen Capture

▶ *Entering Pictures and Other Data by File Name*

You can also copy data from stored files to a *graphic field* or to other fields that allow it. To do so, simply provide the location and name of the graphic, as follows:

1. Move the cursor to the field and make sure you're in Edit mode.

2. If you wish, switch to Field View (press F2, or click the Field View button).

3. Choose Edit ➤ Paste From. You'll see the Paste From Graphic File dialog box like the one in Figure 6.14.

4. Click the name of the graphic you want to use, or use the Drive (or Alias) and Directories lists to locate the graphic, then click on the name of the file you want.

5. Choose OK.

▶ ▶ N O T E

The Edit ➤ Paste From command will only be available if the operation is allowed. For example, you can copy a date, time, or timestamp field from an external file if you're in Form View, but not if you're in Table View. The menu options are dimmed when the operation isn't allowed.

For example, suppose you've scanned several signatures and stored them in TIFF files with each person's name (*wanda.tif*, *keith.tif*, and so forth) on a directory named *c:\empsigs*. When filling in the dialog box for Wanda Granolabar's record, you'd specify *c:\empsigs\wanda.tif* as the name of the file.

FIGURE 6.14

*The Paste From
Graphic File dialog box*

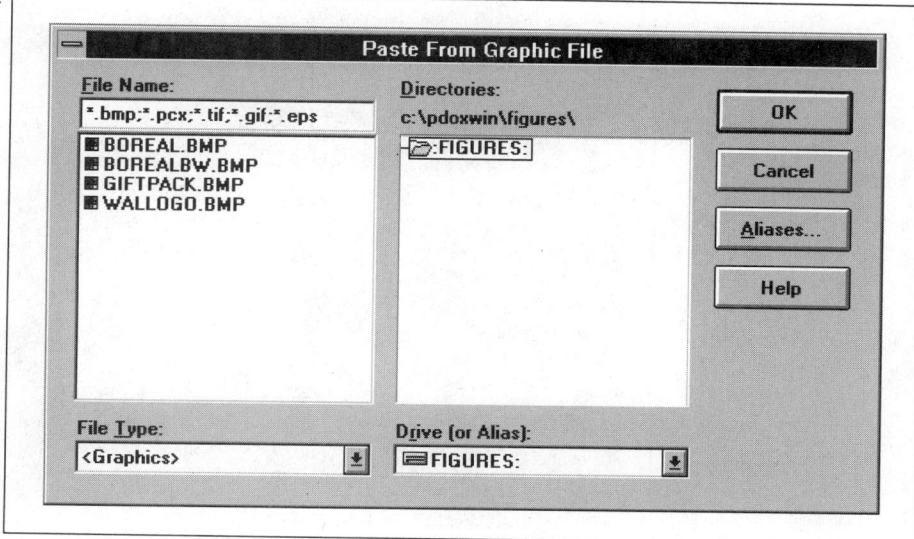

NOTE

**Special fields often display <BLOB...>, which stands for
Binary Large Object, followed by the type of object in
the field. We'll look at several ways to view the
contents of these fields here and in the next chapter.**

After choosing OK in step 5, you're returned to Table View or Form
View. In Table View, double-clicking the Signature field (or using any of
the other techniques to switch to Field View) displays the contents of
that field in a full window, as in Figure 6.15. Double-clicking the picture, pressing F2, or closing the current window will return you to the
table. (Remember that you cannot display a full-window picture in
Form View.)

▶ *Pasting a Picture into a Graphic Field*

You can also cut and paste a graphic image into a field, provided that
the graphic was created, or at least can be displayed in, some other

FIGURE 6.15

Scanned signature (faked, since Wanda is a figment of our imagination) in a graphic field

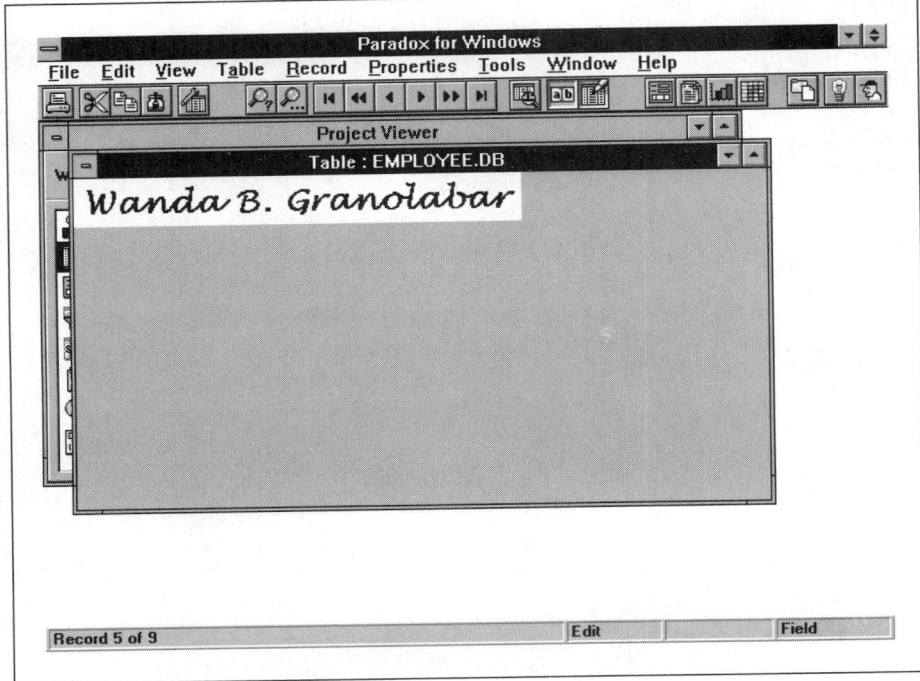

application, which we'll refer to as the *source application*. The source application must be able to display the graphic and copy it to the Windows Clipboard. That way, you can simply select the image that you want to store, copy (or cut) it to the Clipboard, then paste it into the graphic field. Here are the steps:

1. Run the source application, and bring the image that you want to store in your Paradox table to the screen.

2. Select the image, or a portion of the image, that you want to copy to your Paradox table.

For example, Figure 6.16 shows a photograph that we originally scanned into a bitmap (.bmp) file, which was sized to approximately 2.5 × 1.5 inches during the scanning process. To prepare for pasting the photo into the Paradox table, we ran the Windows 3.1 Paintbrush application, opened the bitmap image, then defined a cutout using the Pick tool.

FIGURE 6.16

A photo displayed in the Window Paintbrush accessory, selected before being copied to the Clipboard

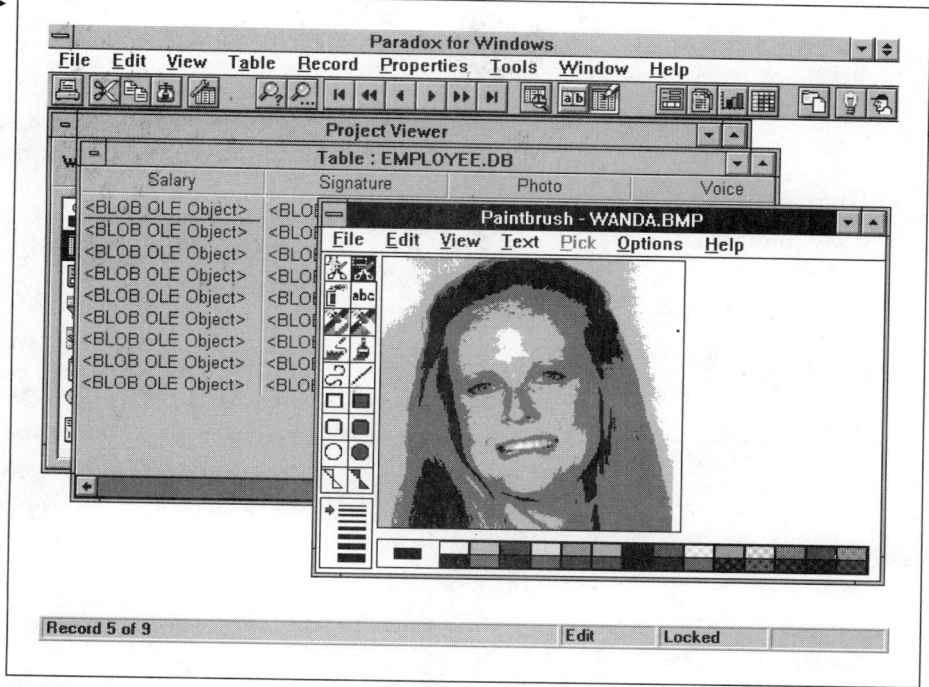

 ► ► **TIP**

Any time you're scanning pictures, signatures, or anything else for use in a table, it's best to crop, scale, and size the image while scanning. It's easier to manage scanned images if they're roughly equal in size before you put them into a Paradox table.

To copy the cutout portion of the Paintbrush picture into a Paradox table, continue with these steps:

3. Choose Edit ➤ Copy from the source application's menu to copy the picture to the Windows Clipboard.

4. Minimize or close the source application to get it out of the way.

5. Switch to your Paradox for Windows table.

6. Move the cursor to the graphic field in the record of the table where you want to copy the image.

7. Make sure you're in Edit mode.

8. Choose <u>E</u>dit ➤ <u>P</u>aste from the Paradox menus, or press Shift+Ins, or click the Paste From Clipboard button in the Toolbar.

Initially, you'll see only a small portion of the picture in your table. But if you move to the field and switch to Field View (or just double-click the field), the field will expand, as in Figure 6.17.

▶▶**N O T E**

Figure 6.17 assumes that the Photo field is the graphic field type, rather than the OLE field type. If Photo *is* the OLE field type, the photo would appear in the Paintbrush application rather than in the Paradox window—more on OLE in a moment.

FIGURE 6.17 ▶

We pasted the selected image from Paintbrush into the graphic Photo field of a slightly-revised Employee table. Double-clicking the field displays the photo in a window.

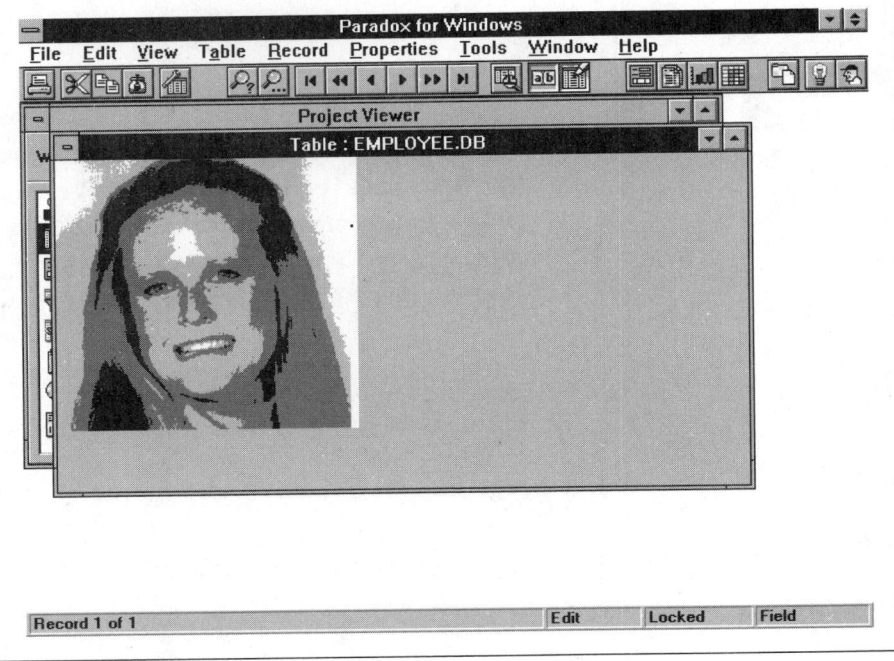

After viewing the picture, double-click, or press F2, or close the window to return to your table.

▶▶ *Copying Paradox Fields to Non-Paradox Files*

You can copy the contents of many types of fields—including binary, formatted memo, graphic, and memo fields—to a non-Paradox file. Later, you can open that file in another application and make whatever changes you wish, without affecting the original Paradox table.

 ▶ ▶ N O T E

> The **Edit** ➤ **C**opy To command will only be available if the operation is allowed. For example, you can copy a date, time, or timestamp field to an external file from Form View, but not from Table View. The menu options are dimmed when the operation isn't allowed.

To save the contents of a Paradox table field in a file, follow the steps below.

1. Move the cursor to the binary, formatted memo, graphic, or memo field you want.

2. If you're copying a binary or graphic field or you're using Form View, skip to step 4.

3. Switch to Field View (press F2) and select all the text of the formatted memo or memo field (for example, choose Edit ➤ Select All). Or, you can select a portion of text to copy by dragging the mouse pointer through it.

4. Choose Edit ➤ Copy To. You'll see a dialog box like the one in Figure 6.18.

FIGURE 6.18 ►

The Copy To Graphic File dialog box appears when you copy a graphic field. The Copy To File dialog box for copying memo fields is similar.

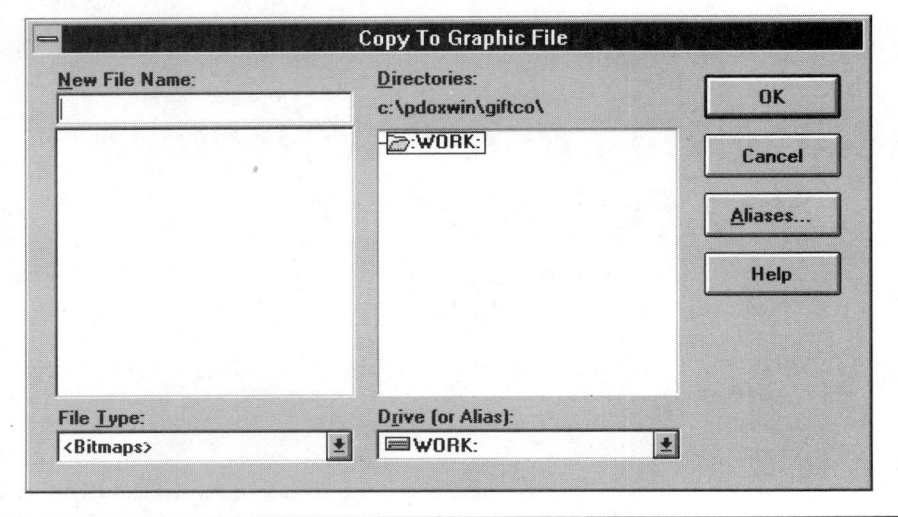

5. In the <u>N</u>ew File Name text box, type the full path and file name for the new file. You can also use the D<u>r</u>ive (or Alias) list box and <u>D</u>irectories list to switch to the directory where you want to save the file, and then type in the file name (see Chapters 3 and 15 for details). If you omit the file extension, Paradox will use the default extension for the type of data you're saving.

6. Choose OK to save the new file.

You can save memo or formatted memo fields to files with .pxt, .txt, or .rtf extensions. The extension you specify will determine the format of the text and the applications you can use to open and edit the file later, as listed below:

.pxt   Paradox text format. If you save memo field text in this format, you can later read that text into another memo field by choosing <u>E</u>dit ► Paste <u>F</u>rom.

.txt   Standard DOS text format (no formatting) that you can read into just about any DOS or Windows application, such as DOS Edit or Windows Notepad.

.rtf   Rich Text Format that includes some formatting,
          and can be read by Windows applications that
          support RTF, such as Windows Write and Word
          for Windows.

When you save a graphic field, Paradox automatically assigns a .bmp
(bitmap graphics) file name extension to the file. After saving the file,
you can open it in any application that accepts .bmp format files, such
as Windows Paintbrush.

▶▶ *Using OLE Fields and DDE Links*

As discussed in Chapter 4, Object Linking and Embedding (OLE) and
Dynamic Data Exchange (DDE) let Windows applications share objects. With OLE, the shared objects can be virtually anything: text from
a word processing application, spreadsheet data or charts, any graphic
image, or a sound (.wav file). With DDE, the shared objects can be text
or numbers only (typically from a spreadsheet or word processing application, or from Paradox alpha and numeric fields).

In both schemes, a Paradox table can act either as a client or as a server.
(Remember, the *client* application receives its data from the server; the
server application sends its data to the client.) You can copy an object
from any DDE or OLE server application *to* an alpha field or OLE field
in a Paradox table. When you copy to an alpha field, you create a DDE
link; when you copy to an OLE field, you're using OLE.

You can also copy an object *from* a field in a Paradox table *to* a DDE client application; and you can copy an entire Paradox table *to* an OLE2
client application such as a word processing document or spreadsheet.

If the object you're copying from is in a saved file, OLE can either *link*
or *embed* that object into the client application. (In DDE, the object always must come from a saved file, and linking is your only option.)

▶▶ N O T E

> **When you copy a Paradox table into an OLE2 client application, the table is always "live." Therefore, changes you make while in Paradox are reflected in the client application; similarly, table changes made in the client application will affect the original table in Paradox.**

With *embedded* objects (other than Paradox tables), the copy exists independently of the original object—changes to the copy don't affect the original object and vice versa. By contrast, a *linked* object is simply a pointer to the original object. Thus, changes to the copy affect the original object and vice versa.

Confused about when to use DDE and when to use OLE? Maybe these pointers will help. Use DDE to send fields from a Paradox table to another application, or to send data from another application to a Paradox table or query. You can also use DDE to link a Paradox table to a Paradox query result (see Chapter 16). OLE is used to embed files from an OLE server application into a Paradox table, or to embed an entire Paradox table into an OLE2 client document.

As you'll soon learn, there are many ways to link and embed data. This can be be perplexing and vexing at first glance, but after you've played with OLE, OLE2, and DDE for a while, you'll discover the method you like best and you'll enjoy the benefits of sharing objects among many different Windows applications.

▶▶ N O T E

> **OLE1 (or OLE) is the first generation of Object Linking and Embedding; OLE2 is the second generation of this handy object sharing tool. OLE2 support is new in Paradox 5 for Windows.**

▶ *Copying an Object to an OLE or Alpha Field*

The following steps show how to put information into an OLE field or an alpha field of a table. We'll assume that the table you want to put the data into is open on the Desktop. Later on, you'll see some practical examples of OLE and DDE in action.

1. If you haven't already done so, start the server application from the Windows Program Manager. If the application is already running, you can just switch to it using the Task List (Ctrl+Esc) or Alt+Tab.

2. In the server application, open or create the document that contains the data you want to store in your Paradox table.

3. If you intend to create a DDE or OLE link and haven't already saved your file, use File ➤ Save in the server application to give it a file name.

▶ ▶ **W A R N I N G**

DDE doesn't work properly with new or "untitled" data that has not been given a file name yet. Moreover, you cannot link an object into an OLE field unless the object is already saved in a file.

4. If appropriate in the server application, select the object (or a portion of the object) that you want to copy to your Paradox table, using proper selection techniques for that application.

5. Choose Edit ➤ Copy from the server application's menu to copy the object to the Windows Clipboard.

6. Switch back to Paradox for Windows.

7. Move the cursor to the OLE field (to embed or link an OLE object) or alpha field (to link the DDE object) in the Paradox table where the copied object should appear.

8. Make sure you're in Edit mode (press F9 or click Edit Data in the Toolbar).

9. Do one of the following:

- To *embed* the object into the field (OLE only), choose Edit ➤ Paste, or press Shift+Ins, or click the Paste From Clipboard button in the Toolbar.
- To *link* the object into the field (OLE or DDE), choose Edit ➤ Paste Link.

▶ ▶ **N O T E**

> **If you choose Edit ➤ Paste in an alpha field, the data will simply be copied from the Clipboard, as described earlier under "Data Entry Shortcuts."**

You now have the original object in your server application, plus either an embedded copy of that document or a link to that document in your client application.

Remember: If you *embedded* the object in your Paradox table (Edit ➤ Paste in step 9), that object will behave independently of the original object you pasted from the server application. You can change the copy in your Paradox table without affecting the original copy of the object. Likewise, if you change the original copy of the object outside of Paradox, that change will *not* be reflected in your Paradox table.

On the other hand, if you *linked* the object (Edit ➤ Paste Link in step 9), any changes you make to the copy in your Paradox table *will* be reflected in the original copy. Likewise, any changes you make to the original object outside of Paradox will be reflected when you edit the object from your Paradox table.

▶ ▶ **N O T E**

> **Paradox Help offers useful tips for linking and embedding objects under the topics *DDE* and *OLE*. You also can consult the manuals and online Help for the client application for more details; try searching for the online Help topics *DDE*, *OLE*, or *link*.**

▶ *Inserting an Object*

Here's another way to create an OLE object and insert it into your Paradox table in just a few quick steps, using the Edit ➤ Insert Object commands. This may be the easiest way to do the job.

Begin in Edit mode as usual, and move to the OLE field you want to put the object in. Now follow the steps below:

1. Choose Edit ➤ Insert Object to open a dialog box like the one shown in Figure 6.19. (In Form View, you can inspect the field and choose Insert Object from the menu that appears.)

2. Do one of the following:

- If you want to create a new object from scratch, choose Create New. Then scroll to and highlight the type of object you want to create. For example, you can highlight *Paintbrush Picture*.

- If you want to create the object from an existing file, choose Create From File, then specify the complete path name to the file in the File text box; or use the Browse button to locate the file. If you want to link the object (rather than embed it), check the Link check box.

3. Choose OK.

If you chose Create New in step 2, the server application will launch and you can create or modify the object as needed. When you're finished, choose File ➤ Exit & Return.... If you're asked whether you want to update, choose Yes. You'll be returned to Paradox.

▶ *Storing a Package in a Field*

Instead of storing a complete picture or other object in a field, you can store an icon or *package* that represents the object. A package can contain just about anything: a picture, a sound, a spreadsheet, a word processing document—even an entire application.

To store a package in a Paradox table, move the cursor to your OLE field and choose Edit ➤ Insert Object (or right-click the field in Form View and choose Insert Object). Select Create New, highlight the *Package* entry in the Object Type list, and choose OK. Now create or import

FIGURE 6.19 ►

The Insert Object dialog box lets you create new objects or insert existing objects, and then embed or link them in your table.

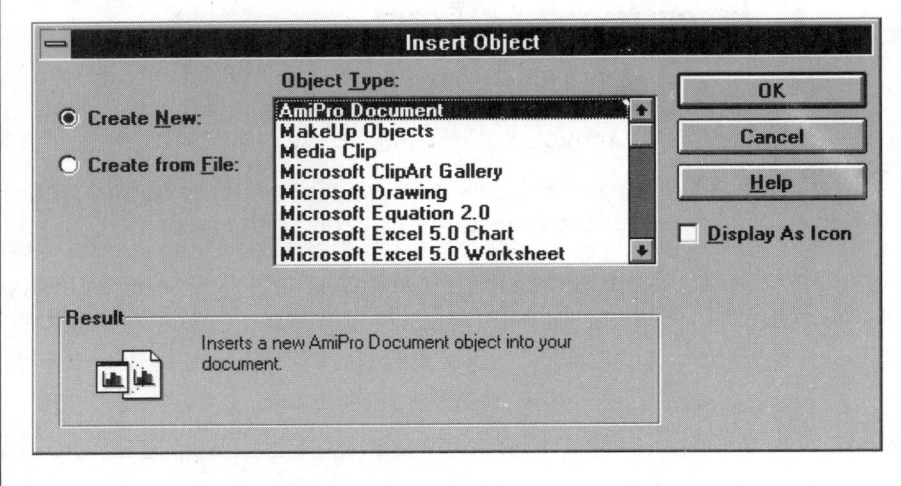

the package using the Windows 3.1 Object Packager (see your Windows documentation if you need help with that). Once you've created the package, choose File ➤ Exit ➤ Yes in Object Packager to copy the package to the OLE field and return to Paradox.

► *Putting a Paradox Table into an OLE2 Document*

You can put an entire Paradox for Windows table into a word processor or spreadsheet application that can act as an OLE2 client. An easy way is to use the Insert Object technique listed below:

1. Open Paradox for Windows.

2. Switch to the OLE2 client and position the insertion point where the table should appear.

3. From client application menus, choose Insert ➤ Object (or whatever sequence of menu commands provides similar capabilities).

4. In the Object Type list that appears, select *Paradox Table*, then choose OK.

5. You'll be taken to Paradox's Open Table dialog box. Select the file name of the Paradox table you want to insert, and choose OK.

6. A table editing window will appear. If you wish, you can change the data and adjust the table's appearance and window size (as discussed in Chapter 7); this appearance will be used in the client document.

7. When you're ready to return to the OLE2 client, close the Table view window (for example, press Ctrl+F4).

You'll be returned to the OLE2 client application, with your table looking just great!

Want more? Here's another way to put a Paradox table into an OLE2 client document:

1. Start the OLE2 client application and Paradox. Then switch to Paradox and open your Paradox table.

2. Choose Edit ➤ Select All. Then choose Edit ➤ Copy (or press Ctrl+Ins or click the Copy To Clipboard button in the Toolbar).

3. Switch to the OLE2 client application (for example, Microsoft Word 6 for Windows) and put the insertion point where you want the table to appear.

4. In the client application, choose one of the following to put the table into your document. The appropriate commands to use will depend on the application:

- Choose Edit ➤ Paste or Edit ➤ Paste Link.
- Choose Edit ➤ Paste Special ➤ Paste or Edit ➤ Paste Special ➤ Paste Link. Then highlight *Paradox For Windows 5 Table Object*, and choose OK.

When you return to the client application, you'll see the Paradox table in the document.

▶ *Viewing an Embedded or Linked Object*

Once you've put an OLE or DDE object in a Paradox table, you can work with it in Field View. Field View is handy if you want to edit the text reference (for example, the path name or cell reference) in a DDE link or you want to get a full-window look at a linked or embedded OLE object. Keep in mind that switching to Field View *does not* launch the server application or open the object.

1. If you plan to make changes, make sure your table or form is in Edit mode (press F9 or click the Edit Data button in the Toolbar).

2. Move the cursor to the field you want to work with.

3. Do one of the following:

- If you want to alter the path name or other reference information for an alpha DDE object, press F2, or click the Field View button in the Toolbar, or choose View ➤ Field View. As a shortcut, you can double-click an alpha DDE field to open Field View.

- If you're in Table View and want a full-window look at an OLE object, switch to Field View (for example, press F2).

4. When you're done using Field View, press F2, or click the Field View button, or choose View ➤ Field View again.

▶ Editing an Embedded or Linked Object

Although it's sometimes handy to work with an embedded or linked object in Field View, you'll often want to launch the server application and open the object for editing. Here are the steps to follow:

1. Make sure your table or form is in Edit mode (press F9 or click the Edit Data button in the Toolbar).

2. Move the cursor to the field you want to work with.

3. Do one of the following:

- In Table View, press Shift+F2 (this works for DDE or OLE fields).

- In Table View or Form View, double-click an *OLE field* (this doesn't work for DDE fields).

- In Table View, switch to Field View (F2). Then inspect (right-click) the object and choose an Open or Edit command from the pop-up menu.

- In Form View, inspect (right-click) the object and choose an Open or Edit command from the pop-up menu.

NOTE

> The <u>E</u>dit menu provides still more options for editing a linked OLE object or changing its links. To use these features, start from Edit mode and click the linked OLE field you want to update. If you want to edit the field, choose <u>E</u>dit ➤ Linked ... Ob<u>j</u>ect followed by <u>E</u>dit or <u>O</u>pen. If you want to change or break the link, or to control when Paradox updates the link, choose <u>E</u>dit ➤ Lin<u>k</u>s, click on the appropriate object name in the <u>L</u>inks list, and select options from the Links dialog box (for more details click the <u>H</u>elp button in this dialog box).

What happens next depends on whether you chose DDE or OLE, which type of OLE server you used to create the object (OLE1 or OLE2), and whether you linked or embedded the object. But as long as your computer has enough memory and your applications are working the way they're supposed to, you'll be able to use the source application to view and edit the object. There, you can use the normal techniques within that application to edit or print the object.

NOTE

> You don't need to worry too much about which version of OLE created your embedded or linked object. You'll quickly figure out what to do.

Here's what you'll see:

- For DDE, OLE1, and linked OLE2 objects, Windows will launch the application in its own window and will open the appropriate file.

- For embedded OLE2 objects, you'll do your editing "in-place" (that is, inside the OLE client). For example, if Paradox is the client, all the tools and menus you need will appear inside the Paradox Desktop and the area inside the OLE field will be the working area for the OLE application. Only the File and Window menus will be standard Paradox menus; the rest will belong to the OLE application. You can just click outside the embedded object to restore the server's normal menu bar and tools.

- For embedded OLE1 objects, the source application's title bar usually indicates the type of object you're editing, but doesn't show a file name. This reminds you that you aren't editing the original object.

- For linked OLE1 or OLE2 objects, the source application's title bar shows the file name of that object as a reminder that you are editing the original.

When you're done working with the object, exit the server application as follows:

- If you were taken to the server application window, choose File ➤ Exit (or whatever command is appropriate in that application); or double-click the server's Control-menu box. You'll be returned to the client application.

- If you are editing in-place, click outside the OLE field or object. The menus and tools will resume their normal appearance and behavior. (Be patient: the transformation back to normal may take a moment.)

 ▶ ▶ **N O T E**

The source application must be available in your computer if you want to access linked or embedded data. The original *document* must also remain available if you've linked it.

If you put a Paradox table into an OLE2 client, you can switch to the client and use any of these techniques to open the table for editing:

- Double-click the table. This usually will give you in-place editing.

- Choose Edit ➤ Paradox 5 Object or right-click the table in the document. Then, to edit the object in-place, choose the Edit option from the menu that appears; to launch Paradox in a new window, choose the Open option from the menu.

When you in-place edit a Paradox table in an OLE2 client document, you'll need to remember a few limitations:

- You can't inspect the table's properties.
- You can't enter memo view.
- You can't use certain menu commands.
- If you delete the Paradox table from disk, it will also disappear from the OLE2 client document.

▶ *Some OLE and DDE Examples*

Now that you know the basic techniques for working with DDE and OLE, let's look at some examples that illustrate the power of object sharing. Figure 6.20 shows several applications on the Windows desktop, including Paradox for Windows. In this example, we used Paradox as a DDE server and linked values in the Salary and Last Name fields of our employee table to cells in a Microsoft Excel worksheet. We then used OLE to link a Paintbrush photo into the Photo field of our employee table.

NOTE

The Emp-DDE table shown in Figures 6.17 and 6.20 is similar to the Employee table shown earlier in this chapter. The main difference is the Salary field, which we changed to a field type of Currency and then filled in with some outrageous and totally bogus salaries.

To display the applications in Figure 6.20, we used standard Windows and Paradox techniques to do the following:

- Opened Paradox for Windows and Microsoft Excel.
- Opened the Paradox Emp-DDE table and increased the height of the sample Paradox record by dragging the underline at the bottom of the left-most column downward a bit. (You'll learn more about controlling the appearance of data in Chapter 7.)

Entering/Editing
Table Data

▶ ▶

Ch.
6

FIGURE 6.20 ▶

*A Paradox employee ta-
ble (named Emp-DDE),
a Microsoft Excel work-
sheet, and a Paintbrush
document. The OLE
Photo field in Emp-
DDE stores data from
Paintbrush; the DDE
cells A1 and A3 in the
worksheet reflect data
in the current record of
the Paradox table's
Last Name and Salary
fields.*

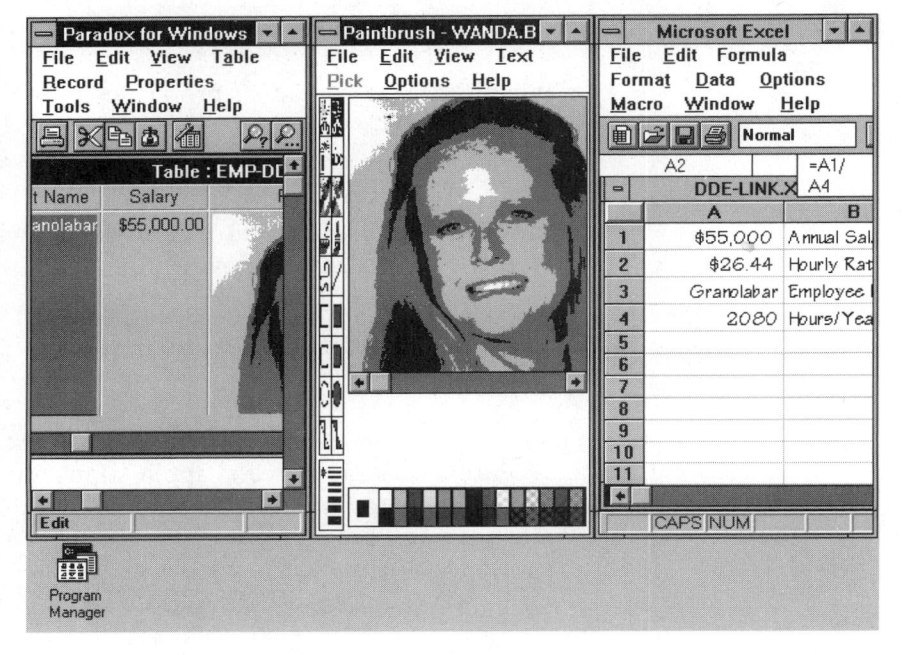

- In the Paradox table, we double-clicked the Photo field for Wanda Granolabar's record. This opened Paintbrush automatically and positioned the cursor in Ms. Granolabar's record.

- In Excel, we opened the worksheet named DDE-Link.XLS. Notice that values in cells A1 and A3 come from Wanda Granolabar's record in the Paradox table. Cell A4 just shows the number of work hours in a year. Cell A2 calculates the hourly rate (A1/A4) for the current employee record in the Paradox table.

- We minimized the Program Manager window, then opened the Windows Task List (Ctrl+Esc) and chose the Tile option. This placed the applications side by side.

Now, look at Figure 6.21 to see what happened when we moved the cursor to Jamey Burns' record in the Paradox table, double-clicked the Photo field, and then rearranged the screen a bit. Notice that the Excel worksheet was updated automatically to reflect the salary and name information for Ms. Burns, and the Paintbrush photo window now shows Ms. Burns' likeness.

▶ ▶ **T I P**

> If you don't want the data to change instantly as you
> scroll from record to record, you can choose **V**iew and
> deselect (uncheck) the **N**otify On option. When you
> want to resume the live updates, just choose **V**iew ➤
> **N**otify On again.

FIGURE 6.21 ▶

*After we moved to
another record in the
Paradox table, the Excel
worksheet instantly
reflected the new infor-
mation. We then double-
clicked the Photo field
for this record to see
Ms. Burns' likeness in
Paintbrush.*

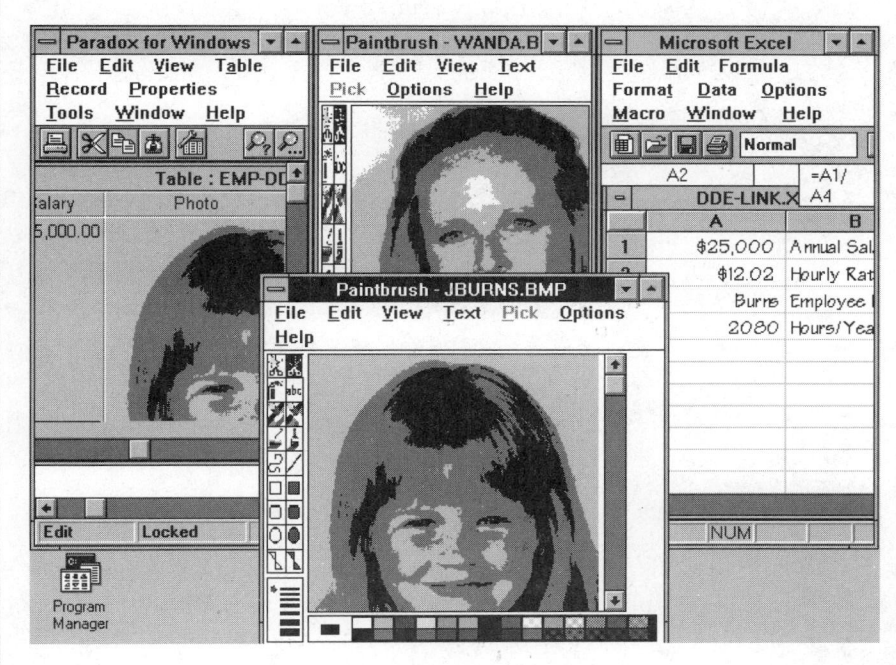

It's easy to link data from the Paintbrush application into the Emp-
DDE table, and to link data from Paradox into the Excel worksheet.
Here's how we began:

- In Paradox, we opened the Emp-DDE table, switched to Edit
  mode, and filled in the name and salary information for each
  employee.

The next step was to set up our Excel worksheet, as follows:

- In Excel, we opened a new worksheet, entered the *Annual Salary, Hourly Rate, Employee Name,* and *Hours/Year* text labels in column B, and the number of annual work hours (2080) in cell A4.

- Then we switched back to Paradox, selected the Salary field (any record will do), and chose Edit ➤ Copy. Next we switched back to Excel, put the cursor into cell A1, and chose Edit ➤ Paste Link.

- Switching back to Paradox again, we selected the Last Name field (again, any record will do), and chose Edit ➤ Copy. Switching back to Excel, we put the cursor into cell A3, and chose Edit ➤ Paste Link.

▶ ▶ **N O T E**

> In Excel, the formula for cell A1 looks like this: {=PDOXWIN|':WORK:EMP-DDE.DB'!Salary}. The formula for cell A3 looks like this: {=PDOXWIN|':WORK:EMP-DDE.DB'!'Last Name'}. This certainly is weird, but that's DDE for you. You never need to change these formulas (and probably shouldn't), but now at least you know what they're for.

- In Excel we entered the formula *=A1/A4* into cell A2 of the worksheet and saved our work.

Next stop, the Paintbrush photos. First we scanned all our employee photos and saved them as bitmap (.bmp) files. Then we followed the steps below:

- In Paintbrush, we used File ➤ Open to open the photograph, which we'd previously scanned and saved as a bitmap file.

- Then we used the Pick tool in Paintbrush to define a cutout of the photograph, and chose Edit ➤ Copy from the Paintbrush menu bar.

- Finally, we clicked the appropriate Photo field in the Paradox table, and chose Edit ➤ Paste Link from the Paradox menu.

We repeated the three steps above for each employee in the table. (As an alternative, we could have linked our photos by using the Edit ➤ Insert Object ➤ Create From File options described earlier.)

In Figure 6.22, you see a different twist. Here we used OLE2 to embed an entire Paradox table into a Microsoft Word 6 for Windows document. First we opened Paradox and a Word document (which is our OLE2 client). Then, we opened our Paradox table, chose Edit ➤ Select All, and then chose Edit ➤ Copy. Switching back to Word, we positioned the cursor where we wanted the table to appear, and chose Edit ➤ Paste.

▶ ▶ **N O T E**

Please see the documentation for your OLE2 client for specific information about linking and embedding objects.

FIGURE 6.22 ▶

A Paradox table embedded in a Microsoft Word 6 for Windows document via OLE 2

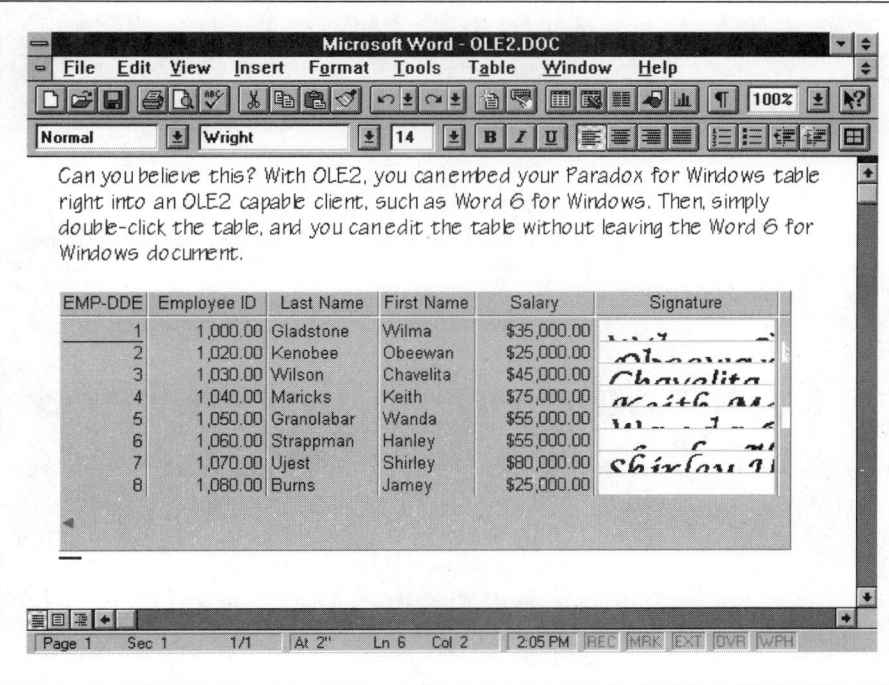

Figure 6.23 shows what happened after we double-clicked the Paradox table within the Word document. Notice how the Paradox menu bar and Toolbar replaced the one for Word. From here we can scroll through and edit our table just as though we were in Paradox (with the limitations mentioned previously). To restore Word's tools, we can just click outside the Paradox table.

FIGURE 6.23 ▶

To edit an embedded OLE2 object in the server application while you're in the client, just double-click the object. The server's menu bar and tools will appear in place of the client's menu bar and tools. You can return to the client's normal menu bar and tools by clicking outside the linked object.

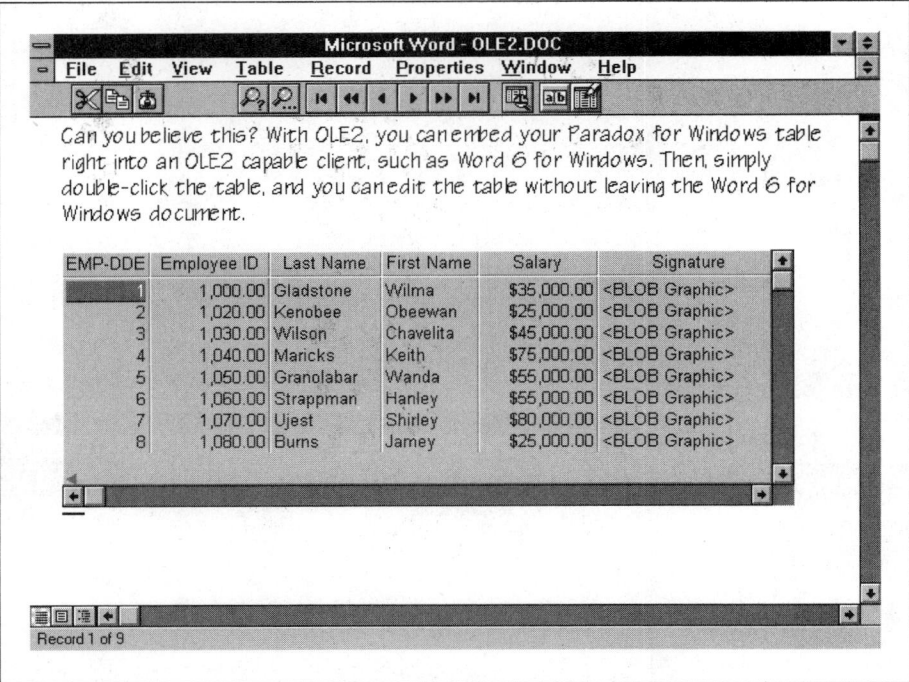

▶▶ *Using Lookup Tables to Enter Data*

A lookup table is yet another way to speed and verify data entry and editing. The lookup table can contain any number of valid entries for a field. For instance, you could define a lookup table of all the valid two-letter state abbreviations in the United States, or all the valid product codes in your inventory. Once you've created a lookup table, you can use it in three ways:

- To verify entries as they're entered into a table.

- To look up a valid entry for a field.

- To copy data from the lookup table into the corresponding fields of the table you're editing.

Notice that there are two tables involved. The *lookup table* contains a list of valid entries. The other table, which we'll call the *data-entry table*, is the one in which you're actually entering data. For instance, if you're entering data into the CustList table and you want to prevent anyone from entering invalid two-letter state abbreviations, CustList is the data-entry table and the table of state abbreviations is the lookup table.

▶ *Defining a Lookup Table*

When creating a lookup table, you need to remember the following rules and guidelines:

- The field you want to use to verify entries against must be the first field in the lookup table.

- Preferably, this first field should be the primary key for the lookup table.

- Any fields that you want to copy from the lookup table into the data-entry table must have the same field name, field type, and size in both tables.

We'll look at some examples in a moment.

▶ *Defining the Relationship between Tables*

After you've created your lookup table, you'll need to restructure the data-entry table and define the relationship between the data-entry table and the lookup table. During that process, you'll be given a choice of Lookup Types:

Just Current Field   Data from one field in the lookup table will be copied only into the field being edited in the data-entry table.

All Corresponding Fields   Data from multiple fields in the lookup table will be copied into multiple corresponding fields of the data-entry table. (Corresponding fields are those that have the same name and field type in the two tables).

You can also choose either of two types of Lookup Access:

Fill No Help The lookup table verifies entries, but the person entering data in the data-entry table can't view the lookup table.

Help And Fill The lookup table verifies entries, *and* the person entering data can pop open the lookup table to look up a valid entry.

Table 6.7 summarizes how different pairs of selections affect the relationship between the data-entry table and the lookup table.

▶ **TABLE 6.7**: *Lookup Table Data-Entry and Editing Validation Options*

LOOKUP TYPE AND ACCESS	VALIDATE ENTRY?	VIEW LOOKUP TABLE?	COPY CURRENT FIELD?	COPY ALL MATCHING FIELDS?
Just Current Field Fill No Help	Yes	No	No	No
Just Current Field Help And Fill	Yes	Yes	Yes	No
All Corresponding Fields Fill No Help	Yes	No	No	Yes
All Corresponding Fields Help and Fill	Yes	Yes	Yes	Yes

▶ A Simple Lookup Table Example

Creating and using a lookup table is much easier to do than it is to explain. So let's skip the generalities and take a look at a useful example—creating a table of valid two-letter state abbreviations as a lookup table for entering data into our sample CustList table.

▶▶**W A R N I N G**

You *wouldn't* want to use a lookup table of state abbreviations if your CustList table included addresses outside the United States, since any non-U.S. state or abbreviation would be rejected as an invalid entry.

Creating the States Table

Your first step is to create a table, which we'll name *States,* on the same directory as your CustList table. A lookup table is just like any other table, so you use the standard techniques to create it.

> **NOTE**
>
> **You can use *any* table as a lookup table. For instance, if you already have a table named *Products* that includes information about all your products, you can use *that* table as a lookup table for entering orders. More examples are presented in Chapter 17.**

In this example, assuming your working directory is already the same as your CustList table, choose File ➤ New ➤ Table, then choose OK to accept Paradox for Windows as the table type. This table needs only two fields, named *State* and *State Name,* as shown below.

	FIELD NAME	TYPE	SIZE	KEY
1	State	A	2	★
2	State Name	A	15	

Notice that the State field has the same name, field type, and size as the State field in the CustList table (this is required). That field is also keyed for quick access. The State Name field will contain the spelled-out state name to help the person using the table find the appropriate state name. No validity checks are required in this table.

After creating the table structure, choose Save As and give the table a name—*States* in this example.

Filling in the States Table

The next step is to fill in the States table with all the valid two-letter state abbreviations and corresponding state names. Thus, if the States table isn't already open, choose File ➤ Open ➤ Table, and choose *States.db.* Then switch to Edit mode (press F9 or click the Edit Table button) so you can enter some records.

As you fill in records, Paradox automatically alphabetizes them by the two-letter state abbreviations and rejects any duplicates, since the table is keyed on the State field. If you include Guam (GU), Puerto Rico (PR), and the Virgin Islands (VI), you'll end up with 54 records in the States table. Figure 6.24 shows the first 16 records in the table.

After filling in the States table, close it by double-clicking its Control-menu box or choosing <u>W</u>indow ➤ Close <u>A</u>ll.

FIGURE 6.24 ▶

The first 16 records in the States table

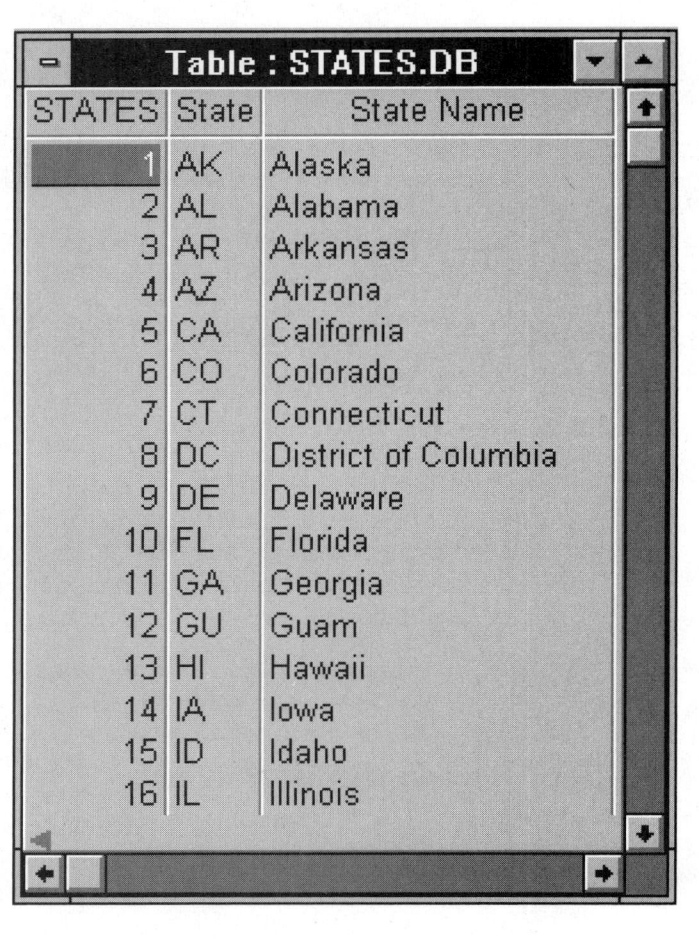

Activating the Lookup Table

The next step is to restructure CustList so that it knows to use the States table as a lookup table. To get started, open CustList and choose Table ➤ Restructure Table (or click the Restructure button in the Toolbar).

Next, click on the State field in the Restructure dialog box to move the cursor to it. Then click the drop-down list button under Table Properties and choose *Table Lookup* (*not* Table Language—a common mistake). Click on Define to get to the Table Lookup dialog box (Figure 6.25).

FIGURE 6.25 ▶

The Table Lookup dialog box filled in to use States.db as a lookup table for the State field in the CustList table. Notice that we've selected the Just Current Field and Help and Fill options.

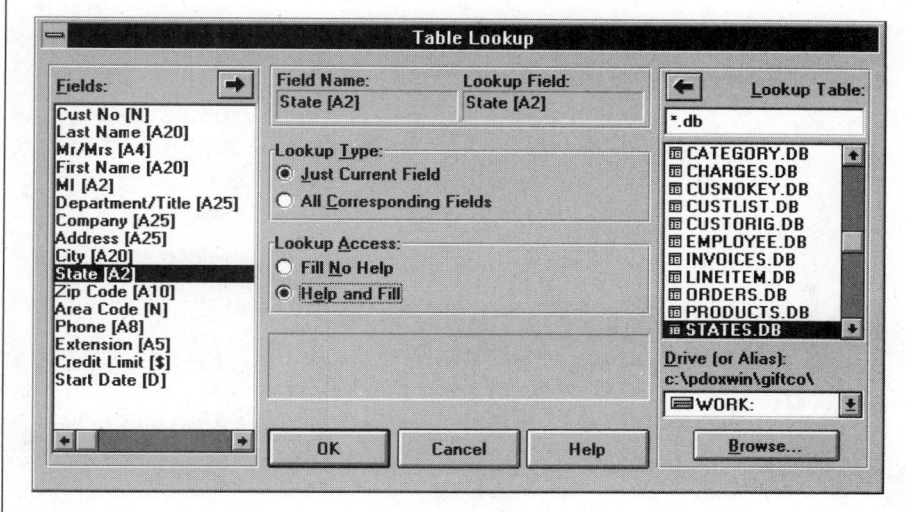

The left side of this dialog box lists the names, types, and sizes of the fields in the table you're restructuring—CustList in this example. For instance, *State (A2)* indicates that the State field is an alpha field with a length of two characters. Since this is the field you want to look up valid entries for, make sure it is the currently selected field. Click that field name, then click the → button next to Fields to make sure that the field name appears under *Field Name* near the top of the dialog box (or just double-click *State (A2)*).

The right side of the dialog box lists names of other tables in the same directory. In this example, you want to use States as the lookup table.

Click on *STATES.DB*, then click the ← button next to Lookup Table (or just double-click on *STATES.DB*). Paradox automatically places *State (A2)* under the Lookup Field option, since this is the first field in the States table.

Finally, under Lookup Type, choose Just Current Field, since we're verifying and copying only the State abbreviation from the lookup table to the CustList table. Under Lookup Access, choose Help And Fill so that the person entering data can look up state abbreviations as needed. Figure 6.25 shows the Table Lookup dialog box, with all the correct selections made.

After finishing with the dialog box, choose OK to return to the table structure. Then choose Save to save the new table structure.

Using the Lookup Table

Now, suppose you decide to add some new records to the CustList table or make some changes to it. Simply open that one table, CustList, and switch to Edit mode, in the usual manner. When the cursor is in the State field, the message below appears in the status bar:

Press Ctrl+Space for lookup help

Pressing Ctrl+spacebar pops open the lookup table, as in Figure 6.26.

FIGURE 6.26 ▶

The lookup table appears on the screen when you press Ctrl+spacebar with the cursor in the State field.

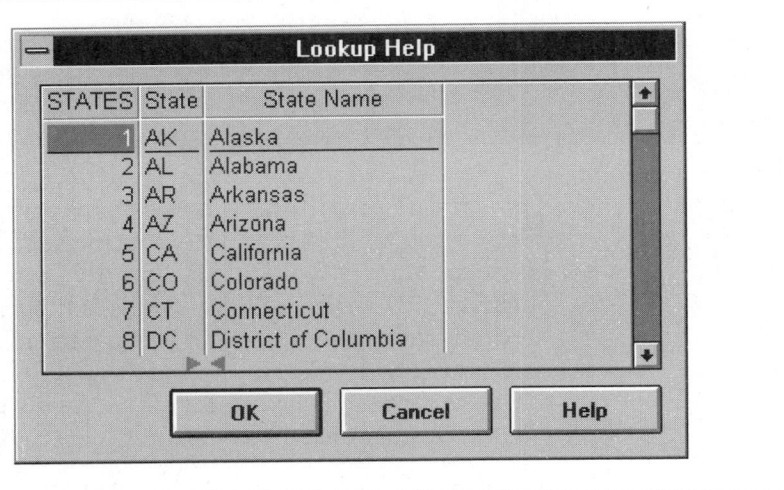

Now you can scroll through the table using the scroll bar at the right of the table or the ↑, ↓, PgUp, and PgDn arrow keys. When you find the two-letter state abbreviation you want, just click it and choose OK, or highlight the abbreviation you want and press ↵. The abbreviation is copied into the field, and the lookup table disappears.

TIP

You can also drag the lookup table by its title bar to move it, and use the Locate (Ctrl+Z) and Locate Next (Ctrl+A) shortcuts to look up a value in any field of the lookup table. You can choose Cancel or press Escape to close the lookup table without making a selection.

Pressing Ctrl+spacebar is entirely optional. If you want, you can still type in the two-letter state abbreviation when you get to the State field. However, if you type an invalid abbreviation (one that isn't in the State field of the States table) then try to move on to the next field, Paradox will reject your entry and display this error message in the status bar:

Unable to find lookup value.

As with any validity check, you won't be able to move the cursor out of the State field until you've entered a valid two-letter state abbreviation. You can press Ctrl+spacebar and choose a valid entry.

For added convenience during data entry, you can use referential integrity with table lookup. For example, we structured the Orders table to have a referential integrity relationship with CustList. We also assigned CustList as the lookup table for the Cust No field in Orders and chose the All Corresponding Fields and Help And Fill table lookup options. Combining referential integrity with table lookup not only ensures the proper relationships between CustList and Orders records, it also fills in Ship To data instantly whenever we enter a valid customer number in the Orders table. Unbelievably slick, and well worth the trouble!

►►**N O T E**

See Chapter 5 for information on multitable database design and referential integrity.

You'll see more examples of lookup tables in Part 5 of this book.

►► Using Move Help When Referential Integrity Is in Effect

When entering data into a child table field that is tied to a parent table through referential integrity, you can either type the appropriate value, or you can request "Move Help." The value you enter must be present in the parent table; otherwise, Paradox will reject the entry. Move Help would be handy when you're entering, into the Orders table, the customer number of the customer who placed the order.

To request Move Help, first switch to Edit mode, then put the cursor in the related field (the Cust No field in the Orders table, for example). Now choose <u>R</u>ecord ➤ <u>M</u>ove Help or press Ctrl+Shift+spacebar. Figure 6.27 shows the Move Help dialog box for the Cust No field of the Orders table.

►►**T I P**

Move Help and Lookup Help are quite similar. However, Move Help comes along for the ride whenever you set up referential integrity, and it can only fill in the value for the related field. By contrast, Lookup Help can fill in additional fields from the lookup table automatically, as long as the field names and types match.

FIGURE 6.27

This dialog box appears after pressing Ctrl+Shift+spacebar in the Cust No field in the Orders table.

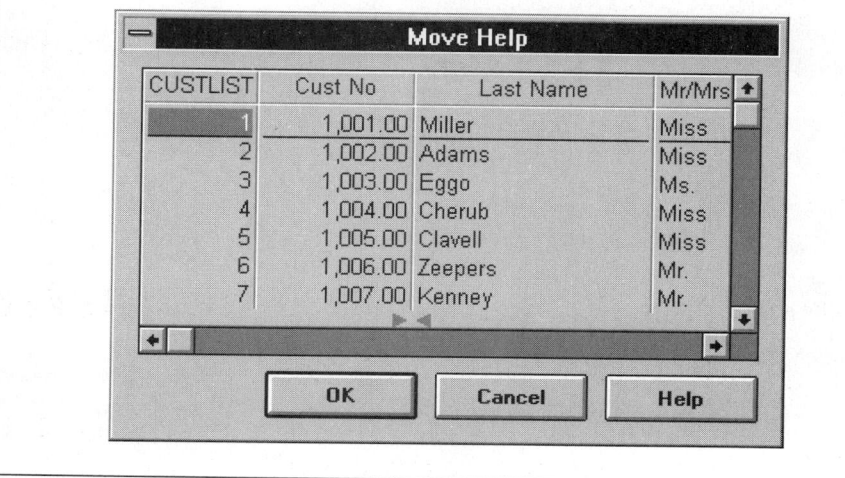

If you want to locate a specific record in the Move Help dialog box, press Ctrl+Z. You'll see the Locate Value dialog box. Select the field you want to search, choose a search method (if you wish), type the value you want to find, then choose OK. To find another occurrence of the same field value, press Ctrl+A. After locating the record you want, choose OK in the Move Help dialog box. Move Help will automatically fill in the value for the current field.

In this chapter you've learned about the many options and techniques for entering and editing data in a table. In the next chapter, we'll take a look at techniques for controlling the appearance of data on your screen, and discuss some techniques for printing data.

▶ ▶ CHAPTER 7

Viewing and Printing Table Data

▶▶ FAST TRACK

▶ **To change the properties of a Table View header area,
data area, or grid** **318**

inspect the area you want to change by right-clicking. Alternatively, you can click on the area you want to change, then right-click or press F6, or choose the Grid, Data, or Heading options from the Properties menu.

▶ **To inspect all the columns at once** **319**

press Ctrl+Shift+M.

▶ **To inspect all the column headings at once** **319**

press Ctrl+Shift+H.

▶ **To set up the printer before printing reports** **359**

choose File ➤ Printer Setup.

▶ **To print a Quick Report of the Table or Form window** **361**

choose File ➤ Print or click the Print button in the Toolbar in the Table or Form window. From Table View, you can preview the report if you like. To do so, click the Quick Report button in the Toolbar, or choose Tools ➤ Quick Report (or Tools ➤ Default Report), or press Shift+F7; then click the Print button in the Toolbar.

▶ ▶ **W**henever you open a table, Paradox initially displays that table in the default Table View, where field names appear across the top of the table in the same order that they're listed in the table structure. Each column is roughly the width you assigned when creating the table structure or the width of the field name, whichever is larger.

The default Table View *inherits* certain properties from settings in the Windows Control Panel. For example, the colors used in the table and the format of dates, numbers, and money (currency) values are all determined by settings in the Windows Control Panel. You can change any of those settings to get the appearance you want for the current Table View.

 ▶ ▶ **T I P**

You can change the default properties by creating a table named *Default* in your private directory (see Chapter 14).

But you're not stuck with the Table window's initial appearance. You can customize it in many ways, as you'll learn in this chapter.

▶ ▶ *Personalizing Table View*

Paradox gives you two quick and easy ways to customize Table View:

Direct manipulation   Click the left mouse button and drag "hot spots" to move and size objects.

Property inspection Right-click the object you want to change, and choose properties, such as fonts and colors, from menus or floating dialog boxes.

We'll look at the direct manipulation techniques first.

▶▶ *Changing Table View Directly*

You can use standard Windows techniques to size and move the entire Table View window. For example, drag the title bar to move the window or drag any border to size it; or use the Minimize and Maximize buttons, and Control-menu box to size and move the window that contains the Table View.

You can also change the table's appearance within the window by clicking and dragging various *hot zones,* shown in Figure 7.1.

▶ *Saving and Restoring Table View Settings*

Before customizing Table View, you'll probably want to know how to save and undo the settings. This way, you can experiment to your heart's content without becoming stuck with a view you don't like. Here are some quick ways to save, restore, and delete the current Table View settings:

- When you find a Table View that you like and you're sure you want to keep it, choose Properties ➤ View Properties ➤ Save to save those settings instantly. (You may also want to save current settings just before trying any options you're not comfortable with yet.)

- If you make a mess of things, choose Properties ➤ View Properties ➤ Restore. Any changes made since the last time you saved will be undone.

- To undo all changes and return to the default Table View, choose Properties ➤ View Properties ➤ Delete, then choose OK.

▶ *Changing the Order of Columns*

It's easy to change the order of columns in Table View. This might be handy if you grouped several fields, such as Last Name, First Name,

FIGURE 7.1 ►

*Hot zones for directly
manipulating Table
View with the left
mouse button*

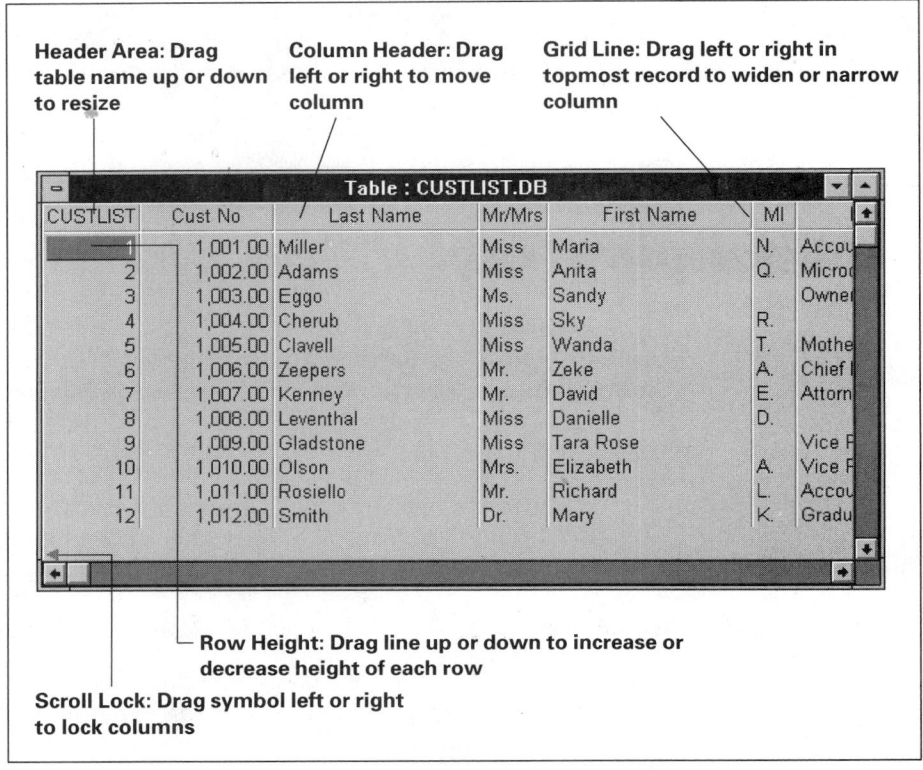

Zip Code, and Address, at the top of the table structure in order to define a primary key, but then wanted to *display* those columns in a more natural order, such as Address, City, State, then Zip Code.

You can use either of two methods to change the order of columns.

- Move the mouse pointer to the header of the column you want to move (that is, to the field name at the top of the column) until you see the icon shown at the left. Then hold down the left mouse button, drag the icon to the new location for the column, and release the mouse button.

- Alternatively, you can move the cursor to any column and press Ctrl+R to rotate that column to the last column position. Each time you press Ctrl+R, the current column becomes the last column in the Table window.

▶ *Changing Column Widths*

You can also widen or narrow any column in Table View. This is handy for displaying more or less text in alpha and memo fields and controlling how many columns appear across the screen. For instance, in Figure 7.2 we narrowed several columns in the CustList table so we could see more information on the screen.

You may notice that the Department/Title field is so narrow that some of the text is clipped off in the longer fields. Not to worry—all the data is still there. Narrowing a column in Table View only changes how much you can *see*. While editing a narrowed field, you'll still be able to scroll through the entire contents of the field.

To change the width of a column, follow the steps below.

1. Move the mouse pointer to the vertical grid line at the right side of the column you want to resize, in the topmost record in view (next to or just below the field name). The mouse pointer changes to a two-headed arrow when properly placed, as in the example shown at left.

2. Hold down the mouse button and drag the icon to the right to widen the column or to the left to narrow the column.

3. Release the mouse button when the column is the desired width.

FIGURE 7.2 ▶

Narrowing some columns in the CustList table lets you see more data on the screen

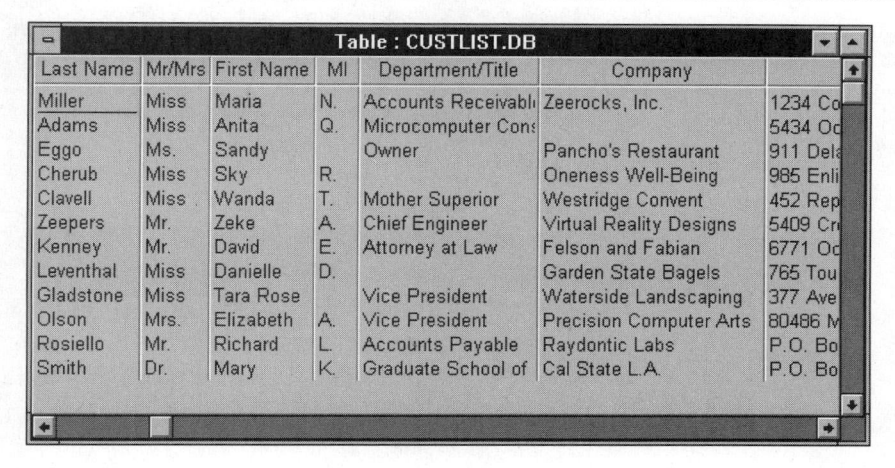

▶▶**N O T E**

If you make a money or numeric column too narrow to show all the data, Paradox will display a series of asterisks (***) rather than the number. To fix this, just widen the column again. Asterisks also appear when part of a numeric column is scrolled off the right edge of the window. Scrolling the rest of the column into view will remove those asterisks.

▶ *Changing the Row Height*

You can also change the height of each row (record) in a table. This is particularly handy if your table contains graphics or memos and you want to see more of their contents as you scroll through the table. Figure 7.3 shows the sample Employee table with each row made tall enough to display the graphic in the Photo field and much of the text in the formatted memo field. (We also changed some column widths.)

FIGURE 7.3 ▶

Changing the row height in Table View is particularly helpful if your table contains graphics and memos and you want to view more of these fields as you scroll through records.

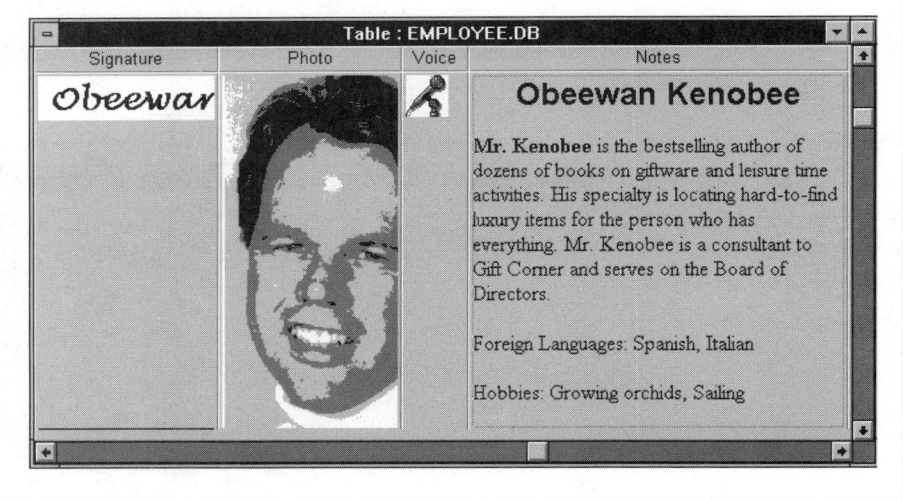

TIP

If only the <BLOB...> message appears in a graphic or OLE field, you can right-click the field and check the **Complete Display** property. However, be aware that scrolling through the records will be slower if you do so.

To change the height of each row in the table, proceed as follows:

1. Move the mouse pointer to the left-most column of the first record in the table. For example, if the table is currently scrolled all the way to the left, position the mouse pointer on the record number 1 field, just below the table name.

2. Now move the pointer down slightly, so that it touches the horizontal line under the first field of the left-most column. When you've positioned it correctly, the mouse pointer will change to the vertical two-headed arrow shown at left.

3. Hold down the mouse button and drag the arrow down to make the rows taller, or up to make the rows shorter. As you drag, a dotted line will appear across the window to show the height of the row.

4. Release the mouse button when the first row is the height you want. The first row and all the other rows will automatically adjust to this height.

▶ Preventing Fields from Scrolling

Normally, as you scroll to the right through a table, columns at the left edge will scroll out of view. For example, if you scroll to the Credit Limit field in the last column of the CustList table, the customer's name scrolls off the left edge of the window, as in Figure 7.4. If you can't see the customer's name as you edit the Credit Limit field, you risk changing the wrong customer's credit limit—a potentially unpleasant situation for your company and your customer.

FIGURE 7.4 ▶

The customer's name scrolls off the left edge of the window when you move the cursor to the right-most column of the CustList table.

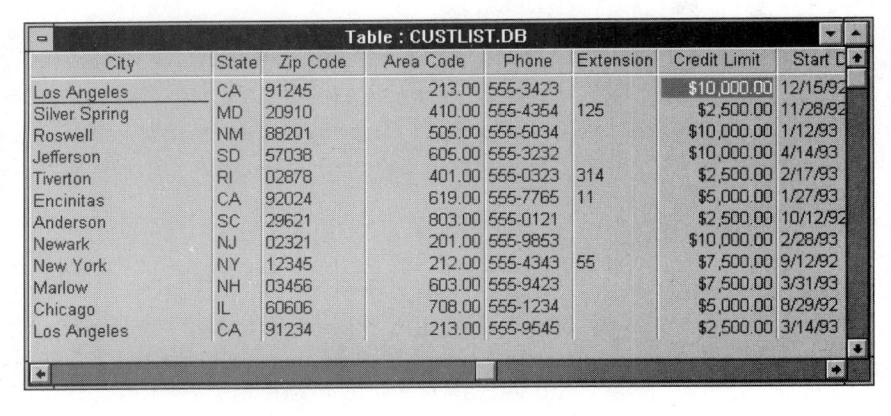

City	State	Zip Code	Area Code	Phone	Extension	Credit Limit	Start D
Los Angeles	CA	91245	213.00	555-3423		$10,000.00	12/15/92
Silver Spring	MD	20910	410.00	555-4354	125	$2,500.00	11/28/92
Roswell	NM	88201	505.00	555-5034		$10,000.00	1/12/93
Jefferson	SD	57038	605.00	555-3232		$10,000.00	4/14/93
Tiverton	RI	02878	401.00	555-0323	314	$2,500.00	2/17/93
Encinitas	CA	92024	619.00	555-7765	11	$5,000.00	1/27/93
Anderson	SC	29621	803.00	555-0121		$2,500.00	10/12/92
Newark	NJ	02321	201.00	555-9853		$10,000.00	2/28/93
New York	NY	12345	212.00	555-4343	55	$7,500.00	9/12/92
Marlow	NH	03456	603.00	555-9423		$7,500.00	3/31/93
Chicago	IL	60606	708.00	555-1234		$5,000.00	8/29/92
Los Angeles	CA	91234	213.00	555-9545		$2,500.00	3/14/93

Table : CUSTLIST.DB

To prevent columns from scrolling off the window, simply lock those columns into position, as follows:

1. If necessary, drag or rotate the columns you want to prevent from scrolling to the leftmost part of the table.

2. If the Table window isn't already scrolled all the way to the left, use the scroll bars (or press Home) to get to the left-most column.

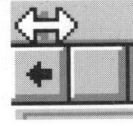

3. Move the mouse pointer to the *scroll lock*, a small triangle ◀ just above the left edge of the horizontal scroll bar on the Table window. The mouse pointer will change to a two-headed horizontal arrow, as shown at the left.

4. Hold down the mouse button and drag the scroll lock to the right or left. As you drag, the scroll lock icon will jump to just below the vertical grid line at the right of a column.

5. Release the mouse button when the column or columns you want to prevent from scrolling are to the left of the scroll lock.

Now, whenever you scroll the Table window to the left or right, the columns you locked into place will be prevented from scrolling and will always remain visible at the left edge of the window. For example, Figure 7.5 shows the CustList table with the cursor in the Credit Limit field after moving the Last Name and First Name fields to the leftmost columns of Table View and placing a scroll lock at the First Name column.

FIGURE 7.5

The Table window after moving the Last Name and First Name columns to the far left, locking those columns, and moving the cursor to the Credit Limit field at the right edge of the window

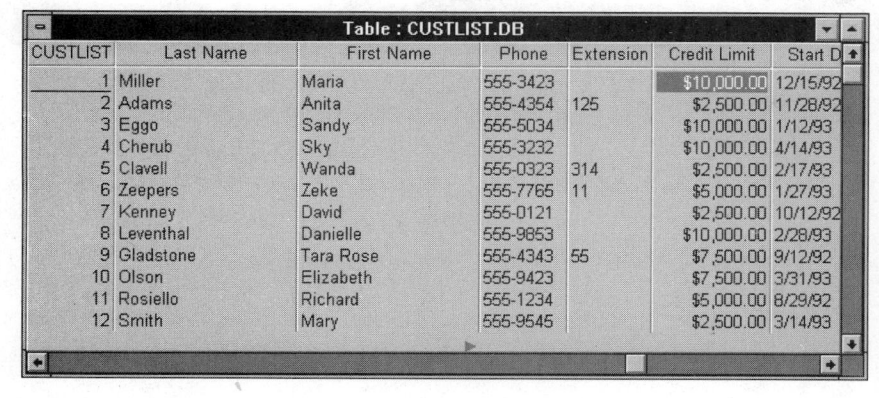

To remove (or change) the scroll lock, first move back to the left-most column of Table View using the horizontal scroll bar or ← key, until the scroll lock symbol becomes two triangles ◄►. Then drag that symbol to the far left edge of Table View or to wherever you want to put the scroll lock.

N O T E

> **You cannot change the position of the scroll lock unless the Table window is scrolled all the way to the left, so that the scroll box in the horizontal scroll bar is at the left edge of the window.**

▶ *Changing the Table Header Height*

To change the height of the header area at the top of a table, move the mouse pointer to the table name at the upper-left corner of the table. The mouse pointer changes to a vertical 2-headed arrow. Hold down the mouse button and drag the arrow icon up to narrow the header area or down to widen it. As you drag, the header area will be shaded to indicate the header height. Release the mouse button when the table header is the desired height.

▶▶ *Changing Table View Properties*

You can change the properties of a Table View header area, data area, or grid, as shown in Figure 7.6. To change the properties of any area, simply inspect (right-click) the area you want to change; or click the area first, then right-click or press F6. You can also use the shortcut keys or the Properties menu, summarized in Table 7.1.

FIGURE 7.6

You can change the properties of the header area, data area, or grid in Table View by moving the mouse pointer to the area and clicking the right mouse button.

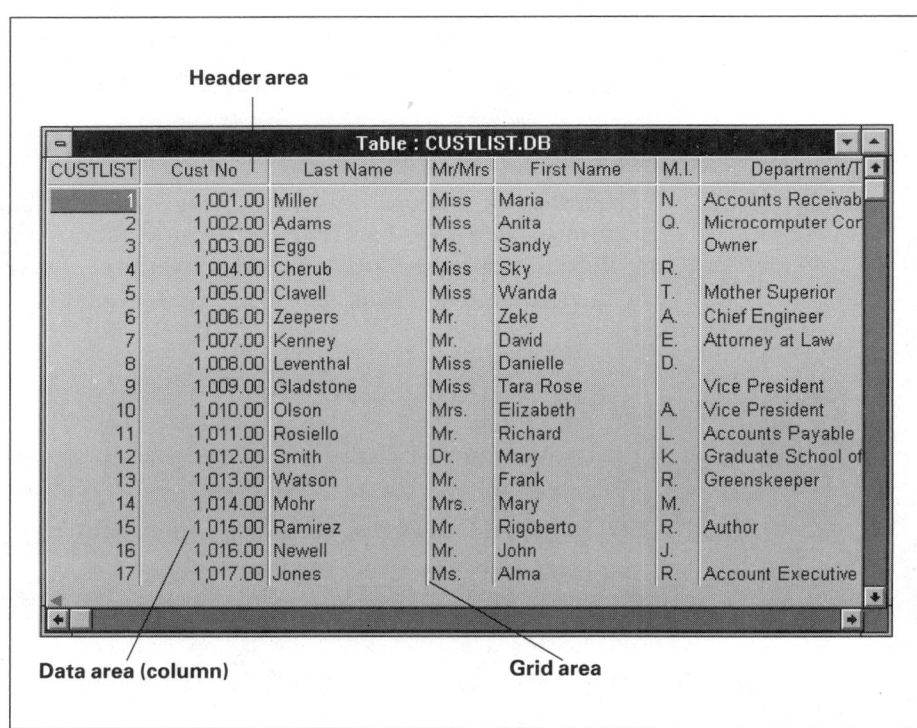

Header area

Data area (column)   Grid area

Once you've selected an area, you'll see a menu of options for changing it. The options available depend on the area you're inspecting, but will generally include several options described below.

▶ **TABLE 7.1:** *Optional Keystrokes for Inspecting Data, Header, and Grid Areas in a Table View*

TO INSPECT	PRESS...	OR CHOOSE...
Current column	Ctrl+M	Properties ➤ Data Properties
All columns	Ctrl+Shift+M	
Current header	Ctrl+H	Properties ➤ Heading Properties
All headers	Ctrl+Shift+H	
Grid	Ctrl+G	Properties ➤ Grid Properties

▶ *Changing the Alignment*

To change the alignment of data within a column or within the column header, follow these steps:

1. Inspect (right-click) the column (data area) or header you want to change, or press Ctrl+Shift+M to inspect all the columns, or Ctrl+Shift+H to inspect all the headers.

▶ ▶ **T I P**

> **The title of the property menu tells you what you're inspecting; for example, *Last_Name* (the Last Name column), *Last_Name_Heading* (header for the Last Name column), *All* (all columns), or *All_Heading* (all column headers).**

2. Choose Alignment from the property menu that appears. You'll then see this menu:

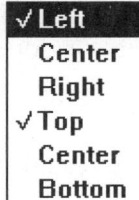

▶ ▶ N O T E

In this chapter, the term "numeric" applies to number, short, long integer, and autoincrement field types. The terms "currency" and "money" apply to the money field type.

3. Choose any option listed below:

Left   Aligns text along the left edge of the column (the default for alpha and date fields).

Center   Centers text horizontally within the column (the default for field names at the top of each column).

Right   Aligns text along the right edge of the column (the default for money and numeric values).

Top   Aligns text at the top edge of the row.

Center   Centers text between the top and bottom edges of each row.

Bottom   Aligns text along the bottom edge of each row.

You can combine horizontal and vertical alignments. For instance, you can inspect a column and choose Alignment ➤ Left to left-align data in that column, then re-inspect the same column and choose Alignment ➤ Center (the lower Center option) to center the field contents vertically.

▶ *Changing the Colors*

Jazzing up the background color of the header area, grid, or data area is easy with these steps:

1. First right-click the header or column you want to color. Or, press Ctrl+Shift+M to color all the data columns, or Ctrl+Shift+H to select all column headings.

2. Choose Color from the property menu. You'll see a Color palette.

3. If you want to change just the background color, choose a color and skip the remaining steps.

4. If you click the snap button at the top of the Color palette, you'll see the floating palette below.

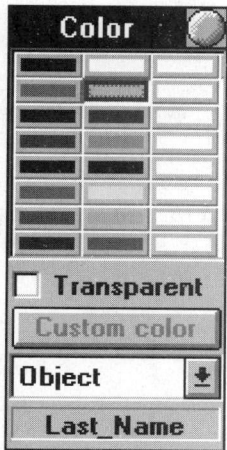

▶ ▶ **N O T E**

The third column of white colors is for creating your own colors, as described in Appendix E. Notice too that the bottom of the floating dialog box reminds you what you're coloring.

5. Now you can use any of these methods to choose existing colors from the palette:

- To change the foreground color (text), choose *Font* from the drop-down list box, then choose a color.

- To change the background color, choose *Object* from the drop-down list box in the palette, or click in the column you want to color, then click on the color you want.

►►**N O T E**

The Transparent option in the Color palette is not relevant to coloring Table View. It is useful in coloring custom forms, as you'll see in Chapter 11 and Appendix E.

While the floating palette is on the screen, you can click in the Table window, then click any column or heading, or press Ctrl+Shift+M (all columns) or Ctrl+Shift+H (all headers) to choose another area to color. The message at the bottom of the dialog box changes, indicating what your next color selection will affect.

►►**T I P**

Try clicking one of the colors on the palette and then use the arrow keys to see the effects of selecting various colors.

When you're happy with the colors you've selected, click the snap button to close the floating palette.

► Changing the Font

It's easy to choose a screen font for the header or data area in Table View. The steps are virtually identical to changing the color or any other property.

►►**N O T E**

Changing the font in Table View will have no effect on printed output. You can control printed fonts by defining a custom report format (Chapter 12).

1. To begin, inspect (right-click) the column or heading you want to change the font of, or press Ctrl+Shift+M to change the font of all columns or Ctrl+Shift+H to change the font of all headings.

2. Choose *Font*. You'll see the font menu shown below.

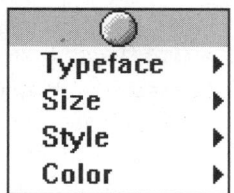

3. You can choose one of the options from the Font menu, and then select a typeface, size, style, or color and skip the remaining steps. Or, click the snap button to get the floating Font palette shown below. As usual, the bottom of the palette shows which area of Table View your choices will affect.

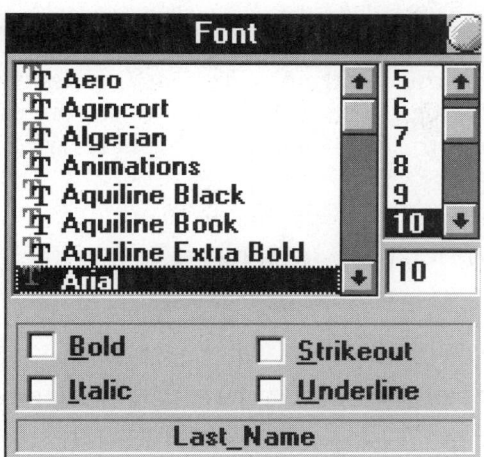

N O T E

Only fonts that you've installed for use in Windows will appear in the list of available fonts.

4. Choose any combination of typefaces, sizes, and styles.

► ►**TIP**

You can click in the typefaces or sizes list in the floating palette, then use the arrow keys to see the effects of various options.

Remember that you can move the Font palette out of the way by dragging its title bar. To select another area to change without losing the floating palette, just click outside the floating palette; then click the area you want or use the shortcut keys.

When you're done changing fonts, click the snap button on the Font palette.

► Customizing the Grid

The grid is the pattern of lines that appears between the columns (and, optionally, the rows) of the table. All the tables shown so far in this chapter use the following default grid settings:

- The grid background is gray.
- Horizontal grid lines appear in the heading area.
- Vertical grid lines appear between columns.
- No grid lines appear between rows.
- The horizontal and vertical lines are gray.
- The grid line spacing is 3D (three-dimensional).
- The current record marker line is hidden.

To change the grid, first inspect it by right-clicking any part of the grid or by pressing Ctrl+G. You'll see the property menu shown below. From here, you can customize many aspects of the table's grid background, grid lines, and current record marker, as described in the sections that follow.

Changing the Background Color of the Grid

To change the grid's background color, inspect the grid and choose
Color from the property menu. You'll see the familiar list of colors.
Select a color as described earlier under "Changing the Colors."

T I P

**To make the grid background disappear, give it the
same color as the data columns and header area and
choose a grid line spacing of None (or any option other
than 3D).**

Changing the Grid Lines

To change the appearance of the grid lines, choose *Grid Lines* from the
Grid property menu. You'll see the options shown below.

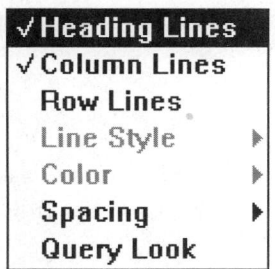

▶ ▶ **N O T E**

You cannot change the grid's line style or color if you've selected Grid Lines ➤ Spacing ➤ 3D.

The first three items (Heading Lines, Column Lines, and Row Lines) and the last item (Query Look) are toggles. If the item is checked, the property is activated. Choosing one of these options switches it to the opposite state ("off" if it is currently "on," "on" if it is currently "off").

- To change the style of the grid lines, choose Grid Lines ➤ Line Style from the Grid property menu. Click on the line style you want from the list of line styles that appears, or click the snap button to get a floating Line Style palette. As with the floating Color and Font palettes, you can move the floating Line Style palette by dragging its title bar. When you're done changing the line style, click the snap button on the Line Style palette.

- To change the color of the grid lines, choose Grid Lines ➤ Color from the Grid property menu. Click on the color you want from the list of colors that appears.

- To define the number of grid lines shown side by side, choose Grid Lines ➤ Spacing from the Grid property menu. Then choose Single, Double, or Triple to select one, two, or three lines for the grid, or choose 3D for a three-dimensional look. If you prefer a compressed display with only a tiny amount of space between rows and columns, choose a Spacing of None.

- To display column headings in a "query" style, choose Grid Lines ➤ Query Look. The top example below shows the headings with their "normal" look, while the bottom example shows the "query" look.

Table : CUSTLIST.DB				
CUSTLIST	Cust No	Last Name	Mr/Mrs	
1	1,001.00	Miller	Miss	M
2	1,002.00	Adams	Miss	A

Table : CUSTLIST.DB				
CUSTLIST	Cust No	Last Name	Mr/Mrs	
1	1,001.00	Miller	Miss	M
2	1,002.00	Adams	Miss	A
3	1,003.00	Eggo	Ms.	S

Changing the Current Record Marker

Initially, your table appears without a current record marker. If you inspect the grid and choose Current Record Marker, you'll have three options: Show, Line Style, and Color.

▶▶**NOTE**

You must check the Show option if you want the Color or Line Style options to have any effect. Show is also a toggle that is turned on (checked) or off (unchecked) each time you select it from the menu.

- Choose Show (if it isn't already checked) to display the current record marker. Then, if you want to change the marker's color or line style, inspect the grid and choose Current Record Marker again.

- To change the line style of the marker, choose Line Style, then select a line style from the Line Style palette.

- To change the color of the marker, choose Color, then select a color from the Color palette.

Once you've turned on the current record marker, you'll see that it extends all the way across Table View and moves from record to record as you scroll up and down through the table.

▶ ▶ **T I P**

If you still can't see the current record marker after doing all these steps, don't throw your computer out the window. The row height may just be too deep in a window that is not sized large enough. Maximize the Table window so you *can* see the marker and then reduce the row height.

▶ *Example of a Customized Table View*

Figure 7.7 shows the Table View for the sample CustList table after we changed some color, font, and grid properties. Read on to see how we got these results.

- We pressed Ctrl+Shift+M to select all data columns, chose Color, then clicked the white color.

- Next we pressed Ctrl+Shift+H to select all headers, chose Color, and clicked the white color again.

FIGURE 7.7 ▶

Sample CustList table after changing color, font, and grid properties

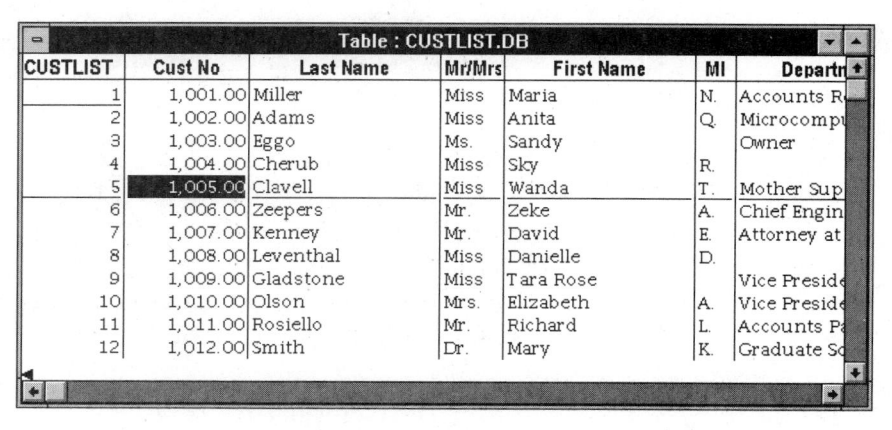

- We pressed Ctrl+G to select the grid, chose Color, and again selected the white color.

- Next we pressed Ctrl+Shift+H to select all headers, chose Font, then clicked the snap button. Then we chose Arial Narrow, Bold, 12 pt from the Font palette.

N O T E

The fonts used in this example are Windows TrueType fonts.

- We made the CUSTLIST column wider by dragging (to the right) the vertical line beside the column heading.

- We clicked outside the Font box and pressed Ctrl+Shift+M to select all columns. From the floating Font dialog box, we chose Lucida Fax 10 point, then clicked the snap button to close the Font palette.

- Next we inspected the grid again (Ctrl+G) and chose Grid Lines ➤ Spacing ➤ Single.

- Finally, we inspected the grid one more time (Ctrl+G) and chose Current Record Marker ➤ Show. The marker appears beneath the fifth record in the figure.

▶ *Changing the Format of Numbers*

Money and numeric values in a table are initially displayed with the format currently defined in the International settings of the Windows Control Panel.

W A R N I N G

Changing the International settings in the Windows Control Panel affects the format of dates and numbers in all Paradox for Windows tables, as well as in other Windows applications.

If you want to change the appearance of money values or numbers in a particular column, inspect that column and then choose Number Format from the property menu that appears. You'll see this menu:

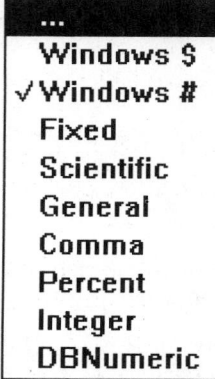

Your options (in alphabetical order) are as follows:

Comma   Displays numbers with two decimal places, trailing zeros, and with thousands separated by a comma. Negative values are enclosed in parentheses.

DBNumeric   Displays numbers in the format specified by your Paradox IDAPI configuration file. Initially, this format uses two decimal places, leading zeros, trailing zeros, and thousand separators. Negative numbers are preceded by a minus sign.

▶▶**N O T E**

The Paradox IDAPI configuration file (usually named IDAPI.CFG) provides specific information about your database environment and preferences. If necessary, you can change the settings using the IDAPI Configuration Utility described in Chapter 14.

Fixed   Displays numbers with two decimal places and trailing zeros, but without thousand separators. Negative numbers are preceded by a minus sign.

General   Displays numbers with two decimal places without trailing zeros or thousand separators. Negative numbers are preceded by a minus sign.

Integer   Displays whole numbers only, without thousand separators. Negative numbers are preceded by a minus sign. When you convert to Integer format, decimal values are rounded. However, if you later convert to another format that displays decimals, they will reappear.

Percent   Displays numbers with one decimal place, followed by the percent sign (%), but without thousand separators. Negative numbers are preceded by a minus sign.

Scientific   Displays numbers in exponential notation: a decimal number from 1 to 10 (with four decimal places), multiplied by an exponent of 10. Negative numbers are preceded by a minus sign.

Windows #   Uses the format defined for numbers in the International option of the Windows Control Panel (the default for numeric fields).

Windows $ Uses the currency symbol and format defined in the International option of the Windows Control Panel (the default for money fields).

WARNING

If existing numbers cannot fit into the column after you change the number format, Paradox displays asterisks instead of the numbers. You'll need to widen the column to see the numbers in their new format.

After choosing a format, you'll be returned to the Desktop and the numbers in the column you inspected will reflect the new format. Table 7.2 shows examples of how three numbers—entered as 35.75, 2500, and –2500—appear in each of the predefined formats. In the table, the Windows # and Windows $ use the United States defaults for numbers and currency.

▶ **TABLE 7.2:** *Sample Numbers in the Predefined Number Formats*

ENTERED AS...	35.75	2500	−2500
Comma	35.75	2,500.00	(2,500.00)
DBNumeric	35.75	2,500.00	−2,500.00
Fixed	35.75	2500.00	−2500.00
General	35.75	2500	−2500
Integer	36	2500	−2500
Percent	3575.0 %	250000.0 %	−250000.0 %
Scientific	3.5750e+1	2.5000e+3	−2.5000e+3
Windows #	35.75	2,500.00	−2,500.00
Windows $	$35.75	$2,500.00	($2,500.00)

Figure 7.8 shows the modified CustList Table View with some columns rearranged and narrowed so you can see both the Cust No and Area Code columns. Notice that Cust No and Area Code are now displayed as integers. To change the format of those fields, we right-clicked the Cust No column and chose Number Format ➤ Integer. Then we right-clicked the Area Code column, and chose Number Format ➤ Integer again.

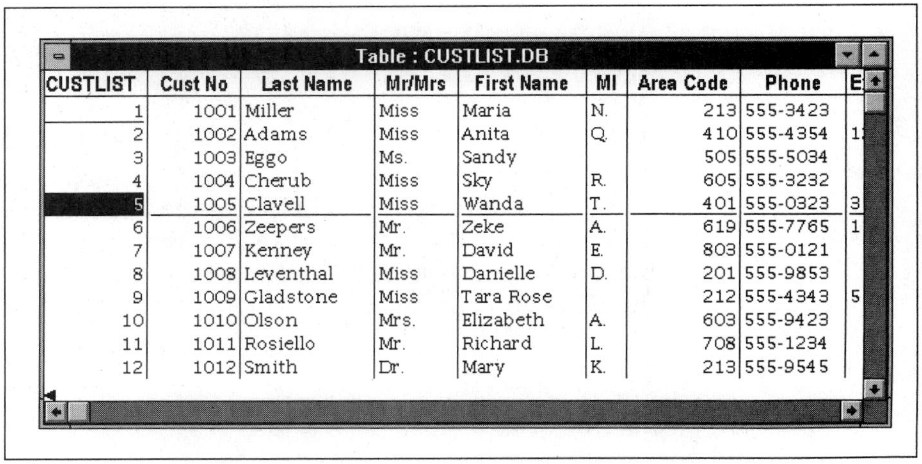

FIGURE 7.8

The sample CustList table after changing the Cust No and Area Code columns to Integer format

CUSTLIST	Cust No	Last Name	Mr/Mrs	First Name	MI	Area Code	Phone	E
1	1001	Miller	Miss	Maria	N.	213	555-3423	
2	1002	Adams	Miss	Anita	Q.	410	555-4354	1
3	1003	Eggo	Ms.	Sandy		505	555-5034	
4	1004	Cherub	Miss	Sky	R.	605	555-3232	
5	1005	Clavell	Miss	Wanda	T.	401	555-0323	3
6	1006	Zeepers	Mr.	Zeke	A.	619	555-7765	1
7	1007	Kenney	Mr.	David	E.	803	555-0121	
8	1008	Leventhal	Miss	Danielle	D.	201	555-9853	
9	1009	Gladstone	Miss	Tara Rose		212	555-4343	5
10	1010	Olson	Mrs.	Elizabeth	A.	603	555-9423	
11	1011	Rosiello	Mr.	Richard	L.	708	555-1234	
12	1012	Smith	Dr.	Mary	K.	213	555-9545	

Table : CUSTLIST.DB

▶ Creating Custom Number Formats

If you don't like any of the predefined number formats, you can create your own. Here's how to begin:

1. Inspect the money or numeric column that you want to reformat, and choose Number Format, as previously described.

2. Click the header (...) at the top of the menu. If you're inspecting a money field, you'll see the dialog box shown in Figure 7.9. If you're inspecting a number field, you'll see the dialog box in Figure 7.10 instead.

3. To create a new format, first choose the existing format (from the right side of the dialog box) that most closely matches the format you want to create. For example, if you want to define a format that's similar to Windows # format but encloses negative numbers in parentheses, choose *Windows #* from the Existing Formats list.

4. Click the Create button.

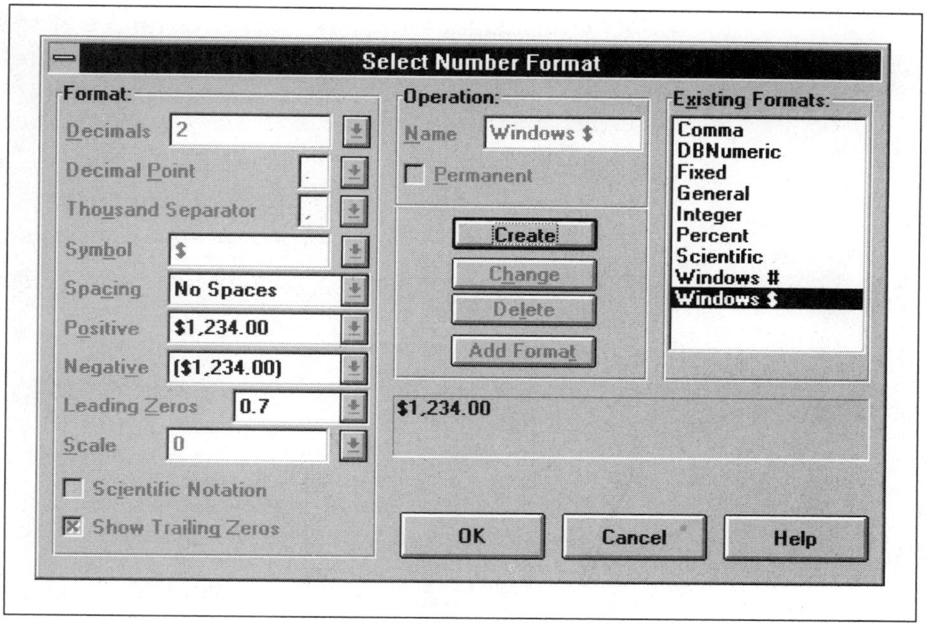

FIGURE 7.9

The Select Number Format dialog box for money ($) fields

FIGURE 7.10 ▶

The Select Number Format dialog box for number (N) fields

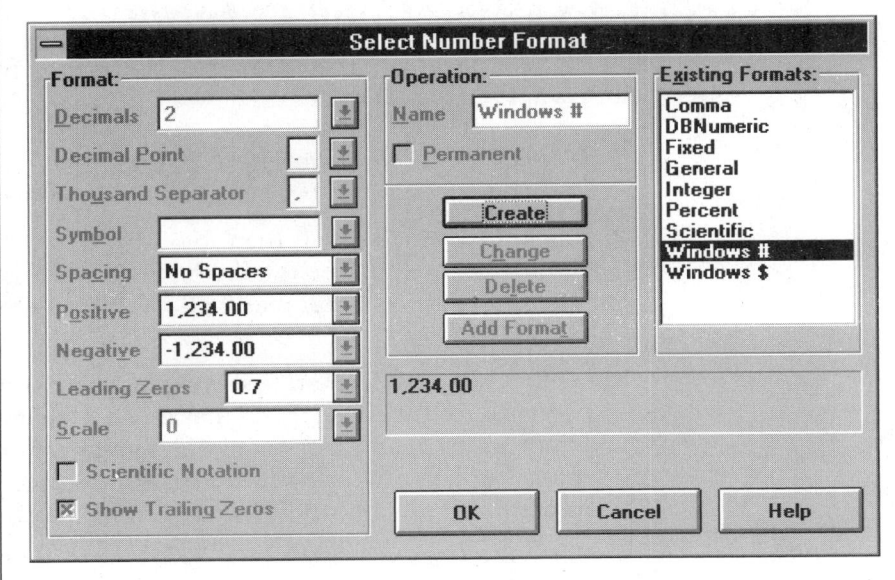

5. Type a name for the new format into the Name text box. For example, type **Win # with ( )** to describe a Windows # format with parentheses for negative numbers. The name you enter must be unique; that is, it cannot match any name listed under Existing Formats.

6. If you want the format you're creating to be available in future Paradox sessions, select (check) the Permanent check box.

7. Now you can choose any combination of options under Format at the left side of the dialog box (see "Setting Number Format Options," below, for details).

8. When the format is the way you want it, click the Add Format button. Paradox adds the new format to the list of Existing Formats and automatically highlights the new format.

9. Leave the new format highlighted in the Existing Formats list and choose OK. You'll be returned to the Desktop, and the column will be formatted according to the new specifications.

To use the new format in another column, just right-click that column and choose the format from the property menu that appears.

Setting Number Format Options

The Format options at the left side of the dialog box are summarized below.

Decimals   Defines the number of decimal places displayed to the right of the decimal point. You can type in the number of places or select the number of decimals from the list box.

Decimal Point   Defines the decimal point character. Choose a period or comma from the list box, or type in your own decimal point character.

Thousand Separator   Defines the character used as the thousand separator. Choose a space, period, or comma from the list box, or type in your own thousand separator.

Symbol   Defines the symbol or symbols displayed with the number. The predefined symbols are $, inch, lb, kg, cm, mi, and DM. You can type in any symbol or symbols you wish, or select a symbol from the list box.

Spacing   Defines whether a space appears between the number and the symbol preceding it. The list box options let you choose *No Spaces*, a space before *Negatives* only, a space before *Positives* only, or a space before *Both* negative and positive numbers.

Positive   For positive numbers, defines the position for the symbol (defined via the Symbol option), and controls whether the plus sign precedes or follows the number, or the DB symbol follows the number. This option also displays a sample positive number that reflects any other settings you've made to the number format so far.

Negative   For negative numbers, defines the position for displaying the symbol (defined via the Symbol option), and controls whether parentheses enclose the number, a minus sign precedes or follows the number, or the CR symbol follows the number. This option also displays a sample negative number that reflects any other settings you've made to the number format so far.

Leading Zeros   Defines how many digits will appear to the left of the decimal place. The list box options are .7 (no leading zeros), 0.7 (one leading zero), 00.7 (two leading zeros), 000.7 (three leading zeros), 0000.7 (four leading zeros), and 00000.7 (five leading zeros). If you enter fewer than the defined number of digits to the left of the decimal place, Paradox pads the number with leading zeros. For example, if you set leading zeros to *0000.7* and type in the number **47** during data entry, Paradox will display the number as 0047.

Scale   Displays the number as a multiple of a power of 10. Choose an entry from the Scale list box or type in your own number. For example, choosing *3* displays numbers as a multiple of 1000 (10^3); thus, a number entered as **1000** appears as 1 million, which is 1000×1000. Choosing *−3* displays numbers as multiples of .001 (10^{-3}); thus a number entered as **1000** appears as 1, which is $1000 \times .001$.

Scientific Notation   When checked, displays numbers in exponential notation (for example, 1.e+1). When unchecked, it displays numbers in decimal notation (for example, 10).

Show Trailing Zeros   When checked, displays numbers with as many trailing zeros as are needed to fill in the number of Decimals (decimal places) you've defined. For example, if you checked Show Trailing Zeros, defined 4 Decimals, and entered the number 47.4, the number would appear as 47.4000.

Keep in mind that when you define a number format, you're changing only the *appearance*, not the actual value, of a number. For example, if you set Decimals to 0, you won't see the "cents" in money amounts. To display cents again, simply choose a format with two or more decimal places.

Changing or Deleting a Custom Number Format

If you need to change or delete a custom number format, return to the dialog box by right-clicking any number or money column in Table View, choosing Number ➤ Format, and clicking ... at the top of the menu that appears. Click the name of the format you want to change or delete.

► ► **N O T E**

You can only change or delete custom formats that you've defined. The Change and Delete buttons and Format options are dimmed when one of the predefined formats is selected.

To *change* the highlighted format, click the Change button and choose new settings from the Format options at the left side of the dialog box. When you're finished making changes, click the Accept button, then choose OK to return to the Desktop.

To *delete* the highlighted format, click the Delete button. If you deleted a format used in the current column, highlight the correct format in the Existing Formats list. Then click OK to return to the Desktop.

Deleting a custom format usually has no effect on numbers currently displayed in that format. That is, numbers still appear as though that format existed. If you want to change the format of one of those columns, inspect the column, then choose any one of the available number formats.

► ► **W A R N I N G**

If the current column has the number format you're deleting, its format *will* change to whatever format is automatically highlighted when you click the Delete button. Therefore, before leaving the dialog box, be sure to choose the format you want.

► Changing the Format of Dates

Initially, any field that you've defined as the date field type appears in the format defined for dates in the International settings of the Windows Control Panel. However, as with numbers, you can change the date format for any column within your table. As you may have guessed by now, the way to get started is to right-click any column that has the date field type, then click Date Format. You'll see this menu.

```
      ...
  √ Windows Short
    Windows Long
    mm/dd/yy
    DBDate
    ISO Date
```

Here, in alphabetical order, are the built-in date format options:

new

DBDate Displays dates in the format specified by your IDAPI configuration file (see Chapter 14). Initially, this format is the same as mm/dd/yy format, described next.

new

ISO Date Displays four-digit numbers for the year, followed by the two-digit month number, followed by the two-digit day number, each separated by a period (.). (ISO is an acronym for International Standards Organization.)

mm/dd/yy Displays two-digit numbers for the month, followed by the day, followed by the year, each separated by a slash (/).

Windows Long Uses the long date format defined in the International option of the Windows Control Panel.

Windows Short Uses the short date format defined in the International option of the Windows Control Panel (the default date format).

Paradox assumes that two-digit year (yy) values are in the twentieth century. For dates not in the twentieth century, you must specify all digits of the year. For example, to specify June 6, 1492, you must enter it as **6/6/1492**.

After choosing a date format, you'll be returned to the Desktop, and the dates in the table column you inspected will reflect the new format. Table 7.3 shows examples of how three dates—entered as **6/6/95, 11/9/1492,** and **10/29/2001**—will appear in each of the predefined formats. The Windows Short and Windows Long formats shown in the table use the United States default formats for dates.

▶ **TABLE 7.3:** *Sample Dates in the Predefined Date Formats*

ENTERED AS...	6/6/95	11/9/1492	10/29/2001
DBDate	06/06/95	11/09/1492	10/29/2001
ISO Date	1995.06.06	1492.11.09	2001.10.29
mm/dd/yy	06/06/95	11/09/1492	10/29/2001
Windows Long	Tuesday, June 06, 1995	Wednesday, November 09, 1492	Monday, October 29, 2001
Windows Short	6/6/95	11/9/1492	10/29/2001

▶ ▶ **N O T E**

If the column isn't wide enough to display dates in the format you've selected, the dates will be truncated in the column. Just widen the column to fix that problem.

Creating Custom Date Formats

If you don't like the predefined date formats, you can define and select your own date formats using the methods previously described for number formats. The basic steps are as follows:

1. Inspect a date column in Table View, choose Date Format from the property menu that appears, then click the header (...) at the top of the menu. You'll see the Select Date Format dialog box shown in Figure 7.11.

2. To create your own date format, first highlight or click on a format in the Existing Formats list that is closest to the new format you want to define.

3. Click the Create button.

4. Type a name for the new format into the Name text box. The name of the date format must be unique.

FIGURE 7.11 ▶

The Select Date Format dialog box lets you choose and define custom date formats.

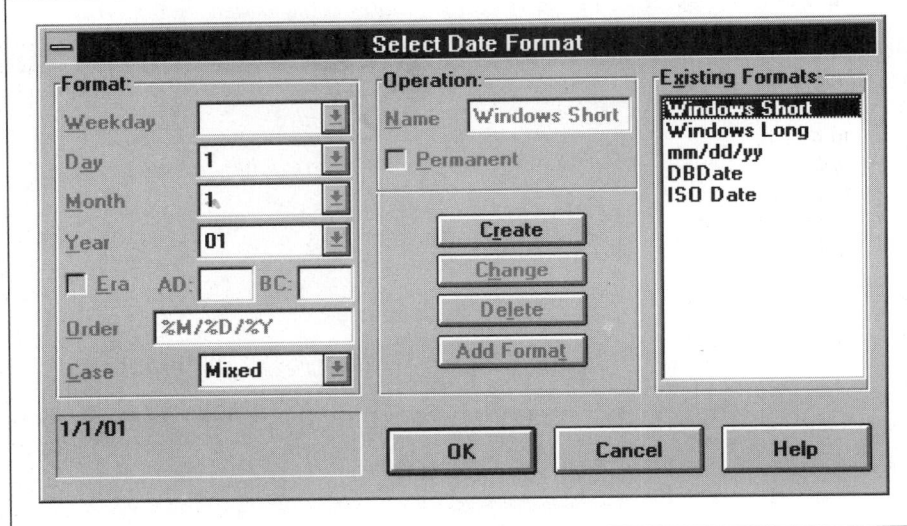

5. If you want to make the new date format available in future Paradox sessions, click the <u>P</u>ermanent check box.

6. Choose any combination of style options listed under Format at the left side of the dialog box (see "Setting Date Format Options," below, for details on these options). Figure 7.12 shows an example, which we've named *Long, no day,* which starts with the Windows Long format, then removes the *%W,* from the front of the <u>O</u>rder option. Notice how the sample date near the lower-left corner of the dialog box displays a date in the format January 01, 1901.

7. When you're satisfied with the format, choose Add Forma<u>t</u>, then choose OK. Paradox adds the new format to the list of E<u>x</u>isting Formats, returns you to the Desktop, and reformats the current column according to the new specifications.

Setting Date Format Options

Here's a summary of what each Format option in the left side of the Select Date Format dialog box offers:

Weekday Specifies whether the weekday is abbreviated or spelled out (for example, *Tuesday* versus *Tue*).

FIGURE 7.12

*The Create Date Format dialog box with a new format, entitled **Long, no day**, defined. The sample date at the lower-left corner of the dialog box shows how a date will look in this format.*

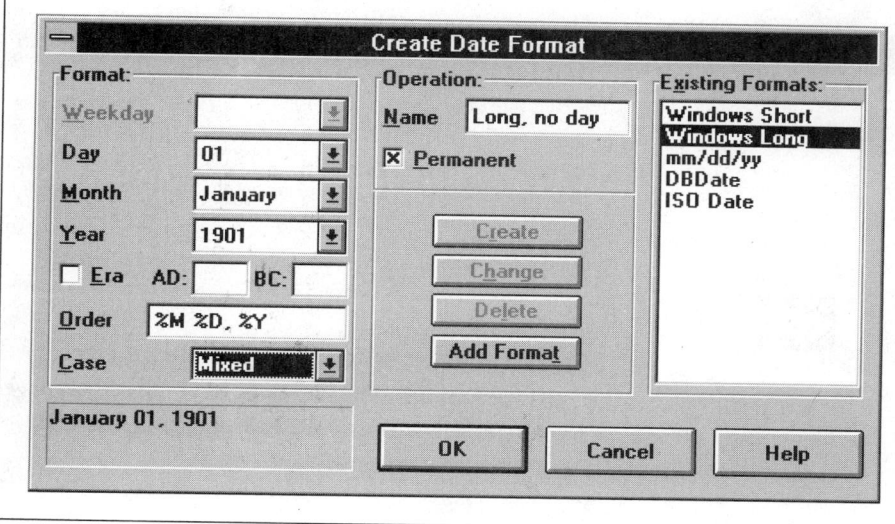

Day   Specifies whether the day number is displayed with or without a leading zero (for instance, *1* or *01*).

Month   Specifies whether the month appears as a number (with or without a leading zero), an abbreviated name, or a spelled-out name (*1*, *01*, *Jan*, or *January*).

Year   Specifies whether years in the twentieth century appear as two-digit numbers (with or without a leading zero) or four-digit numbers (*1*, *01*, or *1901*, for example).

 ▶▶ **N O T E**

> **The Weekday (%W), Day (%D), Month (%M), and Year (%Y) components are hidden unless you include them in the Order text box. If you base your new or changed date format on Windows Long, the Order box will automatically include all four components of the date.**

Era   Defines whether the era designator follows the date (for example, *01/01/94 A.D.*). When Era is selected (checked), the designator A.D. or B.C. will appear after the date; when Era is not checked, no designator will appear. You can change the AD and BC designator text if you wish.

Order   Defines the order for the Weekday (%W), Month (%M), Day (%D), Year (%Y), and Era (%E), and any separator characters. You can edit the contents of this text box to your liking. For example, entering **%M %D, %Y (%W)** will display dates in the order *January 01, 1901 (Tuesday)*; *Jan 1, 1901 (Tue)*; and so forth, depending on the other settings in the Format area.

▶ ▶ **N O T E**

> **Changes you make to the Order text box are not reflected in the sample date at the lower-left corner of the dialog box until you click one of the other format options or press the Tab key.**

Case   Specifies the case used for weekdays and months. Your options are Mixed (as in *Tuesday January 01, 1901*), Lower (*tuesday january 01, 1901*), or Upper (*TUESDAY JANUARY 01, 1901*).

Changing or Deleting a Custom Date Format

The steps for changing a custom date format are basically the same as those described earlier for changing a custom number format. That is, go to the Select Date Format dialog box, click the name of the custom date format you want to change or delete, then choose the Change or Delete button as appropriate. Remember, you can only change or delete custom date formats—not the pre-defined formats.

Now that you've seen how to change the formats for numbers and dates in a table, we can breeze through the steps for changing formats for time, timestamp, and logical fields. The next several sections explain the most important aspects of choosing and customizing these types of fields.

▶ Changing the Format of Times

As for dates, time fields initially appear in the format defined for times in the Control Panel's International settings. To change the time format in a table column, right-click any column that has the time field type, then click Time Format. You'll see a menu with the usual ... at the top, and these three standard time options (listed here in alphabetical order):

DBTime   Displays times in the format specified by your IDAPI configuration file (Chapter 14). Initially, this format is the same as the hh:mm:ss am format described next. Example: The time 1:20:24 pm would appear as *01:20:24 PM*.

hh:mm:ss am   Displays two-digit numbers for the hours, followed by the minutes, followed by the seconds, each separated by a colon (:). The AM or PM designator follows the seconds. Example: The time 1:20:24 pm would appear as *01:20:24 PM*.

Windows Time   Uses the time format defined in the International option of the Windows Control Panel. Initially, this is the same as the hh:mm:ss am format, but without leading zeros for hours. Example: The time 1:20:24 pm would appear as *1:20:24 PM*.

After choosing a time format, you'll be returned to the Desktop, and the times in the table column you inspected will reflect the new format.

When entering times into a time field, you *must* use whatever time format you've selected for the column. Thus, if the column's time format is Windows Time, you must type times in that exact format (though you *can* omit leading zeros). Paradox would, for example, reject the entry **1:20:24** (am/pm designator is missing) or **1:20 PM** (seconds are missing). Only **1:20:24 PM** (or **01:20:24 PM**) would do.

Creating, Changing, and Deleting Custom Time Formats

You probably won't be surprised to find out that you can create, change, and delete custom time formats by using the basic methods already described for number and date formats. That is, inspect a time column in Table View, and choose Time Format from the property menu that appears. Click the header (...) at the top of the menu to open the Select Time Format dialog box shown in Figure 7.13.

To create a new format, highlight or click on a format (in the Existing Formats list) that resembles the new format you want to define, then click the Create button. Type a unique name for the new format into the Name text box. If you want to set up a permanent format, click the Permanent check box. Now choose the appropriate time format

FIGURE 7.13

*The Select Time For-
mat dialog box lets
you create, change,
delete, and choose
custom time formats.*

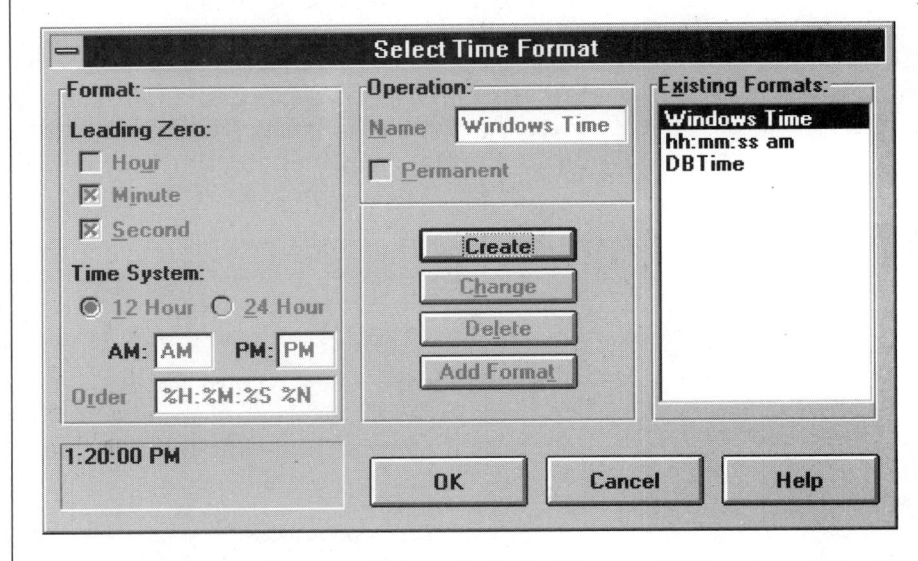

options from the left side of the dialog box. When you're done, click
Add Format.

To change or delete an existing format, highlight or click on that format, then click the Change button or the Delete button. As usual, you
cannot change or delete the pre-defined formats.

When you're finished using the Select Time Format dialog box,
choose OK.

Setting Time Format Options

When creating or changing custom time formats, you can set the following Format options in the left side of the Select Time Format dialog box:

Leading Zero To display leading zeros for hours, minutes, or
seconds, select the appropriate Hour, Minute, or Second checkbox. To hide leading zeros in those portions of the time, deselect
(clear) the appropriate checkbox.

Time System Specifies whether the time displayed uses a 12
Hour or a 24 Hour clock. If you select 12 Hour, you can specify
the text for the AM or PM designator.

> **▶▶NOTE**
>
> **The Hours (%H), Minutes (%M), Seconds (%S), and AM/PM (%N) components are hidden unless you include them in the Order option text box. If you base your new or changed time format on Windows Time or hh:mm:ss am, the Order box will automatically include all four components of the time.**

Order   Defines the order for the Hours (%H), Minutes (%M), Seconds (%S), AM/PM (%N), and any separator characters. You can edit the contents of this text box to your liking.

> **▶▶NOTE**
>
> **Your changes to the Order text box are not reflected in the sample time at the lower-left corner of the dialog box until you click one of the other format options.**

▶ *Changing the Format of Timestamp Fields*

Timestamp fields (timestamps) combine the time and date features you've already learned about. Initially, timestamps appear in the format defined for times and dates in the Control Panel's International settings. To change the timestamp format in a table column, right-click a column that has the timestamp field type, then click Timestamp Format. You'll see a menu with the usual ... at the top, and these three standard timestamp options (listed here in alphabetical order):

DBTimeStamp   Displays timestamps in the format specified by your IDAPI configuration file (Chapter 14). Initially, this format is a *date* (as for DBDate), followed by a space, followed by a *time* (as for DBTime). Example: The time 1:20:24 pm on January 1, 1995 would appear as *01/01/95 01:20:24 PM*.

h:m:s am m/d/y   Displays hh:mm:ss am time, followed by a comma (,) and the mm/dd/yy date. Example: The time 1:20:24 pm on January 1, 1995 would appear as *01:20:24 PM, 01/01/95*.

Win. TimeStamp   A combination of h:mm:ss am time (as for Windows Time), followed by a comma (,), followed by d/m/yy date (as for Windows Short). Initially Win. TimeStamp uses the time and date format defined in the International option of the Windows Control Panel. Example: The time 1:20:24 pm on January 1, 1995 would appear as *1:20:24 PM, 1/1/95.*

You'll be returned to the Desktop, and the table column you inspected will reflect the new format.

As for time data, timestamp data must be entered in whatever timestamp format you've selected for the column. For example, if you've chosen a Win. TimeStamp format, you could enter a time and date like the one below:

4:20:36 PM, 6/9/94

▶ ▶ T I P

You can repeatedly press the spacebar when entering data into a date, time, or timestamp field to fill in the system time and date. See Chapter 6 for more about filling in data automatically.

Creating, Changing, and Deleting Custom Timestamp Formats

The steps for defining, changing, and deleting timestamp formats are essentially the same as for other types of formats. That is, inspect a timestamp column in Table View, choose Timestamp Format from the property menu, then click the header (...) at the top of the menu. Figure 7.14 illustrates the Select Timestamp Format dialog box that appears next.

Now follow the general steps given previously for time and date fields. When you're ready to return to the Desktop, choose OK.

▶ Changing the Format of Logical Fields

A logical field stores data that can have either of two values, such as True or False, Yes or No, Male or Female. When typing data into a

FIGURE 7.14

The Select Timestamp Format dialog box lets you create, change, delete, and choose custom timestamp formats. Notice that this dialog box includes both time and date components.

Select Timestamp Format

Time Format:

Leading Zero:
- ☐ Hour
- ☒ Minute
- ☒ Second

Time System:
- ◉ 12 Hour   ○ 24 Hour

AM: `AM`   PM: `PM`

Order `%H:%M:%S %N,`

Date Format:

Weekday ` `
Day `1`
Month `1`
Year `01`

☐ Era   AD: ` `   BC: ` `

Order `%M/%D/%Y`

Case `Mixed`

Existing Formats:
- Win. Timestamp
- h:m:s am m/d/y
- DBTimestamp

Operation:

Name `Win. Timestamp`

☐ Permanent

| Create | Delete |
| Change | Add Format |

`1:20:00 PM, 1/1/01`

| OK | Cancel | Help |

logical field, you must use whatever format is currently defined for the field. For example, if the current format is True/False (the default choice), you could enter **True** (or just **T**) for True; or **False** (or **F**) for False. With a True/False format, you could *not* type **Yes** (or **Y**), **No** (or **N**), **Male** (or **M**), or **Female** (or **F**).

▶▶TIP

> **When entering data into a logical field, you can usually type just the first letter of the currently selected logical format. For example, if you type T in a logical field that's in True/False logical format, then move the cursor to another field or record, Paradox will automatically fill the logical field with True.**

The steps for changing the format of a logical field should have a familiar ring by now: Right-click any column that has the logical field type, then click Logical Format. You'll see a menu with the usual ... at the top, and these three standard logical options:

True/False   Displays True or False.

Male/Female   Displays Male or Female.

Yes/No   Displays Yes or No.

After choosing an option, you'll be returned to the Desktop and the current column will take on the logical format you selected.

Creating, Editing, and Deleting Custom Logical Formats

As for other field types, you can define and select your own logical formats. Start in Table View, and inspect a logical column. Choose Logical Format from the property menu, then click the header (...) at the top of the menu. You'll see the Select Logical Format dialog box shown in Figure 7.15.

Now create, change, or delete logical formats using the same techniques that work for other field types. Use the two Format options on the left side of the dialog box to fill in the text that will mean "True" or "False." For instance, if you're defining the logical format named

FIGURE 7.15 ▶

The Select Logical Format dialog box lets you create, change, delete, and choose custom logical formats.

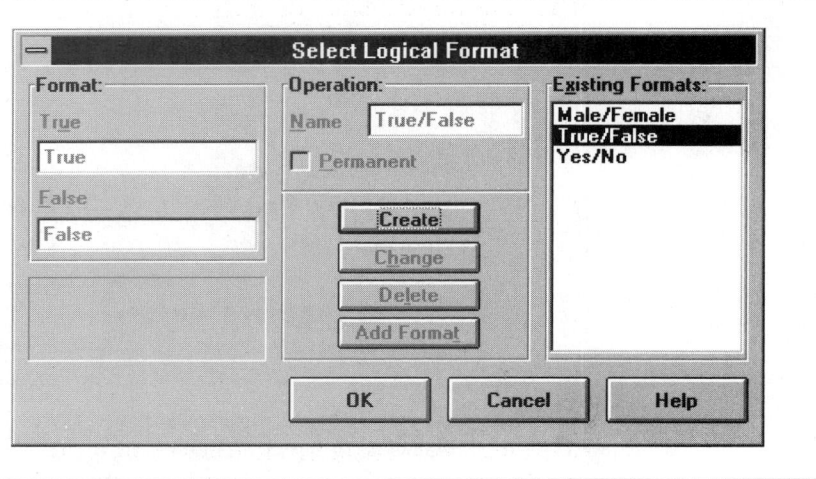

Hot/Cold, you could type **Hot** in the True text box and **Cold** in the False text box.

For added convenience during data entry, make sure the first letters of your True and False values are unique. This way you can type just the first letter of the logical value you want, then move the cursor to another field for automatic fill-in of the remaining text. For example, if you've defined the value "Hot" for True and "Cold" for False, you could type just **H** or just **C** and then move the cursor to another field. By contrast, if you had assigned "Fiery" for True and "Frigid" for False, you'd have to type (at least) **Fi** (for Fiery) or **Fr** (for Frigid) before Paradox would let you move the cursor to another field.

When you're finished using the Select Logical Format dialog box, choose OK.

▶ Changing the Appearance of Memo, Graphic, and OLE Fields

When you inspect a graphic or OLE field, you'll see the menu options shown below. Inspecting a formatted memo or memo field displays only the Complete Display, Color, and Font options. We've already described the Alignment, Color, and Font options. The other options—Complete Display and Magnification—are discussed below.

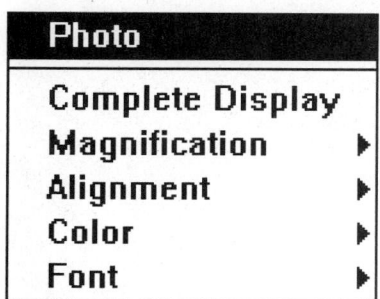

Changing the Complete Display Options

Normally, as you scroll through a table, Paradox displays the <BLOB...> message in the graphic and OLE fields, and shows only a small amount of unformatted text for the memo or formatted memo field of every record except the current record. Right-clicking one of these fields and choosing the Complete Display option lets you change that. Like many properties, Complete Display is a toggle.

- When Complete Display is not checked, Paradox displays the contents of the field in the current record only. All other records display the <BLOB...> message (or partial memo text) in that field. This is the default setting.

- When the option is checked, Paradox displays the contents of the field in all records.

 ▶▶**TIP**

Scrolling through records can be slower when the Complete Display option is checked. Deselecting the Complete Display property will speed things along considerably.

Changing the Magnification

Choosing the Magnification option, available for graphic and OLE fields, takes you to this menu:

Best Fit
25%
50%
✓100%
200%
400%

Your options are as follows:

Best Fit   Shrinks the graphic or OLE object to best fit the current width and height of the field. The proportions of the original object are retained.

25% or 50%   Shrinks the object to one quarter (25%) or one half (50%) its original size.

100%   Restores the object to its original size.

200% or 400%   Expands the object to twice (200%) or four times (400%) its original size.

Figure 7.16 shows some sample records in the Employee table after rearranging the columns, changing their width and height, then checking the Complete Display option in the Photo OLE field, the Signature graphics field, and the Notes formatted memo field, and setting the Magnification option to Best Fit in the Photo and Signature fields.

FIGURE 7.16

Sample data in the Employee table after adjusting column positions, widths, and heights, then checking the Complete Display property and setting the Magnification property to Best Fit

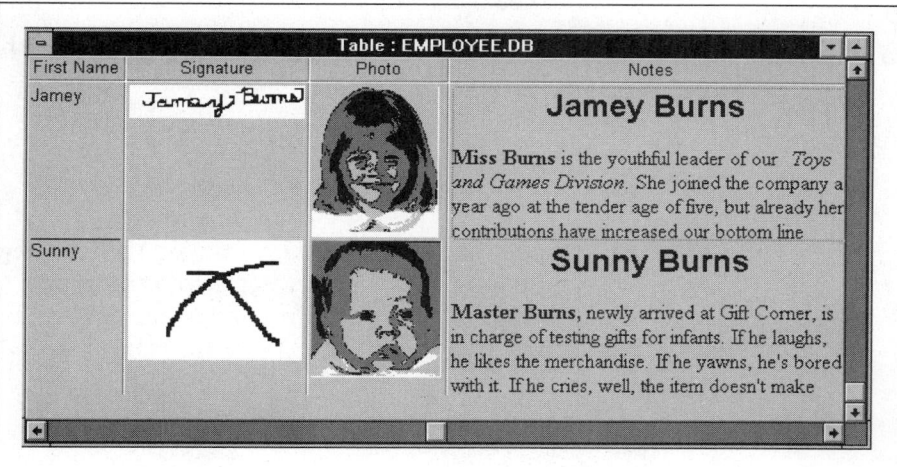

▶ *Changing Data Dependent Properties*

The Color and Font property options let you change the color of text or background for all records in a selected table column, regardless of the value in any field. By contrast, the Data Dependent property lets you use a different color or font to display fields that have a certain value or fall within a certain range of values. Changing the color or font of data based on values makes it easy to manage information on an exception basis, since the exceptional values will stand out. (In Chapter 9 you'll learn how to use queries to isolate records with specific values in one or more fields.)

▶ ▶ N O T E

> The Data Dependent option is not available for binary, bytes, formatted memo, graphic, memo, and OLE field types.

Suppose you want to monitor old, unpaid invoices. The example in Figure 7.17 shows a table named *Invoices*, in which we changed the data dependent colors as follows:

- Invoice dates before 9/30/93 have white text on a black background.
- Invoice dates between 10/1/93 and 10/31/93 have black text on a white background.
- Amount Paid values of 0 have a white background.

To create a data dependent property, follow these steps:

1. Inspect the field you want to assign a data-dependent property to, and choose Data Dependent from the property menu. You'll see the Data Dependent Properties dialog box (Figure 7.18).

2. If you want to create a new range that is similar to one already in the Ranges list, click on that range in the list.

FIGURE 7.17 ▶

Data dependent coloring draws attention to invoices in 1993 (or earlier) with September (or earlier) and October dates, as well as invoices with zero amounts in the Amount Paid column.

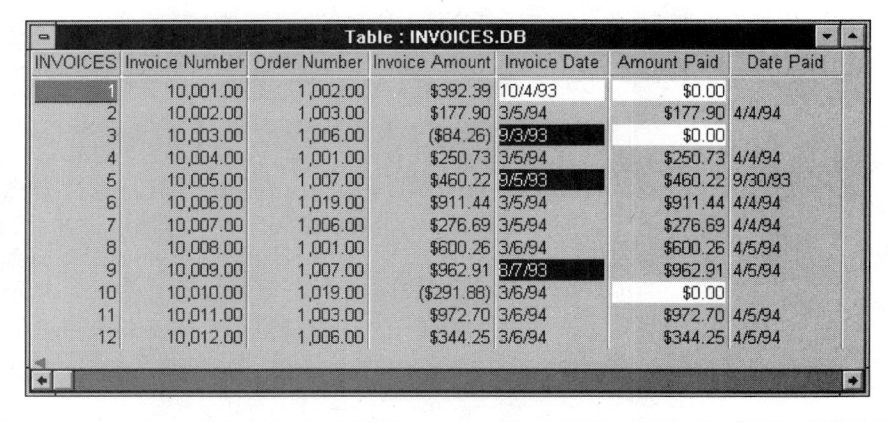

INVOICES	Invoice Number	Order Number	Invoice Amount	Invoice Date	Amount Paid	Date Paid
1	10,001.00	1,002.00	$392.39	10/4/93	$0.00	
2	10,002.00	1,003.00	$177.90	3/5/94	$177.90	4/4/94
3	10,003.00	1,006.00	($84.26)	9/3/93	$0.00	
4	10,004.00	1,001.00	$250.73	3/5/94	$250.73	4/4/94
5	10,005.00	1,007.00	$460.22	9/5/93	$460.22	9/30/93
6	10,006.00	1,019.00	$911.44	3/5/94	$911.44	4/4/94
7	10,007.00	1,006.00	$276.69	3/5/94	$276.69	4/4/94
8	10,008.00	1,001.00	$600.26	3/6/94	$600.26	4/5/94
9	10,009.00	1,007.00	$962.91	8/7/93	$962.91	4/5/94
10	10,010.00	1,019.00	($291.88)	3/6/94	$0.00	
11	10,011.00	1,003.00	$972.70	3/6/94	$972.70	4/5/94
12	10,012.00	1,006.00	$344.25	3/6/94	$344.25	4/5/94

Table : INVOICES.DB

FIGURE 7.18

The Data Dependent Properties dialog box lets you display certain ranges of values in a column in a different color and font.

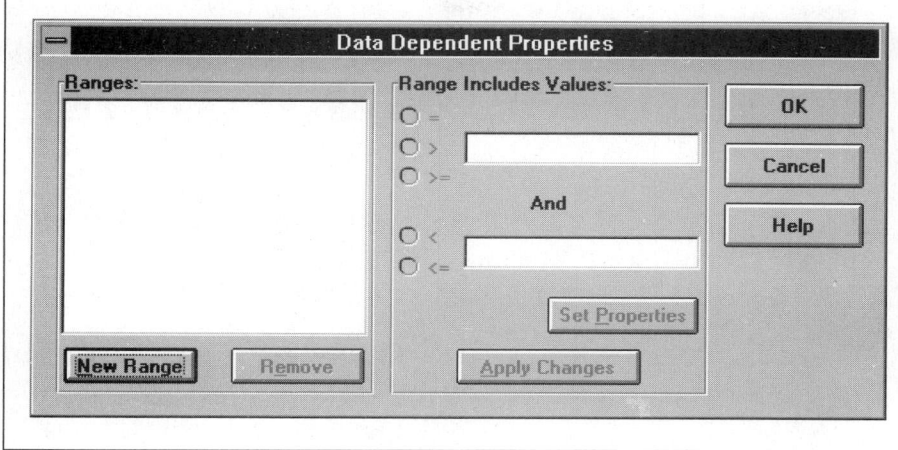

3. Click New Range to add a new range. For some field types, the range is initially set to **> <blank>** (greater than a blank space) or to whatever range is highlighted in the Ranges list.

4. In the Range Includes Values area, choose the operator that defines the type of relationship you're looking for (for example, =, >, >=, <, <=), as summarized in Table 7.4.

5. In the text box next to the operator you chose, type in the comparison value that is appropriate for the field you're working with. The value you enter should conform to the currently selected format for the field (although Paradox will automatically convert some formats, such as dates and money amounts, into the correct format). Examples: In a logical field in True/False format, you could enter **True** to look for True values (but you couldn't enter **Yes,** because *Yes* isn't appropriate for a True/False format). In a date field, you could type **5/16/95** or **May 16, 1995** or **05/16/95** (Paradox would convert those values to the current date format automatically). In a text field, you could type **M** next to the >= operator to highlight words beginning with the letters M through Z.

6. If you want to define a range of values to highlight, repeat steps 4 and 5 for options above and below the **And** operator. (We'll present some examples in a moment.)

7. Click the Set Properties button.

▶ **TABLE 7.4:**   *Operators for Defining Data-Dependent Properties*

OPERATOR	COMPARISON	EXAMPLE	MEANING
=	Equals	=12/1/94	Exactly December 1, 1994
>	Greater than	>12/1/94	Any date after December 1, 1994
>=	Greater than or equal to	>=12/1/94	December 1, 1994 or later
<	Less than	<12/1/94	Any date before December 1, 1994
<=	Less than or equal to	<=11/30/94	November 30, 1994 or earlier
AND	Combine ranges	>=11/1/94 And <= 11/30/94	All dates in November of 1994

8. Choose Color or Font to select color or font properties for values in the range you specified.

9. Click Apply Changes to apply the range, font, and color changes to the new range and display those changes in the Ranges area of the dialog box.

10. Choose OK to apply the range to the table column you're inspecting and return to the Desktop (or choose Cancel to exit the dialog box without making any changes to either the ranges or the column).

▶ ▶ **WARNING**

If you forget to click Apply Changes before exiting the dialog box, your range changes won't take effect.

Let's take a look at how we changed the sample Invoices table earlier. First, we right-clicked the Invoice Date column, chose Data Dependent, clicked New Range, and set up a data-dependent range to highlight dates that are greater than a blank and less than 9/30/93. Then we colored the Sample area as white text on a black background and clicked Apply Changes. Figure 7.19 illustrates the Data Dependent Properties dialog box after these steps.

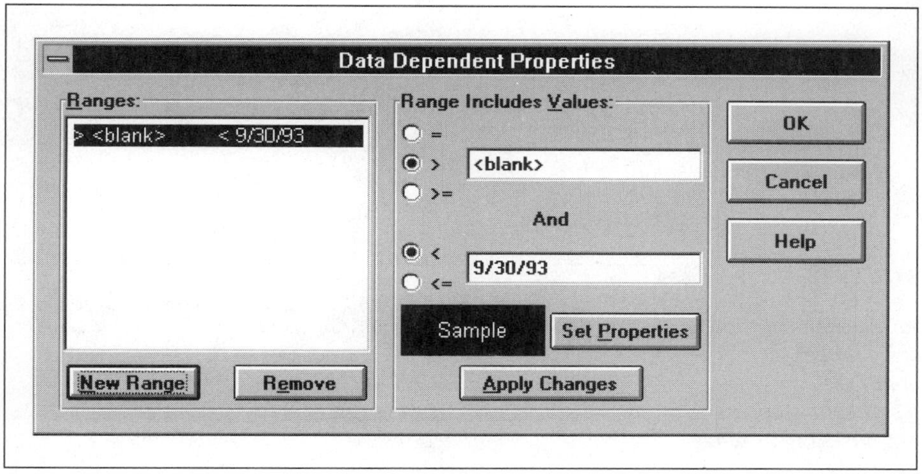

FIGURE 7.19

Data dependent properties for displaying dates before September 30, 1993 as white text on a black background

Without leaving the dialog box, we clicked New Range again to set up a second data dependent range. This time we specified >=*10/1/93 And* <=*10/31/93* as the range, and colored the Sample box as black text on a white background. After we clicked Apply Changes again, both ranges were listed down the left side of the dialog box, as shown in Figure 7.20.

After choosing OK to return to Table View, we right-clicked the Amount Paid column, chose Data Dependent, clicked New Range, and specified = *0* (that's a zero, not the letter *O*) as the range, as shown in Figure 7.21. We colored the background white and left the font unchanged to display data in that range as black text on a white background. Finally, we clicked Apply Changes, and clicked OK to return to the table.

FIGURE 7.20

Two data dependent ranges defined for a single field: one for dates before September 30, 1993, another for dates in October 1993

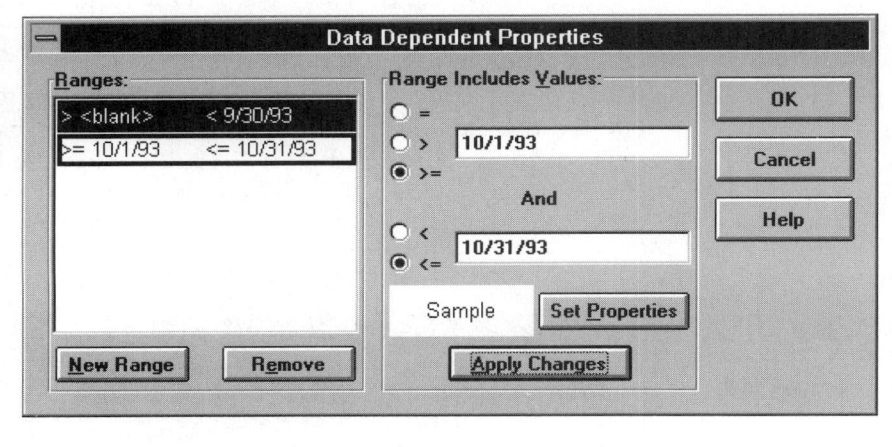

FIGURE 7.21

Data dependent range for a number (or money) column set up to highlight numbers that are equal to zero

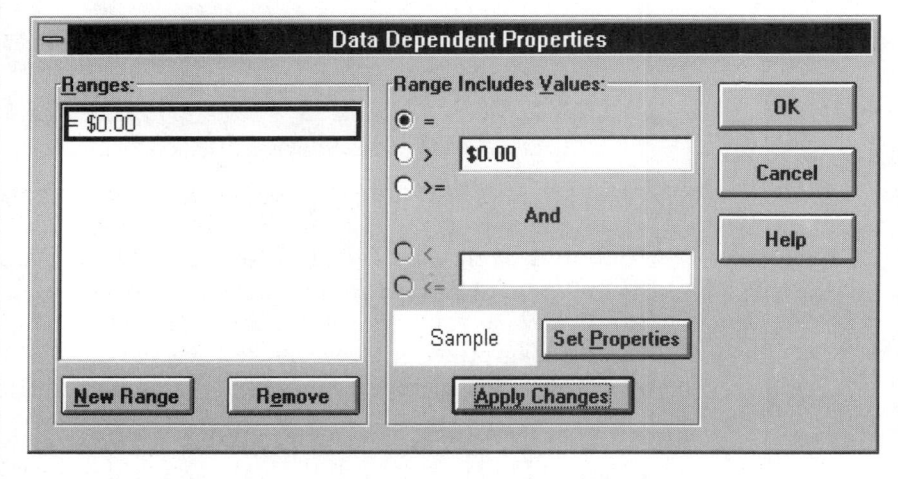

Changing and Deleting Data Dependent Properties

It's easy to change or delete a data dependent range for a column. Just inspect the column and choose Data Dependent to open the Data Dependent Properties dialog box.

- To change any range, click on it under <u>R</u>anges, then change the options under Range Includes <u>V</u>alues or click Set <u>P</u>roperties to update the font or color; when you're done changing the range, click <u>A</u>pply Changes.

- To remove a range, click the range you want to delete, then click the <u>R</u>emove button.

Choose OK when you're ready to return to Table View.

▶▶ *Saving a Modified Table View*

As mentioned earlier, you can save Table View settings at any time using the <u>P</u>roperties ➤ <u>V</u>iew Properties ➤ <u>S</u>ave options. If you don't do this, or if you make additional changes to Table View after choosing these commands, you'll see the dialog box shown in Figure 7.22 when you close the table or exit Paradox. If you choose <u>Y</u>es, your current view settings will be in effect the next time you open the table. If you choose <u>N</u>o, the current view settings will not be saved.

FIGURE 7.22 ▶

This dialog box appears when you close a table or exit Paradox with unsaved Table View settings. Choosing <u>Y</u>es saves the current view settings. Choosing <u>N</u>o abandons the current view. Choosing Cancel leaves the current table open.

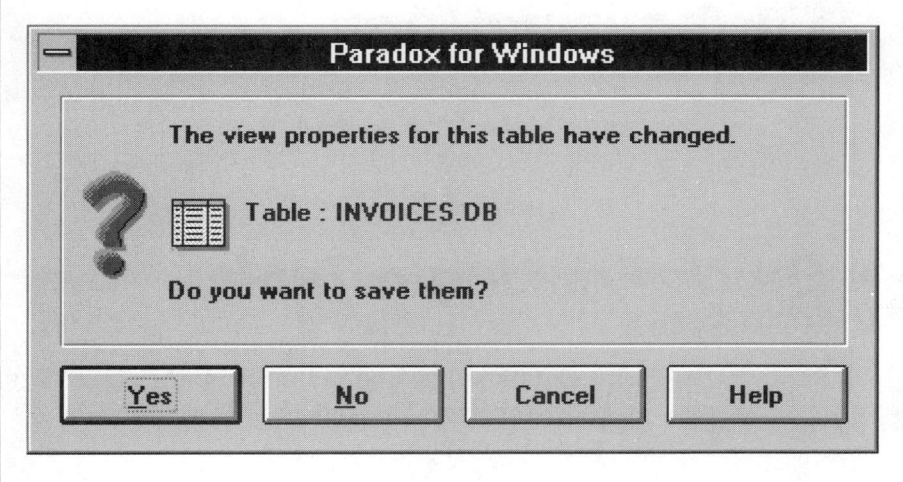

Paradox for Windows

The view properties for this table have changed.

Table : INVOICES.DB

Do you want to save them?

Yes   No   Cancel   Help

►►**N O T E**

> **Table settings are saved in a file that has the same name as the table and the extension .tv.**

If you want to delete all the view settings for a table and completely restore the default view, choose Properties ➤ View Properties ➤ Delete. Then, if you're sure you want to delete the property file, choose OK when prompted.

►►**W A R N I N G**

> **Never delete Paradox files through the Windows File Manager or DOS prompt. Doing so can damage your data permanently because Paradox may be unable to find all the files it needs to manage tables and other objects in your database. Please see Chapter 15 for details on managing Paradox for Windows files.**

►► *Customizing Form View*

Unlike Table View, Form View does not support direct manipulation or property inspection. Instead, you use the Form Design window, discussed in Chapters 10 and 11, to design custom forms.

►► *Quick-Printing a Table*

Chapter 12 explains how to design custom reports that let you arrange printed data in just about any way imaginable. But if all you need is a quick, unformatted look at your Table View data, a Quick Report will do the job nicely.

The Quick Report will not reflect any property changes you've made to Table View. Instead, the report data will have all the "raw" Paradox default settings. Figure 7.23 shows the first page of a Quick Report of the sample CustList table. Notice that the numeric Cust No field is printed in the default Windows # format.

In the next few sections we'll take a look at some of your printing options.

FIGURE 7.23

A Quick Report for the sample CustList table with overflow columns clipped off

Cust No	Last Name	Mr/Mrs	First Name	M.I.	Department/Title	
1,001.00	Miller	Miss	Maria	N.	Accounts Receivable	Zeerocks, Inc.
1,002.00	Adams	Miss	Anita	Q.	Microcomputer Consultant	
1,003.00	Eggo	Ms.	Sandy		Owner	Pancho's Res
1,004.00	Cherub	Miss	Sky	R.		Oneness Well
1,005.00	Clavell	Miss	Wanda	T.	Mother Superior	Westridge Co
1,006.00	Zeepers	Mr.	Zeke	A.	Chief Engineer	Virtual Reality
1,007.00	Kenney	Mr.	David	E.	Attorney at Law	Felson and F
1,008.00	Leventhal	Miss	Danielle	D.		Garden State
1,009.00	Gladstone	Miss	Tara Rose		Vice President	Waterside La
1,010.00	Olson	Mrs.	Elizabeth	A.	Vice President	Precision Co
1,011.00	Rosiello	Mr.	Richard	L.	Accounts Payable	Raydontic La
1,012.00	Smith	Dr.	Mary	K.	Graduate School of Busine	
1,013.00	Watson	Mr.	Frank	R.	Greenskeeper	Whispering P
1,014.00	Mohr	Mrs.	Mary	M.		
1,015.00	Ramirez	Mr.	Rigoberto	R.	Author	
1,016.00	Newell	Mr.	John	J.		Newell Constr
1,017.00	Jones	Ms.	Alma	R.	Account Executive	Ashland Flow
1,018.00	Schumack	Dr.	Susita	M.	Neurosurgeon	Physician's H
1,019.00	Smith	Dr.	Savitha	V.		Slybacks Pap
1,020.00	Smith	Mr.	John	Q.		
1,021.00	Smythe	Ms.	Janet	L.		
1,022.00	Dewey	Mr.	Frank	R.	Senior Partner	Dewey, Cheat
1,023.00	Adams	Mr.	Andy	A.	President	ABC Corporat
1,024.00	Wilson	Dr.	Ted		Psychology Department	Pine Valley U
1,025.00	Zastrow	Dr.	Ruth		Internal Medicine	Scripps Clinic

Friday, June 10, 1994 — CUSTLIST — Page 1

▶ Setting Up the Printer

Initially, Paradox will use the default printer and printer settings defined in the Printers option of the Windows Control Panel when you print a report. However, you might want to change the predefined printer settings for the current Paradox session if...

- You want to print to a printer other than the default printer defined in the Windows Control Panel.

- You want to change the default printer settings temporarily.

► ► **N O T E**

> **Changes you make to the printer settings in Paradox for Windows affect the current Paradox session only. To change the settings for all future Paradox sessions, you must use the Printers option of the Windows Control Panel.**

To change the printer or the printer settings, here's what you need to do:

1. Choose File ➤ Printer Setup from the Paradox Desktop menu bar. You'll see the Printer Setup dialog box, similar to Figure 7.24 (yours will show printers installed for use with Windows on your system).

2. If the printer name you want to use isn't already highlighted in the Printer Setup dialog box, click on it.

3. If you need to modify the current printer settings, choose the Modify Printer Setup button. You'll see a Setup dialog box similar to the one in Figure 7.25 (though relevant to your printer).

FIGURE 7.24 ►

The Printer Setup dialog box appears when you choose File ➤ Printer Setup.

Printer Setup

Printers:

Agfa 9000 Series PS -- LPT1:
HP LaserJet III -- LPT1:
Microsoft At Work Fax -- FAX:
Varityper VT-600 -- LPT1:
WINFAX -- COM1:

Modify Printer Setup...

OK   **Cancel**   **Help**

FIGURE 7.25 ▶

The Setup dialog box appears when you choose the Modify Printer Setup button in the Printer Setup dialog box. This is the same dialog box that appears when you choose Printers from the Windows Control Panel and click the Setup button.

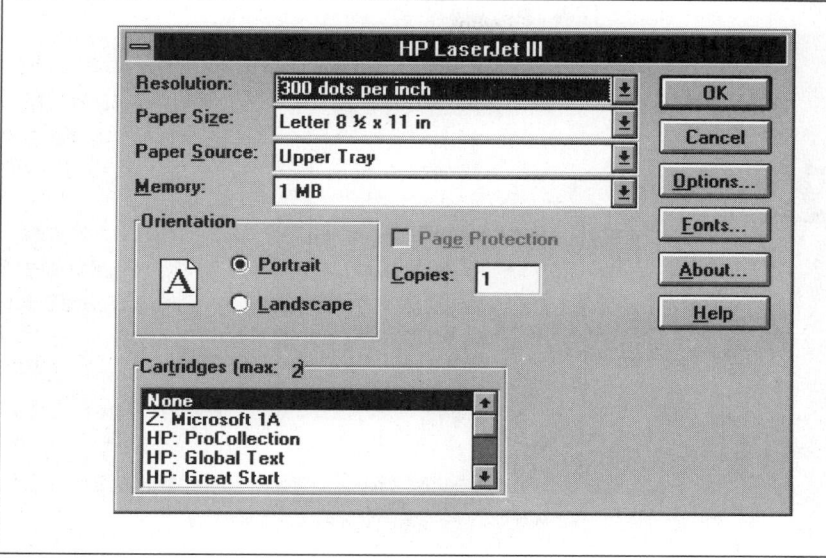

4. Make any necessary changes to the printer settings, then choose OK. You'll be returned to the Printer Setup dialog box.

5. Choose OK again if you want to save the current printer setup.

▶ Printing a Quick Report

You can print a Quick Report of Table View or Form View. From Table View, Paradox offers two ways to print a Quick Report: you can preview it on your screen first, and then print; or you can skip the preview and go directly to printing. The steps below tell all:

1. Open the table you want to report on. If more than one window is opened on the Desktop, activate the window you want by clicking on it.

2. If you want to print all the records in the table, switch to Table View. To print data from a single record, switch to Form View and scroll to the record you want to print.

3. If you're in Table View and want to preview the report before you print it, click the Quick Report button in the Toolbar (shown at left), or choose Tools ➤ Quick Report (or press Shift+F7), or

choose <u>T</u>ools ➤ Default Re<u>p</u>ort. A Report: New window will appear, with the report visible on the screen (see Figure 7.26). You can scroll through the report using the Toolbar buttons or the scroll bars at the bottom and right side of the window.

▶▶**N O T E**

> Technically speaking, the "quick report" options use *preferred* report settings, which you set by choosing <u>P</u>roperties ➤ <u>P</u>referred ➤ <u>R</u>eport in Table View. The "default report" options use Paradox's default report settings. If you haven't defined a preferred report for the table, Paradox will use the default report settings; therefore, a table's "quick report" and "default report" often look the same. You'll learn more about creating preferred reports in Part 3.

4. When you're ready to print the report, just click the Print button in the Toolbar (shown at left), or choose <u>F</u>ile ➤ <u>P</u>rint. The dialog box in Figure 7.27 appears when you print from Table View; the one shown in Figure 7.28 appears when you print from Form View.

5. Choose the page range, page number of the first page, number of copies to print, collation, and overflow handling options as described in the following sections.

6. Choose OK. Sooner or later (depending on how big the table is), your report will start printing.

7. If you previewed the report in step 3, you can close the Report: New window without saving your changes (choose <u>F</u>ile ➤ <u>C</u>lose ➤ <u>N</u>o).

Choosing a Page Range and First Page Number

You can print all the pages of data for the current table or form, or just a specified range of pages. To print all pages, select the <u>A</u>ll option in the Print File dialog box.

To print a range of pages, click the Page <u>R</u>ange option in the dialog box. Then click the <u>F</u>rom text box (or press the Tab key) and type the number of the first page you want to print. Next click the <u>T</u>o text box

FIGURE 7.26

To preview your Quick Report before you print it, open the table and click the Quick Report button in the Toolbar. A Report: New window like this one will appear on the screen.

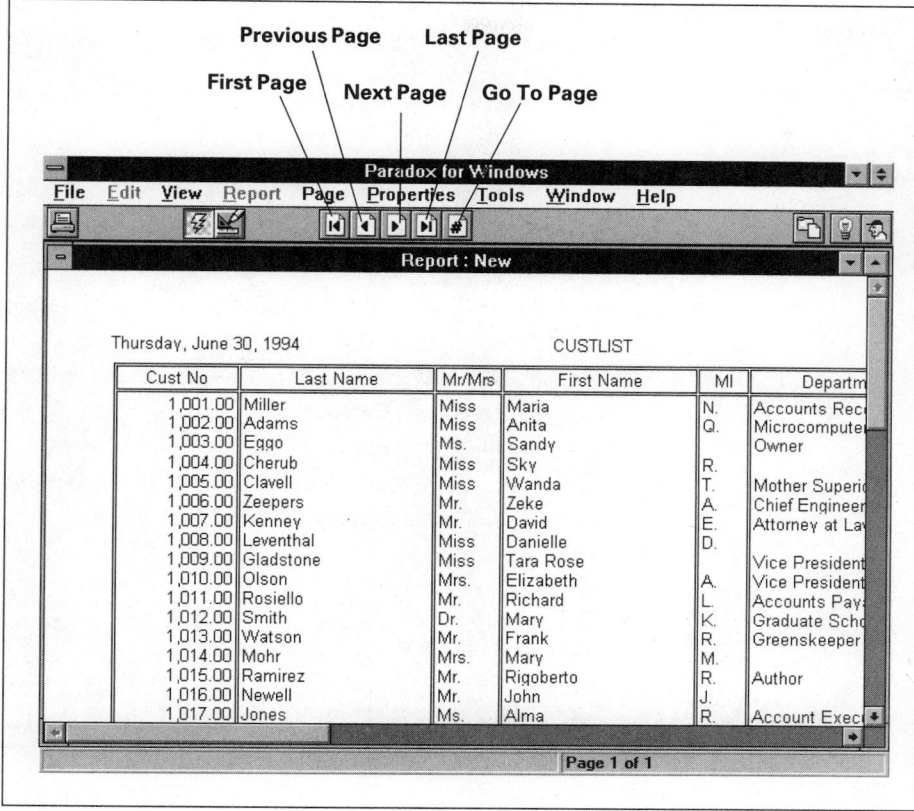

(or press the Tab key) and type the number of the last page you want to print.

If you'd like to change the report's starting page number, click the Number On First Page text box (or press Tab until you highlight the text box), and type the number that should appear on the first page. (Paradox will number subsequent pages consecutively, starting with the page number you typed plus 1.)

Choosing the Number of Copies and Collation

Paradox normally prints one copy of the report. If you want to print more than that, change the number in the Copies text box. By default, the Collate option in the Copies area of the dialog box is checked so the report comes out collated. That is, when printing several copies of

FIGURE 7.27 ►

This dialog box appears when you choose File ➤ Print or click the Print button in the Toolbar from Table View or from the Report: New window.

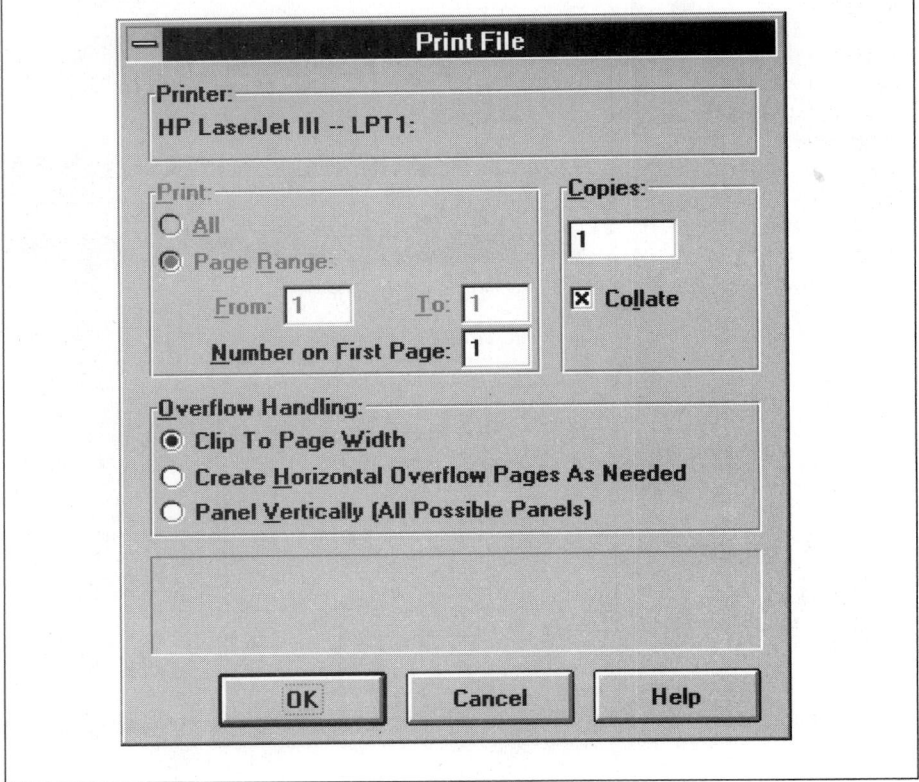

the report, Paradox prints them in this order: Page 1 of the first copy, Page 2 of the first copy, Page 3 of the first copy...; then Page 1 of the second copy, Page 2 of the second copy, Page 3 of the second copy...; and so forth.

If you remove the checkmark from the Collate option (by clicking Collate), the report will not be collated. In that case, the report order is as follows: Page 1 of the first copy, Page 1 of the second copy...; then Page 2 of the first copy, Page 2 of the second copy...; then Page 3 of the first copy, Page 3 of the second copy...; and so forth.

FIGURE 7.28

This dialog box appears when you choose File ➤ Print or click the Print button in the Toolbar from Form View.

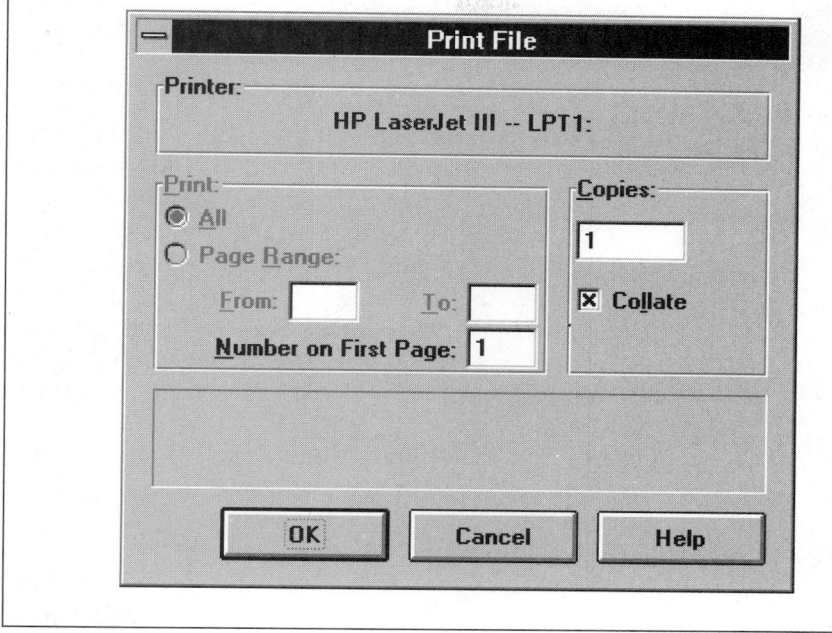

Handling the Overflow Pages

Many tables are too wide or too long (or both) to fit on a single printed page. The Overflow Handling options in the Print File dialog box let you control how Paradox handles the overflow pages. Your options are described below.

N O T E

Overflow handling options aren't available (or needed) when printing reports in Form View.

Clip To Page Width   Clips (cuts off) any data that doesn't fit across the page. The report in Figure 7.23 was printed with this option.

Create Horizontal Overflow Pages (As Needed)   Prints additional pages whenever necessary to fit all the data. Additional horizontal panels (columns) are printed *only* if they contain data. The pages come out in this order: Page 1, Panel 1; Page 1, Panel 2; Page 1, Panel 3; and so forth; then Page 2, Panel 1; Page 2, Panel 2; Page 2, Panel 3; and so forth. After printing, you can trim the report, then paste the pages side by side to see a complete report.

Panel Vertically (All Possible Panels)   Prints additional panels for each page of a report that is too wide to fit on a single page, regardless of how many pages actually contain overflow data. Panels are printed vertically first, then horizontally. The pages come out in this order: Page 1, Panel 1; Page 2, Panel 1; Page 3, Panel 1; and so forth. Then Page 1, Panel 2; Page 2, Panel 2; Page 3, Panel 2; and so forth. Finally, Page 1, Panel 3; Page 2, Panel 3; Page 3, Panel 3; and so forth. Again, you can trim and paste the pages together to see the entire report.

Don't forget that Quick Report is just a quick and easy way to do a "data dump" of your table. Chapter 12 will show you how to print great-looking formatted reports.

In this chapter you've seen many ways to customize the Table View of your data through direct manipulation and property inspection. You've also learned how to print simple reports from your tables. When you're ready to design fancy forms and reports, you can dive into Part 3 of this book. But before plunging ahead, take a look at the next chapter, "Sorting Your Tables." There you'll learn how to organize and sort data in your tables and forms.

► ► CHAPTER **8**

Sorting
Your Tables

——

▶ ▶ FAST TRACK

▶ **To achieve a sort-within-a-sort**   **372**

place more than one field in the Sort Order list.

▶ **To sort (order by letter, number, or date) the table that**
is currently on your Desktop   **375**

choose Table ➤ Sort, or inspect (right-click) the table
name in the Project Viewer window and choose Sort, or
choose Tools ➤ Utilities ➤ Sort and select the table you
want to sort. This takes you to the Sort Table dialog box.
Fill in the options in the dialog box, then choose the OK
button to begin sorting.

▶ **To preserve the order of records in the original table**   **375**

sort to a new table by choosing the New Table option in
the Sort Table dialog box.

▶ **When listing multiple fields to sort on**   **378**

in the Sort Table dialog box, list the primary sort key first,
the secondary sort key second, and so forth.

▶ **To arrange records in smallest to largest order**   **382**

choose an ascending (+) sort direction in the Sort Order list.

▶ **To arrange records in largest to smallest order**   **382**

choose a descending (–) sort direction in the Sort Order list.

▶ **When you've finished with a sorted temporary table**   **387**

you may want to delete it to avoid having multiple copies
of the same table on disk.

▶ **If your table has a primary key, you can speed and
simplify sorting operations**   **387**

by creating secondary indexes of commonly used sort orders.

▶ **To create a secondary index**   **389**

change the structure of the table (Table ➤ Restructure Table or Tools ➤ Utilities ➤ Restructure). In the Restructure dialog box, choose Secondary Indexes under Table
Properties. Then choose the Define button, and define
your sort keys. Choose OK and then Save to return to the
Desktop.

▶ **To use a secondary index to sort a table**   **396**

choose Table ➤ Filter or click the Filter button in the Toolbar, then click the name of the secondary index you want
and choose OK.

▶ ▶ **S**orting, in database management terminology, means the same thing that it does in plain English—to put things into some kind of order. For example, if your table contains names and addresses, you might want to sort records into alphabetical order by names so you can print an alphabetized list. Or, you might want to sort the records by zip code for bulk mailing.

▶ ▶ N O T E

If a table has a primary index, its records are always ordered according to the key field or fields. Otherwise, records appear in the order in which they were entered.

Sorting leads naturally to the grouping of like information. For example, suppose you have a table that contains invoice information, including the date each invoice is due. If you sort the records by date, the bills due in January will naturally precede those due in February, which in turn precede those due in March. Similarly, if your table contains sales information, sorting that table by product code would naturally place the sales of product A-100 above the sales of product A-200, and so on.

▶ ▶ Sorts-within-Sorts

In many cases, you'll want to sort your table on more than one field, to produce a sort-within-a-sort. For example, suppose you have a large table of names and addresses that includes about ten Smiths. If you were to sort that table by last names, all the Smiths would be grouped to-gether like this:

Last Name	First Name	MI
Smiley	Windsor	J.
Smith	Michael	K.
Smith	Anton	A.
Smith	Zeke	A.
Smith	Jennifer	J.
Smith	Wally	P.
Smith	Anita	R.
Smith	Michael	D.
Smith	Antonio	L.
Smith	Vera	
Smith	Susan	M.
Smithsonian	Caroline	J.

Notice that the first names of all the Smiths are in random order (Michael Smith comes before Anton Smith, and so on). To sort the names alphabetically by first name within identical last names (as in a phone book), you would want to sort on Last Name *and* First Name, producing this result:

Last Name	First Name	MI
Smiley	Windsor	J.
Smith	Anita	R.
Smith	Anton	A.
Smith	Antonio	L.
Smith	Jennifer	J.
Smith	Michael	M.
Smith	Michael	D.
Smith	Susan	M.
Smith	Vera	

Last Name	First Name	MI
Smith	Wally	P.
Smith	Zeke	A.
Smithsonian	Caroline	J.

Now all the last names *and* first names are in proper alphabetical order. Notice that the second sort field acts as a "tie breaker." That is, when two individuals have the same last name, the secondary sort order (first name) is used to break the tie.

In the sort order shown above, the Last Name field is the *primary sort key* and the First Name field is the *secondary* (or second) sort key.

Now the only "mistake" in this sorted list is that Michael M. Smith comes before Michael D. Smith. That's easily fixed by sorting on three fields—Last Name, First Name, and MI (middle initial)—to produce the following result:

Last Name	First Name	MI
Smiley	Windsor	J.
Smith	Anita	R.
Smith	Anton	A.
Smith	Antonio	L.
Smith	Jennifer	J.
Smith	Michael	D.
Smith	Michael	M.
Smith	Susan	M.
Smith	Vera	
Smith	Wally	P.
Smith	Zeke	A.
Smithsonian	Caroline	J.

We achieved this sort order by making Last Name the primary sort key, First Name the secondary sort key, and Middle Initial (MI) the third sort key.

When sorting Paradox for Windows tables, you can specify as many sort keys as you wish, so there is really no limit to the number of ways you can order and group information in a table. Since sorting is generally quick and easy, it's no big deal to sort names and addresses into zip code order to print form letters and mailing labels, then sort them into alphabetical order by name to print an alphabetical list.

▶▶ *Using Table ➤ Sort to Sort Tables*

There are several different ways to sort a table on the fly (we'll list other methods at the end of the chapter). Perhaps the simplest is to use the Table ➤ Sort option.

With this technique, you open the table and get to the Sort Table dialog box.

1. If the table you want to sort is not currently open on the Desktop, use File ➤ Open ➤ Table. Other ways to open the table include clicking the Open Table button in the Toolbar, or double-clicking the table's name in the Project Viewer (if these tools are visible).

2. Choose Table ➤ Sort to open the Sort Table dialog box. If you assigned a primary key in the table's structure (Chapter 4), the Sort Table dialog box will resemble Figure 8.1, where we've used our trusty CustList table once again. If you didn't assign a primary key, the Sort Table dialog box will resemble Figure 8.2.

Once you've opened the Sort Table dialog box, you need to make some decisions about how to handle the sort.

▶ *Sorting to the Same Table or a New Table*

If the table you're about to sort has no primary key, you can sort records within the current table or place the sorted records in a new table. The disadvantage of sorting to the same table is that you cannot return the records to their original order. That's because each record will be assigned a new sequence number (record number) in the sorted table, based on its new position in the table.

FIGURE 8.1

This Sort Table dialog box appears when you choose Table ➤ Sort for a table that has a primary index. The key icon reminds you that the table is keyed, and the Same Table option is dimmed (unavailable).

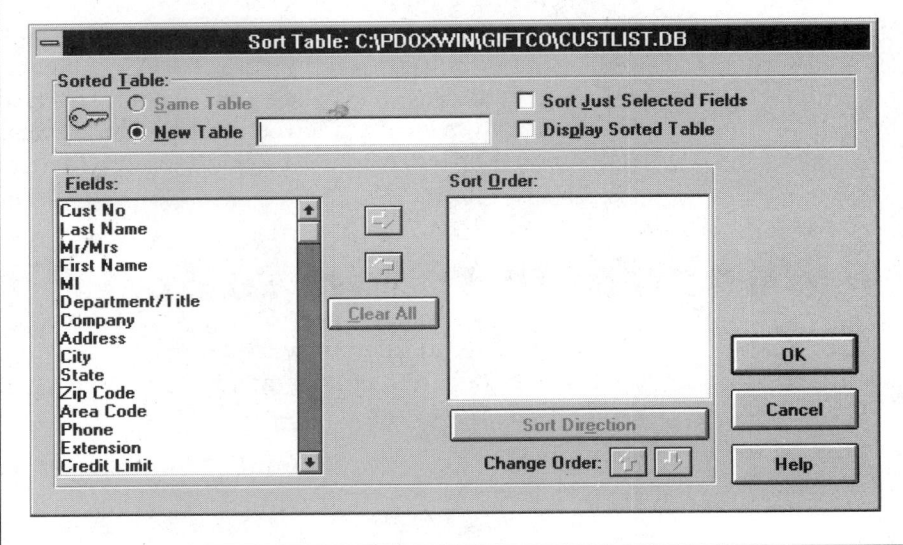

FIGURE 8.2

This Sort Table dialog box appears when you choose Table ➤ Sort for a table that doesn't have key fields defined. No key icon appears, and you can sort to either the Same Table or to a New Table.

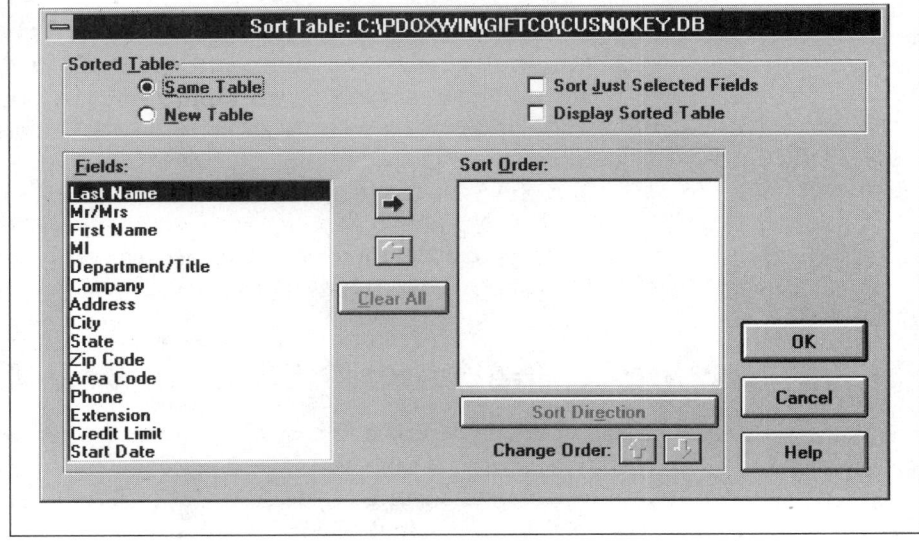

If you sort to a new table, however, the original table isn't changed at all—it retains its original order. The new table will have the same field names, types, and sizes as the original table. However, this new copy of the table will have no primary key, nor will it have any of the properties you might have assigned to the original table's Table View. It will be perfect, however, for printing sorted reports, labels, form letters... whatever, using techniques discussed in Chapter 12.

▶ ▶ N O T E

> **If the table structure includes a primary key, you *must* sort to a different table, unless you use a secondary index to perform the sort, as described later in this chapter.**

To sort to a separate table, name the new table by following these steps:

1. Choose the <u>N</u>ew Table option, near the top left of the Sort Table dialog box.

2. Type a name for the sorted table, such as **Tempsort** (for temporary sort table), into the <u>N</u>ew Table text box. The table you're sorting to must not be open on the Desktop.

▶ ▶ W A R N I N G

> **If you specify the name of an existing table in step 2, Paradox will ask if you want to overwrite it when you perform the sort. Answer <u>Y</u>es if you're sure you want to overwrite the existing table, or <u>N</u>o to return to the Sort Table dialog box.**

3. If you want to see the sorted table as soon as the sort is finished, choose the Dis<u>p</u>lay Sorted Table option to the right of the file name, as in Figure 8.3.

Sorting Your Tables

Ch. 8

FIGURE 8.3 ►

*This Sort Table dialog box tells Paradox to send sorted output from the CustList table to a new table named **Tempsort** and to display the results on the Desktop as soon as the sort is finished.*

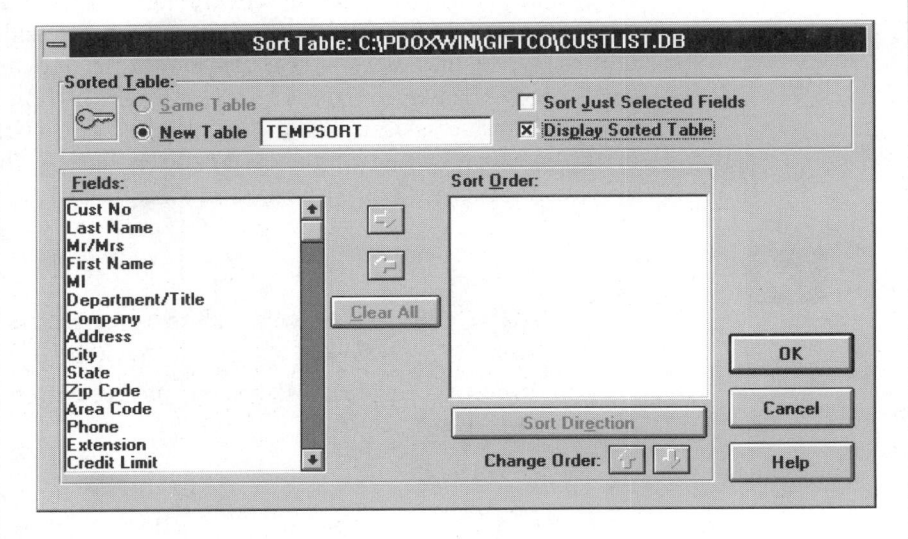

► Choosing Fields to Sort On

As discussed earlier, sorting on multiple fields allows you to create sorts-within-sorts. You can sort on as many fields as you wish, and you must decide which field will be the primary sort key, which field (if any) will be the secondary sort key, and so forth.

►►NOTE

You cannot sort on binary, bytes, formatted memo, graphic, logical, memo, or OLE fields.

Suppose you want to sort by Last Name, then by First Name within identical last names, then by Middle Initial within identical Last and First Names. In that case, Last Name would be the primary sort key, First Name the second sort key, and Middle Initial the third sort key.

Or maybe you want to sort alphabetically by city, then by zip code within each city. City would be the primary sort key, and Zip Code would be the secondary sort key.

To specify a field to sort on, simply copy it from the F̲ields list on the left side of the Sort Table dialog box to the Sort O̲rder list on the right side of the dialog box, starting with the primary sort key. You can use any of the techniques listed below to add field names to the Sort O̲rder list.

- Click on the name of a field you want to sort on, then click the → button (or simply double-click the field you want to sort on). You can repeat these steps to add as many field names as necessary to the list.

- As a shortcut, you can copy several adjacent field names to the Sort O̲rder list by dragging. Just click the first field name you want to copy, hold down the mouse button, and drag the mouse pointer through the fields you want to copy. The selected fields will be highlighted in the F̲ields list. Release the mouse button and click the → button in the dialog box.

- If you want to copy non-adjacent field names to the Sort O̲rder list, click on the first field, then hold down the Ctrl key while clicking the remaining fields. When you've highlighted all the fields you want to copy, click the → button.

▶ ▶**TIP**

You can press Alt+A, instead of clicking the → button, to add selected fields to the list.

The fields are added to the Sort O̲rder list in whatever order you choose them. Figure 8.4 shows an example in which Last Name is the primary sort key, First Name is the second sort key, and MI is the third sort key.

▶ ▶**NOTE**

If you select a range of fields that extends over fields that can't be sorted, or over fields you've already added to the Sort O̲rder List, Paradox will ignore those fields.

Sorting Your Tables

Ch. 8

FIGURE 8.4 ►

Records will be sorted alphabetically by Last Name, by First Name within identical last names, and by Middle Initial within identical last and first names.

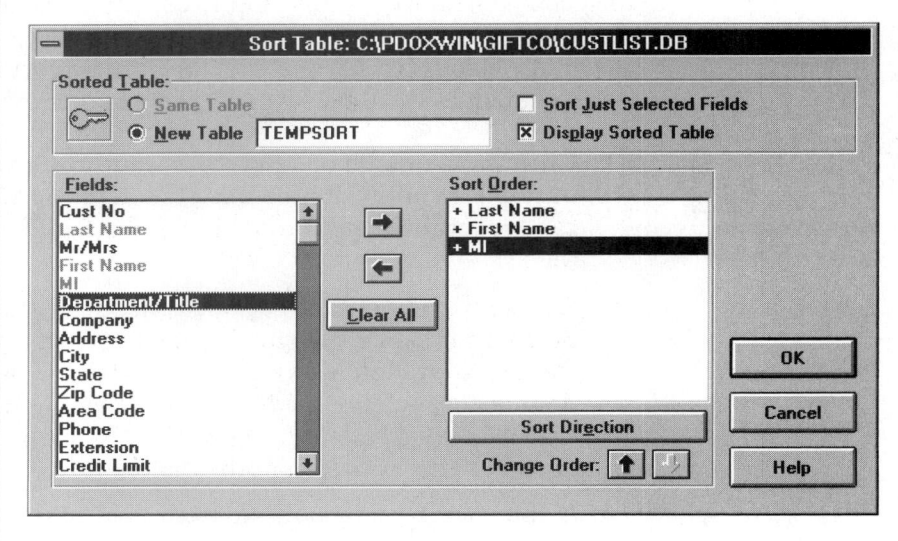

► Inserting and Removing Sort Keys

Remember that the order of field names in the Sort Order list determines the eventual sort order. For instance, in the list below, Start Date is the primary sort key (because it's listed first) and Last Name is the secondary sort key. Thus, the resulting sort would display records chronologically by Start Date (earliest date to latest date), with last names alphabetized for each date.

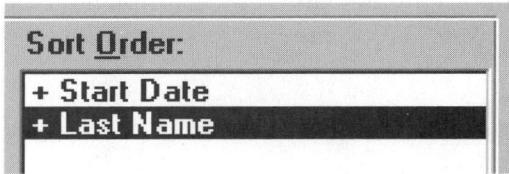

The field list below specifies a completely different sort order, even though it contains the same field names. Last Name is the primary sort key and Start Date is the secondary sort key. Thus, the sort will order records alphabetically by Last Name, then by Start Date within identical last names.

Once you've copied field names to the Sort Order list, you can use any of several techniques to rearrange the list.

- To move an existing field name in the Sort Order list to a new location, click the field name, then use the Change Order buttons (↑ and ↓) to move the selected field name up or down.

- To move adjacent fields in the Sort Order list, drag the mouse pointer through the field names you want to move. Then use the Change Order buttons (↑ and ↓) to move the selected field names up or down.

- To insert a new field name below an existing field name, select the field name (or names) that you want to insert from the Fields list. Then click the position in the Sort Order list that is above where you want the name(s) to appear. Finally, click the → button or press Alt+A to complete the job.

- To remove a single field name from the Sort Order list, click that field name, then click the ← button or press Alt+R.

- To start over from scratch and remove all the field names from the Sort Order list, click the Clear All button or press Alt+C.

Clear All

Whenever you add a field to the Sort Order list, Paradox dims that field name in the Fields list, to let you know that you can't add the field to the Sort Order list again (because it's already there). Conversely, whenever you remove a field from the Sort Order list, Paradox returns the field name to its normal appearance in the <u>F</u>ields list, to again let you know that you can add it to the Sort <u>O</u>rder list.

▶ ▶ **N O T E**

Since you cannot sort binary, bytes, formatted memo, graphic, logical, memo, and OLE fields, they'll always be dimmed and unavailable in the <u>F</u>ields list.

▶ Choosing Ascending or Descending Order

Any field in your Sort Order list can be sorted in either ascending or descending order. Ascending order is smallest to largest: *A* to *Z* for text, smallest number to largest number for numeric fields, earliest date to latest date for date fields. Descending order is the opposite: *Z* to *A*, largest number to smallest, latest date to earliest.

Initially, Paradox assumes you want to sort each field in ascending order. To change the sort direction, click the field name you want to reverse in the Sort Order list, then click the Sort Dir<u>e</u>ction button (shown below), or just double-click the field name in the Sort <u>O</u>rder list. The indicator next to the field name changes to the opposite direction, that is, from + (ascending order) to − (descending order).

Sort Dir<u>e</u>ction

Let's look at an example that uses both directions for sorting. We'll use the Credit Limit field from the CustList table as the primary sort key, in descending order; we'll make the Last Name and First Name fields the second and third sort keys, each in ascending order, as in Figure 8.5.

After you perform the sort (as described in a moment), and rearrange the columns in Table View to focus on these three fields, the resulting order would resemble Figure 8.6. Notice how the credit limits are in largest to smallest order, but within each credit limit, names are alphabetized in ascending order.

FIGURE 8.5 ▶

Here we've opted to make Credit Limit the primary sort key, in descending (largest to smallest) order. Within each credit limit, customer names will be alphabetized in ascending (A to Z) order.

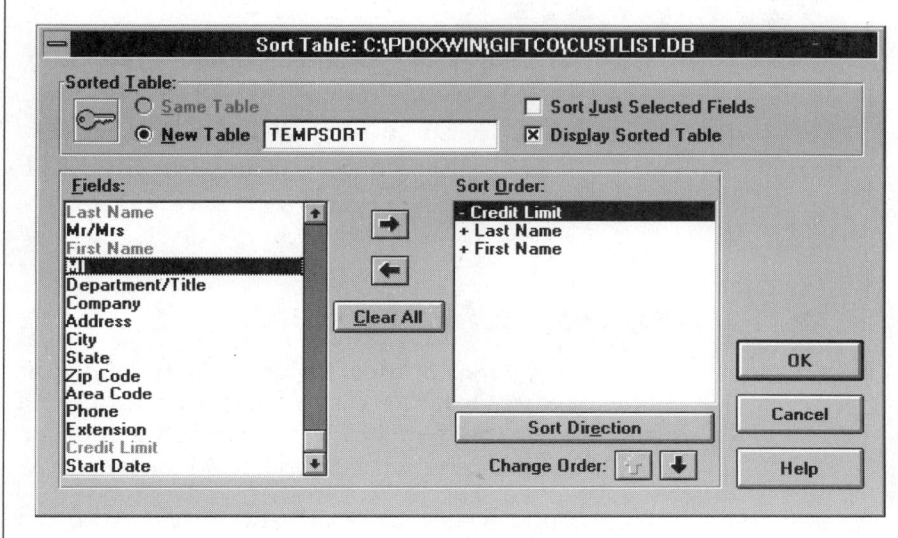

FIGURE 8.6 ▶

Results of the sort operation shown in Figure 8.5, where Credit Limits are sorted in descending order and names are sorted in ascending order within each Credit Limit

TEMPSORT	Credit Limit	Last Name	First Name	MI	Department/Title
1	$10,000.00	Cherub	Sky	R.	
2	$10,000.00	Eggo	Sandy		Owner
3	$10,000.00	Leventhal	Danielle	D.	
4	$10,000.00	Miller	Maria	N.	Accounts Receivable
5	$10,000.00	Mohr	Mary	M.	
6	$10,000.00	Smythe	Janet	L.	
7	$7,500.00	Gladstone	Tara Rose		Vice President
8	$7,500.00	Jones	Alma	R.	Account Executive
9	$7,500.00	Newell	John	J.	
10	$7,500.00	Olson	Elizabeth	A.	Vice President
11	$7,500.00	Ramirez	Rigoberto	R.	Author
12	$7,500.00	Watson	Frank	R.	Greenskeeper
13	$5,000.00	Adams	Andy	A.	President
14	$5,000.00	Dewey	Frank	R.	Senior Partner

Sorting Your Tables

▶ ▶

Ch.

8

►►**N O T E**

> **Paradox for Windows doesn't rearrange columns in Table View automatically. In Figure 8.6, we dragged the Credit Limit field to the left edge of Table View and rotated other columns to the right edge after completing the sort.**

► *Sorting Just Selected Fields*

Normally, Paradox adds any unselected fields from the table to the end of your Sort Order list just before it sorts your table (though you don't actually see that happen). This is simply a convenience, to make those fields act as additional "tie breakers" for records with identical values.

If you don't want Paradox to add unselected fields to the Sort Order list automatically, click the Sort Just Selected Fields option in the Sort Table dialog box.

► *Performing the Sort*

When you've finished with the Sort Table dialog box and double-checked that any existing table specified in the New Table text box can safely be overwritten, click the OK button. If you've changed your mind about doing the sort, choose Cancel to return to the Desktop without sorting your table.

If you typed in the name of an existing table file when filling in the New Table text box, Paradox will display a warning before it begins the sort, asking if you want to overwrite the existing table. If you answer Yes to the prompt, Paradox will overwrite any existing information in that table with sorted data. Be absolutely certain that you want to overwrite the specified table file before performing the sort.

TIP

Your best bet might be to *always* give the file name *Tempsort* to your temporary sort order tables, and use that file name only for such tables. That way, you need never worry about inadvertently overwriting an important table!

You might notice a brief delay as Paradox sorts the table. Of course the actual time required to complete the sort depends on the size of the table being sorted and the speed of your computer.

If you chose the Display Sorted Table option in the Sort Table dialog box, the sorted table will cover the original table. You can rearrange the windows by resizing them, dragging them, or choosing Tile or Cascade from the Window menu. In Figure 8.7, we chose Window ➤ Cascade to show the currently open windows; then we dragged the Tempsort table down and to the right. If you did not choose the Display Table option,

Sorting Your Tables

Ch. **8**

FIGURE 8.7 ▶

After rearranging the open Windows with Window ➤ Cascade *and then dragging the lower window down a bit, the CustList table appears in the background window in its primary key order by Cust No. The sorted table, named* **Tempsort***, appears in the foreground window sorted alphabetically by last name, first name, and middle initial, as shown in Figure 8.4. We rotated the Mr/Mrs field to the right so you could see the alphabetized names.*

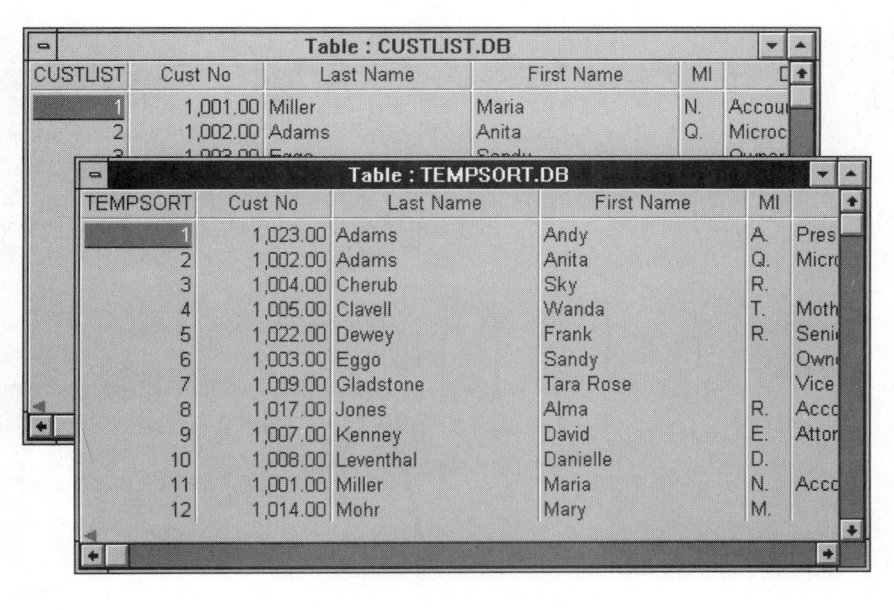

you'll need to open the sorted table (for example, by choosing File ➤ Open ➤ Table).

The sort order affects only the order of *records*, not the order of fields. For example, if you sort on the Zip Code field, you would still need to scroll over to the Zip Code field to see that the records have indeed been sorted. It's easy to rearrange the order of fields in Table View using techniques described in Chapter 7. That can make the new sort order more apparent on your screen.

Don't forget that when you sort records to a separate table (such as *Tempsort*), the resulting table is entirely separate from the original table. If you make any changes or additions to the sorted table, those changes will not be reflected in the original table. Therefore, you'd just be wasting time if you scrolled through the sorted copy of the table making changes and corrections!

 ▶▶**T I P**

You can always tell exactly which table you're viewing by taking a glance at the table name in the title bar or upper-left corner of Table View.

▶ *How the Sort Order Affects Form View*

If you switch to Form View while viewing the sorted table, you'll only see one record at a time, of course, and the order of the fields will be as defined in the table's structure. As you scroll through records using the Toolbar buttons or the Record menu options, the records will appear in the current sort order.

 ▶▶**N O T E**

To control the order of *fields* in a custom form, you must design the form accordingly, as explained in Chapters 10 and 11.

In practice, you'll probably want to use the sort order to print table data in some kind of formatted report. For example, you might print an alphabetized list of names and addresses, or you could print form letters and mailing labels after sorting records by zip code.

That's no problem, once you learn how to create formatted reports. We'll get to that topic in Chapter 12.

▶ *Closing the Temporary Sort Table*

To avoid the confusion of having multiple sorted and unsorted copies of the same table, it's best to close the sorted version of the table (*Tempsort* in our example) when you're done using the sorted records. To do so, make sure the sorted table is in the currently active window. Then double-click that window's Control-menu box (or press Ctrl+F4).

 ▶ ▶ **T I P**

> As an extra precaution, you can delete the temporary table when you're done with it, using **T**ools ➤ **U**tilities ➤ **D**elete or by right-clicking the table in the Project Viewer and choosing **D**elete. See Chapter 15.

Sorting Your Tables

▶ ▶

Ch.
8

▶ ▶ *Using Secondary Indexes to Sort Tables*

T**a**ble ➤ **S**ort is just one way to sort a table. Although it's a quick and straightforward way to get the job done, T**a**ble ➤ **S**ort does have certain disadvantages:

- Sorting a huge table can be quite time-consuming.
- If the table is huge (say, a couple of megabytes), and you sort to a separate table (which is required if the table has a primary key), the sorted copy of the table will gobble up *another* couple of megabytes.
- When you sort to a different table, you might inadvertently make changes, corrections, or additions to the sorted copy which won't be recorded in the original table.

One way around all these disadvantages is to use a secondary index file (usually called a *secondary index*). The secondary index defines an alternate order for viewing the table's records; however, unlike the sort operation discussed previously, the secondary index does not change the original location of records.

Secondary indexes offer several advantages over sorting. They allow you to view records in sorted order with little delay, require only a small amount of extra disk space to store the index file, and can speed up query operations (see Chapter 9). What's more, any changes made to the table while viewing it through the secondary index affect the *original* table, not just some expendable copy. So you see, you really can sort your table and change it too.

There is one small catch, however: You can only define a secondary index for a table after you've defined a primary index. In other words, you can only define a secondary index for a table that has one or more fields marked with an asterisk (*) in the Key column of the table's structure (as discussed in Chapter 4).

▶ Understanding How Indexes Work

When you use either a primary or secondary index to view a table, Paradox stores a copy of the index (or as much of it as it can fit) in memory (RAM). That index is organized much like the index at the back of a book—sorted into alphabetical (or some other) order. The position of each record in the table is included in the index in much the same way that the index at the back of a book includes page numbers indicating where topics are located.

 ▶ ▶ **N O T E**

A primary index file contains field values and record numbers for a table's primary key. A *secondary index* file contains field values and record numbers of *non-key* fields. Primary and secondary indexes are always sorted according to the values in the indexed fields.

Suppose you define an index that's based on the Last Name and First Name fields in a table. When you open the table and ask to find the record for John Smith, Paradox looks up the name John Smith in the index in memory. This takes only a fraction of a second, because Paradox doesn't need to use the disk drive to read through the index.

When Paradox finds John Smith in the index, it will determine that John Smith is in the 495th record. It can then "skip over" the first 494 records when it accesses the disk, thereby saving a considerable amount of time.

Without help from an index, Paradox must read through each record of the table on disk, until it happens to find the one it's looking for. For instance, if you ask Paradox to find the record for John Smith, and John Smith is the 495th record in the table, Paradox will read through the first 494 records, until it finds John Smith. This is like trying to find information in a book by flipping through all the pages until you stumble upon the topic you're looking for.

All this terminology can be confusing. It helps to remember that the term *primary key* refers *specifically* to the field or fields marked with an asterisk (*) in the Key column of the table's structure. The *primary index* is the file that stores primary key values and associated record numbers. The *secondary index* is the file containing non-key values (that is, values of fields that are not primary keys) and associated record numbers. The terms *primary sort key* and *secondary sort key* simply refer to the fields that define the main order and tie-breaker of records in a sort operation.

▶ Preparing for Secondary Indexes

A table can have more than one secondary index. You define secondary indexes in the table's structure. Here's how to get started:

1. To avoid confusion, close all open windows on the Desktop by choosing <u>W</u>indow ➤ Close <u>A</u>ll.

2. Choose <u>T</u>ools ➤ <u>U</u>tilities ➤ Res<u>t</u>ructure, highlight the table that you want to define a secondary index for, and choose OK. You'll be taken to the Restructure Table dialog box for that table.

Sorting Your Tables

Ch.
8

NOTE

You can also define secondary indexes when creating a table via the Create Table dialog box (File ➤ New ➤ Table). However, you must define the primary index before you can define any secondary indexes.

3. Check to make sure that you've already defined a primary key for the table. That is, at least one field must have an asterisk in the Key column. (If not, set up a primary key now, or choose Cancel because you won't be able to proceed very far.)

WARNING

If the table you're restructuring doesn't have a primary key, don't just randomly pick one out of a hat. Instead, make sure you understand the many important roles of the primary index (Chapter 4) as well as the effects of assigning a primary key to a table that already contains data (Chapter 15).

4. Click the drop-down list button under Table Properties and choose *Secondary Indexes*.

In Figure 8.8, we're ready to define secondary indexes for the sample CustList table. Notice that *Secondary Indexes* appears under Table Properties and that this table does indeed already have a primary key: the Cust No field at the top of the field roster.

▶ *Defining the Secondary Indexes*

Here's how to start defining your secondary indexes.

1. Click the Define button. You'll be taken to the Define Secondary Index dialog box.

FIGURE 8.8 ▶

Getting ready to define secondary indexes for the sample CustList table, which already has a primary key based on the Cust No field

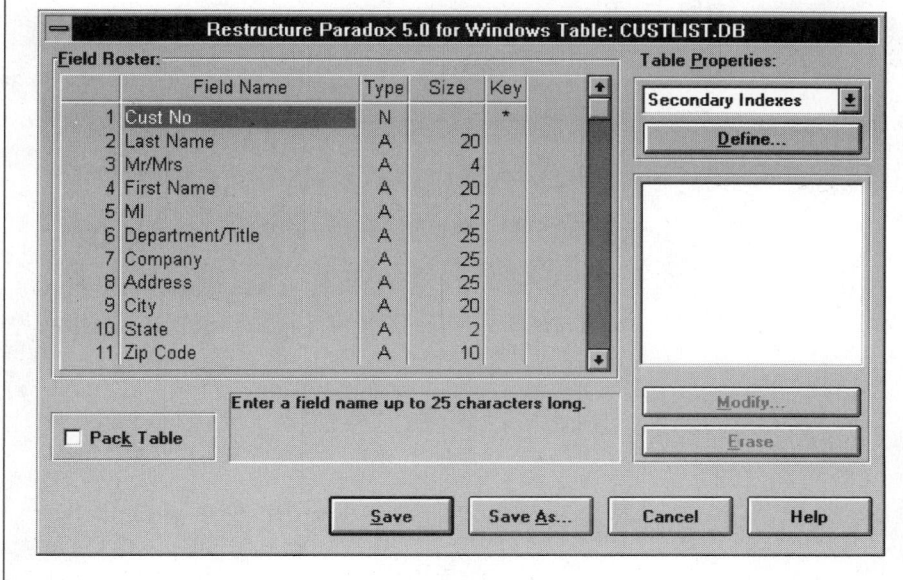

2. Use the techniques described earlier in this chapter to copy a field (or fields) from the Fields list to the Indexed Fields list. For example, in Figure 8.9 we copied the Last Name, First Name, and MI fields (in that order) to the Indexed Fields list.

As with any sort order you define, the first field in the Indexed Field list defines the primary sort key, the next field defines the secondary sort key, and so forth. Thus, the field order in Figure 8.9 will sort records by last name, then by first name, then by middle initial within identical last names.

Notice that this dialog box contains the Add Field (→) and Remove Field (←) buttons, the Change Order ↑ and ↓ buttons for rearranging field names, and a Clear All button. These all work exactly as they do in the Sort Table dialog box described earlier. You also have a few additional choices, under Index Options, which we'll describe next.

FIGURE 8.9 ▸

Here we've copied the Last Name, First Name, and MI fields from the Fields list to the Indexed Fields list.

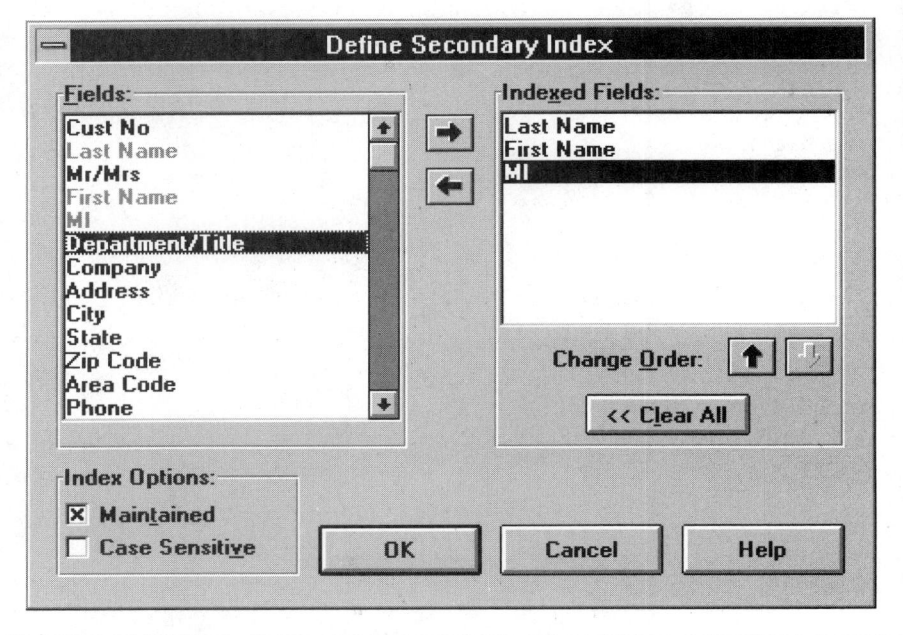

▸▸ **N O T E**

> A *composite* secondary index consists of two or more fields. Each table can have up to 16 composite secondary indexes and as many single-field secondary indexes as there are fields in a table.

About the Maintained Option

The Maintained option determines how Paradox manages the secondary index behind the scenes. If you select (check) this option, Paradox will update the secondary index as you add, change, and delete records in the table. This puts a little overhead on the general editing operations, which in turn can slow them down a tad. However, you probably won't notice the slowdown.

If you deselect the Maintained option, Paradox will update the secondary index only when it's needed during a sort operation or query, or when linking tables via secondary indexes. This puts the slight overhead onto those operations, rather than in your general editing operations.

Chances are, you'll be less likely to notice any slowdown if you check the Maintained option. You can always change your mind later and deselect the option to put the overhead on other operations.

About the Case-sensitive Option

The Case-sensitive option determines whether Paradox distinguishes between upper- and lowercase letters. If you select this option, uppercase letters will take precedence over lowercase letters in the sort order. If you *deselect* this option, making the sort *case-insensitive*, upper- and lowercase letters will be considered the same. Figure 8.10 illustrates the difference between case-sensitive and case-insensitive sort orders.

FIGURE 8.10

A case-sensitive sort places words beginning with lowercase letters after words beginning with uppercase letters. A case-insensitive sort ignores upper and lowercase distinctions.

Case-sensitive Sort Order	Case-insensitive Sort Order
Adams	Adams
Miller	d'Elgin
Zabriski	Miller
d'Elgin	Zabriski

T I P

Checking Case-sensitive makes the secondary index perform an ASCII sort; deselecting Case-sensitive forces a standard "dictionary" sort.

If you want to alphabetize records in the normal "dictionary" fashion, *deselect* the Case-sensitive option (this is the default setting). Notice that we've selected the Maintained option and deselected the Case-sensitive option in Figure 8.9.

Sorting Your Tables

Ch.
8

Saving the Secondary Index

When you've defined your sort fields and index options, follow these steps to save the secondary index:

1. Choose OK. If you've assigned more than one field to the secondary index, you'll see the Save Index As dialog box shown below.

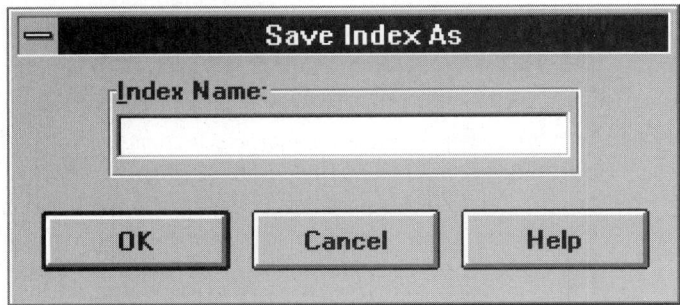

2. If you've included only one field in the secondary index, the name of that field automatically becomes the name of the secondary index, and you can skip the next two steps.

3. Type in a descriptive name for this index, such as **Alphabetical_By_Name.** The name can have up to 25 printable characters (spaces aren't allowed). However, it *cannot* be the same as a field in the table. For instance, you couldn't name this sample index *Department/Title*, since *Department/Title* is the name of a field in the table.

4. Choose OK.

You can repeat the steps above to create as many secondary indexes for the table as you need, up to the limits mentioned previously. For instance, Figure 8.11 shows another secondary index that can be used to sort records alphabetically into city order, and by zip code within cities.

Figure 8.12 shows yet another secondary index. This index orders records by area code and phone number—handy for telemarketing or working with customers within various area codes.

When you've finished defining secondary indexes for a table, just choose <u>S</u>ave from the Restructure Table dialog box to return to the Desktop.

FIGURE 8.11 ▶

A secondary index defined for sorting records alphabetically into city order, and by zip code within each city

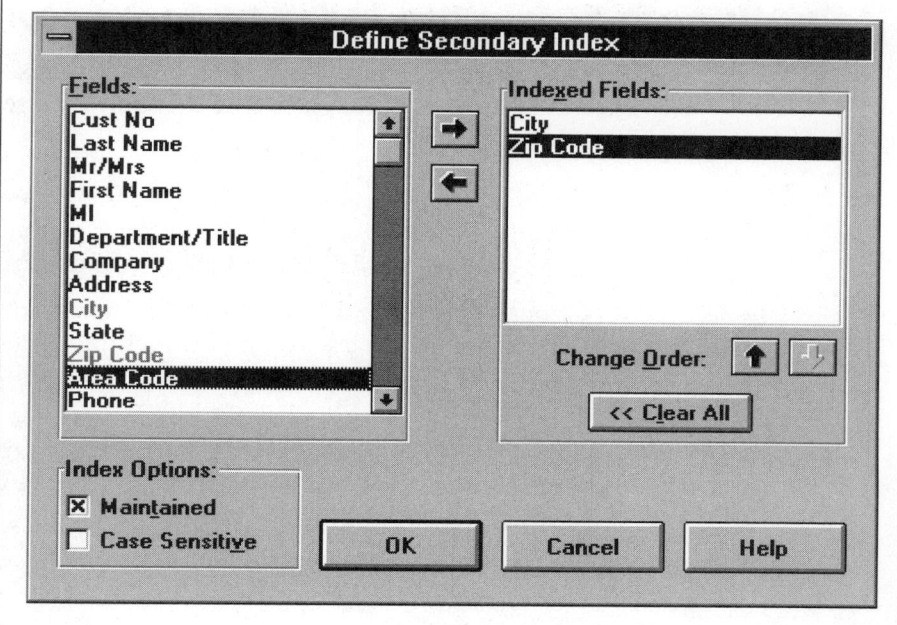

FIGURE 8.12 ▶

A secondary index used to sort records by area code and phone number

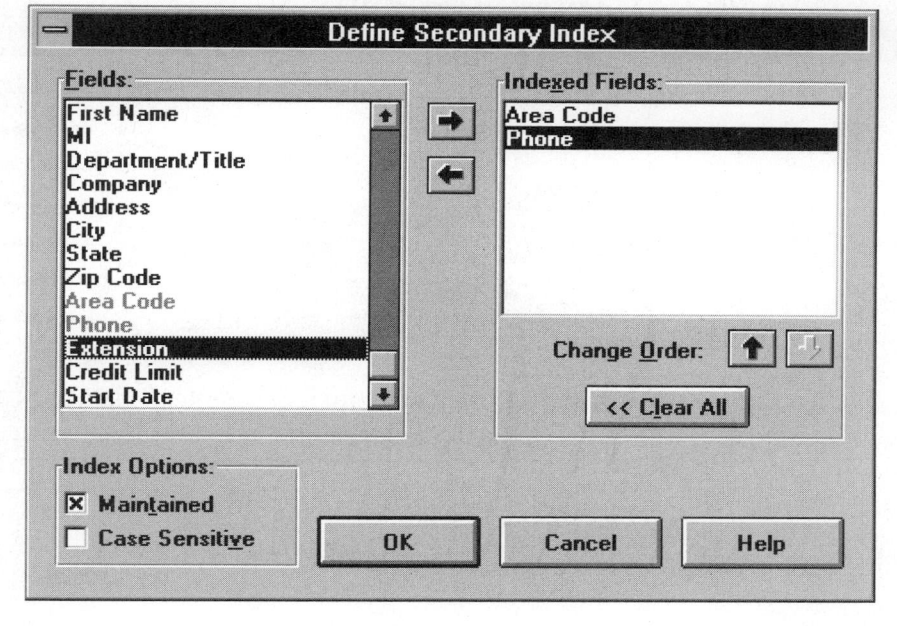

Sorting Your Tables

Ch. **8**

▶ *Using a Secondary Index to Sort Records*

Once you've defined one or more secondary indexes, you can use the "Filters" feature of Paradox to sort the table by a secondary index. Here's how:

1. If you haven't already done so, open the table you want to sort with the File ➤ Open ➤ Table options, or the Open Table button, or by double-clicking the table name in the Project Viewer.

2. Choose Table ➤ Filter, or click the Filter button in the Toolbar (shown at left). You'll see the Filter Tables dialog box, shown in Figure 8.13. The names of any secondary indexes you've created will appear below the primary index.

3. The Table List area shows the name of the table you're working with. If more than one table name appears in the Table List, click on the table name you want to sort.

FIGURE 8.13 ▶

Choosing Table ➤ Filter lets you choose a secondary index to sort records.

Filter Tables
Table List: CUSTLIST.DB
☒ **Order By:**
*Cust No (Primary, Case Sens
Alphabetical_by_Name
Area_Code_and_Phone
City_and_Zip
dBase Index File:
Range
Filters on Fields:
Cust No *
Last Name
Mr/Mrs
First Name
MI
Department/Title
Company
Address
City
State
OK   Cancel   Help

▶ ▶ N O T E

> Additional options in the Filter Tables dialog box let you select which records to display in the table. We'll talk about this aspect of filters under "Using a Filter to Isolate Data" in Chapter 9. If you're sorting a form or report (via For**m** ➤ **F**ilter or **R**eport ➤ **F**ilter), the **T**able List will show all the tables in the data model. Chapter 5 explains data models. You'll learn more about forms, reports, and data models in Part 3.

4. Make sure the **O**rder By box is selected (checked).

5. Choose an index by clicking its name. (The primary key for the table is marked with an asterisk. Any secondary indexes you created are listed below that.)

6. Choose OK to return to Table View.

Records will appear instantly, sorted in the order specified by the secondary index you chose. Of course, the *fields* in Table View will be in their original order, so you may need to scroll to another field or rearrange the columns to detect the sort order. In Figure 8.14, for instance, we chose the sample *Alphabetical_by_Name* secondary index as the sort order, then dragged the Last Name, First Name, and MI columns to the left side of Table View. Clearly, the records are sorted by name.

The title bar of the window indicates that we're viewing records from the original CustList table, not a sorted copy of that table. Therefore, any additions, changes, or deletions you make in this Table View will be made in the original table. Also, if you print a Quick Report, the records on the printout will be in the sort order currently on your screen.

▶ ▶ N O T E

> When you view a table using a secondary index, the physical location of the records in the table does not change. When you sort a table, the physical location of records does change.

FIGURE 8.14 ▶

Records sorted into alphabetical order by name using the secondary index defined in Figure 8.9. The title bar shows you that the records are from the original table, not a sorted copy of the table.

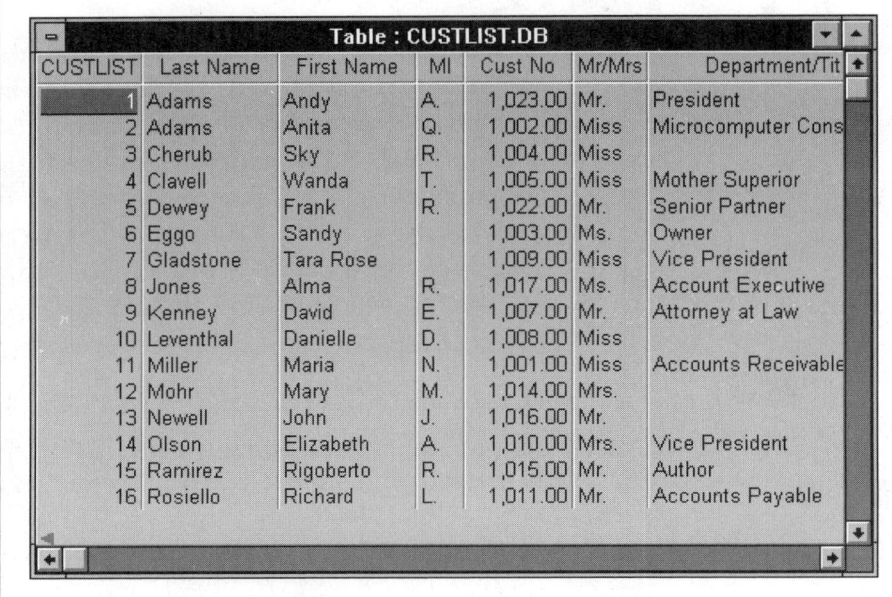

CUSTLIST	Last Name	First Name	MI	Cust No	Mr/Mrs	Department/Tit
1	Adams	Andy	A.	1,023.00	Mr.	President
2	Adams	Anita	Q.	1,002.00	Miss	Microcomputer Cons
3	Cherub	Sky	R.	1,004.00	Miss	
4	Clavell	Wanda	T.	1,005.00	Miss	Mother Superior
5	Dewey	Frank	R.	1,022.00	Mr.	Senior Partner
6	Eggo	Sandy		1,003.00	Ms.	Owner
7	Gladstone	Tara Rose		1,009.00	Miss	Vice President
8	Jones	Alma	R.	1,017.00	Ms.	Account Executive
9	Kenney	David	E.	1,007.00	Mr.	Attorney at Law
10	Leventhal	Danielle	D.	1,008.00	Miss	
11	Miller	Maria	N.	1,001.00	Miss	Accounts Receivable
12	Mohr	Mary	M.	1,014.00	Mrs.	
13	Newell	John	J.	1,016.00	Mr.	
14	Olson	Elizabeth	A.	1,010.00	Mrs.	Vice President
15	Ramirez	Rigoberto	R.	1,015.00	Mr.	Author
16	Rosiello	Richard	L.	1,011.00	Mr.	Accounts Payable

Table : CUSTLIST.DB

▶ Returning to the Original Sort Order

When you want to return to the original sort order, just repeat the steps above (that is, choose T<u>a</u>ble ➤ <u>F</u>ilter) to return to the Filter Tables dialog box. Then select the primary index (the one marked with an asterisk) and choose OK.

▶ Changing or Deleting a Secondary Index

To change a secondary index or delete it, follow the same basic steps you used to create the secondary index. That is, restructure the table and choose *Secondary Indexes* from the Table <u>P</u>roperties drop-down list. Then click the name of the secondary index you want to change or delete.

If you want to change the secondary index, click the <u>M</u>odify button. You'll be taken to the Define Secondary Index dialog box, where you can add, delete, or rearrange fields and change Index Options, as described previously. Choose OK to return to the Restructure Table dialog box after making your changes.

If you want to delete an index, click the name of the index you want to delete, then click the Erase button.

Finally, to save your changes and return to the Desktop, just click the Save button.

▶ ▶ **N O T E**

If you want to change the *name* of a composite secondary index (rather than its fields or Index Options), you must delete the secondary index, save the table structure, then create a new secondary index on the same fields with the name you want.

▶ *File Names for Indexes*

Any secondary index that you create for a table is actually stored in two files, each with the same name as the table, but with the extensions .xg*n* and .yg*n* where *n* is a number, starting at zero, that is assigned as you create the secondary index. For instance, the first secondary index you create for the CustList table is stored in the files *custlist.xg0* and *custlist.yg0*. The next index you create would be stored in files named *custlist.xg1* and *custlist.yg1*.

▶ ▶ **N O T E**

When copying a table to floppies or sending them by modem, be sure to include all index files. For instance, if you use DOS to copy the CustList files, a simple *copy custlist.** command, followed by the destination drive and directory, will do the trick.

▶▶ Still More Ways to Sort Tables

The Table ➤ Sort options are probably the easiest for sorting all the records in a table. However, Paradox for Windows offers other ways to sort tables, as summarized below.

Queries   Let you isolate specific records in a table and sort those records simultaneously into any order you wish (see Chapter 9).

Tools ➤ Utilities ➤ Sort   This is another way to reach the Sort Table dialog box. Choose Tools ➤ Utilities ➤ Sort, and then choose the table you want to sort.

Inspecting a Table in the Project Viewer   Offers yet another way to reach the Sort Table dialog box. Open the Project Viewer by clicking the Project Viewer button in the Toolbar, or choosing Tools ➤ Project Viewer. If necessary, select your working directory, then click the Tables icon in the Project Viewer. Now just inspect (right-click) the table name you want to sort and choose Sort from the menu that appears (see Chapters 3 and 15).

In this chapter we've covered techniques you can use to sort the records in a table. In the next chapter, we'll talk about ways to query, or search, your table to isolate just the records and fields you want.

▶ ▶ CHAPTER **9**

Querying
Your Tables

———

►► *F*AST *T*RACK

▶ **To save a query in a file for later use**   **444**

choose File ➤ Save or File ➤ Save As, or click the Yes
button in the dialog box that appears when you close the
Query window. To reuse a saved query, choose File ➤
Open ➤ Query, or click the Open Query button in the
Toolbar. Or open the Project Viewer window and click the
Query icon, then select the file name of the query you
want. Make any necessary changes, then run the query.

▶ **To change the sort order of records, or to create a
"live" or "read only" view of the query results**   **450**

click the Answer Table Properties button in the Toolbar, or
choose Properties ➤ Answer Options in the Query window.

▶ **To change the sort order of records in the Answer table**   **456**

click the Sort Answer Table button in the Toolbar, or
choose Properties ➤ Answer Sort in the Query window.

▶ **To update a table globally**   **459**

use the CHANGETO or DELETE operator.

▶ **To perform a "filter" query with "live" data**   **467**

open the table and choose Table ➤ Filter or click the Filter
button in the Toolbar. If you want to sort the results,
double-click an index name. If you want to limit the results
to certain values or a range of values, indicate the values
(filter criteria) you want and choose OK. To define a filter
for a single field, inspect the field in Table View or Form
View, choose Filter, type the filter criteria you want, and
choose OK.

▶ ▶ **W**ith small tables, it's easy to see your data at a glance and to make changes record by record. But when you're working with large tables, or with many related tables, you need something more powerful. That's where queries come in.

With a query, you can easily pull out records that meet some criterion or criteria. For example, you might want to view only New York residents, or people in California with credit limits over $5000. Perhaps you want to send a form letter to people whose starting date was one year ago, or maybe you just want to look up a particular address.

 ▶ ▶ **T I P**

For some hands-on practice using queries, take the "Creating A Query" lesson from the "Queries, Forms, And Reports" Coaches. See Chapter 3 for more about Coaches.

You can also use queries to perform basic calculations, delete certain types of records, and much more. Paradox for Windows offers a technique known as *query by example*, or QBE, that lets you search for information and ask questions about tables. Using query by example is a four- or five-step process in which you...

- Choose the object you want to query. (This can be one or more tables, another query, a saved data model, or a data model for a form or report.)

- Specify the fields you want to view in the results of your query by using checkmarks.

- Enter *query criteria* to specify any records you want to include in the results of the query.

- Specify any calculations you want to perform.

- Perform, or *run*, the query.

The results of queries that request information usually are placed in a new table named *Answer* (though you can change this, as you'll learn later). The Answer table will contain only the fields and records you've requested.

TIP

> **Filters provide a simple technique for isolating records in "live" data. See "Using a Filter to Isolate Data," near the end of this chapter, for more information.**

You can also run queries that let you find records in a table, delete records from a table, change values in fields, and insert new records in a table.

▶▶ *Querying a Table*

You define and run your queries in the *Query* window. To open the Query window, follow these simple steps:

1. Use any of the following methods to get started:

- Choose File ➤ New ➤ Query.
- If the Desktop is empty or contains the Project Viewer only, inspect (right-click) the Open Query button in the Toolbar (shown at left) and choose New.
- If the Project Viewer window is open, inspect (right-click) the Queries icon and choose New.

2. A Select File dialog box will appear, listing all the tables in the current working directory.

Querying Your Tables

Ch.

9

▶ ▶ **N O T E**

> **In this chapter, we'll assume you're creating single-table queries. Chapter 16 will cover multitable queries, queries that are based on data models, and other advanced techniques that involve complex groupings and calculations.**

3. Choose the object you want to query as follows:

- To query one table, highlight its name in the list below the File Name text box (or just type the name of the table into the File Name text box).

- To query multiple tables, click the name of the first table you want in the list, then hold down the Ctrl key and click additional table names.

- To base the query on another query or on the data model for a form or report, click the File Type drop-down list, then click <Queries> or <Forms> or <Reports>, as appropriate. In the list that appears below the File Name box, click the file name of the query, form, or report you want.

- To create a data model for the query, or to base the query on a saved data model, click the Data Model button, and fill in the Data Model dialog box, as explained in Chapter 16.

4. When you're finished choosing the object to query, choose OK.

A new Query window appears on the screen, partially overlapping any other windows. The table name and field names from the table you'll be querying appear across the top of the window. These make up the *query table*. You'll also notice that the menu bar includes a Query command and that the Toolbar has changed, as shown in Figure 9.1.

You can size and move the Query window as you would any other. For instance, in Figure 9.1 we moved the Query window to just below the Toolbar and reduced its height.

FIGURE 9.1 ▶

After you create a new query and choose a table, the field names for that table appear across the top of the query table, and a new menu bar and Toolbar appear.

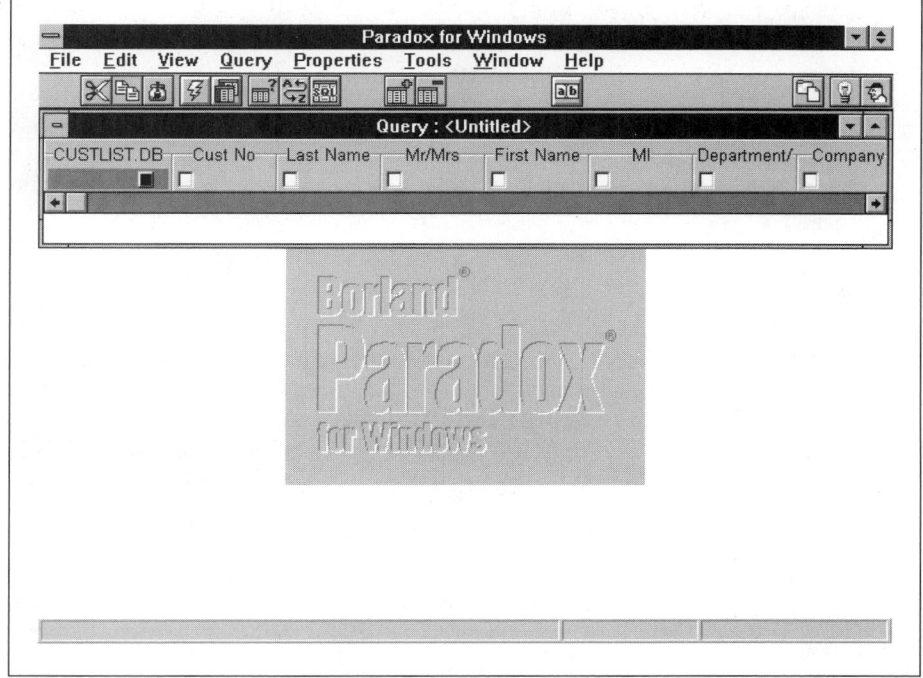

You can also move, rotate, widen, and narrow the columns in the query table using the same techniques as in Table View, as discussed in Chapter 7. We've done this throughout the chapter so the figures will give you a better look at our query designs.

 ▶ ▶**N O T E**

> **The query table has the same fields in the same order as the table it represents. However, the query table doesn't reflect any changes to the table's properties (such as changed column order).**

▶ *Selecting Fields to View*

Now that you've opened the Query window, the next step is to tell Paradox which fields you want to see in the query results. Notice the empty check boxes beneath the table name and each field name in Figure 9.1. Only fields that contain a checkmark will appear in the results of the query. Initially, all the check boxes are empty, so you need to choose the fields you want to see.

Paradox provides several ways to check fields, and several types of checkmarks. If you want to use your mouse, proceed as follows:

1. Move the mouse pointer to the check box of the field you want to show in the query results. (Use the horizontal scroll bar to scroll to field names outside the window.)

2. Hold down the mouse button to view your options, as shown below.

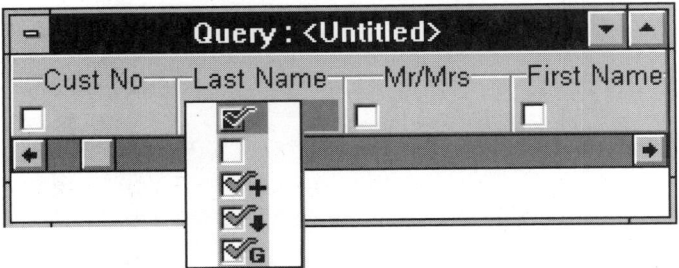

3. With the mouse button depressed, drag the highlight to the checkmark you want, then release the mouse button. As a shortcut, you can choose a checkmark by clicking an empty check box. To "uncheck" a checked field, click the check box again or choose the empty check box from the options shown.

  **TIP**

Normally a plain checkmark appears when you click an empty check box. But if you're planning to create many "live" queries (as discussed later), you might prefer to set the default checkmark to a check plus. To change the default checkmark, click the Query window and choose <u>P</u>roperties ► Query Options; then choose either Check <u>P</u>lus or <u>C</u>heck and choose OK. See Chapter 16 for more on query options.

If you prefer to use the keyboard, follow these steps:

1. Use the Tab (or →) and Shift+Tab (or ←) keys to scroll to a field name.

2. Press F6 to insert the default checkmark (usually a plain check). Or, press Shift+F6 repeatedly until the checkmark you want (or the empty check box) appears in the field.

Checking All the Fields

You can use the methods described above to check fields one at a time. If you want to check all the fields in the table, use the check box just below the table name. Choosing an option from that check box adds the selected checkmark to all the fields in the table.

► ►**T I P**

> To "uncheck" all the fields in the Query window, choose the blank check box under the table name.

We'll look at each type of checkmark next.

Using Check Plus

The check plus displays all the records for a field, even if the records have duplicate values. For example, if you used the check plus in the State field of the CustList table, then ran the query, the results would resemble Figure 9.2. Notice that CA appears several times in the Answer table's State field, and that the Answer table contains 25 records (because the CustList table in this example contains 25 records).

► ►**N O T E**

> Throughout this chapter, we've rearranged windows, query table columns, and query results to show the queries and results more clearly, and to make the book look more attractive.

FIGURE 9.2 ▶

The check plus displays all the records in a field, even if the records have duplicate values. Here we used check plus to display all the states in the sample CustList table.

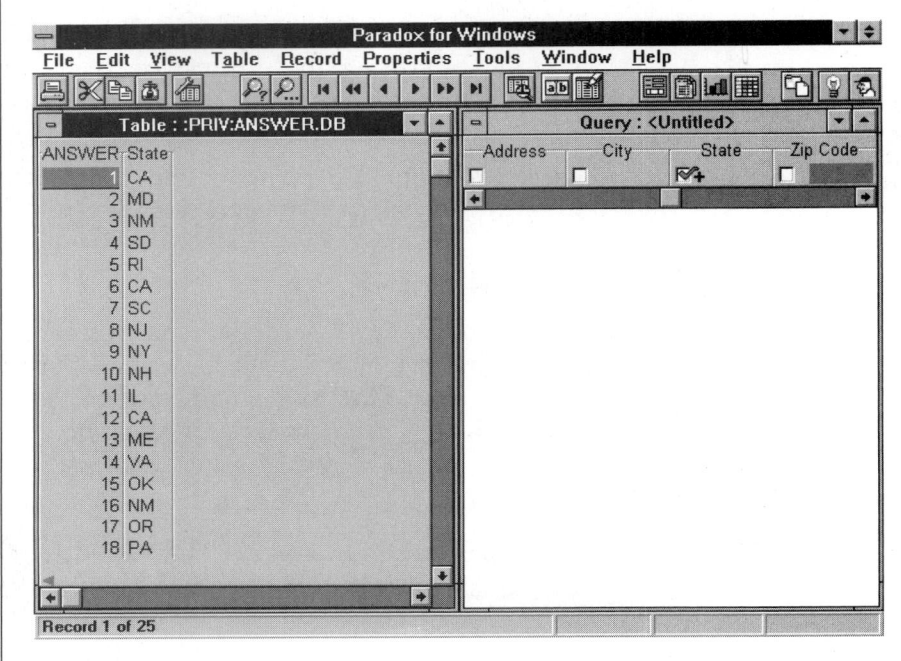

Check plus is a very common checkmark to use because it displays all records and can be used to create "live answer" tables. You'll see some examples a little later in this chapter.

Using the Plain Checkmark

The plain checkmark displays only unique values in a field. It displays them in ascending (*A* to *Z*) sorted order, so it's useful for viewing summary information.

For example, if you were to check only the State field in the query for the CustList table, the results would resemble the Answer table shown in Figure 9.3. Each state is listed only once; that is, no duplicate states appear. Also, the status bar shows 17 records in the Answer table, which corresponds to the 17 unique states in the table.

FIGURE 9.3

Placing a plain check in the State field sorts the states in ascending order, listing each state only once. Compare this result with Figure 9.2.

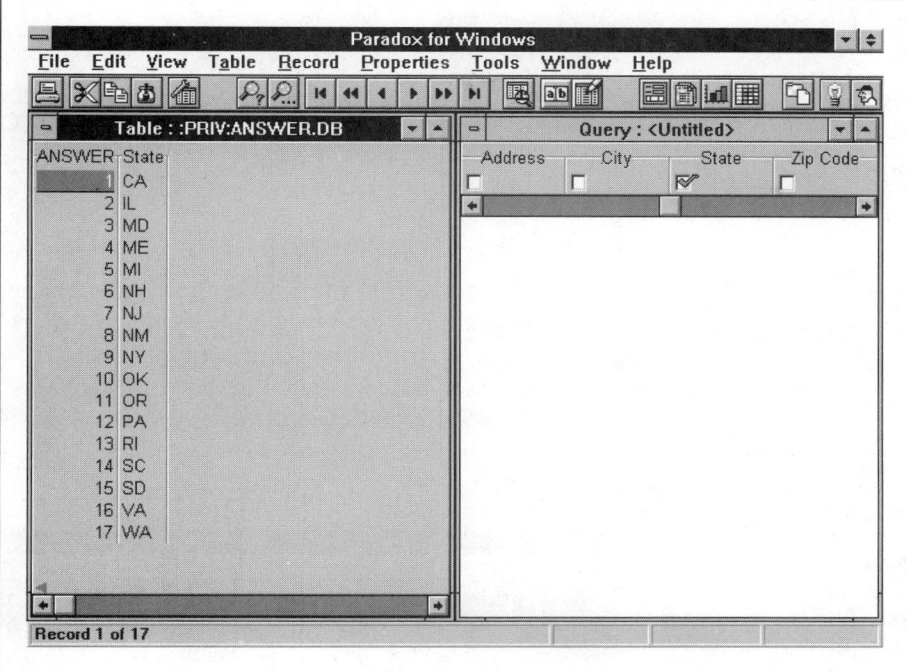

N O T E

When you check multiple fields in the query table, the left-most column in the Answer table (not the query table) determines the primary sort order. We'll describe ways to control sort order under "Controlling the Answer Table's Appearance," later in this chapter.

With the plain checkmark, you can quickly see which states are in the CustList table, in alphabetical order, without having to wade through duplicate state names.

> ▶▶**WARNING**
>
> **When you use a plain checkmark in several fields, only records that have identical values in *all* the checked fields are considered duplicates.**

Using Check Descending

The check descending mark is similar to the plain checkmark, except that it displays records in descending sort order, rather than ascending order. That is, it displays only unique values, and lists them in largest-to-smallest (or *Z* to *A*) order. Figure 9.4 illustrates the results of a query that uses check descending in the State field.

FIGURE 9.4

Placing a check descending mark in the State field sorts the states in descending order and, like the plain checkmark, lists each state only once.

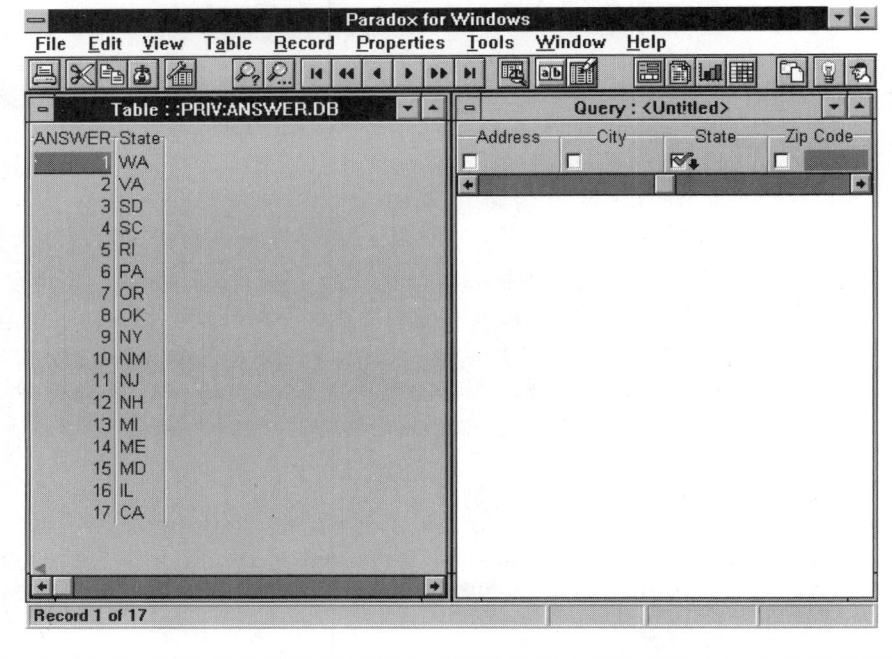

▶ *Running the Query*

 To run a query, just click the Run Query button (shown at left) in the Query window's Toolbar, or choose <u>V</u>iew ➤ <u>R</u>un Query, or press F8. After a brief delay, the requested fields appear in a table named *Answer*. Keep in mind that the Answer table contains *copies* of records from the original table.

 ▶▶ **N O T E**

> The <u>P</u>roperties ➤ Answer Opt<u>i</u>ons command in the Query window lets you control where the query results are sent. See "Changing the Answer Table's Name" and "Querying Live Data," later in the chapter for more details.

When the Answer table appears, the menu and Toolbar switch to those for Table View, so you can use those commands and buttons and treat the Answer table as you would any other table. When you click the Query window or close the Answer table, the menu and Toolbar switch back to those used to design queries.

▶ *If Your Query Fails*

Before we go any further into queries, let's talk about how to get out of a jam if you create a query that Paradox cannot understand. If a query fails because you didn't specify it correctly, you'll see an error message similar to the example shown in Figure 9.5.

After reading the error message, choose the OK button to return to the Query window. There you can make any changes or corrections necessary to make the query run correctly.

 ▶▶ **T I P**

> One of the most common causes of errors in a query is simply forgetting to check any fields to display before running the query!

Querying Your Tables

Ch. 9

FIGURE 9.5 ▶

If the query cannot run for some reason, an error message appears. To return to the Query window, choose OK.

Error

Attempted to prepare an empty query.

[OK]   [Help]

▶▶ *Using the Answer Table*

The Answer table that appears after you run a query contains only a *copy* of records from the table used to set up the query. Here's a quick overview of techniques you can use with the Answer table should you decide to experiment with some queries:

- To move the Answer table so you can see the underlying query, drag the Answer table's title bar to another location. Or, use the Tile and Cascade options on the Window menu, as we've done to create many of this chapter's illustrations.

- You can manipulate the Answer table the same way you would manipulate any Table View, as described in Chapter 7.

 ▶▶ T I P

Paradox will remember the Answer table's size and position on the screen until you close the Answer table.

- If you use the plain checkmark or check descending to display multiple fields, the Answer table will list records sorted by the leftmost field. However, Paradox does not sort records when you use check plus. You can sort the Answer table using the Table ➤ Sort options discussed in Chapter 8.

- You can also "pre-design" the Answer table's appearance and sort order using techniques described under "Controlling the Answer Table's Appearance," later in this chapter.

- To print the Answer table, click the Quick Report button or Print button in the Toolbar (shown at left), or choose File ➤ Print (see Chapter 7).

- To view or print a formatted report using data from the Answer table, choose File ➤ Open ➤ Report and highlight the name of the report format you want to use. Then choose Change Table, specify *answer.db* in the private directory (typically *:priv:answer.db*), and click OK twice. You'll learn more about this in Chapter 12.

- You can move or copy records in the Answer table to another table using options discussed in Chapter 15.

- To return to the Query window, just click on the Query window. You can also choose Window from the menu bar and then click the Query option near the bottom of the menu that appears. Or, press Ctrl+F6 until you return to the Query window.

- To close the Answer table, double-click its Control-menu box, or click the Control-menu box and choose Close, or click on the Answer table window and press Ctrl+F4.

- Use the same methods to close the Query window. If you don't plan to reuse the query in the future, choose No when asked about saving it.

► ► **WARNING**

> If you close the Query window and then create a new query that also sends results to the Answer table, be sure to close the Answer table before running your new query. Otherwise, you may receive a "Table is already in use" message when you run the query. If the error message appears, just choose OK to clear the message box, then close the Answer table and run the query again.

Although Answer has much in common with ordinary tables, it does have two features that set it apart. First, Answer is a temporary table

Querying Your Tables

Ch. 9

that is overwritten each time you run a query. If you want to prevent the results of a query from being lost the next time you run a query, you'll need to rename the Answer table before you run the query (as explained later in this chapter), or after running the query (see Chapter 15).

► ►**WARNING**

Never replace an existing table with the Answer table, unless you're sure you don't want the table that will be replaced.

The second thing that makes the Answer table different from other tables is that it is stored in a private directory reserved for temporary objects. However, you'll still be able to open and use *Answer* as though it were in your working directory.

Perhaps the most important thing to remember when viewing an Answer table is that it contains only a *copy* of data from the original table. If you notice a mistake while viewing the Answer table, *don't make the correction in the Answer table because the correction won't appear in the original table.* To make a correction or change to the data, open the original table (File ➤ Open ➤ Table) and make your changes there.

► ►**TIP**

If you run queries that are specifically meant to help you find mistakes in your data, you might prefer to use the "live table" (rather than the Answer table) for your query results. This way, any corrections you make *will* appear in the original table. See "Querying Live Data," later in the chapter.

►► Using Queries to Select Specific Records

So far, you've learned how to start a query, select *fields* to view in the query results, and then run the query. You can also specify certain *records* to view in a query. For example, you may want to see names and addresses of residents in a specific state or zip code area. Or, you might want to see sales transactions for a particular product or range of dates. To search for specific records, you enter a *query criterion* that defines those records.

▶ Entering Query Criteria

Entering a query criterion into a query table field is a lot like entering data into a Table View field. First, move to the field you want to search (use the scroll bars, mouse, arrow keys, or Tab and Shift+Tab keys), then just type your query criterion. You can type criteria into as many fields as you wish and make changes and corrections the same way you change data stored in fields in a table. When you're ready to carry out the query, just press F8 or click the Run Query button.

As you'll see in the sections that follow, there's almost no limit to the types of records you can ask for in a query.

▶▶ Searching for Exact Values

If you want to search for an exact value in a field, simply type that value into the appropriate field. For example, Figure 9.6 shows the Query window with **CA** typed into the State field of the query table and several fields selected with checkmarks. The Answer table below the Query window, which appears after choosing Run Query, shows only records that have CA in the State field.

▶ ▶ N O T E

> See "Searching for Punctuation Marks and Other Symbols," later in this chapter, for limitations on including commas, periods, and other special symbols in your query criteria.

Even though we used plain checkmarks in the query table, CA appears several times in the Answer table. That's because only records that have identical values in *all* the checked fields are considered duplicates.

FIGURE 9.6 ►

To display only records that have CA in the State field, type CA in the State field of the query table, then choose Run Query.

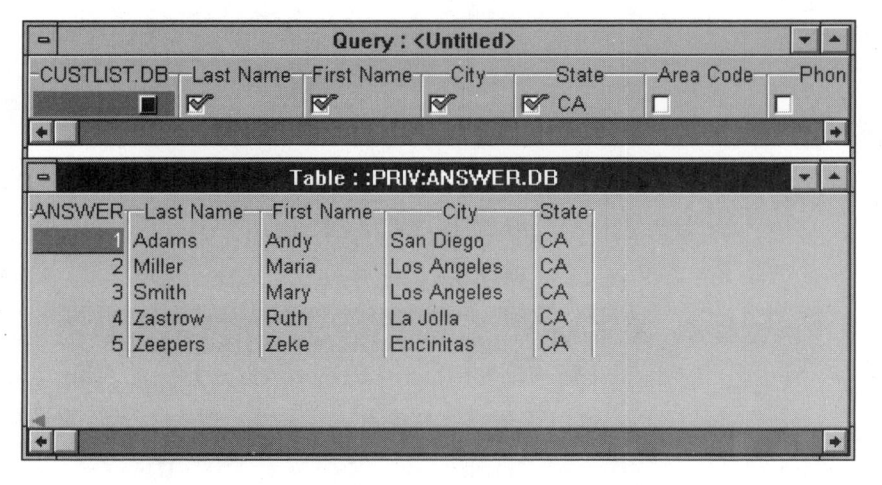

Here you can see that no two records in the Answer table are exactly the same.

Be aware that an exact match requires a match that is literally exact, including the same spacing, upper- and lowercase letters, and length. For example, had we placed *ca* rather than *CA* in the State field of the query table before performing the search, the Answer table would have been empty. Why? Because all the two-letter abbreviations in the State field are uppercase, not lowercase.

Similarly, a search for Smith in the Last Name field would find *only* Smith exactly—not SMITH, smith, Smithsonian, Smith & Wesson, Blacksmith, or any other name with "Smith" embedded in it. However, you *can* search for inexact matches, as we'll discuss later in the chapter.

►► *Searching for a Range of Values*

Often, you'll want to view records in which some value is less than or greater than some other value. Perhaps you want to view records for people who have credit limits of $5000 or more, or for people with start dates on or before a specific date. You can use the comparison operators listed below to perform such queries.

Operator	Meaning
=	Equal to
<	Less than
>	Greater than
<=	Less than or equal to
>=	Greater than or equal to

W A R N I N G

Do not use commas to separate thousands in the query table. As you'll see, the comma plays a special role in queries.

Figure 9.7 shows a sample query that uses the >= operator to display records that have a value of $7500.00 or more in the Credit Limit field. The Answer table displays the appropriate records when you run the query.

FIGURE 9.7

Query and resulting Answer table displaying records with a value of $7500.00 or more in the Credit Limit field

ANSWER	Last Name	First Name	City	State	Credit Limit
1	Cherub	Sky	Jefferson	SD	$10,000.00
2	Eggo	Sandy	Roswell	NM	$10,000.00
3	Gladstone	Tara Rose	New York	NY	$7,500.00
4	Jones	Alma	Ashland	OR	$7,500.00
5	Leventhal	Danielle	Newark	NJ	$10,000.00
6	Miller	Maria	Los Angeles	CA	$10,000.00
7	Mohr	Mary	Herndon	VA	$10,000.00
8	Newell	John	Bernalillo	NM	$7,500.00
9	Olson	Elizabeth	Marlow	NH	$7,500.00
10	Ramirez	Rigoberto	Wyandotte	OK	$7,500.00
11	Smythe	Janet	Seattle	WA	$10,000.00
12	Watson	Frank	Bangor	ME	$7,500.00

(Query : <Untitled> — CUSTLIST.DB, Last Name, First Name, City, State, Credit Limit >=7500)

Querying Your Tables

Ch.
9

When setting up the query in Figure 9.7, we initially forgot to remove the CA criterion from the State field. When we ran the query, the results showed only our California customers with large credit limits. What happened? The answer was simple once we gathered our wits enough to delete that CA condition in the State field. When designing your own queries, make sure you erase any old query criteria that you don't want to use in the query you run next. You can change or delete a query criterion using the same techniques used to change or delete data in a field. For instance, you can double-click a query criterion and then edit it in Field View; or you can highlight the criterion and press the Delete key to remove it.

If you want a more specific range, such as values that are greater than or equal to some value *and* less than or equal to some other value, enter two search criteria, separated by a comma, in the field. For example, the query criterion in the Credit Limit field of Figure 9.8 specifies that the Answer table should include only records with a value that is greater than or equal to $2500.00 and less than or equal to $5000.

FIGURE 9.8

Query to display records that have a value between $2500 and $5000 (inclusive) in the Credit Limit field

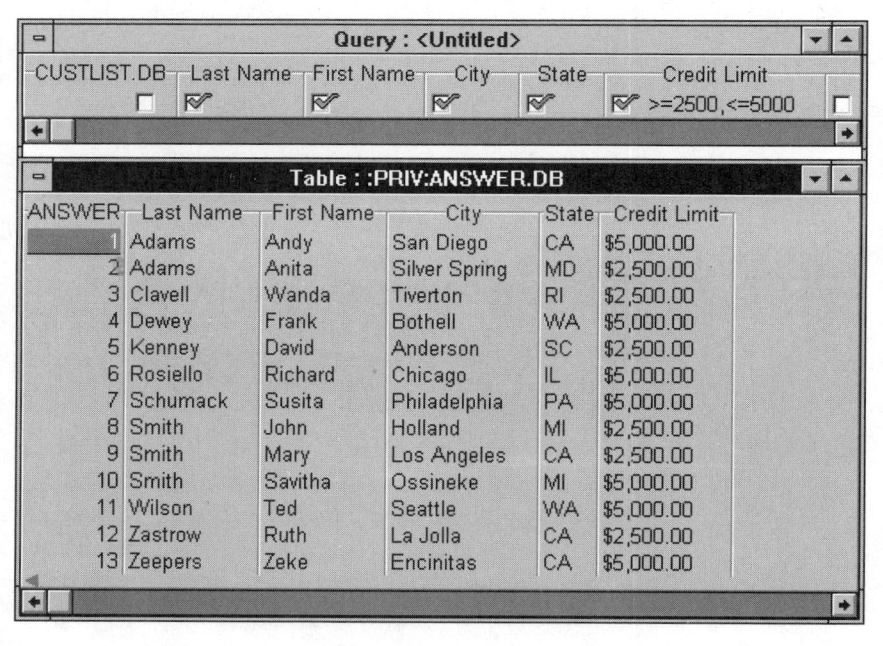

ANSWER	Last Name	First Name	City	State	Credit Limit
1	Adams	Andy	San Diego	CA	$5,000.00
2	Adams	Anita	Silver Spring	MD	$2,500.00
3	Clavell	Wanda	Tiverton	RI	$2,500.00
4	Dewey	Frank	Bothell	WA	$5,000.00
5	Kenney	David	Anderson	SC	$2,500.00
6	Rosiello	Richard	Chicago	IL	$5,000.00
7	Schumack	Susita	Philadelphia	PA	$5,000.00
8	Smith	John	Holland	MI	$2,500.00
9	Smith	Mary	Los Angeles	CA	$2,500.00
10	Smith	Savitha	Ossineke	MI	$5,000.00
11	Wilson	Ted	Seattle	WA	$5,000.00
12	Zastrow	Ruth	La Jolla	CA	$2,500.00
13	Zeepers	Zeke	Encinitas	CA	$5,000.00

You can also use the comparison operators to isolate alpha fields that fall within a range of letters. Use >= to specify the lowest acceptable letter and < to specify one letter higher than the largest acceptable letter. For example, the query below would display records for people whose last names start with the letters *A* through *M*.

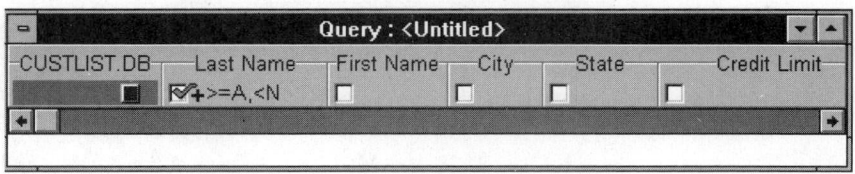

The reason you use <N, rather than <=M, in the second half of a search for names starting with the letters A through M is that the letter M followed by any other letter is "greater than" the letter M by itself. Thus, the query criterion >=A,<N includes all names from the letter A by itself up to "Mzzzzzzzzzzzzzzzz…" while >=A,<M would (for example) exclude MacDonald. Any name starting with the letter N or higher is excluded from the resulting Answer table.

Recall that we originally defined the Zip Code field in the CustList table as an alpha field, rather than a numeric field, to ensure that we could include leading zeros, hyphens, and letters in that field.

When you're searching the field for a range of values, however, it doesn't matter that the field is alpha. For instance, to isolate records with zip codes in the range of 92000 to 92999-9999, you would use the following query criterion:

You can also search a date field for records that fall within a range of dates. For example, the query criterion >=*10/1/92*,<=*12/31/92*, shown in Figure 9.9, displays records that have dates in the fourth quarter of 1992 (October 1 to December 31) in the Start Date field.

Querying Your Tables

Ch.
9

FIGURE 9.9

This query displays records with start dates in the fourth quarter of 1992.

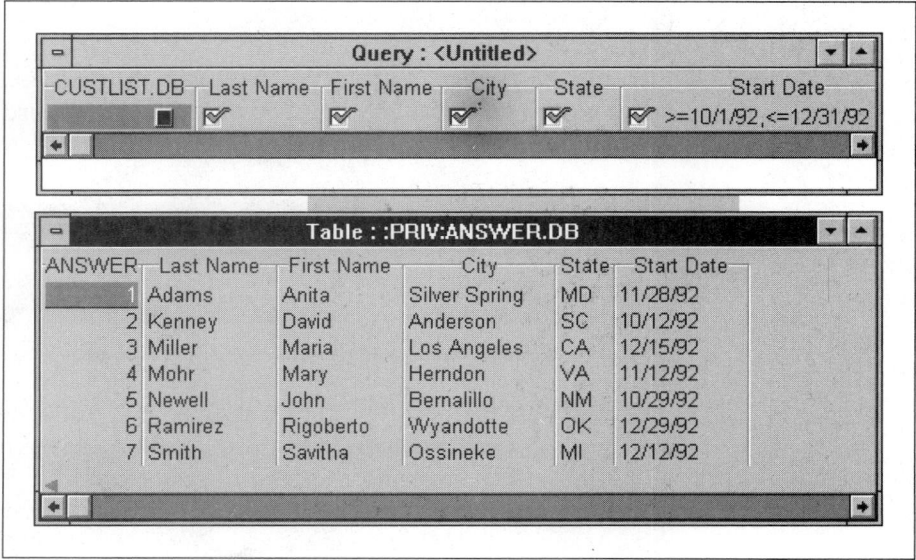

►► *Searching for Inexact Matches*

Sometimes you might want to view records that match a particular pattern or contain a certain sequence of characters. In an inventory system, for example, you may want to view all records that have the characters J2 within the part number. Or, if you want to look up an individual named Smith but aren't sure how to spell it, you can view records that are spelled *like* Smith. The operators used for these types of searches appear below.

Operator	Meaning
..	Matches any sequence of characters, including blank spaces.
@	Matches any single character.
LIKE	Matches items similar to the criterion.
NOT	Preceding the criterion, matches items that do not match the criterion.
BLANK	Matches items that have no data in the field.
TODAY	Compares items with the current date.

> **NOTE**
>
> **Although we've shown the operators in uppercase, you can type them in uppercase, lowercase, or mixed case. For example, *Like*, *LIKE*, and *like* are all treated the same in a query.**

▶ Finding Embedded Text

You can use the .. operator to represent any sequence of characters or numbers (including blank spaces) in a search criterion. For example, suppose you want to view records for people who live on a particular street. You can't ask for all records that contain just a street name, such as Ocean View, because the words "Ocean View" will be embedded somewhere in the middle of the address (for example, 234 Ocean View Dr.). However, you could use the .. operator to stand for the numbers preceding the street name, followed by the words Ocean View, followed by .. again to stand for any other characters. Figure 9.10 shows such a query and its results. Notice that records with the words "Ocean View" embedded in the Address field are included.

FIGURE 9.10 ▶

A search for records with "Ocean View" somewhere in the Address field

ANSWER	Last Name	First Name	Address	City	State
1	Kenney	David	6771 Ocean View Dr.	Anderson	SC
2	Smith	Savitha	767 Ocean View Lane	Ossineke	MI

Query : <Untitled>
CUSTLIST.DB — Last Name — First Name — Address — City — State
..ocean view..

Table : :PRIV:ANSWER.DB

Querying Your Tables

Ch.
9

►►N O T E

The .. operator always makes a search case-insensitive. For instance, in Figure 9.10, even though we asked for ..ocean view.., the query found Ocean View. Likewise, a search for ..smith.. would find SMITH and smith, as well as Smithsonian, Smith & Wesson, and Blacksmith.

The more characters you include in the search criterion, the more specific the search. For example, the query below would list people who live on Crest Dr., but not Crest Ave., Crest St., Crest Blvd., etc.

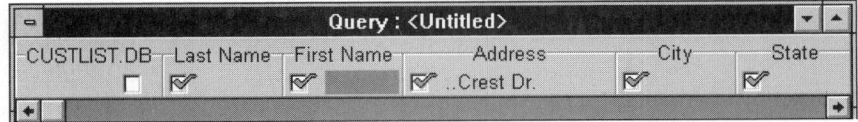

Using few characters in the search criterion tends to broaden the results. In this next example, the query criterion A.. will isolate records of all the people whose last names begin with the letter A.

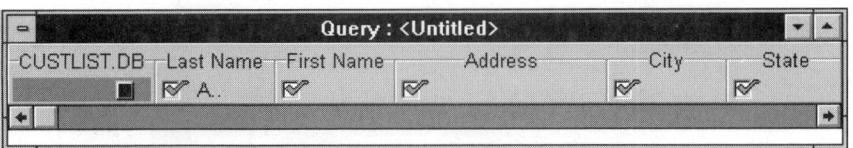

You can also use the .. operator to isolate records for a particular month in a date field. For example, the query below uses .. in place of a specific day in the Start Date field to isolate records with start days on any day of October 1992.

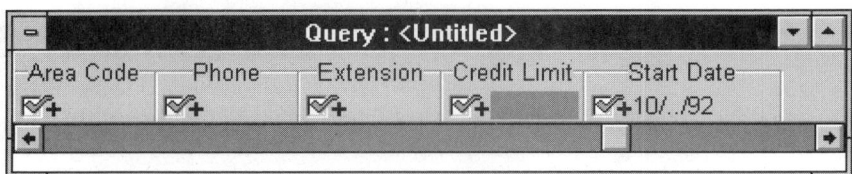

Be sure to type leading zeros in query criteria that include the .. operator and month or day numbers less than 10. For example, type **..**/**05**/**94**
(not **..**/**5**/**94**) to match dates on the fifth day of any month in 1994. If
you prefer not to type leading zeros, you must use the IDAPI Configuration Utility to change the LEADINGZEROM and LEADINGZEROD
settings for the system date format (see Chapter 14).

▶ ▶**N O T E**

**When using a wildcard to find a date, the pattern you
define with the wildcard operator must reflect the
current International setting for dates in the Windows
Control Panel, and the system date formats defined in
the IDAPI Configuration Utility (Chapter 14).**

Searching for embedded, rather than exact, text is always a good way to
broaden a search if your initial search fails. For example, suppose you
search for the name Davis in the Last Name field, and the Answer table
doesn't include all the Davises that you know are somewhere in the table. That's because searching for Davis alone didn't pick up Davis, Jr.
and Davis, III, which do not exactly match Davis.

If you change your search criterion to ..davis.. and run the query, you
might get the results you're looking for, as in the example below. Using
the .. wildcard operator in ..davis.. expands the search to Davis preceded by, or followed by, any other characters.

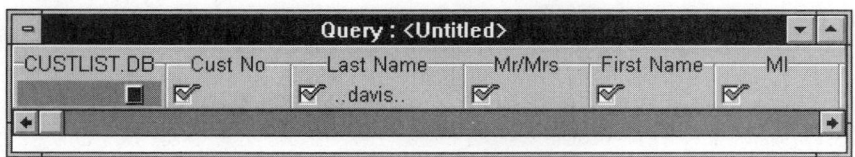

Finding Text in Memos

The .. operator is also useful for finding records with a word embedded
in a formatted memo or memo field. (In fact, you *must* use this operator if you want to search memo fields.) Use the .. operator before and

after the word you're searching for. For instance, the query in Figure 9.11 searches the Employee table for records that have the word "expert" in the formatted memo field named *Notes*.

► *Matching a Single Character*

The @ operator is used to match a single character, as opposed to any series of characters. This is handy when you're not sure of the exact spelling of a word or phrase you're looking for. For instance, a search for Sm@th in the Last Name field would isolate records that contain *Sm*, followed by any single character, followed by *th*. Thus, names such as Smith and Smyth would be included in the Answer table.

FIGURE 9.11 ►

This query searches for records that have the word expert in the Notes field of a sample Employee table. We've adjusted the row height and column width of the resulting Answer table and selected the Complete Display property so that you can see all of the text of the Notes field.

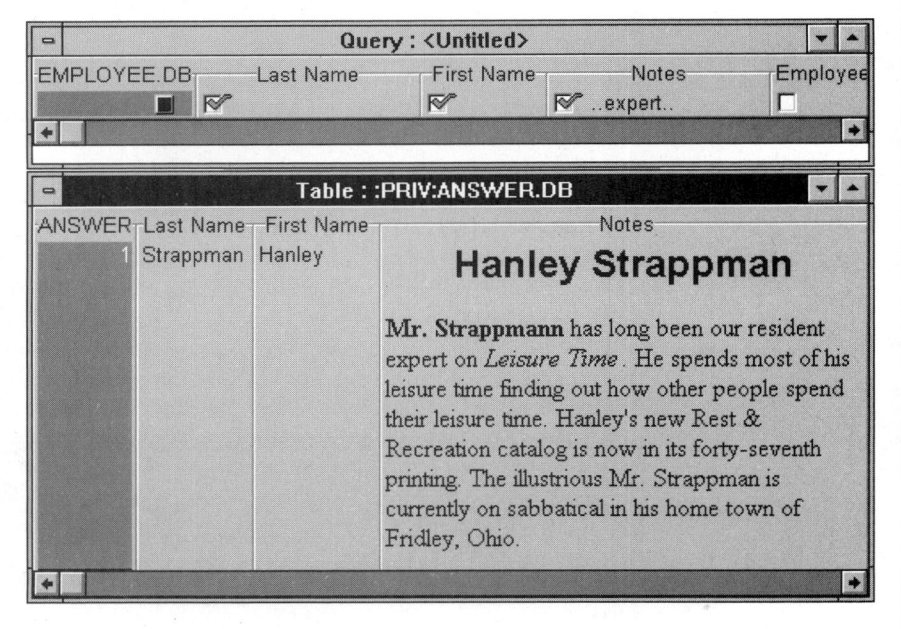

A search for Sm@th.., as below, would find Smith, Smythe, Smithsonian, Smathers, and others that have a single letter embedded between the *m* and the *t*, with or without any characters following the *h*.

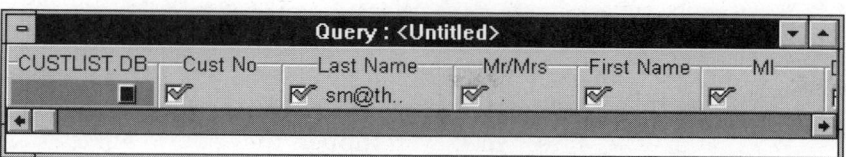

 ▶▶ N O T E

> The @ and .. operators are not allowed in binary, graphic, logical, or OLE fields. Although you can use the @ operator in formatted memo and memo fields, you must also include the .. operator. For instance, in the Notes column of the Employees query table, you could enter ..Sm@th.. to find Smith, Smythe, Smithsonian, and so on.

▶ *Searching for Inexact Spellings*

Sometimes you might want to search for an item of data, without knowing exactly how it is spelled. The LIKE operator comes in handy by searching for text that is spelled like the word you provide. Just type the word **Like,** followed by a blank space, in front of the value you want to search for when specifying your search criterion. The LIKE operator is also case-insensitive and may find records that would otherwise have gone unnoticed.

The query below uses the search criterion *Like abzig* in the Last Name field. This can find last names that are similar to "abzig" in spelling, including Abzug.

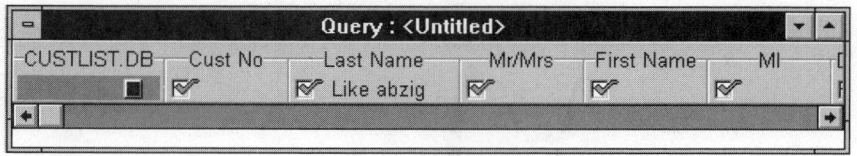

When using the LIKE operator, remember the following points:

- Only records that have the same first letter as the query condition will match. For instance, the search criterion *LIKE kwik* will not find *Quick* even though they sound alike.

- If a record contains at least half of the letters in the query condition, and in the same order, it probably will match. For example, *LIKE la jla*, will find La Jolla, but *LIKE la hoya* will not.

- LIKE is not allowed in binary, formatted memo, graphic, memo, or OLE fields.

► *Searching for Everything Except Some Value*

The NOT operator reverses the meaning of any query criterion. For example, to show only non-California residents in your Answer table, use the query criterion *NOT CA*. Or, to make sure that upper- and lowercase are treated equally, you could use *not ..ca*, as shown in Figure 9.12. No record in the query result has CA in the State field.

FIGURE 9.12 ►

*A search for the records in the CustList table that have some value **other than** CA in the State field eliminates all CA residents from the Answer table.*

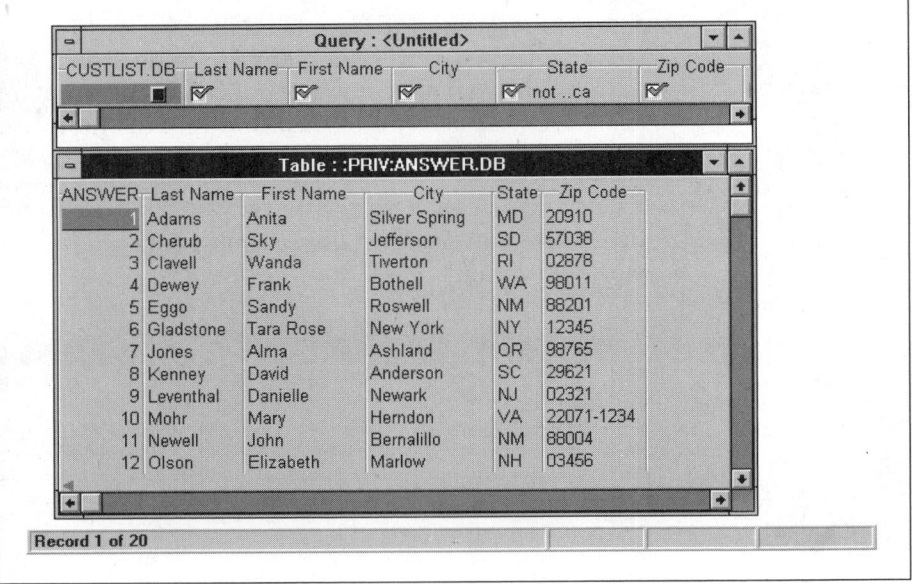

► Searching for Blank Fields

If you want to search for records that have no entry in a particular field, use the BLANK operator. For example, the query below isolates records that have an empty Company field.

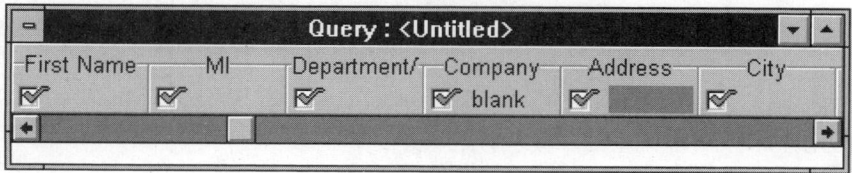

To *exclude* blank records from the results of a query, use *NOT BLANK*. For example, the following query does the exact opposite of the query shown above. Instead of displaying only records that have an empty Company field, it displays only records that do not have an empty Company field.

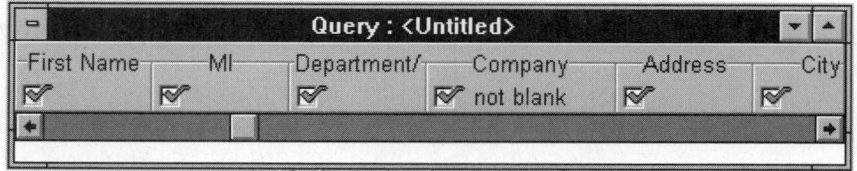

does not seem to work with other queries

► Searching for Relative Dates

The *TODAY* operator represents the current system date in your computer. Typically the system date is maintained by a clock within the computer. You can set the current date using either the Date/Time option in the Windows Control Panel, or the DATE command at the DOS command prompt.

 ► ► **T I P**

> **The Windows Control Panel is located in the Main group in the Windows Program Manager.**

Querying Your Tables

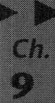

Ch.
9

You can use the TODAY operator alone to isolate records that match the current date exactly. For example, the query criterion below isolates records in the CustList table that have the same Start Date as the current system date.

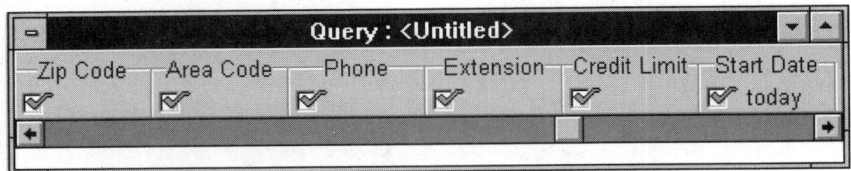

A more common use of the TODAY operator is to find records with dates that fall within some range of days relative to today's date. You can use the comparison operators described earlier (<, >, <=, >=) and the arithmetic operators listed below to help isolate ranges of dates.

OPERATOR	MEANS
+	Adds a number of days to the date.
–	Subtracts a number of days from the date.

Table 9.1 shows sample query criteria used in a date field to isolate ranges of dates relative to the current system date. If your table contains accounts payable or accounts receivable data, such query criteria can help you isolate payables and receivables records within certain ranges of dates.

▶ **TABLE 9.1:** *Examples Using the TODAY Operator to Search for Dates Relative to the Current System Date*

CRITERION	DATES INCLUDED IN ANSWER TABLE
TODAY	Exactly today's date
<=TODAY	Today and all dates prior to today
>=TODAY	Today and all dates after today
<=TODAY,>=TODAY–30	Dates within the last 30 days, including today
>=TODAY,<=TODAY+30	Today and all dates within the next 30 days
>=TODAY–60,<=TODAY–30	Dates between 30 and 60 days ago
<=TODAY+60,>=TODAY+30	Dates between 30 and 60 days from today

Remember that the TODAY operator searches only for records that have some day in relation to the current date. You can also use comparison operators and the .. operator to search for dates. For example, the query criterion *>=7/1/93, <=9/30/93* isolates records in the third quarter of 1993 (July 1, 1993 through September 30, 1993). If you're currently in the month of July 1994, and want to isolate records with dates from about a year ago, you could use the query criterion *07/../93* to find records for July 1993.

▶▶ *Performing AND / OR Searches*

Sometimes you'll want your queries to produce only records that meet *all* the query criteria. For instance, when you are specifically trying to find information about Andy Adams in San Diego, you should set up your query to find only records that contain Adams in the Last Name field *and* Andy in the First Name field *and* San Diego in the City field.

Other times, you might want to find records that match *any* of the search criteria. For instance, to isolate records for people residing in any of several states, you would set up your query to isolate records that have NY *or* NJ *or* PA in the State field.

The basic techniques you use in the Query window to specify AND and OR relationships among query criteria are summarized below.

- To specify an AND relationship among multiple fields, place the query criteria on the same row.

- To specify an OR relationship among multiple fields, place the query criteria in separate rows.

- To specify an AND relationship in a single field, separate the query criteria with a comma.

- To specify an OR relationship in a single field, separate the query criteria with the word OR.

> ▶ ▶ **T I P**
>
> **To add a row to the query table, press ↓ or F12. To delete a row from the query table, move the cursor to that row and then press Ctrl+Del.**

▶ Using AND Relationships across Several Fields

When you want to isolate records that match several search criteria in different fields, place those search criteria in the same row. For example, the query shown in Figure 9.13 asks for records that have exactly "Adams" in the Last name field *and* exactly "Andy" in the First Name field. The resulting Answer table displays the only record in the CustList table that matches these criteria.

FIGURE 9.13 ▶

An AND search to isolate records that have Adams in the Last Name field and Andy in the First Name field. Only one record in the sample CustList table matches these criteria.

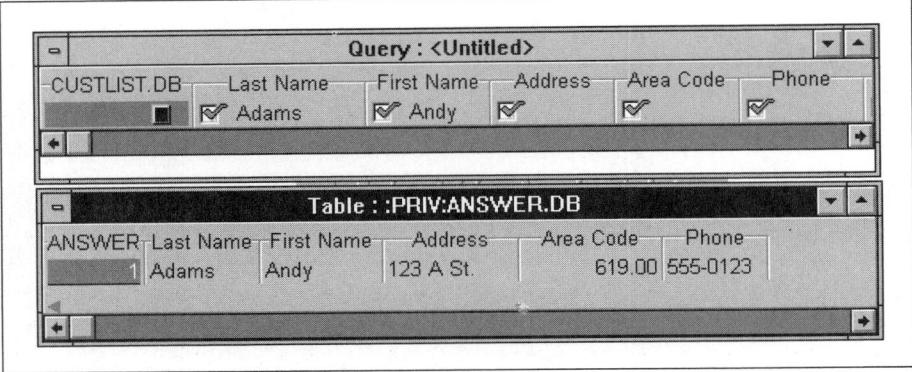

The sample query below will search for records that contain Kenney in the Last Name field, *and* Dav followed by any letters (for example, David, Dave) in the First Name field, *and* SC in the State field.

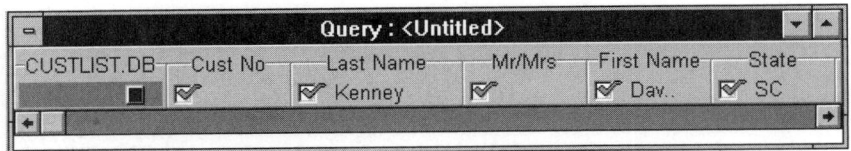

▶ Using AND Relationships in a Single Field

If you want to specify an AND relationship among search criteria in a single field, separate the query criteria with a comma. In most cases, using multiple search criteria only makes sense when searching for ranges using comparison operators. You've already seen several examples of these.

For instance, the query criterion *>=2500, <=5000* in the Credit Limit field isolates records that contain some number that is greater than or equal to $2500 *and* less than or equal to $5000. The query criterion *>=6/1/94, <=12/31/94* in a date field isolates records containing dates that are greater than or equal to 6/1/94 *and* less than or equal to 12/31/94.

You might also want to search for records that contain a combination of words. For example, the query criterion *..spanish..,..french..* shown below would find records that contain both the words "Spanish" *and* "French" in the Notes field of the Employee table. Records that contain only "French," only "Spanish," or neither are excluded from the Answer table.

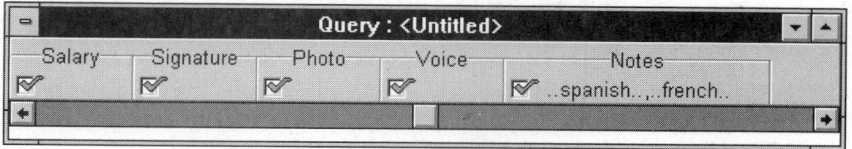

▶ Using OR Relationships across Several Fields

If you want to search for several different values in a field (or several fields), place the query criteria on separate lines. While working in the query table, you need only press ↓ (or F12) to create a new row. For example, the query below finds records that have *either* San Diego in the City field *or* 92 followed by any other characters in the Zip Code field.

Notice how the two query criteria are on separate rows.

The query below searches for people with a last name like Smith who live in Washington *or* California. You might think of each row in the query table as representing a single question.

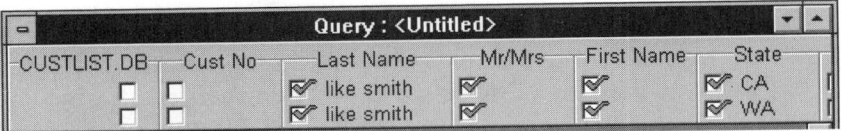

When performing this query, Paradox looks at each record in the table and asks,

- Does this record have a name like Smith in the Last Name field *and* WA in the State field?

- Does this record have a name like Smith in the Last Name field *and* CA in the State field?

If it can answer Yes to *either* of those questions, Paradox displays that record in the Answer table.

Now compare the query above to this example:

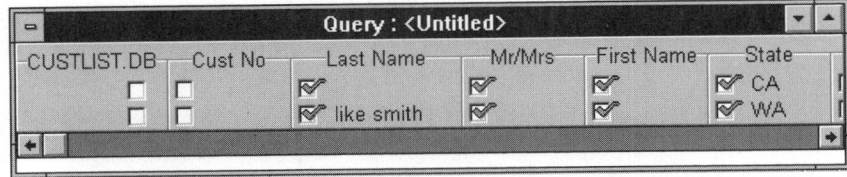

This query would produce an Answer table that contains *all* California residents (regardless of last name) and only Smiths in WA. Why? Because the query asks these two questions when deciding whether or not to display a record in the Answer table:

- Does this record have CA in the State field?
- Does this record have a name like Smith in the Last Name field *and* WA in the State field?

For Paradox to be able to answer Yes to the first question, and thereby display the record in the Answer table, a record need only have CA in the State field. That's because there is no query criterion in the Last Name field in the first row.

▶ *Using OR Relationships in a Field*

If you want to search for any one of several given values in a field, you can stack the values in separate rows (as in the "like Smith in Washington or Like Smith in California" example shown earlier). Alternatively, you can use the *OR* operator to separate the values you want to search for. For instance, if you want to isolate records that have NY, *or* PA, *or* NJ in the State field, you could set up the query as it appears below.

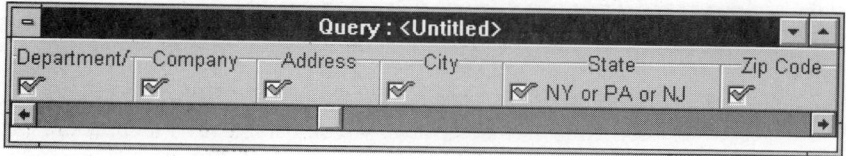

Or you could set it up like this:

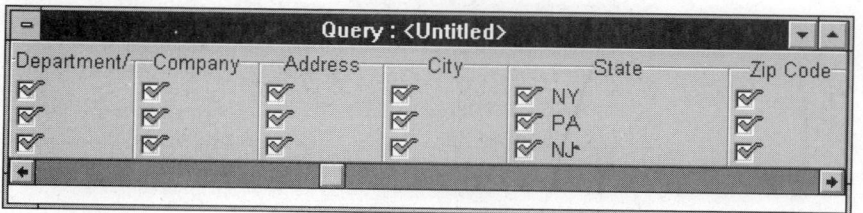

Either way, the results are the same (although the first method, in which all the OR conditions are on the same line, is quicker to set up). The Answer table displays records with NY, PA, or NJ in the State field.

Querying Your Tables

▶ ▶

Ch.

9

> **▶▶ N O T E**
>
> **When setting up a query that will return "live" results, you *must* place all the OR conditions for the same field on one line. Stacked OR conditions for the same field aren't allowed. We'll discuss live queries later in the chapter.**

Returning to an earlier example, if you wanted to isolate records that have either "Spanish" *or* "French" in the Notes field, you could either stack the query conditions or separate them with the OR operator, like this:

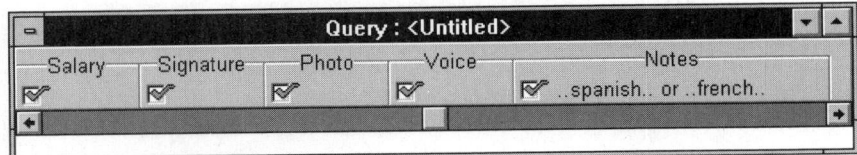

▶ Troubleshooting Queries

When building criteria that use AND logic and OR logic at the same time, keep in mind that the way you think about the query in plain English may *not* be the way to express it in a query. For example, you might think to yourself, "I want to view CA and WA residents." Then you define the query as below.

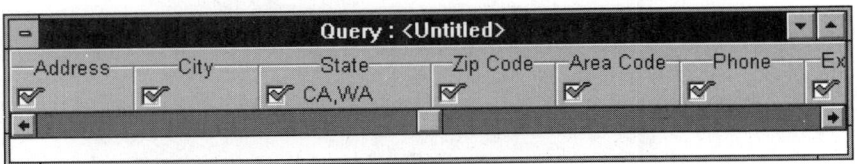

When you run the query, however, the Answer table will be empty, regardless of how many CA and WA residents actually exist in the table. Why? Because it's impossible for the State field in any single record to contain both CA *and* WA. Therefore, Paradox cannot answer Yes when it asks, "Does this record have CA in the State field *and* WA in the State field?"

To isolate records for California and Washington residents, you need to set up the query to look for records that have either CA or WA in the State field, like this:

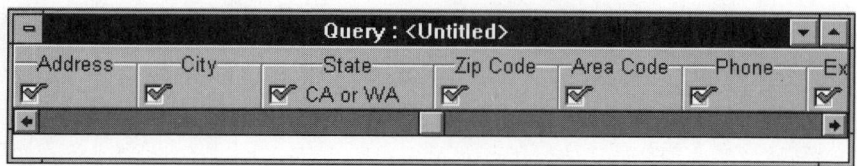

Now Paradox asks two questions as it checks each record: Does this record have CA in the State field? Does this record have WA in the State field? If it can answer Yes to either question, the record is included in the Answer table.

▶ Searching for Punctuation Marks and Other Symbols

Punctuation marks like commas and periods, and operators such as OR, NOT, BLANK, and TODAY are always interpreted as special symbols in a query.

Suppose you want to search for a record that has *Davis, Jr.* in the Last Name field. If you simply enter the query criterion into the Last Name field of the query table as

        Davis, Jr.

and run the query, the Answer table will be empty. Why? Because Paradox interprets the comma as the AND operator, rather than just as a comma.

If you want to include an operator or special word in a query criterion, but want it treated as a literal character rather than an operator, simply enclose the query criterion in quotation marks.

For example, if you change the query criterion to

        "Davis, Jr."

Paradox will know you're looking for Davis, Jr., not for records that contain both Davis and Jr.

▶▶**N O T E**

> **Company names often contain commas, as in *Trans-America, Inc.* To search for that company name, you'd need to use quotation marks, as in this example: "TransAmerica, Inc."**

Similarly, if you wanted to isolate records for people living in California, Oregon, or Washington, you'd have a problem. The two-letter abbreviation for Oregon is OR, which is the same as the OR operator.

The query below takes care of the problem by enclosing the two-letter abbreviation for Oregon in quotation marks. Running this query will successfully isolate records that have CA *or* OR *or* WA in the State field.

Using quotation marks in queries keeps Paradox from converting special symbols and reserved words (such as BLANK, OR, NOT, and TODAY) into commands; instead, they'll be treated as items to look up.

 ▶▶**N O T E**

> **When typing a search criterion in double quotation marks, be sure to use the exact upper- and lowercase characters you want to match. Alternatively, you can use the .. operator to make the search case-insensitive.**

Table 9.2 lists all the symbols, operators, and reserved words that you can use in queries, and tells where each is discussed. Remember that if you want to search a field for any of the characters or words shown in the first column of that table, the search criterion must be enclosed in quotation marks. Although a single period (.) is not listed as a symbol, operator, or reserved word in Table 9.2, you must enclose it in quotation marks when it precedes or follows the .. operator.

▶ **TABLE 9.2:** *Symbols, Query Operators, and Reserved Words*

SYMBOL OR WORD	FUNCTION	CHAPTER(S)
Check Mark Symbols		
☑+	Display all values, including duplicates, in the Answer table	Chapter 9
☑	Display only unique values in the Answer table	Chapter 9
☑↓	Display values in descending sorted order	Chapter 9
☑G	Specify group for set operations	Chapter 16
Comparison Operators		
=	Equal to (optional)	Chapter 9
>	Greater than	Chapter 9
<	Less than	Chapter 9
>=	Greater than or equal to	Chapter 9
<=	Less than or equal to	Chapter 9
Arithmetic Operators		
+	Add numbers or join alphanumeric values	Chapters 9, 16
–	Subtract	Chapters 9, 16
*	Multiply	Chapter 16
/	Divide	Chapter 16
()	Give precedence	Chapter 16

Querying Your Tables

Ch. **9**

▶ **TABLE 9.2:** *Symbols, Query Operators, and Reserved Words (continued)*

SYMBOL OR WORD	FUNCTION	CHAPTER(S)
Wildcard Operators		
@	Matches any single character	Chapter 9
..	Matches any series of characters	Chapter 9
Special Operators		
LIKE	Similar to	Chapter 9
NOT	Does not match	Chapter 9
BLANK	Contains no value	Chapter 9
TODAY	System date	Chapter 9
OR	One condition *or* another (or both) must be met	Chapter 9
,	Both conditions must be met	Chapter 9
AS	Field name to use in Answer table	Chapter 16
!	Display all values, regardless of match	Chapter 16
Reserved Words		
CALC	Display result in new calculated field in Answer table	Chapter 16
CHANGETO	Globally change matching values	Chapter 9
FIND	Locate matching records within table	Chapter 9
INSERT	Insert records with specified value	Chapter 18
DELETE	Delete records with specified values	Chapter 9
SET	Define set of matching values for set comparisons	Chapter 16

► **TABLE 9.2:** *Symbols, Query Operators, and Reserved Words (continued)*

SYMBOL OR WORD	FUNCTION	CHAPTER(S)
Summary Operators		
AVERAGE	Average of values on field	Chapter 16
COUNT	Number of matching items	Chapter 16
MAX	Highest value in field	Chapter 16
MIN	Lowest value in field	Chapter 16
SUM	Total of values in field	Chapter 16
ALL	Calculate summary based on all values in a group, including duplicates	Chapter 16
UNIQUE	Calculate summary based on unique values in group	Chapter 16
Set Comparison Operators		
ONLY	Display only those values matching values in defined set	Chapter 16
NO	Display only those values that do not match any members in defined set	Chapter 16
EVERY	Display only values that match every member of defined set	Chapter 16
EXACTLY	Display only values that match all members of defined set and no others	Chapter 16

►► *Querying OLE Fields*

In general, OLE fields are not good candidates for a query. However, sometimes you can search for text in OLE fields, much as you would search for text in memo fields. For example, if you pasted the contents of a résumé written in Microsoft Word into a Paradox OLE field, you could use a query to search for a specific skill you're interested in. Or, if you pasted a Microsoft Excel spreadsheet into an OLE field, you could search for a specific value or label.

Here are some tips for using queries to search for values in OLE fields:

- You can query an OLE field that contains text or numbers.

▶▶ **N O T E**

When you embed an object in an OLE field, a copy of that object is stored in the field (in the .mb file), so Paradox can search the contents of the field.

- When specifying the query criterion, always place the .. operator before and after the text or numbers you want to search for. Text and numbers are treated the same in OLE fields. For example, to search for "typing 65 wpm" enter **..typing 65 wpm..** as the query criterion. Similarly, to search for 100 in an OLE field that contains spreadsheet data, type **..100..** as the query criterion. To search for 25,000 in an OLE field, enclose the number in quotes (for example, **.."25,000"..**) to prevent Paradox from misinterpreting the comma.

- You can use the @, AND, BLANK, NOT, and OR operators, but cannot use LIKE or TODAY. Nor can you use comparison operators <, <=, >, and >=.

You're better off using a formatted memo or memo field if you need to store a large body of text in each record of a table and also require flexibility in querying that field. Similarly, you may want to avoid storing numbers in an OLE field.

▶▶ *Saving a Query*

If you want to use the same query again, you certainly won't want to go to the trouble of re-creating it each time. Once you've designed the query so that it accurately displays the fields and records you want to see, you can save it by following the steps below.

1. Click anywhere on the Query window to select it.

2. Choose File ➤ Save.

3. Enter a valid DOS file name in the New File Name text box, but omit the extension. (Paradox automatically adds .qbe to the file name you enter.)

4. Choose OK.

▶ Reusing a Saved Query

Here's how to reuse a previously saved query:

1. Choose File ➤ Open ➤ Query. Or, if you're starting from the Desktop, click the Open Query button on the Toolbar, or right-click the Queries icon in the Project Viewer and choose Open. The Select Query dialog box will open.

2. In the lower-left corner of the dialog box, make sure the Design option is selected.

3. Select the name of the query you want to use, either by double-clicking or by clicking and choosing OK.

▶ ▶ **T I P**

As a shortcut, you can open the Project Viewer window (see Chapter 3) and click its Queries icon. Then, if you want to open a query in design mode, right-click the query name you want and choose Open, or just double-click the name. If you want to run the query immediately, right-click the query name and choose Run.

4. The Query window appears on the screen. You can make any changes you want to the query, or just run it as-is by clicking on the Run Query button or pressing F8.

▶ ▶ **T I P**

If you want to run the query immediately, without going to the Query window first, select V̲iew Data instead of D̲esign in step 2 above.

As you'll discover in Parts 3 and 4 of this book, queries can also be handy as the basis for "smart" reports and forms that show just the data you want.

▶▶ *Controlling the Answer Table's Appearance*

Normally, when you run a query, Paradox displays the fields in the Answer table in the same order that they were defined in the original table structure—even if you rotate or drag fields in the query table. What's more, the sort order of records in the Answer table is also based on the original table structure, which can be confusing when you're trying to use checkmarks to control the sort order of records in your Answer table.

For instance, in Figure 9.14 we've moved the Start Date field to the first column of the query table, checked it, and asked to see only records with 1993 dates in them (*../../93*). The resulting Answer table, however, displays records in their original column order, with Start Date at the right end of the Answer table. Records are sorted by the left-most column in the Answer table's structure—Last Name in this case.

To control the exact appearance of the Answer table, you use the P̲roperties ➤ Answer Options and P̲roperties ➤ Answer Sor̲t options on the menu bar, or the equivalent buttons in the Toolbar (these are available only while a Query window is the active window on the Desktop).

Before you can design the Answer table, however, you need to check the fields you want to see and specify all of your query criteria. In fact, it's a good idea to run the query at least once to make sure it will

FIGURE 9.14

Even though Start Date is in the leftmost column of the query table, Start Date is still in the last column of the Answer table. Records are sorted by Last Name—the left-most column in the Answer table.

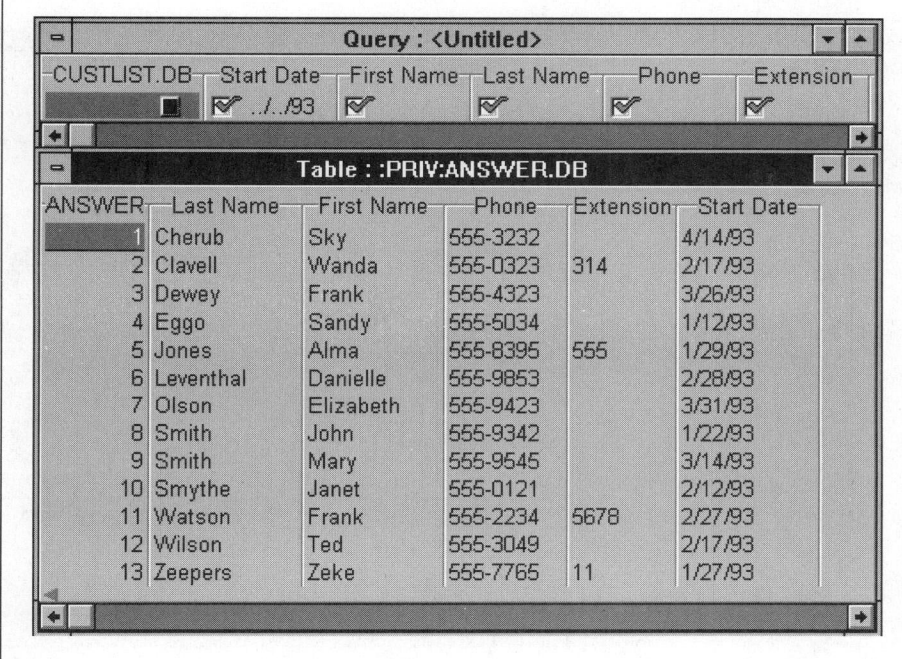

display the fields and records you want, *then* go back and fine-tune the Answer table. Here's how to get started.

1. If you've just run the query and the Answer table is open, close the Answer table by double-clicking its Control-menu box or by pressing Ctrl+F4. The Query window should now be the currently selected window.

2. Choose Properties ➤ Answer Options or click the Answer Table Properties button on the Toolbar (shown at left). You'll see the dialog box shown in Figure 9.15.

3. Fill in the Answer Options dialog box. (Don't worry, we'll explain all this in the sections that follow.)

4. When you're ready to return to the Query window, choose OK.

Now, let's look at several options in this dialog box.

Querying Your Tables

Ch. 9

FIGURE 9.15 ▶

The Answer Options dialog box lets you control the properties of the Answer table. As you'll learn later, this dialog box also lets you choose a "live" view of the table you're querying.

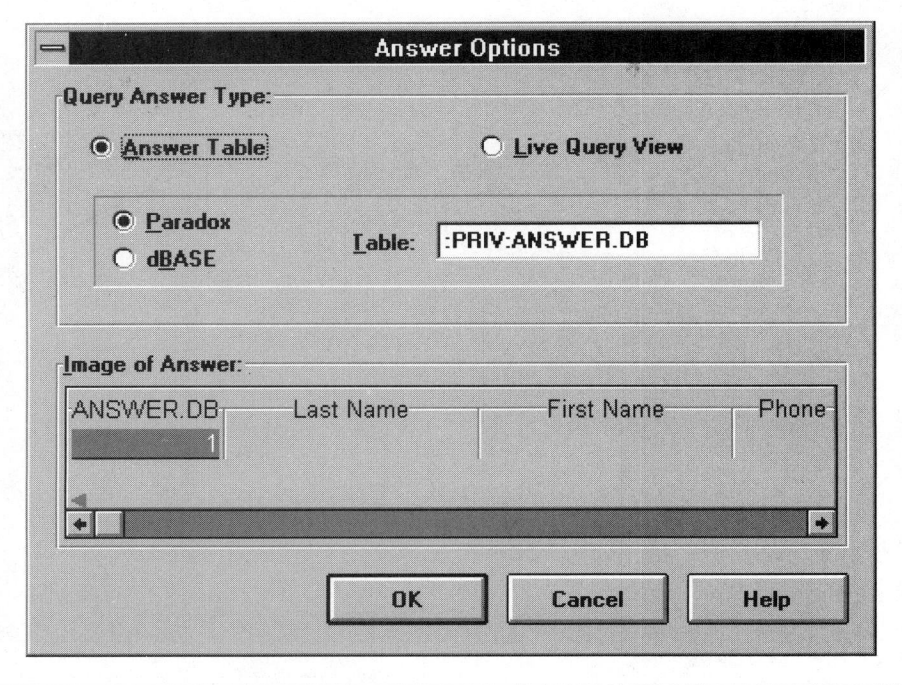

▶ Changing the Name of the Answer Table

In the Query Answer Type area of the Answer Options dialog box, you can choose between two types of tables to hold your query results:

Answer Table Choosing this option places the query result in a *separate* table. This is what we've been doing all along, because Answer Table is the default setting. By default, the separate table is stored in Paradox format in the temporary table named answer.db on your private directory (the private directory alias is :priv:).

Live Query View Choosing this option displays query results in the *original* table that you're querying, rather than in a copy. Depending on how you've set up the query, some or all of the fields may be "live" so that you can change the data in them if necessary.

We'll look at the Live Query View in a moment. For now, let's focus on the Answer Table option.

Naming the Answer Table

If the Answer Table option is selected, you can use the Table text box to specify a different path or table name for storing the query results. Initially, the Table text box suggests :PRIV:ANSWER.DB as the temporary Answer table. Recall that this table is replaced each time you run a query, and it is deleted when you exit Paradox. If you prefer to store the results to a permanent Paradox table rather than the temporary Answer table, choose Table and enter the path name (or alias name) and table name you want to use.

For instance, if you enter **:gift_corner:dateord.db** as the Answer Table, then run the query, the query results will be stored in a table named *dateord.db* in the *c:\pdoxwin\giftco* directory (assuming your *:gift_corner:* alias points to that directory). Unlike the temporary Answer table, this new table will not be erased when you exit Paradox, so you can use its data in multiple sessions. This can also make it easier to print reports from the query results, as we'll explore in Chapter 12.

▶ ▶ **T I P**

> It's always best to use alias names, rather than full path names, whenever possible. This makes it easier to move your database objects to other directories or disks without problems. For example, specifying *:gift_corner:dateord.db* in the Table text box is preferable to using *c:\pdoxwin\giftco\dateord.db*. See "Creating an Alias for a Directory" in Chapter 3 for more about alias names and their many benefits.

Be aware that when you run this query again, Paradox will automatically replace the data currently in the table with the new query results. So, make sure you don't provide the name of a table that already contains important data. For instance, you wouldn't want the results of a query to overwrite the original table, since the resulting query will usually only contain a portion of all the data in the original table.

> ✎ ▶ ▶**N O T E**
>
> **If you receive a "Table is already in use" message when you run a query, chances are that you or someone else has the answer table open. To solve the problem, just close the answer table and run the query again. On a network, you may need to wait until other users have closed the answer table.**

Choosing the Answer Table Type

The Paradox and dBase options below Answer Table in the Answer Options dialog box let you decide whether to store the query results in a Paradox table or a dBASE table. This, of course, is only relevant if you use Paradox to manage dBASE data—a topic we'll explore in Appendix D.

▶ Querying "Live" Data

When Paradox puts the query results in a separate table, such as the Answer table, any changes you make to that table *will not* be reflected in your original data. Instead, you must open the table you used in the query and then make your corrections.

If you are thinking that sounds like a lot of trouble, you're right. Fortunately, you have another choice: You can create a query that displays "live" results, which you can change. Suppose you want to update the credit limits of some customers who live in a posh community of California, presumably because they can afford it. Your job would be much faster if you didn't have to wade through all the California data in order to make your changes. The sample query below would limit your view to the group of records you want. Notice that this query uses the check plus checkmark, a requirement for displaying live data.

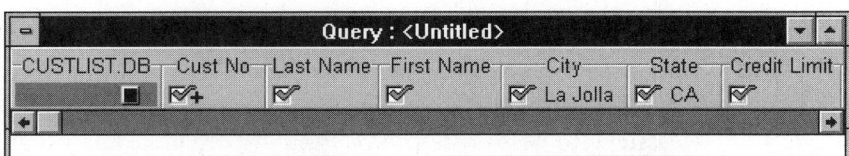

Now you just need to tell Paradox to put the results in a live answer table, called "Live Query View." Paradox will display the original table on which you've based the query and let you edit some or all of the fields in that table.

To create this live view, follow the steps below:

1. Create your query using the standard steps. You must mark at least *one* field with a check plus, as shown in the example above. You'll also need to follow the additional guidelines given in the next section. You can give your query a test run in the Answer table if you wish, by pressing F8 or clicking the Run Query button in the Toolbar.

► ► T I P

Live Query View queries are really just a way to use the Query window to set up a *filter*. You'll use similar techniques to define the conditions in both Live Query Views and filters. (See "Using a Filter to Isolate Data," later in the chapter.)

2. Click on the Query window and choose Properties ➤ Answer Options (or click the Answer Table Properties button in the Toolbar). You'll see the Answer Options dialog box shown earlier in Figure 9.15.

3. Choose Live Query View.

4. Choose OK.

Now run the query normally (for example, press F8 or click the Run Query button). The results will appear in a table named View, and "Query View:..." will appear in the title bar to remind you that you're looking at a subset of the table, not the entire table. You'll also see a small "field view" symbol next to column headings for fields that you can edit, as illustrated in Figure 9.16.

You can now press F9 or click the Edit Data button and edit the existing records normally (you can even add new records to the table). When you're done editing, you can close the table by double-clicking its Control-menu box or pressing Ctrl+F4.

Querying Your Tables

Ch.
9

FIGURE 9.16 ►

To create a live answer table of data that can be edited, use the check plus in your query and select the Live Query View option in the Answer Options dialog box. In Table View, live fields are marked with special symbols next to the field name in the header.

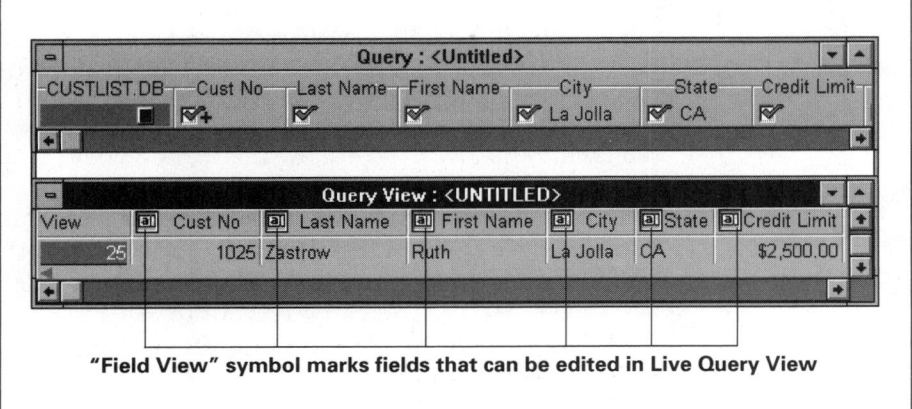

"Field View" symbol marks fields that can be edited in Live Query View

►►**N O T E**

If you want to create a Quick Form, Default Form, Quick Report, or Default Report from the live query result, you must save your query first. Switch back to the Query window, save your query, then run the query again. Now you can create your form or report from the results table by choosing appropriate options from the Tools menu or by clicking the Quick Form or Quick Report buttons in the Toolbar.

Some Queries Do Not Create Live Query Views

Not all Live Query View queries can produce "live" answers, even if you've used the check plus and selected Live Query View in the Answer Options dialog box.

If Paradox cannot create a live query view, it will display a warning message when you run the query. (Choose OK or press ↵ to clear the message.) In this case, your results table will be "read only." You can scroll through it and customize its appearance as you wish. However, you cannot change any data in the table, and no "field view" symbols will appear in the column headings.

► ►**TIP**

> **Read-only view conserves disk space, since Paradox doesn't need to show the query results in a separate table stored on disk. For this reason, it is ideal as the basis for reports (though it's certainly *not* useful for data entry forms). You'll learn how to create reports from query results in Part 3.**

The following situations will prevent your Live Query View from producing "live" data that you can change:

- The query does not include at least one check plus checkmark.
- The query is set up to produce any kind of calculated result. That is, the query cannot include AVERAGE, CALC, COUNT, MAX, MIN, SUM, or any mathematical operators (see Chapter 16).
- The query includes the @ or .. wildcard operators.
- The query involves more than one table (see Chapter 16).
- The query involves multiple rows. If you want to create OR queries that involve the same field, use the OR operator on a single line. For example, to list customers in California or New York or Washington, put a check plus and the following condition in the STATE field of the Query window:

  CA or NY or WA

- The query is sorted via the Properties ► Answer Sort or the Sort Answer Table button in the Toolbar. We'll discuss sorting the Answer table in a later section.
- The query includes example elements (you'll learn about example elements in Chapter 16).

► ►**NOTE**

> **You cannot use the Table ► Sort option to sort the results of a Live Query View.**

You don't need to memorize which types of Live Query View queries produce live answers and which don't. Instead, just remember this: Live answer tables include the "field view" symbols in their column headings; read-only answer tables do not have this symbol.

 ▶ ▶ N O T E

> In Chapter 16 you'll learn about another type of live query, which uses DDE (Dynamic Data Exchange) to update the Answer table's results automatically as you scroll through a linked table in Table View.

▶ Controlling the Properties of the Answer Table

To control the width and order of columns in the Answer table, as well as the other properties (such as color, font, grid lines, and so forth), you manipulate the query table image that appears under Image Of Answer in the Answer Options dialog box. Using the same techniques you'd use to manipulate data in a regular Table View, you can:

- Move columns by dragging them or by using the Rotate key (Ctrl+R).

- Size columns by dragging the grid line left or right.

- Change the color and font using inspection, or by using Ctrl+Shift+M (all columns), Ctrl+Shift+H (all headings), or Ctrl+G (grid).

- Drag the scroll lock marker to prevent columns from scrolling.

NOTE

You cannot change the Image Of Answer for Live Query View queries, and Paradox will ignore any existing image settings if you switch the Query Answer Type from Answer Table to Live Query View. If you want to change the appearance of the Query View, simply run the Live Query View query and then use normal Table View techniques to customize the results.

In Figure 9.17, for instance, we checked the fields we wanted to include in our query and moved the checked columns into view. Then we opened the Answer Options dialog box, dragged the Start Date field to the left-most column of the Answer table image, resized some columns, and set the Area Code to display an Integer number format. We also set the heading, column, and grid colors to white and the grid line spacing to double.

FIGURE 9.17

Use the Image of Answer area to determine the size, column order, and other properties of the Answer table.

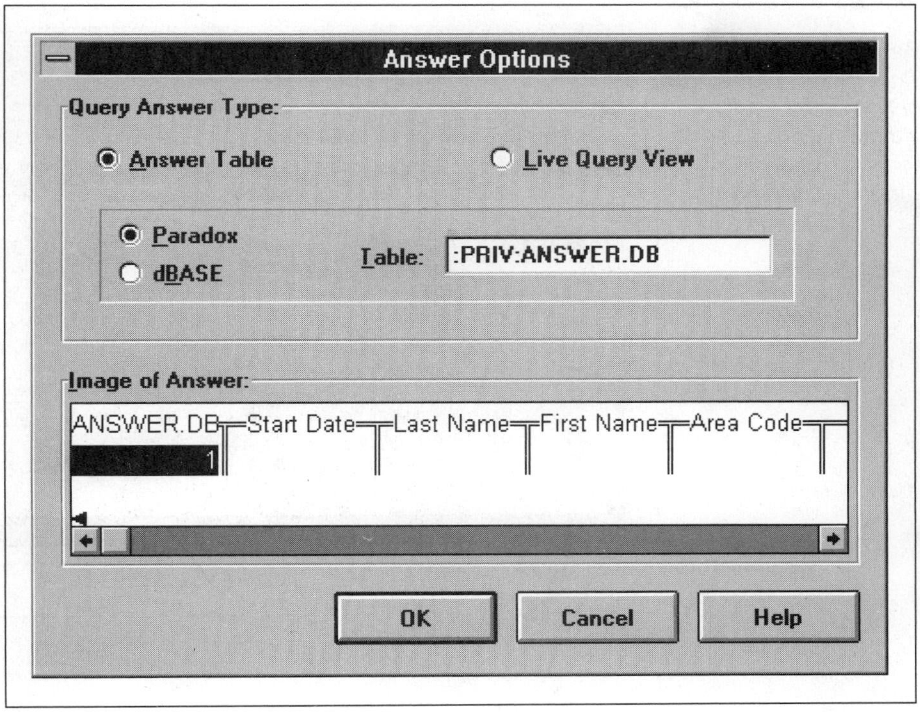

When you've finished changing the Answer Options dialog box, choose OK to return to the Query window. You can then run the query as usual to view your modified Answer table.

Figure 9.18 shows the Answer table after making the changes shown in Figure 9.17. Notice that Start Date is now the first column in the table and that the Answer table has a white background and double grid lines.

▶ Controlling the Sort Order of the Answer Table

Suppose you want to list records in numeric order by area code, and within area code by phone number, regardless of the order in which fields appear in the Answer table or the query table.

 Just click in the Query window and choose <u>P</u>roperties ➤ Answer Sor<u>t</u> or click the Sort Answer Table button in the Toolbar (shown at left).

FIGURE 9.18 ▶

After you change the image of the Answer table in Figure 9.17 and run the query, the Answer table appears with the same properties as that image.

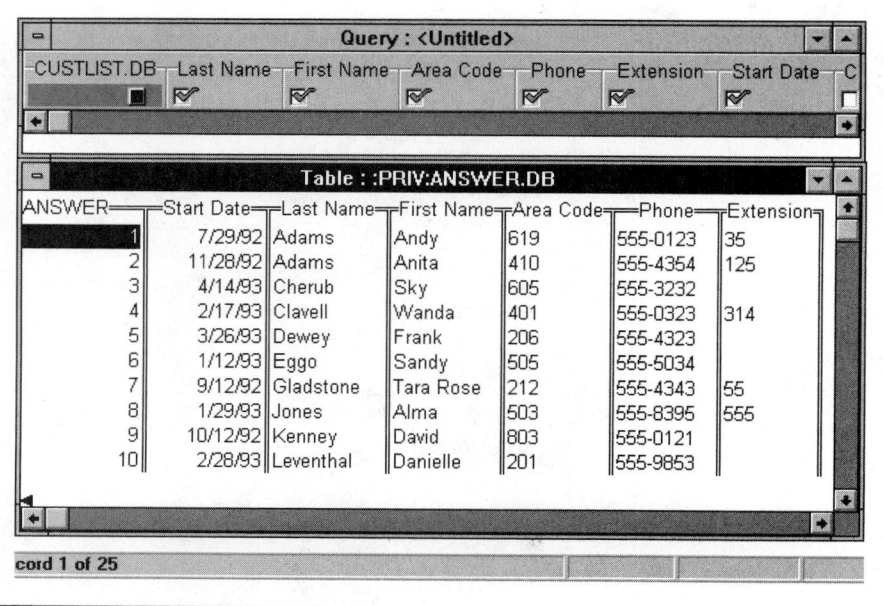

This opens the Sort Answer dialog box, which works exactly like the Sort dialog box described in Chapter 8. In the Available Fields list, click the name of any field you want to use for a sort order, then click the → button to copy the field name to the Sort By list. You can also use the ↑ and ↓ buttons to change the order of fields in the Sort By list, and use the ← button to move a field name back into the Available Fields list. As usual, the first name in the Sort By list will be the primary sort key, the next name the secondary sort key, and so forth.

In Figure 9.19 we've chosen to sort records by area code, then by phone number within each area code.

FIGURE 9.19 ▶

To define a sort order for records in the Answer table, click in the Query window and choose Properties ▶ Answer Sort. Fill in the Sort Answer dialog box using techniques discussed in Chapter 8 for the Sort dialog box.

When you've finished making changes, click OK to return to the Query window. Then run the query as usual. Figure 9.20 shows the resulting Answer table after filling in the Sort Answer dialog box as illustrated in Figure 9.19. Notice that records are sorted into area code order.

▶ Saving the Answer Table Properties

The Answer table image settings that you choose in the Answer Options dialog box are saved as soon as you choose OK in that dialog box. That is,

FIGURE 9.20

Records in the Answer table are sorted by area code and by phone number within each area code.

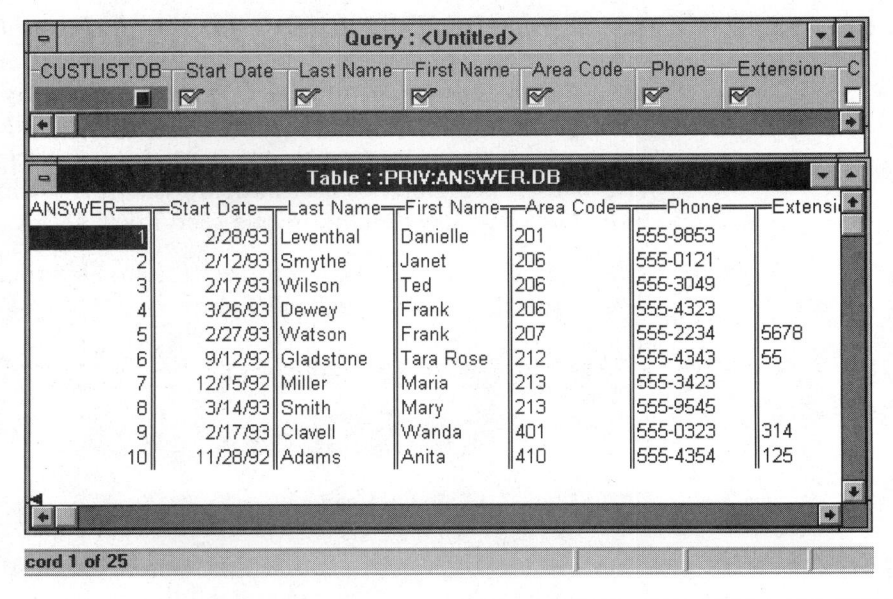

the Answer Options image settings will affect *every* query that creates an Answer table, even if you don't save the query you're working on.

By contrast, the Answer table properties you choose in the Answer Sort dialog box will affect the current query *only*, and they'll be "forgotten" unless you resave the query after making changes. So, when you close the query and see the dialog box asking if you want to save the current version of the query, be sure to choose Yes if you want to keep your sort options.

**TIP**

To quickly remove all the Answer table image settings and return the Answer table to its default appearance, run any query that produces an Answer table, or click in an open Answer table's window, or open the Answer table (it's usually named :priv:answer.db). Then choose Properties ➤ View Properties ➤ Delete ➤ OK.

▶▶ *Using Queries to Update Data*

So far, we've focused on using queries to *isolate* specific types of data. That is, all our sample queries have allowed us to pull out particular fields and records from a table, and view only that information in the resulting Answer table or Live Query View. But you can also use queries to *update* data in a table automatically, as we'll discuss in the next few sections.

▶▶ *Using Queries to Make Global Changes to a Table*

Here is a technique that may someday save you many hours of tedious work. Through a process known as *global editing*, you can use a *CHANGETO query* to automatically change the contents of a field to a new value in records that meet a particular criterion.

For example, suppose two different people have entered data into your table. One typed in **Los Angeles** for all Los Angeles residents; the other typed **L.A.** This creates problems, because queries that search for Los Angeles records miss those with L.A. and vice versa. Even though an OR search could take care of this, it would be better to have consistent entries.

There are countless other examples where CHANGETO queries are useful. For instance, you can use them to increase all the unit prices of products in a particular category by 15% (or any other amount), as you'll learn in Chapter 16. You can also use CHANGETO queries to flag records that have been through some procedure, as illustrated in Chapter 18.

▶ *Playing It Safe with Queries That Change Data*

When using queries that change data, remember that Paradox can change many records in the blink of an eye. If you're not careful, you might make the wrong change to a huge number of records. For instance, you might *intend* to change the contents of the City fields of a table so that they contain Los Angeles rather than L.A. But if you're not careful, you might tell Paradox to change *all* the cities to Los Angeles. Whoops!

Backing Up a Table before Global Editing

To play it safe, always back up your table before you run a query that changes (or deletes) multiple table records. If you don't, your only recourse following an accident will be to retype a field or fields for each record. Not a pleasant task if there are 10,000 records in the table! Here's how to back up a table:

1. Choose Tools ➤ Utilities ➤ Copy.

2. In the Copy File From text box, enter the name of the table you want to back up (or just click the name of the table).

3. In the To text box, enter a name for the backup copy. For instance, in Figure 9.21 we've chosen to copy the *CustList.db* table to a backup table named *CustOrig.db* (for Customer Original).

4. Click the OK button.

FIGURE 9.21

The Copy dialog box filled in to copy the table CustList.db to a table named CustOrig.db

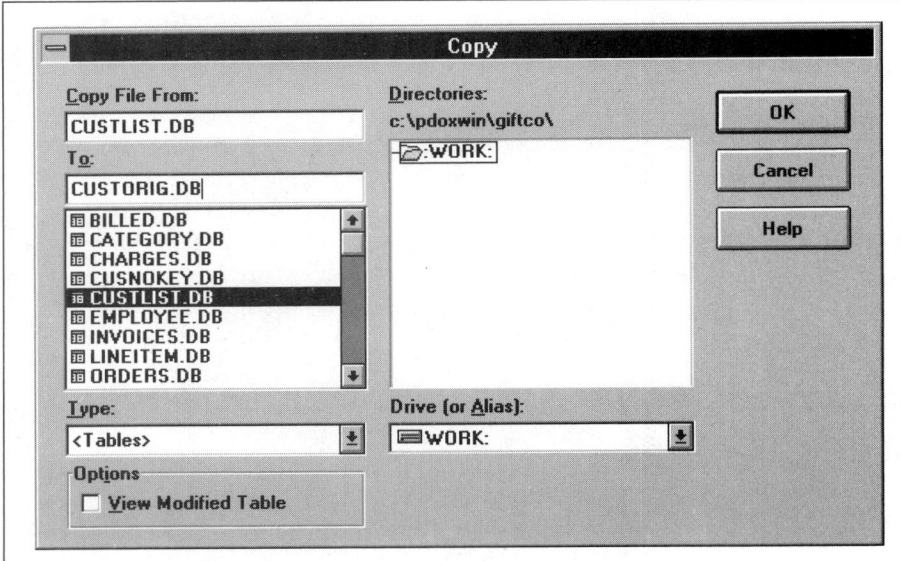

▶ ▶ **T I P**

When you use Paradox for Windows rather than some other file manager to copy a table, Paradox automatically copies any auxiliary files for the table as well, such as the memo file (.mb) and the primary index (.px).

Now you can safely make any changes you want. If you inadvertently make unwanted changes, simply follow the steps above, but reverse the table names. That is, make *CustOrig.db* the source file and *CustList.db* the destination file. (For more information on copying tables and using other file utilities, see Chapter 15.)

▶ Designing a CHANGETO Query

Designing a CHANGETO query is similar to designing any other query, except that you can't use checkmarks. Instead, first enter the query criteria required to isolate the records you want to change.

▶ ▶ **N O T E**

Live Query View is not allowed with CHANGETO queries. This isn't surprising since CHANGETO queries don't allow checkmarks, and Live Query View requires at least one check plus checkmark.

In the Query window below, we've entered **L.A.** in the City field because we plan to change those records to *Los Angeles*.

MI	Department/	Company	Address	City
☐	☐	☐	☐	☐ L.A.	

Query : <Untitled>

Before you do anything else, you might want to run the query just to see which records will be changed in the upcoming steps. That is, check all the fields you want to look at (including the field you'll be changing),

Querying Your Tables

Ch. 9

click the Run Query button, then take a close look at the Answer table to make sure you want to change all the records that appear. If necessary, you can refine and run the query several times until you're sure the query isolates *only* the records you want to change.

When you're sure the records in the Answer table are the ones you want to change, follow these steps:

1. *Uncheck* all the fields in the test query. To do this quickly, move to the left-most column of the query table (press Ctrl+Home), and press F6 until you uncheck all the fields.

2. Move the cursor to the field you want to change. Then add the command *CHANGETO,* followed by a blank space, followed by the new value. If the field you want to change contains a search criterion, precede CHANGETO with a comma and a space.

For example, in the query below, we've told Paradox to isolate records that have L.A. in the City field and change the contents of the City field for those records to "Los Angeles."

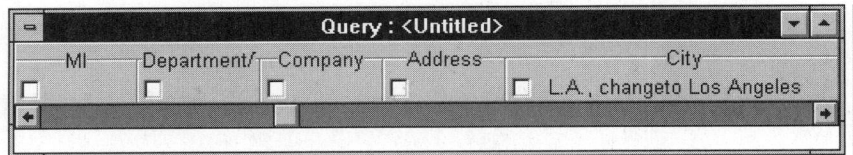

Again, it's crucial to specify which records you want to change. For instance, had we entered *only*

CHANGETO Los Angeles

in the Query window, Paradox would have instantly put "Los Angeles" into the City field of every single record in the table. Ouch! It's not always easy to recover from a mistake like that.

 ► ► **N O T E**

> **If the field you're changing has any validity checks, the new values you place in that field with CHANGETO must satisfy those validity checks.**

When you run a query that contains CHANGETO, Paradox does not display an Answer table. Instead, it displays a temporary table named *Changed*. This table displays all the records that have been changed (and only those records), with the original unchanged data. For instance, if our CustList table happened to contain two records with L.A. in the City field, the resulting Changed table would look like Figure 9.22.

FIGURE 9.22

The Changed table that appears after you run a CHANGETO query contains a list of records that the query changed—with the original unchanged data still in the records.

NOTE

> **If you try to change records that are tied through referential integrity to other tables in your database, Paradox will create a table named *Errorchg* and will not change the records. The Errorchg table will include a copy of the records that Paradox couldn't change. See Chapters 5 and 16 for more about related tables.**

You can close the Changed table, then reopen the original table to verify the changes.

Last-Ditch Approach to Undoing a CHANGETO Query

There is a way to recover from a bad CHANGETO query, even if you didn't make a backup of the table. Below is the basic technique, in case you get into a jam.

►►**W A R N I N G**

This method can be risky in tables that don't have a primary key, so use this recovery technique only when you don't have a recent backup.

1. Leave the *changed.db* table open on your desktop.

2. Choose Tools ➤ Utilities ➤ Add.

3. Click on the *changed.db* table name (most likely appearing as *:PRIV:CHANGED.DB* near the bottom of the table list) to enter that table name into the Add Records From text box.

4. In the To text box, choose or type the name of the original table you changed (*CustList.db* in the previous example).

5. Under Options, choose Update.

6. Click the OK button.

After you do that, you can close all the open windows (choose Window ➤ Close All), then reopen the original table. The records should now contain their original values. (Again, see Chapter 15 for more information on file utilities.)

►► *Using Queries to Delete Records*

By placing the DELETE operator in the left-most column of the query table, you can globally delete a group of records that meets your search criteria. Once again, *extreme* caution is crucial, since a single DELETE query can wipe out hundreds or thousands of records from a table before you've finished saying "oh darn!" So make a backup copy of your table just before doing a DELETE query.

►►**N O T E**

The DELETE operator is located on the menu below the query table name. As for CHANGETO, you *cannot* use it when any field is checked.

Even after making your backup, the safest way to proceed with a DELETE query is as follows:

1. Start a new query as you normally would, but don't check any fields.

2. Enter the search criterion that identifies the records you want to delete. For instance, below we've created a query that will isolate records with CA in the state field.

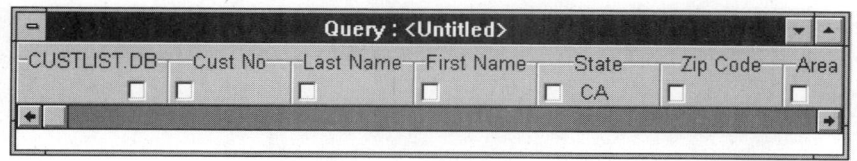

3. If you want to see which records will be deleted, use the check or check plus to check the field that contains your search criterion and any other fields you want to see, then run the query. The resulting Answer table shows which records will be deleted in later steps.

4. As necessary, repeat steps 2 and 3 until the query correctly isolates the records you want to delete.

5. Move to the left-most column of the query table (press Ctrl+Home), and press F6 until you uncheck all the fields. Then type **d,** or hold down the mouse button (or press the spacebar) and choose <u>De</u>-lete from the menu that appears. For example, the query below will delete all records that have CA in the State field.

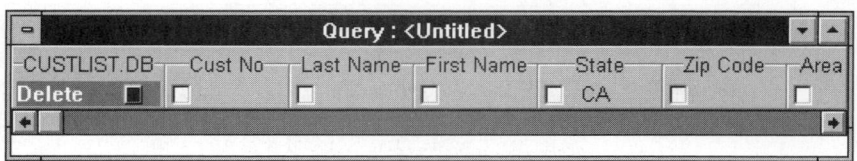

6. Run the query as usual.

When Paradox completes the query, a new temporary table, named *Deleted*, appears on the screen, as in the example shown in Figure 9.23, where we deleted all records that have CA in the State field. This table shows you which records have been removed from the table. If you're satisfied with the deletion, you can close all the windows on the Desktop and open the original table at your leisure. (As with the Answer table, the Deleted table is removed automatically when you exit Paradox.)

▶ ▶ **N O T E**

> **If you try to delete records that are tied to other tables through referential integrity, Paradox will create a table named *Errordel* and will not delete the records. The Errordel table will include a copy of the records that Paradox couldn't delete.**

FIGURE 9.23 ▶

*After we ask Paradox to delete all records that have CA in the State field, Paradox - displays the deleted records in a table named **Deleted**.*

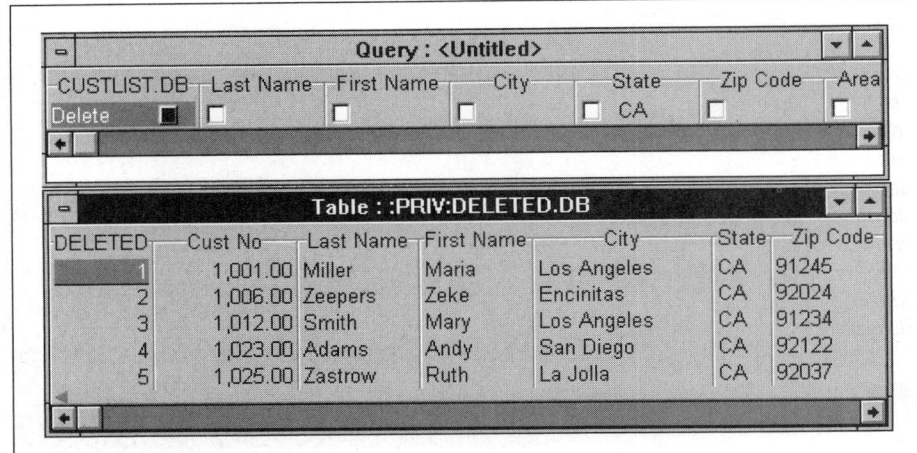

▶ *Recovering from a Bad DELETE Query*

Suppose you run a DELETE query, and upon reviewing the Deleted table decide that you've deleted the wrong records, or too many records, from the original table. Here's a quick way to put those records right back into the table:

1. Choose <u>T</u>ools ➤ <u>U</u>tilities ➤ <u>A</u>dd.

2. Click *Deleted.db* (probably listed as *:PRIV:DELETED.DB*) at the bottom of the tables list to put that table name in the <u>A</u>dd Records From text box.

3. In the To text box, enter the name of the original table that you deleted the records from. Or, click in the To text box, then click the name of the original table in the tables list.

4. Under Options, choose Append. For example, Figure 9.24 shows the Add dialog box filled in to copy deleted records from the Deleted table back into the CustList table.

5. Click the OK button.

If the original table is keyed, the deleted records will be back in their original sort order position within the table. If the original table has no primary key, those records will be at the bottom of the original table because you "appended" them from the *Deleted.db* table to the original table.

FIGURE 9.24 ▸

If you discover you've deleted the wrong records shortly after running a DELETE query, you can use the Add dialog box to append the records from the temporary Deleted table back into the original table.

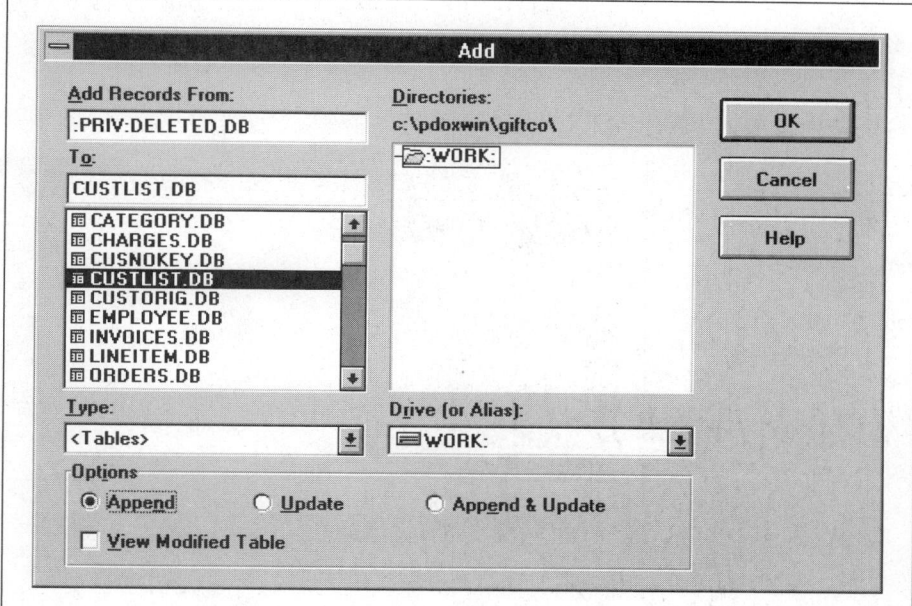

▸▸ *Using a Filter to Isolate Data*

The query by example (QBE) technique presented so far in this chapter provides the greatest flexibility for working with groups of records. But you can also use primary and secondary indexes to sort records (as discussed in Chapter 8) and you can use filters to isolate specific records. Though not as flexible as QBE, these filter queries do offer two big advantages: They always display "live data" in the original table rather than in an Answer table, and they're very easy to set up. So, if you need to change the data you're viewing, you can do so right on the spot.

To create a filter, follow these steps:

1. Open the table you want to work with.

2. Choose Table ➤ Filter, or click the Filter button in the Toolbar (shown at left). You'll see a Filter Tables dialog box like the one shown in Figure 9.25.

3. The Table List area shows the name of the table you're working with. If more than one table name appears in the Table List, click on the one you want to use.

FIGURE 9.25

The Filter Tables dialog box lets you choose a primary or secondary index for sorting (if available in the current table), and isolate particular values within the table.

Filter Tables

Table List:

CUSTLIST.DB

☒ **Order By:**
*Cust No (Primary, Case Sens
Alphabetical_by_Name
Area_Code_and_Phone
City_and_Zip

dBase Index File:

[Range]

Filters on Fields:

Cust No *	
Last Name	
Mr/Mrs	
First Name	
MI	
Department/Title	
Company	
Address	
City	
State	

[OK] [Cancel] [Help]

▶▶ **N O T E**

If you're filtering a form or report (via Form ➤ Filter or Report ➤ Filter), the Table List will show all the tables in the data model. See Chapters 5 and 16 for more about data models.

4. If you want to sort the table and you've defined primary or secondary indexes for it, make sure the Order By box is selected (checked). Then double-click the name of the index that controls the sort order for the table's records (the index names appear just below the Order By option on the left side of the dialog box).

▶▶ **N O T E**

Your table doesn't need a primary or secondary index if you just want to isolate live data. However, it does need a primary or secondary index if you want to sort live data or use the Range button described later. The table's primary index is marked with an asterisk, just below the Order By option. Any secondary indexes are listed below that. See Chapter 8 for more about creating indexes and using them to sort tables.

5. The Filters On Fields list shows all the fields in the selected table. If you double-clicked an index name in step 4, the indexed fields will appear at the top of list, marked with asterisks.

6. Specify your selection criteria in the Filters On Fields list. You also can use the Range button to quickly isolate a range of values in the key fields. The following sections explain more about this step.

7. When you're ready to apply the filter and isolate the records, choose OK in the Filter Tables dialog box.

In Figure 9.26 we chose the Area_Code_and_Phone index described in Chapter 8. Notice that the Area Code and Phone fields appear at the top of the Filters On Fields column and are marked with asterisks.

Querying Your Tables

▶▶

Ch.
9

FIGURE 9.26 ▶

The Filters On Fields column shows all the fields in the table. If you've selected an index, the indexed fields—Area Code and Phone in this example—appear at the top of the column, marked with asterisks.

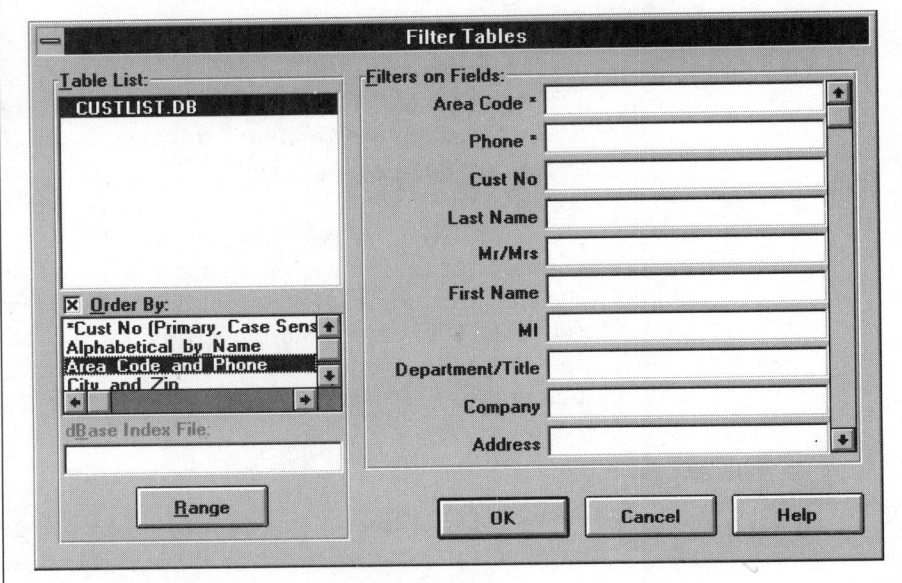

A "filtered" view of your table will appear on the screen. Each field will appear in the table, but you'll only see records that match your search criteria. The records will be sorted according to the index you selected (if any). All the data is live, so you can change it if you need to.

If you're not happy with the filtered results, simply choose Table ▶ Filter, or click the Filter button in the Toolbar, fix your criteria in the Filter Tables dialog box (or remove them altogether), and choose OK.

Paradox will remember the most recent filter criteria until you close the table; then it will discard the filter. The next time you open the table, all records will again be visible.

▶ *Filling in the Filters On Fields List*

In many ways, filters are similar to Live Query View queries. The tips below will help you enter specific values into the text boxes in the Filters On Fields list:

- You can skip (leave blank) any fields that you don't want to restrict to specific values. To move the cursor from text box to text

Wild cards don't seem to be allowed (handwritten)

box in the Filters On Fields list, press Tab or Shift+Tab, or click in the appropriate text box.

- You can type in an exact value or use comparison operators, including =, <, >, <=, >=, NOT, AND (or comma), OR, BLANK, and TODAY. For example, the following expressions would be valid in the Last Name field:

Smith
<Smith
>=A and <N

- You can use parentheses to group values that you're comparing (see Figure 9.27).

- Searches are case sensitive. For example, if you've entered state abbreviations in uppercase letters, be sure to type them in uppercase letters in the State text box (for example, type **CA,** not **ca**).

- Use quotation marks to prevent Paradox from confusing a value with an operator. For instance, to isolate people in the states of Oregon or California, type the following into the State text box:

"OR" or CA

- When you enter conditions into more than one field of the Filters On Fields list, you are setting up an AND condition. That is, the results will include only those records that have all the field values you've specified.

- If you want to reference another field in your filter expression, enclose the field name in square brackets. You can use field names on the left side of a comparison operator, but not on the right side. For example, to show customers in New York or customers in Los Angeles, you could type **[State]=NY OR [City]="Los Angeles"** into any field of the Filters On Tables list. Similarly, to show records in which the zip code is between 92000 and 92999-9999, or the credit limit is less than $6000, you could type this expression:

([Zip Code]>=92000 AND [Zip Code]<="92999-9999") OR [Credit Limit]<6000

Querying Your Tables

Ch.
9

Although filters are similar to queries, they do have the limitations listed below:

- You can use the .. operator at the end of a filter condition, but not before it. For example, to select records in which the address contains the word *Drive*, enter **drive..** as the filter condition for the Address field. However, the condition *..drive..* would not be allowed.

- You cannot use the @ operator. For instance, in the Last Name field, the value *Sm@th* would not be allowed.

- You cannot use LIKE, AS, and SET operators. (AS and SET are covered in Chapter 16.)

- You cannot use operators that change data.

- The fields in the index determine the sort order of records, and you cannot specify another sort order.

Figure 9.27 shows an example that will isolate records for people with last names ranging from A to Mzzzzzzzzzz... who live in the 619 area code or any area code in the range of 200 to 400.

FIGURE 9.27 ▶

This filter would sort records by area code and phone and display only those records of people whose last names are in the range of A to Mzzzzzzzzzz... and who live in the 619 area code or any area code in the range of 200 to 400.

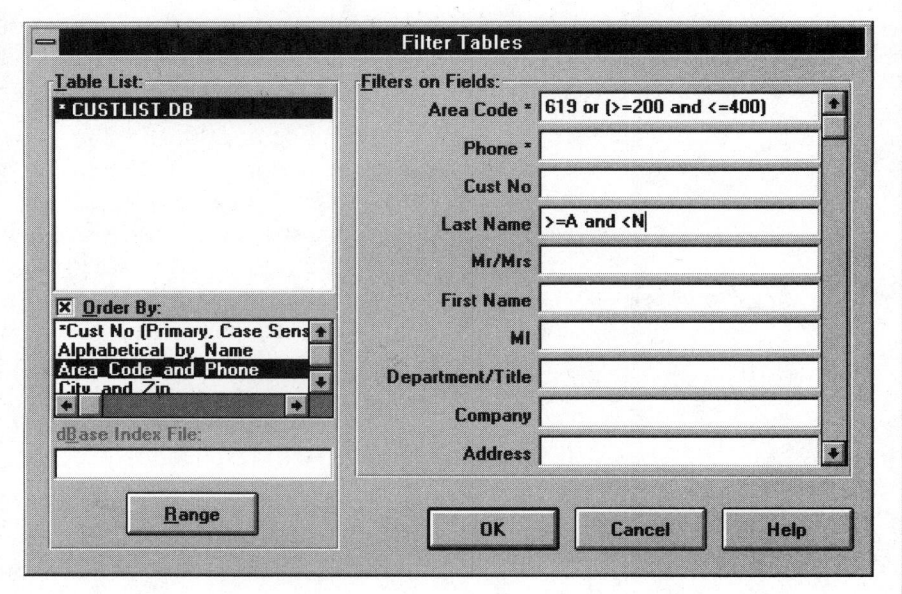

▶ Isolating a Range of Records in an Indexed Table

Figure 9.27 illustrates how to isolate records that fall into some range of values. You can use *comparison operators* to define a range, whether the table has an index or not.

If your table has a primary or secondary index, however, you can use the *index* to isolate a range of records very quickly. (Using an index can be much faster than using the comparison operators to isolate a range.) To begin, go to the Filter Tables dialog box, make sure Order By is checked, and double-click the index you want. In the Filters On Fields list, set up any filter criteria you want for fields that *are not* in the index. Next, click the Range button. The Set Range For Index dialog box will appear, as illustrated in Figure 9.28.

FIGURE 9.28 ▶

The Set Range For Index dialog box lets you search for a single value or a range of values using the selected index. The search will be very fast, but your options for defining the search are quite limited.

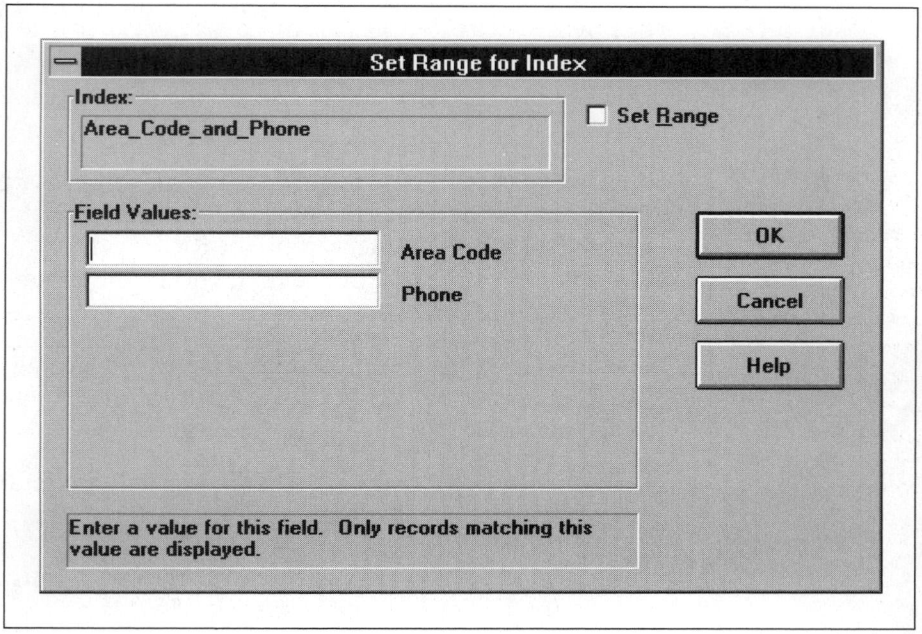

Set Range for Index

Index:
Area_Code_and_Phone   ☐ Set Range

Field Values:
[   ] Area Code
[   ] Phone

OK
Cancel
Help

Enter a value for this field. Only records matching this value are displayed.

▶ ▶ **N O T E**

> **If you haven't created a primary or secondary index for the current table, the index list will be empty and the Range button will be dimmed and unavailable.**

Now you can enter the specific values to isolate in the text boxes next to the field names. The following rules apply:

- You can only type in an exact value. No fancy QBE operators such as .., @, <, >, NOT, AND, OR, LIKE, BLANK, or TODAY. For instance "Smith" is OK, but "Sm@th", "..smith..", "NOT Smith", and so forth are all invalid in the Set Range For Index dialog box.

- You cannot skip any fields in the Field Values list.

- The fields in the index determine the sort order of records.

For instance, in Figure 9.28 you could fill in just the Area Code text box or both the Area Code and Phone text boxes. But you cannot leave the Area Code text box blank and fill in the Phone text box.

Alternatively, you can specify a range of values for one of the indexed fields. To do that, first fill in the lowest value for the field you want to search, then select (check) the Set Range option. A second text box for the field will appear. Put the high end of the range in this second (bottom) text box.

For example, in the Set Range For Index dialog box shown in Figure 9.29, we've chosen Set Range and specified records with area codes in the range of 600 to 699 as the range to view.

When using composite indexes (indexes that contain multiple fields) to specify ranges, there's one more rule to remember:

- If you are combining exact matches with ranges, the range match must be the last one in the set of fields.

For example, if the index you're using contains the three fields City, State, and Start Date, you could set an exact match on the first field (Los Angeles), an exact match on the second field (CA), and a range on the last field (1/1/94 to 3/31/94).

FIGURE 9.29

This Set Range For Index dialog box will isolate records that have area codes in the range of 600 to 699 (inclusive).

Set Range for Index

Index:
Area_Code_and_Phone   ☒ Set Range

Field Values:

| 600 | Area Code |
| 699 | (High) |

OK

Cancel

Help

Enter largest value for the range field.

▶▶ **TIP**

If you accidentally enter your range into the wrong text box below Field Values, delete the text you entered, then put the cursor in the text box that should contain the low value. Now deselect Set Range, select Set Range again, and fill in the text boxes correctly.

Specifying a Partial Match

When designating a range in an alpha field, you can also specify an inexact match, where only the first character or characters of the field need to match the value you're searching for. Figure 9.30 illustrates a Set Range For Index dialog box where we chose the Alphabetical_by_Name index and entered **A** as the field value to search for in the Last Name index. Then we chose Set Range and entered **N** into the second text box to appear. Then we chose Match Partial Strings to tell Paradox we want to view only records that start with the letters *A* through *N*.

FIGURE 9.30 ▶

This Set Range For In-dex dialog box will isolate records for cus-tomers whose last names begin with the letters A through N.

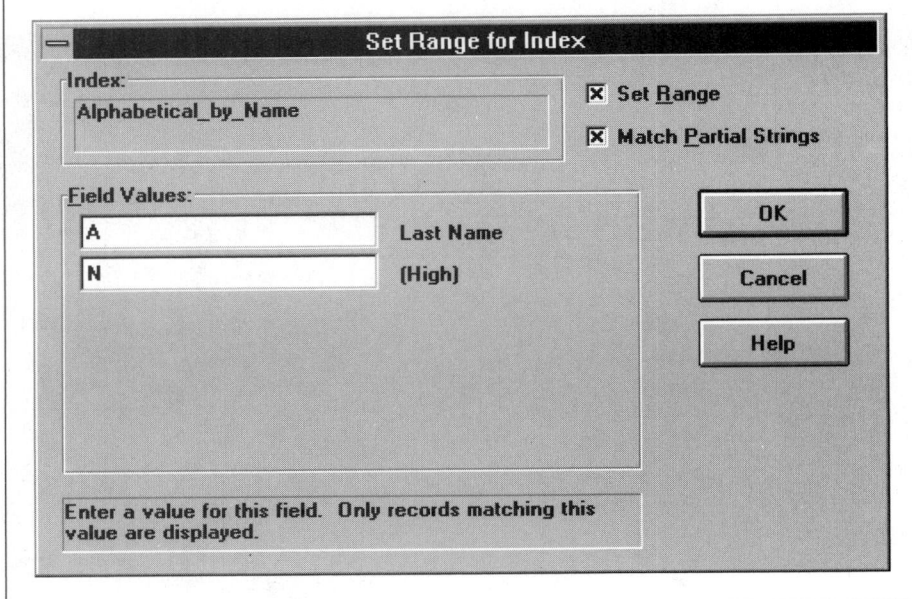

▶ Applying the Filter

Once you've filled in the Filter Tables dialog box or the Set Range For Index dialog box, choose OK once (from the Filter Tables dialog box) or twice (from the Set Range For Index dialog box) to apply the filter. Records appear in the original table, and any records that do not match the search criteria become temporarily invisible. In fact, even the record count at the bottom of the screen acts as though the records don't exist.

Because this is the original table and live data, you can make any changes right on the spot. If you change a record so that it no longer matches the search criterion, it will seem to disappear. Any other task you perform, such as printing data, will also ignore the invisible data.

To bring the invisible records out of hiding, choose Table ➤ Filter again. Delete any field values in the Filters On Fields list and remove any Field Values from the range (or just choose another index). Alternatively, you can close the table and reopen it.

When changing or removing entries in the Filters On Fields list, be sure to use the vertical scroll bar and examine *all* the fields in the list. A filled-in field may lurk at the very bottom of the list and prevent all of your records from reappearing the next time you apply the filter.

▶ *Filtering One Field at a Time*

Here's a quick way to filter records in just one field:

1. Start in Table View or Form View, and put the cursor in the field you want to filter.

2. Inspect (right-click) the field and choose Filter from the menu that appears. You'll see a Field Filter dialog box like the one below:

3. Type the filter text, using any technique discussed earlier under "Filling in the Filters On Fields List." For example, you can type an exact value and you can use comparison operators such as >, <, >=, <=, AND, comma, OR, BLANK, and TODAY; however, you cannot use the .., @, and LIKE operators.

4. Choose OK to apply your filter.

The results will be the same as if you had chosen Table ➤ Filter and filled in just one field in the Filters On Fields list. Remember that Paradox will display the filtered version of your records until you change the filter or you close the table.

▶ ▶ **N O T E**

> **Setting up a one-field filter is just a shortcut alternative to using the Table ➤ Filter commands. Your one-field filters will appear automatically in the Filter Fields dialog box the next time you choose Table ➤ Filter or click the Filter button.**

If you'd like to add a filter to another field (or change an existing filter), simply repeat the steps above for the field you're interested in. Remember that adding a filter to another field sets up an AND condition, just as when you add another condition to the Filter On Fields list in the Filter Tables dialog box described earlier.

To remove the filter on a field, repeat the first two steps above, erase the text in the Filter Field dialog box, and choose OK.

▶ ▶ **T I P**

> **If you accidentally create a filter that hides all the records in your table, don't panic. Instead, choose Table ➤ Filter or Form ➤ Filter, revise (or remove) your filter criteria as required, and choose OK. As an alternative, you could just close the table or form and reopen it (this would discard filters on all the fields).**

In this chapter, you've learned the basics of using queries to search for and change data in a table. If you've been reading the chapters of this book in sequence, you now know how to use the most essential features of Paradox for Windows.

Chapter 10 begins Part 3 of this book, where you'll learn how to design fancy forms, reports, and graphs for entering and presenting data in attractive, easy-to-use, and easy-to-understand formats.

Viewing and Printing Data

PART THREE

Tools for Creating Design Documents

▶▶ FAST TRACK

▶ **To create a design document**   **491**

choose File ➤ New ➤ Form (to create a form) or File ➤
New ➤ Report (to create a report). Then, click one of the
following buttons: Form Expert, Report Expert, or Label
Expert (to let an automated "expert" guide you through
setting up a form, report, or mailing labels); Blank (to
start with a completely blank document); or Data Model /
Layout Diagram (to choose a table, query, or data model,
and then select the initial fields and field layout, style, and
style sheet). Regardless of how you create the initial design
document, you can customize it by switching to the Design
window and using the tools it provides.

▶ **To preview your design**   **513**

click the View Data button in the Toolbar or press F8.

▶ **To print your design or data**   **514**

click the Print button in the Toolbar. See Chapters 10 and
11 for additional information.

▶ **To save your design**   **515**

choose File ➤ Save.

▶ **To assign a design to the Quick buttons**   **516**

open the table you want to associate with the button. Then
choose Properties ➤ Preferred, followed by Form, Report,
Graph, or Crosstab. Or, right-click the appropriate Toolbar
button and choose the document from the dialog box that
appears.

▶ ***To open an existing design document***   *517*

> choose File ➤ Open ➤ Form or File ➤ Open ➤ Report.
> Choose a file name, an Open mode, and other options as
> needed. Then click OK. To open a document quickly, click
> the Form or Report icon in the Project Viewer; then double-
> click the name of the document you want, or right-click
> the document name and choose an option from the prop-
> erty menu.

▶ ***To select design objects***   *527*

> first choose the Selection Arrow in the Toolbar. Then click
> on the object or use the Shift+click and Shift+drag tech-
> niques to select multiple objects. To select all objects within
> the currently selected object, choose Edit ➤ Select All.

▶ ***To arrange and resize multiple objects automatically***   *532*

> select the objects, then choose options from the
> Design menu.

▶ ***To change the properties of objects***   *535*

> select the objects, right-click (or press F6), then choose
> options from the property menu that appears. To change
> *penetrating* properties of objects, hold down the Ctrl key
> while right-clicking the mouse, or press Shift+F6.

▶ ***To create and place objects***   *545*

> click the appropriate tool in the Toolbar, then click in the
> Design window and drag the outline to define the size you
> want. You can then reposition or resize the object, or
> change its properties.

*I*n Chapter 1 you saw several examples of jazzy forms and reports for presenting table data on-screen or in printed form. And, if you completed Lessons 4 and 5 in Chapter 2, you've already designed a simple custom form and report of your own. But what you've seen so far is just the tip of the iceberg, for the design possibilities in Paradox for Windows are limited only by your imagination.

In this chapter, we'll cover basic techniques used to design forms and reports. You'll learn how to

- Create a new design document.

- Choose a table, query, or data model to associate with your design.

- Specify an initial layout for the design.

- Customize the design by adding, removing, and rearranging design objects and changing their properties.

- Preview, print, and save a design document.

▶ ▶ **N O T E**

If you haven't completed Lessons 4 and 5 in Chapter 2, please do so before reading this chapter. The concepts presented in this chapter will make a lot more sense once you've gotten your fingers wet.

In Chapters 11 and 12, we'll cover more specific techniques for designing forms and reports. Then, in Chapter 13, you'll learn how to create graphs and crosstabs of table data. Chapter 17 covers more advanced topics, including calculated fields and multitable design documents.

As you look through this chapter, don't be daunted by its size. Focus on the basics presented here, try some features on a new form that you use just for practice, then go back and read the details when you need them. Be sure to experiment freely with the many design tools available—experimentation is truly your best teacher.

► ►**TIP**

> **For some hands-on practice in setting up forms and reports, click the Coaches button in the Toolbar, select the "Queries, Forms, And Reports" Coach, and try out the "Creating A Standard Form" and "Creating A Standard Report" lessons. See Chapter 3 for more about Coaches.**

► ► *What Is a Design Document?*

Forms and reports are called *design documents* in Paradox for Windows. *Forms* are usually designed to display table data, either for viewing or for data entry. A cleverly designed form can make data entry efficient, easy, and fun. Figure 10.1 shows a form for our Employee table, complete with three-dimensional frames, scroll bars around the note text, the Gift Corner logo and form title, and the employee's photograph and signature. You'll see many more examples of custom forms in Chapter 11.

Reports are usually intended for printed data. You can design simple reports which display data in a "raw" form, or you can create complex summary reports that group and summarize data by various fields, and even include graphs. Figure 10.2 shows a sample customer report, sorted into alphabetical order by the customer's name.

► ► *What Is a Design Object?*

All design documents (except completely empty ones) contain *design objects*. Certain design objects, called *data elements*, relate specifically to your data. These include tables, records, fields, graphs, and crosstabs. Other design objects, called *design elements*, are used to spruce up the design document. These include boxes, lines, ellipses, graphics, OLE

FIGURE 10.1 ▶

A data entry form for the Employee table

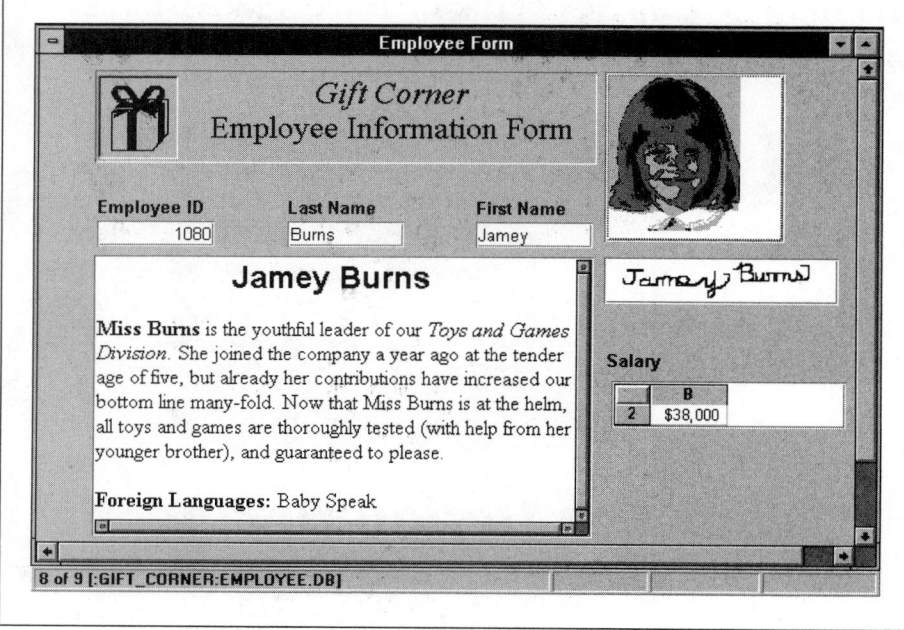

objects, and text. We'll refer to both data elements and design elements simply as *objects*.

A big part of customizing a design is adding, deleting, and rearranging design objects in the document. The most exciting part of designing a document involves changing the *properties*—the appearance and behavior—of objects in the design. Each type of object has its own set of associated properties, such as color, font, alignment, and so forth. We'll be discussing object properties throughout this chapter and the three chapters that follow.

▶▶ *If in Doubt, Try It Out*

If you've ever used a Windows drawing or painting package, you know that creating the perfect picture is largely a matter of picking a drawing tool, dragging it across the screen to define a shape or line, then adding a splash of color or some other enhancement. After a good deal of experimentation—and some creative insights—your drawing is complete.

FIGURE 10.2

A report from the CustList table

Wednesday, July 27, 1994   6:39:54 AM   Page 1

Gift Corner
Customer Information Report

Adams, Mr. Andy
President   **Phone:** 619 / 555-0123 Ext: 35
ABC Corporation
123 A St.
San Diego, CA 92122
Start Date: 7/29/92   **Credit Limit:** $5,000.00   **Customer #:** 1023

Adams, Miss Anita
Microcomputer Consultant   **Phone:** 410 / 555-4354 Ext: 125
5434 Oceanic Way
Silver Spring, MD 20910
Start Date: 11/28/92   **Credit Limit:** $2,500.00   **Customer #:** 1002

Cherub, Miss Sky
Oneness Well-Being   **Phone:** 605 / 555-3232
985 Enlightenment Way
Jefferson, SD 57038
Start Date: 4/14/93   **Credit Limit:** $10,000.00   **Customer #:** 1004

Clavell, Miss Wanda
Mother Superior   **Phone:** 401 / 555-0323 Ext: 314
Westridge Convent
452 Reposo Alto
Tiverton, RI 02878
Start Date: 2/17/93   **Credit Limit:** $2,500.00   **Customer #:** 1005

Dewey, Mr. Frank
Senior Partner   **Phone:** 206 / 555-4323
Dewey, Cheatham, and Howe
1121 Cass St, Suite 33
Bothell, WA 98011
Start Date: 3/26/93   **Credit Limit:** $5,000.00   **Customer #:** 1022

Designing a document in Paradox is a lot like using Paintbrush or any Windows drawing application; therefore, before tackling the tools in the Design window, you should already know something about using your mouse to draw lines and boxes, select objects, and move objects around on the screen. (You'll find Paintbrush in the Accessories window of Program Manager.)

The key to designing a Paradox for Windows document is to take a free-form, non-procedural approach. Just let your imagination run free instead of trying to do everything step by step. Try various tools, select and rearrange objects, change object properties, and so on, until you arrive at a design that suits your fancy. Just remember these watchwords as you work:

> If in doubt, try it out! And don't forget that online help is just an F1 keypress away.

▶▶ *General Steps for Designing a Document*

Paradox offers two ways to design a new document. The first method uses Experts, which guide you through the design process step by step. Experts are quick to use but offer less flexibility in setting up an initial design. We'll cover the form Experts in Chapter 11, and show you how to use the report and mailing label Experts in Chapter 12.

▶▶ **T I P**

If you're in a hurry to try the Experts now, just click the Expert button in the Toolbar, or choose <u>H</u>elp ➤ E<u>x</u>perts. Alternatively, you can choose an Expert when you create a new design document, as explained later. Once the Expert appears, simply read the prompts carefully and make your choices.

The second method, which we'll cover in detail, involves designing the document from scratch. Here are the basic steps for designing a document. We'll elaborate on these steps throughout this and following chapters.

1. Open a new design document.

2. Choose a table, query, or data model to associate with your document.

3. Choose a design style—single record, tabular, multi-record, or blank.

4. Select the fields to include, the initial layout (by columns or by rows), and whether to label fields.

5. Choose a style sheet to control the initial appearance and behavior of new objects in the document.

6. Add, delete, and rearrange design objects and change the object properties to get the look you want.

7. Preview or print the document to see the results.

8. Repeat steps 6 and 7 as needed.

9. Save the design.

10. If you wish, assign the design to one of the Quick buttons in the Toolbar for Table View.

►► *Creating a New Design Document*

The steps for creating a new design document are similar, whether you're creating forms or reports. The next two sections explain how to get started.

► *Starting a New Form*

You can begin a new form in any of the following ways:

- Choose File ➤ New ➤ Form from the menus.

 - Right-click the Open Form button in the Toolbar, if it's available, and choose New.

- Right-click the Forms icon in the left side of the Project Viewer and choose New.

You'll see the New Form dialog box shown here:

From here, you can click one of the following buttons, depending on what you want to do next:

Blank   Creates a blank form that isn't associated with any table, query, or data model. You'll rarely want to choose this button, unless you're creating a form that consists of buttons or menu options for an application. (More about this in Chapter 19.)

Form Expert   Takes you through the steps for defining a form that is based on one table or two related tables. (We'll discuss form Experts in Chapter 11.)

Data Model / Layout Diagram   Lets you choose a table, query, or data model upon which to base the form, and then define the form's initial fields and layout. In this chapter, we'll assume you've chosen the Data Model / Layout Diagram button to get started.

▶ Starting a New Report

To begin a new report, use any of these methods:

- Choose File ➤ New ➤ Report from the menus.

- Right-click the Open Report button in the Toolbar, if it's available, and choose New.

- Right-click the Reports icon in the left side of the Project Viewer and choose New.

The New Report dialog box, shown below, appears next:

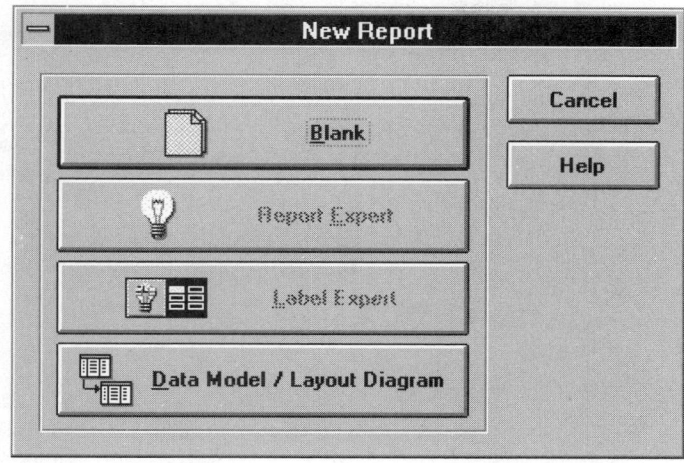

You can click one of the following buttons (notice how similar these are to the options in the New Form dialog box):

Blank   Creates a blank report that isn't associated with any table, query, or data model. You may never need to use this button.

Report Expert   Takes you through the steps for defining a report that is based on one table or two related tables. See Chapter 11.

Label Expert   Takes you through the steps for setting up mailing labels. See Chapter 11.

Data Model / Layout Diagram   Lets you choose a table, query, or data model upon which to base the report, and then define the report's initial fields and layout. Again, we'll assume you've chosen this option.

▶▶ *The Data Model Dialog Box*

If you clicked <u>D</u>ata Model / Layout Diagram button in the New Form or New Report dialog box, you'll see the Data Model dialog box next. Initially, this dialog box lists tables in the current working directory, as in Figure 10.3.

FIGURE 10.3 ▶

The Data Model dialog box lets you name the table, query, or data model to use as a basis for the design document.

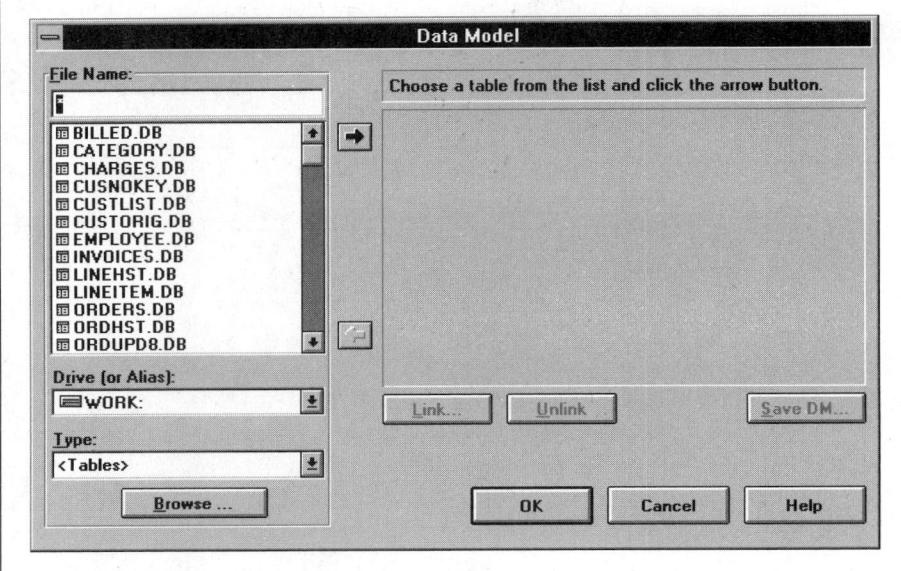

▶ Defining the Data Model

The *data model* tells Paradox which data you want to work with in your document. Your data model can use any of the following:

- A single table
- Multiple related tables
- A query
- A data model that is stored in a separate file
- No tables or queries

▶▶ **N O T E**

Chapter 5 explained how to create and save data models using the Data Model Designer. We'll discuss multitable data models in Chapter 17.

▶ *Designing with a Single Table*

As shown in Figure 10.3, the left side of the Data Model dialog box is similar to the Open Table dialog box discussed in Chapter 6. To add a table to the data model, double-click the table name you want in the left side of the dialog box, or click once on the table name and then click the → button. The table name will move to the data model area at the right of the dialog box.

If you choose the wrong table, simply click the table in the right side of the dialog box, then click the ← button (or press Alt+D) and choose the correct table name.

You also can use the D<u>r</u>ive (or Alias) list box and <u>B</u>rowse buttons to choose tables that aren't in your current working directory. When you're finished defining the data model, choose OK.

 ▶▶**T I P**

> **You can return to the Data Model dialog box at any time by clicking the Data Model button in the Design window Toolbar or any dialog box in which that button appears. Or, you can choose For<u>m</u> ➤ Data <u>M</u>odel or <u>R</u>eport ➤ Data <u>M</u>odel from the Design window menus.**

▶ *Designing with Saved Queries*

As you know, queries provide a powerful way to select certain fields and records from your table. You can take advantage of queries by designing a document based on a saved query.

 ▶▶**N O T E**

> **In Chapter 16 you'll learn how to perform calculations in queries, making saved queries even more useful as the basis for reports.**

Suppose, for example, that you want to design a telephone directory report listing the names, area codes, and phone numbers of all your customers sorted by customer name. Using techniques discussed in Chapter 9, you could set up a query like the one in Figure 10.4. From the Query window, choose Properties ➤ Answer Sort and sort the Answer table by Last Name, First Name, and MI. Then close the Query window and save it as usual.

FIGURE 10.4 ►

Query to select fields from the CustList table and sort the Answer table

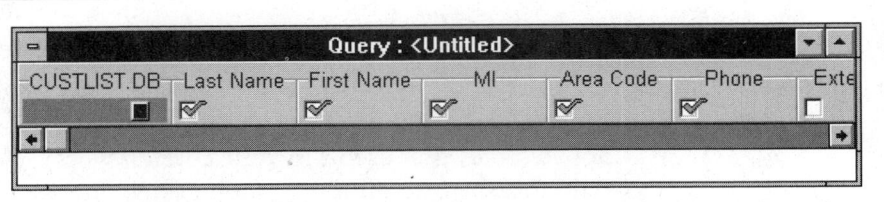

Now, to base your document on the saved query, go to the Data Model dialog box as described above. Then, instead of choosing a table name, click the Type drop-down list box and choose <Queries>. Select the query you want from the left side of the dialog box and choose OK. Complete the design (as described in this and following chapters) and save your document.

Each time you run the report in the future, Paradox will first run the query, generating a new Answer table. That way, your phone list will always be up to the minute and sorted with no extra effort on your part.

 ► ►**W A R N I N G**

Most queries do not work on "live" table data, so you shouldn't use them as the basis for data entry forms. In general, it's best to use queries for reports, not forms. However, as you learned in Chapter 9, you *can* create live queries that are useful for data entry forms. Unfortunately, live queries are limited to one table only, must use the check plus checkmark, cannot sort the query results, and must adhere to some other sticky little rules.

▶ Designing with Data Models

You also can base your design document on a saved data model (see Chapter 5). If you'd like to use a saved data model, go to the Data Model dialog box, click the Type drop-down list box and choose <Data Models>. Select the data model you want from the left side of the dialog box and choose OK. Then complete the design and save it.

▶ Creating a Blank Design

Normally, you'll want to associate the design document with an existing table or query. However, if you wish, you can create a blank document that isn't bound to any table's data. To do so, simply choose OK in the Data Model dialog box without first choosing a table or query. (Or, click the Blank button that appears in the New Form or New Report dialog box.) If you opt to create a blank design, Paradox will skip the Design Layout dialog box described a little later in this chapter.

▶▶**TIP**

You can always bind your design to a table or query later by clicking the Data Model button in the Toolbar. However, you'll save time by choosing a table, query, or data model to begin with.

▶ Inspecting Tables in the Data Model

Inspecting a table name in the right side of the Data Model dialog box leads to several useful options. The options available when designing *forms* are listed below.

Fields   Displays the field names for the table you're inspecting. This list is for reference only.

Filter   Lets you sort and filter the records displayed in the form. When the Filter Tables dialog box appears, select a secondary index (if you wish) and any values or ranges you want to use, then choose OK to return to the Data Model dialog box. (See Chapter 8 for details on secondary indexes and Chapter 9 for details about the Filter Tables dialog box.)

Read-Only   Prevents users from making any changes to this table.

Strict Translation   When checked (the default setting), Paradox limits data entry to characters that are available in the DOS character set for the selected language driver. For example, when this option is checked, typing the copyright symbol (©) into a field will cause Paradox to reject the entry and display the message "Character(s) not supported by Table Language" in the status bar. When the option is not checked, Paradox will let you enter characters that aren't in the set, but will convert the character to one that is in the set when you move the cursor out of the field.

Auto-Append   When this option is checked (the default setting), you can add new records automatically. Just switch to Edit mode, move the cursor to the last record, press Ins, PgDn, or F12 (or click the Next Record button in the Toolbar or choose Record ▶ Next), and then type the new record's data. When the option is not checked, you must press the Ins key (or choose Record ▶ Insert) to insert new records.

When you inspect a table name in the data model for a *report*, Paradox will list the field names for the table you're inspecting. This list is for reference only.

▶▶ *Choosing an Initial Design Layout*

The Design Layout dialog box appears after you choose OK from the Data Model dialog box. There you can specify an initial layout for your design, including:

- A general field layout and style for the design
- Which fields will appear
- Whether fields will be labeled or not
- Which style sheet will control the initial appearance of objects in the design

Keep in mind that the options in the Design Layout dialog box are mainly a convenience for setting up your initial design. You don't have to change any of the settings unless you want to. However, after designing a few reports or forms, you'll appreciate the time saved by making a few choices up front.

The changes you make in the Design Layout dialog box are reflected immediately in the sample design area, so you can see what the document will look like before you get to the Design window. Note that the appearance of the Design Layout dialog box and the options available depend on the table you selected, whether you're designing a form or report, and the basic style you've chosen. For instance, Figure 10.5 shows the default Design Layout dialog box for a form, while Figure 10.6 shows the default Design Layout dialog box for a report. Both examples are based on the now-familiar Employee table.

N O T E

> If your data model involves multiple tables that are involved in one-to-many relationships, the Design Layout dialog box will include a Show **D**etail Tables button, which lets you control the style for displaying detail tables. You'll learn about that in Chapter 17.

FIGURE 10.5

The default Design Layout dialog box for a form based on the sample Employee table

Design Layout
Field Layout: ⦿ By **C**olumns ○ By Ro**w**s	Show La**y**out	Show **F**ields
Style: ⦿ **Single Record** ○ **T**abular ○ **M**ulti-Record ○ Blan**k**	Employee ID : / LastName : / FirstName : / Salary : / Signature : / Photo : / Voice :	Notes :
Multi-Record Layout: ○ Horizontal ○ **V**ertical ⦿ **B**oth		
☒ **L**abel Fields		
Style Sheet: C:\PDOXWIN\DEFAULT.FT	OK Cancel Help	

FIGURE 10.6 ►

FIGURE 10.6 ►

The default Design Layout dialog box for a report based on the sample Employee table

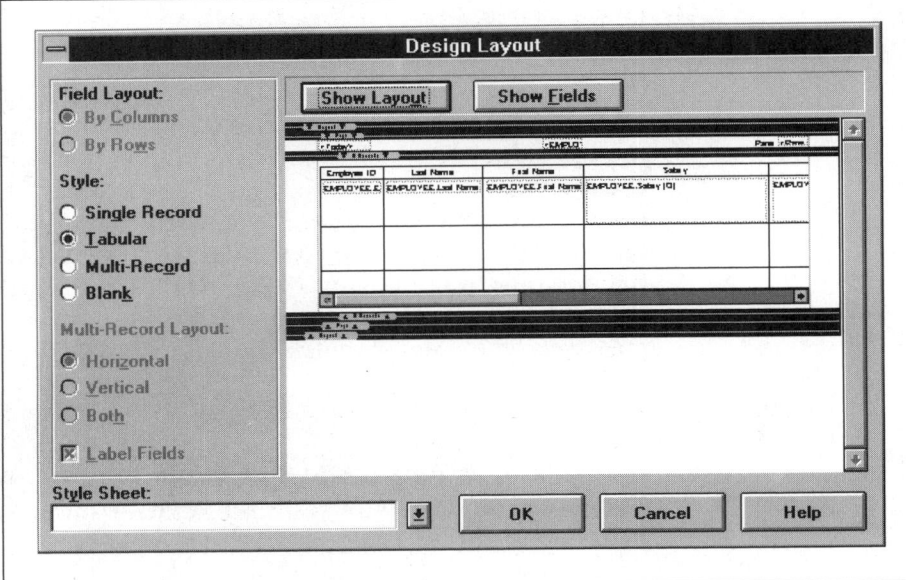

Make any changes you want in this dialog box as described in the sections that follow. When you're happy with the initial layout, choose OK to get to the Design window, where you can customize the design to your heart's content.

► ► **W A R N I N G**

Although you'll rarely need to do so, you can return to the Design Layout dialog box later by choosing Design ► Design Layout from the Design window. However, be aware that if you change the design layout, your existing design will be *completely replaced*. Paradox will give you a chance to back out before taking this action. When the warning message appears, choose Yes *only* if you're sure you want to replace your design; otherwise choose No to cancel the changes.

▶ *Hiding or Showing Field Labels*

A field label is a text object that contains the field name. Paradox for Windows initially displays all fields in a document with field labels.

To display field data without field labels, select the Label Fields option in the Design Layout dialog box to remove the checkmark. You'll save considerable time by figuring out early whether you want *most* of the fields to appear with or without labels. Later, when you reach the Design window, you can inspect individual fields to turn labels on or off.

 ▶ ▶ N O T E

> The Label Fields option is always checked and cannot be changed for a Tabular or Blank design style.

▶ *Choosing a Design Style*

Paradox for Windows offers several styles for displaying a design, including the following:

Single-Record   Displays one record of the table at a time.

Tabular   Displays several records of the table in a table frame.

Multi-Record   Displays several records of the table in a multi-record object.

Blank   Doesn't display any records of the table.

To choose one of these styles, click the appropriate option in the Style area of the dialog box.

 ▶ ▶ N O T E

> The remaining figures in this chapter show examples of form designs; the concepts illustrated are basically the same for reports.

Tabular Design Style

The simplest design style is *Tabular,* which resembles the Quick Report format discussed in Chapter 7. As shown by the sample design layout in Figure 10.7, the rows and columns look just like the table itself, with a horizontal scroll bar added. Reports initially have a tabular style.

FIGURE 10.7 ▶

A tabular design style for the Employee table

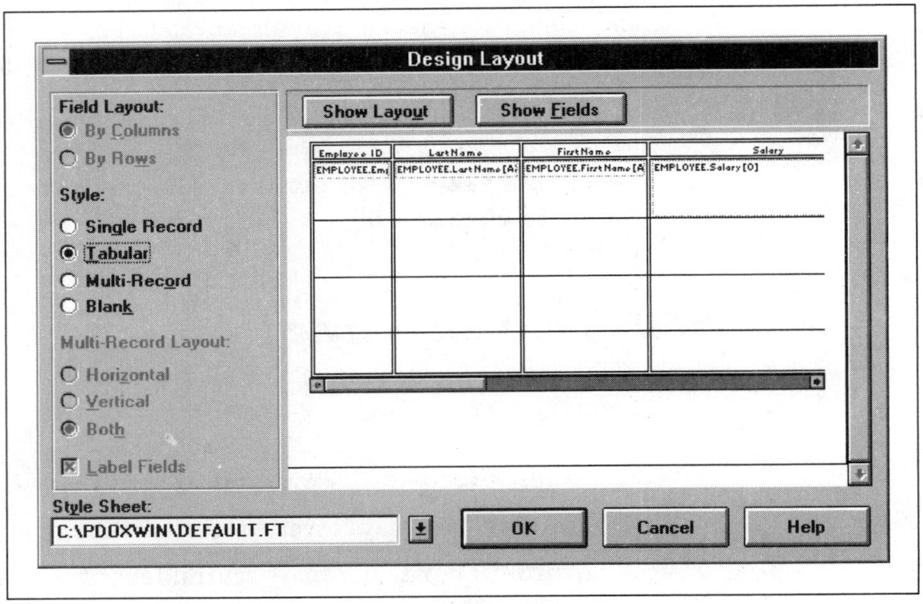

Single-Record Design Style

The *Single-Record* design style displays one record at a time. It is the default layout for a form. You can either arrange the fields by columns (top-to-bottom) or by rows (left-to-right). To arrange fields by columns, choose By Columns in the Field Layout area of the Design Layout dialog box (see Figure 10.5, above). To arrange them by rows, choose By Rows in the Field layout area (see Figure 10.8, below).

Multi-Record Style

The *Multi-Record* design style displays several records in the table at one time and is especially handy for creating mailing labels. (Chapter 12 shows how to design multi-record mailing labels, with an Expert.)

FIGURE 10.8

The Single-Record design style arranged in rows

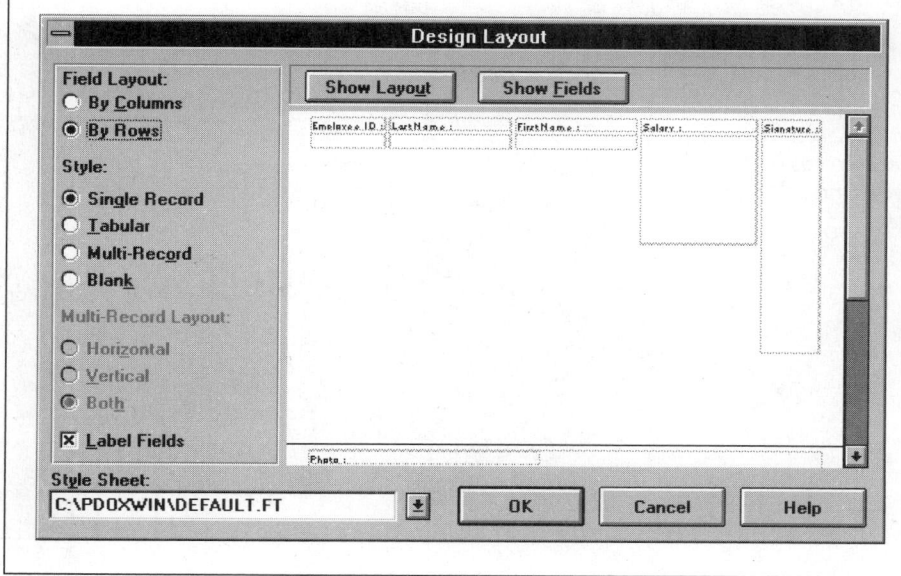

Notice in Figure 10.9 that the fields of a record appear in the first record region of the sample area. As for the Single-Record layout, you can choose whether the field layout within a record is By Columns or By Rows.

You can also specify how you want repeated records to appear on the page by choosing options in the Multi-Record Layout area of the dialog box. Your choices are as follows:

Horizontal   Records repeat across the page (this is the default multi-record layout for a report).

Vertical   Records repeat down the page.

Both   Records repeat both across and down the page (this is the default multi-record layout for a form).

Figure 10.9 shows the Employee design after choosing *Both* to repeat records across and down the page. (An error message will warn you if Paradox cannot fit all the fields into the multi-record layout. Choose OK to clear the message. Paradox will then place as many fields as will fit into the sample area.)

FIGURE 10.9 ▶

A multi-record design style for an Employee table form. The Both option selected here re-peats records both across and down the page.

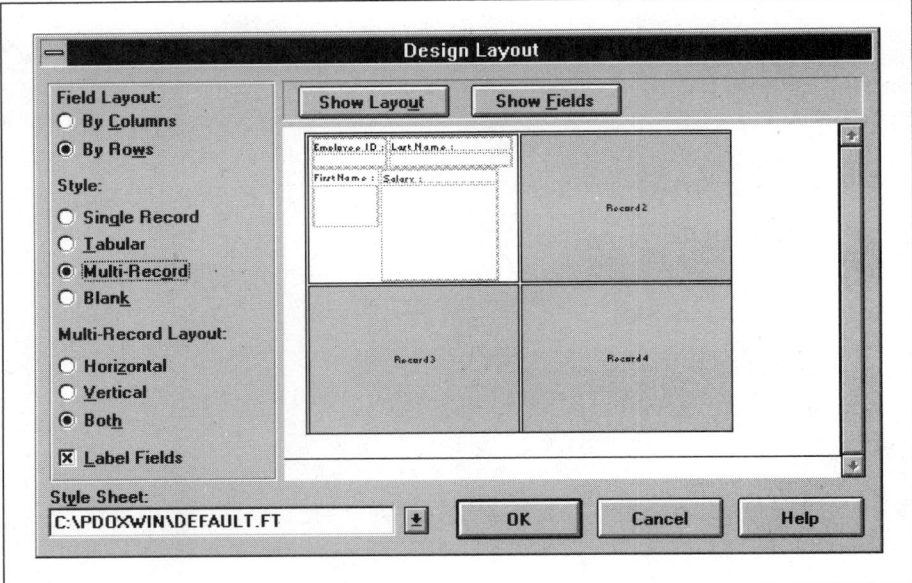

> **N O T E**
>
> **You specify only the initial multi-record layout in the Design Layout dialog box. From the Design window you can specify the number of records across and down a page and the spacing between them. You can also change your initial choices about the layout of repeated records.**

Blank Style

The *Blank* design style erases all fields from the design. Of course, you can always use tools on the Design window's Toolbar to add tables, records, and fields later, but with a blank design they won't be placed automatically. Note that the blank design style is *not* the same as a completely blank form, which is not associated with any table at all. The blank style is handy when you want to include very few fields in the form or report or when you're creating graphs and crosstabs.

▶ Selecting Fields to Display

Initially, all the fields appear in the Design Layout dialog box (and in your design) in the order they are defined in the table structure. Of course, you can remove, rearrange, or add fields when you get to the Design window (as described later), but it's often easier to do this while defining the initial design layout.

To get a jump on things and save yourself many a mouse click and drag, click the Show Fields button in the Design Layout dialog box. The left side of the Design Layout dialog box will change to show the names of tables in your data model and the fields in the currently selected table, as in Figure 10.10. Notice that the Table drop-down list shows the table (or tables) you've chosen for the design, while the Selected Fields list shows the currently selected fields.

To remove or reorder fields in the design, first select the appropriate table from the Table drop-down list. (This won't be necessary if your design

Creating Design Documents

Ch. 10

FIGURE 10.10 ▶

The Selected Fields list initially contains all the table fields in the order they appear in the table structure.

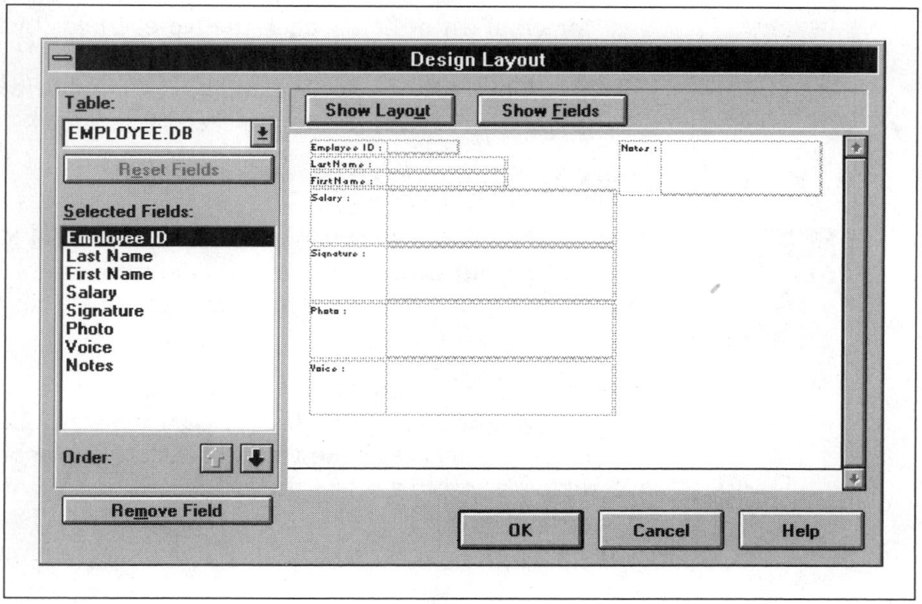

includes only one table.) Then use the tips below to delete or reorder fields in the Selected Fields list and in your design:

- To select one field in the Selected Fields list, click on it. The field name will be highlighted.

- To select a bunch of adjacent fields, drag the mouse through the fields you want. (To select all the fields at once, press Ctrl+/.)

- To select more than one non-adjacent field, hold down the Ctrl key while clicking an *unselected* field name in the list (this is called *Ctrl+clicking*).

- To deselect a selected field, Ctrl+click that field. To deselect all but one field, click any field.

- To remove fields from the Selected Fields list, select the field or fields, then click the Remove Field button.

- To reposition a field, select it, then click the ↑ or ↓ button as needed to move the field up or down in the list.

- If you've removed too many fields and want to start over with the original list of fields, click the Reset Fields button.

When you're finished selecting and rearranging fields, click Show Layout.

► *Selecting a Style Sheet*

Style sheets offer a slick way to control the initial look and behavior of objects on your design documents. Paradox offers several built-in style sheets, and you can either enhance these or set up your own.

To select the style sheet that Paradox will use when it creates your document (and when you add new objects to your design), go to the Design Layout dialog box. If necessary, click the Show Layout button so the Style Sheet drop-down list is visible at the bottom-left corner of the dialog box. Now select the style sheet you want from the Style Sheet drop-down list. Figure 10.11 shows what happened after we chose the *Shadows* style sheet that comes with Paradox for Windows.

Creating Design Documents

Ch. 10

▶ ▶ **N O T E**

Style sheets have a file extension of .ft for forms and .fp for reports; they usually reside in the *c:\pdoxwin* directory or your current working directory. The Style Sheet dialog box will list any style sheets in the *\pdoxwin* directory and current working directory.

▶ ▶ **T I P**

You can switch to a different style sheet anytime you're in the Report Design or Form Design window. To do this, choose <u>P</u>roperties ➤ <u>F</u>orm ➤ <u>S</u>tyle Sheet or <u>P</u>roperties ➤ <u>R</u>eport ➤ <u>S</u>tyle Sheet, select the style sheet name you want, and choose OK. Any new objects you create will take their initial appearance from the selected style sheet; existing objects will not change. There's more about style sheets in "Working with Style Sheets," near the end of this chapter.

FIGURE 10.11 ▶

Use the Style Sheet drop-down list in the Design Layout dialog box to select a style sheet for your design.

Design Layout

Field Layout:
- ◉ <u>B</u>y Columns
- ○ By Ro<u>w</u>s

Style:
- ◉ <u>S</u>ingle Record
- ○ <u>T</u>abular
- ○ <u>M</u>ulti-Record
- ○ Blan<u>k</u>

Multi-Record Layout:
- ○ <u>H</u>orizontal
- ○ <u>V</u>ertical
- ◉ <u>B</u>oth

☒ <u>L</u>abel Fields

[Show Layout] [Show <u>F</u>ields]

Employee ID :
Last Name :
First Name :
Salary :
Signature :
Photo :
Voice :
Notes :

Style Sheet:

C:\PDPXWIN\SHADOWS.FT [▼]   [OK]   [Cancel]   [Help]

►► *Overview of the Design Window*

When you choose OK in the Design Layout dialog box, the Design window appears (see Figures 10.12 and 10.13). From here you can customize every aspect of the document's appearance. You can add, remove, and rearrange objects, or you can change the appearance or behavior of any design object by inspecting it and choosing options from its property menu. You can also preview, print, and save the design.

FIGURE 10.12 ►

The default Form Design window for the Employee table. Notice the Form menu and the Button tool on the Toolbar.

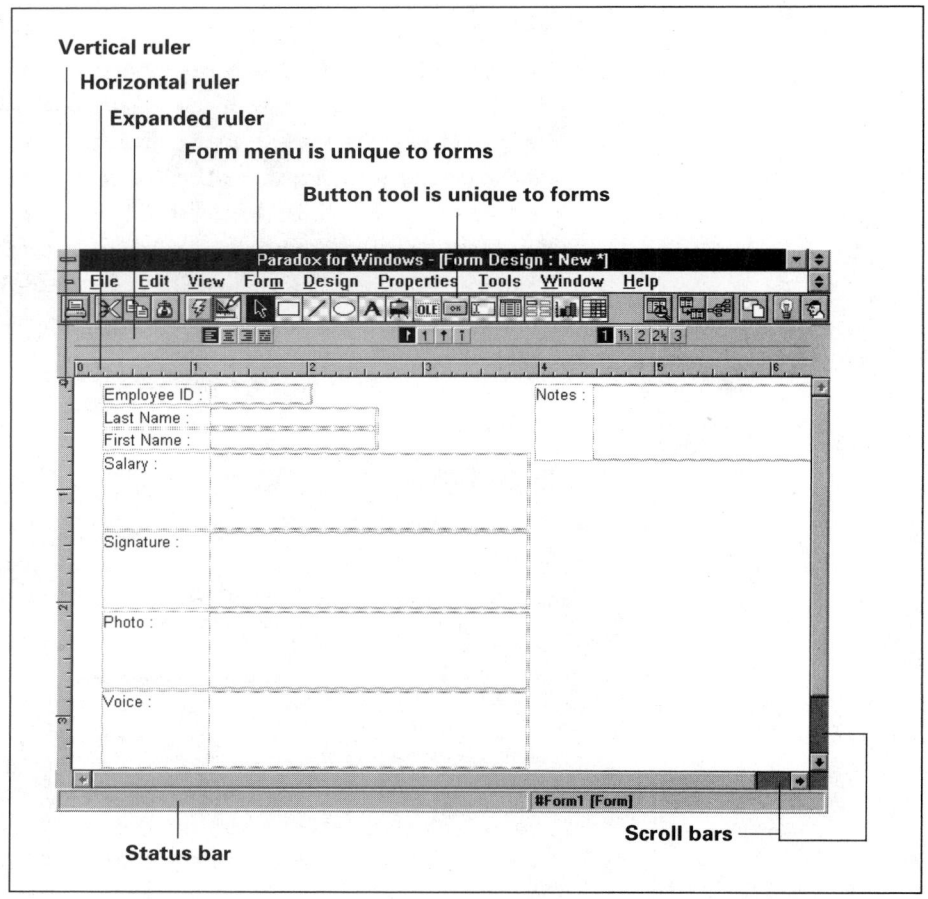

Creating Design Documents

Ch.

FIGURE 10.13

The default Report Design window for the Employee table. Notice the Report menu, the Add Band tool on the Toolbar, and the report, page, and record bands in the design area.

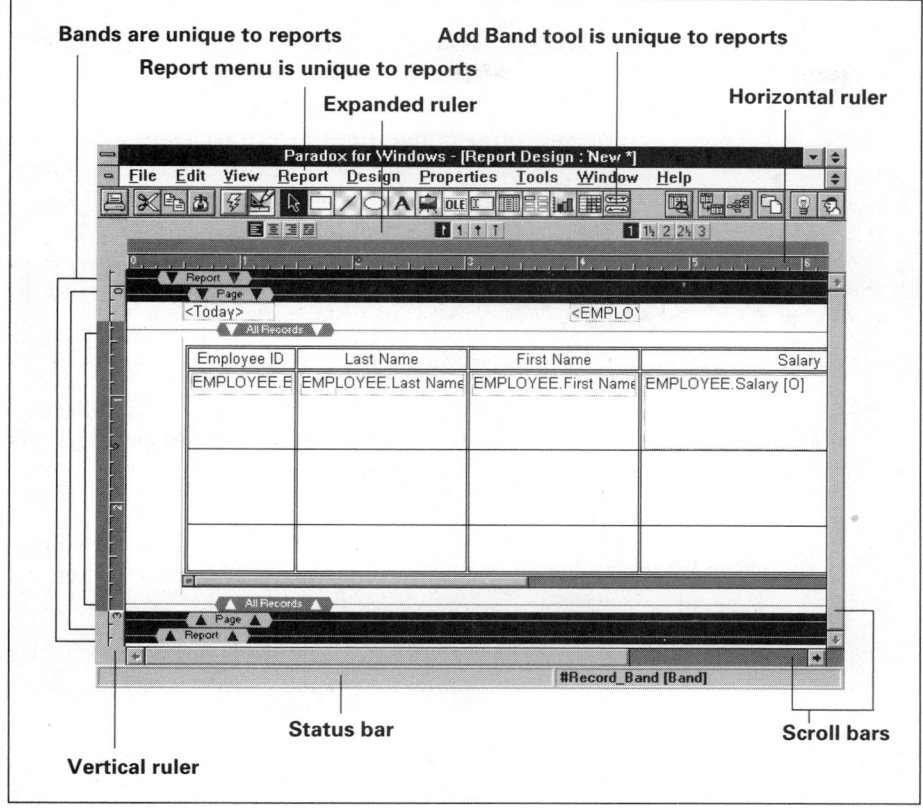

Bands are unique to reports

Report menu is unique to reports

Add Band tool is unique to reports

Expanded ruler

Horizontal ruler

Vertical ruler

Status bar

Scroll bars

Figures 10.12 and 10.13 show Paradox Design windows for an Employee form and report, respectively. As you can see, the two Design windows have much in common, though there are some differences, as indicated by labels on the figures.

▶ ▶NOTE

Don't worry if your screen doesn't display all the rulers shown in Figures 10.12 and 10.13. As you'll learn later, the rulers and other areas of the Design window can be turned on or off as needed.

The menus in the Design window provide additional options for designing, previewing, printing, and saving your document, as well as for rearranging document windows, getting help, and changing various properties. The Toolbar buttons let you add new objects to the document and offer convenient alternatives to choosing options from the menus. Table 10.1 shows each button and briefly describes its function.

▶ **TABLE 10.1:** *Summary of Toolbar Buttons in the Design Window*

BUTTON	BUTTON NAME	DESCRIPTION AND MENU OR KEYBOARD EQUIVALENT (IF ANY)
	Print	Prints the design (if you're in the Design window) or data (if you're previewing). Same as choosing File ➤ Print options (see Chapters 10 and 11).
	Cut To Clipboard	Cuts the currently selected text or object to the Clipboard. Same as choosing Edit ➤ Cut or pressing Shift+Del.
	Copy To Clipboard	Copies the currently selected text or object to the Clipboard. Same as choosing Edit ➤ Copy or pressing Shift+Ins.
	Paste From Clipboard	Pastes data from the Clipboard to the design document. Same as choosing Edit ➤ Paste or pressing Shift+Ins.
	View Data	Displays the form or report on screen with the actual data from your table. Same as choosing View ➤ View Data, View ➤ Run Report, or pressing F8.
	Design	Returns to the Design window. Same as choosing View ➤ Design Form, View ➤ Design Report, or pressing F8.
	Selection Arrow	Selects objects in the design document.
	Box Tool	Adds boxes to the design document.

▶ **TABLE 10.1:** *Summary of Toolbar Buttons in the Design Window (continued)*

BUTTON	BUTTON NAME	DESCRIPTION AND MENU OR KEYBOARD EQUIVALENT (IF ANY)
	Line Tool	Adds lines to the design document.
	Ellipse Tool	Adds ellipses to the design document.
	Text Tool	Adds text objects to the design document.
	Graphic Tool	Adds graphic objects to the design document.
	OLE Tool	Adds OLE objects to the design document.
	Button Tool	(Forms only) Adds buttons to a form. You can use ObjectPAL to assign actions that the button will perform when clicked (see Chapter 19).
	Field Tool	Adds table fields to the design document.
	Table Tool	Adds entire table frames to the design document.
	Multi-Record Tool	Adds repeating records to a design document.
	Graph Tool	Adds graphs to a design document (see Chapter 13).

▶ **TABLE 10.1:** *Summary of Toolbar Buttons in the Design Window (continued)*

BUTTON	BUTTON NAME	DESCRIPTION AND MENU OR KEYBOARD EQUIVALENT (IF ANY)
	Crosstab Tool	Adds crosstabs to a form (see Chapter 13).
	Add Band	(Reports only) Adds bands to a report (see Chapter 12).
	Filter	Takes you to the Filter Tables dialog box, which lets you sort records and isolate records that will appear (see Chapters 8 and 9). Same as choosing Form ➤ Filter or Report ➤ Filter.
	Data Model	Returns to the Data Model dialog box. Same as choosing Form ➤ Data Model or Report ➤ Data Model.
	Object Tree	Displays a hierarchical chart of your design. You can inspect the properties of any object in the Object Tree. Same as choosing Tools ➤ Object Tree.
	Open Project Viewer	Displays the objects in the Project Viewer window (see Chapter 15). Same as choosing Tools ➤ Project Viewer.
	Expert	Displays the Expert Control Panel, which lets you create a new form, mailing label, or report document (see Chapters 11 and 12). Same as choosing Help ➤ Experts.
	Coaches	Opens the interactive Coaches, which can take you through the steps for creating a standard form or report (see Chapter 3). Same as choosing Help ➤ Coaches.

▶ ▶ **T I P**

> **The button name appears in the status bar whenever you move the mouse pointer to the button icon in the Toolbar.**

In the Design window, you can preview the form or report, print and save the document, close it, and open it again to make further changes. Before diving into the nitty-gritty of document design, let's take a quick look at these topics.

▶ ▶ *Previewing Your Document*

 You can preview your design at any time to see how it will look with the data filled in. To do so, simply click the View Data button in the Toolbar (shown at left), or press the F8 key. Alternatively, you can choose View ➤ View Data (if you're designing a form) or View ➤ Run Report (if you're designing a report).

You'll see the form or report document filled in with actual data from your table, along with any objects you added to the design. Figure 10.14, for example, shows a simple form for the Employee table previewed on the screen. Notice that we scrolled to the fifth record in the table. (To display the data in the Notes field completely, simply move the cursor to that field and scroll up and down as needed. To display all the data in a formatted memo field or memo field, even when the cursor isn't in the field, you must set the Run Time ➤ Complete Display property, as described in the next chapter.)

 ▶ ▶ **T I P**

> **When previewing a form design, you're actually in Form View and have all the usual Form View capabilities (see Chapter 6).**

FIGURE 10.14 ▶

A simple Employee form after clicking the View Data button and using the Form View Toolbar buttons to scroll to the fifth record in the table

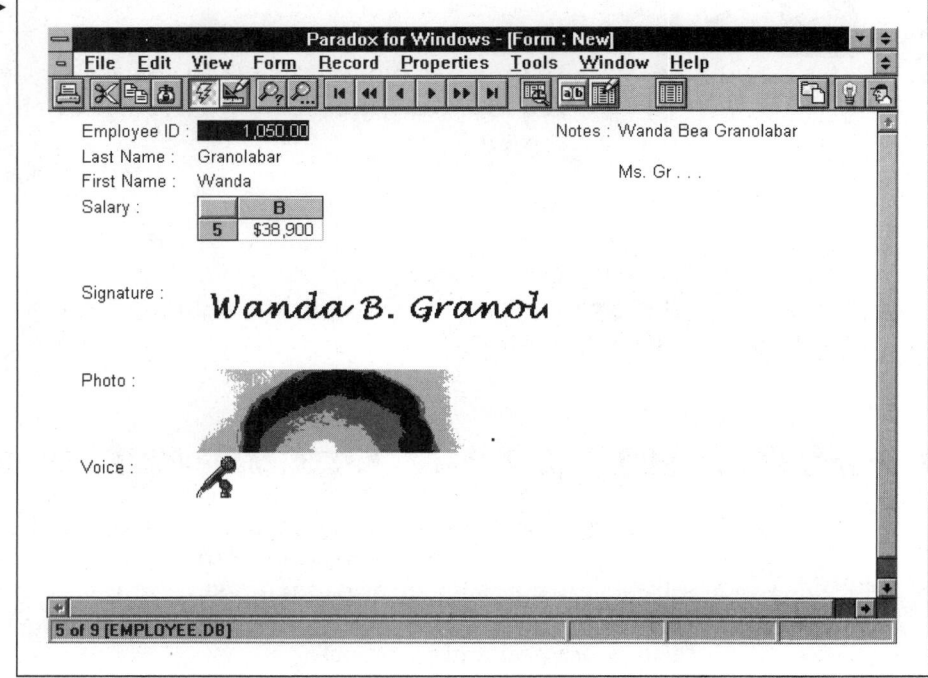

 When you're ready to make more changes to your design, return to the Design window by clicking the Design button in the Toolbar (shown at left) or by pressing F8 again. You can also choose <u>V</u>iew ▶ <u>D</u>esign Form (for forms) or <u>V</u>iew ▶ <u>D</u>esign Report (for reports). Remember, you can only change your design from the Design window.

▶▶ *Printing Your Document*

Printing a report or form is quite easy. You can print either the design itself or the actual data in the format defined by your design.

 To print the *design* of a form or report, make sure you're in the Design window (click the Design button if necessary). Then to print a form design, click the Print button shown at left. To print a report design, choose <u>F</u>ile ▶ <u>P</u>rint ▶ <u>D</u>esign.

To print the form or report with its data filled in, switch to the Form View or Report View window by clicking the View Data button, then click the Print button. (You also can print a report from the Design window by choosing File ➤ Print ➤ Report.)

See Chapters 11 and 12 for other ways to print designs and documents.

▶▶ *Saving Your Document*

It's a good idea to save your design document when:

- You're finished designing it.
- You've spent lots of time customizing the design and want to save the changes made so far.
- You're about to try a new design technique and want to preserve your work in case the experiment is a bust.

To save changes to a new document, make sure you're in the Design window, then choose File ➤ Save. When the Save File As dialog box appears, enter the file name or complete path name for the document, *without an extension,* in the New File Name box and choose OK. If the file already exists, Paradox will ask if you want to overwrite it. Choose Yes if you're sure you want to overwrite the existing file, or No to return to the Save File As dialog box.

 ▶▶ **N O T E**

> **Forms have a file name extension of *.fsl*, while reports have an *.rsl* extension.**

When you use File ➤ Save to save changes to an existing document, Paradox saves your changes without further prompting. If you want to save the document under a *different* name, choose File ➤ Save As instead.

▶▶ Assigning the Design to Quick Buttons

Once you've saved a design, you can assign it to a table's Quick Form, Quick Report, Quick Graph, or Quick Crosstab button in the Toolbar. This makes it a *preferred document.*

▶▶ **N O T E**

Graphs (described in Chapter 13) must be saved as forms if you want to use them with Quick buttons.

To assign a preferred document to a table, follow the steps below.

1. Choose File ➤ Open ➤ Table (or use any of the shortcuts you've learned for opening a table). Then follow the usual steps to open the table you want to associate with the form, report, graph, or crosstab.

2. Choose Properties ➤ Preferred, then Form, Report, Graph, or Crosstab. Or, right-click the Quick Form, Quick Report, Quick Graph, or Quick Crosstab button in the Toolbar.

3. Choose the file you want to assign as preferred, then choose OK.

4. Choose Properties ➤ View Properties ➤ Save.

From now on, whenever you click the Quick button in the Toolbar (or choose one of the "Quick" options on the Tools menu), Paradox will use the preferred design to display the data. To assign a different document to the Quick button, simply repeat the steps above.

▶▶ **N O T E**

If you want to return to Paradox for Windows' standard form, report, graph, or crosstab, you must delete the table's View Properties file (.tv) via Properties ➤ View Properties ➤ Delete. *Caution:* This removes *all* the table's View properties (see Chapter 7).

▶▶ *Opening an Existing Design*

Of course, you needn't finish an entire design in one sitting. If you want to take a break, just save your changes and close the Design window. When you're ready to return to the design, follow these steps:

1. Click the Open Form button (to open a form) or Open Report button (to open a report), if it's available on the Toolbar. Or, right-click the Forms or Reports icon in the Project Viewer and choose Open. Or, choose File ➤ Open ➤ Form or File ➤ Open ➤ Report, as appropriate.

2. The Open Document dialog box appears, as shown in Figure 10.15.

3. Choose the file name you want from the File Name area. When opening forms, only files with an .fsl extension appear in the File Name list. When opening reports, you'll only see files with an .rsl extension.

FIGURE 10.15 ▶

The Open Document dialog box lets you select a document, open a form as a report (or vice versa), or change the table associated with the document.

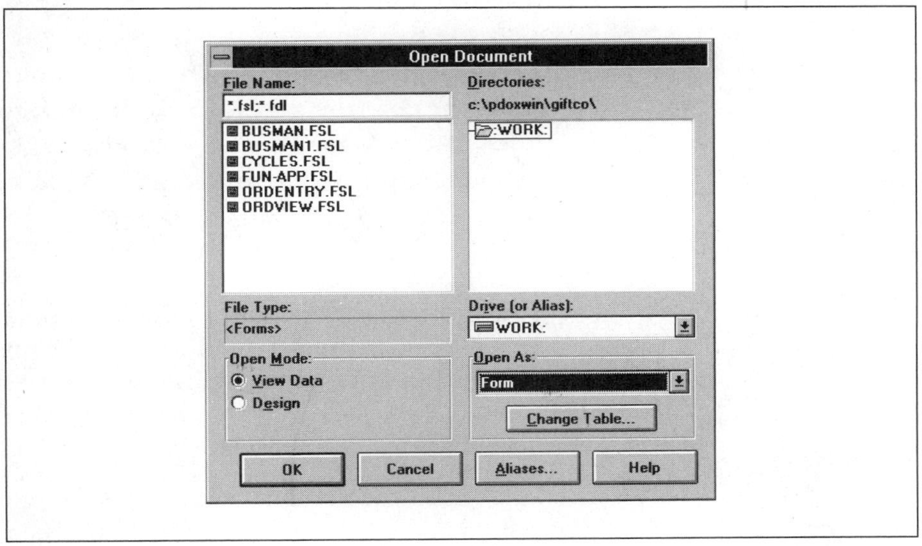

4. If you wish, choose an Open <u>M</u>ode. Your choices are as follows:

View Data   Displays the document on-screen with data filled in.

Design   Opens the document in the Design window.

Print   Prints the data instead of opening a window. This option is available for reports only and is not shown in Figure 10.15.

5. Choose additional options as described in the following sections.

6. Choose OK.

If you opened the document in <u>V</u>iew Data mode, which usually is the default choice, you can click the Design button or press F8 to return to the Design window. From there you can make any changes necessary. When you're done, save the design.

►   ►**T I P**

> To use an existing design as the basis for a new one, open the document in Design mode, then choose <u>F</u>ile ➤ Save <u>A</u>s, type a new file name, and choose OK. Make whatever changes you wish in the Design window, then choose <u>F</u>ile ➤ <u>S</u>ave to save your changes. You can also use the Copy feature, which is discussed in Chapter 15, to copy existing designs to new files.

Want to try a shortcut for opening a design document? If so, open the Project Viewer (see Chapter 3), then click the Forms or Reports icon in the left side of the Project Viewer. Now, to open your form or report in View Data mode, just double-click the appropriate file name in the right side of the Project Viewer window.

If you'd rather open the document in a different mode, right-click the file name (or click the file name and press F6), then choose an appropriate option from the property menu shown below (the menu for forms won't include a <u>P</u>rint or Print <u>W</u>ith option). For example, you can choose De<u>s</u>ign to open the Design window, or View With to choose a different table (as discussed in the next section). You can learn more about the Project Viewer in Chapters 3 and 15.

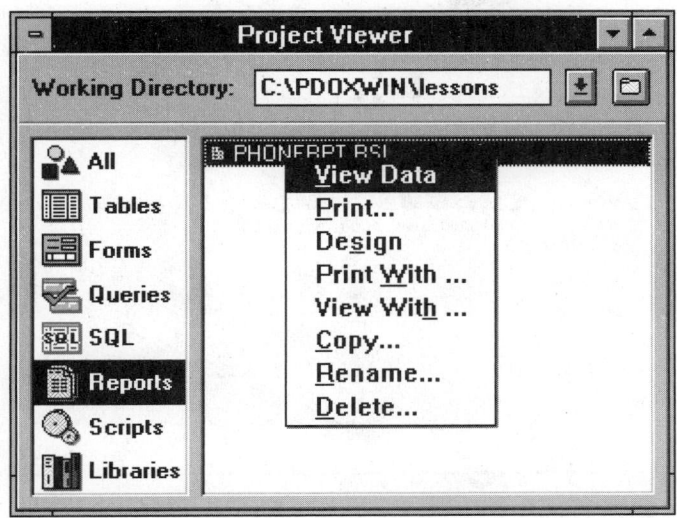

▶ Choosing a Different Table

When opening a form or report, you can choose a table other than the one used to design the document. For example, suppose you design a form for the CustList table that's just perfect for a similarly structured table of inactive customers (perhaps named *OldCust*). Instead of designing the form for the OldCust table from scratch, you can simply open the original form with a different table. To do so, click the Change Table button in the Open Document dialog box, or right-click the document name in the Project Viewer window and choose View With (or Print With). Then specify a different table.

When you use the "change table" technique, Paradox tries to place the corresponding fields from the table in the form or report. You can then change and save the design if you wish. (If you use File ➤ Save, the changes will be made to the original document; if you use File ➤ Save As, you can save the changes to a copy.)

Paradox may be unable to match every field name in the design with a corresponding field in the table if the new table's structure doesn't exactly match the structure of the table used to design the document. After you choose OK to open the document, Paradox will display a dialog box like the one below for each missing field.

Choose OK if you don't mind having undefined fields in your form or report, or choose Cancel to back out of the operation.

▶ ▶ **N O T E**

> **Unless all the fields from the new table match fields in the existing table, you'll probably need to switch to the Design window and define or delete some field objects.**

▶ *Opening Forms as Reports and Vice Versa*

With Paradox for Windows, you can open a form as a report or a report as a form. This would come in handy if you designed a report that you really liked and wanted to use it as a form—or vice versa.

To change a form into a report, or vice versa, click the Open As drop-down list in the Open Document dialog box, and then choose *Report* or *Form*, as appropriate. When you use the Open As option, Paradox copies the original document to a new one, leaving the original untouched.

When you use this feature, keep the following points in mind:

- Some objects behave differently in forms and reports. In particular, you may need to modify summary and calculated fields (see Chapter 17 for information on these types of fields).

- When converting a form to a report, the form fields appear in the *record band* of the report. Similarly, when converting a report to a form, only the fields in the record band come across to the form.

- Some form layouts may not be valid for reports.

- If the report includes a page break in the record band, Paradox creates a multipage form. Likewise, Paradox places a page break in the appropriate spot in the report's record band if you're opening a multipage form as a report.

 ▶▶ **N O T E**

> **Chapter 11 discusses multipage forms, and Chapter 12 covers record bands and page breaks.**

▶▶ *Tips for Using the Design Window*

Now that you know the basics of creating and saving documents, let's look at some techniques for customizing documents in the Design window.

Following are a few tips to keep in mind when you begin using the Design window.

- Maximize the Design window to see more of your design (click the Maximize button or double-click the Design window's title bar).

- Use the Zoom feature to zoom in on part of the design or to reduce the design and get a better overall view. See "Zooming In and Out," below.

- Use grids, rulers, and the show size and position features to help you align, size, and separate objects. See "Tracking an Object's Size and Position" and "Using Grids," below.

- Preview your design frequently to check your progress.

- Use the floating Toolbar (Chapter 3) if you need more viewing room or want to move the Toolbar tools to a more convenient spot on the Desktop. (Choose Properties ➤ Desktop.)

- If necessary, use the Undo command to back out of your most recent change. (Choose Edit ➤ Undo or press Alt+Backspace.)

 ▶ ▶ T I P

If your design is hopelessly botched, simply close the Design window and choose No when asked if you want to save your changes. Then re-open the document and begin again.

▶ Zooming In and Out

Unless you have a big-screen monitor, you probably won't be able to see the whole design at once. The scroll bars provide one way to bring a portion of the design into view; zooming provides another. You can zoom in for a close-up view of part of your design, or zoom out for a bird's eye view of the entire design. To zoom, choose View➤ Zoom, then choose any of the options listed below.

25 % or 50 % Reduces the design to 25 or 50 percent of its normal size.

100 % Displays the design at its normal size.

200 % or 400 % Expands the design to 200 percent or 400 percent its normal size.

Fit Width Sizes the design to the width of the window.

Fit Height Sizes the design to the height of the window.

Best Fit Sizes the design to both the width and height of the window.

▶ Tracking an Object's Size and Position

Whenever you move the mouse pointer around the window, the pointer position is tracked on the rulers by small, colored markers. When you select an object in the design, segments of the rulers change color to indicate the dimensions and exact position of the object. Similarly, the ruler segments change length as you resize an object, and they move whenever you drag an object to a new position in the window. Thus, the rulers can help you determine the exact position or measurement of objects in the design document.

If you've turned on the show size and position feature, the status bar also will indicate an object's size and position in the Design window. For example, in Figure 10.16 we turned on the horizontal and vertical rulers and activated show size and position. We then clicked on the Salary field to select it. Notice how the shaded areas on the rulers match the width and height of the selected object. Similarly, the object's position (.25" horizontal and .67" vertical) and size (3.69" wide by .69" high) appear at the right edge of the status bar.

Displaying and Hiding Rulers

You can display or hide the horizontal, vertical, or expanded rulers on the Design window by choosing options from the Properties menu.

- Choose Properties ➤ Horizontal Ruler to turn the horizontal ruler on or off.

- Choose Properties ➤ Vertical Ruler to turn the vertical ruler on or off.

- Choose Properties ➤ Expanded Ruler to turn the expanded ruler on or off. (The expanded ruler lets you align text, set tabs, and choose line spacing for text, as described later.)

 ▶▶**N O T E**

> **Like many options in the Design window menus, the ruler options are toggles. When checked (selected), the ruler is turned on (visible). When unchecked (deselected), the ruler is turned off (hidden). Turning off the rulers gives you more workspace in the Design window.**

FIGURE 10.16 ▶

The horizontal and vertical rulers in the Design window indicate the width and height of a selected object.

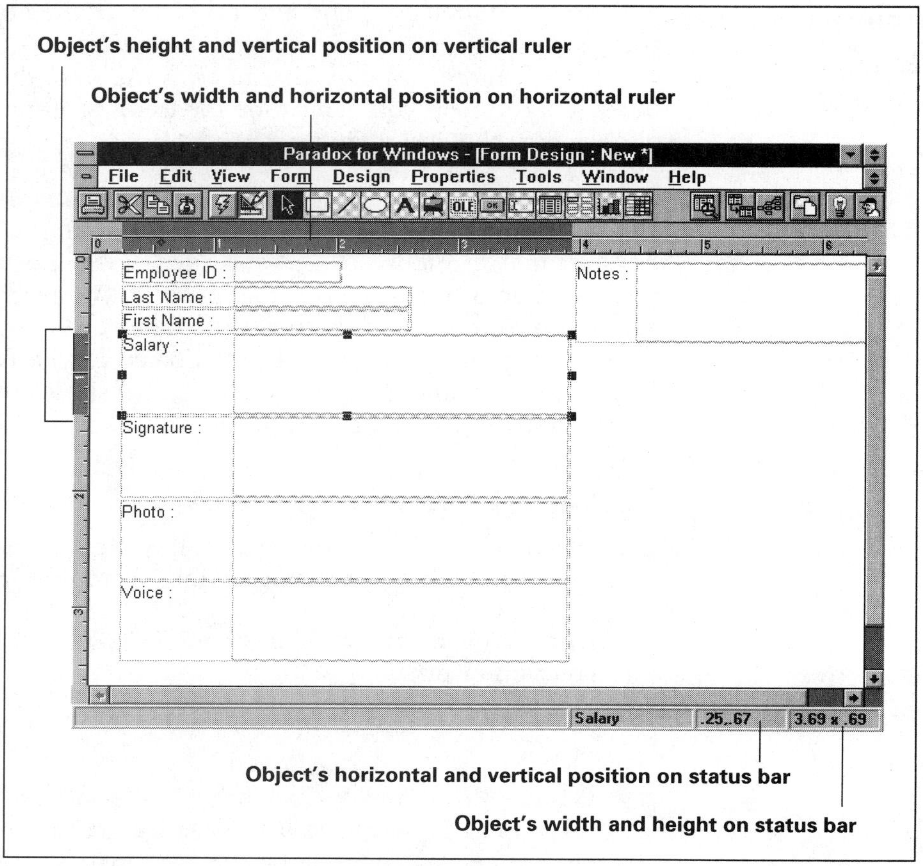

Object's height and vertical position on vertical ruler

Object's width and horizontal position on horizontal ruler

```
Paradox for Windows - [Form Design : New *]
File   Edit   View   Form   Design   Properties   Tools   Window   Help
```

| 0 | 1 | 2 | 3 | 4 | 5 | 6 |

Employee ID :
Last Name :
First Name :
Salary :

Signature :

Photo :

Voice :

Notes :

| Salary | .25,.67 | 3.69 x .69 |

Object's horizontal and vertical position on status bar

Object's width and height on status bar

Displaying and Hiding the Size and Position

Like the rulers, the show size and position feature is a toggle, and it's available on the Properties menu. Simply choose Properties ➤ Show Size And Position to turn the size and position status bar information on or off.

▶ Using Grids

Paradox for Windows can display a background of horizontal and vertical grid lines and dots, as in Figure 10.17, to help you place and resize

FIGURE 10.17

The Employee form with grid lines visible

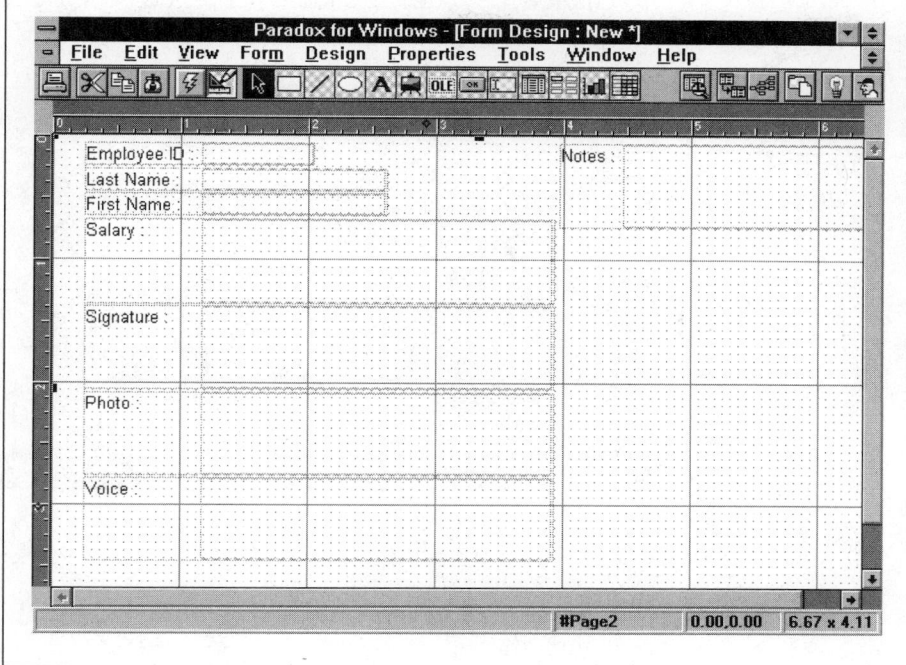

objects with precision. To display the grid, choose Properties and make sure Show Grid is checked. Deselect the Show Grid option to hide the grid lines. Notice that lines show the grid's major divisions, while dots show the grid's minor divisions.

If you want all objects to align on major or minor grid lines whenever you place, resize, or move them, check the Properties ➤ Snap to Grid option. Remove the checkmark to turn off the feature. With grid snap on, objects will snap to the grid whether or not the grid is visible.

Changing the Grid Settings

The grid settings control the unit of measure and divisions in both the ruler and the grid. The default unit of measure is inches, with major divisions at one-inch intervals and sixteen minor divisions per inch.

To change the settings, choose Properties ➤ Grid Settings. You'll see the Grid Settings dialog box, as shown below.

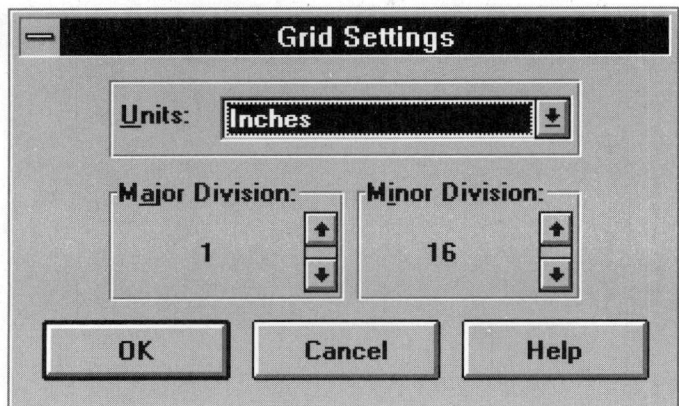

Make any of the changes listed below, then choose OK.

- To change the measurement units, open the Units drop-down list box, then choose *Inches* or *Centimeters*.

- To change the distance between the major grid lines, click the arrow buttons below the Major Division heading. Clicking ↑ increases the distance between major divisions; clicking ↓ decreases the distance.

- To change the distance between minor grid lines, click the arrow buttons below Minor Division. Clicking ↑ decreases the distance between divisions (creating more divisions); clicking ↓ increases the distance (creating fewer divisions).

▶ Saving and Restoring Zoom, Rulers, and Other Design Window Properties

When you close the Design window, most settings on the View and Properties menus return to their defaults. These settings include the current zoom, rulers, grid, size and position, and band labels (reports only).

To save these settings for use with all future forms or reports that you open in the Design window, choose <u>P</u>roperties ➤ Fo<u>r</u>m Options ➤ <u>S</u>ave Defaults (for forms) or <u>P</u>roperties ➤ Report <u>O</u>ptions ➤ <u>S</u>ave Defaults (for reports). If you've made changes to the default settings and want to restore the most recently saved settings, choose <u>P</u>roperties ➤ Fo<u>r</u>m Options ➤ <u>R</u>estore Defaults (for forms) or <u>P</u>roperties ➤ Report <u>O</u>ptions ➤ <u>R</u>estore Defaults (for reports).

▶▶ *Selecting Design Objects*

You must select objects before you can move, resize, delete, or otherwise manipulate them in the Design window. When you select an object, "handles" appear around it. As you pass the mouse pointer over a handle, the pointer changes shape to indicate the direction you can move that handle. The example below shows a selected box and all the possible directions of movement.

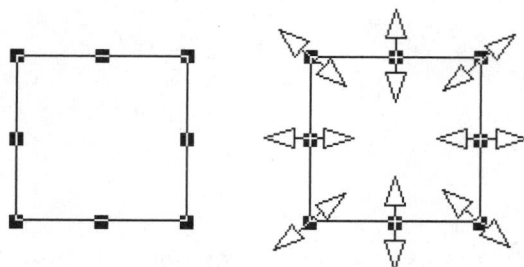

 To begin selecting an object, click the Selection Arrow tool in the Toolbar (shown at left), if it isn't already selected (darkened). Then, to select a single object, simply click on the object.

▶ *Selecting from the Outside or Inside*

When you click an object that is contained within another object, Paradox will select either the outside or the inside object first, depending on the current Designer Properties settings. For example, suppose you have a line within a box, as below.

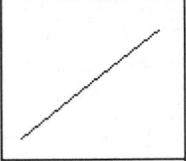

When you click on the line, Paradox's default action is to select the *outermost* object first (the box, in this example). You must click again to select the object inside it (the line). Likewise, if you had a line, within a circle, within a box, as below, the first click would select the box, the next would select the circle, and the last would select the line. Thus, the next innermost object is selected each time you click.

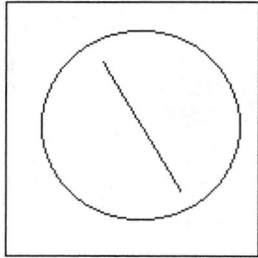

If you don't like this way of selecting objects, choose Properties ➤ Designer, click Select From Inside to check the option, then choose OK. Once you've done this, you can select whatever object you click. (To restore the default setting, simply choose Properties ➤ Designer ➤ Select From Inside to remove the checkmark, and choose OK.)

Whenever you select an object that is contained by another object, you can press Esc to select the next outermost object. Thus, if you've selected the line within the circle in the previous example, you can press Esc to select the circle. You can also press Tab or Shift+Tab to cycle through and select individual objects in your design.

▶ Selecting Multiple Objects

Paradox offers several ways to select more than one object at a time. To begin, click the Selection Arrow in the Toolbar (if the tool isn't selected already), then choose the most convenient multi-selection method.

- Hold down the Shift key while clicking each object you want to select. To deselect an object, simply click it again while holding down the Shift key. This technique is called *Shift+click*.

- To select several objects that are close together, position the mouse pointer slightly outside the first object you want to select. Now hold down the Shift key, hold down the left mouse button, and drag to create a box outline around the objects. When you release the left mouse button, all the objects surrounded by the outline will be selected. This is called *Shift+drag* or *marquee selection*.

- To select all the objects inside the currently selected object, choose Edit ➤ Select All. If no object is currently selected, Paradox will select all objects on the page (if you're designing a form), or all objects in the current band (if you're designing a report).

You can deselect all the currently selected objects by pressing the Esc key repeatedly until no more objects are selected.

▶ Moving, Resizing, and Deleting Selected Objects

After selecting an object, you can perform many operations on it, including moving it to another position in the design, resizing it, or deleting it.

To *move* selected objects, point the mouse inside the selected area (not on any handle), then drag the whole object in the desired direction. You can also use the arrow keys to move selected objects by small, precise increments up, down, left, or right. If Properties ➤ Snap To Grid is on, the object will move to the closest grid line when you press an arrow key.

You can *resize* one selected object at a time by dragging a handle in the appropriate direction. Drag a corner handle to change both the height and width of an object. Drag the top or bottom center handle to change the object's height. Drag the left or right center handle to widen or narrow the object. We'll talk about ways to resize several selected objects at once in the next section.

Deleting objects is easy: Simply select the objects and press the Del key.

 ▶ ▶**T I P**

> **If you make a mistake moving, resizing, or deleting an object, choose <u>E</u>dit ➤ <u>U</u>ndo or press Alt+Backspace right away.**

▶▶ *Shortcuts for Managing Multiple Objects*

Paradox offers some real timesavers for organizing and resizing several selected objects at once. These options are all found on the <u>D</u>esign menu shown below.

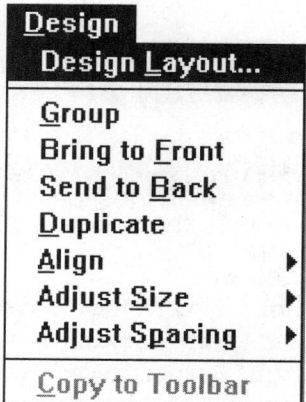

 ▶ ▶**N O T E**

> **Remember to select the objects you want before using the options described in the following sections.**

▶ *Aligning Objects*

Often you'll want certain objects to line up with respect to one another. So, instead of painstakingly moving each object to its proper position, just select the objects you want to line up, then choose <u>D</u>esign ➤ <u>A</u>lign, followed by one of these options:

Align Left Aligns the left edges of the selected objects.

Align Right Aligns the right edges of the selected objects.

Align Center Aligns the selected objects along an imaginary line that passes vertically through the center of all the objects.

Align Top Aligns the top edges of the selected objects.

Align Bottom Aligns the bottom edges of the selected objects.

Align Middle Aligns the selected objects along an imaginary line that passes horizontally through the center of all the objects.

Figure 10.18 shows examples of objects aligned with these options.

FIGURE 10.18 ▶

The <u>D</u>esign ➤ <u>A</u>lign option lets you line up several selected objects at once.

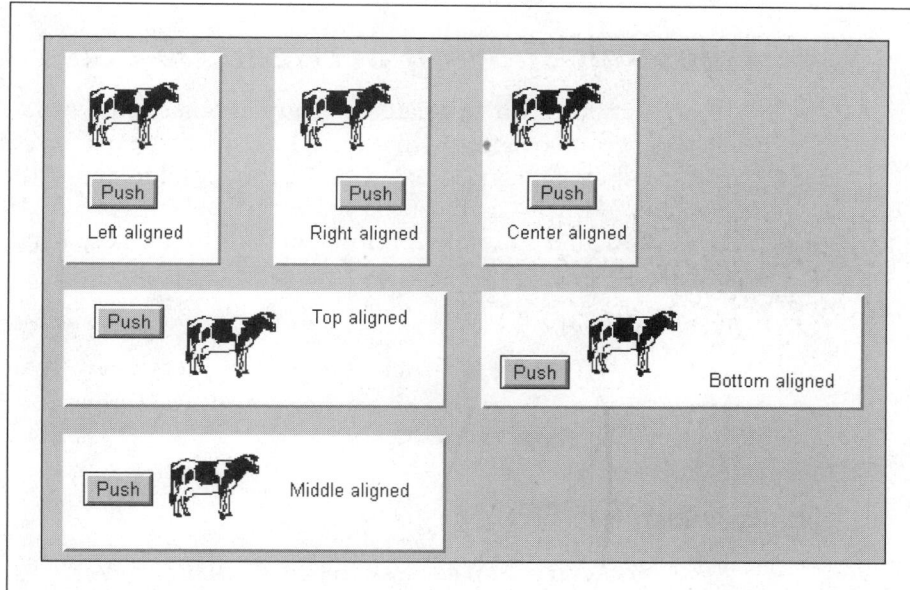

Creating Design Documents

▶ ▶

Ch.

10

▶ *Resizing Several Objects at Once*

The Adjust Size options let you adjust the size of multiple selected objects to achieve a symmetrical look. This is handy when your design contains several fields or other objects that should be exactly the same size.

To resize several objects at once, select the objects, then choose Design ➤ Adjust Size followed by one of these options:

Minimum Width   Makes all objects as wide as the narrowest of the group.

Maximum Width   Makes all objects as wide as the widest of the group.

Minimum Height   Makes all objects as tall as the shortest of the group.

Maximum Height   Makes all objects as tall as the tallest of the group.

If Paradox cannot resize some of the objects you selected, it will ignore those objects and resize the rest as specified.

▶ *Adjusting Spacing between Objects*

Suppose you've created a group of objects and want the spacing between them to be exactly the same. Just select the objects, then choose Design ➤ Adjust Spacing. Next choose Horizontal to adjust the space horizontally or Vertical to adjust the space vertically. Figure 10.19 shows some before and after examples of horizontal and vertical spacing.

 ▶▶ **N O T E**

Adjust Spacing moves objects even if you've pinned them to the design (pinning is described later).

▶ *Grouping Objects*

You can group several objects so they behave as a single object. When you select the group, a single set of handles will surround the whole

FIGURE 10.19

Use Design ➤ Adjust Spacing to adjust the horizontal and vertical spacing between selected objects. Notice that Paradox preserves the overall width or height of the group of objects, as indicated by the arrows in the figure.

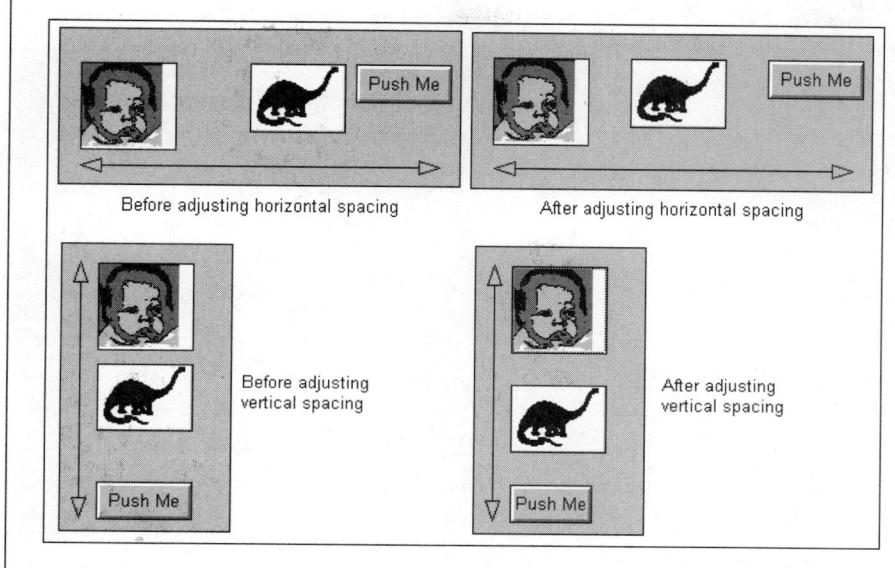

group. You can then work with the group as a whole. Note that even after you've created a group, you can still select individual objects in the group by clicking repeatedly.

To create a group, select the objects, then choose Design ➤ Group. A fine outline will appear around the selected objects. To separate a group into its individual objects, select the group by clicking on it, then choose Design ➤ Ungroup, or right-click the group and choose Ungroup from the property menu.

▶ Stacking Objects

Objects in a design document can be in layers, on top of or underneath other objects. To change the layering of objects or groups of objects, choose Design ➤ Bring To Front or Design ➤ Send To Back.

For example, in the left side of Figure 10.20 the circle is obscuring a graphic that's behind it. To move the circle behind the graphic, we selected the circle, then chose Design ➤ Send To Back, producing the result shown in the right side of the figure.

FIGURE 10.20 ▶

In the left side of the figure, the circle covers the graphic. After selecting the circle and sending it to the back, the graphic is fully visible.

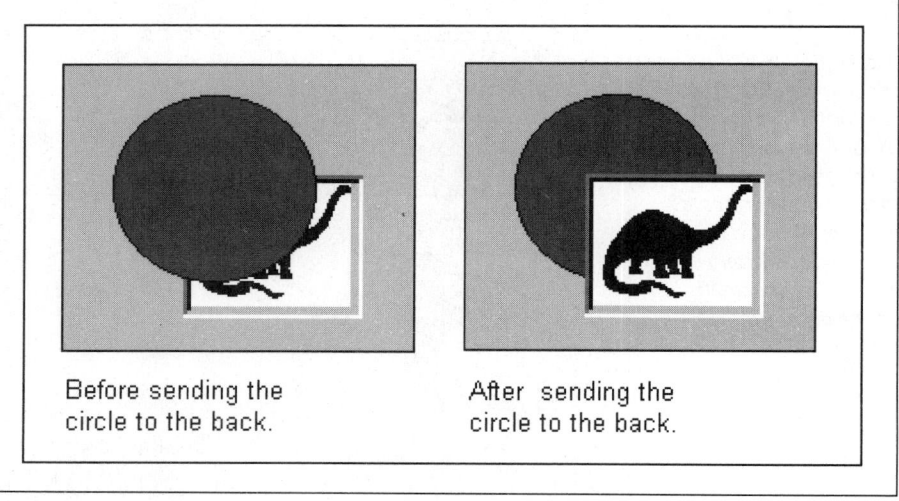

Before sending the circle to the back.

After sending the circle to the back.

▶ *Duplicating Objects*

Paradox offers two ways to copy selected objects. If you want to place selected objects on the Clipboard first, follow these steps:

1. Select the object or objects you want to duplicate.

2. Choose Edit ➤ Copy (or click the Copy To Clipboard button in the Toolbar, or press Ctrl+Ins).

3. Click in the Design window where you want the copy to appear.

4. Choose Edit ➤ Paste (or click the Paste From Clipboard button or press Shift+Ins).

If you prefer to bypass the Clipboard and perform the copy in a single step, select the object or objects you want to duplicate, then choose Design ➤ Duplicate. Paradox will put a copy of the object or objects in the document, adjacent to the original.

▶▶ *Inspecting Objects and Changing Properties*

Every object in your document has its own set of properties, which are easily changed by inspecting the object in the Design window and selecting options from the property menu that appears. Rather than bogging you down with details of all the properties in this chapter, we'll explain basic inspection and property-changing techniques that work for *any* object in a document and discuss a few of the most important *Design* and *Run Time* properties. When you're ready for more details about individual properties, you can:

- Try them out for yourself—the best approach!
- Highlight the property you're interested in on the property menu, then press F1.
- Refer to Appendix E.

▶ *Understanding Normal and Penetrating Properties*

Before you can change the appearance or behavior of an object in the Design window, you must inspect it. Paradox offers two ways to inspect objects: *normal inspection* and *penetrating inspection*. In the *normal* method, you right-click a single (unselected) object or right-click one or more selected objects. This leads to the property menu for the object or objects.

▶ ▶ **T I P**

> Instead of right-clicking, you can select one or more objects and then press F6 or choose <u>P</u>roperties ➤ <u>C</u>urrent Object.

After right-clicking a box, we got the property menu in Figure 10.21.

Now, if we select both the box and the Last Name field and then right-click the box, we'll still get a property menu for the box. However, if we right-click the Last Name field, we'll get the field's property menu instead, as shown in Figure 10.22.

FIGURE 10.21

This property menu appears after right-clicking a box.

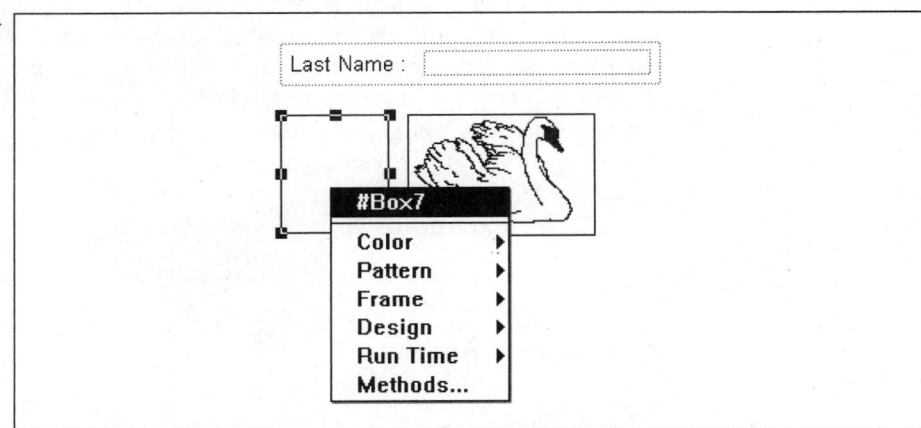

FIGURE 10.22

The property menu for a field appears when we right-click the field.

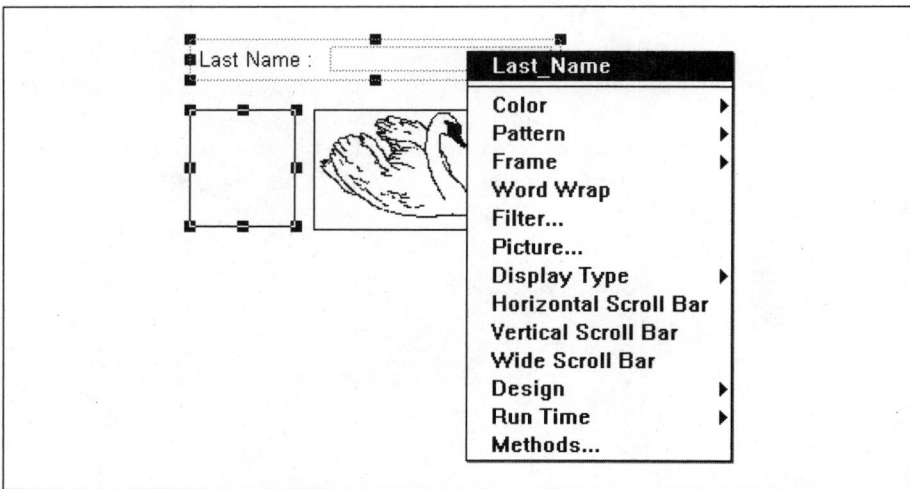

In the *penetrating* method, you first select the object or objects you want to inspect. Then hold down the Ctrl key while right-clicking (this is called *Ctrl+right-clicking*) or press Shift+F6. This leads to a *penetrating property menu* composed of properties available for all the selected objects—that is, the *union* of all properties.

In Figure 10.23, for example, we selected the box and the Last Name field, as before, but this time we Ctrl+right-clicked the box to display a menu of properties that includes box and field properties.

FIGURE 10.23 ▶

Ctrl+right-clicking leads to a property menu showing the union of all properties available for the selected objects. Notice the menu heading: "Objects in Selection."

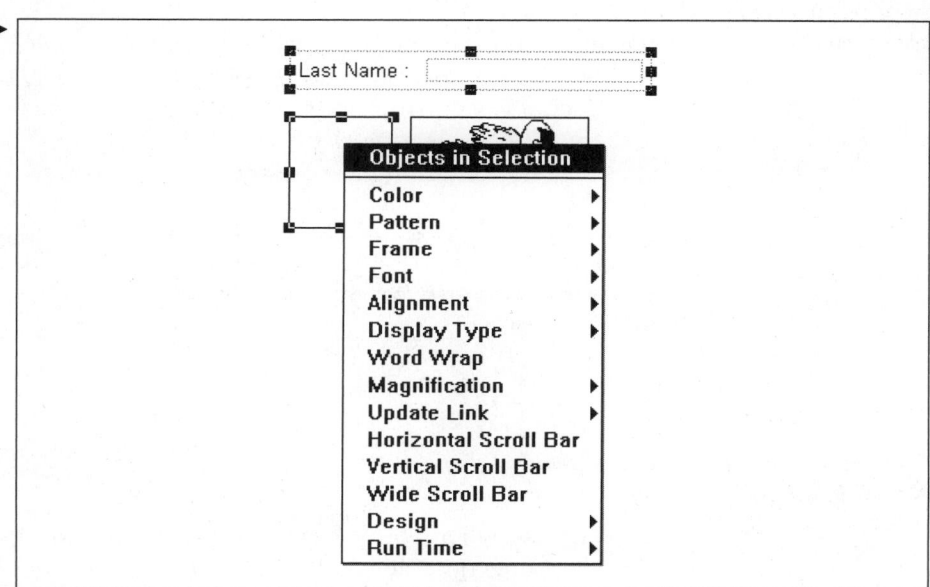

 ▶ ▶ **T I P**

Changing penetrating properties changes not only the selected objects but also any objects inside them.

▶ Choosing Property Menu Options

To change a property, use one of the inspection methods discussed above, then choose the appropriate option from the menu (some options lead to additional menus). As usual, you can click the option you want, type the first letter of the option, or use the ↑ and ↓ keys to high-light the option and then press ⏎. (To clear the property menu without selecting an option, press the Alt or Esc key.)

 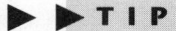

►►T I P

> **To display help for a property menu option, use the arrow key to highlight the option you're interested in and press F1.**

It's important to note that when you use the *normal* method to inspect and choose a property, Paradox applies the property to all selected objects for which it is valid, but not to any objects contained inside the selected objects. Thus, selecting the box and Last Name field objects, right-clicking, and changing the Frame property produces the result below.

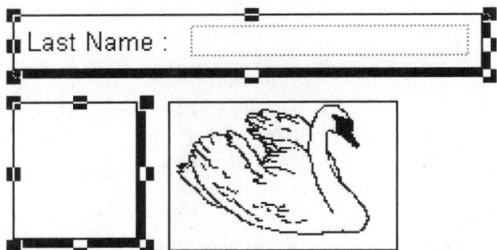

By contrast, when you use the *penetrating* method Paradox applies the chosen property to all selected objects—and to all objects contained in selected objects—for which it is valid. Therefore, if we select the same box and Last Name field objects, Ctrl+right-click, then change the Frame property, we get the result shown below.

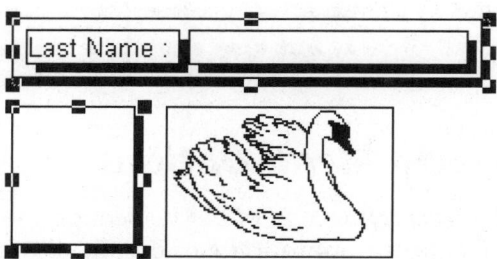

Table 10.2 summarizes the differences between normal and penetrating object properties.

 ►►**TIP**

> To change the properties of all objects on the form or report, press Esc until no objects (including the page) are selected. Then Ctrl+right-click to open a menu of all properties that can be used by *any* object on the form or report. When you change a property, Paradox will apply it to every object that can use it.

► **TABLE 10.2:** *Differences between Normal and Penetrating Object Properties*

NORMAL OBJECT PROPERTIES	PENETRATING OBJECT PROPERTIES
To inspect: Right-click one object. Or select one or more objects, then right-click or press F6.	**To inspect:** Select one or more objects, then Ctrl+right-click or press Shift+F6.
Property menu header lists the type of the object you inspected (for example, #Box3).	Property menu header shows "Objects in" followed by whatever was selected when you inspected the object(s).
Properties shown apply only to the object you inspected, even if multiple objects are selected.	Properties shown are the *union* of all available properties for the selected object(s).
Changes affect the selected object(s) only, but none of the objects inside them.	Changes affect the selected object(s) *and* any objects inside them.

► Using the Object Tree

If you create a large and complex design, you may have trouble inspecting exactly the portion you want, or you may be unable to remember what an object does or what you named it. This is where the *Object Tree* comes in handy. The Object Tree lets you step back from the design and take a look at the big picture of all the objects placed within it. You can use the Object Tree to select an object, inspect it, and even change its properties without having to scroll through the whole design.

To view a design's Object Tree, click the Object Tree button in the Tool-bar (shown at left). The Object Tree includes all objects in the design if no objects or multiple objects are selected. If you've selected just one object, the Object Tree includes that object only.

Figure 10.24 illustrates the Object Tree for the sample Employee form in Figure 10.1. Notice the hierarchical arrangement of objects. For example, the Employee_ID field consists of two parts: the text label (#Text23) and the editing area (#EditRegion24).

To select an object in the document, click its name in the Object Tree window. This highlights (darkens) the name in the Object Tree window and places selection handles around the corresponding object in the document, as in Figure 10.24. (If necessary, move the Object Tree win-dow out of the way and scroll around the design document until you can see the selected object.)

To inspect the properties of an object, right-click (or Ctrl+right-click) the object name in the Object Tree window. The property menu for that object will appear.

FIGURE 10.24 ▶

The Object Tree for the Employee form. In this example we clicked on the Em-ployee_ID field in the Object Tree window to select it in the design.

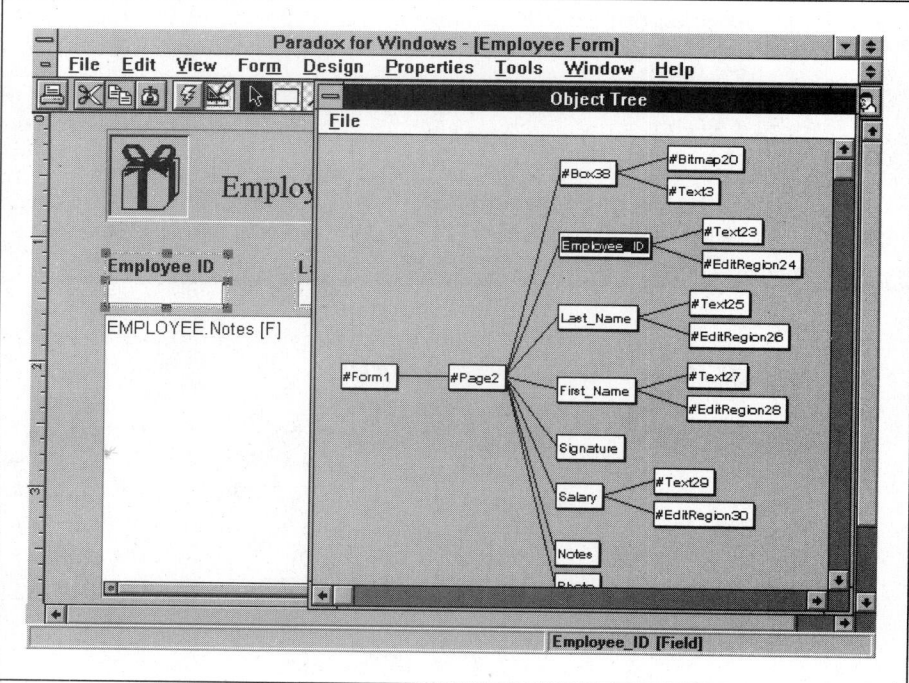

If you would like to print a copy of the Object Tree, choose File ➤ Print from the Object Tree's menu bar.

When you're finished using the Object Tree window, close it any of the following ways: Double-click its Control-menu box, or click the window and press Alt+F4, or choose File ➤ Close from the Object Tree's menu bar.

▶ ▶**TIP**

> **You can select several objects by holding down the Shift key while clicking objects in the Object Tree window. To change the properties of the selected objects, right-click or Ctrl+right-click the mouse.**

▶ *Using Floating Property Palettes*

Paradox for Windows displays visual properties—Color, Line Style, Font, and Frame—on *palettes* instead of menus. To select an option from a palette, simply click on the option or appearance you want.

Initially, the palettes are temporary and disappear when you make a selection. However, if you want to leave a palette on the screen, just click the snap button at the top of the palette. This creates a *floating palette* that you can move about on the Desktop by dragging the title bar. The floating palette remains on the Desktop until you click the snap button again.

▶ ▶**NOTE**

> **You've already seen the palettes in action in Chapter 7.**

▶ *Changing Design Properties*

Most object property menus include a *Design* option, which affects objects in the Design window only. (Design properties have no effect when you preview or print the document.) Depending on the type of object you're inspecting, the following options appear after you choose Design from a property menu. These are toggle options, which are either checked or unchecked.

Pin Horizontal   When checked, you can move the object up and down within the design, but not from side to side.

Pin Vertical   When checked, you can move the object from side to side within the design, but not up and down.

Contain Objects   When checked, the object can contain embedded objects, so that moving or deleting the container also moves or deletes the embedded object.

Size To Fit   When checked, objects such as labeled fields, graphics, OLE objects, and table frames can expand or contract automatically in the Design window as needed.

Selectable   When checked, you can select the object by clicking on it. When deselected, you cannot select the object with a mouse click (though you can still select objects inside the object and you can still inspect the object by right-clicking).

> ▶▶**N O T E**
>
> **Pinning prevents you from accidentally moving an object with your mouse once you've positioned it where you want it. However, certain actions, such as aligning objects via the Design ➤ Align options, will move objects even if they are pinned.**

Understanding Containers and Embedded Objects

When working with design objects, you should understand the relationship between containers and objects embedded within containers. A *container* completely surrounds and controls the behavior of all objects embedded within its frame. Thus, when you move or delete a container object, the embedded objects are automatically moved or deleted along with the container.

All objects that can use the Design ➤ Contain Objects property initially have that property turned on (checked). Thus, you only have to place an object inside another object's frame to create a contained relationship.

You can place an object inside a container in any of the following ways:

- Create the object within the frame of another object.
- Move an existing object so that it is completely contained within another object's frame.
- Move or enlarge the container to surround another object completely.
- Paste an object into another object.

If you want to break the relationship between a container and its embedded objects, inspect the container object, then deselect Design ➤ Contain Objects in the property menu. Or, select the contained object and drag it outside the frame of the container; the relationship is broken as soon as one part of the embedded object is dragged outside the container's frame.

Certain container relationships are unbreakable. For example, when working with labeled field objects, you can't move the field label (a text object) or the field edit region (where you enter data) outside the container. That's because a field object, by definition, contains all three parts: the container, the edit region, and the field label.

 ▶▶ **N O T E**

The field label appears only if the Display Type ➤ Labeled property is checked.

Here are some rules about containers and embedded objects:

- Deleting or moving a container deletes or moves the objects within it.
- Deleting or moving an embedded object has no effect on the container.
- Even when an object is embedded inside a container, you can select the object by clicking it.
- You can move a pinned object's container as long as you haven't pinned the container itself.

- Moving or resizing an object to surround a pinned object *does not* cause the pinned object to be contained.

Sizing Objects to Fit their Contents

When the Design ➤ Size To Fit property is checked, a field, table, graphic, or OLE object automatically grows or shrinks to fit the size of its contents. When the property isn't checked, the object does not change size automatically, and you can resize it yourself with the mouse.

When Size To Fit is checked, the effect is slightly different for each type of object, as summarized below.

Tables If the table doesn't have room to grow, Paradox adds a horizontal scroll bar to the table and turns off Size To Fit. When you resize a table manually with Size To Fit on, Paradox automatically resizes the columns (if all columns fit in the design).

Fields Size To Fit remains on even if Paradox doesn't have room to resize the field object. When Size To Fit is on, Paradox resizes fields automatically when you change properties such as the font, definition, display type, and frame style—even if you've already resized the field manually.

Graphic and OLE objects Size To Fit remains on even if Paradox doesn't have room to resize the object. You can't resize a graphic or OLE object manually when Size To Fit is on.

 ▶▶**T I P**

Paradox 5 for Windows can display wide or narrow scroll bars. To choose a wide scroll bar, inspect any object that can have a scroll bar and select (check) Wide Scroll Bar. To return to the default narrow scroll bar, inspect the object and deselect Wide Scroll Bar. The narrow or wide scroll bar appears only if the Vertical Scroll Bar or Horizontal Scroll Bar option is also checked in the object's property menu.

▶ *Changing Run Time Properties*

The *Run Time properties* of an object take effect when you *run* (print or view) a document. Therefore, although you change the Run Time properties in the Design window, you won't actually see their effects until you click the View Data button in the Toolbar or print the document. Not surprisingly, the Run Time properties available depend on the type of document you're designing and the object you're inspecting. Chapters 11 and 12 and Appendix E cover Run Time properties in more detail.

▶ *Renaming Design Objects*

An object's name appears at the top of its property menu, in the Object Tree, and on the status bar when the object is selected. By default, field objects use their field names; table and multi-record objects use their table names; and design objects are named according to their object type, with a sequential number added (for example, *#Text4* and *#EditRegion5*). You can change an object's name, if you wish, as follows:

1. Inspect the object by right-clicking (or click it and press F6).

2. Click the header at the top of the property menu or press ↵.

3. Type a new name for the object in the Object Name dialog box, then choose OK.

 ▶ ▶ **N O T E**

> **You might wish to rename an object if you'll be referring to it in calculations (Chapter 17) or in ObjectPAL methods (Chapter 19). Otherwise, you needn't bother.**

▶▶ *Creating New Objects*

You use the tools on the Design window Toolbar, shown in Figure 10.25, to create and place objects such as boxes, graphics, fields, tables, and so forth. Table 10.1 (shown earlier) offers a quick summary of each tool.

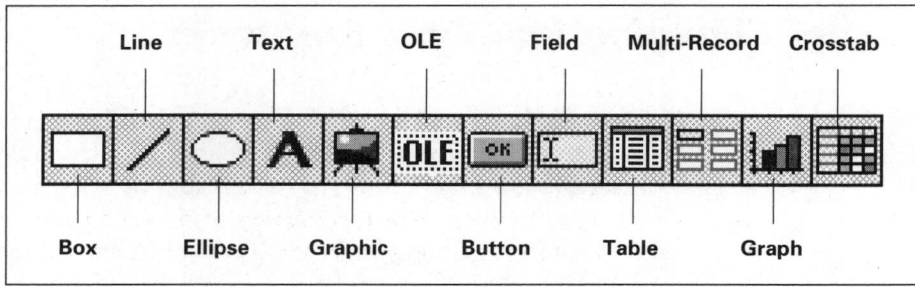

To place a new object in your design, click the tool you want, then click and drag in the Design window. When the object is the size and shape you want, release the mouse button. Normally the mouse pointer reverts to a selection arrow after you place an object. If you want to create more than one object of the same type, hold down the Shift key while clicking the tool. The tool will remain active until you select another tool.

 ►►**TIP**

> **The object is selected as soon as you release the mouse button. You can then move, delete, or resize the object, or change its properties.**

► *Changing Properties of Toolbar Tools*

You can change the properties of any design tool in the Toolbar, so that new objects you create already have the properties you want. For example, if you want all boxes to appear in red, you can change the Color property of the Box tool. Or, if you want to change the default text font to *Times New Roman*, you can change the Font property of the Text tool.

▶ ▶ **T I P**

> **Paradox initially uses the default system font for fields (but not labels or text objects) in a design document. To change the default system font, choose Properties ➤ Desktop ➤ Change, select the font you want, choose OK twice, then exit Paradox and restart it. Be aware that changing the default system font also changes the font used in tables and queries.**

Paradox for Windows offers two ways to change the Toolbar tools. The first method involves inspecting the Toolbar tool itself; the second involves copying properties from an object to the Toolbar.

To inspect the Toolbar button itself, right-click the appropriate tool in the Toolbar. Then change whatever property you want. Repeat these steps as needed.

To copy properties from an object to the corresponding Toolbar tool, create (or select) the object you want to use. For example, if you want to change the default properties for the Box tool, create a box, then inspect the box object and change its properties to your liking. Finally, choose Design ➤ Copy To Toolbar. Paradox will automatically copy the selected object's properties to the appropriate Toolbar tool.

Regardless of how you change the properties of the Toolbar, all subsequent design elements will have the new default properties. However, the change will not affect any objects already placed in the design.

▶ ▶ **T I P**

> **To change the default properties of a page, inspect the page (by right-clicking an empty area of your design). Then change the properties and choose Design ➤ Copy To Toolbar.**

The properties you set for a tool remain in effect for all design documents until you exit Paradox. If you want to save them permanently, choose Properties ➤ Form ➤ Style Sheet (for forms) or Properties ➤ Report ➤ Style Sheet (for reports). Next, either specify a new file for the tool properties, or highlight an existing file. Then click the Save button and choose OK. For more about style sheets, see "Working with Style Sheets" near the end of this chapter.

▶ Creating Boxes, Lines, and Ellipses

The simple drawing tools listed below let you add graphical elements to your design.

Box   Draws squares and rectangles in your design.

Line   Draws horizontal, vertical, and diagonal lines. Each line can appear with or without arrowheads (depending on the Line Ends property), and it may be straight or curved (depending on the Line Type property).

Ellipse   Draws circles and ellipses.

Simply select the tool you want in the Toolbar, drag in the Design window to define the object's size and shape, and then release the mouse button.

▶ Creating Graphics

To place graphics in your design, you use the Graphic tool (shown at left). You can either paste a graphic from the Clipboard or from a .bmp, .pcx, .tif, .gif, or .eps file.

Begin by choosing the Graphic tool in the Toolbar and dragging in the Design window to define the size and shape of your graphic. The words "Undefined Graphic" appear inside the frame, as illustrated below.

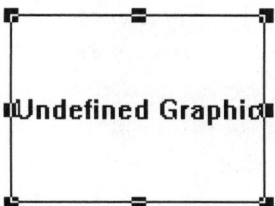

To place the graphic in the frame, inspect the object and choose Define Graphic from the property menu. Then, proceed as follows:

- To copy the graphic from the Clipboard, choose Paste.
- To copy the graphic from a file, choose Paste From and select a file.

T I P

> **Paradox automatically turns on (checks) the graphic's Design ➤ Size To Fit property. Before resizing the graphic, you must inspect it and turn off (uncheck) this property. To make the entire graphic fit inside the frame, inspect it and choose Magnification ➤ Best Fit.**

You can crop graphics within their frames if you haven't checked the Magnification ➤ Best Fit property. If a graphic can be cropped, you'll see a hand tool after clicking on the graphic (you may need to click more than once). When the mouse pointer changes to a hand tool, simply click and drag to move the graphic within the frame, as shown below.

➤ Creating OLE Objects

 OLE objects can display data from other applications (graphics, sound, spreadsheets, and text) right in your design document. (You'll find a discussion of OLE in Chapter 6.) To create an OLE object, start by choosing the OLE tool (shown at left) and dragging in the Design window to define the object's size. From here, you can choose either of two basic methods for defining what's inside the OLE object.

NOTE

Do not confuse an OLE field in your table with an OLE object in your design document. An OLE field in a table contains data that can change from record to record. By contrast, an OLE object on a design document is for decoration only, and does not change as you scroll from record to record.

Here's the first method for defining the OLE contents.

1. Switch to an OLE server.

2. If you want to link the server data to the design document, open an existing server document, or create and save one.

3. Cut or copy the data you want to the Clipboard.

4. Switch back to the Paradox Design window, inspect the OLE object, and choose Define OLE from the property menu.

5. Now do either of the following, depending on whether you want to embed or link the data:

   - To embed the data into the OLE object, choose the P̲aste... option (for example, choose P̲aste PBrush if Paintbrush data is on the Clipboard).

   - To link the object, choose Paste L̲ink.

TIP

Paradox for Windows automatically turns on the OLE object's Design ➤ Size To Fit property. Before resizing the OLE object, you must inspect it and turn off this property. To make the entire OLE object fit inside the frame, inspect it, then choose Magnification ➤ Best Fit.

new

If you prefer to define the OLE data on the fly, or you just like the "Insert Object" method, follow the steps below:

1. Inspect the OLE object, then choose Define OLE ➤ Insert Object from the property menu.

2. When the Insert Object dialog box appears, do either of the following:

   - To define a new object on the fly, choose Create New, highlight the type of object you want in the Object Type list, and choose OK. Now, create your object normally. When you're finished, choose File ➤ Exit & Return... and answer Yes; or, if the server application supports OLE2, simply click outside the object.

   - To create the object from an existing file, choose Create From File. Then type in the file name you want, or use the Browse button to locate the file. If you wish to link the file, select (check) Link. Choose OK.

Regardless of which method you choose, you'll see the OLE object within its frame when you return to the Design window.

new

Here are some ways to edit OLE and OLE2 objects that you've placed in your design:

   - To edit an OLE object, double-click it in the Design window. Or, inspect the object and choose the Edit... option from the property menu.

   - To edit an OLE2 object within its frame (without leaving Paradox), inspect the object in the Design window and choose Edit.... When you're finished editing, click outside the object frame.

   - To edit an OLE2 object in a separate server application window, inspect the object and choose Open.... When you're finished editing, choose the usual File ➤ Exit commands.

You can control when Paradox will update the contents of a linked OLE object, as outlined below:

   - To force Paradox to update a linked OLE object right now, inspect the object and choose Update Now.

- To control whether Paradox updates a linked OLE object manually or automatically, select the object, then choose Edit ➤ Links from the Design window menus. When the Links dialog box appears, click the link you want to update in the Links list. Finally, choose either Automatic or Manual and then choose Close. When you select Automatic, Paradox will update the object whenever it detects that the object has changed. When you select Manual, Paradox updates the object only when you inspect it and choose Update Now (or when you open the Links dialog box, click the link in the Links list, click the Update Now button, and choose Close).

▶ Creating Buttons

 You use the Button tool (shown at left) to create buttons on your form (buttons aren't available for reports). After defining a button, it looks like this:

From this point, you can change the label and assign a specific function to the button using ObjectPAL methods, so that clicking the button performs an action. We'll talk about buttons in Chapter 19.

▶ Creating Graphs and Crosstabs

 The Graph tool (shown at left) is used to create charts and graphs from your Paradox table. Choose the Graph tool and drag it in the Design window to define the overall size and shape of the graph. Before Paradox can display a graph, you must tell it what information to use. That's the topic of Chapter 13, which covers both graphs and crosstabs.

 Crosstab objects summarize (cross-tabulate) information according to one or more columns, then display the summary in a tabular format similar to a spreadsheet. Use the Crosstab tool (shown at left) to define a crosstab by clicking and dragging. As with graphs, the crosstab starts out undefined.

►► *Working with Text Objects*

Text objects are really just invisible boxes you type text into. Depending on the properties you select, the text object can either be fixed in size or grow to hold all the text you enter. If you've worked with formatted memo fields, you already know most of the techniques for editing and formatting text. But thanks to Paradox for Windows' expanded ruler, you can go beyond simple memo editing features by setting tabs and margins, text alignment, and line spacing.

► *Creating a Text Object*

You can create a text box in either of two ways, depending on whether you want a fixed- or variable-size object initially.

A *fixed-size* text object doesn't automatically grow or shrink horizontally or vertically to fit the amount of text it contains. Therefore, you must resize the object manually if you want it to show all the text within the box.

 You create a fixed-size text object by using the click and drag technique. That is, click the Text tool in the Toolbar (shown at the left), click in the design where you want the text to begin, and then drag the outline to define the size and shape of the object. After placing the object, type your text within the frame. Click elsewhere in the design when you're done.

Unlike fixed text objects, *variable-size* or *fit text* objects grow or shrink to fit the amount of text they contain. To create a fit text object, follow the steps below.

1. Click the Text tool in the Toolbar.

2. Click in the design where you want the text to begin.

3. Type the text and press ⏎ when you reach the desired width of the object. Then continue typing, pressing ⏎ only when you want to end a paragraph or create a blank line. Paradox will automatically wrap the text at the right border and expand the box downward as you type.

4. Click elsewhere in the design when you're finished.

Regardless of how you create a text object, the Word Wrap property is on initially. Therefore, as you type in text, the text wraps automatically when it reaches the right side of the object. If you turn Word Wrap off, you can enter only a single line of text into the object.

Of course, you're not stuck with the initial settings for the behavior of a text object. To make changes, simply inspect the object and choose any of the property options listed below.

Word Wrap   When checked, this option turns on Word Wrap. If you turn off Word Wrap, you can enter only one line of text in the object.

Design Sizing ➤ Fixed Size   When this is checked, the text object stays the same size, and text wraps at the right edge and scrolls up and down within the object. You can resize fixed-size text objects manually as needed.

Design Sizing ➤ Fit Text   When this option is checked, the text object grows or shrinks to fit the text you type. With Word Wrap on, the first time you press ↵, the right margin is set and any new text automatically wraps at the right margin. If Word Wrap is off, you can enter only one line of text; the object will adjust horizontally to fit the line of text. You can resize a fit text object only if Word Wrap is on, and then only horizontally.

Design Sizing ➤ Grow Only   When this is checked, the text object grows to fit the text but does not shrink if the text does not fill the object. As with the Fit Text option, if Word Wrap is off, the object is only one line wide but will grow horizontally to fit the text you enter.

 ▶ ▶ **T I P**

> **If your fixed-size text object is too small to hold all the text you've typed in, inspect the object and turn on the Vertical Scroll Bar property. You can then use the scroll bar to view all the text. Scroll bars are available only for form documents.**

▶ *Formatting the Text*

You can change the font, alignment, and line spacing of an entire text object or of selected text within the object.

To change the format of part of the text, select the text by dragging or using Shift+arrow, then right-click and choose options from the property menu. To change the format of an entire text object, inspect the object without first selecting any text. You can change the Font (Typeface, Size, Style, and Color), Alignment, and Line Spacing properties, as discussed in Chapter 7.

▶▶ **N O T E**

The expanded ruler provides shortcuts for changing the alignment, tabs, and line spacing. These are discussed later in this chapter.

▶ *Editing Text*

You use the standard Windows editing techniques to position the insertion point, type text, and select text in a text object. The only difference is that you may need to click more than once before the insertion point appears in the text object, depending on whether the object is currently selected. You can also cut, copy, and paste text using options on the Edit menu or by clicking the Cut To Clipboard, Copy To Clipboard, and Paste From Clipboard buttons in the Toolbar.

▶▶ **T I P**

To select a word in a text object, double-click the word. To select all the text when the insertion point is in a text object, press Ctrl+Home, then hold down the Shift key while pressing Ctrl+End.

Just as you can search for and replace text in a memo or formatted memo field, you can also use the Search And Replace feature in a text object. To get started, inspect the text object and choose Search Text from the property menu; or put the insertion point in the text box, press Ctrl+Home (to start the search at the top), and choose <u>E</u>dit ➤ <u>S</u>earch Text from the menus. Type the search text or pattern, type optional replacement text, and begin the search as described in Chapter 6.

► *Using the Rulers*

Paradox for Windows' rulers provide some powerful word processing capabilities. For example, the expanded ruler contains useful shortcuts for aligning text, adjusting line spacing, and setting tabs. And the horizontal ruler lets you change the location of tabs, adjust the margins, and set the indent for the first line of a paragraph.

► ► **N O T E**

To display the expanded, horizontal, and vertical rulers (respectively), choose <u>P</u>roperties ➤ <u>E</u>xpanded Ruler, <u>P</u>roperties ➤ <u>H</u>orizontal Ruler, and <u>P</u>roperties ➤ <u>V</u>ertical Ruler. (The horizontal and expanded rulers are also available in Form View, where you can use them in Edit mode to customize the appearance of formatted memo fields.)

Figure 10.26 shows all three rulers and some sample text. The rulers in the figure are labeled to show various buttons and markers available for changing the appearance of text. Notice how the buttons in the expanded ruler darken to show the current alignment and line spacing of text at the insertion point. Similarly, the tab well of the horizontal ruler indicates the current margins, paragraph indent, and tab settings.

Before using the rulers to change settings, indicate the amount of text you want to change, as described below.

- Select text to change settings only within that text.
- Place the insertion point at the beginning of a paragraph to change the settings in that paragraph only.
- Place the insertion point at the beginning of a blank line to change settings for new text that you type.

Creating Design Documents

FIGURE 10.26

The expanded ruler lets you set alignment, tab stops, and line spacing. The tab well of the horizontal ruler shows current settings for text at the insertion point and includes markers for the left margin, paragraph indent, tab settings, and right margin.

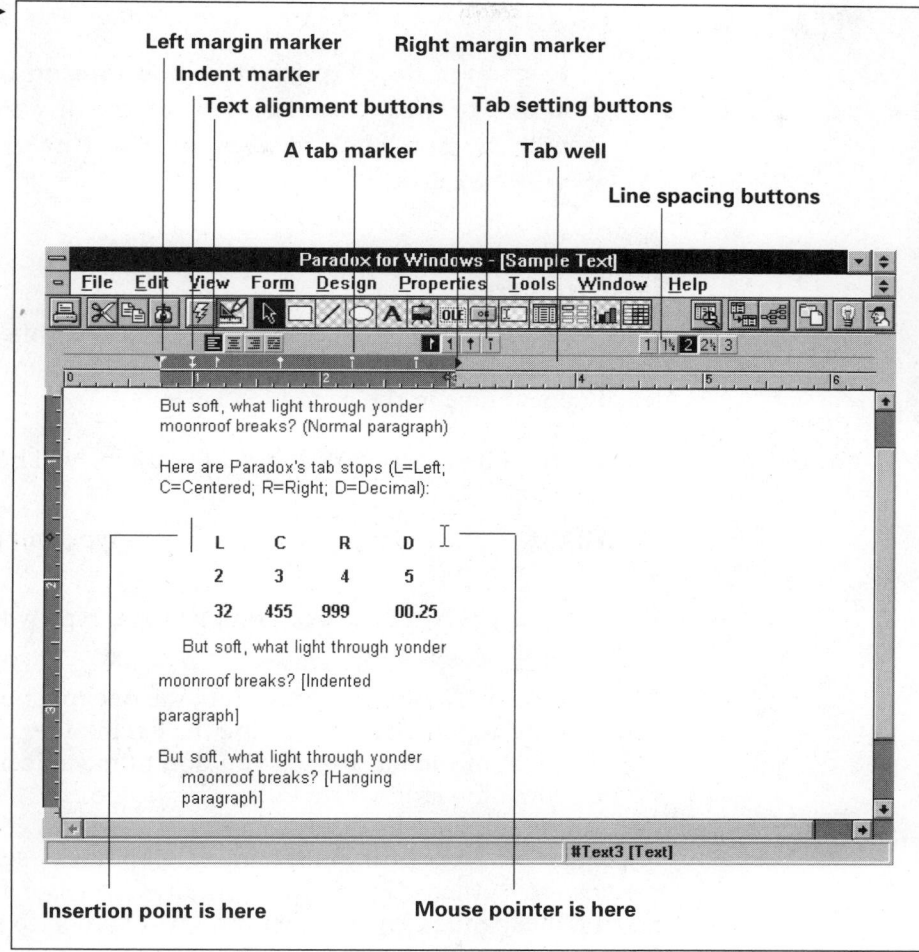

Left margin marker
Indent marker
Text alignment buttons
A tab marker
Right margin marker
Tab setting buttons
Tab well
Line spacing buttons

Insertion point is here
Mouse pointer is here

Changing Alignment and Line Spacing

The alignment and line spacing buttons provide a handy alternative to inspecting text. After specifying the amount of text you want to change, simply click the appropriate button in the expanded ruler. For example, click any of the first four buttons in the expanded ruler to change the alignment to left, center, right, or justified, respectively. Click any of the last five buttons in the ruler to change the line spacing to 1, $1\frac{1}{2}$, 2, $2\frac{1}{2}$, or 3, respectively.

> To change the alignment or line spacing of *all the text* in one or more text objects, select the object or objects, then click an alignment or line spacing button in the expanded ruler.

Setting Tabs

When the horizontal and expanded rulers are visible, you can set four types of tabs, as described below. These tab types are listed in their order of appearance in the expanded ruler.

Left   When you press Tab, text you type will be left-aligned at the tab stop.

Right   When you press Tab, text you type will be right-aligned at the tab stop.

Center   When you press Tab, text you type will be centered around the tab stop.

Decimal   When you press Tab, the decimal point will appear at the tab stop and text following the decimal point will appear to the right of the tab stop. If you don't type a decimal point, the Decimal tab stop will act like a Right tab.

To place a tab stop, position the insertion point or select the text as described above, then click the Left, Right, Center, or Decimal tab button in the expanded ruler (the button will darken to indicate your selection). Now click in the tab well (above the horizontal ruler) where you want the tab stop to appear. If necessary, drag the tab marker left or right to position it more precisely.

To remove a tab stop, click it, then drag it downward and out of the tab well. (You cannot delete or reposition the little T-shaped tab stop markers, since these are preset by Paradox.)

Changing Margins

The default margins are the left and right borders of the selected text object. To change the margin setting, select the text or position the insertion point, then drag the left or right margin icon to its new location.

Adding Paragraph Indents

You can use the indent marker to create indented paragraphs and hanging paragraphs (see Figure 10.26 for examples). To place an indent, drag the indent marker to the desired location in the tab well. Initially, the indent and margin markers are at the same position, so you'll need to drag the indent marker by its *bottom* to move it (dragging it at the top moves the margin marker).

For an indented paragraph, place the indent marker to the *right* of the left margin marker. For a hanging paragraph, place the indent marker to the *left* of the left margin marker.

TIP

Dragging the left margin marker moves both the left margin and the indent together. Dragging the indent marker moves only the indent.

▶▶ *Working with Field Objects*

Initially, your design will already contain fields, unless you chose a blank design style. However, you can add more fields and change field properties anytime you want.

NOTE

A field is composed of the field itself, an optional text label, and the frame that surrounds them.

Paradox offers several types of fields, including the following:

- Normal table fields
- Special fields (including current date, time, page number, and total number of pages)
- Calculated fields
- Summary fields

The basic field types are discussed in this chapter, while the more advanced calculated and summary fields are covered in Chapters 13 and 17.

▶ Creating a Field

To place a field in the design, click the Field tool in the Toolbar (shown at the left), then click in the design where you want to position the field, and drag to define the frame.

▶ Defining a Field

To define the field, inspect it and choose Define Field from the property menu. You'll see a list, as in Figure 10.27, of available fields from the tables you included in the data model. Click the field name you want.

FIGURE 10.27 ▶

To define a field, inspect it and choose Define Field from the property menu, then click the name of the field you want.

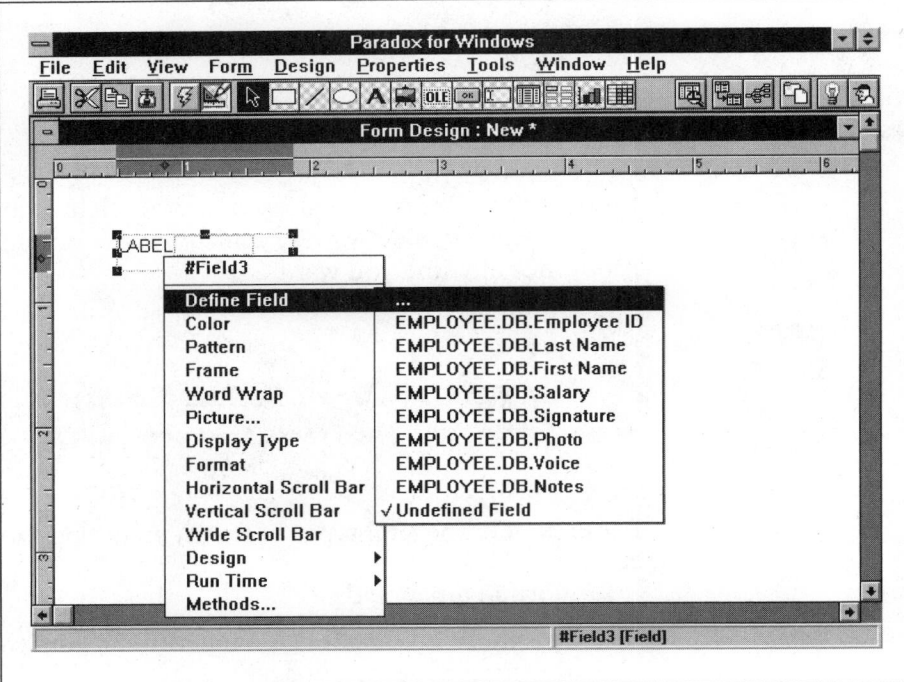

If the field you want is not on the list, click the list header (...) or press ↵ to display the Define Field Object dialog box shown in Figure 10.28. You can click the drop-down arrow next to the table name to display a list of all fields in that table and some special fields that provide information about the table. Select a field by double-clicking.

FIGURE 10.28 ▶

The list of fields for the table appears when you click the drop-down arrow next to the table name.

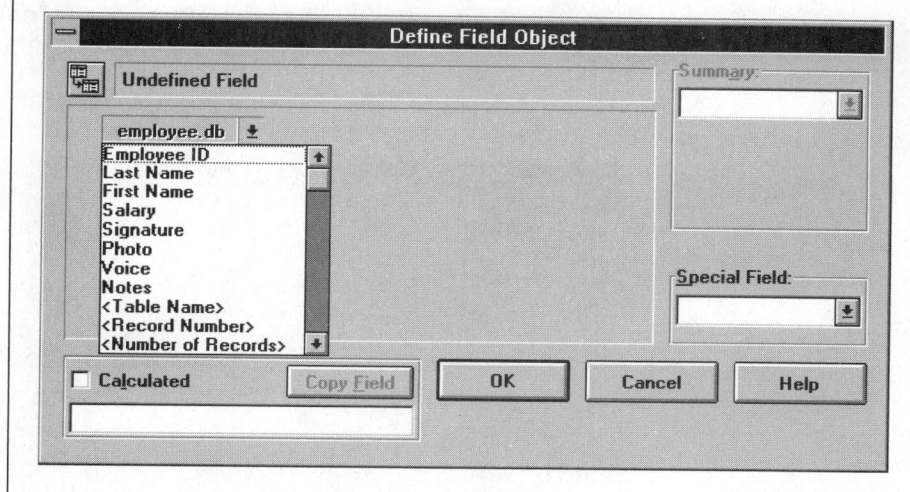

NOTE

The last four items in the drop-down list refer to the table itself: the table name (*<Table Name>*), the current record number (*<Record Number>*), the total number of records (*<Number of Records>*), and the number of fields in the table structure (*<Number of Fields>*, scrolled off the list in Figure 10.28).

You can also select a special field that describes the design as a whole by clicking the Special Field drop-down list. These fields, shown in Figure 10.29, display the current date (*Today*), the current time (*Now*), the current date and time (*Timestamp*), the current page number (*Page Number*), and the total number of pages in the document (*Number of Pages*). Click to choose the item you want.

▶▶**N O T E**

Timestamps are new in Paradox 5. When you choose View Data in a form design, the Timestamp field (or Now field) will be updated automatically with every tick of your computer's clock. In a report design, the Timestamp field (or Now field) will show the exact time you clicked the View Data (or Print) button.

FIGURE 10.29 ▶

Fields that relate to the design as a whole appear in the Special Field list.

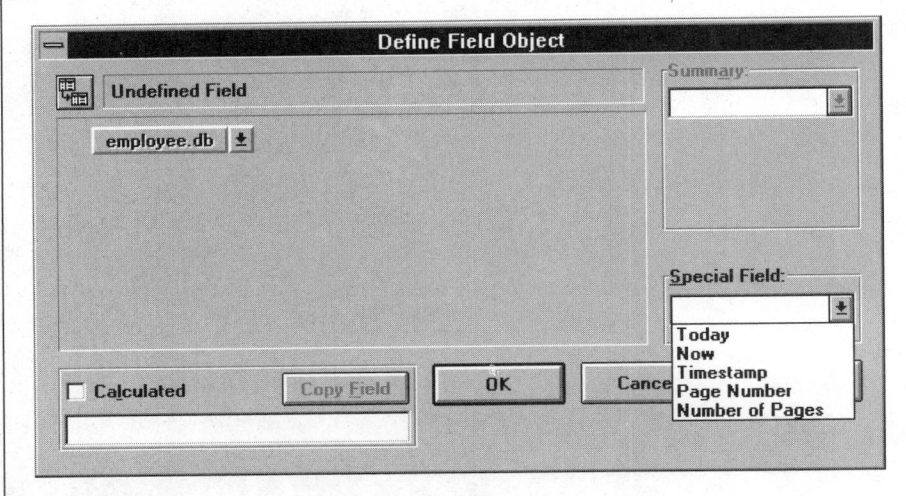

When you're finished defining the new field, click OK. Now you can change the field's properties, resize it, move it, and so forth.

▶ Adding or Removing Field Labels

By default, new fields are labeled when you create them. You can edit the field label as you would any text object. To remove the field label altogether, inspect the field and choose Display Type ➤ Unlabeled from the property menu. To label the field again (with its default label), inspect the field and choose Display Type ➤ Labeled.

Creating Design
Documents

Ch.
10

►►N O T E

> Initially, the label has the Design Sizing ➤ Fit Text
> option turned on and Word Wrap turned off.

► Formatting Field Data

You can control the field format by inspecting the field and choosing
Format from the property menu. From there, you can choose predefined number, date, and other formats or create your own customized
formats, as discussed in Chapter 7.

► Formatting Graphic Fields

Graphic fields have two special and quite interesting properties: *Magni-*
fication and *Raster Operation*. The Magnification property leads to the
Best Fit, 25%, 50%, 100%, 200%, and 400% options described in
Chapter 6.

The Raster Operation property controls interactions between a bitmap
image and the background on which it is painted. These interactions
are logical operations performed on the colors of the image, including
Source Copy, Source Paint, Source And, Source Invert, Source Erase,
Not Source Copy, Not Source Erase, and Merge Paint.

The raster operations are more easily shown than explained, so take a
look at Figure 10.30, which depicts several examples of the same
graphic pasted onto a light gray background. As indicated by the labels
below each example, we chose a different Raster Operation property
for each pasted graphic.

►►N O T E

> To see a dramatic color example of the Raster
> Operation properties at work, open the Rasterop form
> in the *pdoxwin**examples* directory that's created when
> you install Paradox.

FIGURE 10.30 ▶

In this example we pasted several copies of the same graphic onto a light gray background, then chose different Raster Operations for each copy.

▶▶ *Working with Table Objects*

When you choose a tabular style for your form or report, or when you create a table with the Table tool, you actually get a table *frame*, not a table. A table frame is composed of the following elements:

- Field objects from the source table
- Text objects, which provide labels for the fields
- A grid for the fields and labels representing the table
- Columns of fields
- Rows of records
- Headers showing the row of field labels

You can customize these components by inspecting the object properties using many of the techniques discussed in Chapter 7.

▶ Creating a Table Object

 To add a table object to the design, just click the Table tool in the Toolbar (shown at the left), then click in the design and drag to define the size of the table. The table frame you outline will include a grid marking rows and columns, as in Figure 10.31, along with labels and undefined fields.

FIGURE 10.31 ▶

After using the Table tool to place a table in the design, you will see a table frame with undefined fields.

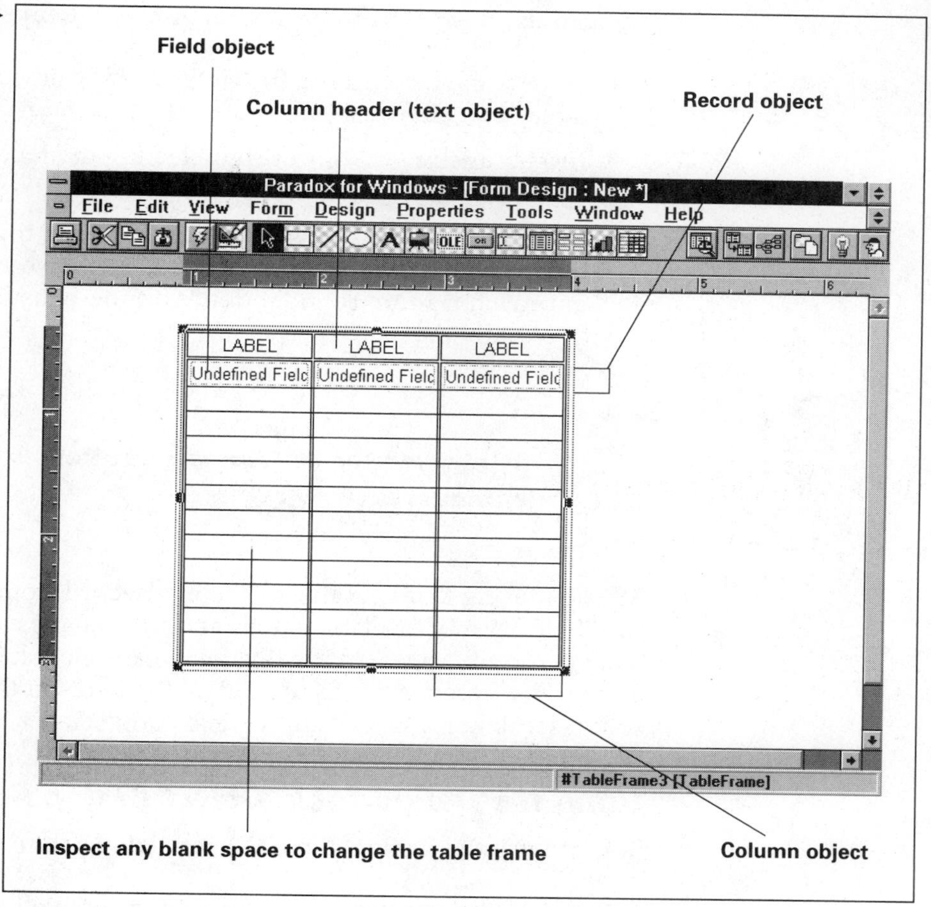

Field object

Column header (text object)

Record object

Paradox for Windows - [Form Design : New *]

<u>F</u>ile   <u>E</u>dit   <u>V</u>iew   <u>F</u>orm   <u>D</u>esign   <u>P</u>roperties   <u>T</u>ools   <u>W</u>indow   <u>H</u>elp

LABEL	LABEL	LABEL
Undefined Field	Undefined Field	Undefined Field

#TableFrame3 [TableFrame]

Inspect any blank space to change the table frame

Column object

▶ ▶ **T I P**

> You can inspect and change properties of the table as a whole, any column (field), any row (record), the grid, any label, or any undefined field.

▶ *Defining a Table Object*

You can use any of the following methods to define your table object:

- Inspect the table frame (by right-clicking any blank space on the table) and choose *Define Table*.

- Inspect the record object (by selecting the record object, then right-clicking) and choose *Define Record*.

- Inspect each field individually (by selecting the field object, then right-clicking) and choose *Define Field*. As you might expect, this approach is more roundabout and time-consuming than the first two methods.

▶ ▶ **N O T E**

> The method for defining a table field is the same as for defining a field object.

After choosing Define Table or Define Record from the property menu, you'll see a list of available tables and the usual list header (...). If the table you want appears in the list, you can select it by clicking the table name. The frame expands to hold all the fields in the table, with a horizontal scroll bar added if all the fields don't fit.

Using the Define Table Object Dialog Box

You can use the Define Table Object dialog box to:

- Add fields not already included in the table frame.
- Remove fields from the table frame.
- Rearrange fields in the table frame.

- Change the main table assigned to the data model.

- Add a table to the existing data model.

To open this dialog box, inspect the table or record, then click the header (...) of the property menu or press ↵. The dialog box will resemble Figure 10.32.

FIGURE 10.32

The Define Table Object dialog box. In this example, we opened the drop-down list to show the available fields for the Employee table.

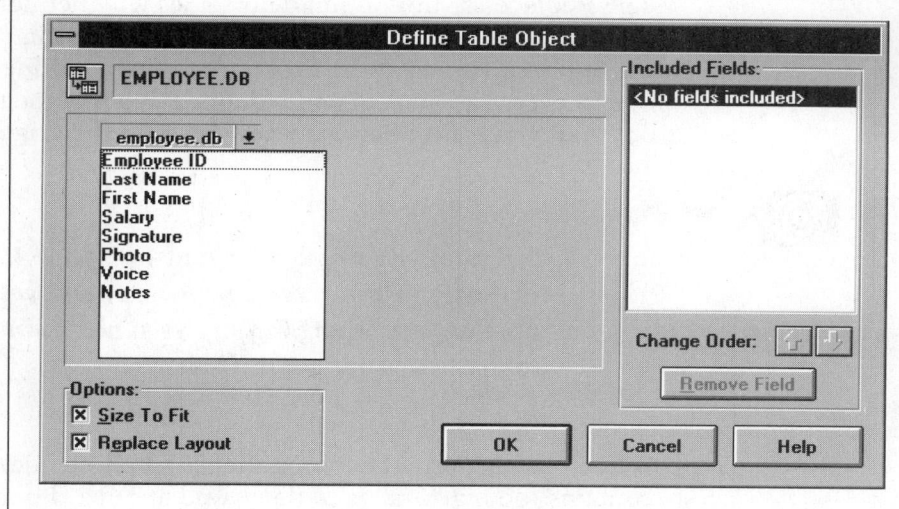

The names of all tables currently in the data model appear in the table name area of the dialog box, each with a drop-down arrow next to it. You can click the drop-down arrow to see a list of all fields in the table, then select the fields you want to include in the table object (selected fields will appear in the Included Fields list). You can use the ↑ and ↓ Change Order buttons to change the order of the fields, and the Remove Field button to remove fields. Or, use techniques described earlier under "Selecting Fields to Display" to select, rearrange, or remove fields in the Define Table Object dialog box.

If you want to change the main table or add another table to the data model, click the *Data Model* button at the upper-left corner. When the Data Model dialog box appears, complete it as described earlier in this chapter, then choose OK. Adding a table to a blank design makes the table the main table for the document. Adding a table to a design that's already associated with a table creates a multitable design, and you must define the relationship between multiple tables in the Data Model dialog box (see Chapter 17).

The Size To Fit option in the Define Table Object dialog box controls whether the table frame expands to include all the fields you have selected. Check it to have the table expand, or uncheck it to have the table frame keep its original size and shape.

The Replace Layout option determines whether fields will be added to or will completely replace the contents of the existing table frame. Check the option if you want the fields in the Included Fields list of the dialog box to overwrite any currently defined fields in the table. Uncheck this option if you want to append new fields to the original design layout.

▶▶ **WARNING**

Checking the Replace Layout option deletes all objects currently in the record or header and rebuilds the table object. Anything in the table frame, including ObjectPAL code, will be lost.

When you're finished defining the table object, click OK. If the table contains too many fields to be viewed at once, a horizontal scroll bar will appear automatically.

Changing Table Properties and Appearance

As always, you can change properties of an entire table or parts of a table by inspection. For an especially neat three-dimensional effect, inspect the table and check the Grid ➤ Grid Style ➤ 3D property. Then, add to the drama by choosing a light-gray background for the table. If you want to place horizontal dividing lines between records, inspect the table and check the Grid ➤ Record Divider property.

Scroll bars can be especially useful when your table is too wide or too deep to be viewed all at once. To add scroll bars, inspect the table frame, then choose Horizontal Scroll Bar or Vertical Scroll bar from the property menu. If you prefer to see wider scroll bars—rather than the scrawny ones that appear by default—inspect the frame and select Wide Scroll Bar. (Sorry, scroll bars aren't available in reports.)

If you'd like to detach the header from the rest of the table, inspect the table and choose Detach Header. Then drag the header (or the main body of the table) to create a gap between the table header and the data. If you change your mind and want to reattach the header, inspect the lower portion of the table (not the header) and choose Attach Header.

Not only can you inspect various table properties, but you can also manipulate the table with your mouse using the techniques discussed in Chapter 7. For example, you can drag the vertical or horizontal grid lines to adjust the width of columns and rows or drag the columns to rearrange them.

Removing and adding columns takes only a few mouse clicks. The first step is to select a column by clicking at the lower edge of the column until the mouse pointer changes to a small ↑ and the column is highlighted. (To select another column, hold down the Shift key and click on the column you want.) Now, if you want to delete the selected columns, press the Del key. To insert a column, select the column that should appear to the *right* of the new column and press the Ins key. Then select the undefined field that appears, inspect it, and choose Define Field.

For some interesting effects, try stacking more than one field in a column. To do so, first resize the record area of the column by adjusting its width and height. Then, either drag existing field objects from other columns into the desired column, or create new field objects in the column and change their Display Type property to Unlabeled (if you wish). And don't forget that you can place *other* types of objects—graphics, boxes, lines, ellipses, and even other tables and graphs—within a table. Just resize the record area as needed and place the objects where you want them.

▶▶ *Working with Multi-Record Objects*

Multi-record objects display several records at a time, using a layout that repeats horizontally and vertically on the page. These objects are especially nice for creating mailing labels (see Chapter 12 for an example).

► Creating a Multi-Record Object

To create a multi-record object, choose the Multi-Record tool in the Toolbar (shown at left), then click and drag as usual. The Design window will display a blank master record in the top left and gray repeating regions to the right and below (Figure 10.33 shows the Design window after we defined and customized the appearance of the multi-record object). The entire multi-record object is surrounded by a container.

To resize the records, select the master record and drag its selection handles to the desired size. Paradox automatically resizes the repeating regions as well.

► Defining a Multi-Record Object

When you're ready to define the fields for a multi-record object, inspect the object or the record at the upper-left corner and choose Define

FIGURE 10.33 ►

A multi-record object with three fields from the Employee table. After choosing the three fields in the Define Multi-Record Object dialog box (described in a moment), we moved and resized them, set the Magnification property for the Photo field to Best Fit, and then selected the master record.

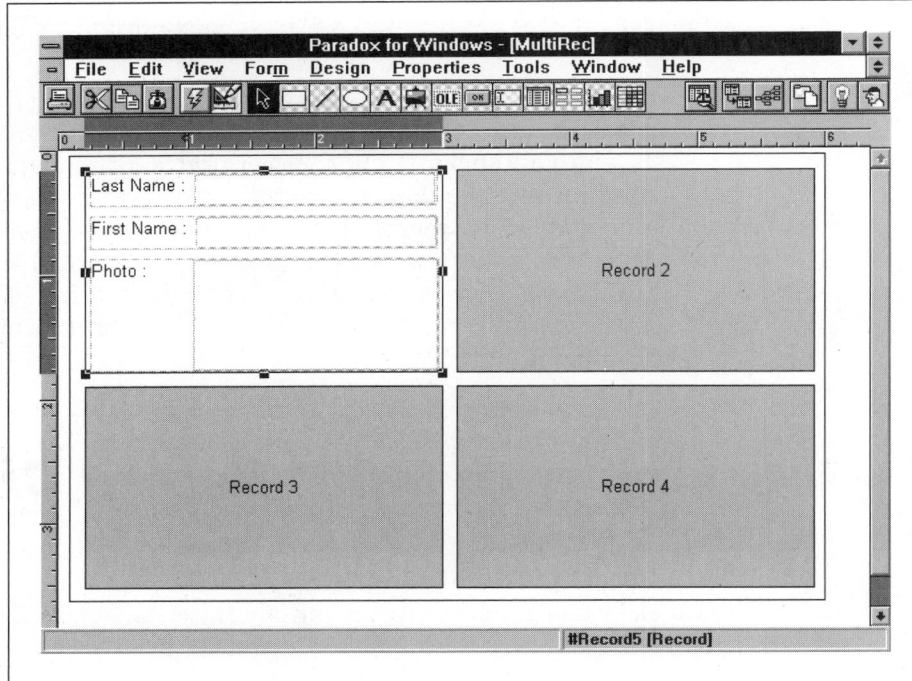

Record from the property menu. Then choose a table from the list, or click the header (...) or press ⏎ to open the Define Table Object dialog box described previously.

> ▶ ▶ **N O T E**
>
> **You can also use the Field tool in the Toolbar to place fields individually, though this can be more time consuming.**

▶ *Changing a Multi-Record Layout*

The Design Layout dialog box gives you some control over the initial appearance of multi-record layouts. Sometimes, however, you will want to change the number of records across or down, the spacing between records, or the order in which records appear. Changing the record layout might be handy, for example, if you've used the mailing label Expert (described in Chapter 12) to set up some mailing labels, but your forms don't exactly match the ones the Expert supports.

Before you change the record layout, you may need to do some preliminary steps, which are listed below:

- If you plan to increase the number of records across or the space between records in a row, you should reduce the width of the master record at the top-left corner of the multi-record object.

- If you plan to increase the number of records down or the space between records in a column, you should reduce the height of the master record.

To reduce the width or height of the master record, you can rearrange (or even delete) some fields or reduce their width. Once that's done, you can resize the master record as needed. (The message *#Record* will appear when you select the correct record for resizing.)

▶ ▶ N O T E

All this rigmarole for adjusting the record size before changing the record layout can help avoid messages from Paradox about not being able to fit the records into whatever layout you request.

With the preliminaries out of the way, you can change the record layout as follows:

1. In the Design window, click on the master record in the multi-record object until *#Record* appears in the status bar.

2. Inspect this master record and choose Record Layout from the property menu. You'll see the Record Layout dialog box shown below.

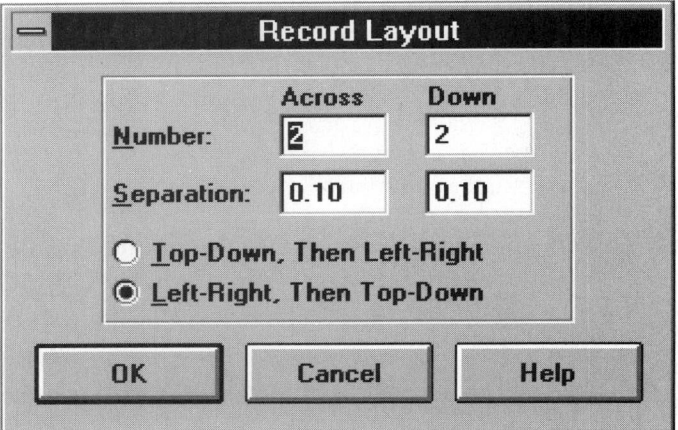

3. Make whatever changes you need in the dialog box. You can adjust the number of records across or down, the separation between records (in inches) across or down, and whether the records are arranged in top-down then left-right order, or in left-right then top-down order.

4. When you're finished making changes, choose OK.

If the page offers enough room for your new record layout, Paradox will rearrange the multi-record objects in the Design window accordingly.

If there isn't enough room on the page, an error message will let you know what number of labels *will* fit across and down. Choose OK to clear the message and return to the Record Layout dialog box. You can then choose a layout that will fit and then click OK, or you can click Cancel and resize the master record object as explained above.

▶ *Changing the Field Layout in a Multi-Record Object*

Recall that the Design Layout dialog box lets you choose which fields will appear in the design and whether they will be labeled. Once you reach the Design window, you can place additional fields, rearrange fields, delete them, and remove field labels as you like. Alternatively, you can make these changes in the convenient Layout MRO dialog box shown below:

Layout MRO
Object Layout: [Show Layout]   [Show Fields]
◉ By Columns
○ By Rows
☒ Label Fields

Last Name :
First Name :
Company :
Address :
City :
State :
Zip Code :

[OK] [Cancel] [Help]

To open this dialog box, inspect the master record in the multi-record object and choose Field Layout. Then, if you want to change the field layout, click the Show Fields button and update the Selected Fields list just as you would in the Design Layout dialog box. If you want to change whether fields are arranged By Columns or By Rows or add or remove labels, click Show Layout (if necessary) and update the Object Layout area as for the Design Layout dialog box. When you're done, choose OK to return to your design.

▶ Changing Multi-Record Properties

You can change the appearance of records within the multi-record object or the entire multi-record object. If you click on and then inspect the *master record*, your property changes will affect all the records within the object. If you click on and then inspect one of the gray *repeating record*s, the property changes will affect the background and perimeter of the multi-record object.

▶▶ *Working with Style Sheets*

Style sheets offer a terrific way for you to customize the design tools so that any form or report has a consistent appearance. For instance, you might want all fields to appear with a drop-shadow frame and sea-green background; all tables to have a 3D grid and gray background; and all boxes to have a thick red frame.

One way to accomplish this goal would be to draw all the objects, select them, inspect them, and apply the properties you want. But that's a time-consuming drag (no pun intended).

A better method would be to copy all the custom properties you want to the appropriate buttons in the Toolbar (as explained earlier in "Changing Properties of Toolbar Tools"), and then save those properties in a style sheet. Then, you can reuse that style sheet whenever you want to create objects with a certain look. You could also use any of several predefined style sheets that come with Paradox.

Keep in mind that style sheets only affect new objects that you place in your design. Existing objects will not change if you select another style sheet.

▶ Using a Style Sheet

There are several ways to choose a style sheet.

- First, you can select a style sheet file from the Style Sheet drop-down list in the Design Layout dialog box. (This dialog box appears after you create a new form or report, choose Data Model / Layout Diagram, and complete the Data Model dialog box. It also appears when you choose Design ➤ Design Layout in the Design window.)

- Second, you can select a style sheet file anytime you're in the Design window. Just choose Properties ➤ Form ➤ Style Sheet or Properties ➤ Report ➤ Style Sheet. Then click the name of the style sheet you want to use and choose OK.

- Third, you can select a style sheet when you use an Expert to create a form or report.

Paradox will use the current style sheet whenever you create new objects in your design.

▶ Saving a Style Sheet

It's easy to save a new style sheet or to update an existing style sheet with customized design tool properties. Here are the steps to follow:

1. Modify the design tools in the Toolbar using the methods discussed earlier under "Changing Properties of Toolbar Tools."

2. Choose Properties ➤ Form ➤ Style Sheet or Properties ➤ Report ➤ Style Sheet.

3. When the Style Sheet dialog box appears, do one of the following:

    - To update an existing style sheet with any changes you've made to the design tool properties, highlight that style sheet in the list and choose Save.

    - To create a new style sheet with all the current design tool properties, choose Save As, type a new file name (without an extension), and choose OK. Form style sheets will be saved with a .ft extension, while report style sheets will have a .fp extension.

4. To return to the Design window and select the currently highlighted style sheet, choose OK. To return to the Design window without selecting the highlighted style sheet, choose Cancel.

 ►►**TIP**

> If you've created a style sheet accidentally, you can delete it. Open the Project Viewer and change your working directory to the one where your style sheet is stored (typically, either *c:\pdoxwin* or the working directory in effect when you saved the style sheet). Click the All icon in the left side of the Project Viewer window, then right-click the style sheet's file name in the right side of the window. Finally, choose **D**elete and **Y**es. (You should not delete the built-in style sheets that come with Paradox, since they are quite attractive.)

► *Making a Style Sheet Accessible to All Projects*

Normally when you save a style sheet, it's placed on the working directory of your project. Hence, that style sheet is only available while you're working on that particular project. To make a custom style sheet accessible to all your projects, you need to move it to the Paradox (*c:\pdoxwin*) directory. Here's how:

1. Choose **T**ools ► **U**tilities ► **R**ename, and then go to the directory that contains the style sheet you want to move.

2. Under **T**ype, choose <Screen Style Sheets> or <Printer Style Sheets>, depending on which type of sheet you want to move.

3. Click in the **R**ename File From text box. Now, type the name of your style sheet (e.g. *mystyle.ft*), or click its name in the list below the T**o** text box.

4. In the T**o**: text box, type the new destination location and file name (e.g. **c:\pdoxwin\mystyle.ft**).

5. Choose OK.

▶ Choosing a Default Style Sheet

You can choose which style sheet Paradox will use automatically, whenever you don't explicitly choose a style sheet. We'll cover this topic, and other aspects of customizing the default form and report preferences, in "Setting Form and Report Preferences" near the end of this chapter.

▶▶ *Setting Design Window Preferences*

Earlier in this chapter, you learned how to change the selection order of objects. This procedure, and a few others that affect drawing, are called *designer properties* because they affect the behavior of the Design window.

To get started, choose Properties ➤ Designer from the Design window menus. The Designer Properties dialog box shown in Figure 10.34 appears on your screen.

▶▶ **N O T E**

The Designer Properties dialog box is just the tip of the "have it any way you want" iceberg. As you discovered earlier, you can save the default zoom, rulers, grid, and other properties by choosing Properties ➤ Form Options ➤ Save Defaults or Properties ➤ Report Options ➤ Save Defaults.

▶ Using Select From Inside

The Select From Inside option affects how contained objects are selected. When the option is off (unchecked), outermost objects are selected before inner objects. When the option is on (checked), you'll select the object you click even if it's contained within another object.

▶ Using Frame Objects

Normally, objects appear with faint dotted-line frames so they're easier to locate on the screen. If you prefer to have frames appear only when

FIGURE 10.34 ▶

*The Designer Proper-
ties dialog box controls
the behavior of the
Design window.*

you've changed an object's Frame property, turn the F̲rame Objects option off (uncheck it).

 ▶ ▶ **N O T E**

**The dotted-line frames never appear when you preview
or print your document.**

▶ *Using Flicker-Free Draw*

If your screen flashes when you move or resize objects, especially in designs with a dark background, you can check the Flicker-Free D̲raw option to reduce the flickering. However, keep in mind that flicker-free
draw can slow things down when you're moving or resizing objects. Try
experimenting with this option's settings to see what works best with
your screen.

▶ *Using Outlined Move/Resize*

The O̲utlined Move/Resize option determines the appearance of an object as you move or resize it. When this option is checked, only an outline of the object moves, expands, or contracts. When the option is
unchecked, the object itself appears as it is moved or resized. For speed-
ier displays, check this option.

▶▶ *Setting Form and Report Preferences*

Many of us are control freaks, and Paradox certainly is happy to accommodate us. If you'd like to control the way Paradox sets up and opens forms and reports, choose Properties ➤ Desktop and click the Forms And Reports button. You'll see the Forms/Reports Preferences dialog box pictured in Figure 10.35. You can select the options you want from this dialog box and then choose OK twice to return to the Desktop.

We'll take a quick look at each area in this dialog box. Remember that you can always click the Help button, or press F1, if you'd like more details.

▶ *Choosing a Starting Point for New Forms and Reports*

You can control what initially happens after you choose File ➤ New ➤ Form or File ➤ New ➤ Report (or any of the shortcuts that do the same thing). Normally Paradox will display the New Form or New

FIGURE 10.35 ▶

Use the Forms/Reports Preferences dialog box to customize the way Paradox starts new forms and reports.

Forms/Reports Preferences

New Forms / Reports:
- ⦿ No Default
- ○ Always Blank
- ○ Always Use Expert
- ○ Always Use Data Model

Open Default:
- ☐ Open Forms in Design Mode
- ☐ Open Reports in Design Mode

Form Screen Page Size:
- ☒ Size to Desktop

Width: _____
Height: _____

- ⦿ Inches
- ○ Centimeters
- ○ Pixels

Designer Style Sheets:

Screen Style Sheets
PXTOOLS.FT ▼

Printer Style Sheets
PXTOOLS.FT ▼

[OK] [Cancel] [Help]

Report dialog box, which lets you choose a blank document, use an Expert, or set up a data model for your new document. But you can change that behavior by selecting an option in the New Forms / Reports area:

- To always create a blank document, select <u>A</u>lways Blank. Paradox will immediately open a blank Design window when you create a new document, bypassing all other preliminary screens.

- To always use a form or report Expert, select Always Use <u>E</u>xpert. Paradox will open the appropriate Expert immediately.

- To go directly to the Data Model dialog box (followed by the Design Layout dialog box), choose Always <u>U</u>se Data Model.

- To again display the New Form or New Report dialog box when you create a new document, select <u>N</u>o Default. This option is the most flexible.

▶ *Choosing a Default Open Mode*

Paradox usually will open your form or report in View Data mode when you choose <u>F</u>ile ▶ <u>O</u>pen ▶ <u>F</u>orm, <u>F</u>ile ▶ <u>O</u>pen ▶ <u>R</u>eport, or any of the equivalent shortcuts. If you prefer to open forms or reports in Design mode, select (check) Open <u>F</u>orms In Design Mode or Open <u>R</u>eports In Design Mode, as appropriate. These options are in the Open Default area of the Forms/Reports Preferences dialog box.

▶ *Choosing a Default Style Sheet*

The Designer Style Sheets area of the Forms/Reports Preferences dialog box lets you choose which style sheet will be used automatically when you create a new form or report. Paradox will use the default style sheet if you don't explicitly request a different one when creating a new document.

The <u>S</u>creen Style Sheets drop-down list shows you all the style sheets that are available for forms, while the <u>P</u>rinter Style Sheets drop-down list shows you all the style sheets for reports. Simply choose the style sheet you want to use as the default for each type of document. Of course, you can always override the default style sheet by selecting a different one when you create the document, or anytime you're in the document's Design window.

> ►►**N O T E**
>
> **The drop-down lists will include the built-in style sheets that come with Paradox, plus any style sheets that you've created in the current working directory.**

► *Choosing a Default Screen Page Size*

The Form Screen Page Size area lets you customize the default size of a new form. If you want the initial size to match the size of the Desktop, select (check) Size To Desktop. If you prefer to define a custom width and height, deselect Size To Desktop. Then select a unit of measurement (Inches, Centimeters, or Pixels) and type in a value for the default Width and Height.

This chapter has provided an overview of tools and techniques for designing custom forms and reports. In the next two chapters, we'll take a closer look at techniques for designing forms and reports, and provide many examples that you can try for yourself.

► ► **CHAPTER** **11**

Creating
Custom Forms

——

▶▶ FAST TRACK

▶ ***To add a blank page to the end of a form*** **622**

> choose For<u>m</u> ➤ <u>P</u>age ➤ <u>A</u>dd. To create a new page from
> an existing page, select the page and copy it to the Clip-
> board. Click on the page that should fall after the new
> page, then paste from the Clipboard.

▶ ***To delete a page from a form*** **624**

> select the page, then press the Del key. Be careful!
> (Immediately choose <u>E</u>dit ➤ <u>U</u>ndo if you delete a page
> accidentally.)

▶ ***To rotate the current page to the end of a
multipage form*** **626**

> choose For<u>m</u> ➤ <u>P</u>age ➤ <u>R</u>otate.

▶ ***To display multipage forms in a tiled arrangement*** **626**

> choose options from the For<u>m</u> ➤ <u>P</u>age ➤ <u>T</u>ile menu. The
> tile setting is saved along with the form.

▶ ***To print the form*** **638**

> switch to Form View if you want to print the current rec-
> ord; or switch to the Form Design window if you want to
> print the form design (without any data filled in). Then
> click the Print button in the Toolbar or choose <u>F</u>ile ➤
> <u>P</u>rint and complete the Print File dialog box.

Whenever you switch from Table View to Form View (by clicking the Quick Form button in the Toolbar or pressing F7), Paradox lets you view or edit data one record at a time. Unless you develop your own custom forms, Paradox will produce a standard form, called the Quick Form, similar to the one in Figure 11.1.

▶▶ **N O T E**

If you define a preferred form for the table, Paradox will use that form instead of the standard form. Chapter 10 explained how to create preferred forms.

In many situations, the Quick Form is just fine. But custom forms can be much better when you need to display instructions to the user during data entry, or when you want the on-screen form to resemble a paper form. For example, you can design a custom form that looks like a purchase requisition, a sales order, or even a check.

When designing a form, you can organize data in a single-record format, where one record appears on each page, or in a tabular or multi-record format, where multiple records appear on each page. You can also add graphs, crosstabs, and many other enhancements to the form.

In this chapter, we'll show you how to create single-page and multipage data entry forms complete with three-dimensional effects, scroll bars, protected data fields, special fields for displaying the time and date, and more. You'll also learn how to use the Experts to create forms with just a few keystrokes. In Chapter 13 you'll learn how to add graphs and crosstabs to your forms.

FIGURE 11.1

The Quick Form generated by Paradox for the sample CustList table

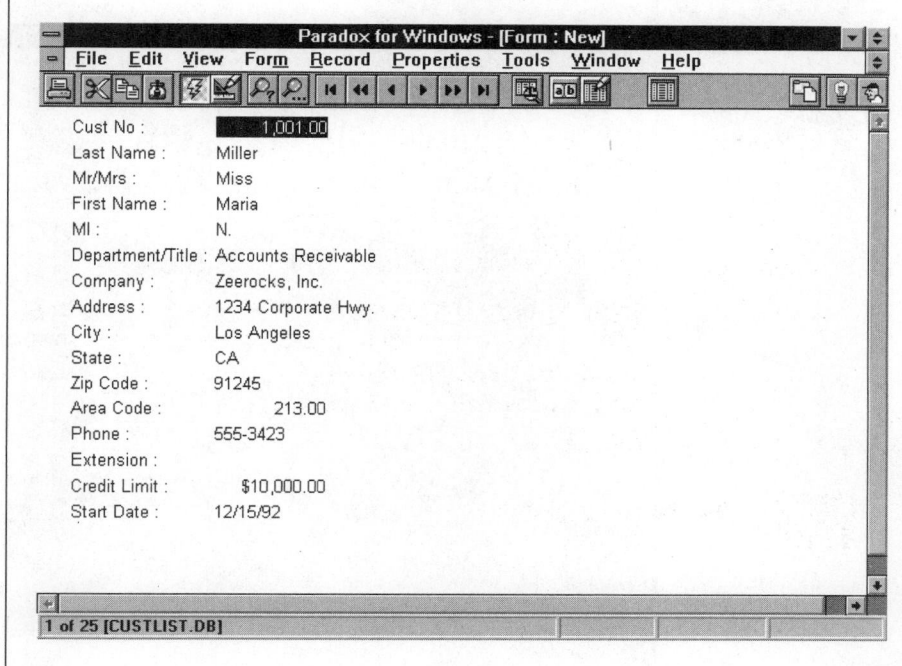

NOTE

Before continuing with this chapter, be sure to complete Lesson 4 in Chapter 2 and at least skim through Chapter 10. Lesson 4 provides some hands-on guidance for designing a simple form, while Chapter 10 covers general techniques for designing forms and reports.

Figure 11.2 shows a custom form for editing the Credit Limit field of the CustList table. Notice that the custom form features many flourishes that make it more attractive and easier to use than the plain-vanilla Quick Form. These embellishments include the following:

- The frame styles and thicknesses give the form a three-dimensional look.

FIGURE 11.2 ▶

*A custom form for up-
dating the Credit Limit
field of existing custom-
ers in the CustList table*

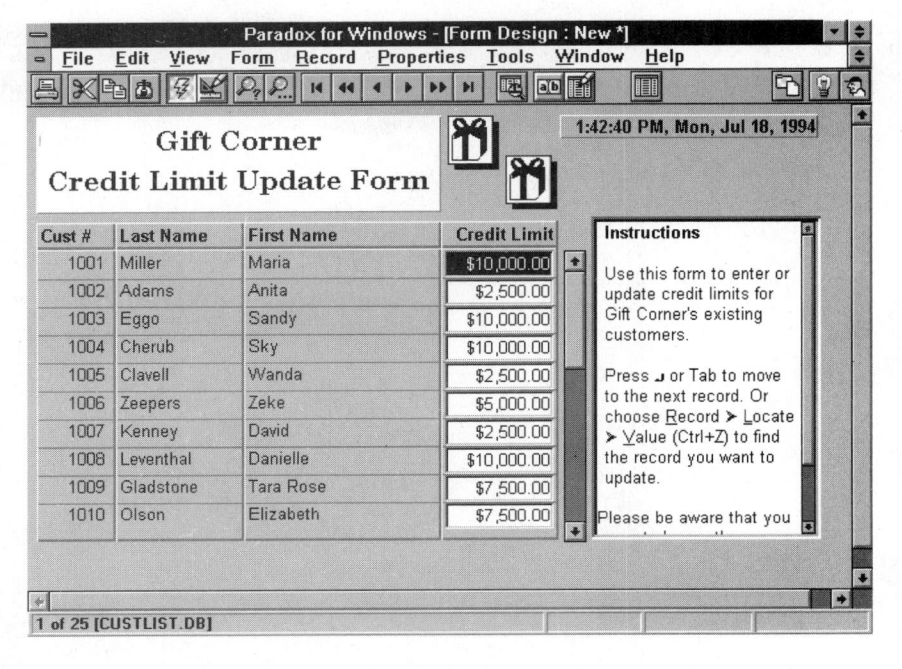

- Heading text clearly states the purpose of the form: *Credit Limit Update Form*.

- The company's logo, a wrapped gift, appears.

- The current time and date appear at the upper-right corner of the form.

- The records are arranged in a tabular format so the user can work with several records at once. We've also added a vertical scroll bar, a three-dimensional grid, and a record divider.

- The Cust No field header was changed to *Cust #*. The Cust No field's number format was changed to integer.

- The Credit Limit field sports a three-dimensional look and a contrasting background that identifies it clearly as the field to be edited. The user cannot place the cursor in any field except Credit Limit, and all fields except Credit Limit are Read Only.

- A text object explains the purpose of the form and how to move the cursor through it. The vertical scroll bar makes it easy for the user to browse through the instructions.

NOTE

Many of the fancy effects shown in Figure 11.2 were created automatically by the style sheet we chose when setting up the form. However, we'll also show you how to set up the special effects manually, just in case you choose not to use a style sheet.

Later on in this chapter, we'll describe some of the specific techniques used to produce these effects.

▶▶ *Planning a Custom Form*

Careful planning can help prevent data-entry errors, so it is important to think about your form design before creating it with Paradox. If you are modeling the custom form on a data collection sheet or other paper form already in use, try to employ the same arrangement of fields and informational areas. This will give your custom form the look and feel the user is accustomed to.

TIP

If your existing paper forms need an overhaul, now is the time to improve them so you can avoid problems encountered in the past.

▶▶ *Getting Help from an Expert*

If you're in a hurry to create a great-looking form in just a minute or so, why not let the Experts be your guide? Using an Expert is quick and easy—and self-explanatory—so we'll just get you started with the steps. As you're working, you can get additional help by clicking the Help button in any Expert dialog box.

▶ Creating a New Form

To use an Expert to create a new form, follow the steps below:

1. Start the Expert in any of the following ways:

- Click the Expert button in the Toolbar (shown at left).
- Choose Help ➤ Experts.
- Choose File ➤ New ➤ Form (or any of the equivalent short-cuts on the Toolbar or Project Viewer), and click the Form Expert button in the New Form dialog box. Then skip to step 3.

2. Click the *Form* button in the Expert Control Panel dialog box.

▶ ▶ **N O T E**

If your system includes Experts from third-party developers, you can click the Next>> and <<Prev buttons in the Expert Control Panel to locate those add-on Experts.

3. When the first Paradox Form Expert dialog box appears, select the type of form you want. You can either click on the button that illustrates the desired form design or click the numbered option that describes it. To continue with the next step, click the Next>> button.

4. To complete your form, follow the prompts on the dialog boxes that follow. The guidelines below should help you sail through easily:

- To figure out what to do in any dialog box, read the prompts carefully.
- To continue to the next dialog box after making your selections, click the Next>> button.

- To return to the previous dialog box (in case you change your mind about selections you've already made), click the <<Prev button.

- To cancel the Expert and return to the Desktop without creating a form, click the Cancel button.

- To get help at any time, click the Help button.

- When you reach the final dialog box, click the Create button to design your form automatically and open it in Form View.

Once the form appears in Form View, you can use it right out of the box, or you can customize it by clicking the Design button in the Toolbar (or by pressing F8 or choosing View ➤ Design Form). When you're ready to save your creation, simply close the form's window, answer Yes when asked about saving the document, type in a file name, and choose OK.

▶ ▶ **T I P**

See "Customizing the Experts," at the end of this chapter, to learn how you can tweak the Experts and make them even more useful.

Creating Custom Forms

▶ ▶

Ch. **11**

▶▶ *General Steps for Designing and Using a Custom Form*

The Experts provide a perfect starting point for many forms, and they may be all you'll ever need. But if you'd like more control over your forms, then the remaining topics in this chapter can help.

Remember that Chapter 10 covers the basics for designing forms from scratch, and you should look there for information on starting new forms, creating, selecting, and inspecting objects, and so forth. Listed below is a whirlwind review of steps for designing and working with custom forms.

1. Choose File ➤ New ➤ Form from the menus; or inspect the Open Form button in the Toolbar or right-click the Forms icon in the Project Viewer and choose New.

2. Click the <u>D</u>ata Model / Layout Diagram button. Then, select a table, query, or data model as the basis for the design. If you wish, you can inspect the table in the right side of the Data Model dialog box, then choose the <u>F</u>ields, Fi<u>l</u>ter, <u>R</u>ead-Only, <u>S</u>trict Translation, and <u>A</u>uto-Append options. When you're finished using the Data Model dialog box, choose OK.

3. In the Design Layout dialog box, specify the design layout. Initially, Paradox assigns the Single-Record layout to forms and organizes fields By <u>C</u>olumns.

4. If you want to remove or reorder fields, click the Show <u>F</u>ields button in the Design Layout dialog box, then remove (or rearrange) fields as needed. Choose Show Layo<u>u</u>t when you're done.

5. If you want to start with all the fields labeled, leave the <u>L</u>abel Fields option checked. Otherwise, remove the checkmark to remove labels from all the fields.

6. If you want to choose a style sheet, open the St<u>y</u>le Sheet drop-down list and select the style sheet you want.

7. Choose OK in the Design Layout dialog box to open the Form Design window.

8. Customize the design as you wish, then preview it by clicking the View Data button in the Toolbar or pressing F8. Return to Design View as necessary (by clicking the Design button in the Toolbar or pressing F8) and make further changes.

9. Choose <u>F</u>ile ➤ <u>S</u>ave to save the form, then close the Design window if you wish.

10. If you want Paradox to use this form when you click the Quick Form button in Table View, open the table to be associated with this form, then right-click the Quick Form button. Select the form name and choose OK from the dialog box that appears. Now choose <u>P</u>roperties ➤ <u>V</u>iew Properties ➤ <u>S</u>ave to save your changes.

11. To open an existing form, choose <u>F</u>ile ➤ <u>O</u>pen ➤ <u>F</u>orm. Then choose the file name of the form, change the table if you want to view a different table's data with this form's layout, choose an Open <u>M</u>ode (either <u>V</u>iew Data or D<u>e</u>sign), and choose OK. You can also double-click a form name in the Project Viewer, or right-click the form name and choose <u>V</u>iew Data, De<u>s</u>ign, or View <u>W</u>ith from the drop-down menu.

▶ ▶ T I P

> **To use the currently assigned Quick Form as the basis for a new design, click the Quick Form button in the Table window, then click the Design button in the Toolbar or press F8.**

▶▶ *Choosing a Page Layout*

Initially, any forms you design are set up for the screen. If you'd like to change this, choose Form ➤ Page ➤ Layout in the Form Design window. Figure 11.3 shows the Page Layout dialog box for a form.

FIGURE 11.3 ▶

The default Page Layout dialog box for a form

Page Layout

Design For:
○ Printer
◉ Screen

Orientation:
◉ Portrait
○ Landscape

Screen Size:
640 x 480

Custom Size:
Width: 6.67
Height: 4.60

Units:
Centimeters
Inches

OK   Cancel   Help

When designing for the screen, you can change the width and height of the screen you're designing for as well as the units of measure. The Screen Size shown is the one that Paradox detects for your current screen driver.

If you prefer to design for the printer, click Printer in the Design For area. The dialog box will now include a list of paper sizes for you to choose from and allow you to switch the Orientation from Portrait to Landscape, as shown in Figure 11.4.

When you're finished with the Page Layout dialog box, choose OK.

FIGURE 11.4 ►

The Page Layout dialog box for a form, after selecting Printer in the Design For area and changing the orientation to Landscape. (Notice that the paper icon is flipped horizontally.)

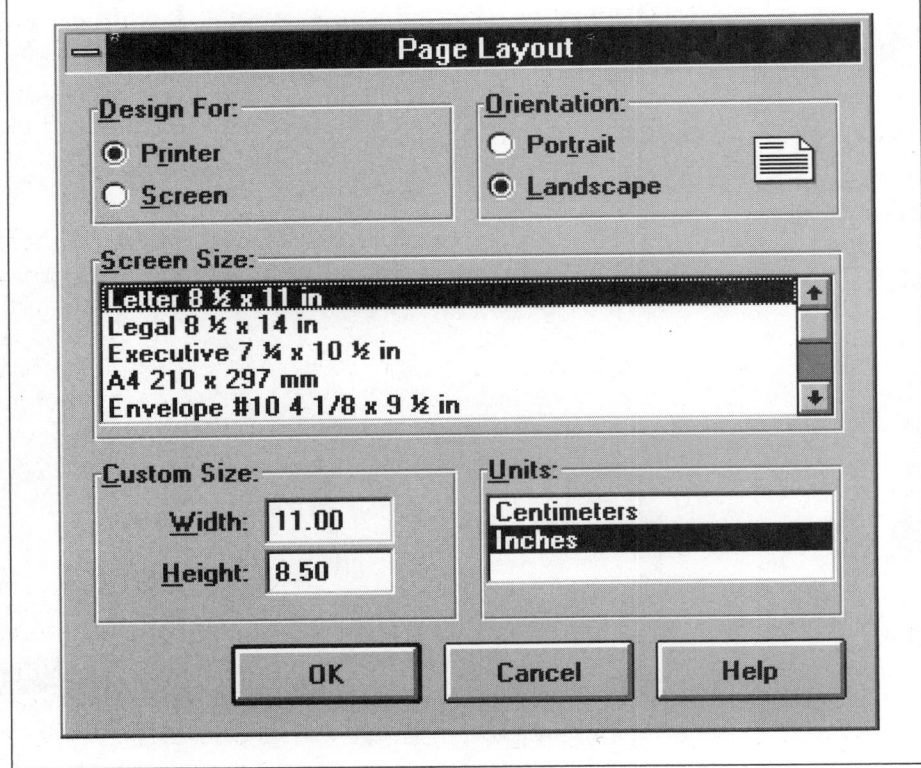

▶▶NOTE

If you design for the printer, only fonts installed for the active printer will be available. Paradox will do its best to match the screen fonts displayed in the Form window to the printed output. Don't worry too much if what you see on screen doesn't quite match the printed output. After all, when you design for the printer, it's the printed output that counts.

▶▶ *Working in the Design Window*

In the Design window, you can create, position, and resize objects and change object properties, such as color, font, fill pattern, and alignment. Chapter 10 discusses general techniques for using the Design window.

Keep in mind that complex designs can be time-consuming to create. You'll need to experiment with various object arrangements and properties until you've coaxed the document into ultimate perfection. Therefore, it's a good idea to choose File ➤ Save as soon as you successfully complete a portion of the design. That way, if you make a series of changes you're not happy with, you can simply close the window without saving those changes. When you open the document again, it will contain the last acceptable version and you can continue from there.

▶▶TIP

You can save yourself considerable time by starting with a form created by an Expert, or by making smart choices in the Design Layout dialog box for field layout, style, multi-record layout, label fields, style sheets, and selected fields.

Creating Custom Forms

▶ ▶

Ch. **11**

▶▶ *Creating the Sample Credit Limit Update Form*

The best way to learn form design is to go ahead and try it. So through-out this chapter, we'll show you steps for creating forms similar to those in the figures. Of course, you shouldn't feel restricted to any pre-cise sequence of steps—or to our designs for that matter. After all, you may have much better design ideas of your own.

Let's start by looking at the steps used to set up the form shown back in Figure 11.2.

▶ *Placing Objects in the Sample Form*

To begin the design, choose File ➤ New ➤ Form, click Data Model / Layout Diagram, select the CustList table in the Data Model dialog box, then choose OK. In the Style area of the Design Layout dialog box select Tabular. In the Style Sheet drop-down list, select *c:\pdoxwin\control3d.ft*. Next click the Show Fields button to specify the fields you want to include in the design. When the Selected Fields dia-log box appears, remove all field names *except* Cust No, Last Name, First Name, and Credit Limit. Click OK to open the Form Design window.

Now continue with the steps listed below. When you finish, your screen will resemble Figure 11.5.

1. Maximize the Form Design window by clicking its Maximize but-ton or double-clicking its title bar.

2. If the expanded ruler doesn't appear below the Toolbar (see Fig-ure 11.5), choose Properties ➤ Expanded Ruler.

3. Drag the table object to the lower-left corner of the window. Then drag the table's vertical grid lines to narrow the Cust No and Last Name fields.

4. Inspect the table object and select (check) the Vertical Scroll Bar option in the property menu.

5. To use a wide vertical scroll bar, inspect the table object again and select (check) the Wide Scroll Bar option.

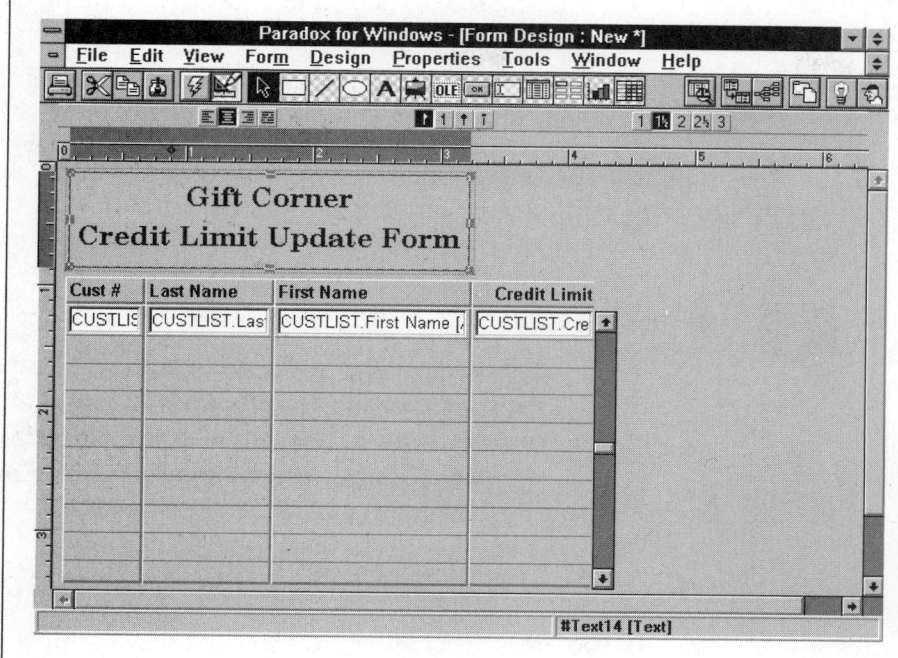

FIGURE 11.5

After completing the 12 suggested design steps, the Design window includes the form title and the table.

6. Click the Cust No text object in the table header until selection handles appear around it, then use Shift+click to add the Last Name and First Name text objects to the selection. Inspect the selected objects and choose Alignment ➤ Left from the property menu. Next, click on the Credit Limit text object in the table header, inspect it, and choose Alignment ➤ Right.

7. Click on the Cust No text in the table object until the insertion point appears, then edit the text to change Cust No to *Cust #*.

8. Inspect the Cust No field (not the header) in the first record of the table object and change the Format ➤ Number Format property to Integer.

9. Use the Text tool to draw the outline of the form's title above the table object (refer to Figure 11.5), then type **Gift Corner**, press ↵, and type **Credit Limit Update Form**.

10. Press Esc to select the text box you just created, then click the $1\frac{1}{2}$ button in the expanded ruler to set line spacing to 1.5 lines.

11. Inspect the text box and choose Alignment ➤ Center from the property menu.

12. Inspect the text box again, choose Font, then click the snap button to open the floating Font palette. Now change the font as desired (we chose Century Schoolbook 16-point bold type). Click the snap button to close the Font palette.

The Form Design window should now resemble Figure 11.5.

▶▶ **T I P**

Remember that you can preview your design at any time by clicking the View Data button in the Toolbar or pressing F8. To return to the Form Design window, click the Design button in the Toolbar or press F8 again.

▶ *Adding Special Field Objects to the Form*

In the previous chapter, you learned how to add special fields, such as the record number, total number of records, current page number, date, time, and timestamp to your design. Paradox for Windows automatically updates these special fields whenever you view or edit data in the form.

Notice the special field in the upper-right corner of Figure 11.2. This field is a *Timestamp* (for displaying the current system date and time).

To create a special field, click the Field tool in the Toolbar and draw a field at the appropriate location in your design. Then inspect the field and choose Display Type ➤ Unlabeled. Inspect the field again and choose Define Field from the property menu, then click the header (...) of the list. Now open the Special Field drop-down list in the Define Field Object dialog box and select the field you want. When you're finished, choose OK.

> **NOTE**
>
> **We'll discuss the other Display Type options in the section called "Special Techniques for Displaying Fields."**

Go ahead and create the <Timestamp> special field, using Figure 11.6 as a guide for placement. To format the field for the results shown in the figure, follow the steps below.

1. Inspect the <Timestamp> field, choose Format ➤ Timestamp Format from the property menu, then click the ... header and define a custom date format as shown in Figure 11.7. Choose OK when you're finished.

2. With the <Timestamp> field still selected, inspect it and choose WordWrap (to turn word wrap off). Inspect the field again and choose Alignment ➤ Right. Then inspect the field once more

Creating Custom Forms

Ch. 11

FIGURE 11.6

The custom form after adding the <Timestamp> field

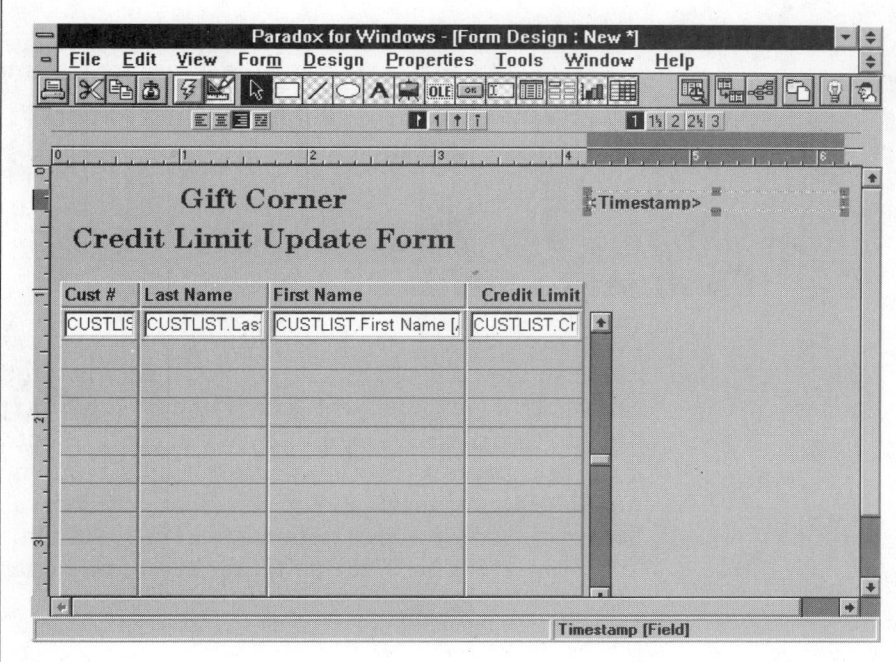

FIGURE 11.7 ►

*Our <Timestamp> field's custom **Form Timestamp** format is based on the Win. Timestamp format, includes a revised Order of %W, %M %D, %Y for the Date Format, uses short names for Weekday and Month, and uses the full four-digit year.*

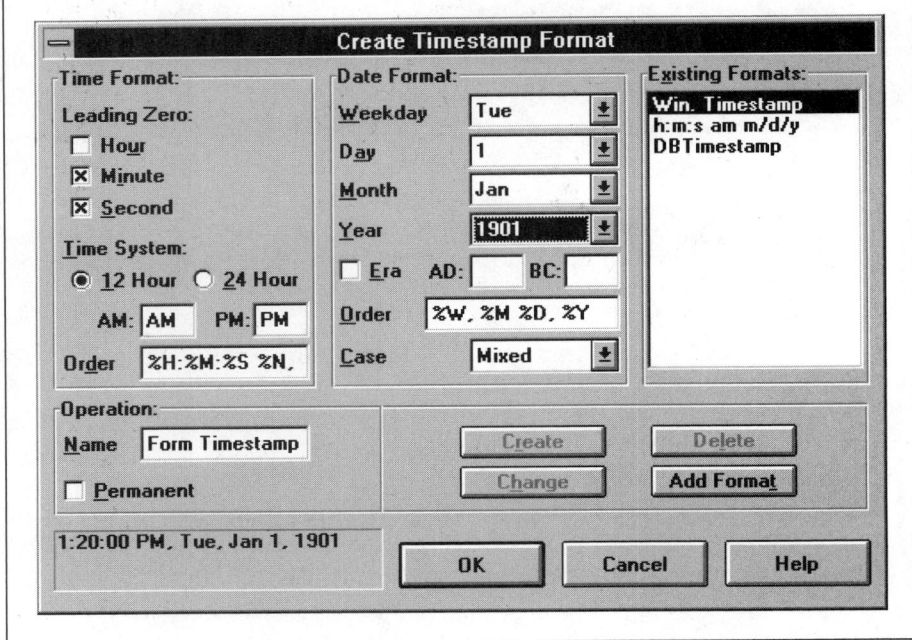

and choose Font ➤ Style ➤ Bold. Finally, widen the field as needed to accommodate the entire time stamp.

3. Next, select the text object ("Gift Corner...") and the <Time-stamp> field and choose <u>D</u>esign ➤ Align <u>T</u>op.

► *Skipping over Fields and Preventing Changes to Fields*

As mentioned in Chapter 10, Run Time properties control the behavior of an object when you view or edit data in a form. For example, you can turn off (uncheck) the Run Time ➤ Tab Stop property to prevent the cursor from landing on a field during data entry. That way, even if the user presses the Tab or ↵ key or clicks the mouse in a field where the Tab Stop property is turned off, the cursor will not stop at that field. Similarly, you can define a field as Read Only, so that even if the Tab property is on (checked), the user cannot change the field.

If you're designing the sample form shown in Figure 11.2, you can try some Run Time properties now. Select the Cust No, Last Name, and First Name *fields* in the table (*not* the header labels). Then inspect those objects and choose Run Time ➤ Tab Stop to uncheck the Tab Stop option. For extra safety, inspect those objects again and select Run Time ➤ Read Only.

➤ ➤ N O T E

> **See Appendix E for a complete list of Run Time properties.**

Now, just so the user *really* gets the message that these fields aren't changeable, inspect the fields again and change their Color property to gray; then inspect the fields once more and change their Frame ➤ Style property to the top entry in the list (no frame).

➤ *Displaying Text and Memo Fields*

As you know, formatted memo fields, memo fields, and text objects can contain a lot of text. In a form design, therefore, you'll probably want to restrict the display of a memo field or text object to a prescribed area of the screen, while allowing all the text to be viewed and edited. The trick is to add vertical and horizontal scroll bars by inspecting the object and choosing Vertical Scroll Bar or Horizontal Scroll Bar from the property menu.

To create the instruction text in Figure 11.2, follow the steps below. When you're finished, the Form Design window will resemble Figure 11.8.

1. Create a fixed-size text object to the right of the table, inspect it, and choose Vertical Scroll Bar from the property menu.

2. Inspect the text object, change the typeface to something like Arial 10-point, without bold. Inspect the text object again and change the Font ➤ Color to black. Now type the instruction text. (You can't see all the text in Figure 11.2, but don't worry about that—just make up your own ending.)

3. Select the *Instructions* heading text, inspect it, and choose Font ➤ Style ➤ Bold. To underline the <u>R</u> in Record and the <u>L</u> in Locate, select the appropriate letter, inspect it, and choose Font ➤ Style ➤ Underline.

4. Add some white space at the left and right edges of the text by selecting all the text and then using the horizontal ruler's tab well to move the left margin, first-line paragraph indent, and right margin in just a touch (see Chapter 10 for instructions on doing this). The tab well in Figure 11.8 shows the settings we chose.

► ►**N O T E**

We used the Character Map, described in Chapter 6, to create the special ↵ character (from the TrueType Symbol font) and the arrow character (from the Wingdings font).

FIGURE 11.8 ►

The Form Design window after adding the text object and making some adjustments to the position and size of objects in the design

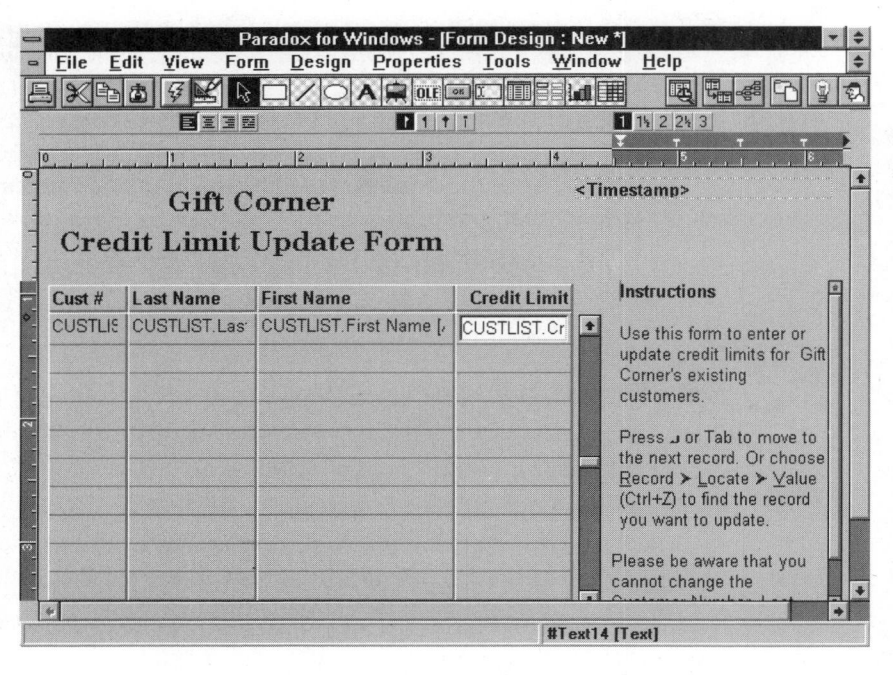

▶ *Duplicating an Object*

If you want more than one copy of an object or field in your design, you can either draw the object or field again, or you can copy it. Obviously, copying is the better choice because it's faster and it copies any properties assigned to the object.

▶▶ **WARNING**

After copying or duplicating fields, be sure to change the property of any copies to Read Only and turn off the Tab Stop property as discussed earlier.

Following are the steps used to create the two gift box graphics shown in Figure 11.2. Our form, after these steps are complete, appears in Figure 11.9.

FIGURE 11.9 ▶

The Credit Limit Update form after creating a graphics box and duplicating it and dragging the objects into position

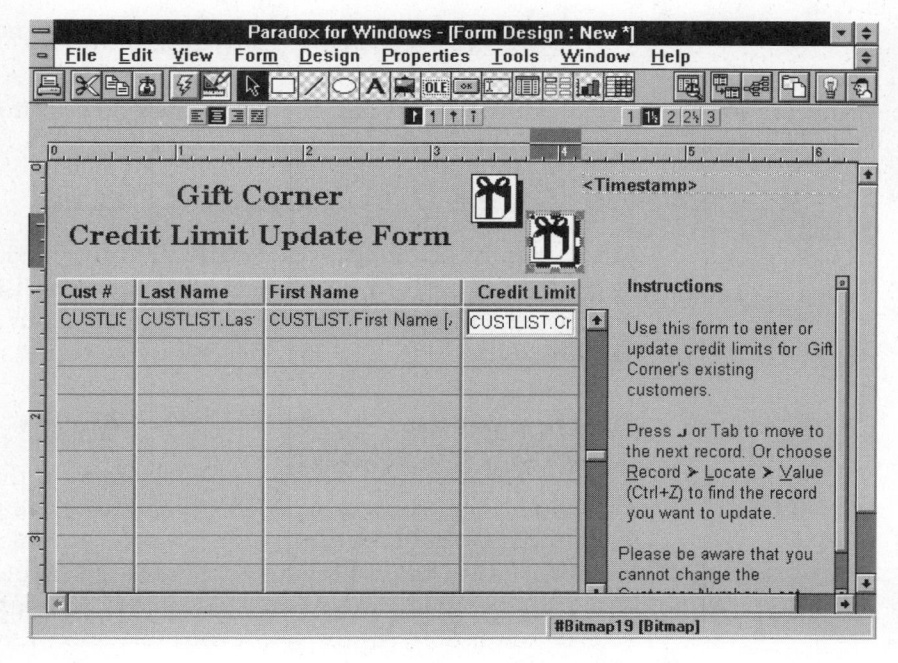

1. Switch to the Program Manager, open Paintbrush in the Accessories group, and maximize the window. Then choose Edit ➤ Paste From and select the file containing the graphic (you can pick any available graphic that suits your fancy). When the graphic appears, use the Pick tool to outline the portion of the graphic you want to copy. When you're done, choose Edit ➤ Copy and close the Paintbrush window without saving the image. (For information on using Paintbrush, refer to your Windows documentation.)

2. Return to the Paradox Form Design window, click the Graphic tool in the Toolbar, draw the outline for the graphic, then right-click the graphic, and choose Define Graphic ➤ Paste from the property menu.

3. Inspect the graphic object and choose Magnification ➤ Best Fit from the property menu. This fits the entire graphic within the graphic object box and automatically turns off the Design ➤ Size To Fit property.

4. To change the graphic's frame, inspect the graphic box, choose Frame ➤ Style, then click the style you want. We selected the drop-shadow, which is the fifth frame from the bottom.

5. If you need to resize the graphic box, do so now.

6. With the graphic object selected, choose Design ➤ Duplicate from the menu bar, then drag the objects into position.

▶ Creating Three-Dimensional Effects

At this point, the design is attractive, but not yet dazzling. Fortunately, moving from drab to dazzling is easily accomplished by adding three-dimensional effects to your design. Of course, our *Control3D* style sheet has already added some 3D effects, but we can easily create others.

Turning Off Size To Fit

If you're following the design steps presented in this chapter, it's time to turn off the Design ➤ Size To Fit option for all the field and table objects (it has already been turned off for the graphic objects). Although the effect won't be immediately obvious, this step will prevent the objects from changing size when you add the 3D effects. To deselect the Size To Fit option, simply select the table and the <Timestamp> field objects, then right-click one of the selected objects and uncheck Design ➤ Size To Fit.

▶ ▶ **T I P**

> **While it's not strictly necessary to turn off Size To Fit after you've sized objects, doing so eliminates the need to resize them after changing frame styles, frame thickness, fonts, field definitions, and so forth.**

Selecting a Background Color

The first step to 3D nirvana is to select a background color for the entire page. The *Control3D* style sheet did this for us already. However, if you did not choose this style sheet or you just want to experiment, click the page (*#Page* appears in the status bar when the page is selected), then right-click, choose Color from the property menu, and click on the color you want. The examples so far have used a light gray background, but any pale color can be effective.

▶ ▶ **T I P**

> **When you change the color of an object, Paradox initially assigns an opaque color. Opaque colors are best for creating three-dimensional effects. You can switch to a transparent color by selecting the Transparent option in the floating Color palette. See Appendix E for information on opaque and transparent colors and creating custom colors.**

Creating 3D Frames

After turning off the Design ➤ Size To Fit option and making sure the background color is set to gray, you can create 3D frames for objects in the design by following the steps below. The final results appear in Figure 11.10.

FIGURE 11.10 ▶

The Design window after putting convex frames around the form's title and <Timestamp> fields and placing a thick concave frame around the **Instructions** *text object*

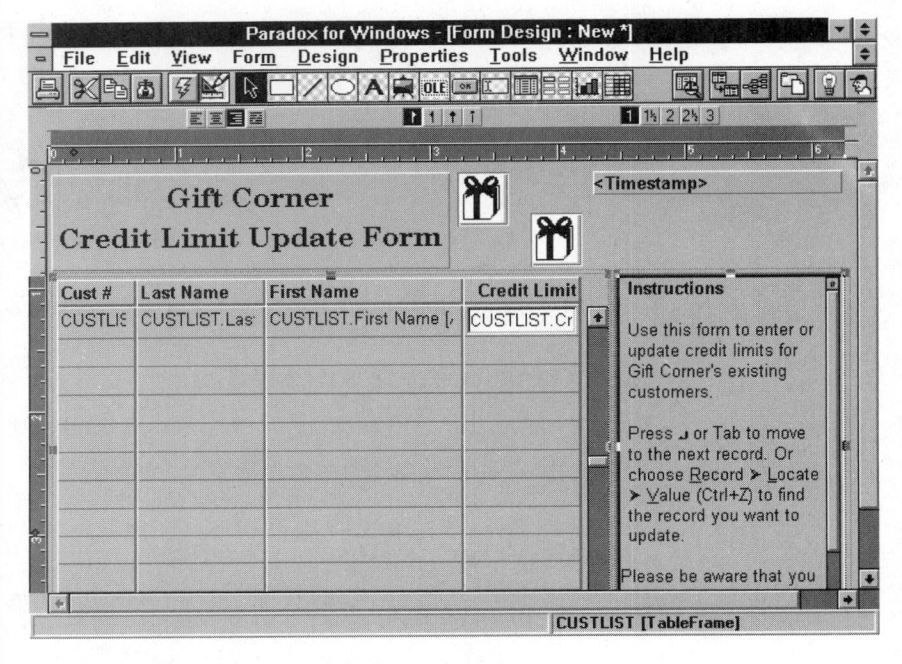

1. Select the text object containing the form's title *(Gift Corner...)* and the <Timestamp> field.

2. Inspect the selected objects and choose Frame ➤ Style to reveal the frame style palette.

3. Choose the third-to-last frame style, which gives the framed objects a raised (convex) effect.

4. Now inspect the *Instructions* text object, choose Frame ➤ Style, and choose the second-to-last frame style for a sunken (concave) effect.

Here's a trick to try if you're having trouble locating fields after creating a gray or colored background. Simply return the background color to white while you're creating 3D effects, then change the background back to gray (or another color).

> **TIP**
>
> **You can determine the current Color, Pattern Style, Line Style, Thickness, Frame Style, and so forth by inspecting an object and choosing the property you want to find out about. The current settings are highlighted in red on the palette.**

If you want a deeper indentation for the *Instructions* text object, as in our example, inspect that object again and choose Frame ➤ Thickness followed by one of the line thicknesses. We selected the second sample from the top to produce the results shown in Figure 11.10.

Creating 3D Tables

Adding a three-dimensional look to tables is a snap. Of course, our style sheet already did this for us. But if you'd like to learn the secrets of adding 3D effects to any table, here are the steps. First, inspect the table, then choose Grid ➤ Grid Style ➤ 3D from the property menu. If you also want a horizontal divider between each row of records, inspect the table again, then turn on (check) the Grid ➤ Record Divider option. We added the record divider to our own form. Note that the record divider won't be obvious unless you switch to Form View.

Creating Highlighted Backgrounds

Data entry will be easier if your form draws the user's eye to important information and fields. For example, the form in Figure 11.2 uses a contrasting color (white) as the background for the *Instructions* text and for the Credit Limit field—the only field you can update. It also uses a white background for the form's title, just to make it stand out better.

To add these finishing touches to the sample form, first select the objects whose background color you want to change. (The Credit Limit field was automatically set to white by our style sheet, so we just needed to select the *Gift Corner...* and *Instructions* text objects in our example.) Next, inspect the objects, then choose Color from the property menu and click on the color you want (we chose white). Figure 11.11 shows the final result in the Design window.

FIGURE 11.11 ▶

*In this example, we se-
lected the form's title
(**Gift Corner...**) and Instructions text objects,
inspected their proper-
ties, chose Color, then
selected a white color
(which allows the text
to show through). The
Credit Limit field was
automatically set to
white by the **Con-
trol3D** style sheet.*

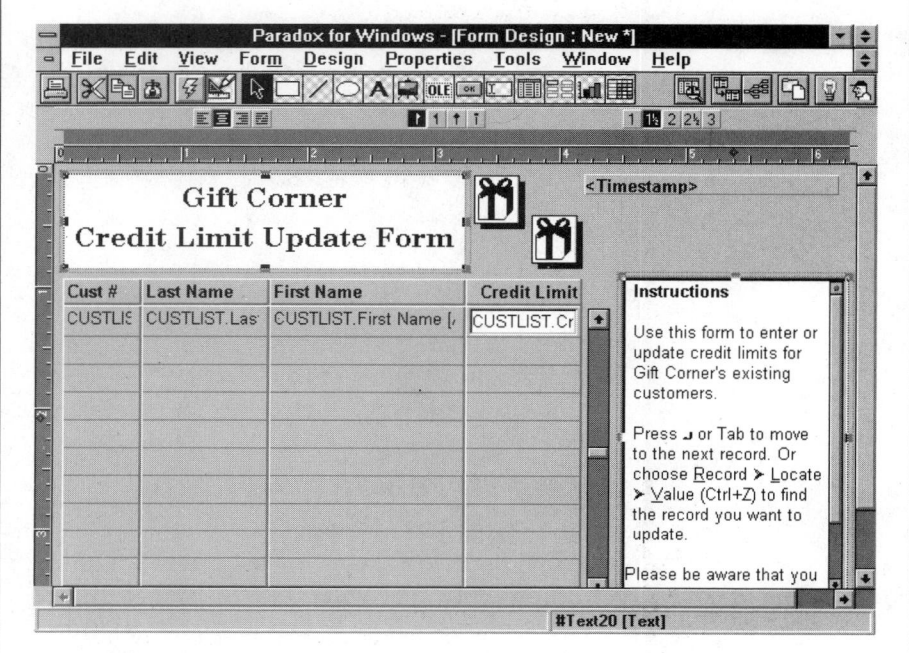

> ▶▶▶**N O T E**
>
> **Another way to make fields stand out is to choose one
> color for the fields and another color for field labels.
> You might also want to use one color for optional
> fields and a contrasting color for required fields.**

The final step is to save the form by choosing File ▶ Save, typing a
new file name, and choosing OK. To preview your handiwork, click the
View Data button or press F8. If you're finished with the document,
close its window by double-clicking the Control-menu box or pressing
Ctrl+F4. Or, if you'd like to edit data right away, make sure you're in
Form View, then press F9 to switch to Edit mode.

►► *Special Techniques for Displaying Fields*

Paradox for Windows offers several ways to display and enter a field's data within a form. You're already familiar with the standard labeled field, which you get automatically whenever you create a new field object. You also know how to remove labels from fields either by removing the Labeled Fields checkmark in the Design Layout dialog box or by inspecting the field and choosing Display Type ➤ Unlabeled. However, there's a lot more you can do. The following field properties can help prevent spelling and other data entry errors and make it easy to enter values without having to type them in:

new

Filter Lets you filter values in a single field, so that only records matching the filter condition will appear in the form. This option isn't available for formatted memo, graphic, memo, or OLE field types. (You can also choose Form ➤ Filter from the Form View or Form Design menus, as explained in Chapter 9.)

new

Picture Lets you define a picture for the field, so that data entries conform to the picture. This option isn't available for formatted memo, graphic, memo, or OLE field types. (See Chapter 4.)

Display Type Lets you choose whether a data entry field appears with or without a label, as a drop-down edit or list box, as radio buttons, or as a check box. Only the Labeled and Unlabeled display types are available for formatted memo, graphic, memo, and OLE field types. We'll explain this topic in a moment.

Format Lets you choose the display format for the data. For example, you can choose the number format or logical format. This option isn't available for formatted memo, graphic, memo, or OLE field types. (See Chapter 7.)

► *Choosing the Display Type*

Whenever you inspect a field and choose Display Type from the property menu, the following options appear (though unavailable options will be dimmed):

Figure 11.12 shows the Form window for a sample order entry form in which we used each available display type to simplify data entry, reduce errors, and limit the number of choices the user must make. You can

FIGURE 11.12 ►

The Form window for an order entry form using normal fields, plus the special drop-down edit, list, radio button, and check box field types

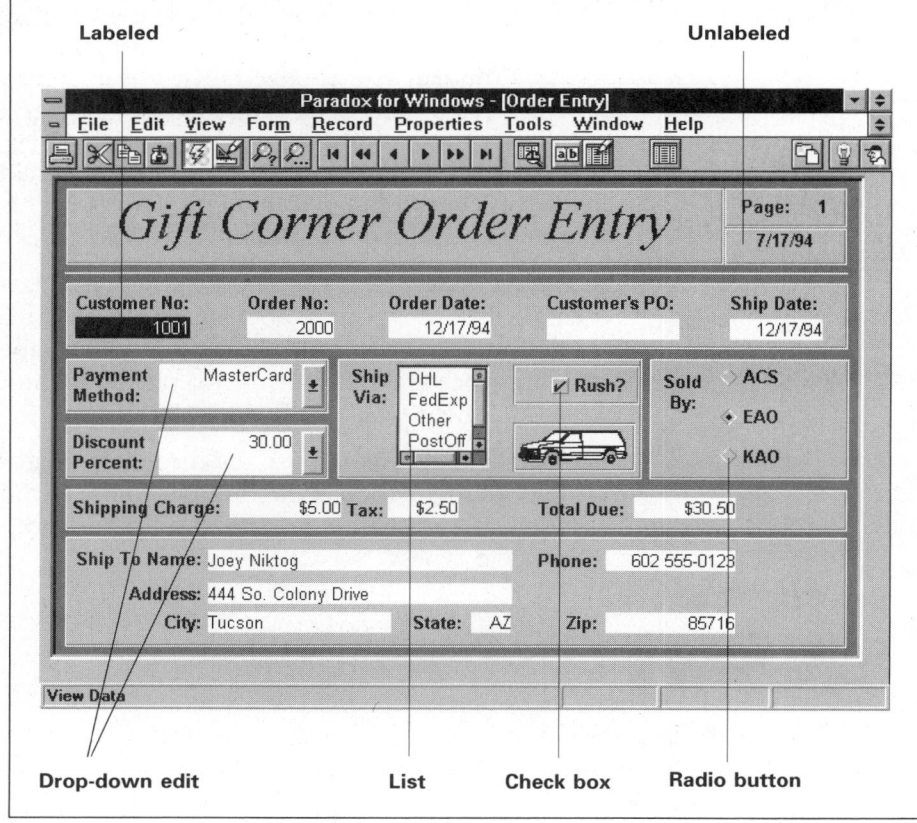

see a simpler example of each special field display type in Figures 11.13 and 11.14. Figure 11.13 shows the Form window, while Figure 11.14 shows the Form Design window.

> **N O T E**
>
> The *ordentry.fsl* form in the *\pdoxwin\sample* directory that comes with Paradox for Windows includes examples of various field display types.

Figures 11.13 and 11.14 illustrate the basic field display types in a more "vanilla" form. Notice that radio button fields can appear in three different flavors: radio button (the default), push button, and check boxes. Likewise, check box fields can appear as check boxes (the default), radio buttons, or push buttons.

FIGURE 11.13

The Form window for a sample form that uses drop-down edit, check box, list, and radio button display types. In this example, we clicked the drop-down edit list so you can see the values in the field.

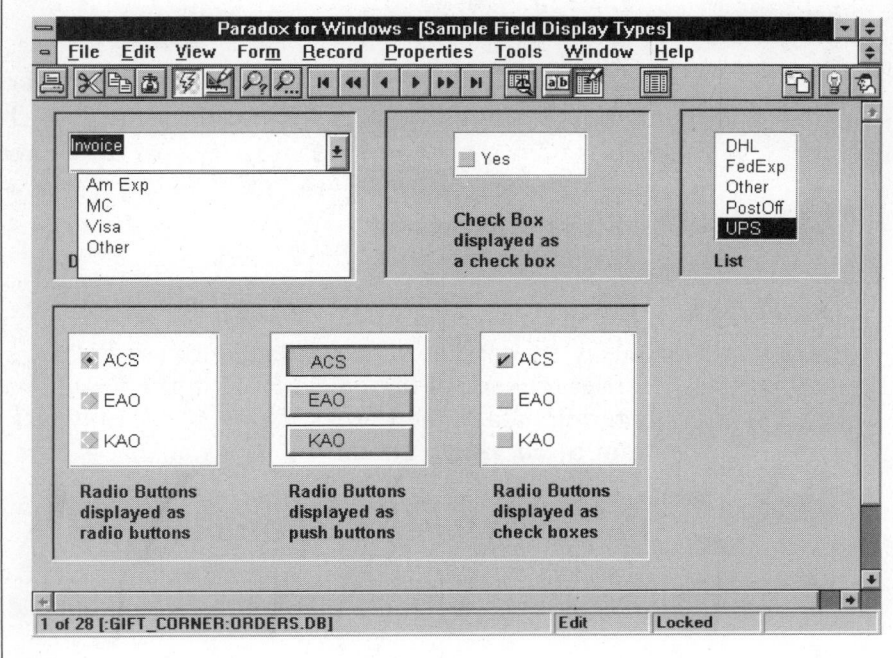

Creating
Custom Forms

Ch.
11

FIGURE 11.14

The Form Design window for the form shown in Figure 11.13.

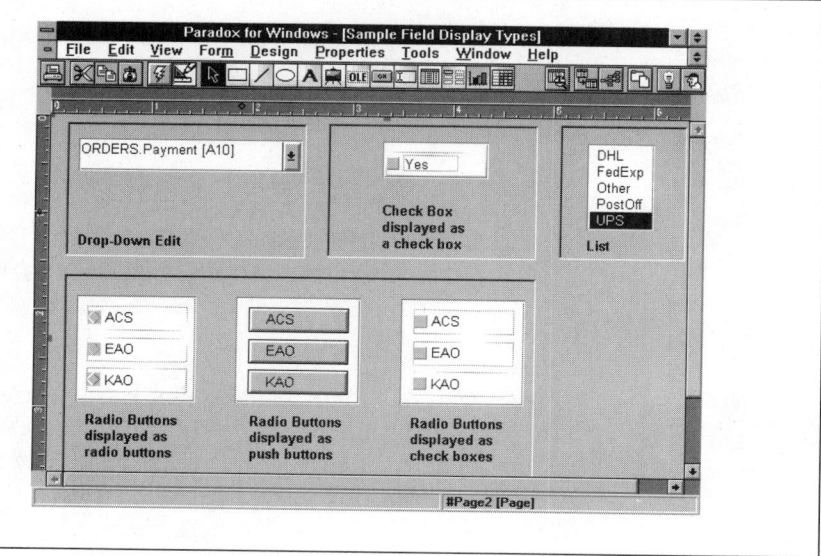

> **WARNING**
>
> **The same field should never appear more than once on a real data-entry form unless you also choose the Run Time ➤ Read Only property for duplicate fields. The examples in Figures 11.13 and 11.14 are for illustration purposes only—not for actual data entry.**

Drop-down edit, list, and *radio button* fields are especially handy when only a few possible values are valid for a field. You specify the valid entries for each of these field types in the Design window. Then, when entering data in the Form window, you simply pick the values you want by clicking on them.

Tips for Defining Field Display Types

Although each field display type has its own visual characteristics (as you'll see in a moment), all require you to keep the following in mind:

- The field width must be wide enough to accommodate any values you specify.

- Values you specify when defining the field must meet requirements of any validity check for the field. For example, if your field requires a picture of ??? (three letters), you mustn't specify values like *100*, *3 blind mice*, and so forth in your list of possible values. Although you'll be able to define such field values when setting up the field, Paradox will reject them during data entry.

- Values you specify must be the proper type for the field. For example, you can't define a value of *20%* for a number field (because "%" is text, not a number). Again, you won't discover that the values aren't right until someone tries to choose them during data entry.

- Values you specify when defining the field's Display Type property also must meet requirements of any Format property defined for the field. This is especially true for logical fields. If necessary, inspect the logical field in your form design, select Format ➤ Logical Format, and select or define a logical format in which the True and False values match the ones defined in your field's Display Type. For example, suppose you inspect a logical field and choose Display Type ➤ Check Box, then specify a value of *Rush* when checked, and *No Rush* when blank. You must then be sure to inspect the field again and select (or define and select) a Format ➤ Logical Format property (for example *Rush/No Rush*) that also uses *Rush* for True and *No Rush* for False.

▶ ▶ T I P

You can easily convert one Display Type to another. Simply select the field object, inspect it, choose Display Type, and then select the display type you want. If a dialog box appears, complete it as described in the following sections.

Now, let's take a closer look at how to create and use the four special display types: Drop-Down Edit, List, Radio Buttons, and Check Box.

Creating Custom Forms

Ch.
11

Drop-Down Edit Fields

Drop-down edit fields are especially versatile during data entry because you can type values directly into the field, or you can choose values from a drop-down list. (The value you type doesn't have to match any of the values in the drop-down list.) Thus, in the sample form of Figure 11.12, we could either type in the payment method or discount percent we want, or we could click the drop-down arrow in the field, then click the value we want in the list. Figure 11.13 showed an opened drop-down edit field.

To create a drop-down edit field, inspect the field and choose Display Type ▶ Drop-Down Edit from the property menu. You'll see the Define List dialog box shown in Figure 11.15.

Follow the steps below to define values that will appear in the drop-down list when it is clicked during data entry.

1. Type in the items you wish to have the user select, one at a time, in the Item box. Press ↵ after typing each item. Each time you press ↵, the new item will appear in the Item List area.

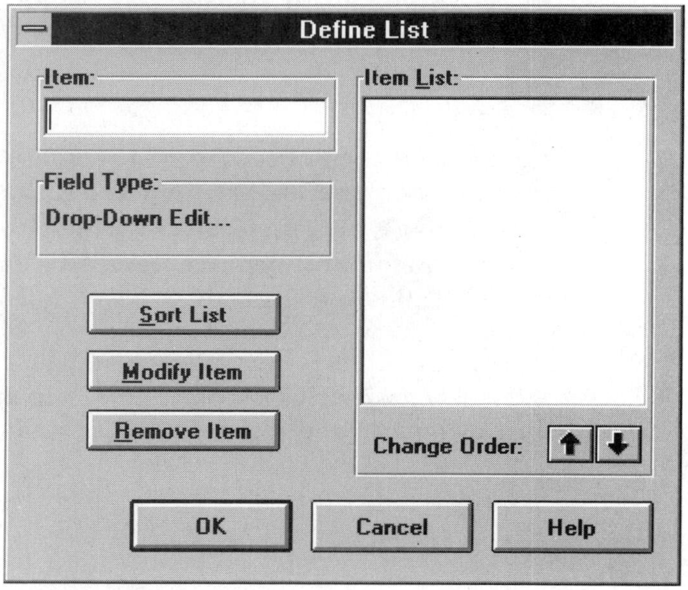

FIGURE 11.15 ▶

The Define List dialog box

2. Do any of the following if you need to alter the Item List:

- To sort the field values in alphabetical order, click the Sort List button.

- To change an item in the list, click the item in the Item List area of the dialog box, then click the Modify Item button. After making changes in the Item text box, press ↵.

- To move an item in the list, click on the item in the Item List area, then click the ↑ or ↓ Change Order buttons as needed.

- To delete an item, click on the item in the Item List area, then click Remove Item.

3. When you're finished entering the fields, choose OK.

 ► ►**N O T E**

> **Since the drop-down edit display type does not include a label, you should use the Text tool to create a label that describes the field.**

If you need to change the definition of a drop-down edit field, simply inspect the field and choose Display Type ➤ Drop-Down Edit again.

List Fields

During data entry, a list field, like the one shown back in Figure 11.13, lets you choose a value from a list. However, unlike drop-down edit fields, list fields do not allow you to type a value into the field; instead you must select one of the values from the list by clicking on or highlighting the value you want. Lists can prevent typing and spelling errors, and limit the values that can appear in a field.

To create a list display type, inspect the field and then choose Display Type ➤ List. You'll see a Define List dialog box that is almost identical to the one in Figure 11.15 (the only difference is that the Field Type area displays *List...* instead of *Drop-Down Edit...*). Follow the steps above to define your list. If you need to change values in the list, inspect the list field and choose Display Type ➤ List again. Or, inspect the list itself—select the list field, click inside the field, then right-click—and choose *List*.

> **▶▶ N O T E**
>
> **Like the drop-down edit display type, the list display type does not include a label. You can use the Text tool to create labels for list fields.**

Radio Button Fields

Radio button fields offer the same capabilities as list fields, but are visually different. When entering data into a field displayed as radio buttons, you simply click the button you want.

To create a radio button display type, inspect the field, choose Display Type ➤ Radio Buttons, then use the techniques described under "Drop-Down Edit Fields" to fill in the Define List dialog box (see Figure 11.15).

By default, Paradox creates radio buttons that look like this in the Design window:

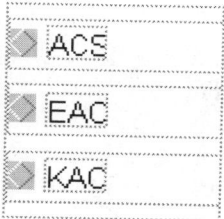

You can change the button type and style by selecting the individual buttons and inspecting them. When you inspect buttons, you'll see a Button property menu, as shown below.

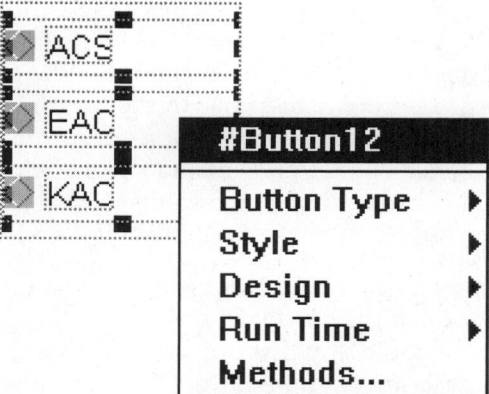

In this menu, you can choose Button Type, which leads to the Push, Radio, and Check Box options.

If you've chosen a Radio or Check Box button type, you can further customize the appearance by choosing Style, and then one of these options:

Borland   The default style, shown in Figures 11.13 and 11.14.

Windows   A round or square option button style.

Windows 3d   A round or square option button style with a 3D look.

If you've chosen a Push button type, you can select a Center Label option, which will center the label text object within the button.

You can also inspect any of the labels within the buttons or change their text, as you would for any text object.

Check Box Fields

As mentioned earlier, a check box can have two states—checked and unchecked—and is useful only for fields that can have one of two possible values, such as Yes or No. Of course, a perfect candidate for check boxes is the new Logical field type (just be sure to also select a matching Logical Format, as explained in the earlier section on "Tips for Defining Field Display Types").

To create a check box, first inspect a field, then choose Display Type ➤ Check Box. You'll see the Check Box Values dialog box shown in Figure 11.16. In the top text box, enter the value the field should have when it is *checked* during data entry. In the bottom text box, enter the value the field should have when it is *unchecked* during data entry. For example, if the check box represents a Logical field, you can set the Value When Checked option to the value *Yes* and the Value When Blank option to the value *No*. Choose OK after typing in your values.

Initially, the label in the check box contains whatever value you entered in the top text box of the Check Box Values dialog box. You can change this value as you would any text object, and it's a good idea to do so if the label isn't descriptive enough. Just keep in mind that the check box label is independent of the contents of the field. The *field* contains either the value you entered into the top text box or the value you entered into the bottom text box of the Check Box Values dialog box; however, the field *label* can display anything you want.

You can change the Button Type and Style properties of check box fields, just as you can for radio buttons. Simply select and inspect the check box button itself (you'll see *#Button* in the status bar) and make your choices.

Now that you know the basic methods for designing forms that contain only one page, let's turn our attention to some special techniques used for multipage forms.

FIGURE 11.16

The Check Box Values dialog box

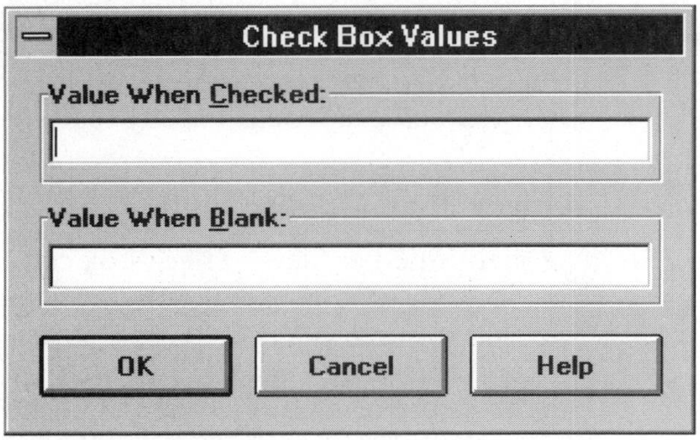

▶▶ *Designing a Multipage Form*

When a table contains too many fields to fit in one window, or your form design becomes too crowded, you can add pages. Figures 11.17 and 11.18 show each page of a two-page data entry form for an expanded table of information about *Gift Corner's* employees. The table is named *empladdr.db*.

▶▶ **NOTE**

The Empladdr table is the same as the Employee table described earlier in this book, with the addition of Address (25), City (20), State (2), Zip (10), and Phone (13) fields. All the new fields are alpha and have the sizes indicated in parentheses.

FIGURE 11.17 ▶

The first page of the Employee Update form, with instructions for moving to the next page, information about the current page number and total number of pages, the current date and time, and a read-only field containing the employee's salary.

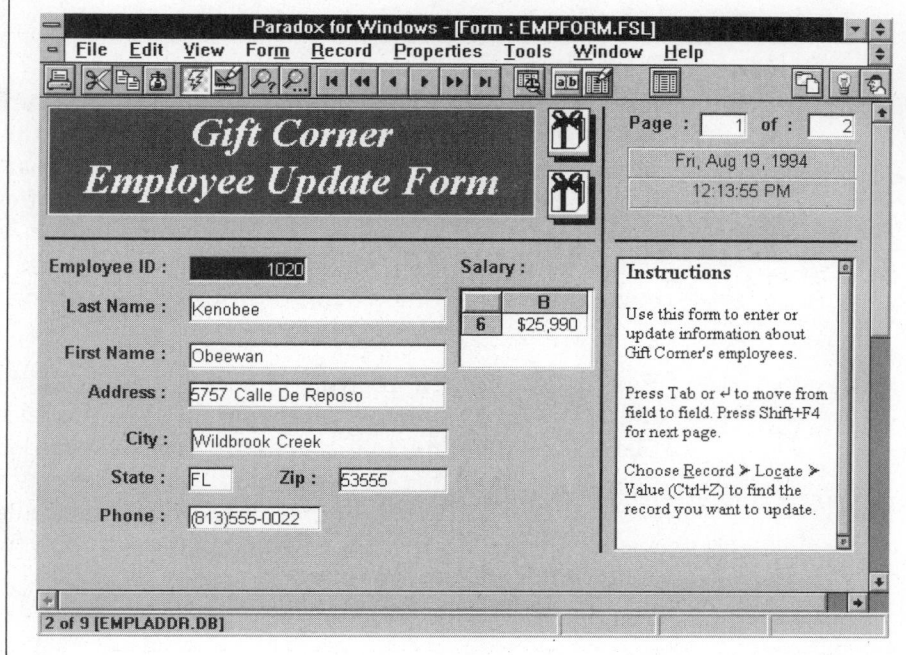

FIGURE 11.18 ►

The second page of the Employee Update form, with a reminder about how to move to the previous page, the current page number, total number of pages, current date and time, and read-only fields showiing the current employee's first and last names.

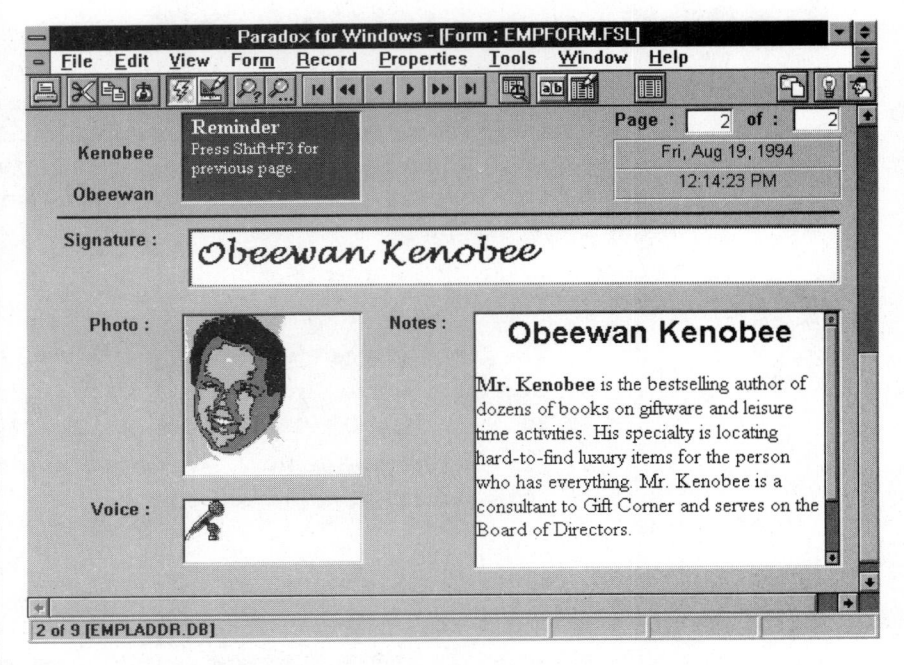

Notice in Figure 11.18 that the employee's last name and first name appear at the top left corner of the second page, so the user knows whose record is currently in view. To prevent the user from entering data into those fields accidentally, we changed their properties to Read Only and turned off the Tab Stop. At the upper-right corner, we added fields for the current page number, total number of pages in the form, and the current date and time. We also provided instructions for moving from page to page.

Finally, we checked the Run Time ➤ Complete Display property for the Notes field (a formatted memo field). This causes Paradox to display the field completely, whether or not the cursor is positioned in the field. The Run Time ➤ Complete Display property is basically the same as the Complete Display property that is available when you inspect a formatted memo, graphic, memo, or OLE field in the Table View window. (See Chapter 7.)

▶ ▶ T I P

> **In multipage forms it's important to let the user know the current page number and the total number of pages in the form so that no fields are overlooked during data entry.**

The initial steps for creating a multipage form are identical to those for creating a single-page form. After selecting the table name in the Data Model dialog box, we chose OK, then opened the Style Sheet drop-down list and clicked the *c:\pdoxwin\control3d.ft* style sheet name, then chose OK again to continue to the Design window.

▶ Using the Zoom Feature with Multipage Forms

Normally, each page of your form occupies the full screen and is displayed at its normal size, which is 100% magnification. However, with multipage forms, you'll often want to zoom in or out of your design by choosing View ➤ Zoom from the Design window menus, then selecting a magnification. The 25%, 50%, Fit Height, and Best Fit options are especially handy when working with multipage documents because they provide a bird's-eye view of several pages at once. Figure 11.19, for example, shows the Design window after we created a new form for the Empladdr table (using the *c:\pdoxwin\control3d.ft* style sheet), added a page, chose View ➤ Zoom ➤ Best Fit, and removed the rulers from the window.

Choosing smaller magnifications that let you see multiple pages at once can be a real timesaver. You can select multiple fields on any (or several) of the pages, then inspect and change the properties of all selected fields at once. You can also drag selected fields to other pages and easily perform cut, copy, and paste operations across pages.

Regardless of the magnification you choose, you can use the vertical scroll bar to display additional pages. Later in this chapter, we'll describe techniques that let you navigate through multipage documents.

FIGURE 11.19 ►

A new two-page form shown at Best Fit magnification with all rulers turned off. We used the Control3D style sheet to set up the initial look of this form.

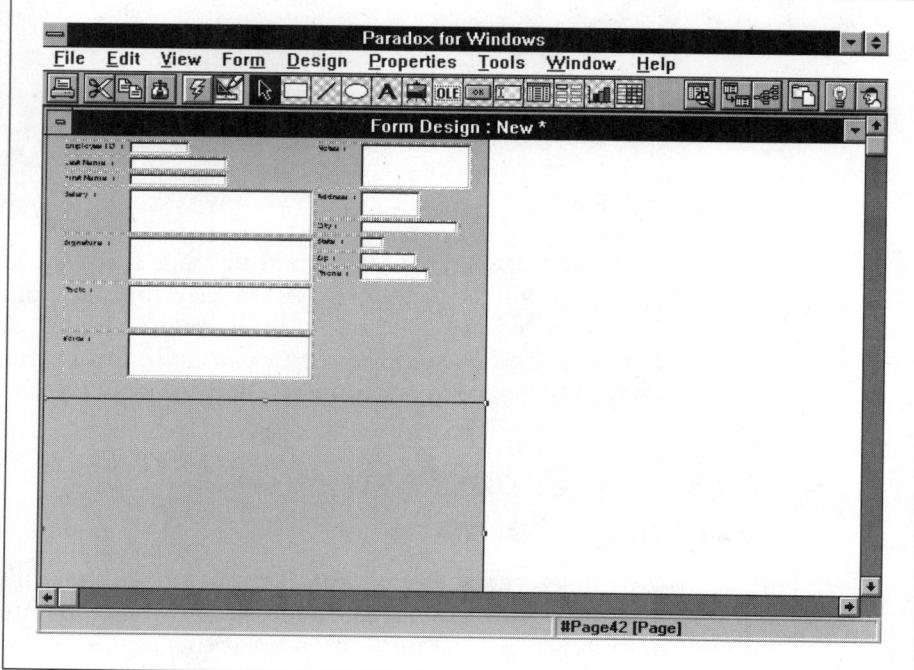

► Adding Blank Pages to the End of a Form

Adding pages to the end of a form is very easy. Just choose Form ➤ Page ➤ Add. Paradox always adds the page after all existing pages, and the new page is selected automatically.

After adding a blank page, you can place new objects on it, or you can move to a different page, cut or copy objects from that page to the Clipboard, then return to the new page and paste the objects into the design. You can also drag objects from other pages to the blank page.

► Creating New Pages from Existing Pages

Paradox for Windows lets you create a new page that's exactly the same as an existing page of a form. Here's how:

1. Select the entire page by clicking on it in the Form Design window (*#Page* will appear in the status bar).

Click the Copy To Clipboard button in the Toolbar, or press Ctrl+Ins, or choose Edit ➤ Copy.

Click on the page that should *follow* the copied page, then click the Paste From Clipboard button, or press Shift+Ins, or choose Edit ➤ Paste.

A new page containing all the design objects of the original page will be added.

T I P

To place a blank page between existing pages, add a blank page to the end of the form by choosing Form ➤ Page ➤ Add, then cut the page to the Clipboard, click on the page that should follow the blank page, and paste the page from the Clipboard.

▶ Copying and Moving Fields from Page to Page

You don't have to re-create objects laboriously on each new page of a document. Instead, you can use the Clipboard to copy design objects from one page to another. To do so, select the objects you want, then click the Copy To Clipboard button in the Toolbar (or choose Edit ➤ Copy or press Ctrl+Ins). Next, move to the page you want to copy the objects to, click the spot where you want the objects to appear (*clicking is very important!*), then click the Paste From Clipboard button (or choose Edit ➤ Paste or press Shift+Ins).

For example, when designing the form in Figures 11.17 and 11.18, we chose Form ➤ Page ➤ Add to create the second page as soon as the Design window appeared. Then we returned to the first page, selected the Last Name and First Name fields, copied them to the Clipboard, moved to the second page, clicked where we wanted the fields to appear, then pasted the fields onto the design. We also changed the Read Only and Tab Stop properties as described earlier.

You can use either of two methods to move fields from one page to another. The first method is similar to copying: Select the fields you want to move, click the Cut To Clipboard button (or choose Edit ➤ Cut or press Shift+Del). Now move to the appropriate page, click where the fields should appear, and then click the Paste From Clipboard button (or choose Edit ➤ Paste or press Shift+Ins).

The second way to move fields from page to page is much easier. First, zoom out so you can see both the source page (which you want to move fields *from*) and the target page (which you want to move fields *to*). Then simply select and drag the fields from the source to the target page. For example, to move the Signature, Notes, Photo, and Voice fields to the second page of our sample Employee Update form, we simply selected those fields, then dragged them to the blank page.

▶ Deleting a Page

You can delete any page of a multipage form (though you need to be careful about this). Click on the page you want to delete, then press the Del key or choose Edit ➤ Delete.

 ▶▶**N O T E**

You can choose Edit ➤ Undo or press Alt+Backspace if you immediately regret deleting a page.

▶ Navigating a Multipage Form

As mentioned earlier, you can use scroll bars in the Design window to move from page to page of your form, and you can click on the page you want if you've used the Zoom feature. The Form ➤ Page menu, shown below, provides additional options for moving from page to page in a form design.

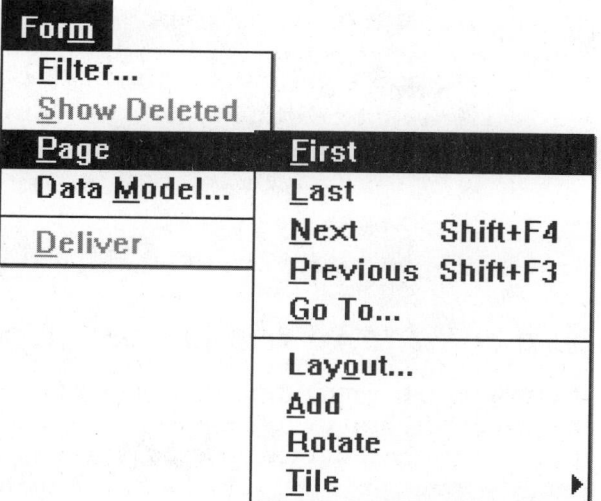

In the For<u>m</u> ➤ <u>P</u>age menu, your choices are as follows:

First Moves to the first page of the form.

Last Moves to the last page of the form.

Next Moves to the next page of the form. As a shortcut, you can press Shift+F4.

Previous Moves to the previous page of the form. As a shortcut, you can press Shift+F3.

Go To Displays the Go To Page dialog box shown below. To choose a page number, either type the page you want into the <u>P</u>age Number text box, or click the ↑ or ↓ button to decrease or increase the page number. Then choose OK.

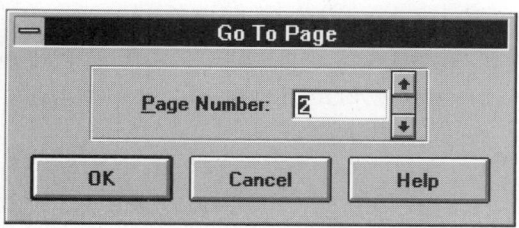

▶▶**N O T E**

The above options are also available when you're viewing or editing data in the Form window. In the Design window, when you use these techniques to move to a page, Paradox automatically selects the page you move to.

▶ *Rotating a Page to the End of the Form*

As an alternative to cutting and copying pages, you can rearrange the pages of your form by rotating pages to the end. To do so, select any page except the last, then choose Form ➤ Page ➤ Rotate. The currently selected page will move to the end of the form.

▶ *Tiling a Multipage Form*

Normally, the pages of your form are lined up vertically in the Design window, so that you can use the vertical scroll bar to move from page to page. However, you can choose options on the Form ➤ Page ➤ Tile menu to view the pages in a different arrangement, as summarized below.

Stack Pages   Stacks pages one on top of the other, with the current page on top. You cannot use scroll bars to move from page to page when this option is selected. Instead, you must choose appropriate options from the Form ➤ Page menu (or the equivalent function keys), as described earlier under "Navigating a Multipage Form."

Tile Horizontal   Tiles pages horizontally across the screen. You can use the horizontal scroll bar to move from page to page when this option is selected.

Tile Vertical   Tiles pages vertically, in the default manner. You can use the vertical scroll bar to move from page to page when this option is selected.

> **▶ ▶ N O T E**
>
> **The Tile setting in effect when you save the form will
> be used when viewing or editing data.**

▶▶ *Designing the Sample Multipage Form*

You might like to try your hand at designing the sample multipage
form shown in Figures 11.17 and 11.18. To begin, choose File ➤
New ➤ Form, click Data Model / Layout Diagram, then select your
table and choose OK in the Data Model dialog box. Then select the
c:\pdoxwin\control3d.ft style sheet from the Style Sheet drop-down list in
the Design Layout dialog box, and choose OK.

When you get to the Design window, add a second page to the form by
choosing Form ➤ Page ➤ Add. Now choose View ➤ Zoom and reduce the magnification (or choose Best Fit or Fit Height), then use the
copy and paste techniques described earlier to copy the Last Name
and First Name fields to the top of the second page. Select the newly
copied Last Name and First Name fields, inspect them, and change the
Run Time ➤ Read Only and Run Time ➤ Tab Stop properties as described earlier. Also change their Display Type property to Unlabeled.

If you can see both pages at once, select and drag the Signature, Photo,
Notes, and Voice fields to the second page of the form; otherwise, cut
and paste to move those fields to the second page. Next, rearrange
and resize the fields into the approximate configurations shown in Figures 11.17 and 11.18. (We selected the labels on the left side of the
multipage forms and chose Design ➤ Align ➤ Align Right, so that the
colons would line up neatly.)

Now, refer to the general guidelines presented in Chapter 10 and in
this chapter, and proceed with the two sections below to complete the
design. Feel free to experiment and make corrections as needed, and
be sure to switch back and forth between the Design window and the
Form window (by pressing F8 or using the View Data and Design buttons in the Toolbar) to see how the form will look with data filled in.
Zoom in and out as needed.

▶ *Designing the First Page of the Sample Multipage Form*

Use the following guidelines to complete the first page of the sample form shown in Figure 11.17:

- Create a text object for the title, then type the two title lines, pressing ↵ after the first one. Select and inspect the text object and change the font to Times New Roman, 24-point, Bold, Italic. Then change the text object's background Color to red, its Font ➤ Color to white, and its Alignment to Center. Change the Frame ➤ Style property to the embossed frame style (last selection in the palette).

- Create the two gift graphics (or whatever graphics suit your fancy), as for Figure 11.9.

- Add the four special fields shown in the upper-right corner; these are current page (Page Number), total number of pages (Number of Pages), current date (Today), and current time (Now).

- Change the Alignment property for the <Today> and <Now> fields to Center. Change the <Today> field's Format ➤ Date Format property to use the short month name and short day name.

 ▶▶ **N O T E**

If you cannot find the Alignment property when you inspect the selected <Today> and <Now> fields, try turning off the Word Wrap property. Then inspect the fields again and choose Alignment ➤ Center.

- To create the 3D effects in the special page number, date, and time fields, select and inspect the fields, then choose the embossed style at the bottom of the Frame ➤ Style property palette.

- Move the <Today> and <Now> fields close together so that the bottom of the <Today> field just touches the top of the <Now> field.

- Use the Line tool to create the vertical and horizontal lines. Change the Line ➤ Thickness property for those lines to the second thickness listed.

TIP

Before drawing lines, try zooming to a smaller magnification so you can define the full length of the lines with a single drag of the mouse.

- Create the *Instructions* text object as for Figure 11.8, modifying the text to describe the form you're designing. Change the Frame ➤ Style property to the sunken appearance (the second-to-last selection on the palette), add a vertical scroll bar, and change the Color to white.
- Change the Run Time properties for the Salary field to Read Only and turn off the Tab Stop.

NOTE

Recall that Salary is an OLE field designed to contain data from a Microsoft Excel spreadsheet. We chose not to allow updates to the employee's salary.

- Change the Format ➤ Number Format property for the Employee ID field to Integer.
- Adjust and rearrange the fields as needed.

▶ Designing the Second Page of the Sample Multipage Form

When designing the second page of the sample form in Figure 11.18, follow these guidelines:

- Select the page number, total number of pages, current date, and current time fields in the first page of the form and copy them to the Clipboard.

- Use any of the techniques described earlier to move to the second page of the form. For example, press Shift+F4, or zoom to 50% or Best Fit, and click on the second page's frame.

- Click in the upper-right corner of the page, where you want the copied fields to appear, then paste from the Clipboard.

- Select the Last Name and First Name fields, inspect them, and choose Font ➤ Style ➤ Bold; inspect them again and choose Alignment ➤ Right.

- Create the text object containing the Reminder text as for the *Instructions* text object on the previous page. As before, choose the second-to-last Frame ➤ Style property, but omit the vertical scroll bar. For some added drama, inspect the object, and change its Color to red; inspect it again and change its Font ➤ Color to white.

- Draw the horizontal line and change its Thickness to the second sample in the list.

- Inspect the Notes field and select the Vertical Scrollbar property. Then click the Notes field again to select its *EditRegion;* then right-click and select (check) the Run Time ➤ Complete Display property.

- Inspect the Photo field's EditRegion and select the Magnification ➤ Best Fit property.

- Make any necessary adjustments, then save the form (we used the name *Empform*).

▶▶ *Changing Form Design Window Properties*

As you know, the Properties menu in the Design window offers several options for controlling the appearance of the Form Design window, including Snap To Grid, Show Grid, Horizontal Ruler, Vertical Ruler, Expanded Ruler, and Show Size And Position. The View menu includes the Zoom option. After setting these properties to your liking, you can save them by choosing Properties ➤ Form Options ➤ Save Defaults. If you change your mind and want to restore properties to their previous settings, you must do so *before* exiting Paradox, by choosing

Properties ➤ Fo̱rm Options ➤ R̲estore Defaults. These defaults are stored in your *pdoxwin.ini* file (see Chapter 14).

➤ ➤ **T I P**

> **You can also use the P̲roperties menu in Form View to turn the horizontal and expanded rulers on or off. When the horizontal and expanded rulers are on, you can use them in Edit mode to adjust the tab stops, indents, and margins for text in a formatted memo field.**

➤ ➤ *Changing Form Window Properties*

Paradox offers several advanced options for controlling the final appearance of your forms in the Form window. For example, you can decide whether you want your form to appear as a window or a dialog box, and you can define the title and border for the form. To control the appearance of the Form window, start from the Design window and follow these steps:

1. Choose P̲roperties ➤ F̲orm ➤ W̲indow Style, or press Esc until no objects are selected, press F6, then choose Window Style. You'll see the Form Window Properties dialog box as in Figure 11.20.

2. Choose a basic style for your form (either W̲indow or D̲ialog Box) in the Window Style area of the dialog box. Then choose additional options as discussed in the following sections.

3. Choose OK to save your changes and return to the Form Design window.

4. Save your form and close it.

➤ ➤ **N O T E**

> **To see the full effect of changing the Window Style, you must close the form and reopen it in Form View. It isn't enough to simply switch from Design View to Form View after changing these properties.**

Creating Custom Forms

➤ ➤

Ch. **11**

FIGURE 11.20 ▶

The Form Window Properties dialog box

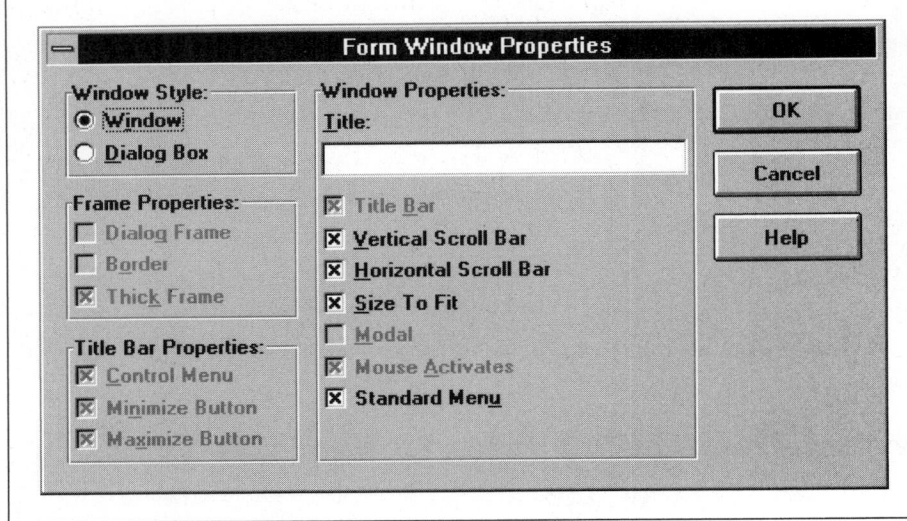

Table 11.1 summarizes the options available after choosing the window or dialog box style in step 2. Those options will be described in more detail below.

▶ **TABLE 11.1:** *Summary of Properties Available for the Window and Dialog Box Window Style*

PROPERTY	WINDOW	DIALOG BOX
Frame Properties		
Dialog Frame		X (if Border isn't checked)
Border		X (if Dialog Frame isn't checked)
Thick Frame		X (if Dialog Frame isn't checked)
Title Bar Properties		
Control Menu		X (if Title Bar is checked)
Minimize Button		X (if Title Bar is checked)
Maximize Button		X (if Title Bar is checked)

▶ **TABLE 11.1:** *Summary of Properties Available for the Window and Dialog Box Window Style (continued)*

PROPERTY	WINDOW	DIALOG BOX
Window Properties		
Title	X	X
Title Bar		X
Vertical Scroll Bar	X	X
Horizontal Scroll Bar	X	X
Size To Fit	X	X (always enabled)
Modal		X
Mouse Activates		X
Standard Menu	X	

The next time you open the form in Form View, your form will have the properties you chose. Keep in mind that except for changes to the window's title, these options have *no* effect on the form's appearance in the Form Design window.

You should be very careful about the options you choose in this dialog box, because some combinations may cause users confusion about how to close the form. And when users don't know how to close a form, they'll be tempted to reboot the computer—an operation that's potentially hazardous to data. Please read the following sections carefully before making changes.

 ▶ ▶ **T I P**

> **When there's no obvious way to close a form in the Form window, pressing Alt+F4 usually will do the trick. (Note that pressing Alt+F4 in the *Form Design* window exits Paradox, so make sure your data appears in the form before pressing these keys.)**

► *Changing Window Style*

When you switch to Form View, Paradox normally displays your form in a window that has the properties selected in Figure 11.20. So far, all our examples of Form windows have used the default window style (though in some cases, we've altered the Title).

As an alternative to the familiar window style, you can display your form in a dialog box that has these general properties:

- It opens in the center of the screen.
- It lies on top of normal windows and the Paradox menu bar.
- You *cannot* resize it, but you can move it if you include a title bar.
- You can switch to other applications by pressing Alt+Tab or Ctrl+Esc, or via the Control-menu box, if it's available.
- To move from page to page on the form, you must use the Shift+F4 and Shift+F3 shortcut keys.
- You can close the dialog box by pressing Alt+F4 or using the Control-menu box, if it's available.

The following sections explain how to customize the dialog box to your liking. Keep in mind that the most "friendly" dialog box style includes a title bar (with an informative title), the Control-menu box, a Minimize button, and a Maximize button.

When you use the dialog box window style, you should also be sure to make the following changes to your form:

- If your form is too wide or too long to fit on your screen, it should also include horizontal or vertical scroll bars.
- If you're including a vertical scroll bar, choose Form ➤ Page ➤ Layout and reduce the form's width by about .25 inch to make room for the scroll bar.
- If you're designing a multipage form, choose Form ➤ Page ➤ Tile ➤ Stack Pages. You'll then need to use the Shift+F4 and Shift+F3 keys, respectively, to move to the next or previous page in the multipage form.

> ▶▶ **TIP**
>
> **Attention ObjectPAL programmers! To make the multipage form easier to navigate, add a button to each page of the form and change the button's label accordingly (for example, change it to *Next Page* or *Prev Page*). Then, for each button, attach a *pushbutton method* and type an appropriate *MoveToPage (n)* command (where *n* is the page number you want to move to). See Chapter 19 for more about ObjectPAL.**

The example in Figure 11.21 follows these general guidelines. Figure 11.22 shows the settings used in the Form Window Properties dialog box to produce this form style.

FIGURE 11.21

A sample dialog box containing a title bar, Control-menu box, Minimize and Maximize buttons, and horizontal and vertical scroll bars

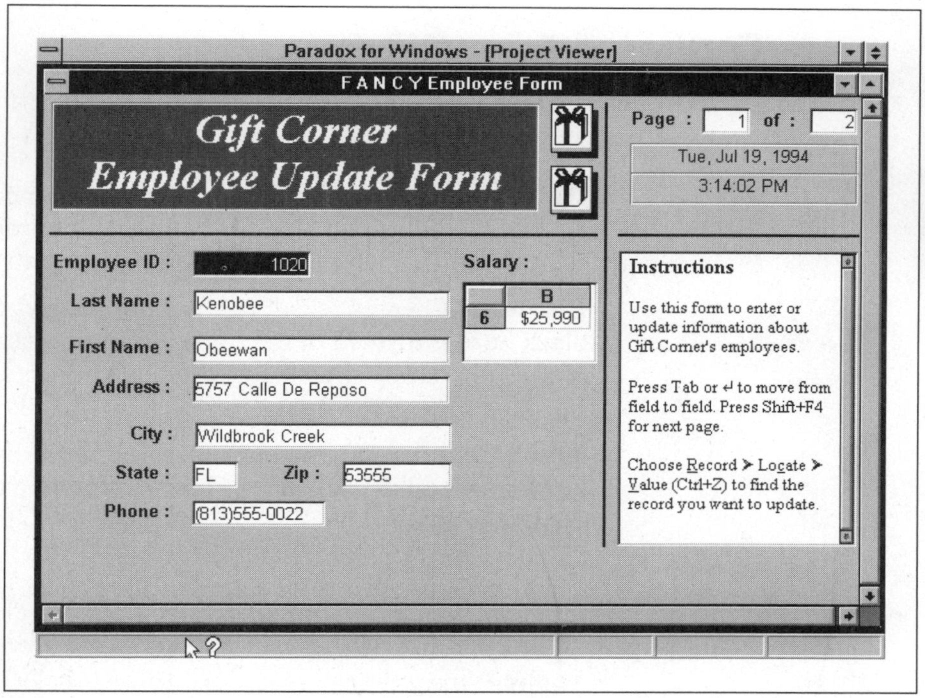

FIGURE 11.22 ▶

*Form Window Proper-
ties settings used to
produce the form style
in Figure 11.21*

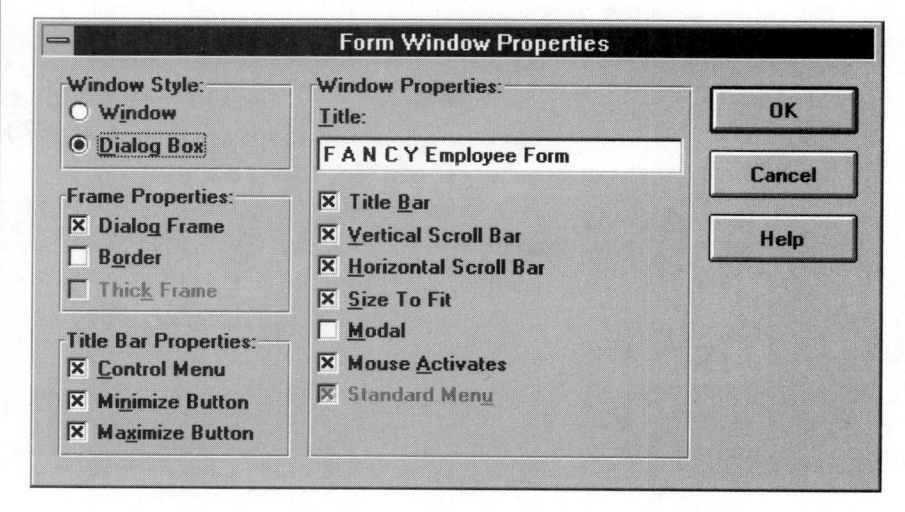

▶ *Changing Frame Properties*

The frame style options summarized below are available only if you've chosen a Dialog Box style.

Dialog Frame   When checked, this option displays the form in a normal Windows dialog box, where the border, colors, and other settings are determined in the Windows Control Panel.

Border   When checked, this option displays the form with a black border instead of the normal Windows style. You cannot display a title bar or choose any title bar properties if you select the Border frame property.

Thick Frame   When checked, this option displays the dialog border as a thick black line. Thick Frame is available only if you've selected Border.

 ▶▶**T I P**

To create a dialog box without a border, deselect both the Dialog Frame and Border options.

▶ *Changing Title Bar Properties*

The title bar properties determine whether your dialog box will include a Control menu (Control-menu box), Minimize button, or Maximize button. When checked, the selected element appears in the dialog box; when unchecked, the element does not appear.

When you choose the Window style, all three elements are included automatically and they cannot be turned off.

▶ *Changing Window Properties*

The Window Properties area of the dialog box controls a variety of attributes of the Dialog Box or Window style. Here's a summary of these options:

Title   Type whatever title you want into the <u>T</u>itle text box. If Title <u>B</u>ar is also checked, this title will appear in the title bar of the window or dialog box, and under the icon if you minimize the form. To have Paradox display the file name of the form, leave the Title text box empty. To create a blank title bar, type a space in the text box.

Title Bar   When checked, this option displays the title bar in your form. In the Window style, this option is automatically selected and cannot be turned off.

Vertical Scroll Bar   When checked, this option displays a vertical scroll bar. You should include a vertical scroll bar if any page of your form is longer than the screen.

Horizontal Scroll Bar   When checked, this option displays a horizontal scroll bar. You should include a horizontal scroll bar if any page of your form is wider than the screen.

Size To Fit   When this option is checked, Paradox opens the form in a window of whatever size you chose in the Page Layout dialog box. If this option is not checked, the form opens in the Windows default size. When you select the <u>D</u>ialog Box style, <u>S</u>ize To Fit is always enabled.

Modal   When checked, this option prevents you from working elsewhere in Paradox until you close the form (you can, however, work in other applications). This option is available only for the Dialog Box style.

Mouse Activates   This option is used only in Dialog Box forms and is useful only if you've attached ObjectPAL methods to your form. (See Chapter 19 for an introduction to ObjectPAL.)

Standard Menu   This option is used only in Window forms and is useful only if you've written your own Form window menu in ObjectPAL and attached it to your form.

▸▸ *Printing a Form*

Although forms are designed primarily for on-screen display, you can print a form or its design.

▸ *Printing the Form Design*

Once you have designed a data entry form, you might want to print the blank form design to use as a data collection tool or for reference when designing future forms. Using the actual form for manual data collection reduces the chances of introducing errors into your table.

To print the form design, switch to the Form Design window, if you're not there already. Then click the Print button in the Toolbar, or choose File ▸ Print. You'll see the Print File dialog box (discussed in Chapter 7). From here, you can choose All to print all pages of a multipage form, or choose Page Range and define a range to print only the specified pages of a multipage form. Choose OK to begin printing.

▸▶**N O T E**

> **Depending on your form design and the type of printer you have, field names in the printed design may appear garbled if Paradox cannot fit them in the space allotted. This is no cause for concern, and it will not affect the appearance of your form on the screen.**

▶ *Printing Records in Your Form*

You can use your form layout to print the current record (or the current set of records if your form contains a multi-record object or table frame). To do so, make sure you're in the Form window (your data should appear in the form) and choose File ➤ Print or click the Print button in the Toolbar. Choose a page range, or choose All to print every page of a multipage form. Specify the number of copies you want and decide whether or not you want the copies collated, as described in Chapter 7. Then choose OK to begin printing.

▶ ▶ **T I P**

If you want to print more than one record at a time using the form's layout, open the form as a report (see Chapter 10).

▶ ▶ *Delivering a Form*

After designing and saving the perfect form, you may not want to let anyone else change it. To prevent other people from changing your form, open your form in the Form Design window, save your changes (if you made any), then choose Form ➤ Deliver. Paradox will create a form with the same name as your original form and an .fdl extension. For example, if your original form is named *custform.fsl*, the delivered version will be called *custform.fdl*. You can then give the .fdl file (not the .fsl) to others. They'll be able to use the form, but cannot switch to the Design window to change it (the Design button appears in the Toolbar as usual, but displays the status bar message "Cannot modify this document" when clicked).

▶ ▶ **W A R N I N G**

Be sure to keep the original .fsl file around, or *you* won't be able to change the form.

If you need to change the form later, simply modify the original form file (with the .fsl extension), save your changes, choose Form ➤ Deliver again, then distribute the updated .fdl file.

▶▶ *Customizing the Experts*

Advanced users and third-party developers can customize the forms, reports, and mailing labels Experts if necessary. For example, you can add new Experts, change the prompts and icons used for existing experts, add new style sheets to control the initial look of documents that the Experts create, and customize the error messages.

The behavior of an Expert is controlled by tables, forms, and other objects in the *c:\pdoxwin\experts* database. This database is installed automatically when you do a complete Paradox installation (see Appendix A). To view the database objects, open the Project Viewer and change your working directory to *c:\pdoxwin\experts* by using the Browse button.

Providing a detailed explanation about how to create your own Experts is beyond the scope of this book; however, we *can* tell you how to make some simple tweaks. If you need more information about designing Experts, please contact Borland directly.

 ▶ ▶ W A R N I N G

It's best not to change the Experts that come with Paradox. Nonetheless, if you *are* tempted to play with the Experts, be sure to make a complete backup of the Experts database. That way, if your experiments go awry, you can restore the botched objects from your backup copies.

▶ *About the Expert Tables*

If you switch to the Experts database directory and then open the Project Viewer and click the Tables icon, you'll see a list of tables that control the behavior of Paradox's forms, mailing labels, and reports Experts (as shown below).

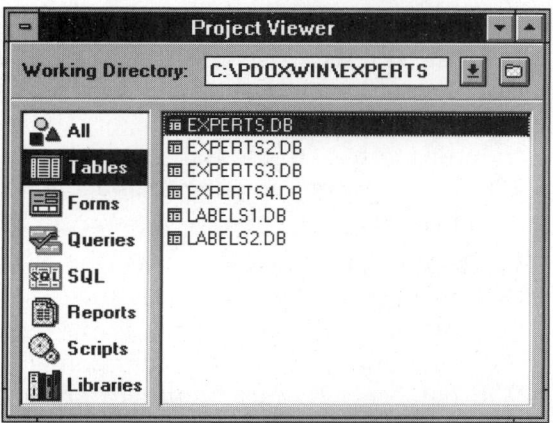

Here's a quick rundown of each table.

EXPERTS.DB   Controls which Experts, bitmap buttons, and prompts appear in the opening Expert Control Panel. The Expert-FormName field in the table specifies the file name of the master form that steps you through creating forms, mailing labels, or reports.

EXPERTS2.DB   Controls the available style sheets for the form and report Experts. If you'd like to plug one of your own custom style sheets into the Experts, design and save the style sheet as explained in Chapter 10. Then edit the Experts2 table. Using the existing records as your guide, type a long description into the LongName field, type **Screen** (for form style sheets) or **Printer** (for report style sheets) into the Type field, type the alias name for the directory where the style sheet is stored into the Path field, and type the style sheet's file name into the FileName field.

EXPERTS3.DB   This table controls information used by the delivered forms in the Experts database. Don't touch the information here unless you thoroughly understand the consequences of doing so. (Unless you're a third-party developer, you won't need to touch this table and you won't know how to change it anyway.)

EXPERTS4.DB Includes error codes and error messages for things that can go wrong when you're using an Expert. Again, you probably won't want to change this table unless you're a third-party developer.

LABELS1.DB Lists the categories of labels that the mailing label Expert can create. If you want to design custom mailing labels, you could add a new category to this table and add corresponding entries to the Labels2 table described next. See Chapter 12 for more about creating mailing labels and using the Mailing Label Expert.

LABELS2.DB Describes the category, type, and dimensions of each mailing label format that the Expert can create. To set up a new custom label, enter values for Category, Type, Top Margin, Side Margin, Vertical Pitch, Horizontal Pitch, Label Height, Label Width, Corner Radius, Number Across, Number Down, and Inches (True or False). If *Inches* is True, measurements for margins, pitch, height, width, and radius are in inches; otherwise, they're in pixels. Your Category entry in the Labels2 table must match a Category entry in the Labels1 table.

▶ *About the Expert Forms*

As an alternative to running the Experts using the methods given near the start of this chapter, you can run the appropriate forms in the Experts working directory. This might come in handy while you're tweaking the Experts for your own use. For example, to start the Expert Control Panel form, switch to the *c:\pdoxwin\experts* working directory, click the Forms icon in the left side of the Project Viewer, and double-click the delivered form named *expmain.fdl*.   •

 ▶▶ N O T E

> **Delivered forms cannot be changed. See the earlier section on "Delivering a Form" to learn how the Borland developers delivered the Expert forms to you.**

The example below shows all the delivered forms in the Experts database.

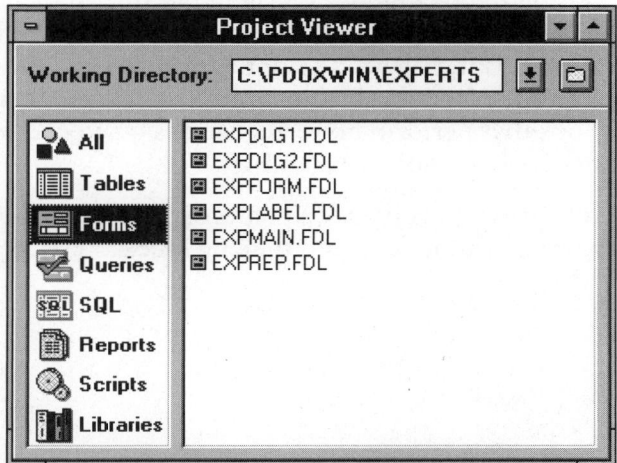

▶ ▶**W A R N I N G**

Do not open the *expdlg1.fdl* and *expdlg2.fdl* forms directly. If you do open Expdlg1 by accident, choose <u>W</u>indow ➤ Close <u>A</u>ll to clear it from the screen. If you open Expdlg2 accidentally, click its <u>C</u>ancel button.

You can open the following forms while you're in the Experts database working directory:

EXPFORM.FDL   Opens the first dialog box for the Form Expert.

EXPLABEL.FDL   Opens the first dialog box for the Mailing Label Expert.

EXPMAIN.FDL   Opens the Expert Control Panel, which lets you choose any Expert you want.

EXPREP.FDL   Opens the first dialog box for the Report Expert.

Creating
Custom Forms

Ch.
11

Using the techniques presented in this chapter and your own imagination, you should now be able to create sophisticated and attractive forms. But, believe it or not, Paradox for Windows offers even more features for form design, including multitable forms, calculations, and buttons that perform powerful actions when clicked. We'll explore these topics in Chapters 17 and 19.

In the next chapter, we'll cover special techniques for designing reports, form letters, and mailing labels.

▶ ▶ CHAPTER **12**

Designing and Printing Formatted Reports

—

►► Fast Track

▶ *To sort reports*   **678**

inspect the record band, choose Sort, and complete the
Sort Record Band dialog box using techniques discussed
in Chapter 8. If you are using group bands, the group
bands also control the sort order for the report. You can
also control sort order by designing your report from a
sorted table or query (if you're not using group bands).

▶ *To place objects within a text object*   **680**

position the insertion point where you want the new object to appear, select the appropriate tool from the Toolbar, then click and drag the mouse to define the size of the
object. (To place a field object quickly, position the insertion point, then press F5.) After placing a field object,
inspect it, and choose Define Field.

▶ *To prevent unwanted blank space in a document*   **704**

make sure the Run Time ➤ Fit Width and Run Time ➤
Fit Height properties are checked for fields and the Run
Time ➤ Line Squeeze and Run Time ➤ Field Squeeze
properties are checked for the text objects that surround
fields.

▶ *To print a report*   **718**

click the Print button in the Toolbar. If you're previewing the
report, you can also choose File ➤ Print; or, if you're designing the report, you can choose File ➤ Print ➤ Report.

▶ *To print a report design*   **718**

from the Report Design window, choose File ➤ Print ➤
Design.

▶ ▶ *I*n this chapter we'll build on concepts presented in Chapters 10 and 11, focusing on techniques for designing and printing reports, form letters, mailing labels, and envelopes. If you've designed custom forms before (perhaps by reproducing the sample forms in Chapter 11 or completing Lesson 4 in Chapter 2), you should have little trouble mastering the techniques presented here. However, if you haven't yet worked through Chapters 10 and 11, please do so before tackling the more advanced topics presented in this chapter.

 ▶▶**T I P**

If you want to create instant reports and mailing labels with no muss or fuss, skip to the sections "Using the Report Expert" and "Using the Mailing Label Expert."

Typically, you'll use a *report* to print summary information about your data. For instance, you can print a telephone directory of all customers sorted by area code, or you might want to create an employee directory complete with photos, signatures, and résumé. Perhaps you'd like to produce a list of customer credit limits, sorted by state. The possibilities are limitless.

 ▶▶**N O T E**

Chapter 17 discusses advanced topics related to report design, including how to use summary and calculated fields and how to create multitable reports.

You can also design *mail merge documents*, or form letters, that are customized for each person on a mailing list. You can send new credit customers a letter of welcome that includes the customer's name and address, the amount of credit granted, and when the credit limit becomes effective—along with an appropriate sales pitch to encourage customers to use that credit right away. You can even design personalized mailing labels or envelopes for each customer.

> **N O T E**
>
> **The term *mail merge document* is frequently used to describe form letters, mailing labels, and envelopes. Although mail merge documents are really just reports in Paradox for Windows, they do involve some specialized techniques that we'll discuss later in this chapter.**

►► *Special Techniques for Designing Reports*

The general steps for designing documents (especially forms) were presented in Chapters 10 and 11, and these are fundamental to report design. However, a few design techniques are unique to reports and mail merge documents, including the following:

- Using report bands to control placement of report titles, page headers and footers, and records, and to control the sort order
- Grouping related records together
- Using object properties that are unique to report design
- Using text objects to squeeze fields together in mail merge documents

- Sorting the records in the table, without using group bands.

▶▶ *Printing a Quick Report*

The most basic type of report is the *Quick Report,* a simple list of data in tabular form, with labels printed at the top of each column. The Quick Report is often sufficient for checking the accuracy of data or for looking up pieces of information. However, it's rather boring to look at.

To print a Quick Report from the Table View window, click the Quick Report button in the Toolbar (or press Shift+F7, or choose Tools ➤ Quick Report), then click the Print button in the Toolbar to open the Print File dialog box and print the results (see Chapter 7).

Figures 12.1 and 12.2 illustrate some of the most important differences between Quick Reports and customized reports. Note that a Quick Report includes all the fields in a table, regardless of whether they contain information of immediate interest. Any fields that cannot fit on a single page are either cut off (clipped) or printed on overflow pages, depending on options that you select in the Print File dialog box. When printing Figure 12.1, we chose the default option (Clip to Page Width), so Figure 12.1 shows only the left-most fields of the table.

The custom report shown in Figure 12.2 includes only the fields we want in the order we want them, and is grouped by area code and alphabetized by customer last name within each area code. Although we

FIGURE 12.1 ▶

The Quick Report printed from CustList's Table View after clicking the Quick Report button in the Toolbar

Cust No	Last Name	Mr/Mrs	First Name	MI	Department/Title	
1,001.00	Miller	Miss	Maria	N.	Accounts Receivable	Zeerocks, Inc.
1,002.00	Adams	Miss	Anita	Q.	Microcomputer Consultant	
1,003.00	Eggo	Ms.	Sandy		Owner	Pancho's Res
1,004.00	Cherub	Miss	Sky	R.		Oneness Well
1,005.00	Clavell	Miss	Wanda	T.	Mother Superior	Westridge Co
1,006.00	Zeepers	Mr.	Zeke	A.	Chief Engineer	Virtual Reality
1,007.00	Kenney	Mr.	David	E.	Attorney at Law	Felson and F
1,008.00	Leventhal	Miss	Danielle	D.		Garden State
1,009.00	Gladstone	Miss	Tara Rose		Vice President	Waterside La
1,010.00	Olson	Mrs.	Elizabeth	A.	Vice President	Precision Co
1,011.00	Rosiello	Mr.	Richard	L.	Accounts Payable	Raydontic La
1,012.00	Smith	Dr.	Mary	K.	Graduate School of Busine	Cal State L.A.
1,013.00	Watson	Mr.	Frank	R.	Greenskeeper	Whispering P
1,014.00	Mohr	Mrs.	Mary	M.		
1,015.00	Ramirez	Mr.	Rigoberto	R.	Author	
1,016.00	Newell	Mr.	John	J.		Newell Constr
1,017.00	Jones	Ms.	Alma	R.	Account Executive	Ashland Flow
1,018.00	Schumack	Dr.	Susita	M.	Neurosurgeon	Physician's H
1,019.00	Smith	Dr.	Savitha	V.		Slybacks Pap
1,020.00	Smith	Mr.	John	Q.		
1,021.00	Smythe	Ms.	Janet	L.		
1,022.00	Dewey	Mr.	Frank	R.	Senior Partner	Dewey, Cheat
1,023.00	Adams	Mr.	Andy	A.	President	ABC Corporat
1,024.00	Wilson	Dr.	Ted		Psychology Department	Pine Valley U
1,025.00	Zastrow	Dr.	Ruth		Internal Medicine	Scripps Clinic

didn't do so in Figure 12.2, we could have started a new page each time the area code changed. This would simplify distribution of the report if we wanted each of our sales reps to be responsible for calling customers in a specific area code.

We also added the Gift Corner logo and company name, customized the report title, used contrasting colors, and placed a horizontal line, the date, and the page number at the bottom of each page.

FIGURE 12.2

A custom report of the CustList table showing customer name, phone number, extension, city, and state grouped by Area Code, Last Name, and First Name

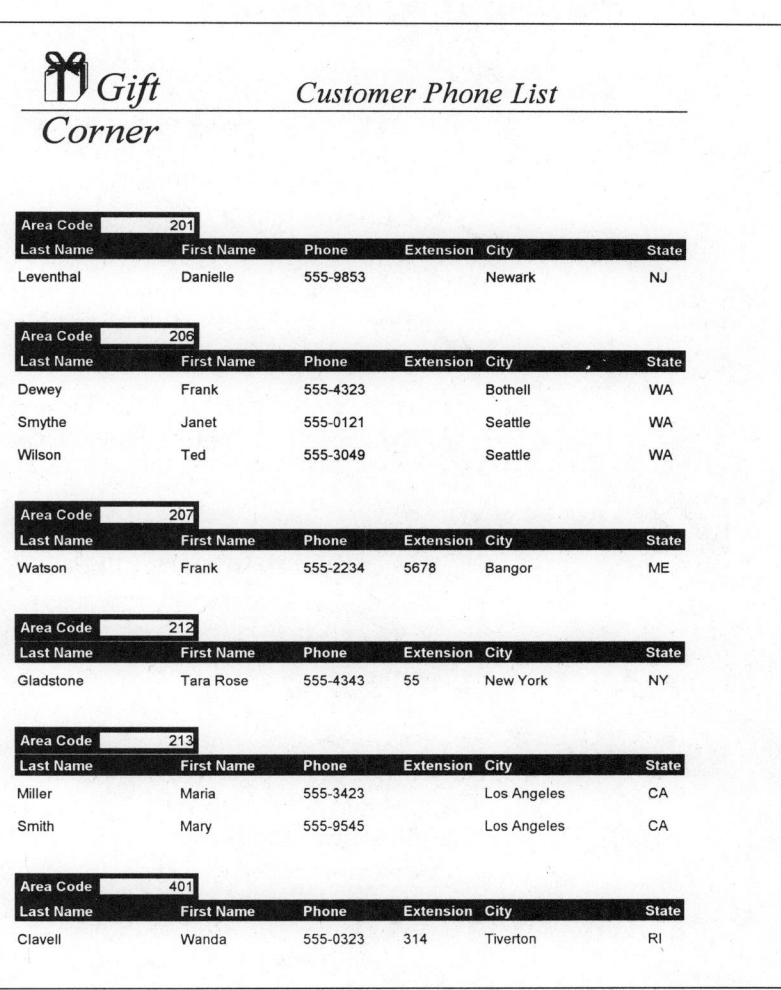

Area Code 201					
Last Name	First Name	Phone	Extension	City	State
Leventhal	Danielle	555-9853		Newark	NJ

Area Code 206					
Last Name	First Name	Phone	Extension	City	State
Dewey	Frank	555-4323		Bothell	WA
Smythe	Janet	555-0121		Seattle	WA
Wilson	Ted	555-3049		Seattle	WA

Area Code 207					
Last Name	First Name	Phone	Extension	City	State
Watson	Frank	555-2234	5678	Bangor	ME

Area Code 212					
Last Name	First Name	Phone	Extension	City	State
Gladstone	Tara Rose	555-4343	55	New York	NY

Area Code 213					
Last Name	First Name	Phone	Extension	City	State
Miller	Maria	555-3423		Los Angeles	CA
Smith	Mary	555-9545		Los Angeles	CA

Area Code 401					
Last Name	First Name	Phone	Extension	City	State
Clavell	Wanda	555-0323	314	Tiverton	RI

Customer Phone List

▶▶ *Using the Report Expert*

The report Expert can help you create nice-looking reports almost instantly. The steps for using the report Expert are like those given in Chapter 11 for the form Expert, but we'll repeat them below to save you some page-flipping.

▶ *Creating a New Report*

Here's how to use an Expert to create a new report:

1. Start the Expert in any of the following ways:

- Click the Expert button in the Toolbar (shown at left).
- Choose Help ➤ Experts.
- Choose File ➤ New ➤ Report (or any of the equivalent shortcuts on the Toolbar or Project Viewer), and click the Report Expert button in the New Report dialog box. Then skip to step 3.

2. Click the *Report* button in the Expert Control Panel dialog box. (We'll discuss the mailing labels Expert later in this chapter.)

▶▶ **N O T E**

If your system includes Experts from third-party developers, you can click the Next>> and <<Prev buttons in the Expert Control Panel to locate those add-on Experts.

3. When the first Paradox Report Expert dialog box appears, select the type of report you want. You can either click on the button that illustrates the desired report design or click the numbered option that describes it. To continue with the next step, click the Next>> button.

4. To complete your report, follow the prompts on the dialog boxes that follow and use the guidelines below:

- To figure out what to do in any dialog box, read the prompts carefully.
- To continue to the next dialog box after making your selections, click the <u>N</u>ext>> button.
- To return to the previous dialog box (in case you change your mind about selections you've already made), click the <<<u>P</u>rev button.
- To cancel the Expert and return to the Desktop without creating a report, click the <u>C</u>ancel button.
- To get help at any time, click the <u>H</u>elp button.
- When you reach the final dialog box, click the <u>C</u>reate button to design your report.

When the Expert is done and the report appears on the screen, you can click the Print button in the Toolbar to print it. Or, if you want to customize it further, click the Design button in the Toolbar (or press F8 or choose <u>V</u>iew ➤ <u>D</u>esign Report) and make whatever change you like. When you're ready to save your creation, simply close the report's window, answer <u>Y</u>es when asked about saving the document, type in a file name, and choose OK.

 ▶ ▶ **T I P**

> **See "Customizing the Experts" at the end of Chapter 11 to learn about tailoring the Experts.**

▶▶ *General Steps for Designing and Using a Custom Report*

The Expert can provide a perfect starting point for many reports, and it may do the trick for most reports. But if you'd like more control over your reports, be sure to read this chapter further. (If you just want to learn how to use the mailing label Expert, skip to "Using the Mailing Label Expert," later in this chapter.)

The steps below summarize how to design and work with custom reports. (See Chapters 10 and 11 for more detailed instructions.)

1. Choose File ➤ New ➤ Report from the menus; or inspect the Open Report button in the Toolbar or right-click the Reports icon in the Project Viewer and choose New.
2. Click the Data Model / Layout Diagram button. Then, select a table, query, or data model as the basis for the design. If you wish, you can inspect the table in the right side of the Data Model dialog box, to review the list of its fields. When you're finished using the Data Model dialog box, choose OK.
3. In the Design Layout dialog box, specify the design layout. Initially, Paradox assigns the Tabular layout to reports.
4. If you want to remove or reorder fields, click the Show Fields button in the Design Layout dialog box, then remove (or rearrange) fields as needed. Choose Show Layout when you're done.
5. If you've selected a Single Record or Multi-Record style, decide whether you want labeled or unlabeled fields.
6. If you want to choose a style sheet, open the Style Sheet drop-down list and select the style sheet you want.
7. Choose OK in the Design Layout dialog box to open the Report Design window.
8. Customize the design as you wish, then preview it by clicking the View Data button in the Toolbar or pressing F8. Return to Design View as necessary (by clicking the Design button in the Toolbar or pressing F8) and make further changes.
9. Choose File ➤ Save to save the report, then close the Design window if you wish.
10. If you want Paradox to use this report when you click the Quick Report button in Table View, open the table to be associated with this report, then right-click the Quick Report button. Select the report file name and choose OK from the dialog box that appears. Now choose Properties ➤ View Properties ➤ Save to save your changes.

Nov 08 Cannot do this on Mesh as I get "Cannot rebind to chosen table"

11. To open an existing report, choose File ➤ Open ➤ Report. Then choose the file name of the report, change the table if you want to view a different table's data with this report's layout, choose an

Open Mode (View Data, Design, or Print), and choose OK. You can also double-click a report name in the Project Viewer, or right-click the report name and choose View Data, Print, Design, Print With, or View With from the property menu.

▶▶ **TIP**

> **To use the currently assigned Quick Report as the basis for a new design, click the Quick Report button in the Table window, then click the Design button in the Toolbar or press F8.**

▶▶ *Choosing a Page Layout*

Initially, any reports you design are set up for the printer. If you'd like to change the page layout settings, choose Report ➤ Page Layout in the Report Design window. Figure 12.3 shows the Page Layout dialog box for a report.

FIGURE 12.3

The default Page Layout dialog box for a report

Page Layout

Design For:
- ● Printer
- ○ Screen

Orientation:
- ● Portrait
- ○ Landscape

Custom Size:
- Width: 8.50
- Height: 11.00

Paper Sizes:
- Letter 8 ½ x 11 in
- Legal 8 ½ x 14 in
- Executive 7 ¼ x 10 ½ in
- A4 210 x 297 mm
- Envelope #10 4 1/8 x 9 ½ in

Units:
- Centimeters
- Inches

Margins:
- Left: 0.50
- Right: 0.50
- Top: 0.50
- Bottom: 0.50

OK   Cancel   Help

Formatted Reports

Ch. **12**

▶▶ **T I P**

The report Expert lets you choose a printer, page orientation, and paper size for your instant report.

When you design a report for the printer, the dialog box includes a list of paper sizes to choose from. You can choose any of these options, or you can define a custom size by entering the Width and Height you want. You can also change the Units of measure, the paper orientation (Portrait or Landscape), and the Left, Right, Top, and Bottom margin settings.

If you prefer to design for the screen, click the Screen option in the Design For area. The same basic options are available, with the exception of Paper Sizes (this changes to Screen Size) and Orientation.

When you're finished with the Page Layout dialog box, choose OK.

▶▶ **N O T E**

When designing for the printer, only fonts installed for the currently active printer are available. Paradox will do its best to match the screen fonts displayed in the Report window to the printed output. When designing for the screen, you can use any available screen fonts.

▶▶ *Understanding Report Bands*

Not surprisingly, most of the techniques for placing design objects, changing their properties, and creating special effects in reports are exactly as described in Chapters 10 and 11. However, unlike forms, reports contain separate sections, called *bands*, that control where objects will appear in the final report. The four types of bands in reports are described below.

Report Band   Contains data to be printed at the beginning and end of the report.

Page Band   Contains data to be printed at the top and bottom of each page.

Group Band   (optional) Lets you group the records of the table. See "Grouping Your Data," later in this chapter, for more on group bands.

Record Band   Contains the table's records.

▶ *Displaying Band Labels*

You can choose Properties ➤ Band Labels to display or hide the band labels in the design window. Figure 12.4 shows band labels turned on (checked), while Figure 12.5 shows band labels turned off (unchecked).

When band labels are on, each section of the report is separated by a boundary line containing a label with the name of the band and two arrows that point in the direction of the record band. (The arrows point down in headers and up in footers.) When the band labels are hidden,

FIGURE 12.4 ▶

The Report Design window with the Properties ➤ Band labels option checked (turned on)

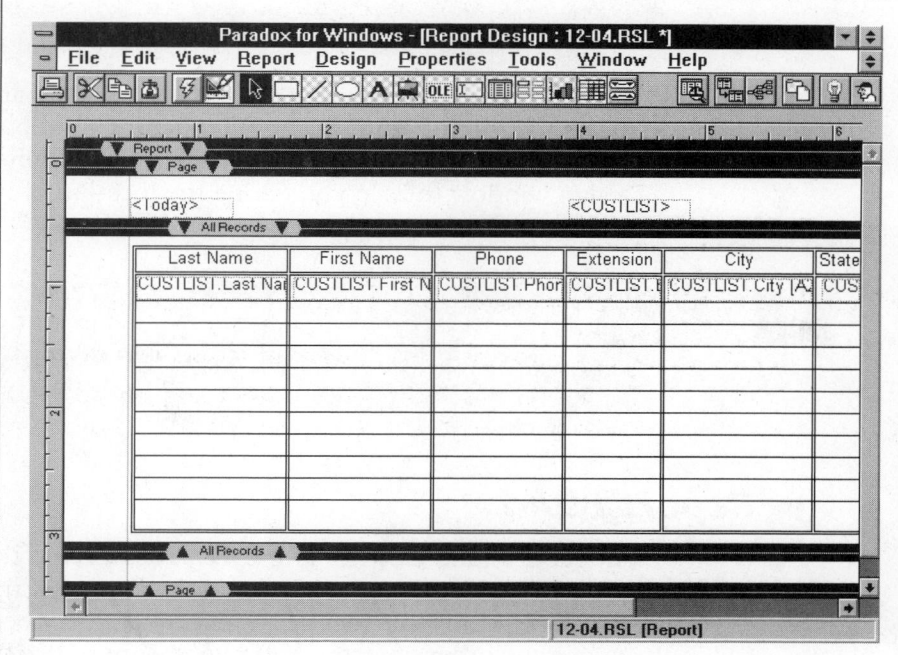

Formatted Reports

Ch. **12**

FIGURE 12.5

The Report Design window with the Properties ➤ Band labels option unchecked (turned off)

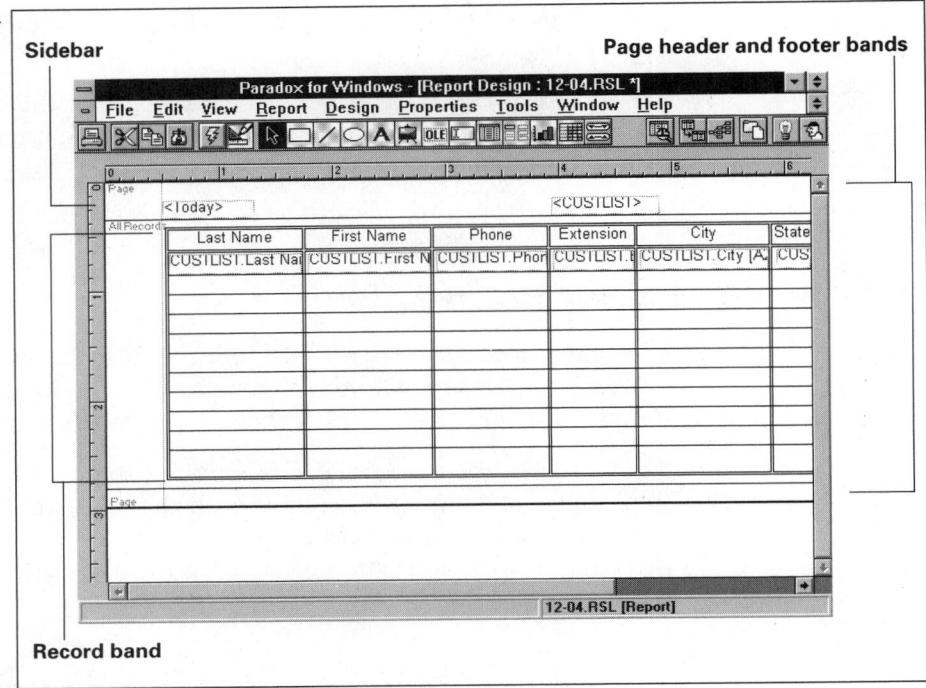

the labels disappear (though thin boundary lines and band names are still visible, as in Figure 12.5). Band labels and boundary lines never appear when you preview or print the report. They're only used in the Design window to help you define the location of information on various parts of the report.

 ▶ ▶ **T I P**

Turning off the band labels can give you a better idea of what the final report will look like.

▶ *Report Band*

The report band consists of the *report header* and the *report footer.* The report header appears at the top of the Design window. Any objects placed in this area appear only once, at the very beginning of the report (before any other objects). You might want to use the report header for a report title, an abstract, an introduction, or your company logo. Initially, the report header is empty.

The report footer appears at the bottom of the Design window, and like the report header it is initially empty. Any objects placed in the report footer appear at the end of the report, after everything else has been printed.

▶ Page Band

The *page band* contains objects to be printed at the top and bottom of each page of the report. Like the report band, it consists of a header and a footer. The page header appears just below the report header, and any objects placed there are printed at the top of each page. Note that Paradox automatically inserts into the page header special fields for the current date <Today>, the table name, and the word "Page" followed by the current page number <Page number>.

TIP

The report Expert lets you choose what information will appear in the page bands.

The page footer appears just above the report footer. Objects placed in the page footer are printed at the bottom of each page.

TIP

You can choose View ➤ Zoom ➤ Best Fit, then select the predefined page number, table name, and page number objects and drag them from the page header to the page footer.

▶ Record Band

The *record band* contains the records of the table you're reporting on. The data objects initially placed into the record band depend on the style of report you chose in the Design Layout dialog box. Of course, you have complete freedom to add other objects to the record band and to delete any objects placed there.

The style sheet you select in the Design Layout dialog box (or the default style sheet assigned via <u>P</u>roperties ➤ <u>D</u>esktop ➤ Forms And <u>R</u>eports) also will affect the appearance of new objects in your design. For example, if we had chosen the *c:\pdoxwin\borland.fp* style sheet that comes with Paradox when we filled in the Design Layout dialog box for Figures 12.4 and 12.5, the table object and page band objects would be shaded instead of white.

▶ Resizing Bands

Paradox places the page, report, and record bands for you, and you cannot remove them. However, you can leave bands blank, and you can resize them with your mouse to add or remove extra space. (There is no keyboard method for resizing bands.)

> **Depending on your hardware, you may find it easier to resize bands when the band labels are turned off. Experiment to find the best method.**

Here are the basic steps for resizing a band:

1. Select the band you want to resize by clicking on it. The name of the band you selected will appear at the right edge of the status bar. If band labels are turned on, the selected band will change color when you've selected it. (To deselect a band, press Esc.)

2. Move the mouse pointer (*without clicking*) to the top or bottom of the selected band until the pointer changes to a two-headed vertical arrow.

   - If you move the pointer to the top of the selected band, you can adjust the space above any objects in the band.

   - If you move the pointer to the bottom of the selected band, you can adjust the space below any objects in the band.

3. Now drag the band up or down. As you drag the band, the status bar at the lower-left corner of the window indicates which band you're resizing and displays the current measurements of the band. For example, the message

Resizing #Page_Footer: 8.50 by .25

means that you're resizing the page footer band, which is currently 8.50 inches wide by .25 inch high. As you drag the band up or down, the height will increase or decrease. Increasing the band height adds white space, decreasing it removes white space.

4. When the band is the correct height, release the mouse button. If you make a mistake in resizing the band, just choose <u>E</u>dit ➤ <u>U</u>ndo or press Alt+Backspace immediately.

▶ ▶ **N O T E**

> **You cannot resize a band to make it smaller than the objects it contains. To close a band completely, delete any objects it contains, then resize it (be sure to scroll to the right edge of the window when looking for objects to delete). If necessary, use <u>P</u>roperties ➤ <u>Z</u>oom to zoom out so that you can see the entire design at once.**

Table 12.1 contains a complete list of rules for resizing all the bands, including group bands, which are described later in this chapter.

▶ **TABLE 12.1:** *Rules for Resizing Bands*

Report Header, Page Header, or Group Header Bands...	
To Change...	**Select the Band You Want, Then Drag**...
Space above objects in the band	Upper band line (near top edge of the band) up or down. Dragging up increases the space above objects, dragging down decreases the space.
Space below objects in the band	Lower band line (near the label of the next band) up or down. Dragging up decreases the space below objects, dragging down increases the space.

► **TABLE 12.1:** *Rules for Resizing Bands (continued)*

Record Bands...	
To Change...	**Select the Record Band, Then Drag...**
Space above objects in the band	Upper record band up or down. Dragging up increases the space above objects, dragging down decreases the space.
Space below objects in the band	Lower record band up or down. Dragging up decreases the space below objects, dragging down increases the space.
Report, Page, or Group Footer Bands...	
To Change...	**Select the Band You Want, Then Drag...**
Space above objects in the band	Upper band line (near the previous band's label) up or down. Dragging up increases the space above objects, dragging down decreases the space.
Space below objects in the band	Lower band line (near the bottom of the band) up or down. Dragging up decreases the space below objects, dragging down increases the space.

At first you might find resizing bands a bit tricky, but with some practice you'll get the hang of it. Here are some secrets to accurate band resizing:

- Turn band labels on or off, depending on which method you prefer.

- Be sure to click the band you want (look at the status bar for feedback). Then wait for the mouse pointer to change to a two-headed arrow before dragging the selected band. This way you'll know exactly which band line you'll be dragging.

- Watch the left edge of the status bar as you drag to determine whether you're increasing or decreasing the band height.

- If you make a mistake and resize the wrong band, choose Edit ➤ Undo or press Alt+Backspace right away.

- Refer frequently to the guidelines in Table 12.1.

▶ *Placing and Using Objects in Report Bands*

You create, define, inspect, and otherwise manipulate objects in reports just as you do in forms. Thus, to add an object, you select a tool in the Toolbar, click in the band where you want the object to appear, then drag to define the object.

 ▶▶**TIP**

> **If the band is too narrow for the object, you can resize the band before placing the object. Resizing is usually optional, however, because Paradox increases the band size automatically when necessary.**

Following are some useful points to remember when working with objects in a report:

- To select all the objects in a band, click in the band, then choose Edit ➤ Select All. Because each band is treated separately, you cannot select all objects in the report at once.

- To move an object from one band to another, select the object and drag it to the new location.

- To copy or cut an object from one band to another, select the object, then click the Cut To Clipboard or Copy To Clipboard button in the Toolbar. Click in the band where you want the object to appear, then click the Paste From Clipboard button in the Toolbar.

- Certain object properties are different in forms and reports. For example, although scroll bars are available to help you design a report, they never appear when you run reports. We'll discuss the most important properties in this chapter, then summarize the rest in Appendix E.

▶▶ *Grouping Your Data*

Paradox offers two ways to sort your records. First, it lets you define *group bands*, which you can use to group (sort) your data. Groups can be based on the following:

- The value in a certain field (for example, by state or area code), which effectively sorts the data by that field. When you preview or print the report, the groups will be sorted in alphabetic or numeric order depending on the type of field you selected.

- A range of data. For example, you can group records based on the first four characters of the customer's last name, by $2500 increments in the customer's credit limit, or by the day, week, month, or quarter of the customer's start date.

- A specified number of records. For example, the report could print a line or leave some extra space after every ten records.

 The second method is even easier: Simply inspect the record band, choose the Sort property, and complete the Sort Record Band dialog box using the same methods you learned in Chapter 8. You can sort on any field in the table. When you're finished, choose OK. If you use record sorting with group bands, the group bands are sorted first, then the records are sorted within each group.

▶ Using Nested Groups

When using group bands, you can define many levels of grouping, where the outermost group specifies the main (primary) sort order, the next group specifies the secondary sort order, and so forth. When one group band lies within another one, it is said to be *nested*.

In Figure 12.6 the outermost group band is based on the Credit Limit field. Nested within that group band is a group band based on the State field. This arrangement tells Paradox to print records in Credit Limit order, with records grouped by State within identical credit limits. We used record band sorting to organize the records further by Last Name, First Name, and MI (Middle Initial) within each Credit Limit and State. Figure 12.7 shows a sample printout using this design.

FIGURE 12.6

The outermost group band, Credit Limit, defines the primary sort order. The next group band, State, defines the secondary sort order.

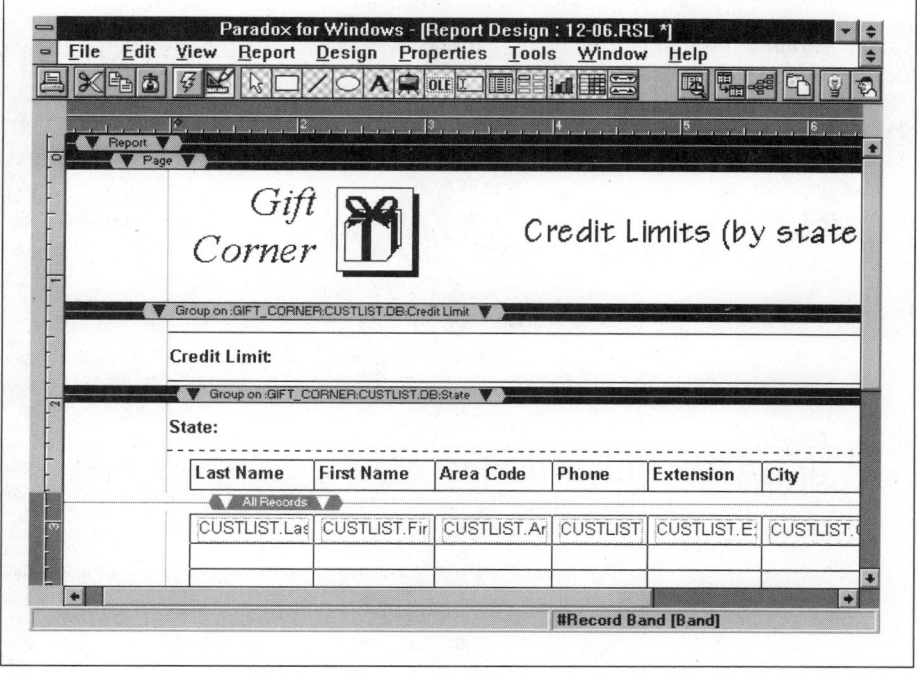

NOTE

Group bands are not ideal for sorting multi-record reports because Paradox will start a new multi-record object each time the group changes. This will happen even if you've removed any objects from the group bands and sized the bands as small as possible. If you need to produce sorted records in a multi-record report, inspect the record band, choose Sort, and complete the Sort Record Band dialog box.

FIGURE 12.7 ►

A sample printout from the report design shown in Figure 12.6. Notice that records are in order by credit limit, and within identical credit limits, by state.

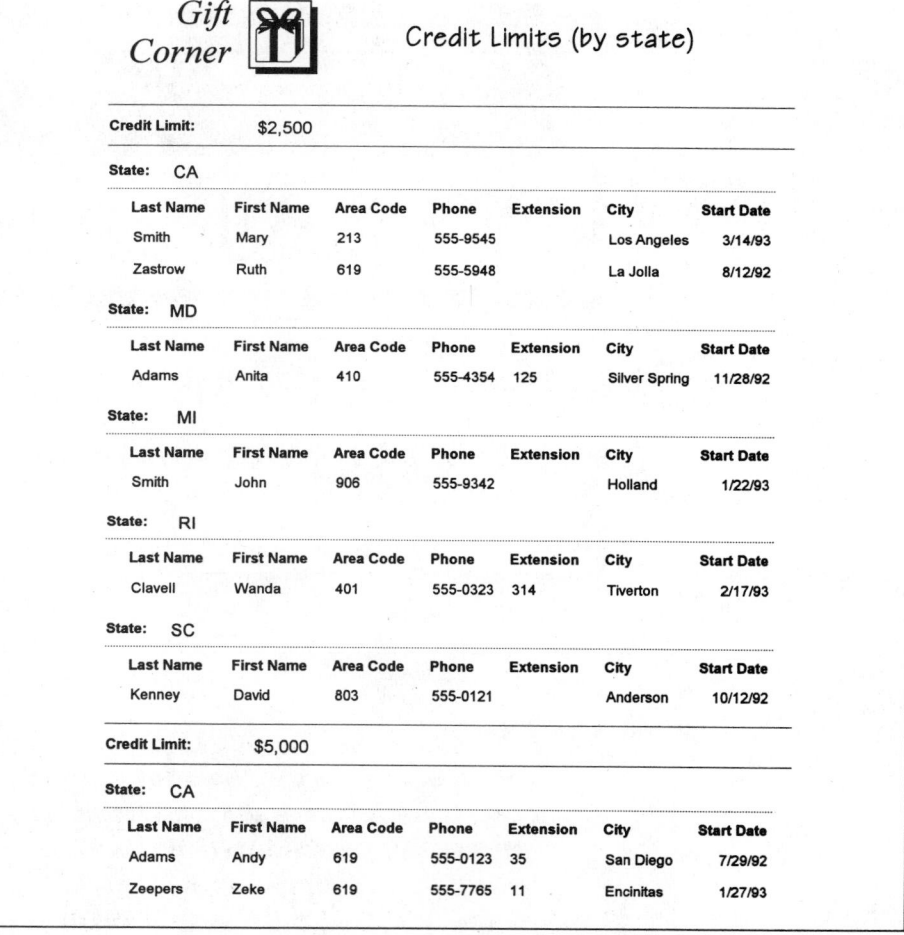

► Adding Group Bands

To add a group band to your report design, follow the steps below.

1. If you've already added one or more groups, click the group header band that's one level higher than the band you want to add. If the report doesn't have any bands yet, you can move on to step 2 without clicking a band.

2. Click the Add Band button in the Toolbar (shown at left), or choose Report ➤ Add Band. You'll see the Define Group dialog box shown in Figure 12.8.

3. Choose the type of grouping you want as described in the following sections of this chapter.

▶ ▶ N O T E

As you make selections, the Band Label at the top of the Define Group dialog box reflects your choices.

4. Choose OK. The newly defined group band will appear in the Report Design window, as in Figure 12.9.

Each group you define consists of a group header, which is identified as a ▼ **Group on** ▼ band above the record band, and a group footer, which is identified as a ▲ **Group on** ▲ band below the record band. If you choose to group by a field without specifying a range or number of records, Paradox will automatically insert a labeled field object for the

FIGURE 12.8 ▶

The Define Group dialog box

```
┌──────────────────────────── Define Group ─────────────────────────┐
│ ┌──┐                                                               │
│ │▦ │  Band Label:  Group on CUSTLIST.DB:Cust No                   │
│ └──┘                                                               │
│  ● Group By Field Value                                           │
│    Table:              Field:            ☐ Range Group:           │
│   ┌────────────┐   ┌──────────────┐   ┌────────────────────┐     │
│   │ CUSTLIST.DB│   │ Cust No     ↑│   │                    │     │
│   │            │   │ Last Name    │   ├────────────────────┤     │
│   │            │   │ Mr/Mrs       │   │ Day                │     │
│   │            │   │ First Name   │   │ Week               │     │
│   │            │   │ MI           │   │ Month              │     │
│   │            │   │ Department/Title │ Quarter            │     │
│   │            │   │ Company      │   │ Year               │     │
│   │            │   │ Address      │   │                    │     │
│   │            │   │ City         │   │                    │     │
│   │            │   │ State       ↓│   │                    │     │
│   └────────────┘   └──────────────┘   └────────────────────┘     │
│  ○ Group By Record        Number of Records: [        ]           │
│       ┌────────┐   ┌────────┐   ┌────────┐                        │
│       │   OK   │   │ Cancel │   │  Help  │                        │
│       └────────┘   └────────┘   └────────┘                        │
└────────────────────────────────────────────────────────────────┘
```

Formatted Reports

Ch. **12**

field you choose into the group band header (see Figure 12.9). Otherwise, the band header and footer will just contain empty space, which creates a gap between groups of records. You can add any objects you wish to a group band, or you can remove the object and close up the group bands by resizing them.

▶ ▶ **T I P**

Group headings and footings can include basic math calculations and summaries such as subtotals. See Chapter 17 for details.

Regardless of how you group the records, Paradox performs the following steps for each group:

- Prints any blank space or objects in the group header.
- Prints the records in the group.

FIGURE 12.9 ▶

The Report Design window after defining a group band on the Area Code field. When printed, this report's sort order will be similar to the example in Figure 12.2. To sort the report by customer name within area code, inspect the record band and use the Sort Record Band dialog box to sort the records by Last Name, First Name, and MI (Middle Initial).

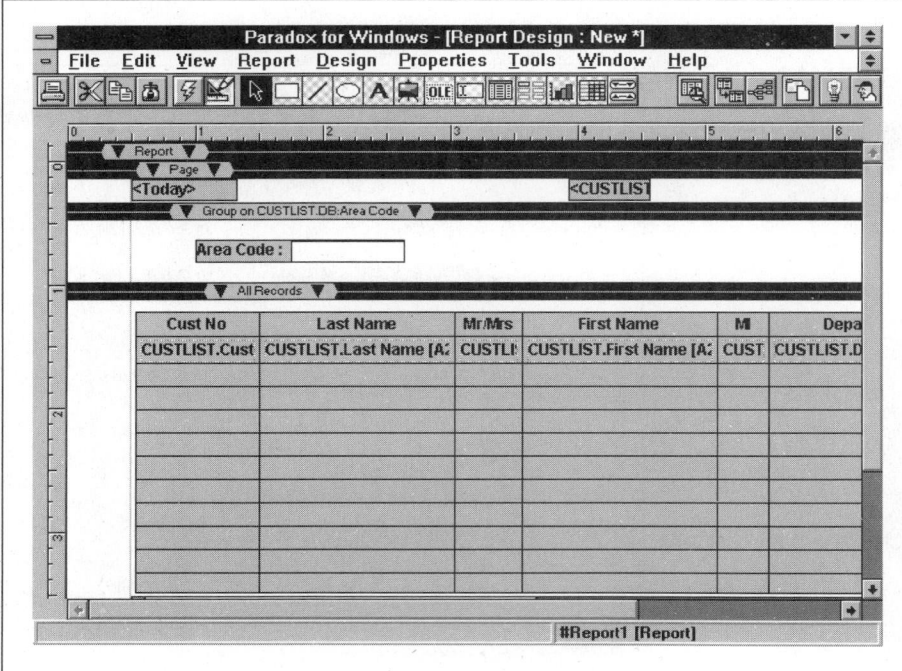

- Prints any blank space or objects in the group footer.

Now, let's look at the various grouping options available in the Define Group dialog box shown back in Figure 12.8.

Grouping on a Field Value

When you group on a field value, Paradox places all records having the same value for that field into the same group. When that field value changes, Paradox starts a new group. For example, in Figure 12.2 we grouped by Area Code and displayed the area code in the group header. Thus, the records appear in the order shown below.

> Area Code 201 heading
>   All the records in the 201 area code
>
> Area Code 206 heading
>   All the records in the 206 area code
>
> Area Code 207 heading
>   All the records in the 207 area code
>
> and so forth...

To group by a field value, click the Group By Field Value option in the Define Group dialog box (if it isn't already selected), then double-click the field you want to group by.

Grouping on a Range

You can also group records according to a range of values. To do so, click the Group By Field Value option in the Define Group dialog box (if necessary), click the field you want to group by, then check the Range Group option in the dialog box and type or choose a value.

The way you define a group range depends on the type of field you selected. For example, if you selected an alpha or memo field, you can type the number of characters to group by into the text box below Range Group. The default value is 1, which means that all values in the group must have the same first character, but the remaining characters can be different. If you prefer to group by the first few characters of a field, type the number of characters into the text box. For example, if you group by the first three characters of the Zip Code field (by entering **3** into the text box), you might see groups like these:

88201
88255
88256

91234
91245

92024
92037

If the field you're grouping by is numeric, you can type an interval size into the text box. For example, if you chose Credit Limit as the field to group on, and specified 2500 as the range, records would be sorted by the Credit Limit field, with credit limits between 0 and 2500 in the first group, credit limits between 2501 and 5000 in the second group, credit limits between 5001 and 7500 in the next group, and so on.

If you group by a date field, you can click a date option in the list that appears below the Range Group area. These date options are:

Day   Records with identical dates are placed in groups. For example, records with a Start Date of 1/1/95 are in one group, records with 1/2/95 are in the next group, and so forth.

Week   Records are grouped by week (from Sunday to Saturday). For example, records with dates from 1/1/95 (a Sunday) to 1/7/95 (a Saturday) are in one group; records with dates from 1/8/95 (a Sunday) to 1/14/95 (a Saturday) are in the next group, and so forth.

Month   Records are grouped by month. With this option, all the January 1995 dates would appear in one group, February 1995 dates in the next group, and so forth. Any records with January 1996 dates would follow records dated in December of 1995.

Quarter   Records are grouped by quarter. For example, all records in the first quarter of 1995 (January, February, and March) form one group, records in the next quarter of 1995 (April, May, and June) form the next group, records in the third quarter of 1995 (July, August, and September) form the next group, and records in the fourth quarter of 1995 (October, November, and December) form the next. Any records in the first quarter of 1996 would follow records in the last quarter of 1995.

Year Records are grouped by year. Records with 1995 dates are in one group, records with 1996 dates are in the next group, and so on.

Figure 12.10 shows the Define Group dialog box with the Start Date range defined by Quarter.

FIGURE 12.10 ▶

The Define Group dialog box with the Start Date range defined by Quarter

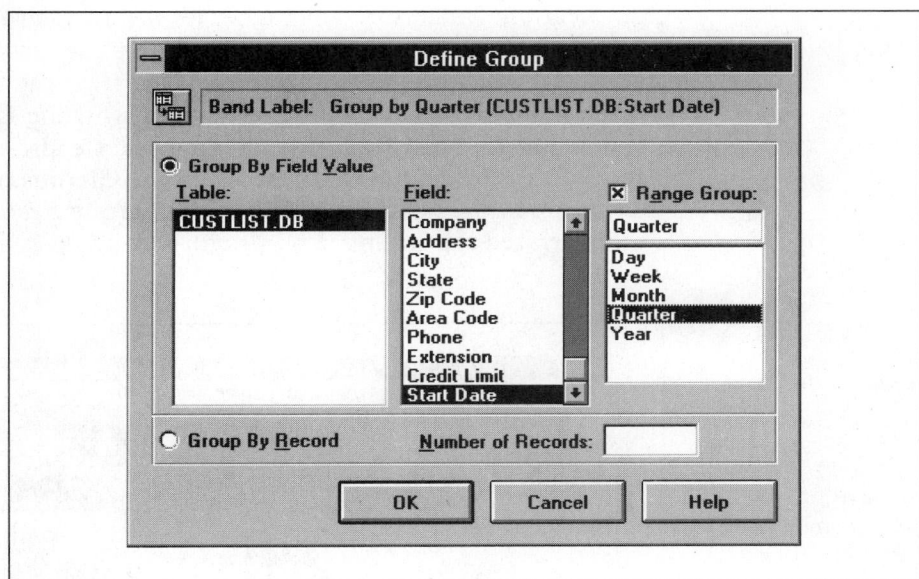

Grouping on a Record Count

To group on a record count, click the Group By Record option in the Define Group dialog box, then type the Number Of Records you want in each group.

The Group By Record option doesn't actually sort records. Instead, it organizes records into equal-sized groups in the printed report. For example, if you enter 5 as the number of records to group by, Paradox will place a blank space between groups of five records.

Formatted Reports

Ch. **12**

► Deleting and Rearranging Group Bands

To remove a group band, simply select it and press the Del key. The band and any objects in it will disappear.

If you've defined several groups in your report and want to rearrange them, click the *group header* of the band you want to move, move your mouse pointer to an empty area of the header, and drag the band to its new location. Make sure any higher level sorting groups appear above the lower level groups. For example, to group the records in Figure 12.6 by state, then by credit limit within each state, drag the group header for the State group above the group header for the Credit Limit group, as shown in Figure 12.11. (In this example, we also moved the table header from the State group header to the Credit Limit group header, and swapped the horizontal lines in each group header.) The first page of this printed report appears in Figure 12.12.

FIGURE 12.11 ►

We revised the example in Figure 12.6 so that the outermost group band (primary sort order) is State. The next group band, Credit Limit, defines the secondary sort order. We also moved the table header from the State band to the Credit Limit band and rearranged the horizontal lines.

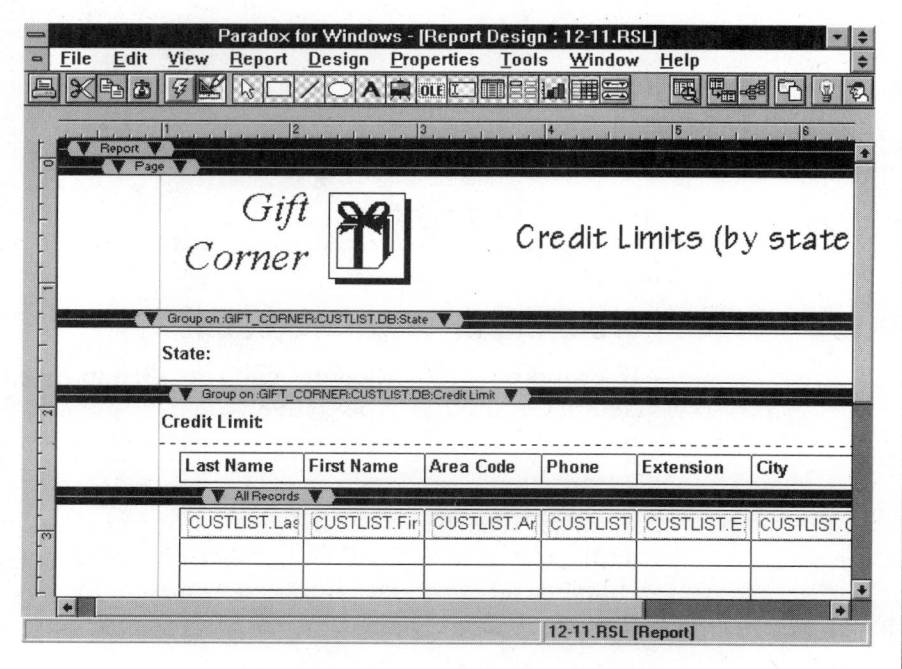

FIGURE 12.12

Page 1 of the printed output from the report design shown in Figure 12.11. Notice that records are now in order by state, and within state, by credit limit.

Gift Corner   Credit Limits (by state)

State: CA

Credit Limit: $2,500

Last Name	First Name	Area Code	Phone	Extension	City	Start Date
Smith	Mary	213	555-9545		Los Angeles	3/14/93
Zastrow	Ruth	619	555-5948		La Jolla	8/12/92

Credit Limit: $5,000

Last Name	First Name	Area Code	Phone	Extension	City	Start Date
Adams	Andy	619	555-0123	35	San Diego	7/29/92
Zeepers	Zeke	619	555-7765	11	Encinitas	1/27/93

Credit Limit: $10,000

Last Name	First Name	Area Code	Phone	Extension	City	Start Date
Miller	Maria	213	555-3423		Los Angeles	12/15/92

State: IL

Credit Limit: $5,000

Last Name	First Name	Area Code	Phone	Extension	City	Start Date
Rosiello	Richard	708	555-1234		Chicago	8/29/92

State: MD

Credit Limit: $2,500

Last Name	First Name	Area Code	Phone	Extension	City	Start Date
Adams	Anita	410	555-4354	125	Silver Spring	11/28/92

Tuesday, July 19, 1994   Page 1

Formatted Reports

Ch. 12

▶ *Redefining a Group*

You can redefine a group at any time by inspecting the group band you want to change, then choosing Define Group. From the list of field names that appears, choose a different field for the group, or click on the header (...) to open the Define Group dialog box.

▶ ▶ **N O T E**

> **Redefining a group doesn't automatically redefine the field in the group header. You'll need to do that separately.**

▶ Choosing the Sort Direction

Normally, Paradox assumes you want to print grouped records in ascending sorted order. If you want Paradox to sort the group bands in descending order, inspect the header or footer of the group band you want to change, then choose Sort Order ➤ Descending. To switch the sort direction back to Ascending, inspect the header or footer again, and choose Sort Order ➤ Ascending.

You can also sort individual fields in the record band in ascending or descending order. Just inspect the record band, choose Sort, and put the appropriate fields into the Sort Order list in the Sort Record Band dialog box. To toggle the sort between ascending and descending order, click the field you want to change in the Sort Order list and then click the Sort Direction button; or just double-click the appropriate field. (See Chapter 8 for more details.)

▶ ▶ **N O T E**

> **If your report also includes group bands that are grouped by field value, those group band field names will not appear in the Fields list of the Sort Record Band dialog box. That's because the group band sort fields take precedence over any sort order you define for the record band.**

▶ Sorting without Grouping

The easiest way to sort without grouping is to inspect the record band, select the Sort property, and fill in the Sort Record Band dialog box.

But if you'd rather use group bands, you should remember that it is the blank space and any objects placed in the group header and footer bands that create the visual breaks between groups. If the group header and footer bands are empty, the records will still be sorted, but no blank lines or objects will appear between the groups. This means that you can use group bands to sort records without grouping them, simply by deleting any objects in the group header and footer bands and resizing (closing) the group header, group footer, and record bands to squeeze out any extra blank space.

When using group bands to sort records in a tabular report, your report may look better if you inspect the table, choose Detach Header, and move the table header into the page band, or into an appropriate band above the record band. For example, you could move the header into the Credit Limit band as shown in Figure 12.11. After moving the table header, you may also want to move the table up within the record band. Finally, resize the record band to remove excess space below the table frame.

▶ ▶ N O T E

Resizing or dragging the table frame also resizes or moves a detached table header. Likewise, resizing or dragging a detached table header resizes or moves the table frame.

If you want even more control over the table headings than a detached table header offers, try this: Make sure all the table's columns fit within the band and that none are clipped off at the right edge. If necessary, narrow or remove some table columns. Inspect the table and choose Detach Header. Next select the table header (if it isn't selected already) and choose Edit ➤ Select All; this will select all the text fields in the header. Now click the Copy To Clipboard button in the Toolbar or press Ctrl+Ins. Press Esc to select the table header, then press Del to delete it. Next, click in the band where you want the left-most header text field to appear (widen the band if necessary), and click the Paste From Clipboard button in the Toolbar or press Shift+Ins. If you wish, draw a box around all the text fields in the new header. You can then adjust the spacing of the text fields or the color and frame of the surrounding box as needed.

▶ ▶ **T I P**

Choosing a grid style of None for the table frame often gives attractive results when you're designing your own table headers.

▶ Controlling the Sort Order for Reports

Remember that Paradox offers four ways to sort reports:

- You can use the Table ➤ Sort or Tools ➤ Utilities ➤ Sort menu options (Chapter 8), or you can use a query that produces a sorted Answer table (Chapter 9), then print the report from the sorted table.

- You can base the report directly on a saved query that produces a sorted Answer table (Chapters 9 and 10).

- You can define group bands that group and sort the report, as described above.

- You can inspect the record band, select the Sort property, and complete the Sort Record Band dialog box using the techniques described in Chapter 8.

You'll have little trouble defining the perfect sort order for your reports if you keep this important point in mind: Group band sorts override sorts performed outside the report by queries and table sort operations. Thus, there's no point in sorting your table ahead of time if your report will contain group bands.

Remember that if you're using group bands in a report design and also want to sort records by other fields in the table, you should set up the group bands, then sort the record band. For example, to sort the grouped reports in Figures 12.2, 12.7, and 12.12 by customer name, you would first define the higher level bands such as Area Code (Figure 12.2), Credit Limit and State (Figure 12.7), or State and Credit Limit (Figure 12.12). Next, inspect the record band, choose Sort, and add the Last Name, First Name, and MI fields to the Sort Order list in the Sort Record Band dialog box. That's how we sorted reports in this chapter by name within some other grouping. For reports involving table objects (see Figures 12.2, 12.11, 12.12, and 12.16), we also detached the table headers and then moved the headers into the group band above the Last Name group band.

▶▶ *Adding a Page Break to a Report*

With Paradox for Windows, it's easy to insert page breaks in a report. For example, you might want to print a page break after the report's title page. Or, you might want to start a new page whenever the area code changes in a telephone directory report. In mail merge documents, page breaks are used to start each letter on a new page.

There are two ways to add page breaks to your design:

- You can add a page break at a group band and restart numbering at one (1).

- You can add a page break anywhere, without restarting the page numbering.

▶ *Restarting the Page Numbers*

To add a page break whenever Paradox prints a particular group band and restart page numbering at one, inspect the band where you want the page break to occur, and select (check) the Start Page Numbers option on the property menu. If you change your mind, just repeat the step to remove the checkmark from the Start Page Numbers property.

▶ *Putting a Page Break Anywhere*

If you want to add a page break without restarting the page numbering at one, make sure the vertical ruler is visible (choose Properties ➤ Vertical Ruler if necessary), then click in the sidebar area where you want the page break to appear. A horizontal line will appear across the Report Design window and a marker will appear in the sidebar to indicate the position of the page break, as in Figure 12.13.

You can drag the page break marker in the sidebar area up or down to reposition the page break. (Do not drag the horizontal line itself, or you'll resize the band instead of moving the page break.)

FIGURE 12.13 ▶

You can insert a page break by clicking in the sidebar of a report design. In this example, Paradox will start a new page whenever the area code changes.

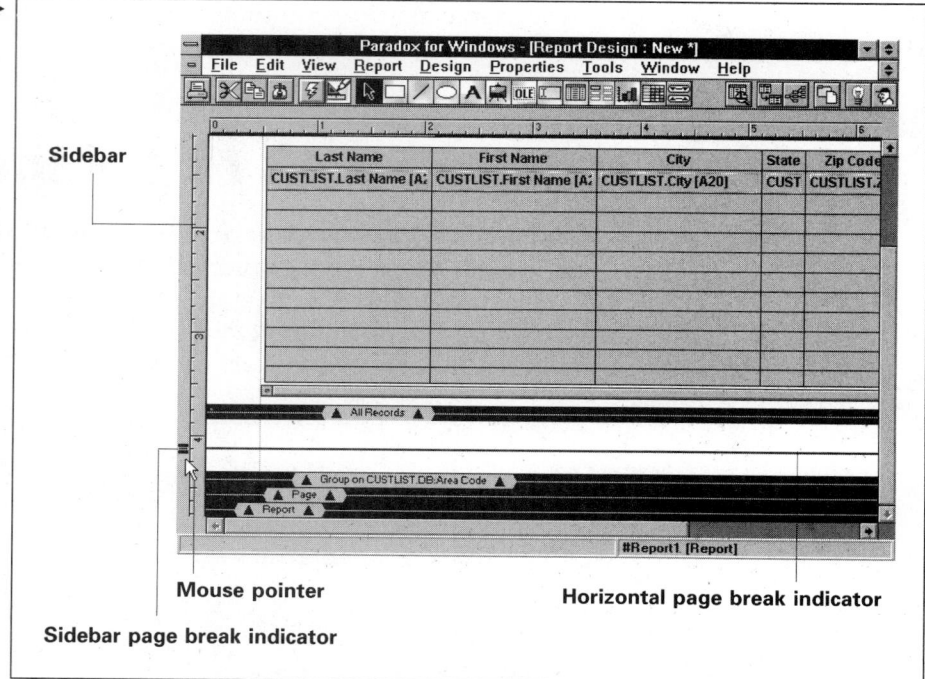

▶▶ N O T E

You cannot place a page break in the page band or within an object.

To delete a page break, drag the marker to the right, out of the sidebar. When you release the mouse button, the marker and horizontal line will disappear.

▶▶ *Inserting Fields in Text*

In general, you work with text in reports the same way you work with text in forms. In itself, that's not too remarkable—but when you insert fields within a text object, things really start to cook. For example, suppose you perform these steps:

1. Define a report for the CustList table (or any table containing names and addresses). When you get to the Design Layout dialog box, choose a Blan<u>k</u> style and choose OK.

2. Use the Text tool to place a text object in the record band, sizing it to about the width of your screen.

3. Now type **Dear** and press the spacebar.

4. Press F5 to place an undefined field within the text object at the cursor position. Now press the spacebar again and press F5 once more.

5. Type a colon (:), press ↵ a couple of times, then type a few sentences. (You can add more fields, if you wish, by pressing F5.)

6. Press Esc to select the text object. (This makes it easier to complete step 7.)

7. Select and inspect the first undefined field, select Define Field, and choose the Mr/Mrs field from the property menu. Then inspect the second undefined field and choose the Last Name field. Your screen will resemble Figure 12.14, though the actual appearance will depend on the style sheet you've chosen.

Now preview the report by clicking the View Data button in the Toolbar. *Voilà!* You see the beginnings of a form letter like the one in Figure 12.15. Notice how the field data integrates smoothly with the text. All it needs now is some more text, a page break to separate each letter, and perhaps a few embellishments.

▶ ▶ **N O T E**

Don't be concerned if the screen display doesn't match the printed output. The fonts that you see are a "best guess" of the printer fonts that will appear when you print the report. This can be disconcerting as you de-sign your report, but if you preview your work frequently and print occasionally, you'll have an easier time.

FIGURE 12.14 ▶

Fields embedded in a text object in the Report Design window

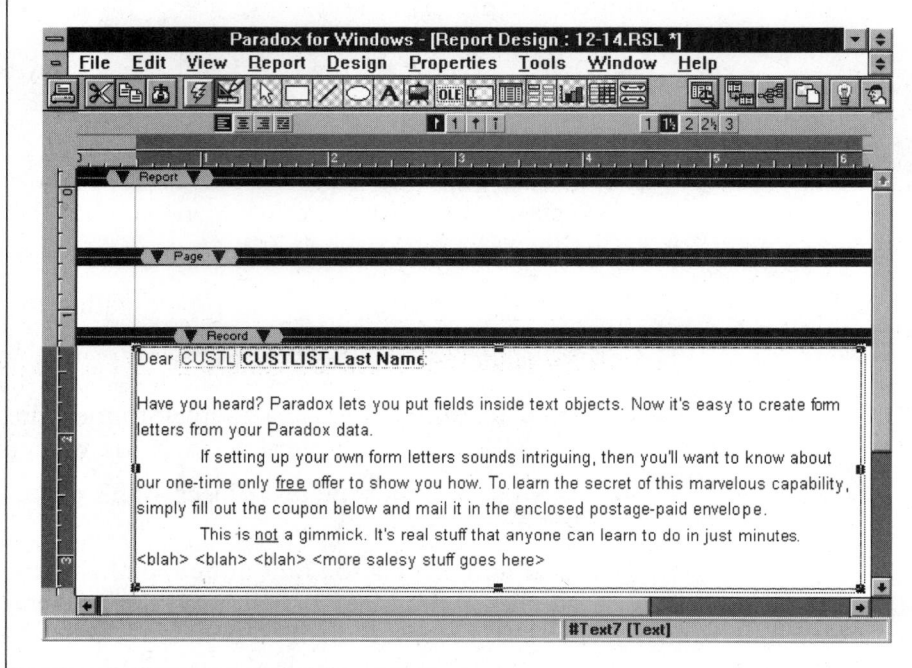

In "Designing a Mail Merge Document," later in this chapter, we'll talk more about how you can use the basic technique of embedding fields in a text object to create fancy form letters.

 ▶▶ **T I P**

This technique also works in forms, though you have less control over the spacing between text and field objects.

▶▶ *Controlling Headers, Footers, and Repeated Data*

Let's turn our attention now to the many ways you can control how and when Paradox prints the following sections of a report.

- Report headers
- Page headers and footers
- Group headers
- Repeated group values in the record band
- Objects in group headers
- Table headers

FIGURE 12.15

The sample form letters produced by the design in Figure 12.14.

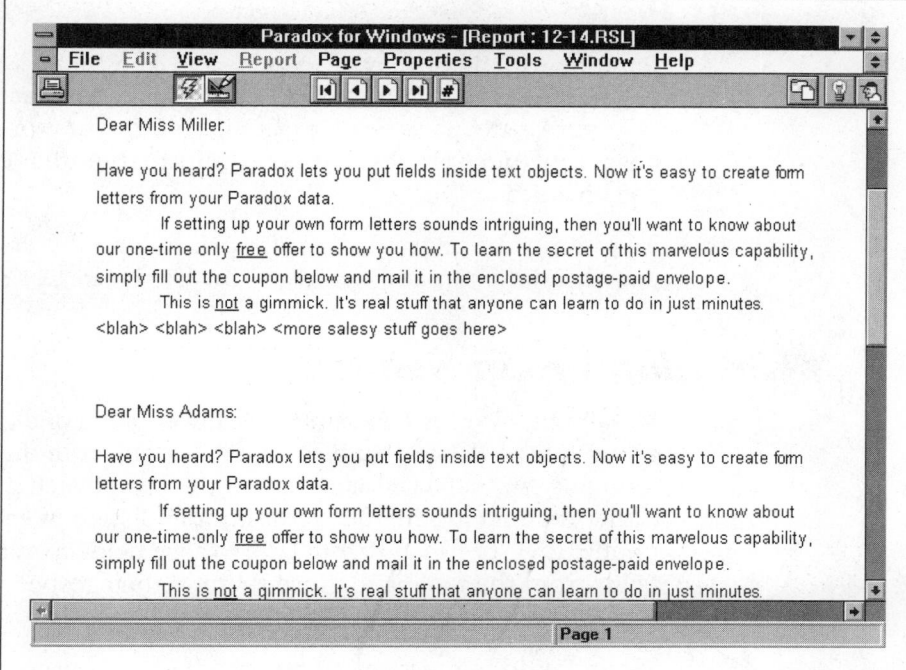

▶ *Printing Report Headers*

Normally, the report header objects print before the page header on the first page of the report. If you prefer to have the report header appear *after* the first page header, inspect the report header band and *uncheck* the Precede Page Header property.

Formatted
Reports

Ch.
12

▶ ▶ N O T E

Changing the Precede Page Header property has no effect on the Report Design window (since the bands don't move); however, when you preview the report, you'll see the order you've specified.

▶ Printing Page Headers and Footers on the First Page

Paradox usually prints the page header and footer objects on the first page of the report, but you can change this. For example, you may wish to suppress the page header or footer on the first page if your report header includes graphics or other information that clashes with the page header or footer.

To prevent the page header from printing on the first page, inspect the page header band and *uncheck* Print On 1st Page.

▶ Printing Group Headers

Recall that every group band actually consists of a group header and a group footer. When you place a field or object in the group header, Paradox prints that information at the top of each group. For instance, rather than including the credit limit and state in each record of a telephone directory that's grouped by those fields, you could omit the fields from the table and place them in their respective group bands instead, as we did in Figure 12.12.

When Paradox must split a group of records across two or more pages, it normally prints the group header again at the top of the next page. If you prefer to print the group headings only at the beginning of the group, inspect the group band and choose Headings ▶ Group Only. To return to the default setting, where headings appear both at the top of the page and at the beginning of the group, inspect the group band and choose Headings ▶ Page And Group.

▶ Printing Repeated Group Values

When your record band contains fields that are also used to group the data, you may wish to suppress repeated values within the group. For example, if you're grouping data by state and have included the State field in the record band, you can have Paradox display the state in each record or only when the state changes.

Normally, Paradox prints repeated values in every record. To print only the *first* occurrence of repeated data, choose Properties ➤ Report ➤ Remove Group Repeats (this checks the Remove Group Repeats option). For example, in Figure 12.16 we created a simple report, grouped it by the State field, Last Name, and First Name, then checked the Properties ➤ Report ➤ Remove Group Repeats option. Notice how the state names CA, MI, and NM appear only in the first record of each group of records for those states. Likewise, duplicate customer names are not repeated (see "Smiths" in the MI group).

▶ Conditionally Printing Objects in Group Headers

You can control when Paradox displays objects in the group's header band by inspecting objects in the header band and changing the Conditional property. The Conditional options are as follows:

Print At Group & Page   (default setting) Paradox displays the group header object at the beginning of each group, and at the top of the page only when the group breaks across pages.

Print Only At Group   Paradox displays the group header object at the beginning of each group, and at the top of each page only if the group begins at the top of the page.

Print Only At Page   Paradox displays the group header object at the top of the page whenever a group breaks across pages, but never displays the object at the beginning of each group. This option is handy if you've added an object to the group header that indicates the group is continued. For example, you could add a text object that says "Area Code continued from previous page."

FIGURE 12.16 ▶

In this report, which is grouped by State, Last Name, and First Name, the Properties ▶ Report ▶ Remove Group Repeats option is checked to prevent duplicate state and customer names from printing.

Wednesday, August 24, 1994			CUSTLIST		Page 1

Last Name	First Name	Phone	Extension	City	State
Adams	Andy	555-0123	35	San Diego	CA
Miller	Maria	555-3423		Los Angeles	
Smith	Mary	555-9545		Los Angeles	
Zastrow	Ruth	555-5948		La Jolla	
Zeepers	Zeke	555-7765	11	Encinitas	

Last Name	First Name	Phone	Extension	City	State
Rosiello	Richard	555-1234		Chicago	IL

Last Name	First Name	Phone	Extension	City	State
Adams	Anita	555-4354	125	Silver Spring	MD

Last Name	First Name	Phone	Extension	City	State
Watson	Frank	555-2234	5678	Bangor	ME

Last Name	First Name	Phone	Extension	City	State
Smith	John	555-9342		Holland	MI
	Savitha	555-0323	7	Ossineke	

Last Name	First Name	Phone	Extension	City	State
Olson	Elizabeth	555-9423		Marlow	NH

Last Name	First Name	Phone	Extension	City	State
Leventhal	Danielle	555-9853		Newark	NJ

Last Name	First Name	Phone	Extension	City	State
Eggo	Sandy	555-5034		Roswell	NM
Newell	John	555-9089		Bernalillo	

Last Name	First Name	Phone	Extension	City	State
Gladstone	Tara Rose	555-4343	55	New York	NY

Last Name	First Name	Phone	Extension	City	State
Ramirez	Rigoberto	555-0987		Wyandotte	OK

Last Name	First Name	Phone	Extension	City	State
Jones	Alma	555-8395	555	Ashland	OR

▶ *Repeating a Table Header across Pages*

When a table breaks across the pages of a report, you can choose whether or not to repeat the header at the top of each page. Normally, headers are repeated, but if you want to prevent this, inspect the table and uncheck the Repeat Header property.

▶ ▶ **N O T E**

> **Repeat Header will not be available if you checked the table's Detach Header property.**

▶▶ *Using Run Time Properties*

Paradox gives you lots of control over the behavior of objects and report bands when you print or preview a report. As for forms, the available properties depend on the type of object you're inspecting. To change Run Time properties, inspect an object or band, choose Run Time, then select the property you want from the submenu.

▶ ▶ **N O T E**

> **Few Run Time properties have an obvious effect in the Report Design window.**

▶ *Breakable and Shrinkable*

All bands have the *Breakable* and *Shrinkable* run time properties. When Run Time ➤ Breakable is checked, Paradox can move some objects in the band to a new page if they don't all fit at the bottom of the current page. When this option is unchecked, Paradox keeps all objects in the band together, moving them to the next page if there isn't enough room for all of them at the bottom of the current page.

When Run Time ➤ Shrinkable is checked, Paradox will squeeze out extra white space below the last object in a band that falls at the bottom of a page. Shrinking may be necessary when all objects in the band will fit on the page but there isn't enough room to print the white space following those objects.

Formatted Reports

▶ ▶

Ch.
12

▶ ▶ N O T E

By default, both Breakable and Shrinkable are checked, and Paradox attempts to shrink the band before breaking it.

Many objects also have a Breakable and Shrinkable property. If you uncheck Run Time ➤ Breakable for an object, the object will be pushed to the next page if it doesn't fit at the bottom of the current page. With the option checked, the object can be broken at the bottom of the page, with the remainder printed at the top of the next page. Similarly, checking Run Time ➤ Shrinkable allows Paradox to clip off the white space at the bottom of an object if the object would be small enough to print at the bottom of the page without the white space below it.

▶ ▶ N O T E

When both Shrinkable and Breakable are checked, Shrinkable takes precedence over Breakable. Paradox will never break a record across two pages.

▶ *Pinning Objects at Run Time*

Certain objects, such as tables, fields, multi-record objects, and graphs, fill with data when you run a report—growing or shrinking as necessary. As objects resize, they push or pull other objects on the page. You can prevent an object from being pushed horizontally or vertically by checking the Run Time ➤ Pin Horizontal or Run Time ➤ Pin Vertical properties (initially these properties are turned off). For example, in Figure 12.17 the Pin Horizontal property is unchecked for the dart graphic, but checked for the gift box graphic. This means that the dart will float horizontally as the address field shrinks or grows, while the gift box graphic stays put.

FIGURE 12.17 ▶

The dart graphic is not pinned horizontally, but the gift box is. Notice how the dart is pushed to the right as the address expands or shrinks, while the gift box stays at the same horizontal position. (Word wrap is turned off in the address field.)

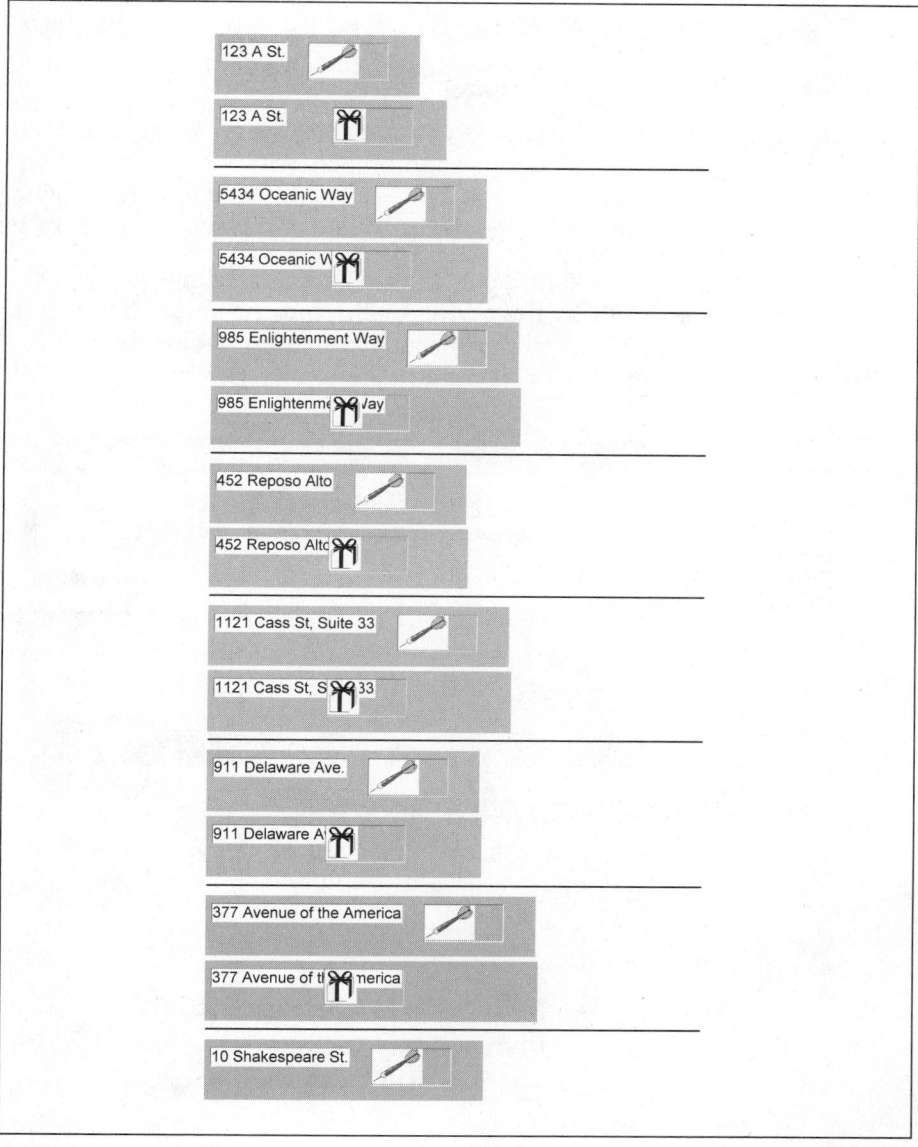

Be aware that pinning an object that might otherwise be pushed can cause an expanding object to cover up the pinned object, as in Figure 12.17. One way to solve this problem is to place the pinned object in back by selecting it and choosing Design ➤ Send To Back. You could also move the pinned object further to the right, so that it's less likely to get in the way.

▶ *Aligning Pushed Objects and Keeping Them Together*

Recall that you can use the Design ➤ Align options in the Design window menus to align objects with respect to one another. However, some objects may be pushed out of alignment when you run the report. You can solve this problem with invisible lines or boxes.

For example, in Figure 12.18 the dinosaur graphic is pushed to the right by the address field, but the empty box is not. To keep those objects together, place a vertical line the length of the two objects just to the left of the objects, as shown below.

Now inspect the line and check the Run Time ➤ Invisible property (the line will appear dotted on the screen). When you print or preview the report, the results will appear as in Figure 12.19.

▶▶ **T I P**

If you want to display the line, don't check Run Time ➤ Invisible for the line. The objects to the right of the line will still be pushed together.

You can also use horizontal lines to push objects. For example, the horizontal line in the design below will push both the dinosaur and the empty box as the table expands. Without this line, only the dinosaur

FIGURE 12.18

*Objects may not align
as expected when you
run your report*

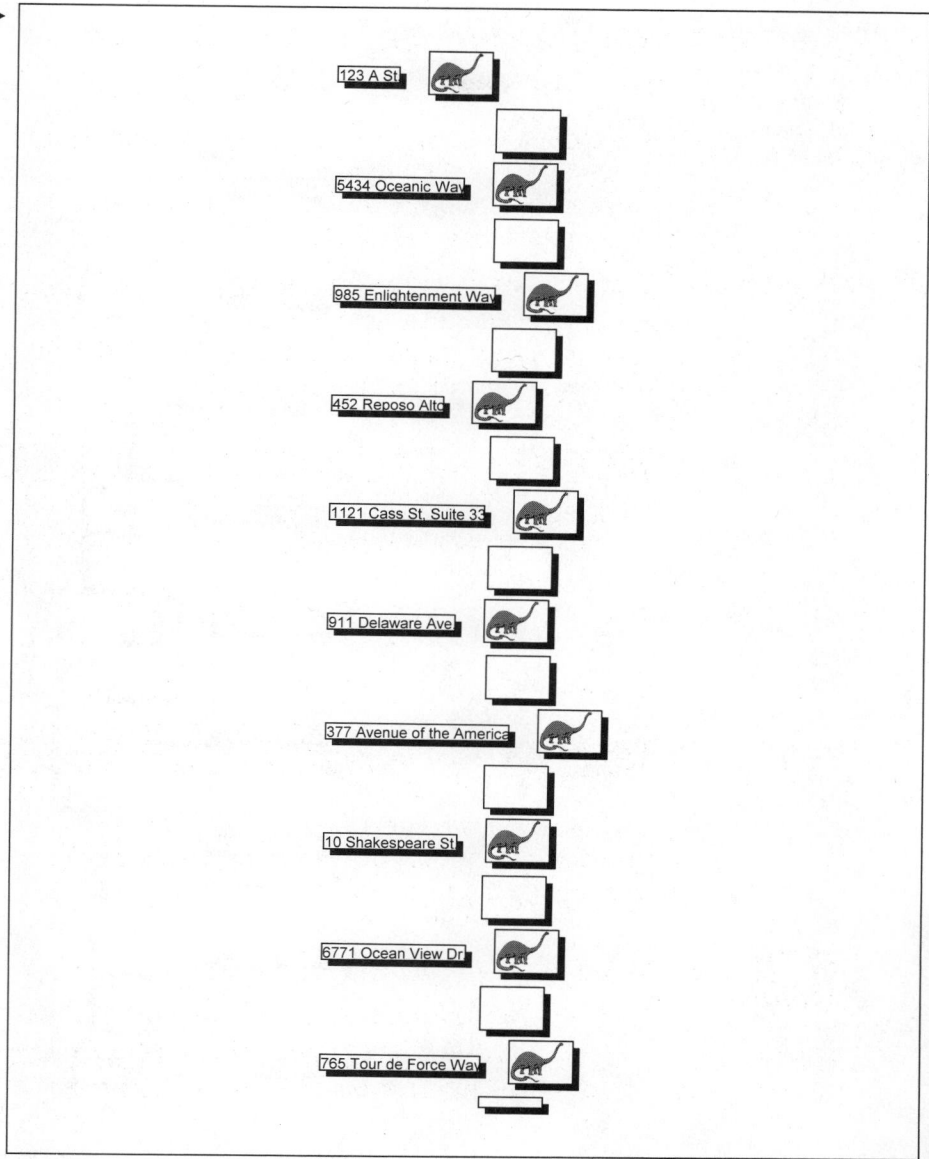

FIGURE 12.19 ▶

The report in Figure 12.18, after using an invisible line to control alignment

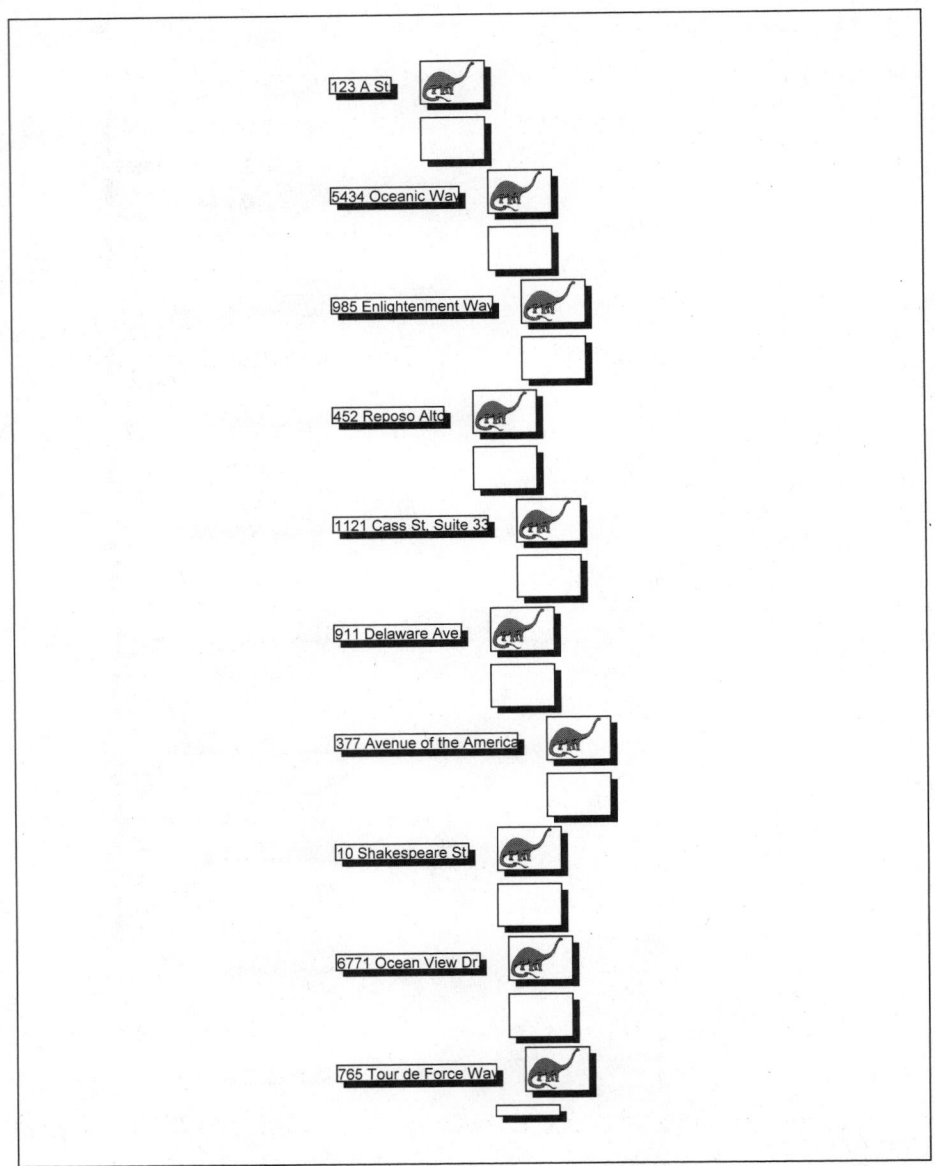

will move down to accommodate the expanding table. (We've left the Invisible property unchecked so that you can see the horizontal line.)

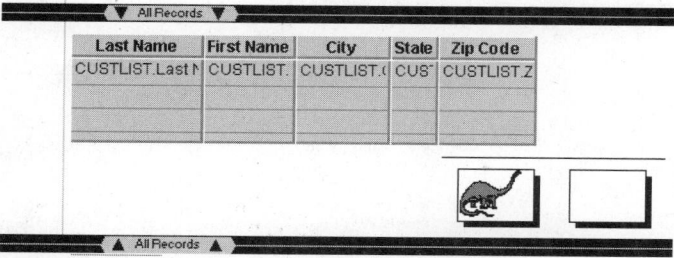

If you'd like to have Paradox push *and* pull objects together, try surrounding them with an invisible box and turn off the box's Run Time ➤ Breakable property.

▶ Fitting Height and Width

Paradox for Windows can grow or shrink boxes, text, ellipses, and field objects to fit their contents when you run a report, or it can keep these objects their original size.

If you turn off the Run Time ➤ Fit Height or Run Time ➤ Fit Width properties, the objects will retain their original height or width when you run the report. Turning these properties on (the default settings) allows Paradox to shrink or expand the height or width to fit their contents.

Figure 12.20 shows what happens when you preview a design in which the Run Time ➤ Fit Height property is turned off for the gray box to the right of the vertical line, and turned on for the box to the left. Notice how the boxes on the left expand to fit the word-wrapped address field. The vertical line shows the original height of the box.

▶ Showing Records and Columns in Tables and Multi-Record Objects

To control how Paradox displays repeated records of a table or multi-record object, choose the Run Time ➤ Show All Records property. When Show All Records is turned on (the default setting), Paradox expands the object vertically down the page, creating as many pages as

FIGURE 12.20 ▶

The right side of the figure shows the effects of turning Run Time ➤ Fit Height off.

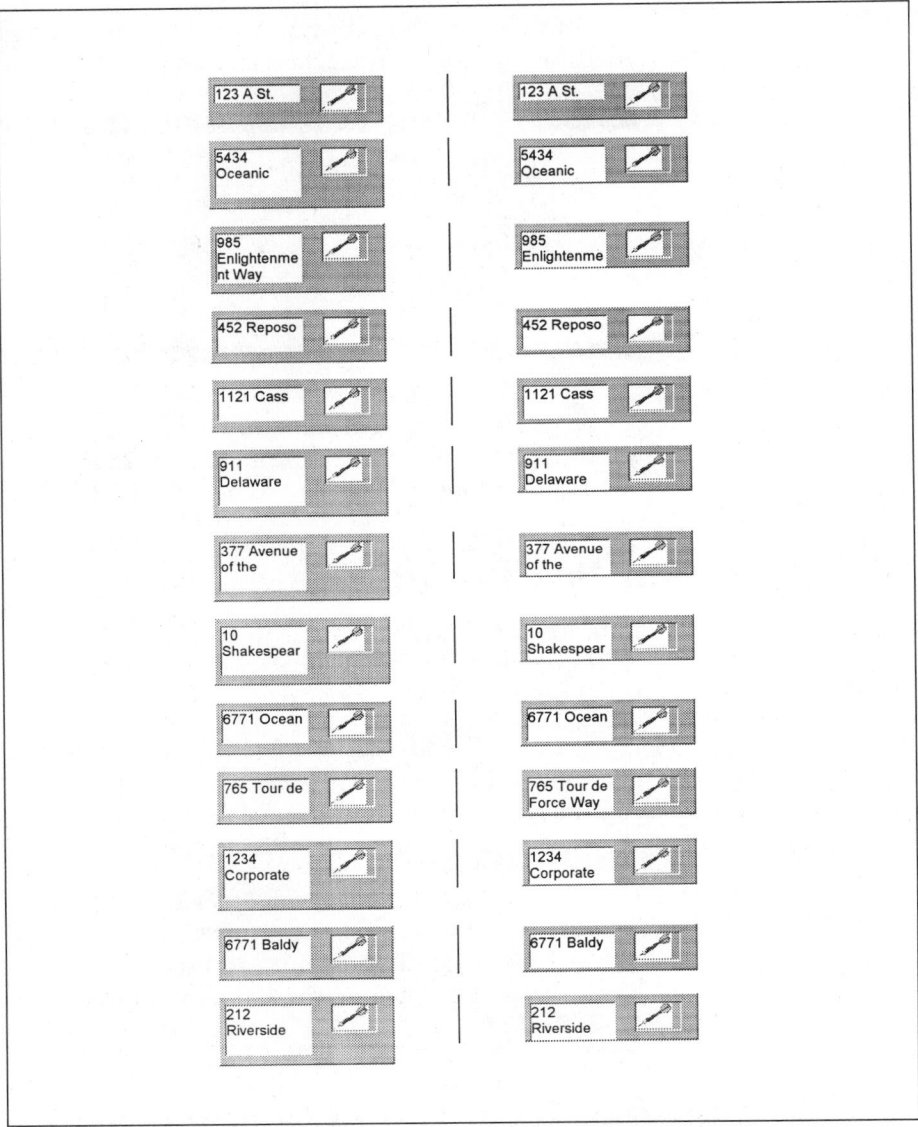

necessary to display all the records. When you turn this property off, Paradox does not expand the object; instead it repeats the object in the same size and shape until all records are displayed.

Run Time ➤ Show All Records is on for the multi-record object shown in Figure 12.21, but off for the multi-record object in Figure 12.22.

FIGURE 12.21 ▶

*A multi-record object
with Run Time* ➤
*Show All Records
turned on*

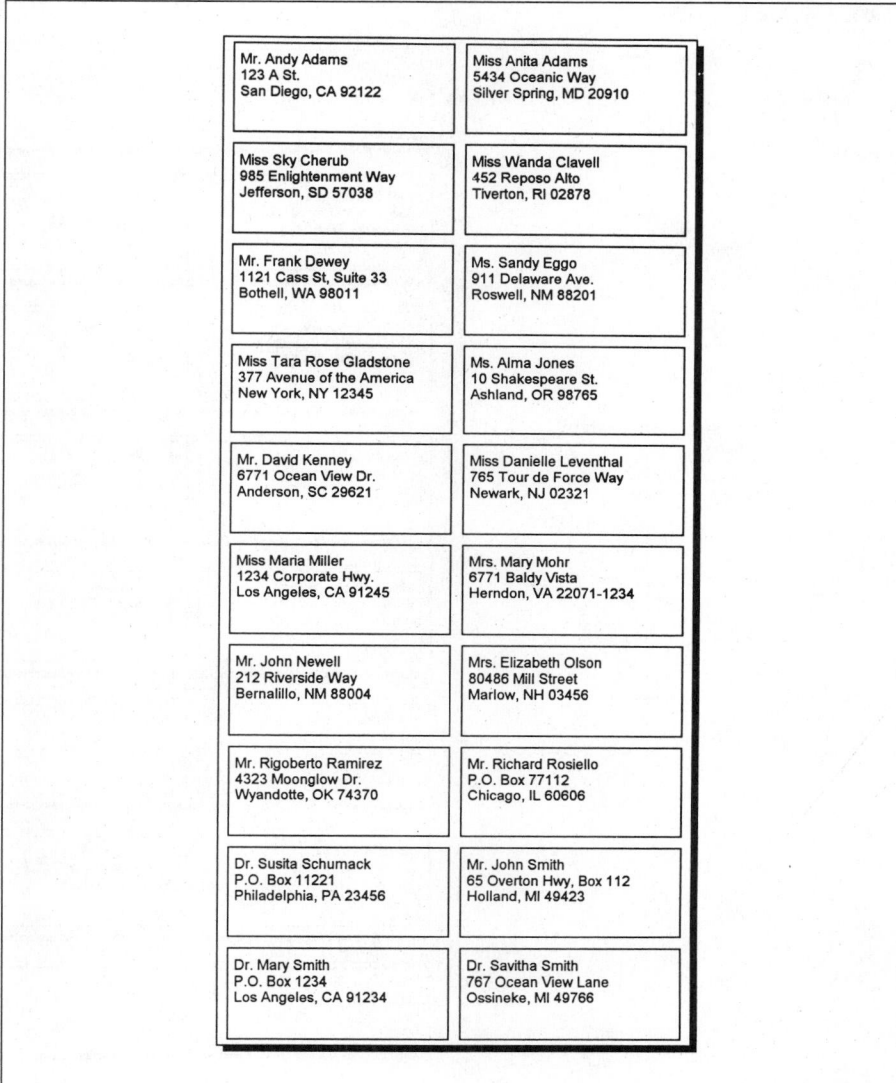

You can also turn the Run Time ➤ Show All Columns property on or off for table frames. When on (checked), the table frame expands to include all the columns. When off, Paradox clips any columns that exceed the page width.

FIGURE 12.22

A multi-record object with Run Time ▶ Show All Records turned off

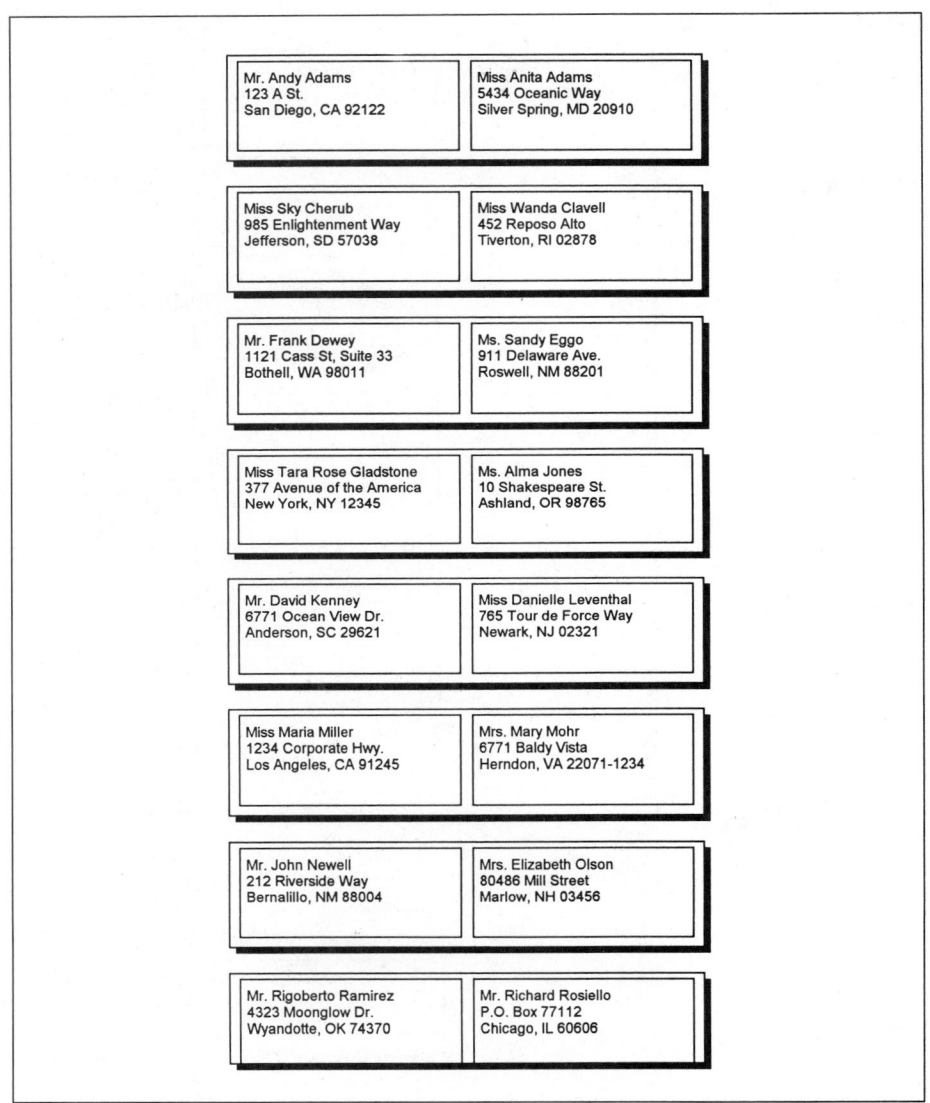

▶ Deleting Empty Records

Normally, Paradox won't print blank records in table and multi-record objects. If you would like to have *all* records printed (even if they're blank), inspect the record object in the table frame or multi-record object and uncheck Delete When Empty. The sample report in Figure 12.23

shows a multi-record object with the Delete When Empty property checked. Figure 12.24 shows what happens when this property is not checked and you preview or print the report.

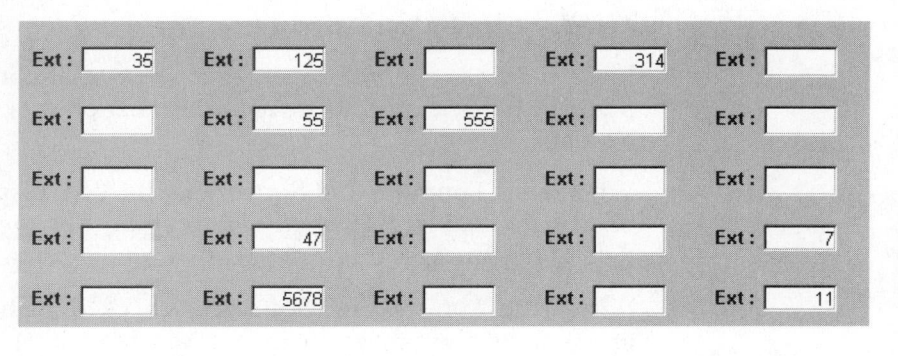

N O T E

> *#Record* **will appear at the right edge of the status bar when you've selected a record object in the Design window.**

▶ Special Properties of Text Objects

Text objects have some special properties that are particularly useful when you're designing form letters, mailing labels, and envelopes. The default run-time settings are usually perfect for mail merge, so we'll just summarize them here. You'll see more examples of these properties later in "Designing a Mail Merge Document."

Formatted Reports

▶ ▶

Ch.
12

Controlling Widows and Orphans

Contrary to what you might think, widow and orphan control is not a new government program to keep women and children off the streets. A *widow* is actually a single line of text at the top of the page that has been separated from the paragraph it ends. An *orphan* is a single line of text at the bottom of a page that has been separated from the paragraph it begins.

Paradox will prevent orphans and widows if you inspect a text object and check its Run Time ➤ Orphan/Widow property (this is *not* on by default). If you're designing form letters that might expand to more than one page, it's a good idea to turn this property on.

Controlling Field and Line Squeeze

Field and line squeeze properties are very useful in mail merge documents, where fields embedded within text objects may vary in length or be blank.

When Run Time ➤ Field Squeeze is checked, text to the right of a field object is pulled in or pushed out automatically to fit the width of the field. This prevents unsightly gaps within lines that contain empty fields.

When Run Time ➤ Line Squeeze is checked, blank fields that appear on a line by themselves are ignored, instead of being printed as blank lines. This option is handy when printing mailing labels and form letters with inside addresses that contain some empty fields.

 ▶▶ **T I P**

Paradox will squeeze out extra space between fields that may be blank if you enclose them in a text box.

▶▶ Designing a Mail Merge Document

As mentioned earlier in this chapter, letters, mailing labels, and envelopes fall into the single category of *mail merge documents*. The only thing that's really special about mail merge documents is that they consist primarily of fields embedded within text objects. Objects placed within the text wrap along with the text and appear as part of the body of text when you print or view the document.

For example, the form letter in Figure 12.25 welcomes new credit customers to a business. Although most of the text is the same for each addressee, the inside address, salutation, credit limit, and start date near the top of the letter contain data that is specific to each individual, and the customer's name appears again in the second paragraph of the

FIGURE 12.25 ▶

The welcome letter that is sent to new credit customers

Gift Corner

8891 Gaudy Ave * West Fantasee, CA 92222
1-800-555-GIFT

April 21, 1995

Mr. Willy O. Wontee
P.O. Box 23981
Tucson, AZ 85711

Dear Mr. Wontee:

Welcome aboard, Mr. Wontee! *The Gift Corner* is pleased to have you as one of our new credit customers. Your credit limit of $10,000.00 is available as of Saturday, April 15, 1995.

Now that you're firmly established as one of our valued customers, you may want to peruse our exciting new catalog, which is chock full of great gift items. For example, you'll find some terrific ***Toys for Boys***, including hot new race cars in price ranges that are as torrid as the engines under the hoods of these babies. If you're looking for something a bit more tame, try our ***Jungle Creatures Collection*** -- stuffed animals that look like the real thing! And Mr. Wontee, if those on your gift list are itching for a holiday, take a look at our ***Exotic Vacation Packages***. We'll guarantee some unforgettable memories! We'll even throw in a free camera, film, and developing so those memories will never be lost.

 Free!

*S*o why not call your Account Representative here at *The Gift Corner* today? We'll send you a complimentary gift, just for picking up the phone and talking to us. You can reach us 24-hours a day, toll-free at **1-800-555-GIFT**. Don't delay...Call us today!

Sincerely yours,

Frank Lee Unctuous

Frank Lee Unctuous
Account Manager

Formatted Reports

▶▶

Ch.

12

letter. (To help you locate the areas where actual field values appear, we've underlined them in Figure 12.25.) Notice how smoothly these fields are integrated into the form letter.

Figure 12.26 shows the top portion of the Report Design window for the welcome form letter. In this illustration, you can see how the field names from the CustList table are interspersed throughout the text. The completed design for this report appears later in Figure 12.33.

The steps for beginning mail merge documents are nearly identical to those for creating regular reports. The only difference is that you should select a Blank or Single-Record style in the Design Layout box if you're creating a form letter or envelope, or a Multi-Record style if you're designing mailing labels.

FIGURE 12.26 ▶

The welcome letter in the Report Design window. We reduced the size of the screen and removed the rulers so you can see more of the document.

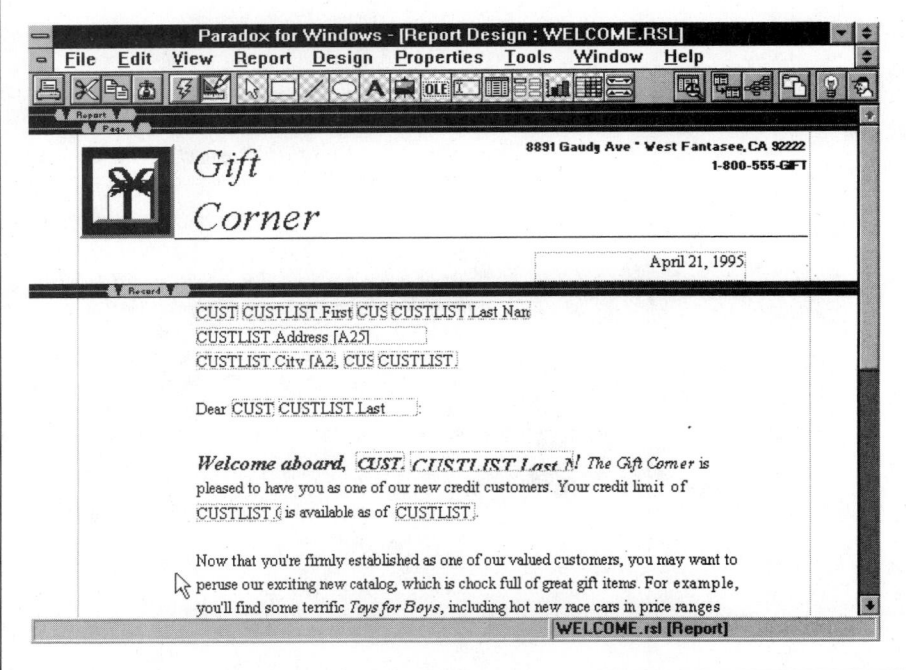

►►TIP

> **Thanks to the new mailing label Expert, setting up mailing labels is a breeze. You'll find out more about this handy Expert later in the chapter.**

We'll focus next on techniques for designing form letters. Later in this chapter, you'll learn how to create mailing labels and custom envelopes.

►►TIP

> **If you plan to send letters to only a few people on your list, rather than to everyone in a table, you can extract names with a query. You can also use the query to sort your letters.**

► Getting Started with Form Letters

To begin a form letter, choose File ➤ New ➤ Report, click Data Model / Layout Diagram, select a table, query, or data model as usual, then choose OK. In the Design Layout dialog box, choose Blank, then choose OK. After reaching the Report Design window, you can set up the report headers, page headers, and groups (if needed), or you can do this after you've designed the body text of the form letter.

The next step is to place a text object in the record band by selecting the Text tool and dragging in the report band to define the width of your letter. You needn't worry about how tall the text object is, since Paradox will expand it automatically as you add text and fields to it. Figure 12.27 shows a new text object placed in our design.

►►TIP

> **After typing a few characters, you may want to inspect the text object and choose Vertical Scroll Bar or Design Sizing ➤ Fit Text to facilitate text entry.**

FIGURE 12.27 ▶

*A text object defined in
the record band of the
Report Design window*

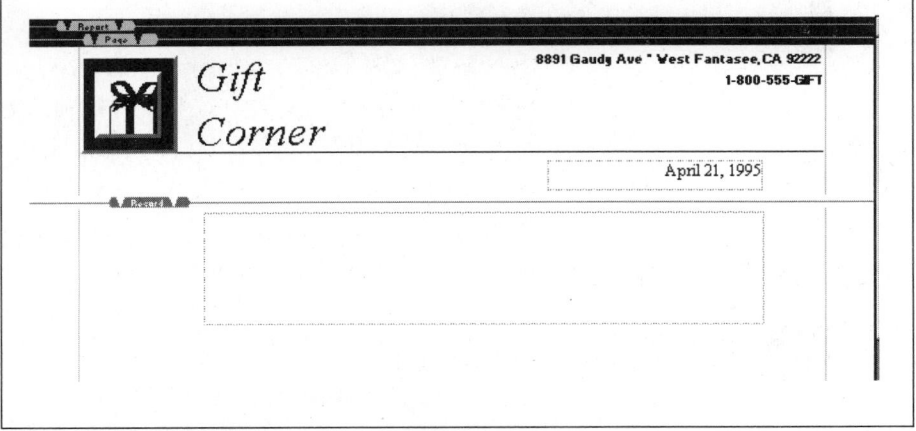

Now click in the text object until you see the insertion point. If you want the letter to start with an inside address, don't type anything— just skip to the next section to find out how to place fields and objects. Otherwise, type the text you want to appear before the first field or object within the body text.

▶ Placing Fields and Objects in a Form Letter

You can place fields or other objects into the text of a form letter either before or after you've typed in text. Here are the basic steps:

1. Position the insertion point where you want the new object to appear. You can either click the mouse at the appropriate location or use the cursor positioning keys (the arrow keys, Home, End, Ctrl+Home, Ctrl+End, and so forth).

2. Select the tool you want from the Toolbar, then click and drag the mouse to define the size of the object. If you're placing a field object, just press F5 as a shortcut.

▶ ▶ **T I P**

> **To place a field or object on a line by itself, press ↵ at the end of the line above where the object should appear. Then place the field or object and press ↵ again. After you define a field object, check its Delete When Empty property and make sure the surrounding text object's Line Squeeze run time property is checked.**

Typically, when designing a form letter, you type some text into the document, then place a field or other object wherever you want it to appear within the text. For example, to enter the salutation in the first line of the welcome letter in Figure 12.26, we followed these steps:

- We typed **Dear**, pressed the spacebar, pressed F5, pressed the spacebar, pressed F5, typed a colon, then pressed ↵ twice.

- After creating each line of the salutation, we pressed Esc to select the text object, then we selected and inspected each field individually and defined it as usual.

▶ ▶ **N O T E**

> **We could use the Field tool to place the fields, then define each field name, and change its Display Type property to Unlabeled as soon as we place the field. However, the method described above is quite a bit faster.**

From here, you simply repeat the process of typing text until you need to add a field or object. Then press F5 to add a field or use the Toolbar to place other objects. If you discover that you forgot to add an object to the text, it's no problem. Simply move the insertion point to the appropriate position and place the object.

▶ *Working with Embedded Objects*

Objects embedded in text retain their usual characteristics—that is, you can select them and inspect their properties. However, you should think of them as "super" characters. For example,

- If the insertion point is just to the left of an object, pressing the → key will move the insertion point to the right of the object. Similarly, pressing the ← key while the insertion point is immediately to the right of an object positions the insertion point just to the left of the object.

- You can delete an object by positioning the insertion point just after the object and pressing the Backspace key. Or, position the insertion point just before the object and press the Del key. (If you inadvertently delete an object, immediately choose Edit ➤ Undo or press Alt+Backspace.)

- Press ↵ to add blank lines after existing text and objects and before new text and objects.

- Just as when typing characters into the document, you can only add objects just before or after existing text or within existing text. Thus, if your text object contains only two short lines, you cannot place an object at the lower-right corner of the text object.

While you're working in a text object that contains embedded fields, you may need to go back and select one of the objects, perhaps to redefine it, resize it, or change its properties. When the mouse pointer is an insertion point, you can't simply click on an object since doing so merely repositions the insertion point. To get around this problem, press the Esc key, then click on the object you want. You can then Shift+click to select additional objects within the text. As usual, handles will appear around the selected object. You can then resize the object, inspect and change its properties, delete the object by pressing the Del key, or copy or cut it to the Clipboard.

Although you can drag a selected object to a new position in the text, it's difficult to do so accurately. Therefore, it's best to select the object, cut or copy it to the Clipboard, position the insertion point where you want the object to appear, then paste the object from the Clipboard. (If you'd rather, you can delete the object and create it again in its new position.)

▶ Preventing Unwanted Blank Spaces

Certain field properties cooperate with text properties to provide smooth insertion of fields within text. For example, checking a field's

Run Time ➤ Fit Width and Run Time ➤ Fit Height properties makes the field object shrink or expand to fit the data it contains. At the same time, the Run Time ➤ Line Squeeze and Run Time ➤ Field Squeeze text properties eliminate any undesirable white space surrounding inserted fields. (As mentioned earlier, Field Squeeze closes up the text around the field data, while Line Squeeze causes Paradox to ignore blank lines.)

When you place an embedded field on a line by itself (for example, by clicking in the surrounding text object, pressing ↵, pressing F5, then pressing ↵ again), be sure that the field's Delete When Empty property and the text object's Line Squeeze run time property are checked. This will prevent unwanted blank space if the field is empty in some records.

If you have problems fitting text around field data, or your document contains unwanted blank spaces or lines, you might want to inspect these text and field properties to see if they are set correctly.

▶ *Putting Text Objects Around Fields*

Although it's usually easier to create a text object first, and then embed fields or other objects inside, you *can* draw a text object around existing fields. This technique is sometimes useful for setting up mailing labels and envelopes; however, you'll probably prefer to use the mailing label Expert to design these types of documents.

Here are the basic steps for putting text objects around fields:

1. Drag the fields you want to enclose so that they are near one another. Also make sure there's enough space around the fields to draw the text object around them (select and drag the fields up, down, left, or right as necessary).

2. Select the Text tool in the Toolbar and drag its outline so that all the field objects are completely enclosed (the fields will instantly squeeze together inside the text object).

3. Position the insertion point in the text object, and add spaces, commas, new lines (↵), and other punctuation between the fields as needed.

4. Select the enclosed fields, inspect them, and check their Run Time ➤ Fit Width and Run Time ➤ Fit Height properties (if they aren't checked already). Also make sure the Delete When Empty

property is checked. Then inspect the text object and check its Run Time ➤ Field Squeeze and Run Time ➤ Line Squeeze properties (if they aren't checked already).

▶ Sorting Your Output

Any of the sorting techniques presented earlier will sort mail merge documents. Thus, you can sort the table first, base your mail merge design on a query, use group bands, or sort the record band.

 ▶ ▶ W A R N I N G

Be sure to sort your letters and envelopes in the same order. Otherwise, you'll have to match each printed letter with its correct envelope manually.

▶ Creating Mailing Labels

Many people use database packages to print mailing labels from tables, and Paradox for Windows' multi-record objects are ideal for printing on the many varieties of labels used with laser and dot matrix printers. Figure 12.28 shows a page of printed labels for the CustList table, while the design that the mailing label Expert created for these labels appears in Figure 12.29.

 ▶ ▶ N O T E

Don't be concerned that the fields are difficult to read in the Design window. To see the field names clearly, use the Object Tree (Chapter 10) or click on each field and look in the status bar.

There are two ways to create mailing labels:

- The easy way, with the mailing label Expert.
- The hard way, by creating the labels from scratch.

Mr. Andy A. Adams
President
ABC Corporation
123 A St.
San Diego, CA 92122

Miss Anita Q. Adams
Microcomputer Consultant
5434 Oceanic Way
Silver Spring, MD 20910

Miss Sky R. Cherub
Oneness Well-Being
985 Enlightenment Way
Jefferson, SD 57038

Miss Wanda T. Clavell
Mother Superior
Westridge Convent
452 Reposo Alto
Tiverton, RI 02878

Mr. Frank R. Dewey
Senior Partner
Dewey, Cheatham, and Howe
1121 Cass St, Suite 33
Bothell, WA 98011

Ms. Sandy Eggo
Owner
Pancho's Restaurant
911 Delaware Ave.
Roswell, NM 88201

Miss Tara Rose Gladstone
Vice President
Waterside Landscaping
377 Avenue of the America
New York, NY 12345

Ms. Alma R. Jones
Account Executive
Ashland Flowers
10 Shakespeare St.
Ashland, OR 98765

Mr. David E. Kenney
Attorney at Law
Felson and Fabian
6771 Ocean View Dr.
Anderson, SC 29621

Miss Danielle D. Leventhal
Garden State Bagels
765 Tour de Force Way
Newark, NJ 02321

Miss Maria N. Miller
Accounts Receivable
Zeerocks, Inc.
1234 Corporate Hwy.
Los Angeles, CA 91245

Mrs. Mary M. Mohr
6771 Baldy Vista
Herndon, VA 22071-1234

Mr. John J. Newell
Newell Construction
212 Riverside Way
Bernalillo, NM 88004

Mrs. Elizabeth A. Olson
Vice President
Precision Computer Arts
80486 Mill Street
Marlow, NH 03456

Mr. Rigoberto R. Ramirez
Author
4323 Moonglow Dr.
Wyandotte, OK 74370

Mr. Richard L. Rosiello
Accounts Payable
Raydontic Labs
P.O. Box 77112
Chicago, IL 60606

Dr. Susita M. Schumack
Neurosurgeon
Physician's Hospital
P.O. Box 11221
Philadelphia, PA 23456

Mr. John Q. Smith
65 Overton Hwy, Box 112
Holland, MI 49423

Dr. Mary K. Smith
Graduate School of Busine
Cal State L.A.
P.O. Box 1234
Los Angeles, CA 91234

Dr. Savitha V. Smith
Slybacks Paperbacks
767 Ocean View Lane
Ossineke, MI 49766

Ms. Janet L. Smythe
P.O. Box 3384
Seattle, WA 98762

Mr. Frank R. Watson
Greenskeeper
Whispering Palms Golf Clu
8775 Concha de Golf
Bangor, ME 01876

Dr. Ted Wilson
Psychology Department
Pine Valley University
P.O. Box 463
Seattle, WA 98103

Dr. Ruth Zastrow
Internal Medicine
Scripps Clinic
4331 La Jolla Scenic Dr.
La Jolla, CA 92037

Mr. Zeke A. Zeepers
Chief Engineer
Virtual Reality Designs
5409 Crest Dr.
Encinitas, CA 92024

We'll describe the easy way here, and skip the hard way because it is such a pain. Your best bet is to use the mailing label Expert to get started, and then tweak the resulting design if you need to adjust field or text object properties, or you're using a label size that isn't supported, or you want to decorate your labels in some way. See "Tweaking Your Mailing Label Design," later in the chapter.

FIGURE 12.29 ▶

A multi-record report design for the CustList mailing labels shown in Figure 12.28.

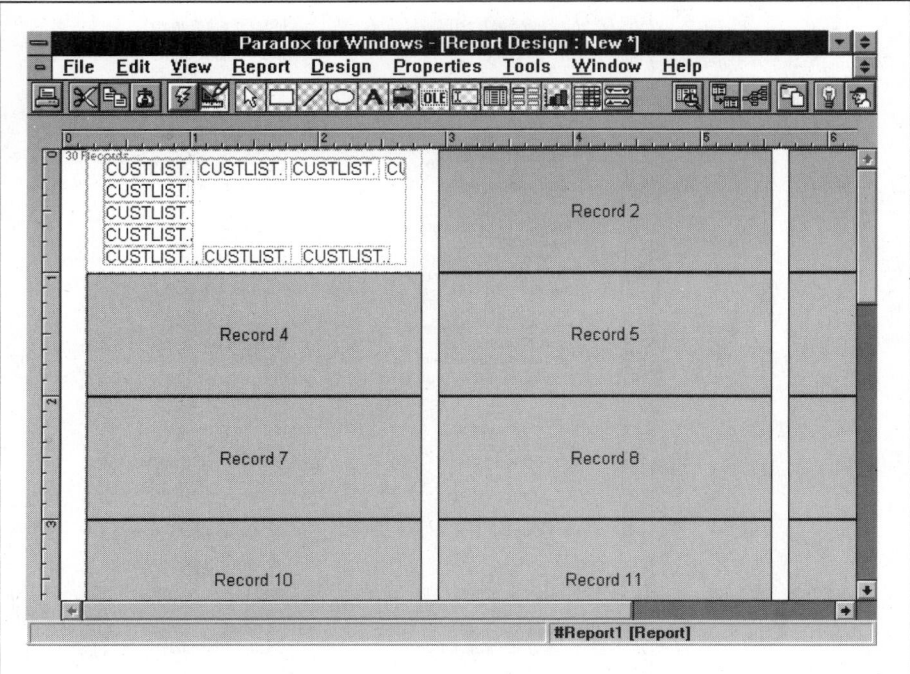

> ▶▶**WARNING**
>
> **Be sure to use mailing labels that are suitable for your printer. In particular, avoid using continuous forms designed for dot matrix printers with laser printers, because laser printers get very hot and can be damaged if the adhesive backing of the labels melts. Avery offers many types of labels that are ideal for laser printers.**

▶ *Using the Mailing Label Expert*

The mailing label Expert is one of Paradox for Windows' best new features. A few quick mouse clicks and you're done! We'll go through the steps in a moment, but first, you should know about a few things that you *cannot* do with the Expert:

- You cannot base the mailing labels on a query or data model. If you need to massage the information in the mailing labels, first create a query (and base it on a data model if you like), run the query to produce an Answer table, and then create your mailing labels from the Answer table. See Chapter 9 for details about queries.

- You cannot sort the output while using the Expert. But that's easy to solve. After the Expert completes its job, return to the Design window, inspect the record band, select the Sort property, and define the fields you want to sort by. Alternatively, you can base the mailing labels on a table that you've already sorted (Chapter 8) or on a query that produces a sorted Answer table (Chapter 9).

- You are limited to the predefined Avery mailing labels that come with the Expert. Fortunately, however, the supported label formats are commonly used, so you'll probably find a format to meet your needs. But even if your label size isn't supported, you can begin with the mailing label Expert and then customize the design later, as discussed later under "Tweaking Your Mailing Label Design."

▶ ▶ N O T E

If you'll be using non-supported label sizes frequently, you can fine-tune the Expert to use a label format of your choosing. You will need to know the following vital statistics about your labels: Top Margin, Side Margin, Vertical Pitch, Horizontal Pitch, Label Height, Label Width, Corner Radius, Number Across, and Number Down. See "Customizing the Experts" in Chapter 11 for details.

Now that all the preliminaries are out of the way, let's go through the steps for creating a set of mailing labels from our CustList table. (Remember that you can click the <u>H</u>elp button anytime you're in the Expert if you need more information.)

1. Click the Expert button in the Toolbar (shown at left), or choose <u>H</u>elp ➤ E<u>x</u>perts.

2. When the Expert Control Panel appears, click the Mailing Labels button.

3. In the first Mailing Label Expert dialog box, choose a category from the Label Categories drop-down list, then choose an Avery label type from the Label Types list. Click the Next>> button. (For our example, we chose the *Avery Address Labels* category and the *5160-Address* label type.)

▶▶ N O T E

The mailing label Expert supports Avery mailing labels only. Each box of Avery labels lists the product code number (for example, 5160), the dimensions of each page, and the dimensions of each label.

4. In the second Mailing Label Expert dialog box, highlight the table that contains the data for your mailing labels. Or, click the Select A New Directory Or Alias Button, use the Directory Browser to locate the directory or alias where the table is stored, choose OK, and then highlight the table you want. Click the Next>> button. (We chose the *CustList* table for our example.)

5. In the third Mailing Label Expert dialog box, choose the Font you want, select a font Size, and select the attributes you want (Bold, Italic, Strikeout, or Underline). Click the Next>> button. (We chose *Arial 10-point* font for our sample labels.)

▶▶ W A R N I N G

Be sure to select a font that will allow all the data to fit on your mailing labels.

6. In the fourth Mailing Label Expert dialog box, click the picture that shows the order in which the labels will print on the page. If necessary, click the picture that tells Paradox how you'll be feeding the label sheet into your printer. Click the Next>> button. (Our example used the default Left To Right arrangement.)

7. In the fifth and final Mailing Label Expert dialog box, you'll need to place fields from the Fields list and any punctuation you want into the <u>L</u>abel Region box. Figure 12.30 illustrates a completed dialog box after we placed the Mr/Mrs, First Name, MI, Last Name, Department/Title, Company, Address, City, State, and Zip Code fields from our CustList table. The next section explains how to use this dialog box, to reproduce the result in Figure 12.30.

8. When you're finished defining the <u>L</u>abel Region, click the C<u>r</u>eate button.

> **WARNING**
>
> **The fields you select must fit the measurements of your labels, so don't pick too many!**

Faster than you can say "Create it in a jiffy," your mailing labels will appear in the Report window. Now you only have to click the Print button in the Toolbar to complete the job. If you wish to customize the labels, simply click the Toolbar's Design button and use the usual techniques to tweak the labels to perfection.

FIGURE 12.30

The final Mailing Label Expert dialog box, after filling in the fields and text for the <u>L</u>abel Region box

---

Paradox Mailing Label Expert - Step 5 of 5

Place fields to indicate their position on the label, then click on Create to generate the label report. To place fields, click the label region, then double-click on the field name. To place text, click the label region and type.

<u>F</u>ields:

- Cust No
- Last Name
- Mr/Mrs
- First Name
- MI
- Department/Title
- Company
- Address
- City
- State
- **Zip Code**
- Area Code

<u>L</u>abel Region:

{Mr/Mrs} {First Name} {MI} {Last Name}
{Department/Title}
{Company}
{Address}
{City}, {State} {Zip Code}|

[<u>A</u>dd Field >>]

[<u>C</u>ancel] [<u>H</u>elp]   [<< <u>P</u>rev] [C<u>r</u>eate]

Formatted
Reports

Ch.
12

Filling in the Label Region

Placing fields and text into the Label Region box is a snap. Here are the basic techniques you can use:

- To put a field into the Label Region box, click in the Label Region where you want the field to appear. Then double-click the field name in the Fields list; or click the field name in the Fields list, then click the Add Field button. The field will appear in the Label Region.

- To add text to the Label Region box (for example, a space, comma, line break, or other text), click in the Label Region box where you want the text to appear, then type your text.

- To delete text or a field in the Label Region box, click where you want to make a change (or use the normal cursor positioning keys such as ←, →, ↑, ↓, Ctrl+←, Ctrl+→, Home, or End). Then press Backspace as needed to delete text to the left of the insertion point, or press Del to delete text to the right of the insertion point. Or, select the text you want to delete and then press Backspace or Del.

 ▶ ▶**T I P**

If you select the fields and type the text in the order you want them to appear, you can skip the steps of positioning the insertion point in the Label Region box.

Here are the steps we followed to place our sample fields in the dialog box shown in Figure 12.30:

- Double-click the *Mr/Mrs* field in the Fields list, then press the spacebar.

- Double-click the *First Name* field in the Fields list, then press the spacebar.

- Double-click the *MI* field in the Fields list, then press the spacebar.

- Double-click the *Last Name* field in the Fields list, then press ↵ to insert a line break.

- Double-click the *Department/Title* field in the Fields list, then press ↵ to insert a line break.

- Double-click the *Company* field in the Fields list, then press ↵ to insert a line break.

- Double-click the *Address* field in the Fields list, then press ↵ to insert a line break.

- Double-click t' ` *City* field in the Fields list, then type a comma and press th ͺacebar.

- Double-clicκ the *State* field in the Fields list, then press the spacebar twice.

- Double-click the *Zip Code* field in the Fields list.

- Click the Create button to create the labels.

If you inadvertently delete one of the curly braces that enclose the field names in this dialog box, Paradox will print that information as a constant literal in each label. For example, you will see {*Street* in every address rather than the information you entered in the Street field. To fix the problem, just re-insert the missing curly braces ({ }).

▶ *Tweaking Your Mailing Label Design*

Once the mailing labels appear in the Report window, you can switch back to the Design window and enhance them further. Here are some suggestions to get you started:

- If your labels contain unwanted blank lines, select the text object that's inside the master record, inspect it, and select (check) its Run Time ▶ Line Squeeze property.

- To adjust the number of labels across or down, change the space between labels, or alter the order in which records appear, inspect the master record in the multi-record object and choose Record Layout. See "Changing a Multi-Record Layout" in Chapter 10 for more details.

- To quickly adjust which fields appear in the label, inspect the master record in the multi-record object and choose Field Layout. See "Changing the Field Layout in a Multi-Record Object" in Chapter 10.

Formatted Reports

Ch.
12

- To add a frame around the labels, first select the text object in the master record (*#Text* appears in the status bar). Then inspect the record, choose Frame ➤ Style, and click the frame style you want. For instance, the second frame style in the palette will put a box around each label. You can also add graphics and other decorations to the master record.

- To sort the labels by any field, inspect the record band, select the Sort property, and complete the Sort Record Band dialog box.

- Use any other techniques discussed in Chapters 10–12 to tune up the properties of various objects in the labels.

▶ Creating Envelopes

If your laser printer can print envelopes, either with an envelope tray or manual feed, you can design a report to print custom envelopes. Figure 12.31 shows an envelope printed with Paradox for Windows that includes a company logo, return address, and the customer's mailing address. The design for this envelope appears in Figure 12.32.

Designing for a standard number 10 envelope ($9^1/_2$ inches by $4^1/_8$ inches) is relatively easy if you start with the mailing label Expert and then adjust the design to accommodate an envelope. Here's how to begin:

1. Click the Expert button in the Toolbar and choose the Mailing Labels button.

FIGURE 12.31 ▶

A sample envelope, including company logo, return address, and the customer's mailing address

Gift Corner
8891 Gaudy Ave * West Fantasee, CA 92222
1-800-555-GIFT

Miss Maria N. Miller
Accounts Receivable
Zeerocks, Inc.
1234 Corporate Hwy.
Los Angeles, CA 91245

FIGURE 12.32

The design of the sample envelope shown in Figure 12.31

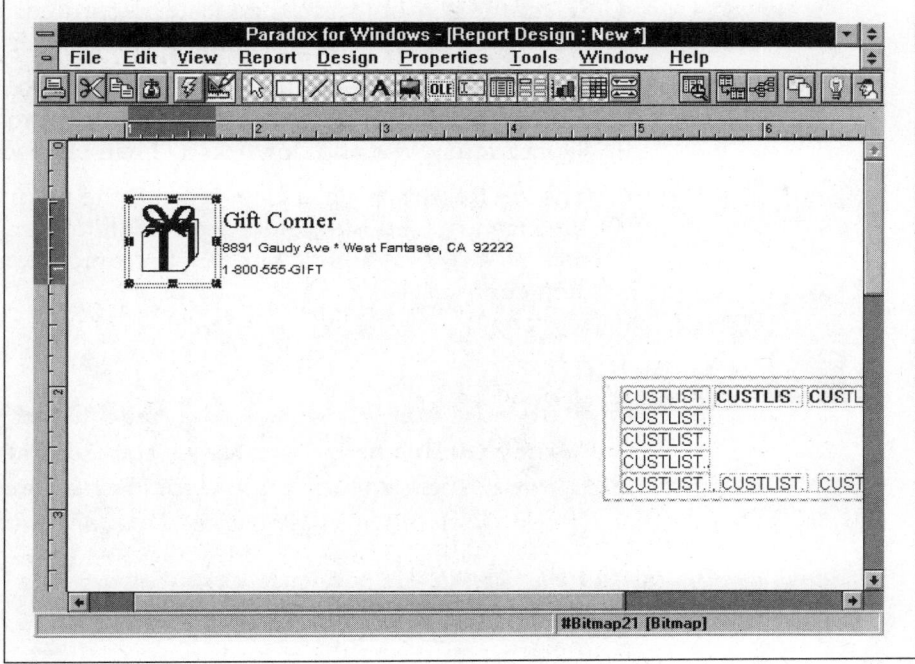

2. Complete the mailing label dialog boxes as outlined below:

   - In the first dialog box, choose the default label (*5160 - Address*), and choose Next>>.
   - In the second dialog box, choose the table you want to use and choose Next>>.
   - In the third dialog box, choose the font you want (remember not to make it too large), then choose Next>>.
   - In the fourth dialog box, choose Next>> to use the default label sheet feed and printing order.
   - In the last dialog box, fill in the fields you want, as described earlier under "Filling in the Label Region," then click Create.

3. When the Report window appears, click the Design button in the Toolbar. You'll be taken to the Design window.

4. Select the text object in the master record, inspect it, then select (check) the Run Time ➤ Line Squeeze property.

5. Select the master record, inspect it, choose Record Layout, then set the <u>N</u>umber of records across and down to 1 and change the <u>S</u>eparation across and down to 0. Then choose OK.

6. Choose <u>R</u>eport ➤ <u>P</u>age Layout from the menus and define your page layout. Choose <u>L</u>andscape orientation and an envelope size such as #10 or A4. Set your top, bottom, left, and right margins, then choose OK.

▶ ▶ **N O T E**

Because many laser printers have "dead zones" where they cannot print, you may need to adjust the margins in the Page Layout dialog box. For example, we changed all the margins to .5″ to accommodate the dead zone on our Hewlett-Packard LaserJet III printer.

7. If you want to sort the records, inspect the record band, choose Sort, complete the Sort Record Band dialog box, and choose OK.

8. Select the multi-record object that surrounds your envelope's fields and position it so that the top-left corner begins at about the 2.25-inch mark on the vertical ruler and the 4.75-inch mark on the horizontal ruler.

9. Place the inside address and any graphic logos near the upper-left corner of the record band. We put the top-left corner of our logo at about the 1-inch mark on the horizontal ruler and the $^{1}/_{2}$-inch mark on the vertical ruler, as in Figure 12.32.

When you've completed your design, save it, then preview and print the envelopes. (If you're trying this procedure for the first time, we suggest that you print just one envelope to make sure everything looks OK.)

►►NOTE

If printing doesn't begin right away, check to see whether your laser printer is prompting you to insert an envelope. You may need to push a "Continue" button or perform some other action to start printing. See your printer manual for details.

On some printers (for example, a Hewlett-Packard LaserJet III) that use manual envelope feeders, the envelope may be printed too high and text might be cut off or positioned improperly. The tips below can help you solve this problem:

- Choose Report ➤ Page Layout and change the paper size back to Letter $8\,^1/_2\,x\,11\,in$. Leave all the other settings the same.

- Reposition the return address and addressee objects as needed. On our LaserJet III, we had to move the objects down about 1.5 inches and to the right about .5 inch. The measurements you use will depend on your printer and the envelope design.

- Continue experimenting and printing a single envelope until your adjustments look just right, then print the whole shebang.

►►WARNING

The settings in the Page Layout dialog box are remembered throughout the current Paradox session, unless you change them. So be sure to verify those settings before you print or design another report.

►► *Changing Report Design Window Properties*

View ➤ Zoom and the Properties menu in the Design window provide several options for controlling the appearance and behavior of the window. After setting the properties, you can save them by choosing Properties ➤ Report Options ➤ Save Defaults. If you change your mind

Formatted Reports

►►
Ch.
12

immediately, you can choose Properties ➤ Report Options ➤ Restore Defaults to undo the most recent Save Defaults. The property settings become permanent when you exit Paradox.

▶ ▶ **N O T E**

Although you can't restore properties after exiting Paradox, you can easily reset any property you wish, then choose Properties ➤ Report Options ➤ Save Defaults again.

▶▶ *Printing Report Documents*

Paradox offers several ways to print reports and designs. These are outlined in the sections below.

▶ *Printing Your Report Design*

You may find it handy to print the report design, which shows all the objects and bands in the report. To begin, make sure you're in the Report Design window, then choose File ➤ Print ➤ Design.

The Print File dialog box appears with the page options preselected to print only the first page (and without Overflow Handling options). Click OK to begin printing the design as it appears in the Design window. Figure 12.33 shows the design for the sample form letter presented earlier in this chapter. As with forms, field names in the printed report design may appear garbled if Paradox cannot fit them in the space allotted. This appearance is normal, and it will not cause problems when you print your report.

▶ ▶ **N O T E**

The page break at the bottom of the record band does not appear in Figure 12.33, though it is present in the actual form design. Page breaks force Paradox to start each record's form letter on a new page.

FIGURE 12.33 ▶

*A sample design for
the form letter in
Figure 12.25*

Gift
Corner

8891 Gaudy Ave * West Fantasee, CA 92222
1-800-555-GIFT

April 21, 1995

▼ Record ▼

CUST CUSTLIST.First CU   CUSTLIST.Last Na
CUSTLIST.Address [A25]
CUSTLIST.City [A2 , CU   CUSTLIST

Dear CUST CUSTLIST.Last   :

*Welcome aboard, **CUST CUSTLIST.Last**   !* *The Gift Corner is*
pleased to have you as one of our new credit customers. Your credit limit of
CUSTLIST. is available as of CUSTLIST .

Now that you're firmly established as one of our valued customers, you may want to
peruse our exciting new catalog, which is chock full of great gift items. For example,
you'll find some terrific *Toys for Boys*, including hot new race cars in price ranges
that are as torrid as the engines under the hoods of these babies. If you're looking for
something a bit more tame, try our *Jungle Creatures Collection* -- stuffed animals
that look like the real thing! And CUST CUSTLIST.Last Na , if those on your gift
list are itching for a holiday, take a look at our *Exotic Vacation Packages*. We'll
guarantee some unforgettable memories! We'll even throw in a free camera, film, and
developing so those memories will never be lost.

Free!

*S*o why not call your Account Representative here at *The Gift Corner* today? We'll
send you a complimentary gift, just for picking up the phone and talking to us. You
can reach us 24-hours a day, toll-free at **1-800-555-GIFT**. Don't delay...Call us
today!

Sincerely yours,

Frank Lee Unctuous

Frank Lee Unctuous
Account Manager

▶ Printing Your Records

Paradox for Windows offers several ways to print a report in the layout specified by its design. Your options are as follows:

- Click the Print button in the Toolbar of either the Report Design or Report window.
- Choose File ➤ Print ➤ Report from the Design window.
- Choose File ➤ Print from the Report window.

If you don't want to change the design or view the data before printing, you can also print from the Open Document dialog box that appears when you choose File ➤ Open ➤ Report, or click the Open Report button in the Toolbar, or right-click the Reports icon in the Project Viewer and choose Open. After selecting the report name, simply choose the Print option in the Open Mode area of the dialog box, change the table, if you wish, then choose OK. For a quicker way to print, you can inspect the report's file name in the Project Viewer, and then choose Print or Print With from the property menu.

▶ ▶ **T I P**

You can use the buttons in the Toolbar or options on the Page menu of the Report window to move to and view any page in your report.

All of the methods listed above produce the Print File dialog box. Choose the appropriate print options, as described in Chapter 7, then choose OK to begin printing.

▶ Restarting the Print Job

As a general rule, any report that you print and distribute should contain the latest and greatest information. However, if you operate in a multi-user (network) environment, someone else might edit the data before the report has finished printing.

Fortunately, Paradox lets you decide how to proceed if data changes while your report is printing. To select an option, choose Report ➤ Restart Options from the Report Design window. You'll see the Restart Options dialog box shown below.

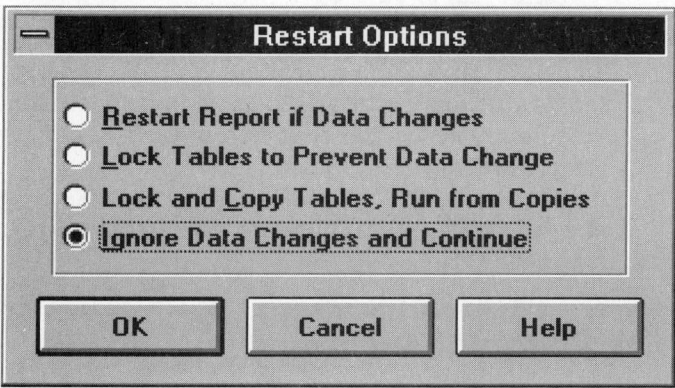

Your Restart options are described below.

Restart Report If Data Changes   Starts printing the report over again if data changes, regenerating queries if necessary. This option is the best choice if you're sure no one will be editing your table data while the report is printing. (This option is not available for dBASE tables.)

Lock Tables To Prevent Data Change   Prevents other users from editing the table while your report is printing. Paradox immediately releases the lock when printing is complete. If the lock fails, you should stop the report, then start it again later.

 ▶▶ **N O T E**

Lock Tables To Prevent Data Change is the least polite of the restart options, and you should use it sparingly to remain in the good graces of other network users.

Lock And Copy Tables, Run From Copies   Locks everyone out just long enough to copy the tables to disk. Paradox uses the copied version of your table(s) to print the report, deleting the

Formatted
Reports

▶ ▶

Ch.
12

copies when printing is complete. This option is more considerate of other users since copying to disk is faster than printing an entire report. However, reports on large tables can require a lot of disk space, and it's still possible that someone could change the original table data while your report is printing from the copy.

Ignore Data Changes And Continue   This is the fastest option, because the report continues even if someone changes the data during printing. This option is useful for rough reports where accuracy and consistency are not a top concern, and it is the default setting.

Choose the option that's best for your report (and your colleagues), then choose OK.

▶ *Tips for Faster Printing*

The speed of printing reports can be influenced by many factors, especially in a multi-user environment. Here are some tips to speed up report printing:

- Turn on the Windows Print Manager whenever you're printing to a local printer, or when printing small to medium-sized reports on a network.

- Turn off the Windows Print Manager when you're printing a large document on a network. This prevents Paradox from sending the report to the Print Manager first, saving both time and memory.

▶▶ *Delivering a Report Document*

Like forms, reports can be delivered so that users can print and preview them, but not make any changes. To prevent others from changing your report design, open it in the Report Design window, save any changes, then choose Report ➤ Deliver. Paradox will create a report with the same name as the original, but with an .rdl extension. For example, if your original form is *custrept.rsl*, the delivered version will be named *custrept.rdl*. You can then give the *.rdl* file to other users.

► ► **W A R N I N G**

> **Don't discard your original *.rsl* file, or *you* won't be able to change the report.**

If you need to change the report later, just modify the original report file (with the *.rsl* extension), save your changes, choose <u>R</u>eport ➤ <u>De</u>liver again, then distribute the updated *.rdl* file once more.

In this chapter, you've learned special techniques for creating custom reports, form letters, mailing labels, and envelopes. The most important differences between report and form design involve the use of report bands to separate your data into sections and group data, the expanded Run Time properties available for report objects, and the extra field- and line-squeezing that result when you surround fields and other objects within a text object.

In the next chapter, you'll learn how graphs and crosstabs can be used to analyze, summarize, and present large amounts of data in an attractive and useful form. After mastering the skills presented in Chapters 10 through 13, you'll be well on your way to designing just about any document you can imagine. When you're ready to create advanced forms and reports, turn to Chapter 17 to learn how to set up multitable design documents and how to use summary and calculated fields.

Graphing
Your Data

▶ ▶ Fₐₛₜ Tᵣₐcₖ

▶ ***To control whether titles, axes, labels, and legends
appear*** **754**

      inspect the graph, select Options, and select one of the
Show options on the menu.

▶ ***To add a crosstab to a document*** **774**

      click the Crosstab tool in the Design window Toolbar, click
in your design, and drag to define the size of the crosstab.

▶ ***To create a new "crosstab-only" document*** **775**

      click the Quick Crosstab button in the Table window's
Toolbar. Or, create a new form or report and choose a
Blan̲k style in the Design Layout dialog box. When you
reach the Design window, use the Crosstab tool to place
the crosstab. In crosstab-only reports, it's best to place the
crosstab in the report header or report footer band.

▶ ***To inspect an entire crosstab object*** **776**

      select the crosstab, move the mouse pointer to an empty area
at the upper-left corner of the crosstab, then right-click.

▶ ***To inspect a crosstab "hot zone"*** **776**

      select the crosstab, move the mouse pointer to an empty
area inside the boundaries of the hot zone, and right-click.

▶ ***To define the Categories, Column, and Summaries for a
crosstab*** **777**

      inspect the crosstab, choose Define Crosstab, click the
header (…) of the list that appears, and fill in the Define
Crosstab dialog box.

Paradox offers you a whole new way to analyze and summarize your table data, either visually in *graphs* or in spreadsheet formats called cross-tabulations (or *crosstabs* for short). Graphs and crosstabs are handy for digging out the hidden treasures of information that are so often buried under mountains of data.

The techniques used to design graphs and crosstabs are extensions of concepts presented in Chapters 10 through 12. Just remember that graphs and crosstabs are simply objects within a design document—like boxes, tables, fields, and so forth. Once created, they can be moved, resized, copied, deleted, and customized in plain or fancy flavors.

In this chapter, you'll discover how easy it is to plot data on graphs and to refine graphs to your own specifications. You'll find a rich variety of business graphs, including bar graphs, pie charts, line graphs, and others you may never have seen before. When we get to crosstabs, you'll learn how to group, summarize, and analyze your data in a handy spreadsheet format.

▶▶NOTE

Graphs and crosstabs can be used in both forms and reports. (In previous versions of Paradox, crosstabs were available only in forms.)

▶▶ *Summarizing Data with Graphs*

Graphs present information visually, in keeping with the idea that one picture is worth a thousand words. With Paradox for Windows, you can choose from 17 different types of graphs. You can choose from bar and line graphs, stacked bars, columns, pie charts, three-dimensional ribbons and surfaces, and more, depending on the data and what you want to do with it. Just be aware that not every type of graph makes sense for each set of data.

Throughout this chapter, we'll base our sample graphs and crosstabs on two tables containing financial information. The structure of the first table, *SalesReg*, is shown in Figure 13.1, and its sample data appears in Figure 13.2. The structure of the second table, *FinSum*, appears in Figure 13.3, and Figure 13.4 shows its data.

▶▶N O T E

We displayed the table structure by opening the appropriate table in the Table window and choosing Table ➤ Info Structure from the menus. You'll learn more about displaying a table structure in Chapter 15.

Let's take a moment to look at some of the types of graphs that Paradox for Windows has to offer.

FIGURE 13.1 ▶

The structure of the SalesReg table

Structure Information Paradox 5.0 for Windows Table: SALESREG.DB				
Field Roster:				

Field Roster:

	Field Name	Type	Size	Key
1	Sales Person	A	10	
2	Product Number	A	5	
3	Units Sold	N		
4	Total Sales	$		
5	Date Sold	D		

Table Properties:

Validity Checks ▼

☐ 1. Required Field

2. Minimum

3. Maximum

4. Default

5. Picture

Save As...   Done   Help

FIGURE 13.2 ▶

Sample data for the SalesReg table

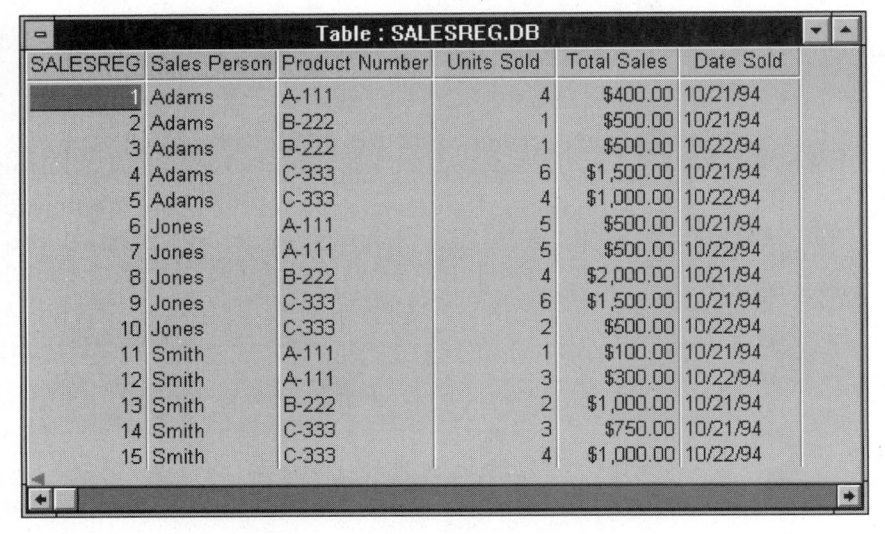

FIGURE 13.3 ▶

The structure of the Fin-Sum table

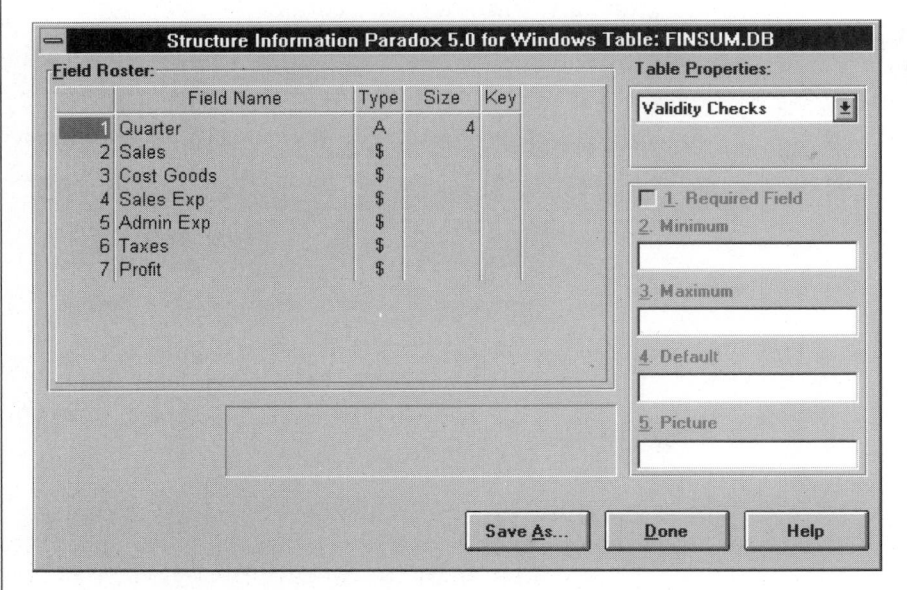

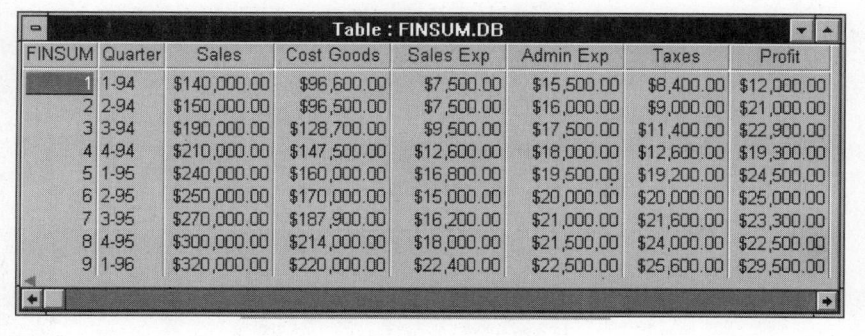

FIGURE 13.4

*Sample data for the
FinSum table*

►► *Exploring Graph Types*

The purpose of a graph is to display information in a form that's easy
to understand: a feat that requires creativity on your part and versatil-
ity from the graphic tools you use. Fortunately, the tools provided by
Paradox for Windows are up to the challenge. These offer eight types of
two-dimensional graphs and nine types of three-dimensional graphs, all
of which you can customize as you like. Each type of graph is described
briefly below, and several of the graph types are illustrated in Figures 13.5 and 13.6.

It's easy to switch from one type of graph to another, so you should experiment to find the best graph for your data. To change the graph
type, simply inspect the graph, choose Graph Type from the property
menu, and select the graph you want.

► *Two-Dimensional Graph Types*

The following two-dimensional graph types are available in Paradox for
Windows.

XY Graph   Uses the values assigned to the X (horizontal) and Y
(vertical) axes to plot points with a line connecting them. XY
graphs show the relationship between two or more variables. For
example, an XY graph can show how sales relate to profit in the
FinSum table.

FIGURE 13.5 ▶

Examples of the many types of 2D graphs you can display in Paradox for Windows. These graphs display data from the SalesReg and FinSum Tables.

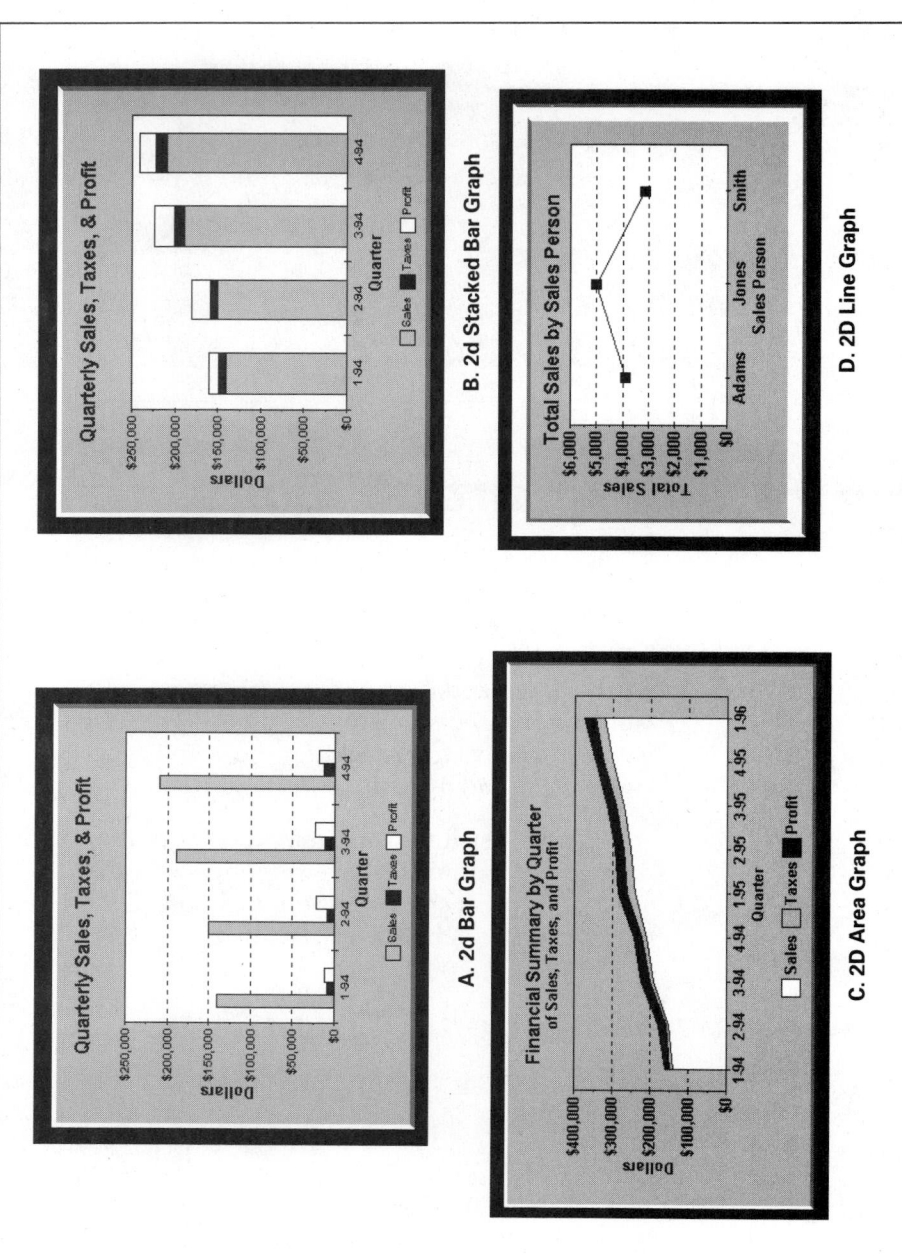

2D Bar (default graph type) Uses a single vertical bar to represent each data element (Figure 13.5A). 2D bar graphs can be useful for comparing values over a period of time.

2D Stacked Bar Shows the value of each series of data relative to the total by stacking series elements. The stacked bar graph in

FIGURE 13.6 ▶

A few of the many types of 3D graphs you can design in Paradox for Windows. These graphs display data from the SalesReg and FinSum tables.

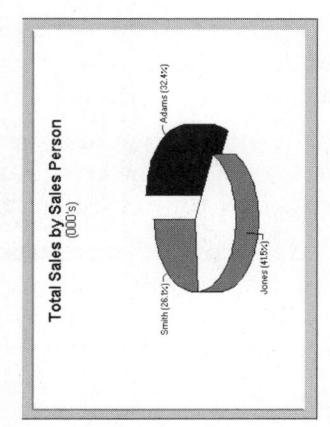

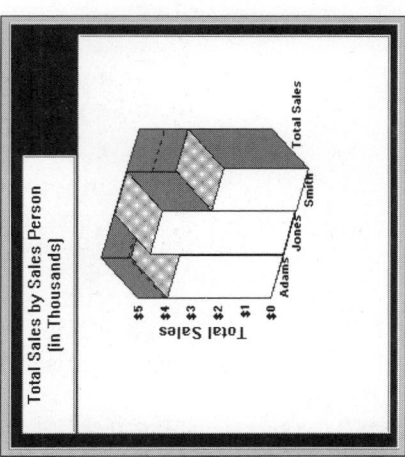

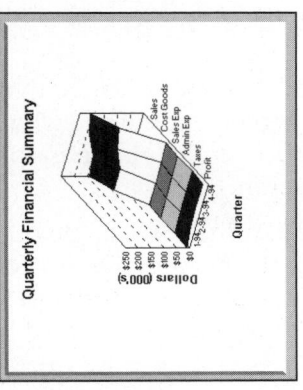

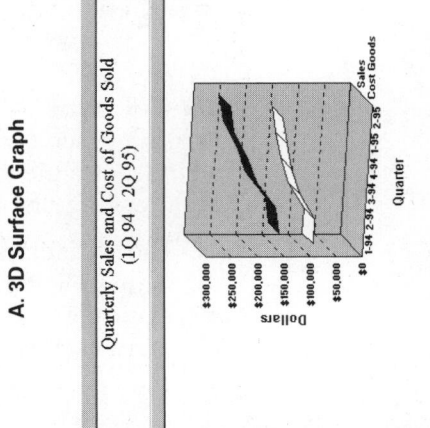

Figure 13.5B illustrates the relative impact of sales, taxes, and profit for each quarter.

 ►►**N O T E**

A *series* is a single field from a table that is plotted on a graph.

2D Rotated Bar   Reverses the X and Y axes, with the bars laid out horizontally. Rotated bar graphs are often used to represent and compare performance over time.

2D Area   Presents the information of a stacked bar graph with the smoothness of a line graph. The area graph is often used to show changes in values over time (see Figure 13.5C).

2D Line   Often used to show the changes in a value (or values) over time, so that you can easily see the dips and rises in your data. The x-axis on a line graph is often a progression of time, but can be used to plot any series of values (see Figure 13.5D).

 ►►**N O T E**

As discussed later in this chapter, line graphs can include a variety of marker types, no markers at all, or markers only. Furthermore, on 2D bar and 2D line graphs, you can change the graph type of any individual series to bar, line, or area.

2D Columns   Similar to pie charts in that they show the values in a single series as percentages of the whole. Instead of slicing up a circle, as a pie chart does, a column graph stacks slices vertically on a rectangular column.

2D Pie   Displays the values of a single series as percentages of the whole, slicing up the percentages in a circle. Each pie chart plots one series of values only (that is, a single field from the table), and each slice represents one record in the table.

▶ *Three-Dimensional Graph Types*

The three-dimensional graph types all display data series on a three-dimensional grid (an x-, y-, and z-axis). The series can be bars, areas, ribbons, pies, columns, or steps, as described below.

3D Bar, 3D Stacked Bar, and 3D Rotated Bar Resemble the corresponding 2D bar graphs except that the bars appear on a three-dimensional grid.

3D Area Resembles the corresponding 2D area graph, except the areas appear on a three-dimensional grid.

3D Surface A three-dimensional version of a line graph, with the lines flowing smoothly into one another (see Figure 13.6A). This format can give you a better view of the contours of your data, and is especially useful for seeing the effects of several data components at once. You must specify at least two y-axis fields to display a 3D surface graph.

3D Columns Resemble the corresponding 2D column graph, except the column appears on a three-dimensional grid.

3D Pie Resembles the corresponding 2D pie chart, except the slices appear on a three-dimensional grid (see Figure 13.6B).

3D Ribbon Essentially a line graph on a 3D grid, with each line flattened out into a segmented ribbon. Like line graphs, these work well to show trends and patterns over time (see Figure 13.6C).

3D Step Similar to a 3D bar graph, except that the bars of a series touch, as shown in Figure 13.6D. The effect of a 3D step graph can be more dramatic than a 3D bar graph, but sometimes the steps obscure data behind them.

▶▶ *Anatomy of a Graph*

Once you understand the anatomy of a graph, you'll have a better idea of which parts can be customized through property inspection. So let's take a moment to go over the terms used to describe the elements of a graph.

Figure 13.7 shows a customized graph with the most important elements labeled. This graph began as a 2D line graph, but we changed the Taxes series to bars for variety and altered the default markers for the Admin Expense series. We also changed the color of each series, the graph, and the graph background, customized the title of the graph and each axis title, and added a subtitle.

Depending on the type of graph you choose, Paradox will use any or all of the elements described below.

Axes The horizontal (x) and vertical (y) lines that establish the range of values plotted on the graph. Normally, the x-axis categorizes the data and the y-axis measures the values. This is true for

FIGURE 13.7 ▶

A sample graph with the elements labeled

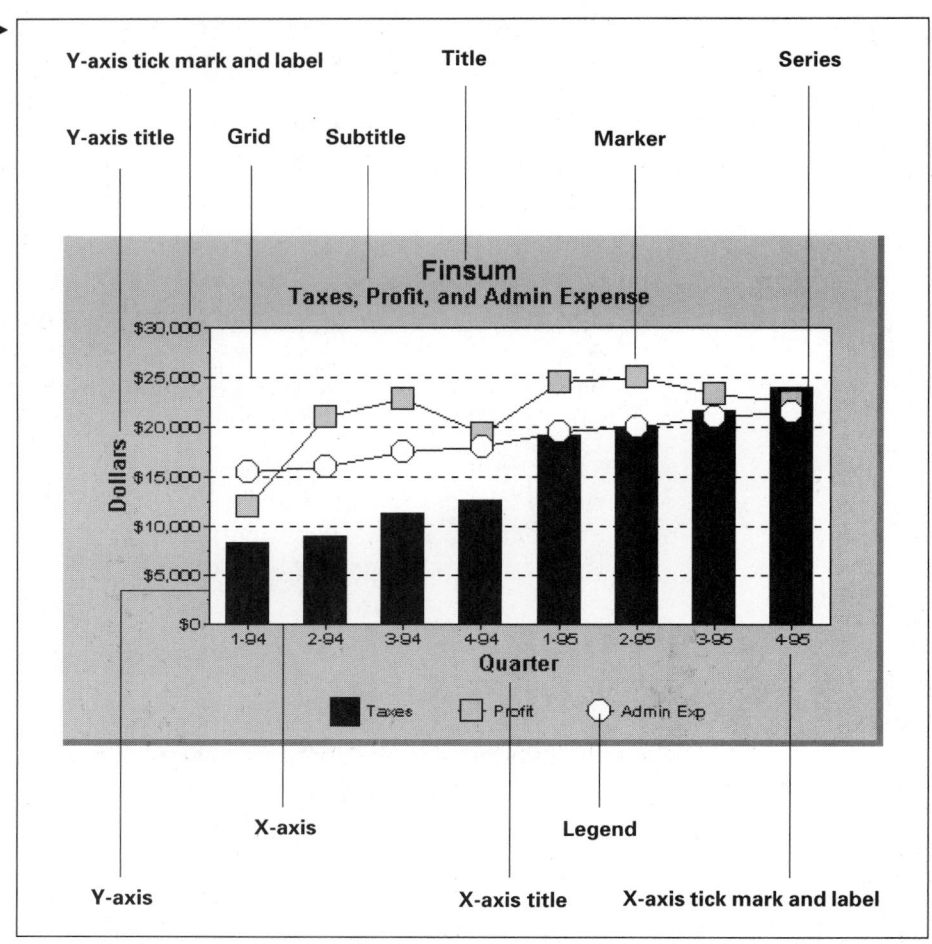

all Paradox graphs except pie charts and columns (which have no axes) and rotated bar graphs (where the x- and y-axes are reversed). Data on the x-axis appears in sorted order from smallest value to largest.

NOTE

Three-dimensional graphs also have an imaginary z-axis projecting outward from the graph.

Series   A single field that you plot against the y-axis. The first y-axis field definition is called the *first series*, the second, the *second series*, and so forth.

Titles   Text that appears at the top of the graph and along the axes. By default, Paradox uses the table name as the graph title and field names for axis titles. However, the graph title and axis titles can contain any text you want. You may also enter a subtitle, which will appear below the graph title.

Legend   The visual key that identifies the series in a graph. You can hide or show the legend as well as change its location and appearance.

Tick marks   Small marks along an axis that divide it into segments of equal length. These make the graph easier to read and they indicate the scale. In some types of graphs, horizontal grid lines extend from each tick mark on the y-axis (you can remove these if you wish).

Labels   Text appearing near each tick mark to identify values on the axes.

Scale   Definition of the range of values on the axes and the increments used to divide the axes by tick marks.

Slice   Representation of a single graphed value on a pie or column chart.

▶▶ *Understanding Graph Data Types*

Paradox for Windows offers three ways to analyze data in a table: *tabular*, *1-D summary*, and *2-D summary*. These are called the *data type* of the graph because they refer to the way Paradox analyzes data before plotting it.

▶▶ **N O T E**

> **Do not confuse the graph's data type with the graph type. The *data type* describes how the data is analyzed, whereas the *graph type* describes the picture used to display the results of the analysis.**

▶ *Tabular Data Type*

The tabular data type simply lays out the field values in a visual way, plotting each value as it is stored in the table. Thus, the height of a bar or line, or the width of a pie slice corresponds to an exact field value. For example, the tabular graph in Figure 13.8, taken from the Sales-Reg table, shows the number of units sold by Adams. Notice that each

FIGURE 13.8 ▶

This tabular bar graph shows the number of units sold in each of Adams' sales transactions.

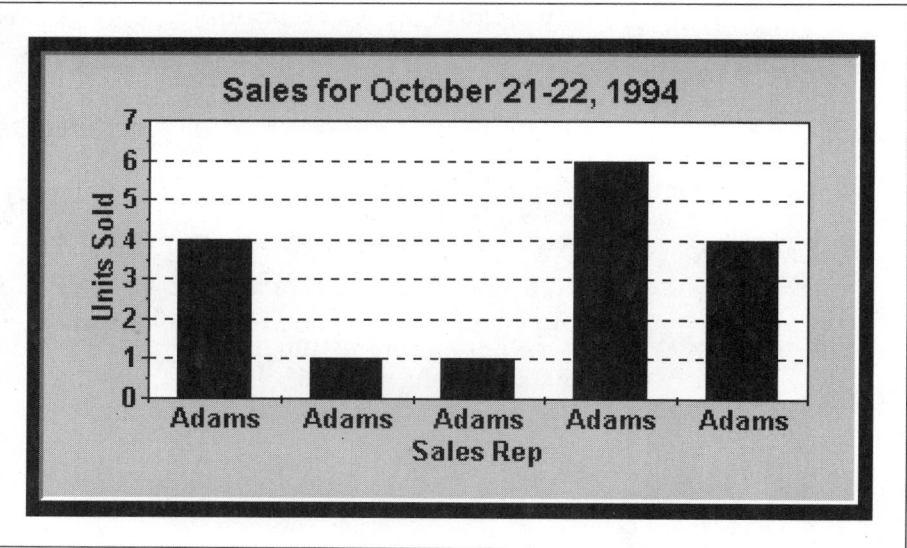

sales transaction is a separate bar, and the height of the bar indicates the number of units sold.

▶ ▶ **N O T E**

> **Tabular graphs are the default data type. You can define one x-axis field and as many numeric y-axis fields as you wish in a tabular graph.**

▶ *1-D Summary and 2-D Summary Data Type*

While tabular graphs are useful for presenting small amounts of data, they lead to cluttered and complicated graphs with no summarized (totaled) results when used with large tables. A better way to graph data in the SalesReg table would be to group and summarize the records first. For example, you might want to graph each salesperson's total sales. Or, you might want to go one step further and graph each salesperson's total sales *for each product*. Here's where 1-D summary and 2-D summary graphs can help.

▶ ▶ **N O T E**

> **You could also use a query to summarize your data, and then graph the results. Chapter 16 explains how to pose queries that perform calculations on numeric data.**

In a *1-D summary* graph, the x-axis field contains values to be grouped together, so that all records with the same values in the x-axis field are placed in the same group. In essence, the table is sorted by the x-axis field. The y-axis field or fields in a 1-D summary graph are used to display the results of some calculation within each group. For example, to calculate and graph the total number of units sold by each salesperson in the SalesReg table shown in Figure 13.2, we would create a 1-D summary graph, making Sales Person the x-axis field and Units Sold the y-axis field.

A *2-D summary* graph is the same as a 1-D summary graph, except that it lets you group data by a second field. Thus, we could graph the total units sold by each salesperson for each product in the table. To do so, we would create a 2-D summary graph, specify Sales Person as the x-axis field, Units Sold as the y-axis field, and Product Number as the field to group by.

▶ ▶NOTE

In previous versions of Paradox for Windows, only the tabular graph type was allowed in reports. In Paradox 5 for Windows, however, your reports can display tabular, 1-D summary, and 2-D summary graphs.

In most cases, you will probably use graphs to generate totals (or sums). However, 1-D and 2-D summary graphs can perform any of several operations on the field used as the summary value.

As you read the descriptions of each operation below, take a look at the sample 1-D summary graphs in Figure 13.9 and the 2-D summary graphs in Figure 13.10. Notice that the y-axis in the sample graphs is labeled to indicate the summary operator used to produce the graph. Although the 2-D summary graphs in Figure 13.10 are nearly identical to the 1-D summary graphs in Figure 13.9, they've been broken down further by product number. So, instead of displaying only one value in each group on the x-axis, the 2-D summary graphs show three values for each salesperson: one value for each of the three product numbers. The legends and subtitles in Figure 13.10 identify Product Number as the field used to group the data.

Sum   For each record of each group on the x-axis, *Sum* totals the non-empty values in the corresponding y-axis field. For instance, the Sum example in Figure 13.9 graphs the total units sold by Adams (16 units), followed by the total units sold by Jones (22 units), followed by the total units sold by Smith (13 units).

In Figure 13.10 the sums are broken down by product number. Thus the first group in the Sum example of Figure 13.10 shows the total units of product A-111 sold by Adams (4), the total units of product B-222 sold by Adams (2), and the total units of product C-333 sold by Adams (10). The next group shows the total

FIGURE 13.9

A series of 1-D summary bar graphs showing how each summary operator graphs the unit sales per salesperson. The y-axis in each graph is labeled with the type of summary operator used to produce the graph.

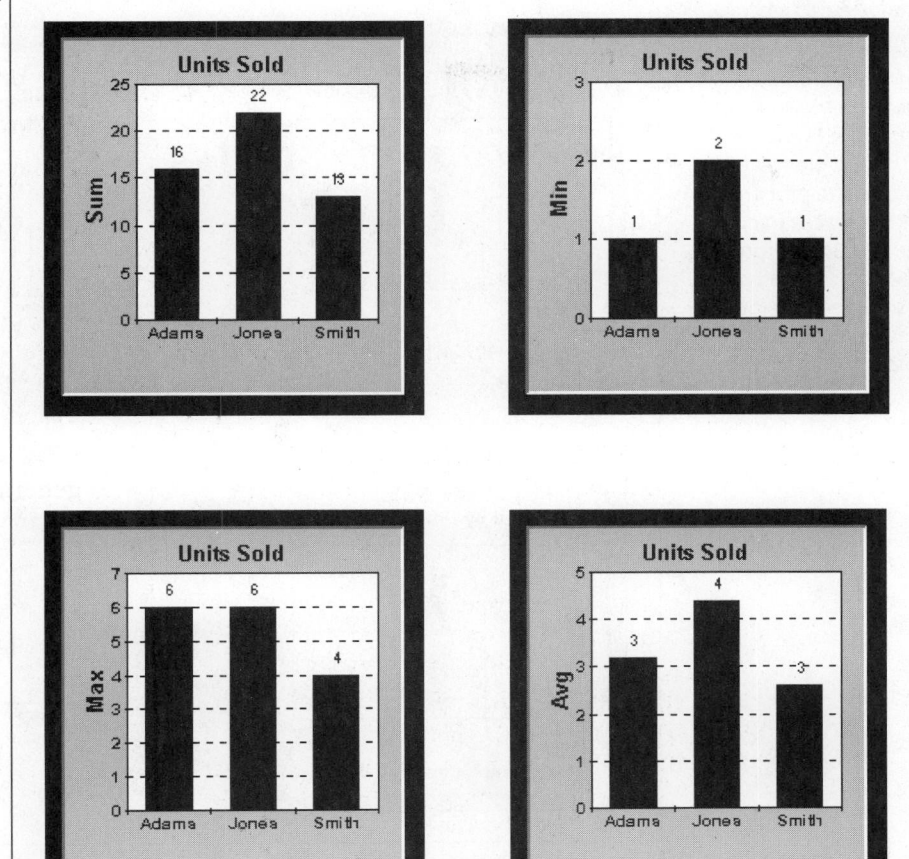

units of each product sold by Jones, and the last group shows the total units of each product sold by Smith.

Min For each value on the x-axis, *Min* graphs the smallest of all the individual values found in the corresponding y-axis field. In the 1-D summary example, this is the smallest number of units sold by each salesperson. In the 2-D summary example, the Min operator graphs the smallest number of units sold by each salesperson for each product number.

FIGURE 13.10 ▶

A series of 2-D summary bar graphs based on the same data as in Figure 13.9, with data grouped by salesperson and product number. Again, the y-axis in each graph is labeled with the type of summary operator used to produce the graph.

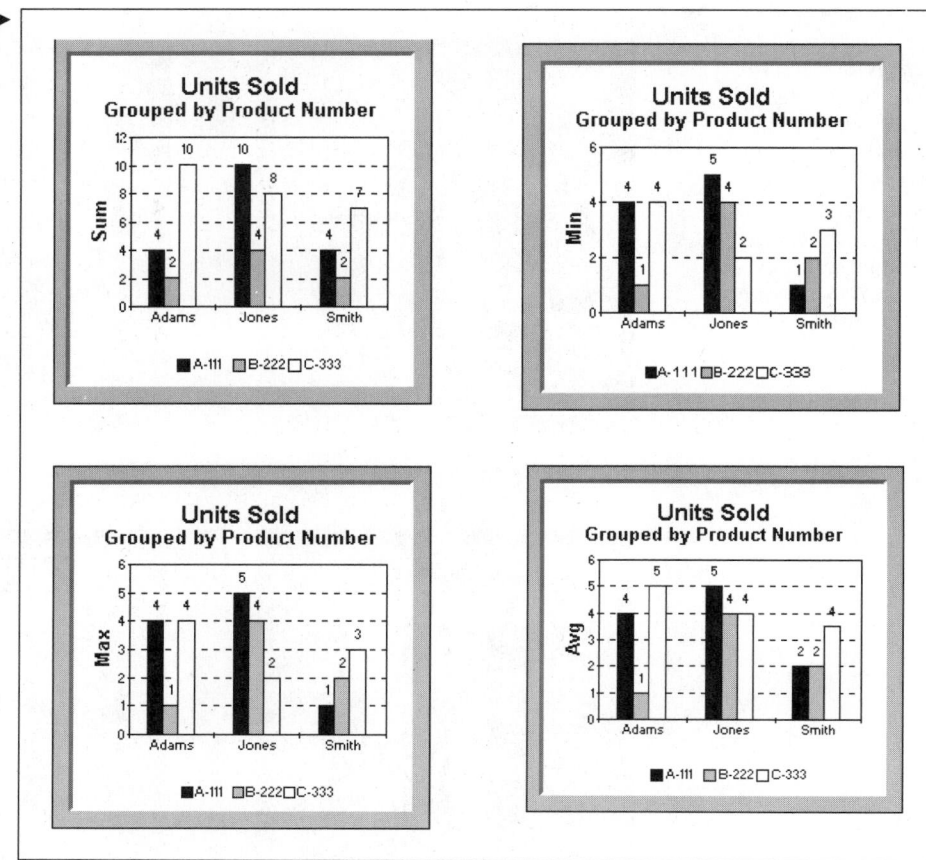

Max   For each value on the x-axis, *Max* graphs the largest of all the individual values found in the corresponding y-axis field. In the 1-D summary example, this is the largest number of units sold by each salesperson. In the 2-D summary example, you'll see the largest number of units sold by each salesperson for each product number.

Count   For each value on the x-axis, *Count* tallies the number of corresponding non-empty y-axis values. In the 1-D summary example, this would be the count in the SalesReg table for each salesperson. In the 2-D summary example, this is the count for each salesperson for each product number.

▶ ▶ **N O T E**

> In the SalesReg table, all records contain values in the
> Units Sold field, so the counts are equal to the number
> of transactions for each salesperson. In the 1-D
> summary, each salesperson has a Count of 5, for a total
> of 15 transactions. In the 2-D summary, Adams has 1
> transaction for product A-111 and 2 transactions each
> for B-222 and C-333; Jones and Smith have 2
> transactions each for A-111 and C-333 and 1 for B-222
> (for a total of 15).

Avg   For each value on the x-axis, *Avg* graphs the average of all
the individual values found in the corresponding y-axis field. In
the 1-D summary example, this is the average number of units
sold by each salesperson. In the 2-D summary example, Avg
graphs the average number of units sold by each salesperson for
each product number. The average is the sum of the non-empty
values divided by the count of the non-empty values.

Std   For each value on the x-axis, *Std* graphs the standard deviation of all the individual values in the corresponding y-axis field.
Std is meaningful only with very large samples.

Var   For each value on the x-axis, *Var* graphs the statistical variance of all the individual values found in the corresponding y-axis
field. Like Std, Var is meaningful only with very large samples.

Here are some rules to keep in mind about 1-D and 2-D summary
graphs:

- You can define one x-axis field and multiple y-axis fields in a 1-D
  summary graph.

- You can define one x-axis field, one group-by field, and one y-axis
  field for a 2-D summary graph.

- Some field types cannot be used for the x-axis, grouped by, or
  y-axis values (these will be dimmed and unavailable in various dialog boxes and property lists).

▶▶ *Designing a Graph*

As with other aspects of document design, setting up graphs isn't a strictly sequential process. Once you've created the basic graph object, you can define its properties in just about any order. In this chapter, we'll summarize the basic procedures for creating graphs. Then, with these techniques in mind, you can take the approach that suits you best.

Regardless of how you define your graph, Paradox will make some initial choices concerning the graph title, axis titles, labels for tick marks, scaling, and so forth. For example, the default title for the graph is the table name; there is no subtitle or legend; the axis titles are taken from field names, where appropriate; tick mark labels are derived from the data values in the x- and y-axes; and the tick mark scale and increments are calculated automatically, based on the data being plotted. You can customize any of these settings, as you will learn later in this chapter.

▶ *Creating a Graph*

 To add a graph to an existing form or report document, click the Graph tool in the Design window Toolbar (shown at left), then click in your design and drag the mouse to define the initial size of the graph.

For example, the form in Figure 13.11 includes a table object showing three fields from the FinSum table and an undefined 2D bar graph whose size was outlined using the Graph tool. Keep in mind that the graph shown in the Design window is simply a replica or *template* of the actual graph, which will probably look quite a bit different when you preview or print it.

 ▶ ▶ **T I P**

> If anyone changes data that's used in a graph you're currently displaying in Form View, Paradox will update the affected data in the graph as soon as the user moves the cursor to another record in the table and you refresh the graph in Form View. The quickest way to refresh the graph is to press F8 twice (this switches between the Form Design and Form View windows). If the graph is on the same form as the table you're updating, it will be refreshed as soon as you move the cursor to another record.

FIGURE 13.11 ►

A newly created graph initially appears as an undefined 2D bar graph.

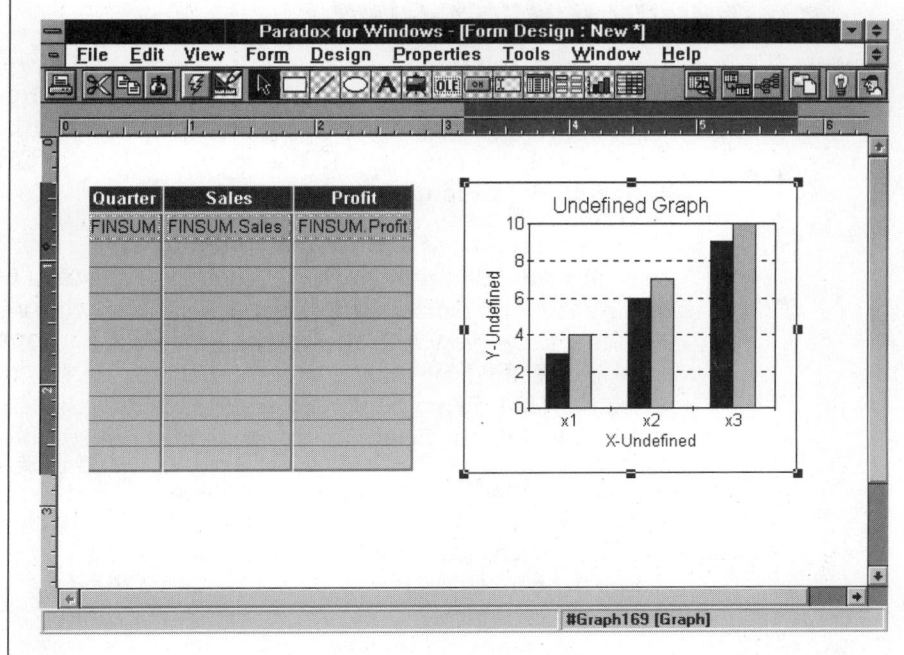

You can also create a new form or report that includes the graph only—with no other fields from the table. To do this, simply choose File ➤ New ➤ Form or File ➤ New ➤ Report, click the Data Model / Layout Diagram button, choose your table in the Data Model dialog box, then select a Blank style in the Design Layout dialog box and click OK. Next, use the Graph tool as described above to place the graph into your design.

 ► ► **T I P**

> **When creating graph-only reports, your best bet is to place the graph in the report header or report footer band. If you accidentally put a 1-D or 2-D summary graph in the record band, the graph will be repeated once for each record in the table! You cannot define 1-D or 2-D summary graphs in the page band.**

▶ Creating a Quick Graph

If you're in Table View and haven't yet assigned a preferred graph to the table, there's another way to create a graph: Simply click the Quick Graph button in the Toolbar (shown at left) to begin defining a graph for the table immediately. (This opens the Define Graph dialog box shown later in Figure 13.13.)

We'll explain how to use the Define Graph dialog box in a moment. For now, just note that the Quick Graph button creates a new form and takes you right to the Define Graph dialog box. This works just as if you had chosen File ▶ New ▶ Form, clicked the Data Model / Layout Diagram button, specified the table currently open on the Desktop, chosen a blank design style, drawn a graph object, inspected it, chosen Define Graph, and then clicked the ... header in the property menu. Truly a timesaver!

If you've already assigned a preferred graph to the table, clicking the Quick Graph button in Table View will immediately display the graph in a new Form window. You can then click the Design button in the Toolbar or press F8 if you want to change the design.

▶ ▶ **T I P**

To create a preferred graph, open the table, right-click the Quick Graph button in the Toolbar, choose the form that contains your graph, and click OK. Then choose Properties ▶ View Properties ▶ Save to save your changes.

▶ Inspecting the Entire Graph Object

Like other objects in a design, graphs can be customized in a variety of ways. It should come as no surprise that you define and customize a graph by changing *properties* of the graph object or one of its hot zones.

We'll explain how to inspect a hot zone in the next section. For now, let's look at the basic techniques for inspecting the graph object itself:

● Select the graph by clicking it. Then press F6, or move the mouse pointer to an empty area just inside the selection handles of the graph and right-click.

- Or, click the Object Tree button in the Toolbar (see Chapter 10), then right-click the graph object (labeled *#Graph*).

Figure 13.12 shows the property menu for a default graph object. From this property menu, you can choose Define Graph (explained in a moment) to define your graph, or you can choose any of the other options to customize the graph. (Note that some options are not available for reports.)

FIGURE 13.12 ▶

The Graph property menu appears when you inspect the graph.

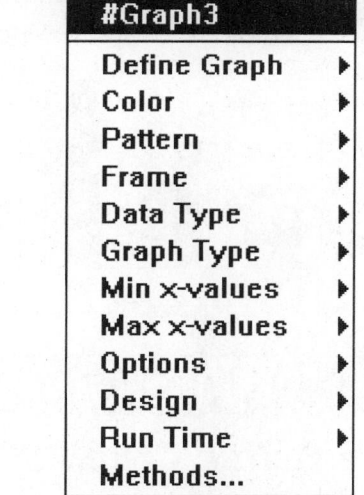

```
#Graph3
  Define Graph      ▶
  Color             ▶
  Pattern           ▶
  Frame             ▶
  Data Type         ▶
  Graph Type        ▶
  Min x-values      ▶
  Max x-values      ▶
  Options           ▶
  Design            ▶
  Run Time          ▶
  Methods...
```

▶ ▶ **N O T E**

> In this chapter, we'll focus on properties that are unique to graphs. Please refer to Chapter 10 for general information on changing properties, and to Appendix E for a complete list of properties.

▶ *Inspecting the Graph Hot Zones*

Graphs contain many hot zones that you can inspect and change. These include the title box, axes, data series, legend box, background, and other areas that depend on the type of picture you're using to display the graph. At first you might have trouble locating the hot zones, but with practice you'll soon become an expert.

To locate a hot zone and change its properties, select the graph by clicking it, then move the mouse pointer to the area you want to inspect. When the mouse pointer changes to a small ↑, right-click to open the property menu. In the example below, we moved the mouse pointer to the first data series hot zone (indicated by the ↑ in the first bar above the *x3* label on the x-axis).

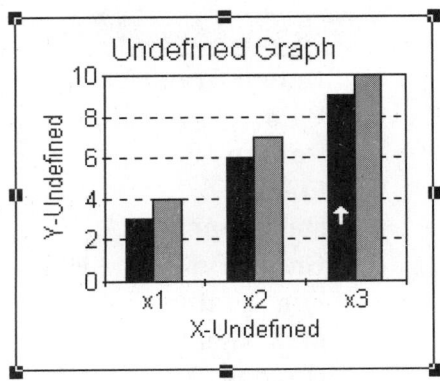

▶ *Using the Define Graph Dialog Box*

You can define the table, graph data, x- and y-axis fields, and any groups in a single step, or you can inspect individual areas of the graph. It's probably easiest to start with the "all at once" approach described below. Later we'll explain how to set up the graph definition on a piecemeal basis.

To define a graph, inspect the entire graph object (not a hot zone) as described previously and choose Define Graph. You'll see a list of the tables defined in the Data Model dialog box, plus the list header (…). Now you have two choices: You can define a default graph, or you can define the table, fields, and graph data type more precisely.

To define a *default* graph for the table, simply click the table name in the property list. Paradox will create a 2D bar graph, in which the leftmost numeric field in the table defines the x-axis, and the remaining numeric fields, in left-to-right order, become the y-axis fields. From here, you can preview the graph or you can inspect various elements of the graph—including the graph itself—to customize further.

If you prefer not to define a default graph, click the header (...) or press ↵. You'll see the Define Graph dialog box shown in Figure 13.13.

FIGURE 13.13

The Define Graph dialog box lets you define the table, fields, data type, and groups all at once.

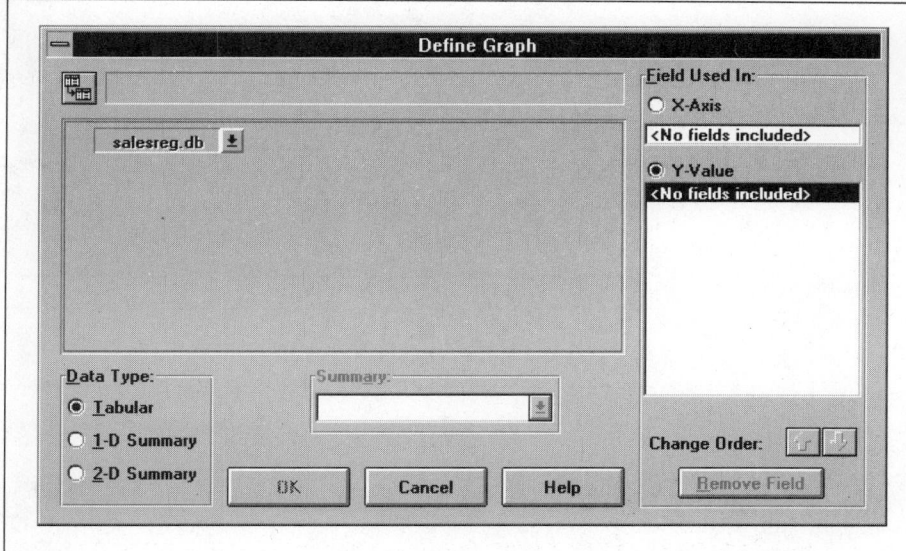

From here, the steps are as follows:

1. If you wish to add or delete a table, click the Data Model button at the upper-left corner of the dialog box and choose the table you want, as described in Chapter 10. Click OK when you're finished. The Data Model button is handy for graphing a table *other* than the one you first specified in the Data Model dialog box.

2. In the Data Type area, click Tabular, 1-D Summary, or 2-D Summary.

- If you chose 1-D Summary, the Define Graph dialog box will change to resemble Figure 13.14.

- If you chose 2-D Summary, the dialog box will resemble Figure 13.15 instead.

FIGURE 13.14 ▶

The Define Graph dialog box after choosing 1-D Summary in the Graph Type area. Notice that the Y-Value area moves down in the dialog box.

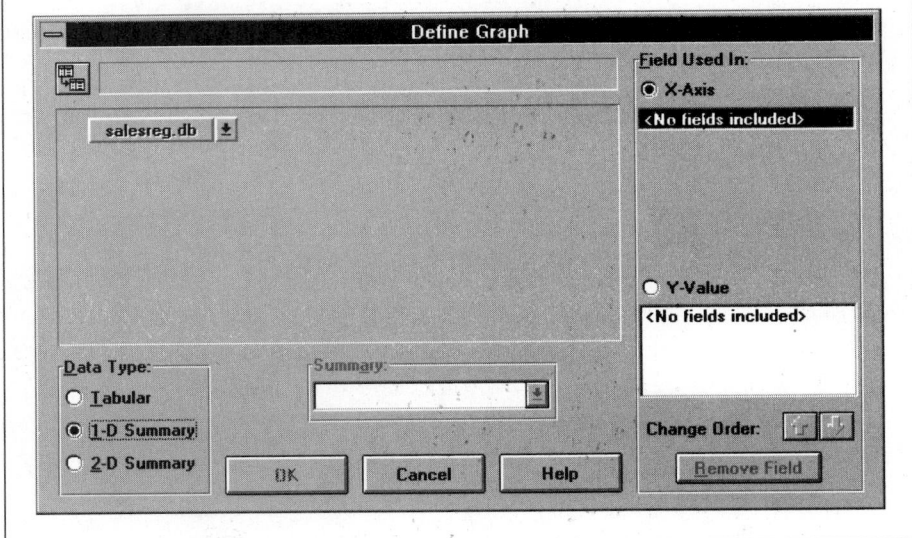

FIGURE 13.15 ▶

The Define Graph dialog box after choosing 2-D Summary in the Graph Type area. Notice that the Y-Value area moves down and a new Grouped By area appears in the dialog box.

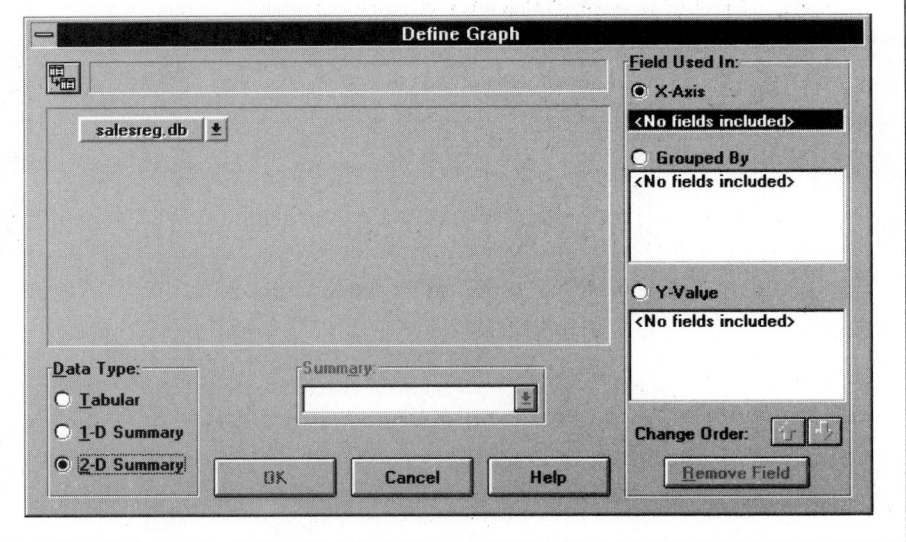

3. To define the X-Axis, Y-Value, or Grouped By fields, click the appropriate option in the Field Used In area of the dialog box.

4. Click the drop-down arrow next to the table, then click the appropriate field or fields. The selected fields will appear beneath the option you chose in step 3.

5. Make any of the changes listed below.

   • To change the summary operator for a field (1-D and 2-D summary graphs only), click the Y-Value field you want to summarize in the Field Used In area, then click the Summary list box and select the summary operator you want.

   • To rearrange the order of fields, click the field you want to move in the Field Used In area, then click the ↑ and ↓ Change Order buttons as appropriate.

   • To remove a field, click the field in the Field Used In area, then click the Remove Field button.

6. When you're finished, choose OK.

▶ Defining the X- and Y-Axis Fields

If you'd like to define fields for the x- or y-axis individually, inspect the axis title or tick marks for the axis you want to change. The x-axis property menu for a 2D bar graph appears below.

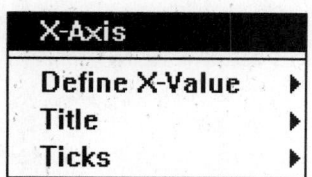

And here's the y-axis property menu for a 2D bar graph:

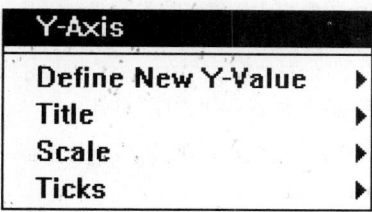

Now, choose Define X-Value or Define New Y-Value and choose a field name from the list that appears. If you want to plot more than one series on the y-axis, inspect the y-axis title or tick marks again, choose Define New Y-Value, and choose another field name.

▶▶**N O T E**

The fields available depend on the data type and graph type; unavailable fields will be dimmed.

▶ Changing the Graph Data Type

Recall that the default graph data type is Tabular, which simply uses the selected pictorial format to display values as they appear in the table. You can change the data type of the graph at any time by inspecting the graph object, choosing Data Type, then selecting the data type you want (Tabular, 1D Summary, or 2D Summary).

▶▶**N O T E**

You can also use the Define Graph dialog box, discussed earlier, to change the data type of a graph.

▶ Changing the Graph Type

As you define your graph, you may want to experiment with different graph types to determine which format presents your data in the clearest and most attractive way. Changing the graph type is easy: Simply inspect the graph object, choose Graph Type, and select the graph type you want from the menu that appears. Later on in this chapter, we'll provide some tips to help you choose the most effective representation for your graphs.

Figure 13.16 shows the menu of graph types. The graph types available depend on the graph's data type and the fields you've selected for the x-axis and y-axis. For example, you can't choose an XY graph type if one of the axes contains alphanumeric data.

Once you choose a graph type, the Design window immediately changes to reflect your selection.

FIGURE 13.16 ►

*You can choose
any of 17 different
graph types to dis-
play your data.*

XY Graph
√ 2D Bar
2D Stacked Bar
2D Rotated Bar
2D Area
2D Line
2D Columns
2D Pie
3D Bar
3D Stacked Bar
3D Rotated Bar
3D Area
3D Surface
3D Columns
3D Pie
3D Ribbon
3D Step

► *Redefining Graph Elements*

Most elements in the graph object have *Define* properties, which let you
redefine the element. For example, the property menu for a title includes a Define Graph property. Similarly, the x-axis property menu
has a Define X-Value option, while the y-axis menu includes a Define
New Y-Value (or Define Y-Value) property.

When you choose Define from a property menu, a list of options appears. You can either choose one of the options or click the header area
of the list (…) and make choices from a dialog box.

 ► ►**TIP**

**To save time, you can open the Define Graph dialog
box and define the fields and data type in one step.**

▶ *Using the Graph Object's Options Property*

You can determine whether your graph will display a title and subtitle, a legend, grid, axes, and data labels. If you find that a graph is too cluttered, consider removing one or more of these elements. If you'd like the graph to convey more information, you can display these elements. Either way, you will need to inspect the graph object, choose Options, and select one of the options below.

Show Title When checked, this option displays the graph title and subtitle. When it is unchecked, the title and subtitle are removed from the graph.

Show Legend When checked, this option displays a legend. When it is unchecked, no legend appears.

Show Grid When checked, this option displays grid lines that begin at each y-axis tick mark on the graph. Unchecking the option removes the grid lines from the graph. Note that grid lines will not appear unless *Show Axes* is also checked.

Show Axes When this option is checked, tick marks and tick labels appear on the graph. When the option is unchecked, tick marks, tick labels, and any grid lines will disappear from the graph.

Show Labels When checked, this option displays labels showing the value of each data series. When Show Labels is unchecked, no data labels appear.

Rotation This option controls the rotation of 3D graphs (described later in this chapter).

Elevation This option controls the elevation of 3D graphs (described later in this chapter).

Note that the available options and their default settings depend on the type of graph you're defining.

▶ ▶ **N O T E**

If you want to customize the titles, legend, or tick marks, be sure the corresponding Show Title, Show Legend, or Show Axes option is checked.

► Customizing Graph Titles and Subtitles

If you want to display a special title at the top of the graph, first inspect the title hot zone near the top of the graph, and choose Title or Subtitle. You'll see the following property menu (2-D summary graphs also have a Define Group option).

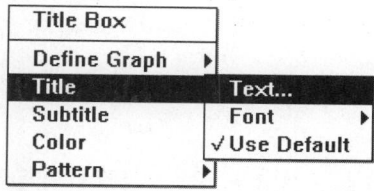

- To customize the title or subtitle text, choose *Text*, type your text in the dialog box that appears, and choose OK.

- To change the font, choose *Font* followed by the Typeface, Size, Style, or Color options.

- To return customized title or subtitle text to the default, or vice versa, choose *Use Default*. When the option is checked, Paradox uses the default title or subtitle, with whatever font attributes you've chosen. When the option is unchecked, Paradox uses the customized text you've supplied.

 ► ► T I P

If you don't need a subtitle but you do want some extra space to appear below the graph's title, inspect the title hot zone, choose Subtitle ► Text, press the spacebar (to create a blank subtitle), and choose OK.

The title and subtitle options don't provide a great deal of flexibility and they limit the number of characters you can type. If you need fancier titles and subtitles than the above options allow, or you want to place the titles outside the graph object, turn off the titles altogether by inspecting the graph object and unchecking Options ► Show Title.

Then use the Text tool in the Toolbar to draw a text object where you can type in the text you want. You can change the properties of the text object if you want to customize the title further.

▶ Customizing Axis Titles

Changing titles on the x-axis and y-axis is just as easy as customizing the graph titles: Inspect the appropriate x-axis or y-axis hot zones, choose *Title*, then choose *Text*, *Font*, or *Use Default*, as described above.

 ▶ ▶ **N O T E**

To locate the axis hot zone, select the graph, then move the mouse pointer near the axis title or the tick marks. The mouse pointer changes to ↑ when it hits a hot zone.

▶ Customizing Tick Labels

Customizing the tick mark labels is also easy. Inspect the appropriate axis title or tick mark area and choose *Ticks* from the property menu. The available options depend on the data type of the axis labels and the axis you're changing, but they'll typically include one or more of the following:

Font Provides options for changing the Typeface, Size, Style, and Color of the label.

Number Format Lets you change the number format for the tick mark labels (see Chapter 7).

Alternate Available for the x-axis only. Checking this option staggers the x-axis labels to prevent them from overlapping. Choose this option if the x-axis labels are too long to allow space between each one.

▶ Scaling the Axes

The *Scale* option on the property menu for an axis allows you to control the range of numeric values displayed. Although you can always define the scale for a y-axis that is plotting numeric values, x-axis scaling is available only for XY graphs.

N O T E

Choosing the Scale property leads to the following options: Auto-Scale, Logarithmic, Low Value, High Value, and Increment.

By default, Paradox figures out how to scale the graph axes based on the data being plotted. For example, if the smallest value to be plotted is 1000 and the largest value is 5100, Paradox automatically sets up the y-axis to extend from 0 to 6000. Automatic scaling is in effect when the Scale ➤ Auto-Scale property option is checked.

If you uncheck the Scale ➤ Auto-Scale property, you can set your own minimum (Low) and maximum (High) values that display or accentuate a trend or value. When defining scaling, make sure the range you select includes all the values to be graphed; otherwise the resulting graph may show inaccurate results. For instance, if you set the high end of the y-axis to 2000, data values larger than 2000 will always appear at the top of the graph. Thus, a value of 5000 would appear as 2000.

When the Scale ➤ Auto-Scale property is not checked, you can also customize the Increment used to separate the tick marks along the axis. For example, if you set a Low Value of 0 and a High Value of 5000, Paradox will automatically place tick marks at 1000, 2000, 3000, and 4000 on the y-axis. However, if you change the tick mark increment value for the y-axis to 2000, Paradox will place tick marks at 2000 and 4000.

To define your own scaling, first inspect the axis you want to scale, then uncheck the Scale ➤ Auto-Scale option. The Low Value, High Value, and Increment options will be available the next time you choose the Scale property. Now, for each component of the scale that you want to change, inspect the axis, choose Scale, select Low Value, High Value, or Increment, type the value you want into the dialog box that appears, and choose OK. (We used manual scaling to adjust the High Value for many graphs shown in this chapter.)

Logarithmic Scaling

Regardless of whether Paradox is scaling your data automatically or you are scaling it manually, you might want to use logarithmic scaling when plotting series with wide ranges of magnitude. In a logarithmically scaled axis, each major division of the axis represents ten times the value of the previous division. For example, the first tick mark is .1, the next is 1, the next is 10, the next is 100, and so forth.

To choose logarithmic scaling, inspect the axis, then check the Scale ➤ Logarithmic option. To return to normal scaling, uncheck the option.

▶▶**N O T E**

If you uncheck Auto-Scale and check Logarithmic, Paradox will automatically set positive values (> 0) for Scale ➤ Low Value and Scale ➤ High Value. Make sure that these values remain positive if you define low and high values of your own. Also remember that Paradox will not let you use logarithmic scaling if any Y-Values in your table are negative or zero.

▶ Controlling the Amount of Data Shown in the Graph

When viewing your graph, you may find that it's too cluttered to show the specific data points or trends you're interested in. Fortunately, you can limit data values in any of the ways described below.

- Base your graph on a saved query. A carefully constructed query can reduce confusion by eliminating unnecessary data points from the graph.

- Use 1-D summary and 2-D summary graphs (or crosstabs, described later in this chapter) to summarize your data.

- Specify the number of values to display along the x-axis of your graph and the number of groups that appear in a 2-D summary graph.

To use the last method, inspect the graph object, then choose one of the following options:

Min X-Values   Lets you specify the minimum number of x-axis values that can appear in a graph. After choosing Min X-Values, choose a number from the list (1 to 8) or click the header area, type your own value, and choose OK.

Max X-Values Lets you specify the maximum number of x-axis values that can appear. Again, you can choose a value from 1 to 8, or click the header area to type in your own value.

Max Groups Defines the maximum number of group-by values in 2-D summary graphs. Choosing this option limits the number of bars that appear in each group on the x-axis. Again, you can choose a value from 1 to 8, or click the list header and type in your own value. The graph in Figure 13.17 shows total sales for each salesperson in the SalesReg table, grouped by the Product Number field, with Max Groups set to 2.

FIGURE 13.17 ▶

This 2-D summary graph is limited to displaying only two groups.

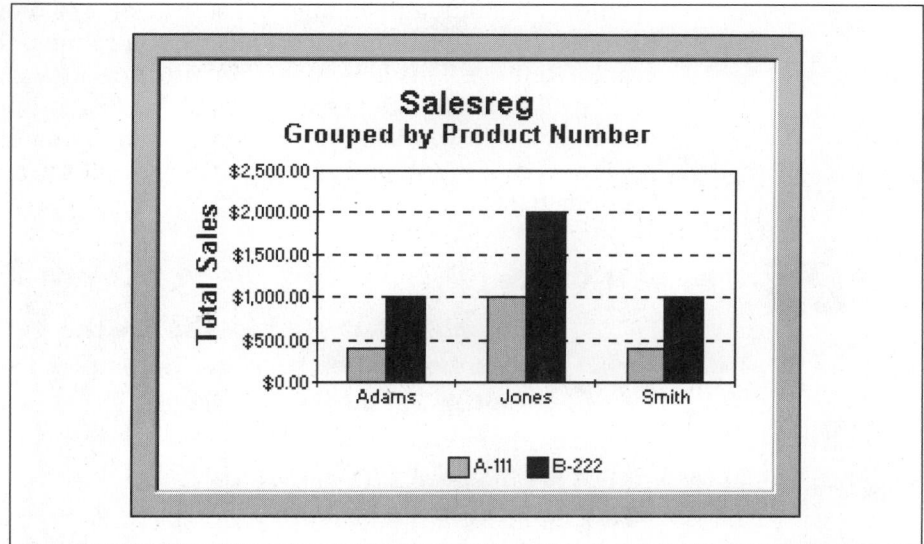

▶ *Customizing the Graph Series*

In addition to customizing the overall features of a graph, you can customize individual series. To do so, inspect the hot zone for the series you want to change. For example, if you want to change the appearance of the first series in a 2D line graph, click the graph object and move the pointer near the line you want to change. Then, when the mouse pointer changes to ↑, right-click. You'll see a property menu similar to the one below.

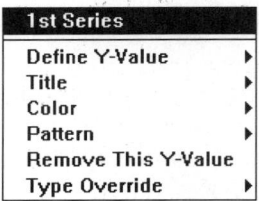

All series property menus let you redefine the field used for the series (Define Y-Value), and change the series color (Color) or pattern (Pattern); all but 2-D summary graphs let you remove the series from the graph (Remove This Y-Value). The title option will appear only if you've also checked the Options ➤ Show Legend property for the graph (see "Customizing the Legend"). The remaining options depend on the type of graph and series you're inspecting, as explained in the sections below.

 **N O T E**

Remember that you can also use the Define Graph dialog box to delete, redefine, and reorder the fields used for Y-values in the graph.

Type Override

The series property menus for 2D bar and 2D line graphs include a Type Override option to change the graph type used to represent an individual series. For example, in a 2D bar graph, each series normally appears as a bar; in a 2D line graph, each series is represented by a line. By choosing the Type Override option, you can change an individual series to 2D line, 2D bar, or 2D area. To return the series to its original representation, choose Type Override ➤ None from the property menu.

The Type Override option is especially useful if you want to draw attention to one or more data series. For example, suppose we want to compare sales with the cost of goods in our FinSum table. We used Type

Graphing
Your Data

Ch.
13

Override in the 2D bar graph of Figure 13.18 to emphasize this comparison by displaying the Sales series as a 2D line.

FIGURE 13.18

A combined graph based on the Sales and Cost of Goods fields from the FinSum financial summary table

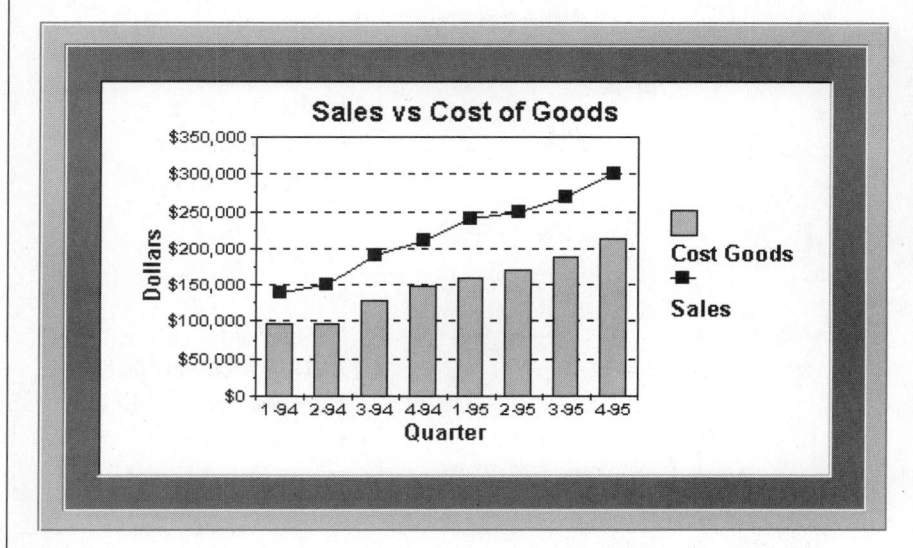

Markers

Paradox for Windows offers a variety of styles for marking individual data points in line graphs. The default marker style is a filled box, but you can change this by inspecting the series whose marker style you want to change, then choosing Marker ➤ Style from the property menu. The marker styles are shown in Figure 13.19.

In addition to changing the marker style, you can change the marker size. Just inspect the series you want to change, then choose Marker ➤ Size and select a weight from 0 Weight (no marker) to 72 Weight (huge!). The default weight is 18.

Line Styles

You can change the line style, color, and thickness of a 2D line by inspecting the series you want to change, choosing Line, then choosing Line Style, Color, or Thickness.

FIGURE 13.19 ▶

Marker styles for lines in a graph

√ Filled Box
Hollow Box
Filled Down-Triangle
Hollow Down-Triangle
Filled Circle
Hollow Circle
Filled Triangle
Hollow Triangle
+
Boxed +
×
Boxed ×
Filled Triangles
Hollow Triangles
Vertical Line
Horizontal Line

 ▶ ▶ **T I P**

To display a series with markers but without a line connecting them, inspect the series, choose Line ➤ Line Style, then choose the top (blank) line style from the Line palette.

▶ Customizing the Legend

A legend provides a key to each series on the graph. Paradox for Windows legends automatically use the fields in the table to identify each series plotted on the graph. For example, the legend in the 2-D summary graph in Figure 13.20 identifies the first series as sales of product A-111, the second as sales of B-222, and the third as sales of C-333. Figure 13.20 also illustrates how placing a graph and a table side-by-side on the same form can help make sense of the data.

*The graph legend iden-
tifies each data series.
In this example, we
placed the graph and
table side-by-side to
illustrate how summa-
rized data in a graph
can help you get a
quick understanding of
detailed tabular data.*

Sales Rep	Prod #	Units	Total $	Date Sold
Adams	A-111	4	$400	10/21/94
Adams	B-222	1	$500	10/21/94
Adams	B-222	1	$500	10/22/94
Adams	C-333	6	$1,500	10/21/94
Adams	C-333	4	$1,000	10/22/94
Jones	A-111	5	$500	10/21/94
Jones	A-111	5	$500	10/22/94
Jones	B-222	4	$2,000	10/21/94
Jones	C-333	6	$1,500	10/21/94
Jones	C-333	2	$500	10/22/94
Smith	A-111	1	$100	10/21/94
Smith	A-111	3	$300	10/22/94

new

Although the legend labels initially use the field values to identify each series, you can change this easily. First, make sure the legend is visible (if necessary, inspect the graph and check Options ➤ Show Legend). Then inspect the appropriate data series in the graph or the appropriate data series *marker* in the legend, and choose Title. From here, you can select Text (to define your own for this series) or *Use Default* (to restore the default label).

You can also change the appearance and position of the legend. To do so, first make sure the legend appears on the graph in the Design window (if necessary, inspect the graph object and choose Options ➤ Show Legend). Then click the graph object, move the mouse pointer to a *text label* in the legend (*not* to a legend marker) and right-click. The Legend Box property menu will appear, as below.

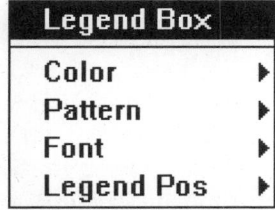

From here, you can change the background color or pattern of the legend, or the font of the legend labels. To position the legend box at the right or bottom of the graph, choose *Legend Pos.*

 ►► **T I P**

> **If you're having trouble locating the hot zone for a series, turn on the legend, then move the mouse pointer to the legend *marker* (not the legend label) for the series you want to change. As usual, you can right-click when the mouse pointer changes to ↑.**

► *Changing Rotation and Elevation in 3D Graphs*

The rotation and elevation properties of a 3D graph work together to create a three-dimensional effect. Rotation turns the graph around the y-axis, while elevation turns the graph around the x-axis. You can change the rotation and elevation of any 3D graph except 3D columns and 3D pie. To do so, inspect the graph object, choose Options, then choose *Elevation* or *Rotation* and select the number of degrees you want to elevate or rotate the graph. You can choose 0, 15, 30, 45, 60, 75, or 90 degrees.

 ►► **N O T E**

> **The default elevation for a 3D graph is 60 degrees; the default rotation is 30 degrees.**

Figure 13.21 shows the effect of rotation and elevation on a 3D stacked bar and a 3D ribbon graph. Some combinations will work better than others.

FIGURE 13.21 ▶

*Various combinations
of rotation and eleva-
tion on a 3D stacked
bar graph and a 3D
ribbon graph. We've
unchecked the Options
➤ Show Axes property
in these examples.*

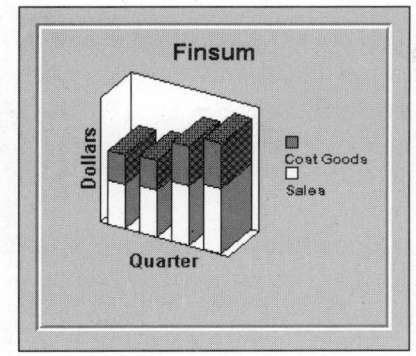

Rotation 30 Elevation 60 (default)

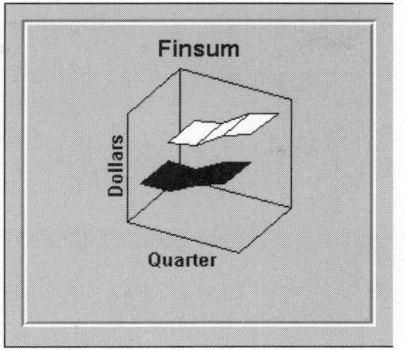

Rotation 30 Elevation 60 (default)

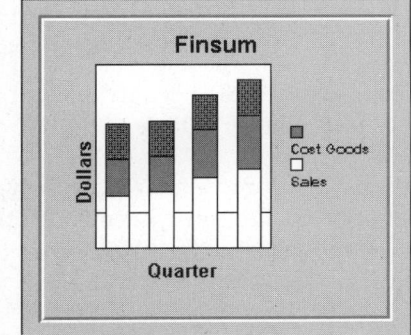

Rotation 0 Elevation 60

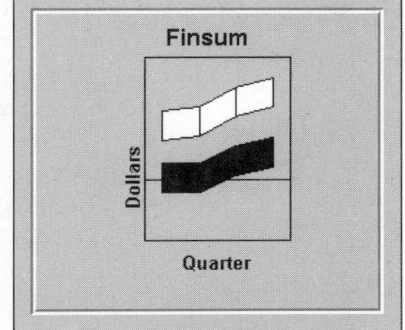

Rotation 0 Elevation 60

▶ *Adding Colors or Patterns to the Graph Background*

We've already talked about how to customize individual data series properties, including the color and pattern. You can also change the color or
pattern of background areas of a graph, including the background of the
entire graph and the background area containing the data series.

To change the background color or pattern of the entire graph, inspect
the *graph object*, then choose Pattern or Color. To change the color or
pattern of an area containing the data series, inspect the *hot zone* for
the area you want to change, then choose Color or Pattern.

▶ ▶ **T I P**

The header of each property menu will indicate which object you've inspected. For example, if you inspect the background for a 2D Bar graph, the word *Background* will appear on the property menu's header.

Keep in mind that the areas you can change depend on the type of graph you're designing, as summarized below.

Background Area	Type Of Graph
Entire graph	All
Background	All 2D bar, area, and line graphs except 2D columns and 2D pie.
Left Wall, Back Wall, or Base Floor	All 3D graphs except 3D columns and 3D pie

Figure 13.22 shows three representative graph types—a 2D bar, a 3D area, and a 3D pie—on the Design window and points out the areas you can inspect to change the background color or pattern.

▶ Special Techniques for Pie Charts and Column Graphs

Many of the enhancements that can be added to graphs do not apply to pie charts and column graphs because they have no axes and can display only a single series (data from a single field). However, Paradox for Windows offers other ways to customize pie charts and column graphs.

Label Format

You can change the labels on pie slices by inspecting the graph object, choosing Label, and then selecting any of the options below.

Font   Presents Typeface, Size, Style, and Color options.

Number Format   Presents number format options (available only when you've selected Label Format ➤ y-Value).

FIGURE 13.22

You can change the color or pattern of various background areas in a graph. The areas you can change depend on the type of graph.

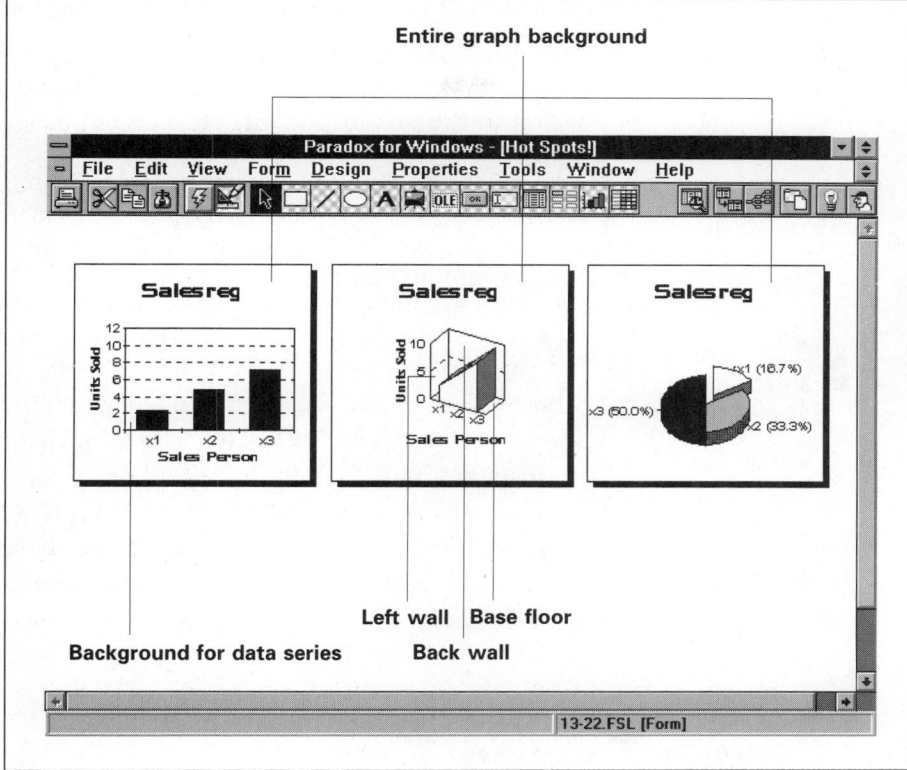

Label Format ➤ No y-Value   Displays only the x-axis value for the slice.

Label Format ➤ y-Value   Labels each slice with the x-axis value and the actual table value, if it fits.

Label Format ➤ y in Percent   Labels each slice with the x-axis value and the percentage of the whole series the slice represents. (This is the default setting.)

Slices

You can fill or color each slice in a pie chart or column graph individually, and you can *explode* individual slices in a pie chart for emphasis. Inspect the slice you want to change, then do any of the steps below.

● Choose *Color* to change the color of the slice.

- Choose *Pattern* to change the fill pattern of the slice.

- Choose *Explode* to separate the slice from the rest of the pie. You can explode any or all slices in a pie. To bring an exploded slice back into the pie, inspect the slice and choose Explode again.

Figure 13.23 shows the 1994 quarterly profit from the FinSum table as a pie chart. Note that each slice is a different color, and the pie slice for the fourth quarter of 1994 is exploded. We set the Label Format property for the graph to No y-Value.

▶▶**NOTE**

In Figure 13.23, we used the Form ▶ Filter command and entered the following filter condition for the Quarter field: "1-94" or "2-94" or "3-94" or "4-94"; as an alternative, we could have based the form on a query that selected only those records with ..-94 in the Quarter field. See Chapter 9 for more about queries and filters.

▶▶ Graph Design Tips

You've now learned all the techniques necessary for designing graphs in Paradox for Windows. In this section, you'll find tips to help you develop graphs that are professional-looking and easy to understand.

The most crucial decision you'll make when designing graphs is to pick the graph type that most clearly represents your data. For example, consider using a line graph to illustrate trends. When you want to show how each element contributes to a total, an area or stacked bar graph might do the best job. If your goal is to compare values, standard bar graphs and rotated bar graphs are good choices. And finally, when you're trying to show the relative contribution of different parts to a whole, a pie chart or column chart is ideal.

If you're not sure which graph is best for a particular purpose, experiment until you find the right graph. To switch to a new graph type, just inspect the graph and choose Graph Type, specify a different graph type, and then click the View Data button in the Toolbar to see the results.

FIGURE 13.23

Quarterly profit for 1994 represented as a pie chart. This example is based on a filter that isolated records with "1-94" or "2-94" or "3-94" or "4-94" in the Quarter field of the FinSum table.

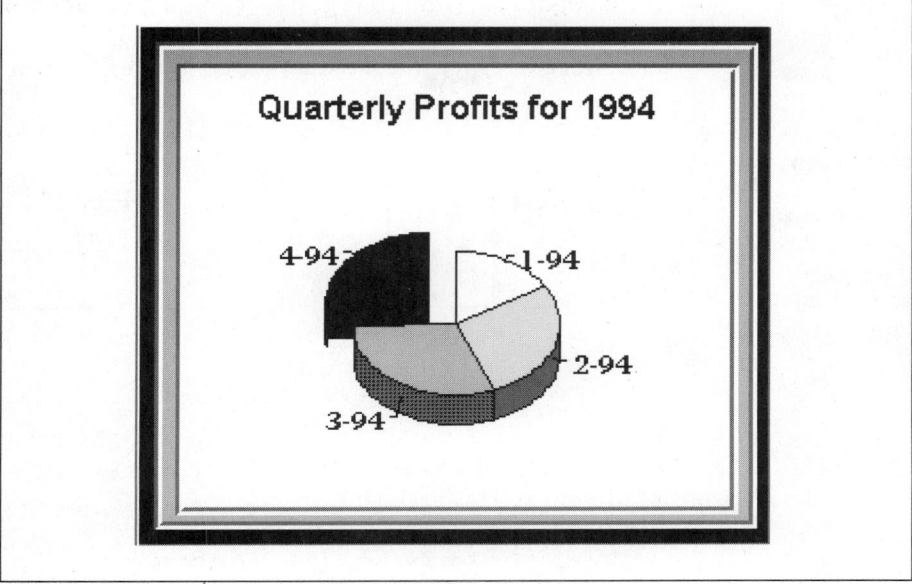

Avoid cluttering your graphs with unnecessary data or labels, as this will obscure the message you're trying to convey. For example, if your objective is to show commissions for sales people in the Western region, there's no need to show commissions for sales people in the Eastern and Overseas regions unless you want to compare commissions by region. If necessary, use one or more of these techniques to reduce the amount of data:

- Base the graph on a query.
- Use a 2-D summary or 3-D summary graph.
- Use the Filter feature in the Data Model dialog box (forms only) or the For<u>m</u> ➤ <u>F</u>ilter or <u>R</u>eport ➤ <u>F</u>ilter menu options.
- Reduce the number of x-axis values displayed.

Be sure to make important information stand out in your graphs. For example, explode the most important slice or slices in a pie chart, use bright colors or more noticeable patterns for key data items, or choose a different font to highlight vital information.

Finally, don't forget that graphs can be combined with information in forms, reports, and form letters. Figure 13.24, for example, integrates an effective graph into a form letter to emphasize a point.

FIGURE 13.24

This form letter includes a graph informing investors that sales continue to rise.

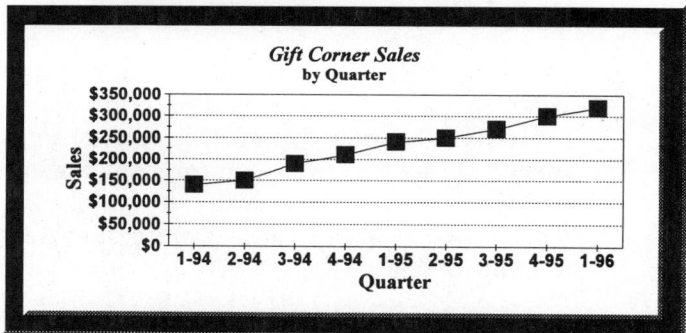

Gift Corner

8891 Gaudy Ave * West Fantasee, CA 92222
1-800-555-GIFT

March 18, 1996

Miss Maria N. Miller
1234 Corporate Hwy.
Los Angeles, CA 91245

Dear Miss Miller,

The Gift Corner is enjoying its greatest sales performance in years. As you can see from the graph below, our sales have risen steadily over the past several quarters.

Gift Corner Sales by Quarter

And there's more good news! We project continued growth with even greater gains, thanks to new product lines that will hit the market over the next year. Furthermore, our profitability is expected to climb dramatically due to the big tax cut on corporate profits recently enacted by Congress.

Miss Miller, we're proud to count you among our loyal investors and trust that you'll be as pleased by our financial results as we are. If you have any questions, please don't hesitate to call me at the toll-free number on our letterhead.

Sincerely,

Gondola Claplock

Gondola Claplock
Manager, Investor Relations

Now, let's turn our attention to crosstabs, which let you analyze and summarize data using tables instead of pictures.

▶ ▶ *Summarizing Data with Crosstabs*

Cross tabulations (or *crosstabs* for short) are very useful for reducing and arranging data from a large table into a smaller table that's easier to understand. Like 1-D and 2-D Summary graphs, crosstabs can classify data by one or more categories, summarize the data within these categories, and sort the summarized information. Instead of displaying the results in a graph, the results of a crosstab appear in a spreadsheet format.

In Figures 13.25 and 13.26, you see two crosstabs for the sample Sales-Reg table. Both crosstabs summarize the total number of units sold by date, though one displays the dates vertically along the left side of the crosstab, while the other displays the dates horizontally across the top. The orientation depends on how you define the crosstab fields.

FIGURE 13.25 ▶

A one-dimensional crosstab showing the total quantity of each product sold on each date. In this example, the dates are arranged vertically down the left side of the crosstab.

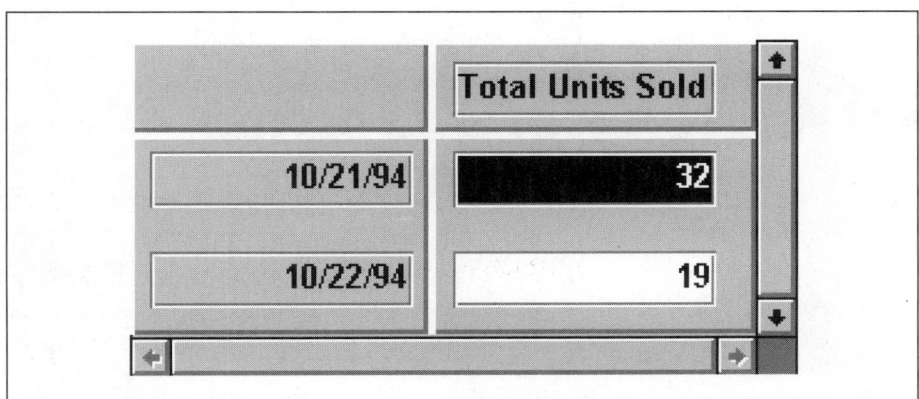

FIGURE 13.26 ▶

Another one-dimensional crosstab of the total number of each product sold on each date. In this example, the dates appear horizontally across the top of the crosstab.

One-dimensional crosstabs, like those in Figure 13.25 and Figure 13.26, group data by only one category (for example, by date). Two-dimensional crosstabs can group by more than one category. Figure 13.27 shows a crosstab with sales broken down by salesperson (rows) for each date (columns).

FIGURE 13.27 ▶

A two-dimensional crosstab summarizing Total Sales by Sales Person and Date Sold

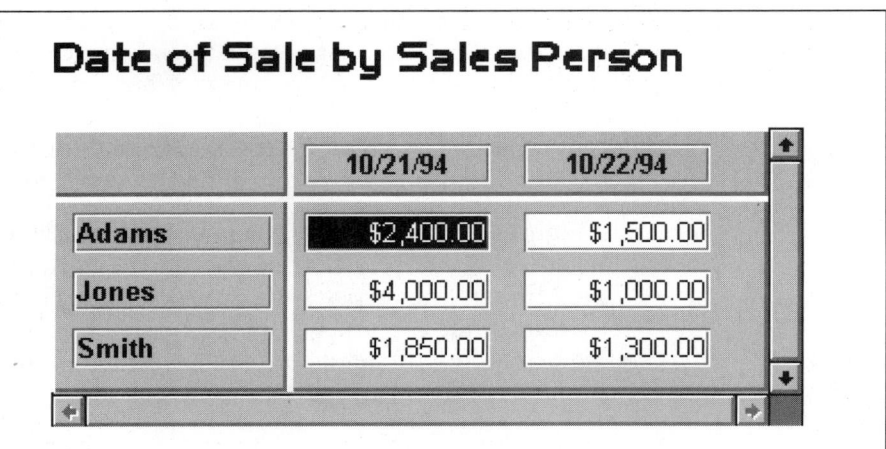

▶▶ *Anatomy of a Crosstab*

The three main components of a crosstab are described below.

Column   Specifies the field to group by; the values in this field are used as column labels in the crosstab. In Figure 13.27 the column field is Date Sold. This component corresponds to the x-axis in 1-D summary and 2-D summary graphs.

Categories   Become the row labels in the crosstab. In Figure 13.27, the category field is Sales Person. The Categories component (which is optional) corresponds to the Grouped By field of a 2-D summary graph.

Summaries   Display the results of a calculation at the intersection of each row and column in the crosstab. In Figure 13.27, the summary field is Total Sales. The Summaries component corresponds to the y-axis in a 1-D summary or 2-D summary graph.

You may define only one Column field for a crosstab, but you can have as many Categories and Summaries as you wish. (However, the number of summary fields times the number of column values cannot exceed 250.)

▶▶ *Understanding Crosstab Summary Operators*

Crosstabs can use the same summary operators as 1-D and 2-D summary graphs. These operators are described briefly below.

Sum   Shows totals for each non-empty row and column pair.

Min   Shows smallest of all individual values for each row and column pair.

Max   Shows largest of all individual values for each row and column pair.

Count   Counts the number of non-empty records for each row and column pair.

Avg   Shows the average of all individual non-empty values for each row and column pair.

Std   Shows the standard deviation of all individual values for each row and column pair (meaningful only with large samples).

Var   Shows the statistical variance of all individual values for each row and column pair (meaningful only with large samples).

▶▶ *Designing a Crosstab*

A crosstab, like a graph, is simply an object in your document design. The steps for designing crosstabs are a lot like those for designing graphs.

▶ Creating a Crosstab

To add crosstabs to existing documents, click the Crosstab tool in the Design window Toolbar (shown at left), then click in your design and drag to define the initial size of your crosstab. A crosstab with undefined Categories, Column, and Summaries fields will appear on the Design window as in Figure 13.28.

▶▶**N O T E**

In previous versions of Paradox for Windows, crosstabs were allowed in forms only; but in Paradox 5 for Windows, you can use them in both forms and reports.

FIGURE 13.28 ▶

The crosstab initially appears with undefined Categories, Column, and Summaries fields.

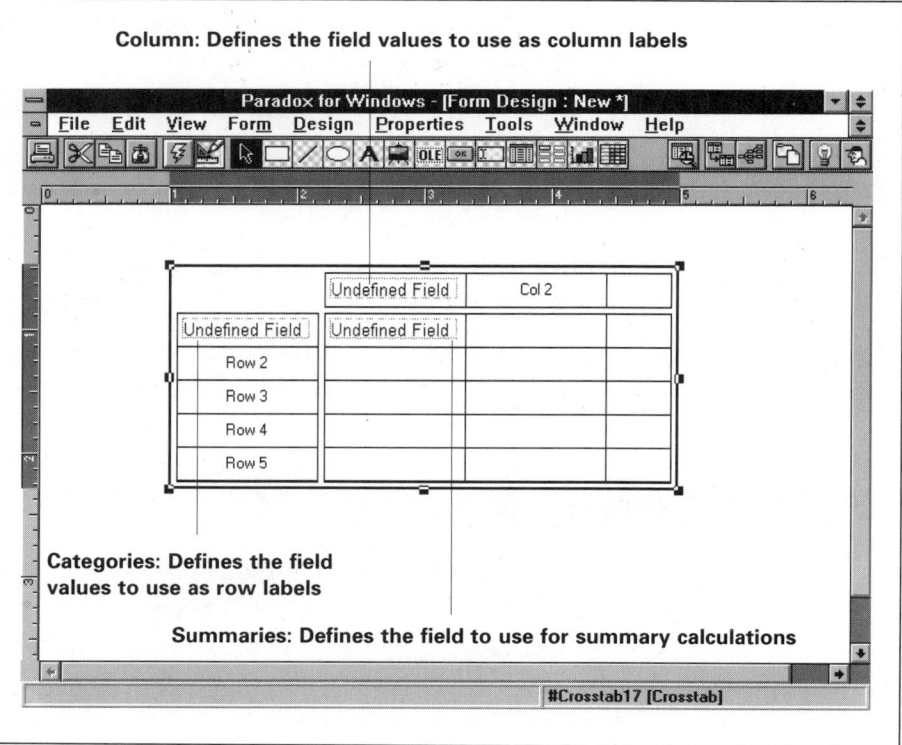

As for graph objects, the crosstab shown on the Design window is only a *template* of the actual crosstab that will appear when you preview or print the document.

After outlining the basic crosstab, you'll need to define it. The steps for defining crosstabs are described a bit later in this chapter.

If you want to, you can create a new form or report that includes just the crosstab. Choose <u>F</u>ile ➤ <u>N</u>ew ➤ <u>F</u>orm or <u>F</u>ile ➤ <u>N</u>ew ➤ <u>R</u>eport, click the <u>D</u>ata Model / Layout Diagram button, choose your table in the Data Model dialog box, then select a Blan<u>k</u> style in the Design Layout dialog box and click OK. Next, use the Crosstab tool as described above to place the crosstab into your design.

▶ ▶ **TIP**

> **When creating crosstab-only reports, it's best to place the crosstab in the report header or report footer band. If you accidentally put a crosstab in the record band, the crosstab will be repeated once for each record in the table! You cannot define crosstabs in the page band.**

As with graphs, if anyone changes data that is used in a crosstab you're currently displaying in Form View, Paradox will update the affected data in the crosstab as soon as the user moves the cursor to another record in the table and you refresh the crosstab in Form View (for example, by pressing F8 twice). If the crosstab is on the same form as the table you're updating, it will be refreshed as soon as you move the cursor to another record.

▶ Creating a Quick Crosstab

You can use the Quick Crosstab button in Table View either to create a new crosstab form or to display a form containing a crosstab.

If you're in Table View and haven't assigned a preferred crosstab to the table, click the Quick Crosstab button in the Toolbar (shown at left). You'll be taken to the Define Crosstab dialog box, which is described later in this chapter.

If you've already created a preferred crosstab for the table, clicking the Quick Crosstab button will display the crosstab in a new form. You can then click the Design button in the Toolbar or press F8 to change the design.

▶▶ **T I P**

To create a preferred crosstab, open the table, right-click the Quick Crosstab button in the Toolbar, choose the form that contains your crosstab, and click OK. Then choose Properties ➤ View Properties ➤ Save to save your changes.

▶ Inspecting the Entire Crosstab Object

When you're ready to define the fields of a crosstab or change its properties, you must inspect the crosstab object or its hot zones.

Inspecting the crosstab object leads to the property menu shown in Figure 13.29. This menu lets you define all the fields for the crosstab and change the properties of the crosstab object.

You can use either of the following techniques to inspect the crosstab object:

- Select the crosstab by clicking it. Then press F6 or move the mouse pointer to an empty area at the upper-left corner of the crosstab (just inside the selection handles) and right-click.

- Use the Object Tree to inspect the crosstab object, its Column, Categories, and Summaries, or any of its fields. This is often easier than inspecting the crosstab hot zone.

▶ Inspecting the Crosstab Hot Zones

You can inspect the Categories, Summaries, or Column hot zones whenever you want to add a category, summary, or column to the crosstab, or you want to change the properties of an individual category, summary, or column.

FIGURE 13.29

The Crosstab property menu

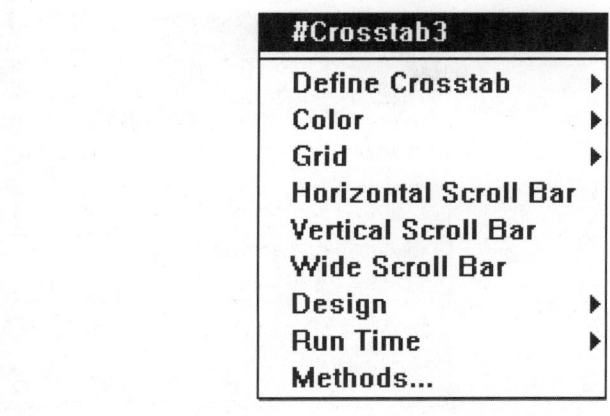

```
#Crosstab3

Define Crosstab        ▶
Color                  ▶
Grid                   ▶
Horizontal Scroll Bar
Vertical Scroll Bar
Wide Scroll Bar
Design                 ▶
Run Time               ▶
Methods...
```

To inspect one of these hot zones, click on the crosstab, move the mouse pointer to an empty area inside the boundaries of the hot zone you want to change, and then right-click. Figure 13.30 shows the hot zones for a selected crosstab object.

You can also inspect an individual field within the crosstab and change its properties. To do so, simply click the field, then right-click or press F6.

▶ Defining Crosstab Fields One by One

You can define crosstab fields individually, or you can specify them all at once. The simplest crosstab uses field names from your table as the Column, Categories, and Summaries fields. To define these fields, select the undefined field object you want, then right-click or press F6. Next choose Define Field from the menu and select a field name from the list.

When you specify a Summaries field, Paradox automatically determines the default operator for that field. Sum is the initial default for all numeric fields, while Count is the default for non-numeric fields. If you want to use one of the other summary operators (Min, Max, Count, Avg, Std, or Var) for a numeric field, you must open the Define Crosstab dialog box, described below.

FIGURE 13.30 ▶

*Hot zones on a se-
lected crosstab object*

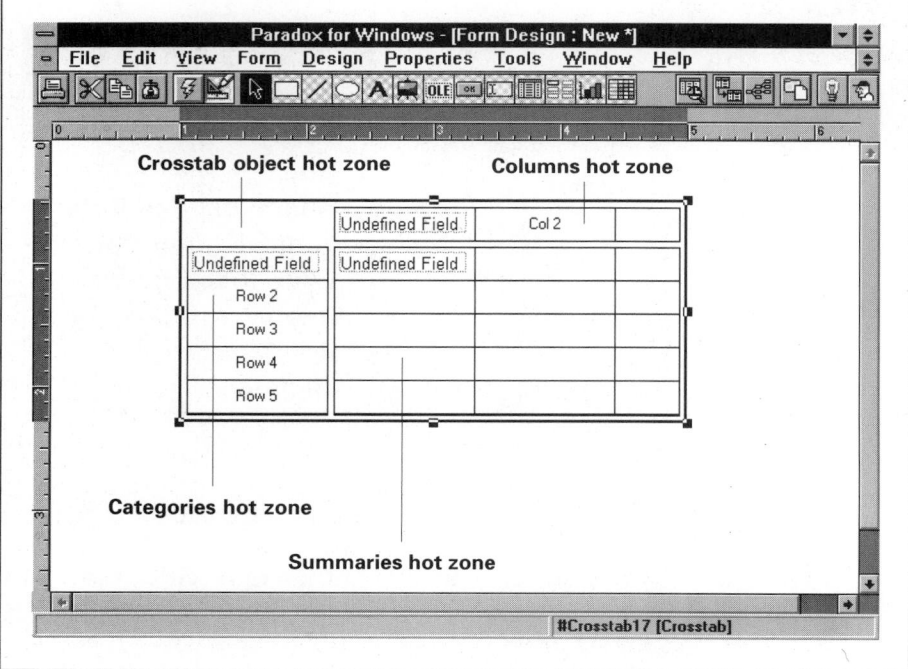

If you prefer to specify all fields for the crosstab at once, inspect the
crosstab object, choose Define Crosstab from the property menu,
then...

- Click the table name if you want Paradox to assign the first three
  fields in your table to the Column, Categories, and Summaries
  fields of the crosstab, respectively.

- Click the list header (...) or press ◄┘ if you want to: specify each
  field individually; reorder, remove, or add fields; or change the
  summary operators for fields in the crosstab.

Clicking the list header leads to the Define Crosstab dialog box shown
in Figure 13.31.

FIGURE 13.31

The Define Crosstab dialog box is similar to the Define Graph dialog box described earlier in this chapter.

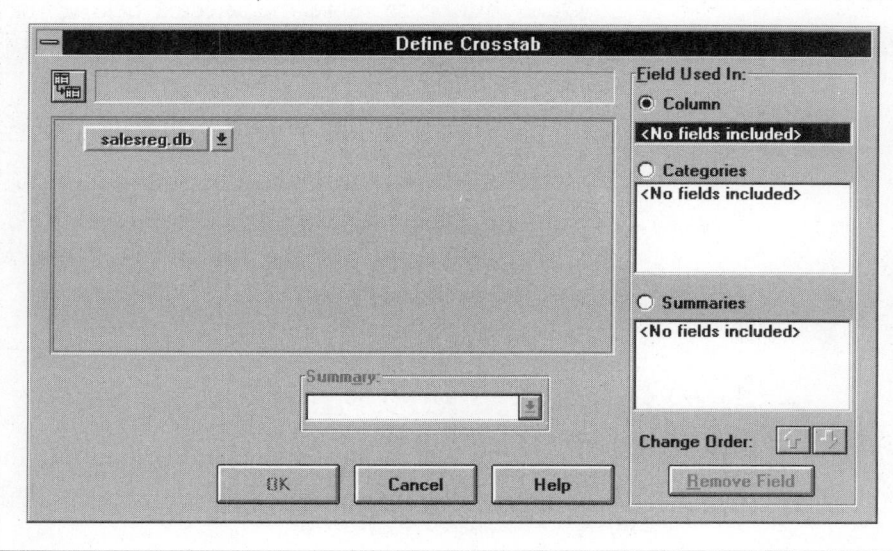

▶ *Using the Define Crosstab Dialog Box*

Here are the steps for defining all fields and summary operators of your crosstab at once:

1. If you want to add a table to the data model, click the Data Model button in the upper-left corner of the dialog box, choose a table, and click OK. (This step is optional.)

2. For each field that you want to define, click the appropriate option in the Field Used In area of the dialog box. Then click the drop-down arrow to the right of the table name and click the field you want to assign. (You can click several fields when assigning Categories or Summaries.)

3. If you want to change the summary operator for a field, click the field you want to change in the Summaries list. Then click the Summary drop-down list and click on the operator you want.

4. If you want to remove a field, click the field in the Fields Used In area of the dialog box, then click the Remove Field button.

5. If you want to change the order of a field in the Categories or Summaries list, click on the appropriate field, then click the ↑ or ↓ Change

Order button to move the selected field up or down in the list.

6. When you're finished, click OK.

▶ ▶ **N O T E**

Remember that the Column field appears across the top of the crosstab, the Categories fields appear down the left side, and the Summaries fields are in the main part of the crosstab.

▶ Adding a Category Field

You may want to summarize your table data by more than one category. For example, you could analyze the sales made by each salesperson, broken down by product.

To add a field (category) in the row area, inspect the Categories area of the crosstab object (where the numbered rows appear) and choose Add A Category. Select the field you want, or click the list header (...), fill in the Define Field Object dialog box, and choose OK.

▶ ▶ **N O T E**

You can also use the Define Crosstab dialog box to add a category.

When you run a crosstab with multiple categories, Categories the field names appear in the left-most column of the crosstab object, and the table data is sorted first by the top category, then by subsequent categories. If you want to reposition these fields, return to the Define Crosstab dialog box, click the field you want to reorder in the Categories list, and use the ↑ and ↓ Change Order buttons.

Figure 13.32 shows a crosstab with multiple categories. Here, total sales for each date are categorized by salesperson *and* product number. Notice the separate rows for each unique combination of category values: Adams and A-111, Adams and B-222, Adams and C-333, and so forth. Figure 13.33 shows the design window used to produce this crosstab.

The crosstab in Figure 13.32 includes the following features:

- The Column is the Date Sold field of the SalesReg table.
- The Categories are the Sales Person and Product Number fields.
- The Summaries field is the Total Sales field, and the Sum operator is used.
- We added wide vertical and horizontal scroll bars, which allow scrolling through the crosstab when it is displayed in the Form window. We changed the grid style of the crosstab to 3D.

▶ ▶ **N O T E**

The grid lines and the row and column numbering disappear from the crosstab in the Design window when the Grid ➤ Grid Style ➤ 3D property is selected.

FIGURE 13.32 ▶

This crosstab shows product sales grouped by Date Sold and categorized by Sales Person and Product Number.

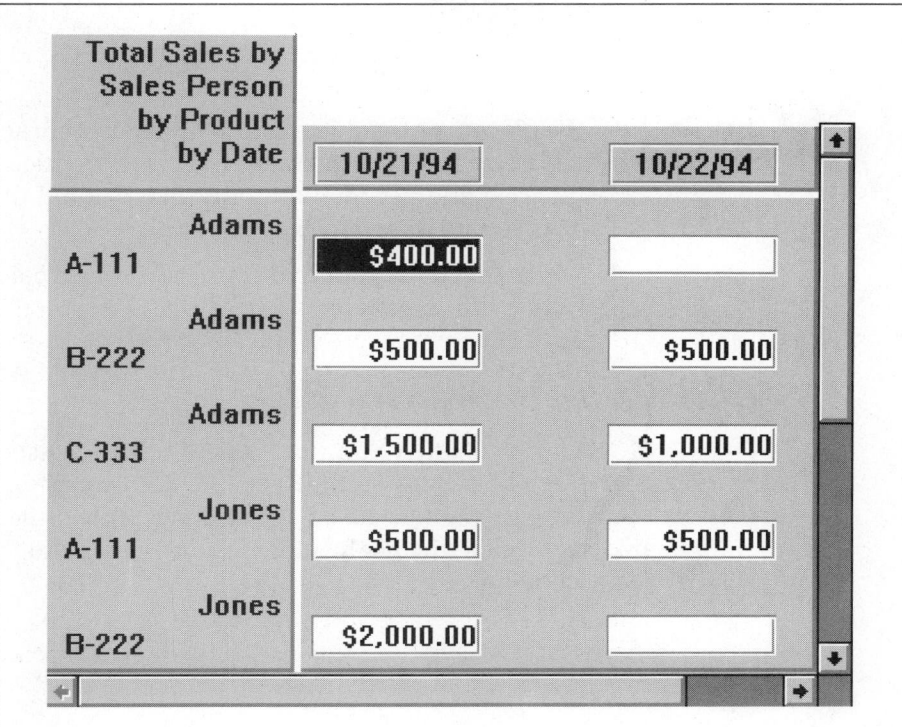

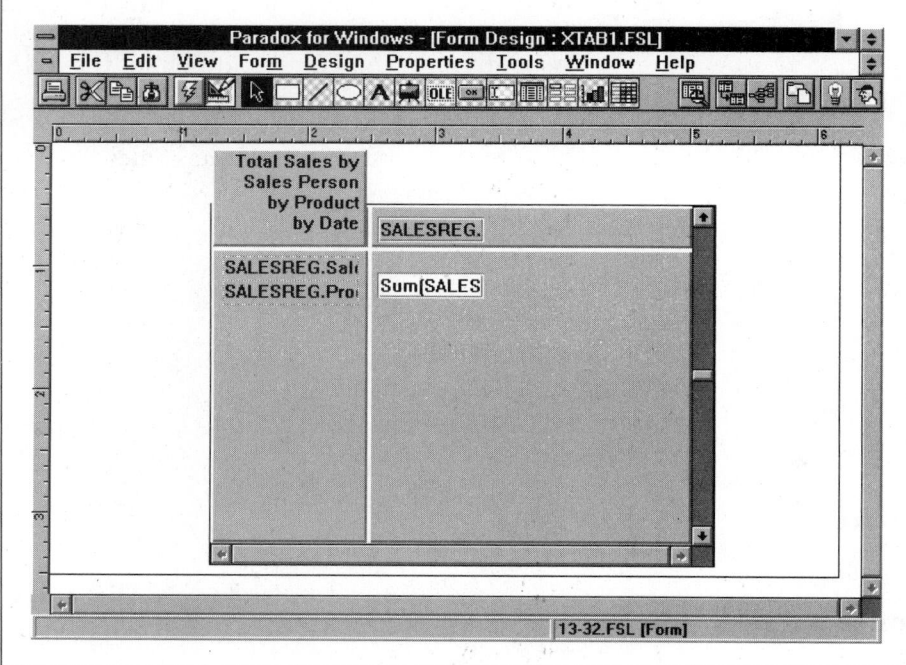

- We placed a text object at the upper-left corner of the crosstab table and typed each line of the crosstab title. We right-aligned the title text and used a bold font, then colored the text box gray and changed its frame style.

- We changed the font and frame styles and colors of the field objects in the crosstab.

▶ Adding a Summaries Field

If you need to add a Summaries field to the crosstab, inspect the Summary area of the crosstab object (the empty area in the body of the crosstab), then choose Add A Summary. Select the field you want from the list, or click the list header (...) and complete the Define Field Object dialog box.

▶ ▶ **N O T E**

> **You can also use the Define Crosstab dialog box to add a Summaries field.**

Suppose you want to sum the total units sold and compute total sales by each salesperson in the SalesReg table. In this case, you need two Summaries fields: one for the total number of units sold by each salesperson and one for the dollar value of all sales by each salesperson.

Figure 13.34 shows a crosstab that does the job. Here the Column field is the Date Sold, the Categories field is Sales Person, and the two Summaries fields are Units Sold and Total Sales. Figure 13.35 shows the Form Design window for the crosstab in Figure 13.34.

FIGURE 13.34 ▶

A crosstab, categorized by Date Sold, and summarized by Units Sold and Total Sales for each Sales Person

$$	Units Sold and Total Sales by Sales Person and Date		$$

Units Sold ↘ Total Sales ↘		10/21/94	10/22/94
Adams		11	5
		$2,400	$1,500
Jones		15	7
		$4,000	$1,000
Smith		6	7
		$1,850	$1,300

FIGURE 13.35 ►

The Form Design window for the crosstab in Figure 13.34

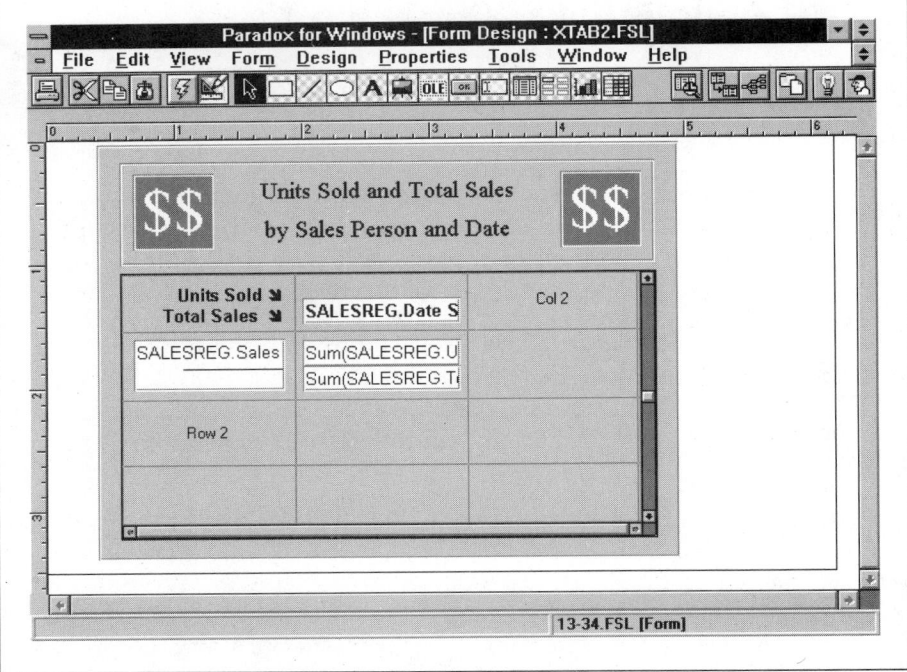

Most of the techniques used to enhance the crosstab in Figure 13.34 should be familiar to you by now, but here are some highlights:

● We placed a gray box around the entire crosstab.

● We placed a text object with the overall title for the crosstab inside the box and added two text objects containing the $$ characters in a large font. The typeface is Times New Roman.

● We added a short horizontal line below the Sales Person field and the Units Sold field to separate the units sold from the total sales figures for each salesperson.

● We added a text object in the upper-left corner of the crosstab to explain the contents of the two Summaries fields. The arrows are available in the Wingdings TrueType font; they were placed using the Character Map (see Chapter 6).

● We added three-dimensional effects by changing the color, frame style, and frame thickness of various objects.

▶ *Redefining a Column*

You can change the grouping of information in a crosstab simply by changing the field used for the crosstab columns. For example, recall that Figure 13.27 showed daily sales for each salesperson grouped by date sold. We changed the grouping to Product Number simply by redefining the column, as in Figure 13.36. (Of course, we also modified the title to reflect the data shown.)

FIGURE 13.36 ▶

The crosstab from Figure 13.27 with the column changed from Date Sold to Product Number, and the title modified accordingly

Product Sales by Sales Person

	A-111	B-222	C-333
Adams	$400	$1,000	$2,500
Jones	$1,000	$2,000	$2,000
Smith	$400	$1,000	$1,750

To redefine the column field, inspect the Column area (any empty area in the numbered columns), choose Define Column Field from the property menu, and select an available field.

▶ ▶ **N O T E**

As always, you can also inspect the crosstab object, choose Define Crosstab, click the list header (...) to open the Define Crosstab dialog box, and change the field used in the Column area.

▶ *Adding Titles to Crosstabs*

Unlike graphs, crosstabs do not have legends that clarify which fields are being displayed, how things are summarized, and why. Nor do they have any specific title or subtitle areas. Therefore, it's especially important to add titles and labels to your crosstabs using the Text tool in the Toolbar. For example, the row label in Figure 13.35 is a text object, as are the titles in all the crosstab examples in this chapter. You can use any of the techniques discussed in Chapters 10 and 11 to customize the text object properties.

▶ ▶ **T I P**

If you place a box, line, ellipse, text, graphic, or OLE object in the same cell with the Categories or Summaries field, the object will be repeated throughout the crosstab.

▶ Customizing Crosstab Objects

As with graphs, most areas of the crosstab object can be inspected and customized. You can use property inspection to change crosstab colors and grid style, add or remove scroll bars, change Design and Run Time properties, and redefine Column, Categories, and Summaries fields. All crosstab properties are changed in the standard way: Inspect the appropriate object or hot zone and choose from the property menu.

When changing color in a crosstab, keep in mind that the area you inspect in a crosstab determines which area is colored. For example, coloring the crosstab object itself changes the entire background color of the crosstab. However, inspecting the Categories, Summaries, or Column area and changing the color affects only the area you inspected. Thus, you can control the color of the row labels (Categories), the body of the crosstab (Summaries), and the column labels (Columns). Similarly, inspecting a field in the crosstab and changing its color affects that field only.

Here are two other valuable facts concerning properties:

● Although the Grid, Horizontal Scroll Bar, Vertical Scroll Bar, and Methods properties appear on the property menus for all the hot zones, they affect the entire crosstab—not just a single area.

● Only the hot zone for the crosstab object itself includes a Design property, which you can use to pin the crosstab vertically or horizontally within your form design.

▶ *Changing the Dimensions of Crosstabs*

Crosstabs are a special kind of table object, with the usual grid lines, rows, and columns normally found in tables. You can use many of the direct manipulation techniques described in Chapter 7 to change the dimensions of crosstabs.

For example, to change the width of all the crosstab table columns, select the crosstab object and move the mouse pointer to the vertical grid line at the right edge of the first column. When the pointer changes to a two-headed horizontal arrow, drag the grid line to the left or right.

To change the height of all the rows, select the crosstab object, move the mouse pointer to the horizontal grid line at the bottom edge of the first row, and when the pointer changes to a two-headed vertical arrow, drag the grid line up or down.

To change the width of the Categories column (which contains the row labels), select the crosstab object and move the mouse pointer to the vertical grid line between the numbered rows and the first column. When the two-headed horizontal arrow appears, drag to the left or right.

To change the height of the Column row (which contains the column labels), select the crosstab object and move the mouse pointer to the horizontal grid line just below the numbered columns. When you see the two-headed vertical arrow, drag up or down.

T I P

Be sure to change the height or width of fields and text objects to accommodate changes to the dimensions of the crosstab table.

You can also drag the borders or corners of the crosstab frame to show more or fewer rows and columns.

▶▶ Combining Crosstabs and Graphs

Sometimes a crosstab or a summary graph alone isn't enough to provide the clearest understanding of your data. But who says you can't use both at once? Simply place a 1-D or 2-D summary graph beside a crosstab of the same data on your form, and you'll be able to spot trends easily while viewing numbers that explain those trends.

For example, the crosstab in Figure 13.37 summarizes total sales for each salesperson by date sold, while the 2-D summary graph next to the crosstab displays the same information graphically. In the graph on the right, you can quickly see that sales were stronger on 10/21/94 (thanks primarily to stellar performance by Jones on that day), and you can instantly compare the daily sales for each salesperson. The crosstab ties the visual display to exact dollar amounts of total sales by each person. Figure 13.38 shows the Form Design window for Figure 13.37.

FIGURE 13.37 ▶

A combined form with both a crosstab and a 2-D summary graph. The form presents total sales for each salesperson by date sold.

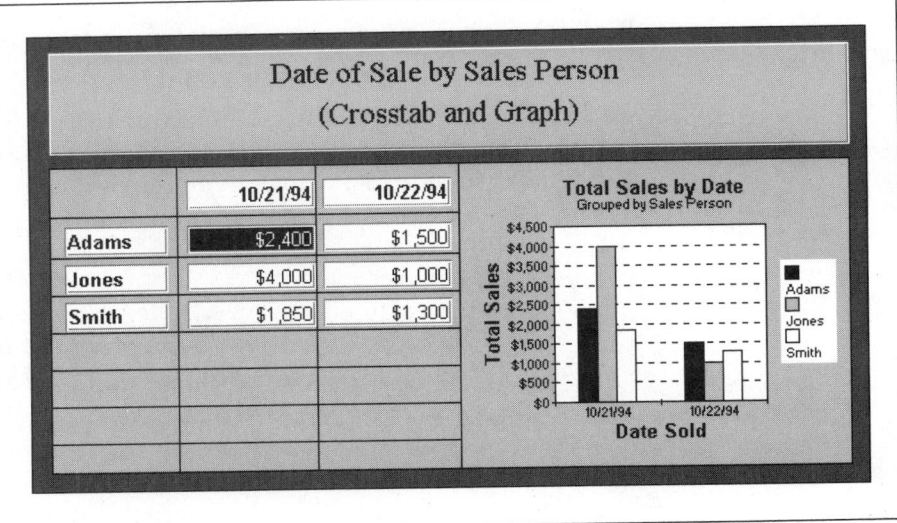

This chapter introduced you to the rich variety of graphs available for presenting your data, and to crosstabs, which summarize your data in a tabular format. When deciding whether to use a graph or a summary (or both) to display your data, keep in mind that 1-D summary and 2-D summary graphs and crosstabs are closely related: Both can

FIGURE 13.38

The Form Design window for the form in Figure 13.37

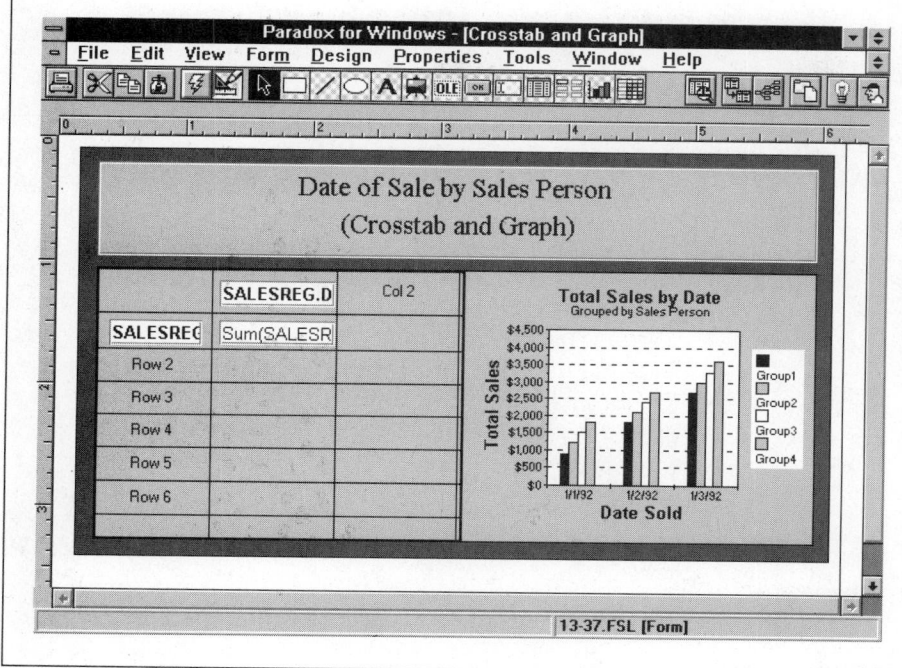

classify data by categories, summarize data within categories, sort the summarized information, and display the results. The main difference is that graphs show pictures—trends, patterns, and so forth—whereas crosstabs report hard numbers.

You've now completed Part 3 of this book. In the next chapter, we'll begin Part 4 by looking at the many ways you can customize the Paradox for Windows environment to suit your requirements and working style.

Managing Your Projects

PART FOUR

Customizing
Paradox for Windows

FAST TRACK

▶ **To change the default table properties** **803**

create a table named *Default* in your private directory, then define one field for each type of data you plan to store in any table. Add at least one row of data to *Default*, change its Table View properties to the default appearance you want, then choose <u>P</u>roperties ➤ <u>V</u>iew Properties ➤ <u>S</u>ave and close the table.

▶ **To change IDAPI configuration settings** **808**

double-click the IDAPI Configuration Utility icon in the Paradox for Windows program group. In the IDAPI Configuration Utility window that appears, click the "page" tab for the setting you want to change or choose an appropriate option from the <u>P</u>ages menu. Carefully make changes in the selected page. (If you need help along the way, click the <u>H</u>elp button or choose options from the Help menu.) Make changes *only* if you thoroughly understand their implications. When you're finished, double-click the Control-menu box or choose <u>F</u>ile ➤ E<u>x</u>it in the IDAPI Configuration Utility window.

▶ **To change the location of your Paradox for Windows local directories and IDAPI configuration file** **815**

double-click the Local Settings Utility icon in the Paradox for Windows program group, fill in or change the text boxes as needed, and choose OK.

► ► **W**hen you install Paradox for Windows, many settings are determined automatically. For example, screen colors, printer, available fonts, and date and number formats are defined in the Windows Control Panel and Windows Setup applications. Other settings are controlled either from within Paradox for Windows or through stand-alone utility applications that are placed in the Paradox for Windows program group during installation.

Unlike the weather, which we have to put up with, default settings can easily be changed. In this chapter, you'll learn how to customize Paradox for Windows. (For information about customizing Paradox for Windows on a network, refer to Appendix B.) Of course, changing default settings is entirely optional. If you are satisfied with the way Paradox runs on your computer, you can leave the default settings as they are.

As you browse through this chapter, keep in mind that some settings can be changed in more than one way. For example, Paradox for Windows takes its initial date and number formats from settings in the Windows Control Panel; however, you can also define custom formats within Paradox by changing the properties of date and number fields in tables, forms, and reports (see Chapter 7) or by revising the IDAPI Configuration Utility settings (as described later in this chapter).

► ► *"When Do My Settings Take Effect?"*

Some changes, such as switching to a new working directory, changing properties in the Table window, and updating Desktop properties, take effect immediately. Others are implemented when you restart Paradox. Still others, such as updates made from Windows Setup, take effect only after you restart Windows. But regardless of when the change takes effect, the new setting becomes the default for all future Paradox for Windows sessions—until you change the default again.

►► *Getting Information about Your Settings*

From time to time, you may need information about your computer system resources. Such information might come in handy when calling Borland's technical support hotline, or when refining default settings to maximize Paradox's performance on your computer. Windows and Paradox for Windows both provide access to system information.

► *Displaying Your Paradox for Windows Version Number*

Like most Windows applications, Paradox for Windows can display signature information (that is, your name and company name), and program version number. To view this information, choose Help ➤ About. You'll see the About Paradox for Windows dialog box.

To display an Internal version number, press Alt+I while viewing the dialog box. The number will appear in the lower left-hand corner. Choose OK or press ↵ or spacebar to exit the dialog box.

► *Displaying Paradox for Windows System Settings*

The Tools ➤ System Settings options shown below provide information about your Paradox for Windows system.

```
Auto Refresh...
Blank As Zero...
Drivers...
IDAPI...
```

Auto Refresh displays, and lets you determine, how often Paradox updates your current view of data on a network (see Appendix B for details).

Blank As Zero is a toggle option that controls how Paradox treats blank fields during calculations. See "Calculating with Blank Fields," later in this chapter, for details.

The remaining options are covered in the following two sections.

Displaying Database Driver Settings

Paradox for Windows can connect to various database drivers, which are installed with Paradox for Windows. (See Appendix A for installation instructions.) As long as you're connected to a driver, you can create, update, and display a table for that driver. For example, when connected to the Paradox and dBASE drivers, you can create and update Paradox for DOS, Paradox for Windows, and dBASE tables.

To view the list of available drivers, choose <u>T</u>ools ➤ System Settings ➤ <u>D</u>rivers. Choose OK when you're finished viewing the list.

Displaying the IDAPI Settings

IDAPI is an acronym for Independent Database Application Programming Interface: the database engine that allows Paradox for Windows to share tables and files with other applications, such as dBASE for Windows and Quattro Pro for Windows. An application that uses the IDAPI engine is said to be "IDAPI-hosted."

 ▶▶**N O T E**

In previous versions of Paradox for Windows, the database engine was named *ODAPI* (Object Database Application Programming Interface), not to be confused with *okapi*, which is an endangered animal.

To display the current IDAPI settings, choose <u>T</u>ools ➤ System Settings ➤ <u>I</u>DAPI. You'll see the IDAPI System Information dialog box shown in Figure 14.1. See "Using the IDAPI Configuration Utility," later in this chapter, or click the Help button in the dialog box to find out what the settings mean and how to change them. When you're done viewing the settings, click OK.

FIGURE 14.1 ▶

The IDAPI System Information dialog box

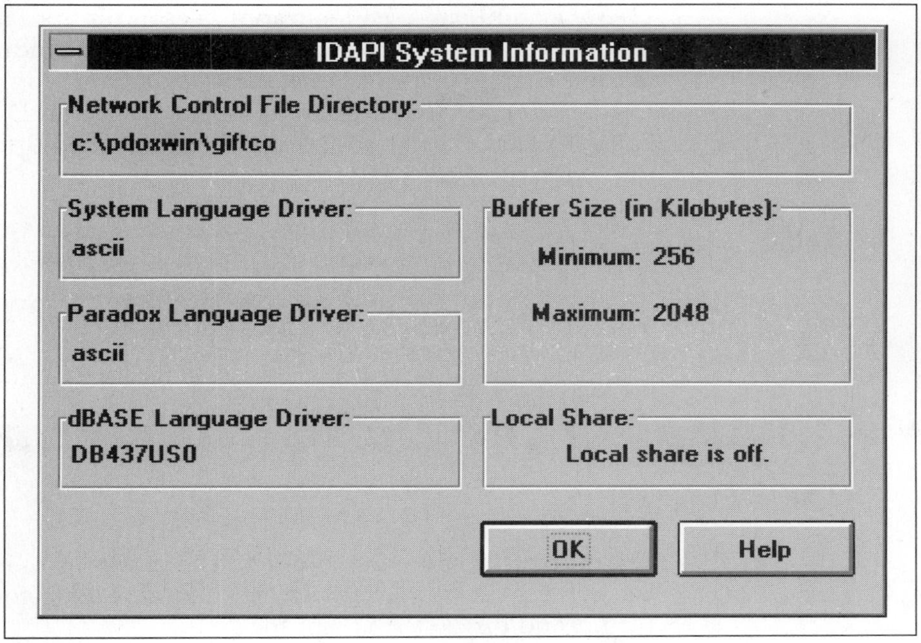

```
┌─────────────────────────────────────────────────────────┐
│ ▬            IDAPI System Information                     │
├─────────────────────────────────────────────────────────┤
│  ┌─Network Control File Directory:──────────────────────┐ │
│  │  c:\pdoxwin\giftco                                    │ │
│  └──────────────────────────────────────────────────────┘ │
│                                                            │
│  ┌─System Language Driver:──────┐ ┌─Buffer Size (in Kilobytes):─┐ │
│  │  ascii                       │ │     Minimum:  256           │ │
│  └──────────────────────────────┘ │                             │ │
│  ┌─Paradox Language Driver:─────┐ │     Maximum:  2048          │ │
│  │  ascii                       │ └─────────────────────────────┘ │
│  └──────────────────────────────┘                              │
│  ┌─dBASE Language Driver:───────┐ ┌─Local Share:──────────────┐ │
│  │  DB437USO                    │ │   Local share is off.     │ │
│  └──────────────────────────────┘ └───────────────────────────┘ │
│                              ┌────────┐   ┌────────┐            │
│                              │   OK   │   │  Help  │            │
│                              └────────┘   └────────┘            │
└─────────────────────────────────────────────────────────┘
```

▶ ▶ *Using Windows Setup and Control Panel to Customize Your Computer*

Like most Windows applications, Paradox for Windows learns about your machine configuration and preferred Windows settings by reading initialization files, which are maintained by the Setup and Control Panel applications in the Main group of the Windows Program Manager. You'll find instructions for using these applications in your Windows documentation.

You must run *Setup* when first installing your Windows system, and again whenever you change the monitor, keyboard, mouse, or network in use. Paradox cannot take advantage of newly installed hardware unless you've properly configured it through Setup or other applications supplied by the hardware vendor.

Control Panel provides many options for configuring and customizing your Windows system. The changes you make are stored in the *control.ini* and *win.ini* initialization files in the *c:\windows* directory. These files are consulted each time you start Windows or Paradox for Windows. The Control Panel options that are most important for customizing the Paradox environment are Color, Date, Time, Fonts, International, Keyboard, Mouse, Network, and Printers.

 ▶ ▶ **T I P**

> **To change printer settings temporarily, choose File ➤ Printer Setup from the Paradox for Windows menus.**

▶▶ *Changing the Default Directory Settings*

If you store files in many different directories, you may wish to change the default *working directory* where Paradox looks for tables, reports, forms, and other permanent files.

 ▶ ▶ **N O T E**

> **Paradox can only switch to a directory that you've already created through the MD (or MKDIR) command in DOS or the File ➤ Create Directory command in Windows File Manager. Paradox itself cannot create or remove directories.**

To change your working directory, follow these steps:

1. Choose File ➤ Working Directory to open the Set Working Directory dialog box.

2. Type the name of the working directory. Be sure to include both the drive and directory name or the alias name (for example, **c:\pdoxwin\giftco** or **:Gift_Corner:**), and be sure that the specified directory exists. You can also use the Browse button or Aliases drop-down list to locate the directory you want.

3. Choose OK.

4. If asked whether you're sure you want to close all Desktop windows and continue, choose OK.

 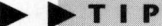

> **You can also change the working directory by using the Project Viewer window's Working Directory drop-down list or Browse button. As an alternative to changing your working directory, you can use the Drive (or Alias) drop-down list and Browse button in various dialog boxes to locate files.**

You can also choose a *private directory* for your network workstation. Each network workstation must have its own private directory for storing temporary tables such as *Answer* and *Changed* to avoid conflicts with other network users' temporary tables. Typically, this is the \pdoxwin\private directory on the local hard disk (if your computer has one) or your home directory on the network drive.

If you're running Paradox on a single-user computer, you'll still have a private directory, which you can change if necessary.

To change the private directory, follow the steps below.

1. Choose File ➤ Private Directory. You'll see the Private Directory dialog box.

2. Type the name of the private directory. Again, be sure to include both the drive and the directory name (or use an alias), and be sure that the directory you specify exists. If you prefer, you can use the Browse button to select a directory.

3. Choose OK.

4. If asked whether you're sure you want to close all Desktop windows and continue, choose OK.

▶ ▶ **N O T E**

Private directory file names will appear at the bottom of the file list in any Open or Save dialog box and in the Project Viewer window (if you've selected the All or Tables icon). You can also access the private directory by clicking the *:PRIV:* alias in any D̲rive (or Alias) drop-down list or typing *:PRIV:* instead of a drive and directory name.

See Chapters 3 and 15 for more details about aliases and working directories.

▶▶ *Calculating with Blank Fields*

You can control how Paradox for Windows treats blank fields during calculations by choosing T̲ools ➤ S̲ystem Settings ➤ B̲lank As Zero. When the Blank = Zero dialog box appears, select (check) or deselect (uncheck) the T̲reat Blank Fields As Zeros option using the guidelines described below, and then choose OK. Blank As Zero works on Paradox number fields (BCD, long integer, money, number, and short number), and dBASE number and float number fields. (We'll explain how to perform calculations in Part 5 of this book.)

When you *check* the T̲reat Blank Fields As Zeros option, blank fields used in calculations are treated as if they contain a numeric value of zero. To understand how this works, imagine that you want to calculate the extended price, including sales tax, for each record in a query, report, or form. Further suppose that you've specified a Tax Rate of 7.75 (for 7.75%), a Unit Price of $35.00, and a blank value for the quantity ordered (Qty). With Treat Blank Fields As Zeros selected, Paradox will treat the blank quantity ordered field as if it contained a zero. In the calculation below, a zero would be placed in the extended price field, which is probably *not* the result you want.

[Qty] * [Unit Price] * (1 + ([Tax Rate]/100))

When Treat Blank Fields As Zeros is not checked, any calculation that uses a blank field value will end up with a blank result. In the calculation above, the extended price field would therefore remain blank. The unchecked setting assumes that if a field is empty, its contents are probably either intentionally or accidentally omitted. Rather than assuming the blank field is meant to be zero, Paradox refuses to perform the calculation so you don't end up with an incorrect result.

Deciding which option to use for blank fields is a matter of personal preference, but remember that you are more likely to get incorrect results in a calculation if you treat blank fields as zeros.

▶ ▶**T I P**

To make blank or zero values stand out in the Table window, inspect the fields you're interested in, choose Data Dependent from the property menu, and select a contrasting background color or font for blank or zero values (see Chapter 7).

▶ ▶ *Changing the Default Table Properties*

Paradox for Windows offers many ways to customize the properties of the Table window. You can change screen colors, column widths, column order, number and date formats, fonts, data-dependent properties, and more. After customizing the Table window, you can save the changes by choosing Properties ➤ View Properties ➤ Save.

▶ ▶**N O T E**

Whenever you change a table's properties or assign a preferred form, report, graph, or crosstab in the Table window, Paradox updates the table's *.tv* or *.tvf* file.

Suppose you want to right-align all date, logical, time, and timestamp fields; show logical fields in Yes/No format; use single lines for the grid; display all data on a white background; show table headings and text fields in a bold font; adjust the initial widths for each field type; use

Complete Display on formatted memo, graphic, memo, and OLE fields; and define a new row height. Changing the properties of each table in your database to meet these specifications would certainly be a royal pain.

Fortunately, Paradox for Windows lets you establish and store default Table View properties. You simply create a table named *Default* in your private directory and assign the properties you want to use as your new defaults. In the future, any table that doesn't already have its own Table View property file (*.tv*) will automatically use the settings from the Default table. The tedium of inspecting and changing properties for each new table is gone forever. (Of course, you can always override the new default Table View properties for specific tables whenever you want, as explained in Chapter 7.)

Follow these steps to establish the Default table and its properties:

1. Choose File ➤ Working Directory, type the name of your private directory (typically **c:\pdoxwin\private** or simply **:priv:**), and choose OK. If you're asked about closing windows on your Desktop, choose OK again.

2. Choose File ➤ New ➤ Table, select the table type you want (usually Paradox for Windows), and click OK. The Table Type you choose determines whether the default table is for Paradox or dBASE.

3. Define a field for each data type that you want to customize (see Chapter 4), then click the Save As button. The structure shown in Figure 14.2 is useful for any Paradox for Windows table.

4. When prompted for the table name, type **default**, then choose OK.

 ▶ ▶N O T E

> A Paradox for Windows default table is named *default.db*. A dBASE default table is named *default.dbf*.

Now open the Default table, switch to Edit mode (press F9), add one or more rows of sample data, then customize the table however you like. Figure 14.3 shows the Default table with custom grids, row heights, data formats, and other modified properties. We've opened a

FIGURE 14.2

A sample structure for a Default table. Because you cannot customize the format of BCD, binary, or bytes field types, we didn't bother to define fields for these types of data.

Field Name	Type	Size
Alpha	A	10
Autoincrement	+	
Date	D	
Formatted Memo	F	20
Graphic	G	20
Logical	L	
Long Integer	I	
Memo	M	20
Money	$	
Number	N	
OLE	O	20
Short	S	
Time	T	
TimeStamp	@	

FIGURE 14.3

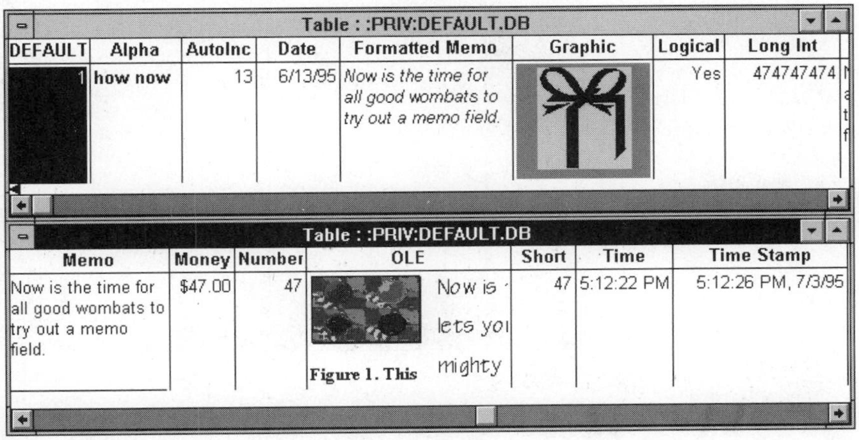

Two copies of the Default table in the Table window. In this example, we modified the grid, background colors, row height and headings, and defined custom properties for various fields. The top copy of the table shows the first seven fields, while the bottom copy shows the remaining seven.

DEFAULT	Alpha	AutoInc	Date	Formatted Memo	Graphic	Logical	Long Int
1	how now	13	6/13/95	Now is the time for all good wombats to try out a memo field.		Yes	474747474

Memo	Money	Number	OLE	Short	Time	Time Stamp
Now is the time for all good wombats to try out a memo field.	$47.00	47	Now is lets yo mighty Figure 1. This	47	5:12:22 PM	5:12:26 PM, 7/3/95

second copy of the table and scrolled it to the right so that you can see additional fields. Thus, the top Default table shows the first seven fields, while the bottom Default table shows the remaining seven fields.

When you're ready to save the properties, choose Properties ➤ View Properties ➤ Save. If you created a Paradox for Windows table, the default Table View properties file will be *default.tv*. The dBASE Table View properties file is *default.tvf*.

Now close the Default table, switch to your preferred working directory, and open your tables as usual. Any tables that don't already have a *.tv* (or *.tvf*) file will get their properties from the *default.tv* (or *default.tvf*) file in your private directory. For example, notice how the Employee table shown in Figure 14.4 has inherited the properties of the Default table in Figure 14.3.

As for any Paradox table, you can change the *default.db* (or *default.dbf*) table's properties, structure, or data at any time. If you want to return to Paradox's built-in properties, simply delete the *default.tv* (or *default.tvf*) file: Open the Default table in your private directory, choose Properties ▶ View Properties ▶ Delete, and choose OK.

FIGURE 14.4 ▶

The Employee table displayed with the properties established by the Default table. We narrowed some columns to display additional fields, but made no other changes to properties that Employee inherited.

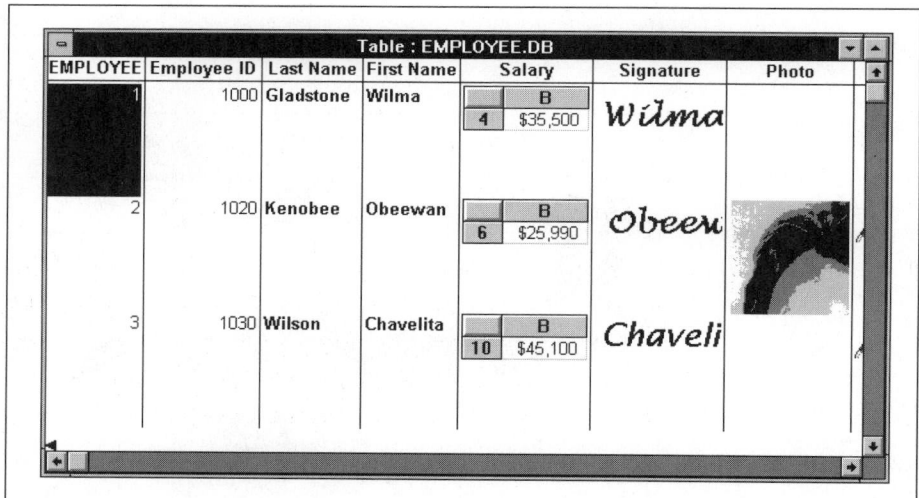

▶▶ Changing the Default Designer Settings

You use the Form and Report Designers to define custom forms, reports, and charts for your data. As explained in Part 3 (especially Chapter 10), there are many ways to customize the default appearance and behavior of object design tools and the designers themselves. Rather than repeat the details here, we'll just summarize the methods for customizing the designers in the next two sections.

▶ *Changing the Behavior of Design Tools*

Use the techniques below to change how the object design tools behave when you use them to create new objects:

- To customize a design tool's default behavior, use either of these techniques. Inspect the tool and choose options from the PROTO menu to customize its properties. Or, select an object that has the properties you want, and then choose <u>D</u>esign ➤ <u>C</u>opy To Toolbar. Your changes are effective for the current Paradox session only, unless you save them in a *style sheet*.

- To permanently save the properties of design tools in a style sheet, choose <u>P</u>roperties, then <u>F</u>orm or <u>R</u>eport (as appropriate), then <u>S</u>tyle Sheet. In the Style Sheet dialog box, type in or highlight a style sheet name, then choose <u>S</u>ave or Save <u>A</u>s. Choose OK to close the dialog box.

▶ ▶ **N O T E**

> **Style sheets for forms have a *.ft* file extension, whereas style sheets for reports have a *.fp* extension. The style sheets that come with Paradox are stored in the *c:\pdoxwin* directory. Style sheets that you create are stored in the current working directory.**

- To use an existing style sheet in the current design document, choose <u>P</u>roperties, then <u>F</u>orm or <u>R</u>eport (as appropriate), then <u>S</u>tyle Sheet. In the Style Sheet dialog box, type in or highlight a style sheet name, then choose OK. The design tools will now take on the default behaviors specified in the style sheet. (You can also specify a style sheet when you create your design document.)

► ►**T I P**

Some settings for the form, report, and label Experts are stored in tables in the *pdoxwin\\experts* directory. You can customize the Experts to some extent by carefully updating the appropriate Experts, Experts2, Labels1, and Labels2 tables. See Chapters 11 and 12.

► Changing the Behavior and Appearance of the Designers

Here's how to change the default appearance and behavior of the Form and Report Designers:

- To customize the appearance of objects that you draw, select, or move in the Design window, choose Properties ➤ Designer, then check or uncheck any of these options: Select From Inside, Frame Objects, Flicker-Free Draw, and Outlined Move/Resize. When you're finished, choose OK. These properties take effect immediately and stay set in future Paradox sessions (until you change them again).

- To control the appearance and behavior of the drawing surface, choose Properties and then check or uncheck options below Form Options or Report Options in the Properties menu. These options include Band Labels (reports only), Snap To Grid, Show Grid, Grid Settings, Horizontal Ruler, Vertical Ruler, Expanded Ruler, and Show Size And Position. Your selections remain in effect for the current form or report only, unless you save them as described next.

- To save changes to the appearance and behavior of the drawing surface, choose Properties, then Form Options or Report Options (as appropriate), then Save Defaults. Your properties will be saved in the *pdoxwin.ini* file that is located in your *windows* directory.

►► Using the IDAPI Configuration Utility

The IDAPI Configuration Utility allows you to change the initial settings for IDAPI, the system that allows Paradox to share tables and files with other IDAPI-hosted applications such as Quattro Pro for Windows, Oracle, Sybase, and dBASE for Windows.

> **NOTE**
>
> **To display the current settings without changing them, choose Tools ➤ System Settings ➤ IDAPI from the Paradox for Windows menus.**

The initial IDAPI settings are established when you install Paradox; once set, they rarely need changing. In fact, most users will never need to run the IDAPI Configuration Utility, since it is designed primarily for Paradox network administrators and programmers who must customize a Paradox system or "tweak" it to meet special needs. We'll describe it briefly here, just to get you started.

> **WARNING**
>
> **In general, the IDAPI Configuration Utility should be used by *advanced users only*, because incorrect settings can cause problems with your system.**

To run the IDAPI Configuration Utility, follow these steps:

1. Close any open IDAPI applications, including Paradox for Windows.
2. Switch to the Windows Program Manager (press Alt+Tab as needed, or press Ctrl+Esc and double-click *Program Manager* in the Task list).
3. Open the Paradox for Windows program group (if it's not already open).

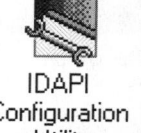
IDAPI Configuration Utility

4. Double-click the IDAPI Configuration Utility icon (shown at left). You'll see the IDAPI Configuration Utility window illustrated in Figure 14.5.
5. Click the tab for the "page" that you want to change, or choose an option from the Pages menu. For example, to change the date settings, you'd click the *Date* tab near the bottom of the window or choose Pages ➤ Date Formats from the configuration utility's

FIGURE 14.5 ►

*The IDAPI Configura-
tion Utility window
with the PARADOX
driver selected*

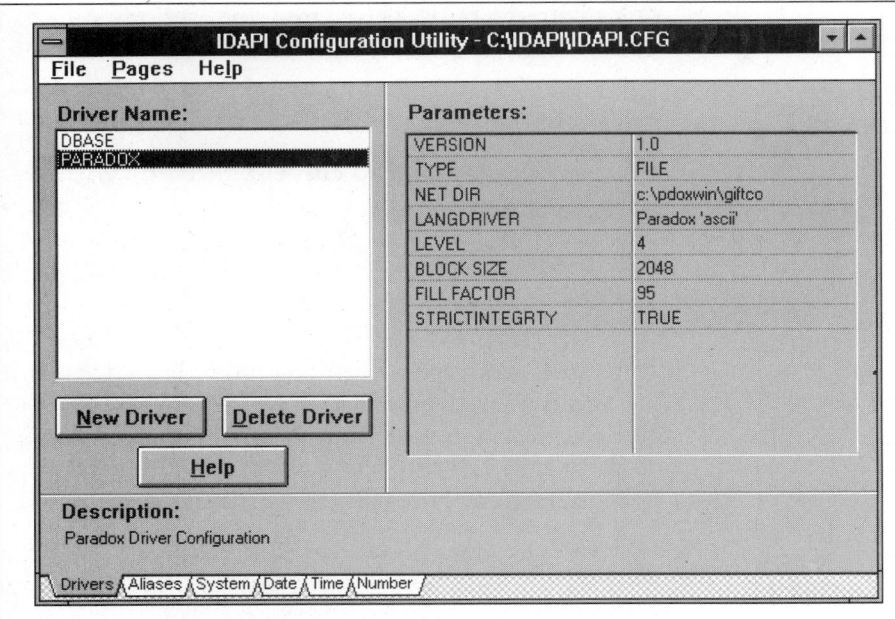

menu bar. There's more information about each page in the next
section.

6. Once you've selected the page you want to change, click the appropriate options, type values into the text boxes, and click option
buttons, as appropriate. When you click in a list box or text box on
a configuration setting page, you'll see a brief explanation of the
selected item just above the tabs near the bottom of the window.

You can get more information about changing IDAPI settings in any of
these ways:

● Click the Help button in any IDAPI Configuration Utility window.

● Choose Help ➤ Contents from the IDAPI Configuration Utility
menu bar, then click the underlined jump word or the icon for
whatever page you are changing.

● Use Windows Notepad to review the *readme.txt* file in your Paradox directory (*c:\paradox\readme.txt*).

When you've finished making changes, choose File ➤ Exit from the IDAPI Configuration Utility menus, or just double-click the IDAPI Configuration Utility window's Control-menu bar. If you're asked about saving the changes, choose Yes if you want to keep them or No if you don't. Your changes will take effect the next time you start your IDAPI application (for example, the next time you restart Paradox for Windows).

Any changes you make in the IDAPI Configuration Utility are usually stored in *c:\ idapi\idapi.cfg*, which Paradox reads at startup. You can use the Local Settings Utility, described later in this chapter, to change the default location of *idapi.cfg*.

▶ What Each IDAPI Configuration Utility Page Is For

The following list offers a brief description of each page in the IDAPI Configuration Utility window. For more details about each option on a given page, just choose the appropriate page, highlight the item you're interested in, and click the Help button.

Drivers Controls the way an IDAPI application creates, sorts, and handles data. To use this page, select the Driver Name you want in the left side of the Drivers page, then select and update the Parameters as needed. For example, to specify the directory where Paradox will find the network control file (pdoxusrs.net), select PARADOX under Driver Name, then click NET DIR and type in the appropriate network directory (or use the ... button to browse through the directories). The Drivers page also allows you to add new SQL drivers and to delete drivers.

▶ ▶ W A R N I N G

Paradox will not work correctly if the NET DIR setting points to a nonexistent directory.

Aliases Lets you change alias path names, add new aliases, or delete existing aliases. This is an alternative to using the File ➤ Aliases option in Paradox.

System   Controls various startup settings for an IDAPI application. These include whether local file sharing is on or off, how IDAPI will use system memory, the default system language driver, and the maximum number of file handles IDAPI will use.

Date   Controls the appearance and interpretation of date values. For example, this setting controls the appearance of dates in DBDate and DBTimestamp format (see Chapter 7), and governs how Paradox will interpret dates when you use them in query criteria (see Chapter 9).

Time   Controls the appearance and interpretation of time values. For example, this setting controls the appearance of times in DBTime and DBTimeStamp format (see Chapter 7).

Number   Controls the appearance and interpretation of number values. For example, this setting controls the appearance of numbers in DBNumeric format (see Chapter 7).

►► *Understanding Paradox for Windows Initialization Files*

As the name suggests, *initialization files* determine settings that take effect when you start Paradox for Windows. For example, initialization files control the appearance and settings of Paradox windows, and set the current working directory and Desktop configuration. Because Paradox updates most initialization settings automatically, most users will never need to know how they work.

► *IDAPI Initialization File*

The IDAPI initialization file (*c:\ idapi\idapi.cfg*) is a binary file that keeps track of initial settings for the IDAPI engine. This file is updated whenever you make changes through the IDAPI Configuration Utility or permanently save or delete an alias via the File ► Aliases option in Paradox for Windows.

The IDAPI settings remain in effect while any application that uses IDAPI is running. For example, if you run Quattro Pro for Windows and then start Paradox for Windows, Paradox will use the IDAPI settings that were loaded with Quattro Pro for Windows. To display the current IDAPI settings, choose Tools ➤ System Settings ➤ IDAPI.

▶ Windows Initialization File

The Windows initialization file (*c:\windows\win.ini*) tracks the location of your working and private directories, default command-line options for starting Paradox, the location of the *idapi.cfg* file, and several Workgroup Desktop (Object Exchange) settings. This text file also contains general Windows defaults.

The *win.ini* file is updated when you install Paradox, and when you change the working and private directory for Paradox or use the Local Settings Utility (described later).

N O T E

Although most updates to *win.ini* are automatic, you must add default command-line options manually. Appendix A provides information about command-line options, which temporarily override settings in the initialization files when you start Paradox from a command line.

▶ Paradox Initialization File

The Paradox initialization file (*c:\windows\pdoxwin.ini*) contains your preferences for the Paradox for Windows Desktop, Desktop properties such as the title and Toolbar appearance, the Form and Report window properties, default system font, and any custom date and number formats you define. This text file is updated automatically whenever you exit Paradox.

If necessary, you can restore many default Desktop settings by renaming (or deleting) the *pdoxwin.ini* file. The next time you start Paradox, it will automatically create a new *pdoxwin.ini* file with the original default settings.

After re-creating the *pdoxwin.ini* file, you may need to restore some settings. For example, choose Properties ➤ Desktop and update the default Background Bitmap location to *c:\pdoxwin\pdoxwin.bmp* and its position to Center Bitmap. You also may want to choose Properties ▶ Project and check Open Project Viewer On Startup.

▶ *Paradox Working Directory Initialization File*

The working directory initialization file, *pdoxwork.ini*, describes the contents of a working directory's Project Viewer window when you're viewing references only (View ▶ Only References). Paradox updates (or creates) this text file whenever you switch to a new working directory or exit Paradox. You can use its settings to override defaults in *pdoxwin.ini*.

 ▶▶**N O T E**

> **Another file, *pdoxwork.cfg*, stores information about the current working directory's project aliases. You'll learn how to set up and use projects and project aliases in Chapter 15.**

▶ *Control Panel Initialization File*

Paradox for Windows inherits many configuration settings from Windows itself, including the default colors for windows and menus, printer information, your network type (if any), international settings for documents and tables, and the formats and values of the system Date and Time variables.

Changes to these settings are made through the Windows Control Panel and are stored in the *c:\windows\control.ini* text file.

▶ *Changing the Initialization Files*

Most changes to Paradox for Windows initialization files are made automatically through Paradox for Windows menu options, the Windows Control Panel, and the stand-alone Paradox utility applications. These methods are always the easiest and *safest* ways to update your preferences.

On rare occasions, however, you may need to use a text editor, such as the Windows Notepad or DOS Edit command, to view or edit the *win.ini, pdoxwin.ini,* and *pdoxwork.ini* files. If you do use a text editor, please be *extremely* careful. An editing mistake can corrupt the file and make it unusable, not only for Paradox for Windows but also for other Windows applications that may need it. As a precaution, always back up your .ini files before changing them. The best advice is: If you're not sure how to edit the files safely, leave them alone.

▶▶WARNING

Paradox provides tools for updating the *idapi.cfg,* *default.db, default.dbf,* and *style sheet* files. *Never* edit these files with a text editor because you can damage your copy of Paradox and the data in your tables.

▶▶ *Changing Your Paradox for Windows Local Settings*

The default working directory, private directory, and location of the IDAPI configuration file are defined when you install Paradox. You can change the local and private directories from within Paradox at any time (those changes take effect immediately).

Local Settings Utility

You can also use the Local Settings Utility to change all three settings at once from outside Paradox for Windows. To use this utility, switch to Program Manager, then double-click the Local Settings Utility icon (shown at left) in the Paradox for Windows group window. The Paradox for Windows Local Settings dialog box appears, as shown in Figure 14.6.

Edit the current settings as necessary, then choose OK. Your changes will update the *win.ini* file and take effect the next time you start Paradox for Windows.

FIGURE 14.6

The Paradox for Windows Local Settings dialog box

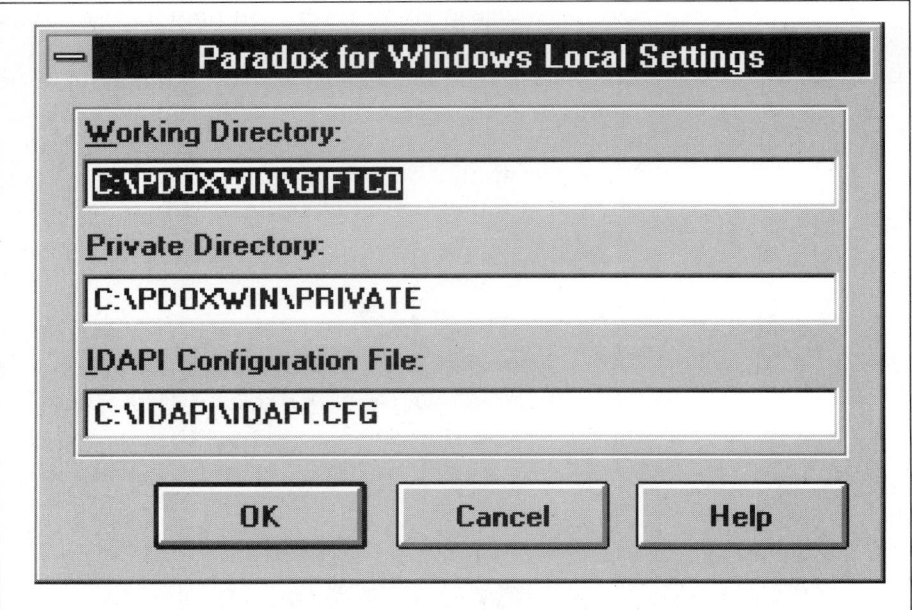

Paradox for Windows Local Settings

Working Directory:

C:\PDOXWIN\GIFTCO

Private Directory:

C:\PDOXWIN\PRIVATE

IDAPI Configuration File:

C:\IDAPI\IDAPI.CFG

[OK]   [Cancel]   [Help]

N O T E

The Local Settings Utility provides the only method, other than manual editing, for updating the location of the IDAPI configuration file.

In this chapter we've discussed many ways to customize the default settings for Paradox for Windows. As mentioned at the outset, changing default settings is entirely optional. If you are happy with the way Paradox is running on your computer, you can leave the default settings alone.

The next chapter presents tools for managing Paradox for Windows files. We'll delve into the Project Viewer and explain how to work with projects. We'll also show you how to rename, copy, and delete files (including tables), move and copy records from one table to another, protect your data, and restructure tables.

► ► CHAPTER **15**

Managing Your Files and Projects

▶▶ FAST TRACK

▶ **To use the Alias Manager to add or delete aliases**   **824**

choose File ➤ Aliases. After defining public aliases, you
can use them to access a database from any directory on
your computer. Project aliases are available only when
you're using the same working directory that was used to
create the project alias.

▶ **The Paradox for Windows browse features**   **828**

let you locate objects on your computer by clicking on
alias names, directory folders, and file names in dialog
boxes that prompt for file or directory names. (If necessary, click the Browse button or the file folder button in
the Project Viewer to open a browser dialog box.) Once
you've highlighted the directory and/or file you want,
choose OK to complete your selection.

▶ **You can use the Project Viewer window and projects**   **834**

to keep related objects together. Each Paradox working directory has its own project, which you can view with the
Project Viewer.

▶ **To open or activate the Project Viewer**   **834**

click the Open Project Viewer button in the Toolbar; or,
if the Desktop is empty, choose Tools ➤ Project Viewer.
Initially, the Project Viewer shows objects in the current
working directory only; however, you can manually add
objects from any other directory. You can inspect most objects in the Project Viewer.

▶ ***To manage tables and files***   ***844***

         choose <u>T</u>ools ➤ <u>U</u>tilities or inspect an object in the Project Viewer window; then select <u>C</u>opy, <u>R</u>ename, or <u>D</u>elete.

▶ ***To add or delete many records at once***   ***850***

         choose <u>T</u>ools ➤ <u>U</u>tilities or inspect a table in the Project Viewer window; then select <u>A</u>dd, <u>E</u>mpty, or S<u>u</u>btract.

▶ ***To get information about a table***   ***859***

         choose <u>T</u>ools ➤ <u>U</u>tilities or inspect a table in the Project Viewer; then select I<u>n</u>fo Structure. If you want to save information about the structure in another table that you can report on, choose Save <u>A</u>s, specify a table name (for example, *Struct*), and choose OK. After viewing the table information, click <u>D</u>one.

▶ ***To change the structure of an existing table***   ***866***

         choose <u>T</u>ools ➤ <u>U</u>tilities or inspect a table in the Project Viewer; then select Res<u>t</u>ructure. Techniques used in the Restructure Table dialog box are similar to those used to create new tables. Be careful! Restructuring can result in data loss and key violations.

▶ ***To add passwords to a table***   ***882***

         choose *Password Security* from the Table <u>P</u>roperties list of the Restructure Table dialog box, then define a master password for the entire table. For more security, you can define auxiliary passwords.

As you develop more Paradox for Windows objects—tables, forms, reports, and so forth—you'll need to manage them efficiently. In this chapter, you'll learn how to perform some important file management tasks, including

- managing aliases and projects
- locating and managing tables, records, and other files
- getting information about Paradox tables
- restructuring existing tables
- adding password protection to tables
- repairing damaged tables

▶▶ **NOTE**

Please refer to Appendix C for information on importing and exporting data between Paradox and other applications.

▶▶ Using Aliases

In Paradox, a database is a collection of files—tables, forms, reports, and so forth—located in a directory on your local hard disk or on a network. As explained in Chapter 3, an *alias* is a nickname that provides quick access to your database.

Suppose you have stored a database in the directory *c:\pdoxwin\giftco*. If you assign an alias, such as *Gift_Corner*, to that directory, that alias will appear in the Drive (or Alias) list of any dialog box that displays a list of file names. From then on, you can simply click the alias name instead of typing a path name. To view the names of files stored in another directory, simply click the Drive (or Alias) drop-down arrow and click the alias name you want.

NOTE

Paradox automatically provides two aliases. The :WORK: alias stands for the current working directory. The :PRIV: alias represents your private directory (usually *c:\pdoxwin\private*).

Aliases provide several advantages:

- They offer a handy, error-free alternative to typing complete path names.
- They allow you to access database files from any directory on your computer.
- You can give aliases meaningful names that are easier to remember than path names. For example, the alias *Chap1_Figures* is easier to remember than a long path name like *d:\pdoxwin\masterng\chap01\figures*.
- You can change the path name of an alias at any time. When you do so, any forms, reports, and other Paradox objects that refer to that alias name will automatically refer to the new directory path.

WARNING

If there's even a remote chance that you'll need to move your databases to another drive or directory, use *alias names*—rather than path names—whenever you specify the location of a database object. Failure to do this can prevent you from moving databases successfully and may render Paradox objects unreadable until you move them back to their original drives and directories.

- You can use aliases instead of full path names when referring to files in ObjectPAL applications. This lets you move applications to other directories without having to recode all references to files. See Chapter 19 for more information about ObjectPAL applications.

▶ *Using the Alias Manager*

The Alias Manager allows you to view or change the path names of existing aliases, to delete aliases, and to add new ones. To open the Alias Manager dialog box, choose File ➤ Aliases. You'll see a dialog box like the one in Figure 15.1.

▶ ▶ **T I P**

You can also open the Alias Manager by clicking the Aliases button in any dialog box that offers it. For example, choosing File ➤ Open ➤ Table leads to the Open Table dialog box, where you can click the Aliases but-ton to use the Alias Manager. When you're finished with the Alias Manager, you'll return to whatever dialog box you came from (in this case, the Open Table dialog box).

▶ *About Public and Project Aliases*

You can set up two types of aliases:

Public aliases   These are available from any working directory, and to any application that uses IDAPI. By default, public aliases are saved to the file *c:\idapi\idapi.cfg* (or to whatever file you specify).

Project aliases   These are available only from the working directory used to create the project alias, and only to Paradox applications. When you change working directories, Paradox removes the current project aliases from memory and loads in any project aliases from the new working directory. If a project alias has the same name as a public alias, Paradox will ignore the project alias in favor of the public alias. Project aliases are stored to the *pdoxwork.cfg* file in the working directory.

FIGURE 15.1

*The Alias Manager
dialog box*

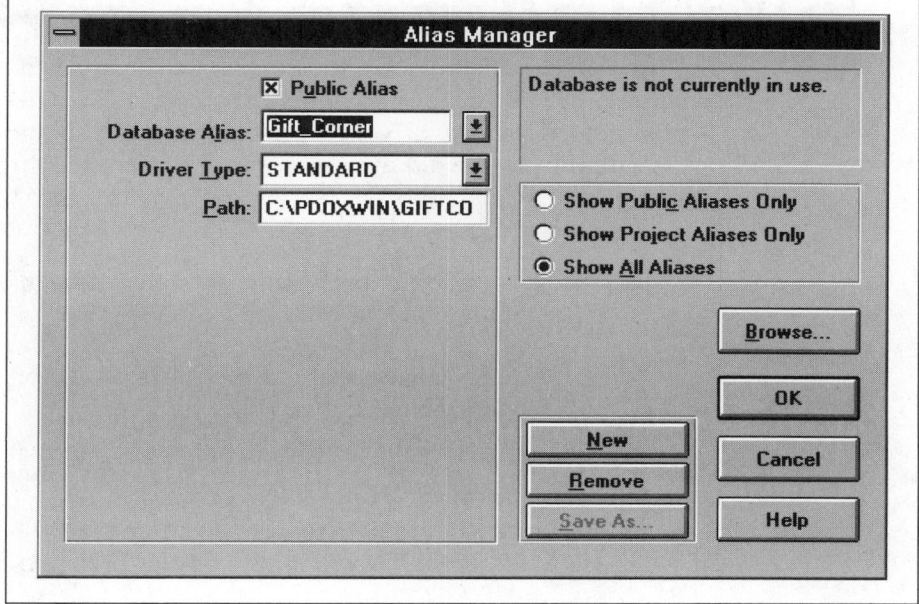

As you can see, public aliases are less restrictive than project aliases. Which type you create depends on the application you're designing, whether you want aliases to be available in any working directory, and whether you want other IDAPI applications to "know about" your Paradox aliases.

You can select which aliases will appear when you open the Database Alias drop-down list of the Alias Manager dialog box, as follows:

- To show both public and project aliases, select the Show All Aliases option. This is the default setting.

- To show public aliases only, select the Show Public Aliases Only option.

- To show project aliases only, select the Show Project Aliases Only option.

▶ Viewing or Changing an Alias Path Name

Recall that aliases make it easier for you to move databases to other directories as needed. If you've moved Paradox files from one working directory (or disk drive) to another, you also should change any aliases that point to the old directory, so they reference the new directory. This way, any forms, reports, queries, or programs that use the alias will continue to work properly.

To view or change the path name for an existing alias, open the Alias Manager dialog box and proceed as follows:

1. Choose the appropriate "Show aliases" option from the right side of the dialog box, as described previously.

2. Click the Database Alias drop-down arrow to display the list of aliases.

3. Click the alias you want to view or change. The path name assigned to the alias will appear in the Path text box.

4. If you want the alias to point to a different directory, change the path name in the Path text box. Or click the Browse button, then click the directory you want in the Directory Browser dialog box and choose OK. The directory must already exist.

5. Save your changes as described below under "Saving Alias Changes."

 ▶▶ N O T E

> To change a database alias *name*, you must delete the alias as described below, then create a new one with the desired name.

▶ Adding an Alias

To add a new alias, open the Alias Manager dialog box, then follow these steps:

1. Choose the appropriate "Show aliases" option from the right side of the dialog box.

2. If you want to use an existing alias as a model for the new one, click the Database Alias drop-down arrow and select the alias.

3. Click the New button.

4. Type a name for the new alias in the Database Alias text box. The alias name must be unique, and can include any combination of letters, numbers, and spaces. Spaces are automatically converted to underscore (_) characters.

5. If you want to change the path name, type the complete path name in the Path text box (for example, **c:\pdoxwin\graphics**).

6. To create this alias as a project alias, deselect (uncheck) the Public Alias option. To create the alias as a public alias, be sure the Public Alias option is selected (checked).

7. Save your changes as described below.

▶ Deleting an Alias

To delete an alias from the Alias Manager dialog box, select the appropriate "Show aliases" option from the right side of the dialog box, then click the Database Alias drop-down arrow, click the name of the alias you want to delete, and click the Remove button. Finally, save your changes as described below. Removing an alias has no effect on the directory that the alias referenced.

▶ Saving Alias Changes

You can save your changes in the Alias Manager dialog box either for the current Paradox session only, or for all future Paradox sessions. Use the buttons listed below to get the job done.

Keep New If you have just created a new alias, the New button changes to Keep New. You can click Keep New to save the current alias without closing the Alias Manager dialog box. This makes it easy to do several alias management tasks without leaving the Alias Manager each time.

OK When you're ready to save your changes and close the Alias Manager, choose OK. You'll be asked if you want to save your public aliases and project aliases. If you choose Yes, your changes will be saved permanently and will be available anytime you use

Managing Files and Projects

Ch. 15

Paradox; if you choose <u>N</u>o, your changes will be temporary only and will be deleted when you exit Paradox.

Save As Choosing Save <u>A</u>s is similar to choosing OK and answering <u>Y</u>es to prompts about saving your changes permanently. The differences are that you'll have a chance to save your changes to different configuration files, and you'll remain in the Alias Manager dialog box. After choosing Save <u>A</u>s, you can type in or highlight a new configuration file name, then choose OK. If you chose an existing configuration file name, you'll be asked for permission to overwrite the file. Choose <u>Y</u>es.

►►**N O T E**

If you created or changed both public and project aliases, you'll first be asked to save your changes to the public aliases in *idapi.cfg* and then to the project aliases in *pdoxwork.cfg*.

►► *Browsing for Directories and Files*

The computer's file system is organized into a tree structure of directories, subdirectories, and files. The highest level of the tree is called the *root* directory; all other directories branch out below the root directory. A directory within a directory is called a subdirectory. Like most Windows applications, Paradox makes it easy to browse through and locate objects (files) and directories on your computer.

Two types of browsers appear in Paradox:

File browser When Paradox is requesting a file name, you'll see a *file browser* like the one shown in Figure 15.2. This dialog box lets you choose a drive, directory, and file simply by clicking or double-clicking appropriate places in the dialog box. Alternatively, you can type a file name (or alias and file name) into the <u>F</u>ile Name text box at the upper-left corner.

FIGURE 15.2

File browsers let you locate and fill in a file name that's located in any directory on your computer. To open this dialog box, we chose File ➤ Open ➤ Table.

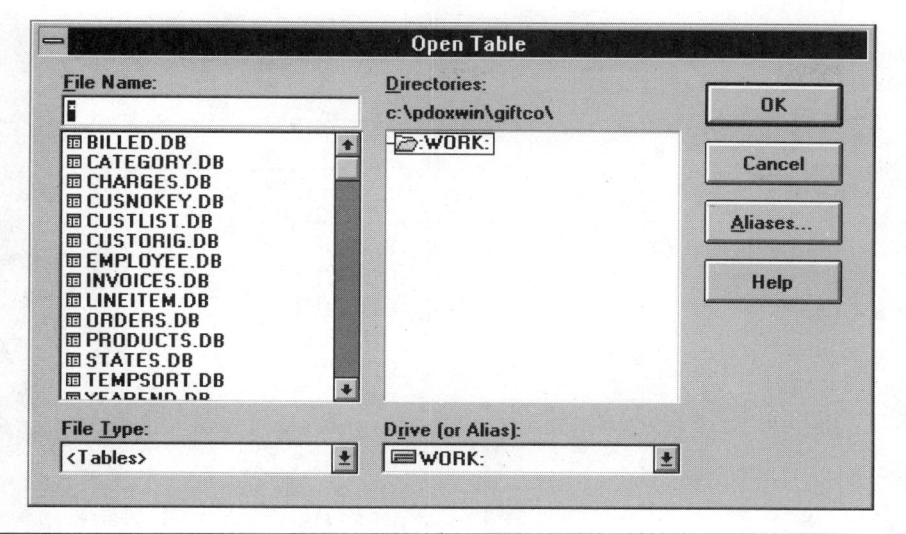

Directory browser When Paradox needs you to fill in a directory name, you'll see a simpler *directory browser*, like the one in Figure 15.3. As you'd expect, you can click on the directory you want or type its name (or alias) into the Directories text box.

▶▶ **NOTE**

Some dialog boxes that prompt for directory or file names don't display the browser automatically; in that case, simply click the Browse button if it's available. (If you're using the Project Viewer, the Browse button looks like a small file folder.)

After typing in or clicking on the file or directory location you want, choose OK. You'll either be returned to the dialog box you came from, or Paradox will immediately take some action on the selected file.

If you wish to return to the dialog box you came from without selecting a file or changing the directory, choose Cancel.

The following sections provide more information about the browsers.

FIGURE 15.3 ▶

Directory browsers let you locate and fill in directory names quickly. To display this dialog box, we chose File ► Working Directory and clicked the Browse button.

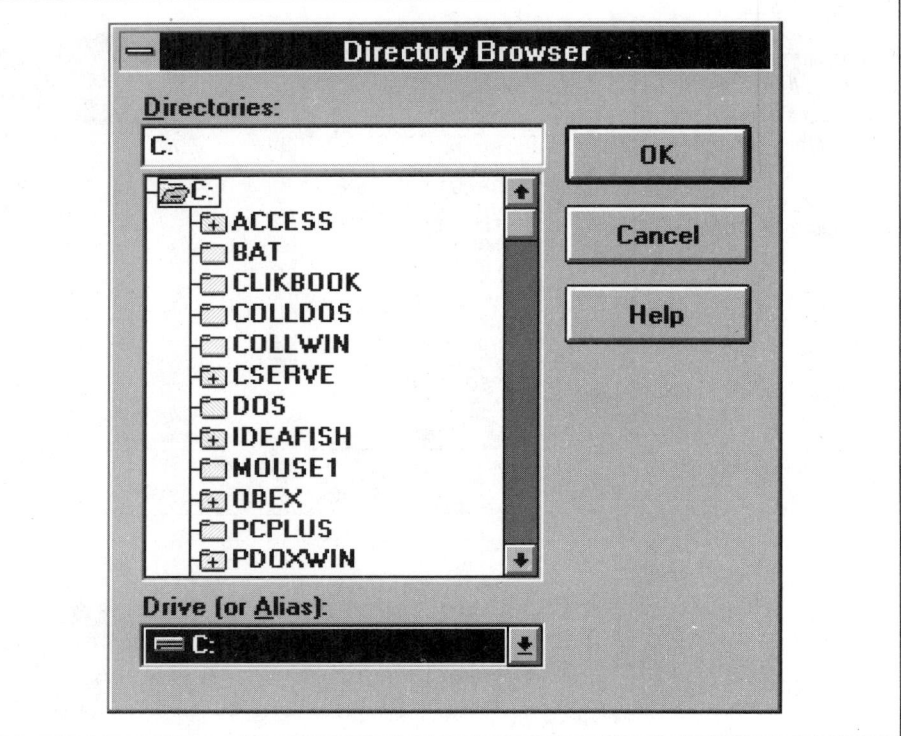

► Using the Aliases List

Anytime an Aliases or Drive (or Alias) drop-down list appears in a browser, you can click the drop-down arrow, then click an alias name. This will switch you to the appropriate directory or drive and fill in the directory name automatically.

To switch to the root directory of a disk drive, simply open the alias list, then scroll up or down to the appropriate drive letter (for example, A:, B:, C:, D:, or E:) and click the drive's alias.

► *Using the File Type List*

The File Type drop-down list in the browser lets you restrict the file list to a specific type of file. The types of files available depend on which dialog box you were using when you began browsing, and you'll only find this option in file browsers. For example, after choosing File ► Open ► Table, only the <Tables> type is available in the File Type list. Table 15.1 describes all the available file types.

► **TABLE 15.1:** *File Types Included in the Type List*

FILE TYPE	DESCRIPTION
<All>	All file types (*.*).
<Data Models>	Paradox data models (*.dm). See Chapters 5, 10, 16, and 17.
<Forms>	Paradox forms (*.fsl, *.fdl). See Chapters 10 and 11.
<Graphics>	Graphics files (*.bmp, *.pcx, *.tif, *.gif, *.eps). See Chapter 6.
<Libraries>	ObjectPAL libraries (*.lsl, *.ldl). See Chapter 19.
<Printer Style Sheets>	Paradox style sheets for printed reports (*.fp). See Chapters 10 and 12.
<Queries>	Paradox query files (*.qbe). See Chapters 9 and 16.
<Reports>	Paradox reports (*.rsl, *.rdl). See Chapters 10 and 12.
<Screen Style Sheets>	Paradox style sheets for onscreen forms (*.ft). See Chapters 10 and 11.
<Scripts>	ObjectPAL script files (*.ssl, *.sdl). See Chapter 19.
<SQL>	SQL script files (*.sql).
<Style Sheet>	Paradox style sheets (*.ft, *.fp). See Chapters 10, 11, and 12.
<Tables>	Paradox and dBASE tables (*.db, *dbf).
<Text>	Text files (*.pxt, *.txt, *.rtf). See Chapter 6.

▶ ▶ T I P

To work with *all* the file types that Paradox recognizes, type the wildcard *.* in the File Name text box and press ⌐. Or, open the Project Viewer window, and click the All icon in the left side of the window. We'll discuss the Project Viewer window later in this chapter.

▶ Using Wildcards to Find Files

The standard DOS wildcard characters listed below provide another way to restrict the list of files shown in file browsers. You can type the wildcard characters when specifying the file name or extension (or both) in a File Name text box (see Figure 15.2), then press ⌐. Paradox will then list only the files that match the wildcard you entered.

- The asterisk (*) represents a whole word or a group of characters. For example *.*exe* represents all files with an *.exe* extension. The wildcard *c*.** represents all files beginning with the letter *c* and having any extension.

- The question mark (?) represents a single character. For instance, *?????.** lists files with up to five letters and any extension.

The wildcard works in conjunction with the aliases and file type specifications. As an example, *c*.** normally specifies all files beginning with the letter *c* and having any extension. However, if you've also specified *Gift_Corner* as the alias and a <Tables> file type, you'll only see file names of tables that begin with the letter *c* in the *c:\pdoxwin\giftco* directory (assuming the Gift_Corner alias points to this directory).

▶ Cruising the Directories

Cruising the directories in a browser is an easy job. If you're using a directory browser, simply click the directory folder you want, or use the Drive (or Alias) drop-down list to select it. The directory name will appear in the Directories text box.

If you're using a file browser, you can use the following techniques to select a directory and file:

- If you wish, use the D̲rive (or Alias) drop-down list to choose a specific drive or directory in the right side of the browser. The D̲irectories list on the right side of the dialog box will reflect your choice.

- To switch to any directory shown in the right side of the browser, click the desired folder icon or directory name. The file names for the selected directory will appear in the left side of the browser.

- To select a file in the left side of the browser, click its name.

In Figure 15.4, we selected *C:GONDOLAC* in the D̲rive (or Alias) drop-down list, then clicked the *pdoxwin* folder, then clicked the *giftco* folder to display the tables in the *c:\pdoxwin\giftco* subdirectory. Notice how the dialog box shown in Figure 15.4 reflects the currently selected directory name (just below the D̲irectories option), the currently selected File T̲ype, and the current D̲rive (or Alias).

When you're finished using the directory or file browser, choose OK to close the dialog box and accept your directory or file selection.

FIGURE 15.4 ▶

To display the sub-directories below a directory, click the appropriate folder icon.

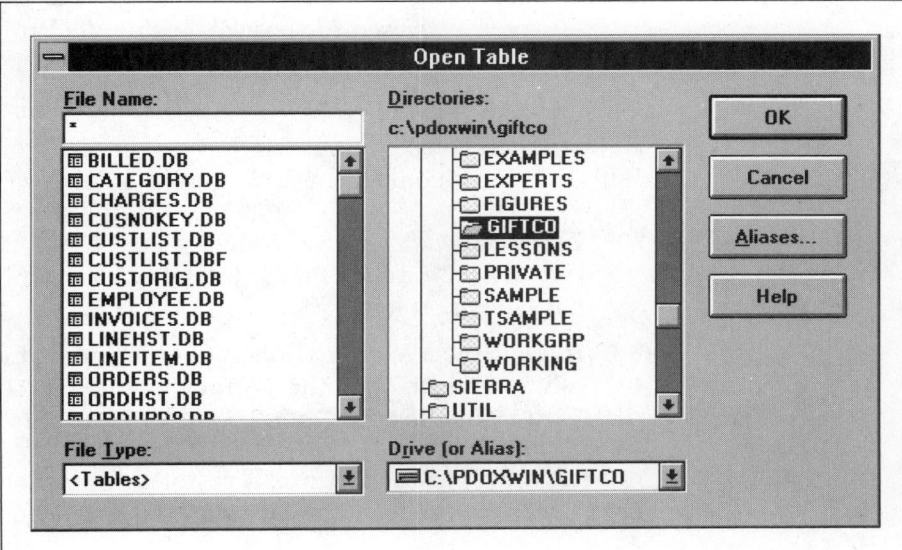

►►**N O T E**

> **If you would like the browsers to indicate which branches have subdirectories below them, choose _P_roperties ➤ _D_esktop and click the _A_dvanced button. Then select (check) _I_ndicate Expandable Directory Branches and choose OK twice. With this option selected, expandable directory folders will be marked with a plus (+). When you click an expandable directory folder, its subdirectory folders will appear and the plus will change to a minus (–). To collapse an expanded directory, double-click it; the subdirectories will be hidden again and the minus will change back to a plus. (To immediately expand the directory again, you'll need to double-click it.)**

►► *Using the Project Viewer Window*

The Project Viewer is one of Paradox's most powerful and convenient tools for managing both Paradox and non-Paradox objects in any directory. Chapter 3 covered the basics of using the Project Viewer window. In this chapter, we'll focus on ways to use the Project Viewer to manage groups of related objects called *projects*.

To open the Project Viewer window on the Desktop, use whichever method is most convenient from the list below:

- If the Project Viewer window isn't open yet, choose _T_ools ➤ Project _V_iewer, or click the Open Project Viewer button in the Toolbar (shown at left).

- If the Project Viewer window is open, but is hidden behind another window, open the _W_indow menu and choose Project Viewer, or click the Open Project Viewer button in the Toolbar.

You can move, resize, maximize, restore, minimize, and close the Project Viewer as you would any window. Here are some additional ways to use the Project Viewer window:

- To change the working directory, click the drop-down list button next to Working Directory and select the directory you want to use. Or, click the file folder (Browse) button in the Project Viewer to open the Directory Browser, then click the directory you want and choose OK.

► ►**T I P**

The Working Directory drop-down list holds the ten most recently-used working directories.

- To control whether the Project Viewer appears automatically whenever you start Paradox, choose <u>P</u>roperties ➤ <u>P</u>roject. Then, if you want to see the window at startup, select (check) <u>O</u>pen Project Viewer On Startup; to hide the window at startup, deselect the option. Finally, choose OK. Your settings will take effect the next time you start Paradox for Windows.

Figure 15.5 illustrates a sample Project Viewer window after we selected the Tables icon from the left side and right-clicked the CUSTLIST.DB table name. Table 15.2 provides an alphabetical list of all the options you'll encounter when inspecting objects and icons in the Project Viewer window. However, exactly *which* of those options is available depends on the type of object you're working with at the moment.

► ►**T I P**

You can also inspect an object in the right side of the Project Viewer by clicking that object and then pressing F6 (or choosing <u>P</u>roperties ➤ <u>C</u>urrent Item).

In the next few sections, we'll take a closer look at techniques for managing projects.

Managing Files and Projects

Ch.
15

FIGURE 15.5 ▶

Inspecting a table object in the Project Viewer opens the menu shown here.

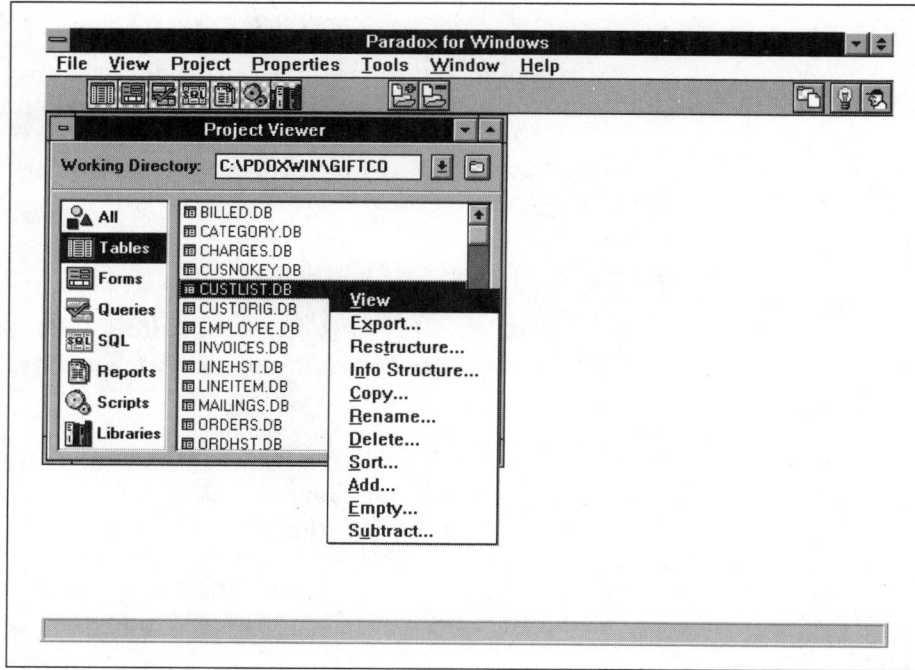

▶ **TABLE 15.2:** *Options Available When Inspecting Objects in the Project Viewer*

PROPERTY	EXPLANATION
Add	Add records from this table to another table.
Copy	Copy this object to a new object.
Delete	Delete this object.
Delimited Text Import	Import this text file into a table in delimited text format. See Appendix C.
Design	Open the Design window for this object. See Chapters 10–13 and 19.
Empty	Remove all records from this table.
Export	Export this table to another application. See Appendix C.

▶ **TABLE 15.2:** *Options Available When Inspecting Objects in the Project Viewer (continued)*

PROPERTY	EXPLANATION
Fixed Length Import	Import this text file into a table in fixed length text format. See Appendix C.
Import	Import this spreadsheet file into a table. See Appendix C.
Info Structure	Display information about the table's structure.
Open	Open this query. See Chapter 9.
Play	Play the ObjectPAL script. See Chapter 19.
Print	Print this report document. See Chapter 12.
Print With	Request the table to use, then print this report document. See Chapter 12.
Rename	Change the name of this object.
Restructure	Change the structure of this table.
Run	Run this query. See Chapter 9.
Run *application*	Run this application.
Run *application* W/Params	Run this application with command-line parameters. When prompted, type the parameters (but do not type the program name), then choose OK.
Sort	Sort this table. See Chapter 8.
Subtract	Remove records from a target table if they match records in this table.
View	Open this table in Table View. See Chapter 7.
View Data	Display the data in the format defined by this document. See Chapters 10–13.
View With	Request the name of the table to use, then display the data in the format defined by this document. See Chapters 10–13.

▶▶ *Managing Projects*

The Project Viewer window provides a convenient way to view, organize, and access related objects. Taken together, the group of related objects in a given working directory is called a *project*.

When you open the Project Viewer window, it automatically displays the names of objects in the current working directory. It will also show the names of objects that you've added to the project manually; those objects can be in the current directory, different directories, or even different network servers, so you can work with them easily without changing their physical location or your working directory. (You'll learn how to add objects soon.) Figure 15.5 showed a sample Project Viewer window for the *c:\pdoxwin\giftco* directory opened on the Desktop.

▶▶**N O T E**

When you manually add an object to a project, Paradox creates a *reference* to the object. A reference is simply a pointer to an object. It is not the object itself.

The Project Viewer isn't limited to showing only Paradox objects. In fact it can reference *any* type of file stored on your computer or network, including Paradox objects and non-Paradox objects such as spreadsheets, text files, and executable programs. Table 15.3 lists the file extensions of all Paradox for Windows objects.

▶ **TABLE 15.3:** *File Extensions for Paradox for Windows Objects*

EXTENSION	TYPE OF OBJECT
.cfg	Configuration file
.db	Paradox table
.dbf	dBASE table
.dbt	Memos for a dBASE table
.fdl	Delivered form
.fp	Style sheet for reports

EXTENSION	TYPE OF OBJECT
.fsl	Saved form
.ft	Style sheet for forms
.ftl	Temporary form document
.hlp	Help file
.ini	Initialization file
.lck	Lock file
.ldl	Delivered ObjectPAL library
.lsl	Saved ObjectPAL library
.ini	Initialization file
.mb	Memos for a Paradox table
.mdx	Maintained index of a dBASE table
.ndx	Non-maintained index of a dBASE table
.px	Primary index of a Paradox table
.qbe	Saved query
.rdl	Delivered report
.rsl	Saved report
.rtl	Temporary report document
.ssl	Saved ObjectPAL script
.stl	Temporary ObjectPAL script document
.tv	Table View settings for a Paradox table
.tvf	Table View settings for a dBASE table
.val	Validity checks and referential integrity for a Paradox table
.x*nn*	Secondary index for a Paradox table (where *nn* is a number)
.y*nn*	Secondary index for a Paradox table (where *nn* is a number)

Managing Files and Projects

Ch.
15

To open a project, simply open the Project Viewer window, make sure it's the active window (for example, by clicking on it), and switch to the working directory that contains the project. After opening a project, you can do the following:

- Choose which objects appear in the Project Viewer window.
- Add references to the project.
- Delete references from the project.
- Inspect or double-click objects in the right side of the Project Viewer window. Inspect icons in the left side of the Project Viewer window.

These operations are explained in the following sections.

► *Choosing Objects to View*

Normally, the Project Viewer window displays all the objects, including objects you added manually. Here are techniques you can use to control the Project Viewer window's contents. (Be sure the Project Viewer window is opened and active before trying the procedures below.)

- To display *all* files in your current working directory and private directory—whether they're Paradox objects or not, click the All icon in the left side of the Project Viewer window, or choose <u>V</u>iew ➤ <u>A</u>ll.

- To display only a certain type of Paradox object, click the appropriate icon in the left side of the Project Viewer window, or choose <u>V</u>iew followed by an appropriate option (<u>T</u>ables, <u>F</u>orms, <u>Q</u>ueries, SQL, <u>R</u>eports, S<u>c</u>ripts, or <u>L</u>ibraries).

- To switch between displaying only the references that you've added to the project manually and *all* objects in your working directory, choose <u>V</u>iew ➤ <u>O</u>nly References. When <u>O</u>nly References is checked, you'll see only references that *you've* added; when the option is not checked, you'll see all objects in the project, including those references you added.

► ►**T I P**

> If objects in your working directory seem to have
> vanished suddenly, pull down the <u>V</u>iew menu and make
> sure that <u>O</u>nly References is *not* checked. If it is, select
> that option to remove the checkmark. If it isn't checked,
> close the menu without selecting an option (press the
> Alt key or click outside the menu).

► *Adding References to a Project*

Recall that the Project Viewer window automatically shows the names
of objects in the working directory. You can also manually add references to objects that are located anywhere on your computer or network. This makes the "remote" objects easier to find and use without
copying them to the working directory or switching to another directory. Keep in mind that adding a reference does *not* physically move or
copy the object to the current working directory; it simply makes that
object visible in the Project Viewer.

► ►**N O T E**

> References that you add to the project are stored in
> the [Folder] section of the *pdoxwork.ini* file that
> Paradox creates in each working directory. Chapter 14
> provides more details about the *pdoxwork.ini* file.

If you want to add a reference to the open Project Viewer window, follow the steps below.

1. Click the Add Reference button in the Toolbar (shown at left), or
choose Pro<u>j</u>ect ► <u>A</u>dd Reference. The Select File dialog box appears.

▶▶ **N O T E**

> The Add Reference button is available whenever the Desktop is empty or the Project Viewer window is· active (that is, opened and in front). The Project menu is available *only* when the Project Viewer window is active.

2. Use any of the methods below to select the files you want to add to the Project Viewer window:

- To add one object, double-click the file name, or click the file name and choose OK.

- To add objects for several adjacent file names, drag the mouse pointer through the file names in the list (or hold down the Shift key while clicking each adjacent file name), then choose OK.

- To add objects for several non-adjacent file names, hold down the Ctrl key while clicking each non-adjacent file name in the list, then choose OK.

- To add an object for a file in a directory outside your working directory or private directory, use the Drive (or Alias) and Directories lists to switch to that directory. Then select objects as described above.

When you return to the Project Viewer window, the selected file names will appear in the right side of the Project Viewer window. Files added from a directory outside your working or private directory will appear in file lists of the working directory, just as if they were part of the working directory.

▶▶ **T I P**

> To limit your view to the references you added manually, choose View and check the Only References option. To view all objects, whether you added them or not, choose View and uncheck the Only References option.

▶ *Removing References from a Project*

When you no longer want to see an object in the Project Viewer window, you can remove it. The method you use depends on whether the object is a Paradox object, and whether it is stored in the current working directory:

- If the object is a Paradox object in the current working directory, you can delete the object from the Project Viewer *only* by deleting the actual file that is stored on disk. See "Deleting Paradox for Windows Files" later in this chapter.

▶ ▶ N O T E

You cannot delete non-Paradox objects from Paradox for Windows. To do that, you must use Windows File Manager, DOS, or another file management application.

- If you added a reference to a Paradox object that is stored in another directory, you can remove the object reference from the project using the techniques described below. Removing an object reference has no effect on the file saved on the computer's disk. The file still exists; it just won't appear in the Project Viewer window unless you switch to the working directory where that file is stored.

If you added a reference to a Paradox object that's stored in another directory, you can delete that reference as follows:

1. Click the Remove Reference button in the Toolbar (shown at left), or choose Project ▶ Remove Reference. The Remove Reference button is available whenever the Desktop is empty or the Project Viewer window is active.

2. Select the file or files you want to remove. To remove just one file from the project, double-click the file name or click the file name and choose OK. To remove several files, use the drag, Shift+click, or Ctrl+click methods discussed in the previous section, and then choose OK.

When you return to the Project Viewer window, the object will no longer appear in file lists of the working directory; however, you can use the browser or change the working directory to locate it.

▶ Inspecting Objects in the Project

With related database objects nicely organized in the Project Viewer window, activating an object—that is, opening a table or form, printing a report, or starting an application—is simply a matter of double-clicking the object in the right side of the Project Viewer window, or inspecting the object and selecting an option from the menu that pops up (see Table 15.2). Double-clicking an object in the Project Viewer window selects the first option on the menu. Inspecting an object allows you to select any property on the object's menu.

 ▶▶ T I P

As an alternative to inspecting an object, you can highlight it in the Project Viewer and then either press F6 or choose Properties ➤ Current Item.

You can also inspect icons in the *left side* of the Project Viewer window. If you right-click any icon (except the All icon), a menu will let you choose to create a New object of that type or Open an existing object of that type. This provides a handy alternative to inspecting the various "Open" buttons in the Toolbar.

▶▶ Managing Tables and Files

From time to time, you may need to rename, copy, or delete tables and other files. You may also want to add and remove records from one table if they match records in another, and you may want to empty a table of all its records. In the following sections, we'll discuss ways to manage tables and files. Later we'll explain ways to manage records.

When performing file management, table management, and record management operations, keep the following points in mind:

- Paradox cannot normally perform management operations on objects that are locked by network users (including yourself). If objects are locked, you may see an error message indicating that Paradox cannot complete your request because someone is currently working with the object.

- For best results, close forms, reports, other Paradox windows, and other applications that reference objects you want to work with.

- For utmost safety, use Paradox for Windows tools—not DOS commands or the Windows File Manager—to perform file management operations on Paradox for Windows tables and related files. Paradox file management tools handle tables and their associated files automatically; however, DOS commands and the File Manager do not. Managing files from outside Paradox could, therefore, result in incomplete or damaged tables and databases. (An exception to this guideline is explained below, in the section "Copying Tables with Referential Integrity Relationships.")

▶ *Renaming Paradox for Windows Files*

The Rename option allows you to assign a new name to an existing Paradox for Windows file. Before renaming files, however, you should consider the potential pitfalls listed below:

- The new name cannot be the same as the original name *unless* you're renaming to a different drive or directory.

- Once renamed, a table cannot be found by associated objects such as forms, reports, and queries. Unfortunately, Paradox does not offer any options for finding renamed tables when you open a query that's looking for the old table name. You can, however, inspect a form or report in the Project Viewer, choose the View With or Print With menu option, and select the renamed table. Or you can open a form or report and use the Change Table button to select a table name. (If you forget to use Change Table, Paradox will give you a chance to supply the table name.) See Chapter 10 for more about opening forms and reports.

- You cannot use Rename to change a table's type. A Paradox table must be renamed as a Paradox table (*.db*), and a dBASE table must be renamed as a dBASE table (*.dbf*). (Use *Copy*, described later, if you need to change a table's type.)

- You cannot rename a table that is identified as the parent table in a referential integrity relationship. Referential integrity is discussed in Chapter 5.

With these points in mind, you can follow the steps below to rename a Paradox for Windows file.

1. Choose Tools ➤ Utilities ➤ Rename.

2. If you want to rename a file other than a table, click the Type drop-down list and choose a file type.

3. Type the name of the file you want to rename into the Rename File From text box, or click in the Rename File From text box and highlight the file in the file name list.

4. Type the new name for the file into the To text box. If you want to move the file to a drive or directory other than the working directory, you must include the complete drive and directory path, or its alias (for example, *:Gift_Corner:NewCust.db*).

5. If you want to view the renamed table, click the View Modified Table option.

6. Click the OK button.

As a shortcut, you can choose Table ➤ Rename (if the table you want to rename is opened on the Desktop), or inspect the file object in the Project Viewer window and choose Rename from the menu. Type the new name for the file and choose OK.

When you rename a *table*, Paradox will also automatically rename all the auxiliary files associated with the original table.

> **▶▶WARNING**
>
> **Forms, reports, queries, and applications will continue to look for the table under its original name. Paradox will give you a chance to search for the table if it can't be found under the original name when you open a form or report; however, it doesn't provide that option for other types of files (such as queries).**

▶ Copying Paradox for Windows Files

When you copy a Paradox for Windows file, you create an exact duplicate of the original. Copying is useful for making backups of important data, creating a new table with the same structure and data as the original table, and changing the type of a table from Paradox to dBASE or dBASE to Paradox.

The steps for copying a Paradox for Windows file are as follows:

1. Choose Tools ➤ Utilities ➤ Copy.

2. If you want to copy a file other than a table, click the Type drop-down list and choose a file type.

3. Type the name of the file you want to copy into the Copy File From text box, or click in the Copy File From text box and highlight the file in the file name list.

4. Type the new name for the file into the To text box, making sure to include the file extension. If you want to copy the file to a drive or directory other than the working directory, you must include the complete drive and directory path, or the alias name (for example, *:Gift_Corner:NewCusts.db*). If you want to copy a table over an existing table, you can click in the To text box, and then highlight the existing table's name in the file name list (be *very careful* to choose the correct table to overwrite).

5. If you want to view the copied table, click the View Modified Table option.

6. Click the OK button. If the destination file already exists, Paradox will ask if you want to overwrite it. Choose <u>N</u>o to return to the dialog box without overwriting the existing file, or <u>Y</u>es if you want to replace the existing file with the one you're copying.

As a shortcut, you can inspect the file object in the Project Viewer window and choose <u>C</u>opy from the menu. Type the new name for the file and choose OK. If the new file already exists, you'll be asked if you want to overwrite it.

When you copy a *table*, the copied table usually will include all the index and validity check files associated with the original table, but none of the forms, reports, or queries designed for the original table. (See "Copying Tables with Referential Integrity Relationships" for some exceptions.)

 ► ►**T I P**

> To use the copy instead of the original table when opening a form or report, click the <u>C</u>hange Table button in the Open Document dialog box. Or inspect the form or report in the Project Viewer and choose View With or Print With. See Chapter 10 for more information.

Copying to a New Table Type

To copy a Paradox for Windows table to a dBASE table, or a dBASE table to a Paradox for Windows table, simply include the appropriate extension when specifying the new file name. Enter a *.db* extension to create a Paradox table or a *.dbf* extension to create a dBASE table.

Paradox automatically adjusts field types when you copy to a different table type. See Appendix C for more information.

Copying Tables with Referential Integrity Relationships

Referential integrity relationships are not always preserved when you use the Paradox Copy command to copy parent and child tables. The tips below will help you decide how to copy tables when referential integrity is involved.

- If you're copying tables in the *same* directory, the Paradox Copy command will preserve the referential integrity relationship for the copy of the *child* table (since two child tables can refer to the same parent table), but it will delete referential integrity from the copy of the *parent* table (since a single field of a child table cannot refer to more than one parent table).

- If you're copying tables to *different* directories, the Paradox Copy utility *will not* preserve referential integrity across directories. You can use Restructure to rebuild the relationships after copying.

- To always preserve the referential integrity relationships, you can use the DOS Copy command or Windows File Manager. Be sure to copy *all files* for *all tables* in the relationship. This is most important when distributing an application or moving it onto a network.

 ▶▶ **N O T E**

> **The files involved in a referential integrity relationship have the following extensions: *.db*, *.px*, *.tv*, *.mb*, *.x??*, *.y??*, and *.val*. You can specify the file names and extensions individually, or you can use a wildcard to copy all the related files at once. For example, typing the DOS command copy orders.* c:\pdoxwin\newdir\orders.* would copy all the files for the Orders table from the current directory to the directory named c:\pdoxwin\newdir.**

▶ *Deleting Paradox for Windows Files*

You can use the Delete option to delete Paradox for Windows files. Keep in mind that once tables and files are deleted, they *cannot* be recovered through Paradox. Before deleting an object, you should be very sure that it isn't required by other Paradox objects—forms, reports, queries, applications, and so forth—since deleting objects needed by other files can damage your database.

▶ ▶ **N O T E**

If you delete an object accidentally and realize the mistake immediately, you may be able to recover the object with the DOS *Undelete* command or some other file utility that's designed to recover deleted files. But don't rely on undelete to bail you out. You should always keep current backups of every Paradox file!

If you're certain that you want to delete a Paradox for Windows file, follow the steps below.

1. Choose Tools ➤ Utilities ➤ Delete.

2. If you want to delete a file other than a table, click the Type drop-down list and choose a file type.

3. Type the name of the file you want to delete in the Delete File text box.

4. Click the OK button.

5. When asked if you're sure you want to delete the file, choose Yes to delete the file, or No to return to the dialog box without deleting the file.

As a shortcut, you can inspect the file object in the Project Viewer window and choose Delete from the menu. When asked to confirm the deletion, choose Yes to delete the file or No to leave the file alone.

When you delete a *table*, Paradox removes the table and its associated indexes, table property files, and validity check files.

▶▶ *Managing Records*

The Add, Subtract, and Empty options discussed below provide handy tools for copying and moving records from one table to another, and removing all records from a table without deleting the table itself.

► Adding Records from One Table to Another

You can use the Add feature to copy or add records from one table to another without having to retype them. *Add* is also useful for combining information from several tables into a single table.

To add records to a table, proceed as follows:

1. Choose Tools ➤ Utilities ➤ Add, or inspect the table you wish to copy records from in the Project Viewer window and choose Add from the menu. You'll see the Add dialog box shown in Figure 15.6.

2. If the Add Records From text box isn't filled in already, type in the file name and extension of the table you're copying *from,* or click in that text box and highlight the table name from the file name list.

3. Type the file name and extension of the table you're copying *to* into the To text box, or click in that text box and highlight the table name from the file name list. The destination table must already exist.

FIGURE 15.6 ►

The Add dialog box

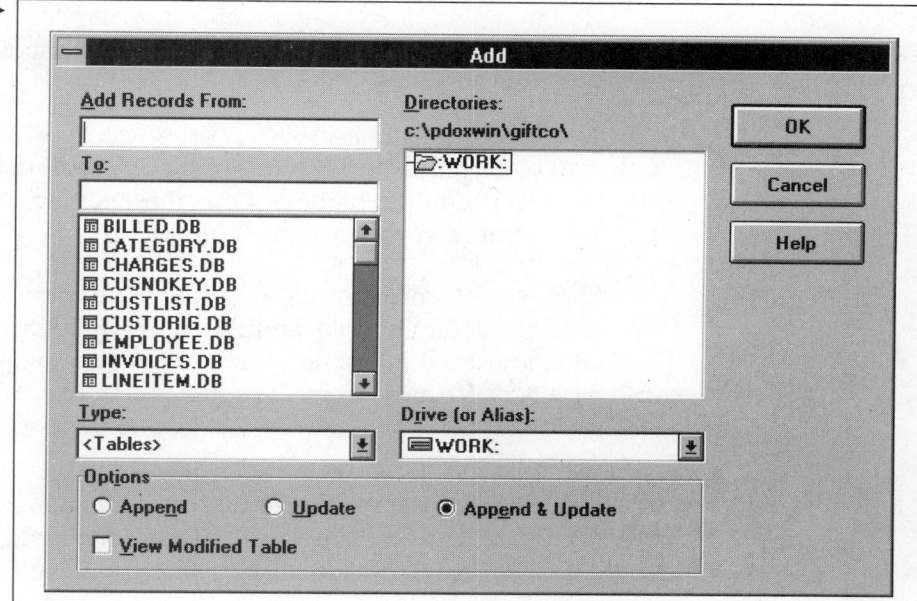

4. Choose Append, Update, or Append & Update, as described below.

5. If you want to open the target table after copying it, select (check) View Modified Table.

6. Click the OK button.

Choosing an Update Option

When adding records from one table to another, you must tell Paradox how to update the target table. The behavior of the update options depends on whether the table has a primary index (see Chapter 4). Here are the update options you can choose in the Add dialog box.

Append Records from the source table are added to the target table. *Append* is the only option allowed for tables without primary indexes (that is, non-keyed tables).

- If the target table is non-keyed, records are added after existing records.

- If the target table is keyed, records in the source table that do not violate the key conditions are inserted in their proper sort order. Records that violate the key conditions are stored in a temporary *Keyviol* table in your private directory. You can edit the records in *Keyviol* to eliminate the duplicate keys, then add them to the target table.

  If *Keyviol* already exists, Paradox creates *Keyviol1*, then *Keyviol2*, and so forth, up to *Keyvio99* to hold the newer records. You should rename or copy these temporary tables if you want to keep permanent copies.

Update Records from the source table overwrite matching records of the target table, and the original records from the target table are saved in the temporary *Changed* table in your private directory. Records from the source table that don't match those in the target table are ignored. This option is available only if the target table is keyed.

If *Changed* already exists, Paradox creates *Changed1*, then *Changed2*, and so forth, up to *Change99* to hold the newer records. The *Changed* tables are deleted when you exit Paradox. You should rename or copy these temporary tables if you want to keep permanent copies.

Append & Update   Combines the add and update options to add new records to a table and update existing records in the target table (following the above rules). This option is available for keyed tables only and is the default choice.

Keep in mind that *Add* never changes the source table. However, you should watch out for some minor catches when using this option:

- The two tables should have compatible structures. For example, you cannot add records from a table containing Last Name, First Name, and Address fields to a table containing Amount, Qty, and Date fields. If you wish to combine tables with incompatible structures, you should use multitable queries (see Chapter 16) and rename the Answer table to create a new table with a new structure.

- If two compatible tables are combined, but the receiving table has a key field, records that violate the rule of uniqueness in the key field are stored in the *Keyviol* table. You can edit or delete records in the *Keyviol* table, then use the *Add* option once again to add records from the *Keyviol* table to the receiving table.

► ► **N O T E**

If you do try to add tables with incompatible structures, Paradox will give you a chance to trim the incompatible data. If you choose not to trim the data, the problem records will be stored in a *Problems* table. The error messages and options available to you when adding data from one table to another are similar to those for restructuring a table, as described later in the section "Restructuring a Table."

► *Subtracting Records from a Table*

You already know how to remove individual records from a table by pressing Ctrl+Del while in Edit mode (Chapter 6) or using the Delete operator in a query (Chapter 9). However, for bigger jobs that involve keyed tables with compatible structures, you can use the Subtract command. *Subtract* removes from the target table all records with key field values that exactly match corresponding key fields of records in the source table. *Subtract* has no effect on the source table.

▶▶ **N O T E**

> *Subtract* **works only when the two tables have compatible structures and both are keyed. You cannot use** *Subtract* **on dBASE tables (use a Delete query instead).**

Let's take a look now at the steps for subtracting records in one keyed table from records in another keyed table:

1. Choose <u>T</u>ools ➤ <u>U</u>tilities ➤ S<u>u</u>btract, or inspect a table object in the Project Viewer window and choose S<u>u</u>btract from the property menu. The Subtract dialog box shown in Figure 15.7 will appear.

2. If the <u>S</u>ubtract Records In text box isn't filled in already, type the file name and extension of the table containing the records you want to subtract into the <u>S</u>ubtract Records In text box; or click in that text box and highlight the table name in the file name list.

FIGURE 15.7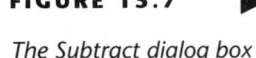

The Subtract dialog box

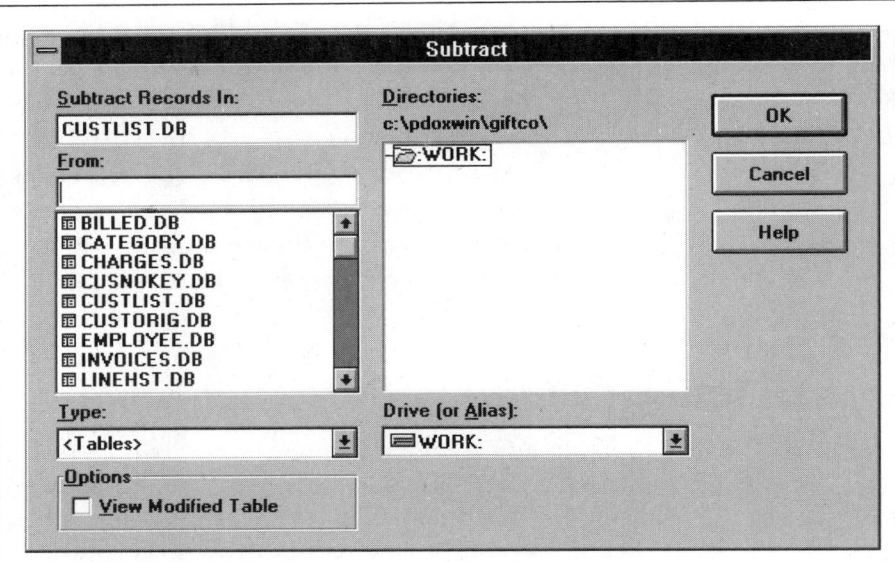

3. Type the file name and extension of the table you want to remove records from in the <u>F</u>rom text box, or click in the <u>F</u>rom text box and highlight the table name in the file name list.

4. To open the target table after deleting records, click <u>V</u>iew Modified Table.

5. Click the OK button.

6. When asked if you're sure you want to delete records from the target table, choose <u>Y</u>es if you want to delete the records, or <u>N</u>o to return to the Subtract dialog box without deleting any records.

Using Subtract to Remove Completed Transactions

To understand just how useful Subtract can be, suppose you have an accounts-receivable system in which you bill clients at the end of the month for purchases made during the previous month. You store these charges in the Charges table shown in Figure 15.8.

At the end of November, you could set up the query shown at the top of Figure 15.9 to pull out all records with purchase dates in October. Before running the query, choose <u>P</u>roperties ➤ Answer Options, select <u>A</u>nswer Table, and change the <u>T</u>able to *billed.db* in the working directory (for example, *:work:billed.db*). Be sure to change the path name as well as the file name. You can also use the Answer Options dialog box to adjust the appearance of the billed.db query results table (see Chapter 9).

FIGURE 15.8 ▶

The Charges table

CHARGES	Cust No	Part Number	Quantity	Unit Price	Purchase Date
1	1001	GC-123	1	1,116.95	11/12/94
2	1001	GC-292	2	171.95	10/1/94
3	1002	GC-234	6	27.95	10/15/94
4	1003	GC-291	5	3,367.97	10/30/94
5	1004	GC-234	2	27.95	11/11/94
6	1005	GC-235	1	2,133.95	11/7/94
7	1009	GC-300	4	278.95	10/9/94

Table : CHARGES.DB

Managing Files and Projects

Ch. 15

FIGURE 15.9 ►

A query for charges in the month of October, and the resulting Billed table

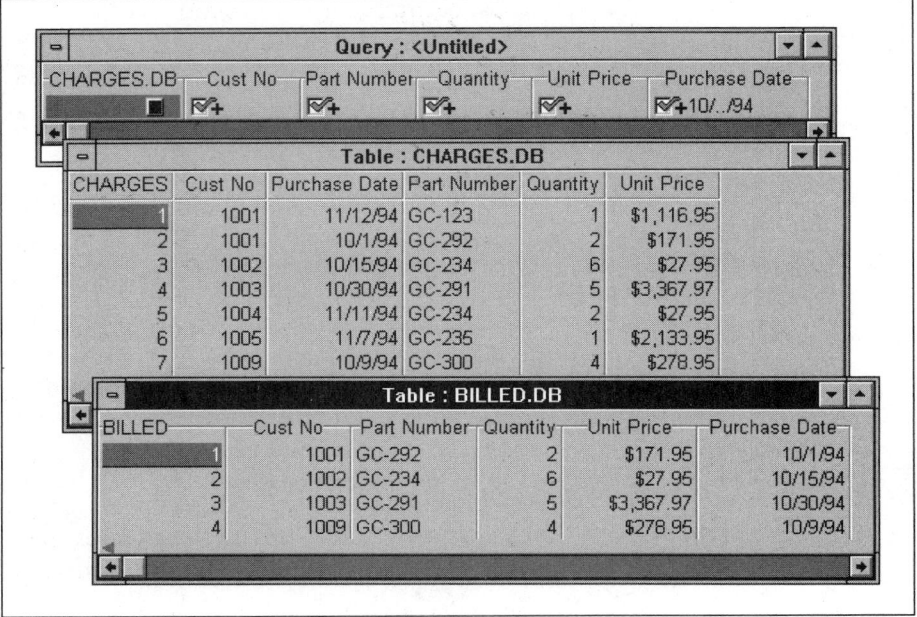

NOTE

Instead of choosing Properties ➤ Answer Options, as suggested above, you could run the query, then use the Rename command to change the Answer table file name to *Billed* (in the working directory).

As shown in Figure 15.9, the Billed table contains only transactions for October. You can print invoices from the Billed table using an invoice report designed for any table that has the same structure and field names as *Billed*. To print the report, choose File ➤ Open ➤ Report, click Print in the Open Mode area of the Open Document dialog box, and highlight the report you want to print. Then click the Change Table button, select the Billed table, and choose OK twice.

After billing the October transactions, you can use *Subtract* to remove them from the Charges table. The Billed table contains the transactions to be subtracted. In the Subtract dialog box, specify *Billed* in the Subtract Records In text box and *Charges* in the From text box. When the subtraction is complete, the Charges table will no longer contain charges for October.

Using Subtract for Bulk Mailings and Error Recovery

Now that you've seen a complete example, it should be easy to imagine other applications for the table utility options. Here are two ideas to get you started.

Suppose you're planning a special mailing to introduce an extra-hot, low-priced item that everyone is sure to want. Assuming your list of in-active clients is stored in a table named *Inactive*, you can perform a query on that table to isolate customers who haven't ordered within the past year. Using Properties ➤ Answer Options in the Query window or the Rename command, rename the resulting Answer table to *PastYear*. Then use *Add* to add the names from PastYear (the source table) to a master mailing list table named *MailMast*. Next, create a form letter to introduce the new product, and print copies of it. After the mailing is complete, use *Subtract* to remove the inactive customers from the master mailing list. (You can add these customers again after they purchase your new product.)

Here's a way to recover from a common—and potentially serious—mistake. Imagine that you ran a query to delete many records from a table, then suddenly realized you didn't intend to delete those records at all. Recall that during a Delete query, Paradox moves deleted records into the *Deleted* table in your private directory. If you discover the mistake immediately (or you have renamed the Deleted table), you can restore the deleted records. Choose the Add command, then specify Deleted as the source table and your original table as the target table. Paradox will retrieve the deleted records and your original table will be as good as new.

▶ ▶ **N O T E**

> **To delete records globally, place the Delete operator just below the table name in the query table. Specify selection criteria to use for deletions, then click the Run Query button in the Toolbar. See Chapter 9 for more information on DELETE queries.**

▶ *Emptying a Table*

You can use the Empty command to remove all records from a table. This is particularly useful for databases in which updated transactions are copied to a history file using Add, then deleted from the current transactions table (see Chapter 18).

Be careful with the Empty command! Once records are emptied from a table, they cannot be retrieved. Paradox doesn't create a Deleted table when you use Empty, and you cannot use DOS Undelete or other utilities to recover records.

To empty a table, follow these steps:

1. Choose <u>T</u>ools ➤ <u>U</u>tilities ➤ <u>E</u>mpty, or Ta<u>b</u>le ➤ <u>E</u>mpty (in Table View), or inspect a table object in the Project Viewer window and choose <u>E</u>mpty from the menu. If you see the Empty dialog box shown in Figure 15.10, continue with step 2. If you see a Warning box instead, skip to step 4.

2. Type the table's file name and extension into the <u>E</u>mpty Table text box.

3. Click the OK button.

FIGURE 15.10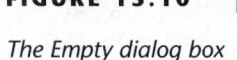

The Empty dialog box

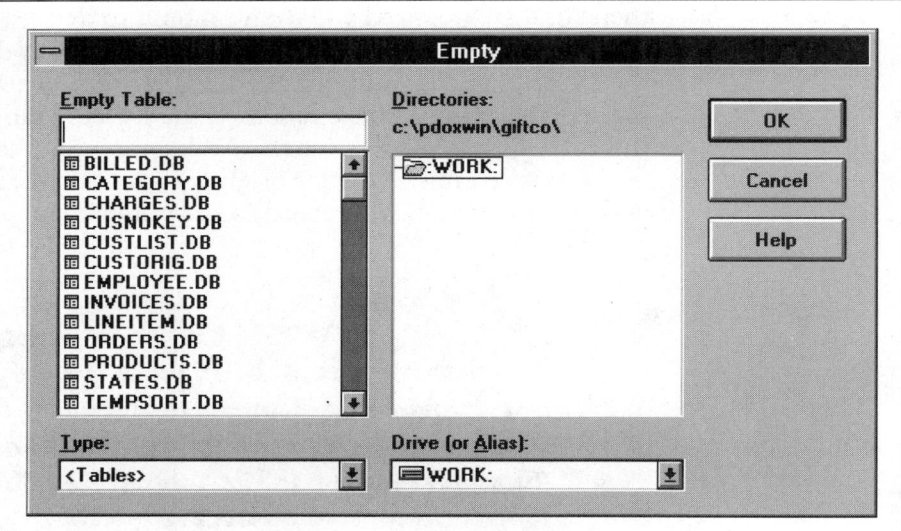

4. When the Warning dialog box asks if you're sure you want to empty the records, choose <u>N</u>o to leave the table unchanged or choose <u>Y</u>es to delete the records.

▶▶ *Getting Information about Your Table*

You can display the structure of any table and later print the table's structure in a default or custom report format.

To display the table's structure, choose <u>T</u>ools ➤ Utilities ➤ I<u>n</u>fo Structure, or T<u>a</u>ble ➤ <u>I</u>nfo Structure (in Table View), or inspect a table object in the Project Viewer window and choose I<u>n</u>fo Structure from the menu. If the Select File dialog box appears, select a table name, then choose OK.

Paradox will display the table structure in a Structure Information dialog box resembling the one in Figure 15.11. This dialog box is similar to the Create Table dialog box (see Chapter 4) and the Restructure

FIGURE 15.11 ▶

A sample display from the Info Structure option

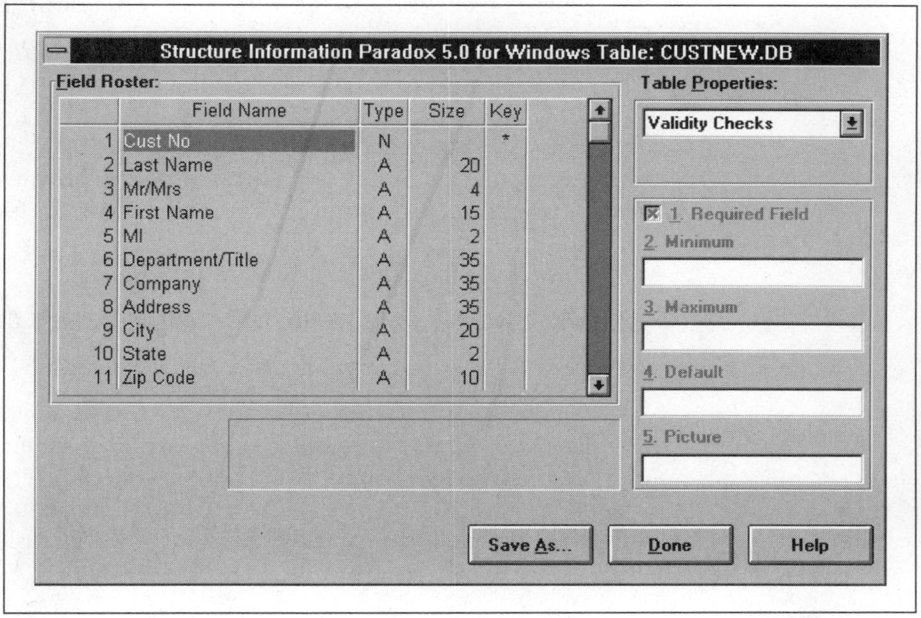

	Field Name	Type	Size	Key
1	Cust No	N		*
2	Last Name	A	20	
3	Mr/Mrs	A	4	
4	First Name	A	15	
5	MI	A	2	
6	Department/Title	A	35	
7	Company	A	35	
8	Address	A	35	
9	City	A	20	
10	State	A	2	
11	Zip Code	A	10	

Structure Information Paradox 5.0 for Windows Table: CUSTNEW.DB

Table Properties: Validity Checks

☒ 1. Required Field
2. Minimum
3. Maximum
4. Default
5. Picture

Save As...   Done   Help

Managing Files and Projects

Ch. **15**

Table dialog box (discussed later in this chapter); however you can only *view* the structure of the table, not change it.

You can use any of the following techniques to navigate the Structure Information dialog box:

- To display the properties of a field, click the field. If the property you're interested in isn't selected in the Table Properties list box, click the Table Properties drop-down button and choose the property you want. For example, in Figure 15.11, the mouse is positioned in the first field (Cust No), *Validity Checks* is selected in the Table Properties list, and the Required Field is checked (indicating that Cust No is a required field).

- If a Detail Info button appears, click the item that you want to know more about in the list above the button (for example, click a secondary index name), then click Detail Info to open a dialog box with more detailed information about the property. When you're finished viewing the information, click Done or OK to return to the Structure Information dialog box.

- If you want to save the current structure as a table that you can report on, click Save As, type a new table name, and choose OK. Be sure to provide an unused table name or one that isn't currently storing important data! (There's more about this later.)

- When you're finished viewing the structure information, click the Done button.

Figure 15.11 shows the structure for a Paradox table named *CustNew*, which is similar to our trusty CustList table. However, to make things more interesting, we added these features to CustNew:

- *Cust No* is a key field and is required.

- *State* has a default value of CA and a lookup table named *States*.

- *Area Code* is required and has a picture value of #{0,1}#.

- *Credit Limit* has a default value of 10,000.00, a minimum value of 1,000.00, and a maximum value of 25,000.00.

Now, you may be thinking "The Structure Information dialog box is very nice, but how do I get a *printed copy* of the table's structure?"

Unfortunately, there's no push-button answer to this question, but a solution *is* available. First, use the Save As button in the Structure Information dialog box to save the table structure you're viewing in another table. When prompted for a new file name, enter a name that's *different* from any table that already contains important data. For example, name it *Struct*, or *Test*, or *X* or anything else that you're unlikely to be using for "real" data. Choose OK to return to the Structure Information dialog box, and then choose Done.

Once you've created the structure information table, you can view and print it like any other table. Let's look at that next.

▶ *Exploring the Structure Information Table*

After closing the Structure Information dialog box, you can open the structure information table as you would any normal table. Figure 15.12 illustrates a sample table named *Struct*, which contains information about the structure of our hypothetical CustNew table.

Each record in the structure information table for a Paradox for Windows table describes one field in the table you requested information about. Within each record, the fields are as follows:

Field Name   Contains the name of the field being described.

Type   Contains the type of the field: # (BCD), $ (Money), + (Autoincrement), @ (Timestamp), A (Alpha), B (Binary), D (Date), F (Formatted Memo), G (Graphic), I (Long Integer), L (Logical), M (Memo), N (Number), O (OLE), S (Short), T (Time), or Y (Bytes).

Size   Contains the size of the field.

Key   Contains an asterisk (*) for key fields; non-key fields are blank.

_Invariant Field ID   Contains a numeric identifier for the field. This ID remains the same (invariant) even if you change the original order of the table's fields.

_Required Value   Contains an asterisk (*) if the field is required; non-required fields are blank.

_Min Value   Contains the minimum allowable value for this field, if one was defined.

FIGURE 15.12 ▸

The fields in the Struct table document the structure of our sample CustNew table.

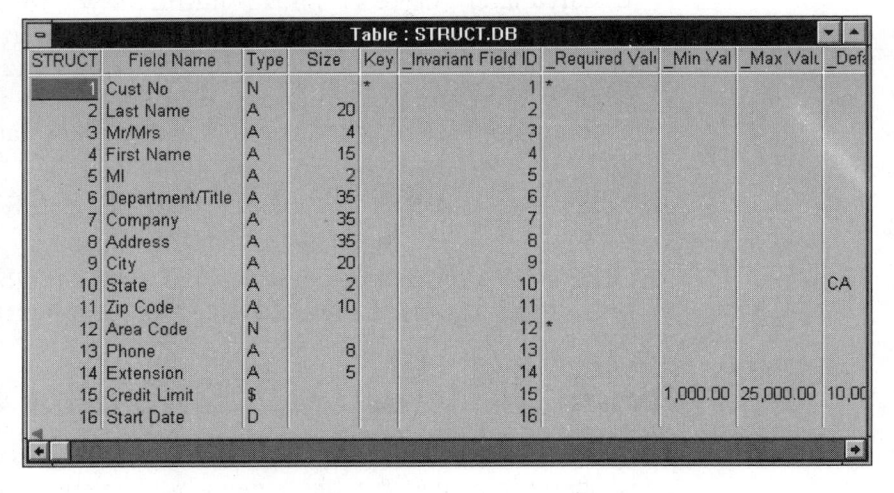

STRUCT	Field Name	Type	Size	Key	Invariant Field ID	Required Valu	Min Val	Max Valu	Defa
1	Cust No	N		*	1	*			
2	Last Name	A	20		2				
3	Mr/Mrs	A	4		3				
4	First Name	A	15		4				
5	MI	A	2		5				
6	Department/Title	A	35		6				
7	Company	A	35		7				
8	Address	A	35		8				
9	City	A	20		9				
10	State	A	2		10				CA
11	Zip Code	A	10		11				
12	Area Code	N			12	*			
13	Phone	A	8		13				
14	Extension	A	5		14				
15	Credit Limit	$			15		1,000.00	25,000.00	10,0
16	Start Date	D			16				

_Max Value   Contains the maximum allowable value for this field, if one was defined.

_Default Value   Contains the default value for this field, if one was defined.

_Picture Value   Contains the picture for this field, if one was defined.

_Table Lookup   Contains the name of the lookup table for this field, if one was defined.

_Table Lookup Type   Contains a number describing the type of lookup table used. The number is 0 (zero) or blank if no lookup table is used, and non-zero if a lookup table *is* used.

You can change the appearance of your structure information table using direct manipulation or property inspection in the Table window (see Chapter 7). You can also define custom forms or reports for it.

▶ *Printing the Structure Information Table*

If you simply need a quick report of the structure information table, you can open the table on the Desktop, then click the Print or Quick Report button in the Toolbar. Although the quick report is the easiest way to print a table's structure, you'll probably find the report to be incredibly unattractive.

Fortunately, you can create and save a custom report (or form) for the structure information table, using techniques covered in Chapters 10 through 12. After creating the report or form, you can reuse it any time you want to print or view the structure information table.

NOTE

> **The structure information tables generated for Paradox and dBASE tables are different; therefore, you'll need to design one report and form for the Paradox table and another for the dBASE Struct table.**

Figure 15.13 shows a customized report for an Answer table that's based on our sample *Struct* table. We used a simple query (see Figure 15.15) to limit the report to just the Cust No, State, Area Code, and Credit Limit fields from CustNew, both to conserve space and to focus on the most interesting fields.

Here are the basic steps we used to create the report in Figure 15.13:

1. In the Project Viewer, we clicked the Tables icon, inspected the CustNew table (though any Paradox table will do), then chose Info Structure. Next, we clicked Save As, typed a new table name (**Struct** in this example), then chose OK and clicked Done to return to the Desktop.

2. We chose File ➤ New ➤ Report, clicked the Data Model/Layout Diagram button, chose *struct.db* in the Data Model dialog box, and chose OK. In the Design Layout dialog box we chose Single Record and By Columns, then OK (see Chapter 10).

3. We then created the report design shown in Figure 15.14, saved it with the name *Structur,* and closed it.

4. With the Structur report complete, we next designed a query to place selected records from the Struct table into the Answer table. To begin, we chose File ➤ New ➤ Query, and selected *struct.db* as the table to query. We used the OR operator to select the values

FIGURE 15.13 ►

A sample report, based on the Structur query, of the Struct table

07/05/94   Table Structure Report for: STRUCTUR   Page 1

Field Name : Cust No

Type : N   Size :   Key : *

_Invariant Field ID : 1   _Required Value : *

_Min Value :   _Max Value :   _Default Value :

_Picture Value :

_Table Lookup :   _Table Lookup Type : 0

Field Name : State

Type : A   Size : 2   Key :

_Invariant Field ID : 10   _Required Value :

_Min Value :   _Max Value :   _Default Value : CA

_Picture Value :

_Table Lookup : STATES.DB   _Table Lookup Type : 1

Field Name : Area Code

Type : N   Size :   Key :

_Invariant Field ID : 12   _Required Value : *

_Min Value :   _Max Value :   _Default Value :

_Picture Value : #{0,1}#

_Table Lookup :   _Table Lookup Type : 0

Field Name : Credit Limit

Type : $ Size :   Key :

_Invariant Field ID : 15   _Required Value :

_Min Value : 1,000.00 _Max Value : 25,000.00 _Default Value : 10,000.00

_Picture Value :

_Table Lookup :   _Table Lookup Type : 0

we wanted from the Field Name column, then placed a check plus in all the columns, as shown in Figure 15.15. Next, we saved the query with the name *Structur* and clicked the Run Query button in the Toolbar to test the results.

FIGURE 15.14

The design for the sample report in Figure 15.13

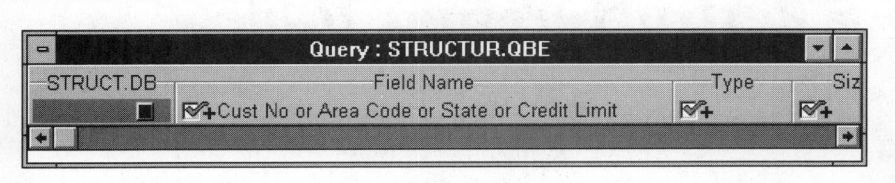

FIGURE 15.15

A query to limit the output of the report to just the Cust No, Area Code, State, and Credit Limit fields

TIP

To report on the entire structure information table, simply skip the query steps. To place records from another table's structure into the Answer table, generate the structure information table for the table you're interested in, modify the query to select the appropriate field names, then run the query.

5. When we were ready to use the Structur report, we clicked the Reports icon in the Project Viewer, and inspected the *structur.rsl* report object. To use the query instead of the Struct table for which it was designed, we chose Print With from the property menu. (If you prefer to view the report first, choose View With instead.) In the Select File dialog box, we opened the File Type drop-down list and selected <Queries>, then double-clicked *structur.qbe* in the file name list. When the Print File dialog box appeared, we chose OK. (If you chose View With, click the Print button in the Toolbar, and then choose OK.)

 ▶▶ **T I P**

> **You can assign your custom report as the preferred report for Struct. To do so, open Struct in the Table View window, right-click the Quick Report button, select the report name you want (for example, *structur.rsl*), then choose OK. Now you can view a great-looking report of the entire Struct table, simply by clicking the Quick Report button in the Toolbar.**

▶▶ *Restructuring a Table*

Once you've created a table, added some data to it, and used it for a while, you may decide to change something about its basic structure. For example, you might want to add a field for storing the customer's fax number to the CustList table, or you may need to lengthen a field such as Company or Address.

Restructuring a table is almost identical to creating one. However, restructuring can lead to data loss and key violations and, therefore, should not be undertaken unless you understand its potential effects.

Before restructuring a table, it's a good idea to back it up using the Copy command or another backup utility. That way, if the restructuring creates unexpected (or unsatisfactory) results, you can restore the original data with little fuss or lost time. If you prefer, you can save the original table with a new name (as described later) to leave the original table untouched.

▶ *Restructuring Pitfalls and Limitations*

Before looking at the actual steps involved in restructuring a table, you should consider the following points:

- You cannot use *Restructure* to change a Paradox table to a dBASE table, or a dBASE table to a Paradox table. Use the Copy command instead.

- You cannot use *Restructure* to change a table's name. Use the Rename command instead.

- Adding keys to a table that previously had no keys, or had different keys, may cause key violations where data already in the table violates the new key. For example, a key violation will occur if more than one record has the same value for a newly defined key field. Paradox removes (from the original table) any records that violate the key and places them in a temporary *Keyviol* table in your private directory. The Keyviol table will appear on the Desktop after the restructuring is complete. You can change the records in Keyviol to comply with the new key requirements, then use the Add command to return the records to the original table.

- If you change a field's type and the data in that field cannot be converted to the new type, Paradox will ask you to confirm the change. If you choose not to allow the change, Paradox will move records that cannot be converted into a temporary *Problems* table in your private directory. The Problems table will appear on the Desktop after the restructuring is complete. As with key violations, you can correct the problem records and then add them to the original table.

- If you add or change a validity check, lookup table, or referential integrity rule (see Chapters 4 and 5), and existing data doesn't comply with it, Paradox will let you place the non-compliant records in the *Keyviol* table. Again, you can correct the records and return them to the original table.

- You may be prevented from restructuring parent or child tables that are related through referential integrity rules (see Chapter 5). If you're not sure whether a table is involved in a referential integrity relationship, choose the Info Structure command described earlier, select *Referential Integrity* from the Table Properties list, and use the Detail Info button. Please see Chapter 5 for more information on referential integrity.

Note that if a Problems table already exists, Paradox will create *Problem1*, then *Problem2*, and so forth, up to *Proble99*. Similarly, if Keyviol already exists, Paradox will create *Keyviol1*, *Keyviol2*, and so forth, up to *Keyvio99*. You should rename or copy these temporary tables if you want to keep permanent copies.

▶ ▶ **N O T E**

> **Don't forget to fix problems or key violations, or rename the Problems and Keyviol tables before moving on to the next task or exiting Paradox.**

Watch Out for Restructured Tables and Queries

You should take extra care to consider the effects of table restructuring on queries that use fields in your restructured table. The bottom line is this: *If you rename or delete fields in a table, you cannot open or run any query that uses those renamed or deleted table fields in any way.* When you try to open or run such a query, an error message will tell you that Paradox can't find the missing field.

▶ ▶ **N O T E**

> **Adding new fields should not cause problems in your queries. When you open a query, you'll notice empty check boxes for the new fields (as you might expect).**

Fortunately, there are two solutions to the problem:

- You can delete the old queries and recreate them from scratch (a painful proposition at best).

- You can restore the original field names to the table structure. Then remove example elements (Chapter 16), checkmarks, and query criteria from any fields you intend to rename or delete (Chapter 9). Now restructure your table again with the fields you want; then revise the queries as needed.

▶ *General Steps for Restructuring a Table*

To change a table's structure, follow these steps:

1. Close any windows for documents that reference the table you want to restructure. This prevents error messages caused by locked tables.

2. Use any of the following methods to get started:

- Choose <u>T</u>ools ➤ <u>U</u>tilities ➤ Res<u>t</u>ructure.
- Inspect a table object in the Project Viewer window and choose Res<u>t</u>ructure from the menu.

- If the table is open in Table View, choose T<u>a</u>ble ➤ Restructure <u>T</u>able or click the Restructure button in the Toolbar (shown at left). This option is the least desirable, because Paradox cannot always restructure a table if it is open on the Desktop.

3. If the Select File dialog box appears, select the name of the table you want to restructure and choose OK.

4. Use the Restructure Table dialog box to revise the table's structure as needed.

5. Save your changes as described in the next section.

Figure 15.16 shows a sample Restructure Table dialog box. As for the Create Table dialog box discussed in Chapters 4 and 5, you can use the arrow keys or mouse to move the cursor around and make changes. Use the Ins and Ctrl+Del keys to insert and delete fields. The Table Properties list allows you to change validity checks, table lookup, secondary indexes, referential integrity, and table language, as described later in this chapter.

▶ ▶ **N O T E**

The Restructure Table dialog box for dBASE tables is slightly different from the one shown in Figure 15.16. See Appendix C for more information on restructuring dBASE tables.

FIGURE 15.16 ▶

The Restructure Table dialog box

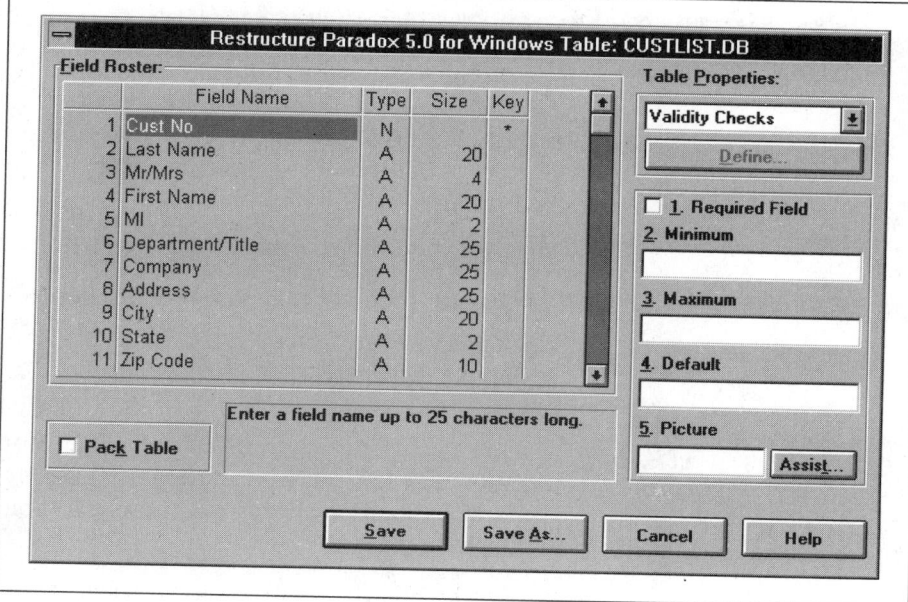

▶ Saving the Restructured Table

When you're satisfied with the new table structure, you can click either the Save or Save As button:

The Save button overwrites the old structure with the new structure. The Save As button provides a more cautious way to save your changes because it creates a new table with the structure you've defined, leaving the old table intact. If you're not sure what potential problems and data loss might arise as a result of restructuring a table, it's best to use Save As rather than Save. After adding corrected records from the Keyviol and Problems tables to the new table (if necessary) and inspecting it carefully, you can delete the old table, then use Tools ▶ Utilities ▶ Rename to change the name of the new table to the old table name.

When you click Save As, you'll see the Save Table As dialog box. Follow these steps to complete the dialog box:

1. In the New File Name text box, type the new file name and extension for the table. The extension must be the same as for the original table.

2. To display the new table after restructuring is complete, make sure Display Table is checked.

3. To add as much data from the old table as suits the structure of the new table, make sure Add Data To New Table is checked. If you prefer to create an empty table and add data later, click Add Data To New Table to deselect it.

4. Click OK.

If the new name you specified in step 1 is the same as an existing table's name, you'll be asked whether to overwrite the existing table. Choose Yes to overwrite the table, or No to return to the Save Table As dialog box without overwriting the table.

▶ *Understanding the Restructure Warnings*

If the restructure will result in data loss or other problems, you'll see a Restructure Warning dialog box similar to the one shown in Figure 15.17 after choosing Save or Save As.

The top of the Restructure Warning dialog box displays a question about a specific field in the table. To take the action the question suggests, click Yes. To avoid the action, click No. Records that no longer meet the requirements for the table will move to the Problems or Keyviol table.

The remaining check boxes allow you to set options that guide Paradox's future handling of restructuring problems for this table. You can check any of the options discussed below to avoid further questions about fields that require special handling.

> **Field Trim**   Check this option to specify the trimming method for all fields. Then select Trim All Fields to have Paradox trim (truncate) characters from the end of field values that exceed the new field length, or select Trim No Fields to have Paradox move all records containing data that exceeds the new field length into the Problems table.

> **Skip Confirmation for Each Deleted Field**   Check this option to delete fields without further confirmation.

> **Validity Checks**   Check this option to specify whether or not all fields must satisfy the validity checks. Then select Apply To

FIGURE 15.17 ▶

The Restructure Warning dialog box

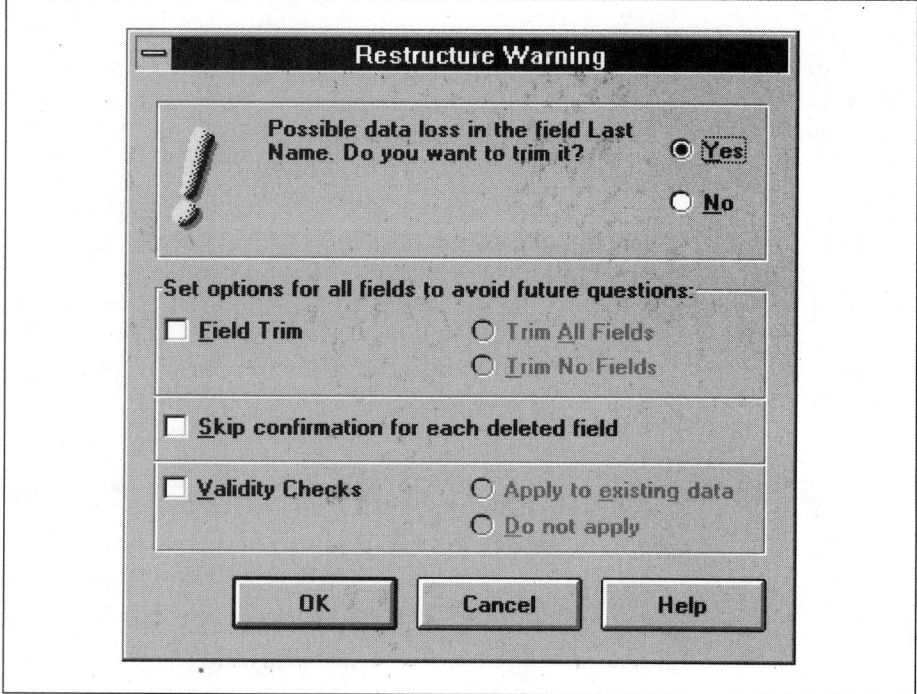

Existing Data to have Paradox move records that no longer meet the conditions of new validity checks, lookup tables, or referential integrity rules to the Keyviol table; or select Do Not Apply to allow existing records to violate validity checks and remain in the original table.

▶▶**N O T E**

> **The default settings shown in Figure 15.17 minimize potential data loss. So if you're unsure about how to proceed with a restructure, just stick with those default settings.**

After selecting options in the Restructure Warning dialog box, choose OK to continue restructuring or choose Cancel to stop restructuring and return to the Restructure Table dialog box.

> **Paradox 5 for Windows can automatically interpret tables from older Paradox versions, and it will automatically upgrade a table to Paradox 5 format whenever you restructure it to include a field that has one of these new field types: Autoincrement, BCD, Bytes, Logical, Long Integer, Time, or Timestamp. When you save a table that must be upgraded, Paradox will ask permission first. Choose OK only if you're sure that you won't need to work with that table in an older version of Paradox.**

▶ Changing Your Mind

If you make a mistake when defining a new structure for a table and want to return to the original structure, click the Cancel button in the Restructure Table dialog box. Paradox will cancel the changes you made and return to the Desktop.

Now, let's take a look at specific ways to change the structure of a table.

▶ Adding a Field

To add a field to the table, click on the field that's just below the point where you want the new field to appear, then press the Ins key. A blank line will open up above the highlighted field. Now type the new field name, field type, and size (if necessary). Remember to mark new *primary key* fields with an asterisk (*) and place them before any non-key fields.

When you add fields to an existing table, Paradox does not automatically update forms, reports, or queries associated with that table. You must open the Form or Report Design window for the document and use the Field tool to add new fields to the design.

► Deleting a Field

To delete a field from the Restructure Table dialog box, simply click on that field and press Ctrl+Del. Deleting a field erases all data stored in that field, which means a great deal of data could be lost if the wrong field were deleted. When you save the table structure after deleting a field, Paradox will display the Restructure Warning dialog box and ask for confirmation. Choose <u>Y</u>es if you want to delete the field, or <u>N</u>o to leave the field and its data in the table.

► ►**N O T E**

The confirmation warning won't appear if you click the Save <u>A</u>s button and remove the checkmark from the Add Data To Ne<u>w</u> Table option before choosing OK.

Deleted fields lose their definitions in any form or report documents associated with the table. The next time you open the document, Paradox will warn you that missing fields will be undefined. To solve this problem, return to the Form or Report Design window for the document, redefine or delete the undefined fields, then save the revised design.

► ►**W A R N I N G**

If you delete a field that's used in a query, Paradox will not be able to open that query in the future.

► Renaming a Field

To change the name of a field, simply click on the appropriate field name in the structure and type in the new name.

The next time you open a form or report containing a field that you've renamed, Paradox will reconcile the name change automatically.

⊚ ▶ ▶ W A R N I N G

If you rename a field that's used in a query, Paradox will not be able to open that query in the future.

▶ *Changing a Non-Key Field to a Key Field*

You can change a non-key field to a key field by placing an asterisk (*) in the Key column of the dialog box. However, make sure that all the key fields appear at the top of the field roster in the proper sort order. If necessary, rearrange the fields as described below. (See Chapter 4 for more information on primary keys.)

Remember that converting an existing non-key field to a key field can result in key violations. Records that do not comply with the new key will be moved to the Keyviol table.

▶ *Rearranging Fields*

To rearrange fields in the field roster, use your mouse to point to the left-most column (field number) of the field you want to move. Then hold down the left mouse button, drag the field to its new position, and release the mouse button. (Horizontal lines will appear above and below the field to be moved, and the mouse pointer will change to a two-headed vertical arrow as you begin dragging the field.)

▶ *Changing the Length of a Field*

Lengthening an alpha field (for instance, from a size of 20 to 25) will not usually cause any problems, though you might have to change the format of a custom form or report later to accommodate the new width.

Shortening an alpha field (for example, from 25 to 20) may cause data loss if the table contains data that is longer than the new width. When you shorten an alpha field, Paradox will display the Restructure Warning dialog box shown back in Figure 15.17.

▶ *Changing the Type of a Field*

You can change many field types (for example, alpha, numeric, money, and date), though you may run into the same problems as when shortening an alpha field. Paradox will warn you of any potential data loss and give you the Restructure Warning options described earlier in this chapter.

Generally, you won't want to change the type of data in a field. However, if you've made an error at the outset, it's easy enough to do. If you remember to put numeric values in autoincrement, money, or numeric fields, dates in date fields, times in time fields, combined times and dates in timestamp fields, and all other text and numbers in alpha fields, you will probably never have to change a field type.

Remember that Paradox also offers the S field type for *short numbers*. A short number field can contain whole numbers (no decimal places) in the range of −32,767 to 32,767. Until you are an experienced Paradox user, you should avoid this field type. It has the advantage of conserving memory, but the small range of acceptable numbers makes it very restrictive. For example, the number 1.1 is unacceptable because it has a decimal place, and the zip code 40001 is unacceptable because it is too large.

Table 15.4 summarizes the possible consequences of changing field types.

▶ *Changing Table Properties*

The procedures for changing validity checks, table lookup, secondary indexes, referential integrity, and other properties are the same as for defining them in the first place. However, you must take extra care that data already in your table will meet the revised criteria. The general steps for changing a table property in the Restructure Table dialog box are listed below.

1. If you want to add or change validity checks or a lookup table for a field, select the field you want to change.

2. Click the Table Properties drop-down arrow, then choose the property you want to change. Your options are as follows:

> **Validity Checks**   Provides constraints or checks on the values entered for this field. (See Chapter 4.)

▲ **TABLE 15.4:** *Consequences of Changing Field Types*

	TO #	TO $	TO +	TO @	TO A	TO B	TO D	TO F	TO G
From #	Y	Y							
From $		Y			Y				
From +		Y	Y						
From @				Y	Y		Y		
From A		P		P	Y		P		
From B						Y			
From D				Y	Y		Y		
From F					Y	Y		Y	
From G					Y	Y			Y
From I	Y	Y			Y				
From L	Y				Y				
From M					Y	Y		Y	
From N		Y			Y				
From O						Y			
From S		Y			Y				
From T				Y	Y				
From Y					Y	Y	Y	Y	Y

▲ **TABLE 15.4:** Consequences of Changing Field Types (continued)

	TO I	TO L	TO M	TO N	TO O	TO S	TO T	TO Y
From #	Y	Y		Y		Y		
From $	Y	Y		Y		Y		
From +	Y	Y		Y		Y		
From @							Y	
From A	P	Y	Y	P		P	P	Y
From B								
From D								
From F			Y					
From G								
From I	Y	Y		Y		Y		
From L	Y	Y		Y		Y		
From M		Y	Y					
From N	Y	Y		Y		P		
From O					Y			
From S	Y	Y		Y		Y	Y	
From T							Y	
From Y			Y		Y			Y
	TO I	**TO L**	**TO M**	**TO N**	**TO O**	**TO S**	**TO T**	**TO Y**

NOTE Blank means the conversion is not allowed under any conditions.

. P means the conversion is allowed, but will undoubtedly generate the Problems table.

Y means the conversion is allowed, but may result in some trimming.

(Field types #, +, @, I, L, T, and Y are new in Paradox 5.)

▲ **TABLE 15.4:** *Consequences of Changing Field Types (continued)*

EXPLANATION OF FIELD TYPE ABBREVIATIONS	
FIELD TYPE ABBREVIATIONS	**DESCRIPTION**
#	BCD
$	Money
+	Autoincrement
@	Timestamp
A	Alpha
B	Binary
D	Date
F	Formatted Memo
G	Graphic
I	Long Integer
L	Logical
M	Memo
N	Number
O	OLE
S	Short
T	Time
Y	Bytes

Table Lookup   Assures that a value entered into this field is a legitimate value for a corresponding field in another table. (See Chapters 5 and 6.)

Secondary Indexes   Defines indexes on non-key fields in the table. These indexes are used for sorting and speeding up query operations that link multiple tables. (See Chapter 8.)

Referential Integrity   Ensures that ties between like data in this table and other tables cannot be broken. (See Chapter 5.)

Password Security   Assigns master and auxiliary passwords to a table (described in "Using Passwords to Protect Tables," below).

Table Language   Assigns the language driver that controls sorting, capitalization, and text comparison operations. (Chapter 14 offers information about the IDAPI Configuration Utility, which establishes the default table language.)

Dependent Tables   Displays the names of child tables that are linked to this table through referential integrity. This option is for reference only.

3. Complete the specifications for the property you chose.

Please see "Restructuring Pitfalls and Limitations," earlier in this chapter, for an explanation of how Paradox handles data values that no longer comply with the table properties you set.

▶ Borrowing a Structure from an Existing Table

When defining a new table, you can borrow the table's structure from an existing table (see Chapter 4). However, the Borrow feature is not available in the Restructure Table dialog box. Fortunately, there's an easy way around this limitation. In the Restructure Table dialog box, simply click Save As. Then type a new table name in the Save Table As dialog box, click Add Data To New Table to *remove* the checkmark from that option, change the Display Table option if you wish, then choose OK. The table structure and related files (but none of its data) will be copied to the new table.

▶ *Packing a Table*

In dBASE tables, records aren't permanently deleted from the disk until you *pack* the table. The Pack Table option in the Restructure Table dialog box allows you to pack dBASE tables. To pack a dBASE table, go to the Restructure Table dialog box, select (check) Pack Table, then choose Save or Save As. If you chose Save, Paradox will permanently delete the records from the original table. You cannot "undo" this procedure!

If you chose Save As, Paradox will not copy the deleted records to the new table it creates (the original table remains unchanged).

▶▶ *Using Passwords to Protect Tables*

When you *password protect* a table, users cannot perform any operation on that table without first supplying the correct password. You can establish a password for the table as a whole, and you can assign specific types of rights to the table or to individual fields. Passwords are especially useful for adding security to shared tables on a network.

Before jumping into the procedure for defining a password, please note the following points:

- The password can be up to 15 characters long, including spaces.

- Case matters. That is, the password *Hello* is *not* the same as *hello*, *HELLO*, or HeLlO. Therefore, pay attention to case as you enter your password.

- The password does not appear on the screen as you type it. Instead, you'll see a series of asterisks, one for each character you typed. This is a safety precaution to prevent others from watching what you enter on the screen.

- You cannot view a password-protected table or change or remove the password if you do not know the password. Therefore, you should write down your password, then swallow it (or better yet, store it in a safe place where you can find it easily).

- If your data is sensitive enough to deserve password protection, you should avoid obvious passwords like your first name, initials, nickname, the names of pets, spouses, friends, and so forth.

Managing Files and Projects

▶ ▶

Ch. 15

▶ Adding a Password

To define a password for a table, close the table (if it's currently open), then follow the steps for creating or restructuring the table (see Chapter 4 and "Restructuring a Table" in this chapter). When you reach the Create Table or Restructure Table dialog box, follow the steps below.

1. Choose *Password Security* from the Table Properties list.

2. Click Define to open the Password Security dialog box.

3. Type the password you want in the Master Password text box. The master password secures all rights to the table.

4. Type the same password in the Verify Master Password text box.

5. If you want more specific security, you can click the Auxiliary Passwords button and fill in the Auxiliary Passwords dialog box, as described later in this chapter.

6. Choose OK to return to the Create Table or Restructure Table dialog box.

7. Choose Save or Save As to save your changes.

 ▶▶ **N O T E**

If the passwords entered in steps 3 and 4 aren't identical, you'll need to correct at least one of them.

Keep in mind that if several tables are assigned the same master or auxiliary passwords, entering the password for one table will provide access to all tables with that password. This can be both a blessing and a curse.

On the positive side, this feature can save time because you can assign the same password to several related tables. When you open the tables, Paradox will request the password for only one table of the group.

The downside, of course, is that you risk assigning the same password to unrelated (and potentially sensitive) tables. For example, you wouldn't want a table of salaries to have the same password as a table of volunteers for the company picnic.

▶ *Changing or Removing a Password*

If you've defined a password for a table, you can change or remove it at any time.

To change a password, follow the steps below.

1. Go to the Restructure Table dialog box and choose Password Security from the Table Properties drop-down list box.

2. Click the Modify button. You'll see the Password Security dialog box shown in Figure 15.18.

3. If you wish to change the master password, click the Change button, type the new password in the Master Password text box, then confirm the change by retyping the same password in the Verify Master Password text box.

4. If you wish to change auxiliary passwords, click the Auxiliary Passwords button and fill in the Auxiliary Passwords dialog box (described in the next section).

FIGURE 15.18 ▶

The Password Security dialog box for an existing password

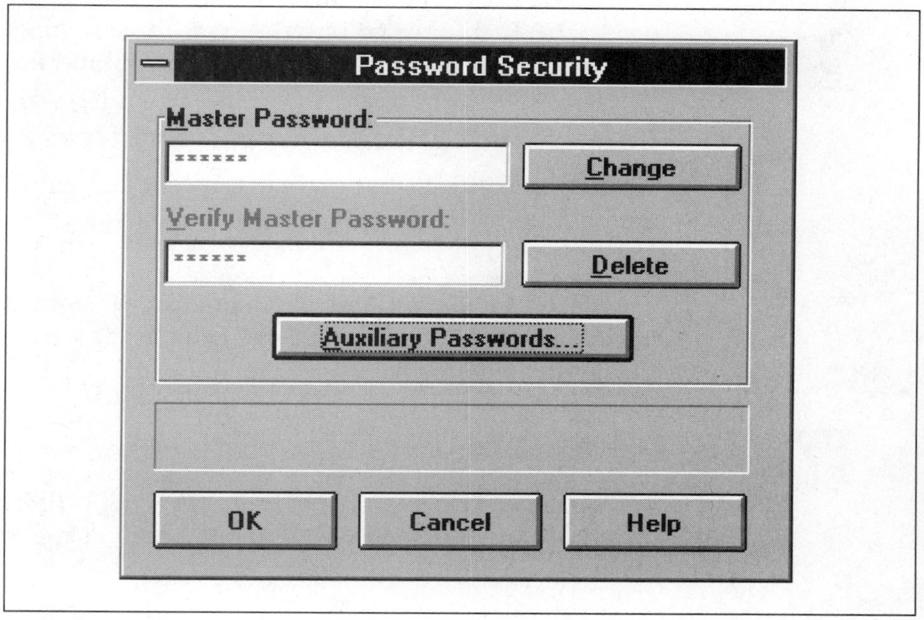

Password Security

Master Password:
`******`   Change

Verify Master Password:
`******`   Delete

Auxiliary Passwords...

OK   Cancel   Help

Managing Files and Projects

Ch.
15

5. Choose OK to return to the Create Table or Restructure Table dialog box. Or, if you change your mind and want to return to the previously saved passwords, click the Revert button and choose OK.

6. Choose Save or Save As to save your changes.

To delete the master password and its associated auxiliary passwords, repeat steps 1 and 2 above, then click the Delete button. Choose OK to return to the Create Table or Restructure Table dialog box and then choose Save or Save As.

▶ Defining Auxiliary Passwords

The master password provides all rights to the table and its fields. You can also assign auxiliary passwords that restrict the rights granted for the entire table or individual fields in the table. When the user opens the table with an auxiliary password, only the limited rights will be available. For example, you can create an auxiliary password that allows users to read a table but prevents them from changing it.

Clicking the Auxiliary Passwords button in the Password Security dialog box opens the Auxiliary Passwords dialog box shown in Figure 15.19. Before we go into the steps for assigning auxiliary passwords, let's take a closer look at table rights and field rights.

Understanding Table Rights and Field Rights

Table rights control what users can do with an entire table and all of its fields. Table 15.5 explains the table rights you can assign through auxiliary passwords.

To select a table right, specify an auxiliary password (as described below), then click the option in the Table Rights area of the Auxiliary Passwords dialog box.

 ▶▶ N O T E

> Each auxiliary password can confer only one of the table rights listed in Table 15.5.

FIGURE 15.19

The Auxiliary Passwords dialog box after we've defined one auxiliary password and started to define another

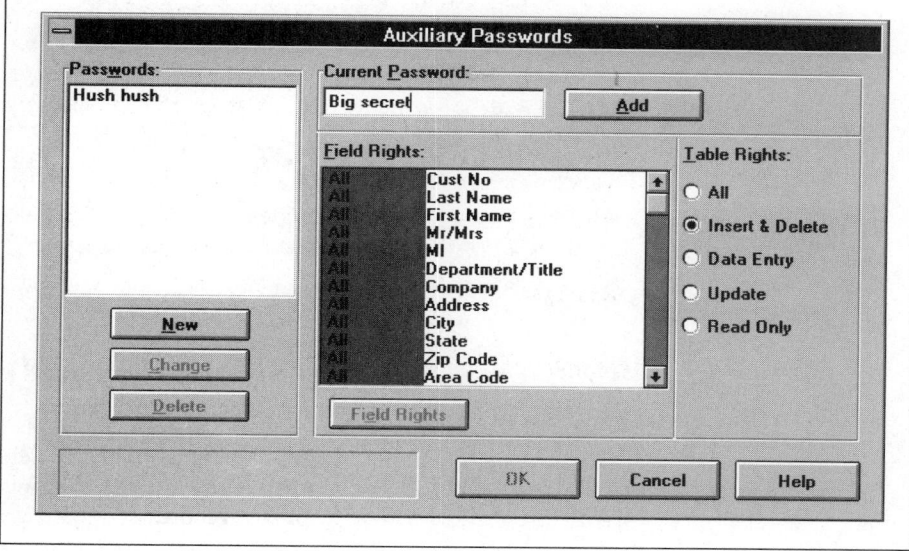

▶ **TABLE 15.5:** *Table Rights You Can Assign through Auxiliary Passwords*

TABLE RIGHT	WHAT IT DOES
All	Provides all rights to any function of the table, including the ability to restructure or delete it. (Users cannot change or delete passwords.)
Insert & Delete	Allows users to insert or delete records, but not to delete the table. This is the default setting.
Data Entry	Allows users to enter data in the table, but not to delete, restructure, or empty the table.
Update	Allows users to view fields and change non-key fields of a table, but not to insert or delete records or change key fields.
Read Only	Allows users to view the table, but not to change it in any way.

Managing Files and Projects

Ch.
15

Field rights provide another level of protection for individual fields in the table. Available field rights are listed in Table 15.6.

► **TABLE 15.6:** *Field Rights You Can Assign through Auxiliary Passwords*

FIELD RIGHT	WHAT IT DOES
All	Provides all rights on the field, within the limits of the specified table rights.
Read Only	Allows users to view, but not change, the data in the field.
None	Prevents users from viewing or changing the data in that field. Paradox hides the field values when the table is opened. (In Table View, users won't even see a column for the field.) This is useful for sensitive data like salary information within an employee record.

To select a field right, specify an auxiliary password, click the field you want to change in the Field Rights area of the Auxiliary Passwords dialog box, then click the Field Rights button to cycle through each available right of ReadOnly, None, or All. Alternatively, you can double-click a field to cycle through the rights.

Assigning and Changing Auxiliary Passwords

To specify new auxiliary passwords for a table, go to the Auxiliary Passwords dialog box and follow these steps:

1. If the cursor is not in the Current Password text box, click the New button.

2. Type the auxiliary password into the Current Password text box.

3. Select a table right to associate with this password.

4. Assign the field rights for the password.

5. Click Add to add the password to the Passwords list.

6. Repeat steps 1 through 5 to specify as many auxiliary passwords as you need.

7. Choose OK twice to save the master passwords and auxiliary passwords and return to the Create Table or Restructure Table dialog box.

8. Choose <u>S</u>ave or Save <u>A</u>s to save your changes.

> **WARNING**
>
> **Unlike master passwords, auxiliary passwords will appear on your screen when you define them. So be sure to close your window shades, shoo everyone out of your office, put on your secret decoder ring, and perform these steps in utmost secrecy.**

If you want to change an existing auxiliary password in the Auxiliary Passwords dialog box, click the password in the Pass<u>w</u>ords list, click <u>C</u>hange, make the changes you want, then click Acce<u>p</u>t to accept them or <u>R</u>evert to return the password to the list unchanged. To remove an auxiliary password, click the password in the Pass<u>w</u>ords list, click <u>C</u>hange, then click <u>D</u>elete.

▶ *Using a Password-Protected Table*

When you attempt to work with a password-protected table, Paradox will display the Enter Password(s) dialog box shown below.

You must type in the correct password in order to proceed. Asterisks will appear on the screen as you type, so type carefully. When you've entered the correct password, choose OK or press ↵. If you do not enter the correct password, Paradox will continue displaying the Enter Passwords(s) dialog box until you either type the correct password or choose Cancel to return to the Desktop.

 ▶▶**TIP**

You can enter passwords for several tables at once by typing a password and clicking Add for each password you wish to add. When you're finished, choose OK.

Remember that entering the master password gives you full access to the table. Entering an auxiliary password gives you only the rights defined for that password in the Auxiliary Passwords dialog box.

▶ Clearing Passwords from Memory

Once you enter the magic password to open (or put a password on) a password-protected table, you can access that table as often as you wish during the current Paradox session. You won't have to reenter the password. When you exit Paradox, however, the password is released and you'll need to enter it again before you can reopen the table.

This is convenient, since reentering the password each time you need a table can ruin your good mood in a hurry. But there is a drawback: If you walk away from your computer during a session, anyone who sits down at your computer can access all your password-protected tables without reentering the passwords.

You can easily release a password without exiting Paradox for Windows. Choose Tools ➤ Utilities ➤ Passwords, and when the Enter Password(s) dialog box appears, type the password you want to remove from memory and click Remove. To remove all passwords from memory at once, click Remove All. When you're finished with the dialog box, click OK.

After you clear passwords, Paradox will require you (or anyone masquerading as you) to reenter the passwords to access the tables again.

▶▶ *Repairing Damaged Tables*

Paradox tables may become damaged through power failures, hardware failures, or rebooting your computer while Paradox is active in memory. Although such damage is rare, it can be utterly devastating, especially if the damaged table contains huge amounts of data.

Fortunately, first aid is available through a table repair program named *TUtility*. To use this program, close all the open windows on your Paradox Desktop (choose Window ➤ Close All), then choose Tools ➤ Table Repair and complete the TUtility dialog box. After selecting the name of the table to repair, you can view or edit its structure (or borrow a structure from another table). You can also choose a file format for the table and verify the table's integrity. If you want to rebuild the table, click the Rebuild Table button. When you're ready to close the TUtility dialog box, double-click its Control-menu box or press Ctrl+F4.

Keep in mind that TUtility should *never* be considered a substitute for backing up your Paradox databases, especially since it can only be used to repair damaged Paradox *tables*. TUtility cannot repair forms, reports, queries, or other non-table objects.

This chapter has covered the many tools provided to help you manage Paradox for Windows files. So ends Part 4 of our odyssey into Paradox for Windows. In the next chapter, we'll take a look at advanced query and calculation techniques that are especially useful for managing related tables.

Managing Files
and Projects

Ch.
15

Managing Related Tables

PART FIVE

CHAPTER 16

Advanced Queries and Calculations

▶▶ FAST TRACK

▶ ***To use the contents of a field in a calculation***   **928**

place an example element in the field that contains the value you want to use, then place the same example element in the calculation expression.

▶ ***To perform statistical summary calculations on a table***   **932**

use any of the reserved words SUM, AVERAGE, MIN, MAX, and COUNT.

▶ ***To compare groups (sets) of records in one table to sets of records in another table***   **941**

use a *SET query* with any of the reserved words ONLY, NO, EVERY, or EXACTLY.

▶ ***To control the default behavior of queries***   **960**

choose Properties ➤ Query Options, select the options you want, and choose OK. You can choose what happens when someone else changes a table you're querying; whether auxiliary tables are created during a CHANGETO, INSERT, or DELETE query; the default checkmark type; and how Paradox handles queries against remote tables.

▶ ***To save the default View and Query Options settings***   **963**

choose Properties ➤ Save As Default. To restore default settings to whatever they were when you saved them last, choose Properties ➤ Restore Default.

Chapter 5 introduced multitable database designs and data models, while Chapter 9 showed basic query techniques. In this chapter, we'll focus on using queries to combine data from multiple tables. We'll also discuss techniques for performing calculations with queries and for setting up "live" DDE links between a table and a query.

► ► N O T E

As you read this chapter, keep in mind that forms and reports can also perform mathematical calculations. We'll get to those topics in Chapter 17.

► ► *Sample Tables*

Most examples in this chapter will use the Products, Category, Orders, LineItem, and CustList tables introduced near the end of Chapter 5 (see Figure 5.13). Of course, we understand that no two businesses do everything exactly alike. Unlike socks and bathrobes, our one-size-fits-all database design won't work perfectly for every business. But it does illustrate a design that a retail or mail order business with both cash and charge orders might use. Moreover, it sticks to the basic principle of avoiding repetitive groups of fields and redundant data. Once you grasp the basic concepts illustrated here, you should have little trouble expanding your database design to meet your own business needs.

Let's take a quick look at the sample tables and data we'll be using in this chapter.

▶ *The Products Table*

The Products table stores information about each product we sell. Figure 16.1 shows the structure for this table, along with a brief description of each field. The bottom half of Figure 16.1 shows sample data for the first few fields of this table.

FIGURE 16.1

Top: Structure of the sample Products table with brief descriptions of each field. Bottom: Sample data in the Products table. Each product has a unique identifying code.

Field Name	Type	Description
Prod Code	A8 *	Uniquely identifies each product
Description	A30	Describes the product
Category ID	N	Identifies the product's category
Unit Price	$	Our cost for one item of this product
In Stock	N	Quantity currently in stock
On Order	N	Quantity currently on order
Reorder Point	N	Reorder point

Prod Code	Description	Category ID	Unit Price
GC-006	Van	114	$9,500.00
GC-086	Yacht - 180 ft	102	$900,000.00
GC-093	Camera and Case	110	$100.95
GC-105	Buckingham Palace Tour	113	$13,500.00
GC-111	Guernsey Cow	107	$225.00
GC-112	Never-Die Bulb	105	$150.00
GC-122	Mountain Bicycle	111	$5,000.00
GC-125	Bowling Ball and Pins	111	$325.00

▶ *The Category Table*

The Category table describes each category of product sold. The table's structure and a description of each field appear in Figure 16.2. The bottom half of the figure shows some sample data.

▶ *The Orders Table*

The overall information about each order, including the customer's Ship To address and phone number, is stored in the Orders table. Since each order must have a unique identifying number, the Order No field is keyed. Details of individual items in the order are stored in the LineItem table, as you'll see in a moment.

The structure and field descriptions for the Orders table appear at the top of Figure 16.3 (we've omitted the Ship To fields to conserve space). The bottom of Figure 16.3 shows sample data for a few fields of the table.

FIGURE 16.2 ▶

Top: Structure of the sample Category table with descriptions of each field. Bottom: Sample data in the Category table. Each category has a unique Category ID.

Field Name	Type	Description
Category ID	N *	Uniquely identifies each category
Category Name	A30	Describes the category

Category ID	Category Name
101	Airplane
102	Boat
103	Computer Equipment
104	House
105	Housewares
106	Livestock - Ancient
107	Livestock - Domestic
108	Livestock - Wild
109	Novelty
110	Photo Equipment

FIGURE 16.3 ▶

Top: Structure of the sample Orders table, with brief descriptions of all fields except Ship To name, address, and phone. Bottom: Sample data in the Orders table.

Field Name	Type	Description
Order No	N *	Uniquely identifies each order
Cust No	N	Who placed the order
Date Sold	D	Date of sale
Ship Via	A10	Shipping method (e.g., FedEx)
Payment	A10	Payment method (e.g., Invoice)
Sold By	A3	Salesperson's initials
Customer's PO	A10	Purchase order number
Shipping Charge	$	Shipping charge
Date Shipped	D	Shipping date (blank if unfulfilled)
Invoice Date	D	Date of invoice (blank until invoiced)
Tax Rate	N	Tax rate (e.g., 0.0775)
Terms	A10	Payment terms (e.g., Net 30)
Amount Paid	$	Amount paid on the order
Rush	L	Rush the order? (Yes or No)

(Ship To name, address, and phone fields are not shown)

Order No	Cust No	Date Sold	Ship Via	Payment	Sold By
2000	1002	12/01/94	UPS	Invoice	ACS
2001	1001	10/22/94	UPS	Check	ACS
2002	1007	10/22/94	UPS	Check	EAO
2003	1002	10/22/94	Emery	Invoice	EAO
2004	1003	10/22/94	UPS	MC	EAO
2005	1007	10/22/94	FedEx	Check	EAO

One question that might arise is "What do you do to a record after an order is fulfilled?" You could just delete the record, but then you would have no history of the transaction. To avoid this, we use the Date Shipped field. While the order is outstanding, this field is blank; but as soon as the order is fulfilled, we place the date into the field. That way, we can use this field to track *outstanding* orders (Date Shipped is blank) and *fulfilled* orders (Date Shipped is not blank).

The Payment field of the Orders table indicates the customer's payment method. When this field has a value of "Invoice," we'll need to send the customer an invoice. Whenever we enter an order, the Invoice Date field will be blank to indicate that the customer hasn't been invoiced yet. When we ship the order and send an invoice, we'll fill in the invoice date. To determine which orders require invoicing, we would simply look for records with a Payment of "Invoice" and a blank Invoice Date.

NOTE

For simplicity, we'll use the Order Number as the invoice number.

▸ *The LineItem Table*

The LineItem table tracks detail items for each order. We use the Order No field to link each detail record with its associated order in the Orders table. The Prod Code field links each item in an order to a particular product. The structure of the LineItem table appears at the top of Figure 16.4; sample data appears at the bottom of the figure.

A negative value in the Qty field represents a returned item. Placing a returned item in the LineItem table as a "negative" sale provides a record of the transaction, and also keeps the In Stock quantities in the Products table accurate during automatic updating. (We'll discuss automatic updating in Chapter 18.)

Now, a database purist might argue that invoice transactions (those with an "Invoice" payment method), direct sales (those without an "Invoice" payment method), and adjustments (negative sales) should be stored in separate tables. Indeed, you *could* create separate tables for each type of transaction; however, there are certain conveniences to

FIGURE 16.4 ▶

Top: Structure of the sample LineItem table, with brief descriptions of each field. Bottom: Sample data in the LineItem table.

Field Name	Type		Description
Order No	N	*	Identifies customer order number
Prod Code	A8	*	Identifies product ordered
Qty	N		Quantity ordered
Unit Price	$		Selling price of one item of this product
Extended Price	$		Calculated by a query as Qty * Unit Price

Order No	Prod Code	Qty	Unit Price	Extended Price
2000	GC-006	3	$9,899.95	$29,699.85
2000	GC-111	2	$270.00	$540.00
2000	GC-122	1	$5,225.00	$5,225.00
2001	GC-111	-4	$270.00	($1,080.00)
2001	GC-129	4	$430.00	$1,720.00
2002	GC-006	3	$9,899.95	$29,699.85
2002	GC-112	-2	$171.00	($342.00)

storing all these transactions in one table. First, it's easier to work with one big table of sales and adjustments than to juggle different "types" of sales in separate tables. Second, automatic updating is easier when all the transactions are stored in one table.

▶ The CustList Table

The CustList table, which keeps track of customers, is the same table we've been using throughout this book. Cust No is keyed in the Cust-List table to ensure unique customer identifiers, and it is used in the Orders table to link orders to the customers who placed them.

Now let's look at ways to combine data from all these tables to get information we need.

▶▶ Combining Data from Multiple Tables

Queries are the basic tool required to *join* (combine) information from multiple related tables. All the query techniques that we covered in

Chapter 9 apply here. However, when querying multiple tables, you need to consider these additional points:

- You must fill out a separate query table for each table.

- You must provide example elements that tell Paradox which field is the common field that links information from one table to information in another.

- You cannot create a direct query view that has "live," or editable, fields. All direct query view fields in a multitable query will be read-only, even if you chose Properties ➤ Answer Options ➤ Live Query View in the Answer Options dialog box.

▶▶ *Understanding Example Elements*

An example element in a query table plays the same role that a variable, or "placeholder," plays in math. The example element holds a value that's likely to change. For instance, we can make the general statement

$$X * Y = \text{Extended Price}$$

where X stands for any Quantity, * means "times" (multiplied by), and Y stands for Unit Price. Regardless of the number you substitute for X (the quantity), and the number you substitute for Y (the unit price), it remains true that X times Y results in the Extended Price.

When used to link multiple tables, the example element plays the additional role of "looking up" data in one table based on the contents of the example element in another table. While running a query of the LineItem table, for example, Paradox might encounter a transaction involving product GC-006. If the Prod Code fields of the LineItem and Products tables are linked in a query, Paradox "knows" to get related information about product GC-006 in the LineItem table by looking up GC-006 in the Prod Code field of the Products table. You'll see some examples in a moment, but first let's discuss the "rules" for entering example elements into query tables.

You can set up example elements in any of the following ways:

- You can create the example elements manually. There are several variations on this theme, as you'll discover in the next several sections.

- You can base your query on a data model that contains linked tables. With this method, Paradox creates the example elements automatically. We'll cover the data model method later, in "Using the Data Model to Link Tables Automatically."

- You can start with a data model and then use the manual methods as needed.

▶ Using the Example Key (F5) to Enter Example Elements

The Example key (F5) offers one way to manually enter example elements into a query table. Here's how to use it:

1. Position the cursor where you want to type the example element in the query table.

2. Press the F5 key.

3. Type the example element, which can be any combination of letters and numbers, but cannot contain blank spaces or be a reserved word. *X, Y, hello, QUESTION1*, and **PRODUCT** are all valid example elements.

4. After typing the example element, move the cursor to any other column.

When using example elements, remember the following ground rules:

- You cannot use example elements in BCD, binary, bytes, formatted memo, graphic, memo, or OLE fields.

- Unlike query (search) criteria and other elements used in query tables, example elements always appear in reverse video or in some color (usually red) that makes them stand out.

- You can link up to 24 tables using example elements (though a 24-table query would be slow and unwieldy to set up).

▶ *Adding and Removing Tables in the Query Window*

 When you're ready to place another table in the Query window, click the Add Table button in the Toolbar (shown at left), or choose Query ➤ Add Table from the menus. When the Select File dialog box appears, click on the name of the table you want to add and choose OK. Paradox will add the new table to the bottom of the Query window.

To add several tables to the Query window at once, click the name of the *first* table you want to add, then Ctrl+click the remaining tables and choose OK. The selected tables will appear below any existing query tables in the window, in alphabetical order by table name. (If necessary, you can choose Window ➤ Tile or Window ➤ Cascade to arrange the query tables neatly on your Desktop.)

 If you wish to remove a table from the Query window, click the Remove Table button in the Toolbar (shown at left), or choose Query ➤ Remove Table. When the Remove Table dialog box appears, click on the name of the table you want to remove and choose OK.

 ▶ ▶ **TIP**

To add or delete names of several adjacent tables in the Select File or Remove Table dialog box, click the first table name, Ctrl+click the remaining names (or drag the mouse through the names you want to select), then choose OK.

Other Ways to Create a Multitable Query

Paradox offers two more shortcuts for setting up a multitable query. First, you can select several tables when you first create the query. Start by choosing File ➤ New ➤ Query. When the Select File dialog box appears, Ctrl+click in the file list to select each table. After selecting all the tables you want, choose OK to continue to the Query window.

Second, you can base your new query on a saved query. This is a real timesaver because the new query will automatically include all the tables, checkmarks, example elements, and criteria from the saved query. Begin as usual, by choosing File ➤ New ➤ Query. Then, type the query name (e.g., **myquery.qbe**) in the File Name text box; or click the File Type drop-down list, select <Queries>, and highlight the query you want in the list that appears. When you're ready to create the query, choose OK.

► *Using Example Elements to Link Tables*

Suppose you want to list products from the Products table, but you also want to include the category name with each product. Since the category name is stored in the Category table, not the Products table, you'll need to combine data from the two tables.

To begin the query, choose File ➤ New ➤ Query. In the Select File dialog box, click the *PRODUCTS.DB* table name, then choose OK to open the Query window.

Now check the Prod Code, Description, and Category ID fields in the Products table by clicking on the empty check box in each field.

To display data from the related Category table, you must place an example element in the Category ID field of the Products query table. This example element will act as the placeholder for the current Category ID when Paradox performs the query. Remember to press F5 before typing the example element.

In the example below, we used the abbreviation *CatID* as the example element. The example element is just a placeholder that has no meaning of its own; you could have used *x* or *abc* or *HOWDY* or *category* or *row1* as the example element instead of *CatID*.

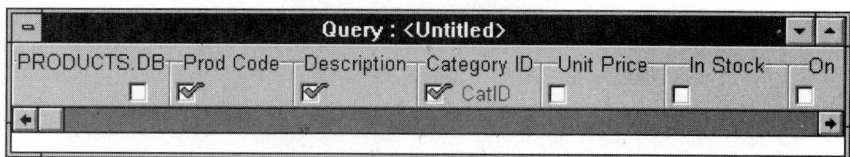

Now you're ready to add the Category table to the Query window. Click the Add Table button in the Toolbar or choose Query ➤ Add Table, select *CATEGORY.DB* from the list, and choose OK. Next you must place the same *CatID* example element in the Category ID field of the Category query table to define the link between the tables. So, click in the Category table's Category ID field, press F5, then type the example element. You must use the same example element in both the Products and the Category query tables so that Paradox will know to match those field values when processing the query.

Now you can check the Category fields you want to see in the resulting Answer table. We'll assume you want to see the Category Name field. When you click the Run Query button in the Toolbar or press F8 to run the query, the resulting Answer table will include all records from the Products table, together with the associated category names from the Category table, as shown in Figure 16.5.

FIGURE 16.5

Query tables for the Products and Category tables. The example element, CatID, in the Category ID field of both tables defines the common field that links the tables. Checkmarks indicate fields to display. The resulting Answer table is shown below the Query window.

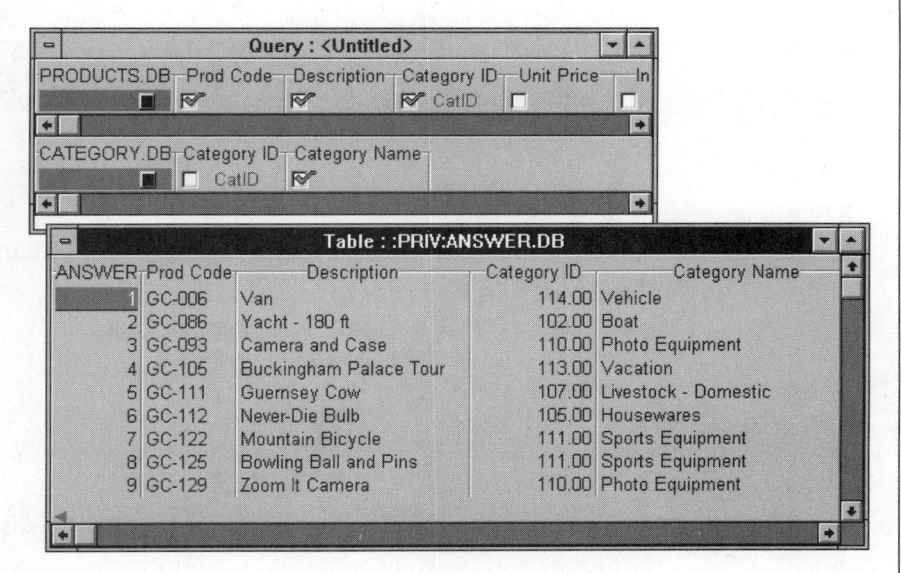

Because **CatID** is an example element and is identical in the two query tables, Paradox "knows" that you want matching information in these two fields when you run the query. For instance, if the current record in the Products table contains 114 in the Category ID field, Paradox must find a record in the Category table that also contains 114 in the Category ID field when running the query.

Notice that we checked the Category ID field in the query table for the Products table, but not in the query table for the Category table. After all, there's no need to see the Category ID twice in the resulting Answer table. Nevertheless, there's no harm in checking the common field in both tables if you wish. In Figure 16.6, for instance, we checked the Category ID field in both query tables. In the resulting Answer table, the field titled *Category ID* is the Category ID from the Products table. The field titled *Category ID_1* is the Category ID from the Category table, which Paradox has included automatically. Even though we don't need to see the Category ID twice in the Answer table, the Answer table in Figure 16.6 demonstrates that Paradox did indeed find the Category ID in the Products table that matches the Category ID in the Category table. (The codes are identical in each record of the Answer table.)

► Copying Example Elements

You can use copy and paste techniques to copy query elements from one query table field to another. Not only does this guarantee accurately typed examples, it can also save you time. Simply select the example element you want to copy, then click the Copy To Clipboard button in the Toolbar or press Ctrl+Ins. Next, click in the query table and field where you want to paste the example element, and click the Paste From Clipboard button or press Shift+Ins.

FIGURE 16.6 ▶

In this example, we checked the Category ID field in both the Products and Category tables. Notice that the Category ID appears twice in the Answer table, proving that Paradox has displayed records from the two tables with matching Category ID codes.

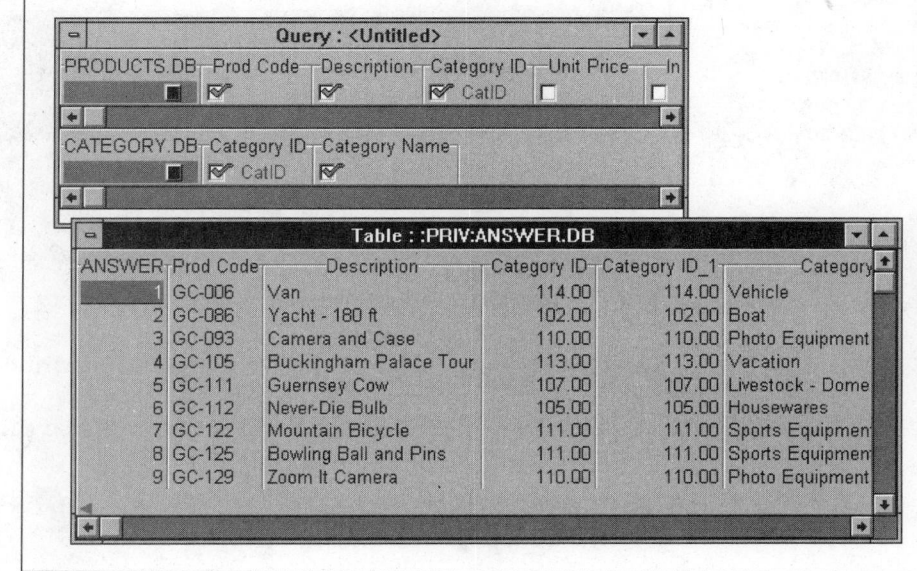

▶ *Using the Toolbar to Place Example Elements*

You've seen how to link tables together manually by pressing the F5 key and typing the example element. However, Paradox for Windows provides another way to link two or more tables. This method uses *Join Tables* example elements. To place Join Tables example elements in the common fields of two tables, follow the steps below.

1. Click the Join Tables button in the Toolbar (shown at left). A "join tables" icon appears at the lower-right of the mouse pointer when you move the pointer to a field in the query table.

2. Click in the field where you want to place the first example element (for instance, the Category ID field of the Products query table). The term *join1*, highlighted or in a different color, usually appears in that field.

3. Now click in the common field of the query table you want to link. The same highlighted example element appears in this field, as shown in Figure 16.7.

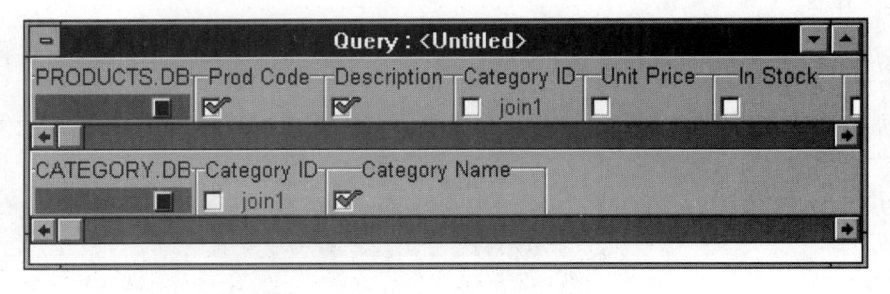

When using Join Tables example elements, remember these points:

- The fields of the tables being linked must be the same type, and they must contain corresponding data.

- The first automatic example element is *join1*, the next is *join2,* the next is *join3*, and so on.

- To cancel the join, simply click the Join Tables button again. If you've already placed an automatic example element in one of the query tables, you can delete it as you would delete any text in a query.

▶ Combining Data from More than Two Tables

You can use the techniques presented in this chapter to query any number of tables. For example, Figure 16.8 links four tables in a single query. The query tables involved contribute the following example elements and checked fields:

Orders	*Join1* (in the Order No field) and *join3* (in the Cust No field) are example elements linking the Orders table to the LineItem and CustList tables, respectively. The Order No field is checked for display.
LineItem	*Join1* (in the Order No field) links the LineItem and Orders table; *join2* (in the Prod Code field) links the LineItem table to the Products table. The Prod Code and Qty fields are checked for display.

FIGURE 16.8

Sample query that takes data from four different tables. Example elements in each query table link the common fields among the tables.

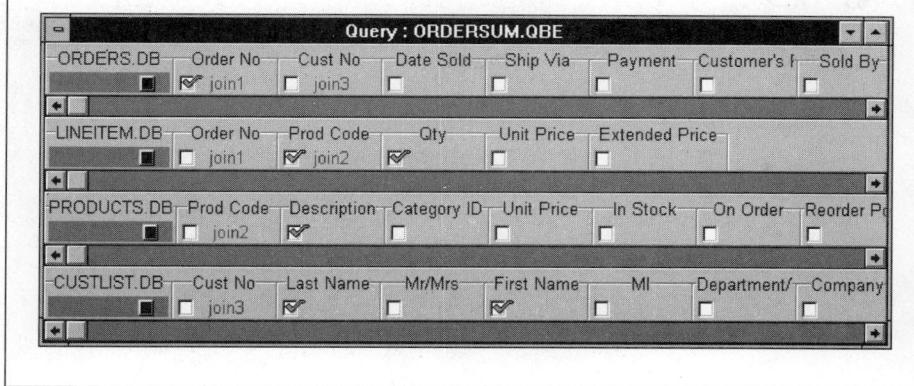

Products	The *join2* example element (in the Prod Code field) links the Products table to the LineItem table. The Description field is checked for display.
CustList	Example element *join3* (in the Cust No field) links the CustList table to the Orders table. Last Name and First Name are checked for display.

When you run the query, Paradox creates the Answer table shown in Figure 16.9. The table includes the order number, product code, quantity ordered, product description, and the name of the customer who placed each order.

▶ ▶ **N O T E**

In Chapter 17 you'll learn how to print invoices from multiple tables.

When you have multiple query tables on the screen, the top-to-bottom and left-to-right order of checked fields in the query tables determines the initial order of fields in the Answer table, as well as the sort order.

Of course, you can arrange the columns in Table View by dragging the columns or pressing Ctrl+R. You can also modify the order of fields in the Answer table or define a sort order for the Answer tables as discussed

FIGURE 16.9

Results of the query shown in Figure 16.8. Fields that were checked in the query tables are displayed in the Answer table.

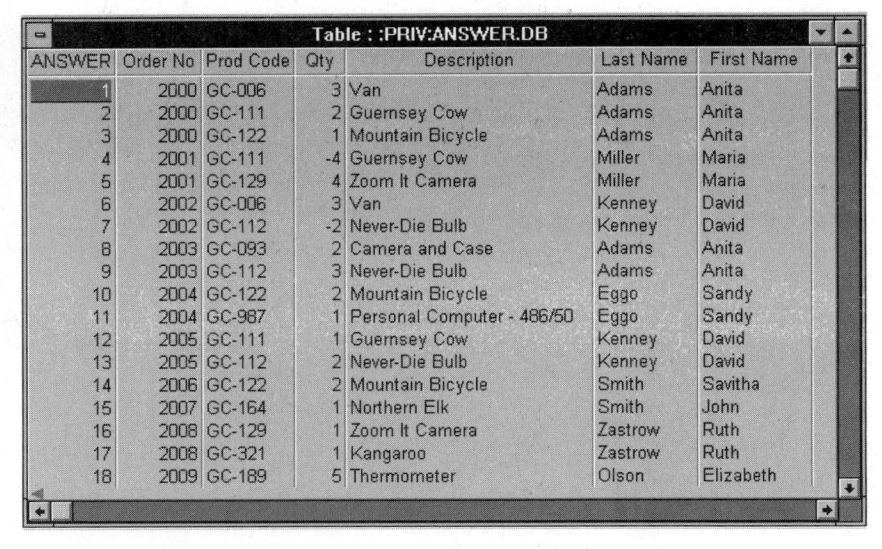

ANSWER	Order No	Prod Code	Qty	Description	Last Name	First Name
1	2000	GC-006	3	Van	Adams	Anita
2	2000	GC-111	2	Guernsey Cow	Adams	Anita
3	2000	GC-122	1	Mountain Bicycle	Adams	Anita
4	2001	GC-111	-4	Guernsey Cow	Miller	Maria
5	2001	GC-129	4	Zoom It Camera	Miller	Maria
6	2002	GC-006	3	Van	Kenney	David
7	2002	GC-112	-2	Never-Die Bulb	Kenney	David
8	2003	GC-093	2	Camera and Case	Adams	Anita
9	2003	GC-112	3	Never-Die Bulb	Adams	Anita
10	2004	GC-122	2	Mountain Bicycle	Eggo	Sandy
11	2004	GC-987	1	Personal Computer - 486/50	Eggo	Sandy
12	2005	GC-111	1	Guernsey Cow	Kenney	David
13	2005	GC-112	2	Never-Die Bulb	Kenney	David
14	2006	GC-122	2	Mountain Bicycle	Smith	Savitha
15	2007	GC-164	1	Northern Elk	Smith	John
16	2008	GC-129	1	Zoom It Camera	Zastrow	Ruth
17	2008	GC-321	1	Kangaroo	Zastrow	Ruth
18	2009	GC-189	5	Thermometer	Olson	Elizabeth

in Chapter 9. In addition, if you'll be printing the contents of the Answer table or displaying it as a form, you can rearrange the fields any way you wish. You don't need to worry about the appearance of the Answer table while you're creating query tables.

► ►T I P

> **See Chapter 7 if you need a reminder about how to move columns and customize the appearance of text and numbers in Table View.**

► Using the Data Model to Link Tables Automatically

Now that you've learned how to add tables and link them manually with example elements, let's explore the automatic way to link tables with example elements. To set up automatic links, you just base the new query on a multitable data model in which you've linked the related tables. The data model can be one that you've already created and saved, or one that you define on the fly when you create the new query.

> **NOTE**
>
> **Chapter 5 explained how to use the Data Model Designer to create and save a data model outside of any query, form, or report.**

Using an Existing Data Model or Query

Here's how to use a previously saved data model to set up a new multi-table query:

1. Begin your new query as described in Chapter 9. For example, choose File ➤ New ➤ Query.

2. When the Select File dialog box appears, click the Data Model button. You'll see a Data Model dialog box like the one shown in Figure 16.10.

3. Click the Type drop-down list, then choose <Data Models>.

FIGURE 16.10

Use the Data Model dialog box to select an existing data model or to create (and optionally save) a data model on the fly.

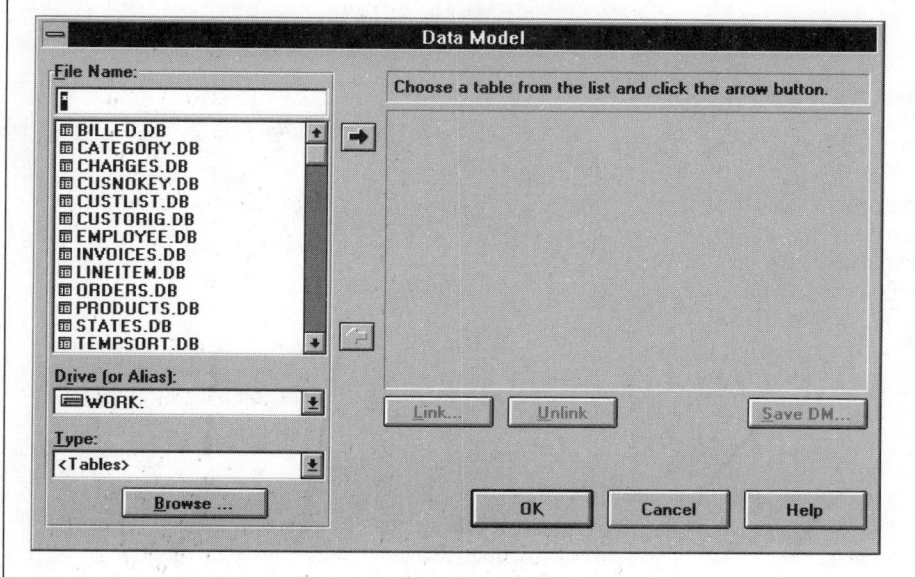

▶▶ **WARNING**

Although the Type drop-down list includes a <Queries> option, you cannot base a data model on a query. Simply ignore the <Queries> option. If you accidentally select a query file in the Data Model dialog box, and then choose OK, you'll get an error message. Choose OK to clear the message, and try creating your query again.

4. In the list of files that appears below File Name in the Data Model dialog box, click the data model file you want. That data model will appear in the Data Model area of the dialog box. The example in Figure 16.11 illustrates the Data Model dialog box after we loaded a data model stored in the data model file named *ordersum.dm*.

5. If you wish, you can update the data model as described in the next section on "Creating a Data Model On the Fly."

6. When you're ready to continue to the Query window, choose OK.

FIGURE 16.11 ▶

*The Data Model dialog box after loading a saved data model named **ordersum.dm**. This data model links the CustList, Orders, LineItem, and Products tables.*

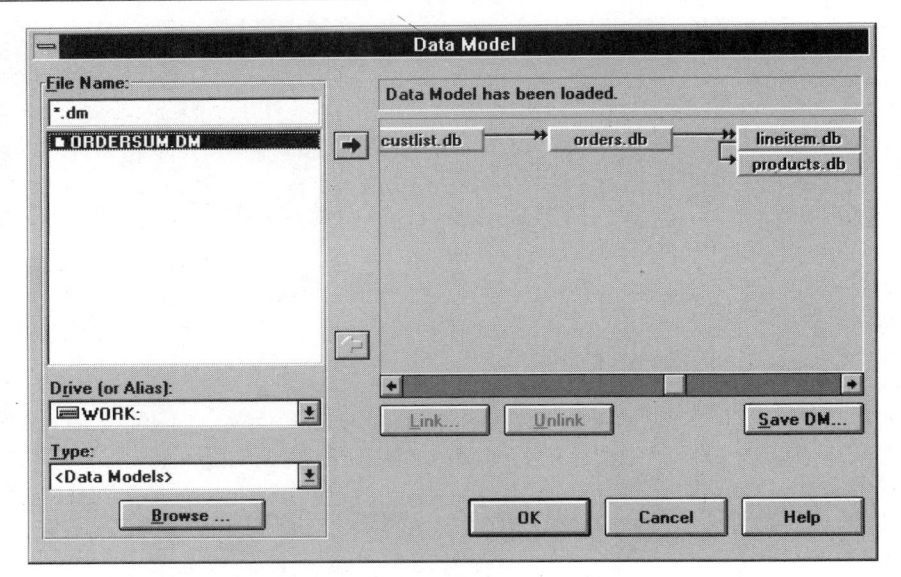

Your query tables will appear in the Query window, just as if you added and linked the tables manually. In Figure 16.12, for example, you can see the results of using the data model from Figure 16.11.

Notice in Figure 16.12 that the first field in the topmost table is checked automatically, and that example elements link the related fields. You can revise and run the query as you would any other.

FIGURE 16.12 ▶

*The query tables pro-
duced by the data
model shown in
Figure 16.11*

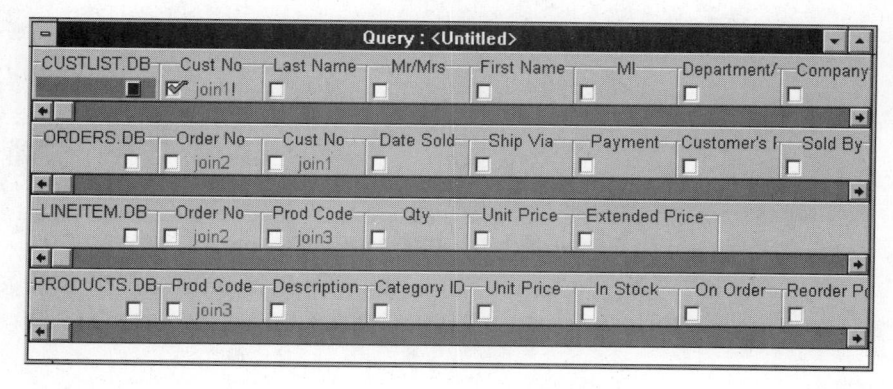

💡 ▶▶**TIP**

**If you accidentally delete one of the example elements
that Paradox created automatically, simply click where
the example element belongs, press F5, and type the
example element as you would any other. For example,
if you deleted the *join1* element, you'd press F5 and
type *join1*.**

You may have noted a small flyspeck in the checked *join1!* example ele-ment of the top-most query table in Figure 16.12. That flyspeck is an *inclusion operator* (!), which Paradox automatically places next to the example element in the topmost linking field. The inclusion operator guarantees that *all* records from the topmost table will be returned when you run the query, not just records that have matching values in the other tables. So, as you can see in Figure 16.13, Paradox returns all customer records from CustList, even for customers who didn't place any orders. (In Figure 16.13 we also checked the Last Name and First Name fields in the CustList query table, the Order No field in Orders, the Qty field in LineItem, and the Description field in Products.)

> **▶▶TIP**
>
> **If you want the query to show only the records in the topmost table that have matching records in the related tables, just delete the ! character from the topmost table in the Query window (be careful not to delete the example element). There's more about the inclusion operator later in the chapter, in the section "Displaying Non-Matching Records."**

Creating a Data Model On the Fly

If you haven't already saved a data model in the Data Model Designer (see Chapter 5), you can set up a data model when you create the

FIGURE 16.13 ▶

The results of running a modified version of the query shown in Figure 16.12

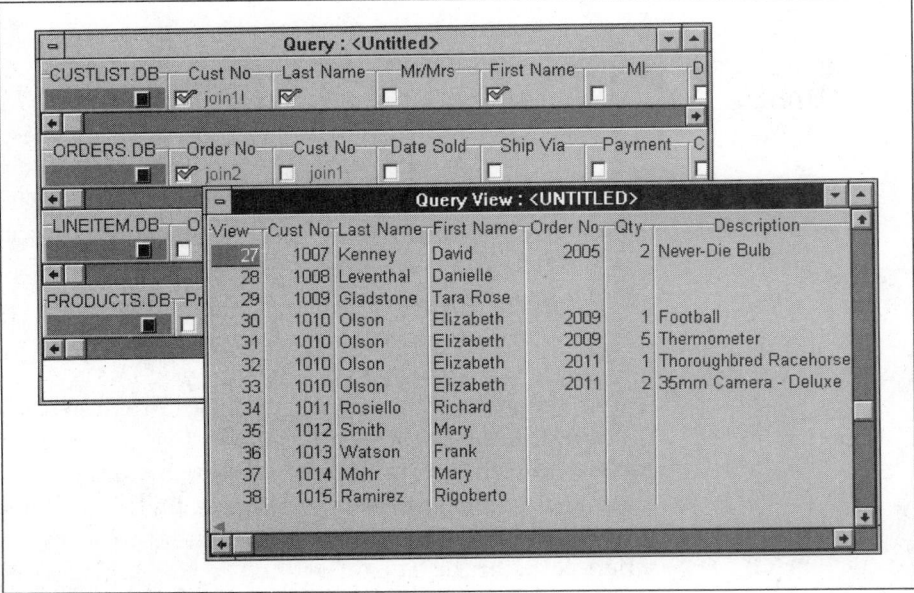

query. Here's how to begin:

1. Start a new query. For example, choose File ➤ New ➤ Query.

2. When the Select File dialog box appears, click the Data Model button. Again, the Data Model dialog box will resemble the example shown earlier in Figure 16.10.

Now you're ready to add tables to the data model. To do so, simply double-click a table name in the File Name list, or click the table name and then click the → button. Repeat this step until you've added all the tables you want.

When you finish adding tables, the Data Model area of the dialog box will resemble the example below.

If you need to remove a table from the data model, start by clicking on it in the data model area in the right half of the Data Model dialog box. The table name will appear "pushed in" and its name will appear just above the data model area. (If the table you want to delete is linked, you must then click the Unlink button to unlink it.) Now click the ← button or press Alt+D. The table will disappear from the data model and return to the File Name list.

Once you've added the tables you want, you can link them, using the same techniques that were presented in Chapter 5. Here is a brief review of the steps (if you need more details, please flip back to Chapter 5, or click the Help button in the Data Model dialog box):

1. Click the master table in the data model area of the dialog box. The mouse pointer changes to a linking tool when you pass it over a table.

2. Click and drag the linking tool from the master table to the detail table, then release the mouse button.

►►TIP

As an alternative to adding all the tables to the data model and then linking them, you may prefer to link each pair of tables as you add them. In multitable designs that include many tables, this technique reduces the need to scroll the data model in the Data Model dialog box to view all the tables you want to link.

If you haven't established referential integrity between the two tables, Paradox will display the Define Link dialog box, and you can complete the dialog box as described in Chapter 5. If you *have* established referential integrity, Paradox will complete the link automatically and bypass the Define Link dialog box. (To return to the Define Link dialog box at any time, click the detail table whose link you want to change, then click the Link button in the Data Model dialog box.)

When you finish creating the data model, the screen will resemble the example shown back in Figure 16.11. If you'd like to save your data model for later use, click Save DM, type in a new file name, and choose OK.

When the data model is complete, choose OK to have Paradox set up your multitable query in the Query window.

►► Using Query Criteria with Multiple Tables

You can add query criteria to any table in a multitable query, including operators such as <, >, LIKE, .., and all the others discussed in Chapter 9. A few important points are listed below.

- Do not press F5 before typing a query criterion (unlike example elements, query criteria should not be highlighted).

- If you want to include a query criterion in a field that contains an example element, follow the example element with a comma (and a space if you wish), then type the query criterion for that field.

Suppose you wanted to display only orders placed by Anita Adams. You could create the query shown in Figure 16.14 so that the CustList query table displays only records that contain Adams in the Last Name field and Anita in the First Name field. Because *Anita* and *Adams* are query criteria and not example elements, we did not press F5 before typing the names; therefore, they are not highlighted. The resulting Answer table lists records for Anita Adams only.

FIGURE 16.14

A query that displays orders placed by Anita Adams.

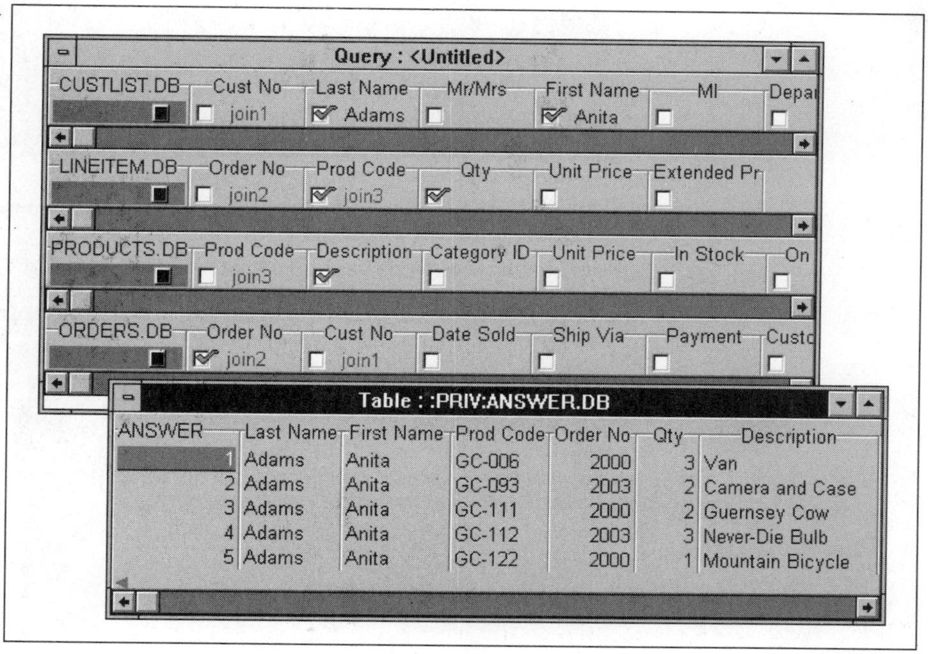

Figure 16.15 shows a slightly more complicated example. Here, the query isolates the transactions for invoice number 2001. This is practically the same as the query shown back in Figure 16.8, but the query criterion 2001 in the Order No field of the Orders table restricts the Answer table to records that contain 2001 in the Order No field. Notice how a comma and a space precede each query criterion, and the query criteria are not highlighted (this distinguishes them from example elements).

FIGURE 16.15 ▶

A multitable query that limits the Answer table to records that have the number 2001 in the Order No field

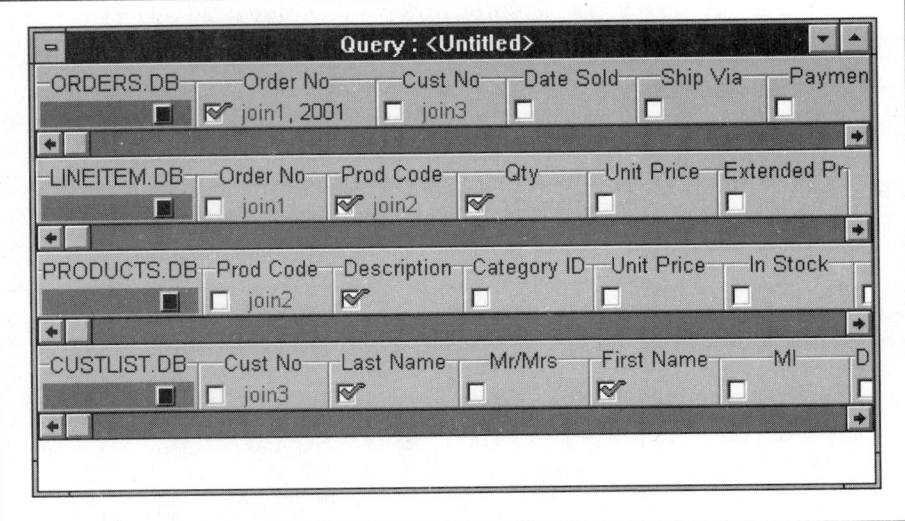

The results of the query shown in Figure 16.15 appear below.

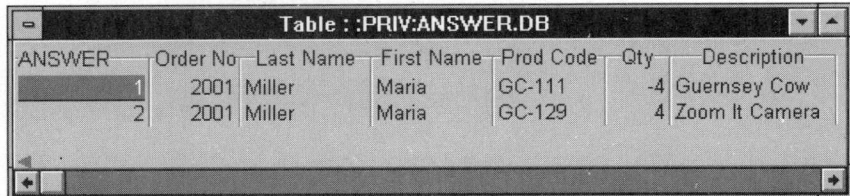

▶ AND and OR Queries with Multiple Tables

AND and OR queries with multiple tables are similar to AND and OR queries with a single table. For an AND query, place the query criteria on the same line. As with a single table, you can add as many selection criteria as you want.

Even if you use different fields on two or more query tables, the relationship among the queries is still treated as an AND question. Suppose you want to know how much photo equipment salesperson ACS has sold (the Category ID for photo equipment is *110*). First, you would set up a query on the Orders table and put **ACS** in the Sold By field to isolate orders for that salesperson.

To limit the display of transactions to sales of photo equipment, add the LineItem and Products tables to the Query window. Next use the Join Tables button in the Toolbar to link the Order No fields of the Orders and LineItem tables, then use the Join Tables button once more to link the Prod Code fields of the LineItem and Products tables. Check the fields you want to view, and type the query criterion **110** in the Category ID field of the Products query table, as shown in Figure 16.16.

FIGURE 16.16 ▶

*A multitable query that asks for transactions involving salesperson ACS **and** products in Category ID 110 (photo equipment). Example element **join1** links the Orders and LineItem tables, and **join2** links the ProdCode field of the LineItem and Products tables.*

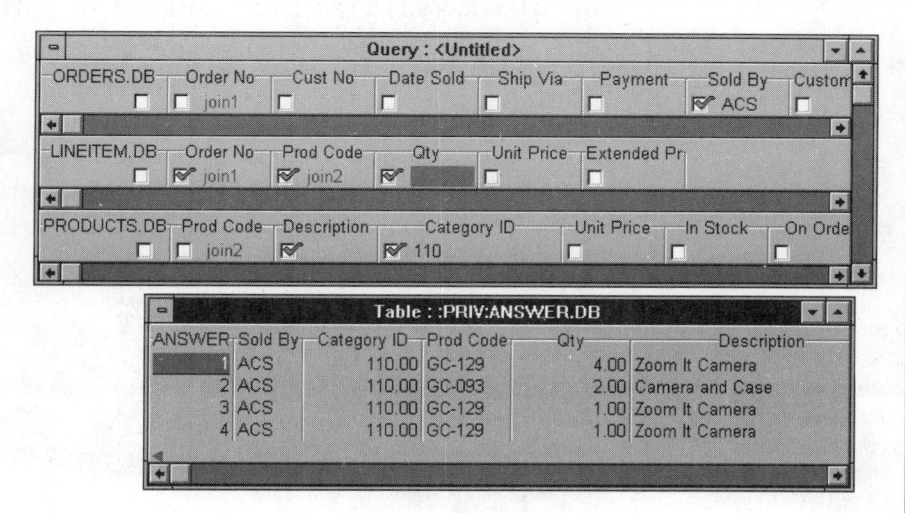

Because both *ACS* and *110* are on the first row of their respective query tables, Paradox will interpret the query as requesting records that have ACS in the Sold By field of the Orders table *and* 110 in the Category ID field of the Products table. As Figure 16.16 demonstrates, the Answer table contains exactly those records.

▶▶**N O T E**

> **To use the *Category Name* in the query criterion instead of the Category ID, add the Category table to the Query window shown in Figure 16.16, link the Category ID fields of the Products and Category tables, erase *110* from the Category ID field in the Products table, and type Photo Equipment into the Category Name field of the Category table. Then run the query.**

OR queries that involve a single field can be handled with the OR operator. The query in Figure 16.17 displays records for salesperson ACS that have either 103 (computer equipment) *or* 110 (photo equipment) in the Category ID field of the Products table.

If you want to ask OR questions with two separate tables, you need to "stack" the questions on separate lines in the query tables. To create a new query line, move the cursor to an existing query line and press ↓.

FIGURE 16.17 ▶

*A multitable query that asks for transactions involving salesperson ACS **and** products in either the computer equipment category (Category ID 103) **or** the photo equipment category (Category ID 110) of the Products table*

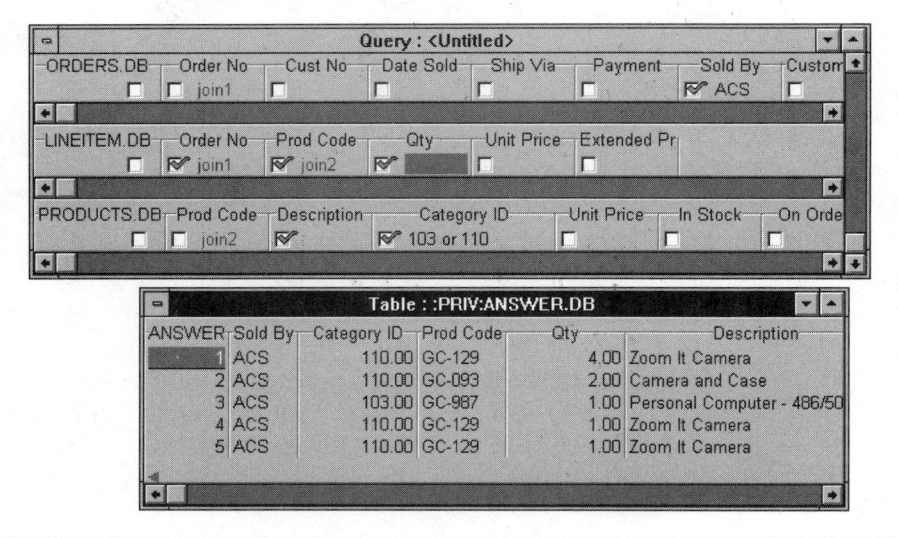

(If you need to delete a query line, move the cursor to the line and press Ctrl+Del.)

When working with OR questions on separate tables, keep in mind these points:

- Each "question" (row) in each query table should have its own linking example element. For instance, if two questions are involved, you'll need two pairs of matching example elements.

- The same fields should be checked in each row of a query table.

This may sound complicated, but an example should clear things up. Suppose we want to list all products sold by ACS (regardless of the category) or any products sold in Category ID 110 (regardless of the salesperson). The query and Answer tables shown in Figure 16.18 illustrate the stacking technique required to extract the information we want. Each query table contains two rows (one for each OR query criterion), and the checkmarks in the two rows of each query table correspond. The example elements are as follows: *Ord1* links the first row of the Orders and LineItem query tables; *Ord2* links the second row of Orders and LineItem; *Prod1* links the first row of the LineItem and Products query tables; *Prod2* links the second row of LineItem and Products.

FIGURE 16.18

A query that asks for records with ACS in the Sold By field (regardless of category) or with 110 in the Category ID field (regardless of salesperson)

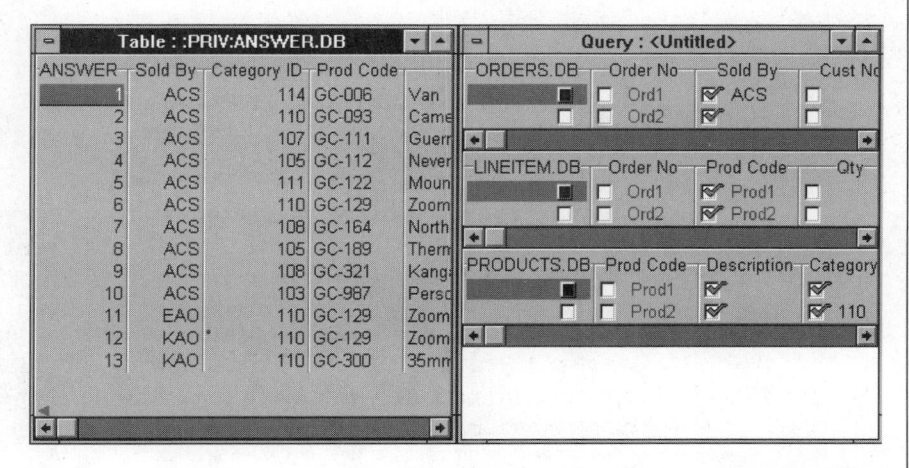

▶ ▶**TIP**

> To show the query and Answer tables side by side, as in Figure 16.18, choose <u>W</u>indow ➤ <u>T</u>ile from the Query window menus.

Because *ACS* is on the first row of the Orders query table and *110* is on the second row of the Products query table, the two are treated as two separate questions. Consequently, the Answer table contains records with *ACS* in the Sold By field (regardless of category) *and* records with *110* in the Category ID field (regardless of salesperson).

▶▶ *Displaying Non-Matching Records*

When you create a query that links two or more tables, Paradox usually displays only those records with matching values in the tables. This point is illustrated in Figure 16.19, where we've used the example element *join1* to link the Cust No fields of the CustList and Orders tables. The Last Name, First Name, Order No, and Date Sold fields are checked for display, and the Answer table shows the results of the query.

Notice in Figure 16.19 that records for customers who did not place orders are excluded from the Answer table. Why? Because when Paradox is running the query, the *join1* example element requires matching values in the CustList and Orders tables; if the values don't match, the records are left out.

Suppose you want to list *all* customers, regardless of whether they've placed orders. Further imagine that you also want to see the order number and date if a customer did place an order.

To display that information, you must use the *inclusion operator* (!) in what is called an *outer join*. When entering the query, type the inclusion operator immediately following the example element, without any blank space between the example element and the operator.

FIGURE 16.19

*This Answer table includes customer name, order number, and date sold. Because the **join1** example element requires matching Cust No fields in the Cust-List and Orders table, the Answer table omits customers who haven't placed orders.*

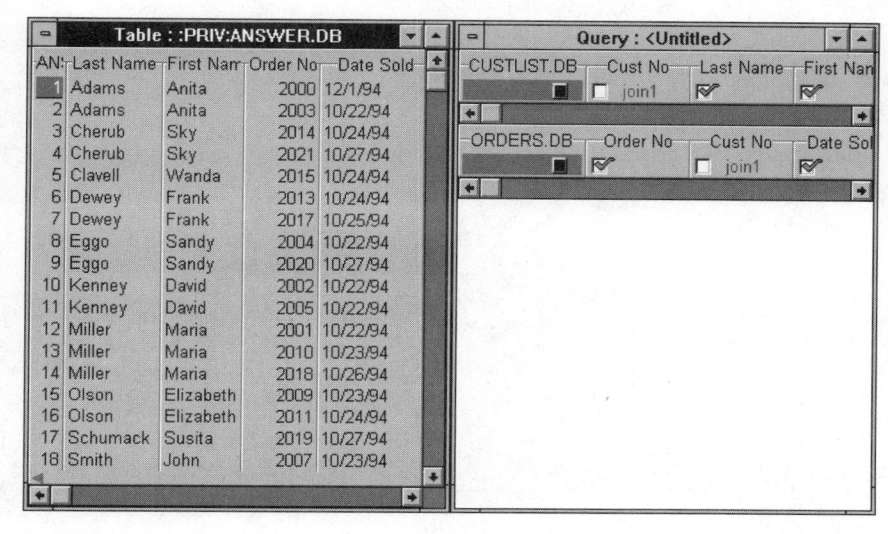

 TIP

> **Because the inclusion operator includes records that have no matching records in a linked table, it can help you discover mistakes made while typing data into common fields. Any non-matching records may be the result of a typographical error.**

In Figure 16.20, we placed the inclusion operator (!) after the *join1* example element in the CustList table. In essence, we're telling Paradox to list every record from the CustList table, whether or not there's a corresponding order for that customer in the Orders table. The resulting Answer table includes *all* the records from the CustList table, with blank order information for customers who have not placed orders.

 NOTE

> **Remember that Paradox automatically inserts an inclusion operator into queries that you've created from multitable data models.**

FIGURE 16.20 ▶

The inclusion opera-tor (!) tells Paradox to display all the records from the CustList table, even if there are no matching records in the Orders table.

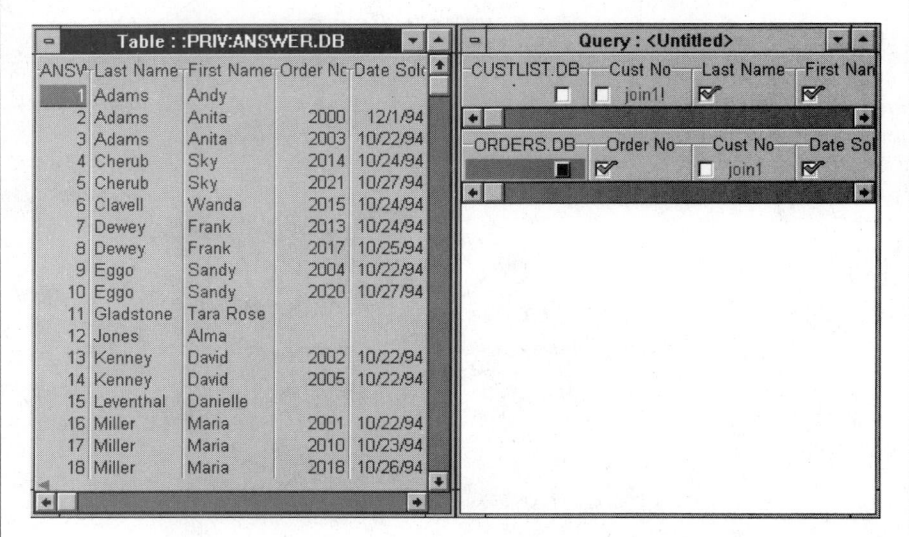

In summary, the basic technique for joining data from multiple related tables into a single table is to link the common fields through identical example elements. As with single-table queries, you can check the fields you want to view in the Answer table, and you can enter query criteria to specify which records to include in the Answer table.

Let's now turn our attention to an entirely different use of queries—performing mathematical calculations. This feature is useful for both single-table and multitable queries.

▶▶ *Using Queries to Perform Calculations*

To perform calculations in queries, you type in an *expression* using any combination of the arithmetic operators listed in Table 16.1.

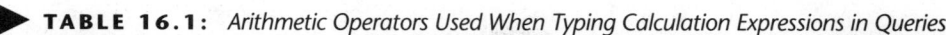

TABLE 16.1: *Arithmetic Operators Used When Typing Calculation Expressions in Queries*

OPERATOR	FUNCTION
+	Addition
–	Subtraction
*	Multiplication
/	Division
( )	Grouping

N O T E

You can also use reports and forms to perform calculations, as described in the next chapter.

All Paradox for Windows calculations observe the standard mathematical *order of precedence*. That is, multiplication and division are done before addition and subtraction.

To understand how order of precedence affects calculations, consider a simple expression such as **10+5*2**. Because multiplication is done before addition, the result of this expression is *20*: five times two, plus ten.

If you want to override the standard order of precedence, you can use parentheses. Any portion of an expression that is enclosed in parentheses will always be calculated first. Thus, the result of the expression **(10+5)*2** is *30*, because Paradox first adds ten and five, then multiplies the result by two.

In Chapter 9 we explained how to use arithmetic operators in queries to locate records that fall within a specified range of dates. By subtracting a certain number of days from the **TODAY** operator, you can isolate records that fall within a range of dates in relation to the current date. For instance, the query below isolates records from the Orders table in which Date Sold is more than 90 days ago.

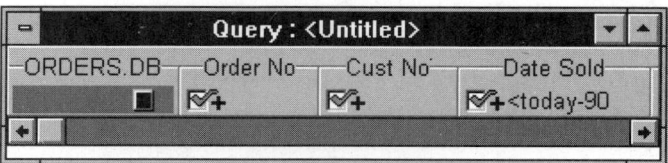

▶ *Using CALC to Display Calculation Results*

The <*TODAY-90* calculation shown above does not present the calculation results in the Answer table. To *display* the results of a calculation, you must precede the calculation with the keyword **CALC**. CALC displays the result of the expression in a new field in the Answer table. Unless you use the **AS** operator to name the field (as explained in a moment), the field takes the calculation expression as its name.

You can use example elements with calculations to display the results of calculations that involve two or more fields, to add a constant to a field, and to project "what-if" situations. Recall that the LineItem table has a Qty field and a Unit Price field. If we want to calculate the extended price for each detail line, we must multiply the quantity by the unit price in each record. Figure 16.21 shows the query we need, along with the resulting Answer table. Note that **QTY** and **PRICE** are example elements entered with the F5 key. After typing the **PRICE** example element, a comma, and a blank space in the Unit Price field, we entered an expression telling Paradox to multiply the quantity by the price (again pressing F5 before entering **QTY** and **PRICE** in the expression).

 ▶▶ **TIP**

> We've used check plus in this query, rather than check, to ensure that records with identical quantities and prices will appear in the Answer table, and won't be discarded as duplicates.

FIGURE 16.21

The extended price calculated using example elements and CALC

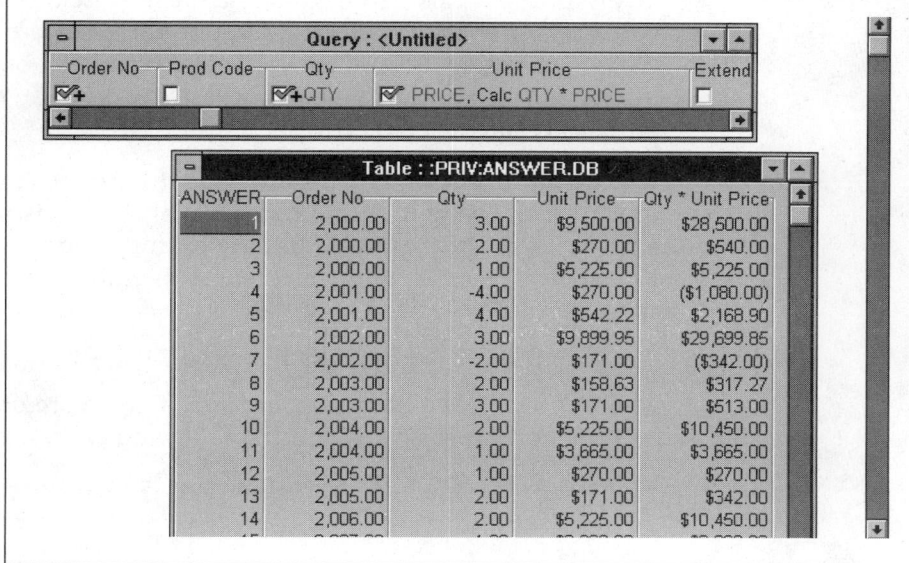

When we run the query, Paradox puts the value in the current record's Qty field into the **QTY** example element, then puts the value in the current record's Unit Price field into the **PRICE** example element. Next it performs the calculation **QTY** times **PRICE**. The result is a new field that displays the extended price of each transaction, as the Answer table in Figure 16.21 shows.

▶ How Paradox Calculates Blank Fields

Normally, if any field that's used in a calculation is blank, the result of the calculation will also be blank. For instance, if either the Qty field or the Unit Price field (or both) were empty in one of the records in Figure 16.21, the result would be blank. If you would prefer that Paradox treat blank fields as the number zero, choose Tools ▶ System Settings ▶ Blank As Zero, select (check) Treat Blank Fields As Zeros, and choose OK (see Chapter 14).

▶ Renaming Calculated Fields

Notice in Figure 16.21 that the last column in the Answer table is named *Qty * Unit Price*. Paradox automatically uses the names of fields involved in the calculation to name the new field in the Answer table. If you'd rather assign a different name to the calculated field, you can use the AS operator. Renaming a calculated field can be useful when you intend to run another query on the Answer table, or use the Answer table to create a report format.

The query in Figure 16.22 shows how to use the AS operator in a query table. Using the LineItem table again, we assigned the example element *X* to the Qty field, and the example element *Y* to the Unit Price field. The *Y* example element is then followed by a comma, a space, and the expression

CALC *X* * *Y* AS Extended

where *X* and *Y* are example elements. That expression is followed by another comma, a space, and the following expression:

CALC *X* * *Y* * 1.0775 AS Total

▶ ▶ T I P

To use multiple CALC expressions in a field of the query table, separate the expressions with commas, as we did in Figure 16.22. And don't forget to press F5 before typing example elements.

In the Answer table, the result of the first calculation is shown in the column named *Extended*. The result of the second expression, which adds 7.75% sales tax to the quantity times the unit price, appears in the column named *Total*.

You can place CALC in any field of the query table—even one that is not used directly in the calculation. Because Paradox *always* includes the calculated field in the query result, you do not need to check it.

▶ Calculations Using Fields from Multiple Tables

Paradox for Windows lets you use a field from another table in a calculation. Figure 16.23 shows a query in which the example element *join1* links the LineItem and Products tables on the common Prod Code field. The example element *QTY* acts as the placeholder for the Qty

FIGURE 16.22

In the Answer table,
the extended price
(Qty times Unit Price)
appears in the column
named **Extended**. The
extended price with
7.75% sales tax added
appears in the column
named **Total**.

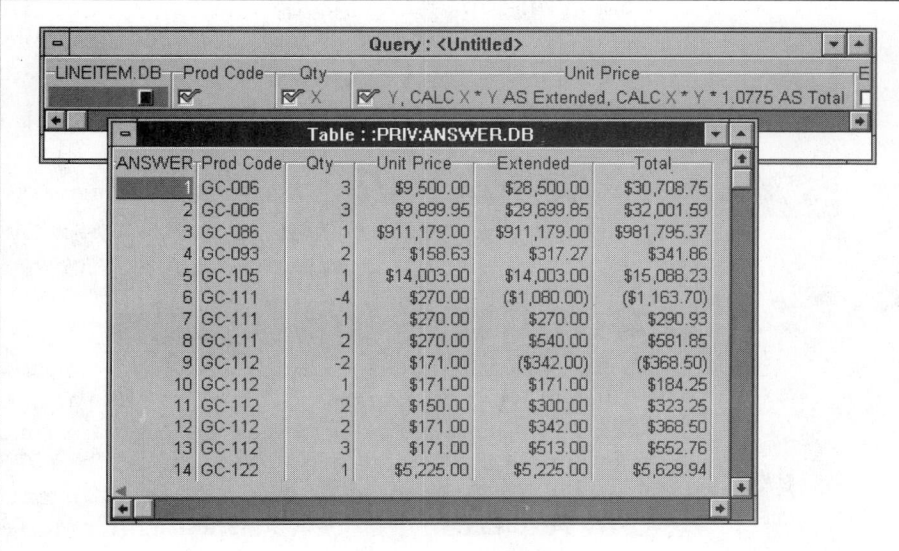

FIGURE 16.23

A query that uses two
tables to perform a
calculation

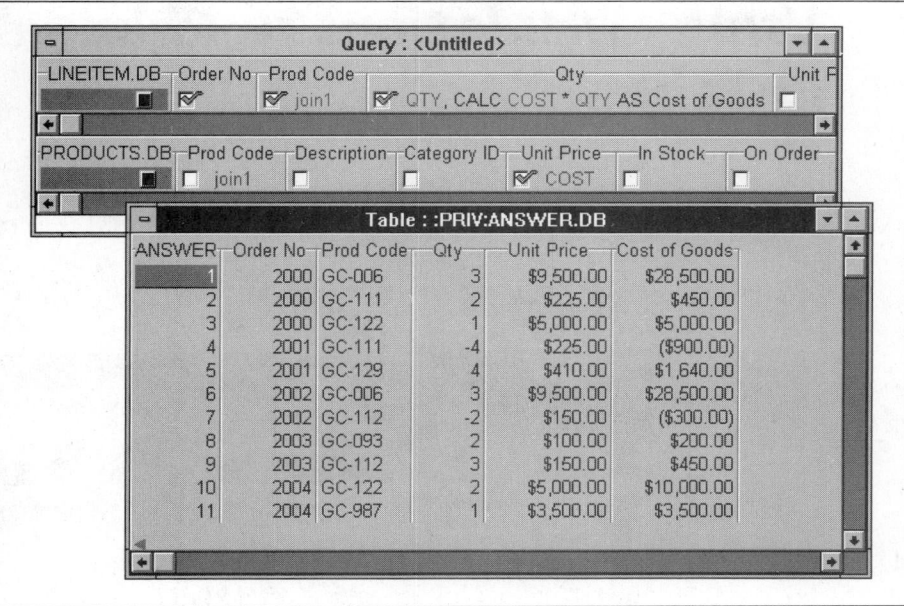

field in the LineItem table; the example element **COST** is the place-holder for the Unit Price field of the Products table. The expression *CALC **COST** * **QTY** AS Cost of Goods* calculates the total cost of goods sold.

▶▶**N O T E**

In the Products table, Unit Price represents our cost for the item; in the LineItem table, Unit Price represents the item's selling price.

Once you've used example elements to link the common fields of two tables, performing a calculation is basically the same as performing calculations in a single table. So, even though the *COST* value comes from the Products table, we can still use that example element in a CALC expression in a query for the LineItem table.

▶▶ *Using Calculations to Change Values in Tables*

In Chapter 9 you learned how to change the value in a field globally using a simple CHANGETO query. You can also use example elements and arithmetic operators with the **CHANGETO** operator. For instance, we can update the Extended Price field in every record of LineItem using the query below.

As in Figure 16.21, the *qty* and *price* example elements are used in the Qty field, Unit Price field, and in the calculation. This time, however, we used CHANGETO to update the LineItem table, instead of using CALC to display a result. As with any CHANGETO query, copies of original records that were changed during the query appear in the temporary Changed table. The actual changes take place in the original table—in this case LineItem.

 ▶▶ **N O T E**

> **You cannot use CALC or checked fields with CHANGETO. Remember, CALC and the checkmarks are used to display calculation results, whereas CHANGETO updates records globally. You cannot combine these actions in the same Query window.**

Now suppose you wanted to increase the selling price of all photo equipment (category 110) in the LineItem table by 15 percent. In the example below, the ***PRICE*** example element holds the unit price for each record. *CHANGETO* ***PRICE*** ** 1.15* multiplies the current price by 1.15 (increasing the unit price by 15 percent).

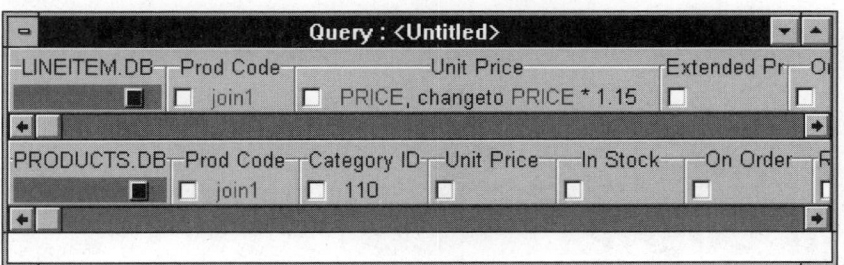

Because the Category ID field contains the value 110, only records in that category will be affected by the query. (Omitting the query criterion in the Category ID field would cause the query to increase the unit price of *every* record in the table by 15 percent). After updating the unit price for photo equipment, you could run the first CHANGETO query shown in this section to recalculate the extended price for each record.

You might be tempted to perform the price increase and extended price calculations in the same Query window, as shown below. However, this will *not* work properly.

The reason this won't work is that Paradox always looks at the *original* records when performing calculations. In this example, the Unit Price field will be updated properly; however, the Extended Price field will be *incorrect* because Paradox hasn't "seen" the increased unit price values at the time it performs the extended price calculation. To solve the problem, run the query to increase the unit price first, then run the extended price calculation query. Alternatively, you can type **CHANGETO *QTY* ★ *PRICE* ★ 1.15** in the Extended Price field of the query table, instead of using the incorrect CHANGETO calculation shown above. This calculation works correctly because the original unit price is increased by the same amount—15 percent—in both the Unit Price and Extended Price calculations.

▶▶ *Performing Summary Calculations in Queries*

You can perform statistical and summary calculations on table data using the *summary operators* listed in Table 16.2. As with the arithmetic operators, these can be used either with or without CALC in a query.

Not all the summary operators can be used with all field types. For example, the **SUM** operator works with numeric data types only, as these are the only ones that it makes sense to sum. The **AVERAGE** operator can also handle the date field type, since Paradox can determine an average date from a range of dates. The **MAX**, **MIN**, and **COUNT** operators work with alpha data, since Paradox can find the "smallest"

▶ **TABLE 16.2:** *Summary Operators Used in Query Forms*

SUMMARY OPERATOR	CALCULATES	FIELD TYPES	DEFAULT GROUPING
AVERAGE	Average of values	#, $, +, @, D, I, N, S, T	All
COUNT	Number of values	#, $, +, @, A, D, I, L, N, S, T, Y	Unique
MAX	Highest value	#, $, +, @, A, D, I, L, N, S, T, Y	Unique
MIN	Lowest value	#, $, +, @, A, D, I, L, N, S, T, Y	Unique
SUM	Total of values	#, $, +, I, N, S	All

NOTE # (BCD), $ (Money), + (Autoincrement), @ (TimeStamp), A (Alpha), D (Date), I (Long Integer), L (Logical), N (Number), S (Short), T (Time), Y (Bytes)

("aardvark") and "largest" ("zzyxx") text values, and can count the number of particular text values ("how many Smiths are there?")

NOTE

You cannot use summary operators with binary, formatted memo, graphic, memo, or OLE fields.

The default grouping for a summary operator determines whether it normally includes all values in a field (including duplicates), or whether it weeds out the duplicates. You can override the default grouping of a summary operator using the **ALL** or **UNIQUE** keywords in the query table, or by using checkmarks, as described later in this chapter.

To understand how the default grouping might affect the outcome of a summary calculation, suppose you have a table with an Invoice Date field that contains 30 records. Of the 30 records, 28 contain the date 10/1/94, 1 contains the date 10/15/94, and 1 contains 10/31/94.

If you used CALC AVERAGE in a query table to calculate the "average" date in all those records, the result would be 10/2/94, since the preponderance of 10/1/94 dates would skew the average toward the earlier date. However, if you used CALC AVERAGE UNIQUE, Paradox would treat all the 10/1/94 dates as one unique value. The resulting average date would be 10/15/94.

On the other side of the coin, the CALC COUNT operator defaults to a UNIQUE grouping, rather than an ALL grouping. Suppose you have a large table containing thousands of names and addresses. If you were to use CALC COUNT in the State field of that table, the result would be no greater than 51, since there would be at most 51 unique "states" in the table (50 states, plus the District of Columbia). However, if you used CALC COUNT ALL in that field, the result would be in the thousands, since every record, including those with duplicate state entries, would be counted.

In the sections that follow, we'll look at some practical examples using CALC queries.

▶ Summarizing All Records

Summarizing a field for all the records of a table is one of the most common applications of summary operators. When you want to include all the records in a table in summary calculations, don't check any fields in the query table.

Recall that the sample CustList table includes a Credit Limit field. Suppose you want to know how much total credit you're extending to all customers, along with the average, highest, and lowest credit limits. The query and Answer table shown in Figure 16.24 answer those questions.

In Figure 16.24, each CALC expression results in a new field in the Answer table. Each new field name starts with the name of a summary operator followed by "of" and the *Credit Limit* field name (*Sum of Credit Limit*, *Average of Credit Limit*, and so forth). Although the query

FIGURE 16.24 ▶

The sum, average, lowest, and highest credit limits in the CustList table

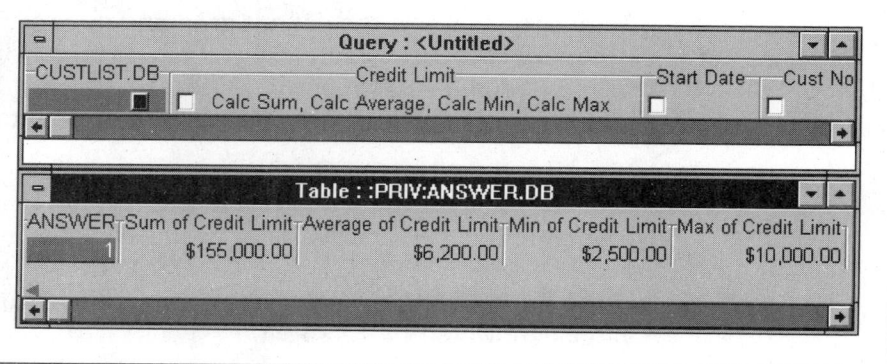

table contains no checked fields, the summary calculations appear because CALC always displays its result in the Answer table.

▶ *Performing Calculations on Groups of Records*

When you use checkmarks with summary operators, the checks behave differently than in other types of queries. With summary operators, a checkmark displays the checked field in the Answer table as expected; however, it also groups identical values in the checked field (or fields) so that summary calculations are performed on each group separately.

The query table in Figure 16.25 illustrates this point. The checkmark in the Prod Code field of the LineItem query table bases calculations on groups of like products. CALC SUM in the Qty field totals the values in the Qty field for each product. The resulting Answer table displays the total number of units sold for each product.

FIGURE 16.25 ▶

The sum of the Qty field for each product code

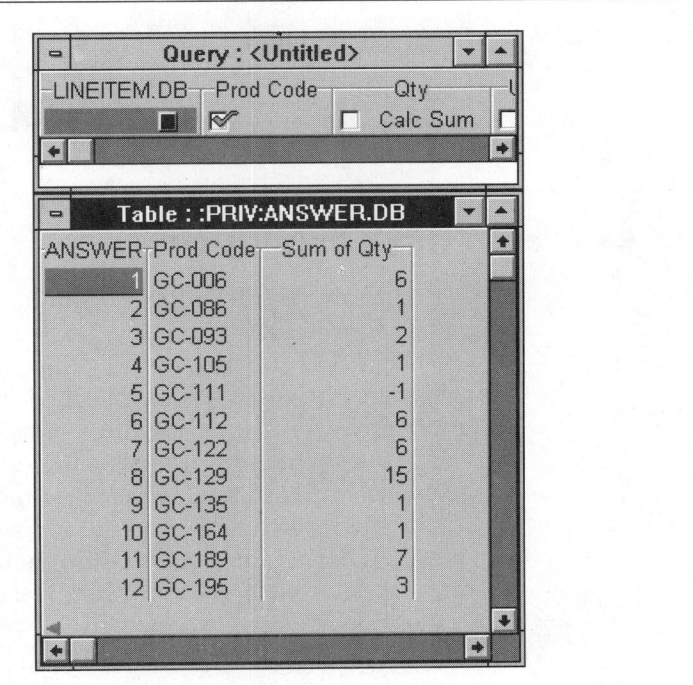

Checking multiple fields in a CALC query breaks down the resulting calculations even further. In Figure 16.26, for example, we checked both the Prod Code field in the LineItem query table and the Sold By field in the Orders query table and placed CALC SUM in the Qty field. The end result is the quantity of each item sold by each salesperson.

FIGURE 16.26 ▸

Quantity of each product sold by each salesperson

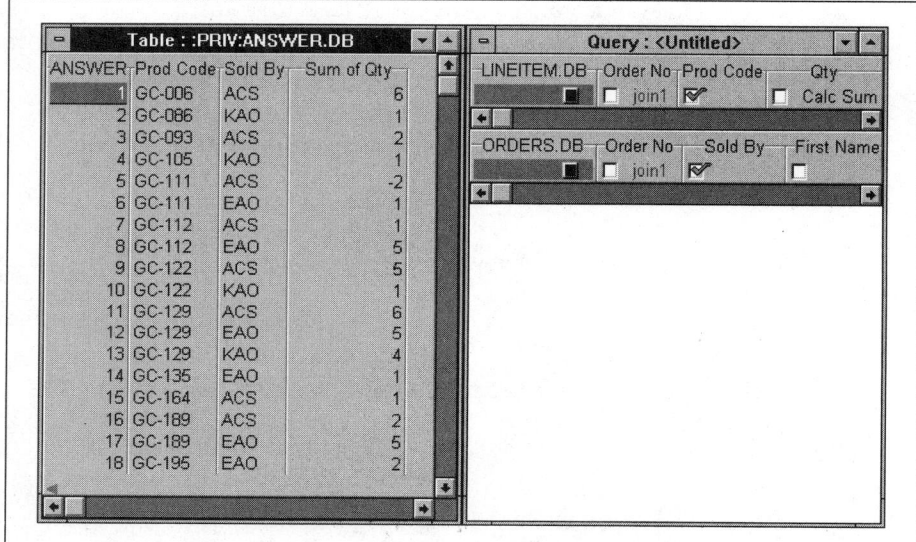

▸ Frequency Distributions

A frequency distribution tells you how many times a certain value appears. For a quick frequency distribution, combine the CALC COUNT ALL operator with a checked field (or fields). In the query shown in Figure 16.27, we checked the State field of the CustList query table for display and grouping. The expression CALC COUNT ALL counts the number of records containing each state. We used ALL in this example so that Paradox would count *all* records with the same state. (If we omitted ALL, Paradox would not count duplicates, and the COUNT of the State field in the Answer table would contain the number 1 for each group with at least one record in it.)

FIGURE 16.27 ▶

Frequency distribution of states represented in the CustList table

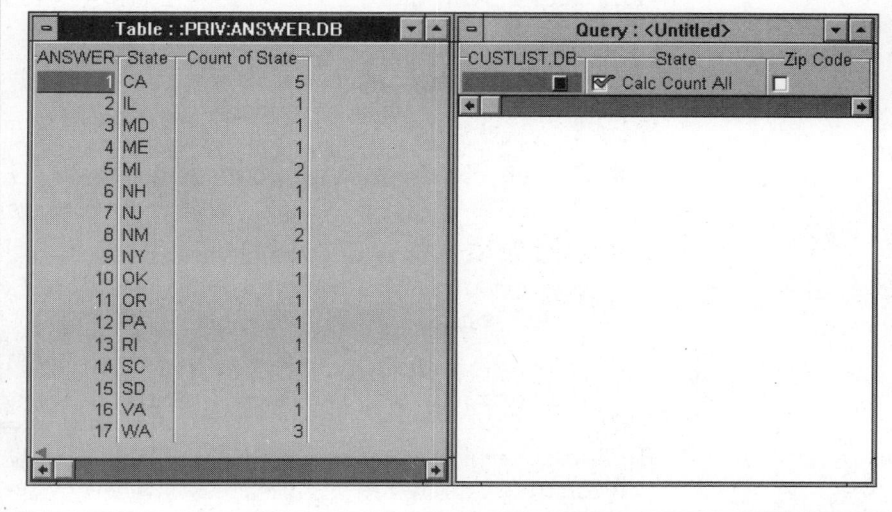

▶ Selecting Records Based on Summary Information

Suppose you want to know "Which products in the LineItem table have a value of 5 or greater in the Qty field?" For answers to questions like this, you use summary operators to select records based on a comparison to a summary calculation.

Here are the general steps for using summary operators in this way:

1. Check the fields that define the groups you want to compare against the summary calculation.

2. If you want to show the summary values, use the CALC keyword followed by the summary operator as usual, then type a comma and a space.

3. Omit the keyword CALC, and use the summary operator in a comparison expression—that is, an expression that uses <, >, =, <=, or >=.

The example in Figure 16.28 follows the three steps above and it answers the question posed earlier.

To understand this query better, you need to break it into its constituent parts:

- The checkmark in the Prod Code field groups the values by product. These values will be compared against the summary calculation.

- CALC SUM in the Qty field sums and displays the units sold for each product. You can omit this expression if you don't wish to display the sum.

- SUM >= 5 selects only records for which total units sold is greater than or equal to 5. The Answer table includes only those records.

To find out which states in the CustList table have only one customer, we ran the query shown in Figure 16.29. In this query, the checkmark in the State field groups the records by state and displays the contents of the

FIGURE 16.28 ▶

This query answers the question "Which products have we sold 5 or more units of?"

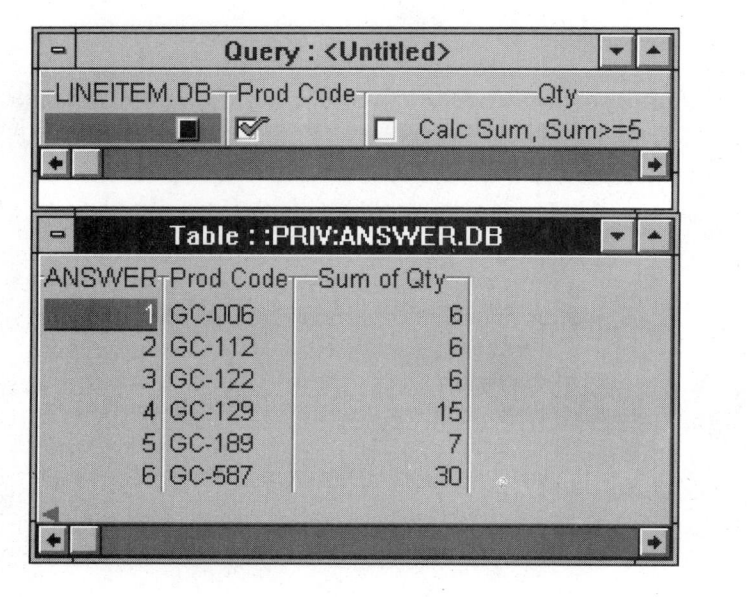

State field. The expression COUNT ALL = 1 counts the number of customers in each state, and displays only records in which the count (including duplicate states) is exactly 1. Here we omitted the CALC COUNT expression, so no field appears for the count. Nonetheless, the Answer table displays states represented by only one customer.

FIGURE 16.29

A query that isolates states in the CustList table represented by only one customer

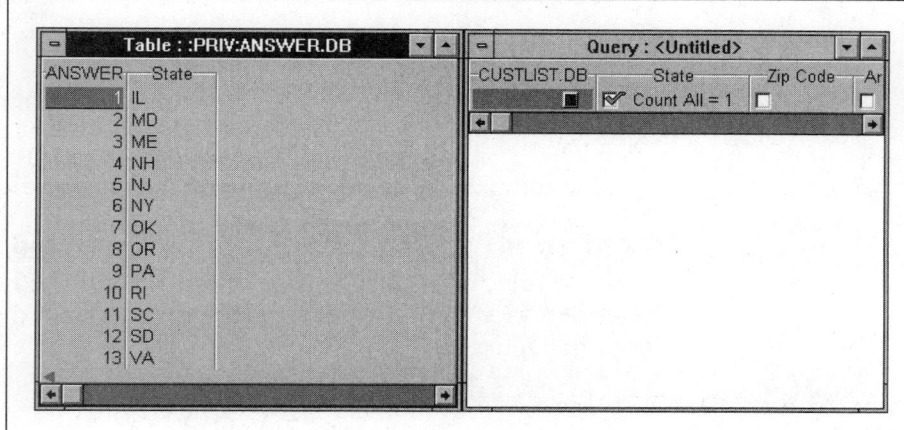

▶▶ *Complex Calculations with Multiple Tables*

To help you understand how with some ingenuity (and patience) you can use calculations to answer questions that require several steps, we'll calculate the total amount owed for each customer's order.

▶▶**TIP**

If you intend to run a sequence of queries on a regular basis (daily, weekly, monthly, and so on) or use them in a form or report, you should save each query. Chapter 9 explains how to save and reuse queries.

The first step is to calculate and update the Extended Price field in the LineItem table, using the query shown below.

After running the query, we saved it with the name *ExtPrice* so that we could reuse it later. (Figure 16.21 showed the results of calculating the extended price of records in the LineItem table.)

Next, you'll need to create a temporary table that holds the subtotal of the Extended Price for each order in the LineItem table, as shown in Figure 16.30. When creating the query, we checked the Order No field to group the calculation by order number and used CALC SUM in the Extended Price field to calculate the total extended price for all line items in each group. We also used the Answer Table Properties button in the Toolbar to rename the Answer table to *:gift_corner:subtotal.db (c:\pdoxwin\giftco\subtotal.db)*, and saved the query with the name *SubTotal* (see Chapter 9). Then we ran the query, which produced the Subtotal table shown in Figure 16.30.

As shown in Figure 16.31, the final query (which we named *OrdTotal*) calculates the total amount owed for each order and displays checked and calculated fields in the Answer table. Notice that the **OrdNo** example element links the Orders and SubTotal query tables, and the **CustNo** example element links Orders and CustList. In the Orders query table, we entered example elements **ship** (for shipping charges), **tax** (for the tax rate—0.0775 in all cases), and **paid** (for amount paid). Then we placed the **SubTotal** example element in the SubTotal field of the SubTotal query table. The final calculation appears below:

CALC **Subtotal** + (**Subtotal** * **Tax**) + **Ship** – **Paid** AS Total

FIGURE 16.30

The Subtotal query calculates the total extended price for each order in the LineItem table and saves the result in a table named **Subtotal**.

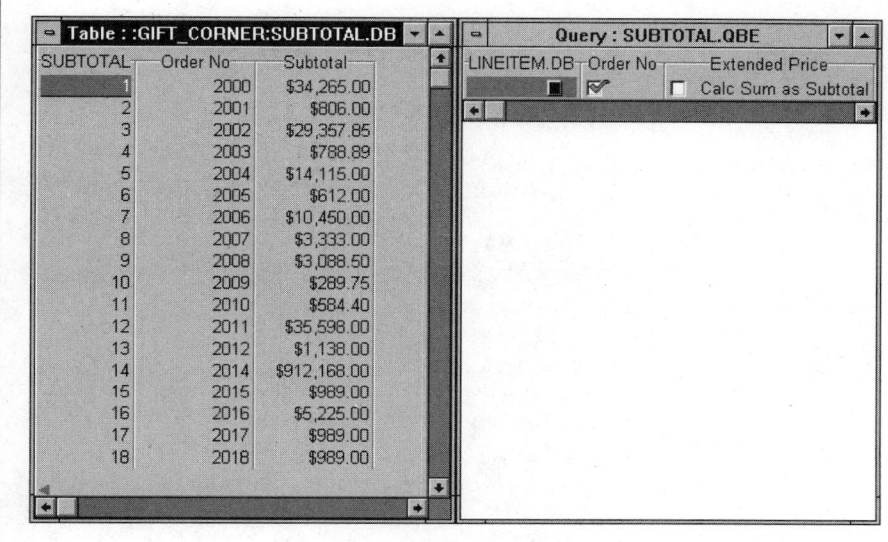

This calculation starts with the subtotal stored in the SubTotal field, adds the tax amount (subtotal times the tax rate), adds the shipping charge, then subtracts the amount the customer has already paid and displays the result in a field named *Total*.

 ▶▶ TIP

> **You can rerun the ExtPrice, SubTotal, and OrdTotal queries (in that order) whenever you want to view the latest order totals.**

▶▶ *Asking about Sets of Records*

SET queries ask questions about categories or sets of records, rather than about individual records. In essence, a SET query lets you answer questions that might otherwise require two or more queries.

FIGURE 16.31   ►

The OrdTotal query calculates the total order amount as SubTotal + Tax + Shipping Charge – Amount Paid.

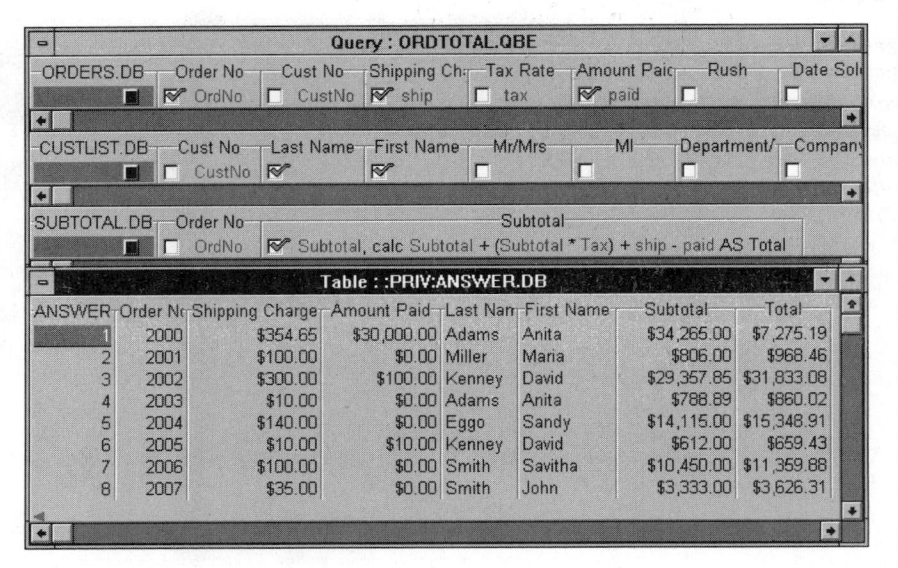

Suppose you want to track the quantity of each product purchased by your customers at the end of the year, and then ask further questions about those purchases. To begin, create the query shown in Figure 16.32 and use the Answer Table Properties button in the Toolbar to rename the Answer table to *:Work:YearEnd* (a table named *YearEnd* in your working directory). The figure illustrates the query and a portion of the YearEnd table that appears when you run the query.

After creating the YearEnd table, you can use SET queries with the set operators **ONLY, NO, EVERY,** and **EXACTLY** to ask questions about which customers did (and which did not) buy products in various categories. These operators are summarized in Table 16.3.

Figure 16.33 illustrates various set relationships, using shapes rather than products. The group of shapes on the left could be called *TestShapes*. We'll call this the *comparison set*. The group on the right in each example is a set of shapes we're comparing to TestShapes.

FIGURE 16.32

The query and a portion of the resulting YearEnd table created by combining fields from the LineItem and Orders tables

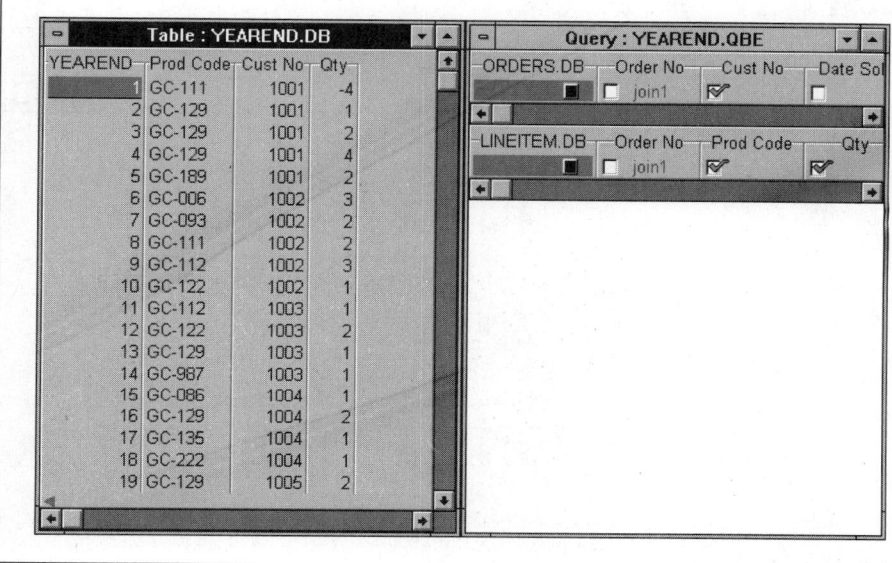

Advanced Queries and Calculations

Ch. **16**

TABLE 16.3: *Set Comparison Operators and Sample Questions*

SET OPERATOR	DISPLAYS	SAMPLE QUESTION
ONLY	Records that have only values of the defined set	Which customers have bought only computer equipment (Category ID 103)?
NO	Records that do not match any values in the defined set	Which customers did not buy any computer equipment?
EVERY	Records that match every value in the set	Which customers bought every product in the photo equipment category (Category ID 110)?
EXACTLY	Records that have exactly the same values as the defined set; no more or less (a combination of **ONLY** and **EVERY**)	Which customers bought every product in the photo equipment category, but no products in any other category?

FIGURE 16.33 ▶

An illustration of set relationships (EVERY, ONLY, EXACTLY, and NO)

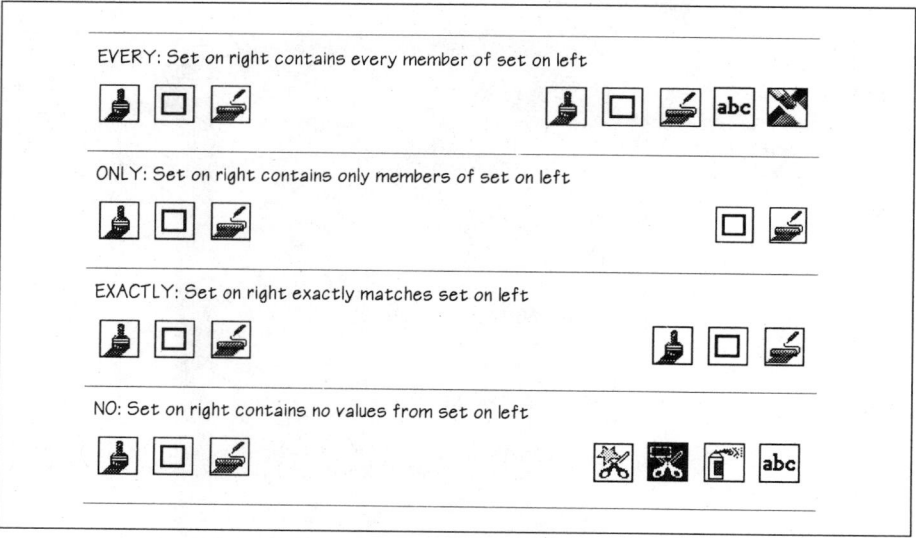

▶ Creating a SET Query

When designing a SET query, follow these general steps (we'll get more specific in a moment):

- Include one or more lines that define the comparison set. These lines will include the **SET** reserved word in the left-most column and an *example element* to group the set. Many comparison sets also include a *selection criterion* to restrict the set to specific values or ranges. (If you omit the selection criterion, the comparison set will be the entire table.)

 ▶▶**TIP**

Defining a set of records is similar to selecting records to include in the Answer table, except that you use example elements instead of checkmarks.

- Include one or more lines that define the second set of records that you want to compare. These lines will include an appropriate *set operator* (EVERY, ONLY, EXACTLY, or NO) and a *checkmark* or **GROUPBY** operator to group the records. Checked fields will appear in the Answer table. (GROUPBY fields are discussed later in this chapter.)

● If you wish, include one or more lines that display related information. These lines will contain linking *example elements* and *checkmarks*.

To illustrate the concepts presented above, we'll create a SET query that asks the question "Which customers bought items in the photo equipment category only (Category ID 110)?" The final query and its results appear in Figure 16.34.

FIGURE 16.34 ▶

This sample SET query displays customers who have purchased products in the photo equipment category (Category ID 110).

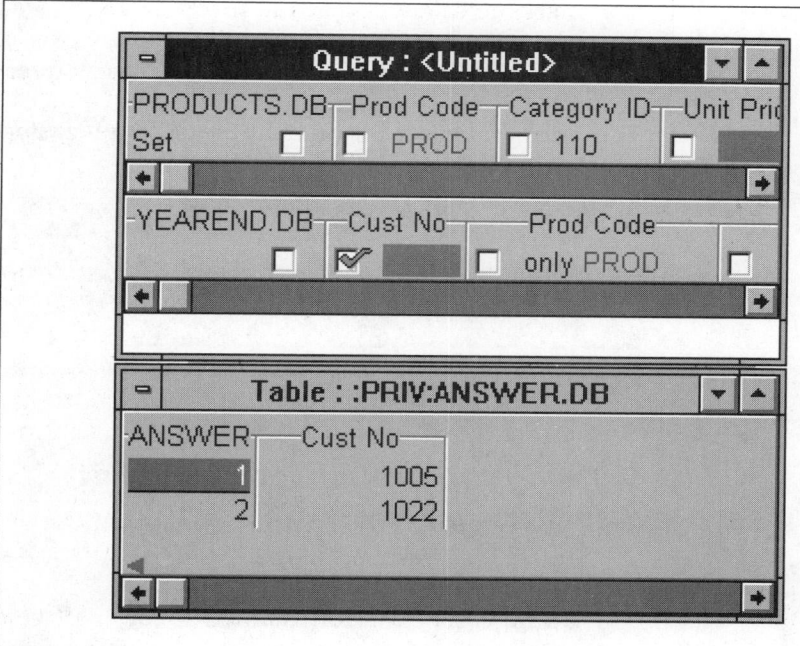

Defining the Comparison Set

Your first step is to define the comparison set, as follows:

1. Open the query table(s) for tables containing the records that will define the set. For example, open a new Query window and select *Products* as the table containing the set.

2. If you wish, enter *selection criteria* that further limit the records to include in the set. If the records are in more than one table, add the tables to the query windows and use example elements to link the tables. To select records in the photo equipment category, we would type **110** into the Category ID field of the Products table.

3. Enter the SET reserved word in the leftmost field of all query lines that define the set. To enter the reserved word, click in the leftmost field of the query table and type **S**. The word "Set" will appear below the table name.

4. Place an example element where you would normally use checkmarks to select and group fields. Since we want to compare groups of products, we would place the example element ***PROD*** into the Prod Code field of the Products query table.

The comparison set for our sample SET query appears below.

Defining the Second Set of Records

Once you've defined the comparison set, you can define the set of records to compare it against, as follows:

1. In the Query window defined so far, add the query table for the set of records to be compared. Continuing with our example, we would add the YearEnd table to the Query window.

2. Type a set operator into the common field that links this new query table to the table or tables containing the comparison set. For example, type **Only** into the Prod Code field of the YearEnd query table.

3. Follow the set operator with a space, then press F5 and type the same example element used in the comparison table (***PROD*** in this example).

4. Check the field that will group the records in this set and that will also appear in the Answer table (Cust No in this example).

▶ ▶ **N O T E**

> The GROUPBY operator, discussed in the next section, provides an alternative to checking fields.

Because our query is seeking customer numbers only, we don't need any additional tables or linking elements; therefore, we can go ahead and run the query now. Figure 16.34 shows the completed query and Answer table. In the figure, the ***PROD*** example element links the two sets, and ONLY is the set operator restricting the retrieved records to Category ID 110. The checkmark in the Cust No column defines that field as the one to display in the Answer table, and also groups the second set of records. That is, the checkmark in the Cust No field says "group together all the records with the same Cust No, then compare that group to the set of records in Products that contain the Category ID of 110."

The resulting Answer table lists customers who bought only photo equipment. (These customers may have bought only one type of photo equipment, or several different types of photo equipment.)

If you want to view customers who didn't buy any photo equipment at all, change the ONLY operator to NO and run the query again. To view customers who bought every type of photo equipment (and possibly products from other categories), use the EVERY operator. Finally, use the EXACTLY operator to see which customers have purchased exactly the products that make up the photo equipment category. The Answer table will include customers who bought every type of photo equipment, and no other product.

▶ ▶ **N O T E**

> You've probably discovered that SET queries aren't easy to put together. Remember that running several queries in sequence will ultimately achieve the same result as a SET query.

▶ Using the GROUPBY Operator

Checkmarks in SET queries with two or more tables specify which field or fields you want to see in the Answer table and define the group of records for the second set. If you want to group records by a field, without displaying that field, you can use the **GROUPBY** operator, rather than a checkmark, in the query table. Then you can use an example element next to the GROUPBY operator to look up data from that field in another table. (The GROUPBY operator can only be used in SET queries.)

 To place the GROUPBY operator in a query table, choose the GROUPBY checkmark (shown at left) from the check box menu for the field, or press Shift+F6 in the field until the GROUPBY operator appears.

In Figure 16.35, we've used the GROUPBY operator to display the *cities and states* in which only photo equipment was sold, rather than the customer number of people who bought photo equipment only.

FIGURE 16.35 ▶

The GROUPBY operator lets you use one field for grouping in a SET query and other fields to display results in the Answer table.

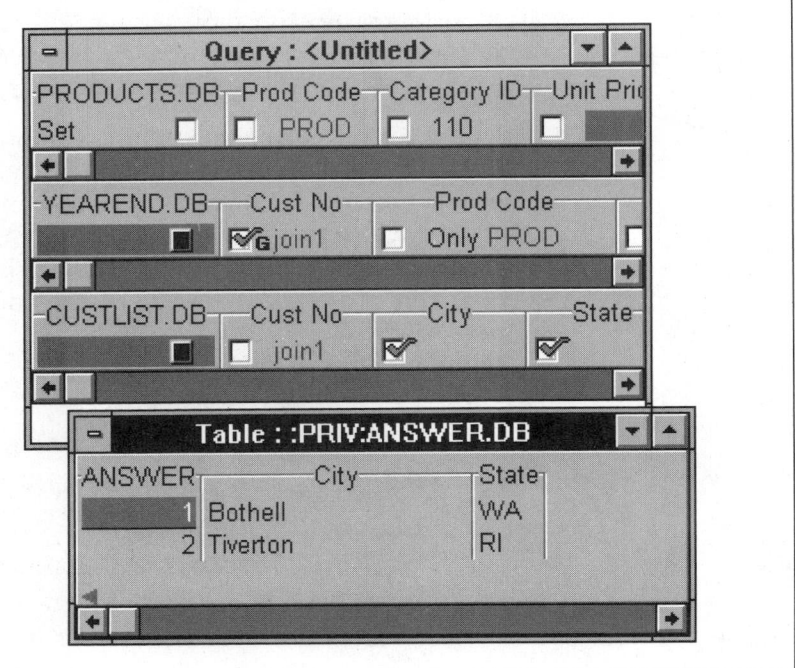

Compare the query in Figure 16.35 to the query in Figure 16.34, and notice the following differences:

- Instead of using a checkmark in the Cust No field to define that field for both grouping and display, the field contains the GROUPBY operator. Cust No is still the group being compared to the photo equipment set, but it will not appear in the Answer table.

- We've added a third table, CustList, to provide the city and state information we want.

- The *join1* example elements in the Cust No fields link the YearEnd and CustList query tables.

- The City and State fields are checked in the CustList table so they will appear in the Answer table.

▶ Comparing Records to Summary Values

In the preceding examples, you saw how SET queries can compare records in one table to a set of records in another table. You can also use SET queries to compare records in a table to a summary calculation within that table, such as an average or a sum. You can use any of the summary operators (AVERAGE, COUNT, MAX, MIN) to perform such an analysis.

Figure 16.36 shows an example using the CustList table. The first line of the query includes **Set** in the leftmost column and the example element named **limit** in the Credit Limit field. Because there are no search criteria in the top line of the query, the set includes all records in the table.

The checkmarks in the Last Name, First Name, and Credit Limit fields of the second query line mark the fields we want to see in the Answer table. The second line also includes the query criterion **> Average** *limit* to restrict the Answer table records to those in which credit limits are greater than the average credit limit. As a finishing touch, we also used the expression **calc AVERAGE** *limit* **as Avg Limit** to calculate and display the average credit limit amount of $6,200.

Note that if we had used **> Min** *limit* in place of **> Average** *limit* and **calc MIN** *limit* **as Min Limit** in place of **calc AVERAGE** *limit* **as**

FIGURE 16.36 ▶

A SET query that finds individuals with higher than average credit limits in the sample CustList table

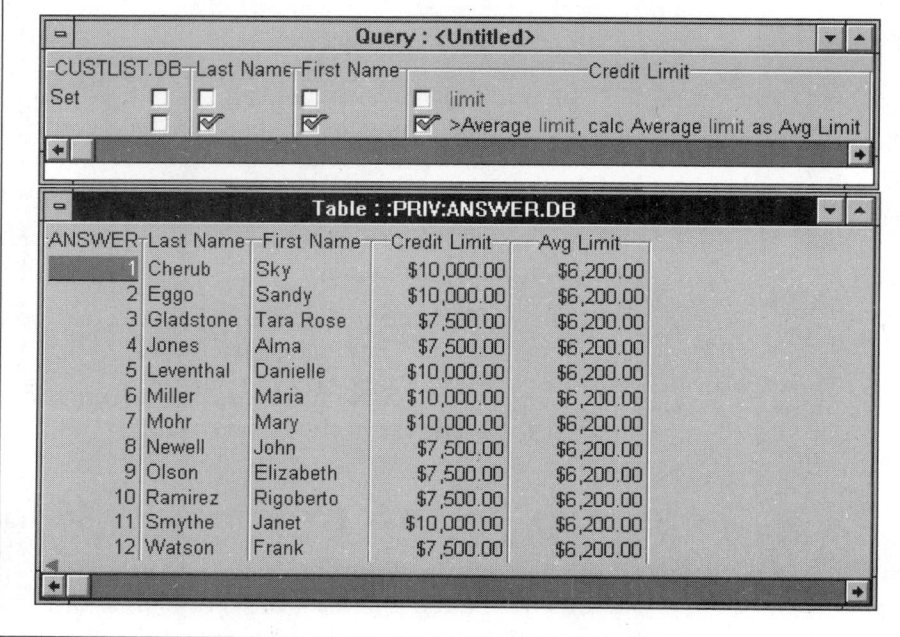

Avg Limit, the Answer table would display records containing values that are greater than the *smallest* credit limit. Using the criterion **Max limit** would display records containing the *highest* credit limits.

▶▶ *Calculating Percentages*

Paradox for Windows does not provide a simple way to calculate percentages. Fortunately, you can work around this problem.

Suppose you want to ask "How much does each product in my YearEnd table contribute to total sales?" One easy way to answer this question is to create a pie chart, which can calculate percentages automatically. To begin, open a new query for the YearEnd table, check the Prod Code field, type **Calc Sum** into the Qty field, and run the query. A sample query and the resulting Answer table appear in Figure 16.37.

Now click the Quick Graph button in the Toolbar, or choose <u>T</u>ools ▶ Quick <u>G</u>raph, or press Ctrl+F7. When the Define Graph dialog box

FIGURE 16.37

*The Answer table shows
the total units sold for
each product in the
YearEnd table.*

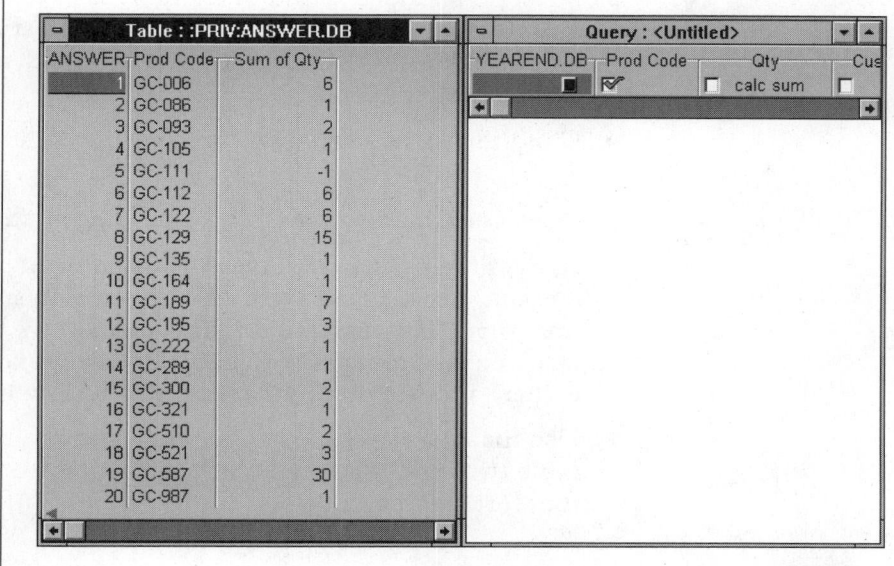

appears, click the drop-down arrow next to the Answer table name and
select *Prod Code* for the X-Axis. Next click the Y-Value option in the dialog box, open the Answer table drop-down list again, and select *Sum of
Qty*. Click OK. A bar graph appears.

To switch to a pie chart, click the Design button in the Toolbar, inspect
(right-click) the graph, and choose Graph Type ➤ 2D Pie. Finally, click
the View Data button in the Toolbar to view the graph. (See Chapter 13
for additional information on creating graphs and pie charts.)

The pie chart will be quite cluttered if your company sells many different products. If you prefer to show the percentages in a form or report,
proceed as follows:

1. First, you need to know the grand total of units sold. To get this
   information, close the Answer table and pie chart form if they're
   still open. Then, open a new Query window for the YearEnd table,
   type **Calc Sum** into the Qty field (don't add any checkmarks),
   and run the query to get the grand total.

2. Jot down the number that appears in the Answer table, then close
   the Answer table window. Let's assume the number is **89**.

3. Now, set up the YearEnd query table shown in Figure 16.37 to get a subtotal of units sold for each product. Just check the Prod Code field, put **CALC sum** in the Qty field, and run the query to get the desired results.

4. Close the Answer table and create a new query, specifying *Answer* as the table to query.

5. Place checkmarks in the Prod Code and Sum of Qty fields.

6. In the Sum of Qty field, type the ***units*** example element, a comma, a space, and the CALC expression shown in Figure 16.38. The expression *CALC **units**/89 as Percent* divides the value in the Sum of Qty field by 89 (the grand total determined earlier) and will place the result in a field named *Percent*.

7. Use the Answer Table Properties button to rename the Answer table (we used the name *:work:percent* to save the Percent table in the working directory*)*.

FIGURE 16.38 ►

Each product's contribution to total units sold is displayed in the right-most column.

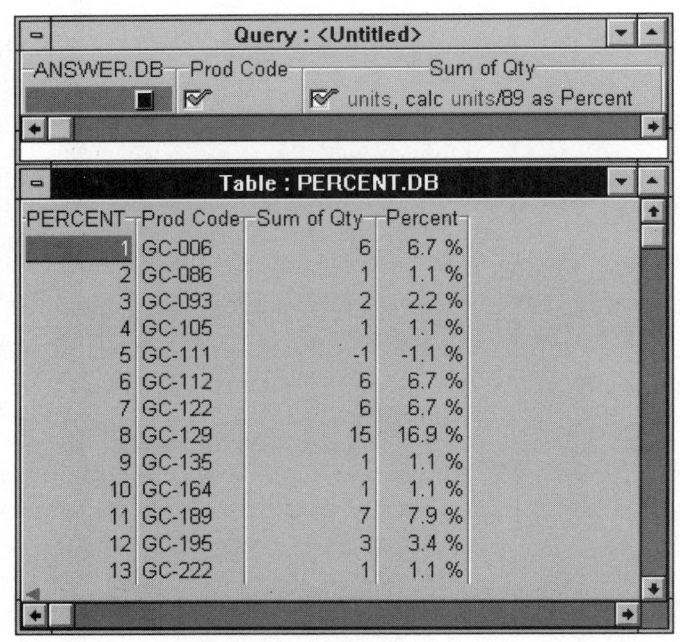

When you run the query, the resulting Percent table will display the information you want. To display the numbers as percents, inspect the Percent column and choose Number Format ➤ Percent. Figure 16.38 shows the final result.

▶▶ *Using DDE to Display "Live" Results in Queries*

Chapter 6 explained how to use DDE (Dynamic Data Exchange) to set up a dynamic link between a field in a Paradox table and various cells in a spreadsheet application. You can use similar techniques to set up a "live" DDE link between a Paradox table and a query.

Imagine that you'd like to know which customers live in a particular state, simply by highlighting that state in the States table. Or maybe you'd like to see what orders a customer has placed, just by highlighting that customer's record in the CustList table. DDE makes it easy to update a query result automatically as you scroll through a DDE server table.

Setting up a DDE query requires several steps, but each one is easy to do. We'll start with the general steps, and then look at the states/customers and customers/orders scenarios presented just above.

▶ *Setting Up a DDE Query*

Here are the general steps for setting up a DDE query:

1. Clear the Desktop (Window ➤ Close All), then create your query normally. The query can use one or more related tables and you can check any fields you want. You also can use criteria to select specific records; however, you should *omit* the criterion for the field that will use a DDE link.

2. Next, open the DDE server table that will supply the criterion as you scroll through its records. For example, choose File ➤ Open ➤ Table, and double-click the table name you want to open. (Stay in Table View, since this technique does not work in Form View.)

3. Starting in any record you wish, highlight the field in the DDE server table that will supply the data for your query criterion. Then choose <u>E</u>dit ➤ <u>C</u>opy to copy the field to the Windows Clipboard.

 ►►**TIP**

If you know which record in the table has a matching value in the table that you're querying, you can highlight that record. Then, when you run the query for the first time (see step 5 below), you'll immediately see results in the Answer table.

4. Switch back to the Query window, click in the column that corresponds to the field you just copied, then choose <u>E</u>dit ➤ Paste <u>L</u>ink. DDE link text will appear in the current column of the query table.

5. Run your query to produce an Answer table (press F8 or click the Run Query button). Don't worry if the Answer table is empty the first time you run the query.

6. To activate the DDE link, switch to the Query window and choose <u>Q</u>uery ➤ <u>W</u>ait for DDE (this places a checkmark next to the <u>W</u>ait for DDE option on the <u>Q</u>uery menu).

7. Now switch back to the DDE server table and scroll through its records to see the results.

 ►►**TIP**

As you work through the steps above, you may want to reorganize the windows on the Desktop by choosing <u>W</u>indow ➤ <u>T</u>ile or <u>W</u>indow ➤ <u>C</u>ascade.

Should you wish to save or change the query, you'll need to deactivate the DDE link. Just return to the Query window and choose <u>Q</u>uery ➤ <u>W</u>ait for DDE (this removes the checkmark from the <u>W</u>ait for DDE option on the <u>Q</u>uery menu).

▶ *A States and Customers Example*

The above steps will seem much easier once you've tried an example or two. Let's start with an easy one, in which you scroll through the States table to see which customers reside in each state. The following steps correspond to the general steps given in the previous section:

1. Choose <u>W</u>indow ➤ Close <u>A</u>ll to clear the Desktop, and answer any prompts that appear. Now create a simple query on the Cust-List table, as shown below:

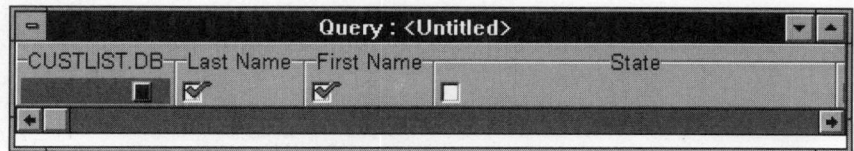

2. Choose <u>F</u>ile ➤ <u>O</u>pen ➤ <u>T</u>able, type **states**, and choose OK.

3. Click in the State field of any record and choose <u>E</u>dit ➤ <u>C</u>opy. If you wish, choose <u>W</u>indow ➤ <u>C</u>ascade or <u>W</u>indow ➤ <u>T</u>ile and then arrange the open windows neatly on the screen.

4. Switch back to the Query window, click in the State column, then choose <u>E</u>dit ➤ Paste <u>L</u>ink. Your screen will resemble Figure 16.39.

5. Press F8 to produce an Answer table. Don't worry if Answer is empty. We'll fix that in a moment.

6. Switch to the Query window and choose Query ➤ <u>W</u>ait for DDE (this activates the DDE link). Rearrange the open windows on the screen once more. For example, choose <u>W</u>indow ➤ <u>C</u>ascade or <u>W</u>indow ➤ <u>T</u>ile, then drag and resize the windows as needed.

7. Now switch back to the States table, scroll through its records, and watch the Answer table carefully to see the results.

Figure 16.40 shows what happened when we highlighted the CA record in the States table. Notice how the Answer table is updated instantly with customers who reside in California. Not bad!

If you want to save the query, switch back to the Query window and choose Query ➤ <u>W</u>ait for DDE (this deactivates the DDE link). Then choose <u>F</u>ile ➤ <u>S</u>ave, type a query name, and choose OK.

FIGURE 16.39 ▶

The States Table View window and the new Query window after pasting the DDE link into the query's State field.

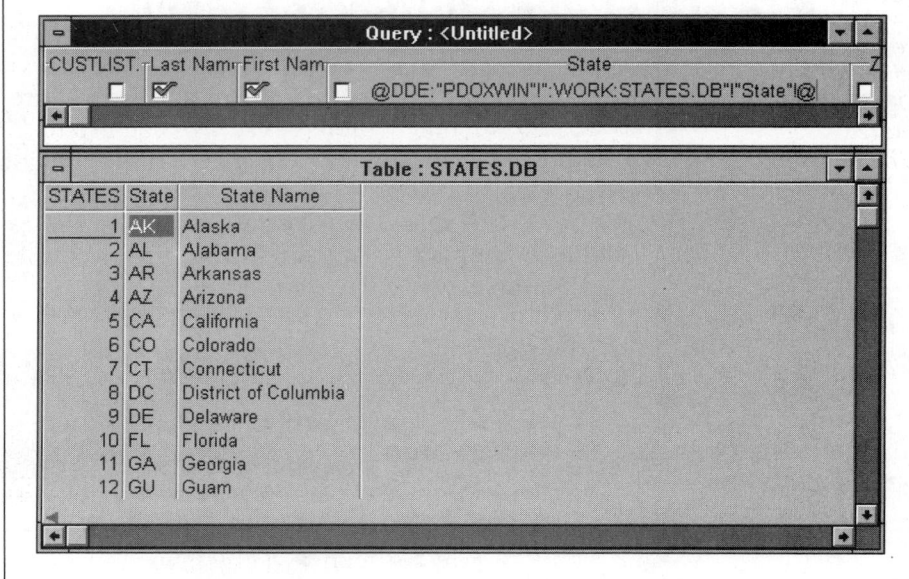

To reuse the query in the future, open it as usual (File ➤ Open ➤ Query), and press F8 to run the query; the States and Answer tables will appear automatically. Now switch back to the Query window, choose Query ➤ Wait for DDE (to activate DDE), and scroll through the States table as before.

There's one "gotcha" that can bite you when using DDE links to supply query criteria. If the data you're scrolling through contains a reserved word (such as AND, OR, NOT, or BLANK), Paradox will display a "Syntax error in expression" message when you scroll to that record. For instance, if you scroll to the "OR" entry for the state of Oregon in the States table, the error message will appear.

Unfortunately, there's no good solution to this problem, other than clicking OK in the message dialog box and moving the cursor to another record. This problem with "reserved words that are really data" is

FIGURE 16.40

The Desktop after activating the "Wait for DDE" and clicking on a state record for which we have customers.

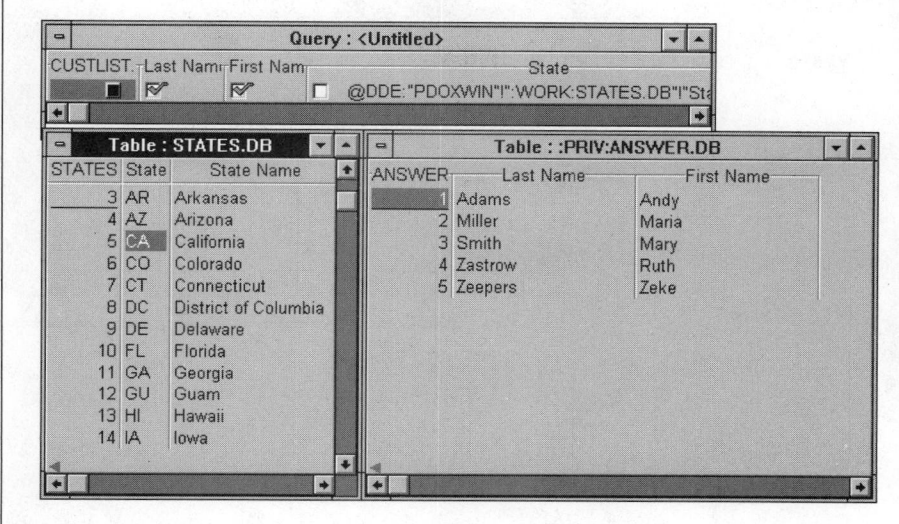

simply a DDE quirk that you'll have to learn to live with. As an alternative to using DDE queries, you can use linked tables in a multitable form or report to show related data such as States and Customers or Customers and Orders (see Chapter 17).

▶ *A Customers and Orders Example*

Now that you've seen a complete states and customers example, we'll breeze through an example that displays orders for a highlighted customer in the CustList table. Here's the "Cliff's Notes" version of the steps:

1. Clear the Desktop (Choose <u>W</u>indow ➤ Close <u>A</u>ll), then create a query on the Orders, LineItem, and Products tables, as shown below.

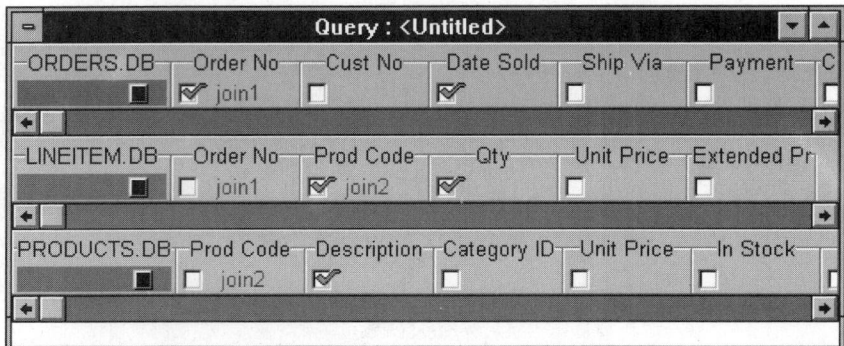

2. Choose File ➤ Open ➤ Table, type **custlist**, and choose OK.

3. Click in the Cust No field of any record and choose Edit ➤ Copy. Rearrange the open windows neatly on the screen.

4. Switch back to the Query window, click in the Cust No column of the Orders table, then choose Edit ➤ Paste Link.

5. Press F8 to produce an Answer table. Again, don't worry if Answer is empty.

6. Switch to the Query window and choose Query ➤ Wait for DDE. Rearrange the open windows on the screen once more.

7. Now switch back to the CustList table and scroll through its records to see the results.

Figure 16.41 shows what happened when we highlighted the record for customer number 1002 in the CustList table. Notice how the Answer table is updated instantly with orders for that customer.

▶▶ *Changing the Query Window Options*

Paradox offers several ways to customize the appearance and behavior of the Query window. First, you can display query tables in the Query window in a tiled or cascaded arrangement. We've used the tiled arrangement throughout this book, since it is the default choice.

FIGURE 16.41 ▶

The Desktop after activating the "Wait for DDE" and clicking on a customer record for which we have orders.

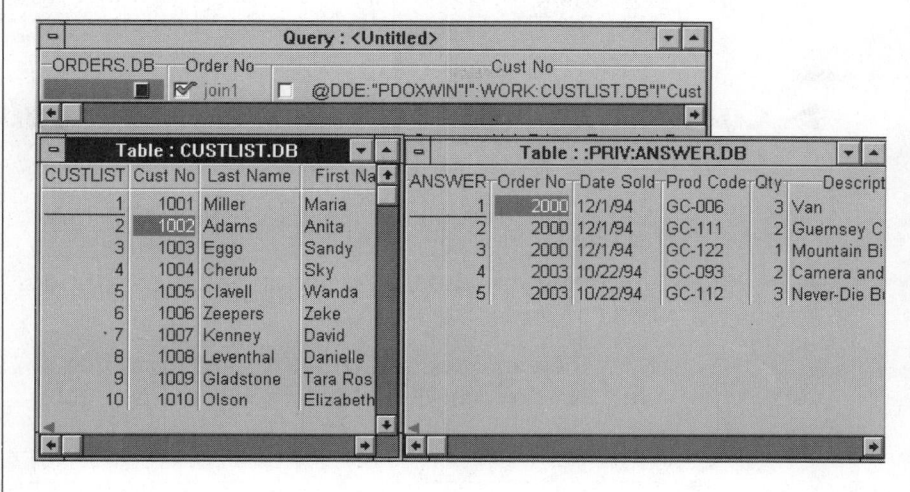

In the cascaded arrangement, each query table floats freely in the Query window, and you can resize and rearrange the query tables as needed. To select the cascaded arrangement, choose <u>V</u>iew ▶ <u>C</u>ascade Tables from the Query window menus. Figure 16.42 shows a new Query window after we added the Products and Category tables, chose <u>V</u>iew ▶ <u>C</u>ascade Tables, and rearranged and resized the windows.

FIGURE 16.42 ▶

A cascaded arrangement of query tables within a Query window

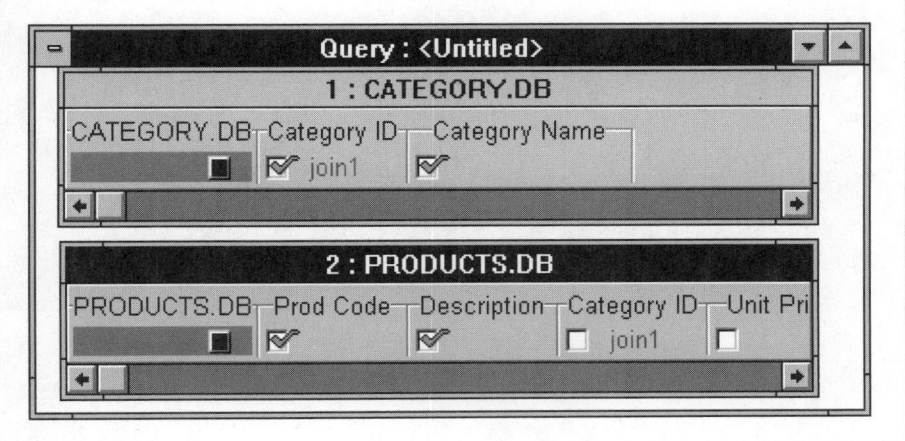

To return to the tiled arrangement shown throughout this book, choose View ➤ Tile Tables.

▶ Controlling How Paradox Handles Tables When You Run a Query

You can set several options that tell Paradox how to run your queries and what kind of checkmarks to use as the default. To begin setting these options, choose Properties ➤ Query Options. You'll see the dialog box shown in Figure 16.43.

Let's look at areas in the Query Options dialog box that control the way Paradox handles tables when you run a query.

FIGURE 16.43 ▶

The Query Options dialog box lets you set options that tell Paradox how to run your queries and what kind of checkmarks to use as the default.

Query Options

Table Update Handling:
- ◯ Restart Query On Changes
- ◯ Lock All Tables To Prevent Changes
- ◉ Ignore Source Changes

Auxiliary Table Option:
- ◯ Fast Queries (No Auxiliary Tables)
- ◉ Generate Auxiliary Tables

Default Checkmark Type:
- ◉ Check
- ◯ Check Plus

Queries Against Remote Tables:
- ◉ Query May Be Local Or Remote
- ◯ Run Query Remotely
- ◯ Run Query Locally

[OK]   [Cancel]   [Help]

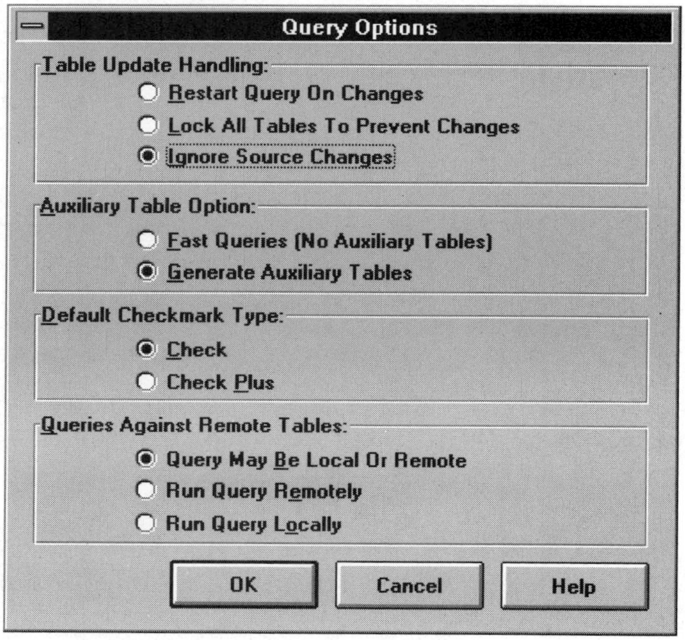

Controlling What Happens When Network Users Update Source Tables

The Table Update Handling area tells Paradox what to do if data in the source table changes while you're running a query in a multiuser (network) environment. In this area, you'll find three options:

Restart Query on Changes   Starts the query over if source data changes while the query is running. This is the fastest option when you know that no one will be changing data in the tables you're querying.

Lock All Tables to Prevent Changes   Locks all other users out of tables that are needed while the query is running. (This option is the least polite to other users.) If Paradox cannot lock a table, the query stops. If a lock fails, you must start the query again.

Ignore Source Changes   Runs the query even if someone changes the source data while it's running. This option, which is the fastest, is useful for "rough" queries where accuracy is not the top concern.

NOTE

The Properties ➤ Query Options in the Query window are similar to the Report ➤ Restart Options available from the Report Design window menus (see Chapter 12).

Controlling Whether Auxiliary Tables Appear

Recall that CHANGETO, DELETE, and INSERT queries normally generate auxiliary tables that show you which data the query changed. The Auxiliary Table Options let you control whether Paradox generates those auxiliary tables when it runs your queries. Here's what they do:

Fast Queries (No Auxiliary Tables)   If you don't want to generate auxiliary tables, select this option. Your queries will run faster. But beware! Choosing this option has one major drawback: You *will not* be able to use the auxiliary tables to back out of a botched CHANGETO, DELETE, or INSERT query, as explained in Chapters 9 and 18.

Generate Auxiliary Tables   When you select this option, Paradox will always generate auxiliary tables during a CHANGETO, DELETE, or INSERT query. Though slower than the Fast Queries option, this one is safer and it is the default setting.

▶ ▶ N O T E

> The Auxiliary Table Option settings have no effect on the Answer or Error tables. Paradox will always create these tables as needed.

▶ *Controlling Queries Against Remote Tables*

What do you think happens when you query SQL tables that are stored on remote servers? Will the remote data be processed on the remote server or on your local hard disk? Paradox will use your settings in the Queries Against Remote Tables area to answer these puzzlers, as follows:

Query May Be Local Or Remote   Select this option if you want Paradox to decide the most efficient place to process your query. This is the default "no-brainer" setting. Just sit back and let Paradox make your decisions.

Run Query Remotely   Select this option if you want Paradox to process your query on the remote server.

Run Query Locally   Select this option if you want Paradox to process your query on the local hard disk.

▶ ▶ N O T E

> When working with remote server tables, you don't need to worry about writing SQL statements—Paradox will handle all the translations automatically. However, if you're into pain and punishment, you can use the SQL Editor to view and type SQL statements yourself. To start the SQL Editor, open or create your query as usual, then choose Query ➤ Show SQL. For more information about the SQL Editor, please see the SQL Editor topic in the online Help and Appendix B.

► *Controlling the Default Checkmark Type*

Recall from Chapter 9 that Paradox offers two main types of checkmarks. The *Check* checkmark shows all unique values for the checked field, in sorted (A to Z) order. The *Check Plus* checkmark shows *all* values in a field, including duplicates, without sorting the results. In single-table queries, Check Plus also allows you to create a direct query view with live, editable fields.

You can use the Default Checkmark Type area in the Query Options dialog box to choose the default checkmark that appears when you click an empty check box or press F6 in the Query window. Your choices are Check (use the plain Check by default) or Check Plus (use the Check Plus by default).

► ►**T I P**

If you plan to create many "live" direct view queries, you can save yourself some time by selecting Check Plus as the default checkmark type.

► *Saving the Query Options*

To save the current Query Options and your choice of tiled or cascaded query tables, choose Properties ► Save As Default. To restore the previous options as the default, choose Properties ► Restore Default.

In this chapter you've learned how to create complex queries that join data from multiple tables into a single table and how to perform math calculations. In the next chapter, we'll show you techniques for creating forms and reports that combine data from multiple tables and perform calculations.

▶ ▶ CHAPTER **17**

Advanced Form
and Report Techniques

—

FAST TRACK

typing field object names, enter the field object name only (without brackets or a period), as in *Qty1* or *MySales*.

▶ **To copy field names into your calculation**   **980**

position the insertion point in the text box below the Calculated check box, select the field from the table's drop-down list, and select a summary operator from the Summary drop-down list (if you wish). Then click the Copy Field button.

▶ **You can perform summary calculations on fields**   **986**

and you can perform calculations within the summaries. For example, the calculation *SUM([LINEITEM.Qty])* would calculate the total number of units ordered. *SUM([LINEITEM.Qty]*[LINEITEM.Unit Price])* * *1.0725* would calculate the total extended price with 7.25% tax. You cannot perform summaries on calculated fields; instead, just repeat the calculation inside the parentheses rather than using the calculated field name.

▶ **To define a multitable document**   **991**

identify the tables you want to use in the Data Model dialog box and define the relationship (if any) between the tables. Or use a previously saved data model or query.

▶ **To draw a link between two tables in the Data Model dialog box**   **995**

drag the mouse from the master table in the data model area to the detail table. If the Define Link dialog box appears, select the master table field to link and the detail index, then choose OK.

▶ ▶ *I*n this chapter you'll learn how to create sophisticated design documents that perform calculations on your data and allow you to display, edit, and print data from multiple tables. The techniques in this chapter may not make your documents prettier, but they'll surely make them "smarter" and more useful.

Before attempting the advanced techniques presented here, you should know how to design forms and reports (Chapters 10 through 12), understand multitable database design (Chapter 5), and be familiar with using queries to perform calculations and link multiple tables (Chapter 16). You may also wish to review the structure and purpose of the CustList, Orders, LineItem, and Products tables presented at the end of Chapter 5 and the beginning of Chapter 16, since we'll use them in examples throughout this chapter.

 ▶ ▶ **N O T E**

> We'll frequently use the term "design documents" in place of "forms and reports" when explaining procedures that apply equally to form and report design.

▶ ▶ *Calculating Data in Design Documents*

You can place summary and calculated fields anywhere in a design document to perform a variety of useful calculations on your data. In many cases, a few strategically placed calculations and the multitable techniques covered later in this chapter can save you the trouble of designing complex queries that store temporary tables on your computer's disk.

Before diving into the topic of calculations, you should understand that summary and calculated fields can *display* or *print* data only; they *never* store data in your tables and they *cannot* be edited. For that job, you must use a query or an ObjectPAL method. For example, you can use a calculated field to multiply quantity ordered by unit price so you can display or print the extended price of a line item in an order. However, you cannot store the result of that calculation in the Extended Price field of a table without using a Changeto query or an ObjectPAL method.

NOTE

In Chapter 19 you'll find out how to use ObjectPAL to update fields with calculation results.

To place a summary or calculated field in a design document, follow these steps:

1. Open a form or report in the Design window.

2. If you want to create a new summary or calculated field, use the Field tool in the Toolbar (see Chapter 10). Alternatively, you can select an existing field and redefine it as a summary or calculated field.

3. Right-click (inspect) the field, and choose Define Field from the property menu.

4. Click the menu header (…) or press ↵.

If you're designing a report, you'll see the Define Field Object dialog box shown in Figure 17.1. If you're designing a form, the Normal, Unique, and Cumulative options in the Summary area will be absent. From here, the remaining steps depend on whether you want to define a *summary field* or a *calculated field*, as outlined in the sections that follow.

FIGURE 17.1 ►

The Define Field Object dialog box for a report. The Normal, Unique, and Cumulative options do not appear when you're defining a field object in a form.

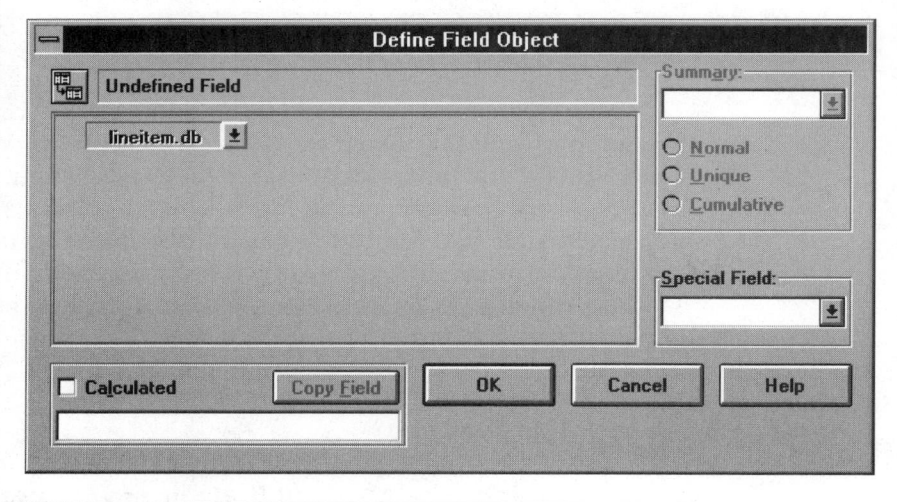

► Defining Summary Fields

Summary fields perform statistical calculations on a set of records in a table. In Chapter 13 you discovered how to use summary operators in graphs and crosstabs, and in Chapter 16 you learned about summary operators used with queries. The operators used with summary fields are basically the same. You can use them to sum (total), count, or average the values in a field; find the minimum or maximum value in a field; or find the standard deviation or variance of values in a field. Table 17.1 lists, in alphabetical order, the summary operators available in design documents. Notice that the First, Last, and Prev operators are available in reports only.

► **TABLE 17.1:** *Summary Operators Used in Forms and Reports*

SUMMARY OPERATOR	CALCULATES
Avg	Average of non-empty values in the set
Count	Number of non-empty values in the set
First	(In reports only) First value in the set

▶ **TABLE 17.1:** *Summary Operators Used in Forms and Reports (continued)*

SUMMARY OPERATOR	CALCULATES
Last	(In reports only) Last value in the set
Max	Highest value in the set
Min	Lowest value in the set
Prev	(In reports only) Previous value in the set
Std	Standard deviation of values in the set
Sum	Total of non-empty values in the set
Var	Statistical variance of values in the set

To define a summary field, open the Define Field Object dialog box as described above, then follow these steps:

1. Click the drop-down arrow next to the table that contains the field you want to summarize, then select the field. (If you plan to use the Count operator, selecting the table's primary key field will give you the most accurate count.)

2. Click the Summary drop-down list and select a summary operator. The summary statement will appear in the box below the Define Field Object title bar, as shown in Figure 17.2.

3. If you're designing a report, you can select the Normal, Unique, or Cumulative summary option, as discussed below (Normal is the default choice). These options appear below the drop-down list of summary operators.

4. When you're finished, choose OK to return to the Design window.

When you return to the Design window, the field's label and name will change automatically, reflecting the summary operator you selected. (Of course, if you defined an unlabeled field, it will stay unlabeled!) Figure 17.3 illustrates the label (*Sum(Qty):*) and the field object name (*Qty*) that Paradox supplied after we selected *Qty* in step 1 and the *Sum* operator in step 2 above. As Figure 17.3 shows, the name of the field object will appear in the status bar when you select the field and

Form Report Techniques

▶

Ch.
17

in the header of the property menu when you inspect the field. (As you'll learn later, you can use field object names in calculated fields.)

FIGURE 17.2

The Design Field Object dialog box after choosing a summary operator and a field to summarize

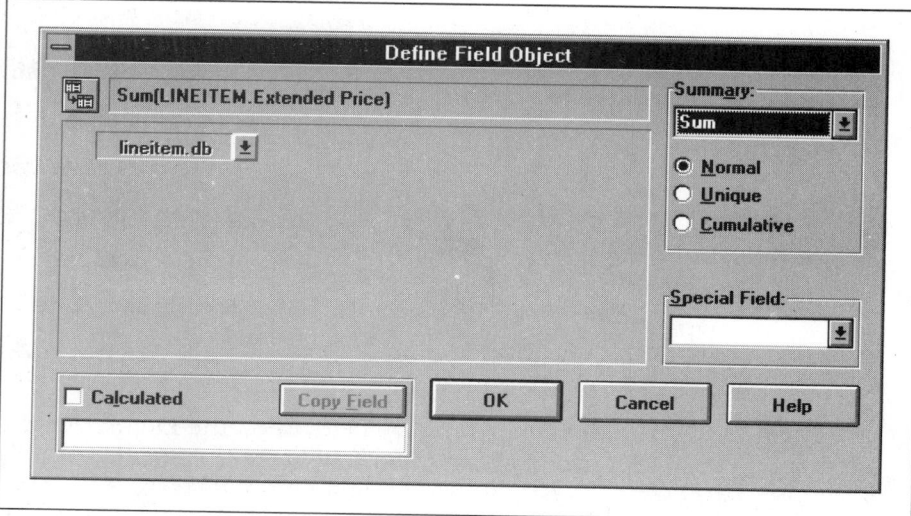

FIGURE 17.3

After you choose a field and a summary operator, Paradox assigns a label and field object name automatically.

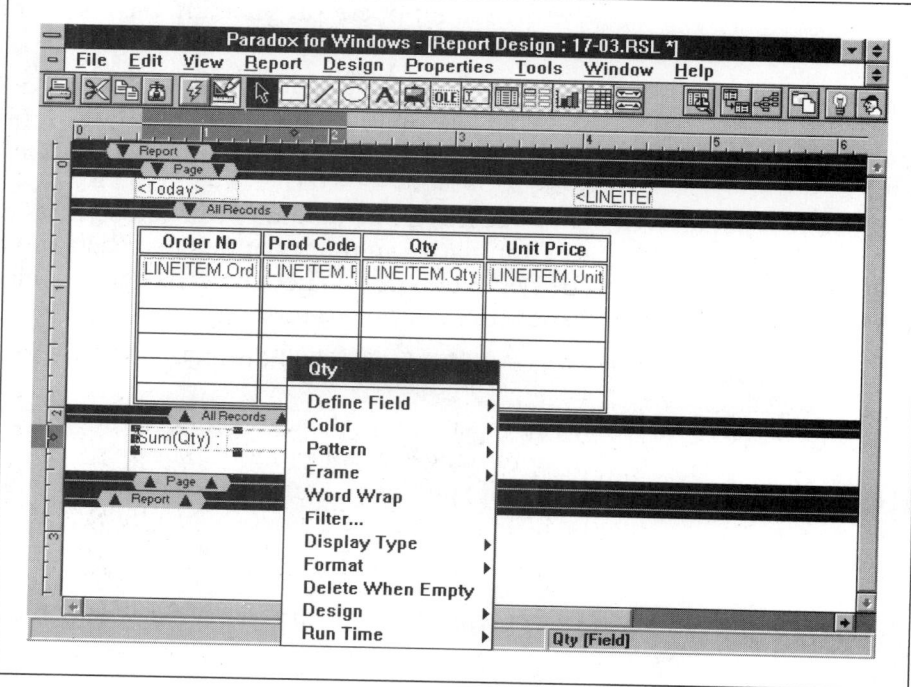

After defining the summary field, you can click the View Data button or press F8 to see the results of the summary operation. In Figure 17.3, for example, the summary field will total the number of units ordered on each page, with the total appearing in the page footer. If you need to change the field you're summarizing or the summary operator, simply return to the Design window, open the Define Field Object dialog box, and repeat the steps above.

Normal, Unique, and Cumulative Summaries

The Normal, Unique, and Cumulative summary options are available in the Define Field Object dialog box for reports only. These options control how Paradox will perform the summary:

Normal Normal summaries consider all non-empty values, including duplicates, in the set of records being summarized. This is the default selection.

Unique Unique summaries consider unique non-empty values only, ignoring duplicates. For example, you could use the Count summary operator with Unique to answer the question "In how many California zip codes do we have customers?" Note that selecting Unique with a Sum or Avg operator will *not* yield accurate results, since duplicate values are ignored.

Cumulative Cumulative summaries return a running total for the operation they are performing. In a cumulative sum, for example, the summary field is set to zero initially, then it keeps a running total from the start of the report through the end of the current set. A cumulative summary is often used in the page footer band to display the running total from the beginning of the report to the end of the current page.

Understanding Scope in Summary Fields

The location of a summary field in a form or report design determines the set or *scope* of records used to calculate the result. If you're designing a report, the type of summary you select (normal, unique, or cumulative) also governs the scope. We could describe all the technical details of scope, but since the concept is really quite intuitive, let's dispense with that and look at an example instead.

Figure 17.4 presents the last page of a report for the LineItem table described in Chapters 5 and 16. This report is grouped by product code (Prod Code) and illustrates three levels of summary (we used the <u>N</u>ormal

FIGURE 17.4

This report is grouped by product code (Prod Code) and shows summary totals at the group level, page level, and overall report level. The group bands are sorted in descending order by product code.

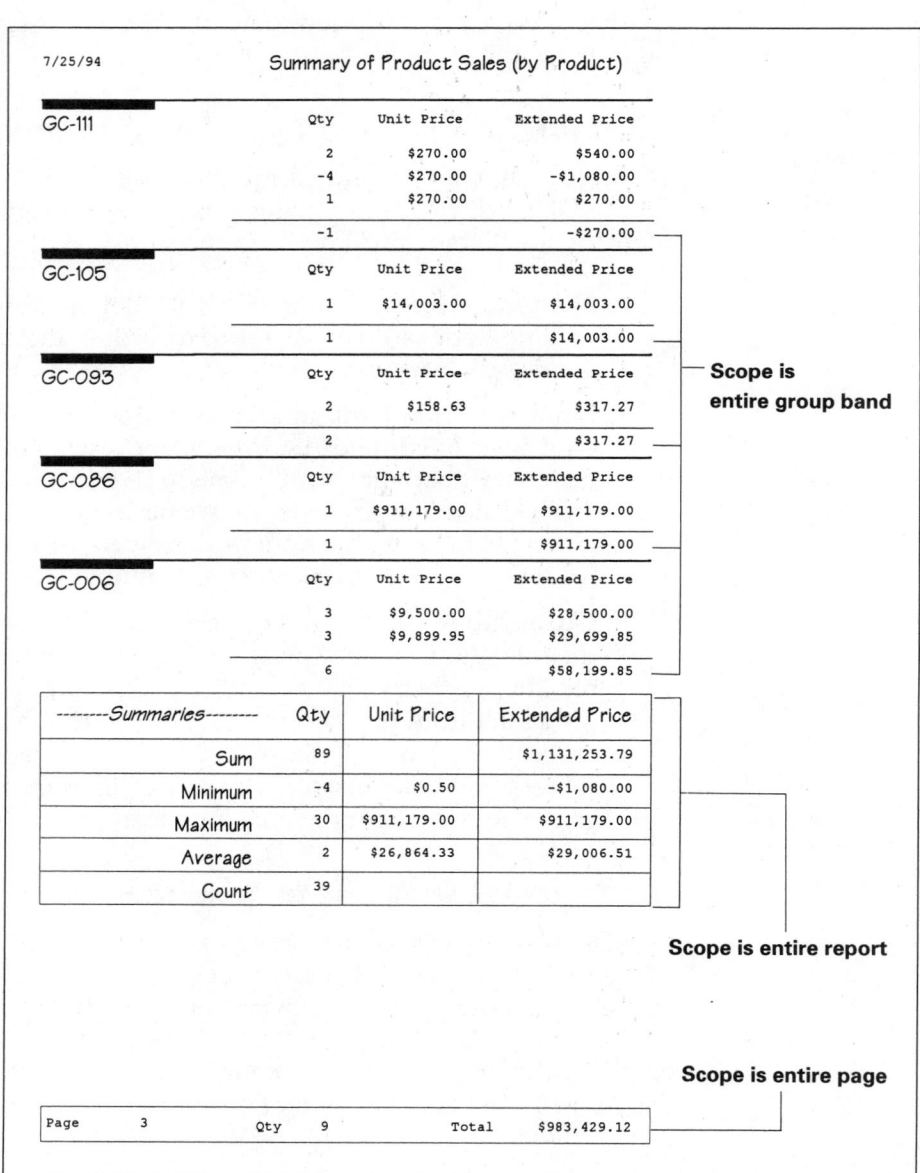

summary method). The first level shows the quantity, unit price, and extended price for each group of products sold. The next level is the page footer, which totals the quantity and extended price for all products on the page. Finally, the "Summaries" section at the end of the report provides an overall summary of the total quantity and extended price for all records; the minimum, maximum, and average quantity, unit price, and extended price for all records; and the count of the individual line items for the entire report.

▶ ▶ N O T E

> **Throughout this chapter, we calculated the extended price values by multiplying the LineItem table's Qty field times the table's Unit Price field, rather than using the Extended Price field. This is faster and more accurate because we don't have to run a query to update the Extended Price field each time we want to use a form or report; instead, we just calculate extended price on the fly. You'll learn how to set up calculated fields later in the chapter.**

Figure 17.5 shows the Report Design window for the report in Figure 17.4. (We chose View ➤ Zoom ➤ Fit Height and hid the rulers to better show all the report elements.) Notice how the bands in the design correspond to the levels of summary information in the printed report. Summary fields in the ProdCode *group band* total the quantity, unit price, and extended price of each product group. In the *page band*, the summary fields total the quantity and extended price for each page. And in the *report band*, summaries provide the total, minimum, maximum, average, and count for all records in the report.

Hiding the Details in a Report

In some situations you might want to see *only* the summary data in a report, without all the details that contribute to the totals. The quickest way to hide details is simply to remove objects from the record band.

FIGURE 17.5 ▶

The Report Design window for the report shown in Figure 17.4

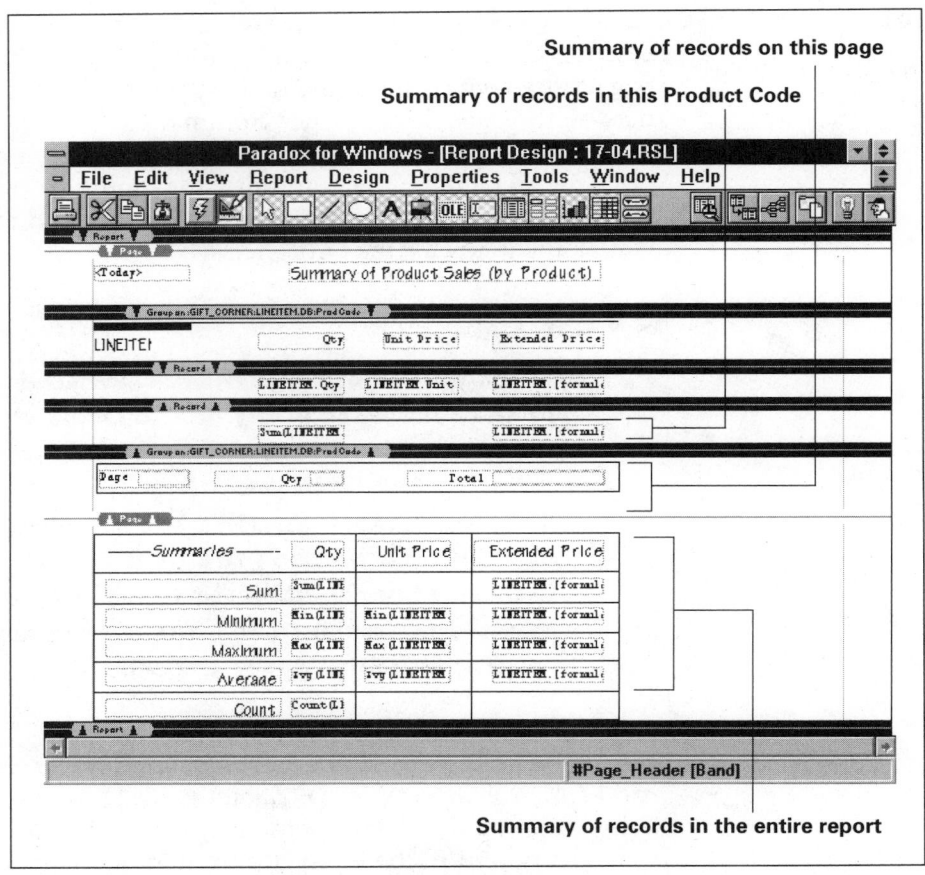

We used this technique in the sample report shown in Figure 17.6 and the corresponding Report Design window in Figure 17.7. To begin, we opened the report design shown in Figure 17.5 and saved it under a new name so that we could use the existing design as the basis for a new one. Next we deleted the Qty field and the Extended Price field object from the record band and moved the Unit Price field object from the record band to the group band, between the two summary fields. (Remember, the unit price is the same for all items with the same product code.) Finally, we closed the record band, removed the horizontal line above the summary fields in the group band, and adjusted the spacing a bit. That's all there was to it!

FIGURE 17.6 ▶

A summary report that omits details of each product sold

7/25/94	Summary of Product Sales (by Product)		
GC-111	Qty	Unit Price	Extended Price
	-1	$270.00	-$270.00
GC-105	Qty	Unit Price	Extended Price
	1	$14,003.00	$14,003.00
GC-093	Qty	Unit Price	Extended Price
	2	$158.63	$317.27
GC-086	Qty	Unit Price	Extended Price
	1	$911,179.00	$911,179.00
GC-006	Qty	Unit Price	Extended Price
	6	$9,899.95	$58,199.85

--------Summaries--------	Qty	Unit Price	Extended Price
Sum	89		$1,131,253.79
Minimum	-4	$0.50	-$1,080.00
Maximum	30	$911,179.00	$911,179.00
Average	2	$26,864.33	$29,006.51
Count	39		

Form Report Techniques

Ch.
17

▶ *Defining Calculated Fields*

In Chapter 16 you learned how to use queries to perform calculations on data in tables. The techniques for specifying calculations in design documents are similar in many ways. However, instead of using example elements to act as place holders in the calculation (as you do with queries), you use *field names* or *field object names* to represent values stored in table fields.

To define a calculated field, start from the Define Field Object dialog box and follow the steps below.

1. Click the Calculated option in the dialog box (an × will appear).

FIGURE 17.7 ▶

*The Report Design for
the report in Figure 17.6*

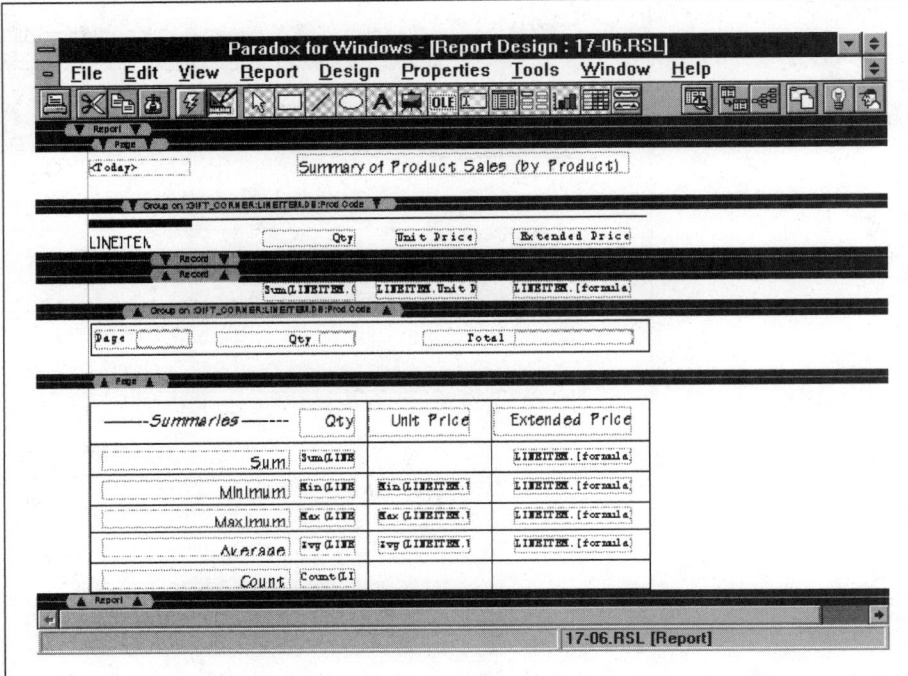

2. Type the calculation in the text box below the Calculated check box. It doesn't matter whether you type the calculation in uppercase letters, lowercase letters, or a mixture of the two. (You'll see some examples in a moment.)

3. When you're finished, choose OK to return to the Design window.

You can use any of the following elements in a calculation:

- Field names, typed in the format **[TABLENAME.fieldname]** or **[TABLENAME."fieldname"]**. For example, *[LINEITEM.Qty]* refers to the Qty field in the LineItem table. It's best to use the Copy Field button, described below, to fill in field names.

▶ ▶ **N O T E**

If the field name contains a period, you must enclose the name in quotation marks, like this: *[CUSTLIST."M.I."]*. If you forget the quote marks, you'll get an error message when you try to close the Define Field Object dialog box.

- You can add the alias name to the field name, in the format **[:ALIAS:TABLENAME.fieldname]** or the format **[:ALIAS:TABLENAME."fieldname"]**. For example, *[:GIFT_CORNER:LINEITEM.Qty]* refers to the Qty field in the LineItem table stored in the directory that has the *Gift_Corner* alias.

- Field object names, such as *Tax*, *#EditRegion5*, and *Qty1*.

- Arithmetic operators: + (addition), − (subtraction), ★ (multiplication), / (division), and parentheses ( ) for grouping.

- Logical operators AND, OR, and NOT.

- Comparison operators < (less than), > (greater than), <> (not equal to), = (equal to), >= (greater than or equal to), and <= (less than or equal to).

- Numeric constants (for example, 1.5).

- Alpha strings enclosed in quotes (for example, "*Hi there*").

- Most ObjectPAL mathematical, statistical, string manipulation, and date/time methods and procedures. For example, the ObjectPAL procedure *today( )-30* calculates the date 30 days prior to the current date. The *ObjectPAL Quick Reference Manual* and on-line help that come with Paradox for Windows document the built-in procedures available. (*Procedures* in ObjectPAL are similar to *functions* in other programming languages.)

- Summary operators (also called *aggregators*). For instance, *Sum([LINEITEM.Unit Price]) ★ Tax1* is a legal calculation that involves the summary operator named Sum.

►►NOTE

The same scope rules illustrated earlier for summary fields also apply to calculated fields. See "Understanding Scope in Summary Fields," earlier in this chapter.

- Custom ObjectPAL procedures inside of an aggregator. For example, if you've defined a custom procedure named *coolCustom-Proc* that operates on a table field, you could use an expression such as *Sum(coolCustomProc([LINEITEM.Qty]))*. This is available in forms only.

- Summaries that contain calculations. For example, *Sum([LINEITEM.Qty]*[LINEITEM.Unit Price])* would calculate the total extended price. The expression *Sum([LINEITEM.Qty]*[LINEITEM.Unit Price]) * 1.0725* would calculate the total extended price with a 7.25% tax tacked on.

►►NOTE

Some restrictions apply to using these summary (or aggregation) expressions, as you'll learn later in "Working with Summary Operators and Calculated Fields."

Using Field Names in Calculations

When used in a calculation, field names must appear in the format

    [TABLENAME.fieldname] or [:ALIAS:TABLENAME.fieldname]

in which *ALIAS* is an alias name, *TABLENAME* is the name of a table in the data model, and *fieldname* is the name of a field in that table.

Although you can enter field names by typing them into the Calculated text box, the easiest and most accurate way to enter a field name is as follows:

1. Make sure the Calculated option is checked in the Define Field Object dialog box.

2. Position the insertion point in the Calculated text box, at the spot where you want the field name to appear in your calculation.

3. Click the drop-down arrow next to the table name and select the field you want.

4. If you wish to perform a summary calculation on this field, click the Summary drop-down list and select the summary operator.

5. Click the Copy Field button.

The field you chose will appear in the text box, in the proper format, and the expression that you copied will be selected. If you wish, you can edit the expression further using standard Windows editing techniques. When you return to the Design window, the word *[formula]* usually will appear in the field.

► ► N O T E

Later in this chapter, we'll talk about some shortcuts for copying calculations and calculated fields.

In Figure 17.8, we selected the Qty field from the LineItem table's drop-down list, clicked the Copy Field button, pressed the End key, and typed an asterisk (*). We then selected the Unit Price field from the LineItem table's drop-down list and clicked Copy Field once more. The result? A calculation that multiplies the value in the Qty field by the value in the Unit Price field of the current record in the LineItem table.

Using Field Object Names in Calculations

When you use a *field name* in an expression, you're telling Paradox to perform the calculation on the actual values in the table. You can also use *field object names* to display table values or calculation results. Calculations will often (but not always) display the same results whether you use a field name or a field object name. Rather than worrying about the exceptions, just keep this rule of thumb in mind: Use *field names* when performing calculations on actual table values, and use *field object names* when performing calculations on other calculated fields. (In a moment, you'll see an example that uses both field names and field object names to calculate percentages.)

FIGURE 17.8

A calculation entered into the Calculated text box

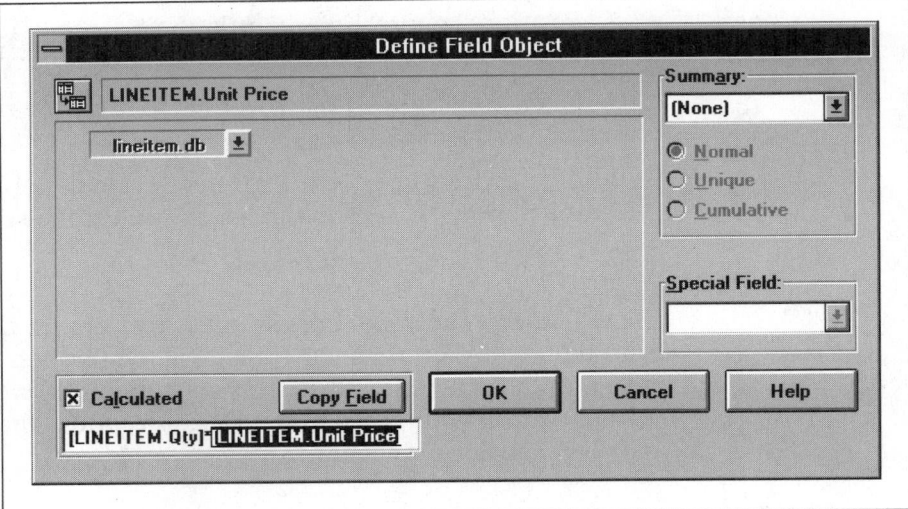

▶ **NOTE**

Remember that field names refer to actual fields in your table. Field object names refer to objects that exist only in the design document, not in your table.

To use a field object name in a calculation, type the *object name*, without dots or brackets, into the Calculated text box. For example, to multiply a field named *Qty1* by 10, you would type **Qty1 ★ 10**. You can use field names and field object names in the same calculation.

Remember that field object names appear on the status line when you select a field object in the Design window, and at the top of the property menu when you inspect an object. This makes it easy to find out the name of a field object.

Field object names are sometimes cryptic and difficult to type (objects may have names like *#EditRegion1*, for example). Fortunately, you can change field object names quite easily. To do so, inspect the field object in the Design window, press ↵ or click the header of the property menu, type a new name for the object (no spaces allowed!), and choose OK.

Form Report
Techniques

Ch.
17

► ►**TIP**

It's a good idea to change the default names of field objects that you intend to use in other calculations. However, you must be sure that *all* object names in a given design document are unique.

Combining Alpha Strings

You can use the + operator to combine alpha strings. Suppose you wish to eliminate unsightly gaps between first and last names in the CustList table by separating the names with a single space, as shown below:

Maria Miller

To achieve this result, create a new field in your design document, then go to the Define Field Object dialog box and click the Calculated option. In the Calculated text box, enter the calculation shown below (use the Copy Field button to help).

[CUSTLIST.First Name] + " " + [CUSTLIST.Last Name]

Notice how the + operators connect each part of the calculation. This calculation says, "Display the customer's first name, add a blank space, then display the customer's last name." Remember to type blank spaces and other text (alpha strings) within double quotation marks. You'll see some examples using the + operator later in this chapter.

► ►**NOTE**

Two double-quotation marks placed together, as in "", represent an empty or null string. However, two double-quotation marks placed around a space, as in " ", represent a single space (this string is *not* blank, empty, or null).

► Calculating Percentages

Recall from Chapter 16 that calculating percentages required several queries and some manual tallying. Such calculations are much simpler when performed in design documents. Figure 17.9 shows a sample report for

Sales Breakdown by Product Code

Product Code	Sales	% of Total Sales
GC-006	$58,199.85	5.15 %
GC-086	$911,179.00	80.57 %
GC-093	$317.27	.03 %
GC-105	$14,003.00	1.24 %
GC-111	($270.00)	-.02 %
GC-112	$654.00	.06 %
GC-122	$31,350.00	2.77 %
GC-129	$8,424.32	.74 %
GC-135	$119.00	.01 %
GC-164	$3,333.00	.29 %
GC-189	$314.65	.03 %
GC-195	$95,000.00	8.4 %
GC-222	$150.00	.01 %
GC-289	$65.00	.01 %
GC-300	$687.70	.06 %
GC-321	$2,594.00	.23 %
GC-510	$1,000.00	.09 %
GC-521	$123.00	.01 %
GC-587	$15.00	0 %
GC-987	$3,665.00	.32 %
Grand Total:	**$1,130,923.79**	

the LineItem table that summarizes sales by product code and displays each product's contribution to total sales as a percentage. The corresponding Report Design window appears in Figure 17.10.

To create the percentage report, we started with a blank design based on the LineItem table. We added a group band (based on the Prod Code field) and placed titles, column headings, and a horizontal line in the page band. We placed two undefined fields in the group band and one in the report band, then selected and inspected the fields in the group band and chose Display Type ➤ Unlabeled from the property menu. Next we added a horizontal line to the report band, then changed the text for the undefined field to **Grand Total:** (in bold) and arranged it neatly in the field. We then resized the bands to squeeze out unwanted white space. Finally, we inspected and defined the fields in the group and report bands. The letters in Figure 17.10 correspond to the field definitions listed below.

FIGURE 17.10

The Report Design window for the report in Figure 17.9. The labels in the figure mark the important fields in the report.

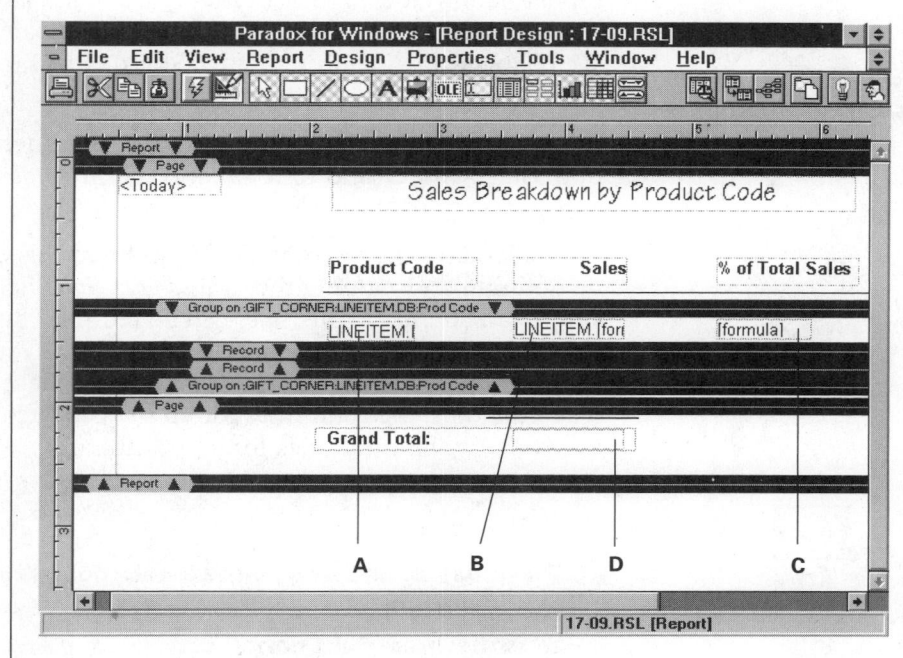

A   Displays the Prod Code field of the LineItem table. This field appeared automatically when we created the group band.

B and D   Display extended price summaries. To define the fields as *Sum([LINEITEM.Qty]*[LINEITEM.Unit Price])* we checked the Calculated box, clicked in the Calculated text box, selected *Qty* from the table's drop-down list, selected the *Sum* operator from the Summary drop-down list, then clicked Copy Field. Next, we pressed End, then ←, then typed an asterisk (*). Finally, we selected *Unit Price* from the table's drop-down list, clicked Copy Field, and chose OK.

The summary field in the Prod Code group band (labeled "B" in Figure 17.10) calculates the total extended price for each product. We changed this field's name to Sales, for use in the percentage calculation (labeled "C" in the figure). The summary field in the report band (labeled "D" in the figure) calculates the total extended price for all products; that is, it calculates the grand total. We changed this field's name to Grand, also for use in the percentage calculation.

For a finishing touch, we changed the Alignment property for both Sales and Grand to *Right* and the Format ▶ Number Format property to *Windows $*.

C   Calculates the percentage. We defined this calculated field *after* defining and naming the *Grand* and *Sales* fields. The formula is simply *Sales/Grand* (the *Sales* calculated field divided by the *Grand* calculated field). This calculation divides the total extended price in the group band by the *Grand* calculated field. In other words, we're dividing the total sales for all the products in a given product code by the total sales for all products.

▶ ▶ **W A R N I N G**

You must define and name a calculated field before you can use it in another calculation. If you try to use an undefined field name, or you type an erroneous calculation, Paradox will display an error message when you try to return to the Design window. You must either correct the calculation or choose Cancel in the Define Field Object dialog box.

After returning from the Define Field Object dialog box to the Design window, we inspected the percentage calculation field and defined a custom number format to display the results. The custom format is based on the standard Percent format, but displays two places to the right of the decimal point instead of just one. (See Chapter 7 for information on defining custom number formats.)

▶ Working with Summary Operators and Calculated Fields

Notice that the percentage calculation in the previous example quite happily performed a calculation on a summary field.

As another example, you can perform summary operations on a calculation that involves multiple fields in the same table. Thus, the following statement is perfectly valid:

Sum([LINEITEM.Qty] * [LINEITEM.Unit Price])

And so is this one:

Sum([LINEITEM.Qty] * [LINEITEM.Unit Price]) * 1.0725

So you see that calculations can be very flexible. However, Paradox does impose a few restrictions that you should know about:

- You cannot reference multiple fields in a summary calculation if those fields don't all come from the same table.

- You cannot nest the summary operators. Therefore, an expression like *Sum(Avg([LINEITEM.Qty]))* is strictly taboo.

There's one other restriction: You cannot perform summary operations on calculated fields like the one that figured out the Sales amount (Qty * Unit Price) in Figure 17.9. Fortunately, this is an easy one to work around if you just repeat the full calculation in your summary expression. For instance, suppose you wanted to compute the grand total of sales, including a 7.25% sales tax, in the report footer. When defining this field, you would place the following expression into the Calculated text box:

Sum([LINEITEM.Qty]*[LINEITEM.Unit Price])*1.0725

The simpler expression *Sum(Sales) *1.0725* isn't allowed. Too bad!

Previous versions of Paradox did not let you combine summary operators and calculations, so it was often necessary to create extra fields—such as Extended Price—to store calculation results. But with Paradox 5 for Windows, it's rarely necessary (or good practice) to store calculation results in your permanent tables.

We did violate this "don't store calculations in tables" rule when we added the Extended Price field to the LineItem table for our sample order entry database. However, this database design *faux pas* allowed us to illustrate Changeto queries that perform calculations on multiple fields (Qty times Unit Price) and store the result in another field (Extended Price). Later in this chapter you'll see a sample invoice and an

Form Report
Techniques

Ch.
17

order entry form that perform all the necessary calculations for overall tax and amount due for each order, without having to store an Extended Price field in the LineItem table.

▶ Using Iif Statements to Make Decisions

You can use the ObjectPAL **Iif** statement in a calculated field to create "smart" design documents that display one value if a condition is true, and another if a condition is false. The general form of the Iif statement is

    Iif(condition, true, false)

where *condition* is the condition you are testing, *true* is the value or field to display if the condition is true, and *false* is the value or field to display if the condition is false. Figure 17.11 shows an example of Iif in action, while Figure 17.12 shows the corresponding Form Design window.

FIGURE 17.11 ▶

A smart form that displays one message if a condition is true and another message if a condition is false. We also chose the Form ➤ Filter options to sort the records by zip code, using the Zip Code index described in Chapter 8.

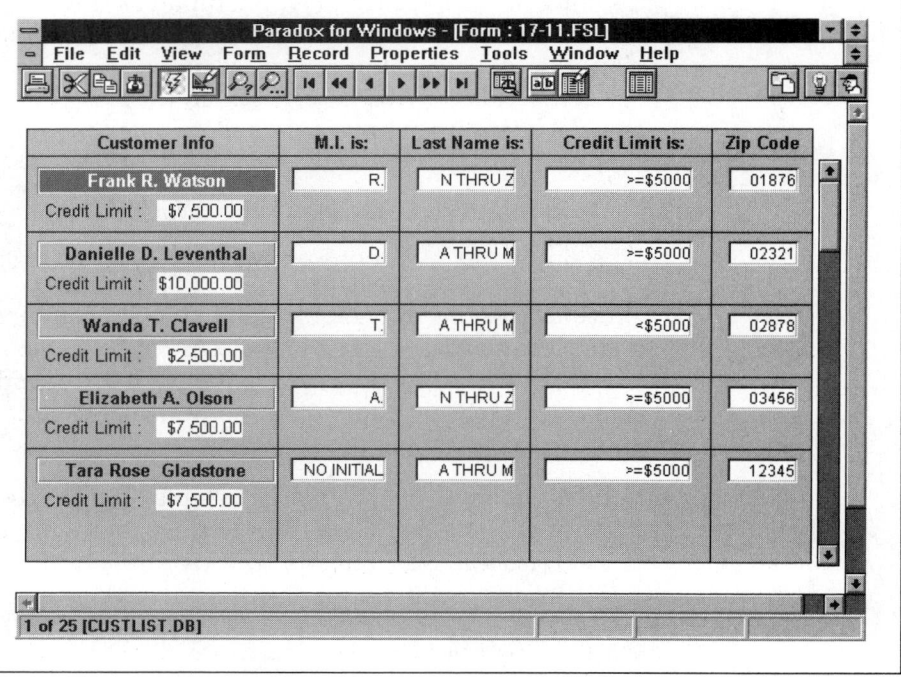

FIGURE 17.12 ▶

The Form Design window for the form in Figure 17.11

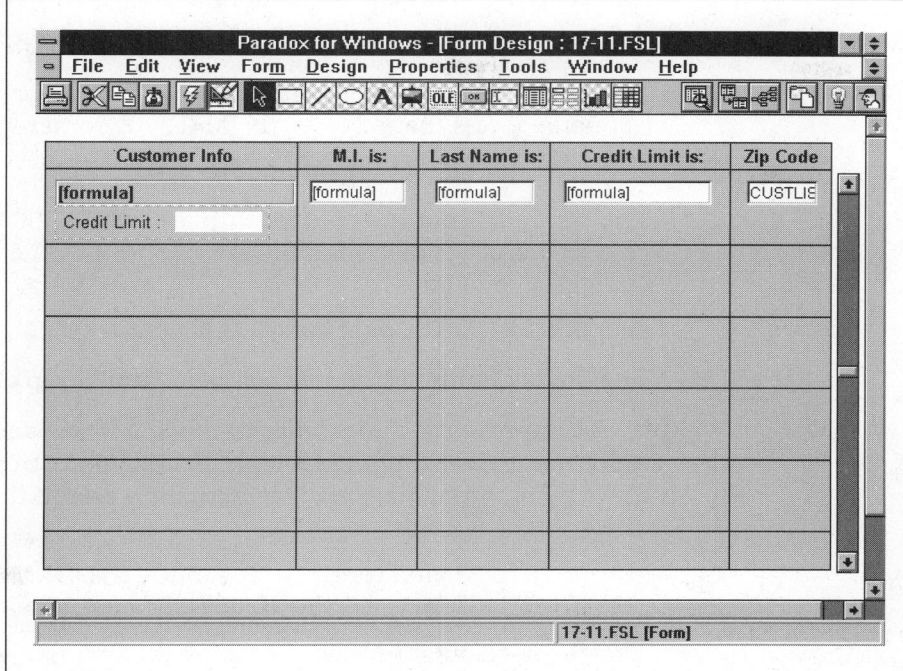

 ▶▶**N O T E**

Like all keywords in a calculation, the Iif keyword can be typed in uppercase, lowercase, or a combination of upper- and lowercase letters.

In the sample form, the column labeled *Customer Info* displays some information about the customer. The customer name is a calculated field combining the first name, middle initial, and last name, with spaces in between, as shown below.

    [CUSTLIST.First Name] + " " + [CUSTLIST.MI] + " " +
    [CUSTLIST.Last Name]

Calculated fields in the next three columns use the Iif statement to determine what to print. In the "M.I. is:" column, we use the Iif statement shown below to display the words "NO INITIAL" if the middle initial is blank, or the middle initial if the customer has a middle initial (that is, if the middle initial is not blank):

Iif([CUSTLIST.MI] = "", "NO INITIAL", [CUSTLIST.MI])

The "Last Name is:" column displays the message "A THRU M" if the last name is less than "N" or "N THRU Z" otherwise, as follows:

Iif([CUSTLIST.Last Name] < "N", "A THRU M", "N THRU Z")

The "Credit Limit is:" column displays ">=$5000" if the credit limit is greater than or equal to $5000 and "<$5000" otherwise. The Iif statement is as follows:

Iif([CUSTLIST.Credit Limit] >= 5000, ">=$5000", "<$5000")

The final column just contains a plain-vanilla Zip Code field.

Iif can improve the appearance of mailing labels and other designs in which some fields might be blank. For example, to print the customer's name with proper spacing or punctuation even if there is no middle initial, try this calculation:

[CUSTLIST.First Name] + " " + Iif([CUSTLIST.MI] <> "",
[CUSTLIST.MI] + " ","") + [CUSTLIST.Last Name]

The above calculation says, "Display the first name followed by a space. Then, if the middle initial is not blank (""), display the middle initial followed by a space; otherwise display nothing. Finally, display the last name."

 ▶ ▶ **T I P**

We also could have used the statement above to display the customer's name in the *Customer Info* column in Figure 17.11.

▶ *Tips for Typing Calculations*

As you've seen, formulas in calculated fields can become quite long, and typing them correctly may take a couple of tries. Here are some tips to help you along:

- We've broken some of the calculation statements shown above into several lines in order to fit them onto the pages of this book. However, you cannot do this when typing them into the Calculated text box. Instead, you must type the calculation on a single line until the statement is complete. You can use the Home, End, ←, and → keys (or the mouse) if you need to move the insertion point through long calculation statements in the text box.

- Whenever you need to enter a field name into a calculation, position the insertion point where you want the field to appear in the Calculated text box, select the field from the table's drop-down list, select a summary operator from the Summary drop-down list (if you wish), then click the Copy Field button.

- You can copy and paste text in the Calculated text box just as you would any other Windows text: Select the text, press Ctrl+Ins or Ctrl+C to copy it, then position the insertion point where you want the copied text to appear and press Shift+Ins or Ctrl+V. This can save you some typing and improve your accuracy.

- If you want to use an existing calculated or summary field as the basis for another field in your design, select the field, then choose Design ➤ Duplicate from the menus. You can move the duplicated field wherever you want it, then inspect and change the calculation if necessary. This technique is a great way to create subtotals and grand totals for the same fields in group bands, page bands, and report bands.

▶▶WARNING

Be sure to use <u>D</u>esign ➤ <u>D</u>uplicate, not copy and paste, when copying calculated or summary fields. Unlike copy and paste, <u>D</u>esign ➤ <u>D</u>uplicate assigns unique names to each field duplicated. If you use copy and paste, you must then assign unique names to the copied fields.

Form Report Techniques

Ch. 17

▶▶ Creating Multitable Design Documents

Multitable design documents let you view, edit, and print data from several tables simultaneously. This feature provides you with tremendous flexibility for data entry and display, and often eliminates the need to run queries that generate temporary tables.

To define a multitable document, you simply identify the tables you want to use in the data model and define the relationship, if any, between the tables. (You'll see several examples of data models later in this chapter.) Multitable documents can contain *linked* tables, *nonlinked* tables, or both.

▶ Understanding Linked Multitable Documents

When tables are *linked*, they are joined by key fields. Figure 17.13, for example, shows an order entry form in which the Orders table is linked to the LineItem table via the Order No key field, and the LineItem table is linked to the Products table via the Prod Code key field.

FIGURE 17.13 ▶

A sample order entry form containing multiple linked tables. The Orders table is linked to LineItem and LineItem is linked to Products. Moving the cursor through the form displays information about specific orders and their associated line items.

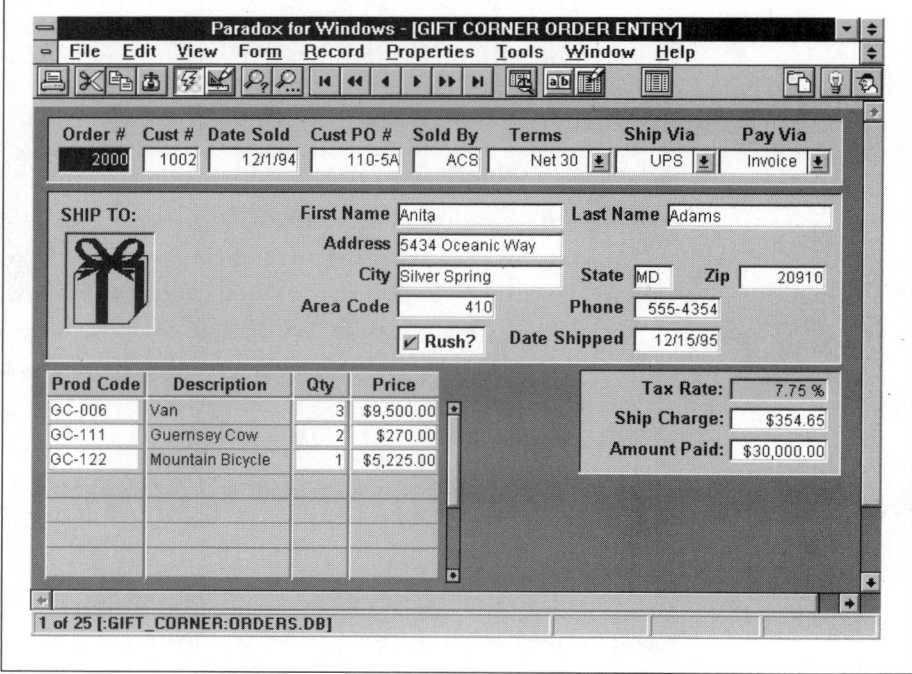

Notice that the form includes order header information (from the Orders table), each line item for the associated order (from the LineItem table), and a description of each product ordered (from the Products table). If we move the cursor to another order in this form (for example, by pressing PgDn when the cursor is in any of the order fields) or enter a new order, the line items and product descriptions will change instantly to reflect the detail information of the new order.

► ►**N O T E**

In our discussion of multitable queries in Chapter 16, we used queries to join these tables. Linking tables in a design document is analogous to joining them in a query.

Remember that you can use referential integrity, default values, and table lookups to make data entry in multiple related tables even more convenient. For instance, when we type a customer number into the appropriate field at the top of the form shown in Figure 17.13, default Ship To information from the CustList lookup table is filled in automatically. Likewise, typing a product code into the line item area of the form fills in the description and price data from the Products lookup table. Default values appear automatically for the Date Sold, Terms, Ship Via, Pay Via, and Tax Rate fields whenever we enter a new order. Of course, we can override the defaults if we wish.

► ►**N O T E**

Chapters 4, 5, and 6 cover techniques for defining default values, lookup tables, and referential integrity in a table structure. Chapter 11 explains how to set up drop-down lists like those for the Terms, Ship Via, and Pay Via fields. Finally, Chapters 5 and 16 discuss the structure of our sample order entry database.

Form Report Techniques

► ►

Ch.
17

▶ Understanding Non-Linked Multitable Documents

Placing multiple *non-linked* tables on a form is handy when you want to keep a small table on the screen for reference during data entry or when you don't want to force the entry in one table to contain a value that's listed in the other table. Non-linked tables are also useful for graphing overall results in forms or reports (see Chapter 13).

Unlike fields in linked multitable documents, the fields in non-linked multitable documents are totally independent. Therefore, moving the cursor through one non-linked table has no effect on other non-linked tables. In Figure 17.14, for example, we've displayed the States table for reference. This table is not linked to any tables on the form, so the user can scroll through it freely and change values without affecting other tables on the form.

FIGURE 17.14 ▶

A form with non-linked tables. The States table is completely independent of other tables on the form. The Cust-List table appears twice in this form to allow convenient scrolling to customer records.

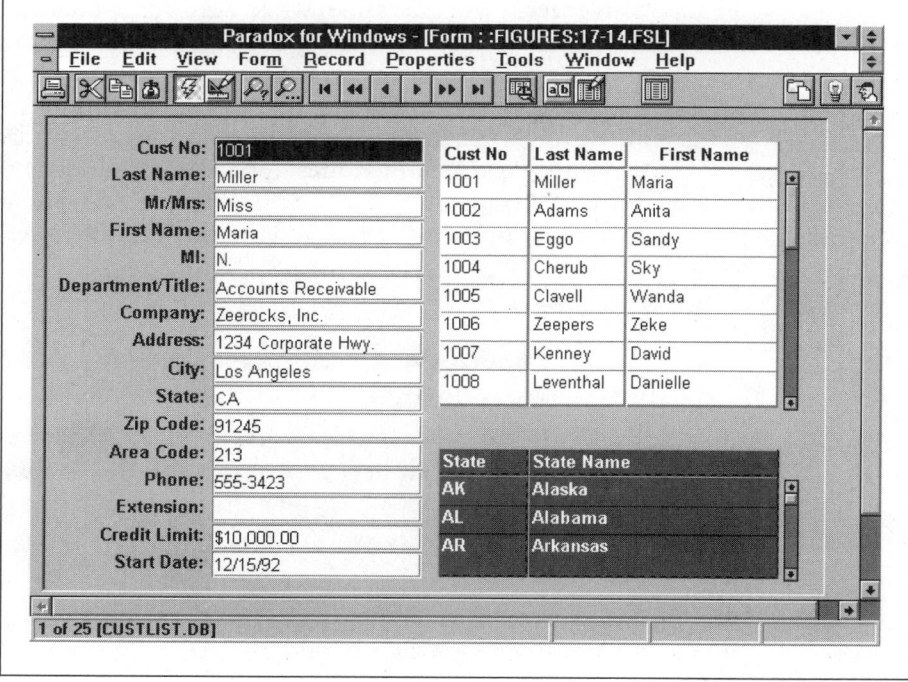

▶▶N O T E

> Things get a bit more complicated when tables are defined with referential integrity or table lookups. For example, if you've defined referential integrity between the CustList and States tables, changing a state abbreviation would change the corresponding abbreviation in the CustList table, whether or not the tables are linked in the form. See Chapter 5 for details on these topics.

Figure 17.14 illustrates a tricky technique you might like to try with your own forms. Notice that the CustList table appears twice, once in a single-record format and again in a tabular format. The CustList table at the right side of the form displays many records at once, so it's easy to locate a particular customer record simply by scrolling. Clicking on or scrolling to a customer record in the right-hand table displays that customer's fields on the left side of the form. Likewise, scrolling to a record in the left-hand table brings the corresponding record in the right-hand table into view. Furthermore, any changes made to the table on the right will be reflected immediately in the table on the left, and vice versa.

▶▶N O T E

> When we add a second instance of CustList to the form design (using the Table tool in the Toolbar), the tables behave as though they were linked tables since they're actually the same table.

▶ *Setting Up the Multitable Data Model*

All the tables you want to use in a multitable document must appear in the data model area of the Data Model dialog box, whether you link them or not. The data model can be one that you've already created and saved, or one that you define on the fly. Let's take a look at both methods for creating the data model.

Using an Existing Data Model or Query

The steps for using a previously saved data model to set up a new multitable design document are similar to those for defining the data model in a query (Chapter 16). Here's a quick summary of what you need to do:

1. Begin your new design as described in Chapter 10 and go to the Data Model dialog box. Or, if you're already in the Design window, click the Data Model button in the Toolbar (shown at left).

2. Click the Type drop-down list, then choose either <Data Models> or <Queries>.

3. In the list of files that appears below File Name in the Data Model dialog box, click the data model or query file you want. That file's data model will appear in the Data Model area of the dialog box.

4. If you wish, you can update the data model as described in the next section on "Creating a Data Model On the Fly."

5. When you're ready to continue with your design, choose OK.

 ▶▶**N O T E**

> **Chapter 5 explained how to use the Data Model Designer to create and save a data model outside of any query, form, or report.**

Creating a Data Model On the Fly

As an alternative (or a supplement) to using a saved data model or query as the basis for your document, you can manually set up a data model in the Data Model dialog box. To get started, go to the Data Model dialog box, as described in the previous section.

To add a table to the dialog box, simply double-click a table in the File Name list, or click the table name and then click the → button. Repeat this step until you've added all the tables you want.

When you finish adding tables, the dialog box will resemble Figure 17.15 (we used a finished version of this data model for the form shown in Figure 17.14). If you don't need to link tables, you can

FIGURE 17.15

The Data Model dialog box for a multitable document, before linking any tables

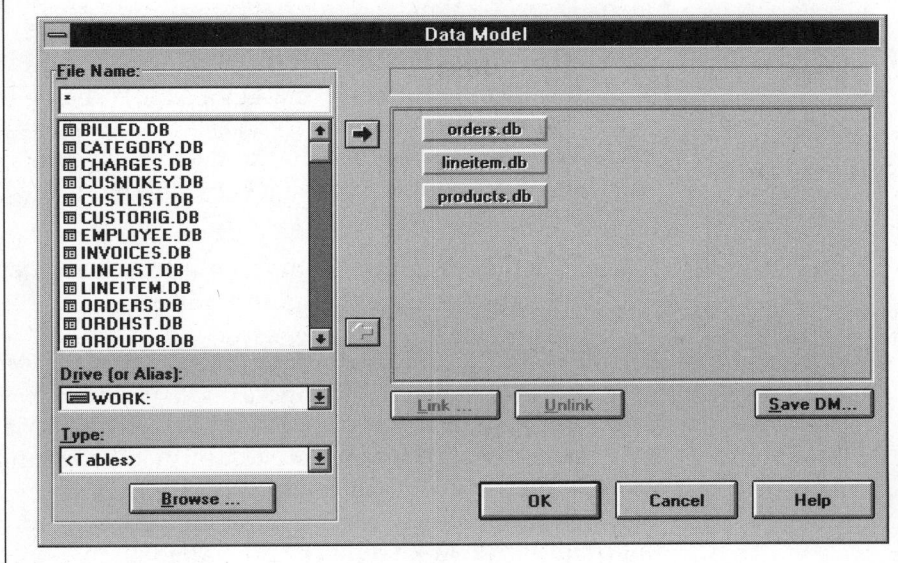

choose OK to continue with your design. Otherwise, remain in the Data Model dialog box and link the tables, as explained a bit later.

TIP

As an alternative to adding all the tables to the data model and then linking them, you may prefer to link each pair of tables as you add them. In multitable designs that include many tables, this technique reduces the need to scroll the data model to view all the tables you want to link.

If you need to remove a table from the data model, start by clicking on it in the data model area in the right half of the Data Model dialog box. The table name will appear "pushed in" and its name will appear just above the data model area. (If the table you want to delete is linked, you must then click the Unlink button to unlink it.) Now click the ← button or press Alt+D. The table will disappear from the data model and return to the File Name list.

Once you've added the tables you want, you can link them, using the same techniques that were presented in Chapter 5. Here is a brief review of the steps (if you need more details, just flip back to Chapter 5, or click the Help button in the Data Model dialog box):

1. Click the master table in the data model area of the dialog box. The mouse pointer changes to a linking tool when you pass it over a table.

2. Click and drag the linking tool from the master table to the detail table, then release the mouse button.

If you haven't established referential integrity between the two tables, Paradox will display the Define Link dialog box. Select the master table field to link, then select the detail index, and choose OK (see Chapter 5 for more details). If you *have* established referential integrity, Paradox will complete the link automatically and bypass the Define Link dialog box. (To return to the Define Link dialog box at any time, click the detail table whose link you want to change, then click the Link button in the Data Model dialog box.)

Be aware that when you define a link, Paradox sets the Read-Only option for each linked table. When the Read-Only option is not checked (the more common situation), you can edit the table; when the option is checked, you *cannot* make changes. To change the setting, open the Data Model dialog box, inspect the table in the data model area, and select Read-Only. (This applies to forms only; you can never edit tables in report designs.)

Repeat the linking steps as needed. When you finish creating the data model, the screen will resemble the example shown in Figure 17.16. If you'd like to save your data model for later use, click Save DM, type in a new file name, and choose OK.

When you're ready to continue with your design, choose OK.

▶ Choosing a Multitable Design Layout

The Design Layout dialog box lets you choose an initial layout for your document's design. If you're creating a new design document, the Design Layout dialog box will appear after you choose OK in the Data

FIGURE 17.16

The Data Model dialog box after linking multiple tables.

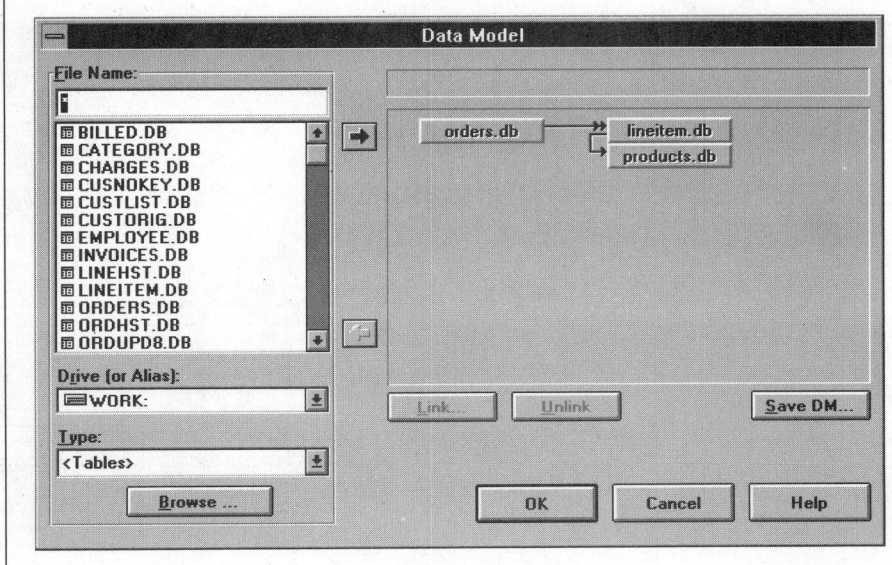

Model dialog box. If you're modifying an existing document, you'll need to choose <u>D</u>esign ➤ Design <u>L</u>ayout to return to the Design Layout dialog box.

▶▶ **W A R N I N G**

> **If you return to the Design Layout dialog box and then choose OK to return to the Design window, Paradox will ask if you want to completely replace your current design. If you choose <u>Y</u>es, your existing layout will be replaced with any new design layout you choose.**

You learned how to use the Design Layout dialog box for single-table data models in Chapter 10. When you define a multitable data model involving one-to-many relationships, you have many more options to choose from, as illustrated in Figure 17.17. In this example, we used the Show <u>F</u>ields button to remove several Orders fields from the form design, allowing more room for the combined LineItem and Products table object. Note that if your data model includes one-to-one relationships *only*, the Design Layout dialog box will be the same as for single-table data models.

FIGURE 17.17 ►

The Design Layout window for the form in Figure 17.13.

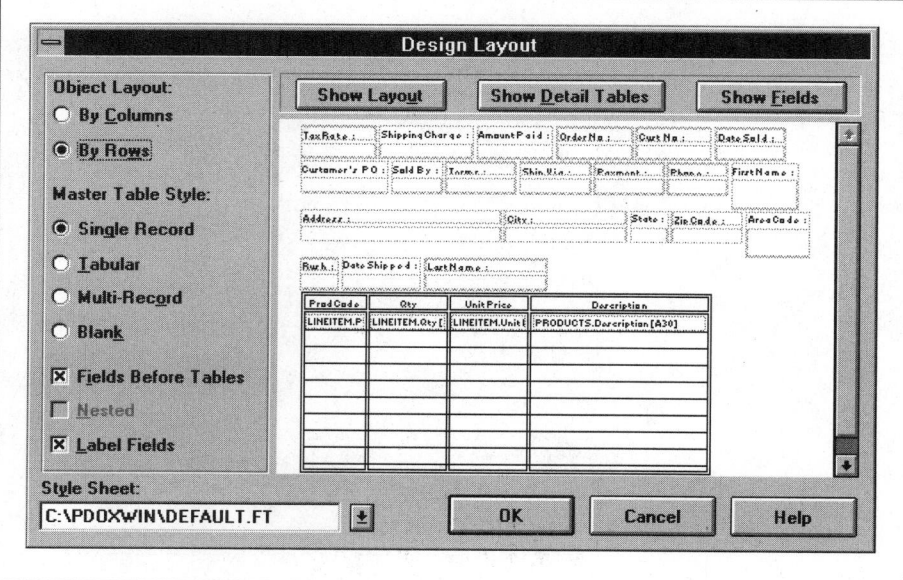

►►►**N O T E**

The Design Layout dialog box has been completely revamped in Paradox 5 for Windows.

►►►**T I P**

It's a good idea to use the Show Fields button and to pick a style sheet *before* changing the Design Layout options so you can evaluate the effects of your choices more easily. This also will reduce the number of "Could not fit field *xxx* in layout" warning messages (where *xxx* is a field name).

Initially, records from the master table are displayed one at a time, and appear in the single-record style. Records in the detail tables are displayed in a table object. Paradox will combine into a single table frame fields of tables having a one-to-one (or many-to-one) relationship. In

Figure 17.17, for example, Paradox combined the LineItem and Products fields into a single table; the Description field of the Products table is visible at the right edge of the table frame. If necessary, you can use the horizontal scroll bar in the table frame to view additional fields.

Here are the basic techniques for working with a multitable layout:

- **To control which fields appear in the design**, click the Show Fields button. You'll see the Table drop-down list, the Selected Fields list, the ↑ and ↓ Order buttons, and the Remove Field button, which let you choose which fields will appear in the design. From here, the techniques for using the dialog box are the same as those described in Chapter 10, except that you have more tables from which to choose fields. If necessaryFigure 17.18 illustrates the Design Layout dialog box for our sample order entry form after we clicked the Show Fields button.

- **To control the general layout of fields within single-record and multi-record objects**, click the Show Layout button and choose options in the Object Layout area. Your choices are By Columns (fields appear in columns down the page) or By Rows (fields appear in rows across the page).

FIGURE 17.18

The Design Layout dialog box for the sample order entry form (Figure 17.13) after we clicked the Show Fields Tables button.

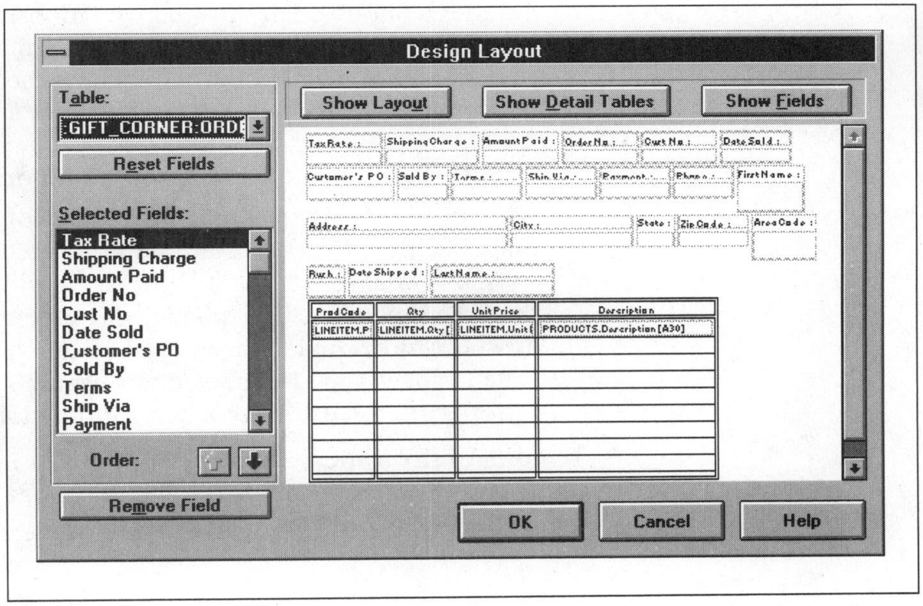

- **To control the appearance of master tables in your design**, click the Show Layout button and choose an option from the Master Table Style area. Your choices are:

  Single Record Displays one master record at a time.

  Tabular Displays many master records at a time in a tabular format.

  Multi-Record Displays many master records at a time in a multi-record format. (To define the number of records across and down and the spacing between them, return to the Design window, inspect the master record in the multi-record object, and choose Record Layout. See Chapter 10 for details.)

  Blank Displays no master or detail records.

  Fields Before Tables Lets you determine whether master tables appear before or after the detail tables. When Fields Before Tables is checked, master table fields appear before detail tables (the default arrangement); when unchecked, the detail tables appear above the master table.

  Nested Lets you nest detail records inside a multi-record master object. This option appears in forms if you've chosen a multi-record master table style, or the data model includes a one-to-many-to-many relationship. When checked, the Nested option places detail records inside a multi-record master object. When unchecked, detail objects remain outside the master objects. (Reports automatically use a nested layout, so this option is not available in the Design Layout dialog box for a report design.)

  Label Fields Lets you decide ahead of time whether to label fields in single-record and multi-record objects. When Label Fields is checked, labels will appear; when unchecked, fields will be unlabeled. Remember that you can inspect individual fields in the Design window and choose the Display Type ➤ Labeled or Display Type ➤ Unlabeled properties to customize labels for individual fields.

- **To control the appearance of detail tables in your design**, click the Show Detail Tables button. Then choose an option from the Detail Table Style area to display detail tables as a Table (tabular) object or a Record (multi-record) object. Depending on the option you chose, and whether you're designing a form or report, you also can choose one of the following multi-record layout options:

Horizontal   The records are displayed side-by-side (horizontally).

Vertical   The records are displayed vertically, with one record below the other.

Both   The records are displayed both side-by-side and vertically.

Figure 17.19 shows the sample order form's Design Layout dialog box after we clicked the Show Detail Tables button.

FIGURE 17.19

The Design Layout dialog box for the sample order entry form (Figure 17.13) after we clicked the Show Detail Tables button.

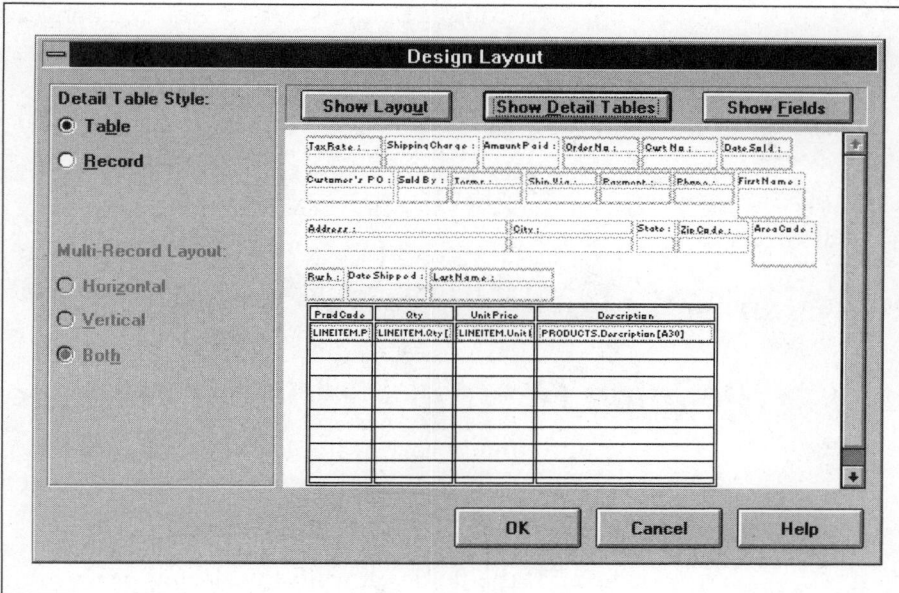

Each time you select an option from the Design Layout dialog box, the sample design area below the title bar will change to reflect your current choices. You can experiment with the initial layout to your heart's content. After choosing the layout that's closest to your intended form or report design, choose OK to reach the Design window.

▶ ▶ **W A R N I N G**

> **Each record in a report design must be structured to fit on a *single* page. Paradox cannot split a record across two or more pages.**

Before making any changes in the Design window, you should click the View Data button in the Toolbar to preview your design. If you aren't happy with your initial layout choices, you can return to the Design window, then open the Design Layout dialog box again (choose <u>D</u>esign ▶ Design <u>L</u>ayout) and try some different options. Remember that once you reach the Design window, any changes made in the Design Layout dialog box will completely replace your existing design. Therefore, it's a good idea not to waste time tweaking a design until you're satisfied with its overall layout.

▶ ▶ **N O T E**

> **When you return to the Design Layout dialog box, you'll see only fields that are currently in the design. You can add or remove fields using the Show <u>F</u>ields button in the Design Layout dialog box.**

▶ *Defining Fields in Multitable Documents*

Defining fields in multitable design documents is basically the same as defining them in single-table documents: Simply inspect the field in the Design window and choose Define Field. The list that appears will include fields from the master and detail tables (preceded by the table name). If the field you want to select appears in the list, click it. If it doesn't appear, click the list header or press ↵ to open the Define Field Object dialog box.

Figure 17.20 presents the Define Field Object dialog box for an order entry form. Notice that the tables are shown with the appropriate links, and they have drop-down arrows next to them. From here, you can use the techniques described in this chapter and in previous chapters to define regular, summary, special, and calculated fields.

FIGURE 17.20

The Define Field Object dialog box for a multitable document

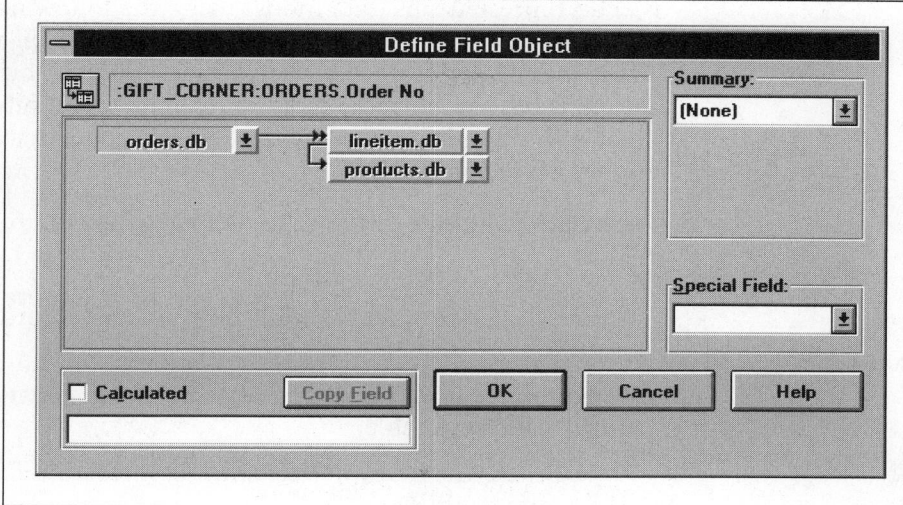

Understanding Scope in Multitable Documents

The various levels in the data model hierarchy and the relationships between master and detail tables affect the scope of summary and calculated fields in multitable documents. Rather than presenting a bunch of complicated rules to explain scope, we'll take a simpler approach and look at some practical examples that illustrate the concepts. First you'll see a handy order summary form that presents each customer's order at a glance. Next is a fancy order entry form that performs a variety of calculations automatically. Finally, you'll see the invoice we promised earlier in this chapter.

A Summary of Orders for Each Customer

Let's begin with the data model shown below:

We can represent this data model using the following shorthand notation: *CustList->>Orders->>LineItem->Products*. This means that CustList is the master table in a one-to-many relationship with Orders; Orders is the master table in a one-to-many relationship with LineItem; and LineItem is the master table in a many-to-one relationship with Products.

The relationships in this data model allow us to summarize values as follows:

- For each customer, we can show associated orders in the Orders table.

- For each order, we can summarize the associated detail records in the LineItem table.

- For each line item, we can show associated information from the Products table.

To understand the effects of this data model on summary field calculations, take a look at the order summary form in Figure 17.21. In this example, you can see all orders placed by customer number 1007, the line item details for the customer's first order (number 2002), and three tidbits of summary information. These are the definitions for the summary fields:

- The total amount paid by customer number 1007 on all orders is *Sum(ORDERS.Amount Paid)*.

- The number of orders placed by customer number 1007 is *Count(ORDERS.Order No)*.

- The Extended Price (Ext Price) for each line item is *[LINEITEM.Qty] * [LINEITEM.Unit Price]*.

- The total extended price for the first order (number 2002) is *Sum([LINEITEM.Qty] * [LINEITEM.Unit Price])*.

If you break out your trusty calculator, you can easily verify the results shown in the figure.

FIGURE 17.21

An order summary form containing the data model CustList->>Orders->>LineItem-> Products and three summary fields

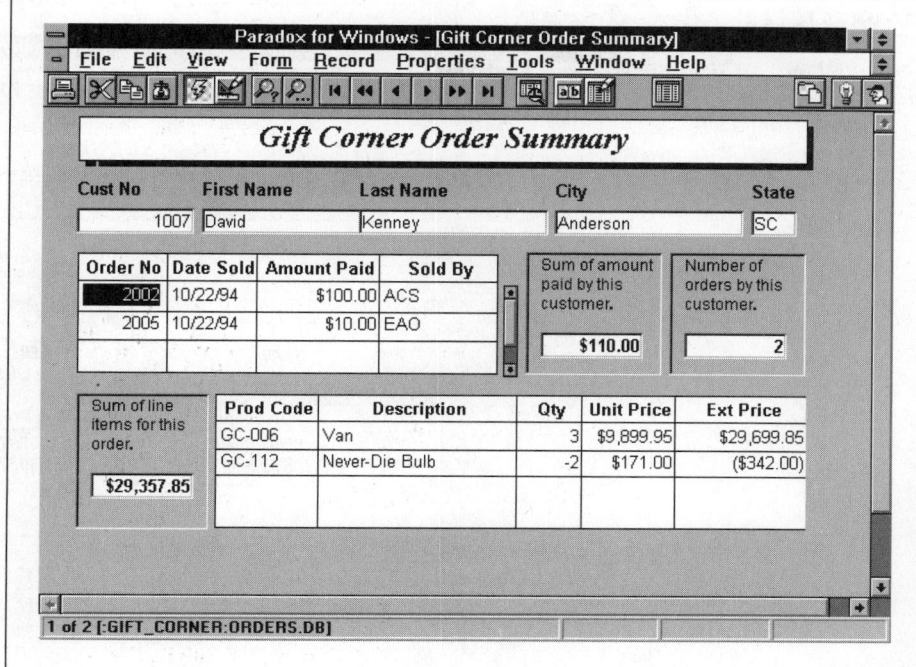

NOTE

Paradox displays information for the *first* record at each level in the data hierarchy until you move the cursor to a different detail record.

Figure 17.22 shows the effect of moving the cursor to the second order (2005) for this customer (1007). As you can see, the line items have changed, and so has the sum of line items for the order. However, the amount paid by the customer and the number of orders placed remain the same, as expected.

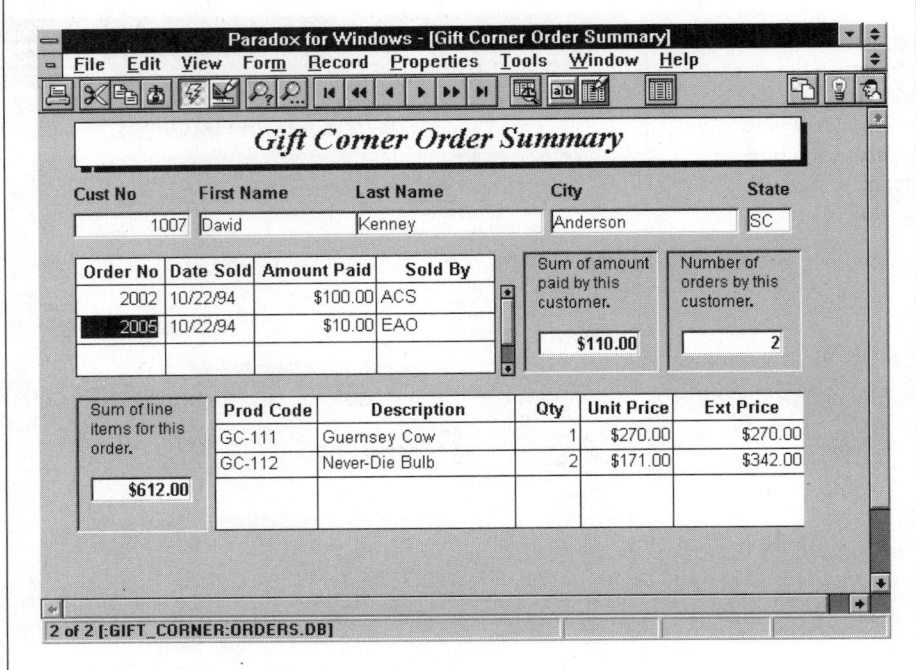

► *An Order Entry Form*

Figure 17.23 illustrates a fancier version of the order-entry form shown previously in Figure 17.13. This form features the data model relationships *Orders->>LineItem->Products* and performs several calculations, which are summarized below.

Next Avail. Order# A calculated field that is defined as *Max([ORDERS.Order No])+1*. This field displays the highest order number currently in the Orders table, plus 1. The user should type this number into the Order # field when entering a new order.

FIGURE 17.23 ▶

A fancier version of the order entry form shown in Figure 17.13. This form shows the next available order number and calculates order subtotals and totals.

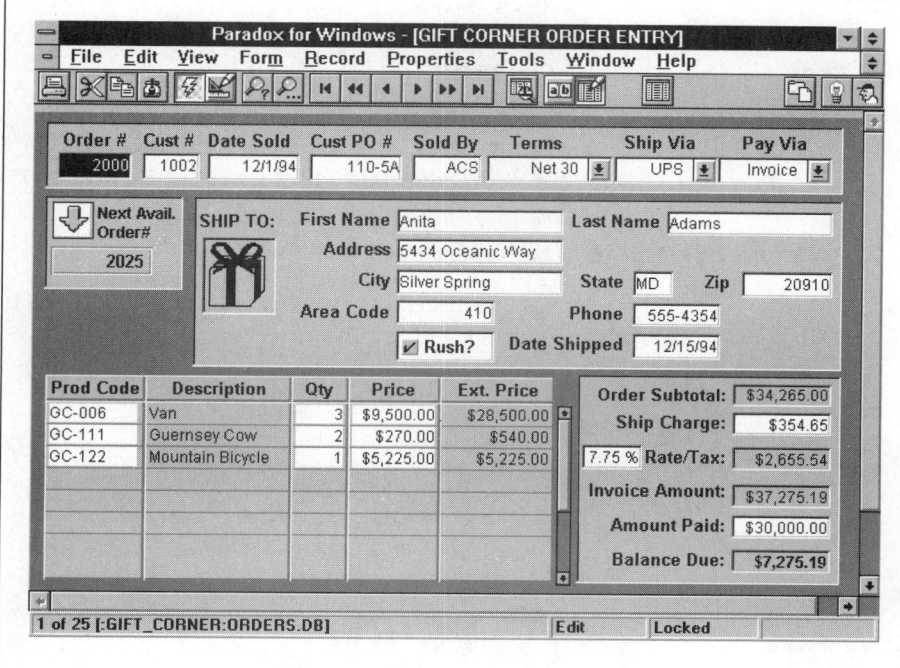

▶ ▶ **T I P**

Instead of making the user type in the order number manually, we could have used the Autoincrement field type to calculate and enter the order number automatically.

Order Subtotal A summary field that is defined as *Sum([LINEITEM.Qty]*[LINEITEM.Unit Price])*. This field totals the extended prices for the current order. We named it *SubTotal*.

Rate/Tax The Tax portion is a calculated field that is defined as *Subtotal * [ORDERS.Tax Rate]*. This totals the extended prices for the current order in the LineItem table and multiplies it by the tax rate stored in the Orders table. We named this field *Tax*. The tax rate appears just to the left of the calculated field.

Invoice Amount A calculated field that is defined as *Subtotal + Tax + [ORDERS.Shipping Charge]*. This field adds the total extended price, the tax, and the shipping charge for the order. We named this field *Total*.

Balance Due A calculated field that is defined as *Total – [ORDERS.Amount Paid]*. This gives us the final balance due for the order.

▶ A Sample Invoice

The sample invoice report shown in Figure 17.24 uses the calculations outlined previously for the order entry form. However, the data model is different, as shown below:

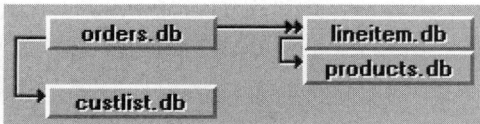

FIGURE 17.24 ▶

A sample invoice

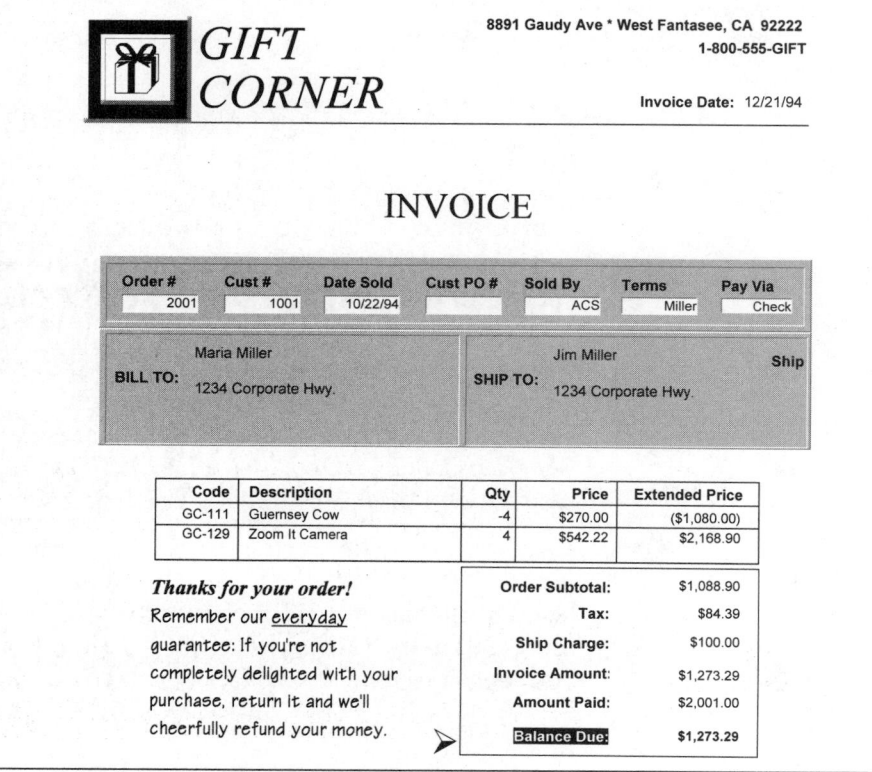

GIFT CORNER

8891 Gaudy Ave * West Fantasee, CA 92222
1-800-555-GIFT

Invoice Date: 12/21/94

INVOICE

Order #	Cust #	Date Sold	Cust PO #	Sold By	Terms	Pay Via
2001	1001	10/22/94		ACS	Miller	Check

BILL TO: Maria Miller
1234 Corporate Hwy.

SHIP TO: Jim Miller
1234 Corporate Hwy.   **Ship**

Code	Description	Qty	Price	Extended Price
GC-111	Guernsey Cow	-4	$270.00	($1,080.00)
GC-129	Zoom It Camera	4	$542.22	$2,168.90

Thanks for your order!
Remember our <u>everyday</u>
guarantee: If you're not
completely delighted with your
purchase, return it and we'll
cheerfully refund your money.

Order Subtotal:	$1,088.90
Tax:	$84.39
Ship Charge:	$100.00
Invoice Amount:	$1,273.29
Amount Paid:	$2,001.00
Balance Due:	$1,273.29

The invoice data model includes the CustList table (which wasn't needed in our order entry form) and shows the Orders table at the top. Placing Orders on top by dragging the mouse from Orders to CustList in the Data Model dialog box creates a many-to-one relationship, ensuring one invoice per order. In this relationship, Orders is the master table and CustList is the detail table (after all, a single customer can place many orders).

The design for this invoice appears in Figure 17.25. Notice that the report is grouped first by the Cust No field of the Orders table, then by

FIGURE 17.25 ▶

The design for the invoice report shown in Figure 17.24

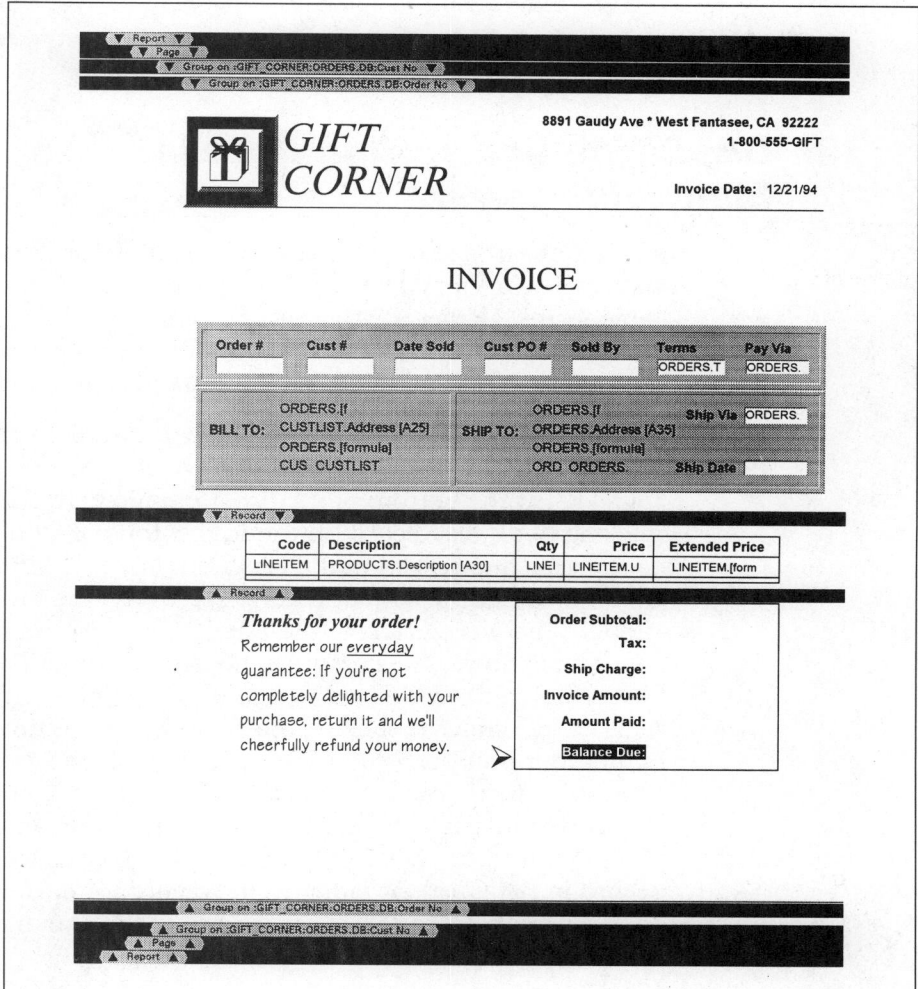

Form Report Techniques

Ch. 17

the Order No field. This keeps all invoices for each customer together. Because the subtotal, tax, invoice amount, and balance due calculations appear in the Order No band of the report, these amounts reflect totals for an individual order.

▶▶ **T I P**

> To print a report design like the one shown in Figure 17.25, return to the Report Design window and choose <u>F</u>ile ➤ <u>P</u>rint ➤ <u>D</u>esign. (Some field names in the printed design may appear garbled if Paradox doesn't have enough room to print them. However, the report should be just fine when you view or print it.)

▶ Displaying and Editing Data in Multitable Forms

In Chapter 6 we covered a variety of techniques for viewing and editing data in Form View. The procedures are generally the same for multitable forms. However, you must remember that the hierarchy of the data model controls the movement of the cursor from record to record within the fields and tables of a multitable form.

To understand how cursor movement works, flip back to Figure 17.22. Now imagine that the cursor is positioned in the field for product code GC-112, at the bottom of the LineItem table. In a single-table form, clicking the First Record button in the Toolbar would move the cursor to the very first record in the LineItem table. In a multitable form, however, all cursor movement takes place within the hierarchy of the data model. Therefore, clicking the First Record button in the order summary form moves the cursor to the first record of the LineItem table *for the current customer and order* (that is, to the record for product code GC-111). Similarly, clicking the First Record button when the cursor is on order number 2005 of the Orders table moves the cursor to the first order *for the current customer* (to the record for order number 2002). Finally, clicking the First Record button when the cursor is on customer number 1007 of the CustList table moves it to the very first record in the CustList table (to the record for customer number 1001). In this example, CustList is at the top of the data model hierarchy, so moving the cursor through this portion of the form is the same as moving it through a single-table form for the CustList Table.

▶▶**N O T E**

> You can use the mouse, cursor movement keys (arrow keys, Tab, Shift+Tab, Home, End, Ctrl+Home, Ctrl+End, PgUp, and PgDn), and Toolbar buttons to move the cursor through a form.

The most important points to remember about moving the cursor through multitable forms are summarized below.

- You can click the mouse in any field to move the cursor to that field (unless the Tab Stop property is turned off, as described in Chapter 11).

- The cursor positioning keys and Toolbar buttons apply to the current level of the data hierarchy only.

- You can press the Super Tab (F4) key to move the cursor to the *next* table or multi-record region; press the Super Back Tab (F3) key to move the cursor to the *previous* table or multi-record region.

As you can see, multitable documents are an incredibly powerful and convenient tool. When updating tables through multitable forms, remember that your changes are always made to the proper table in the data model. Therefore, as long as your data model is set up correctly, you won't need to open many table or form windows simultaneously in order to keep all your data in sync—a single form will do it all.

In this chapter, you learned how to perform summaries and calculations in design documents, and how to create multitable documents. In the next chapter, we'll introduce ObjectPAL techniques that can add even more automation and sophistication to Paradox objects.

Form Report Techniques

Ch. **17**

CHAPTER 18

Updating Tables Automatically

F*AST* T*RACK*

▶ ***Automatic updating is a procedure in which***   **1019**

     data from one table is used to change data stored in a sepa-
rate, related table.

▶ ***When filling in the query forms for an automatic update***   **1024**

     be sure to identify the common field that links the two
tables with matching example elements, entered with the
F5 key or the Join Tables button.

▶ ***In the table that will be receiving data from another
table***   **1024**

     use the CHANGETO command with example elements to
indicate which data from the source table you want to use.

▶ ***In the table that contains the data you want to copy***   **1026**

     or the data you want to use in a calculation, use example
elements to identify fields to be copied or used.

▶ ***When you use the contents of one table to change the
contents of another table***   **1032**

     you need to devise a scheme to prevent processed (posted)
records from being used in more than one update. You can
do so by flagging posted records and implementing an update scheme that uses unflagged records only. Or, you can
move all posted records from the original table to a separate "history table."

▶ *If you want to move posted records from their original table to a history table*   **1034**

use Tools ➤ Utilities ➤ Add to add records to the history table, then use Tools ➤ Utilities ➤ Empty to empty the original table.

▶ *It is important to perform automatic update steps*   **1037**

in the proper sequence. Using saved queries will help avoid unnecessary delays and improve the accuracy of your updates. However, to automate the steps fully, you'll need to learn ObjectPAL, the Paradox for Windows programming language, described in Chapter 19.

▶ *An INSERT query provides an alternative method*   **1047**

for inserting records from one or more source tables into a single target table.

▶ *To define an INSERT query*   **1047**

add the source and target tables to the Query window. For each source table, specify selection criteria, if necessary. In the *target* table, move the cursor to the column under the table name and type the letter **I**. Place linking example elements in the source and target tables to indicate which fields in the source tables should update the target table. Then run the query as usual.

▶ ▶ *I*n this chapter we'll look at ways to update information in one table using information stored in another table. Here we'll pull together many techniques from previous chapters, including designing databases with multiple related tables (Chapter 5); querying single tables (Chapter 9); using CALC, CHANGETO, and example elements in queries to change data and perform calculations on multiple tables (Chapter 16); and using options from the Tools ➤ Utilities menus (Chapter 15). Please refer to these earlier chapters if you need more reminders about how to use the features discussed in this chapter.

We'll also discuss the important topic of keeping track of which records have been used during an automatic updating procedure, and which have not. Since Paradox for Windows has no built-in way to determine whether a given record in a table has already been used or *posted* during an update, you must devise your own scheme to prevent records from being posted more than once. We'll illustrate two commonly used techniques: (1) marking or *flagging* posted records in their original table and (2) moving posted records from their original table to another table (often called a *history table*).

Finally, we'll expand on a topic introduced back in Chapter 5 and show you some additional tricks for starting autoincrement fields at whatever value you want.

This chapter presents examples as "food for thought," which you can use to design your own databases and applications. As we progress through the examples, remember that we are only demonstrating a few possibilities. You can mix and match data from multiple related tables in almost unlimited variations. Let your imagination run free and you'll come up with many more ideas!

> **WARNING**
>
> **It's always a good idea to use "dummy" data, as we're doing in this chapter, to develop and test updating procedures. This prevents you from damaging your "real" data in case one of your test procedures doesn't work as planned. You also should fully back up any tables you're about to change with test procedures, so that you can quickly restore them following botched experiments that create unwanted "Frankenstein monsters" in your data.**

▶▶ An Order Processing and Purchasing Example

Throughout this chapter, we'll use a simple order processing and purchasing system to illustrate our points. The system uses the Orders, LineItem, Products, and Category tables presented in Chapters 5 and 16. Recall that we used referential integrity and table lookups to ensure consistent data in these related tables.

We'll also introduce several new tables, which are described below:

OrdUpd8 Records the date shipped and invoice date of each order we process. Its fields are Order No, Date Shipped, and Invoice Date. To simplify data entry, we've defined Orders as the lookup table for the Order No field of the OrdUpd8 table.

Summary Consolidates each order for reporting and analysis only. The Summary fields are Order No, Cust No, Payment, Date Shipped, and Invoice Date.

Purchase Tracks the product code, quantity received, purchase price, and date received for items we've ordered to replenish our inventory. The Purchase table fields are Prod Code, Qty Recd (Quantity Received), Purchase Price, and Date Recd (Date Received). To simplify data entry, we've defined Products as the lookup table for the Prod Code field of the Purchase table.

We'll also use three history tables to store posted records. *OrdHst* stores history data from the Orders table; *LineHst* stores history data from the LineItem table; and *PurHst* stores history data from the Purchase table. You'll see examples of all these tables later in this chapter.

▶ An Overview of the Order Processing and Purchasing Cycles

Figure 18.1 provides a bird's-eye view of the basic steps required to process customer orders for our products. The steps are summarized below and explained in more detail in the sections that follow.

1. First we enter each customer's order into the Orders and LineItem tables, perhaps using the multitable order entry form presented in Chapter 17.

2. After shipping and invoicing a batch of customer orders, we record the Order No, Date Shipped, and Invoice Date (if any) of each shipped order in the OrdUpd8 table. (Recall from Chapter 16 that the Payment field of the Orders table indicates whether an invoice is necessary.)

FIGURE 18.1 ▶

The order processing cycle

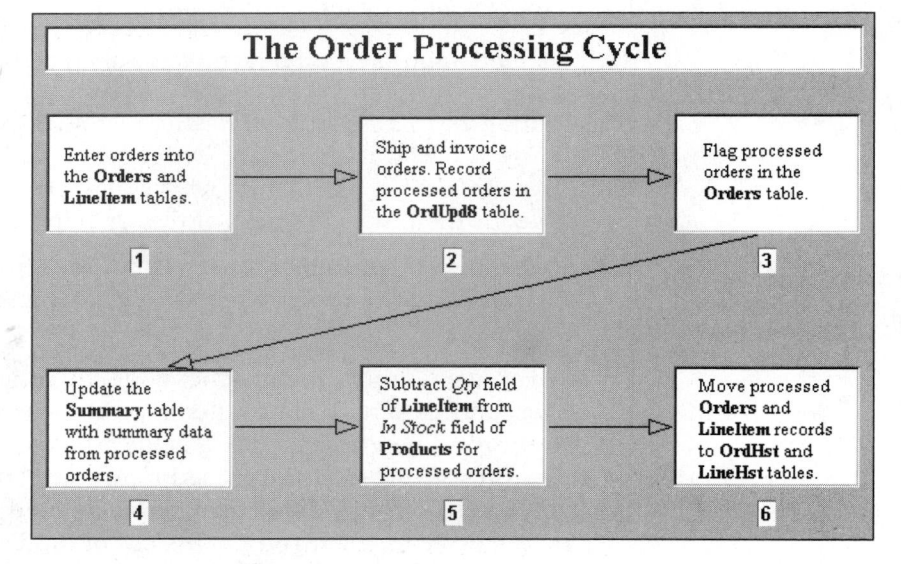

3. Next we mark orders as "processed" by updating (flagging) the Date Shipped and Invoice Date fields of appropriate orders in the Orders table. Flagging these fields will prevent us from shipping the orders again or sending duplicate invoices.

4. We update the Summary table with selected fields from the Orders and OrdUpd8 tables. Although this table is not required for successful order processing, we've included it to illustrate how to copy records from one or more tables to a different table with an incompatible structure.

5. In this step, we update the current in-stock quantities for each product shipped.

6. Finally, we post the processed Orders and LineItem records to appropriate history files (OrdHst and LineHst, respectively), remove the processed records from the Orders and LineItem tables, and clear out the OrdUpd8 table.

Figure 18.2 presents the purchasing cycle, whereby we replenish inventory in our stockroom. Here's a summary of steps involved in this cycle. (We'll describe them further later in this chapter.)

1. First we update the Purchase table with data about each item received in the stockroom.

2. Next we update the quantities and costs of inventory items in the Products table with data from the Purchase table.

3. In this step, we copy processed records from the Purchase table to the PurHst history table, then empty the Purchase table to prevent posted records from being reused.

FIGURE 18.2

The purchasing cycle

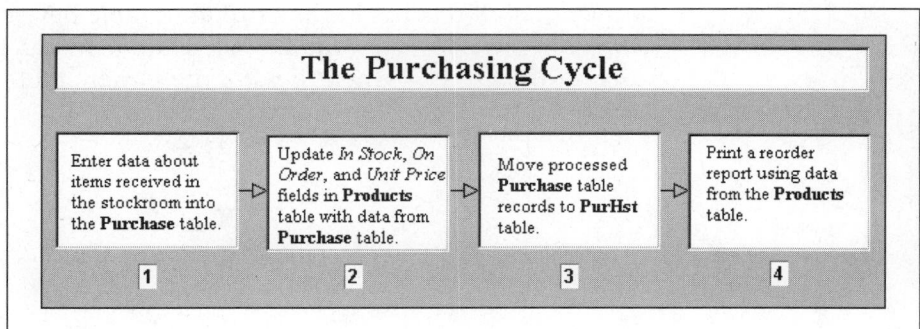

The Purchasing Cycle

| Enter data about items received in the stockroom into the **Purchase** table. | Update *In Stock, On Order,* and *Unit Price* fields in **Products** table with data from **Purchase** table. | Move processed **Purchase** table records to **PurHst** table. | Print a reorder report using data from the **Products** table. |
| 1 | 2 | 3 | 4 |

Updating Tables Automatically

Ch. **18**

4. Finally, we print a reorder report to find out which inventory items in the Products table need replenishing. (We can do this step at any time.)

Now that you have an overview of the basic order processing and purchasing cycles, let's look at techniques for completing each step. Keep in mind that we're illustrating relatively simple approaches to some common business tasks. Bullet-proof commercial order processing and purchasing applications are usually more complex than the ones presented here.

▶▶ *Copying Fields from One Table to Another*

As mentioned earlier, after invoicing and shipping an order (step 1 of Figure 18.1), we'll enter the order number, ship date, and invoice date of those orders into the OrdUpd8 table (step 2 of Figure 18.1). A few sample records for the OrdUpd8 table appear below.

Notice that all records in the OrdUpd8 table have entries in the Date Shipped field. However, the Invoice Date field has entries only for records in which the Payment field of the Orders table contains the value "Invoice."

> ▶▶ **N O T E**
>
> **In this chapter you'll see the benefits of combining a concise transaction table like OrdUpd8 with multitable queries and a few well-chosen options from the Tools ➤ Utilities menus to update many master tables at once in a quick, efficient, and consistent manner.**

Recall from Chapter 16 that we're using the Date Shipped and Invoice Date fields in the Orders table to determine whether an order has been fulfilled (shipped) and invoiced. These two fields are left blank initially to indicate that order processing is incomplete. After we fulfill and invoice an order, it is important to avoid shipping or invoicing it again; therefore, we need a way to mark, or *flag*, orders that have been processed (step 3 of Figure 18.1).

The first step of the marking process is to enter the order number, ship date, and invoice date into the OrdUpd8 table, as described earlier. To complete the marking process, we use the simple *ShipInv* query shown in Figure 18.3.

FIGURE 18.3 ▶

The ShipInv query updates blank Date Shipped and Invoice Date fields in the Orders table with values from the OrdUpd8 table.

We've moved fields, adjusted field widths, and changed default number formats of fields in Query windows and Table windows throughout this chapter so that you can see the queries and results more easily. We've also saved all the queries so we can reuse them as needed (the query name appears on the title bar of each Query window).

In the completed query, we've used the following example elements and query commands:

- *Join1* (entered via the Join Tables button) is the example element linking the common Order No field of the Orders and OrdUpd8 tables.

- *ShipDate* (entered by pressing the F5 key before typing the element name) is an example element representing the date we shipped the order.

- *InvDate* is an example element representing the date we invoiced the order.

- **BLANK, Changeto** *ShipDate* tells Paradox to plug in the Date Shipped value from the OrdUpd8 table if the Date Shipped field in the current Orders record is blank.

- **BLANK, Changeto** *InvDate* tells Paradox to plug in the Invoice Date value from the OrdUpd8 table if the Invoice Date field in the current Orders record is blank.

After you run the query (by pressing F8 or clicking the Run Query button), the Changed table will appear. If you open the Orders table, you'll see that Paradox has indeed copied the appropriate data from OrdUpd8 to Orders, as Figure 18.4 shows.

FIGURE 18.4

After you run the query in Figure 18.3, the Date Shipped and In-voice Date fields in the Orders table contain updated values from the OrdUpd8 table.

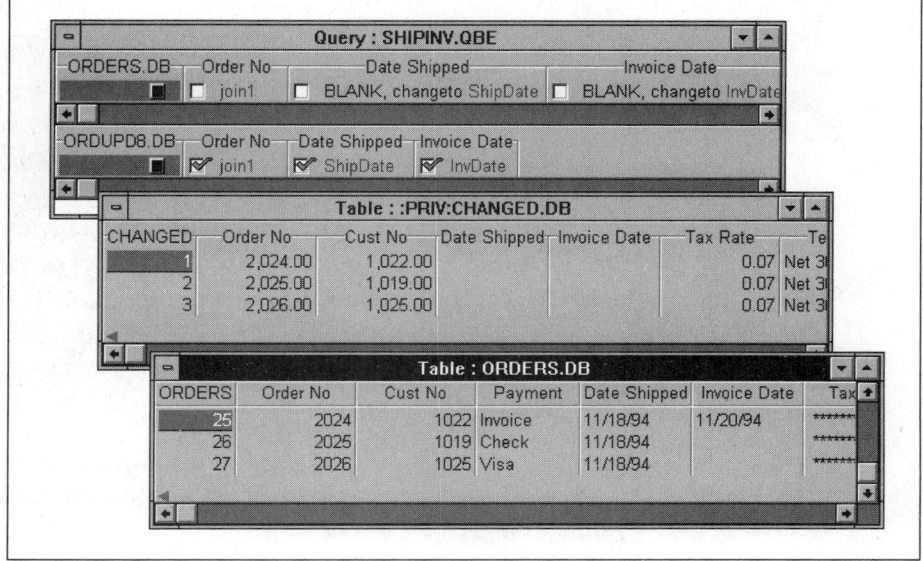

 ▶▶**T I P**

> **It's a good idea to close all windows (choose Window ➤ Close All) before running the next query in a cycle. This precaution helps to avoid those exasperating "Table is already in use" messages that appear when Paradox cannot complete a query because a required table is opened on the Desktop.**

▶▶ *Copying "Incompatible" Records from One Table to Another*

Sometimes you'll want to add records from one or more tables to an-other table. If you're copying just one table's records to another table and the two tables have compatible structures—that is, the field names and data types match—you can use Tools ➤ Utilities ➤ Add, as dis-cussed in Chapter 15. However, if the records come from more than one table, or the structures of the tables are incompatible, it's best to use queries to accomplish your task.

►►NOTE

If you use Tools ➤ Utilities ➤ Add to copy records to a table that has an incompatible structure, some data may be lost. If data loss is likely, Paradox will display a Table Structure Mismatch Warning dialog box that is similar to the Restructure Warning dialog box discussed in Chapter 15, and will give you a chance either to trim the data or back out of the operation.

Suppose you want to summarize data from several tables and add it to a more compact table, such as the Summary table shown below (step 4 of Figure 18.1).

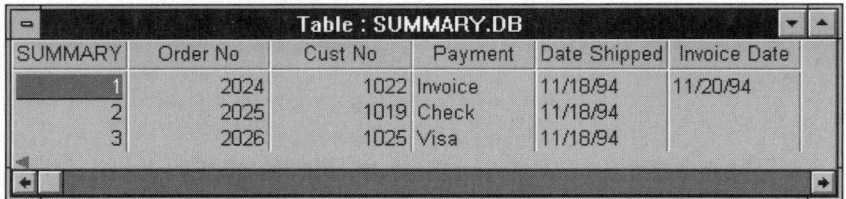

Paradox for Windows offers two methods that are especially useful for adding "incompatible" records from one table to another. The first method uses the Answer table as an intermediary. The second method uses example elements and the INSERT reserved word to insert the records from the source tables into the target table.

The query shown in Figure 18.5 illustrates the first technique. The example element *join1* joins the Orders and OrdUpd8 tables by their common Order No field, and the checkmarks select the fields we want to display. Running the query creates an Answer table with the same structure as the Summary table. Once the query has been run, we could use Tools ➤ Utilities ➤ Add to add records from the Answer table to the Summary table. When the Add dialog box appears, we would select *:PRIV:ANSWER.DB* as the source table and *SUMMARY.DB* as the target table, then click the OK button.

The INSERT reserved word provides an alternative method for inserting records from one or more source tables into a single target table. You can also use INSERT queries to insert records from dBASE tables into Paradox tables, and from Paradox tables into dBASE tables. The steps for creating an INSERT query are as follows:

1. Create a new query (File ➤ New ➤ Query) and add the source table (or tables) and target table to the Query window. (See Chapter 16.)

2. For each source table, specify selection criteria, if necessary.

3. In the *target* table, move the cursor to the leftmost column (under the table name) and type the letter **I**; or click under the table name and choose *Insert* from the list that appears.

4. Link the source and target tables using example elements. Example elements indicate which fields in the source tables should be used to update the target table. If you omit an example element from a field in the target table, that field will not receive any values from the source table.

5. Press F8 or click the Run Query button to run the query.

After you run the query, the appropriate records from the source tables will be inserted into the target table and a temporary table named

Inserted will appear. The Inserted table will include only the records inserted into the target table and will be overwritten every time you run an INSERT query.

▶▶**N O T E**

If necessary, you can use the Inserted table along with the DELETE reserved word to undo an insertion. Be aware that if the INSERT query inserted records that were already present in the target table, the DELETE query will remove the *original* records from the target table as well as the duplicates.

Figure 18.6 shows an INSERT query named *Summary* and the Inserted table that appears after you run the query. In this figure, the example element ***Order*** links the Orders and OrdUpd8 tables and limits the summarized orders to shipped and invoiced orders only. The example elements ***Order***, ***Cust***, ***Payment***, ***ShipDate***, and ***InvDate*** tell Paradox where to insert values from OrdUpd8 into the Summary table.

FIGURE 18.6 ▶

The Summary query uses the INSERT reserved word to insert records from the Orders and OrdUpd8 tables into the Summary table.

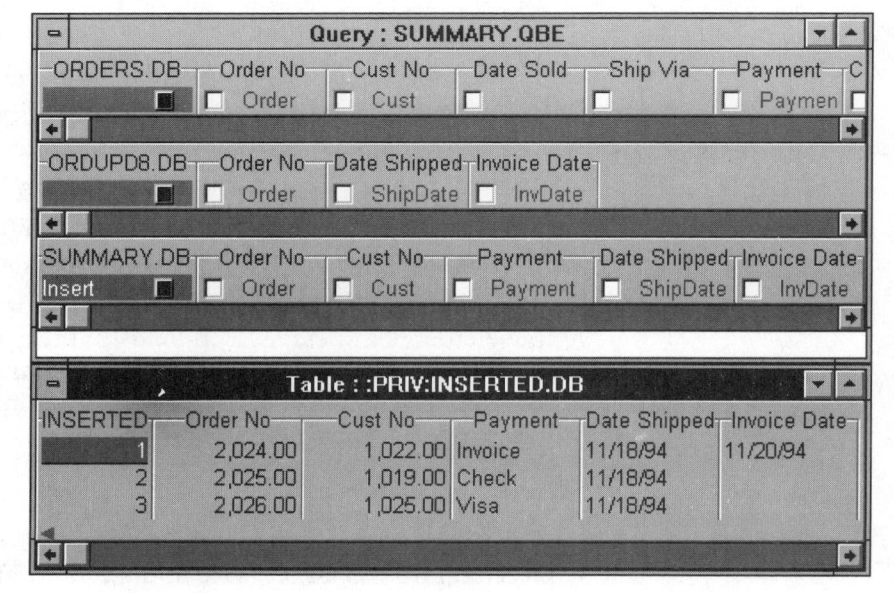

▶▶ W A R N I N G

If you're following along at your own computer, be aware that using *both* the Answer table method and the INSERT query method on the same data will result in duplicate records in your Summary table. You can use a DELETE query to delete the duplicate records, or open the Summary table, press F9, move the cursor to each duplicate record, and press Ctrl+Del.

▶▶ *Changing Values in One Table Based on Another Table*

Perhaps the most common use of automatic updating is to change the contents of one table based on the contents of another table. For instance, in our order processing example, we want to subtract the Qty values for shipped orders in the LineItem table from In Stock quantities in the Products table so that our In Stock quantities will be accurate and up to date (step 5 in Figure 18.1). Performing this step manually would be a real pain; however, it's easy if we use the automatic updating procedures described below.

▶ *Subtracting Quantities Sold from In-Stock Quantities*

To subtract quantities sold from in-stock quantities, we need to complete two steps:

1. Calculate the total quantity of each type of product shipped. That is, for each shipped product in the LineItem table, we must calculate the total value of the Qty field. Again, we'll use the OrdUpd8 table to indicate which items have been shipped and need processing.

2. Subtract the total quantity (Qty) of each item shipped from the In Stock quantity field of the Products table.

To make it easy to test and verify the updating procedure, we'll place some "dummy" values in the Products table. In Figure 18.7, for example, we've set the In Stock quantity to 100, the On Order quantity to 10, and the Reorder Point to 200 for products GC-093, GC-111, and GC-112. (We'll use the On Order and Reorder Point fields later when we discuss the purchasing cycle.)

Now let's suppose that the LineItem table includes the fields and values listed below for order numbers 2024, 2025, and 2026.

Prod Code	Order No	Qty
GC-093	2024	1
GC-093	2025	2
GC-111	2024	2
GC-111	2025	1
GC-112	2025	2
GC-112	2026	2

The query named *CalcSum* in Figure 18.8 shows the first step required to update the In Stock quantities in the Products table: calculating the total quantity sold for each product shipped. Notice that including the OrdUpd8 query table in the Query window limits the calculation to shipped orders only. The example elements *join1* and *join2* link the common fields in the OrdUpd8, Products, and LineItem query tables. The Sold field of the resulting Answer table shows the total quantity sold for each product shipped.

FIGURE 18.7 ►

The Products table with some dummy values entered for products GC-093, GC-111, and GC-112

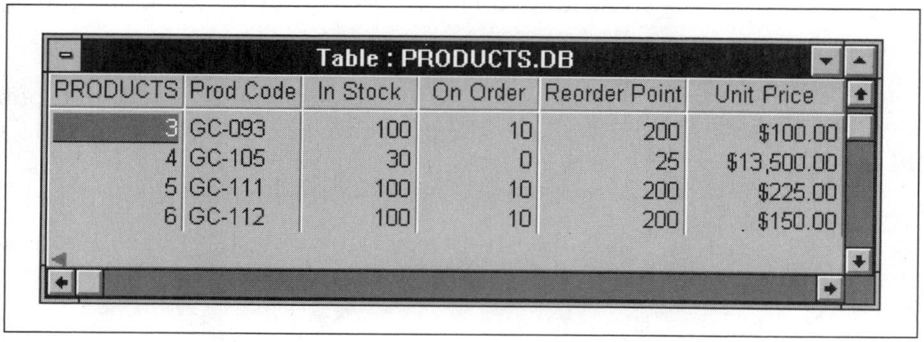

PRODUCTS	Prod Code	In Stock	On Order	Reorder Point	Unit Price
3	GC-093	100	10	200	$100.00
4	GC-105	30	0	25	$13,500.00
5	GC-111	100	10	200	$225.00
6	GC-112	100	10	200	$150.00

Table : PRODUCTS.DB

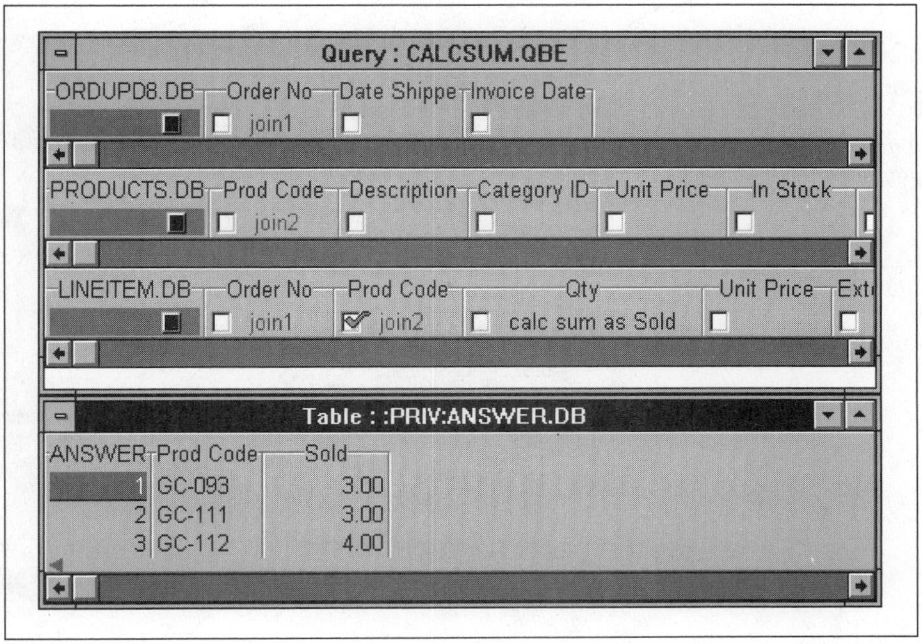

FIGURE 18.8

The CalcSum query shows the total quantity of each product in a field named Sold *in the Answer table.*

The second step of the updating procedure is to subtract the quantities in the Sold field of the Answer table from In Stock quantities in the Products table. To do this update, we created and saved the *Upd8Prod* query shown at the top of Figure 18.9. Here we've used the example element ***join1*** to link the Products and Answer table. The example element ***Current*** represents the current In Stock value in the Products table, and the example element ***QtySold*** represents the value in the Sold field of the Answer table. The CHANGETO command in the query performs the desired calculation and updates the In Stock value.

After we run the query, the changed records are copied to the Changed table as usual. If we open the Products table, we can see that Paradox has indeed subtracted the values in the Sold field from the In Stock quantities in the Products table, as shown at the bottom of Figure 18.9.

FIGURE 18.9 ▶

The Upd8Prod query subtracts the quantity of each product sold from the In Stock quantities

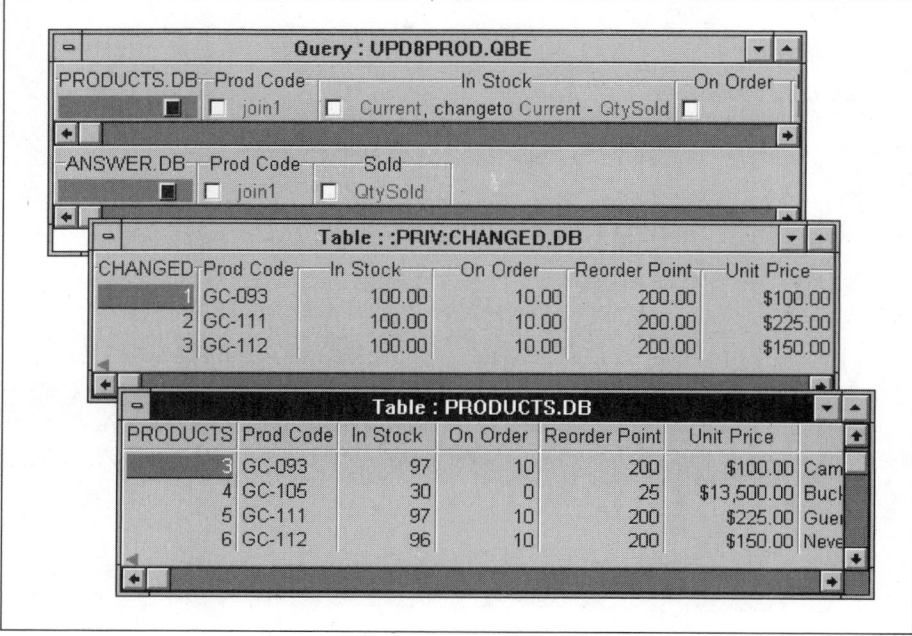

▶▶ *Using History Files*

Now that we've completed the first five steps of the order processing cycle shown in Figure 18.1, we must find some way to ensure that each record in the LineItem table is used only once when subtracting quantities sold from In Stock quantities.

In the previous example, we accomplished this by flagging the Date Shipped and Invoice Date in each record of the Orders table with the dates from the OrdUpd8 table. We also designed the update queries so that only "unflagged" records (those with blank Date Shipped and Invoice Date fields) were updated. Another way to ensure that records are never posted more than once is to move all posted records from the original table to a separate history table.

There are advantages and disadvantages to each approach. The advantage of flagging posted records is that all the records remain in one table. In some ways this makes overall management easier, but the drawback is that the table grows indefinitely, requires extra fields to indicate which records have been processed, and could become huge by the end of a year. Since very large tables can slow down general processing, you will certainly want to consider the disadvantages of flagging records.

By storing live (unprocessed) orders in one table and moving posted orders to a history table, you can keep the table of live orders fairly small and speed up day-to-day processing a bit. You must decide which approach is best on a case-by-case basis when developing applications on your own.

Since history tables usually have the same structure as the original tables, you can easily adapt reports and forms to display and report on historical data.

For the sixth and final step in our order processing cycle, we'll demonstrate the history table method, which involves the following steps:

- Copy all shipped orders from the Orders and LineItem tables to history tables.

- Delete all shipped orders from the Orders and LineItem tables to prevent those records from being used in future updates.

- Clear the OrdUpd8 table so that we won't process shipped and invoiced orders again.

First, you need to create history tables to store the posted records. Since these tables use the same structure as the original tables (Orders and LineItem in this example), you can quickly create an empty history table by following these steps:

1. Choose File ➤ New ➤ Table, then choose OK to begin defining a new Paradox for Windows table.

2. In the Create Table dialog box, click Borrow, click on the name of the table you want to borrow (*ORDERS.DB* in this example), and choose OK.

3. Click the Save As button, type the name of the new history table (**ordhst.db** in this example), and choose OK until you return to the Desktop.

Now Orders and OrdHst have exactly the same structures; the only difference between the two tables is that the OrdHst table is new and completely empty. Repeat the three steps above to create a history table for the LineItem table. This time, specify the table name *LINEITEM.DB* in step 2 and type the name **linehst.db** in step 3.

▶ Moving Posted Orders to the History Tables

Now you're ready to copy all the shipped records from the Orders table to the OrdHst table and from the LineItem table to the LineHst table. Once you've done that, you'll want to remove those records from the original tables so they won't be posted again in the future. The steps are listed below.

1. Clear the Desktop (choose <u>W</u>indow ➤ Close <u>A</u>ll) to prevent "Table is already in use" messages.

2. Run the query shown in Figure 18.10 to copy shipped records from the LineItem table to the Answer table (we named this query *PostLine*). The example element *join1* in the query restricts the selected line items to shipped items only.

FIGURE 18.10 ▶

The PostLine query selects shipped records from the LineItem table and places them in the Answer table. You can then use <u>Tools</u> ➤ <u>Utilities</u> ➤ <u>Add</u> to add the Answer table records to the LineHst table.

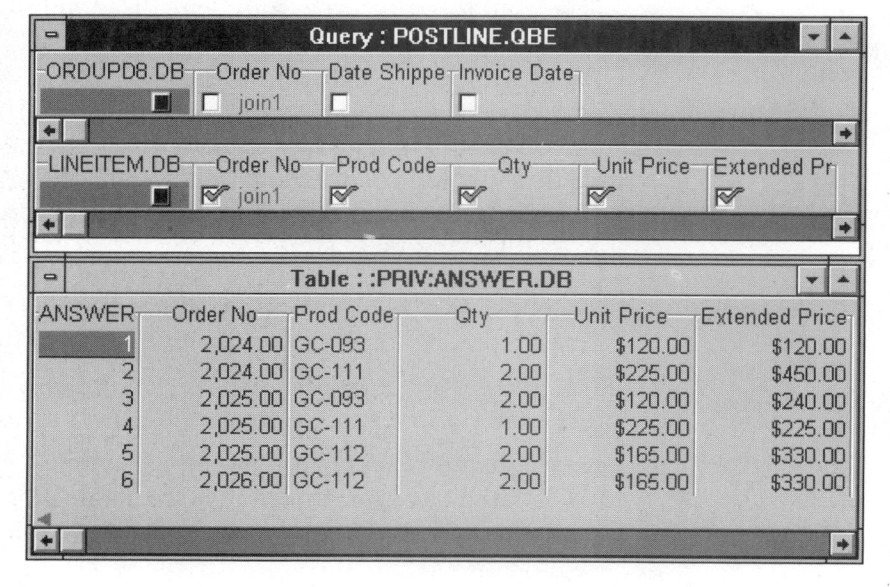

3. Choose <u>T</u>ools ➤ Utilities ➤ <u>A</u>dd, select *:PRIV:ANSWER.DB* as the source table and *LINEHST.DB* as the target table, click Append in the Op<u>t</u>ions area of the Add dialog box, and click the OK button.

4. Clear the Desktop again, then run the DELETE query shown in Figure 18.11 to remove the posted records from the LineItem table (we've named this query *ClrLine*). Paradox stores the deleted records in the temporary Deleted table.

> ▶ ▶ **W A R N I N G**
>
> **If you've set up referential integrity between tables, as we've done between Orders (the parent table) and LineItem (the child table), you must post and remove records from the child table before posting and removing records from the parent table (see Chapter 5).**

FIGURE 18.11 ▶

The ClrLine query removes the posted records from the LineItem table and prevents records from being posted more than once.

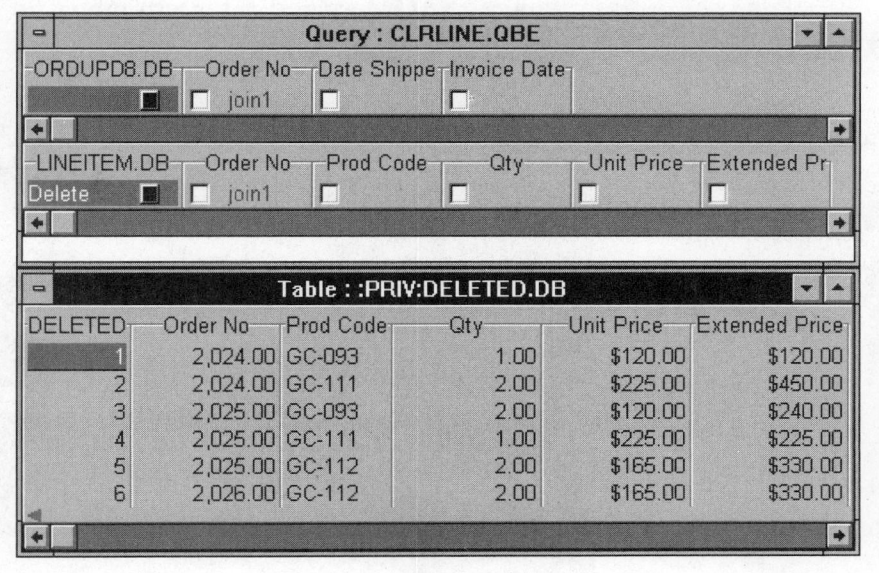

You can now repeat the four steps above to move shipped records from Orders to OrdHst. Briefly, these steps are as follows:

1. Clear the Desktop.

2. Run the query shown in Figure 18.12 to copy shipped orders to the Answer table (we've named the query *PostOrd*). Note that all fields are checked in the Orders table.

3. Choose Tools ➤ Utilities ➤ Add, select *:PRIV:ANSWER.DB* as the source table and *ORDHST.DB* as the target table, click Append in the Options area of the Add dialog box, and click OK.

4. Clear the Desktop, then run the query shown in Figure 18.13 to remove the posted records from the Orders table (this query is named *ClrOrd*).

The final step is to clear out the OrdUpd8 transaction file. Choose Tools ➤ Utilities ➤ Empty, select *ORDUPD8.DB* as the table to empty, click the OK button, and choose Yes.

If you were to peruse the Orders, OrdHst, LineItem, LineHst, and OrdUpd8 tables now, you would find that the OrdHst and LineHst tables contain the posted records that were in the Orders and Line-Item tables, the Orders and LineItem tables no longer contain the posted records, and the OrdUpd8 table is empty.

FIGURE 18.12 ▸

The PostOrd query copies shipped records from the Orders table to the Answer table.

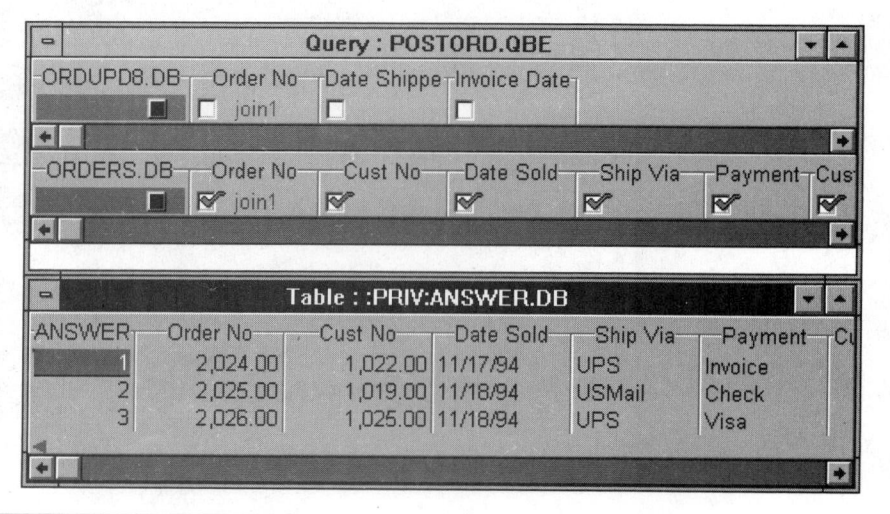

FIGURE 18.13

The ClrOrd query removes the posted records from the Orders table.

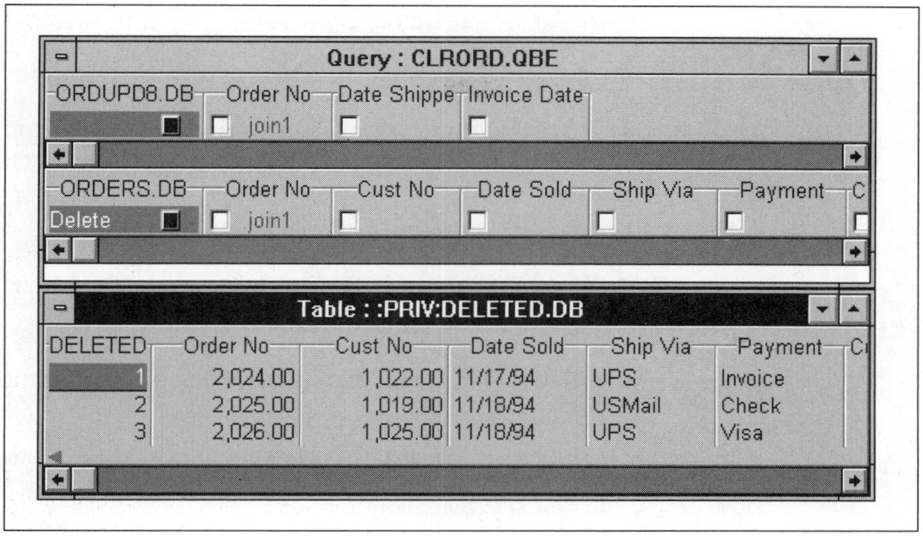

Assuming you saved all the queries required to post records and remove posted records, you need only run those queries and choose the appropriate Tools ➤ Utilities options (in the order given above) when you want to repeat the updates in the future.

▶▶ *Automating Your Work*

As you've seen, automatic updating procedures can involve quite a few steps, and it's very important to do those steps in the proper sequence. Saved queries will certainly help avoid unnecessary delays and improve the accuracy of your updates. However, if you want to automate the steps fully, so that you can perform them with just the click of a button or a few selections from a menu, you'll need to learn ObjectPAL, the Paradox for Windows programming language. We'll introduce that topic in Chapter 19.

▶▶ *Completing the Purchasing Cycle*

Now let's take a closer look at the purchasing cycle that updates the Products table with records in the Purchase table. Recall from

Figure 18.2 that this cycle involves four main steps:

1. Enter received items into the Purchase table.

2. Update the In Stock, On Order, and Unit Price fields in the Products table with data from the Purchase table.

3. Copy processed Purchase table records to a history table named *PurHst*, and then empty the Purchase table.

4. Print a reorder report to determine which items need replenishing in the stockroom.

We'll elaborate on these steps in the following sections.

▶ Entering Received Items into the Purchase Table

After receiving items purchased from vendors in the stockroom, we enter information about those items in the Purchase table, as shown below.

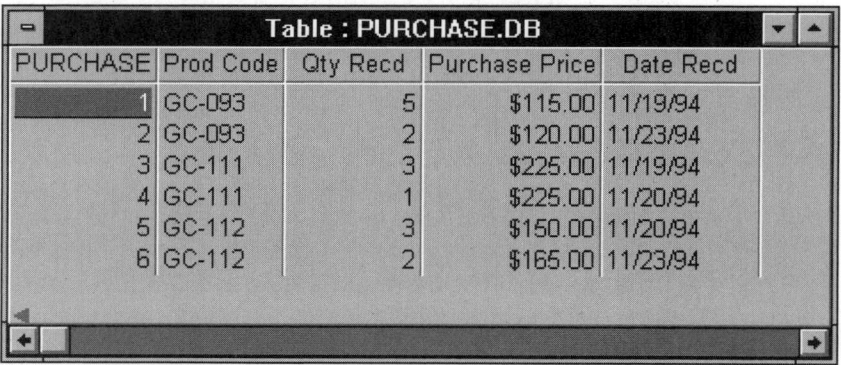

▶ Creating a History Table for Posted Purchases

You'll need a history table to store posted purchase transactions, so follow the steps you used to create the OrdHst and LineHst tables, as explained below.

1. Choose File ➤ New ➤ Table and choose OK.

2. In the Create Table dialog box, click Borrow, select *PURCHASE.DB*, and choose OK.

3. Click the Save As button, type **purhst.db**, and choose OK until you return to the Desktop.

Let's assume that the Products, Purchase, and PurHst tables contain the data shown in Figure 18.14. Note that the PurHst table is currently empty and we've shown only the relevant records in the Products table.

FIGURE 18.14 ▶

Sample data in the Products, Purchase, and (currently empty) PurHst tables

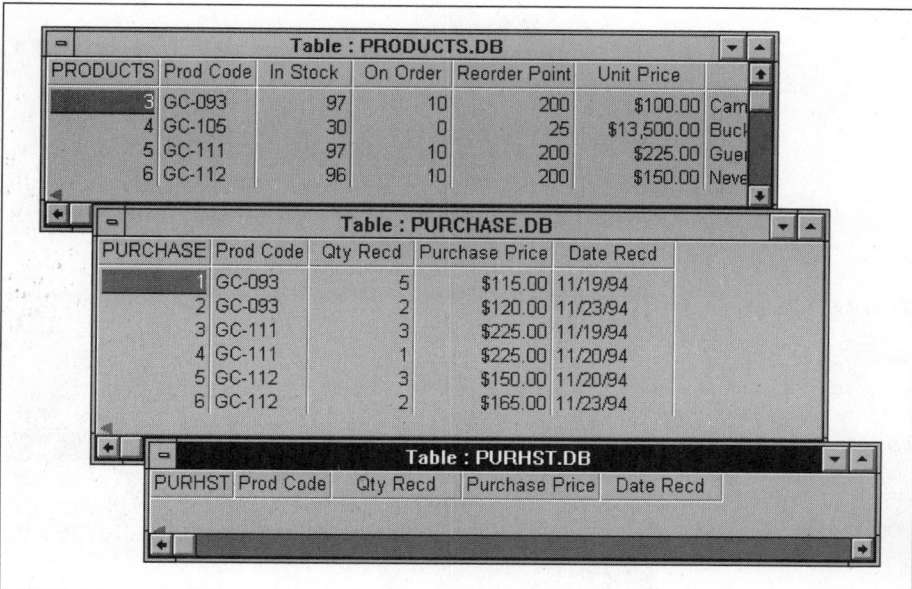

▶ *Adding Received Items to In-Stock Quantities*

Now we're ready to update the master inventory in the Products table with quantities and prices from the Purchase table. We'll need to make the following adjustments:

- Add the quantities of products received to In Stock quantities in the Products table.

- Subtract the quantities of products received from the On Order quantities in the Products table.

- Change the Unit Price field in Products to the highest purchase price in the Purchase table.

- Copy all posted purchase transactions from the Purchase table to the PurHst table.

- Empty the Purchase table.

The procedure is essentially the same as updating Products from the LineItem table, but we've added some new twists to demonstrate additional updating techniques.

To begin, clear the Desktop (choose <u>W</u>indows ➤ Close <u>A</u>ll), then set up and run the query shown at the top of Figure 18.15 (we've named the query *CalcPurc*). Notice that the Prod Code field is checked, *Calc Sum* sums the Qty Recd in a new field named *Qty*, and *Calc Max* calculates the highest Purchase Price in a new field named *Cost*. The resulting Answer table appears at the bottom of the figure.

FIGURE 18.15 ▶

The CalcPurc query calculates the total quantity of each item received in the Purchase table and the highest purchase price of each product.

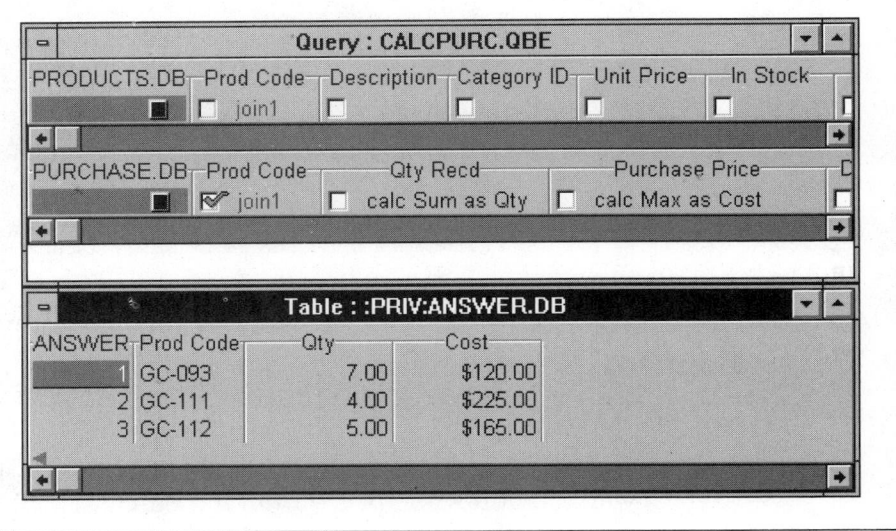

> ## NOTE
>
> **The scheme for updating purchase prices for inventory in real-world situations can become very complex, and many different techniques are used in business. However, to keep things simple in our examples, we've chosen to update the Unit Price field of the Products table with the maximum purchase price calculated for each corresponding product code in the Purchase table.**

Now that you've calculated the total quantity received and the cost of each item, you can use the fields in the Answer table to update the Products table. Clear the Desktop and run the query shown in Figure 18.16 (we've named the query *Upd8Stoc*). Notice that the example element ***join1*** links the Answer and Products tables. The other example elements in the Query window—***Cost***, ***Qty***, ***X***, and ***Y***—are used to perform the calculations and update the Products table fields. After you run the query, the Changed table appears as usual.

> ## NOTE
>
> **We rotated and narrowed the query table columns in Figure 18.16 to fit everything on the screen. Be sure to place the example elements and CHANGETO commands in the correct columns.**

FIGURE 18.16

The Upd8Stoc query updates the Products Table with fields from the Answer Table.

Query : UPD8STOC.QBE				
PRODUCTS.DB	Prod Code	Unit Price	In Stock	On Order
	□ join1	□ changeto Cost	□ X, changeto X + Qty	□ Y, changeto Y - Qty

ANSWER.DB	Prod Code	Qty	Cost
	□ join1	□ Qty	□ Cost

► Moving Posted Purchases to the History Table

Now that you've updated the Products table, you must move all the updated records from the Purchase table to the PurHst table, so they won't be posted in future updates. Here are the steps:

1. Clear the Desktop by choosing Windows ➤ Close All.

2. Choose Tools ➤ Utilities ➤ Add, select *PURCHASE.DB* as the source table, select *PURHST.DB* as the target table, click Append in the Options area of the Add dialog box, and then click OK to add the records from the Purchase table to the PurHst table.

3. Choose Tools ➤ Utilities ➤ Empty, select *PURCHASE.DB*, click the OK button, and choose Yes to empty the Purchase table.

If you were to peruse the Products, PurHst, and Purchase tables now, you'd notice the following:

- The In Stock, On Order, and Unit Price fields in Products have been updated according to values in the original Purchase table.

- The PurHst table contains the posted records from the Purchase table.

- The Purchase table is empty.

Figure 18.17 shows a portion of each of these tables on the Desktop.

► Printing a Reorder Report

After all this automatic updating, it might be nice to know which items need to be reordered. A query that isolates records in which the in-stock plus on-order quantities fall at or below the reorder point will do the trick. The *Reorder* example in Figure 18.18 illustrates this procedure. Notice that ***InStock*** and ***OnOrd*** are example elements used in the calculations. After running the query, you can use techniques discussed in Chapters 10 and 12 to design and print an attractive reorder report based on the Answer table.

Completing the Purchasing Cycle

FIGURE 18.17 ▶

Portions of the Products, PurHst, and Purchase tables on the Desktop after performing the update

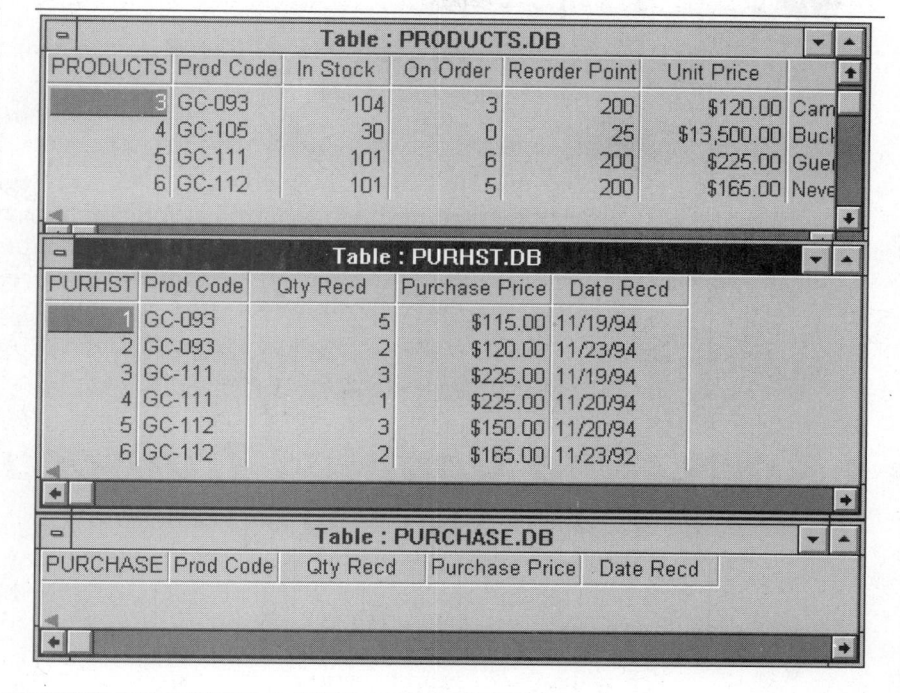

FIGURE 18.18 ▶

The Reorder query selects records in which product quantities have fallen below (or exactly at) the reorder point.

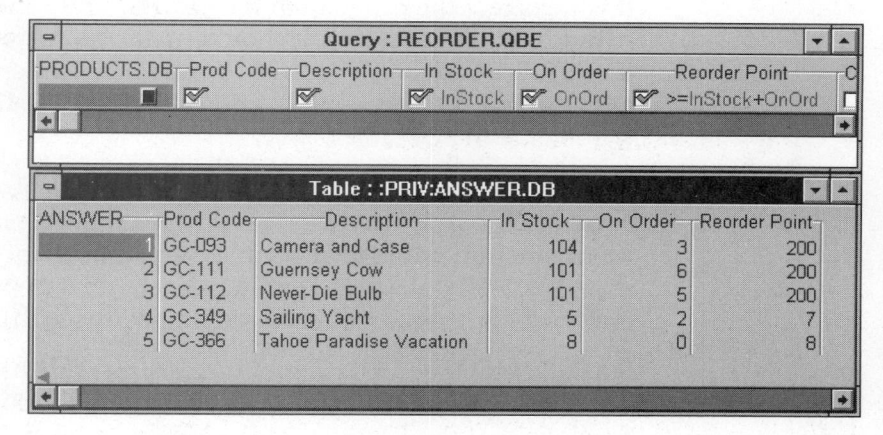

►►**N O T E**

The reorder query will produce an empty Answer table if no products fall at or below the reorder point.

The purchasing cycle is now complete. As you begin to design and develop sophisticated database applications of your own, you'll find that you can use the techniques presented in this chapter to combine and update data among multiple related tables however you wish. And after you've learned how to use ObjectPAL, you'll be able to reduce the whole procedure to a few simple mouse clicks or menu selections.

►► *Correcting Updated Transactions*

One problem always arises when you use automatic updating to change the contents of one table based on the contents of another table: If you discover an error in one of the transactions *after* the update, how do you fix it?

For instance, suppose you discover an error in the quantity ordered for a customer's order *after* you update the Products table and move the original Orders and LineItem records to history files.

If you correct the problem in the OrdHst and LineHst tables directly, Paradox won't know that it should make the correction in the Products table. If you also corrected the Products table manually, that would be OK. However, there would be no "audit trail" indicating that changes were made to any tables.

The best way to correct an error after updating records is to add an *adjustment transaction* to the original tables. For instance, in Figure 18.19 we used a multitable form to make an adjustment transaction showing the return of two Never-Die Bulbs (at $165 a pop they shouldn't be faulty, but apparently a few duds slipped through).

During automatic updating, this adjustment record will be processed just like any other. That is, its Qty field will be subtracted from the In Stock field of the Products table. However, given that Qty is a negative number, the net result will be to *add* the value of 2 to the In Stock quantity. Furthermore, the record will be copied to the OrdHst and

LineItem ⁺ables, just like any other record, so there's a permanent history of the transaction on disk.

FIGURE 18.19

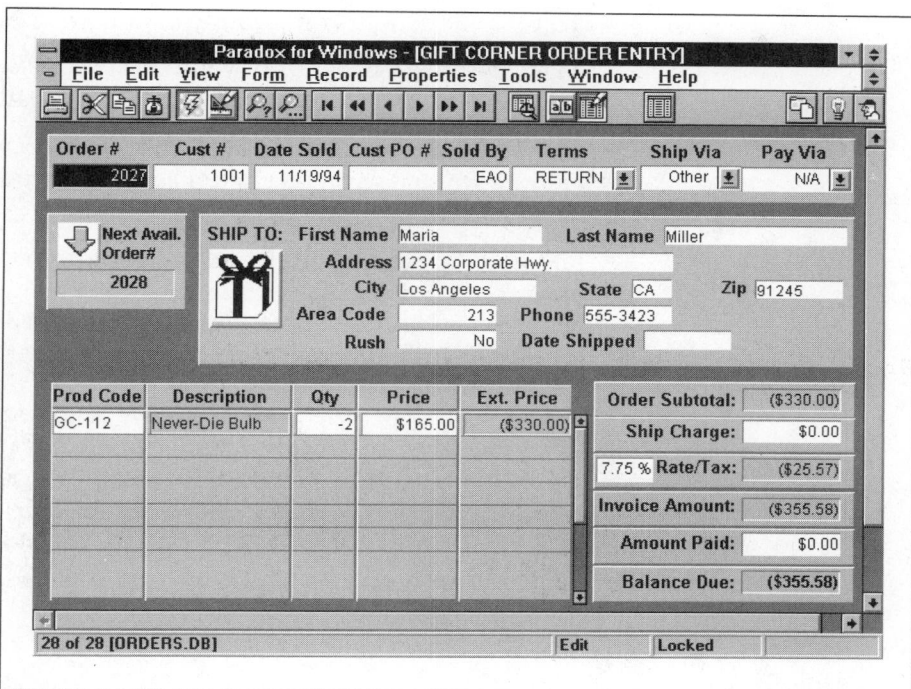

An adjustment transaction on a custom form. The -2 indicates that two items were returned, and the Terms and Pay Via fields briefly explain the negative Qty value.

▶▶ *Resetting Autoincrement Field Values*

In Chapter 5 you learned how to set an autoincrement field in a new table to whatever starting value you wanted. With autoincrement fields, it's really best to plan ahead and set the table up with the starting value you want—before you've put data into your tables. But what if you haven't used an autoincrement field in your table and now want to? Or maybe you've been using autoincrement fields, but now want to start them at some other value.

Making the switch is tricky, and it can require many steps. Moreover, you may end up in hot water if your tables involve referential integrity

Updating Tables Automatically

Ch.
18

relationships (we fried a dummy copy of our database the first time we tried this). Fortunately, it's relatively easy to avoid boiling your data and your brain, if you heed the warnings below:

- Test the procedures on dummy data first.
- Make complete backups of your database *before* you try the steps below. Chapter 15 explains how to copy Paradox files.
- Make complete backups of your database *before* you try the steps below. (We said this twice because it's so important!)
- For tables involved in referential integrity relationships, your detail tables should be empty before you try the steps below. For instance, if you are reassigning customer numbers, be sure to process all outstanding orders and empty the orders and line item tables *first* (as explained earlier in this chapter).

In the sections below, we'll assume you've followed this advice to the letter. For the sake of example, let's assume you've been assigning sequential customer numbers manually and now want an autoincrement field to do the job automatically. (To reset the starting value for data that's already in an autoincrement field, you would also use the procedures given below.)

►►**N O T E**

> **Resetting autoincrement fields is a tricky business in most database managers, not just Paradox. And although autoincrement fields are extremely convenient for some types of data entry, they are much less flexible than numeric and alpha fields when you need to make changes.**

► *Creating the New Table*

To begin, create a new table that has the same structure as your original table, with this exception: The key field (Cust No, in this example) should be a Long Integer. Here's a quick review of the steps to follow:

1. Choose File ➤ New ➤ Table, then choose OK to begin defining a new Paradox for Windows table.

2. In the Create Table dialog box, click <u>B</u>orrow, click on the name of the table you want to borrow (*CUSTLIST.DB* in this example), select (check) all the options in the Options list in the Borrow Table Structure dialog box, and choose OK.

3. Change the Type for the key field (Cust No) to Long Integer (I).

4. Click the Save <u>A</u>s button, type the name of the new customer table (**tempcust.db** in this example), and choose OK.

▶ Entering a Dummy Record to Set a New Starting Value

The next step is to add a new "dummy" record to the new table. Open the TempCust table, press F9 to go into Edit mode, then fill in one dummy record. In the Cust No field, type the desired starting value for your customer numbers, minus 1. For example, type **4700** if you want your real customer numbers to begin at 4701 (as illustrated later in Figure 18.20). You can leave the other fields blank if they aren't assigned the "Required Field" validity check.

▶ Converting the Key Field to an Autoincrement Type

Now you must restructure the new table to convert its Long Integer key field (Cust No) to an Autoincrement field. Close the TempCust table (<u>F</u>ile ➤ <u>C</u>lose), choose <u>T</u>ools ➤ <u>U</u>tilities ➤ Re<u>s</u>tructure, and then double-click the *TEMPCUST.DB* table in the <u>F</u>ile Name list. In the Restructure Table dialog box, highlight the Type column for the Cust No field and change its type from Long Integer to Autoincrement (+), then click <u>S</u>ave to save the table and return to the Desktop.

Next, open the TempCust table again, move the cursor to the first (dummy) record, press F9, and press Ctrl+Del to delete the record. Close TempCust again.

▶ Inserting Records into the New Table

Next, you must create an INSERT query to insert records and values from the existing table (CustList) into the new table (TempCust).

Updating Tables Automatically

Ch. 18

The basic steps are listed below:

1. Choose File ➤ New ➤ Query, select the *CUSTLIST.DB* and *TEMPCUST.DB* tables (by Ctrl-clicking, as discussed in Chapter 16), and choose OK.

2. In the query table for CustList, create example elements for every field, *except* for Cust No. For instance, use the example element *a* for Last Name, *b* for Mr/Mrs, *c* for First Name, and so on, as we did in Figure 18.20. Remember to press F5 before typing each example element.

3. Place the same example elements in the corresponding fields of the TempCust query table.

4. Click in the leftmost column of the TempCust query table (just below the TEMPCUST.DB name) and type **I** to select the *Insert* reserved word.

5. Press F8 to run the query.

Figure 18.20 shows the screen after running the INSERT query and then opening the TempCust table to see the results.

FIGURE 18.20 ▶

A query to insert each field, except Cust No, from the CustList table into the TempCust table.

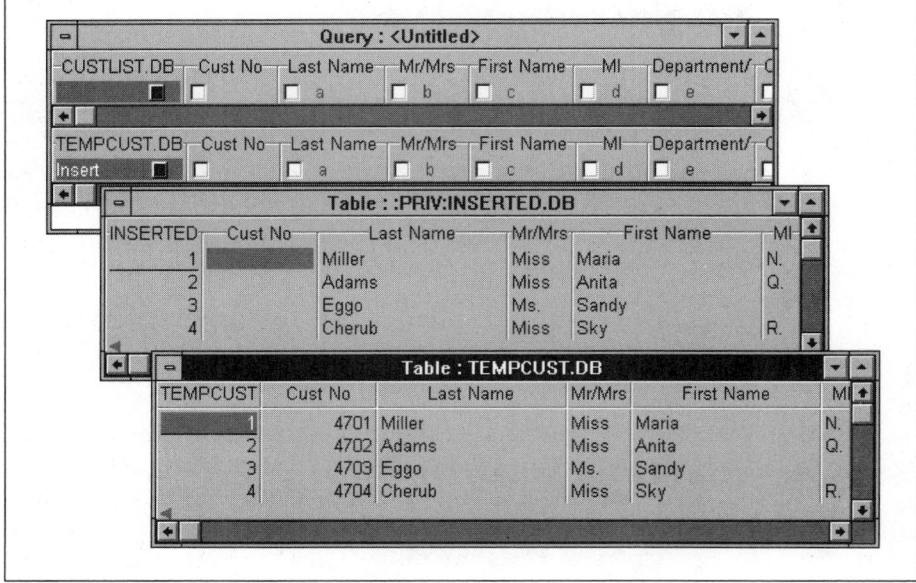

▶ *Finishing the Job*

You're almost done. All that remains is to rename TempCust to Cust-List. Unfortunately, this is rather messy if you've set up referential integrity between CustList and other tables in your database. In our sample database, we defined referential integrity between Orders and CustList (also, between LineItem and Orders). So, we must break the referential integrity links temporarily, rename TempCust to CustList, then reestablish our referential integrity relationships. Here are the steps:

1. Close all windows (<u>W</u>indow ➤ Close <u>A</u>ll).

2. Choose <u>T</u>ools ➤ <u>U</u>tilities ➤ Res<u>t</u>ructure, then double-click *ORDERS.DB* in the file list.

3. In the Restructure Table dialog box, click the Table <u>P</u>roperties drop-down list, then click *Referential Integrity*.

4. Click the referential integrity relationship you want to delete (*Orders to CustList* in our example), then click <u>E</u>rase.

5. Choose <u>S</u>ave to save the revised Orders table structure.

Now, rename TempCust to CustList. To do this, choose <u>T</u>ools ➤ Utili-ties ➤ <u>R</u>ename, type **tempcust.db** in the <u>R</u>ename File From text box, type **custlist.db** in the T<u>o</u> text box, choose OK, then choose <u>Y</u>es.

For the finishing touch, you need to redefine the Cust No field of the Orders table as Long Integer and then restore the referential integrity relationship between Orders and CustList. Follow these steps:

1. Choose <u>T</u>ools ➤ <u>U</u>tilities ➤ Res<u>t</u>ructure, then double-click *ORDERS.DB* in the file list. The Restructure Table dialog box will appear.

2. Change the Type for the Cust No field to Long Integer (I). (If you forget to do this, you won't be able to establish referential integrity between CustList and Orders.)

3. Click the Table <u>P</u>roperties drop-down list, then click *Referential Integrity* and choose <u>D</u>efine. In the <u>F</u>ields list of the Referential Integrity dialog box, double-click *Cust No*. In the <u>T</u>able list, double-click *CUSTLIST.DB*.

Updating Tables Automatically

Ch.
18

4. To save the referential integrity relationship, choose OK, type a referential integrity name (for example, **Orders to CustList**), and choose OK.

5. Choose <u>S</u>ave to save the revised Orders table structure. Respond to any prompts and Restructure Warning messages by letting Paradox continue the operation.

▶ ▶ **N O T E**

You may also need to update other Table Properties, such as Table Lookup.

As you can see, starting autoincrement fields at a new value is not simple, especially if referential integrity and a great deal of data are involved. Your best bet is to plan ahead and set your autoincrement field to an appropriate starting value *before* you've entered a lot of data. Still, isn't it comforting to know that you *can* change your mind and resequence the autoincrement fields if necessary?

In this chapter, we've explored techniques for automatically updating tables and for keeping track of records that have been posted. In Chapter 19 we'll introduce you to ObjectPAL, the Paradox for Windows programming language, which enables you to automate your forms into full-fledged applications.

Automating Your Work with ObjectPAL

▶▶ FAST TRACK

F1. All the standard online tools are available to help you navigate the Help manual. You can also copy sample code from the *Example* section of any Help window into the method you're entering.

▶ **To copy sample code from a Help window into your method** **1071**

click the Copy button in an ObjectPAL Example window. Use your mouse to select the block of code you want, click the Copy button, and then switch to the ObjectPAL Editor window. Place the insertion point where you want the sample code to appear, and press Shift+Ins or Ctrl+V.

▶ **To begin testing a method** **1076**

click the View Data button in the Toolbar of the Form Design or ObjectPAL Editor window, or press F8. The remaining steps depend on the type of object you attached the method to and the event that triggers the method. In general, you can test the method by performing whatever action triggers it. For example, to test a method attached to a button, click the button.

▶ **This chapter describes a "starter set"** **1086**

of ObjectPAL statements. To work with reports, forms, and tables, use the *Open*, *setTitle*, *Maximize*, *postRecord*, and *action(dataBeginEdit)* statements. To execute a query from a file, you must first read it into a variable (with the *readFromFile* command) and then execute the query (with the *executeQBE* command). To display messages to users, use the *msgInfo* and *msgQuestion* statements. To get user input, use the *View* statement. To exit Paradox for Windows, use the *Exit* statement.

ObjectPAL is a full-featured, visual programming language that you can use to automate your work and to build sophisticated Paradox for Windows applications. The language provides hundreds of tools for automating *anything* that can be done in Paradox for Windows—and more.

► ► N O T E

Borland International has made many changes to ObjectPAL in each successive version of Paradox for Windows. To learn about the main differences between versions 4.5 and 5.0 of ObjectPAL, go to the ObjectPAL Contents in Help, and explore the topics under the "Changes and New Features" heading. In some cases you may need to revise existing programs to make them run properly under Paradox 5 for Windows. You'll learn more about using the ObjectPAL Help system later in this chapter.

Not surprisingly, a comprehensive explanation of ObjectPAL would require a hefty book at least as large as the one you're reading now and an equally hefty wheelbarrow to cart it around in. So instead of presenting an exhaustive (and exhausting) catalog of ObjectPAL features and syntax rules, we'll focus on the highlights of the language and take you through some practical examples that automate tasks discussed in previous chapters of this book.

Once you've studied these examples, you should feel more comfortable using the *Guide to ObjectPAL* manual, the *ObjectPAL Quick Reference* manual, and the online *ObjectPAL Reference* that come with Paradox for Windows to help you learn more about ObjectPAL programming.

> ▶ ▶ **N O T E**
>
> ***Guide to ObjectPAL* presents some tutorial examples to introduce the fundamentals of ObjectPAL programming. The *ObjectPAL Quick Reference* offers a concise summary of the ObjectPAL language. In the *ObjectPAL Reference Guide*, you'll find detailed reference material about each built-in method and language statement. The *ObjectPAL Reference Guide* is available online (via the Help system), or in printed form if you order it separately from Borland.**

You certainly don't have to be a programming guru to reap the benefits of ObjectPAL or to understand the material presented in this chapter. However, we do assume that you are familiar with basic programming concepts and that you know how to design custom forms using the techniques presented in Chapters 10 and 11 of this book.

▶ ▶ *Understanding ObjectPAL Terminology*

Before jumping into our examples, we must introduce some essential ObjectPAL terminology, including the terms *object*, *event*, *method*, and *application*.

▶ *What Is an Object?*

As you learned in Chapter 1, just about anything you can create in Paradox for Windows is an *object*. For example, buttons, fields, graphics, tables, queries, forms, and reports are all objects.

Every Paradox object consists of *properties* (such as color, position, font, and frame style) and *methods* (code that defines how the object behaves). The specific properties and methods available depend on the type of the object. For example, the properties and methods for buttons are different than those for table frames. (Please see Chapters 10 through 12 and Appendix E for more about properties.)

▶ What Is an Event?

An *event* is an action that affects an object. Anything you do in Paradox for Windows can generate an event. Common types of events include:

- Pressing a key or clicking the mouse
- Opening or closing a form, report, or table
- Changing a value in a field
- Adding a record to a table
- Clicking a button
- Choosing an option from a menu

▶ What Is a Method?

A *method* is a snippet of ObjectPAL code that defines how an *object* responds to an *event*. Methods are activated (or *triggered*) when specific events occur. For example, the following method maximizes a window on the Desktop when the user arrives in a form:

```
method arrive(var eventInfo MoveEvent)
    maximize()
endmethod
```

Later in this chapter we'll explain each component of a method. For now, however, we just want to give you an idea of what a simple method looks like.

▶▶ **N O T E**

A method in ObjectPAL is similar to a subroutine in a traditional programming language. When a subroutine finishes executing, control normally returns to the calling program. Likewise, when a method finishes executing, control normally returns to the form.

Methods are typically attached to objects in forms (see Chapters 10 and 11), but they can also be stored in stand-alone files called *scripts* and in collections of ObjectPAL code called *libraries*. In this chapter, we'll concentrate on methods attached to objects in forms.

▶ What Is an Application?

An *application* is a system that automates database management tasks. Often, applications perform useful business functions, such as processing accounts receivable, fulfilling customer orders, and checking purchases into the stockroom. Most ObjectPAL applications are built from customized forms that contain buttons to which ObjectPAL methods are attached. The examples in this chapter include an automated order-entry form and a form that automates the order-processing and purchasing cycles discussed in Chapter 18.

▶ Objects Are "Smart" Things

When you were learning to design forms, you probably discovered that objects "know" about the objects inside them. What's more, you undoubtedly noticed that the same types of objects always have the same properties and methods available to them—they even tend to look alike and behave similarly. Thus, a form "knows" about the tables and fields in its data model, and all buttons in a form have the same general appearance and give basically the same response when you click them. For these reasons, we say that Paradox objects are "smart."

▶ How ObjectPAL Differs from Traditional Programming Languages

If you've ever developed an application in a traditional programming language, such as BASIC, FORTRAN, Pascal, or C, you know that the process can be time-consuming and frustrating, since you must write and debug program code for *every* action performed by the application.

When you use Paradox for Windows, however, a large part of your programming is done *automatically* (and correctly!) whenever you place objects on a form and set properties for those objects (see Chapters 10 and 11). Why? Because the standard behavior of each object on the form is defined automatically. ObjectPAL is needed only if you want to automate a series of steps, change the built-in behavior of an object, or exercise greater control over what the user sees and does. For example, you could use ObjectPAL to prompt for the name of a table or form to open; to automate the many steps required to update inventory and history files; or to calculate and update an Extended Price field automatically.

►►**N O T E**

Programmers who are comfortable with Microsoft Visual C++ or Visual BASIC will have little trouble learning ObjectPAL.

To speed the development process further and reduce the amount of programming you must do, ObjectPAL features many built-in methods. It also includes an extensive online Help system with lots of sample code that you can paste in and revise as needed.

Before setting out to develop a substantial application with ObjectPAL, you should understand basic programming techniques, and you should be comfortable using most of the Paradox features discussed in this book. If that sounds like a tall order, keep in mind that you may *never* need to write a speck of ObjectPAL code. Although ObjectPAL is a tremendously valuable tool for automating and simplifying your work, the standard Paradox for Windows features and some custom forms and reports may provide all the power you need.

Our advice is to begin by creating short and simple ObjectPAL methods like the ones presented in this chapter. Then, study the sample application in the *c:\pdoxwin\connect* directory (described next). As you gain experience, you can experiment with increasingly sophisticated ObjectPAL features and develop fancier applications.

►► *Exploring the Connections Application*

The *Connections* application that comes with Paradox 5 for Windows is a feature-filled prospecting and contact-management application that includes a full Help system. Perfect for sales and marketing people who want to manage their communications with prospects and clients, this application is installed automatically when you install Paradox for Windows. You'll find Connections in the directory *c:\pdoxwin\connect* (assuming you did a standard installation).

▶ ▶ **N O T E**

You'll find other simpler applications in the *c:\pdoxwin\examples* directory, which also appears automatically when you install Paradox for Windows.

To use Connections, switch your working directory to *\pdoxwin\connect*, click the Scripts icon in the left side of the Project Viewer window, and then double-click the *start.ssl* file name in the right side of the Project Viewer.

If you'd like to find out what makes the application tick, exit Connections (if you've started it), then try the following:

- To explore the genius behind any Connections form, click the Forms icon in the Project Viewer window, then right-click the form you'd like to study and choose De§ign.

- To find out how the *Start* script works, click the Scripts icon in the Project Viewer window, then right-click the *start.ssl* file name and choose De§ign.

- To explore other objects in the database, click the appropriate icon in the Project Viewer, then right-click the object you're interested in and choose an option from the pop-up menu.

You probably should avoid changing the Connections application's forms, reports, scripts, libraries, queries, and table structures so that you don't break anything important. This is especially true if you or your colleagues will be using Connections to track your business contacts. If you do plan to make changes, be sure to back up the entire *c:\pdoxwin\connect* directory first. Then, should an experiment go awry, you can restore damaged files with fresh copies from your backups. As a last resort, you can also reinstall the Connections application; however, that will cause you to lose any data that you've already stored in Connections.

💡 ▶▶**TIP**

If you haven't installed this handy application yet, or you need to reinstall it, do a *Custom* install and select the Connections Application installation option only. See Appendix A for more details about installing Paradox.

▶▶ *Attaching a Method to an Object*

Typically, you'll attach ObjectPAL methods to a button, a field, a page of a form, or to the form itself. To begin attaching a method, inspect (right-click) the object in the Form Design window and choose Methods, or select the object and press Ctrl+spacebar. Figure 19.1 shows the Method Inspector that appears when you inspect a button and choose Methods. In the figure, we've highlighted the *pushButton*

FIGURE 19.1 ▶

The Method Inspector appears after you inspect an object in the Form Design window and choose Methods.

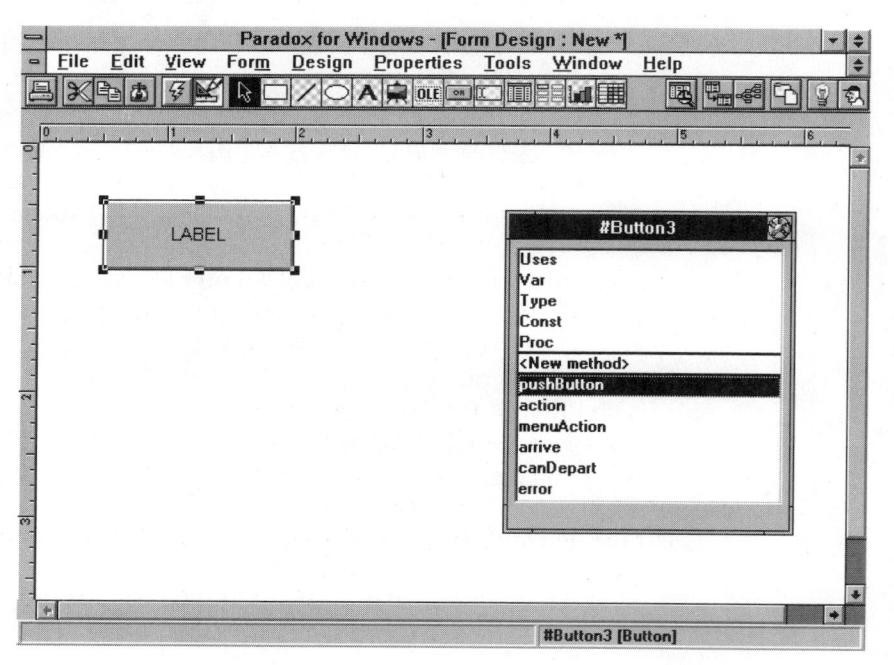

method. This method is triggered when the user pushes (clicks) the button to which the method is attached.

> **N O T E**
>
> **The Method Inspector has been redesigned in Paradox 5 for Windows.**

The most important areas of the Method Inspector are explained below.

- The title bar displays the name of the object to which you're attaching the method.

- The items above the horizontal line let you specify external library routines (Uses), variables (Var), data types (Type), constants (Const), and procedures (Proc) in a separate editing window. We won't be discussing this use of the Method Inspector here. If you'd like to explore this further, click in the Method Inspector and press F1.

- The items below the horizontal line list built-in methods provided by ObjectPAL. The name of the method reflects the type of event that triggers it. We'll focus on these built-in methods in this chapter. You can also design your own custom methods by double-clicking the <New Method> entry.

- The snap button lets you keep the Method Inspector on the screen as you work in the Form Design window, Object Tree, or ObjectPAL Editor window. The Method Inspector will change to reflect the methods available for any object that you select in the Design window or Object Tree. To close the Method Inspector after clicking its snap button once, simply click its snap button again.

The built-in methods displayed in the Method Inspector depend on the object you've inspected and the settings you've chosen in the Properties ➤ ObjectPAL dialog box. The default Properties ➤ ObjectPAL setting is Beginner, which provides a "starter set" of methods. If you choose the Advanced option in the ObjectPAL Preferences dialog box, more built-in methods will be available. When you're first learning ObjectPAL, it's best to stick with the default setting of Beginner to avoid confusion. You can change the Properties ➤ ObjectPAL settings from any Paradox for Windows menu. Table 19.1 briefly describes the "beginner-level" built-in methods available.

Once you've opened the Method Inspector, you can work with its methods in a variety of ways:

- To select an existing method to work with, click on its name in the Method Inspector. To select several adjacent methods, hold down the Shift key while clicking or dragging the mouse pointer through the method names. To select several non-adjacent methods, hold down the Ctrl key while clicking the method names.

- To create a new custom method, double-click the <New method> entry in the Method Inspector, or right-click any method and choose <u>N</u>ew, or press the Insert (Ins) key.

▶ **TABLE 19.1:** *Some "Beginner-Level" Built-in Methods*

METHOD	WHEN CALLED
*action**	Called when an action takes place (e.g., the cursor is moved to another field in a table) or when a method wants some action performed (e.g., switch to Edit mode).
*arrive**	Called after moving to (arriving at) an object such as a form, form page, field, table frame, or multi-record object.
canDepart	Called when trying to move off a field or record.
*changeValue**	Called when a new value is about to be stored. (Available for fields only.)
error	Called when an error occurs. Objects (except the form itself) pass errors to their containers.
menuAction	Called when the user chooses an item from a menu or clicks a Toolbar button that executes a menu action.
mouseClick	Called when the left mouse button is clicked on the object.
*pushButton**	Called when a user clicks on a button. (Available for buttons and fields defined as list boxes only.)

* Illustrated in this chapter

- To open a method for editing, just double-click it in the Method Inspector. Alternatively, you can select one or more methods in the Method Inspector, then press ↵ (or right-click and choose Open from the pop-up menu).

- To delete a method, select the method or methods you want to delete and press the Delete (Del) key; or right-click the method or methods and choose Delete. When prompted for confirmation, choose Yes to delete the method, or No to leave it intact (you'll be prompted once for each method you selected before choosing Delete). If you delete a *custom method (*one that you created), that method is deleted permanently. By contrast, if you delete a built-in method, the method is simply detached from the current object.

- To display help about using the Method Inspector, click in the Method Inspector (or click its title bar) and press F1.

When you open one or more selected methods, an ObjectPAL Editor window will open for each method you selected. Figure 19.2 shows the ObjectPAL Editor window that appears after selecting the *pushButton* method from the Method Inspector. Paradox generates the *Method* and *endMethod* statements automatically to define the method name and its parameters and to end the method you selected. These statements are required and you shouldn't need to change them.

 ▶▶**N O T E**

> ObjectPAL statements are not case-sensitive. Therefore, statements and variable names can be typed in uppercase letters, lowercase letters, or a mixture of both. Thus, *method, METHOD,* and *Method* are all the same to Paradox, as are *endmethod, ENDMETHOD,* and *endMethod.* Text within quotation marks, however, *is* case-sensitive. For instance, the statement *msgInfo("A message","This is a message.")* would produce a different message than *msgInfo("A MESSAGE","THIS IS A MESSAGE.")*

FIGURE 19.2

The ObjectPAL Editor window after selecting the pushButton method from the Method Inspector

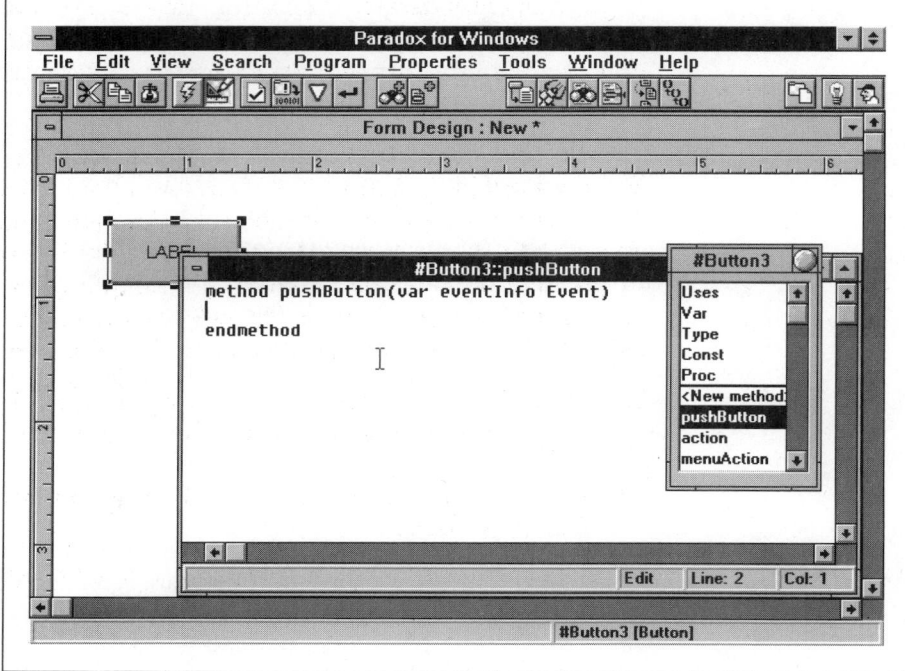

The *Method* statement specifies the method name (for example, *push-Button*), and defines the information being passed to the method within parentheses. Every built-in method has the following information passed to it: the word *Var* (which introduces a parameter), the parameter *eventInfo* (which provides information about the event that triggered the method), and the parameter's data type (e.g., *Event*). The data type will depend on the method you selected and determines which methods you can use with *eventInfo* to get and/or store information about the event.

▶▶ **W A R N I N G**

For the simple tasks discussed in this chapter, you don't need to concern yourself with the parameters in the *Method* statement. Just be sure that you leave the *Method* and *endMethod* statements unchanged when editing a built-in method.

The status bar indicates the current position of the insertion point (it's in line 2, column 1 in the example). You should enter the program code after the *Method* statement and before the *endMethod* statement (that is, between the *Method* and *endMethod* statements).

The ObjectPAL Editor menu bar includes the File, Edit, Properties, Window, and Help menus common to all Paradox windows, plus the View, Search, Program, and Tools menus, which contain options that are unique to the ObjectPAL Editor window. Several ObjectPAL Editor menu options are discussed in this chapter. For additional information on the menu options, pull down the menu, use the arrow keys to highlight the option you're interested in, and press F1.

The general steps for writing and testing a method are listed below and explained in more detail in the sections that follow.

1. Enter the ObjectPAL code for the method into the ObjectPAL Editor window.

2. Check the syntax of the method and make any necessary corrections.

3. Save the method and exit the editor.

4. Test the method.

5. Change or delete the method if necessary.

▶▶ *Entering ObjectPAL Code*

After opening the ObjectPAL Editor window, the simplest way to enter program code is to type it. For instance, you could type **maximize( )** on line 2 of the Editor window. (The *Maximize* statement will cause the form to maximize when the button is clicked in Form View.) Later in this chapter, you'll see many examples of program code entered in the ObjectPAL Editor window.

▶ ▶ **T I P**

> By default, Paradox uses an editor that is similar to the
> Windows Notepad application (notepad.exe) as the
> ObjectPAL Editor. If you'd like to use a different editor
> (which must be able to save text-only files), choose
> **Properties ➤ ObjectPAL**, check the **Alternate Editor**
> option, specify the full path and file name of the edit-
> ing program you want to use, and choose **OK**.

You can use the mouse or the ←, →, Home, and End keys to position
the insertion point for typing. You can also use the editing techniques
summarized below.

- To select text, drag the mouse across the text or hold down the
  Shift key while pressing a cursor-positioning key such as ← or →.
  To select a word, double-click the word. To select an entire line,
  move the mouse pointer to the left edge of the line (the pointer
  will change from an I-beam to an arrow) and click.

- To delete text, use the Backspace or Delete key.

- To undo a change, choose Edit ➤ Undo or press Alt+Backspace.

- To undo all changes made to the method since the last time it was
  saved, choose Edit ➤ Undo All Edits, then choose Yes when
  asked to confirm your choice.

▶ ▶ **T I P**

> You may wish to maximize the Editor window by
> double-clicking the title bar or clicking the Maximize
> button. This allows you to see more of the program
> code at once. You can also use options from the
> **Window** menu to rearrange windows on the screen
> and temporarily switch back to the Form Design
> window.

▶ *Saving Time when Entering ObjectPAL Code*

Rather than typing ObjectPAL code in the ObjectPAL Editor window, you can use any of several shortcuts to enter program code. For example, to copy ObjectPAL code from another method, proceed as follows:

1. Open the ObjectPAL Editor window for the object where you want the new code to appear, as described earlier.

2. Switch to the Form Design window for the form that contains the ObjectPAL code you wish to copy, inspect the object you want to copy *from*, choose Methods, and double-click the name of the method you want to copy. (Methods that have code assigned to them will be marked with an asterisk (*) in the Method Inspector and will be underlined in the Object Tree.)

3. When the ObjectPAL Editor window appears, select the code you want to copy, press Ctrl+Ins or Ctrl+C, and close the Editor window (press Ctrl+F4).

4. Switch to the ObjectPAL Editor window for the method you're copying *to*. Now, position the insertion point where the new code should appear and press Shift+Ins or Ctrl+V.

You can also paste code from a saved text file (typically a file with a *.txt* file extension). To do so, position the insertion point where you want the text to appear, then choose Edit ▶ Paste From. In the Paste From File dialog box, select the text file you want and choose OK.

▶▶**N O T E**

To copy code from your method to a text file, select the code you want to copy, choose Edit ➤ Copy To, then type a file name without an extension, and choose OK. (Paradox will give the file a *.txt* extension.)

One of the handiest shortcuts—copying examples from the ObjectPAL online Help—is covered in the next section.

▶▶ *Using the ObjectPAL Help System*

ObjectPAL's online Help manual provides the quickest, most efficient way to get up to speed with the language. In addition to providing detailed information about each language feature, ObjectPAL's online Help also includes hundreds of program samples that you can paste into your own methods and then revise as needed. In fact, it's a complete online reference manual at your fingertips—and you don't need to worry about whether many trees were killed to supply the information you need.

To use the ObjectPAL online Help, choose Help ▶ ObjectPAL Contents from any Paradox menu. You'll see the ObjectPAL Contents page shown in Figure 19.3.

FIGURE 19.3 ▶

The ObjectPAL Contents page

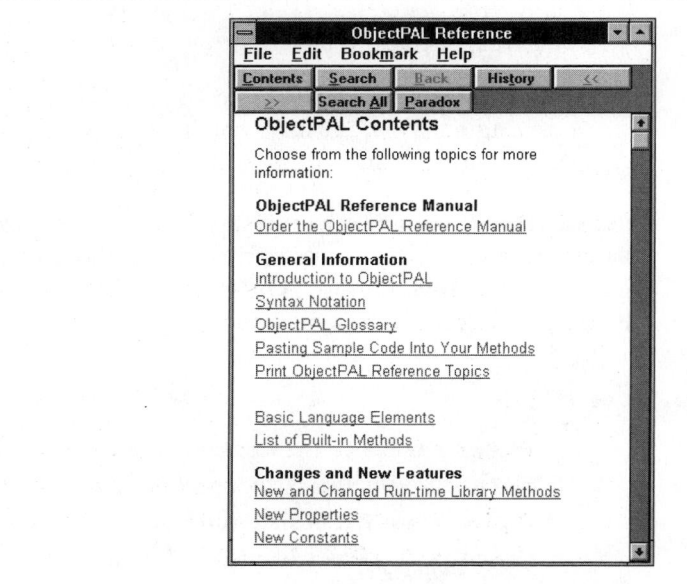

Automating
with ObjectPAL

▶ ▶
Ch.
19

▶ ▶ **N O T E**

You can also reach the Contents page by clicking the <u>O</u>bjectPAL button in any Paradox Help window, or by clicking the <u>C</u>ontents button in any ObjectPAL Help window.

From the ObjectPAL Contents page, you can click on any underlined topic to get more information about essential features of the language. If you want to search for help on a particular topic, click the <u>S</u>earch (or Search <u>A</u>ll) button in any Help window. For details about the built-in methods, click the *List of Built-in Methods* topic in the "General Information" section of the ObjectPAL Contents page. For help on any ObjectPAL command, put the insertion point within the command's text (or select the text) in the ObjectPAL Editor window, and press F1.

To return from any ObjectPAL Help screen to the ObjectPAL Contents page, click the <u>C</u>ontents button. (To return to the standard Paradox for Windows Contents page, click the <u>P</u>aradox button instead.) Other buttons and features in the ObjectPAL Help system are the same as those used in the standard Paradox for Windows Help system covered in Chapter 3.

Figure 19.4 illustrates a sample Help topic describing the ObjectPAL statement used to maximize a window. To display this topic, we typed the word **maximize** in the ObjectPAL Editor window, selected that word, and then pressed F1. What could be easier?

▶ ▶ **N O T E**

Depending on the command you selected before pressing F1, you may need to make further selections in the Search or Search All dialog box.

▶ *Copying the Sample Code*

Like the Maximize topic shown in Figure 19.4, most ObjectPAL Help topics are divided into several sections, including an *Example* section that contains sample code and a *See Also* section listing related topics that you can click on for more information.

FIGURE 19.4

*The Maximize Help
topic*

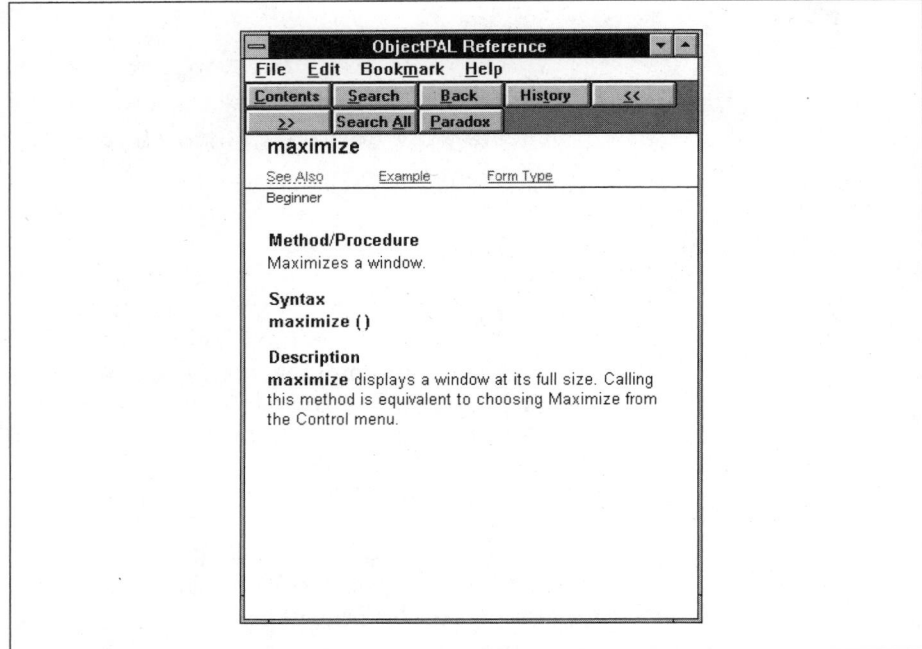

To copy sample code from the Example section of a Help topic into
your ObjectPAL method, follow these steps:

1. Click the underlined *Example* text near the top of the Help topic.
An ObjectPAL Example window will appear, as shown below:

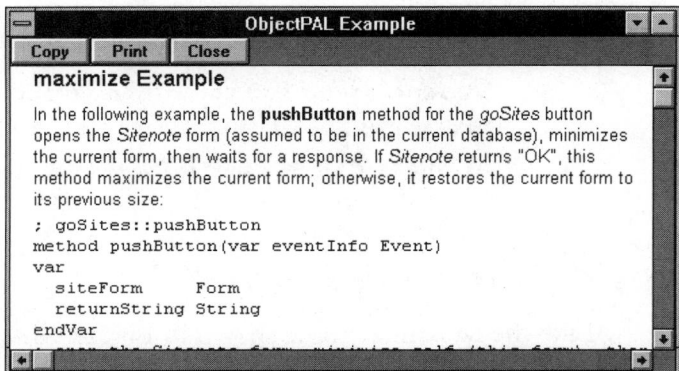

2. Click the Copy button in the ObjectPAL Example window. (If you want a printed copy of the example, click the Print button instead.)

3. Use your mouse to select the block of code you want, and then click the <u>C</u>opy button. If you wish, you can close the ObjectPAL Example window (by clicking its Close button) and the ObjectPAL Reference window (by double-clicking its Control-Menu box or pressing Esc).

4. Switch to the ObjectPAL Editor window and place the insertion point where you want the sample code to appear.

5. To paste the code from the Clipboard, press Shift+Ins or Ctrl+V, or click the Paste From Clipboard button in the Toolbar, or choose <u>E</u>dit ➤ <u>P</u>aste.

6. Revise the pasted code as necessary.

▶ Printing the Online Manual

Sometimes it's easier to review a printed copy of a Help window than it is to review the information online. Paradox offers several ways to get printed information from its online reference manual, as summarized below:

- To print the current Help topic, choose <u>F</u>ile ➤ <u>P</u>rint Topic.

new

- To print a group of ObjectPAL Topics from any ObjectPAL Help window, choose <u>F</u>ile ➤ Print <u>G</u>roup Of ObjectPAL Topics. Alternatively, you can go to the ObjectPAL Contents window and click the topic *Print ObjectPAL Reference Topics*, which is in the "General Information" section. When the Print ObjectPAL Reference Topics screen appears, follow the instructions for selecting and printing the topics you want. Be careful! This could tie up your printer for a while.

▶ ▶ **T I P**

If the ObjectPAL Reference screen you're viewing includes a little printer icon, you can click that icon to go to the Print ObjectPAL Reference Topics screen.

If you think your printer doesn't have enough gas to print all the topics you want, or you're tired of feeding it paper and you don't mind spending a few dollars, you can order a printed version of the ObjectPAL reference material from Borland International. The ordering instructions and a handy order form are online (of course). To print them, go to the ObjectPAL Contents in Help, click the topic *Order the ObjectPAL Reference Manual* (near the top of the page), then choose File ➤ Print Topic from the Help menus.

►► *Checking the Syntax and Compiling the Code*

After you're finished typing the code for your method, you should check the syntax to be certain that you haven't violated any rules of the ObjectPAL language. To check the syntax, use any of these techniques:

- Click the Check Syntax button in the Toolbar (shown at left).
- Choose Program ➤ Check Syntax or press F9.
- Right-click anywhere in the ObjectPAL Editor window, or click in the window and press F6; then choose Check Syntax.

If all the syntax is correct, the status bar will display the message "No syntax errors." If ObjectPAL does find a syntax error, it positions the insertion point near the error in the ObjectPAL Editor window and displays an error message in the status bar. You should then correct the error and recheck the syntax (after all, few people make just *one* mistake).

To quickly view the next error (if any), click the Go To The Next Warning button in the Toolbar, or press Ctrl+N, or choose Search ➤ Next Warning, or right-click the ObjectPAL Editor window and choose Next Warning. When all the syntax errors are gone, you'll see the message "No more errors" in the status bar.

Automating
with ObjectPAL

Ch.
19

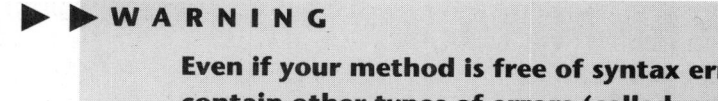

WARNING

> Even if your method is free of syntax errors, it may contain other types of errors (called *runtime* or *logic* errors). These won't be evident until you test the method and it doesn't behave as you intended.

After checking the syntax (or instead of checking the syntax), you can compile the method if you wish. This step is optional, since Paradox will do it automatically whenever you switch to Form View or save your method. *Compilation* is a process that both checks syntax and converts your ObjectPAL language statements into a form that your computer can execute quickly and efficiently. To compile a method, use any of these techniques:

- Click the Compile button in the Toolbar (shown at left).
- Choose P_rogram ➤ Compi_le or press Shift+F9.
- Right-click anywhere in the ObjectPAL Editor window, or click in the window and press F6; then choose Compi_le.
- Choose _File ➤ _Save in the Form Design or Form View window.

If the syntax passes muster, you'll see the comforting message "No syntax errors" in the status bar. Otherwise, the status bar will describe the problem and the insertion point will appear near the trouble spot.

TIP

> When your programs become too long to be viewed at a single glance, your best bet is to review them in printed form, rather than on the screen. A printed copy can help you find and correct errors more quickly, and it provides a handy reference for anyone who must update the method later. To print a copy of the currently open method, choose _File ➤ _Print from the ObjectPAL Editor menus.

►► Saving the Method

When the code is free of syntax errors, you're ready to save the method and exit the ObjectPAL Editor window. To do so, click the Save Source And Exit The Editor button in the Toolbar (shown at left), or simply close the window. Your method will be saved with the object to which it is attached, and you'll be returned to the Form Design window.

**T I P**

To save your changes without leaving the ObjectPAL Editor window, choose File ➤ Save.

►► Testing the Method

After checking the syntax, you should test it in Form View. Not surprisingly, Paradox offers you several ways to do this, as listed below:

- From the Form Design window, click the View Data button in the Toolbar or press F8.

- From the ObjectPAL Editor window, click the View Data button in the Toolbar, or press F8, or choose Program ➤ Run. Or, right-click anywhere in the window, or click in the window and press F6; then choose Run.

If the form wasn't compiled previously, Paradox will compile it and report any errors that occur. You must correct all syntax errors before you can use the form.

After opening the form in Form View, the actual steps for testing the method depend on the type of object you attached the method to and the event that triggers the method. In general, you can test the method by performing whatever action triggers it. (To return to the ObjectPAL Editor window after testing, simply click the Design button in the Form View window's Toolbar or press F8.)

Suppose you attached the *arrive* built-in method containing the *Maximize* statement shown below to the *page* of a form. (Recall from "What

Is an Object," above, that this method maximizes a window on the Desktop.)

```
method arrive(var eventInfo MoveEvent)
    maximize()
endmethod
```

To test this method, simply open the form (in Form View) and the form will be maximized automatically.

> ▶ ▶ **T I P**
>
> **To attach a method to the page of a form, click on an empty area of the page in the Form Design window and press Ctrl+spacebar. To attach a method to the form itself, press Esc until no objects are selected, then press Ctrl+spacebar.**

By contrast, if you attached the *pushButton* built-in method shown below to a *button*, the form would be maximized only when you click the button in the Form window.

```
method pushButton(var eventInfo Event)
    maximize()
endmethod
```

▶ ▶ *Changing and Deleting a Method*

After you define and save a method for an object, the method name will be marked with an asterisk (*) in the Method Inspector. Changing a method is a lot like creating it in the first place. The easiest way is to return to the Method Inspector for the object and double-click the method you want to change. The ObjectPAL Editor window will appear and you can edit the code, check its syntax, and save it as described above.

To delete a method that's attached to an object, click on the method you want to delete in the Method Inspector, press the Delete key (or right-click and choose <u>D</u>elete), then choose <u>Y</u>es when asked to verify the deletion.

Note that deleting a *built-in* method erases the ObjectPAL code you entered for that method and removes the asterisk next to the method name in the Method Inspector; however, it does not remove the method name from the list. By contrast, deleting a custom method removes both the ObjectPAL code and the method name.

►►TIP

> **The Object Tree provides a bird's-eye view of all objects in the Form Design window. Objects that have methods attached to them will be underlined (though the underlining will be difficult to see if you've highlighted the object in the Object Tree). To open the Object Tree, press Esc until no objects are selected, then click the Object Tree button in the Toolbar (see Chapter 10). You can then open the Method Inspector by inspecting an object in the Object Tree and choosing Methods, or by clicking on the object and pressing Ctrl+spacebar.**

Now that you've seen the basic steps for attaching, editing, saving, changing, and deleting methods, let's look at some practical examples. Keep in mind that our goal here is to give you a feel for the ObjectPAL language—not to transform you instantly into an ObjectPAL expert. After trying out the examples presented in this chapter, you'll probably be ready to develop some simple applications on your own. At the very least, you'll appreciate how ObjectPAL can be used to streamline your day-to-day work with Paradox for Windows, and you'll feel comfortable using ObjectPAL's online Help and the language manuals that come with Paradox for Windows.

►► *Adding ObjectPAL Methods to an Order-Entry Form*

In Chapter 17 we presented an order entry form that calculated the Extended Price field automatically. In this chapter, we'll explore a slightly different form that updates the Extended Price field in the LineItem table whenever we change the Qty or Unit Price field for a line item in an order. This form appears in Figure 19.5.

> ▶▶**N O T E**
>
> As mentioned in Chapter 17, you're better off if you do not store calculated fields in tables, since Paradox 5 makes it relatively easy to calculate them on the fly in any design document. Nonetheless, you may want to use ObjectPAL to update a field in a table at some point, so this form provides a good example for illustrating the techniques involved.

To have Paradox maximize the form automatically whenever it's opened, first open the form in the Form Design window, click an empty area of the page, then press Ctrl+Spacebar and double-click

FIGURE 19.5 ▶

A sample order entry form that updates the Extended Price field automatically

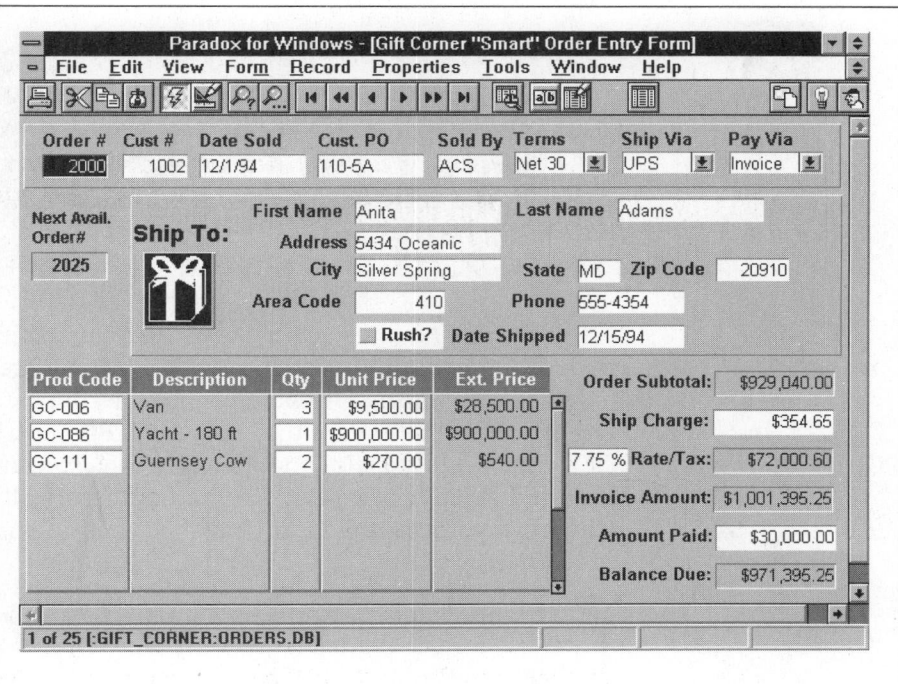

arrive in the Method Inspector. When the ObjectPAL Editor window appears, type **maximize( )** on line 2, check the syntax, then save and close the method.

Next, attach the calculation method to the Qty field as follows:

1. Click the field, press Ctrl+spacebar, and double-click *changeValue* in the Method Inspector. (The *changeValue* method will be triggered whenever you change the value in the field.)

2. When the ObjectPAL Editor window appears, type in the code shown between the *Method* and *endMethod* statements below, check the syntax or compile the code, and save and close the method. (An explanation of the code is given below.)

```
method changeValue(var eventInfo ValueEvent)
    postRecord()              ; post current record
    Extended_Price = Qty * Unit_Price
endmethod
```

Repeat the two steps above for the Unit Price field.

▶ ▶ N O T E

The semicolon in the example above introduces a comment, which is ignored by the compiler, but can be helpful as a reminder to you about what is happening in the code. We'll discuss comments later in this chapter.

To test the methods, click the View Data button in the Toolbar of the Form Design window, switch to Edit mode by pressing F9, then change a value in the Qty field of the order form, and move the cursor to another field. (Moving the cursor lets Paradox know that you've finished changing the field, and activates the *changeValue* method.) The Extended Price field will be updated automatically. Repeat the test by changing a value in the Unit Price field and moving the cursor out of the field.

The statements in the *changeValue* method work as follows:

• The *postRecord()* statement posts the current record so that the next calculation uses the most up-to-date values.

The *Extended_Price = Qty * Unit_Price* calculation multiplies the value in the Qty field of the LineItem table by the Unit_Price field of the LineItem table and stores the result in the Extended_Price field of the LineItem table.

▶▶ **N O T E**

> The *action(DataPostRecord)* command used in previous versions of ObjectPAL has been changed to *postRecord( )*.

Note that in this example we're working with the Qty, Unit_Price, and Extended_Price field objects and the LineItem table frame object, not with the actual fields of the LineItem table. Although the field names were defined in the LineItem table as "Unit Price" and "Extended Price" (with a blank space between words), blanks and other punctuation are replaced by an underscore character (_) when objects are placed in the Form Design window.

▶▶ **T I P**

> The object *name* always appears in the status bar of the Form Design window when you click on the object. You can change the name of an object if you wish. Chapter 17 describes the differences between object names and objects and explains how to rename design objects.

▶ *Understanding Dot Notation*

In the *changeValue* method shown above, we could have written the code a bit differently, like this:

```
method changeValue(var eventInfo ValueEvent)
    LineItem.postRecord()          ; post current record
    LineItem.Extended_Price = LineItem.Qty * LineItem.Unit_Price
endmethod
```

The dot (.) notation is used throughout ObjectPAL to separate elements such as object names, variables, methods, and properties in a statement. For example, the first statement above means "In the LineItem table, post the current record." The second statement means "Multiply the LineItem table's Qty field by the LineItem table's Unit Price field and store the result in the LineItem table's Extended Price field."

►►**N O T E**

Dot notation is also used in calculated fields and summary fields of forms and reports (see Chapter 17).

Earlier in this chapter, we explained that objects are "smart" things that know about the objects inside them. For example, the data model of the multitable order form in Figure 19.5 specifies three tables: Orders, LineItem, and Products. Because the form "knows" about tables in its data model, we can omit the table name and dot when referring to fields in those tables in an ObjectPAL statement. However, if we were to attach another table that wasn't part of this form, we would need to tell ObjectPAL exactly which table we were referring to. (You'll find out how to attach tables later in this chapter.)

►►**N O T E**

The _data model_ is a diagram of table relationships in the form. (See Chapters 5, 10, and 17.)

You also use dot notation to specify the hierarchy of objects. Suppose we designed a form in which a text object named "myText" is contained within a box object named "theBox." The statement _theBox.myText.text_ = _"Hello there!"_ would store _Hello there!_ in the text object within the box. The topics under "General Information" in the ObjectPAL contents Help window will guide you to Help screens that discuss dot notation and other language essentials in more detail.

▶ Using Comments, Blank Lines, and White Space

You may have noticed the semicolon (;) followed by text in the sample methods above. The semicolon introduces program comments in ObjectPAL. You should make liberal use of comments to describe what's happening in a method and to make your programs more understandable. Contrary to popular folklore, comments *do not* slow down program execution.

Any text following a semicolon is considered to be a comment and is therefore ignored by ObjectPAL. If you begin a line with a semicolon, the whole line is treated as a comment. Note, however, that a semicolon within quotation marks is *not* treated as a comment. For example, the semicolon and following text are all part of the string assigned to *myText* in the statement *myText = "Brrrr; it's cold outside!"*.

If you want to create comments that occupy multiple lines, place a semicolon in front of each line of the comment. Alternatively, you can create large blocks of commented text by placing a left brace ({) before the first comment line of the block and a right brace (}) after the last comment line of the block. The braces and all text between them will be treated as comments.

You can also use blank lines, blank spaces, and tabs to make your programs more readable. These elements are ignored, unless they appear in a quoted string. For example, the statement

```
msgInfo("Two Lines","This text
spans two lines.")
```

displays the dialog box shown below.

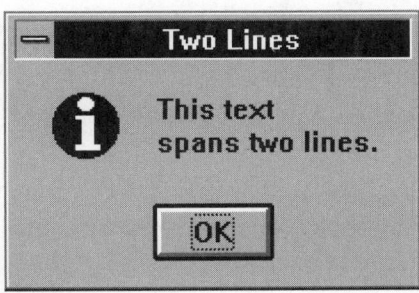

▶▶ Creating an Application to Open Tables, Forms, Queries, and Reports

Now let's take a look at a complete (though simple) application. Figure 19.6 illustrates a form that lets us open tables, forms, and reports, or run queries simply by clicking a button. In the figure you can see what happened after we clicked the *Open Table* button.

Here's how the application works:

1. When we click one of the buttons, a dialog box requests the name of a table, form, query, or report (as appropriate). We then type the name of the desired object into the dialog box (with or without the file extension) and choose OK.

  - If the method fails to find the requested object, it displays an error message dialog box.

FIGURE 19.6 ▶

A simple application after clicking the Open Table button. (After clicking the button, we moved the "Enter a table name" dialog box so that it would not cover any of the buttons on the form.)

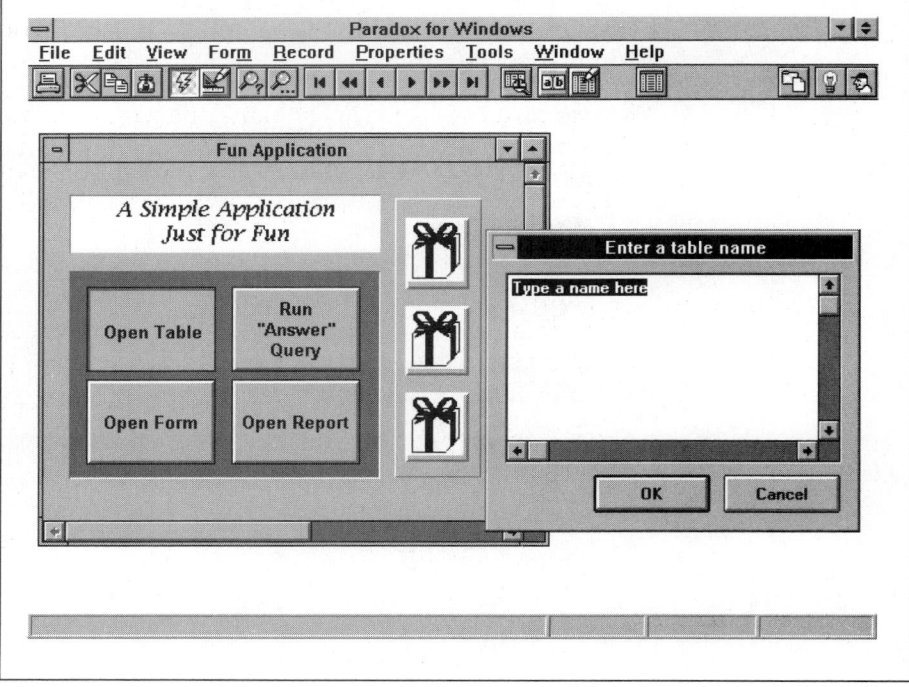

- If the method finds the table, form, or report we requested, it opens the object on the Desktop. If the method finds the query we requested, it runs the query and opens the Answer table on the Desktop.

▶ ▶ **T I P**

> **You can use aliases when entering table, form, query, or report names into the dialog box. For example, to open a report named *areacode* that's stored in a directory with the alias name of *:Gift_Corner:*, simply click the Open Report button, type *:Gift_Corner:areacode* into the dialog box that appears, and choose OK**

2. To return to the application form shown in Figure 19.6, we simply close the Table, Form, or Report window by pressing Ctrl+F4 or double-clicking the Control-menu box.

The ObjectPAL techniques used to create the "action" in this form are listed below.

1. First we created four buttons and edited the button labels.

2. Then we attached a *pushButton* method to each button. The code for each *pushButton* method is presented in the following sections.

▶ ▶ **T I P**

> **To center a label within a button, inspect the button and select (check) Center Label. Button labels are centered automatically when you create a new button. Chapters 10 and 11 explain how to create buttons and edit text objects such as button labels.**

▶ Defining the Open Table Button

The *pushButton* method shown in Figure 19.7 is considerably more complex than the methods you've seen so far. Let's break it down statement by statement.

Defining Variables

A variable is like a pigeonhole in which you can temporarily store an item of information. Before storing a value in a variable, you should declare the variable and define its data type using the *Var...endVar* statement (see Figure 19.7).

Table 19.2 lists some commonly used ObjectPAL data types (there are many more). For more details, choose Help ▶ ObjectPAL Contents, click the *List of ObjectPAL Types* topic under "Run-time Library Types

FIGURE 19.7 ▶

*The **pushButton** method for opening a table.*

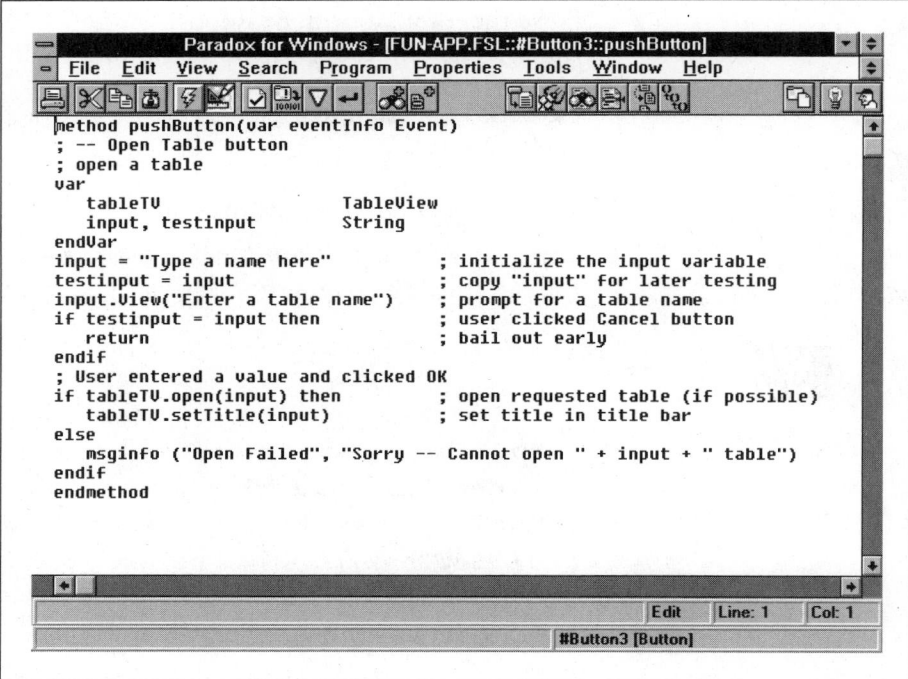

```
method pushButton(var eventInfo Event)
; -- Open Table button
; open a table
var
    tableTV                TableView
    input, testinput       String
endVar
input = "Type a name here"          ; initialize the input variable
testinput = input                   ; copy "input" for later testing
input.View("Enter a table name")    ; prompt for a table name
if testinput = input then           ; user clicked Cancel button
    return                          ; bail out early
endif
; User entered a value and clicked OK
if tableTV.open(input) then         ; open requested table (if possible)
    tableTV.setTitle(input)         ; set title in title bar
else
    msginfo ("Open Failed", "Sorry -- Cannot open " + input + " table")
endif
endmethod
```

and Methods," then use the alphabetical buttons to locate topics of interest. (To flip back to the Alphabetical List of ObjectPAL Types screen after viewing the Help for a particular object type, click the Back button below the menu bar.)

▶ **TABLE 19.2:** *Some Commonly Used Data Types in ObjectPAL*

DATA TYPE	DESCRIPTION
AnyType	A catch-all data type that behaves like a string when assigned a string value, like a number when assigned a number value, and so forth. It cannot be used to store complex objects such as a *TCursor* (see below).
Currency	Stores currency values ranging from $3.4 \star 10^{-4930}$ to $1.1 \star 10^{4930}$, scaled to six decimal places.
Date	Stores date values ranging from January 1, 100 to December 31, 9999.
Form	Refers to the file containing a form.
Graphic	Allows you to manipulate graphic objects.
Logical	Stores the logical value *True* or *False*. Logical variables are useful for answering questions about other objects and operations.
Memo	Stores memo data.
Number	Stores floating-point numbers.
Report	Refers to the file containing a report.
String	Stores up to 32,000 characters. A quoted string can contain up to 255 characters.
Table	Refers to the file containing a table.
TableView	Refers to the data in a Table View window.
TCursor	Points to the data in a table. *TCursor* variables allow you to manipulate data at the table level, record level, and field level without having to display the table.
Time	Stores time data.
UIObject	Includes all the objects you can place on a form. Only UIObjects have built-in methods, have code attached to them, and can respond to events.

Getting User Input

You can use the *View* statement to display a prompt in a dialog box and store the user's response in a variable, as shown below:

```
input = "Type a name here"
testinput = input
input.View("Enter a table name")
```

The first statement above sets the value of the *input* variable to "Type a name here".

The *testinput = input* statement copies the "Type a name here" text into the *testinput* variable. We'll use *testinput* later to find out whether the user closed the dialog box without changing the value, as explained below.

The *View* statement displays the value of *input* in a dialog box with the title "Enter a table name." Any text typed into the dialog box will replace the current value of the *input* variable.

Making Decisions

If statements are used to make decisions in an ObjectPAL method. They work just like the *If* statements found in most other programming languages. For instance, the *If...Then...endIf* and *If...Then...Else...endIf* statements shown in Figure 19.7 behave as follows:

1. The comparison statement *if testinput = input* checks to see whether the values in the *testinput* and *input* variables are the same. If the user types a table name, the values will not match; that is, the value in *input* will contain whatever text the user typed, whereas *testinput* will still have the value "Type a name here". However, if the user clicks the Cancel button, the values will match because the value in *input* is changed only if the user types in a new value and chooses OK.

   - Therefore, if the user clicks Cancel (*testinput = input* is "True"), the program will return to the form (via the *Return* keyword) without executing any other statements. As you can see, *Return* is ideal for bailing out of a program early.

   - If the user enters a value and chooses OK (*testinput = input* is "False"), the program continues to the statement following the *endIf* keyword.

2. The *if tableTV.open(input)* statement tries to open the table specified by the *input* variable.

- If the *open* statement succeeds, the *If* condition is "True" and the *setTitle* statement in the following line places the value of the *input* variable in the title bar of the Table View window (that is, whatever the user typed into the dialog box appears in the title bar). Notice that the *setTitle* statement uses the TableView variable named *tableTV* to access the Table View object.

- If the *Open* statement fails (because the table doesn't exist, for instance), the statement following the *Else* keyword displays an error message (via *msgInfo*).

  **T I P**

> As an alternative to using a variable name in the *open* statement, you can place the name of the object you want to open between quotation marks, as in *tableTV.open("OrdUpd8.db")*.

Displaying a Message

ObjectPAL offers several ways to display messages to the user. For example, the *msgInfo* statement in Figure 19.7 displays a dialog box containing an "i" icon, a title bar, a message, and an OK button. The first argument displays a message in the title bar, and the second argument displays a message in the dialog box itself. For example, if we had typed the non-existent table name **ork** into the dialog box shown in Figure 19.6, we'd see this msgInfo dialog box:

Notice that we used the plus (+) string operator in the *msgInfo* statement to connect (concatenate) the text strings shown in the error message box. (See Chapter 17 for more information on using the + operator.)

▶ *Defining the Open Form Button*

The method for the *Open Form* button appears in Figure 19.8. Notice that this method is almost the same as the *Open Table* method shown in Figure 19.7. In this example, we changed the name and data type of the variable used to access the form and altered the prompts and comments. Thus, the variable name is *formV* and its data type is *Form*.

Instead of typing all the statements, we simply pasted text from the Open Table button's ObjectPAL Editor window into the Editor window for the Open Form button. Then we modified the statements as needed. To speed up editing, we used Search ▶ Replace to make changes globally (see Chapter 6 for information on using Search and Replace).

FIGURE 19.8 ▶

The method for the Open Form button is almost the same as the method for the Open Table button.

```
method pushButton(var eventInfo Event)
; -- Open Form button
; open a form
var
    formV                 Form
    input, testinput      String
endVar
input = "Type a name here"        ; initialize the input variable
testinput = input                 ; copy "input" for later testing
input.View("Enter a form name")   ; prompt for a form name
if testinput = input then         ; use clicked Cancel button
    return                        ; bail out early
endif
; User entered a value and clicked OK
if formV.open(input) then         ; open requested form (if possible)
    formV.setTitle(input)         ; set title in title bar
else
    msginfo ("Open Failed", "Sorry -- Cannot open " + input + " form")
endif
endmethod
```

▶ *Defining the Run "Answer" Query Button*

Figure 19.9 shows the method for the *Run "Answer" Query* button. This button runs a query and then displays the Answer table on the Desktop. If the query cannot be opened (perhaps because it doesn't exist), or the Answer table cannot be opened (perhaps because the query generates a Changed, Deleted, or Inserted table instead of an Answer table), an appropriate message will appear. Because the entire method is too long to fit onto a single screen, we used the handy File ➤ Print command in the ObjectPAL Editor window to print a paper copy of the code.

▶▶ N O T E

You may have noticed that the semicolons and data types for variables in the output from the File ➤ Print command do not line up neatly. If you'd like to print a better looking report, you can save the method to a text file (as described earlier), and then use another text editor to "pretty up" the text and print it with a more finished look in any font you want.

Notice the differences between this method and the one shown in Figure 19.8:

- The prompts and comments specify "query" instead of "form."

- We replaced the *Open* statement with *readFromFile* and *executeQBE* statements. These statements allow you to run any saved query from a method.

- We placed an *If...Then...Else...endIf* statement inside the outer *If...Then...Else...endIf* statement. The statements in the new *If* statement display the Answer table if the table exists; otherwise, they display an error message.

- We used the alias name *:priv:* to refer to the private directory where the Answer table is stored. As mentioned in Chapter 15, you can make applications more portable by using aliases instead of hard-coding full path names. For example, if your application uses the alias name *:Gift_Corner:*, you could use the statement

FIGURE 19.9 ▶

The method for the Run "Answer" Query button. We created this printout using the File ➤ Print command in the ObjectPAL Editor window.

```
method pushButton(var eventInfo Event)
; -- Run "Answer" Query button
; run a query that generates an Answer table, open Answer
var
    tableTV              TableView
    input, testinput     String
    qvar                 Query
endVar
input = "Type a name here"          ; initialize the input variable
testinput = input                   ; copy "input" for later testing
input.View("Enter a query name")    ; prompt for a query name
if testinput = input then           ; user clicked Cancel button
    return                          ; bail out early
endif
; User entered a value and clicked OK
if qVar.readFromFile(input) then    ; read query into variable (if possible)
    qvar.executeQBE()               ; run requested query
    if tableTV.open(":priv:answer.db") then  ; open requested table (if possible)
    else
        msginfo ("No Answer Table!", "Sorry -- cannot open the Answer table")
    endif
else
    msginfo ("Query Failed", "Sorry -- Cannot open " + input + " query")
endif
endmethod
```

tableTV.open(":Gift_Corner:custlist.db") to open the CustList table. As long as all users have a *:Gift_Corner:* alias defined, the application will have no trouble finding the CustList table—regardless of the actual path name referenced by the alias.

 ▶▶ **N O T E**

> **If you do supply full path names when referencing files in your ObjectPAL methods, you must place two backslash characters between each level of the path name. For example, you would specify the path to the CustList table as** *c:\\pdoxwin\\giftco\\custlist.db.*

In the examples shown in this chapter, we're assuming that tables, queries, forms, and reports are located in the user's current working directory (so we need only specify the file name) or the user's private directory. You can use the *setDir* statement if you wish to change the user's working directory through ObjectPAL.

▶ *Defining the Open Report Button*

The method for the *Open Report* button appears in Figure 19.10. As you can see, this method resembles the methods attached to the Open Table and Open Form buttons described previously. Here, however, we've changed the variable name to *RptName*, changed the data type to *Report*, removed the *setTitle* statement, and modified the prompts and comments.

FIGURE 19.10 ▶

The method for the Open Report button

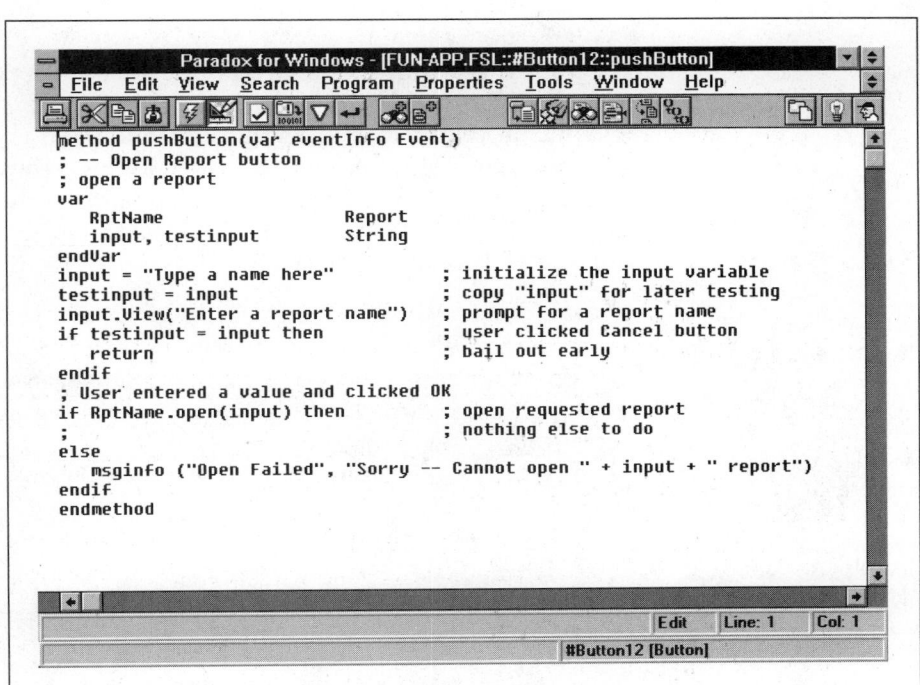

```
method pushButton(var eventInfo Event)
; -- Open Report button
; open a report
var
    RptName                    Report
    input, testinput           String
endVar
input = "Type a name here"          ; initialize the input variable
testinput = input                   ; copy "input" for later testing
input.View("Enter a report name")   ; prompt for a report name
if testinput = input then           ; user clicked Cancel button
    return                          ; bail out early
endif
; User entered a value and clicked OK
if RptName.open(input) then         ; open requested report
;                                   ; nothing else to do
else
    msginfo ("Open Failed", "Sorry -- Cannot open " + input + " report")
endif
endmethod
```

▶▶ *Automating the Order Processing and Purchasing Cycle*

In Chapter 18 you learned how to perform automatic updates via multitable queries, history tables, and the Add and Empty options on the Tools ➤ Utilities menus. As you know, automatic updating can require many steps, each of which must be completed in sequence to ensure that tables are updated correctly. Performing these steps manually can be error-prone and time consuming. Fortunately, you can use ObjectPAL to streamline the entire process, making the job as easy as clicking a few buttons.

Figure 19.11 shows a form that reduces the order processing and purchasing cycles presented in Chapter 18 to a few mouse clicks. To complete the Order Processing cycle, the user simply clicks the buttons on the left side of the form in sequence from 1 to 6. To complete the Purchasing cycle, the user clicks buttons 1, 2, 3, and 4 on the right side of the form.

In a "real" application, we might prefer to combine the third, fourth, fifth, and sixth buttons on the Order Processing side of the form into a single button that performs all these related steps automatically. Likewise, we might wish to combine the second and third buttons on the Purchasing side of the form into a single button. However, to make it easier for you to understand the ObjectPAL methods used in our application, we've broken the steps into separate buttons that correspond to

FIGURE 19.11 ▶

A sample application for the Order Processing and Purchasing cycles presented in Chapter 18. To use the form, simply click the buttons in the sequence indicated on the button labels.

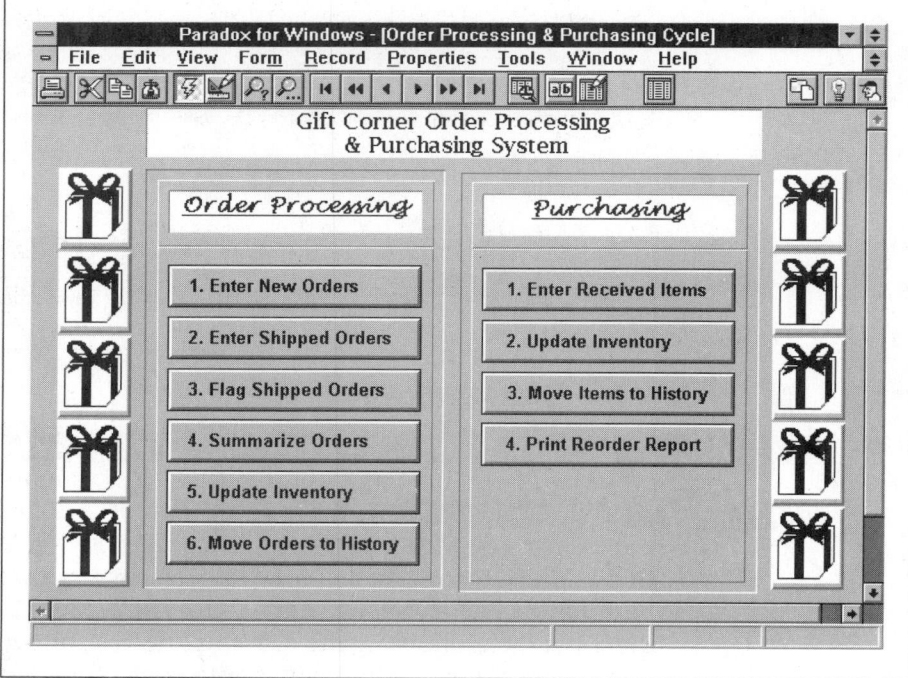

the Order Processing and Purchasing cycles illustrated in Figures 18.1 and 18.2 of the previous chapter.

To begin implementing the application, choose File ➤ New ➤ Form and click the Blank button. This creates a blank form with no tables defined in the data model. Next, use the Button tool to create ten buttons with the labels shown in Figure 19.11, and then add text objects, graphic objects, and boxes to make the form more attractive (see Chapters 10 and 11).

With the basic design complete, the only remaining steps are to attach appropriate ObjectPAL methods to each button. As the following sections will show, these methods use ObjectPAL techniques that you've seen already, as well as some new ones. They also employ previously saved queries, forms, and reports as building blocks for an integrated, easy-to-use application.

 ▶ ▶ **N O T E**

> All buttons in the sample application in Figure 19.11 use the *pushButton* method, which is triggered when the user clicks the button to which the method is attached. To keep things simple, our examples do not check extensively for errors and they do not handle multiuser record-locking.

▶ Defining the Order-Processing Buttons

First we'll take a look at the ObjectPAL method for each button in the Order Processing side of the sample application shown in Figure 19.11.

Entering New Orders

As its label implies, the *1. Enter New Orders* button allows users to enter new orders into the database. Figure 19.12 presents the ObjectPAL method for this button. The *If* statement first tries to open the OrdEntry form discussed earlier under "Adding ObjectPAL Methods to an Order Entry Form." If the *Open* statement succeeds, ObjectPAL places all tables on the form into Edit mode via the *action(DataBeginEdit)* statement, and waits for the user to close the form. If the *Open* statement fails, an appropriate message appears. By now, the *Open* statement

FIGURE 19.12 ▶

The ObjectPAL method for the order processing button named "1. Enter New Orders"

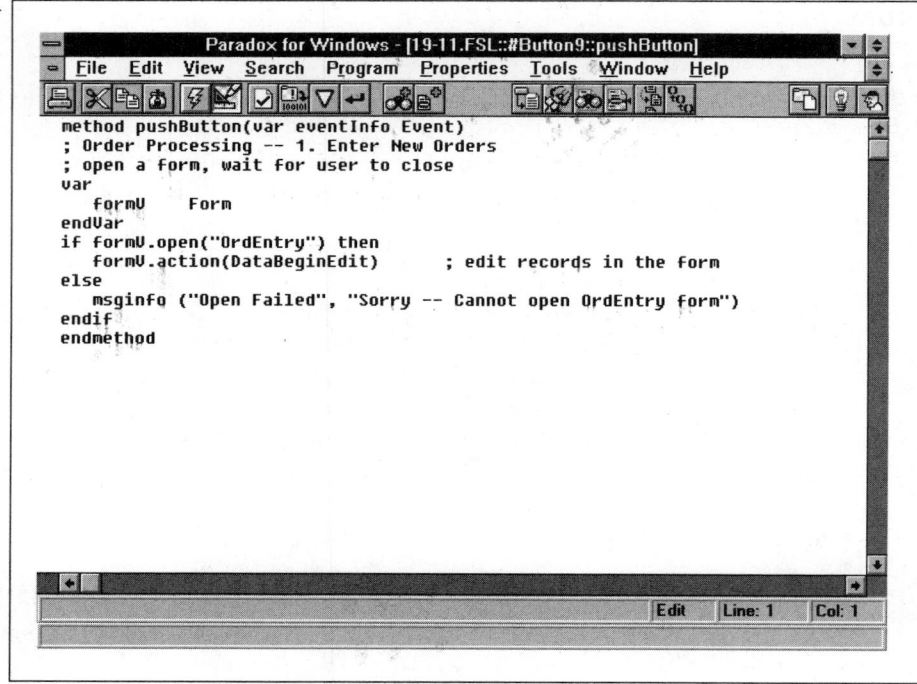

```
method pushButton(var eventInfo Event)
; Order Processing -- 1. Enter New Orders
; open a form, wait for user to close
var
    formU    Form
endUar
if formU.open("OrdEntry") then
    formU.action(DataBeginEdit)       ; edit records in the form
else
    msginfo ("Open Failed", "Sorry -- Cannot open OrdEntry form")
endif
endmethod
```

should be familiar to you. However, one statement—*formV.action (DataBeginEdit)*—is new. This *Action* statement places the active Form View window into Edit mode, just as if the user had pressed the F9 key.

Entering Shipped Orders

The button named *2. Enter Shipped Orders* allows users to record shipped and invoiced orders. Figure 19.13 presents the ObjectPAL method for this button. Notice that this code uses the now-famous statements *Open*, *Action*, and *msgInfo*.

Flagging Shipped Orders

The method for the next button, *3. Flag Shipped Orders*, is illustrated in Figure 19.14. This code includes some new commands, as well as our old standbys. First, it executes the saved query named *ShipInv* (see Figure 18.3 in Chapter 18). Recall that this query updates blank Date Shipped and Invoice Date fields in the Orders table with corresponding fields from the OrdUpd8 table.

FIGURE 19.13

The ObjectPAL method for the button named "2. Enter Shipped Orders"

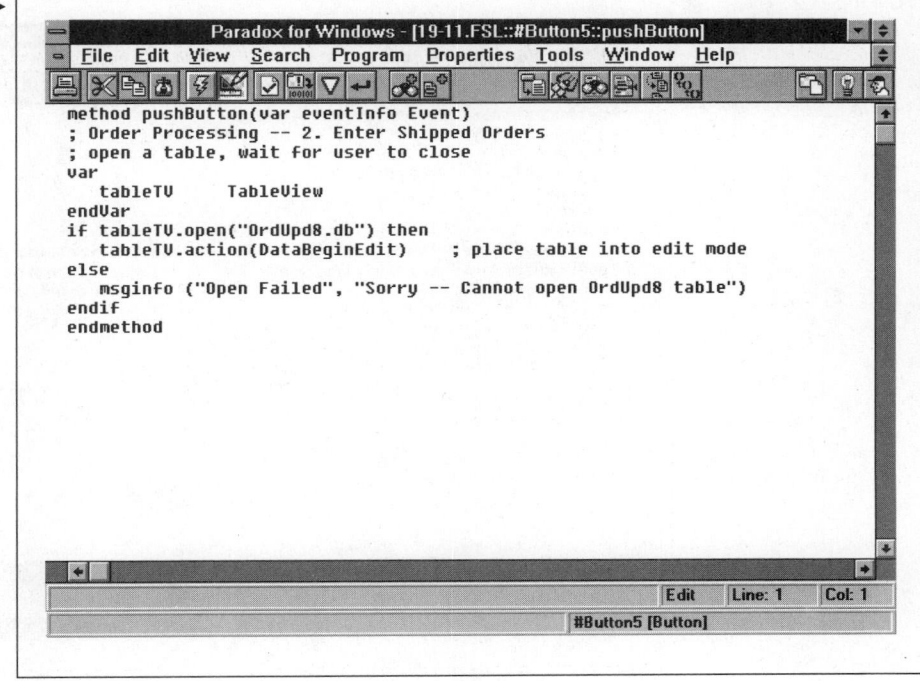

The statement

```
userChoice = msgQuestion("View Changed",
    "Do you wish to view the Changed table?")
```

displays a dialog box and waits for the user to click the Yes or No button. Notice how the arguments in the *msgQuestion* statement correspond to text in the title bar and dialog box shown below.

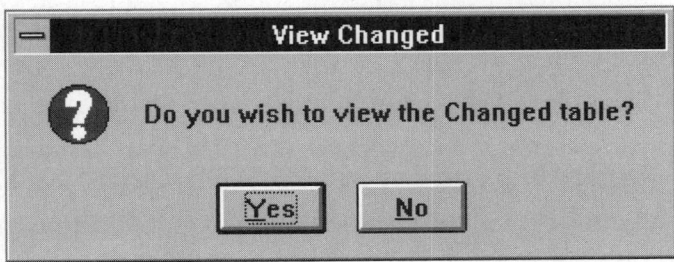

FIGURE 19.14 ▶

The ObjectPAL method for the button named "3. Flag Shipped Orders"

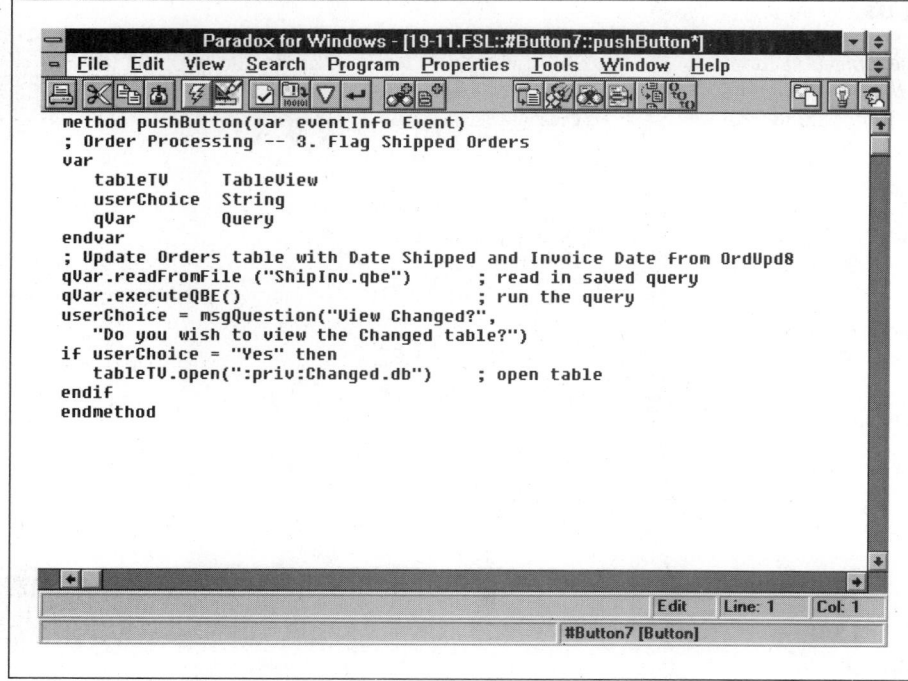

```
method pushButton(var eventInfo Event)
; Order Processing -- 3. Flag Shipped Orders
var
    tableTV     TableView
    userChoice  String
    qVar        Query
endvar
; Update Orders table with Date Shipped and Invoice Date from OrdUpd8
qVar.readFromFile ("ShipInv.qbe")      ; read in saved query
qVar.executeQBE()                      ; run the query
userChoice = msgQuestion("View Changed?",
    "Do you wish to view the Changed table?")
if userChoice = "Yes" then
    tableTV.open(":priv:Changed.db")    ; open table
endif
endmethod
```

If the user clicks the <u>Y</u>es button in the dialog box, the value "Yes" is stored in the string variable named *userChoice* and the Changed table in the user's private directory (*:priv:Changed.db*) appears on the Desktop. If the user clicks <u>N</u>o, the value "No" is stored in *userChoice* and the method ends without displaying the Changed table.

Summarizing Shipped Orders

Figure 19.15 shows the method for the button *4. Summarize Orders*, which updates a summary table of shipped and invoiced orders. This method executes the saved query named *Summary* (see Figure 18.6 in Chapter 18) and allows the user to view the Summary table.

Updating the Inventory with Quantity Shipped

Figure 19.16 illustrates the method attached to button 5 of the Order Processing cycle. Here we're executing two queries in a row—*CalcSum* and *Upd8Prod* (see Figures 18.8 and 18.9 in Chapter 18). The first query calculates the sum of the quantity sold for each product shipped.

FIGURE 19.15

The ObjectPAL method for the button named "4. Summarize Orders"

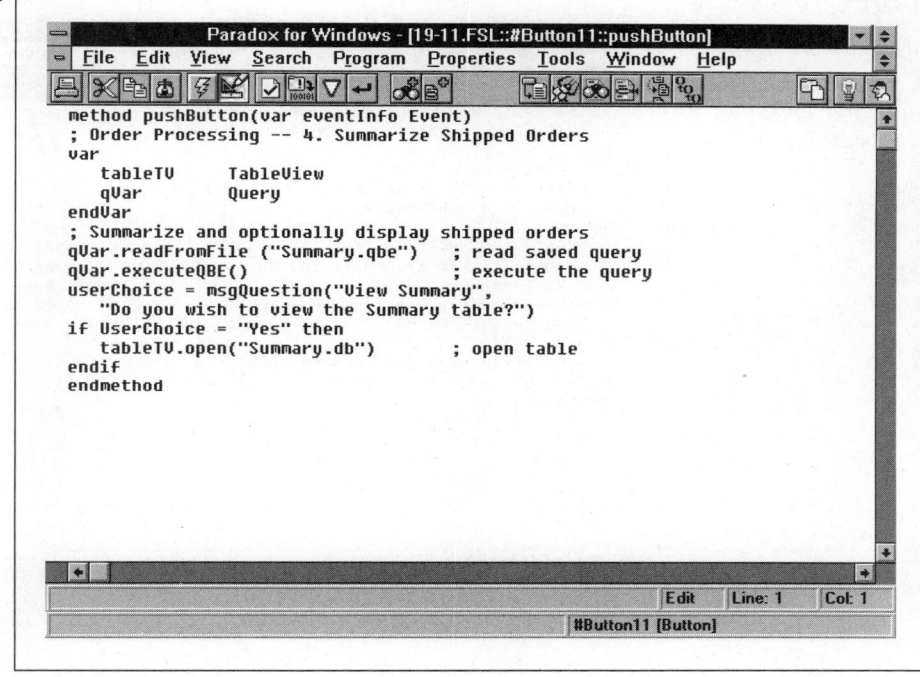

```
method pushButton(var eventInfo Event)
; Order Processing -- 4. Summarize Shipped Orders
var
    tableTV      TableView
    qVar         Query
endVar
; Summarize and optionally display shipped orders
qVar.readFromFile ("Summary.qbe")    ; read saved query
qVar.executeQBE()                    ; execute the query
userChoice = msgQuestion("View Summary",
    "Do you wish to view the Summary table?")
if UserChoice = "Yes" then
    tableTV.open("Summary.db")        ; open table
endif
endmethod
```

The second query subtracts the calculated quantity from the In Stock quantity for each associated item in the Products table.

> **N O T E**
>
> **Notice how similar the method in Figure 19.16 (button 5) is to the method in Figure 19.15 (button 4). Again, we used the copy and paste techniques discussed earlier in this chapter to save time and avoid typing mistakes.**

Moving the Shipped Orders to History

When the user clicks the button *6. Move Orders to History,* processed orders are moved to the history tables named *OrdHst* and *LineHst.* The method for this button appears in Figure 19.17. As for Figure 19.9, we

FIGURE 19.16 ▶

The ObjectPAL method for the Order Processing button named "5. Update Inventory"

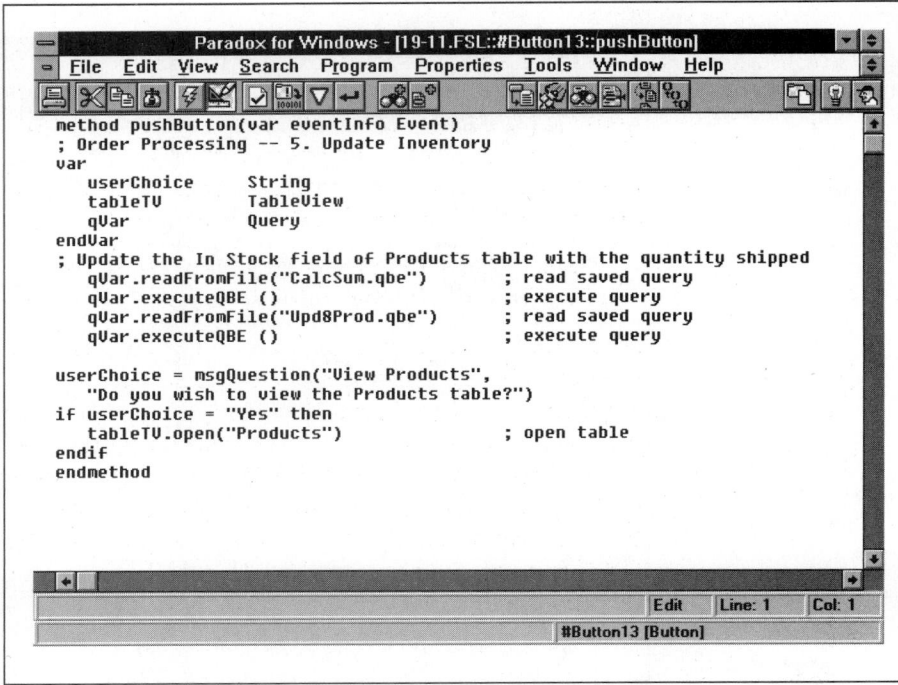

```
method pushButton(var eventInfo Event)
; Order Processing -- 5. Update Inventory
var
    userChoice      String
    tableTV         TableView
    qVar            Query
endVar
; Update the In Stock field of Products table with the quantity shipped
    qVar.readFromFile("CalcSum.qbe")        ; read saved query
    qVar.executeQBE ()                      ; execute query
    qVar.readFromFile("Upd8Prod.qbe")       ; read saved query
    qVar.executeQBE ()                      ; execute query

userChoice = msgQuestion("View Products",
    "Do you wish to view the Products table?")
if userChoice = "Yes" then
    tableTV.open("Products")                ; open table
endif
endmethod
```

FIGURE 19.17 ▶

The ObjectPAL method for the button named "6. Move Orders to History". We created this printout using the File ▶ Print command in the ObjectPAL Editor window.

```
method pushButton(var eventInfo Event)
; Order Processing -- 6. Move Orders to History
var
    ansTbl   Table
    updTbl   Table
    qVar     Query
endVar
; Post line items
    qVar.readFromFile("PostLine.qbe")            ; post the line items to history
    qVar.executeQBE ()
    ansTbl.attach(":priv:Answer.db", "Paradox")    ; attach Answer in private directory
    ansTbl.add("LineHst.db",True,False)          ; append records from Answer
    qVar.readFromFile("ClrLine.qbe")             ; clear records
    qVar.executeQBE ()                    ;
; Post orders
    qVar.readFromFile("PostOrd.qbe")             ; post the orders to history
    qVar.executeQBE ()                    ;
    ansTbl.attach(":priv:Answer.db", "Paradox") ; attach Answer in private directory
    ansTbl.add("OrdHst.db",True,False)         ; append records from Answer
    qVar.readFromFile("ClrOrd.qbe")            ; clear records
    qVar.executeQBE ()                    ;
; Empty OrdUpd8
    updTbl.attach("OrdUpd8.db", "Paradox")       ; attach OrdUpd8 table
    updTbl.empty()                       ; empty OrdUpd8
msgInfo ("Done!", "Done moving orders and line items to history.")
endmethod
```

used the File ➤ Print command in the ObjectPAL Editor window so that you can see all the code in this relatively lengthy method.

The first section of this code is introduced by the comment "; Post line items" and continues through the statement that executes the *ClrLine* query. In this section we execute the saved query named *PostLine* (see Figure 18.10), which creates an Answer table containing shipped records from the LineItem table. The statements

```
ansTbl.attach(":priv:Answer.db", "Paradox")
ansTbl.add("LineHst.db",True,False)
```

associate the table variable named *ansTbl* with the Paradox-style Answer table in the private directory, and then append the Answer table records to the LineHst table. These statements are equivalent to choosing Tools ➤ Utilities ➤ Add from the menus, specifying Answer as the source table and LineHst as the target table, and selecting the Append option. (The *Attach* statement is similar to *Open*, but it does not display the table on-screen.) The last statement in this section executes the *ClrLine* query (see Figure 18.11), which clears the posted records from the LineItem table.

NOTE

The *True* and *False* arguments in the *Add* statement set values for the *append* and *update* conditions. These values tell Paradox to append new records to the LineHst table but not to update existing records. By default, the *append* and *update* conditions are both True (which corresponds to the default setting of Append & Update in the Add dialog box). Because the LineHst table is not keyed, we can append the records only, not update them. For more details, search for the *Add* topic in the ObjectPAL online Help.

The second section of the code starts with the "; Post Orders" comment and ends with the command to execute the *ClrOrd* query. This section posts the shipped records from the Orders table to the OrdHst table, and then clears them from the Orders table. You'll find examples of the PostOrd and ClrOrd queries in Figures 18.12 and 18.13 of Chapter 18.

The last section of code (beginning with "; Empty OrdUpd8") attaches the OrdUpd8 table and then empties it. This is equivalent to choosing <u>T</u>ools ➤ <u>U</u>tilities ➤ <u>E</u>mpty and specifying OrdUpd8 as the table to empty.

▶ Defining the Purchasing Buttons

Now let's turn our attention to the four buttons in the Purchasing cycle. As you'll see, many of the ObjectPAL methods for the Purchasing buttons are similar to those attached to the Order Processing buttons.

Entering Received Items

When purchased items arrive in the stockroom, we can record them by clicking the *1. Enter Received Items* button in the Cycles application form and entering data into the Prod Code, Qty Recd, Purchase Price, and Date Recd fields of the Purchase table that appears. As Figure 19.18 shows, the code attached to this button features the familiar *Open*, *Action*, and *msgInfo* statements.

Updating the Inventory with Quantity Received

The next step is to update inventory quantities and unit prices in the Products table with data from the Purchases table. Figure 19.19 shows the method attached to the button *2. Update Inventory*, which accomplishes this task. Notice how similar this method is to the method for the fifth button on the Order Processing side (see Figure 19.16). The main difference is that the Purchasing button for updating inventory executes the *CalcPurc* and *Upd8Stoc* queries (see Figures 18.15 and 18.16) instead of the *CalcSum* and *Upd8Prod* queries used by the corresponding Order Processing button.

Moving Received Items to History

The method for the button *3. Move Items to History* appears in Figure 19.20. Here we simply attach the Purchase table, add its records to the PurHst table, and empty the Purchase table.

FIGURE 19.18

The ObjectPAL method for the button named "1. Enter Received Items"

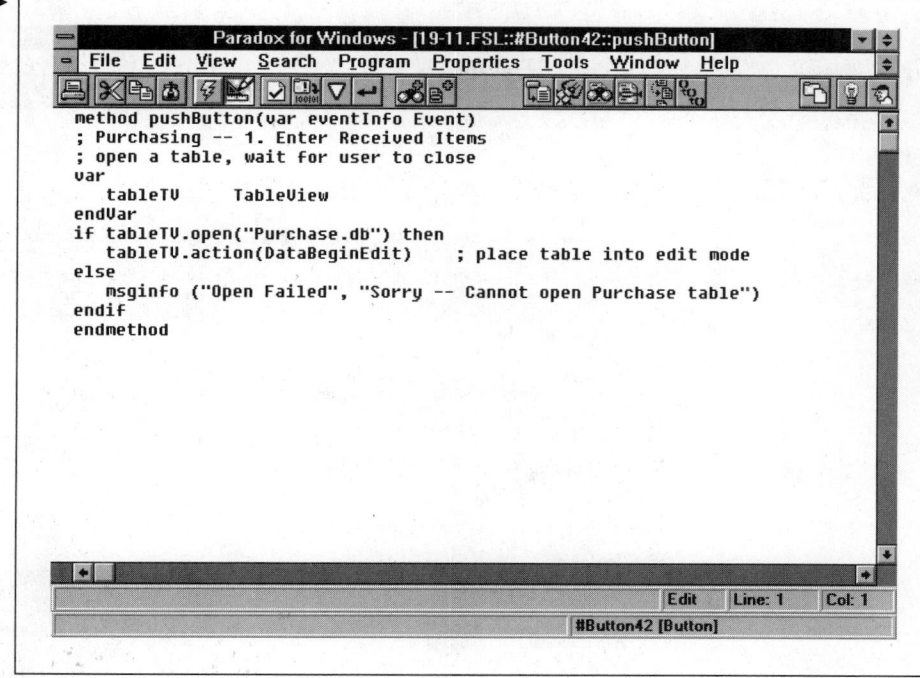

```
method pushButton(var eventInfo Event)
; Purchasing -- 1. Enter Received Items
; open a table, wait for user to close
var
    tableTV        TableView
endVar
if tableTV.open("Purchase.db") then
    tableTV.action(DataBeginEdit)     ; place table into edit mode
else
    msginfo ("Open Failed", "Sorry -- Cannot open Purchase table")
endif
endmethod
```

Printing a Reorder Report

The *4. Print Reorder Report* button in the Purchasing cycle can be used at any time to display (and print) a reorder report. Its method, which appears in Figure 19.21, executes the *Reorder* query (see Figure 18.18) and opens the custom *Reorder* report shown in Figure 19.22. Clicking the Print button in the Toolbar will print the reorder report displayed on the screen.

▶▶ *Using Scripts*

As you know, Paradox for Windows applications are typically developed by attaching ObjectPAL methods to objects in custom forms. You can also run applications from stand-alone files called *scripts*. Like methods attached to objects, scripts contain ObjectPAL program code; however, scripts run on the Paradox for Windows Desktop and are completely independent of any form.

FIGURE 19.19 ▶

The ObjectPAL method for the Purchasing button named "2. Update Inventory"

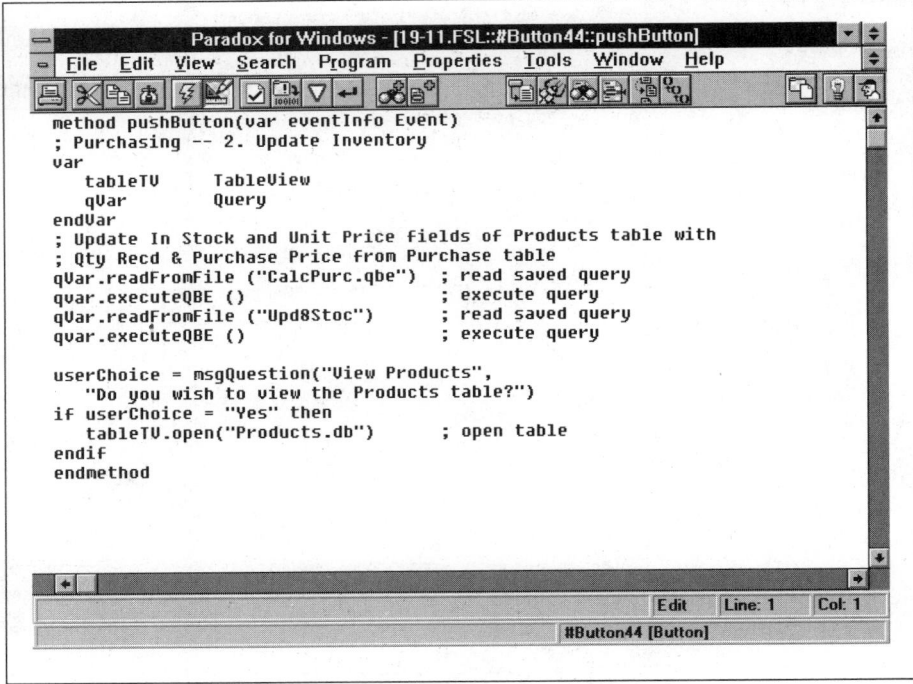

```
method pushButton(var eventInfo Event)
; Purchasing -- 2. Update Inventory
var
     tableTV      TableView
     qVar         Query
endVar
; Update In Stock and Unit Price fields of Products table with
; Qty Recd & Purchase Price from Purchase table
qVar.readFromFile ("CalcPurc.qbe")  ; read saved query
qvar.executeQBE ()                  ; execute query
qVar.readFromFile ("Upd8Stoc")      ; read saved query
qvar.executeQBE ()                  ; execute query

userChoice = msgQuestion("View Products",
     "Do you wish to view the Products table?")
if userChoice = "Yes" then
     tableTV.open("Products.db")     ; open table
endif
endmethod
```

▶ ▶ **N O T E**

> **Paradox for DOS also allows you to create scripts, applications, forms, reports, and queries. Unfortunately, those Paradox for DOS files *cannot* be used with Paradox for Windows. You can, however, view and update Paradox for DOS *tables* from Paradox for Windows (see Appendix C).**

Scripts provide advanced capabilities that may not interest first-time ObjectPAL users, but might be helpful later in your ObjectPAL programming life. For example, scripts can be used to call other scripts; open and work with tables, forms, and reports; run queries; and use methods attached to other objects. If you'd like to peek at a finished script, switch to the *c:\pdoxwin\connect* working directory, click the Scripts button in the Project Viewer, right-click the script named *start.ssl*, and choose De*s*ign.

FIGURE 19.20 ▶

The ObjectPAL method for the Purchasing button named "3. Move Items to History"

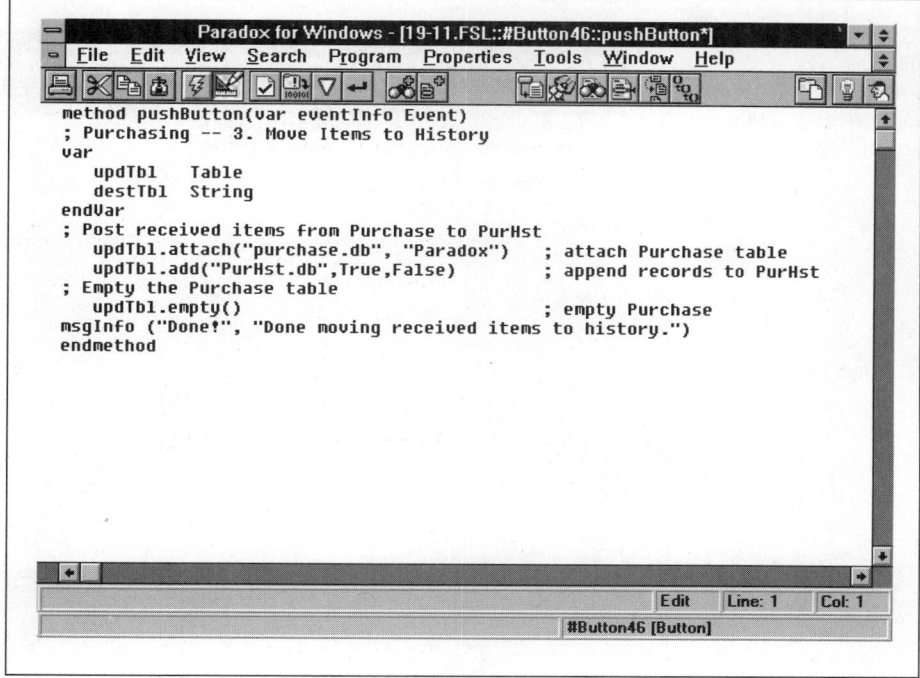

```
method pushButton(var eventInfo Event)
; Purchasing -- 3. Move Items to History
var
    updTbl    Table
    destTbl   String
endVar
; Post received items from Purchase to PurHst
    updTbl.attach("purchase.db", "Paradox")    ; attach Purchase table
    updTbl.add("PurHst.db",True,False)         ; append records to PurHst
; Empty the Purchase table
    updTbl.empty()                             ; empty Purchase
msgInfo ("Done!", "Done moving received items to history.")
endmethod
```

▶ Creating a Script

Creating a script is similar to creating any other object in Paradox. For example, choose File ➤ New ➤ Script. When the ObjectPAL Editor window appears, type the program code and check the syntax as described earlier. To save the script, choose File ➤ Save, specify a file name (no extension), and choose OK. Paradox will add the extension *.ssl* automatically.

▶ Running a Script

To run the script from Paradox for Windows, choose File ➤ Open ➤ Script and double-click the script name in the Open Document dialog box that appears. Alternatively, you can click the Scripts button in the Project Viewer, then double-click the script you want to play (see Chapter 15).

FIGURE 19.21 ▸

The ObjectPAL method for the Purchasing button named "4. Print Reorder Report"

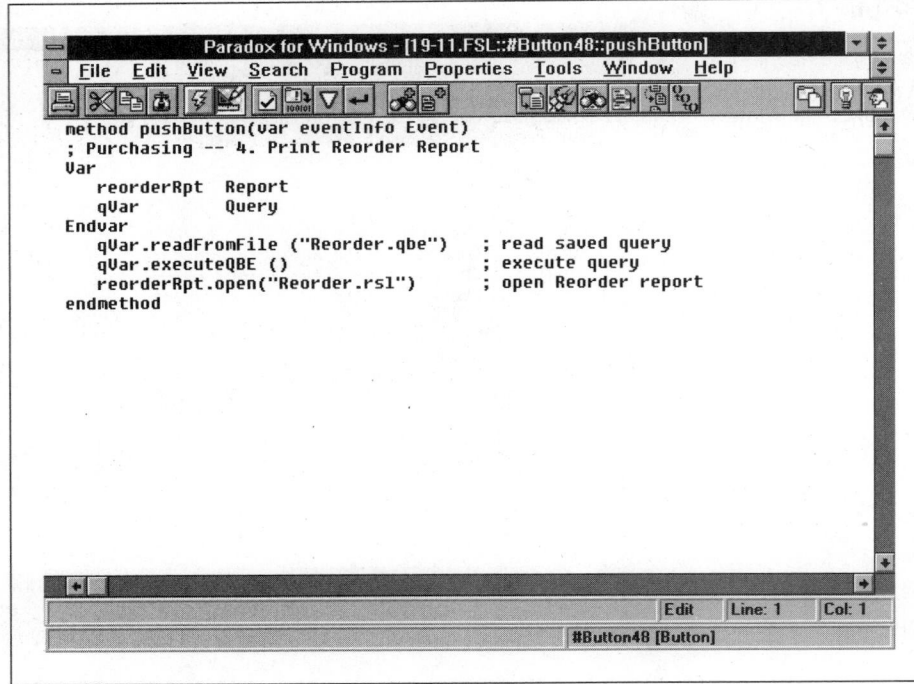

```
method pushButton(var eventInfo Event)
; Purchasing -- 4. Print Reorder Report
Var
    reorderRpt   Report
    qVar         Query
Endvar
    qVar.readFromFile ("Reorder.qbe")    ; read saved query
    qVar.executeQBE ()                   ; execute query
    reorderRpt.open("Reorder.rsl")       ; open Reorder report
endmethod
```

You can also run a script from a command line. To start Paradox for Windows and run a script from the Program Manager, choose File ➤ Run from the Program Manager, type **c:\pdoxwin\pdoxwin** and a space, then type the complete path name of the script and press ↵. For example, the command line

c:\pdoxwin\pdoxwin c:\pdoxwin\giftco\startup.ssl

will start Paradox for Windows and immediately run the script named *Startup*. (The same command line will work when typed at the DOS command prompt or when entered into your *autoexec.bat* file.)

To start the script whenever you double-click the Paradox for Windows icon, return to Program Manager, click (just once) the Paradox for Windows icon in the Paradox for Windows program group, choose File ➤ Properties from the Program Manager menu, add the blank space and complete path of the script to the end of the command in the Command Line text box, and choose OK.

FIGURE 19.22

*A simple report listing
items that are due for
reordering*

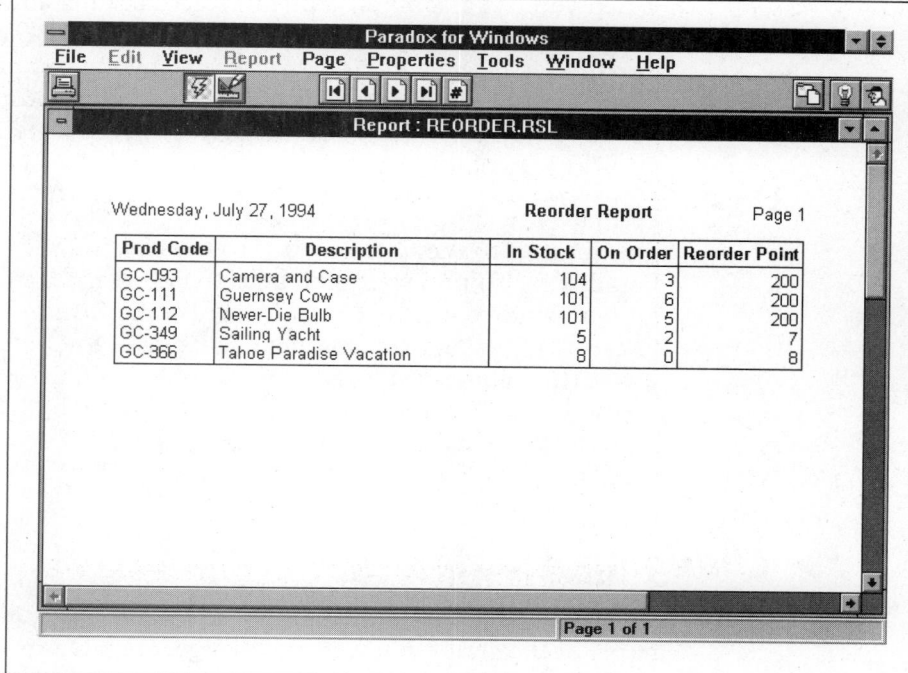

NOTE

**Appendix A provides additional information about
using command line options.**

To understand just how useful a script can be, suppose you created a
form like the one shown in Figure 19.11 and named it *Cycles*. Then
you created a script like the one shown below and saved it with the
name *Startup*:

```
method run(var eventInfo Event)
var
    formV    Form
endVar
; open the Cycles form in the current directory.
formV.open("Cycles")
endmethod
```

When you use a command line to start Paradox and run this script, the *cycles.fsl* form will open immediately. Because the *Startup* script opens the form as soon as Paradox starts up, anyone can perform essential business tasks simply by clicking a few buttons with the mouse. Users needn't know anything about tables, forms, reports, or other Paradox for Windows objects.

To make the application even easier to use, you could add a "Quit Paradox" button to the *Cycles* form, so that clicking the button would exit Paradox for Windows completely. To define the button, open the Form Design window for the *Cycles* form, use the Button tool in the Toolbar to create a new button, and change its label to *Quit Paradox*. Inspect the button, choose Methods, and double-click the *pushButton* built-in method. Finally, type **exit( )** on line 2 of the ObjectPAL Editor window, double-click the window's Control-menu box, and then save the form.

▶ Changing a Script

To change an existing script, choose File ➤ Open ➤ Script, select the name of the script you want to change, click Design in the Open Document dialog box, then click OK; or inspect the script's icon in the Project Viewer window and choose Design.

In this chapter we have introduced ObjectPAL, the rich and powerful programming language supplied with Paradox for Windows. We hope the examples provided here will inspire you to begin creating applications of your own that can be run with push-button ease. Keep in mind that ObjectPAL offers an extensive online Help system and several manuals to assist you in learning the language.

A

Installing
Paradox
for Windows

► ► **B**efore you can use Paradox for Windows, it must be installed on your computer. You need to install Paradox for Windows only once, not each time you use it. This appendix explains how to install the program on a single-user machine. (Appendix B explains how to get more information about installing Paradox on a network.)

► ► *Hardware and Software Requirements*

Before you install Paradox for Windows, please make sure your hardware and software meet the following minimum requirements:

- An IBM or compatible PC with 80386 or higher processor.
- A hard disk with at least 20MB of free space or, better yet, about 29MB for a full installation.
- 4MB of memory (RAM), preferably more.
- EGA or VGA display (preferably VGA). CGA is not supported.
- A mouse or similar pointing device.
- DOS Version 3.1 or later.
- Windows Version 3.1 or later, running in Standard or 386 Enhanced mode. Real mode is not supported.

 ► ► N O T E

> **Paradox also runs on Windows NT and in an OS/2 WIN-OS/2 session, although only Windows 3.1 (and higher) is supported officially.**

▶▶ *Installing Paradox for Windows for the First Time*

To install Paradox for Windows on a single-user computer (using floppy disks), follow these steps:

1. Start your computer and get to the Windows Program Manager.

2. Place *Paradox for Windows Installation Disk 1* into the floppy drive and close the drive door.

3. From the Program Manager menu choose File ➤ Run.

4. If you inserted the installation disk into drive A, type **a:\install**. If you inserted the disk into drive B, type **b:\install**. Now click OK or press ↵.

5. After a few moments you will see the Paradox for Windows Installation dialog box shown in Figure A.1. Choose one of the following options, then click Continue or press ↵. (In the remaining steps, we'll assume you selected the Full option).

> **Full**   Installs all the Paradox for Windows files, including the Paradox program itself; Experts, Coaches, and Help files; sample applications (Samples, Examples, and Connections); IDAPI files needed to run Paradox with other Borland Windows products; and Workgroup Desktop (Object Exchange) features that let you distribute Paradox objects to other users via messaging systems such as MCI, MHS, cc:Mail, and Windows for Workgroups (see Appendix B). If you have at least 29MB of disk space available, the Full option is your best bet for a complete single-user installation.
>
> **Minimum**   Installs the bare-bones Paradox for Windows system only, including the Paradox program, Help files, and IDAPI files.
>
> **Custom**   Lets you choose exactly which files you want to install. This option is especially useful when you need to reinstall just part of the Paradox system, or to install a component that you omitted during an earlier Minimum or Custom installation.

FIGURE A.1 ▶

The Paradox 5 for Windows Installation dialog box

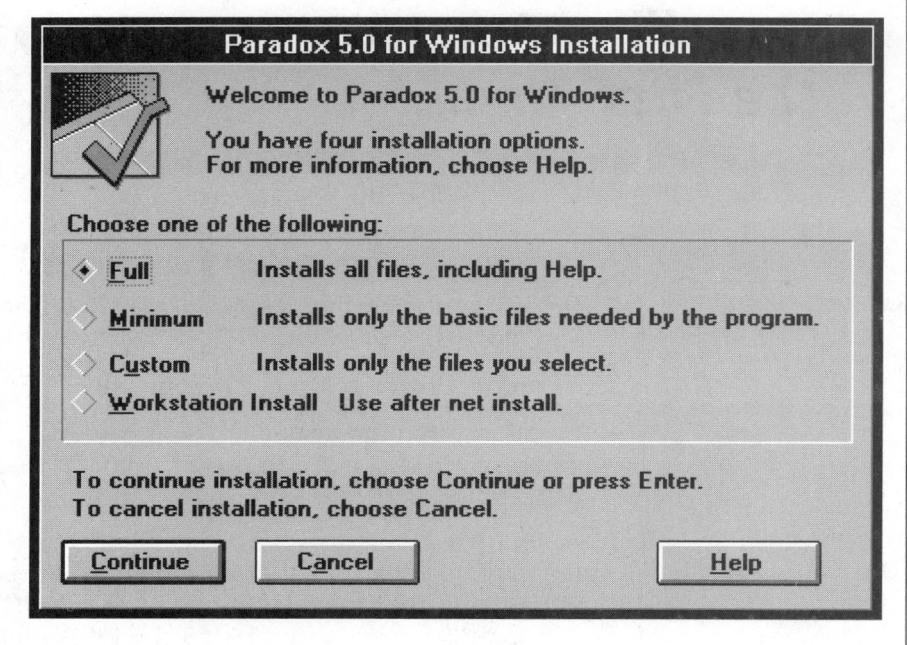

Workstation Install Primarily for the network adminis-trator, this option lets you configure individual worksta-tions to use Paradox on a network. Choose this option only after completing a network server install, and only if you know the locations of the idapi.cfg file, object store di-rectory, object exchange directory, and IDAPI directory. See your Paradox for Windows documentation and Ap-pendix B for more about installing and using Paradox on a network.

 ▶▶▶ **N O T E**

You can cancel the Install program at any time by clicking the Cancel and Exit buttons until you return to Program Manager. For help with any dialog box, click the Help button.

6. When the Paradox 5 for Windows User Registration dialog box appears, complete the steps below:

- In the <u>N</u>ame text box, type your full name and press Tab.
- In the <u>C</u>ompany text box, type the name of your company.
- Choose <u>C</u>ontinue.

7. In the next few dialog boxes, you'll be prompted for the locations to use for various installation directories. The default locations shown in the dialog boxes usually will be the ones you want, so you probably won't need to make any changes. Read the instructions in each dialog box carefully, make whatever changes you need, and choose <u>C</u>ontinue or press ↵ to proceed to the next dialog box.

 ▶ ▶**N O T E**

If you have Paradox 4.5 for Windows, you can overwrite it by accepting the suggested directory locations, or you can install Paradox 5 for Windows to different directories. Most users will want to overwrite their old version of Paradox for Windows.

8. When you've finished specifying directory locations, you'll be ready to install Paradox. Click the <u>I</u>nstall button or press ↵ to continue, or click the C<u>a</u>ncel and E<u>x</u>it buttons to exit without installing. (We'll assume you chose <u>I</u>nstall.)

9. As the installation progresses, you'll be prompted to replace the disk that's currently in drive A or B with the disk indicated in the instructions. Remove the old disk, insert the new one, and then click OK or press ↵ to proceed. (If you accidentally insert the wrong disk, you'll be prompted to insert the correct disk; replace the disk and click OK to continue.)

10. When asked if you want to install the Paradox 5 for Windows Program Manager group, choose <u>C</u>ontinue (to install the group), or <u>S</u>kip (to skip the group window installation). Normally you'll want to choose <u>C</u>ontinue the first time you install Paradox, and

Skip if you're reinstalling Paradox or adding new files (as discussed later under "Installing Specific Files"). However, it never hurts to install the group again, and it takes only a moment.

11. When asked if you want to see the Paradox 5 for Windows "Read Me" file, choose Continue to view this file's important late-breaking news, or Skip if you prefer to skip it for now. When you've finished reading the file, close the window or choose File ➤ Exit.

▶▶ **N O T E**

> **Be sure to read this 'Read Me' file at least once! If you skip it during the initial installation, you can always view it later by double-clicking the *Paradox Readme File* icon in the Paradox for Windows group window (the file opens in Windows Notepad). To print the file in Notepad, choose File ➤ Print.**

When installation is complete, the Install program will return to Windows, and the Paradox for Windows group will contain icons for Paradox for Windows and several related utilities (see Chapter 14).

▶ *Adjusting CONFIG.SYS and AUTOEXEC.BAT*

Before running Paradox for Windows, you may need to change some settings in your *config.sys* and *autoexec.bat* files. In particular, you should

- Change your *config.sys* file settings to at least FILES=60 and BUFFERS=40. (The BUFFERS setting can be reduced to 10 if you use SMARTDRV.)

- Change your *autoexec.bat* file PATH statement to include the Paradox for Windows installation directory (usually *c:\pdoxwin*). Although this step is optional, it makes starting Paradox from the DOS command line easier.

- If you're planning to use Paradox with other IDAPI-hosted applications or to run multiple instances of Paradox, type the command **c:\dos\share** into *autoexec.bat*, on the line *above* any command that starts Windows or any Windows application (or at the end of the file, if you're not starting Windows from *auto-exec.bat*). See the Paradox Readme File for more information about SHARE.

After adjusting *config.sys* and *autoexec.bat*, remove any floppy disks from the drives, reboot the computer (press Ctrl+Alt+Del), and then start Windows as usual.

▶ *Starting Paradox for Windows*

You can start Paradox for Windows by double-clicking its icon in the Paradox for Windows program group of Windows' Program Manager (see Chapters 2 and 3). You can also start Paradox from a command line, as described later in this appendix.

▶▶ *Installing Specific Files*

Paradox for Windows comes with several sample applications and other components that must be installed on your computer before you can use them. Normally, these components are installed automatically when you choose the Full installation described earlier in this appendix. If you chose a Minimum installation, or you just need to reinstall some components, you can do so at any time by following these steps:

1. Repeat steps 1 through 6 as described in the earlier section "Installing Paradox for Windows for the First Time," *except* select Custom in step 5.

2. When you see the Paradox 5 for Windows Installation Options dialog box shown in Figure A.2, choose the files you want to install by clicking on the appropriate option. (Clicking toggles the checkmark off or on.) When an option is checked, the files will be installed; when unchecked, the files will not be installed. Initially, all the options are checked.

3. After checking and unchecking the appropriate files, choose Continue and proceed as explained in steps 7 through 11 of the earlier section "Installing Paradox for Windows for the First Time."

The Paradox 5 for Windows Installation Options dialog box lets you choose which Paradox files to install.

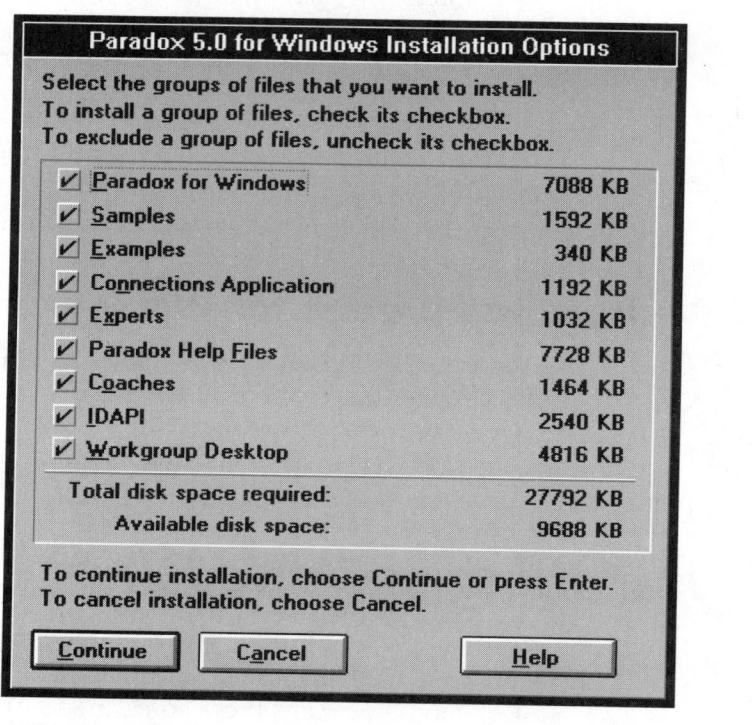

▶▶ *Running Paradox for Windows from the Command Line*

As an alternative to starting Paradox for Windows by double-clicking its icon, you can run the program from a command line. The command line can include options that override certain default settings for the current session only.

Command-line options always begin with a space, and always must appear to the right of the command used to start Paradox for Windows. You can type command lines in uppercase, lowercase, or any combination of the two. For example, the command line shown below starts Paradox with an initial working directory of *c:\pdoxwin\giftco*.

```
c:\pdoxwin\pdoxwin -w c:\pdoxwin\giftco
```

You can combine command-line options, as shown by the next example, which sets the initial working directory as above and immediately runs the script named *startup.ssl* in that directory.

c:\pdoxwin\pdoxwin -w c:\pdoxwin\giftco startup.ssl

If your DOS path does not contain the Paradox for Windows system directory (normally *c:\pdoxwin*), you must include the directory name when specifying the command used to start Paradox. For example, typing **c:\pdoxwin\pdoxwin -c** would start Paradox without any tables, forms, queries, reports, scripts, or libraries open on the Desktop. If your DOS path *does* include the Paradox for Windows directory, you can omit the directory name in the Paradox startup command, like this: **pdoxwin -c**.

Table A.1 describes the Paradox for Windows command line options available.

▶ **TABLE A.1:** *Paradox for Windows Command Line Options*

OPTION	DESCRIPTION
-b	Brings Paradox to the front of your other desktop windows—without trying to start another copy of Paradox—if you accidentally reload Paradox after it is already running. The -b option also suppresses the annoying error message "Could not initialize IDAPI.: Directory is busy." if you try to run a second copy of Paradox without also supplying the -n and -p command-line parameters. (The -b option is new in Paradox 5 for Windows.)
-c	Starts Paradox for Windows without any objects opened on the Desktop (except for the Project Viewer if it is normally opened at startup).
-d *filename*	Specifies an alternate *pdoxwork.ini* file. If you include a full directory path (e.g., *c:\pdoxwin\giftco\mywork.ini*), Paradox will use that file for *every* working directory you switch to.
-i *filename*	Specifies an alternate *pdoxwin.ini* file.
-m	Loads Paradox for Windows as a minimized application. (Alternatively, you can load Paradox as a minimized application by holding down Shift while double-clicking the Paradox for Windows icon.)

▶ **TABLE A.1:** *Paradox for Windows Command Line Options (continued)*

OPTION	DESCRIPTION
-n	Prevents Paradox from saving private and working directory settings in the *win.ini* file.
-o *filename*	Specifies an alternate *idapi.cfg* file.
-p *directory*	Specifies an alternate private directory.
-q	Starts Paradox for Windows without displaying the title screen and "Loading" message.
-w *directory*	Specifies an initial working directory.
startfile	Opens a document and performs its default action.

NOTE
filename is the name of the file to use; the name must include the file extension.
directory is the name of the directory to use.
startfile is the name of a Paradox form, report, table, query, or script to use; the name must include the file extension.

You can type command lines at the DOS prompt or in the <u>C</u>ommand Line text box that appears when you choose <u>F</u>ile ➤ <u>R</u>un from the Windows Program Manager menus. To run the command line automatically when you start your computer, enter it into your *autoexec.bat* file. If you want the command line to run whenever you double-click the Paradox for Windows icon, enter it into the <u>C</u>ommand Line text box that appears when you click the Paradox for Windows icon (once) and then choose <u>F</u>ile ➤ <u>P</u>roperties from the Program Manager menus.

▶ ▶ **W A R N I N G**

> When starting a second instance of Paradox for Windows, use both the -n *command-line* parameter and the -p *directory* parameter. When specifying the private directory, be sure to supply a name that is different from the private directory used by any other instance of Paradox.

Network, OBEX, and SQL Features

►► **W**hen you use Paradox for Windows as part of a workgroup or networked environment, Paradox offers some additional features and behaves somewhat differently than the way it is described in the chapters of this book. This appendix addresses those features and differences.

In the first part of this appendix, we'll cover the ways Paradox works differently when you are on a network. We'll explain how to view user names, lock tables and records, and set the retry period and screen refresh rate on a network. We'll also discuss some data security issues and explain how the Tools ➤ Utilities options behave in a multiuser environment.

In the next two parts, we'll cover the Object Exchange (OBEX) and Borland SQL Links for Windows features.

OBEX allows you to publish data objects to the members of your workgroup (even if they aren't on the same network), and to subscribe to the objects they are publishing to you. These objects can be tables, query results, or groups of files in a single directory.

The Borland SQL Links for Windows features allow Paradox for Windows to become a client to a larger server database, such as ORACLE, InterBase, or SYBASE/Microsoft SQL Server. You'll learn how to simplify some of the common tasks of connecting to and using a server database with the special SQL Tools palette. You also can use this palette with your local Paradox and dBASE tables to do many of the same tasks.

▸▸ **N O T E**

> **In previous versions of Paradox for Windows, the OBEX and SQL Links features were available only in a separate Workgroup Edition. These features now come standard with Paradox 5 for Windows (although you will need to order and install the SQL drivers separately, as explained later in this appendix). See Appendix A for more information about installing Paradox.**

▸▸ *Networking Basics*

When you use Paradox for Windows in a network environment, some features work differently than they do on a stand-alone version. The next few sections explain the essential differences.

▸▸ **N O T E**

> **Installing Paradox for Windows on a network is considerably more complicated than performing the single-user installation discussed in Appendix A. It should be undertaken only by a network administrator or supervisor who has full (or "parental") rights to all directories on the network and a thorough understanding of network concepts. Please refer to the *User's Guide* that comes with Paradox for instructions on installing and configuring Paradox for Windows on a network.**

▸ *Viewing User Names*

In a *multiuser* environment, each user has a "name" that uniquely identifies him or her to Paradox. Unlike many other multiuser databases, Paradox for Windows does not require a separate list of user names and passwords. For instance, if you log in to your Novell NetWare network as *SUSAN*, Paradox for Windows will identify you simply as *SUSAN*.

To view your user name, choose Tools ➤ Multiuser ➤ User Name. After viewing the dialog box that appears, click OK.

To view the names of other network users who are also running Paradox for Windows at the moment, choose Tools ➤ Multiuser ➤ Who. When you're finished viewing the list, click OK.

► Securing Your Data from Prying Eyes

In a multiuser environment, it is important to protect your data from unauthorized access and to control which users can access tables and fields. In Paradox for Windows, you control access to data by assigning passwords and security privileges separately for each table.

Each secure table can have a *master password* that provides full control over the table's security. Tables also can have one or more *auxiliary passwords*, which provide an additional level of security for the table and its fields. For example, a user who enters the password **BASEBALL** may be able to insert or delete records from a Customer table. However, a user who enters the password **FOOTBALL** may only be able to read data from the Customer table, or may only be able to update certain fields.

Chapter 15 explains how to assign and use master and auxiliary passwords via the Restructure and Passwords options on the Tools ➤ Utilities menu.

► Locking Tables and Records

In a multiuser environment, many users may need to read or update data at the same time. The database management system must prevent several people from changing data at the same time (this can corrupt the data), while still allowing multiple users to view the data or work with data in other parts of the database.

Paradox uses a system of locks to control who can do what, and when they can do it. In essence, the locking mechanism acts as a traffic cop, placing *locks* on data when a person needs to perform a certain function and then releasing the locks when the work is done.

Paradox for Windows' automatic locking schemes are usually fine for any user's needs, so you shouldn't have to take any special action. For example, Paradox will *always* lock a record automatically when a user is updating it, and will release the lock automatically when the cursor is moved to another record. Similarly, it will place a special lock called an *Open* lock on a table when anyone opens the table, or when any form, report, query, or other document that uses the table's data is opened.

If necessary, you can lock tables and records explicitly by choosing options from the Paradox Desktop menus or by writing ObjectPAL programs. In this appendix, we'll discuss methods for locking tables and records from the Desktop. For information on locking records through ObjectPAL programs, search for the *Lock* topic in the ObjectPAL on-line Help. (Chapter 19 explains how to use ObjectPAL's Help system.)

Before setting locks, you should understand the implications thoroughly. In particular, be aware that you must explicitly remove any locks that you set from the Desktop menus (as explained below). If you forget to remove the Desktop locks, other users may be unable to view or update the data. Also, be certain that you exit Paradox for Windows and the network properly to avoid leaving tables and records locked accidentally.

WARNING

Never exit by simply turning off your computer. Doing so without properly exiting Paradox can corrupt your data and prevent other people from using Paradox on the network.

Locking a Table from the Desktop

To set an explicit lock on a table, proceed as follows:

1. Choose Tools ➤ Multiuser ➤ Set Locks. You'll see the Table Locks dialog box, as shown in Figure B.1.

2. Select the table for which you wish to set locks.

3. Select the type of lock you want from the Locks area. Each type of lock is described below. To remove all locks that you've placed on the table, select No Lock.

4. Choose OK.

Network, OBEX, and SQL

App. **B**

FIGURE B.1

The Table Locks dialog box allows you to lock a table.

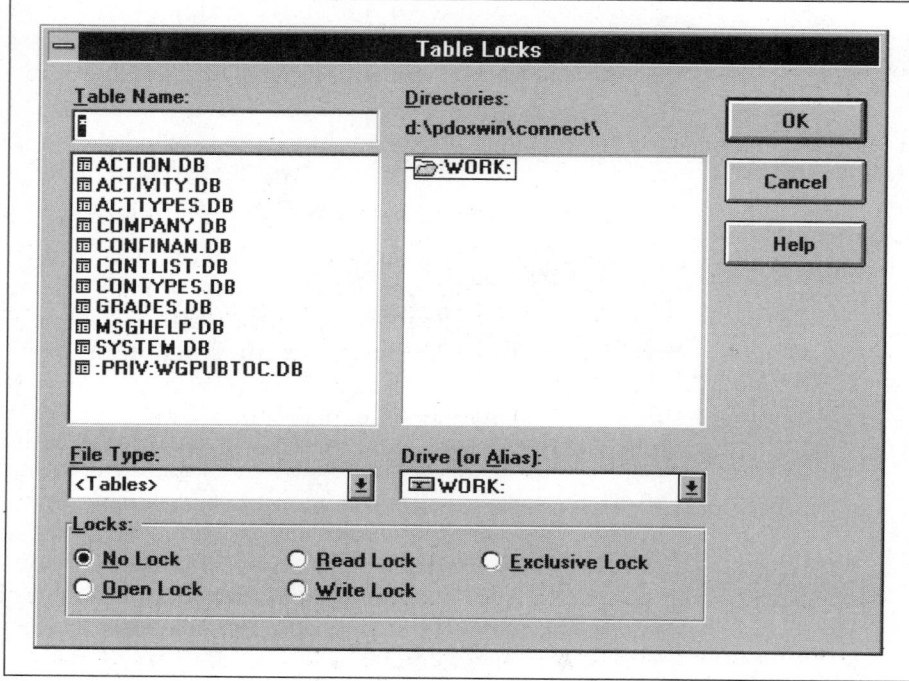

In step 3, above, you can select one of the following locks:

No Lock   Unlocks all locks that you've placed on the table. Note that this has no effect on locks set by *other* users. All users must explicitly remove their own table locks.

Open Lock   Locks the table as though you had opened it (without actually opening the table). An Open lock prevents other users from putting an Exclusive lock on the table. However, another user can still put a Write lock on the table even if you've placed an Open lock on it.

Read Lock   Allows you to read (view) and write to (edit) the selected table. Other users can view the data in the table if they have the required rights, but they cannot write to the table unless they place a Write lock on the same table. If another user does place a Write lock on the table, you'll be unable to write to the table until the Write lock is removed. A table can have more than one Read lock on it at a time.

Write Lock   Allows you to read and write to the table. Other users can read from the table, but they cannot write to it. A table can have only one Write lock on it at a time.

Exclusive Lock   Gives you read and write access to the table. However, others cannot use the table in any way, nor can they create a table with the same name until you release the lock. This lock is the most restrictive and should be used only when absolutely necessary.

Remember that Paradox places an Open lock on a table when anyone opens the table, or when any form, report, query, or other document that uses the table's data is opened. Users (including yourself) must remove Open locks by closing windows that contain the table's data before Paradox or any other user can place an Exclusive lock on it.

Table B.1 summarizes the effects of placing different types of table locks from the Desktop.

▶ **TABLE B.1:**   *Effects of Locking Tables from the Desktop*

LOCK LEVEL	YOUR RIGHTS	OTHER USERS' RIGHTS	LOCKS OTHER USERS CAN PLACE
No Lock	None	All	All*
Open Lock	Read, Write (if no one else has a Read lock)	Read, Write	All except Exclusive if no Record lock is in place; otherwise, only Open
Read Lock	Read, Write (if no one else has a Read lock)	Read	Open, Read
Write Lock	Read, Write	Read	Open
Exclusive Lock	All	None	None

NOTE* No Lock removes Desktop-level locks only; it has no effect on Record locks or Open locks. You cannot obtain an Exclusive lock if the table is locked from the Desktop, through Record locks, or through Open locks.

Network, OBEX, and SQL

App.
B

To view the current locks on a table, choose Tools ➤ Multiuser ➤ Display Locks, select the table you're interested in, and choose OK. The information appears in a temporary Paradox table named *Locks*, and includes the type of locks placed and the name of the user who placed each lock. This feature is not available for dBASE tables.

Locking a Record from the Desktop

Although Paradox tries to lock a record automatically when you begin to change it, you might want to lock a record manually. For example, if you are talking with a customer who is about to provide some information about an address change, you can lock the record so that no one else can jump in and change that customer's data.

To lock a record, open the table or form, switch to Edit mode (press F9 or click the Edit Data button in the Toolbar), move the cursor to the record you want to lock, and then choose Record ➤ Lock or press F5.

If you'd like to immediately post (or save) your changes to the table and still keep the record locked when posting is complete, choose Record ➤ Post/Keep Locked or press Ctrl+F5. This option is handy when your table has a primary key and you want to make sure the key data you've entered is unique. In addition to verifying the uniqueness of the key field, Paradox will put the record in its proper sort position and leave the cursor positioned in the record so you can make more changes.

When you're ready to unlock a record, move the cursor to another record, or choose Record ➤ Unlock, or press Shift+F5.

► ►**N O T E**

Unlocking a record saves the changes to the table. Chapter 6 provides more information about entering and editing data.

▶ *Setting the Network Retry Period*

You can set the length of time (in seconds) that Paradox will try to open a table if you are locked out of it. For instance, if you set the time to 10 seconds, Paradox will retry the open operation for 10 seconds. To set this "retry time," choose T̲ools ➤ M̲ultiuser ➤ Set R̲etry, type the retry time (in seconds) into the Network Retry Period dialog box that appears, and choose OK.

 ▶ ▶ **W A R N I N G**

> **While Paradox is trying again to open the table, you cannot do anything else on your system. Therefore, you should set a short retry period if you don't want to wait very long; or, if you're the more patient type, you can set a longer retry period, such as 30 seconds.**

▶ *Setting the Network Refresh Rate*

The Network Refresh Rate determines how often Paradox updates your current view of data. Since others may be updating tables that are of interest to you, you probably will want Paradox to display the latest data on your screen. To set the Network Refresh Rate, choose T̲ools ➤ S̲ystem Settings ➤ A̲uto Refresh, type the refresh interval (in seconds) into the Network Refresh Rate dialog box that appears, and choose OK. (Of course, Paradox updates your screen immediately whenever *you* make a change.)

 ▶ ▶ **N O T E**

> **The Auto Refresh feature affects Paradox tables only. To refresh other file formats, such as dBASE or SQL tables, press Ctrl+F3.**

Network, OBEX, and SQL

▶ ▶
App.
B

▶ *Using Tool Utilities in a Multiuser Environment*

Many options on the Tools ➤ Utilities menus deal with tables that other network users might be reading or updating at the same time you're accessing them. Therefore, it's worth taking a look at how you, and other network users, might be affected when working with the utilities in a multiuser environment. Please refer to Chapter 15 for general instructions on using the Tools ➤ Utilities options.

▶▶**N O T E**

> In Windows, you or other users can have several views of the same data open at once. Thus, Paradox may consider a duplicate view on your own Desktop to be another "user," and you may be prevented from performing a file utility operation. For best results, close all views of your table before using Tools ➤ Utilities options.

Adding Records from One Table to Another

When you use Tools ➤ Utilities ➤ Add to add records from one table to another, Paradox puts a Read lock on the source table and a Write lock on the target table. (When you use Add with dBASE tables, Paradox places Write locks on both tables.) Until the Add operation is complete, other users cannot change the structure or contents of either table, and they cannot do any operation that requires a Write lock or Exclusive lock on either table. If locks exist on either table before you begin, you must wait until they are cleared.

Copying Tables

When you use Tools ➤ Utilities ➤ Copy to copy a table, Paradox puts a Read lock on the source table and an Exclusive lock on the target table. Until you are finished with the copy, other users cannot change the structure of contents of the source table, and they cannot do any operation on the target table. If someone else has put a Record lock, Write lock, or Exclusive lock on the source table before you begin, you'll have to wait until the locks are cleared.

Deleting Tables

When you delete a table via <u>T</u>ools ➤ <u>U</u>tilities ➤ <u>D</u>elete, Paradox puts an Exclusive lock on the target table. Until the Delete is finished, other people cannot use the target table at all. If other users are working with the table in any way, you cannot delete it until they are done and they remove all the locks.

Emptying Tables

When you empty a table using <u>T</u>ools ➤ <u>U</u>tilities ➤ <u>E</u>mpty, Paradox puts an Exclusive lock on the target table. As for deleting a table, this prevents other people from using the target table until the Empty operation is done.

▶ Renaming Tables

When you rename a table via <u>T</u>ools ➤ <u>U</u>tilities ➤ <u>R</u>ename, Paradox puts an Exclusive lock on the target table. As usual, this prevents other people from using the target table until the Rename is complete. You cannot rename a table while anyone is using it in any way.

Restructuring Tables

No one can access any table that you're restructuring via the <u>T</u>ools ➤ <u>U</u>tilities ➤ Res<u>t</u>ructure option until the restructure is complete. Likewise, if others are using the table in any way, you can't restructure the table until they have closed it.

Subtracting from Tables

When you use <u>T</u>ools ➤ <u>U</u>tilities ➤ S<u>u</u>btract to remove records from one table that exist in another table, Paradox puts a Read lock on the source table (the one that contains the records you are subtracting) and a Write lock on the target table (the one you are subtracting from). As for the Add operation, other users cannot change the structure or contents of either table, and they cannot do any operation that requires a Write lock or Exclusive lock on either table until the Subtract is done. By the same token, you must wait to perform the Subtract operation until all Write locks and Exclusive locks are removed from either table.

▶▶**TIP**

> **Rather than trying to memorize all the rules and regulations presented above, just remember that Paradox won't let you do anything that could be a problem for you or for other users. If you are locked out of an operation, someone else is using the tables you need to work with. Just wait patiently. If the wait seems too long, you can find out who is hogging the tables by choosing Tools ➤ Multiuser ➤ Display Locks as described earlier in this appendix.**

▶▶ *OBEX: The Workgroup Solution*

OBEX is short for **OB**ject **EX**change, Borland's (and Paradox's) workgroup technology. The Object Exchange goes beyond network file sharing by allowing you to share data in any format across a network or mail system. With a network file-sharing environment, everyone sees live updates of exactly the same data or application. With OBEX, you can *publish* a snapshot of your current data to your workgroup (the *subscribers*), get everyone's ideas about what you have published, and then publish just the final result to your boss (another subscriber), who doesn't have to see the steps in the process. You also can use OBEX to send electronic mail (e-mail), without leaving Paradox.

▶▶**NOTE**

> **OBEX uses the terms *publish* and *subscribe* to describe how data objects are shared in the workgroup. When you publish an object, a snapshot of that data becomes available to members of your workgroup. The members can then incorporate the object into their own work by subscribing to it. Whenever you publish a revision to your data object, the subscribers will receive the updated versions.**

If you are on the road, you can use Paradox to access your workgroup objects and electronic mail quite easily. For example, you could log into MCI Mail and pick up the latest version of data to which you subscribe, make some essential changes, and then publish a revision back to the rest of the workgroup. All this happens transparently, just as if you were in the office, hooked up to the network. Need to add a group of engineers in Tokyo to the workgroup? Just add their MCI Mail addresses to the subscriber list, and you're done.

▶ ▶ **N O T E**

> The *Workgroup Desktop* is the collection of tools that automates communication and information exchange among workgroup members. *OBEX* is the software engine that drives the Workgroup Desktop. For simplicity, we'll refer to all these items as OBEX or Object Exchange.

The Object Exchange supports a variety of messaging services, called *transports*, which let you send and receive electronic mail and establish data-distribution with remote users without leaving Paradox. These transports include:

ccMAIL   Messaging services that comply with the widely-supported **V**endor **I**ndependent **M**essaging (VIM) standard. The best-known VIM service is the Lotus cc:Mail electronic mail program.

LAN   Local area networks including 3Com 3+, 3Com 3+Open, AT&T StarGroup 3.5.1, Banyan 5.0, IBM LAN Server 2.0, Microsoft LAN Manager 2.1, and Novell NetWare.

MAPI   Microsoft's **M**ail **A**pplication **P**rogramming **I**nterface (MAPI), which lets you use Windows for Workgroups, Windows NT, and other MAPI-compliant messaging services such as Microsoft Mail.

MCI   MCI Mail, a global electronic mail service. To use MCI, you will need an MCI account, a modem, and access to a telephone system.

Network, OBEX, and SQL

▶ ▶
App.
B

MHS Novell's e-mail systems for local area networks. This includes NetWare **M**essage **H**andling **S**ervice (MHS) version 1.5 and NetWare **G**lobal **M**essaging (NGM).

NOTES Lotus Notes, version 3.0 or later.

WPO WordPerfect Office, version 4.0a or later.

▶ ▶ **N O T E**

In this appendix, we'll show sample screens that use the MAPI transport system that comes with Windows for Workgroups.

A thorough tour of Object Exchange and the Workgroup Desktop would fill a small book of its own. Since this book is already quite large, we will limit our discussion to the essential features of this versatile tool. You'll learn what OBEX can do for you, and how to use OBEX commands to send electronic mail, poll your accounts, publish objects, and subscribe to them. If you'd like more information, you won't be disappointed in your search. Simply turn to the following sources:

- The *Workgroup Desktop Guide*, a separate book that comes with Paradox for Windows.

- The OBEX online Help. Every OBEX dialog box features a Help button that provides context-sensitive Help. You can also peruse the general OBEX topics shown in Figure B.2 by choosing <u>H</u>elp ▶O<u>B</u>EX.

▶ *How OBEX Can Help You: A Scenario*

So, how can OBEX help you share information with people at remote locations? Here is just one possibility, but there are many others. Suppose your company, Worldwide Yaks, has a central order-processing operation in Mongolia in which PCs are connected by a Novell Network and data is stored in a shared Paradox database. Here are some of the activities that take place:

- As orders for yaks and yak products pour in, they are added to an Orders database.

- The Shipping department gets automatic updates by running a query against the Orders database.

FIGURE B.2

The OBEX Help Contents leads you to detailed information about using Object Exchange features.

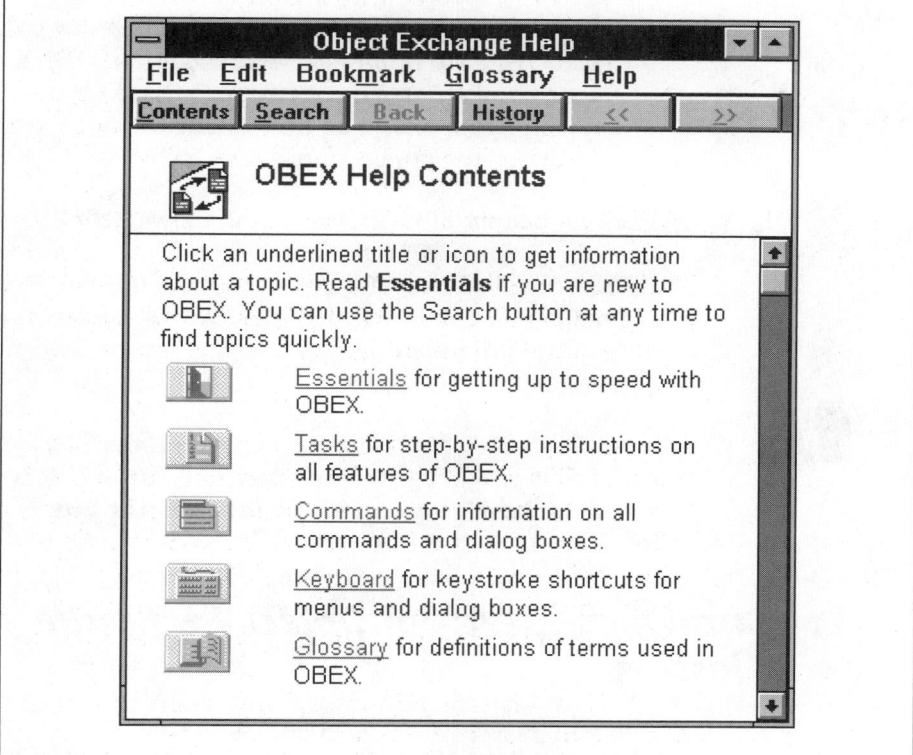

- Shipping uses OBEX to publish a twice-daily report with the shipping status of the orders in the system. The regional offices get this update via MCI Mail.

- Shipping also uses OBEX to publish a more detailed report to Customer Service. This version is published hourly, unless there's a major problem, in which case they publish one immediately.

- The Orders department publishes a daily update of the new customers for each regional and international sales office.

- The Orders department publishes a weekly report for each regional and international sales office. This report shows the current sales figures, plots the weekly and monthly trends, and highlights the top three net gains by region. It is published as a Quattro Pro for Windows spreadsheet, but is based on the Orders data stored in Paradox.

Network, OBEX, and SQL

App.

- The salespeople who are on the road fire up Paradox for Windows from their hotel rooms, plug the modem into the phone line, and use OBEX to poll their MCI accounts. OBEX automatically sends any reports the salespeople have written up to the main office in Mongolia, then downloads the new customers list that the Orders department publishes for them.

The real beauty of OBEX is that it allows people to send and receive information *from anywhere* in the world, *to anywhere* in the world. Time differences, distance, and type of connection are irrelevant and invisible when you combine OBEX, networks, commercial messaging services, and Paradox databases into a complete information system.

▶▶**T I P**

As you'll learn later, you can use OBEX to publish and subscribe to all kinds of files, not just Paradox objects.

▶ Buzzword Alert: An Object Exchange Glossary

The Object Exchange has its own unique set of buzzwords. Most are words you have already seen and are familiar with in other contexts, but their meanings can be a bit different in the Object Exchange. Table B.2 provides a brief list of some important OBEX buzzwords and their meanings. To view a complete online glossary of OBEX terms, choose Help ➤ OBEX, then click the glossary icon near the lower-left corner of the OBEX Help Contents screen (or choose Glossary ➤ Definitions from the OBEX Help menus).

▶ Getting Started

There are two ways to start the Object Exchange: from within Paradox, and from outside Paradox.

From within Paradox, you can choose the following options on the File and Tools menus (you'll learn more about them later):

File ➤ Send   Lets you compose messages, attach files, and send them via electronic mail.

▶ **TABLE B.2:** *An OBEX Glossary*

OBEX WORD	MEANING
OBEX	OBject EXchange—A way to share tables, queries, documents, and even applications in a workgroup.
Object (or Data Object)	The table, query result, worksheet, document, or file set being shared.
File Set	A group of files that are exchanged within a workgroup.
Mail	To send a data object once to a person or group of people without establishing a regular connection.
Poll	To initiate the exchange of data objects to or from your workstation.
Publish	To make a data object available for repeated use by a person or group of people within a workgroup.
Subscribe	To use and save a data object that was published. This establishes a remote, dynamic link to the publisher.
Workgroup	A group of users who exchange data objects.

File ➤ Publish   Lets you distribute one or more data objects to other users, who are called subscribers.

File ➤ Subscribe   Lets you update data that has been published to you.

Tools ➤ OBEX Address Book   Lets you set up a list of addresses for recipients of your e-mail or published data. An *address* is the unique electronic mail or communication system address that tells the transport exactly how to connect with a particular user.

Tools ➤ OBEX Poll   Lets you transmit outgoing objects or pick up incoming ones. You can poll a transport manually, or have OBEX poll it automatically at specified intervals.

Network, OBEX, and SQL

App.

B

From outside Paradox, you can double-click the Object Exchange, Address Book, or Object Exchange Alerter icons in the Paradox for Windows group window shown in Figure B.3. Note that it's rarely necessary to use the icons from outside of Paradox, since the OBEX options on the <u>F</u>ile and <u>T</u>ools menus will load the necessary components automatically. We will not describe these "outsider" icons in detail, but here's a brief summary of what each one can do:

FIGURE B.3

The Paradox for Windows group window includes three icons for using Object Exchange from outside Paradox: Object Exchange, Object Exchange Alerter, and Address Book.

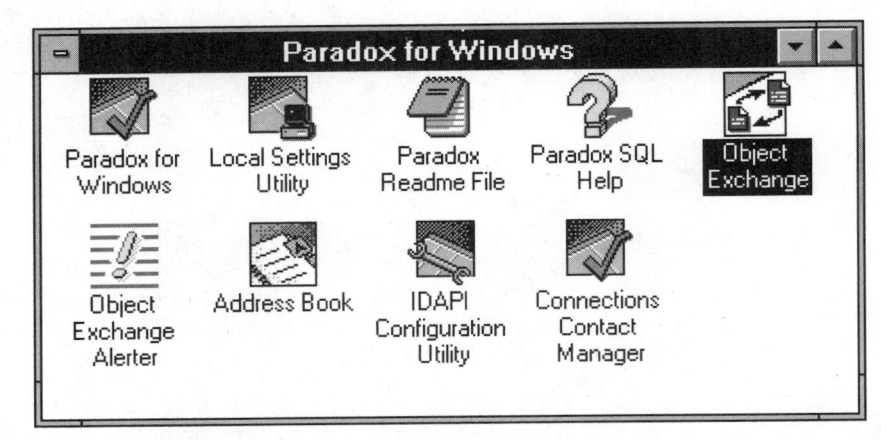

Object Exchange   Lets you set up new accounts, delete accounts, and reconfigure existing accounts. You also can poll accounts and view detailed error messages about events. The Object Exchange is started automatically whenever you use OBEX features from within Paradox.

Address Book   Same as choosing <u>T</u>ools ➤ OBEX <u>A</u>ddress Book from within Paradox.

Object Exchange Alerter   Displays details of the most recent problems OBEX encountered when polling or sending objects.

Be aware that the Object Exchange, Address Book, and Object Exchange Alerter run in their own application windows. If you're using one of these applications and you accidentally click outside the window, the OBEX application window may disappear behind other open windows. You can use any of the standard Windows methods to return the window to the forefront. For example, hold down the Alt key and tap the Tab key until the appropriate window name appears in the center of the screen, or press Ctrl+Esc and double-click the name of the application you want.

TIP

To have a bell sound whenever an important OBEX event occurs, start Object Exchange. Then either click on the minimized Object Exchange icon or open the Object Exchange dialog box's Control-menu and choose Sound. Select the Sound option again if you want to turn off the bell.

To use OBEX effectively, you first need to:

1. Define and configure the accounts to which your workstation (computer) can connect. For example, on a Windows for Workgroups network, you would set up a MAPI account. To access your MCI mailbox, you would also need to set up an MCI account.

2. Set up an address book with the names and message service addresses of people to whom you want to send e-mail or publish data. This step is optional, but it can be a real timesaver.

Once those steps are complete, you can send e-mail, poll your accounts, publish objects to other people, or subscribe to objects that people have published to you. We'll describe each of these steps in the following sections.

▶ Setting Up Your Accounts

Before you can send, poll, publish, or subscribe, you must set up your OBEX accounts. These tell OBEX which transports your workstation will be using.

To begin, start Object Exchange from outside Paradox (by double-clicking the Object Exchange icon in the Paradox for Windows group window) or from within Paradox (by choosing Tools ► OBEX Poll ► Cancel). Now open the Object Exchange dialog box using any of the following methods:

Object Exchange

- Double-click the minimized Object Exchange icon (shown at left) if it appears in the lower-left corner of your screen.

- Press Alt+Tab until *Object Exchange* appears in the center of your screen, then release the Alt and Tab keys.

- Press Ctrl+Esc to open the Task List, then double-click *Object Exchange*.

You'll see the Object Exchange dialog box shown in Figure B.4.

FIGURE B.4

The Object Exchange dialog box. To see details of previous errors, you can click the Show Details button (it will change to a Hide Details button). To hide the details again (as shown in this example), click the Hide Details button.

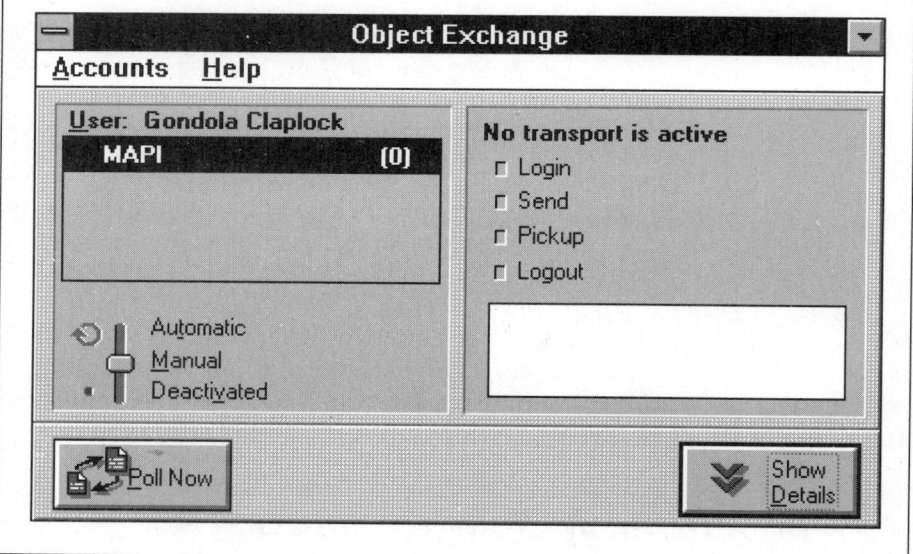

To define a new account in the Object Exchange dialog box, follow these steps:

1. Choose <u>A</u>ccounts ➤ <u>N</u>ew. You'll see the New Account dialog box shown below:

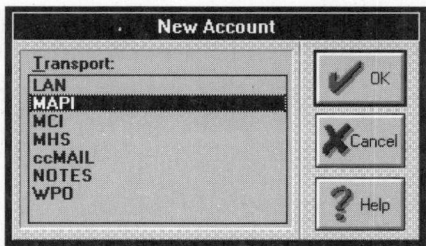

2. Click on the name of the transport you will be connecting to (MAPI, for example) and choose OK. The Configure Account dialog box will appear, as in Figure B.5.

3. Complete the Configure Account dialog box for the transport you selected, as follows:

    • In the left side of the dialog box, fill in the <u>A</u>ccount Name that OBEX will use to identify the account (or accept the default name), then complete the information that identifies your workstation to the transport you selected. The specifics

FIGURE B.5 ▶

The Configure Account dialog box for a MAPI account. The exact appearance of the dialog box will depend on the type of transport you select in step 2.

will depend on the type of transport you selected. Click the Help button in the dialog box for specific instructions.

- In the right side of the dialog box, choose the frequency that will be used for automatic polling. Again, you can click the Help button for more information.

▶▶ WARNING

If you fail to set up your account information properly, OBEX will not work. Please check the online OBEX Help and any documentation that comes with your messaging service for details.

4. Choose OK to return to the Object Exchange dialog box. Your account will appear in the Accounts list underneath your User Name.

Repeat the four steps above for each account you'll be using.

Here are some other OBEX tasks you can perform while using the Object Exchange dialog box:

- To delete an existing account, choose Accounts ➤ Delete, click the name of the account you want to delete, and choose Yes when asked for verification.

- To reconfigure an existing account, choose Accounts ➤ Configure, click the name of the account you want to change, and fill in the Configure Account dialog box as explained in step 3 above.

- To set an account's polling mode, click the account name in the Object Exchange dialog box, then drag the slider button to choose one of the following polling modes:

    Automatic OBEX will poll the account automatically, at whatever frequency you selected when configuring the account. A curved arrow will appear next to the account name.

    Manual Poll manually (the default setting). OBEX will poll the account only when you click the Poll Now button in the Object Exchange dialog box, or you choose Tools ➤ OBEX Poll ➤ Start Poll from within Paradox.

Deactivated   Polling is disabled for the selected account.

- To poll an account manually, click the account name in the list, then click the Poll Now button. The little boxes next to the Login, Send, Pickup, and Logout items in the right side of the dialog box will show you the polling progress.

- To see the details of the most recent transport errors, click the Show Details button. To hide those details again, click Hide Details.

When you're finished with the Object Exchange dialog box, you can double-click its Control-menu box or press Alt+F4 (to exit Object Exchange and remove it from memory) or click its Minimize button (to leave Object Exchange running as a minimized icon).

▶ Setting Up Your Address Book

An *address* tells OBEX exactly where and how to send objects (e-mail and data objects) to a recipient. When you send e-mail or publish data, you must give OBEX the address of the place to send that information.

Not surprisingly, the transmission will fail if the address isn't 100% correct. Providing a bad OBEX address is like supplying the wrong city name, street name, and house number when you give someone directions to your home. Unfortunately, each transport uses a different convention for its addresses, and we cannot describe all of them here. You'll find information about setting up addresses for each transport in the OBEX online Help and in whatever documentation comes with the transport program itself.

There are two basic ways to specify addresses when you send or publish data. You can either type the addresses manually, or you can store them in a convenient address book that can supply the nitty-gritty address details automatically. We'll take you quickly through setting up a simple address book, since this is the method you're likely to use most often.

To add recipients to your address book, start from the Paradox Desktop and follow these steps:

1. Choose Tools ➤ OBEX Address Book. You'll see the Address Book dialog box shown in Figure B.6.

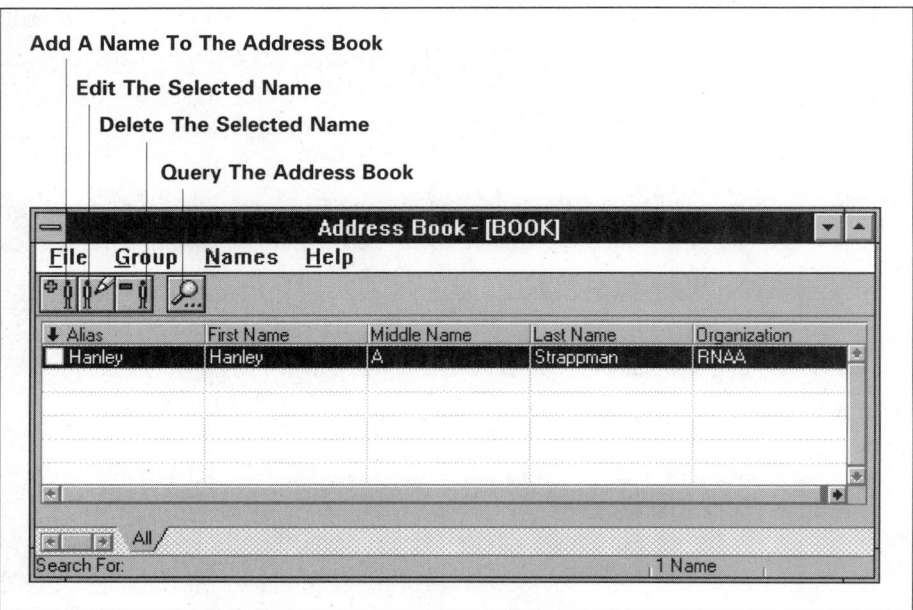

2. Click the Add A Name To The Address Book button in the Toolbar (see Figure B.6), or press the Ins key. You'll see the New Name dialog box. (A completed New Name dialog box appears later in Figure B.8.)

3. In the Alias text box, enter a unique alias that will identify this person. (Once you enter an alias into your address book, you can use it as a shortcut name when sending e-mail messages and publishing objects.)

4. If you wish, fill in the First Name, Middle Name, Last Name, and Organization text boxes with personal information about this recipient.

5. To specify the transport information for your recipient, click the Setup button. This opens the Address Composer shown in Figure B.7.

6. In the Type list, click the name of the transport that will be used to send information to the recipient. For example, in Figure B.7, we chose MAPI.

7. In the Address area, enter the exact address for this person's transport. This step is crucial to the success of your transmissions.

FIGURE B.7

A completed Address Composer dialog box for a potential recipient on a MAPI messaging system

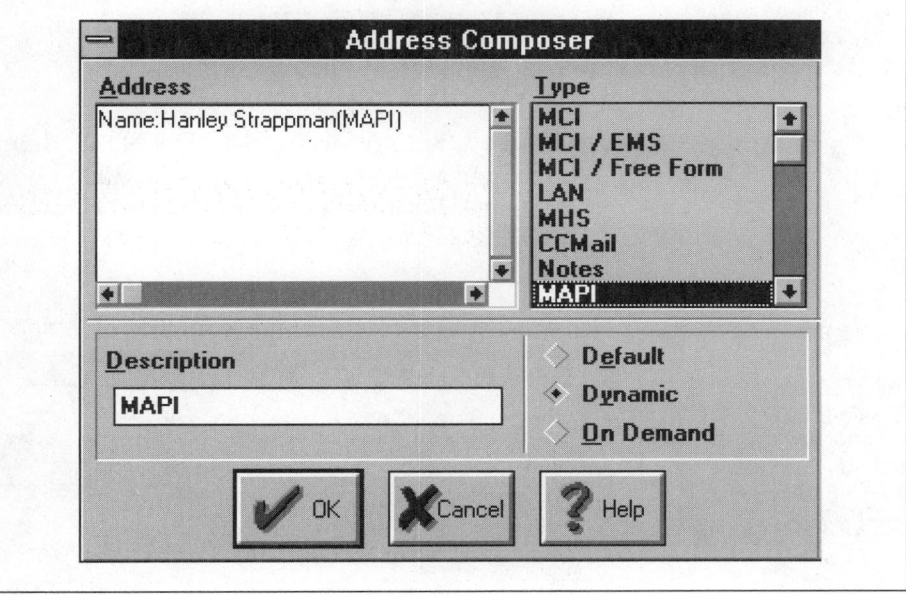

 ▶▶ **T I P**

> If you're not sure how to specify the transport address, online Help is available. First click the Help button in the Address Composer. Next, scroll down to and click the underlined topic *Working with Addresses* (it's in step 3 of the "Entering A New Address" screen). Then scroll down to the bottom of the "Working With Addresses" screen and click the name of the transport you selected from the Type list in step 6 above.

8. If you wish, you can change the address Description, though it's not necessary.

9. If you wish, specify how OBEX should use this address by choosing one of the following options:

> **Default** This will be the person's default address.

Dynamic OBEX will use this address if the default address is not available for this recipient.

On Demand OBEX will use this address only if you specify it in a message.

10. Choose OK to return to the New Name dialog box for this recipient. Figure B.8 shows a completed dialog box for a person named Hanley A Strappman (alias Hanley). Hanley's mailbox user name on Windows for Workgroups (MAPI) is Hanley Strappman.

FIGURE B.8 ▶

The New Name dialog box after filling in the personal information and using the Setup button to define the user's transport address

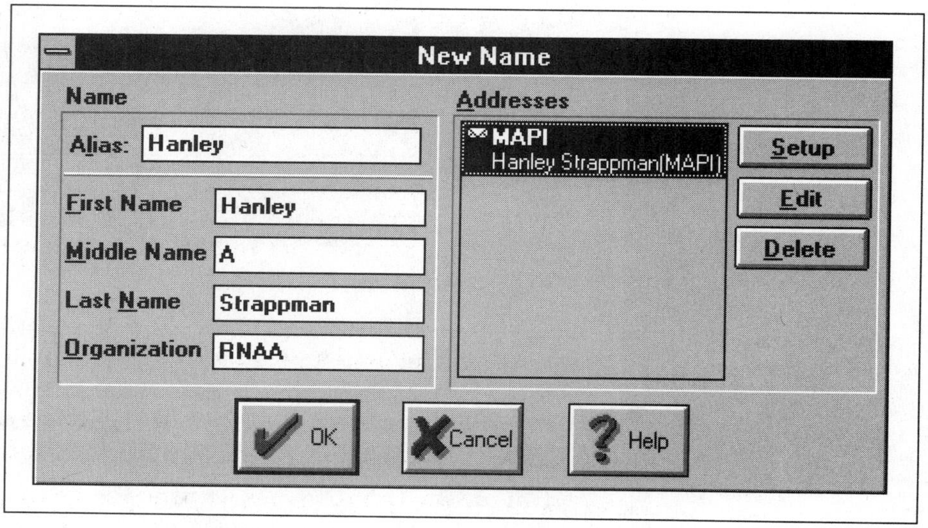

11. When you're finished defining the name, choose OK to return to the address book. The new name will appear in the list, in alphabetical order by Alias.

It's easy to change an existing entry in the Address Book window. Simply double-click the name you want to change, or highlight the name and click the Edit The Selected Name button in the Address Book's Toolbar. From here, you can change the recipient's personal information or Addresses list. To change an address, click the address in the Addresses list, then click Edit button and repeat steps 6–11 above. To create a new address for this recipient, click the Setup button and repeat steps 6–11 above. To delete an address, click that address and then click the Delete button.

The Address Book window also provides additional tools that you can learn about by choosing Help ➤ Contents and then perusing the Address Book Manager's online Help topics. When you're finished using the Address Book, choose File ➤ Exit from the Address Book menus.

▶ Polling an Account

You can manually poll an account anytime you want OBEX to send out and pick up objects. (This isn't necessary if you're using automatic polling and are willing to wait until the next polling cycle begins; however, manual polling is handy whenever you're in a hurry to send or receive something right away.) To poll an account from within Paradox, follow these steps:

1. Choose Tools ➤ OBEX Poll to open the OBEX Poll dialog box.

2. If you have multiple accounts or transports, make sure the ones you want to poll are marked with an × (selected) and that those you don't want to poll are unmarked (deselected). To select or deselect an item, just click it.

3. When you're ready to begin, click the Start Poll button (the button name will change to Cancel Poll while polling is active).

If necessary, you can interrupt polling by clicking the Cancel Poll button. To exit the OBEX Poll dialog box, choose Cancel.

You can also poll from the Object Exchange dialog box as described earlier. Simply open that dialog box, highlight the name of the transport you want to poll, and click the Poll Now button.

▶ ▶ **TIP**

Try manual polling if the objects you sent or the objects you are expecting to receive have not arrived yet.

Network,
OBEX, and SQL

App.

B

▶ *Sending Electronic Mail*

Let's suppose you want to use OBEX to send an electronic mail message to another user, without leaving Paradox. Here are the general steps to follow from the Paradox Desktop:

1. Choose File ➤ Send to open the Object Exchange: Send dialog box pictured in Figure B.9.

FIGURE B.9 ▶

The Object Exchange: Send dialog box lets you send electronic mail to one or more users. In this example, we completed the dialog box and attached a file named c:\bat\clean.bat to the message. The final step is to click the Send button.

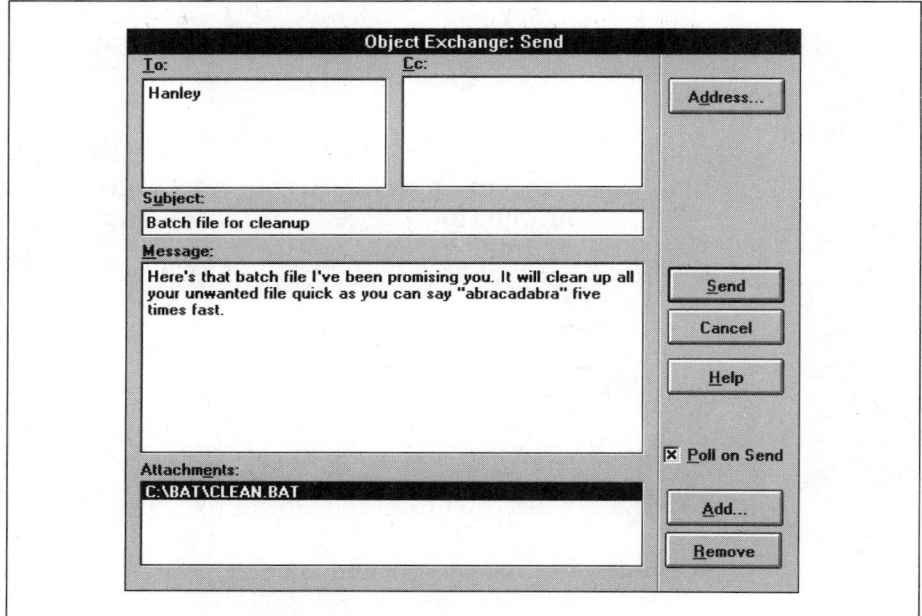

2. In the To box, specify the address of your recipient.

- If you've already set up an address book entry for your recipient, you can type in the recipient's alias (as defined in the address book); or, click the Address button, double-click the recipient's name in the Names list of the Object Exchange: Select Names dialog box that appears, then choose OK.

- If you haven't set up an address book entry for the recipient, you'll need to type the recipient's full address (for example, *Hanley Strappman(MAPI)* is the full address for the recipient shown back in Figure B.8).

- To send the message to more than one recipient, place each recipient's address or alias on a separate line in the <u>T</u>o box. (If necessary, press ↵ after typing a recipient name so that the next name will appear on a new line.)

3. If you wish to send a copy of the message to someone else, click in the <u>C</u>c box and complete it using the same techniques as for step 2 above.

▶ ▶ **T I P**

> As usual, the online Help can assist you with typing addresses correctly. Just click the <u>H</u>elp button in the Object Exchange: Send dialog box, then click the *See Also* topic and choose *Addressing Guidelines.*

4. In the S<u>u</u>bject text box, type a short subject to describe your message.

5. In the <u>M</u>essage box, type the message you want to send.

6. If you want to attach a file to this message, click the <u>A</u>dd button and use the File Browser to locate the file. Simply highlight the file name you want to attach and choose OK (or double-click the file name).

7. Normally Paradox will poll automatically when you send the message. If you don't want this to happen, click the <u>P</u>oll On Send option to deselect it.

8. When you're ready to send the message, click the <u>S</u>end button.

Paradox will send the message to your designated recipients and return you to the Desktop.

Network, OBEX, and SQL

App.
B

▶ *Publishing a Data Object*

When you publish a data object, you control who will see the object and what they will actually see. You also control which versions are made available to them, and when a revision is published.

You can publish three types of data objects—table data, query results, and file sets. Let's take a quick look at each of them.

About Table Data

Publishing a table makes the entire table available. If you change the data in the table, however, the changes are not available to your subscribers until you publish a revision. This is very different from the way a shared table is handled on a local area network. A published table can originate as a Paradox or dBASE table, but will appear to subscribers as a Paradox table. When you publish a table, you can't publish indexes, BLOB files, or OLE objects with it. To distribute these things, you will need to publish a *file set*, as explained later.

About Query Results

Instead of publishing a table, you can publish a query result. Then, whenever you publish a version, OBEX automatically runs the query and publishes the resulting Answer table to your subscribers. Each time you publish a new version, the query runs again.

This method has two advantages over publishing table data. First, the query can be run against multiple databases, either local or remote; and second, the resulting answer table doesn't need to reside on your computer.

About File Sets

If you want to publish more than just tables or queries, you need to use a file set. This lets you send tables, queries, related indexes and BLOB files, referential integrity definitions and table view settings, word-processing documents that depend on the data, or even whole applications. A file set is a group of files that reside in a single directory.

Publishing a New Object

Publishing an object isn't difficult at all, but you do have a number of options. We'll keep our discussion relatively simple here and will not burden you with every possible wrinkle. As always, you can consult the online Help and the *Workgroup Desktop Guide* for further details.

To set up a new data object for publication, follow these steps:

1. Choose File ➤ Publish, then click the New button in the Publications dialog box (you'll see an example of a completed Publications dialog box later, in Figure B.11). This takes you to the New Publication dialog box shown in Figure B.10.

FIGURE B.10

The New Publication dialog box after completing all the sections for a table data object

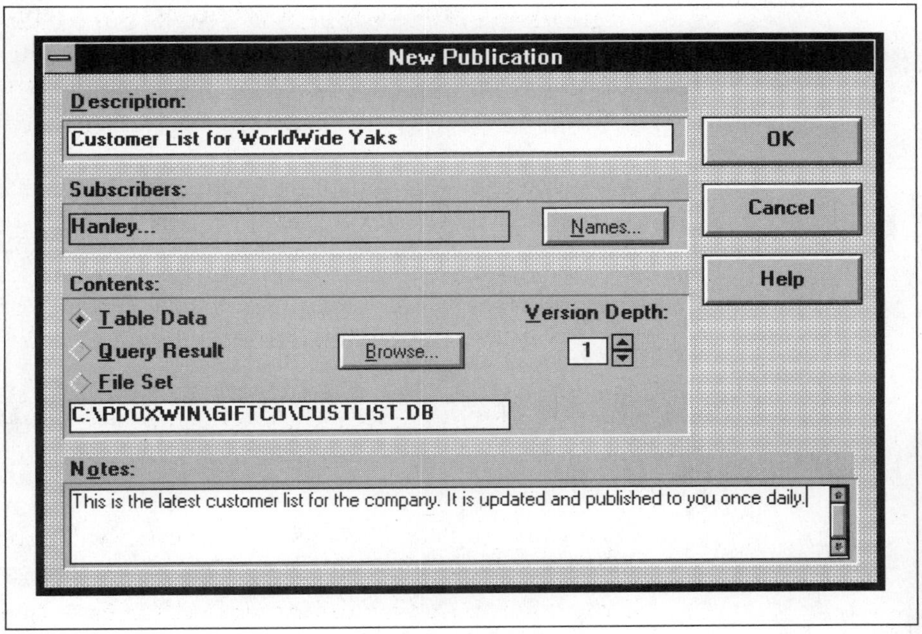

New Publication

Description:
Customer List for WorldWide Yaks

Subscribers:
Hanley...   Names...

Contents:
◆ Table Data
◇ Query Result   Browse...
◇ File Set

Version Depth:
1

C:\PDOXWIN\GIFTCO\CUSTLIST.DB

Notes:
This is the latest customer list for the company. It is updated and published to you once daily.

OK

Cancel

Help

2. In the Description text box, type a description for your new publication. This will appear in the Publications dialog box and in the Use Objects dialog box that your subscribers will see.

Network, OBEX, and SQL

App. B

3. Click the <u>N</u>ames button to open the Object Exchange: Select Names dialog box. Now double-click the names of people who should receive your publication. (As an alternative to double-clicking names, you can click the New <u>A</u>ddress button, type the full network address and transport name in the <u>A</u>ddress text box, and choose OK.) Choose OK to return to the New Publication dialog box.

4. In the Contents area, choose the type of publication you want: Table Data, <u>Q</u>uery Result, or <u>F</u>ile Set.

5. Click the <u>B</u>rowse button and use the File Browser to highlight the object (or objects) you want to publish. Choose OK to return to the New Publication dialog box. (The Contents area will now show the objects you are publishing.)

6. In the N<u>o</u>tes box, type an explanation of the published objects. This will provide your subscribers with useful information about your publication.

7. If you want to choose how many versions will be available to your subscribers, type a value into the <u>V</u>ersion Depth box, or use the triangle buttons to increase or decrease the value. The default value is 1 (which usually is what you want) and the maximum value is 99. For example, a version depth of 4 allows your subscribers to see the most current version, plus the three previous versions.

8. When you're ready to publish the objects, choose OK. You'll be returned to the Paradox Desktop.

9. If you haven't set automatic polling, use the <u>T</u>ools ➤ OBEX Po<u>l</u>l ➤ <u>S</u>tart Poll options (as described earlier) to send the objects on their way.

When you complete the steps above, OBEX will publish the objects to the subscribers (see "Subscribing to a Data Object," later in this appendix).

Using Existing Publications

Once you've defined a publication, you can republish it (or delete it) at any time. Here are the basic steps to follow:

1. Choose <u>F</u>ile ➤ P<u>u</u>blish to open the Publications dialog box shown in Figure B.11.

FIGURE B.11 ▶

The Publications dialog box with several objects that can be published, republished, or deleted as needed

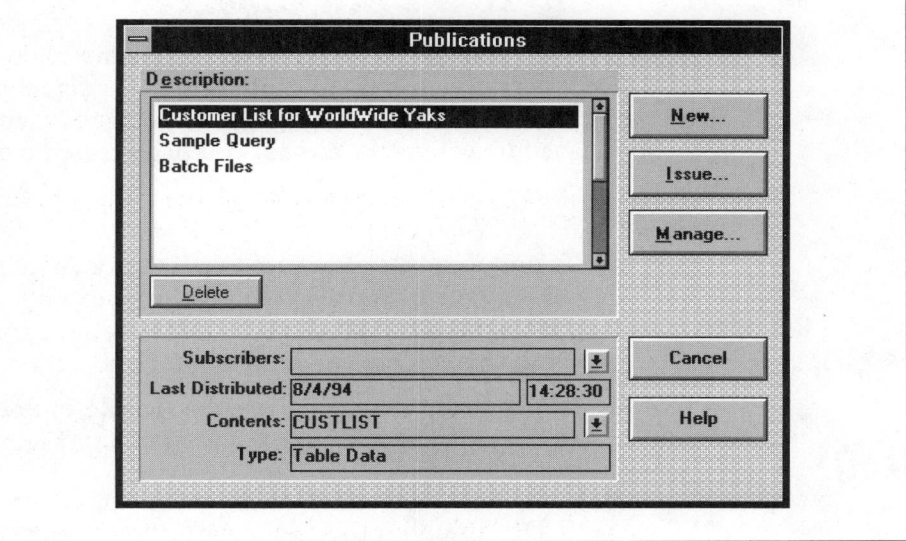

2. Choose a publication to work with by clicking its name in the Description list.

3. From here, you can do any of the following:

- To delete the publication, click the Delete button, then choose Yes when asked for verification. Note that this does not delete your original data, nor does it delete any copies that subscribers have already saved.

- To add or delete subscribers for the selected publication, click the Manage button, complete the Object Exchange: Select Names dialog box, and choose OK.

- To publish this object, click the Issue button, fill in the Issue New Version dialog box with any additional or updated Notes, and choose OK.

4. If necessary, choose the OK or Cancel button until you return to the Desktop.

5. If you issued a publication and want to manually poll the accounts, choose Tools ➤ OBEX Poll ➤ Start Poll.

That's all there is to it.

Network,
OBEX, and SQL

App.
B

▶ Subscribing to a Data Object

When you subscribe to a data object, you simply save the published table, query result, or file set. By saving the object, you become a subscriber and establish a link to the publisher, and you can use the published object just as though you had created it yourself.

Here are the steps for subscribing to an object:

1. If your accounts aren't set to poll automatically, choose Tools ➤ OBEX Poll ➤ Start Poll to get things rolling. (If you turned on the Sound alert for Object Exchange, you may hear a beep when the objects are available for subscribing.)

2. To subscribe to the objects, choose File ➤ Subscribe. You'll see the Use Objects dialog box illustrated in Figure B.12.

3. In the Description list, click on the object you want to subscribe to. Details about the selected object will appear in the Details area. (If you want to see the publisher's notes about this object, click the Notes button, read the notes, then choose OK.)

FIGURE B.12 ▶

The Use Objects dialog box shows objects to which you have subscribed and lets you update those objects with new versions as needed. You also can use this dialog box to delete your links to objects.

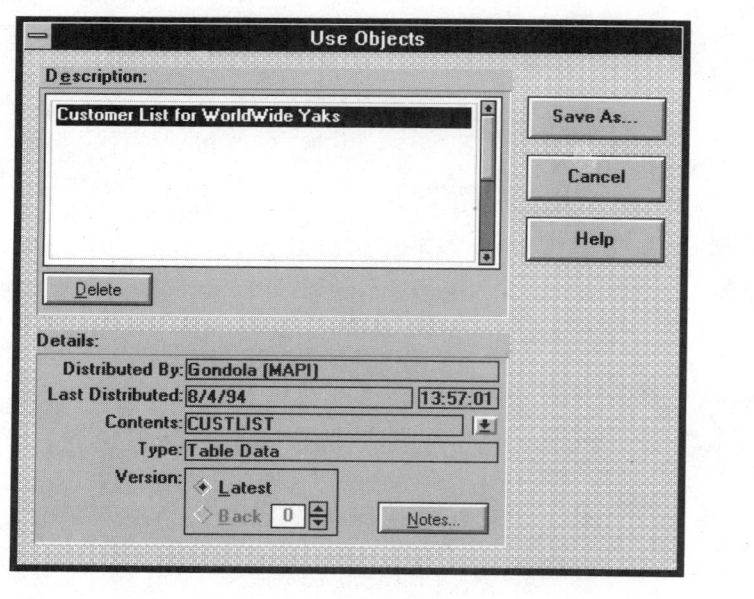

4. To save the selected object, click the Save As button.

5. The appearance of the next dialog box will depend on whether you are subscribing to a table or query or to a file set:

- If you're subscribing to a table or query, specify where you want Paradox to save the object, whether to create a workgroup form that lets you preview the object, and whether to update the object automatically (use the Help button for assistance if you need it).

- If you're subscribing to a file set, specify where you want Paradox to save the object and assign it an alias if you wish.

6. When you're ready to save the object, choose OK.

The update process will begin (be patient, it can take a little time). If you subscribed to a table or query and chose to save a form in step 5 above, a workgroup form like the one in Figure B.13 will appear. (If you chose to update the object manually in step 5, click the Update Now button in the form to create the object now.)

FIGURE B.13

A sample work-group form

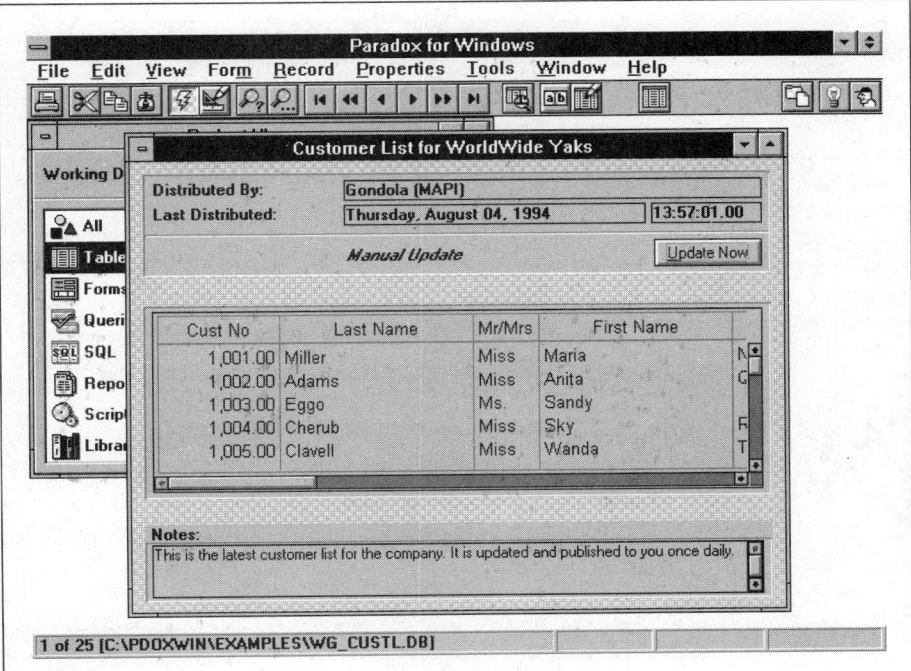

When updating is complete, close the workgroup form (if it is open) and use the newly updated object as you normally would.

If you no longer wish to subscribe to an object, you can choose File ➤ Subscribe, click the name of the object you want to delete, and then click the Delete button in the Use Objects dialog box, choose Yes to verify the deletion, then choose Cancel to return to the Desktop. Deleting a subscription has no effect on the original version held by the publisher, nor will it delete any previously·saved version of the object from your computer.

►► *Borland SQL Links: Connecting Paradox to Your Company's Data*

Borland SQL Links 2.0 for Windows is a collection of drivers that make it easy to connect Paradox (on your PC) to your company's SQL database server (on just about any kind of computer). The beauty of SQL Links is that you don't need to know much about the server to make it work. Once everything is set up, the server is just another database. You can run a query against it, write a report, or create a form for it in much the same way you would a local database. Paradox handles the differences.

 ►►**NOTE**

> **Borland SQL Links for Windows will work with *any* IDAPI-hosted application, including Paradox for Windows and dBASE for Windows, Quattro Pro for Windows Database Desktop, and custom applications that were built using the Borland Database Engine.**

The SQL drivers are not shipped with Paradox for Windows (although the SQL tools, described later, *are available* for Paradox and dBASE tables). You can order the SQL drivers directly from Borland by calling 1-800-331-0877.

Borland offers drivers for the following types of SQL databases:

- Informix 4.1 or later
- InterBase 3.3 (Borland's own relational database server)
- ORACLE 6.0 or greater (the database server with the largest installed base)
- SYBASE/Microsoft SQL Server 4.10 or later

Be aware that even though all SQL servers speak a similar language, each brand of server has different requirements for clients to connect to them. So, if your server isn't one of the products listed above, you will not be able to connect to it until additional links are added.

Of course, a complete discussion of SQL and client/server architecture could be the subject for an entire book. This section is meant to provide you with an overview of what is available, not a complete tutorial. Creating and troubleshooting the connections between client databases and server databases is complicated, but once they are set up, Borland SQL Links for Windows lets you use your server's data almost as if it were local.

▶▶**N O T E**

For more about Borland SQL Links for Windows, click the *SQL Information* topic or icon in the Paradox Help Contents. This topic leads to a host of others that cover SQL in depth, and to some *See Also* information about the SQL Tools (described later in this appendix) and about "upsizing" ObjectPAL applications to access SQL data. The individual SQL Links drivers also come with booklets that provide general information about getting started and details about each driver.

▶ What Is SQL?

SQL, which SQL professionals usually pronounce as "SEE-qual" or increasingly as "ess-q-ell," is short for Structured Query Language. It is a standardized language derived from the Structured English Query Language, which IBM designed some 20 years ago. SQL is used by virtually all large relational databases. Not all versions of SQL are the same, but they are similar. With some effort it is possible for mere mortals to understand and read a simple SQL statement. For example, if you wanted to get a list from the CustList table of customers who live in California, the SQL statement would be something like this:

```
SELECT DISTINCT "CUSTLIST.DB"."Cust No","CUST-
LIST.DB"."Last Name","CUSTLIST.DB"."First Name"
FROM "CUSTLIST.DB"
WHERE
(State = 'CA')
ORDER BY "CUSTLIST.DB"."Cust No","CUSTLIST.DB"."Last
Name","CUSTLIST.DB"."First Name"
```

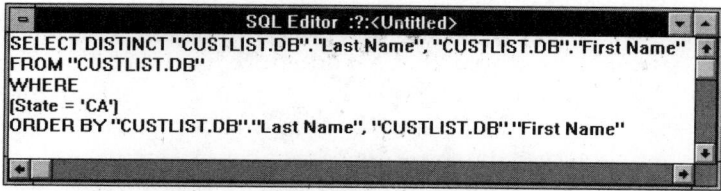

When performing more complex queries, you undoubtedly will prefer Paradox's query-by-example (QBE), which is much easier to decipher and use.

► Client/Server: Besides a Buzzword, What Is It?

Client/server technology offers a way to share power and applications among computers, and to perform the processing where it makes the most sense. This approach matches the right computer—PC, mini, or mainframe—to the task. In a client/server environment, a large application is divided into two parts: the *client* and the *server*. The client software usually is located on a PC, while the server software resides on a larger machine.

Typically, the database server software is a large relational database manager, such as ORACLE, InterBase, SYBASE, or Informix. As a client to these large database servers, Paradox can tap into the power of the server, while providing you with the same Windows-based look and the server, while providing you with the same Windows-based look and feel you are accustomed to. When you use Paradox and Borland SQL Links to get information from the server, the server does most of the work and you don't have to worry about how that work gets done. Paradox automatically converts your QBE query into SQL language statements that the server can understand, then the server processes the query, and reports the result back to Paradox.

In addition to choosing the right machine and database manager for the job, the client/server approach offers another benefit—it is usually more efficient. Network load is reduced because only the transactions themselves cross the network. By contrast, typical LAN-based applications require that entire files are transmitted between the workstation and the file server.

The server's implementation of SQL cannot always support the more complex queries of Paradox's QBE. These queries are processed locally instead, using data from the server. Local processing is required for:

- Queries that access different SQL databases
- Queries that make joins with local databases
- Queries that would require multiple SQL statements

 ▶▶**NOTE**

SQL-literate readers will be happy to know that they can also use SQL statements to query local Paradox or dBASE data. See the last two sections of this appendix and "Controlling Queries Against Remote Tables" in Chapter 16 for more on this topic.

Who Needs to Use Borland SQL Links for Windows?

The short answer to this question is anyone who must access data that's stored on an SQL server. The long answer is a bit more complicated. It is important to understand that the server's *forte* is big databases. If you only need to maintain your address book and a few dozen clients, you will not need or want SQL Links. Just keep this simple information in a Paradox or dBASE table on your local hard drive, or even on a LAN file server. But if you need to keep track of all the trucks your large automotive corporation has built this year, or all the stars in the universe, you definitely need more than Paradox alone to handle the information. You are ready for a relational database server.

Paradox can support the SQL servers listed earlier in this appendix.

▶ SQL Links Requirements

To use Borland SQL Links for Windows with one of the supported database servers, you will need at least:

- An IDAPI-hosted application, including Paradox for Windows, dBASE for Windows, Quattro Pro for Windows Database Desktop, or a custom application that uses IDAPI.
- Borland SQL Links for Windows for the server you want to access.
- Appropriate internetwork protocol software for the client machine.
- Appropriate internetwork protocol software for the server machine.
- Access to the database server you will be connecting to.

Beyond this, you may need specialized network software from the server. ORACLE, for example, requires that you have their Oracle SQL*Net software running on the client machine, in addition to any underlying internetwork protocol software you may need, such as TCP/IP.

Keep in mind that installing the various network protocol software products and configuring them to work correctly with Paradox and the database server can be a complicated job. The process is far more difficult than even a typical network installation of Paradox, and way beyond installing a single-user version of Paradox. You must have full supervisory or *superuser* rights on the server side, and a clear understanding of the network protocols involved before you attempt this. Many of the issues involved are covered in the booklets that come with the SQL drivers. You should also refer to the documentation for the network protocol you will be using.

In the following sections, we will assume that you've managed to solve all these problems and can connect to the SQL server.

▶ *The SQL Tools Palette*

Paradox for Windows includes a special *SQL Tools palette*, which makes using the SQL Links features much easier (this comes with Paradox itself, not with the optional SQL Links drivers). To open the SQL Tools palette, which is shown in Figure B.14, choose Tools ▶ SQL Tools.

FIGURE B.14 ▶

The SQL Tools palette provides an easy-to-use interface to SQL Links.

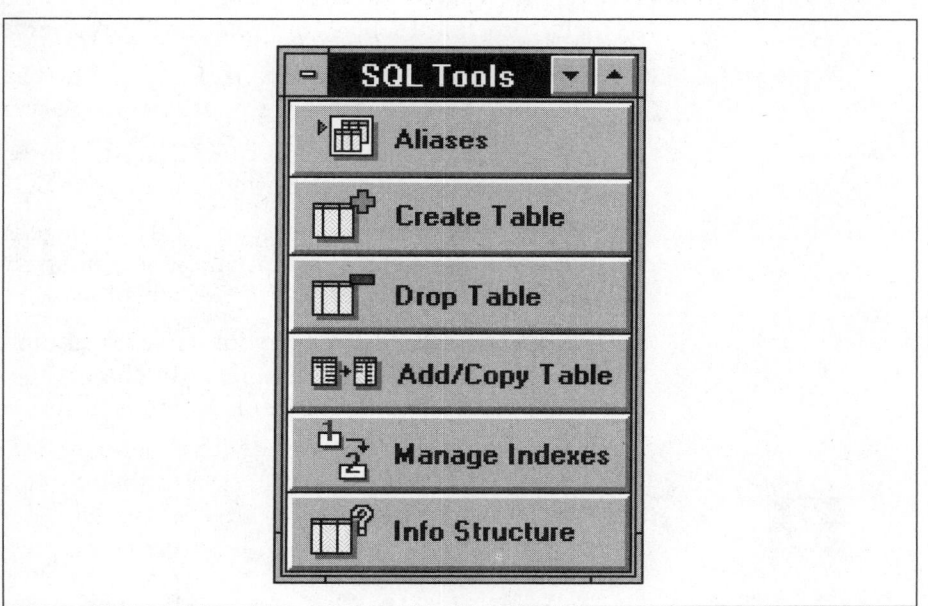

N O T E

You can use the SQL Tools palette to work with dBASE and Paradox tables, as well as SQL tables. However, the normal Paradox tools described in Chapters 3, 8, and 15 are easier to use than the SQL Tools and are recommended for dBASE and Paradox tables.

Here's a brief summary of each button in the SQL Tools palette. We'll look more closely at how these buttons work in a moment:

Aliases   Opens the Alias Manager dialog box, which lets you create and manage aliases to both server databases and local tables. You also can use this button to connect to or disconnect from an SQL server.

Create Table   Opens the SQL Create Table dialog box, which lets you create tables (or "relations") in a server database.

Drop Table   Opens the SQL Drop Table dialog box, which lets you drop (delete) tables or relations in a server database.

Add/Copy Table   Opens the SQL Add/Copy Table dialog box, which lets you add or copy a table to your SQL database.

Manage Indexes   Opens the SQL Manage Indexes dialog box, which lets you create and manage secondary indexes on a server table.

Info Structure   Provides information about the structure of an existing SQL table. (If you need to change the table's structure, use the Paradox SQL Editor, which is described in the *SQL Editor* topic in Paradox Help.)

 ▶▶**T I P**

> **For online Help about any of the buttons in the SQL Tools palette, click the palette, and press F1; when the Help screen appears, click the button you're interested in. Or, click the appropriate button in the SQL Tools palette and then press F1.**

When you're finished using the SQL Tools palette, you can close it by double-clicking its Control-menu box, or by clicking its title bar and pressing Ctrl+F4.

The Aliases Button

The Aliases button on the SQL Tools palette gives you a convenient path into the Alias Manager. Click on the button, and you get the Alias Manager dialog box, which will be similar to the one shown in Figure B.15.

Choose an appropriate driver type from the Driver Type drop-down list (for SQL tables, choose the SERVER option from the list). After you select a driver type, the Alias Manager dialog box will reflect the settings available for the driver you chose.

▶ ▶ **N O T E**

> **The settings in the Alias Manager dialog box reflect and update the information stored in your IDAPI configuration file (see Chapter 15).**

Once you've selected a driver type, you can use techniques similar to those discussed in Chapters 3 and 15 to create aliases for both your server-based databases and your Paradox and dBASE directories. For more details, click the Help button (or press F1) in the Alias Manager, click the *See Also* topic, click the *Creating a New Alias* topic, then click the *Alias Manager Dialog Box (SQL Link)* topic in the first paragraph.

FIGURE B.15 ▶

Use the Alias Manager to create aliases for, connect to, and disconnect from SQL server databases. (The dialog box shown here would display the SQL options if we were to select a Driver Type of SERVER.)

Alias Manager

☒ Public Alias

Database Alias: Gift_Corner

Driver Type: STANDARD

Path: C:\PDOXWIN\GIFTCO

Database is not currently in use.

○ Show Public Aliases Only
○ Show Project Aliases Only
◉ Show All Aliases

Browse...

OK

New
Remove
Save As...

Cancel

Help

Network, OBEX, and SQL

App.

B

The Create Table button

You can use the SQL Create Table dialog box pictured in Figure B.16 to create a new SQL table. To begin, just click the Create Table button in the SQL Tools palette, then specify the Alias Name and Table Name.

FIGURE B.16 ▶

Use the SQL Create Table dialog box to create new SQL tables. For this example we borrowed the strructure of our CustList Table.

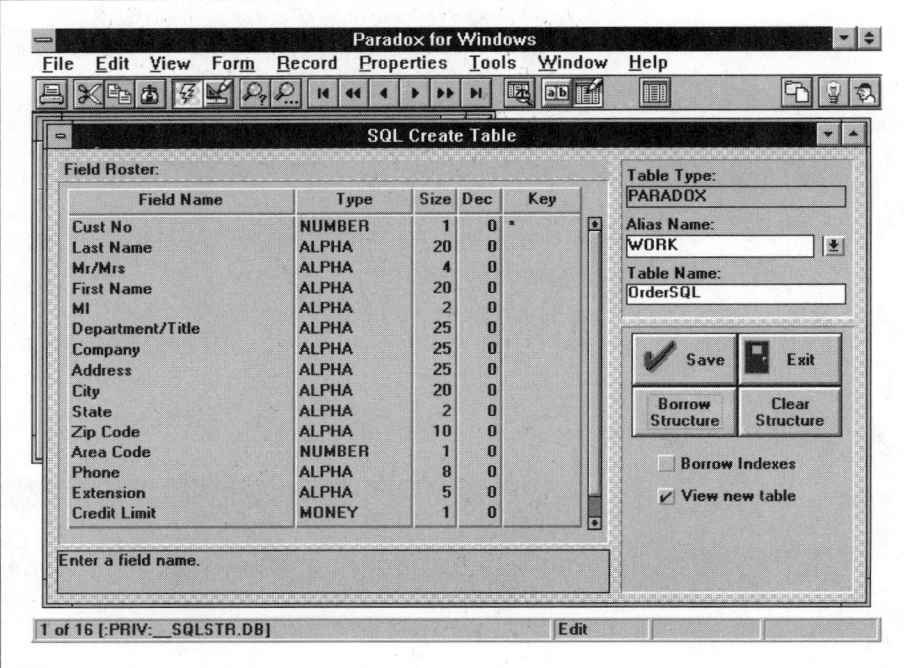

You can create the table structure from scratch, or you can borrow an existing table's structure. The techniques are similar to those discussed in Chapter 4 for setting up Paradox tables. If you want to borrow the new table's structure from an existing table, click the Borrow Structure button. To borrow the existing table's indexes, check the Borrow Indexes box. (If you need to clear the structure you've set up so far, click the Clear Structure button.)

When you're ready to create the table, click the Save button.

The Drop Table Button

Servers don't "delete" tables, they "drop" them (ouch!). The result is the same, however: your table is history, gone, deleted. To drop tables from your server database, click the Drop Table button in the SQL Tools palette. This opens the SQL Drop Table dialog box shown below:

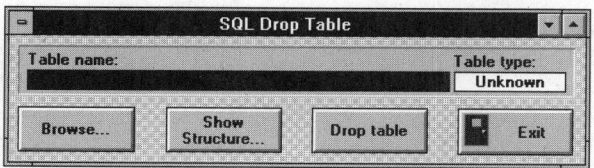

In the Table Name text box, type the table name (or click the Browse button, highlight the table name, and choose OK). To make sure you've chosen the correct table to drop, click the Show Structure button to view the table's structure (click Exit when you're done viewing the structure). Once you're sure you have selected the right table, click the Drop Table button, choose Yes to verify the drop, and kiss your table goodbye. When you're finished dropping tables, click the Exit button in the SQL Drop Table dialog box.

The Add/Copy Table Button

You can use SQL Tools to add records from one table to another. The tables can be part of a database that resides on the server, or they can be local Paradox or dBASE tables.

Suppose you've used a query to select all the vehicles produced in the first week of the new model year. You could then use the Add/Copy Table tool to add the resulting Answer table to an SQL table that will track initial model quality results.

To add records from one table to another, click the Add/Copy Table button in the SQL Tools palette. In the SQL Add/Copy Table dialog box (shown in Figure B.17), click in the From Table text box and specify the table you're adding records *from*; then click in the To Table text box and specify the table you're adding records *to*. You can use the Browse button to help you locate the From and To tables, as needed.

*The SQL Add/Copy
Table dialog box*

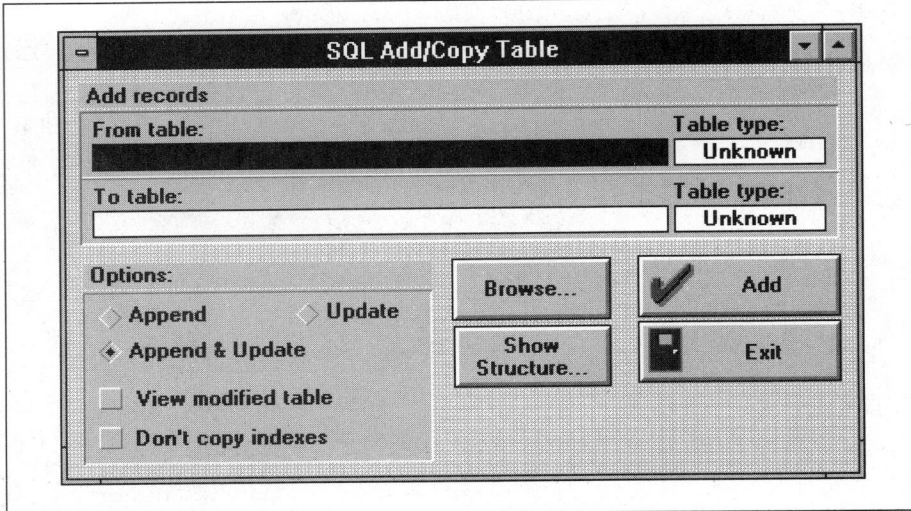

If you'd like to preview the From or To table structure, click in the completed From Table or To Table text box, then click the Show Structure button. You can also specify any options you want in the Options area of the dialog box. (These options are similar to the ones in the Add dialog box described in Chapter 15.) When you're ready to add the records, click the Add button. Choose Exit to return to the SQL Tools palette.

The Manage Indexes Button

Querying large databases on servers can take a long time, depending on how the query is structured, how large the database is, and especially how the indexes are structured on the database. You may be able to speed up a query by creating a secondary index on the database. First, click on the Manage Indexes button in the SQL Tools palette to open the SQL Manage Indexes dialog box. Then click in the Table Name text box and type the name of the table to index, or use the Browse button to fill in the table name. Now click the Indexes button to expand the dialog box as shown in Figure B.18.

Here are the basic techniques to use in this dialog box:

• To define a new index, click the Index Name text box in the bottom-center area (this will highlight any existing index name in that box), then type in a unique index name (no spaces or punctuation).

FIGURE B.18

The SQL Table Indexes dialog box after choosing a table name and clicking the Indexes button

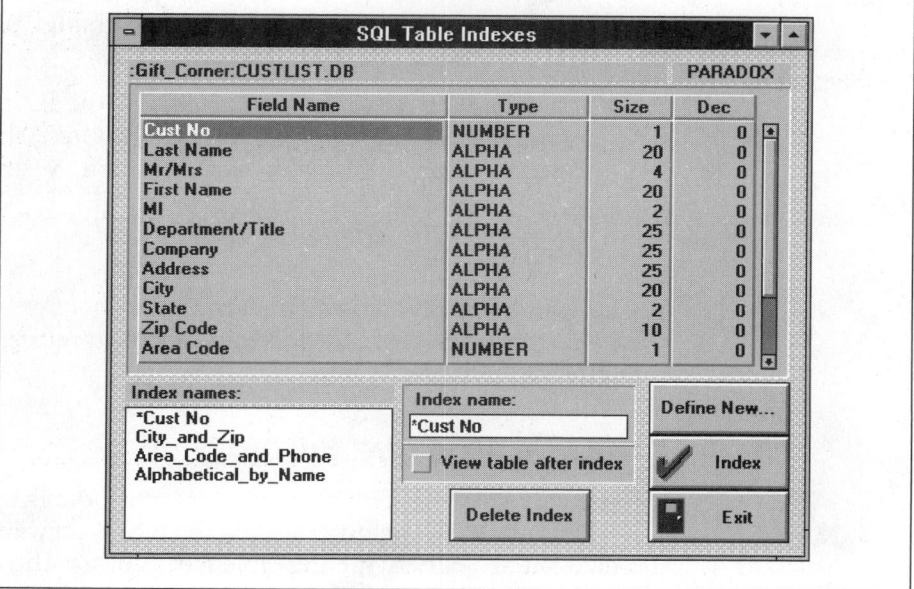

Next, click the Define New button. In the Field Names list that appears, double-click the fields you want to copy to the Indexed Fields list, and use the Change Order (Up and Down) buttons as needed to arrange the Indexed Fields list the way you want it. You can select Index Options by checking or unchecking the Maintained and Case Insensitive boxes as needed. When you're ready to save the index, click Save Index. (If you index on one field only, Paradox will change the index name to the field name.)

- To change an existing index, click its name in the Index Names list in the lower-left corner of the dialog box (the selected index name will appear in the Index Name text box at the bottom-center area), then click the Define New button and make any changes

you wish. When you're ready to update the index, click Save Index. (You cannot use this method to change primary indexes; use the Restructure feature instead.

- To delete an existing index, click it in the Index Names list (the name appears in the Index Name text box), then click Delete Index and choose Yes when asked to verify your change.

- To view the table after indexing is complete, check the View Table After Index check box.

When you're ready to update all the index changes permanently, click the Index button, then choose Exit until you return to the SQL Tools palette.

The Info Structure Button

To quickly view the structure of a table, click the Info Structure button in the SQL Tools palette, then specify the table you want to investigate (as usual, you can either type the table name, or use the Browse button to locate it). When you're ready to view the structure, click the Show Structure button. Click Exit as needed to return to the SQL Tools palette.

▶ Creating and Using an SQL File

You can create an SQL file that contains SQL statements, and then run the statements against your server database. In essence, you're creating a query using the SQL language.

To create a new SQL file, select File ➤ New ➤ SQL File, or right-click the SQL button in the Paradox Toolbar (not the SQL Tools palette) and choose New. This will open the SQL Editor window (see Figure B.19 for a completed example). Type in your SQL statement (you can use Paradox's cut, copy, and paste options as needed). Before running your query, you can use the methods below to set the stage:

- If you don't specify an alias for your table, you may be prompted for one when you run the SQL statement. To select the alias ahead of time, click on the Select Alias button on the Toolbar, or choose SQL ➤ Select Alias from the menus, specify the alias name, and choose OK.

FIGURE B.19

The SQL Editor for a query that shows the last name and first name of customers who live in California. (In this example, we clicked the Run SQL button in the Toolbar to create the Answer table shown below the SQL Editor window.)

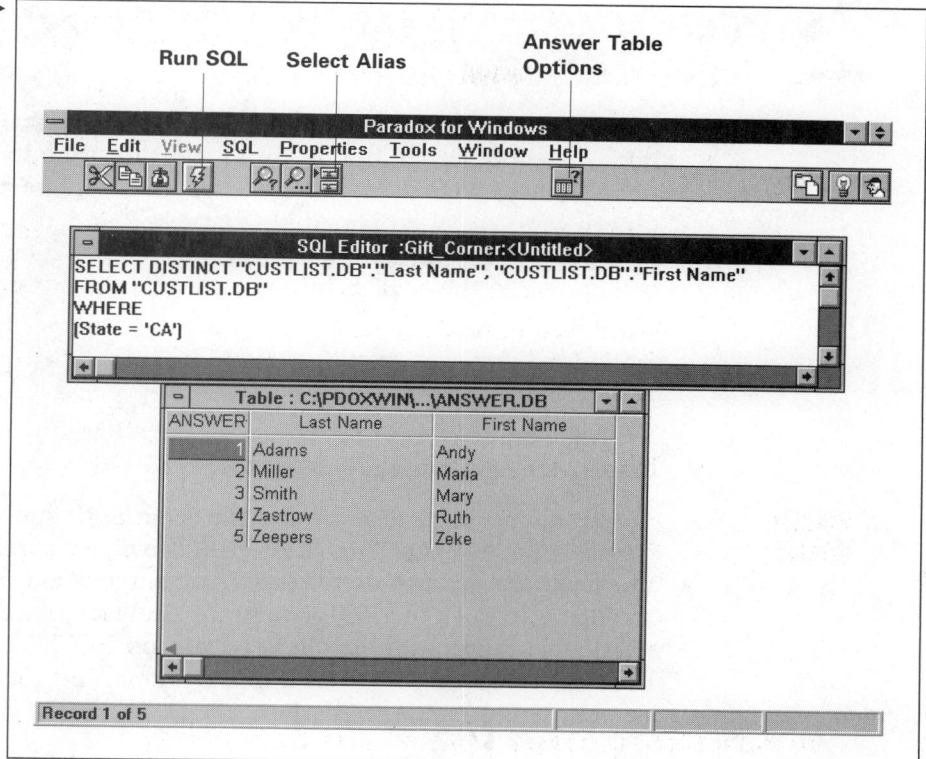

• By default, the Answer table produced by a query will be in your private directory and will be a Paradox table. To change the directory and table type, click the Answer Table Options button in the Toolbar, or choose SQL ➤ Answer Table Options. When the Answer Table Options dialog box appears, fill in the Answer Name and select an Answer Type (either Paradox or dBASE), then choose OK.

When you're ready to run the statement against the remote server database, click the Run SQL button in the Toolbar or press F8 (or choose SQL ➤ Run SQL). Figure B.19 shows a sample query in the SQL Editor window, along with the resulting Answer table.

▶ What SQL Statements Will My Query Generate?

When you use QBE, you can easily see the SQL statements that have been or will be generated by your QBE query, and you can change them if necessary. To view these statements, create your query in the Query window, as explained in Chapters 9 and 16. Then choose Query ▶ Show SQL from the Query window menus. Your SQL statements will appear in the SQL Editor window just as if you had slavishly typed them in.

If you'd like to save your SQL statements to an SQL file that you can use later, choose File ▶ Save from the SQL Editor menus, type a valid DOS file name (omit the extension, since Paradox will add the .sql extension automatically), then choose OK.

When you're ready to reuse this file as an SQL statement, simply choose File ▶ Open ▶ SQL or click the Open SQL Script button in the Toolbar and then double-click the name of the SQL file you want to open. Or, click the SQL icon in the left side of the Project Viewer window and then double-click the appropriate SQL file name. Now use the Select Alias, Answer Table Options, and Run Query buttons in the Toolbar as explained earlier.

Sharing Data with Other Applications

▶ ▶ **P**aradox for Windows provides many tools that allow you to transfer data to and from several application file formats, including delimited text, fixed length text, Quattro Pro for Windows and DOS, Quattro, Lotus 1-2-3, Excel, dBASE, and Paradox 4 for DOS.

Once you've successfully transferred data to a different application, you can use that data just as if you had created it in that application. For example, if you import an Excel spreadsheet to a Paradox for Windows table, you can use the new Paradox table just as if you had created it and added the data in Paradox. Likewise, if you export a Paradox for Windows table to an Excel spreadsheet, you'll be able to use the spreadsheet in Excel as if you created it from scratch in Excel.

 ▶ ▶ **N O T E**

Quattro Pro for Windows and other IDAPI-hosted products will provide direct support for Paradox 5 for Windows table formats. Once you've installed the most recent version of Quattro Pro for Windows, you can usually bypass the Export options if you want to view, query, or edit a Paradox table in that application.

After transferring the data, you may need to "tweak" it to compensate for assumptions Paradox might have made when importing or exporting it. For instance, after importing a text or spreadsheet file to a table, you may need to use *Restructure* to reorganize the table fields or change field names, field types, or field sizes. After exporting a table to a spreadsheet, you may need to use the spreadsheet application to widen or narrow a column.

> ► ►**T I P**
>
> **Before exporting data from Paradox, use queries to isolate specific data, select certain fields, or perform summary calculations.**

Keep in mind that Paradox always converts data through copies of files. In all cases, your original files are left unchanged, while converted data is copied to a new file with a name you provide.

In this appendix, we'll begin by discussing general steps for transferring data; then we'll explain how to transfer data between Paradox and specific applications or file formats.

►► *Exporting Paradox Tables to Other Formats*

The basic steps for exporting Paradox tables to other application file formats are listed below.

1. Choose Tools ➤ Utilities ➤ Export; or, click the Tables icon in the left side of the Project Viewer window, then inspect a table name and choose Export. The Table Export dialog box shown in Figure C.1 appears.

2. Select the name of the table you want to export. If you ran a query that selected specific records or fields to export, specify Answer (or the table you chose in the Properties ➤ Answer Options ➤ Table command) as the table to export.

3. From the Export File Type drop-down list, choose the file format you want to create.

4. Click OK.

5. The next dialog box depends on the file format you selected in step 3. Complete the dialog box as explained in the sections below, then choose OK to begin exporting the table.

FIGURE C.1

*The Table Export
dialog box*

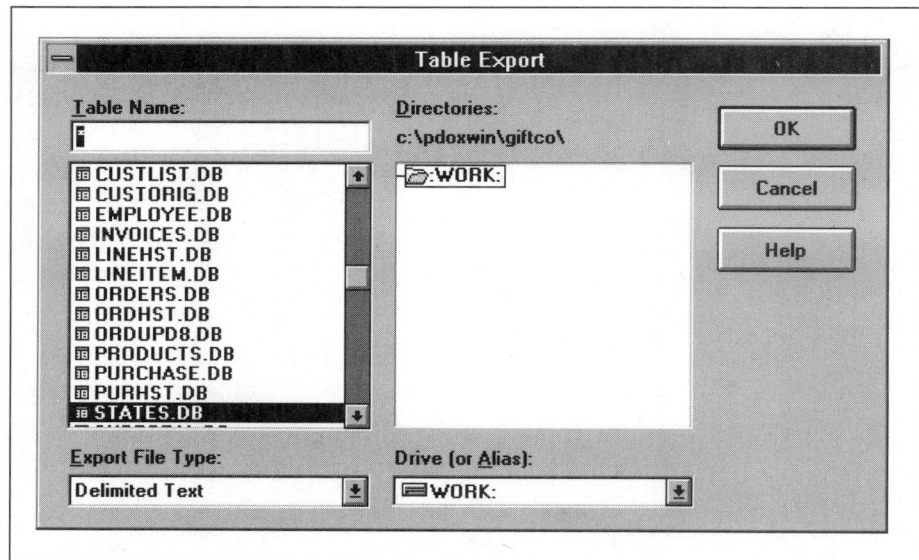

> **NOTE**
>
> **If the file you're exporting to already exists, you'll have the option to cancel the operation or replace the existing file.**

► *Importing Data into Paradox Tables*

You can follow the steps below to import data from other file formats into a Paradox table.

1. Choose Tools ► Utilities ► Import; or, click the All icon in the left side of the Project Viewer window, inspect the file you want to import, and then choose Import (for a spreadsheet), Delimited Text Import (for a delimited text file), or Fixed Length Import (for a fixed length text file). There's more information about these file formats later in this appendix.

• If you chose Tools ► Utilities ► Import, the File Import dialog box shown in Figure C.2 will appear. Paradox initially suggests a file type of *<Delimited Text>* and displays the

FIGURE C.2 ▶

The File Import dialog box appears when you choose Tools ➤ Utilities ➤ Import.

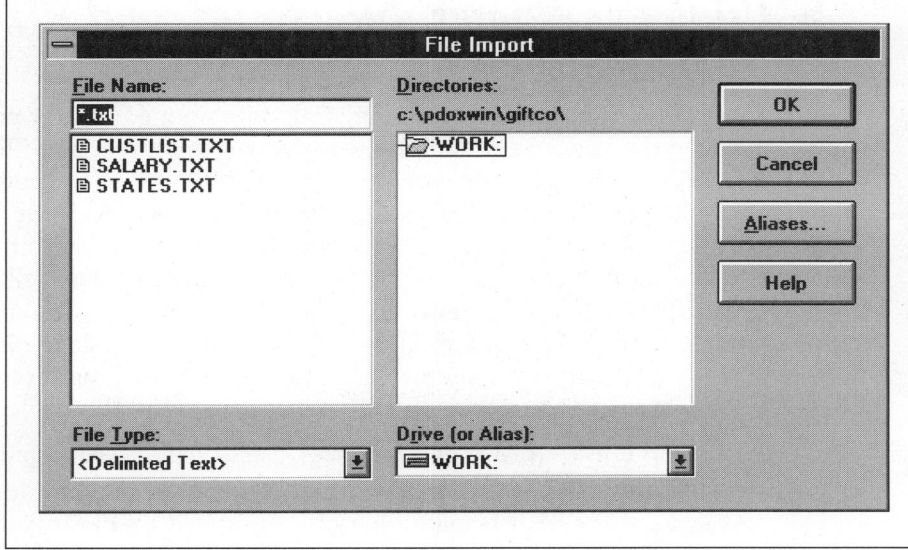

names of all files in the working directory that have a *.txt* extension. Continue with step 2.

- If you inspected a file in the Project Viewer window, skip to step 4.

2. To import files in a format other than delimited text, click the File Type drop-down arrow and select a file type.

3. Select the file you want to import, then click OK.

4. The next dialog box depends on the type of file you're importing. Complete the dialog box as explained below, then choose OK to begin importing the table.

 ▶▶ **N O T E**

If the table you're importing to already exists, you'll have the option to cancel the operation or replace the existing table.

► Using File Names, Directories, and File Name Extensions

When importing or exporting data on a computer with several directories, be sure to include the directory name if it's different from your current working directory (or use the Drive (or Alias) drop-down list and Directories folders to fill in the directory name). For example, to import a Lotus 1-2-3 spreadsheet named *Sales* from the directory named *Lotus* on drive c:, enter the name of the file to import as *c:\lotus\sales*. You can also use an alias in place of a directory name. If you omit the drive and directory name, Paradox will look for files in your private directory, and either your working directory or the directory that contains the file you inspected in the Project Viewer.

If you omit the file name extension when entering a file name, Paradox will assign one automatically based on the file type you specified. Table C.1 lists each file type supported by Paradox and the file name extensions that Paradox expects when importing data or assigns automatically when exporting data.

 ►►**N O T E**

> **Paradox reserves the name *import.db* in your private directory for import operations, and the name *export.db* in your private directory for export operations. Therefore, you should never use these names for permanent tables.**

► Exporting Data to a Spreadsheet

After you select a table to export and a spreadsheet format, you'll see the Spreadsheet Export dialog box shown in Figure C.3. You can edit the name of the table you're exporting in the Table Name text box and the name of the spreadsheet file you're creating in the New File Name text box. Normally, Paradox uses field names from the table to create the first row of labels in the spreadsheet. To omit the labels, click Make Row Headers From Field Names to deselect the option. Click OK to begin exporting the table to your spreadsheet.

▶ **TABLE C.1:** *Data File Descriptions, File Types, and File Name Extensions Supported when Transferring Data to and from Paradox*

DATA FILE DESCRIPTION	FILE TYPE	FILE NAME EXTENSION
Delimited text files	\<Delimited Text\>	.txt
Excel versions 3 and 4 spreadsheet files	\<Excel\>	.xls
Fixed length text files	\<Fixed Length Text\>	.txt
Lotus 1-2-3 version 1.A spreadsheet files	\<Lotus 1.A\>	.wks
Lotus 1-2-3 version 2 and higher spreadsheet files	\<Lotus 2.x\>	.wk1
Paradox for DOS version 4	\<Paradox DOS 4\>	.db
Quattro spreadsheet files	\<Quattro\>	.wkq
Quattro Pro for DOS spreadsheet files	\<Quattro Pro DOS\>	.wq1
Quattro Pro for Windows spreadsheet files	\<Quattro Pro Win\>	.wb1

FIGURE C.3

The Spreadsheet Export dialog box

After exporting the Paradox file to a spreadsheet format, you can start the spreadsheet program and open the new file as you would any other spreadsheet file. The exported file will have the name you assigned, plus the appropriate extension for the spreadsheet format you chose (see Table C.1). Data from the table will appear in the spreadsheet as follows:

- Table fields and records will appear in individual columns and rows.

- Each spreadsheet column will be as wide as the corresponding table field, up to the maximum allowed by the spreadsheet. If a table value is wider than the spreadsheet column display width, the full value will be converted, but will remain partially hidden.

- Dates in the table that are beyond the range of dates allowed in the spreadsheet will have the value *ERROR*.

- Binary, formatted memo, graphic, memo, and OLE fields will be exported with their field names as column headings in the spreadsheet (if Make Row Headers From Field Names was checked), but data for those fields will be blank.

▶ *Importing Data from a Spreadsheet*

Paradox tables store information in even columns (fields) and rows (records), whereas spreadsheets let you arrange text, numbers, and formulas in any manner you wish. However, Paradox cannot reliably import data that are randomly placed about a spreadsheet. Instead, it needs to import even columns (fields) and rows (records), where the top row contains the field names for the table.

If your spreadsheet contains labels or formulas outside of an even row-and-column orientation, or your spreadsheet uses headings, underlines, or other text enhancements, do not attempt to import these into a Paradox table. Instead, extract only the field names and values beneath them into a separate spreadsheet file, then use Paradox to import the extracted file only.

After you select a spreadsheet to import and a spreadsheet format, you'll see the Spreadsheet Import dialog box shown in Figure C.4. You can make any of the changes described below.

- To change the name of the file you're importing, edit the name in the File Name text box.

- To change the name of the table you're creating, edit the name in the New Table Name text box. Do not specify an extension, since this is assigned automatically when you choose the table type.

- To change the type of table you're creating, click the Paradox or dBASE option. Paradox is the default choice.

- By default, Paradox imports the entire spreadsheet file. To specify a range of cells to import, fill in the From Cell and To Cell text boxes. If the spreadsheet has named ranges, you can click the Named Ranges drop-down arrow and choose the range that contains the values you want to import.

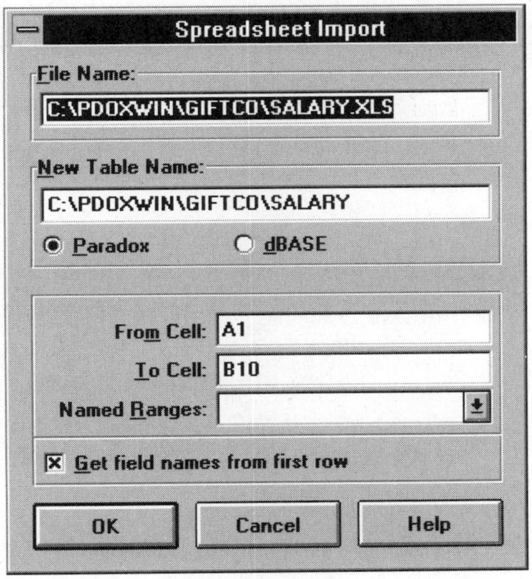

FIGURE C.4

The Spreadsheet Import dialog box

Spreadsheet Import

File Name:
`C:\PDOXWIN\GIFTCO\SALARY.XLS`

New Table Name:
`C:\PDOXWIN\GIFTCO\SALARY`

⦿ Paradox   ○ dBASE

From Cell: `A1`
To Cell: `B10`
Named Ranges:

[X] Get field names from first row

| OK | Cancel | Help |

- Paradox normally uses the top row of the spreadsheet to assign field names for the table. If you deselect <u>G</u>et Field Names From First Row, Paradox will assign names as *FIELD001*, *FIELD002*, *FIELD003*, and so on instead. This is useful if the top row of the spreadsheet or range contains data instead of field names.

Click OK to import the spreadsheet.

When importing data from a spreadsheet, Paradox assigns field types to the data automatically. It scans each spreadsheet column and chooses a field type that can contain every value in the spreadsheet column. For example, if a column contains only numbers, Paradox will use Number. Calculation results will be imported as values, rather than formulas.

▶ Transferring Text Files

Paradox for Windows can export and import delimited text files and fixed length text.

In a *delimited text file*, fields usually are separated by commas, and each record is terminated by a carriage return–linefeed combination. Typically, character data is enclosed in double quotation marks (""). When you use the DOS TYPE command or the Windows Notepad accessory to view a delimited file, it typically resembles the example in Figure C.5.

 ▶▶**N O T E**

Since many applications can use delimited text files, this format provides an excellent way to export Paradox data to word processing applications and other applications that cannot read Paradox or dBASE tables directly.

In a *fixed length text file*, each field has a specified starting position and length. Figure C.6 shows the same CustList table records exported to fixed length text format.

FIGURE C.5 ▶

The records of the Cust-List table exported to delimited text format and displayed in the Windows Notepad. (Some text has scrolled off the right edge of the screen.)

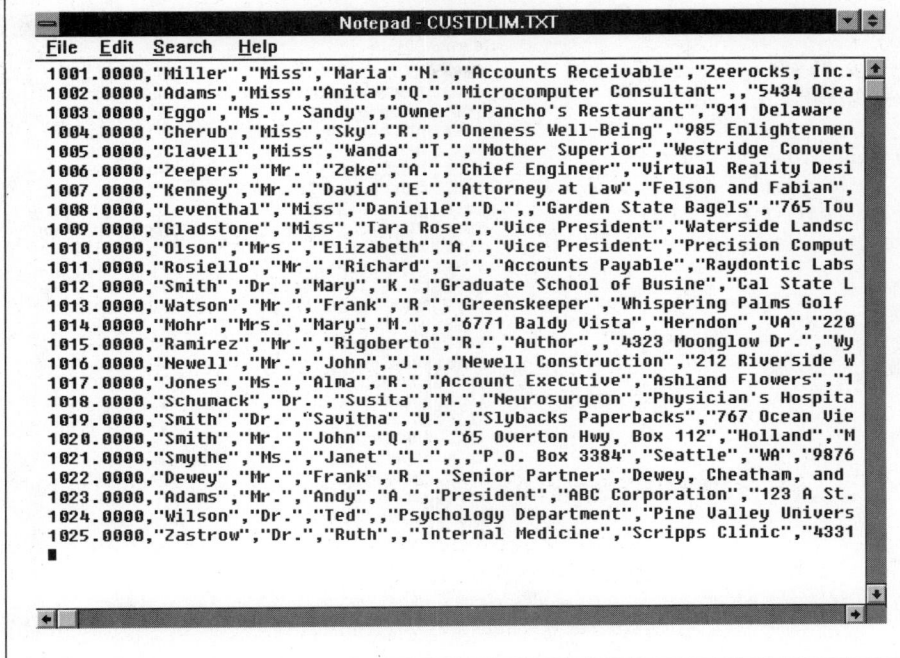

```
                      Notepad - CUSTDLIM.TXT
 File   Edit   Search   Help
1001.0000,"Miller","Miss","Maria","N.","Accounts Receivable","Zeerocks, Inc.
1002.0000,"Adams","Miss","Anita","Q.","Microcomputer Consultant",,"5434 Ocea
1003.0000,"Eggo","Ms.","Sandy",,"Owner","Pancho's Restaurant","911 Delaware
1004.0000,"Cherub","Miss","Sky","R.","Oneness Well-Being","985 Enlightenmen
1005.0000,"Clavell","Miss","Wanda","T.","Mother Superior","Westridge Convent
1006.0000,"Zeepers","Mr.","Zeke","A.","Chief Engineer","Virtual Reality Desi
1007.0000,"Kenney","Mr.","David","E.","Attorney at Law","Felson and Fabian",
1008.0000,"Leventhal","Miss","Danielle","D.",,"Garden State Bagels","765 Tou
1009.0000,"Gladstone","Miss","Tara Rose",,"Vice President","Waterside Landsc
1010.0000,"Olson","Mrs.","Elizabeth","A.","Vice President","Precision Comput
1011.0000,"Rosiello","Mr.","Richard","L.","Accounts Payable","Raydontic Labs
1012.0000,"Smith","Dr.","Mary","K.","Graduate School of Busine","Cal State L
1013.0000,"Watson","Mr.","Frank","R.","Greenskeeper","Whispering Palms Golf
1014.0000,"Mohr","Mrs.","Mary","M.",,,"6771 Baldy Vista","Herndon","VA","220
1015.0000,"Ramirez","Mr.","Rigoberto","R.","Author",,"4323 Moonglow Dr.","Wy
1016.0000,"Newell","Mr.","John","J.",,"Newell Construction","212 Riverside W
1017.0000,"Jones","Ms.","Alma","R.","Account Executive","Ashland Flowers","1
1018.0000,"Schumack","Dr.","Susita","M.","Neurosurgeon","Physician's Hospita
1019.0000,"Smith","Dr.","Savitha","V.","Slybacks Paperbacks","767 Ocean Vie
1020.0000,"Smith","Mr.","John","Q.",,,"65 Overton Hwy, Box 112","Holland","M
1021.0000,"Smythe","Ms.","Janet","L.",,,,"P.O. Box 3384","Seattle","WA","9876
1022.0000,"Dewey","Mr.","Frank","R.","Senior Partner","Dewey, Cheatham, and
1023.0000,"Adams","Mr.","Andy","A.","President","ABC Corporation","123 A St.
1024.0000,"Wilson","Dr.","Ted",,"Psychology Department","Pine Valley Univers
1025.0000,"Zastrow","Dr.","Ruth",,"Internal Medicine","Scripps Clinic","4331
```

 ▶▶**N O T E**

> **Delimited and fixed length text files are also called ASCII files. ASCII is an acronym for American Standard Code for Information Interchange, a sequence of 128 standard characters. ASCII files provide a way to exchange data between different types of applications and computers.**

▶ *Exporting Delimited Text Files*

After selecting a table to export and specifying the delimited text file format, you'll see the Delimited ASCII Export dialog box shown in Figure C.7. You can edit the name of the table you're exporting in the Table Name text box, or the name of the delimited text file you're creating in the New File Name text box.

FIGURE C.6 ▶

The records of the Cust-List table exported to fixed length format and displayed in the Windows Notepad. (Some text has scrolled off the right edge of the screen.)

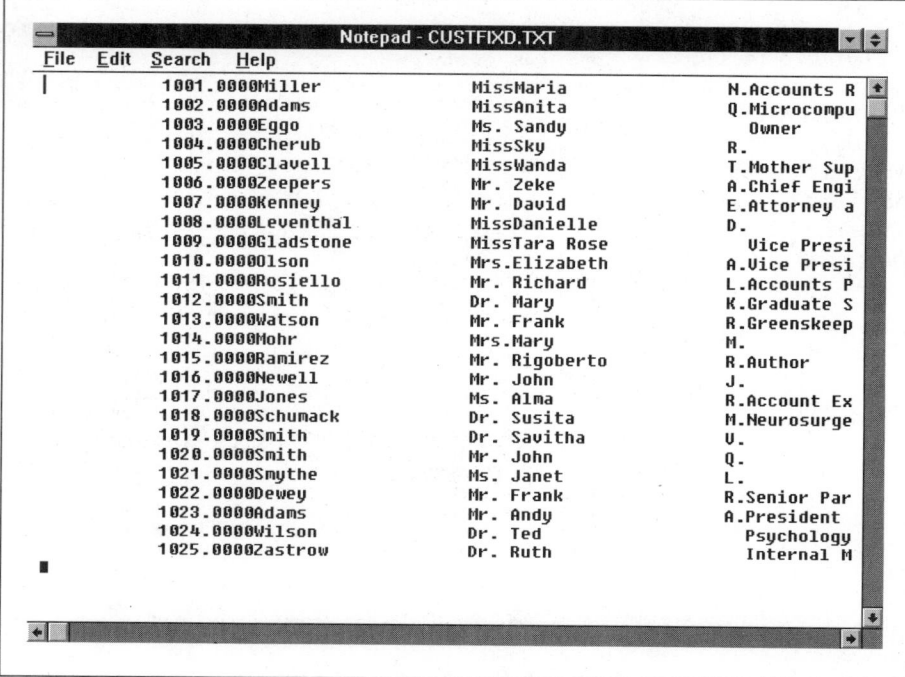

FIGURE C.7 ▶

The Delimited ASCII Export dialog box after changing the file name in the New File Name text box

When creating the delimited text file, Paradox normally separates fields with commas and encloses non-numeric values in double quotation marks (""). Each record is separated by a carriage return and linefeed character. If you want to change the characters used to delimit fields and enclose non-numeric values, click the Options button to open the Text Options dialog box. (See Figure C.9 and the following sections for details on using this dialog box.) After making your selections, click OK to return to the Delimited ASCII Export dialog box.

When you're ready to export the table, choose OK in the Delimited ASCII Export dialog box.

NOTE

Binary, bytes, formatted memo, graphic, memo, and OLE fields cannot be stored as ASCII text and will be ignored.

▶ *Importing Delimited Text Files*

You can also import delimited text files into Paradox tables. When you select a file to import and choose the delimited text file format, you'll see the Delimited ASCII Import dialog box shown in Figure C.8. In this dialog box, you can change the File Name of the file to import and the New Table Name of the table to create. You can also select a Paradox or dBASE table format by clicking the appropriate option.

If you click the Options button, the Text Options dialog box shown in Figure C.9 will appear. You can change the field separator, field delimiter, which fields are delimited, and the character set as described below. When you're finished, choose OK to return to the Delimited ASCII Import dialog box, then choose OK once more to begin importing the file.

The imported data will be stored in a new table with the field names *FIELD001*, *FIELD002*, *FIELD003*, and so on. Paradox scans the entire file to determine the number of fields and the field types the file contains. Field types are determined on a "best guess" basis, date and number formats adhere to the settings in the Windows Control Panel, and any delimited text longer than 255 characters is trimmed to 255 characters and stored in an alpha field.

FIGURE C.8 ▶

The Delimited ASCII Import dialog box

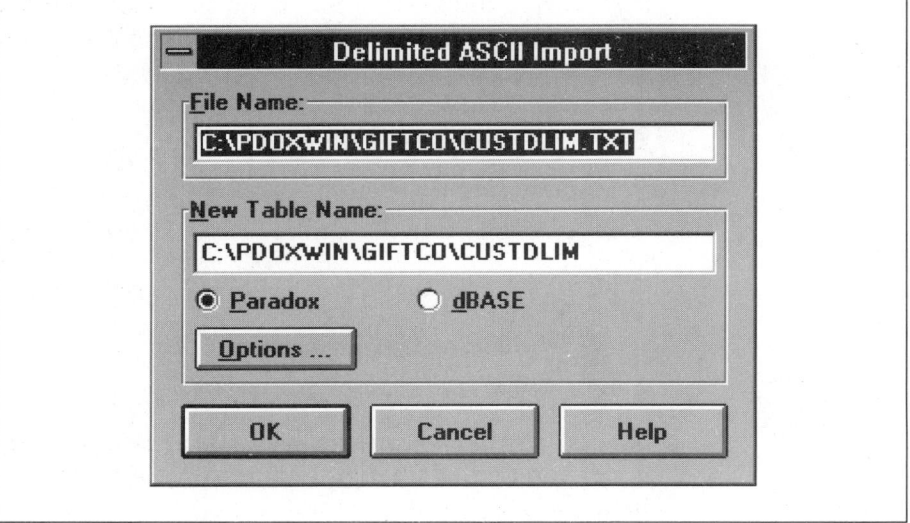

FIGURE C.9 ▶

The Text Options dialog box. After choosing the options you want, click OK to return to the previous dialog box.

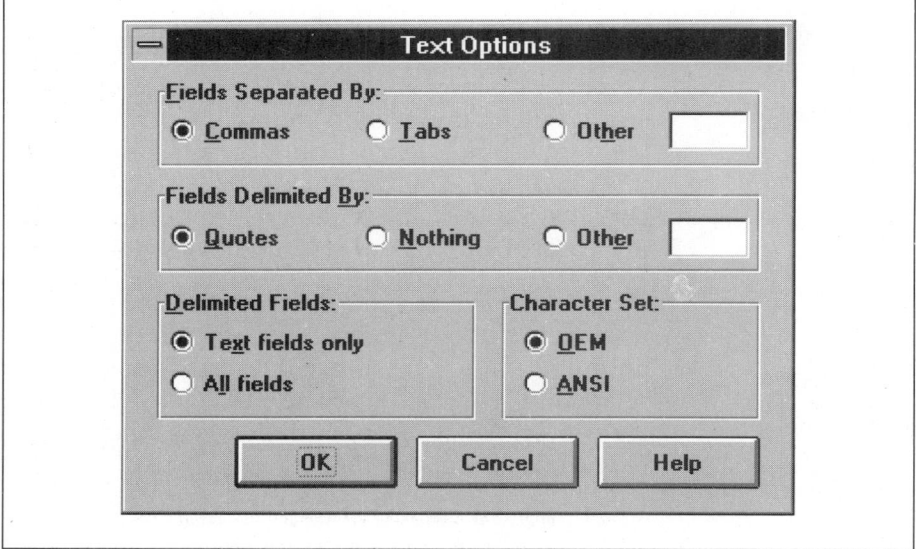

▶ *Using the Text Dialog Box*

You can use the text dialog box shown in figure C.9 to change the field separator, field delimiter, and character set used when exporting or importing delimited ASCII text files. To reach this dialog box, Click the Option button in the delimited ASCII Export or delimited ASCII Import dialog box. We'll look at each option in the dialog box next.

Changing the Field Separator

By default, Paradox separates fields in a delimited text file with commas. To change these separators to tabs, select Tabs in the Fields Separated By area of the Text Options dialog box. To define your own delimiter character, select Other in the Fields Separated By area, press →, then type a character in the text box.

Changing the Field Delimiter Settings

The default character enclosing non-numeric (text) fields is the double quotation mark (""). If you don't want any characters to enclose text fields, select Nothing in the Fields Delimited By area of the Text Options dialog box. To define your own delimiter, select Other, press →, then type a character in the text box.

Normally, Paradox places the field delimiter character around non-numeric text fields only. If you wish to place the delimiter around *all* fields, select All Fields in the Delimited Fields area of the text box.

Changing the Character Set

Although Paradox for Windows can recognize either of two character sets (OEM or ANSI), data in Paradox for Windows and dBASE tables is *always* stored in OEM characters. By contrast, Windows and Windows applications use ANSI characters.

 ▶▶ **N O T E**

> **OEM is an acronym for Original Equipment Manufacturer, and it refers to the character set your computer uses. ANSI is an acronym for American National Standards Institute; it refers to the character set that Windows uses.**

Paradox handles the conversion between OEM and ANSI characters automatically when reading and writing data in tables. However, when exporting or importing text files, you must specify which set to use. If in doubt, stick with the default setting of <u>O</u>EM.

An OEM set (also called a code page) consists of 256 characters, numbered from 0 to 255. Characters 0–127 are the same for every code page. Characters 128-255 (called *extended characters*) differ for every code page. DOS 5.0 and higher come with several different code pages—English, Multilingual (Latin I), Slavic (Latin II), Portuguese, Canadian-French, and Nordic—although only one can be active at a time.

By contrast, only one set of ANSI characters exists. If you choose the <u>A</u>NSI option when importing, characters will be converted from ANSI to OEM. If you choose <u>A</u>NSI when exporting, characters will be converted from OEM to ANSI.

▶▶**N O T E**

> **Characters 32–126 are the same in the two sets; however, other characters are missing altogether, or are in different places in the character sets. Problems may arise during import or export because the two character sets are different.**

▶ Exporting Fixed Length Text Files

When you choose to export a table to a fixed length text file, the Fixed Length ASCII Export dialog box shown in Figure C.10 appears. The usual options are available for changing the name of the table you're exporting from and the file you're exporting to. You can also choose the <u>O</u>EM or <u>A</u>NSI character set options discussed above.

The Field Name, Start, and Length values in the Export table are supplied automatically from the structure of the table you're exporting. You can change these settings if you want more control over the exported file, though you'll rarely need to do so. For instance, you may need to shorten the Length values for one or more fields to accommodate whatever application will be using the exported data (it's best to leave all the other settings in the Export table alone). To change a field length, click in the Length column for the appropriate field name in the Export table, and then type the new length.

FIGURE C.10

The Fixed Length ASCII Export dialog box after changing the file name in the New File Name text box

Fixed Length ASCII Export

Table Name:
CUSTLIST.DB

New File Name:
CUSTFIXD.TXT

Export Specification:
Save
Load
Clear

EXPORT	Field Name	Start	Length
1	Cust No	1	22
2	Last Name	23	20
3	Mr/Mrs	43	4
4	First Name	47	20
5	MI	67	2
6	Department/Title	69	25
7	Company	94	25

Character Set:
⦿ OEM   ○ ANSI

OK   Cancel   Help

NOTE

The Export table controls the starting position and length of text in the *exported* table, not the source table. If you want to select just certain fields or to rearrange fields in the source table, you should run a query that produces the desired structure *before* exporting. Then you can export the customized query results table to the fixed length text file.

You can also use the three Export Specification buttons described below to save, load, and clear export specifications:

- To save the current export specification for later use when exporting other tables, click the Save button, type a new file name, and choose OK.

- To clear the current export specification, click the Clear button. The Export table in the dialog box will be cleared.

- To use a previously saved specification, click the Load button, select a specification table from the list that appears, and choose OK. The Export table will now include the loaded specifications (the loaded specifications will appear below any existing entries).

When you're ready to begin exporting, click OK. Paradox will use the Export table structure to control the location of each field in the exported records.

▶ *Importing Fixed Length Text Files*

The Fixed Length ASCII Import dialog box shown in Figure C.11 allows you to control how data is imported from a fixed length text file into your table. The usual options for changing the import file name and table names, the table type (Paradox or dBASE), and the character set (OEM or ANSI) are available.

When importing a fixed length text file, you must complete the Import table's Field Name, Type, Start, and Length information in the dialog box. Your specifications must exactly match the arrangement of data in your text file. If the specification is incorrect, the imported data will make no sense. When editing the specification, you can insert rows (press Ins), delete rows (press Ctrl+Del), edit field names, and modify the start position and length of any field as needed.

If you wish to load a previously saved import specification, click Load, select a specification table from the list, and choose OK.

As an aid to entering a correct specification, you can print part of your data file and mark the field name, starting position, and length for each field. For example, in Figure C.12, we marked some sample import data for the States lookup table discussed in Chapter 6. In the example, the Start position for the first field (State) is 1 and the Length is 2 (each State abbreviation is always 2 characters long). The Start position for the second field (State Name) is 3 and the length is 20 (the longest State Name, *District of Columbia*, is exactly 20 characters).

If you wish to clear the existing specifications and start over, click the Clear button. As when exporting files, you can save a specification by

FIGURE C.11

The Fixed Length ASCII Import dialog box

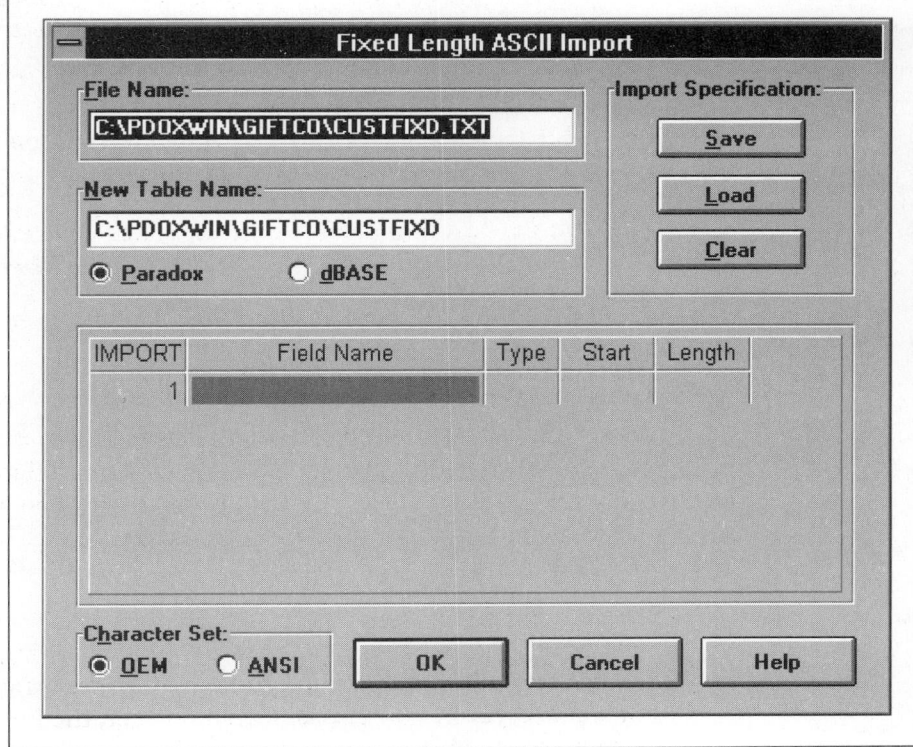

clicking the Save button, typing a new file name for your specification, and choosing OK.

When you're sure the Import specifications match the data you're importing, click OK. Paradox will use the structure you've defined in the dialog box to control the location of each field in the new table.

▶ Exporting Paradox 5 Tables to Paradox 4 for DOS

You can export Paradox 5 tables to Paradox 4 for DOS so that Paradox 4 for DOS users can work with them. Exporting is necessary only if your Paradox 5 tables include autoincrement, BCD, logical, long integer, time, or timestamp field types, which aren't supported in Paradox 4 for DOS.

FIGURE C.12 ▶

We've marked the field name, start position, and length for each field of a data file suitable for importing into the States table.

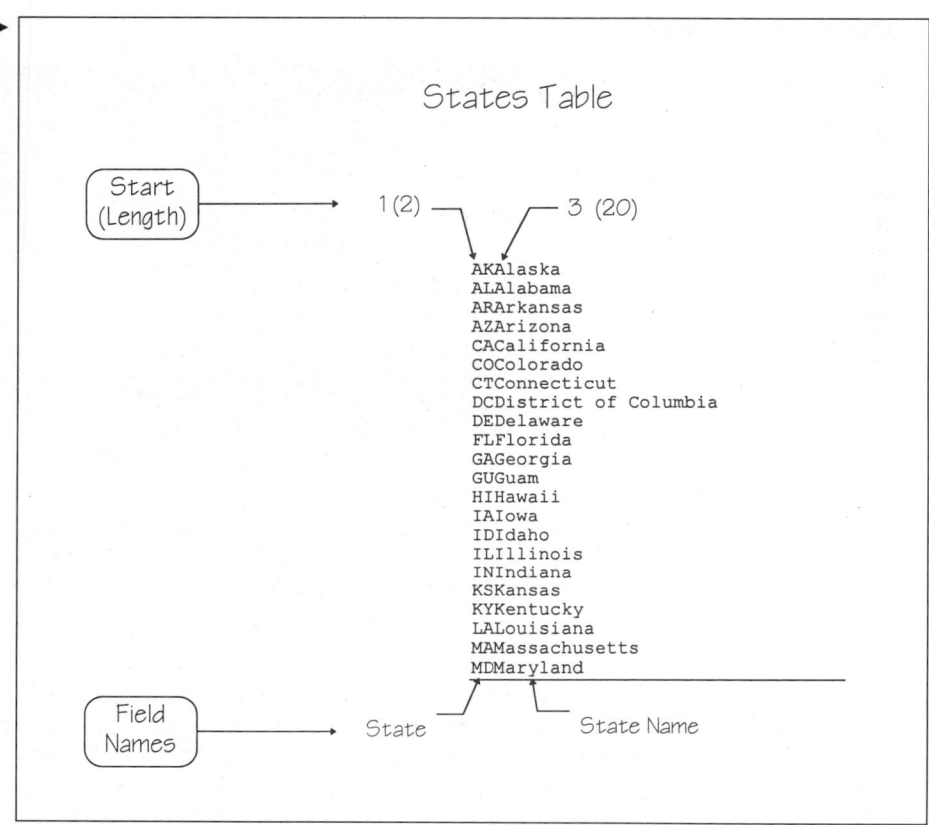

States Table

Start (Length) ⟶ 1 (2)   3 (20)

```
AKAlaska
ALAlabama
ARArkansas
AZArizona
CACalifornia
COColorado
CTConnecticut
DCDistrict of Columbia
DEDelaware
FLFlorida
GAGeorgia
GUGuam
HIHawaii
IAIowa
IDIdaho
ILIllinois
INIndiana
KSKansas
KYKentucky
LALouisiana
MAMassachusetts
MDMaryland
```

Field Names ⟶ State   State Name

> **NOTE**
>
> **Paradox 5 for Windows can open Paradox 4 for DOS tables directly, so no conversion is required. Simply open the Paradox 4 for DOS table as you would any Paradox 5 for Windows table. Paradox can also open dBASE tables directly, and it can create dBASE tables via the copy command discussed in Chapter 15. (There's more about dBASE tables in Appendix D.**

After selecting a table to export and specifying the *Paradox DOS 4* format, you'll see the Paradox DOS 4 Export dialog box shown in Figure C.13. Notice that Paradox automatically supplies the characters "DOS" at the end of the file name in the New File Name text box to

Sharing Data

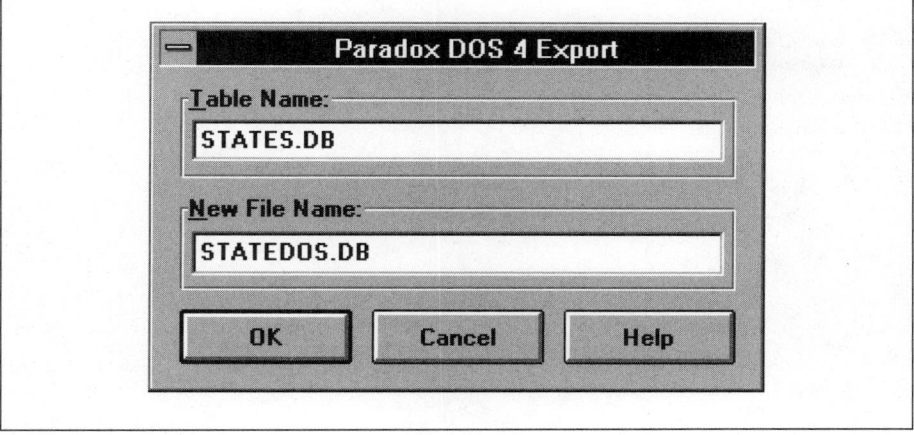

FIGURE C.13

The Paradox DOS 4 Export dialog box. Notice that Paradox automatically adds the characters "DOS" to the file name in the New File Name text box, to prevent you from accidentally overwriting your Paradox 5 source table.

prevent you from overwriting your Paradox 5 table accidentally. As usual, you can specify the Table Name for the table you're exporting, or the New File Name for the Paradox 4 for DOS file you're creating.

When you're ready to export the table, choose OK in the Paradox DOS 4 Export dialog box. During the export, any autoincrement, BCD, and long integer fields in the Paradox 5 table are converted to numeric format in the Paradox 4 for DOS table; and logical, time, and timestamp fields are converted to alphanumeric format.

Using Non-Paradox for Windows Tables

► ► **I**f you are currently using dBASE tables, or you're upgrading from an earlier version of Paradox, you can use Paradox for Windows to open, create, and modify your tables. You can also convert these tables to Paradox for Windows format. This appendix explains how.

 ► ► **N O T E**

> **Like Paradox tables, dBASE tables can be customized and can have default properties defined. dBASE table properties are stored in a *.tvf* file with the same name as the table. (See Chapters 7 and 14.)**

► ► *Using dBASE Tables*

dBASE III+, dBASE IV, and dBASE for Windows tables are entirely compatible with Paradox for Windows, although there are some differences between the dBASE and Paradox formats. For instance, Paradox offers an autoincrement field that isn't available in dBASE. We'll describe special procedures for using dBASE tables in the following sections.

 ► ► **N O T E**

> **Support for dBASE for Windows is new in Paradox 5 for Windows.**

► *Creating dBASE Tables*

The general techniques for creating dBASE tables are the same as those used to create Paradox for Windows tables (see Chapter 4).

However, some of the details differ slightly. To begin creating a dBASE table in Paradox for Windows, proceed as follows:

1. Choose File ➤ New ➤ Table, or right-click the Tables icon in the Project Viewer or the Open Table button in the Toolbar and choose New.

2. Click the Table Type drop-down arrow in the Table Type dialog box and choose *dBASE for Windows, dBASE IV,* or *dBASE III+* from the list.

3. Choose OK to open the Create Table dialog box.

4. Fill in the dialog box as described below.

5. Click Save As, specify a name for the table, and choose OK.

▶ ▶ **N O T E**

> **To restructure a dBASE table, choose Tools ➤ Utilities ➤ Restructure, specify the table name, and choose OK; or inspect the table name in the Project Viewer and choose Restructure. Continue with step 4 above. (See Chapter 15.)**

The dialog box for creating dBASE for Windows tables is shown in Figure D.1. The dialog box for dBASE IV tables is the same, except that the title bar says "Create dBASE IV Table," rather than "Create dBASE for Windows Table." The Create dBASE III+ Table dialog box for dBASE III+ tables is slightly different.

▶ ▶ **N O T E**

> **Validity checks, table lookup, Paradox-style secondary indexes, referential integrity, and password security are not available for dBASE tables. The Table Properties drop-down list includes an Indexes and Table Language option only.**

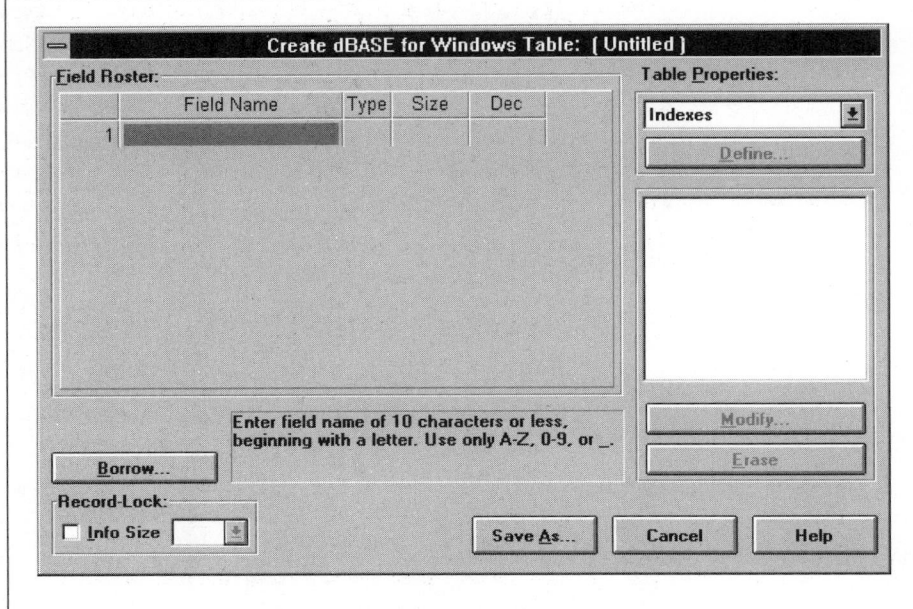

Borrowing a Table Structure

If the Field Roster is empty, you can base your new dBASE table structure on an existing dBASE table. To borrow an existing table's structure, click the Borrow button in the Create Table dialog box. Select the table you want to borrow from. If you also want to use the borrowed table's maintained (.*mdx*) index definitions, check Indexes. Choose OK to return to the Create Table dialog box.

Defining dBASE Fields

When entering dBASE field names in the Field Roster of the dialog box, you must follow these rules:

- Names can have up to ten characters, including letters, digits, and underscores.

- The first character must be a letter.

- No punctuation marks, spaces, or other special characters are allowed.

- Field names must be unique.

After entering a valid field name, define the field type. If the field type allows it, specify the field size (*Size*) and the number of digits to the right of the decimal point (*Dec*). (To display a list of valid field types in the dialog box, move the cursor to the Type column and press the spacebar; or right-click the Type column.) Valid dBASE field types, sizes, and decimal point settings are listed in Table D.1.

▶ **TABLE D.1:** *dBASE III+, dBASE IV, and dBASE for WIndows Field Types and Sizes*

Field Type	Symbol	Field Size	Decimal Point
Binary	B		
Character	C	1–254	
Date	D		
Float	F	1–20	0–18 (must be <= Field Size–2)
Logical	L		
Memo	M		
Number	N	1–20 (1–19 in dBASE III+)	0–18 (must be <= Field Size–2)
OLE	O		

NOTE: *Memo field formats (M) differ between dBASE III+ and later versions of dBASE.*

Float Number (F) format is available only in dBASE IV and later versions.

OLE (O) and Binary (B) formats are available only in dBASE for Windows and later versions of dBASE.

Non-Paradox Tables

▶▶ *App.* **D**

▶▶ **N O T E**

The number of decimal places for a *float* or *number* field must be no more than the field size minus two.

Defining dBASE IV Record Locks

When creating a dBASE for Windows or dBASE IV table that will be used on a network, you may wish to check the Info Size option. When Info Size is checked, Paradox will add to the table a hidden field that shows when a record was locked and which user placed the lock. (Record Lock is not available for dBASE III+ tables.) The record lock field comes out of hiding only when you are locked out of a record.

The amount of information displayed when you try to access a locked field depends on the Info Size you specify to the right of the Info Size check box. The default size of 16 characters tells whether the record has been changed, shows the time and date of the lock, and displays the first 8 characters of the name of the user who placed the lock. You can specify an Info Size of 8 to 24 characters.

Defining an Index for a dBASE Table

Unlike Paradox tables, dBASE tables do not have key fields. However, you can define one or more indexes for a dBASE table. Indexes can be based on a single field or on an expression (composite field).

To define an index, click the Define button in the Create Table or Restructure Table dialog box (see Figure D.1). You'll see the Define Index dialog box shown in Figure D.2.

To create a *single-field index*, select the field you want to index in the Field List, and then select (check) or deselect (uncheck) one or more of the options listed below:

Unique   Select this option to create an index with only one instance of each value. Duplicate values can exist in the table, but will be ignored. Deselect this option to allow the index to contain duplicate values.

Maintained   Select this option to have Paradox update the index whenever the table changes. Deselect this option if you want Paradox to update the index only when you link tables or run a query. Maintained indexes are also called "production indexes." This option is available for dBASE IV and dBASE for Windows tables only.

The Define Index dialog box lets you define single-field and expression indexes for a dBASE table.

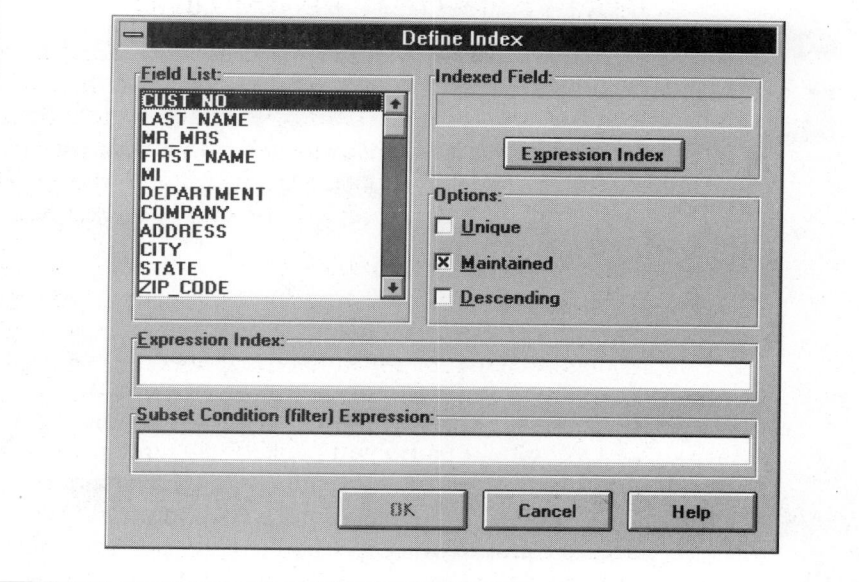

Descending   Select this option to sort index values in descending order (*Z* to *A*). Deselect the option to sort index values in ascending order (*A* to *Z*).

WARNING

Maintained indexes are the recommended index type. Non-maintained indexes are much less desirable because of their many limitations. For example, operations such as adding, subtracting, and emptying tables will invalidate the non-maintained index. Moreover, you must use Table ➤ Filter (Chapter 9) to open a non-maintained index each time you edit or sort the table.

To create an *expression* or *composite* index, click the Expression Index button. The button will be replaced by an Index Field button. Next, enter the expression in the Expression Index text box. For example, the expression *Last_Name+First_Name* would create a composite index on the Last_Name and First_Name fields of a dBASE table.

 ▶ ▶ **T I P**

If you change your mind and want to go back to defining a single-field index, simply click the Index Field button that replaced the E̲xpression Index button in the dialog box.

When entering the expression, you can either type the field names, or you can enter them automatically by placing the insertion point in the Expression Index text box and then clicking the field name in the F̲ield List. The field name you clicked will appear in the text box at the insertion point position. All fields in an expression index must be of the same type. (Please see your dBASE manual for more information on expression indexes.)

You can also base your index on a *subset condition* or filter that evaluates to true or false when tested against values in each record. Records that meet the condition are included in the index. For example, the subset condition *STATE=NY* would create an index for customers who live in New York. That is, if STATE=NY is true for a given record, that record is included in the index; if STATE=NY is false for that record, the record is omitted from the index. Therefore, whenever this index is active, the table will show only those customers who live in New York. All other customer records will be filtered out temporarily (those customer records remain in the table, but they'll be invisible until you choose a different index).

To create a subset condition, click in the S̲ubset Condition (Filter) Expression text box and enter the condition. You may create a subset condition in either a single-field index or an expression index.

To save the index, click OK in the Define Index dialog box. When the Save Index As dialog box appears, fill in the text boxes described below, and then choose OK to return to the Create Table or Restructure Table dialog box.

Index File Name   This text box is available only when you're saving a *non-maintained* index. If you're creating a single-field index,

Paradox will use the field name as the index file name. If you're creating an expression index, you must specify the index file name (*without* the extension) in the text box. The non-maintained index file is assigned an *.ndx* extension automatically.

Index Tag Name   This text box is available only when you're saving a *maintained* index. Enter the name for the index tag, up to 10 characters but no spaces (again, do not type a file extension). For example, **New_York** or **NY_Custs** are valid index tag names.

▶ Restructuring a dBASE Table

You can use any of the techniques discussed in Chapter 15 to restructure a dBASE table, including the Tools ➤ Utilities ➤ Restructure or Table ➤ Restructure options. Remember that changing the field type may mean trimming the data, or may result in records that cannot be converted at all. You'll be asked to confirm any data loss, and any records that cannot be converted will be stored in the temporary *Problems* table in your private directory. Table D.2 shows the effects of converting from one data type to another. See Chapter 15 for more information about restructuring tables.

▶ **TABLE D.2:**   *dBASE III+, dBASE IV, and dBASE for Windows Field Types and Sizes*

	TO B	TO C	TO D	TO F	TO L	TO M	TO N	TO O
From B	Y							
From C		Y	P	P	Y	Y	P	
From D		Y	Y					
From F		Y		Y	Y		Y	
From L		Y		Y	Y		Y	
From M		Y				Y		
From N		Y		Y	Y		Y	
From O								Y

NOTE: Y *means Paradox allows the conversion but may trim data.*

Blank *means the conversion is not allowed.*

P *means the conversion is allowed, but a* **Problems** *table usually will result.*

▶▶ T I P

> If you add production indexes (*.mdx*) or float fields to a dBASE III+ table, Paradox will convert it to a dBASE IV table automatically.

▶ Transferring Data between Paradox and dBASE

To convert a Paradox table to a dBASE table, or vice versa, use the Tools ➤ Utilities ➤ Copy options discussed in Chapter 15. When the Copy dialog box appears, click the source file you want to copy from. Then click in the To text box and type the file name and extension for the new table. To convert a dBASE table to a Paradox table, specify a *.db* extension for the destination file. To convert a Paradox table to a dBASE table, specify a *.dbf* extension for the destination file.

▶▶ T I P

> For a quicker way to copy, right-click the table you want to copy in the Project Viewer, then choose Copy. Specify the file name and extension for the new table and choose OK.

Paradox will change the field types automatically to accommodate the new format. Table D.3 summarizes the effects of copying from a Paradox table to a dBASE table. Table D.4 summarizes the effects of copying from a dBASE table to a Paradox table.

▶▶ N O T E

> Paradox normally creates a dBASE IV table unless the copy yields a binary or OLE field type. In these cases, a dBASE for Windows table results.

▶ **TABLE D.3:** *Effects of Copying from a Paradox Table to a dBASE Table*

FROM PARADOX TYPE	TO DBASE TYPE	SIDE EFFECTS
Alpha	Character	
Autoincrement	Number	Size=11, Dec=0
BCD	Number	Size=20, Dec=4
Binary	Memo	Data cannot be displayed
Bytes	Memo	
Date	Date	
Formatted Memo	Memo	Formatting is lost
Graphic	Binary	
Logical	Logical	
Long Integer	Number	Size=11, Dec=0
Memo	Memo	
Money	Number	Size=20, Dec=4
Number	Number	Size=20, Dec=4
OLE	OLE	
Short	Number	Size=6, Dec=0
Time	Character	Size=11
Timestamp	Character	Size=30

NOTE: *Paradox creates a dBASE IV table, unless the source table contains a binary or OLE field type. In these cases, Paradox creates a dBASE for Windows table.*

Non-Paradox Tables

App. D

▶ *Viewing Deleted dBASE Records*

When you delete a record from a dBASE table, that record is simply *marked* for deletion; it isn't actually removed from your computer's hard disk.

▶ **TABLE D.4:**   *Effects of Copying from a dBASE Table to a Paradox Table*

FROM DBASE TYPE	TO PARADOX TYPE	SIDE EFFECTS
Binary	Graphic	
Character	Alpha	
Date	Date	
Float Number	Number	Removes size
Logical	Logical	
Memo	Memo	Size=1
Number	Number	Removes size
OLE	OLE	

NOTE: *dBASE memo fields are assumed to be in text form. If the memo contains a different type of data, use the Add utility to add the dBASE memo to the appropriate binary, formatted memo, graphic, memo, or OLE field.*

To view records that have been marked for deletion, choose Table ▶ Show Deleted or Form ▶ Show Deleted to check the Show Deleted option. In Table View, deleted records are indicated by a colored deletion marker in the column below the table name. In Form View, the status bar will display "(Record Deleted)" when the cursor lands on a deleted record. To hide the deleted records from view, uncheck the Show Deleted option on the Table or Form menu by choosing that option again.

To delete marked records from the computer's hard disk *permanently*, restructure the table (Tools ▶ Utilities ▶ Restructure), check the Pack Table option in the Restructure Table dialog box, and click Save.

▶ Sorting and Filtering dBASE Records

You can use the Table ▶ Sort feature described in Chapter 8 to sort any dBASE table. The procedures are the same as sorting a Paradox table.

The Filter feature also works with dBASE tables and is nearly the same as for Paradox tables. You can inspect a single field, choose Filter, specify the filter condition, and choose OK. If you want to filter all fields in the table, go to the Filter Tables dialog box, by choosing Table ➤ Filter or Form ➤ Filter when the table is opened in Table View or Form View. When the Filter Tables dialog box appears, select (check) Order By and then select an index tag from the list below the Order By check box. To add another non-maintained index file (*.ndx*) or a maintained (production) index file (*.mdx*), type the file name and extension in the dBASE Index File text box. After selecting the index to use, you can complete the dialog box and choose OK. See Chapter 9 for more about the Filter feature.

▶ Creating Multitable Design Documents with dBASE Tables

The steps for creating multitable forms and reports with dBASE tables are similar to those described in Chapter 17 under "Creating Multitable Design Documents." As for Paradox documents, you start from the Data Model dialog box. Add the tables to the data model and use your mouse to draw the link from the master table to the detail table.

When the Define Link dialog box appears, select the master table field you want to link from the Field list. Then select the index for the detail table from the Index list. Choose OK to complete the link and return to the Data Model dialog box.

Figure D.3 shows the Define Link dialog box for linking *states.dbf* (a master table with a maintained index on the State field) to *custlist.dbf* (a detail table with maintained indexes on the Cust_No and State fields).

As an alternative to defining a field from the Field list, you can click the Master Expression option and type a valid dBASE expression. For instance, the expression *UPPER(State)* would convert the alphanumeric State field values to uppercase. Refer to your dBASE manual for a list of valid master expressions.

You can link dBASE tables only on maintained indexes (*.mdx* files). Furthermore, it's best to use a *unique* index for your master table. The fields being linked in the Define Link dialog box must be the same type, unless you use a master expression in the link.

FIGURE D.3

The States and Cust-List dBASE tables are linked by the State field and State index respectively.

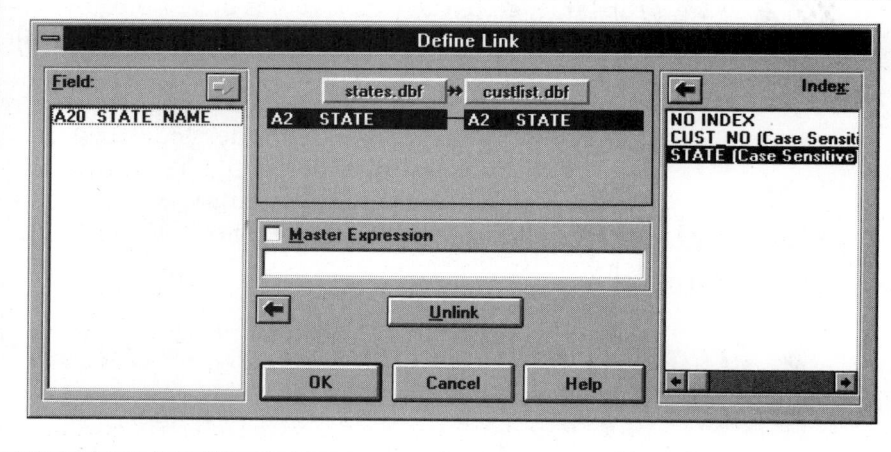

►►**N O T E**

> **When linking dBASE tables, you can link from a field to an expression index or single-field index, or from a master expression to an expression index or single-field index.**

►► *Using Tables from Other Versions of Paradox*

Paradox 5 for Windows recognizes Paradox tables created in different versions of Paradox, including Paradox 3.5, Paradox 4, and Paradox for Windows. In general, later versions of Paradox can open and update tables created by earlier versions. The next few sections cover some fine points about working with tables created in various versions of Paradox. Feel free to skip this section if you're not planning to use older versions of Paradox.

►►NOTE

> **Paradox for Windows does not recognize queries, reports, forms, scripts, or applications created in DOS versions of Paradox.**

► Updating Tables in Different Versions of Paradox

When updating and displaying tables in previous versions of Paradox, keep the following points in mind:

- Paradox 5 for Windows can display and update tables created by *any* previous version of Paradox.

- Paradox 4 can display and update tables created by Paradox for Windows, provided all the field types are supported by Paradox 4. Paradox 4 cannot display or update formatted memo, graphic, OLE, and binary fields.

- Paradox 3.5 or earlier versions cannot display or update tables created by Paradox for Windows, unless the table was specifically created as a Paradox 3.5 table.

► Restructuring Tables

When you use Paradox 5 for Windows to restructure a Paradox 3.5 or Paradox 4 table, that table remains a Paradox 3.5 or Paradox 4 table *unless* you add a field type that is not supported in the older version of Paradox. Here's how it works:

- Adding referential integrity to a Paradox 3.5 table will upgrade it to a Paradox 4 table.

- Adding a binary, formatted memo, graphic, memo, or OLE field to a Paradox 3.5 table will upgrade it to a Paradox 4 table.

- Adding an autoincrement, BCD, bytes, logical, long integer, time, or timestamp field to a Paradox 3.5 or Paradox 4 table will upgrade it to a Paradox 5 for Windows table.

▶ ▶ W A R N I N G

Paradox will ask for permission before upgrading a table. Continue the operation only if the older version of Paradox will never need to access the table you're upgrading. If you still need to use the old-style table with older versions of Paradox, make a copy of that table and then restructure the copy in Paradox 5 for Windows.

If you must use Paradox for Windows tables with older versions of Paradox that cannot read the Paradox for Windows tables, try the following:

1. Create a new Paradox 3.5 or Paradox 4 table (as appropriate). You can borrow the structure from your Paradox for Windows table, but be sure to delete any field types that aren't supported in the older version of Paradox you want to use. The supported field types in each version of Paradox are:

    Paradox 3.5   Valid field types are alpha, date, money, number, and short only.

    Paradox 4   Valid field types include all those for Paradox 3.5, plus binary, formatted memo, graphic, memo, and OLE.

    Paradox 5   Valid field types include all those for Paradox 4, plus autoincrement, BCD, bytes, logical, long integer, time, and timestamp.

2. Create and run an Insert query that inserts appropriate fields from your Paradox for Windows table into the structure you created in step 1. When the query finishes, you'll have an old-style table that's filled with all the allowable data from your Paradox for Windows table.

See Chapters 4, 5, and 15 for more about creating and restructuring tables, and Chapter 18 for information about Insert queries.

> **TIP**
>
> To quickly find out which version of a Paradox table you have, inspect the table in the Project Viewer, choose Restructure, and look at the title bar. After noting the table type, choose Cancel to exit the Restructure Table dialog box.

▶ Ensuring Data Integrity and Validity

Only Paradox for Windows fully supports referential integrity. If you use a Paradox for Windows table with a DOS version of Paradox, you may violate the defined referential integrity (see Chapter 5).

Paradox 4 recognizes and enforces all the passwords and validity checks that are available in Paradox for Windows (see Chapters 4 and 15).

Paradox 3.5 does not support validity checks or referential integrity.

▶ Using Indexes

If you create a composite secondary index for a Paradox for Windows table, Paradox 4 can maintain the index but cannot use it to search for field values.

Both Paradox for Windows and Paradox 4 support case-insensitive indexing, in which uppercase and lowercase characters are considered the same. Paradox 3.5, however, does not allow case-insensitive indexing.

▶ Accessing Tables Concurrently

Paradox for Windows and Paradox 4 for DOS use the same locking mechanism when sharing files on a network. Paradox 3.5 and earlier versions of Paradox, however, use a different locking mechanism. Practically speaking, this means that Paradox for Windows and Paradox 4 for DOS can access tables and directories concurrently. However, Paradox for Windows cannot access tables and directories that are currently in use by Paradox 3.5 or earlier versions.

Non-Paradox Tables

App D

Summary of Design Object Properties

You can change the properties of any object in the Form Design or Report Design windows simply by inspecting the objects and selecting options from the property menus that appear. This appendix briefly describes design object properties and the objects to which they apply. For additional details on the topics listed below, please refer to the chapters indicated:

- Creating design documents, creating objects, selecting objects, and changing object properties (Chapter 10).

- Creating forms and changing properties of objects in form designs (Chapter 11).

- Creating reports and mail merge documents and changing properties of objects in report designs (Chapter 12).

- Creating graphs and crosstabs and changing their properties (Chapter 13).

- Attaching ObjectPAL methods to buttons and other objects in form designs (Chapter 19).

►► *Design Object Properties*

Table E.1 describes object properties for each design object. The Toolbar buttons in Table E.1 indicate which objects have each property. Remember that some design properties apply only to objects in forms, while others apply only to objects in reports. For example, button properties apply to forms only, while report band properties apply to report designs only.

In addition to design properties, objects can have *Run Time* properties, which govern their behavior when you "run" a form or report. Different sets of Run Time properties apply to forms and reports. To see the

Design Object Properties

effects of Run Time properties, click the View Data button in the Tool-bar of the Design window or press F8. Chapter 11 covers the most important Run Time properties for forms, while Chapter 12 explains the essential Run Time properties for reports.

N O T E

Many property settings are "toggles" that are either on (checked) or off (unchecked). The descriptions in Table E.1 assume the toggle settings are on.

▶ **TABLE E.1:** *Summary of Design Object Properties*

PROPERTY	DESCRIPTION	OBJECTS
Add A Category	Add a field (category) in the row area of a crosstab.	
Add A Summary	Add a field to display a calculation result at the intersection of each row and column in a crosstab.	
Alignment	Align text at the left, right, or center of the object border.	
Button Type	Display the button as a Check box, Push button, or Radio button.	
Center Label	Center the label text on the button.	

▶ **TABLE E.1:** *Summary of Design Object Properties*

PROPERTY	DESCRIPTION	OBJECTS
Color	Change the color of an object.	
Columnar	Expand or contract individual records in a multi-record object when you preview or print a report.	
Conditional	Print a group header object at the beginning of each page and/or each group. (Inspect an object in the group band.)	
Data Type	Change data type of a graph design to tabular, 1D, or 2D summary.	
Define Column Field	Define field data for a column in a crosstab.	
Define Crosstab	Define table data and other features of a crosstab.	
Define Field	Define field data for a field object.	

▶ **TABLE E.1:** *Summary of Design Object Properties*

PROPERTY	DESCRIPTION	OBJECTS
Define Graph	Define a complex graph.	
Define Graphic	Define the image for a graphic object.	
Define Group	Define the grouping for a 2D Summary graph or for a report band.	
Define OLE	Define an OLE value for an OLE object.	
Define Record	Define table data to display in the record area of a table or multi-record object.	
Define Table	Define the table to display in a table frame.	
Define X-Value	Define a field for a graph's X-axis.	
Define (New) Y-Value	Define a field for a graph's Y-axis.	
Delete When Empty	Delete this record (or field) from the report if its fields are empty.	

▶ **TABLE E.1:** *Summary of Design Object Properties*

PROPERTY	DESCRIPTION	OBJECTS
Design Sizing ➤ Fixed Size	Prevent the text object from changing size to fit entered text.	
Design Sizing ➤ Fit Text	Expand or contract the text object to fit entered text.	
Design Sizing ➤ Grow Only	Expand, but do not contract, the text object to fit entered text.	
Design ➤ Contain Objects	Allow the object to contain and control objects within its borders.	
Design ➤ Pin Horizontal	Pin object so that it maintains its horizontal position within the design.	All
Design ➤ Pin Vertical	Pin object so that it maintains its vertical position within the design.	All
Design ➤ Selectable	Object can be selected by clicking on it.	All

▶ **TABLE E.1:** *Summary of Design Object Properties*

PROPERTY	DESCRIPTION	OBJECTS
Design ➤ Size to Fit	Expand or contract the object to fit the data it contains.	
Detach Header	Move the table header containing field names away from the body of table data.	
Display Type	Display field values as a Check Box, Drop-Down Edit List, or Radio Button.	
Display Type ➤ Labeled	Display the field value with a label.	
Display Type ➤ Unlabeled	Display the field value without a label.	
Edit …	Edit an OLE object.	
Explode	Explode a slice in a pie graph.	
Field Layout	Define the layout of fields in a multi-record object that is bound to a table.	
Font	Change the typeface, size, style, or color of text.	

► **TABLE E.1:** *Summary of Design Object Properties*

PROPERTY	DESCRIPTION	OBJECTS
Format ➤ Date Format	Change the date field display format.	
Format ➤ Logical Format	Change the logical field display format.	
Format ➤ Number Format	Change the number field display format.	
Format ➤ Time Format	Change the time field display format.	
Format ➤ Time-stamp Format	Change the time/date field display format.	
Frame	Change the frame style, color, or thickness of the object.	
Graph Type	Define the display type for graphed data (e.g., 2D Pie, 2D Bar, 3D Area).	
Grid	Change the line color and style of grid lines; display a divider between multiple records.	

▶ **TABLE E.1:** *Summary of Design Object Properties*

PROPERTY	DESCRIPTION	OBJECTS
Headings	Print a group heading at top of the page and/or group.	
Horizontal Scroll Bar	Display a scroll bar below the object.	
Label	Define the format of labels used in a graph.	
Legend Pos	Define the position of a graph's legend.	
Line	Change the line thickness, color, or style for the object.	
Line Ends	Display an arrow at one or both ends of a line.	
Line Spacing	Set the spacing between lines of text.	
Line Style	Set the line style to solid, dashed, dotted, or combination from palette.	
Line Type	Change the line to straight or curved.	

▶ **TABLE E.1:** *Summary of Design Object Properties*

PROPERTY	DESCRIPTION	OBJECTS
Magnification	Increase or decrease the size of an object within its container.	
Marker	Define the marker style and size for a line in a 2D Line or 2D Bar graph.	
Max Groups	Set the maximum number of group-by values in a 2D summary graph.	
Max X-Values	Set the maximum number of x-axis values in a graph.	
Methods	Attach ObjectPAL methods to an object (form design only).	All
Min X-Values	Set the minimum number of x-axis values in a graph.	
Open ...	Open an OLE object for editing.	
Options	Set parameters for graph axes, elevation, grid, labels, legend, rotation, and titles. (See Chapter 13.)	

▶ **TABLE E.1:** *Summary of Design Object Properties*

PROPERTY	DESCRIPTION	OBJECTS
Pattern	Change the fill pattern or fill color of an object.	
Precede Page Header	Print the report header before printing the page header.	
Print On 1st Page	Print contents of the page band on the first page of the report.	
Raster Operation	Define how source graphic pixels combine with destination pixels.	
Record Layout	Specify the number of records across and down, and the spacing between records in a multi-record object.	
Remove This Y-Value	Remove the selected Y-value from a graph.	
Repeat Header	Print a report header at the top of each page.	

▶ **TABLE E.1:** *Summary of Design Object Properties*

PROPERTY	DESCRIPTION	OBJECTS
Run Time ➤ Breakable	Allow an object to divide at page breaks.	
Run Time ➤ Field Squeeze	Adjust text to remove spaces around embedded fields.	
Run Time ➤ Fit Height	Grow or shrink the object vertically to fit contained objects.	
Run Time ➤ Fit Width	Grow or shrink the object horizontally to fit contained objects.	
Run Time ➤ Invisible	Do not display the object when the report is run.	
Run Time ➤ Line Squeeze	Delete blank text lines.	
Run Time ➤ No Echo	Do not display data entered into this field object.	

▶ **TABLE E.1:** *Summary of Design Object Properties*

PROPERTY	DESCRIPTION	OBJECTS
Run Time ➤ Orphan/Widow	Adjust text to prevent orphans and widows.	A
Run Time ➤ Pin Horizontal	Pin object to maintain its horizontal position on the page at runtime.	All
Run Time ➤ Pin Vertical	Pin object to maintain its vertical position on the page at runtime.	All
Run Time ➤ Read Only	Do not allow user to change data in this field.	
Run Time ➤ Show All Columns	Expand the table frame to fit all table columns.	
Run Time ➤ Show All Records	Expand the object vertically (and horizontally for multi-record objects) to show all records.	
Run Time ➤ Shrinkable	Shrink the object to fit on the page if the object contains no printable data and would otherwise move to the next page.	
Run Time ➤ Tab Stop	Allow user to press Tab on a form to move to this object.	

▶ **TABLE E.1:** *Summary of Design Object Properties*

PROPERTY	DESCRIPTION	OBJECTS
Run Time ➤ Visible	Display the object in the form.	All
Scale	Define the scaling (auto-scale, logarithmic, low value, high value, and increment) for a graph.	
Search Text	Search and replace text values.	
Sort	Define ascending or descending sort order for a record band.	
Sort Order	Define ascending or descending sort order for a report group.	
Start Page Numbers	Begin a new page and reset the page number when the band is reached.	
Style	Define the button style (Borland, Windows, or Windows 3d) for a radio button or check box.	
Subtitle	Define the text or font of a graph's subtitle.	

Design Object Properties

App.
E

▶ **TABLE E.1:** *Summary of Design Object Properties*

PROPERTY	DESCRIPTION	OBJECTS
Thickness	Define the thickness of a line or frame. May appear on property menus as Thickness, Frame ➤ Thickness, or Line ➤ Thickness.	(icons)
Ticks	Define the font or number format of a graph's tick marks.	(icon)
Title	Define the text or font of a graph's title.	(icon)
Type Override	Define a different display type for a selected series in a graph.	(icon)
Update Now	Immediately update a linked OLE object with its source data.	(icon)
Vertical Scroll Bar	Display a vertical scroll bar at the right side of an object.	(icons)

▶ **TABLE E.1:** *Summary of Design Object Properties*

PROPERTY	DESCRIPTION	OBJECTS
Wide Scroll Bar	Use wide scroll bar when the vertical or horizontal scroll bar is selected.	A 🖼 OLE I ▤ ▦ ▦
Word Wrap	Automatically begin a new line when text reaches the right border of the object.	A I

▶▶ *Using the Palettes*

As discussed in Chapter 10, Paradox displays "visual" properties—Color, Line Style, Font, and Frame—on palettes instead of menus. To select an option from a palette, simply click on the option or appearance of your choice.

By default the palettes are temporary and disappear after you make a selection. However, you can leave the palette on the screen just by clicking the snap at the top. This creates a *floating palette* that you can move about on the Desktop by dragging its title bar. The floating palette remains on the Desktop until you click the snap button again. Figure E.1 shows a form design and all the floating palettes on the Paradox for Windows Desktop.

▶▶ **N O T E**

The Thickness property for a line or frame always appears in a temporary palette.

FIGURE E.1

Floating palettes remain on the Desktop until you click the snap button.

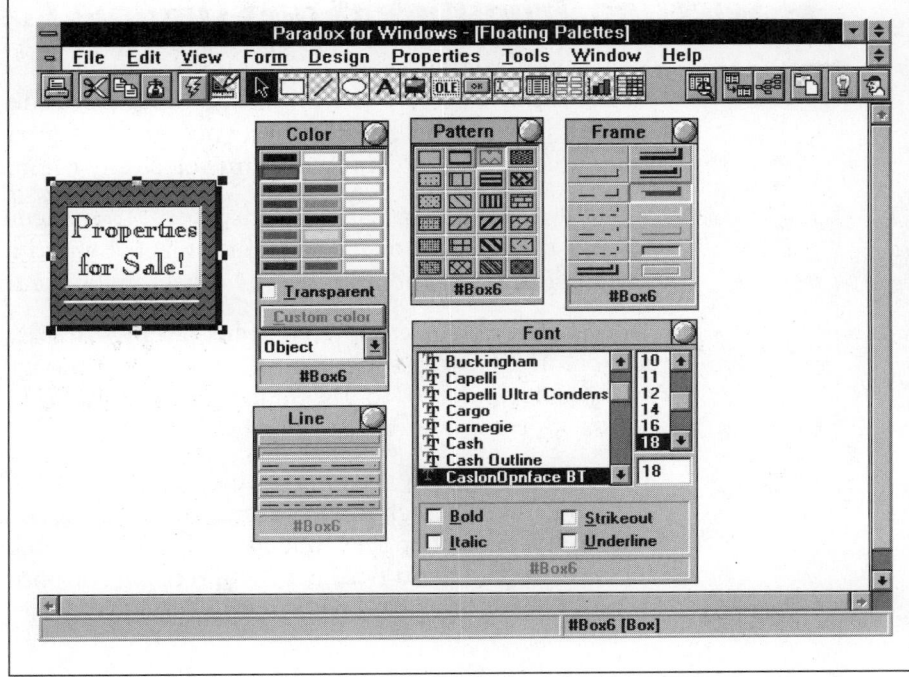

Here's a brief description of each floating palette:

Color   Allows you to change the color of an object, pattern, frame, grid, or font.

Font   Lets you choose a type face, size, and print attribute (bold, italic, strikeout, or underline) for text.

Frame   Lets you change the appearance of the border around an object. To create three-dimensional frames, select any of the last four frame styles on the palette. (See Chapters 10 and 11.)

Line   Allows you to choose a line style (solid, dashed, etc.) To display this palette, inspect a line and choose Line Style.

Pattern   Allows you to change the fill pattern for an object.

▶ Selecting Transparent and Opaque Colors

Nearly all design objects have Color properties that you can change by inspecting the objects and choosing Color from the property menu. When the Color palette appears, you can click on any of sixteen predefined colors, or you can create and select any of nine custom colors.

The color you assign can be transparent, translucent, or opaque. If the color is transparent or translucent, objects behind it will show through; if the color is opaque, the opaque object will obscure objects behind it.

To make an object completely transparent—that is, completely clear and colorless—select the "color" at the bottom-right corner of the *temporary* color palette. To assign an opaque color, select any color from the temporary palette.

The floating Color palette includes a ͟Transparent check box (see Figure E.1). If you check ͟Transparent, the object's color will be *translucent*; that is, it will appear in a color that allows objects behind it to show through. If you deselect the ͟Transparent option, the object in front will obscure anything behind it.

▶ ▶ **T I P**

It's easy to change the color of the background, fill pattern, frame, grid, or font for an object or selected text. Just open the floating Color palette, click the drop-down list, and select the appropriate area to color (Object, Pattern, Frame, Grid, or Font); then click the color you want. See Chapter 7.

▶ Creating Custom Colors

To create a custom color, follow the steps below.

1. Open the floating Color palette and highlight one of the white color samples in the right-hand column. You may create up to nine custom colors in one palette. (To reach the ninth color, click in the right-most column of the floating Color palette and press the → key or press the ↓ key repeatedly until the ninth color sample appears.)

2. Click the <u>C</u>ustom Color button to display the Custom Color dialog box shown in Figure E.2.

3. Select one of the following methods to mix the custom color (any method can be used to create any color):

    RGB Defines the color as a mixture of red, green, and blue.

    HSV Defines the color in terms of hue, saturation, and value (brightness).

    CMY Defines the color as a mixture of cyan, magenta, and yellow.

4. Drag the scroll bars and click the scroll arrows, or type values into the text boxes, to create the color mix you want. A sample of the color will appear above the scroll bars.

5. When the color is to your liking, choose OK to save it on the palette.

You can assign the custom color to any object in a design simply by clicking on the color in the temporary or floating Color palette. Custom colors remain on the palette in future Paradox sessions. To change

FIGURE E.2 ▶

The Custom Color dialog box allows you to define custom colors for design objects.

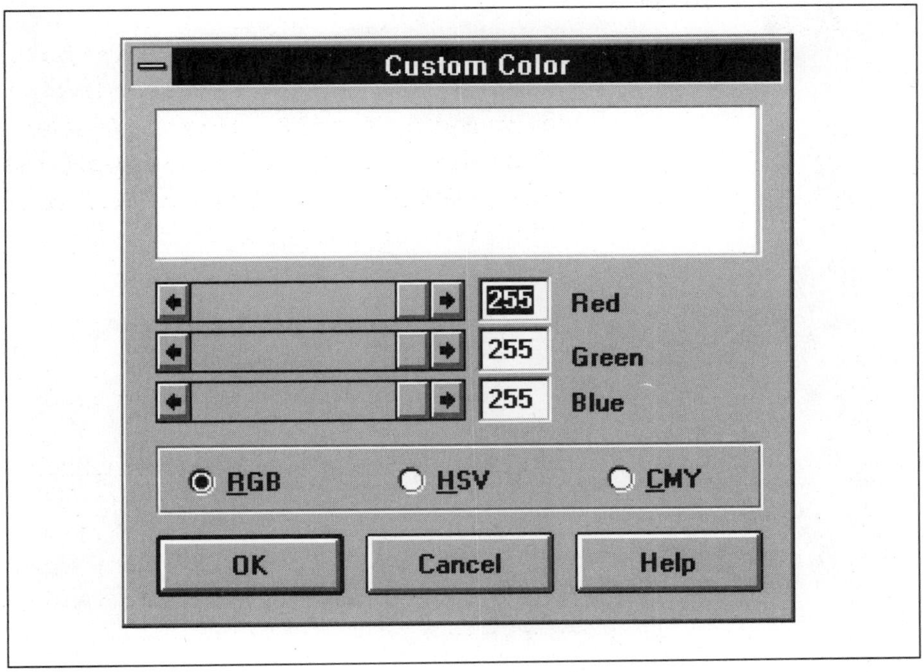

a custom color, highlight the color you want to change in the floating Color palette and repeat steps 2 through 5 above. Changes to the custom color affect the selected objects only; unselected objects will retain their original custom colors.

▶ ▶ **N O T E**

You cannot delete custom colors from within Paradox, but you *can* change them back to white. To permanently delete a custom color, you must exit Paradox, open the *c:\windows\pdoxwin.ini* file in Windows Notepad, and carefully delete the appropriate "CustomColor" entry in the *[Properties]* section of the file. See Chapter 14 for more about the *pdoxwin.ini* file.

▶ Index

Note to the Reader:

Boldfaced numbers indicate the principal discussion of a topic or the definition of a term. *Italic* numbers indicate illustrations.

▶ Numbers and Symbols

▶ U

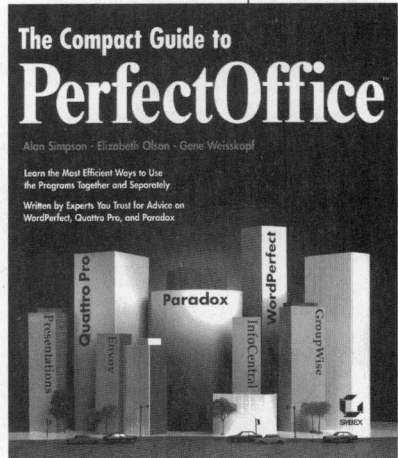

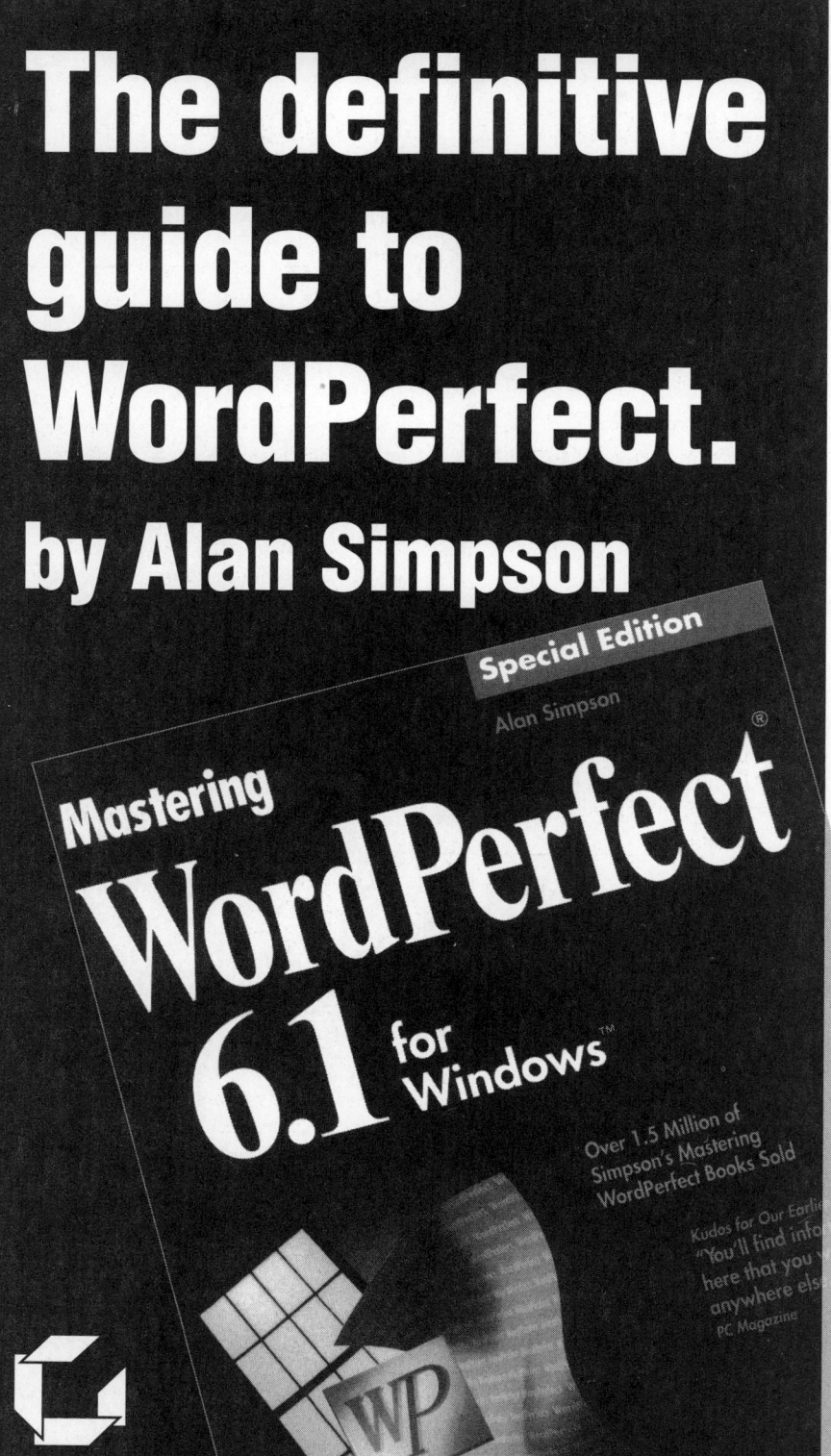

GET A FREE CATALOG JUST FOR EXPRESSING YOUR OPINION.

Help us improve our books and get a *FREE* full-color catalog in the bargain. Please complete this form, pull out this page and send it in today. The address is on the reverse side.

Name _____   Company _____

Address _____   City _____ State _____ Zip _____

Phone (____) _____

1. How would you rate the overall quality of this book?

❑ Excellent
❑ Very Good
❑ Good
❑ Fair
❑ Below Average
❑ Poor

2. What were the things you liked most about the book? (Check all that apply)

❑ Pace
❑ Format
❑ Writing Style
❑ Examples
❑ Table of Contents
❑ Index
❑ Price
❑ Illustrations
❑ Type Style
❑ Cover
❑ Depth of Coverage
❑ Fast Track Notes

3. What were the things you liked *least* about the book? (Check all that apply)

❑ Pace
❑ Format
❑ Writing Style
❑ Examples
❑ Table of Contents
❑ Index
❑ Price
❑ Illustrations
❑ Type Style
❑ Cover
❑ Depth of Coverage
❑ Fast Track Notes

4. Where did you buy this book?

❑ Bookstore chain
❑ Small independent bookstore
❑ Computer store
❑ Wholesale club
❑ College bookstore
❑ Technical bookstore
❑ Other _____

5. How did you decide to buy this particular book?

❑ Recommended by friend
❑ Recommended by store personnel
❑ Author's reputation
❑ Sybex's reputation
❑ Read book review in _____
❑ Other _____

6. How did you pay for this book?

❑ Used own funds
❑ Reimbursed by company
❑ Received book as a gift

7. What is your level of experience with the subject covered in this book?

❑ Beginner
❑ Intermediate
❑ Advanced

8. How long have you been using a computer?

years _____
months _____

9. Where do you most often use your computer?

❑ Home
❑ Work

❑ Both
❑ Other _____

10. What kind of computer equipment do you have? (Check all that apply)

❑ PC Compatible Desktop Computer
❑ PC Compatible Laptop Computer
❑ Apple/Mac Computer
❑ Apple/Mac Laptop Computer
❑ CD ROM
❑ Fax Modem
❑ Data Modem
❑ Scanner
❑ Sound Card
❑ Other _____

11. What other kinds of software packages do you ordinarily use?

❑ Accounting
❑ Databases
❑ Networks
❑ Apple/Mac
❑ Desktop Publishing
❑ Spreadsheets
❑ CAD
❑ Games
❑ Word Processing
❑ Communications
❑ Money Management
❑ Other _____

12. What operating systems do you ordinarily use?

❑ DOS
❑ OS/2
❑ Windows
❑ Apple/Mac
❑ Windows NT
❑ Other _____

13. On what computer-related subject(s) would you like to see more books?

_____

_____

_____

_____

14. Do you have any other comments about this book? (Please feel free to use a separate piece of paper if you need more room)

_____

_____

_____

_____

- - - - - - - - - - - - PLEASE FOLD, SEAL, AND MAIL TO SYBEX - - - - - - - - - - - - - - -

SYBEX INC.
Department M
2021 Challenger Drive
Alameda, CA
94501

Designing and Using Custom Forms

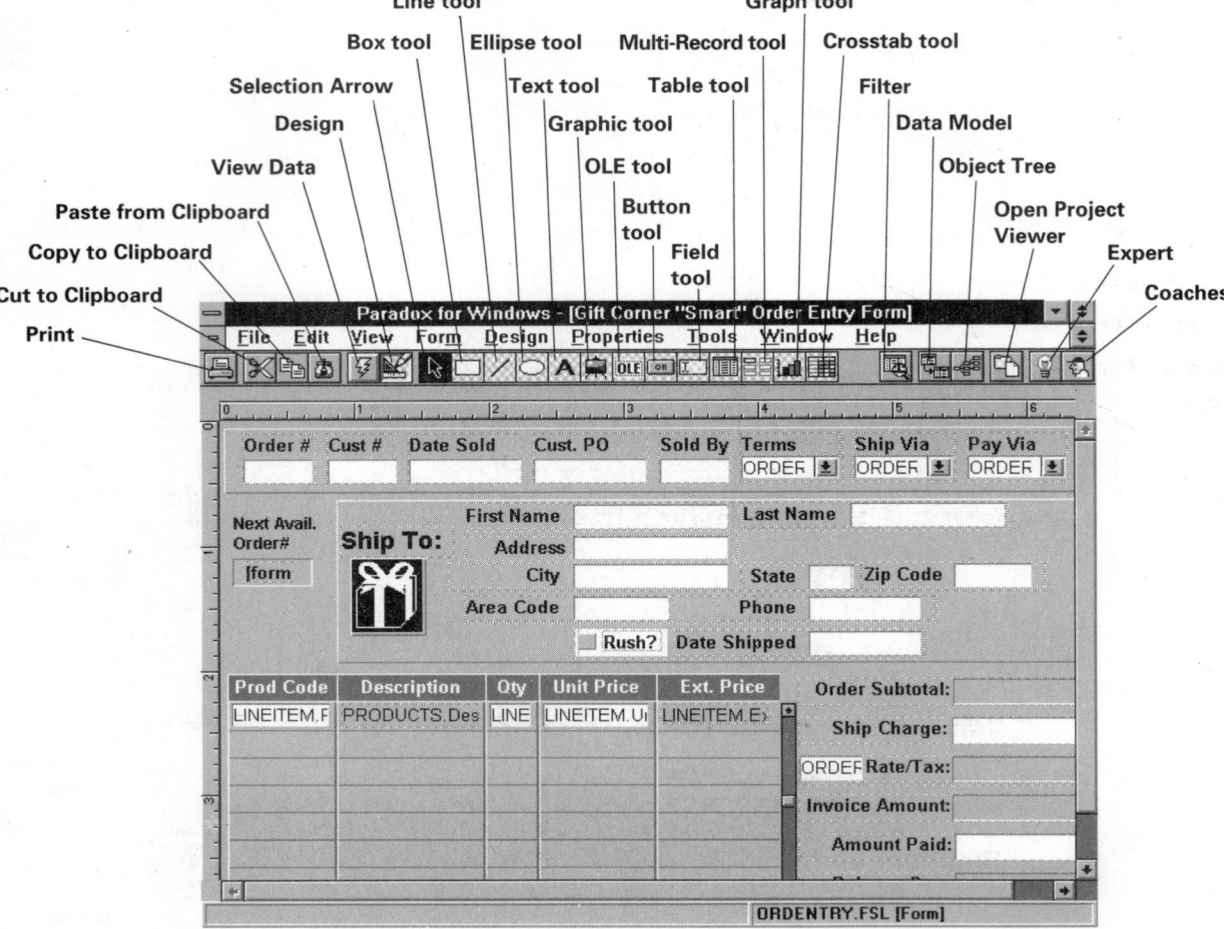

Line tool
Box tool
Ellipse tool
Text tool
Graphic tool
OLE tool
Button tool
Field tool
Multi-Record tool
Table tool
Graph tool
Crosstab tool
Filter
Data Model
Object Tree
Open Project
Viewer
Expert
Coaches

Selection Arrow
Design
View Data
Paste from Clipboard
Copy to Clipboard
Cut to Clipboard
Print

TO DO THIS...	SEE CHAPTER *
Enter and edit data in a Quick Form or custom form	2, 6, 17
Design custom forms	2, 10, 11, 17
Choose tables to include	2, 10, 17
Select and sort data in a form	10
Choose an initial design layout	10
Save and open custom forms	2, 10
Create and copy objects	2, 10, 11
Select objects and change their properties	2, 10
Change properties of design tools in the Toolbar	10
Change the appearance of the Form Design window and Form window	10, 11
Design multipage forms	11
Summarize data with graphs or crosstabs	13
Print a form or form design	11
Perform calculations on fields	17
Make decisions about which data to display	17
Combine data from multiple tables	17
Build "smart" forms to automate your work	19

NOTE: Many techniques for designing forms and reports are identical